m	Hedge ratio (number of options per share of stock)
M	Maturity value of a bond
n	Life of a project; also terminal year of decision horizon
N	Number of states; also shares of stock; number of projects
$N(\cdot)$	Cumulative normal probability used in OPM
p	Price of a security
P	Sales price per unit of product sold; also value of a put
$PV_{r,n}$	Present value; also P_0
$PVA_{r,t}$	Present value of an annuity
p_s	Probability of states-of-the-world
PVIF	Present value interest factor
PVIFA	Present value interest factor for an annuity
q	Number of times compounded within the year; also conversion ratio
Q	Quantity produced or sold
r	Interest rate (usually real rate) or rate of return (profitability rate)
R	Nominal interest rate
$E(R)$	Expected (required) rate of return on new investment (in CAPM)
R^o	Estimated rate of return
R_M	Return on the market portfolio
R_F	Risk-free rate of interest
R_j	Returns to individual firm or security
ρ_{jk} (rho)	Correlation coefficient
s	Subscript referring to alternative states-of-the-world
S	Market value of a firm's common equity; also sales when indicated
σ(sigma)	Standard deviation
σ^2	Variance; also VAR( )
t	Time period or time index
T	Time to maturity in OPM
T_c	Marginal corporate income tax rate; also T
T_{ps}	Capital gains tax rate
T_{pb}	Ordinary personal income tax rate
u	Upward movement in asset price in BOP
V	Market value of a firm; also total variable costs
v	Variable costs per unit
v_{ps}	Value of preferred stock per share
w	Weights in capital structure or portfolio proportions
X	Net operating income of a firm; also equals EBIT = NOI; also exercise price of option; number of foreign currency units per dollar

MANAGERIAL FINANCE

NINTH EDITION

MANAGERIAL FINANCE

NINTH EDITION

J. Fred Weston
Anderson Graduate School of Management
University of California, Los Angeles

Thomas E. Copeland
McKinsey & Company
New York, New York

The Dryden Press
A Harcourt Brace Jovanovich College Publisher
Fort Worth   Philadelphia   San Diego   New York   Orlando   Austin   San Antonio
Toronto   Montreal   London   Sydney   Tokyo

Acquisitions Editor: Michael Roche
Developmental Editor: Millicent Treloar
Project Editor: Cate Rzasa
Art and Design Manager: Alan Wendt
Production Manager: Barb Bahnsen
Director of Editing, Design, and Production: Jane Perkins

Text and Cover Designer: Hunter Graphics
Copy Editor: Cheryl Wilms
Indexer: Leoni McVey
Compositor: York Graphic Services, Inc.
Text Type: 10/12 Times Roman

Library of Congress Cataloging-in-Publication Data

Weston, J. Fred (John Fred), 1916–
   Managerial finance / J. Fred Weston, Thomas E. Copeland. — 9th ed.
     p. cm.
   Includes bibliographical references and index.
   ISBN 0-03-055883-2
    1. Corporations — Finance. I. Copeland, Thomas E., 1946–
II. Title.
   HG4026.W45   1992
   658.15 — dc20   91-17511

Printed in the United States of America
234-016-987654321

Requests for permission to make copies of any part of the work should be
mailed to: Permissions Department, Harcourt Brace Jovanovich, Publishers,
8th Floor, Orlando, Florida 32887.

Address orders:
The Dryden Press
Orlando, Florida   32887

Address editorial correspondence:
The Dryden Press
301 Commerce Street, Suite 3800
Fort Worth, Texas   76102

The Dryden Press
Harcourt Brace Jovanovich

Cover source: Photograph © Herb Comess. All Rights Reserved.

ABOUT THE AUTHORS

J. Fred Weston earned his A.B. in Political Science, his MBA in Business Economics, and his Ph.D. in Finance, all from the University of Chicago. Dr. Weston began his teaching career at the University of Chicago and in 1949 joined the staff of the University of California, Los Angeles, where he has been professor of managerial economics and finance in the Graduate School of Management since 1955 and has served as Chairman of Finance and Chairman of Business Economics. In 1979, Professor Weston was selected one of the five outstanding teachers on the UCLA campus. He is currently the Cordner Professor of Money and Financial Markets.

Dr. Weston was Associate Editor of *The Journal of Finance* from 1948 to 1955, and a member of the journal's editorial board. He has served as President of the American Finance Association, President of the Western Economic Association, and President of the Financial Management Association. He was also a member of the American Economic Association Census Advisory Committee.

Dr. Weston has published extensively in the financial literature. In addition to *Managerial Finance,* he is the author of several other books, including *The Role of Mergers in the Growth of Large Firms, Public Policy toward Mergers* (with Sam Peltzman), *Financial Theory and Corporate Policy* (with Thomas E. Copeland), *Mergers, Restructuring, and Corporate Control* (with Kwang S. Chung and Susan E. Hoag).

Dr. Weston has served extensively as a consultant to business firms and government on financial and economic policies.

Thomas E. Copeland received his B.A. in Economics from Johns Hopkins University, his MBA in Finance from Wharton, and his Ph.D. from the University of Pennsylvania. Between 1973 and 1989 he was a faculty member at UCLA's Anderson Graduate School of Management where he served as Chairman of the Finance Curriculum Area. At UCLA he twice received an award as best teacher in the MBA program. Currently he is a partner and co-leader of the Corporate Finance Practice at McKinsey & Company, Inc. in New York and serves as an adjunct Professor of Finance at the Stern School of Business at New York University. He has been a consultant to more than 50 major companies in 19 different countries.

His other books include *Financial Theory and Corporate Policy,* an advanced level corporate finance text coauthored with J. Fred Weston; *Valuation: Measuring and Managing the Value of Companies,* coauthored with Tim Koller and Jack Murrin; and *Modern Finance and Industrial Economics.* His academic publications include articles about stock splits, theory of market trading activity, receivables policy, bid–ask spreads, leasing, spinoffs, nonprofit organizations, portfolio performance measurement, exchange offers and stock swaps, and experimental economics tests of the value of information. Dr. Copeland is an associate editor of *Financial Management.*

THE DRYDEN PRESS SERIES IN FINANCE

PREFACE

When the first edition of *Managerial Finance* was published in 1962, its hallmark was an emphasis on the use of principles to make sound financial management decisions. From the beginning, *Managerial Finance* analyzed accepted rules and practices to determine whether they simply represented traditional ways of doing things or whether there was some solid rationale behind them. The central aim of *Managerial Finance* has always been to provide a conceptual framework for making sound financial management decisions.

Theory and practice are inseparable. Theory that does not guide sound practice risks being sterile. Practice that cannot be supported by good analytical reasoning is subject to error. Sound theory produces testable predictions and guides sound practice. In a world that is changing with increasing rapidity, sound theory provides managers with the ability to anticipate change, improve adaptability, and enable an organization to be strengthened by change rather than to be weakened by the inability to align effectively with change. Previous editions of *Managerial Finance* have sought to demonstrate in every topic how principles derived from sound theory can be used to guide effective financial decision making.

This ninth edition of *Managerial Finance* seeks to continue to develop this central framework. The ninth edition of *Managerial Finance* is definitely not just an updating. Fifty percent or more of the book represents new or rewritten materials. It reflects the impact of rapid developments and seeks to recognize them in the areas of strategic planning, international finance, the interrelationships between options — forwards — futures — swaps — and to embrace the benefits of technological change embodied in increased computer power at the personal computer level. The preeminence of assembly-line production methods has given way to the advantages of flexible manufacturing systems. Cash and receivables management has been significantly altered by emerging national electronic transfer systems. New approaches to inventory management have been developed including just-in-time (JIT) inventory methods. The technology of financial management has had to be modified to relate to and encompass these changes effectively.

ORGANIZATION OF THE BOOK

In this ninth edition of *Managerial Finance*, we have again reorganized the sequence in which the materials are presented. A number of other finance books now start with the theory chapters. Although theory has always been the central core of *Managerial Finance*, we have resisted placing the theory at the beginning of the book. We continue to believe that the reader is better prepared to understand and make more effective use of theoretical concepts after the requisite foundations have been laid. The theory can then be presented in greater depth and be more meaningful. It can also be utilized in the major decision areas of financial management.

We start with fundamental concepts. Since the heart of finance is decision making about cash flows across time, we present this topic immediately after summarizing the central financial statements that enable financial managers to keep score. We then turn to an overview of financial markets, financial instruments, and the central concepts of market efficiency to round out the background for financial decision making.

The next chapters cover financial analysis, financial planning, and financial control. Following these, we assume a world with no uncertainty and confront the challenges of investment decisions by the firm representing the major source by which value is created. This pushes us to consider how decisions can be made efficient under uncertainty. We analyze risk and return in theory and in its applications. We then discuss options and their many applications. This enables us to return to the investment decision but in a world with uncertainty. The capstone chapter in this section on decision making under uncertainty is ''Managing Financial Risk,'' which covers the interrelationships between options, forwards and futures, and swaps, including the topics of portfolio insurance and duration.

We are then in a position to address the central conceptual issues facing the firm, the impact on the firm's value and cost of capital of financial structure and dividend policy. The central theoretical issues are then focused in the key chapter on value-based management.

The next two sections deal successively with short-term financial management and the financial manager's long-range financial strategies. The final section of the book focuses on two major aspects of the life cycle of the firm. Chapter 27 covers mergers and acquisitions, restructuring, and corporate control. The concluding chapter is conceptually a part of the restructuring orientation of looking at the firm and deals with the broad subject of financial distress and how to manage it effectively.

CHANGES IN THE NINTH EDITION

The ninth edition of *Managerial Finance* has been created in a crucible of turbulent changes in the financial environment and financial practices. As direct participants in these developments, we can write out of our own studies and experiences. We have been active contributors to the literature on these recent revolutions in corporate finance. In addition, we have had the opportunity to test the new concepts and principles in active interaction with corporate executives. Our studies and experience have resulted in the following significant new features in the ninth edition.

1. Provides balanced treatment of ethics and corporate responsibility.
2. Reflects the impact of the November 1987 FASB 95, *Statement of Cash Flows*.
3. Integrates market efficiency principles with the nature of financial markets and evolving new forms of financial contracts.
4. Integrates international finance throughout the book.
5. Is unique and completely up-to-date on tax changes including enactments before and after the Tax Reform Act of 1986 incorporating changes that will affect tax returns in 1992 and subsequent years.
6. Integrates international factors in explaining the determinants of interest rates.
7. Provides innovative reformulation of financial ratio analysis.
8. Contains in-depth analysis and evaluation of major ranking criteria for capital budgeting, including applications of MACRS depreciation rules of the IRS.
9. Demonstrates the applicability of risk and return analysis to financial decision making.
10. Presents material on options so that it can be applied to the material of subsequent chapters.
11. Includes a new innovative chapter on managing financial risk that demonstrates how portfolio insurance, options, forwards–futures, and swaps can be replicated in different combinations.
12. Integrates treatment of financial structure and the cost of capital.
13. Incorporates the latest practices in the spreadsheet approach to value-based management.
14. Provides focused treatment of short-term financial management including recent developments in electronic information transmission.
15. Explains the impact of new inventory control methods on organization systems.
16. Covers recent developments in initial public offerings and going public.
17. Includes authoritative comprehensive coverage on developments in mergers and acquisitions, corporate restructuring, LBOs, share repurchase, ESOPs, and leveraged recaps.
18. Synthesizes the considerable recent literature on financial distress and the use of Chapter 11 of the bankruptcy laws.
19. Includes one or more problems making use of personal computer diskettes in most chapters.

The new *Instructor's Manual* and *Study Guide* for the ninth edition will incorporate all of these fundamental new developments. We hope that the revisions have achieved a unified intellectual framework that will facilitate practical applications in decision making as we enter a new millenium.

FLEXIBILITY IN THE USE OF THE MATERIALS

Much of the book's specific content is the result of our classroom teaching experience over a number of years, including executive development programs. This experience, in addition to our consulting work with business firms on financial problems and policies, has helped us to identify the most significant responsibilities of financial managers, the most fundamental problems facing firms, and the most feasible approaches to practical decision making. Some topics are conceptually difficult but so are the issues faced by financial managers. Business managers must be prepared to handle complex problems, and finding solutions to these problems necessarily involves the use of advanced tools and techniques.

We have not avoided the many unresolved areas of business financial theory and practice. Although we could have simplified the text in many places by side-stepping the difficult issues, we tried to discuss them in balanced analytical terms. We hope that our presentation, along with the additional references provided at the end of each chapter, will stimulate the reader to further inquiry.

We acknowledge that the level and difficulty of the material are uneven. Certain sections are simply descriptions of the institutional features of the financial environment and, as such, can be comprehended easily and rapidly. Other parts — notably the materials on capital budgeting, uncertainty, option pricing, and the cost of capital — are difficult. But such are the activities of financial managers! Also, we hope that by alternating easy and tough material, we will provide a refreshing change of pace for the reader.

Managerial Finance has traditionally been a highly flexible text, and this flexibility continues in the ninth edition. This book can be used in a one-quarter or one-semester introductory course. However, when so used, it will not be possible to cover all of the chapters. Some instructors concentrate on the basic theory chapters for a one-quarter or one-semester course, which would include Chapters 1 to 17 plus 27 and 28, representing about two-thirds of the book. For a one-semester course of 15 to 18 weeks, one or more additional major parts of the book can be added. Other instructors select groups of chapters in the sequence of their individual choice. Still others cover the entire book in a sequence of two quarters or two semesters. We have also found that business executives can work through the book on their own with the assistance of the book's *Study Guide* described below.

We tried to shorten the length of the book but it continues to be encyclopedic for several reasons. We cover the entire field of business finance and deal with all of the financial management functions. Eliminating institutional material and concentrating only on theory and technique would give the student an unrealistic view of finance. Some of the more advanced materials could have been eliminated because they are difficult, but they are essential for sound decision making. These considerations, plus the flexibility in the use of materials, which makes it unnecessary to cover the entire book in one course, caused us to refrain from major deletions. Furthermore, the book has a tradition of functioning as a text or reference work for use in a number of courses and for the practicing financial executive as well.

ANCILLARY MATERIALS

Several items are available to supplement *Managerial Finance*. For the professor, there is a comprehensive *Instructor's Manual,* which contains alternative subject sequences and teaching methods, course outlines, answers to all text questions, solutions to all text problems, and an extensive array of test questions and problems. Also available to the instructor is a comprehensive set of *Transparency Masters,* which feature key concepts and solutions to selected end-of-chapter problems.

For the student, the *Study Guide* provides an outline of the text and presents a comprehensive set of problems similar to those at the end of each chapter. Each problem is solved in detail, so a student who has difficulty working the end-of-chapter problems can be aided by use of the *Study Guide.*

Managerial Finance, ninth edition, can be supplemented with additional materials from The Dryden Press. Supplementary reading materials are available in Philip L. Cooley, *Advances in Business Financial Management: A Collection of Readings,* and Ramon E. Johnson, *Issues and Readings in Managerial Finance.* A casebook that relates well to our materials is Diana R. Harrington, *Case Studies in Financial Decision Making,* second edition.

ACKNOWLEDGMENTS

In its several revisions, this book has been worked on and critically reviewed by numerous individuals, and we have received many detailed comments and suggestions from instructors and students using the book in our own schools and elsewhere. All this help has improved the quality of the book, and we are deeply indebted to the following individuals, and others, for their help: M. Adler, E. Altman, J. Andrews, R. Aubey, P. Bacon, M. Baker, W. Beranek, V. Brewer, W. Brueggeman, R. Carleson, S. C. Carlson, D. Choi, S. Choudhur, P. Cooley, C. Cox, P. Ewald, K. W. Fairchild, D. Fischer, G. Granger, R. Gray, J. Griggs, R. Haugen, S. Hawk, R. Hehre, J. Henry, A. Herrmann, G. Hettenhouse, R. Himes, C. C. Hsia, K. Howe, C. Johnson, M. Johnson, R. Jones, D. Kaplan, M. Kaufman, D. Knight, H. Krogh, M. Lamberson, R. LeClair, W. Lee, D. Longmore, J. Longstreet, H. Magee, P. Malone, R. Masulis, R. Moore, T. Morton, T. Nantell, R. Nelson, R. Norgaard, J. Pappas, G. M. Petry, R. Pettit, R. Pettway, J. Pinkerton, G. Pogue, J. G. Preston, W. Regan, F. Reilly, R. Rentz, R. Richards, C. Rini, R. Roenfeldt, M. S. Scheue, W. Sharpe, K. Smith, P. Smith, R. Smith, D. Sorenson, B. Trueman, M. Tysseland, P. Vanderheiden, J. M. Wachowicz, D. Woods, J. Yeakel, D. Ziegenhein, and D. Zocco.

For providing us with detailed reviews for this edition, we owe special thanks to J. Ronald Hoffmeister, A. Joseph Lerro, S. K. Mansinghka, Michael J. Murray, S. Ghon Rhee, F. R. Searle, Frederick W. Siegel, and Douglas W. Woods.

The Anderson Graduate School of Management at UCLA and our colleagues provided us with intellectual support in bringing this edition to completion. Substantial contributions in the rewriting were made by Daniel Asquith, Duke Bristow, In Ho Lee, and

Kenneth Matheny. For assistance in developing and refining problems and solutions we thank Susan Hoag, Nelson Lim, and Victoria Tang. We owe special appreciation to Marilyn McElroy for her dedication and care in the many revisions of the manuscript and for taking charge of checking the galleys and page proofs.

We are also indebted to The Dryden Press staff — principally, Ann Heath, Millicent Treloar, Cate Rzasa, Michael Roche, and Alan Wendt. During the development and writing of the ninth edition, Dryden and its parent company were going through a very interesting finance case study. Our experience was that the Dryden staff, with a high level of professionalism, maintained their superb quality of creativity and support.

The field of finance will continue to experience significant changes. It is stimulating to participate in these exciting developments, and we hope that *Managerial Finance* will contribute to continued advances in the theory and practice of finance. We welcome comments and suggestions of any kind from our readers.

J. Fred Weston
Anderson Graduate School of Management
UCLA
Los Angeles, California 90024-1481
December 1991

Thomas E. Copeland
Partner
McKinsey & Company, Inc.
55 East 52nd Street
New York, New York 10022

Contents

PART EIGHT
Dynamic Strategies for Increasing Value *1077*

MANAGERIAL FINANCE

NINTH EDITION

Fundamental Concepts of Managerial Finance

Part One provides basic background material. The scope and nature of managerial finance are described in Chapter 1. Chapter 2 discusses the financial statements of the firm and how they relate to each other and to the complex financial reporting environment in which the firm operates. Chapter 3 presents the important concepts measuring growth and present value as the first steps toward the valuation of an enterprise.

The Nature of Finance

What is managerial finance? What is the finance function in the firm? What specific tasks are assigned to financial managers? What tools and techniques are available to them, and how can their performance be measured? On a broader scale, what is the role of finance in the U.S. economy, and how can managerial finance be used to further national goals? The principal purpose of this book is to provide suggested answers to these questions.

THE IMPORTANCE OF MANAGERIAL FINANCE

Managerial finance is an especially exciting subject as we approach the 21st century. The daily newspapers (not just the business press) as well as radio and television carry dramatic stories of the growth and decline of firms, corporate takeovers, and many types of corporate restructuring. To understand these developments and to participate in them effectively requires knowledge of the principles of finance. This book explains these principles and their applications in making decisions.

The importance of finance is underscored by dramatic developments taking place in the financial markets. For example, in September 1989 Campeau Corporation was unable to meet the interest payments due on portions of its debt. Campeau had acquired the Federated Department Stores and Allied Stores earlier in 1989 incurring $10 billion in debt. It sought additional loans to meet the interest payments due on existing loans and tried to sell off such major properties as Bloomingdale's department store chain to reduce debt principal. Campeau's failure to meet its interest payments shocked the entire high yield (''junk'') bond market. In January 1990, Campeau's real estate operations were separated from its retail department store operations, which filed for bankruptcy protection. The critical importance of many aspects of financial management is emphasized by the Campeau history. Examples of successful financial strategies will also be presented throughout the book.

The management and financing problems faced by all types of organizations are similar. Consider the Extrusion Plastics Company (EP) formed to manufacture a line of containers ranging from small holders of kitchen utensils to large heavy-duty plastic boxes used to carry parts in manufacturing operations. EP needs to obtain equipment to form the plastic from its basic ingredients. EP requires a building to house the equipment. It must buy raw materials. It needs workers and salesmen. As it manufactures the products it will have inventories of raw materials, work-in-process, and finished goods. It needs funds to obtain the use of the building and equipment, for raw materials, and for manufacturing operations. It will need to pay its employees. EP finds that it must wait before the sales it makes are actually paid for in cash; while it waits it has accounts receivable. The more it grows, the more funds it needs.

This real life example suggests the two basic financial statements useful for any firm — a balance sheet and income statement. We supply some illustrative numbers.

The Balance Sheet

Cash	$10		Accounts Payable	$ 10	
Accounts Receivable	20		Short-term Debt	20	
Inventories	30		Total Current Liabilities		$30
Total Current Assets		$ 60	Long-term Debt		$20
Property	$10				
Plant	10				
Equipment	20		Shareholders' Equity		50
Total Fixed Assets		$ 40	Total Claims on Assets		$100
Total Assets		$100			

The Income Statement

Sales	$200
Costs	190
Net Income	$ 10

From this brief example of the basic financing problems facing a representative operation, we can describe the major decision areas for the firm and the role of finance.

RESPONSIBILITIES OF FINANCIAL MANAGERS

Some key decision strategy areas of the firm include:

1. Choice of the products and markets of the firm.
2. Strategies for research, investment, production, marketing, and sales.
3. Selection, training, organization, and motivation of executives and other employees.
4. Obtaining funds at a low cost and efficiently.
5. Adjustments to the above as environments and competition change.

Financial managers are involved and must interact with these decisions. The areas that are regarded as primarily finance functions in the firm are:

1. Analysis of the financial aspects of all decisions.

2. How much investment will be required to generate the sales the firm hopes to achieve. These decisions affect the left-hand side of the balance sheet — the investment decisions.

3. How to obtain funds and provide for financing of the assets the firm requires to produce the products and services whose sales generate revenues. This area represents financing decisions or the capital structure decisions of the firm, affecting the right-hand side of the balance sheet.

4. Analysis of specific individual balance sheet accounts.

5. Analysis of individual income statement accounts: revenues and costs. In our highly condensed income statement for the EP Company, sales minus all costs equals net income. There are many kinds of costs — some involve large outlays in advance with costs assigned to operations in subsequent years. (These represent costs that are "fixed" in some sense.) Other costs such as the materials used in making products will rise or fall directly as the number of units produced is increased or decreased (direct or "variable" costs). A major responsibility of financial officers is to control costs in relation to value produced so the firm can price its products competitively and profitably.

6. Analysis of operating cash flows of all types. This aspect has received increasing emphasis in recent years and has given rise to a third major financial statement, the *statement of cash flows,* which can be derived from the balance sheets and income statements.

With the background of this compact case study of the Extrusion Plastics Company, we have a basis for defining the finance function in general terms.

THE FINANCE FUNCTION

While the specifics vary among organizations, the *key finance functions are the investment, financing, and dividend decisions of an organization.*[1] Funds are raised from external financial sources and allocated for different uses. The flow of funds within the enterprise is monitored. Benefits to financing sources take the form of returns, repayments, products, and services. These functions must be performed in business firms, government agencies, and nonprofit organizations alike. *The financial manager's goal is to plan for, obtain, and use funds to maximize the value of the organization.* Several activities are involved. First, in planning and forecasting, the financial manager interacts with the executives responsible for general strategic planning activities.

---

[1]"Dividend decisions" determine how the firm pays a return to all different types of investors for the use of their funds.

Second, the financial manager is concerned with investment and financing decisions and their interactions. A successful firm usually achieves a high rate of growth in sales, which requires the support of increased investments. Financial managers must determine a sound rate of sales growth and rank alternative investment opportunities. They help decide on the specific investments to be made and the alternative sources and forms of funds for financing these investments. Decision variables include internal versus external funds, debt versus owners' funds, and long-term versus short-term financing.

Third, the financial manager interacts with other functional managers to help the organization operate efficiently. All business decisions have financial implications. For example, marketing decisions affect sales growth and, consequently, change investment requirements; hence they must consider their effects on (and how they are affected by) the availability of funds, inventory policies, plant capacity utilization, and so on.

Fourth, the financial manager links the firm to the money and capital markets in which funds are raised and in which the firm's securities are traded.

In sum, the central responsibilities of the financial manager relate to decisions on investments and how they are financed. In the performance of these functions, the financial manager's responsibilities have a direct bearing on the key decisions affecting the value of the firm.

FINANCE IN THE ORGANIZATIONAL STRUCTURE OF THE FIRM

How is the firm organized to carry out the finance functions? The chief financial officer is high in the organization hierarchy of the firm because of the central role of finance in top-level decision making. Figure 1.1 depicts the typical organization structure for large firms in the United States. The board of directors represents the shareholders. The president is often the chief executive or operating officer. One of the key executives is the *senior vice president of finance* or chief financial officer (CFO), who is responsible for the formulation of major financial policies. The CFO interacts with senior officers in other functional areas, communicates the financial implications of major decisions, defines the duties of junior financial officers, and is held accountable for the analytical aspects of the treasurer's and controller's activities.

Specific finance functions are typically divided between two high-ranking financial officers — the treasurer and the controller. The *treasurer* handles the acquisition and custody of funds. The *controller's* function includes accounting, reporting, and control. The treasurer is typically responsible for cash acquisition and management. Although the controller has the main reporting responsibilities, the treasurer provides reports on the daily cash and working capital position of the firm, formulates cash budgets and generally reports on cash flows and cash conservation. As a part of this role, the treasurer maintains the firm's relationships with commercial banks and investment bankers. The treasurer is also usually responsible for credit management, insurance, and pension fund management.

The controller's core function is the recording and reporting of financial information. This typically includes the preparation of budgets and financial statements (except as noted above). Other duties include payroll, taxes, and internal auditing.

FIGURE 1.1   Finance in the Organization Structure of a Large Firm

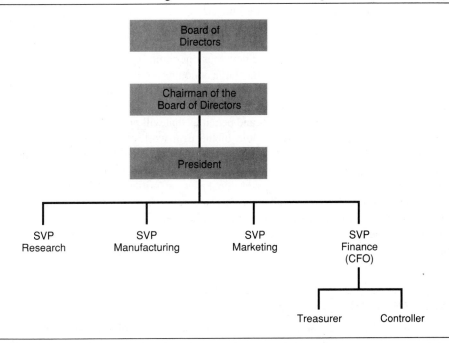

SVP is Senior Vice President.

Some large firms include a fourth corporate officer — the *corporate secretary* — whose activities are related to the finance function. The corporate secretary is responsible for communications relating to the company's financial instruments — record keeping in connection with the instruments of ownership and borrowing activities of the firm (e.g., stocks and bonds). The corporate secretary's duties may also encompass legal affairs and recording the minutes of top-level committee meetings.

Company history and the abilities of individual officers greatly influence the areas of responsibility of these four financial offices. A very able and active financial officer will be involved in all top management policies and decisions, often using the position as a training ground for movement into the top management positions of the company.

In addition to individual financial officers, larger enterprises use *finance committees*. Ideally, a committee assembles persons of different backgrounds and abilities to formulate policies and decisions. Financing decisions require a wide scope of knowledge and balanced judgments. For example, obtaining outside funds is a major decision. A difference of a quarter- or half-percent in interest rates may represent a large amount of money in absolute terms. When such firms as IBM, General Motors, or Kellogg borrow $600 million, a difference of one-half of one percent amounts to $3 million per year. Therefore, the judgments of senior managers with finance backgrounds are valuable in arriving at decisions with bankers on the timing and terms of a loan. Also, the finance committee, working closely with the board of directors, characteristically has major responsibility for administering the capital and operating budgets.

In larger firms, in addition to the general finance committee, there may be subcommittees. A *capital appropriations committee* is responsible primarily for capital budgeting and expenditures. A *budget committee* develops operating budgets, short-term and long-term. A *pension committee* invests the large amounts of funds involved in employee pension plans. A *salary and profit-sharing committee* is responsible for salary administration as well as the classification and compensation of top-level executives. This committee seeks to set up a system of rewards and penalties that will provide the proper incentives to make the planning and control system of the firm work effectively.

All important episodes in the life of a corporation have major financial implications: adding a new product line or reducing participation in an old one; expanding or adding a plant or changing locations; selling additional new securities; entering into leasing arrangements; paying dividends and making share repurchases. These decisions have a lasting effect on long-run profitability and, therefore, require top management consideration. Hence, the finance function is typically close to the top of the organizational structure of the firm.

THE NATURE OF THE FIRM

The "contractual theory" of the nature of the firm has now become widely held.[2] It views the firm as a network of contracts, actual and implicit, which specify the roles of the various participants or stakeholders (workers, managers, owners, lenders) and define their rights, obligations, and payoffs under various conditions. Most participants contract for fixed payoffs. The firm's owners hold residual claims on earnings. Although contracts define the rights and responsibilities of each class of stakeholders in a firm, potential conflicts occur since participants may have personal goals as well.

In the modern corporation, ownership is commonly widely diffused. The day-to-day operations of the firm are conducted by its managers, who usually do not have major stock ownership positions. In theory, the managers are the agents of the owners, but, in fact, they may exercise control over the firm. Thus, potential conflicts of interest may arise between the owners and managers. This is called the "agency problem," the divergence of interests between a principal and his agent.

Jensen and Meckling [1976] discussed many aspects of the agency problem. They described how the agency problem results whenever a manager owns less than the total common stock of the firm. This fractional ownership can lead the managers to work less strenuously and to acquire more perquisites (luxurious offices, furniture and rugs, company cars) than if they had to bear all of the costs.

To deal with agency problems, additional monitoring expenditures (agency costs) are required. Agency costs include (1) auditing systems to limit this kind of management

---

[2]A good summary statement with reference to the origins and development of the theory is found in Alchian [1982] and Alchian and Woodward [1988]. See also Fama and Jensen [1983a, 1983b].

behavior, (2) various kinds of bonding assurances by the managers that such abuses will not be practiced, and (3) changes in organization systems to limit the ability of managers to engage in the undesirable practices.

The board of directors, in theory, monitors managers on behalf of the shareholders. However, some argue that the wide dispersion of ownership of common stock of most large corporations makes it difficult for shareholders to exercise their control through the board of directors. The individual shareholder does not have a large enough stake to justify spending time and money to closely monitor managers and the board of directors. The argument is also made that managers pursue greater firm *size* rather than value maximization in the belief that management compensation is related to sales or total assets.

While there is some basis for this view of managerial control, others point to compensation plans for managers tied to profits and to stock options, which give managers incentives to increase the value of the firm's common stock. In addition, they note that shareholders do, in fact, exercise their ultimate power to replace management. This carrot and stick approach, they contend, is sufficient to keep the agency problem under control.

For large, publicly traded corporations, the stock market also serves as a performance monitor. While stock prices may react to the general economy (for example, changes in the interest rates) or industrywide factors (for example, the impact on the automobile industry of a change in steel prices), the dominant influence is the firm's expected future performance. Thus, if managers are not performing effectively relative to the potential of the assets under their control, a lower stock price will result.

Two additional mechanisms are said to keep managerialism in check. (*Managerialism* refers to self-serving behavior by managers.) One is the managerial labor market, which prices the human capital of managers. The market continuously reassesses the value of managerial human capital on the basis of potential or contracted performance versus actual performance.[3] If the assessment is unfavorable, competition among managers assures that a replacement will be made.

If managerial competition fails, the second control mechanism comes into action. This is the market for corporate takeovers. Poor management will cause the firm's stock price to decline, making the firm attractive to an acquirer who can increase value by improving performance.[4]

GOALS OF THE FIRM

Within the above framework, the *goal of financial management is to maximize the value of the firm,* subject to the constraints of responsibilities to stakeholders. However, there are potential conflicts between a firm's owners and its creditors. For example, consider a firm financed half from the owners' funds and half from debt funds borrowed at a fixed interest rate, such as 10 percent. No matter how high the firm's earnings, the bondholders

---

[3]For a discussion of the role of the managerial labor market, see Fama [1980].

[4]For a more complete discussion of the role of mergers and tender offers, see Chapter 27.

still receive only their 10 percent return. Yet if the firm is highly successful, the market value of the ownership funds (the common stock of the company) is likely to rise greatly.

If the company does very well, the value of its common stock will increase, while the value of the firm's debt is not likely to be greatly increased (but the equity cushion will be enhanced). On the other hand, if the firm does poorly, the claims of the debtholders will have to be honored first and the value of the common stock will decline greatly. Thus, the value of the ownership shares provides a good index for measuring the degree of a company's effectiveness in performance. It is for this reason that the goal of financial management is generally expressed in terms of maximizing the value of the ownership shares of the firm — in short, maximizing share price.

Outside of the United States, particularly in Europe and Japan, the goal of maximizing the share price is not the only goal stated. In Japan, a goal often stressed is capturing the largest market share (being number one in the market). But the purpose is to achieve long-run profitability. And in Europe, where labor sits on the board of directors, social welfare goals are weighed along with corporate goals. Nevertheless, the strongest corporations in the long run are those that generate the highest level of cash flows. The share price reflects these cash flows.

By formulating clear objectives in terms of stock price values, the discipline of the financial markets is implemented. Firms that perform better than others have higher stock prices and can raise additional funds (both debt and equity) under more favorable terms. When funds go to firms with favorable stock price trends, the economy's resources are directed to their most efficient uses. For this reason, the finance literature has generally adopted the basic objective of maximizing the price of the firm's common stock. The shareholder wealth maximization rule provides a basis for rational decision making with respect to a wide range of financial issues faced by the firm.

The goal of maximizing share price does not imply that managers should seek to increase the value of common stock at the expense of bondholders. For example, managers should not substantially alter the riskiness of the firm's product-market investment activities. Riskier investments, if successful, will benefit shareholders. But risky investments that fail will reduce the security to bondholders, causing bond values to fall and the cost of debt financing to rise. As a practical matter, a firm must provide strong assurances to bondholders that investment policies will not be changed to their disadvantage or it will have to pay interest rates high enough to compensate bondholders against the possibility of such adverse policy changes.

Social Responsibility

Another important aspect of the goals of the firm and of financial management is consideration of social responsibility. Maximization of share price requires well-managed operations. Successful firms are at the forefront of efficiency and innovation, so that value maximization leads to new products, technologies, and greater employment; hence, the more successful the firm, the better the quality and quantity of the total "pie" to be distributed.

But in recent years, "externalities" (such as pollution, product safety, and job safety) have increased in importance. Business firms must take into account the effects of their policies and actions on society as a whole. It has long been recognized that the external economic environment is important to a firm's decision making. Fluctuations in overall business activity and related changes in financial markets are also important aspects of the external environment. Also, firms must respond to the expectations of workers, consumers, other stakeholders and interest groups to achieve long-run wealth maximization [Cf. Cornell and Shapiro, 1987]. Indeed, responsiveness to these new and powerful constituencies may be required for the survival of the private enterprise system. This point of view argues that business firms must recognize a wider range of stakeholders and external influences. Throughout this book, we shall assume that managements operate in this manner.

Ethics

Related to social responsibility, the issue of ethics has come to the fore. One reason is dramatic episodes of violations of the securities laws in recent years. The common theme in the insider trading cases of the late 1980s was the illegal use of nonpublic information to obtain large personal gains. Ivan Boesky purchased information from investment bankers about forthcoming takeovers. While the Boesky case and others represent violations of the securities laws, more subtle issues of ethics are also involved. These are matters such as shading on quality, misrepresenting performance of products, misleading advertising (short of being deceptive), etc. The case for strong ethical behavior is based on social and personal reasons. The basic social reasons go back to historical religious teachings, which are consistent with philosophical treatises as well. The philosopher Emmanuel Kant set forth the Categorical Imperative, which states, "Act only on that maxim through which you can at the same time will that it should become a universal law."[5] The principle says that the test of the individual's behavior is to consider the impact of his action if everyone else in the world behaved the same way. This has been expressed in many religions and moral codes for centuries.

The behavior of top executives of a firm establishes the firm's reputation. If the behavior of the firm is not consistently ethical, other stakeholders — workers, consumers, suppliers, etc. — will begin to discount every action and decision of the firm. For example, bonds and common stock of a firm with an uncertain reputation will be viewed with suspicion by the market. The securities will have to be sold at lower prices, which means that the returns to investors will have to be higher to take into account that the issuing firm may be selling a "lemon" — trying to put something over on investors.

Thus, a strong case can be made that executives and the firm establish a reputation for unquestioned ethical behavior. The psychological health of an individual is better, the reputation of the firm is a valuable asset, and the social and economic environment is more conducive to efficient and equitable economic activity. Indeed, the upheavals in the governments of Eastern Europe in 1989–90 resulted from the perceptions that their rulers were self-serving at the expense of the general population.

---

[5]*Encyclopaedia Britannica, Macropaedia*, vol. 10, p. 393, 15th edition, Encyclopaedia Britannica, Inc. 1974, quoting Kant's *Critik der Practischen Vernungt*, 1788 *(Critique of Practical Reason)*.

VALUE MAXIMIZATION AS A GOAL

We have discussed some broad aspects of value maximization as a goal. Now we turn to a consideration of technical distinctions and implementation aspects of the role of financial management in value maximization.

Value maximization is broader than "profit maximization." Maximizing value takes the time value of money into account. First, funds that are received this year have more value than funds that may be received ten years from now. Second, value maximization considers the riskiness of the income stream. For example, the rate of return required on riskless government securities would be lower than the rate of return required on an investment in starting a new business. Third, the "quality" and timing of expected future cash flows may vary. Profit figures can vary widely depending upon the accounting rules and conventions used. But there is considerable evidence that financial markets see through differences in accounting procedures that affect "profit" and perceive underlying determinants of value.

Thus, value maximization is broader and more general than profit maximization and is the unifying conceptual idea used throughout the book. Value maximization is subject to the constraints of the legitimate claims of the different stakeholders. The perestroika (restructuring) taking place in the U.S.S.R. and Eastern Europe relates to the value maximization rule. Value maximization provides criteria for pricing the use of resources such as capital investments in plant and machinery. Without rules for pricing and allocating limited resources, allocations will be arbitrary and inefficient. The arbitrary allocation of resources is perceived as unfair. If limited resources are not allocated by efficiency criteria, production will be inefficient. Value maximization provides a solution to these kinds of problems. But value maximization must be constrained by the expectations of all categories of stakeholders or the social contracts that guide a stable social system will be lacking. Thus, the rules for the sound pricing and allocation of economic resources are essential to a stable social order and thus highly relevant to the profound political changes occurring throughout the world.

Performance Measurement by the Financial Markets

The basic finance functions must be performed in all types of organizations and in all types of economic systems. What is unique about business organizations in a market economy is that they are directly and measurably subject to the discipline of the financial markets. These markets continuously value business firms' securities, thereby providing measures of the firms' performance. A consequence of this continuous assessment of a firm by the capital markets is the change in its valuation level (stock market price). Thus, the capital markets stimulate efficiency and provide incentives to business managers to improve their performance.

The Risk-Return Trade-off

Financial decisions affect the level of a firm's stock price by influencing the cash flow stream and the riskiness of the firm. These relationships are diagrammed in Figure 1.2. Policy decisions, which are subject to government constraints, affect both profitability and risk; these two factors jointly determine the value of the firm.

FIGURE 1.2   Valuation as the Central Focus of the Finance Function

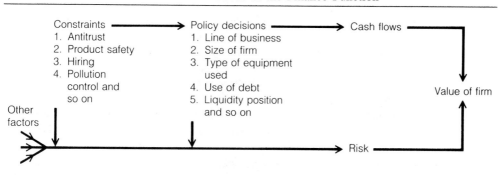

The primary policy decision is made in choosing the industry in which the firm operates. Profitability and risk are further influenced by decisions relating to the size of the firm, its growth rate, the types and amounts of equipment used, the extent to which debt is employed, the firm's liquidity position, and so on. An increase in the cash position reduces risk; however, since cash is not an earning asset, converting other assets to cash also reduces profitability. Similarly, the use of additional debt raises the rate of return, or profitability, on the stockholders' net worth; but more debt means more risk. The financial manager seeks to strike the balance between risk and profitability that will maximize stockholder wealth. Most financial decisions involve *risk-return trade-offs*.

THE CHANGING ROLE OF FINANCIAL MANAGEMENT

When finance first emerged as a separate field of study in the early 1900s, the emphasis was on legalistic matters relating to the various types of securities issued by corporations. Industrialization was sweeping the country, and the critical need was obtaining capital for expansion. Capital markets were relatively primitive, and mechanisms for transfers of funds from individual savers to businesses were not well-developed. Accounting statements of earnings and asset values were unreliable, and stock trading by insiders and manipulators caused prices to fluctuate wildly; consequently, investors were reluctant to purchase stocks and bonds. In this environment, it is easy to see why finance concentrated so heavily on legal issues relating to the issuance of securities.

The emphasis remained on securities through the 1920s; however, important changes occurred during the depression of the 1930s. Business failures during that period caused finance to focus on bankruptcy and reorganization, corporate liquidity, and government regulation of securities markets. Finance was still a descriptive, legalistic subject, but the emphasis shifted from expansion to survival.

During the 1940s and early 1950s, finance continued to be taught as a descriptive, institutional subject, viewed from the outside, rather than from within the firm's management. However, some effort was devoted to budgeting and other internal control procedures and, stimulated by the work of Joel Dean [1951], capital budgeting began to receive attention.

The evolutionary pace quickened during the late 1950s. While the right-hand side of the balance sheet (liabilities and capital) had received more attention in the earlier era, increasing emphasis was placed on asset analysis during the latter half of the decade. Mathematical models were applied to inventories, cash, accounts receivable, and fixed assets. Increasingly, the focus shifted from the outsider's to the insider's point of view, as financial decisions within the firm were recognized to be critical issues in corporate finance. Descriptive, institutional materials on capital markets and financing instruments were still studied, but within the context of corporate financial decisions to maximize firm value.

The emphasis on decision making has continued in recent decades. But fundamental developments in the economic and financial environments have had major impacts on financial management. First were the high inflation rates of the 1970s; second were the changing economic and financial environments of the 1980s. Each will be considered in turn.

The Impact of Inflation on Financial Management

The possibility of recurring inflation has become such a pervasive part of the economic environment that it must be viewed as an important, continuing influence on business financial decisions. During the 1950s and 1960s, prices rose at an average rate of about 1 to 2 percent per year, but in the 1970s, the inflation rate rose to more than 10 percent in some years. In the 1980s, although the U.S. inflation rate was reduced, continuing large government deficits raised concerns about the return of inflation. Thus, the fear of inflation, as much as inflation itself, exerts a strong influence on financial policies. Some major impacts of inflation are briefly sketched here.

Accounting Problems. With high rates of inflation, reported profits are distorted. The sale of low-cost inventories results in higher reported profits, but net cash flows are reduced as firms restock with higher-cost inventories. Similarly, depreciation charges are inaccurate, since they do not reflect the new (higher) costs of replacing plant and equipment. Higher reported profits caused by inadequate inventory valuation and depreciation charges result in higher income taxes and lower cash flows. If a firm plans dividends and capital expenditures based on "paper" profits, it may develop serious financial problems.

Planning Difficulties. Businesses operate on the basis of long-run plans. For example, a firm builds a plant only after making a thorough analysis of expected costs and revenues over the life of the plant. Reaching such estimates is not easy because revenue estimates are subject to the state of the economy and competition, while cost estimates are based on only limited historical experience. During rapid inflation, when revenues and input costs are changing unevenly, accurate forecasts are especially important, yet exceedingly difficult to make.

Demand for Capital.   Inflation increases the amount of capital required to conduct a given volume of business. When inventories are sold, they must be replaced with more expensive goods. The costs of expanding or replacing plants are also greater, and workers demand higher wages. While financial managers are pressured to raise additional capital, the monetary authorities may restrict the supply of loanable funds in an effort to hold down the rate of inflation. The ensuing scramble for limited funds drives interest rates higher still.

Interest Rates.   The rate of interest that any security would yield if there were zero inflation is called the *real rate of interest*. The interest rates that are actually observed in the marketplace are called *nominal rates of interest,* which represent the real rate plus an ''inflation premium.'' The inflation premium reflects the expected future rates of inflation. Accordingly, an increase in the expected rate of inflation is translated into higher interest rates. So higher rates of inflation mean that the cost of obtaining funds by governments, business, and individuals will be increased.

Bond Price Declines.   The prices of outstanding long-term bonds fall as interest rates rise. In the effort to protect themselves against such capital losses, lenders may require that debt instruments carry interest rates that vary with some broader index of interest rate movements. Brazil and other inflation-plagued South American countries have used such indexed bonds for years.

   Inflation is a disturbing and challenging possibility for financial managers. If it returns, financial policies and practices will undergo still further modifications.

The Changing Economic and Financial Environments

Major changes in the economic, political, and financial environments began to explode in the 1980s. These in turn had major impacts on the practice of finance.

International Competition.   While the trends have been under way for decades, full recognition of the international economy took place in the 1980s. In every major industry — autos, steel, pharmaceuticals, oil, computers, other electronics products, for example — the reality of global markets had to be taken into account. In addition to competition from Western European and Japanese companies, even developing countries began to offer challenging competition in manufactured products. The pressures on prices and profit margins presented continued challenges. Investments had to be made wisely; the importance of capital budgeting increased. Profit margins were under pressure so that efficiency had to increase. Some argue that this is a major reason for the increased takeover and restructuring activity of the 1980s. Although foreign firms appear to have higher debt ratios when measured at book values, it is not clear that foreign companies are using more debt when market value ratios are compared.

International Finance.   The improvements in transportation and communications that have resulted in global markets in goods and services have also created a world of international finance. Money and capital flow across national boundaries. Financial transactions in the United States are influenced by international financial markets. When the U.S. stock market crashed on October 19, 1987, similar declines were taking place in the financial markets of most of the other countries of the world as well. The rise in interest rates in Japan and Germany during the first quarter of 1990 put increased pressure on interest rates and bond prices in the United States.

Fluctuating Exchange Rates. In the early 1970s, the major developed countries of the world shifted from a regime of exchange rates fixed by national policy to one in which exchange rates fluctuated in response to the demand and supply of individual currencies. Consider the fluctuations in the number of Japanese yen per U.S. dollar.

	Year End						Summer
	1965	**1970**	**1975**	**1980**	**6/24/84**	**3/27/85**	**1989**
Number of yen per dollar	360.9	357.6	305.15	215.45	235.25	255.40	120.0

The Japanese yen has fluctuated from over 360 to the U.S dollar in 1965 to as low as 120 to the dollar during the summer of 1989. Suppose a Japanese auto producer needs to sell an X-car to dealers at a price of 1.5 million yen to cover all costs plus a required return on equity. The dollar price of the Japanese X-car to provide the required 1.5 million yen varies with the yen-to-dollar exchange rate as follows:

Exchange rate (yen/$)	300	200	100
Required auto price in $	5,000	7,500	15,000

Suppose it costs a U.S. company $10,000 to produce a comparable X-car. Only when the yen has increased in value toward a level of 100 yen per dollar are the costs of the U.S. producer below the price at which the Japanese can sell the X-car. As the exchange rate of yen to the dollar rises, the Japanese producer can cut prices in U.S. dollars to levels at which the U.S. firm can no longer sell and still cover its costs. Alternatively, at U.S. prices that cover U.S. company costs, the Japanese company can elect to match the prices that produce favorable profit margins on its U.S. sales.

The long-run competitiveness of companies in different countries depends primarily on their relative efficiency and costs. But it is clear that fluctuating exchange rates also have an important impact.

Mergers, Takeovers, and Restructuring. The increased international competition has been one of the major factors causing U.S. companies to rethink their strategies to become competitive. Mergers, takeovers, and restructuring represent in part a response to pressures to increase efficiency to meet the new international competition.

Financial Innovations and Financial Engineering. Many financial innovations have taken place in recent years. These have been referred to as financial engineering, representing the creation of new forms of financial products.[6] They include debt instruments

---

[6]See the special issue of *Financial Management,* Winter 1988, on *Financial Engineering;* see also C. W. Smith and C. W. Smithson, *The Handbook of Financial Engineering* (New York: Harper Business, 1990).

with fluctuating (floating) interest rates, various forms of rights to convert debt into equity (or vice versa), the use of higher levels of leverage and lower grade (''junk'') bonds, the use of debt denominated for payment in variously designated foreign currencies, and the development of pools of funds available for investment in new firms or to take over existing firms. These and other innovations will be covered in the chapters that follow.

The Increased Availability of Computers. Increasingly, personal computers make available computational powers, which in earlier decades could be obtained only from relatively large-scale systems. Thus, the ability to develop complex models and spreadsheet analysis has become widely available. It remains important, however, to have a clear understanding of the underlying principles involved. Otherwise, increased complexity will result in less clear understanding and lead to error rather than improved analysis.

In review, the environments of firms have changed dynamically in recent decades. This has affected all aspects of strategic planning in all types of organizations. Since financial markets are especially sensitive and responsive to turbulence in the economic environments, financial decision making has become increasingly challenging. The following chapters seek to assist financial managers in meeting these new challenges and responsibilities.

ORGANIZATION OF THIS BOOK

The aim of this book is to explain the procedures, practices, and policies by which financial management can contribute to the successful performance of organizations. Our emphasis is on strategies involved in the trade-offs between risk and return in seeking to make decisions that will maximize the value of the firm. Each subsequent topic is treated within this basic framework.

The eight major parts of the book are as follows:

- Part One: Fundamental Concepts of Managerial Finance
- Part Two: The Environment for Financial Decisions
- Part Three: Basic Financial Planning and Investment
- Part Four: Decision Making Under Uncertainty
- Part Five: Risk and Valuation
- Part Six: Financial Strategies for Working Capital Management
- Part Seven: The Treasurer's Long-Range Financial Strategies
- Part Eight: Dynamic Strategies for Increasing Value

Part One includes basic background on financial statements and the nature of the finance function and introduces fundamental concepts related to valuation, the basic theme of this book. Part Two discusses financial markets (both domestic and international), organizational forms, and taxation. Part Three covers financial analysis within the context of value maximization and capital budgeting under certainty. In Part Four, we introduce uncertainty: the relationships between risk and return and the models used to quantify them, the effect of risk on discount rates, and the use of options and financial futures to manage risk. Part Five continues the analysis in a world of risk, with capital budgeting under uncertainty, capital structure issues, the cost of capital, dividend policy, and value-based management. Part Six focuses on the strategies available to financial managers for working capital management. Financial planning and control provide a framework for cash, receivables, and inventory management. With the analytic framework established, Part Seven takes a longer view of the decisions facing a corporate treasurer in arranging the long-term financing of the firm: the capital market environments within which financing takes place, the long-term financing instruments available (including recent innovations), leasing, warrants and convertibles, and pension fund management. Finally, Part Eight presents dynamic strategies for increasing a firm's value via mergers, takeovers, and restructuring, and managing financial distress.

SUMMARY

Managerial finance involves the investment, financing, and dividend decisions of the firm. The main functions of financial managers are to plan for, acquire, and use funds to make the maximum contribution to the efficient operation of an organization. This requires familiarity with the financial markets from which funds are drawn as well as with the product/markets in which the organization operates. All financial decisions involve alternative choices between internal versus external funds, long-term versus short-term projects, long-term versus short-term financing, a higher growth rate versus a lower rate of growth. The basic financial statements, which encapsulate the effects of operating and financial decisions, are also explained.

We have set forth the view of the firm as a network of contracts among various stakeholders. The generally accepted goal of the firm is value maximization, which leads to the most efficient use of resources. We discussed potential conflicts between owners and managers, as well as between owners and creditors, and how they might be resolved.

For practical implementation in making financial decisions, stock price maximization is used as a proxy for value maximization. Decisions relating to value maximization involve a trade-off between prospective risks and returns, and must be made within the framework of socially responsible behavior as well as in relation to dynamic external environments, both domestic and international.

The criteria and rules that guide the acquisition and use of resources in a market system perform an important social role. Without decision rules developed from the value maximization principle, the allocation and use of a society's limited resources will be arbitrary and inefficient. This book on managerial finance seeks to implement, at the level of the firm, sound rules and strategies for a socially desirable allocation and use of resources — people, materials, and capital goods.

QUESTIONS

1.1 What are the main functions of financial managers?

1.2 Why is shareholder wealth maximization a better operating goal than profit maximization?

1.3 What is the difference between firm value maximization and shareholder wealth maximization?

1.4   What are the issues in the conflict of interest between stockholders and managers and how can they be resolved?

1.5   What are the potential conflicts of interest between shareholders and bondholders and how can they be resolved?

1.6   What role does social responsibility have in formulating business and financial goals?

1.7   What have been the major developmental periods in the field of finance? What circumstances led to the evolution of the emphasis in each period?

1.8   What is the nature of the risk-return trade-off faced in financial decision making?

1.9   What are some of the effects of high inflation (or the threat of high inflation) on financial decisions?

1.10 What opportunities and threats are created for financial managers by increased international competition?

SELECTED REFERENCES

Alchian, A. A., "Property Rights, Specialization and the Firm," J. Fred Weston and Michael E. Granfield, eds., *Corporate Enterprise in a New Environment*, New York: KCG Productions, Inc., 1982, pp. 11–36.

———, and Woodward, S., "The Firm is Dead; Long Live the Firm: A Review of Oliver E. Williamson's *The Economic Institutions of Capitalism*," *Journal of Economic Literature* (March 1988), pp. 65–79.

Cornell, Bradford, and Shapiro, Alan, "Corporate Stakeholders and Corporate Finance," *Financial Management* (Spring 1987), pp. 5–14.

Dean, Joel, *Capital Budgeting*, New York: Columbia University Press, 1951.

Diamond, Douglas W., and Verrecchia, Robert E., "Optimal Managerial Contracts and Equilibrium Security Prices," *Journal of Finance*, 37 (May 1982), pp. 275–287.

Eaton, Jonathan, and Rosen, Harvey S., "Agency, Delayed Compensation, and the Structure of Executive Remuneration," *Journal of Finance*, 38 (December 1983), pp. 1489–1505.

Fama, Eugene F., "Agency Problems and the Theory of the Firm," *Journal of Political Economy*, 88 (April 1980), pp. 288–307.

———, and Jensen, Michael C., "Separation of Ownership and Control," *The Journal of Law and Economics*, 26 (June 1983a), pp. 301–325.

———, "Agency Problems and Residual Claims," *The Journal of Law and Economics*, 26 (June 1983b), pp. 327–349.

Findlay, Chapman M., and Whitmore, G. A., "Beyond Shareholder Wealth Maximization," *Financial Management*, 3 (Winter 1974), pp. 25–35.

Grossman, S. J., and Stiglitz, J. E., "On Value Maximization and Alternative Objectives of the Firm," *Journal of Finance*, 32 (May 1977), pp. 389–415.

Hakansson, Nils H., "The Fantastic World of Finance: Progress and the Free Lunch," *Journal of Financial and Quantitative Analysis*, 14 (November 1979), pp. 717–734.

Jensen, M. C., and Meckling, W. H., "Theory of the Firm: Managerial Behavior, Agency Costs, and Ownership Structure," *Journal of Financial Economics*, 3 (October 1976), pp. 350–360.

Jensen, M. C., and Ruback, R. S., eds., Symposium on The Structure and Governance of Enterprise, Part I, *Journal of Financial Economics*, 27, 1 (September 1990).

———, eds., Symposium on The Structure and Governance of Enterprise, Part II, *Journal of Financial Economics*, 27, 2 (October 1990).

Lewellen, Wilbur G., "Management and Ownership in the Large Firm," *Journal of Finance*, 24 (May 1969), pp. 299–322.

Seitz, Neil, "Shareholder Goals, Firm Goals and

Firm Financing Decisions," *Financial Management,* 11 (Autumn 1982), pp. 20–26.

Treynor, Jack L., "The Financial Objective in the Widely Held Corporation," *Financial Analysts Journal,* 37 (March/April 1981), pp. 68–71.

Wacht, Richard F., "A Financial Management Theory of the Nonprofit Organization," *Journal of Financial Research,* 7 (Spring 1984), pp. 37–45.

Weston, J. Fred, "Developments in Finance Theory," *Financial Management,* 10 (June 1981), pp. 5–22.

———, "New Themes in Finance," *Journal of Finance,* 24 (March 1974), pp. 237–243.

———, *The Scope and Methodology of Finance,* Englewood Cliffs, N.J.: Prentice-Hall, 1966.

CHAPTER 2

Financial Statements and Cash Flows

Financial statements report the historical performance of a firm and provide a basis, along with business and economic analysis, for making projections and forecasts for the future. The annual report is a document that informs shareholders and is audited in accordance with generally accepted accounting principles. The 10K and 8K are documents provided, under very specific guidelines, to the Securities and Exchange Commission. Tax statements are supplied by the firm to the Internal Revenue Service, to state and local tax authorities (for income and property tax purposes), and to foreign governments (when the firm is multinational).

ROLE OF FINANCIAL STATEMENTS

Chapter 2 describes the key financial statements that record an organization's activity. We have a number of objectives: (1) to provide a language for all that follows, (2) to demonstrate the logic of the interrelationships between financial statements, (3) to introduce some first principles of finance, and (4) to establish the importance of future cash flows as the foundation for measuring the present and future values of an organization.

In some sense, any organization — business firm, government unit, art museum, charitable organization, etc. — is like a competitive game, such as baseball, basketball, or football. It is a team activity. There are rules of the game. We keep score to evaluate performance. Incentives in the form of team spirit and payments stimulate and improve performance.

Financial statements represent the scorecards for recording and evaluating an organization's performance. Financial statements are therefore essential to the efficient management of an organization. They also provide the basis for compensation to the participants or stakeholders. For the owners of the firm, an important part of their compensation is increases in the value of the enterprise. Valuation is the central organizing principle of this book. The goal of maximizing the value of the firm is like scoring the most points in a competitive game. This chapter focuses on explaining the scorecards for business operations.

The financial statements of business are based on accounting rules or conventions. To achieve consistency and comparability, the use of subjective judgments is minimized. But the valuation of an enterprise is based on projections or forecasts of its future performance. This involves the exercise of subjective judgments. Thus accounting statements do not record economic values. Instead, they provide the basic quantitative historical information representing an important set of inputs used in calculating economic values.

A complete description of a firm's financial accounting activities during a year consists of three basic financial statements.

1. A beginning-of-year balance sheet gives a snapshot of the firm at the start of its fiscal year; plus an end-of-year balance sheet provides a snapshot of the ending assets and liabilities.

2. An income statement shows the flows of revenues and costs or expenses during the interval between the beginning- and end-of-period balance sheets.

3. A statement of cash flows lists the sources of the changes in cash and cash equivalents during the same time interval as the income statement.

From the three financial statements and their accompanying footnotes other derivative financial statements such as the reconciliation of the net income from the income statement to the net cash provided by operating activities from the statement of cash flows can be developed.

THE BALANCE SHEET

Table 2.1 presents illustrative balance sheets for company E. The balance sheet for 12/31/X1 represents the end-of-year statement for year X1 and by convention is regarded as the beginning year statement for year X2. Thus we have both beginning- and end-of-year balance sheets. Each provides a snapshot of the firm's financial position at a point in time.

By U.S. accounting rules the balance sheet is set up with assets on the left-hand side. On the right-hand side the sources of financing those assets by either debt or equity funds are listed. By accounting definitions the balance sheet is in "balance" because of the following identity:

$$\text{Assets} \equiv \text{Liabilities} + \text{Equity}$$

By accounting conventions these relationships are based on historical costs. Thus equity is the difference between the recorded costs of assets less the contractual amounts of liabilities. These recorded "book values" are not necessarily the same as market values as we shall explain more fully below.

TABLE 2.1   Company E: Statements of Financial Position

Assets	12/31/X1	12/31/X2	Change
Cash	$ 400	$ 500	$ 100
Marketable securities	100	500	400
Accounts receivable, net	1,500	1,200	(300)
Inventories	1,500	1,800	300
Current assets	3,500	4,000	
Gross plant and equipment	9,000	10,000	1,000
Accumulated depreciation	3,500	4,000	(500)
Net plant and equipment	5,500	6,000	500
Total Assets	$9,000	$10,000	$1,000
Claims on Assets			
Accounts payable	$ 600	$ 1,000	$ 400
Notes payable @ 10%	200	200	0
Accrued wages	200	400	200
Other accruals	100	400	300
Current liabilities	1,100	2,000	900
Deferred taxes	900	1,000	100
Long-term debt @ 10%	2,400	2,000	(400)
Preferred stock	0	0	0
Stockholders' equity			
Common stock (Par = $.10)	1,000	1,000	0
Paid-in capital	1,000	1,000	0
Retained earnings	2,600	3,000	400
Less: Treasury stock	0	0	0
Total stockholders' equity	4,600	5,000	400
Total Liabilities and Equity	$9,000	$10,000	$1,000

The ordering of the list of assets on the left-hand side of the balance sheet is based on liquidity — the length of time required for an ongoing firm to receive cash as it goes through its operating cycles. Cash (realistically, demand deposits at financial institutions) is held primarily to conduct the transactions of the firm. Near cash is held in the form of marketable securities, which can be converted into cash with relatively small risk of a decline in their stated values. Accounts receivable represent the sales made to customers for which the firm has not yet received actual cash payment. Inventories may be in the form of raw materials that will be used in production operations, work-in-process and finished goods.

Note that the long-term assets account (in Table 2.1) is divided into three components. Gross property, plant, and equipment represents the original purchase price of long-term assets. Each year, an estimate of the depreciation of each asset is made and then added to all prior depreciation. The result, accumulated depreciation, is then deducted from gross property, plant, and equipment to arrive at net property, plant, and equipment. Annual depreciation appears as an expense on the income statement (see Table 2.2). Net property, plant, and equipment represents the current depreciated book value of tangible assets. If an asset is sold, its original book value is removed from gross property, plant, and equipment, and its accumulated depreciation is subtracted from that account; if its sale value is above (below) its net book value, then a capital gain (loss) is recorded on the income statement.

Turning to the liabilities side of the balance sheets shown in Table 2.1, we begin with short-term liabilities. Accounts payable represent the amounts owed for purchases from suppliers of goods and services. They represent purchases not yet paid for and are usually referred to as trade credit. Accounts payable do not carry an explicit interest charge, but some argue that an implicit interest charge may be included in the prices paid for purchases.

Notes payable represent short-term debt that carries an explicit interest charge. They usually represent borrowing from commercial banks. The next two items represent accruals that arise because the date at which the balance sheet is drawn up does not coincide with the payment day for obligations that have been incurred. For example, wage earners may be paid at the end of the week, whereas the end of the month or end of the year when the balance sheet is drawn up is not at the end of the week. Other accruals include taxes estimated to be due at some time in the near future. Or the firm may have declared a dividend on its common stock that will be paid some days hence. Current liabilities represent the sum of the short-term liabilities described.

Deferred taxes represent the difference between the measure of the total amount of tax obligations incurred by the firm during the accounting period and the amount of taxes actually paid. The sources of these differences are explained by firms in footnotes to the financial statements in their annual reports. We shall discuss how deferred taxes arise in Chapter 5. Long-term debt represents obligations that will not have to be paid during the forthcoming year. The kinds of long-term debt financing are treated in detail in Chapters 21, 22, and 23.

Preferred stock is a hybrid security having some of the characteristics of both debt and equity. Payments to owners of preferred stock are called preferred dividends. Being of fixed size, they are contractual just like interest payments on debt. However, if cash flow is insufficient to cover preferred dividends, the firm cannot be forced into bankruptcy or reorganization. Instead, the preferred dividends are deferred. Cumulative preferred dividends must be paid before any dividends can be declared to shareholders. Thus, we see that preferred stock is riskier than debt but less risky than equity.

The equity portion of Table 2.1 is subdivided into four items. When new shares are sold, the value per share received by the firm is broken down into common at par and common in excess of par. For example, if the firm receives $20 per share for $1 par value, then $19 per share issued is added to paid-in capital and the remainder is added to common at par. Par value is an anachronistic concept. Many firms have stock with no par value. It used to be that if an investor purchased a share for less than its par value, then in the event of bankruptcy, the investor could be made personally liable for the difference between the purchase price and the par value of the share. The third item in the equity section is retained earnings, which represents the chronological sum of the retained earnings taken each year from the income statement. For a firm founded in 1920, for example, the retained earnings figure will be the accumulation of all earnings retained since 1920.

The final equity item is Treasury stock. It is subtracted from the other equity items because it represents the cost of repurchasing common stock (either via tender offer or open market purchases). The purchase of Treasury stock has the effect of reducing the number of shares outstanding without changing the firm's expected earnings stream. Consequently, earnings per share (and the price per share of the remaining shares) go up following a repurchase of Treasury stock. Share repurchase is intimately related to dividend policy, as shown by the following example. Suppose your firm has $3,000,000 in earnings and that $1,000,000 will be spent either to repurchase shares or paid out as a cash dividend. If dividends are paid, $2,000,000 in retained earnings will be added to the stockholders' equity section of claims on assets. Shareholders will receive $1,000,000 before taxes but must pay personal income taxes on the dividends received. Alternately, if we assume that there is a pro rata (that is, an equal percentage) repurchase of shares from each shareholder, then $3,000,000 is added to retained earnings and $1,000,000 to Treasury stock, which is subtracted from the equity portion of the balance sheet. The net effect on shareholders' equity is the addition of $2,000,000. Thus, cash dividends and share repurchase have the same effect on the book value of shareholders' equity. When the tax code provides for a lower tax rate on capital gains than on dividends received, there is a tax advantage from share repurchases. However, there are other reasons for share repurchases, which we shall discuss in later chapters.

The difference between short-term assets and short-term liabilities is called the *net working capital* of the firm. As long as there are more short-term assets than liabilities, the firm is said to be in a relatively liquid position in the sense that it can pay off all of its short-term obligations without having to liquidate any long-term assets. Part Six of this text discusses the major issues of working capital management. For example, what ratio of short-term assets to short-term liabilities is optimal? What constitutes the optimal management of cash balances, marketable securities, and inventories? And what is the best way to manage accounts receivable and accounts payable?

The choice among sources of financing is one of the most important financial decisions of the firm. The ratio of debt to equity establishes the firm's *capital structure,* and as mentioned earlier, it determines the amount of financial leverage. The firm's cost of financing is called the *weighted average cost of capital* and is a weighted average of the marginal after-tax costs of its sources of capital — its debt and equity. Capital structure and the cost of capital are discussed in Chapter 15. From an investor's point of view, debt is less risky than equity because interest payments are a contractual obligation and because, in the event of bankruptcy, debtholders have prior claim to the firm's assets. Equity payments, that is, the dividend stream, are residual claims on the firm's cash flows. Hence, they are riskier than debt. One can conclude, therefore, that debt capital will require a lower nominal rate of return than equity because it is less risky.

THE INCOME STATEMENT

The income statement measures the *flows* of revenues and expenses during an interval of time, usually one year. The basic income statement equation is:

$$\text{Revenues} - \text{Expenses} \equiv \text{Income}$$

TABLE 2.2   Company E: Statement of Income For the
Year Ended December 31, 19X2

---

1. Revenues (R)	$12,000
2. Cost of sales (CS) (excl. dep.)	6,800
a. Gross income (M)	5,200
3. Marketing expense	3,000
4. General and administrative expense (G&A)	600
b. Earnings before depreciation, interest, and taxes (EBDIT)	1,600
5. Depreciation (Dep.)	500
c. Net operating income (NOI)	1,100
6. Other income, net	120
d. Earnings before interest and taxes (EBIT)	1,220
7. Interest expense (f)	220
e. Earnings before taxes (EBT)	1,000
8. Income taxes @ 40% (T)	400*
f. Net income (NI)	$ 600

---

*Deferred taxes $100

Memo:
Dividends paid (Div.)	$	200
To Retained earnings on the balance sheet	$	400

An illustrative income statement is presented in Table 2.2. In this summarized form of an income statement we set forth eight items of revenue and expense and show six measures or levels of income measurement. The nature of each item will be briefly described.

The income statement begins with the revenues of the firm, (R). The degree of variability in the revenue stream is determined by the nature of the firm's products. For example, consumer products such as food, tobacco, and electricity have relatively low sensitivity to changes in national income, in contrast to products like machinery or steel, which have relatively high sensitivity. For example, if the gross national product (GNP) of the economy rises or falls by 10 percent, the sales of a nondurable consumer good such as food are likely to fluctuate by only 8 or 9 percent since people have to eat even when their income is reduced. In contrast, a 10 percent change in GNP is likely to affect the sales of the steel industry by as much as 20 percent because the durable goods that use steel in their production have relatively long lives and their purchases can be postponed.

Some of the variability in revenues can be reduced by diversification across product lines. Unrelated products are the best candidates for diversification but involve a different kind of problem — does management have sufficient knowledge and experience with the unrelated product activities to manage them effectively?

The cost of sales for a manufacturing operation will generally include the costs of raw materials and parts, labor costs, and manufacturing overhead or fixed cash costs such as the salaries of plant managers and supervisors as well as property taxes on the property and fixed assets. In theory, noncash fixed costs whose major component is usually depreciation on plant and equipment should be included in the cost of sales. However, depreciation is conventionally shown as a separate line in order to facilitate the analysis of cash versus noncash expenses.

The important role of depreciation deserves an explanation. For example, suppose that a firm bought some equipment with a life of five years for $100,000. This investment represents a cash outlay in the year in which the equipment is paid for. The $100,000 is not an expense for that year. The $100,000 cash outlay is distributed as a $20,000 depreciation expense item over each of the five years of the life of the equipment. If the equipment were purchased on the first day of a company's fiscal year, the $100,000 would represent a cash outlay for the year, but the depreciation expense for the year would only be $20,000. During the subsequent four years, there would be no cash outlays but a depreciation expense charged to the income statement of $20,000 for each year. We distinguish between cash costs and noncash costs because the market value of a firm is determined by future cash flows. Depreciation is not a cash flow. Rather, it is an estimate of the decline in the value of physical capital used in production (due to wear and tear or obsolescence).

We have noted a distinction between fixed costs and variable costs, such as materials and wages, whose amount is directly tied to the level of operations. The ratio of fixed costs to variable costs in operations determines the extent to which the gross margin (Item 2a in Table 2.2) is more variable than revenues. The ratio of fixed costs to variable costs is determined in part by the nature of products being produced and in part by the choice of technology employed. For example, a hydroelectric dam could be built by 100,000 men with picks, shovels, and buckets, or by 100 men with bulldozers, cranes, and cement mixers. Economic theory tells us that the choice of technology will be determined by the relative costs of the major inputs, namely capital and labor related to the volume of operations of the firm. The combination of the variability of revenues *(revenue risk),* and the ratio of fixed to variable production costs, determines the degree of *gross margin risk.*

All other costs are deducted from gross income to obtain net operating income. The other costs include marketing expense and general and administrative expenses. When these are deducted from gross income, Line 2a, we obtain earnings before depreciation, interest, and taxes (EBDIT), shown in Line 4b.

As shown in Table 2.2, when depreciation is deducted from EBDIT we obtain net operating income (NOI). The expenses deducted to obtain net operating income include cash and noncash expenses as well as fixed and variable expenses or costs. Considering the ratio of fixed to variable costs or fixed to total costs at this point determines the degree of *operating leverage* employed by the firm, which is discussed in detail in Chapter 8. The combination of revenue risk and operating leverage is called the firm's *business risk,* a measure of the variability of the firm's NOI stream. Managers can modify a firm's business risk through their choice of product-market lines (revenue risk) and by their choice of production technology (operating leverage).

Line 6 in the statement of income is other income on a net basis. It can include income earned on marketable securities and royalties received. Royalties paid would be netted out, but interest expense is shown as a separate item, Line 7 in this illustrative statement of income. This brings us to Line 6d, earnings before interest and taxes (EBIT).

In many discussions NOI and EBIT are used interchangeably. Technically, however, NOI differs from EBIT by the amount of "other income, net." For many major issues of corporate financial theory, the distinction has usually been ignored. Quantitatively the amount of "other income, net" is not usually very large.

We next consider Line 7, interest expense (f). If the amount of funds a firm has borrowed is $1 million, and if the firm has contracted to pay an annual fixed rate of 10 percent per year, it would have an annual fixed interest charge of $100,000. Just as fixed operating costs increase the riskiness of net operating income, fixed interest payments have the effect of increasing the riskiness of the net income stream to shareholders. As the use of debt financing increases along with a greater amount of annual fixed interest charges, the firm is said to have greater financial leverage.[1] The explanation of why financial leverage affects the riskiness of net income is similar to that used for operating leverage. Financial leverage is a major responsibility of the firm's chief financial officer and a major issue in corporation finance.

After subtracting interest expenses from EBIT, we obtain earnings before taxes or taxable income. The amount of income taxes shown in the statement of income generally includes both deferred taxes and taxes actually paid in the current year. Thus from the standpoint of a cash flow analysis, deferred taxes do not represent a cash outflow in the current year. In Table 2.2, we indicate that of the $400 shown as income taxes, only $300 were actually paid and $100 were deferred taxes. (Taxes are discussed more fully in Chapter 5.)

The so-called "bottom line" in the statement of income is net income. It represents the residual stream of earnings owned by shareholders. We have explained why the riskiness of the net income figure is affected by both the business risk and the financial risk of the firm. We have emphasized risk in this early part of the book to establish that management decisions about which lines of business to be in, how much operating leverage to have, and the amount of financial leverage, all affect not only the expected returns to shareholders but also the riskiness of those returns. Thus, the firm can be viewed as a portfolio of asset and liability positions chosen by its management. The risk-return trade-off and how to manage it is a central theme of managing value.

It is the responsibility of the board of directors of the company to determine, on behalf of shareholders, what portion of net income should be paid out to shareholders in the form of dividends. Historically, the percentage of net income paid out as dividends by all corporations as a group has approximated 50 percent in the United States. But dividend policies vary among industries, among firms, and across countries. The portion of net income not paid out as dividends is called retained earnings. The annual amount of retained earnings is added to the retained earnings figure on the balance sheet. Thus the retained earnings line on the balance sheet represents the cumulative retained earnings from income from the firm's inception.

The dividend decision is treated in Chapter 16 where the central issue is whether the market value of the firm's common stock is affected by the firm's dividend policy. Note that financial leverage decisions and dividend policy decisions are related. If a firm de-

---

[1]Outside of the United States, financial leverage is usually called "gearing."

cides to pay out a relatively large fraction of its earnings in the form of dividends, it has less retained earnings to reinvest, raising the probability that it will require more external funds. This then poses the question of the extent to which the external funds will be raised from debt versus equity sources.

ANALYSIS OF CASH FLOWS

The balance sheet represents the financial picture of the firm at a point in time setting forth assets, liabilities, and shareholders' equity. The income statement portrays revenues, costs, and income over a period of time. Neither statement as such presents a picture of the cash flows of the firm.

In November 1987 the Financial Accounting Standards Board of the Financial Accounting Foundation issued its *Statement of Financial Accounting Standards No. 95, Statement of Cash Flows* (FASB 95). Its provisions were to be effective for annual financial statements for fiscal years ending after July 15, 1988, with earlier application encouraged. The illustrative statements provided in FASB 95 are quite complex. Furthermore they do not permit an easy reconciliation of the statement of cash flows with the balance sheets and the income statement from which the statement of cash flows is developed. We, therefore, have developed a simplified statement of cash flows for Company E presented in Table 2.3 based on the data in Tables 2.1 and 2.2.

TABLE 2.3   Company E: Statement of Cash Flows (Direct Method) For the Year Ended December 31, 19X2; Increase (Decrease) in Cash and Cash Equivalents

Cash flows from operating activities:		
Cash received from customers	$12,300	
Cash paid to suppliers and employees	(9,800)	
Other income, net	120	
Interest paid	(220)	
Income taxes paid	(300)	
Net cash provided by operating activities		$2,100
Cash flows from investing activities:		
Capital expenditures	(1,000)	
Net cash used in investing activities		(1,000)
Cash flows from financing activities:		
Proceeds from issuance of long-term debt	(400)*	
Dividends paid	(200)	
Net cash provided by financing activities		(600)
Net increase in cash and cash equivalents		500
Cash and cash equivalents at beginning of year		500
Cash and cash equivalents at end of year		$1,000

*Note: Negative "Proceeds from issuance of long-term debt" indicate repayment of debt principal.

TABLE 2.4   Company E: Reconciliation of Net Income
             to Net Cash Provided by Operating
             Activities (Indirect Method)

Net income		$ 600
Adjustments to reconcile net income to net cash provided by operating activities:		
Cash provided by operating activities:		
Depreciation and amortization	$500	
Increase in deferred taxes	100	
Increase in current liabilities	900	
Total adjustments		1,500
Net cash provided by operating activities		$2,100

Our Table 2.3 follows the format for the statement of cash flows prescribed by FASB 95. Cash flows are divided into three main categories: operating activities, investing activities, and financing activities. These groupings have some logic, but because of the interrelationships among the three categories of activities designated, some arbitrariness is inherently involved.

A rationale for the adoption of the three categories can be formulated. It is informative to know whether the basic operations of a firm generate cash or require a cash infusion. But by this same logic it is inconsistent to include several of the items as cash flows from operating activities that FASB 95 designates. FASB was adopted by a vote of four affirmative with three dissenting. The three dissenters point out that interest and dividends received are returns on investment that should be classified as cash inflows from investing activities. Similarly, interest paid is the cost of obtaining financial resources that should be classified as a cash outflow for financing activities.

As shown by Table 2.3, the result of the three categories of cash flows from operating activities, from investing activities, and from financing activities, is a net change in cash and cash equivalents during the year. When added to cash and cash equivalents at the beginning of the year, the end-of-year cash and cash equivalents figure is obtained. An investment with a maturity of less than three months is defined by FASB 95 as a cash equivalent. The statement of cash flows illustrated in Table 2.3 is what FASB 95 terms the Direct Method. The Direct Method is illustrated in paragraph 131 of FASB 95. In paragraph 132 the Indirect Method is illustrated. Analysis of the two paragraphs shows that the Indirect Method is the same for investing and financing activities and differs only for net cash provided by operating activities. The modification, using the Indirect Method for calculating net cash from operating activities, is actually a reconciliation of the net income figure to net cash provided by operating activities. The nature of this reconciliation is illustrated in Table 2.4 based on the illustrative balance sheet in Table 2.1 and the illustrative income statement in Table 2.2. The adjustment involves adding back to net income all of the noncash outlays such as depreciation, deferred taxes, and other accruals.

TABLE 2.5   Company E: Detail of Major Cash Flow Items

Cash received from customers:	
Revenues	$12,000
Plus decrease in accounts receivable	300
Total	$12,300
Cash paid to suppliers and employees:	
Cost of sales (excl. dep.)	$ 6,800
Plus marketing expense	3,000
Plus general administrative expense	600
Plus increase in inventories	300
Less increase in accounts payable	(400)
Less increase in accruals	(500)
Total	$ 9,800

The two major items under cash flows from operating activities are "cash received from customers" and "cash paid to suppliers and employees" (see Table 2.3). To provide more detailed information, a breakdown of these major cash flow items is set forth in Table 2.5. Cash received from customers includes an adjustment for the change in the working capital item, accounts receivable. The cash paid to suppliers and employees covers most major items of expense including the change in inventories, another current asset item. This category also includes changes in the other current liabilities items.

We have thus far illustrated the nature of the new approach to the analysis of cash flows set forth in FASB 95. We have presented our own set of sample financial statements that illustrate the major principles involved. We next turn to a comparison of this newer approach with the previous practices.

Sources and Uses of Funds Statement

The most widely used tool for analyzing cash flows before FASB 95 was the sources and uses of funds statement. In principle, the sources and uses of funds statement was relatively simple. For example, for our Company E we can readily develop such a statement from the beginning- and end-of-year balance sheets. This is done in Table 2.6. The methodology of calculating sources and uses is straightforward. Increases in assets represent a use. Decreases in assets represent a source of funds. Increases in claims on assets represent a source, decreases in claims on assets represent a use. Note that accumulated depreciation is a deduction from an asset so its increase represents a source of funds. By this logic the changes in assets and in claims on assets during the year are classified as a source or a use. The difference between total sources and total uses shown in Table 2.6 represents the change in cash and equivalents of $500. This is the same change in cash flows that was conveyed by Table 2.3, which illustrates the method prescribed by FASB 95.

TABLE 2.6   Company E: Statement of Changes in Financial Position During 19X2

Assets	12/31/X1	12/31/X2	Source	Use
Cash*	$ 400	$ 500		
Marketable securities*	100	500		
Accounts receivable, net	1,500	1,200	300	
Inventories	1,500	1,800		300
Current assets	3,500	4,000		
Gross plant and equipment	9,000	10,000		1,000
Accumulated depreciation	3,500	4,000	500	
Net plant and equipment	5,500	6,000		
Total Assets	$9,000	$10,000		

Claims on Assets				
Accounts payable	$ 600	$ 1,000	$ 400	
Notes payable @ 10%	200	200		
Accrued wages	200	400	200	
Other accruals	100	400	300	
Current liabilities	1,100	2,000		
Deferred taxes	900	1,000	100	
Long-term debt @ 10%	2,400	2,000		400
Stockholders' equity				
Common stock (Par = $.10)	1,000	1,000		–0–
Paid-in capital	1,000	1,000		–0–
Retained earnings	2,600	3,000	400	
Less: Treasury stock	–0–	–0–		–0–
Total stockholders' equity	4,600	5,000		
Total Liabilities and				
Stockholders' Equity	$9,000	$10,000		
Total Sources and Uses				
Total Sources – Total Uses =				
Δ[Cash and Equivalents] = $500			$2,200	$1,700

---

*Cash and marketable securities are not sources or uses but are what we reconcile in this statement.

Thus we get the same result from using the sources and uses of funds statement as we do under the newer statement of cash flows by FASB 95. Is anything gained by the new approach? From the sources and uses of funds statement in Table 2.6, we observe that the main uses of funds by Company E during the period were to increase inventories, invest in gross plant and equipment, and to pay down some long-term debt. The main sources of funds were from retained income, from depreciation, from reducing accounts receivable, and from increasing accounts payable and accruals. Thus the sources and uses of funds statement provides information that could be used for making further analysis of the patterns of the flows of funds within the company. Indeed, with projected balance sheets and income statements, the financial manager could construct a pro forma or projected

TABLE 2.7 The Cycle of Cash Flow Patterns

Cash Flows	Start-up Firm	Growth Firm	Mature Firm	Declining Firm
Operating activities	$ (20)	$ 200	$ 250	$ 150
Investing activities	(400)	(900)	(200)	30
Financing activities	500	800	(60)	(300)
Net increase in cash and equivalents	$ 80	$ 100	$ (10)	$(120)

sources and uses of funds statement to show how a firm planned to acquire and employ funds during some future period.

FASB 95 represents an advance in that it goes some distance in grouping and thereby analyzing the flows of funds. It thus goes farther in providing a basis for further analysis. It is important, therefore, that individual cash flows be grouped on a logical basis and in this regard we agree with the dissenters in the four-to-three decision that led to the adoption of FASB 95. We agree that interest and dividends received should be classified as cash inflows from investing activities. In addition, interest paid is a cost of obtaining financial resources that should be shown as a cash outflow from financing activities.

With this further improvement in the classification of individual items, we believe that the grouping of cash flows into operating activities, investing activities, and financing activities provides a useful perspective on patterns that firms experience over the life cycle of their activities. We demonstrate this in Table 2.7, which depicts a stylized cycle of cash flow patterns.

During the start-up period for a firm when it is trying to establish both the product and its position in the industry, it may be suffering initial losses from operations. It has heavy investment requirements. Its financing activities are likely to be large enough to cover current needs as well as hoped-for future growth. When the product, industry, and the firm become more strongly established, a growth period is entered. Profitability increases and the firm's operating activities begin to throw off substantial positive cash flows. However, as a firm with rapid growth in sales, its investment requirements are still likely to exceed the cash throw-off from operating activities. The firm with high profitability is now in a position to have strong access to the financial markets. Although investment requirements are very substantial, funds from financing and from operating activities are likely to enable the firm to increase its stock of cash and cash equivalents.

As the firm becomes mature, operating activities throw off more cash at higher levels of sales with reduced profit margins. The need for growth has diminished so that investing activities are reduced. Financing requirements are substantially smaller. The firm is likely to be able to begin paying off some of its debt and pay a higher rate of cash dividends. It can begin to reduce its stock of cash and cash equivalents.

Finally, in the declining phase sales may decline and profit margins may be severely eroded. Hence the cash flow from operating activities is likely to be reduced. Investing activities are likely to be a small source of positive cash flows because some capacity may be reduced. At this stage the firm should be paying off some of its obligations. It is likely to engage in substantial repayments of debt, increased dividend payments, and perhaps engage in share repurchases as the firm begins to shrink in size. The firm is in a position to substantially reduce its stock of cash and cash equivalents.

Our discussion of Table 2.7 has some practical implications. Note that the need for outside financing is likely to be the greatest when the firm is in a period of growth. Large investment requirements and substantial needs for outside financing are healthy indicators if the profitability of the firm is good. But if the firm needs financing because it is losing money, and its existing accounts receivable and inventories are declining in value, this portends disaster. So the information provided by cash flow patterns is necessary, but not sufficient for evaluating the financial health of a firm. Other performance measures are required, particularly the levels of profitability. More detailed analysis of the performance of the firm is presented in Chapter 7. Here our aim is simply to convey the language of finance and business.

A number of other definitions of cash flows can be found in the literature. They reflect the particular requirements of the analysis and the individual interests of the analysts. A widely used definition of operating cash flow is:

$$\text{EBIT} + \text{Depreciation} - \text{Actual taxes paid} = \text{Operating cash flow}$$

This is a definition of operating cash flow widely used in valuation models of the type discussed in Chapter 17. Recall that EBIT can be expressed as:

$$\text{Net income} + \text{Actual taxes}$$
$$+ \text{Interest and other financial charges paid}$$
$$= \text{Earnings before interest and taxes (EBIT)}$$

A cash flow definition using net income as a base does not purely measure cash flows because the net income figure may reflect sales that are not paid in cash and may reflect a number of different types of accrual expenses that do not represent cash outlays. Furthermore, this limited definition of cash flow completely ignores balance sheet cash flows. Nevertheless, this measure of operating cash flow described is widely employed.

Almost any measure of cash flow utilized provides some useful information, but also has limitations. The takeover raider's formula, for example, is defined as pretax income plus depreciation minus maintenance capital spending (but not discretionary capital spending) [Dreyfus, 1988, p. 59]. It reflects the interest of the "entrepreneurial investor" or "raider" in discretionary free cash flow. It is a measure of how much interest expenses could be covered if after a takeover the amount of debt of the firm is increased.

While different analysts will use the cash flow statements provided by FASB 95 in different ways, it has been observed that "analysts will still argue over definitions, but they will be arguing about the same set of numbers" [Dreyfus, 1988, p. 6]. Another observation made was that "analysts perceive that management can't muck around with cash the way it can with accrual accounting" [Dreyfus, 1988, p. 59].

In summary, cash flows are the name of the game. The ways in which cash flows are grouped, however, may be somewhat arbitrary. At a minimum, a statement of cash flow

FIGURE 2.1   Financial Reporting Requirements of the Firm

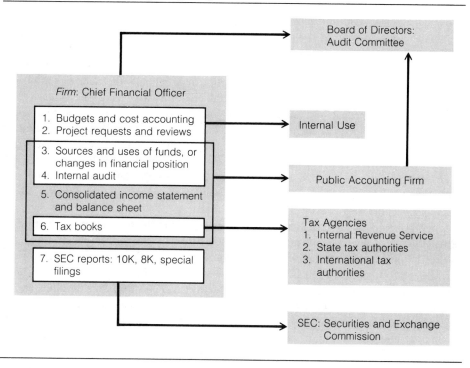

provides an expanded treasure trove of information. The use of this information varies with the needs and interests of financial managers and other financial analysts.

REPORTING REQUIREMENTS

One of the important responsibilities of the chief financial officer is to manage all financial reporting requirements both inside and outside of the firm. Figure 2.1 illustrates the scope of the many types of financial statements that may be necessary.

While carrying out his or her reporting duties, the chief financial officer (CFO) must interact with many different users of financial information. For example, let's look at internal users. The firm's managers must be given budgets, which are governed by cost accounting conventions. In turn, managers supply the CFO with requests for new project funding. Also, ongoing projects are constantly reviewed, sources and uses of funds are monitored, and internal audits are performed to check on the accuracy and validity of data being reported to corporate headquarters.

In addition to these numerous internal reporting requirements, the CFO must supply financial data to shareholders, the board of directors, public accounting firms, the Securities and Exchange Commission (SEC), and various tax agencies, such as the Internal Revenue Service (IRS), state and local tax authorities, and even to international tax authorities. These external users of accounting information each have separate data requirements, and even worse, their demands are not necessarily consistent. For example, the accounting treatment of the annual report can cause earnings per share to increase while cash flows may decrease because taxes have increased on the IRS forms.

First, let's turn our attention to the reporting requirements of shareholders on the annual report. Why require an annual report at all? And why have the annual report audited (at some expense) by an independent public accounting firm? One reasonable answer to these questions is suggested by Watts and Zimmerman [1978]. As a corporation grows in size, it often needs to raise external equity capital. Consequently, there arises a separation between ownership and control. Specialized managers actually operate the firm while external equity capital is supplied by numerous shareholders whose ownership is quite diffuse. In the absence of some kind of monitoring agreement, shareholders would supply new capital only at a high cost because managers could either shirk their duties or consume excess perquisites at shareholder expense. It is in the best interest of both managers and shareholders to agree in advance on some form of independent monitoring if the cost of the monitoring arrangement is less than the costs in the absence of monitoring.

The usual procedure is for shareholders to elect a board of directors, who, in turn, select (1) an audit committee to oversee the external audit of the firm's accounts and to direct the preparation of an annual report to shareholders and (2) a public accounting firm to perform the audit and to approve (or disapprove) the annual report. The audit committee often contains a majority of outside or nonmanagement directors as well as the CFO.

Congress has accepted the ultimate responsibility for the determination of accounting principles. However, in the *Securities Act of 1933,* the authority was delegated to the Securities and Exchange Commission (SEC). Choosing not to become directly involved in the regulation of accounting principles, the SEC has elected to oversee self-regulation by the accounting profession. Public accounting firms are guided by a set of generally accepted accounting principles (GAAP), which are governed by opinions, issued between 1959 and 1973, of the Accounting Principles Board (APB) and by the Financial Accounting Standards Board (FASB), which has been the principal agency outside of the federal government since 1973.

The SEC requires that nearly all publicly held corporations submit a standardized annual report called the 10K, which usually contains more information than the annual report. Firms are required to send the 10K to all shareholders who request it. In addition, there is a quarterly filing called the 10Q. The SEC further requires that whenever a corporation wishes to issue securities to the public, it must file a registration statement that discloses current financial data as well as such items as the purpose for issuing the securities.

Last in order of our discussion, but never least important, are the ubiquitous tax statements which must be filed with the Internal Revenue Service of the federal government, with state tax collection agencies, and with foreign governments. It is not unusual to discover that accounting rules for tax reporting are different from those in the generally accepted accounting principles used in preparation of the annual report. For example, most corporations use some form of accelerated depreciation in order to maximize the present value of the depreciation tax shield on their tax statements. Simultaneously, they use straight line depreciation on the annual report to their shareholders.

INTERNATIONAL COMPARISONS OF FINANCIAL STATEMENTS

Cash flow has the virtue of being tangible. It is always easy to identify cash when you see it. But extracting cash flows from financial statements for the purpose of financial decision making is quite another matter and is complicated by the fact that financial reporting standards and practices differ considerably from country to country.

In Europe, for example, a company's tax books and its annual report are the same. Consequently, for tax reasons, earnings are understated relative to what they would be using commonly accepted U.S. accounting standards. For example, in the United States accelerated depreciation is used for tax purposes but straight line depreciation is used in the annual report thus taxable earnings are often less than reported earnings. In Europe, companies use accelerated depreciation both for their annual report and their tax books. Furthermore, provisions are frequently made to expense against current income anticipated future costs such as pensions, reorganization, or maintenance. The effect is to understate current earnings. Until very recently European companies could, at their discretion, choose whether or not to consolidate foreign subsidiaries. If they did not consolidate, their earnings could be substantially understated. In France, accounting standards allow for the periodic restatement of assets to replacement value. This has no cash impact on the firm except for tax implications. When assets are based on replacement value, earnings are understated relative to U.S. GAAP-derived earnings due to higher depreciation allowances, and stockholders' equity is overstated. The amount by which the assets are written up is usually booked partly to shareholders' equity reserves and partly to deferred taxes.

It is nearly an impossible task to keep track continuously of the changing accounting standards of hundreds of countries. Suffice it to say that one cannot readily assume that accounting numbers in one country have the same meaning as in other countries. The only certainty is that cash flow has an unambiguous meaning across borders and in most countries the accounting reports give enough information to extract cash flow information.

SUMMARY

This chapter has provided an overview of the three key financial statements of the firm: the income statement, the balance sheet, and the statement of cash flows. We have illustrated how the statement of cash flows can be derived from the income statement and the balance sheet. We have emphasized how the new statement of cash flows required by FASB 95 provides additional financial information. Also, we have introduced some of the important issues and definitions discussed later on in the book. We also discussed the complex financial reporting environment in which a U.S. firm operates. The chief financial officer must be familiar with the regulations of the Securities and Exchange Commission, the Financial Accounting Standards Board, the Internal Revenue Service, state tax codes, and international tax codes.

QUESTIONS

2.1   What are the three financial statements necessary for a description of a firm's activities during an interval of time, say, one year?

2.2   What is the limitation of the statement of changes in net working capital position as a measure of cash flows?

2.3   Why are valuation models likely to be based on cash flows rather than on net income?

2.4   What are the three kinds of activities associated with cash flows in the statement of cash flows required by FASB 95?

2.5   What happens to the operating leverage of a firm if it decides to undertake a project that increases fixed costs but decreases variable costs in such a way that total costs do not change?

2.6   Is an increase in accounts payable a source or a use of funds? Why?

2.7   Is an increase in inventories a source or a use of funds? Why?

2.8   Is an increase in accounts receivable a source or a use of funds? Why?

2.9   Who are the primary external users of the firm's financial statements?

2.10 Why is it in the best interests of managers to have the financial statements of the firm audited by an independent public accounting firm?

PROBLEMS

2.1   The accounts of ABC Industries as of December 31, 19X0, are listed alphabetically below — an orderly, but not particularly informative arrangement. Prepare a balance sheet in the format of Table 2.1 using the data provided.

Accounts payable	100
Accounts receivable, net	400
Accrued wages	100
Accumulated depreciation	800
Cash	100
Common stock ($1 par)	200
Deferred taxes	150
Gross property, plant, and equipment	2,000
Inventories	400
Long-term debt	500
Marketable securities	50
Notes payable	50
Other accruals	50
Paid-in capital	300
Preferred stock	100
Retained earnings	700
Treasury stock	100

2.2 The following information is provided about the revenues and expenses of Stark Company for the year ending December 31, 19X0. Use the data to prepare an income statement in the format of Table 2.2 in the text.

General administrative expense	300
Income tax rate	40%
Revenues	7,000
Depreciation	200
Interest expense	80
Other expense	75
Cost of sales (excl. dep.)	3,600
Marketing expense	1,200
Other income	150

Be sure to include all the levels of income measurement shown in Table 2.2. For example, what is net operating income? What is earnings before interest and taxes?

2.3 The Goldstone Company has reported the following income and expense items for 19X3 and 19X4.

	19X3	19X4
Revenues	$40,000	$45,000
Cost of sales (excl. dep.)	20,000	20,000
Marketing expense	6,000	6,500
General administrative expense	1,800	1,800
Depreciation	1,200	2,000
Interest expense	5,000	10,000
Tax rate	40%	34%
Actual taxes paid	2,000	1,000

a. Prepare income statements for 19X3 and 19X4.
b. What is Goldstone's operating cash flow for each year?
c. Discuss the difference between net income and operating cash flow.

2.4 The Roark Corporation has $2,000,000 in long-term debt with an interest rate of 12 percent, and no other interest-bearing debt. It had net revenues of $4,000,000 in 19X6, and its cost of sales (excluding depreciation) was $1,800,000. Depreciation expense was $135,000. Marketing and general administrative expenses were $250,000. From investments it had made in other companies, Roark had income of $100,000 net of expenses. Roark uses a 34 percent tax rate in reports to shareholders; its actual tax rate is 25 percent.
a. What is Roark's gross income for 19X6?
b. What is its net operating income?
c. What are its earnings before interest and taxes?
d. What is its net income?
e. What is its operating cash flow?

2.5 The stockholders' equity accounts for the balance sheet of Wiss Corporation for the year ended December 31, 19X1 are shown below:

Common stock ($1 par)	$1,000,000
Paid-in capital	4,000,000
Treasury stock	(500,000)
Retained earnings	8,000,000

During 19X2, net income was $3,500,000, of which $1,750,000 was paid out in dividends.

a. What is total stockholders' equity at the end of 19X1?

b. What is total stockholders' equity at the end of 19X2?

2.6 The Gallagher Company has provided the following information for 19X0.

Purchases of fixed assets	150,000
Payments received from customers	1,845,000
Proceeds from issuance of long-term debt	60,000
Payments to retire principal on notes payable	1,000
Payments to suppliers	700,000
Payments of interest on long- and short-term debt	33,000
Proceeds from sale of common stock	5,000
Payment of wages to employees	850,000
Payment of taxes	45,000

Use the format and terminology of Table 2.3 in the text to prepare a statement of cash flows.

2.7 Given below are the Tiptop Corporation's income statement and balance sheets ending in the year 19X4. Compute the sources and uses of funds.

Income Statement for the Year 19X4

Revenue	$300,000
Cost of goods sold	−270,000
Selling and administrative expenses	−10,000
Earnings before interest and taxes	20,000
Interest expense	−10,000
Earnings before taxes	10,000
Taxes @ 40%	−4,000
Net income	6,000

Balance Sheets	Dec. 31, 19X3		Dec. 31, 19X4	
Assets				
Cash		$ 10,000		$ 5,000
Accounts receivable		15,000		20,000
Marketable securities		25,000		15,000
Inventories		25,000		35,000
Gross PP&E	150,000		175,000	
Less accumulated depreciation	−40,000		−50,000	
Net PP&E		110,000		125,000
Total assets		185,000		200,000
Liabilities				
Accounts payable		$ 10,000		$ 6,000
Notes due		25,000		24,000
Long-term debt		60,000		70,000
Equity				
Common		50,000		70,000
Retained earnings		50,000		45,000
Less Treasury stock		−10,000		−15,000
Total liabilities		185,000		200,000

2.8 Given the following information, calculate the sources and uses of funds for the XYZ subsidiary:

Income Statement for the Year 19X4

Revenue	$1,000
Cost of goods sold	−600
Selling and administrative expenses	−500
Net operating income	−100
Interest charges	−50
Earnings before taxes	−150
Taxes @ 40%	+60
Net income	−90

Balance Sheets	Dec. 31, 19X3	Dec. 31, 19X4
Assets		
Cash	60	40
Accounts receivable	40	50
Marketable securities	100	0
Inventories	50	100
Gross PP&E	385	405
Less accumulated depreciation	−85	−95
Net PP&E	300	310
Total assets	550	500
Liabilities		
Accounts payable	40	60
Notes due	60	100
Long-term debt	100	90
Equity		
Common	200	200
Retained earnings	150	50
Total liabilities	550	500

2.9 Given below are Topler Company's income statement and beginning and ending balance sheets for the year 19X2.

   a. Calculate the statement of cash flows by the Direct Method and the related reconciliation of net income to net cash provided by operating activities as shown in Table 2.4 and the detail of major cash flows in Table 2.5 of the text.

   b. Also, formulate a sources and uses of funds statement.

   c. What is the amount of the net increase in cash and cash equivalents?

   d. From the pattern of cash flows you observe, what is your judgment of the stage of life cycle of the firm?

Income Statement for the Year Ended December 31, 19X2

1. Revenues (R)	$18,000
2. Cost of sales (CS) (excl. dep.)	12,000
a. Gross income (M)	6,000
3. Marketing expense	2,500
4. General administrative expense (G&A)	1,347
b. Earnings before depreciation, interest and taxes (EBDIT)	2,153

5. Depreciation (Dep.)	500
c. Net operating income (NOI)	1,653
6. Other income, net	10
d. Earnings before interest and taxes (EBIT)	1,663
7. Interest expense (f)	246*
e. Earnings before taxes (EBT)	1,417
8. Income taxes at 40% (T)	567
f. Net income (NI)	850

Memo:

Deferred taxes	$300
Dividends paid	0
To Retained earnings	$850

*Interest expense based on average of beginning-of-year and end-of-year notes payable and long-term debt, both at a rate of 12 percent.

Balance Sheets	Dec. 31, 19X1	Dec. 31, 19X2
Assets		
Cash	300	400
Marketable securities	50	100
Accounts receivable, net	1,000	1,600
Inventories	800	1,000
Current assets	2,150	3,100
Gross plant and equipment	5,000	10,000
Accumulated depreciation	(1,000)	(1,500)
Net plant and equipment	4,000	8,500
Total assets	6,150	11,600
Liabilities		
Accounts payable	500	1,000
Notes payable at 12 percent	100	400
Accrued wages	100	300
Other accruals	100	300
Current liabilities	800	2,000
Deferred taxes	300	600
Long-term debt at 12 percent	1,600	2,500
Preferred stock	0	0
Stockholders' equity		
Common stock ($.10 par)	1,000	1,200
Paid-in capital	1,000	3,000
Retained earnings	1,450	2,300
Less: Treasury stock	0	0
Total stockholders' equity	3,450	6,500
Total liabilities	6,150	11,600

SELECTED REFERENCES

Dreyfus, Patricia, "Go with the (cash) flow," *Institutional Investor* (August 1988), pp. 55–59.

Watts, R., and Zimmerman, J., "Towards a Positive Theory of the Determination of Accounting Standards," *Accounting Review* (January 1978), pp. 112–134.

CHAPTER 3

Decisions across Time

Knowledge of the time value of money is essential to an understanding of most topics in finance. For example, financial structure decisions, project selection, lease versus borrow decisions, bond refunding, security valuation, and the whole question of the cost of capital are subjects that cannot be understood without a knowledge of compound interest. Almost all problems involving compound interest can be handled with only a few basic concepts.

THE NATURE OF FINANCIAL DECISIONS

This chapter on "Decisions across Time" is key to the main theme of our book. Growth is a major source of value, and the analysis of expected future cash flows is the basis of the calculation of value. This theme is implemented throughout the chapters that follow. In this chapter we present the foundations for the analysis of growth and value.

Most decisions we face in our everyday lives, as well as the decisions that confront business firms, involve a comparison of the present with the future. This involves comparing cash flows at different points in time — present outlays versus future benefits, or present consumption versus future payments or foregone future benefits. For example, consider an investment of $1,000 today that pays $1,100 at the end of one year. This returns 10 percent on our investment. If the cost of funds is 12 percent, it is not a good investment because we are not earning our cost of funds. If the funds cost 8 percent, we have made a net gain.

Most financial decisions require comparisons of these kinds. Because funds have earning power, $1,000 today is not the same as $1,000 received a year later. If we have $1,000 today, we can invest it to have more than $1,000 in the future. Financial decisions, therefore, involve the time value of money—decisions across time. Values are determined by the timing of the future cash flows to be received. Funds received next year are worth more than the same amount of funds received in the fifth or tenth year. What is involved is discounted cash flow analysis, representing the fundamental technique for measuring the time value of money. Most financial decisions at both the personal and business levels must take into account the time value of money. The materials in this chapter are, therefore, the key to the important topics of managerial finance.

FUTURE VALUE

A person invests $1,000 in a security that pays 10 percent compounded annually. How much will this person have at the end of one year? To treat the matter systematically, let us define the following terms:

$$P_0 = \text{principal, or beginning amount, at time 0 (that is, \$1,000)}$$

$$r = \text{rate of return or interest rate (that is, 10\%)}^1$$

$$P_0 r = \text{total dollar amount of interest earned at } r$$

$$FV_{r,n} = \text{value at the end of } n \text{ periods at } r.$$

When n equals 1, $FV_{r,n}$ can be calculated as follows:

$$FV_{r,1} = P_0 + P_0 r \qquad (3.1)$$
$$= P_0(1 + r).$$

Equation 3.1 shows that the ending amount ($FV_{r,1}$) is equal to the beginning amount (P_0) times the factor $(1 + r)$. In the example, where P_0 is $1,000, r is 10 percent, and n is one year, $FV_{r,n}$ is determined as follows:

$$FV_{10\%,\ 1\ \text{yr.}} = \$1,000\ (1.0 + 0.10) = \$1,000\ (1.10) = \$1,100.$$

Multiple Periods

If the person leaves the $1,000 on deposit for five years, to what amount will it have grown at the end of that period? Equation 3.1 can be used to construct Table 3.1, which indicates the answer. Note that $FV_{r,2}$, the balance at the end of the second year, is found as follows:

$$FV_{r,2} = FV_{r,1}(1 + r) = P_0(1 + r)(1 + r) = P_0(1 + r)^2$$
$$= \$1,000\ (1.10)^2 = \$1,210.00.$$

Similarly, $FV_{r,3}$, the balance after three years, is found as

$$FV_{r,3} = FV_{r,2}(1 + r) = P_0(1 + r)^3$$
$$= \$1,000\ (1.1)^3 = \$1,331.00.$$

---

[1] In this chapter we use r as the rate of return or interest rate. In later chapters involving topics such as the cost of capital and valuation, the literature uses k instead of r. In one sense, k is a particular kind of rate of return or discount factor. In another sense, r and k could be used interchangeably.

TABLE 3.1   Compound Interest Calculations

Year	(1) Amount at start of year PV	(2) Interest earned $(1) \times (.10)$	(3) Amount at end of year $(1) \times (1 + .10)$ $FV_{r,n}$
1	$1,000.00	$100.00	$1,100.00
2	1,100.00	110.00	1,210.00
3	1,210.00	121.00	1,331.00
4	1,331.00	133.10	1,464.10
5	1,464.10	146.41	1,610.51

In general, $FV_{r,n}$, the compound amount at the end of any future year n, is found as

$$FV_{r,n} = P_0(1 + r)^n. \tag{3.2}$$

Equation 3.2 is the fundamental equation of compound interest. Equation 3.1 is simply a special case of Equation 3.2, where $n = 1$.

The above is straightforward, but some important subtleties need to be drawn out. First, consider simple interest. Under a simple interest contract the investor would have received interest of $100 for each of the years. While contracts are sometimes written to provide for simple interest, the powerful logic behind the idea of compound interest is demonstrated by Table 3.1. If the money is invested for five years, and the interest earned each year is left with the financial institution, interest is earned on the interest. Thus, as shown by Column 2 in Table 3.1, the amount of interest earned under compound interest rises each year. Therefore, the value of the amount at the start of the year on which interest is earned during the year includes the interest earned in previous time periods.

Second, the rate of interest applied to the interest earned is *assumed* to be the 10 percent provided for in the five-year contract. However, it is possible that interest rates would be higher or lower during the five-year period. If so, the contract could provide for adjusting the interest rate upward or downward over the life of the agreement. But the conventional practice in compound interest calculations is to assume reinvestment at the specified interest rate. Thus, the fundamental equation of compound interest set forth in Equation 3.2 has important implications that should be kept in mind when compound interest rate relationships are utilized in the many individual topics of financial management.

Table 3.1 illustrates how compound interest rate relationships can be developed on a year by year basis. We could also use Equation 3.2 to calculate what the future value of $1,000 would be at the end of five years. Any calculator with a y^x function would enable us to quickly calculate the results shown in Table 3.1. It is recommended that at these early stages the relationships between equations, tables, regular calculators, and financial calculators all be explored.

To round out this discussion we, therefore, illustrate how the same result of $1,610.51 as the future value of $1,000 at 10 percent interest can also be obtained from a

TABLE 3.2   Interest Factors as a Function of Interest Rates

Period (n)	$FVIF_{r,n} = (1 + r)^n$			
	0%	5%	10%	15%
1	1.0000	1.0500	1.1000	1.1500
2	1.0000	1.1025	1.2100	1.3225
3	1.0000	1.1576	1.3310	1.5209
4	1.0000	1.2155	1.4641	1.7490
5	1.0000	1.2763	1.6105	2.0114
6	1.0000	1.3401	1.7716	2.3131
7	1.0000	1.4071	1.9487	2.6600
8	1.0000	1.4775	2.1436	3.0590
9	1.0000	1.5513	2.3579	3.5179
10	1.0000	1.6289	2.5937	4.0456

table. Tables have been constructed for values of $(1 + r)^n$ for wide ranges of r and n. (See Table A.1 in Appendix A at the end of the book.)

Letting the *future value interest factor* (FVIF) equal $(1 + r)^n$, we can write Equation 3.2 as $FV_{r,n} = P_0 FVIF(r,n)$. It is necessary only to go to an appropriate interest table to find the proper interest factor. For example, the correct interest factor for the illustration given in Table 3.1 can be found in Table A.1. Look down the period column to 5, then across this row to the appropriate number in the 10 percent column to find the interest factor, 1.6105. Then, using this interest factor, the future value of the $1,000 after five years is

$$FV_{10\%, \ 5 \ yrs.} = P_0 FVIF(10\%, \ 5 \ yrs.) = \$1,000(1.6105) = \$1,610.50.$$

This is the same figure that was obtained by the other methods.

The equation for the future value interest factor ($FVIF_{r,n}$) is:

$$FVIF_{r,n} = (1 + r)^n. \tag{3.3}$$

This equation can be used to calculate how the interest factor is related to the interest rate and time as shown numerically in Table 3.2 and graphically in Figure 3.1.

Table 3.2 and Figure 3.1 demonstrate the power of compound interest. At a 10 percent interest rate our investment doubles in slightly more than seven years. At 15 percent, our investment doubles in less than five years and our investment has more than quadrupled in less than 10 years. The nature of the compound interest relationships is the basis for the *Rule of 72*. If we divide 72 by the interest rate, we obtain the number of years required for an investment to double. At 6 percent, an investment doubles in 12 years; at 9 percent in eight years; at 24 percent in three years. Or if we have the number of years required for an investment to double, we can use the *Rule of 72* to calculate the compound interest rate. If an investment doubles in six years, the interest rate is 12 percent; in 12 years, 6 percent; in three years, 24 percent. So if we are told that a stock price will double in 12 years, that represents only a 6 percent return — relatively modest. If a stock price doubles in three years, that represents a 24 percent rate of return, which is very good.

FIGURE 3.1   Interest Factors as a Function of Interest Rates

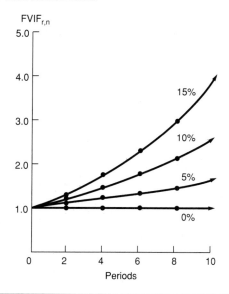

Future Value Interest Factors

PRESENT VALUE

We have observed the power of compound interest to calculate future values. The next concept is the present value concept, which has numerous applications in finance. The present value concept leads directly to the *basic principle of investment decisions,* which is: An investment is acceptable only if it earns at least its opportunity cost. The opportunity cost is what the funds could earn on an investment of equal risk. The *basic principle of investment decisions* may then be stated: An investment is acceptable only if it earns at least the risk-adjusted market interest rate.

An example will illustrate the relationship between future value, present value, and the basic principle of investment decisions under certainty. We have the opportunity to invest $1,000 today for an asset which can be sold one year later for $1,210; the applicable market rate of interest is 10 percent. We can analyze the decision using the future value, present value, and rate of return concepts.

Under future value analysis, we could invest the $1,000 at the market interest rate of 10 percent. At the end of the year, we would have:

$$\$1,000(1 + .10) = \$1,100.$$

But the asset investment would have a value of $1,210, which is higher than the market investment. Alternatively, we can use the concept of present value to compare the two investments.

Finding present values (*discounting*, as it is commonly called) is simply the reverse of compounding, and Equation 3.2 can readily be transformed into a present value formula by dividing both sides by the discount factor $(1 + r)^n$.

$$FV_{r,n} = P_0(1 + r)^n. \tag{3.2}$$

$$\text{Present value} = P_0 = \frac{FV_{r,n}}{(1 + r)^n} = FV_{r,n}\left[\frac{1}{(1 + r)^n}\right] \tag{3.3}$$

$$= FV_{r,n}[(1 + r)^{-n}] = FV_{r,n}PVIF(r,n).$$

The subscript zero in the term P_0 indicates the present. Hence, present value quantities can be identified by either P_0 or $PV_{r,n}$ or more generally as PV.

For our simple examples the present values (PV) of the two investments are:

Market investment $P_0 = \$1,100/1.10 = \$1,000 = \$1,100(.9091)$

Asset investment $P_0 = \$1,210/1.10 = \$1,100 = \$1,210(.9091)$

We can calculate the present value by dividing by one plus the interest rate expressed as a decimal or by multiplying the future value by $1/(1 + r) = (1 + r)^{-1}$. Finally, we note that the market investment has a rate of return of 10 percent, while the asset investment has a return of 21 percent. We have compared two investments using three methods, summarized numerically below and graphically in Figure 3.2.

To summarize the three comparisons, we have:

	Asset Investment	Market Investment
Future value	$1,210	$1,100
Present value at market rate	$1,100	$1,000
Rate of return	21%	10%

By all three methods or criteria, the asset investment is superior to an investment at the market rate. In these comparisons we have explained the concept of present value and illustrated its use. More generally, to obtain the present value we divide by $(1 + r)^n$ or multiply by $(1 + r)^{-n}$.

Tables have been constructed for the present value interest rate factors— $(1 + r)^{-n}$—for various rates, r, and time intervals, n. (See Table A.2 in Appendix A at the end of the book.) For example, to determine the present value of $1,610.51 to be received five years hence where the discount factor is 10 percent, look down the 10 percent column in Table A.2 to the fifth row. The figure shown there, 0.6209, is the present value interest factor (PVIF) used to determine the present value of $1,610.51 payable in five years, discounted at 10 percent.

$$PV_{r,n} = P_0 = FV_{10\%,5 \text{ yrs.}}[PVIF(10\%, 5 \text{ yrs.})]$$
$$= \$1,610.51(0.6209)$$
$$= \$1,000$$

FIGURE 3.2   Time Line Portrayal of Investments

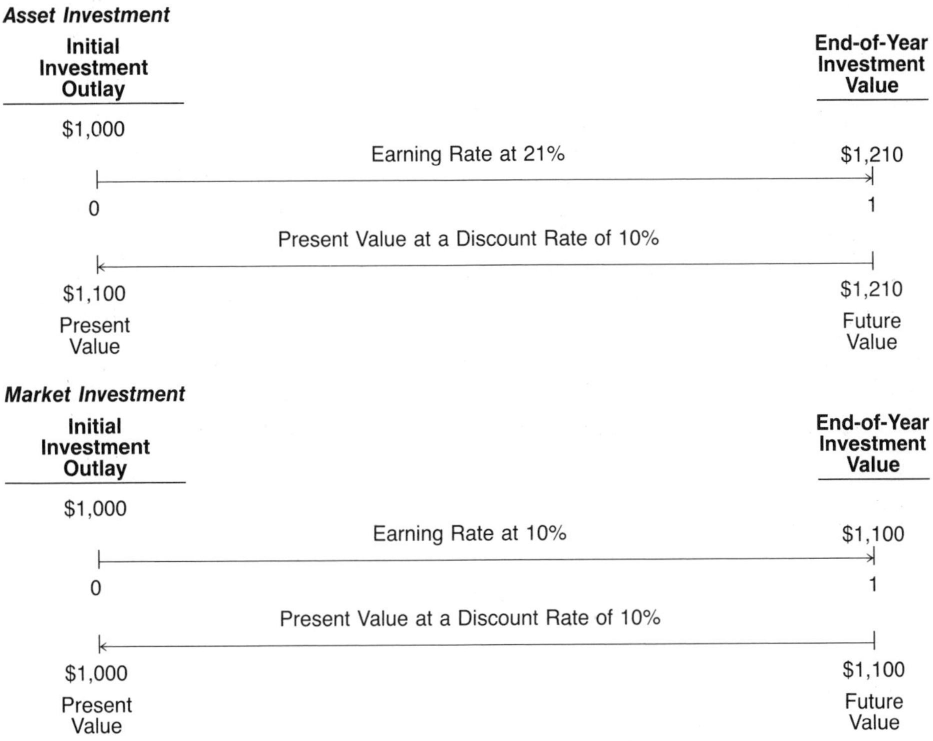

Asset Investment

Initial Investment Outlay		End-of-Year Investment Value

$1,000

Earning Rate at 21% $1,210

0   1

Present Value at a Discount Rate of 10%

$1,100 $1,210

Present   Future
Value   Value

Market Investment

Initial Investment Outlay		End-of-Year Investment Value

$1,000

Earning Rate at 10% $1,100

0   1

Present Value at a Discount Rate of 10%

$1,000 $1,100

Present   Future
Value   Value

Graphic View of Present Values

Table 3.3 and Figure 3.3 portray the nature of the present value relationships. Graphically Figure 3.3 shows how the interest factors for discounting decrease as the discounting period increases. The curves in the figure, plotted from data in Table 3.3, show that the present value of a sum to be received at some future date decreases (1) as the payment date is extended further into the future and (2) as the discount rate increases. If relatively high discount rates apply, funds due in the future are worth very little today; even at relatively low discount rates, funds due in the distant future are not worth much today. For example, $1,000 due in ten years is worth $247 today if the discount rate is 15 percent, but it is worth $614 today at a 5 percent discount rate. Similarly, $1,000 due in ten years at 10 percent is worth $386 today, but the same amount at the same discount rate due in five years is worth $621 today.

To conclude this comparison of present and future values, compare Figures 3.1 and 3.3. Notice that the vertical intercept is at 1.0 in each case, but future value interest factors rise while present value interest factors decline. The reason for this divergence is, of

FIGURE 3.3   Present Value Interest Factors as a Function of Interest Rates

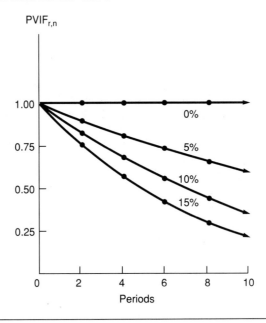

TABLE 3.3   Present Value Interest Factors as a Function of Interest Rates

$$PVIF_{r,n} = \frac{1}{(1 + r)^n} = \left(\frac{1}{1 + r}\right)^n$$

Period (n)	0%	5%	10%	15%
1	1.0000	.9524	.9091	.8696
2	1.0000	.9070	.8264	.7561
3	1.0000	.8638	.7513	.6575
4	1.0000	.8227	.6830	.5718
5	1.0000	.7835	.6209	.4972
6	1.0000	.7462	.5645	.4323
7	1.0000	.7107	.5132	.3759
8	1.0000	.6768	.4665	.3269
9	1.0000	.6446	.4241	.2843
10	1.0000	.6139	.3855	.2472

course, that present value factors are reciprocals of future value factors. To illustrate the application of the discount factors in Table 3.3, suppose you are offered the alternative of either $1,610.50[2] at the end of five years or x dollars today. Assume that there is no risk so that there is no question that the $1,610.50 will be paid in full. Having no current need for the money, you could deposit the x dollars in a financial institution paying 10 percent interest; the 10 percent is your *opportunity cost*. How small must x be to induce you to accept the promise of $1,610.50 five years hence? We can use Table 3.2 to find that future value factor at 10 percent for five years is 1.6105. Divide this into $1,610.50 to obtain a present value of $1,000. Or we can use Table 3.3 to find the present value discount factor at 10 percent for five years to be .6209 which multiplied times $1,610.50 gives us $1,000 (rounded). Thus, if x is less than $1,000, you would prefer $1,610.50 after five years; if $x = $1,000, you would be indifferent between the alternatives; and if $x > $1,000, you would choose x now. The concept of present value is shown graphically as:

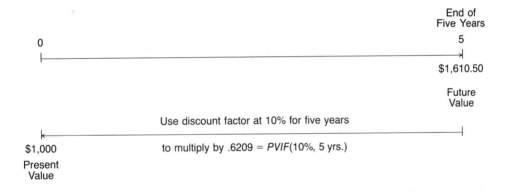

This reinforces the concept of present value. The present value tells us what a future sum or sums would be worth to us if we had those funds today. It is obtained by discounting the future sum or sums back to the starting point, which is the present. Present value analysis clearly involves discounting future cash flows back to the present. It should be understood, however, that the standard practice in finance is to call all compound interest calculations involving future values as well as present values: *discounted cash flow analysis* (DCF).

ANNUITIES

Thus far we have discussed the concepts of future value and present value for a single outflow or inflow. We next consider multiple outflows and/or inflows. These are called annuities.

---

[2]Because the table is carried to only four decimal places the result rounds to $1,610.50 rather than $1,610.51.

FIGURE 3.4   Time Lines for the Future Value of an Annuity @ 10%

Panel A.   Future Value of Ordinary Annuity

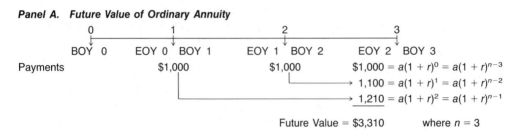

Future Value = $3,310   where $n = 3$

Panel B.   Future Value of Annuity Due

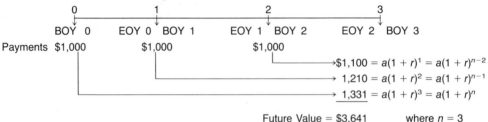

Future Value = $3,641   where $n = 3$

Panel C.

Future Sum of Annuity Due = $(1 + r)$ Future Sum of Ordinary Annuity
$3,641 = (1.10)$3,310

Note: BOY = beginning of year; EOY = end of year.

Future Value of an Annuity

An annuity is defined as a series of payments or receipts for a specified number of periods. The payment or receipt may occur at the end of the year or at the beginning of the year. If it occurs at the end of the year, it is called an *ordinary annuity* (or annuity paid in arrears); if it occurs at the beginning of the year, it is called an *annuity due* (or an annuity paid in advance). Mortgage payments are typically made at the end of the period; lease payments are usually made at the beginning of the period. We will first illustrate the time lines for an ordinary annuity and then for an annuity due. For most problems payments are received at the end of the period so that our emphasis will be on ordinary annuities.

Suppose you were to receive three payments of $1,000 a year for three years — a three-year annuity. If you were to receive such an annuity and invested each annual payment to earn 10 percent interest, what would be the future value of these flows at the end of three years? The answer is illustrated in Figure 3.4, Panel A. A similar time line is shown for the future value of an annuity due. This is shown in Panel B of Figure 3.4. Panel C in Figure 3.4 shows that the future sum of an annuity due is equal to the future sum of an ordinary annuity multiplied by $(1 + r)$. For the ordinary annuity, the first payment is made at the end of Year 1, the second at the end of Year 2, and the third at the end of Year 3. The last payment is not compounded at all; the next to the last is compounded for one year; the first is compounded for two years, that is, for $(n - 1)$ years. When the future values of each of the payments are added, their total is the sum of the annuity. In the example, this total is $3,310.

Expressed algebraically, with *FVA* defined as the future value of an annuity, *a* as the periodic receipt, *t* as the length of the annuity, and *FVIFA* as the future value interest factor for an annuity, the formula for $FVA_{r,t}$ is

$$FVA_{r,t} = a(1 + r)^{n-1} + a(1 + r)^{n-2} + \cdots + a(1 + r)^1 + a(1 + r)^0 \qquad (3.4)$$
$$= a[(1 + r)^{n-1} + (1 + r)^{n-2} + \cdots + (1 + r)^1 + (1 + r)^0]$$
$$= a \sum_{t=0}^{n-1} (1 + r)^t.$$

This expression is called a geometric series. It appears many times in different applications throughout the text. Consequently, it is worth the effort to show how a series with n terms (possibly an infinite number of terms) can be reduced to a simple equation.

Alternatively, multiply both sides of Equation 3.4 by $(1 + r)$ to obtain:

$$(1 + r)FVA_{r,t} = a(1 + r)^n + a(1 + r)^{n-1} + \cdots + a(1 + r) \qquad (3.4a)$$

Then we subtract (3.4a) from (3.4). Note that all of the terms on the right-hand side, except for the first and last, cancel out.

$$FVA_{r,t} - (1 + r)FVA_{r,t} = -a(1 + r)^n + a(1 + r)^0 \qquad (3.4b)$$
$$S_n = a[1 + r + r^2 + \cdots + r^{n-2} + r^{n-1}] \qquad (3.5)$$

The sum of a geometric series can be expressed as shown in Equation 3.6.

$$S_n = a\left[\frac{r^n - 1}{r - 1}\right] \qquad (3.6)$$

For calculating the future value of an annuity at an interest rate of r and the number of periods reflected in t, $(FVA_{r,t})$, the rate of geometric growth is $(1 + r)$. Hence we can write:

$$FVA_{r,t} = a\left[\frac{(1 + r)^n - 1}{1 + r - 1}\right].$$

Solving for $FVA_{r,t}$ results in Equation 3.7, which is the formula for calculating the future value of an annuity.

$$FVA_{r,t} = a\left[\frac{(1 + r)^n - 1}{r}\right] \qquad (3.7)$$

The interest factor in Equation 3.7 can also be written with an abbreviation in letters as shown in Equation 3.8.

$$FVA_{r,t} = aFVIFA(r,t) \qquad (3.8)$$

FVIFA has been given values for various combinations of r and t. To find these, see Table A.3 in Appendix A. To find the answer to the three-year, $1,000 annuity problem, simply refer to Table A.3, look down the 10 percent column to the row for the third year, and multiply the factor 3.3100 by $1,000. The answer using Equation 3.8 is the same as the one derived by the long method illustrated in Figure 3.4.

$$FVA_{r,t} = aFVIFA(r,t)$$

$$FVA_{10\%,3 \text{ yrs.}} = \$1,000(3.3100) = \$3,310$$

Notice that the FVIFA for the sum of an annuity is always larger than the number of years the annuity runs. The reader should verify that the same result can be obtained with a hand calculator, using the formula in Equation 3.7.

PRESENT VALUE OF AN ANNUITY

Many decisions in finance use the concept of the present value of an annuity. It is the basic formulation used in analyzing investment decisions, in valuation calculations, and in many other applications. We start with a simple investment decision. The Abscind Tree Company is considering the purchase of a power saw; the saw will cost $2,000 and generate additional cash flows of $1,000 per year for three years. The cash flows are considered available at the end of each year (ordinary annuity); the applicable discount rate is 10 percent. Will Abscind gain from the investment?

The analysis requires a comparison between the present value of the future cash inflows and the initial investment cash outflow. We use a time line analysis depicted in Figure 3.5, Panel A. The present value of the future cash inflows is $2,486.85. The net present value (NPV) of the investment is the present value of benefits less the present value of costs. In our example, the NPV is $2,486.85 − $2,000 = $486.85. The investment adds value to the firm so it should be made. If the cash inflows were available at the beginning of each year (much less plausible), we would have an annuity due. The analysis is shown in Panel B of Figure 3.5. The present value of the cash inflows is even higher since they are received one year earlier. Again the NPV is positive. (We shall use the NPV concept, which is the basis for value creation, throughout the book.)

More generally, the present value of an annuity ($PVA_{r,t}$) is expressed in Equation 3.9.

$$PVA_{r,t} = a\left(\frac{1}{1+r}\right) + a\left(\frac{1}{1+r}\right)^2 + \cdots + a\left(\frac{1}{1+r}\right)^n \qquad (3.9)$$

$$= a\left[\left(\frac{1}{1+r}\right) + \left(\frac{1}{1+r}\right)^2 + \cdots + \left(\frac{1}{1+r}\right)^n\right]$$

This expression can be put in a form for direct calculation, again using the sum of a geometric series formula as in the previous equation. Now the ratio of growth is $(1/1 + r)$. Accordingly, we have:

$$PVA_{r,t} = a\left(\frac{1}{1+r}\right)\left[\frac{\left(\frac{1}{1+r}\right)^n - 1}{\left(\frac{1}{1+r}\right) - 1}\right]. \qquad (3.10)$$

FIGURE 3.5   Time Lines for the Present Value of an Annuity @ 10 Percent

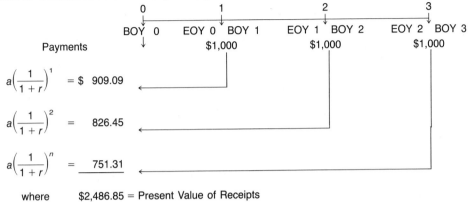

Panel A.   *Present Value of Ordinary Annuity*

$a\left(\dfrac{1}{1+r}\right)^{1}$ = $ 909.09

$a\left(\dfrac{1}{1+r}\right)^{2}$ = 826.45

$a\left(\dfrac{1}{1+r}\right)^{n}$ = 751.31

where $2,486.85 = Present Value of Receipts
$n = 3$

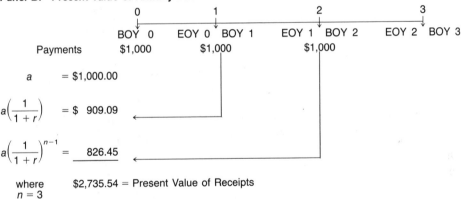

Panel B.   *Present Value of Annuity Due*

a = $1,000.00

$a\left(\dfrac{1}{1+r}\right)$ = $ 909.09

$a\left(\dfrac{1}{1+r}\right)^{n-1}$ = 826.45

where $2,735.54 = Present Value of Receipts
$n = 3$

Panel C.   **Relationship**

Present Value of Annuity Due = $(1 + r)$ Present Value of Ordinary Annuity
$$\$2,735.54 = (1.10)\$2,486.85$$

Note: BOY = beginning of year; EOY = end of year.

This simplifies to:

$$PVA_{r,t} = a\left[\frac{1 - (1 + r)^{-n}}{r}\right]. \qquad (3.11)$$

Alternatively, we can derive Equation 3.11 from the future value formula:

$$PVA_{r,t} = FVA_{r,t}(1 + r)^{-n}$$
$$= a\left[\frac{(1 + r)^{n} - 1}{r}\right](1 + r)^{-n} = a\left[\frac{1 - (1 + r)^{-n}}{r}\right].$$

TABLE 3.4 PVA for Unequal Inflows

Period	Cash Inflow	×	$PVIF_{10\%,n}$	=	PV of Each Cash Inflow
1	100		0.9091		$ 90.91
2	200		0.8264		165.28
3	300		0.7513		225.39
4	500		0.6830		341.50
5	400		0.6209		248.36
6	600		0.5645		338.70
7	200		0.5132		102.64
			Present Value of the Unequal Inflows		$1,512.78

Using *PVIFA,* the present value of an annuity interest factor, we can write: $PVA_{r,t} = a[\text{PVIFA}(r,t)]$.

For our simple numerical example, we have:

$$PVA_{r,t} = \$1,000\left[\frac{1 - (1.10)^{-3}}{.10}\right] = \$1,000\left[\frac{1 - .7513}{.10}\right] = \$2,487.$$

This is the same result as in Figure 3.5, Panel A, except for rounding to the nearest dollar. Notice that the *PVIFA* for the present value of an annuity is always less than the number of years the annuity runs, whereas the *FVIFA* for the sum of an annuity is larger than the number of years. Again, Panel C in Figure 3.5 shows that the present value of an annuity due is the present value of an ordinary annuity multiplied by $(1 + r)$.

Unequal Payments

Thus far we have used constant annual inflows to develop the basic relationships. The concepts can easily be applied to uneven payments by using the simple present value formula. The assumed cash inflows and their present value are shown in Table 3.4. The time line for this example is set forth in Figure 3.6.

PERPETUITIES

Some securities carry no maturity date. They are a perpetuity — an annuity that continues forever. The future value of a perpetuity is infinite since the number of periodic payments is infinite. The present value of an annuity can be calculated by starting with Equation 3.11.

$$PVA_{r,t} = a\left[\frac{1 - (1 + r)^{-n}}{r}\right] \tag{3.11}$$

FIGURE 3.6   Time Line of the PVA for Unequal Inflows

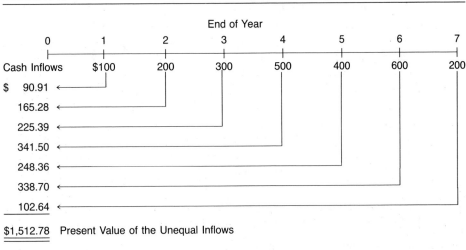

$1,512.78   Present Value of the Unequal Inflows

Notice that the term $(1 + r)^{-n} = 1/(1 + r)^n$ is always less than one for positive interest rates. For example, suppose $r = 10\%$, then

$$(1 + r)^{-1} = .909, \ (1 + r)^{-2} = .826, \ (1 + r)^{-3} = .751, \cdots, \ (1 + r)^{-100} = .000073.$$

As the number of years becomes very large (i.e., infinite) the term $(1 + r)^{-n}$ goes to zero. Thus, if the annuity of constant payments is perpetual, we have as our final result:

$$PVA_{r,\infty} = \frac{a}{r}. \qquad (3.12)$$

So the present value of a perpetuity is the periodic flow, a, divided by the discount factor. Equation 3.12 is a simple expression rich in implications.

Impact of Changing the Discount Rate

Assume that initially $a = \$120$ and $r = 10\%$, the PV is:

$$PV = \frac{\$120}{.10} = \$1,200.$$

If r rises to 12 percent, the PV falls to $1,000. If r falls to 8 percent, the PV rises to $1,500. Thus the PV is very sensitive to the size of the discount factor. This is also generally true for investments even if they do not have infinite lives; however, the impact is largest for a perpetuity.

Interrelationships among the Terms

The formula for a perpetuity also facilitates an understanding of another set of relationships. For all the interest formulas we have three basic terms as shown by Equation 3.13.

$$\text{Value} = (\text{Periodic Flow}) \text{ times } (\text{Interest Factor}) \tag{3.13}$$

For our basic example above, we have

$$\text{Value} = \$120\left(\frac{1}{.10}\right) = \$120(10).$$

If we know any two of the three terms, we can calculate the third. If we have a value of $1,000 and a flow of $120, the discount factor can be solved to be 12 percent. If we have a value of $1,500 and a discount factor of 10 percent, the flow must be $150.

GENERALIZATION OF INTERRELATIONSHIPS

These relationships apply to all of the four basic interest formulas we have discussed in previous sections:

I.   Compound Interest
   A.   Basic Relations
      1a.   Compound sum: *FVIF*
        (Eqn. 3.2) $FV_{r,n} = P_0(1 + r)^n = P_0(FVIF_{r,n})$
      1b.   Present value: *PVIF*
        (Eqn. 3.3) $PV_{r,n} = S_n(1 + r)^{-n} = S_n(PVIF_{r,n})$
      2a.   Sum of annuity: *FVIFA*
        (Eqn. 3.7) $FVA_{r,t} = a\{[(1 + r)^n - 1]/r\} = a(FVIFA_{r,n})$
      2b.   Present value of annuity: *PVIFA*
        (Eqn. 3.11) $PVA_{r,t} = a\{[1 - (1 + r)^{-n}]/r\} = a(PVIFA_{r,n})$

We present some practical illustrations of how we may solve for a third term when we have two of the three factors: present or future value, the periodic flow, and the interest factor.

Determining Interest Rates

In many instances, the present values and cash flows associated with a payment stream are known, but the interest rate is not known. Suppose a bank offers to lend you $1,000 today if you sign a note agreeing to pay the bank $1,762.30 at the end of five years. What rate of interest would you be paying on the loan? To answer the question, we use Equation 3.2.

$$FV_{r,n} = P_0(1 + r)^n = P_0FVIF(r,n). \tag{3.2}$$

We simply solve for the *FVIF* and then look up this value in Table A.1 along the row for the fifth year:

$$FVIF(r,n) = \frac{FV_{r,5 \text{ yrs.}}}{P_0} = \frac{\$1,762.30}{\$1,000} = 1.7623.$$

TABLE 3.5   IBM Financial Data

	1989	1988	1987	1986	1985
Revenue (billions)	$62.7	59.7	55.3	52.2	50.7
Net earnings (billions)	3.8	5.8	5.3	4.8	6.6

Looking across the row for the fifth year, we find the value 1.7623 in the 12 percent column; therefore, the interest rate on the loan is 12 percent.

Precisely the same approach is taken to determine the interest rate implicit in an annuity. For example, suppose a bank will lend you $2,401.80 if you sign a note in which you agree to pay the bank $1,000 at the end of each of the next three years. What interest rate is the bank charging you? To answer the question, we solve Equation 3.11 for $PVIFA$ and then look up the $PVIFA$ in Table A.4:

$$PV_{r,t} = aPVIFA(r,t) \tag{3.11}$$

$$PVIFA(r,t) = \frac{PV_{r,3 \text{ yrs.}}}{a} = \frac{\$2,401.8}{\$1,000} = 2.4018.$$

Looking across the third-year row, we find the factor 2.4018 under the 12 percent column; therefore, the bank is lending you money at a 12 percent interest rate.

A third illustration of finding interest rates is determining growth rates. One method is the endpoints method. For example, on page 45 of IBM's 1989 Annual Report, data for revenue and net earnings are presented as reproduced in Table 3.5.

From the data in Table 3.5, we can calculate (geometric average) growth rates using the future value formula, Equation 3.2:

$$FV_{r,t} = PV_0(1 + r)^n. \tag{3.2}$$

For the revenue stream, the "future amount" after four years of growth is $62.7 million and the "present amount" is $50.7 million. Substituting these into the formula, we have:

$$\$62.7 = \$50.7(1 + r)^4$$

$$\left(\frac{\$62.7}{\$50.7}\right)^{1/4} - 1 = r$$

$$r = 5.45\%.$$

Similarly, for net earnings, we have:

$$FV_{r,t} = PV_0(1 + r)^n$$

$$3.8 = 6.6(1 + r)^4$$

$$\left(\frac{3.8}{6.6}\right)^{1/4} - 1 = r = -12.89\%.$$

Or more generally:

$$g = \left(\frac{X_n}{X_0}\right)^{1/n} - 1 \tag{3.14}$$

where:

g = compound (geometric average) growth rate over the period
X_n = endpoint value
X_0 = beginning value
n = number of periods of growth.

Thus IBM revenue grew at an annual compound rate of 5.45 percent over the years 1985–1989 while net earnings declined by almost 13 percent per year. This suggests that to maintain the growth in revenues IBM had to cut prices, which eroded profit margins over the five-year period. The IBM data illustrate how to calculate growth and decline rates, using compound interest concepts.

Annual Annuity Payments

Suppose that you receive a second mortgage loan for $20,000 at an interest rate of 10 percent. You are required to pay it off in three annual installments to begin at the end of the first year. The solution requires application of the present value of an annuity formula, Equation 3.11. Here, however, we know that the present value of the annuity is $20,000; the problem is to find the three equal annual payments when the interest rate is 10 percent. This calls for dividing both sides of Equation 3.11 by the PVIFA to obtain Equation 3.11a.

$$PVA_{r,t} = aPVIFA(r,t) \qquad\qquad (3.11)$$

$$a = \frac{PVA_{r,t}}{PVIFA(r,t)} \qquad\qquad (3.11a)$$

The interest factor (PVIFA) is found in Appendix A, Table A.4, to be 2.4869. Substituting this value in Equation 3.11a, we find the three equal annual amounts to be $8,042.14:

$$a = \frac{\$20,000}{2.4869} = \$8,042.141.$$

This kind of calculation is also used in setting up insurance and pension plan benefit schedules. For example, if you have accumulated $200,000 and if it were to be paid to you in three annual installments beginning at the end of each year, your annual benefit would be $80,421.41 (ten times the amount in the previous example).

We have provided a number of applications of the relationships between the present or future value, the periodic flow and the interest factor. The same logic can be applied to any other type of discounted cash flow problem that may arise.

Amortized Loans

Corporate bonds are typically payable in full at maturity, with only the interest paid semiannually. Thus a 30-year corporate bond with a face amount of $100,000 and a coupon rate of 12 percent would pay $6,000 in interest each six months for a yearly total of $12,000. The principal of $100,000 would be paid at the end of 30 years. However, business term loans, automobile loans, and home mortgage loans typically provide for

TABLE 3.6 Loan Amortization Schedule ($100,000 @ 12%) 3 Years, Annually

Year	(1) Payment	(2) Interest [.12 × Col. (4)]	(3) Repayment of Principal [Col. (1) − Col. (2)]	(4) End-of- Year Balance
0	—	—	—	$100,000.00
1	$ 41,634.90	$12,000.00	$ 29,634.90	70,365.10
2	41,634.90	8,443.81	33,191.09	37,174.01
3	41,634.90	4,460.88	37,174.02	≈0
	$124,904.70	$24,904.69	$100,000.01	

repayment of principal as each periodic payment is made. These are called *amortized loans*.

An example will illustrate the ideas involved in amortized loans. A firm borrows $100,000, which will be paid off by three equal payments made at the end of the subsequent three years. The applicable annual interest rate is 12 percent. The equal annual payments will combine both interest and repayment of principal so that the loan is completely repaid by the end of the third year. The key concept involved is to determine the amount of the equal annual payments.[3]

We use Equation 3.11a derived previously to determine the annual payment or annuity.

$$a = \frac{PVA_{r,t}}{PVIFA(r,t)}$$

$$= \frac{\$100,000}{PVIFA(12\%, \ 3 \ \text{yrs.})}$$

We can determine from the table for the present value of an annuity that the interest factor is 2.4018; divided into the initial $100,000, it gives us the amount of the equal annual payment of $41,635.44 that has to be made. (If we use a hand calculator and carry the interest factor out to nine places, the equal annual payment is $41,634.90. This is the amount used in the subsequent analysis.)

Remember that the equal annual payment consists of an interest component and a repayment of principal component. The amount of each component varies each year, as illustrated in Table 3.6, which represents an amortization schedule.

Column (1) represents the equal annual payments. Column (2) represents the interest component. The amount for Year 1 is 12 percent of the original amount borrowed. This amount is subtracted from the annual payment to obtain the repayment of principal shown in Column (3). The repayment of principal deducted from the original $100,000 gives the end-of-year balance shown in Column (4) for Year 1. In the subsequent years, interest is calculated on the previous end-of-year balance in Column (4). This new amount of interest is deducted from the equal payment in Column (1) to determine the repayment of

---

[3]Unequal payments could accomplish the same result, but the arithmetic would be somewhat more complicated.

TABLE 3.7   Illustration of Amortization for a Home Mortgage
($100,000 @ 12%) 30 Years, Monthly

Month	(1) Payment	(2) Interest [.01 × Col. (4)]	(3) Repayment of Principal [Col. (1) − Col. (2)]	(4) End-of- Month Balance
0	—	—	—	$100,000.00
1	$ 1,028.61	$ 1,000.00	$ 28.61	99,971.39
2	1,028.61	999.71	28.90	99,942.49
3	1,028.61	999.42	29.19	99,913.30
—	—	—	—	—
—	—	—	—	—
—	—	—	—	—
359	1,028.61	—	—	1,018.43
360	1,028.61	10.18	1,018.43	0
	$370,299.60	$270,299.60	$100,000.00	

principal in Column (3). Column (4) continues to be the balance at the end of the previous year less the repayment of principal during the current year.

The total of the three equal payments made is $124,904.70. This is the total in Column (1). This also represents the sum of the interest payments shown in Column (2) plus the repayment of the $100,000, which is the total of Column (3). In subsequent discussions that involve tax factors, the interest payments for each year in Column (2) represent a deductible cost for the borrower and an addition to taxable income for the lender.

Automobile loans and home mortgage loans typically involve amortization of the principal in equal monthly installments. We will illustrate a home mortgage with the same dollar amount and the same quoted interest rate as in the previous illustration but will change the amortization period to 30 years with equal monthly payments. The expression for the interest factor for the present value of an annuity is taken from Equation 3.11:

$$PVIFA = \frac{1 - (1 + r)^{-n}}{r}.$$

We insert ($.12/12 = .01$) for the monthly interest rate, r, and 360 for the number of months, n. The resulting interest factor is 97.21833. This is divided into $100,000 to obtain the equal monthly mortgage loan payment of $1,028.61. The monthly pattern is illustrated in Table 3.7. The logic of the relation between the columns is exactly the same as for Table 3.6. In the early years, most of the payment represents interest with relatively little left over for repayment of principal. However, as shown, for the final month, most of the payment is repayment of principal with a relatively small amount of interest expense.

The sum of the monthly payments over the entire 30-year period is $370,299.60. Thus, the total of payments made over the 360 periods is almost four times the amount of the original principal of $100,000 borrowed under the home mortgage. However, the lender is simply earning a quoted rate of 12 percent compounded monthly. The dollar amount of interest is so large because the payments are made over the extended 360-month period.

NONINTEGER VALUES OF INTEREST RATES

In the interest tables at the end of the book we have given interest factor values for integer values such as 8 or 9 percent. Sometimes practical problems involve fractional interest rates, such as $8\frac{1}{4}$ percent. Or the interest rate calculation problem you encounter may involve time periods outside the range of the years provided in the tables. (Compounding for periods other than the annual basis given in the tables will be discussed in the following section.) For fractional interest rates, the use of the formulas and a hand calculator enables us to determine the interest factors required. Recall that in the interest rate formulas presented, there was a component (*FVIF, PVIF, FVIFA,* or *PVIFA*) for the interest factor. Assuming that our problem involved alternatively using each of the four types of interest factors for an interest rate of $8\frac{1}{4}$ percent and a ten-year period, the formulas and the resulting values are shown below:

$$FVIF = (1 + r)^n = 1.0825^{10} = 2.2094.$$

$$PVIF = 1/(1 + r)^n = 1/1.0825^{10} = 0.4526.$$

$$FVIFA = [(1 + r)^n - 1]/r = (1.0825^{10} - 1)/0.0825$$

$$= 14.6597.$$

$$PVIFA = [1 - (1 + r)^{-n}]/r = (1 - 1.0825^{-10})/0.0825 = 6.6351.$$

Notice that in performing the calculations, we take $(1.0825)^{10}$ and then simply use this result in a slightly different way for each of the four interest factors that we calculate. Many hand-held calculators are preprogrammed to carry out these kinds of calculations. However, all of these internal programs are based on the logic involved in using each of the four basic compound interest formulas.

Sometimes the problem involves obtaining interest rates when only the interest factors are provided. For example, suppose we make an investment of $663,510, which will yield $100,000 a year for ten years. We want to know the rate of return on that investment. We use Equation 3.11a to find the *PVIFA*:

$$PVIFA = \$663,510 \div \$100,000 = 6.6351.$$

From our calculations above, we recognize that this result is the PVIFA in which the interest rate is $8\frac{1}{4}$ percent. If we are using a preprogrammed hand calculator, we can solve for the required interest rate. With a less sophisticated hand calculator, we would have to obtain the result by trial and error. But with hand calculators of any degree of sophistication, if we keep in mind the expressions for the four basic compound interest relations, we can obtain what we need to solve any real-world problem that might come up. This is even true when compounding is on a basis other than an annual basis, as we shall demonstrate in the following section.

TABLE 3.8   Compound Interest Calculations with Semiannual Compounding

Period	Period Beginning Amount	×	$(1 + r)$	=	Ending Amount ($FV_{r,n}$)
1	$1,000.00		1.05		$1,050.00
2	1,050.00		1.05		1,102.50

SEMIANNUAL AND OTHER COMPOUNDING PERIODS

In all the examples used thus far, it has been assumed that returns were received annually. For example, in the section dealing with future values, it was assumed that the funds earned 10 percent a year. However, suppose the earnings rate had been 10 percent compounded semiannually (that is, every six months). What would this have meant? Consider the following example.

You invest $1,000 in a security to receive a return of 10 percent compounded semiannually. How much will you have at the end of one year? Since semiannual compounding means that interest is actually paid each six months, this fact is taken into account in the tabular calculations in Table 3.8. Here, the annual interest rate is divided by 2, but twice as many compounding periods are used because interest is paid twice a year. Comparing the amount on hand at the end of the second six-month period, $1,102.50, with what would have been on hand under annual compounding, $1,100.00, shows that semiannual compounding is better for the investor. This result occurs because the saver earns interest on interest more frequently. Thus semiannual compounding results in higher effective annual rates. If we require that the annual rates stay at 12 percent, then the semiannual rate would not be $12/2 = 6$ percent but rather $(1.12)^{1/2} - 1 = .0583 = 5.83$ percent.[4] By market convention, however, the yield to maturity based on compounding at intervals of six months is doubled to obtain the annual yield, which understates the effective annual yield.[5]

We can extend this simple example for more frequent compounding within the year. We shall calculate the future sum for one year for multiple compounding within the year for an interest rate of 12 percent and an initial principal of $1 as shown in Table 3.9. We see that daily compounding increases the effective annual interest rate by 0.75 percent.

---

[4]These refinements have been set forth in a series of articles: I. Keong Chew and Ronnie J. Clayton, "Bond Valuation: A Clarification," *The Financial Review,* 18 (May 1983), pp. 234–236; Philip A. Horvath, "A Pedagogic Note on Intra-Period Compounding and Discounting," *The Financial Review,* 20 (February 1985), pp. 116–118; and James T. Lindley, Billy P. Helms, and Mahmoud Haddad, "A Measure of the Errors in Intra-Period Compounding and Bond Valuation," *The Financial Review,* 22 (February 1987), pp. 33–51.

[5]F. J. Fabozzi and T. D. Fabozzi, *Bond Markets, Analysis and Strategies* (New York: Prentice-Hall, 1989), p. 38.

TABLE 3.9 Effective Annual Yields with Multiple Compounding
Within the Year

Annual	$FV_{r,1} = P_0(1 + r)$		$= 1.1200.$ $(q = 1)$
Semiannual		$= P_0\left(1 + \dfrac{r}{2}\right)^2$	$= 1.1236.$ $(q = 2)$
Quarterly		$= P_0\left(1 + \dfrac{r}{4}\right)^4$	$= 1.1255.$ $(q = 4)$
Monthly		$= P_0\left(1 + \dfrac{r}{12}\right)^{12}$	$= 1.1268.$ $(q = 12)$
Daily		$= P_0\left(1 + \dfrac{r}{365}\right)^{365}$	$= 1.1275.$ $(q = 365)$

Equation 3.12 is a generalization of the procedure for within-the-year compounding, where q is frequency, n is years:

$$FV_{r,n} = P_0\left(1 + \frac{r}{q}\right)^{nq}. \tag{3.12}$$

The four interest tables presented can be used when compounding occurs more than once a year. Simply divide the nominal (stated) interest rate by the number of times compounding occurs and multiply the years by the number of compounding periods per year. For example, to find the amount to which $1,000 will grow after five years if semiannual compounding is applied to a stated 10 percent interest rate, divide 10 percent by 2 and multiply the five years by 2. Then look in Table A.1 at the end of the book under the 5 percent column and in the row for the tenth period, where you will find an interest factor of 1.6289. Multiplying this by the initial $1,000 gives a value of $1,628.90, the amount to which $1,000 will grow in five years at 10 percent compounded semiannually. This compares with $1,610.50 for annual compounding.

The same procedure is applied in all the cases covered — compounding, discounting, single payments, and annuities. To illustrate semiannual compounding in calculating the present value of an annuity, for example, consider the case described in the section on the present value of an annuity — $1,000 a year for three years, discounted at 10 percent. With annual discounting or compounding, the interest factor is 2.4869 and the present value of the annuity is $2,486.90. For semiannual compounding, look under the 5 percent column and in the Year 6 row of Table A.4 to find an interest factor of 5.0757. Then multiply by half of $1,000, or the $500 received each six months, to get the present value of the annuity, $2,537.85. The payments come a little more rapidly (the first $500 is paid after only six months), so the annuity is a little more valuable if payments are received semiannually rather than annually.

FIGURE 3.7   Annual, Semiannual, and Continuous Compounding

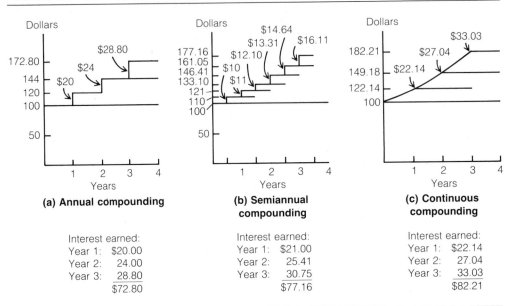

Interest earned:
Year 1: $20.00
Year 2:   24.00
Year 3:   28.80
$72.80

Interest earned:
Year 1: $21.00
Year 2:   25.41
Year 3:   30.75
$77.16

Interest earned:
Year 1: $22.14
Year 2:   27.04
Year 3:   33.03
$82.21

CONTINUOUS COMPOUNDING AND DISCOUNTING

By letting the frequency of compounding, q, approach infinity, Equation 3.12 can be modified to the special case of *continuous compounding*. Continuous compounding is extremely useful in theoretical finance as well as in practical applications. Also as shown in later chapters, computations are often simplified when continuously compounded interest rates are used.

Continuous Compounding

The relationship between discrete and continuous compounding is illustrated in Figure 3.7, for $P_0 = \$100$ and a nominal rate $r = 20$ percent. Figure 3.7(a) shows the annual compounding case, where interest is added once a year; in Figure 3.7(b), compounding occurs twice a year; and in Figure 3.7(c), interest is earned continuously.

Equation 3.12 was used to show compounding for smaller and smaller time intervals.

$$FV_{r,n} = P_0\left(1 + \frac{r}{q}\right)^{nq} \tag{3.12}$$

When we compound continuously, the result is the equation for continuous compounding shown in Equation 3.13.

$$FV_{r,t} = P_0 e^{rt} \tag{3.13}$$

where e is the constant 2.718. Letting $P_0 = 1$, we can rewrite Equation 3.13 as

$$FV_{r,t} = e^{rt}. \tag{3.13a}$$

Expressing Equation 3.13a in log form and noting that ln denotes the log to the base e, we obtain[6]

$$ln\ FV_{r,t} = rt\ ln\ e. \tag{3.13b}$$

Since e is defined as the base of the system of natural logarithms, $ln\ e$ must equal 1.0. Therefore,

$$ln\ FV_{r,t} = rt. \tag{3.13b}$$

For example, if $t = 5$ years and $k = 10$ percent, the product is 0.50. To use Equation 3.13a requires a hand calculator with an e^x key. If your hand calculator has an e^x function, use Equation 3.13a; enter the .5 and push the e^x key to obtain 1.648721. If your hand calculator has a lnx key (but not an e^x key) use Equation 3.13b; enter the .5 and push INV and then the lnx key to obtain the same result. Most calculators have some provision for performing logarithmic functions. For annual compounding, the calculation is $(1.1)^5 = 1.610510$.

Continuous Discounting

Equation 3.13 can be solved for $P_0(= PV_{r,t})$ and used to determine present values under continuous compounding.

$$P_0 = PV_{r,t} = \frac{FV_{r,t}}{e^{rt}} = FV_{r,t}e^{-rt} \tag{3.14}$$

Thus, if $1,649 is due in five years and if the appropriate *continuous* discount rate r is 10 percent, the present value of this future payment is

$$PV = \frac{\$1,649}{1.649} = \$1,000.$$

The present value of an infinite stream of payments growing at a constant rate g with continuous discounting at the rate r can be calculated by using Equation 3.15:

$$PV_{r,\infty} = \frac{a_0}{r - g}. \tag{3.15}$$

---

[6]Recall that the logarithm of a number is the power, or exponent, to which a specified base must be raised to equal the number; that is, the log (base 10) of 100 is 2 because $(10)^2 = 100$. In the system of natural logs, the base is $e \approx 2.718$.

Equation 3.15 is the formula for the present value of a continuous stream of payments growing to infinity at the constant rate g and discounted at rate r.[7] For example, when $a_0 = \$12$, $r = 12\%$ and $g = 4\%$, the (present) value of the stream of inflows is $12/.08 = \$150$.

THE ANNUAL PERCENTAGE RATE (APR)

Different types of financial contracts use different compounding periods. Most bonds pay interest semiannually. Some savings accounts pay interest quarterly, but the new money market accounts at most financial institutions pay interest daily. Department stores, oil companies, and credit cards also specify a daily rate of interest. In addition, to obtain a home mortgage loan, the lender charges points, up front. To compare the costs of different credit sources, it is necessary to calculate the effective rate of interest, or the annual percentage rate (APR), as it is generally called. The APR is always compounded once per year.

To calculate the APR, we should recognize that we are simply making another application of Equation 3.12, where $n = 1$. Equation 3.12 then becomes Equation 3.16:

$$PV_{r,1} = P_0\left(1 + \frac{r}{q}\right)^q. \tag{3.16}$$

The annual effective rate of interest (APR) can be determined as follows:

$$\frac{PV_{r,1}}{P_0} = \left(1 + \frac{r}{q}\right)^q = 1 + \text{APR}.$$

Solving for the APR we have

$$\text{APR} = \left(1 + \frac{r}{q}\right)^q - 1. \tag{3.17}$$

Since we have already calculated $(1 + \text{APR})$ in Table 3.9, the APR in each of the examples is obtained by subtracting 1. For example, the APR rises from 12.36 percent for semiannual compounding to 12.68 percent for monthly compounding.

We can generalize further. At an interest rate of 12 percent, we want to know the future sum of $100 with quarterly compounding for five years. First we use Equation 3.12:

$$FV_{r,n} = P_0\left(1 + \frac{r}{q}\right)^{nq} = \$100\left(1 + \frac{.12}{4}\right)^{5(4)} = \$100(1.03)^{20} = \$180.611.$$

[7]With a continuous stream, the first payments start at the beginning of period zero. With discrete time periods, the first payment occurs at the end of period zero. This latter is the constant growth dividend model discussed in Chapter 16:

$$PV = \frac{d_0(1 + g)}{k - g}$$

where d_0 is the period zero dividend and k is the applicable cost of capital.

Alternatively, we can use the APR in Table 3.9 for quarterly compounding. This is 12.55 percent, which we can use in Equation 3.2:

$$FV_{r,n} = P_0(1 + APR)^n = \$100(1.1255)^5 = \$180.604.$$

Since the results are the same (except for rounding), we can use either method in making calculations. In many transactions, government regulations require that the lender provide the borrower with a written statement of the APR in the transaction. We have described how it can be calculated.

THE RELATIONSHIP BETWEEN DISCRETE AND CONTINUOUS INTEREST RATES

Discrete growth or compounding can always be transformed into an equivalent continuous version. Let d represent a discrete rate of compounding, while c is a continuous compounding rate. In general,

$$ln(1 + d) = c. \tag{3.18}$$

The continuous rate will, in general, be lower than the discrete rate. For example, if the discrete rate of interest is 12 percent, the continuous rate would be $ln(1.12) = 11.33$ percent. This is quite logical, since the interest is working harder when it is compounding every second than when it is compounding only once a year, for example.

Conversely, if a given interest rate is being compounded continuously, the equivalent discrete rate is larger. Thus, if we are using a nominal 12 percent rate but applying it continuously, the equivalent discrete rate will be higher. The appropriate formula to apply requires solving Equation 3.18 for d.

$$d = e^c - 1 \tag{3.19}$$

Compounding a 12 percent nominal rate continuously, the equivalent discrete rate is 12.7497 percent. Note that Equation 3.19 is the continuous compounding equivalent of Equation 3.17, which was the expression for calculating the annual percentage rate under discrete compounding. Thus, we see that the equivalent discrete rate when a nominal interest rate is compounded continuously represents the annual percentage rate (APR).

SUMMARY

A knowledge of compound interest and present value techniques is essential to an understanding of important aspects of finance covered in subsequent chapters: capital budgeting, financial structure, security valuation, and other topics.

The four basic equations with the notation that will be used throughout the book are

1. $FV_{r,n} = P_0 FVIF(r,n) \equiv P(1 + r)^n$

2. $PV_{r,n} = FV_{r,n} PVIF(r,n) \equiv FV_{r,n}(1 + r)^{-n}$

3. $FVA_{r,t} = a FVIFA(r,t) \equiv a[(1 + r)^n - 1]/r$

4. $PVA_{r,t} = aPVIFA(r,t) \equiv a[1 - (1 + r)^{-n}]/r$

With continuous compounding, the first two formulas become:

$$FV_{r,t} = P_0\, e^{rt}$$
$$PV_{r,t} = FV_{r,t}\, e^{-rt}.$$

These interest formulas can be used for either an even or uneven series of receipts or payments. The basic formulas can be used to find (1) the annual payments necessary to accumulate a future sum, (2) the annual receipts from a specified annuity, (3) the periodic payments necessary to amortize a loan, and (4) the interest rate implicit in a loan contract. They are the basis for all valuation formulas. The formulas can also be used with more frequent than annual compounding, including semiannual, monthly, daily, and continuous compounding.

The general formula for within-the-year compounding is:

$$q \text{ frequency, } n \text{ years, } FV_{r,n} = P_0[1 + (r/q)]^{nq}.$$

This expression is used in determining the *APR (annual percentage rate)* implicit in a contract where the *effective interest rate* is not the same as the stated rate because of the frequency of compounding. The formula for the annual percentage rate is:

$$APR = [1 + (r/q)]^q - 1.$$

Finally, the relationship between discrete and continuously compounded discount rates is the following equation:

$$d = e^c - 1$$

where d is also the (higher) APR for a continuously compounded discount rate, c.

QUESTIONS

3.1 When do financial decisions require explicit consideration of the interest factor?

3.2 Explain the relationship of discount rate levels to both present value and future value. Do the same for time to maturity.

3.3 Why do lending firms prefer 360 days per year as a basis for interest calculations, while borrowing firms prefer 365 days?

3.4 Compound interest relationships are important for decisions other than financial ones. Why are they important to marketing managers?

3.5 Would you rather have a savings account that pays 5 percent interest compounded semiannually or one that pays 5 percent interest compounded daily? Why?

3.6 For a given interest rate and a given number of years, is the interest factor for the sum of an annuity greater or smaller than the interest factor for the present value of the annuity?

3.7 Suppose you are examining two investments, A and B. Both have the same maturity, but A pays a 6 percent return and B yields 5 percent. Which investment is probably riskier? How do you know?

PROBLEMS

3.1   Which amount is worth more at 9 percent: $1,000 today or $2,500 after eight years?

3.2   The current production target for the five-year plan of the Logo Company is to increase output by 8 percent a year. If the 1993 production is 3.81 million tons, what is the target production for 1998?

3.3   At a growth rate of 9 percent, how long does it take a sum to double?

3.4   Assuming you had extra cash, how much would you be willing to loan somebody who agreed to pay you $50,000 in five years, if interest rates are 8 percent?

3.5   If, at age 25, you open an IRA account paying 10 percent annual interest, and you put $2,000 in at the end of each year, what will be your balance at age 65?

3.6   You are offered two alternatives: a $2,000 annuity for seven years or a lump sum today. If current interest rates are 9 percent, how large will the lump sum have to be to make you indifferent between the alternatives?

3.7   The Lowell Company's sales last year were $1 million.
   a.   Assuming that sales grow 18 percent a year, calculate sales for each of the next six years.
   b.   Plot the sales projections.
   c.   If your graph is correct, your projected sales curve is nonlinear. If it had been linear, would this have indicated a constant, increasing, or decreasing percentage growth rate? Explain.

3.8   The Hull Company has established a sinking fund to retire a $900,000 mortgage that matures on December 31, 1997. The company plans to put a fixed amount into the fund each year for ten years. The first payment was made on December 31, 1988; the last will be made on December 31, 1997. The company anticipates that the fund will earn 10 percent a year. What annual contributions must be made to accumulate the $900,000 as of December 31, 1997?

3.9   You need $135,500 at the end of 14 years. You know that the best you can do is to make equal payments into a bank account on which you can earn 6 percent interest compounded annually. Your first payment is to be made at the end of the first year.
   a.   What amount must you plan to pay annually to achieve your objective?
   b.   Instead of making annual payments, you decide to make one lump-sum payment today. To achieve your objective of $135,500 at the end of the 14-year period, what should this sum be? (You can still earn 6 percent interest compounded annually on your account.)

3.10   You have just purchased a newly issued $1,000 five-year Malley Company bond at par. The bond (Bond A) pays $60 in interest semiannually ($120 a year). You are also negotiating the purchase of a $1,000 six-year Malley Company bond (Bond B) that returns $30 in semiannual interest payments and has six years remaining before it matures.
   a.   What is the going rate of return on bonds of the risk and maturity of Malley Company's Bond A?
   b.   What should you be willing to pay for Bond B?

    c. How will your answer to Part b change if Bond A pays $40 in semiannual interest instead of $60 but still sells for $1,000? (Bond B still pays $30 semiannually and $1,000 at the end of six years.)

3.11 If you buy a note for $11,300, you will receive ten annual payments of $2,000, the first payment to be made one year from today. What rate of return, or yield, does the note offer?

3.12 You can buy a bond for $1,000 that will pay no interest during its seven-year life but will have a value of $2,502 when it matures. What rate of interest will you earn if you buy the bond and hold it to maturity?

3.13 A bank agrees to lend you $1,000 today in return for your promise to pay back $1,838.50 nine years from today. What rate of interest is the bank charging you?

3.14 If earnings in 1991 are $1.99 a share, while eight years earlier (in 1983) they were $1, what has been the annual rate of growth in earnings?

3.15 You are considering two investment opportunities, A and B. A is expected to pay $300 a year for the first 10 years, $700 a year for the next 15 years, and nothing thereafter. B is expected to pay $1,000 a year for 10 years and nothing thereafter. You find that other investments of similar risk to A and B yield 8 percent and 14 percent, respectively.
    a. Find the present value of each investment. Show your calculations.
    b. Which is the riskier investment? Why?
    c. Assume that your rich uncle will give you a choice of A or B without cost to you and that you (1) must hold the investment for its entire life (cannot sell it) or (2) are free to sell it at its going market price. Which investment would you prefer under each of the two conditions?

3.16 On December 31, Helen Ventor buys a building for $175,000, paying 20 percent down and agreeing to pay the balance in 20 equal annual installments that are to include principal plus 15 percent compound interest on the declining balance. What are the equal installments?

3.17 You wish to borrow $50,000 from your savings and loan for a home mortgage. The quoted interest rate is 11 percent compounded monthly for a 25-year mortgage.
    a. What annual percentage rate is equal to 11 percent compounded monthly?
    b. What will your monthly mortgage payments be (assuming that they are paid at the end of each month)?

3.18 Suppose you open a savings account with $1,800 earned in a summer job. The account's stated interest rate is 11 percent. Calculate your account's balance after one year if interest is paid (a) annually, (b) semiannually, (c) quarterly, (d) monthly, and (e) daily.

3.19 a. What amount will be paid for a $1,000 ten-year bond that pays $40 interest semiannually ($80 a year) and that yields 10 percent, compounded semiannually?
    b. What will be paid if the bond is sold to yield 8 percent?
    c. What will be paid if semiannual interest payments are $50 and the bond yields 6 percent?

3.20 Bank A offers to make you a school loan at an effective annual rate of 9.8 percent. Bank B offers the money at 9.6 percent compounded monthly. Which one should you accept?

3.21 The Hardy Company's common stock paid a dividend of $1 last year. Dividends are expected to grow at a rate of 18 percent for each of the next six years.
  a. Calculate the expected dividend for each of the next six years.
  b. Assuming that the first of these six dividends will be paid one year from now, what is the present value of the six dividends? (Given the riskiness of the dividend stream, 18 percent is the appropriate discount rate.)
  c. Assume that the price of the stock will be $27 six years from now. What is the present value of this "terminal value"? Use an 18 percent discount rate.
  d. Assume that you will buy the stock, receive the six dividends, and then sell the stock. How much should you be willing to pay for it?
  e. What would happen to the price of this stock if the discount rate declined because the riskiness of the stock declined? If the growth rate of the dividend stream increased?

3.22 What annual rate of interest would make you indifferent between it and 10 percent compounded continuously?

3.23 The First Security Bank pays 9 percent interest compounded annually on time deposits. The Second Security Bank pays 8 percent interest compounded continuously.
  a. In which bank would you prefer to deposit your money?
  b. Would your choice of banks be influenced by the fact that you might want to withdraw your funds during the year as opposed to at the end of the year? (Assume that funds must be left on deposit during the entire compounding period in order to receive any interest.)

3.24 If you have an account that compounds interest continuously and has an effective annual yield of 6.18 percent, what is the stated annual interest rate?

3.25 What rate of interest compounded monthly is equivalent to 18 percent compounded continuously?

3.26 For a 20-year deposit, what annual rate, payable quarterly, will produce the same effective rate as 6 percent, compounded continuously?

3.27 You have $32,604 in a 15-year-old account, which has been paying a 12.5 percent nominal rate of interest, compounded continuously. How much was your initial deposit?

3.28 *(Use the computer diskette, File name: 03TVM, Time Value of Money).*
  I am thinking of buying a car with a dealer price of $12,000. As an incentive program, the dealer offers to sell me the car with no down payment and 36 months to pay.
  a. At an interest rate of 15 percent, what will my monthly payments be?
  b. Suppose the manufacturer now engages in an incentive program and reduces the interest rate to an 8.8 percent interest rate. What does this do to my monthly payment?
  c. If you could allocate $120 a month to automobile payments with the interest rate at 8.8 percent, what price car would you buy? At 15 percent interest, what price car would you buy?
  d. Suppose alternatively the manufacturer gave an outright price cut. What price cut would be equivalent to changing the interest rate as above?
  e. Assume that the dealer increases the term of the loan to 60 months. What would my

monthly payment be if I went back to the 15 percent interest rate? The 8.8 percent interest rate?

f.   For questions (a) through (e) above, substitute 10 percent for the 15 percent and 2.5 percent for the 8.8 percent and answer the same questions (a) through (e).

g.   Now explore any other relationships you wish to consider by making up your own questions.

SELECTED REFERENCES

Chew, I. Keong, and Clayton, Ronnie J., "Bond Valuation: A Clarification," *The Financial Review,* 18 (May 1983), pp. 234–236.

Cissell, R.; Cissell, H.; and Flaspohler, D. C., *Mathematics of Finance,* 5th ed., Boston: Houghton Mifflin, 1978.

Fabozzi, F. J., and Fabozzi, T. D., *Bond Markets, Analysis and Strategies,* New York: Prentice-Hall, 1989, p. 38.

Horvath, Philip A., "A Pedagogic Note on Intra-Period Compounding and Discounting," *The Financial Review,* 20 (February 1985), pp. 116–118.

Lindley, James T.; Helms, Billy P.; and Haddad, Mahmoud, "A Measure of the Errors in Intra-Period Compounding and Bond Valuation," *The Financial Review,* 22 (February 1987), pp. 33–51.

Scott, David L., and Moore, W. Kent, *Fundamentals of the Time Value of Money.* New York: Praeger, 1984.

U.S. Department of Commerce, *Handbook of Mathematical Functions.* Edited by M. Abramowitz and I. A. Stegum. Washington, D.C.: Government Printing Office, December 1972.

Vichas, Robert P., *Handbook of Financial Mathematics, Formulas and Tables.* Englewood Cliffs, N. J.: Prentice-Hall, 1979.

PART TWO

The Environment for Financial Decisions

Financial decisions within the firm must take into account the external economic, financial, and social environments. Chapter 4 presents an overview of the total financial network of the modern economy, viewing the functions of financial managers within the perspective of the money and capital markets. The important concept of market efficiency is set forth as a set of forces that need to be understood by financial managers. In Chapter 5, the key elements of the U.S. tax system are summarized. The discussion emphasizes that since a high percentage of business income is paid to the government, taxes have an important influence on many kinds of business decisions, and, particularly, on the form of business organization used by the firm. New developments in organization forms are described. In Chapter 6, we analyze how the markets establish interest rates and interest rate relationships. In particular, we emphasize how the international financial environments influence interest rate levels in individual countries and in relation to other economies.

CHAPTER 4

Financial Markets and Market Efficiency

Financial managers link businesses that invest in physical capital to the financial sector of the economy from which financial capital is supplied via financial institutions and financial instruments. The purpose of financial markets is to allocate financial capital efficiently among alternative physical uses in the economy. The concept of the efficiency of financial markets is implicit in most models of financial decision making. Hence the concept is central to building a conceptual framework required for making rational financial policies and choices.

THE FINANCIAL SYSTEM

The financial manager functions in a complex financial environment because the savings and investment functions in a modern economy are performed by different economic units. Savings surplus units (a "unit" could be a business firm or an individual), whose savings exceed their investment in real assets, own financial assets. Savings deficit units, whose current savings are less than their investment in real assets, incur financial liabilities.

The transfer of funds from a savings surplus unit or the acquisition of funds by a savings deficit unit creates a financial asset and a financial liability. For example, funds deposited in a savings account in a bank represent a financial asset on the account holder's personal balance sheet but a liability account to the financial institution. Conversely, a loan from a financial institution represents a financial asset on its balance sheet but a financial liability to the borrower. A wide variety of financial claims, including promissory notes, bonds, and common stocks, are issued by savings deficit units.

Financial Markets

Financial transactions involve financial assets and financial liabilities. The creation and transfer of such assets and liabilities constitute *financial markets*. The nature of financial markets can be explained by an analogy. The automobile market, for example, is defined by all transactions in automobiles, whether they occur at auto dealers' showrooms, at wholesale auctions of used cars, or at individuals' homes, because they make up the total demand and supply for autos.

Similarly, financial markets are comprised of all trades that result in the creation of financial assets and financial liabilities. Trades are made through organized institutions, such as the New York Stock Exchange or the regional stock exchanges, or through the thousands of brokers and dealers who buy and sell securities off the exchange, comprising the *over-the-counter market*. In recent years computers have facilitated systems for directly matching buyers and sellers. Individual transactions with department stores, savings banks, or other financial institutions also create financial assets and financial liabilities. Thus, financial markets are not specific physical structures remote to the average individual. Rather, everyone participates in the trading process to some degree.

Different segments of the financial markets are characterized by different maturities. When the financial claims and obligations bought and sold have maturities of less than one year, the transactions constitute *money markets*. If the maturities are more than one year, the markets are referred to as *capital markets*. Although real capital in an economy is represented by things — for example, plants, machinery, and equipment — long-term financial instruments are regarded as ultimately representing claims on the real resources in an economy; for that reason, the markets in which these instruments are traded are referred to as capital markets.

Financial Intermediaries

Financial intermediation brings together, through transactions in the financial markets, the savings surplus units and the savings deficit units so that savings can be redistributed into their most productive uses. The specialized business firms whose activities include the creation of financial assets and liabilities are called *financial intermediaries*. Without these intermediaries and the processes of financial intermediation, the allocation of savings into real investment would be limited by whatever the distribution of savings happened to be. With financial intermediation, savings are transferred to economic units that have opportunities for profitable investment. In the process, real resources are allocated more effectively, and real output for the economy as a whole is increased.

The major types of financial intermediaries are briefly described in Table 4.1. Commercial banks are defined by their ability to accept demand deposits subject to transfer by depositors' checks. Such checks represent a widely accepted medium of exchange, accounting for over 90 percent of the transactions that take place. Savings and loan associations traditionally received funds from passbook savings and invested them primarily in

TABLE 4.1 Market Share Changes for Financial Intermediaries

Intermediary	Assets 1990[a] (billions of dollars)	% of Total Intermediary Assets				
		1950	1960	1970	1980	1990[a]
Commercial banks	3,279	52	38	38	37	32
Life insurance companies	1,378	22	20	15	12	13
Private pension funds	1,194	2	6	9	12	12
S&Ls	1,159	6	12	14	15	11
State & local pension funds	753	2	3	5	5	7
Mutual funds	588	1	3	4	2	6
Finance companies	539	3	5	5	5	5
Casualty insurance companies	507	4	5	4	4	5
Money market funds	453	—	—	—	2	4
Mutual savings banks	284	8	7	6	4	3
Credit unions	213	—	1	1	2	2
Total	10,347	100	100	100	100	100

[a]Mid-year for 1990.
Source: *Chicago Fed Letter*, December 1990, p. 1. Compiled from Fed *Flow of Funds Accounts*.

real estate mortgages that represented long-term borrowing, mostly by individuals.[1] Finance companies are business firms whose main activity is making loans to other business firms and to individuals. Life insurance companies sell protection against the loss of income from premature death or disability, and the insurance policies they sell typically have a savings element in them. Pension funds collect contributions from employees and/or employers to make periodic payments upon employees' retirement. Investment funds, also called mutual funds, sell shares to investors and use the proceeds to purchase existing equity securities.

Investment bankers are financial firms that buy new issues of securities from business firms at a guaranteed, agreed-upon price and seek immediately to resell the securities to other investors. Related financial firms that function simply as agents linking buyers and sellers are called investment brokers. Investment dealers are those who purchase for their own account from sellers and ultimately resell to other buyers. While investment bankers operate in the new issues market, brokers and dealers engage in transactions of securities that have already been issued. Other sources of funds are other business firms, households, and governments. At any point in time, some of these will be net borrowers and others net lenders.

The relative size of these institutions is suggested by the data in Table 4.1, which presents the total assets of the major financial intermediaries in the United States in 1990

---

[1]New laws by the early 1980s broadened the lending powers of S&L operations so that they increasingly became department stores of finance. Lack of experience with their new areas of operations, excesses and outright fraud, and the perverse incentives provided by deposit insurance (small investments by owners taking on huge debts resulting in big profits if successful and losses covered by the government if not) resulted in the multibillion-dollar bailouts of the 1990s.

TABLE 4.2 Total Financial Assets and Liabilities, United States
Year-End, 1989 (in billions)

A.	Total Credit Market Debt Owed by		$12,387
	1. U.S. government	$2,268	
	2. Households	3,501	
	3. Farm business	139	
	4. Nonfarm noncorporate business	1,196	
	5. Corporate business	2,065	
	6. State and local governments	634	
	7. Foreign	262	
	8. Government sponsored credit agencies	378	
	9. Mortgage pools	871	
	10. Commercial banks	77	
	11. Bank affiliates	143	
	12. Savings and loan	145	
	13. Mutual savings bank	17	
	14. Finance companies	496	
	15. Real estate investment trusts	10	
	16. Securities credit obligations	184	
B.	**Other Liabilities**		**11,763**
	1. Official foreign exchange	77	
	2. Checkable deposit and currency	889	
	3. Time and savings deposits	2,881	
	4. Other deposits at financial institutions	886	
	5. Life insurance reserves	352	
	6. Pension fund reserves	2,858	
	7. Trade credit	855	
	8. Mutual fund shares	555	
	9. Miscellaneous liabilities	2,276	
C.	**Equities Not Represented by Borrowing**		**6,707**
	Total financial claims (also allocated to sectors as assets)		**$30,857**

Source: Federal Reserve Board, *Flow of Funds Accounts, Financial Assets and Liabilities*, p. 60. *Year-End, 1966–1989.*

and trends in market shares since 1950. These institutions at mid-1990 held assets that summed to $10.3 trillion compared to federal debt of $3.2 trillion. Note also the major shifts in market shares during the four decades.

The major units in the financial economy are governments, households, financial institutions, corporate businesses, farm businesses, and nonfarm noncorporate businesses. Each of these sectors has assets and liabilities. The sum of assets held and claims will be equal for the total economy. In Table 4.2 we present the many categories of financial claims grouped by liabilities of the individual sectors. The total amount of financial liabilities as shown by the table is almost $31 trillion. Of this amount, over $12 trillion or 40 percent is credit market debt, which means that these are financial instruments traded between buyers and sellers in various types of markets such as security exchanges, or by dealers, or directly. The remaining $18 trillion is represented by financial instruments that are not traded in open markets. They include items such as checking deposits, savings deposits, ownership of money market fund shares. Trade credit represents accounts receivable for the sellers of goods (an asset) and accounts payable (a liability) for the buyers of goods. Another type of liability is represented by pension fund reserves that now total almost $3 trillion. Another set of claims is represented by the equities in corporations as well as in noncorporate businesses. The total financial liabilities and claims represent the right-hand side of the balance sheet for the economy. These claims can be allocated to holders for whom they represent assets — the left-hand side of the national economy's balance sheet.

THE ROLE OF GOVERNMENT

Government activities have many influences on the financial markets. Government policies have major influences on the state of the economy, on the money supply, and on the amounts and types of financial instruments outstanding.

The Federal Reserve System

Fundamental to an understanding of the behavior of the money and capital markets is an analysis of the role of the Federal Reserve System. The Fed, as it is called, has a set of instruments with which to influence the operations of commercial banks, whose loan and investment activities, in turn, have an important influence on the cost and availability of money. The most powerful of the Fed's instruments, and hence the one used most sparingly, is the right to change reserve requirements (the percentage of deposits that must be kept in reserve with the Fed). Most often, the Fed will exercise its option to alter the pattern of open-market operations (the Fed's buying and selling of securities), increasing and decreasing the amount of funds in the public's hands.

Changes may also be made in the interest rate the Fed charges its borrowers, mainly the commercial banks. This interest charge is called its discount rate for the following reason. A commercial bank makes loans to its customers, resulting in the creation of debt instruments, such as promissory notes. The bank may, in turn, sell these promissory notes to the Fed. When a commercial bank sells debt instruments to the Fed, they are discounted from face value. To illustrate, suppose a bank sells a promissory note in the amount of $1,210, which the borrower has promised to pay the bank at the end of one year. If the Fed's discount rate at that time is 10 percent, it will pay the bank $1,210 divided by 1.10, or $1,100, the discounted value of the promissory note.

Changes in the discount rate change the interest rates paid by banks and, consequently, the rates they charge their customers. In addition, changes in the Fed's discount rate may have "announcement effects." These changes represent an implicit announcement by Federal Reserve authorities that a change in economic conditions has occurred and that the new conditions call for a tightening or easing of monetary conditions. History shows that increases in the Federal Reserve Bank discount rate have usually been followed by rising interest rate levels and decreases by lowered levels. When the Federal Reserve

System purchases or sells securities in the open market, makes changes in the discount rate, or varies reserve requirements, the supply and price of funds are influenced and the interest rates or returns on most securities change as a result.

Fiscal Policy

The fiscal policy of the federal government may also impact interest rate levels. A cash budget deficit represents a stimulating influence by the federal government, and a cash surplus exerts a restraining influence. However, this generalization must be modified to reflect the way a deficit is financed and the way a surplus is used. To have the most stimulating effect, a deficit should be financed by a sale of securities through the banking system, particularly the central bank, thus providing a maximum amount of bank reserves and permitting a multiple expansion in the money supply. To have the most restrictive effect, the surplus should be used to retire bonds held by the banking system, particularly the central bank, thereby reducing bank reserves and causing a multiple contraction in the supply of money.

The impact of Treasury financing programs varies. Ordinarily, when the Treasury needs to draw funds from the money market, it competes with other potential users of funds, possibly resulting in a rise in interest rate levels. However, the desire to hold down interest rates also influences Treasury and Federal Reserve policy. To ensure the success of a large new offering, Federal Reserve authorities may temporarily ease money conditions, which may soften interest rates. If the Treasury encounters resistance in selling securities in the nonbanking sector, it may sell them in large volume to the commercial banking system, a move that expands its reserves and thereby increases the monetary base. This change, in turn, may lower the level of interest rates. The opposite effects may also occur. If the money supply expands faster than new goods and new investments, there may be too much money chasing too few goods, with inflation as the result. Lenders may then require an inflation component in the nominal interest rates charged, resulting in a rise in interest rates. This more sophisticated reaction to monetary policy has been called a "rational expectations" model in that it takes into account the longer term effects of changes in government policy.

Credit Agencies

The *Federal Reserve Bulletin* lists 27 federal and federally sponsored agencies. These agencies had debt outstanding totaling about $440 billion.[2] The largest categories of debt outstanding by federal agencies are briefly described. Debt outstanding of the Defense Department at early 1991 was about $42 billion representing mortgages assumed by the Defense Department under family housing and home owners assistance programs. An amount of $11 billion represented debentures issued in payment of federal housing administration claims. The Tennessee Valley Authority has debt outstanding of about $23 billion.

The debt outstanding of federally sponsored agencies accounts for $397 billion in total. The Federal Home Loan Banks, which act as a central bank for the savings and loan

---

[2]*Federal Reserve Bulletin*, July 1991, p. A32.

associations, had debt outstanding of about $113 billion. The Federal National Mortgage Association (Fannie Mae) had debt outstanding of $125 billion.

The Federal Home Loan Mortgage Corporation (Freddie Mac) had issued debt of over $31 billion. The Student Loan Marketing Association (Sallie Mae) had debt outstanding of about $36 billion. The three federally sponsored agencies with their relevant associations have common stock that is publicly traded with an active investor interest. Their stock was subject to general market movements as well as the severe declines in the stock prices of financial institutions during 1989–1990. From their 1989 peak levels to early November 1990 Fannie Mae moved from 46 to 27; Freddie Mac from 105 to 34; Sallie Mae from 56 to 33. A *Barron's* article commented on the need to reduce their leverage levels and to tighten their management controls.[3]

The Farm Credit Banks accounted for debt outstanding of about $52 billion. The Financing Corporation, which was established in August 1987 to recapitalize the Federal Savings and Loan Insurance Corporation, undertook its first borrowing in October 1987 and had debt outstanding at early 1991 of over $8 billion. The Resolution Funding Corporation is an arm of the Resolution Trust Corporation (RTC); it was authorized by Congress to borrow up to $30 billion, which it has done. The remainder of the over $200 billion (plus interest) that will be required by the RTC for the S&L rescue operation will be "off the books." The above represents a sample of the many facets of direct lending and sponsored lending by the federal government. They represent important institutions in the financial markets.

TYPES OF FINANCIAL INSTRUMENTS

The basic classification of financial instruments involves three major categories: currency, debt, and equity claims. Currency represents obligations issued by the U.S. Treasury as coins and paper currency. The operations of the commercial banking system result in creating demand deposits (the familiar checking accounts) by which about 90 percent of commercial transactions are conducted. The use of checks on demand deposits, therefore, represents the main form of "money." Debt or credit instruments represent promises to pay to the creditor specified amounts plus interest at a future date or dates. Stock generally means common stock representing the equity or ownership claims on an organization.

The above classification covers the three major types of financial instruments. However, variations on these basic types have produced many different kinds of financial instruments proliferating into a complex variety of forms particularly in recent years with the development of financial engineering.[4] The great variety of financial instruments now observed has resulted because there are several different types of building blocks, each of which can have different characteristics that can be combined in many different ways. We shall briefly describe some basic building blocks here, some of which will be developed in

---

[3]Robert M. Bleiberg, "Sallie, Freddie, Fannie: It's High Time You Put Your House in Order," *Barron's,* November 5, 1990, p. 12.

[4]See the special issue of *Financial Management* on financial engineering, Winter 1988; C. W. Smith and C. W. Smithson, *The Handbook of Financial Engineering,* Harper Business, 1990.

TABLE 4.3   Forms of Financial Contracts

Debt Forms	Pricing Contracts
Zero coupon	Forward contracts
Level coupon	Futures contracts
Floating rate coupon	Swaps
Amortizing	
Options	**Ownership Position**
Calls	Long
Puts	Short

greater detail in subsequent chapters. The basic building blocks can be outlined as shown in Table 4.3.

We shall briefly explain the categories in the above outline in order to provide a vocabulary and overview for materials covered throughout the book.

Debt Forms

Debt instruments can be freely traded in the credit markets or held by the lender. The distinction is not absolute because receivables held by lenders can also be sold. Zero coupon forms of debt have long been used in selling U.S. savings bonds — buy a U.S. savings bond for $15 and receive the face amount $25 at X years in the future. Some debt has a fixed level coupon like fixed rate home mortgages. A floating rate coupon is illustrated by adjustable rate home mortgages (ARMs). The familiar home mortgage also illustrates the concept of amortizing because the periodic (usually monthly) payment made by the borrower includes not only the interest owed but some portion of principle borrowed.

Pricing Contracts

A forward contract requires the purchase or sale of a particular asset at a specified future date at a price set at the time the contract is made.[5] For example, you promise to buy an automobile from someone in two months when you will have gotten together the necessary funds. This protects against a rise in price. Forward contracts may also be entered into to seek to gain from price changes. For example, a forward contract may be made to buy 1,000 bushels of wheat for $3 a bushel at the end of 180 days. If the price of wheat were $4.25 at the end of 180 days, the contract owner will have gained $1.25; if the price were $1.75, the contract owner will have lost $1.25.

A futures contract is equivalent in concept to a forward contract. The purchase of a futures contract obligates the purchaser to buy a specified amount at a designated exercise

---

[5]Forward contracts and futures are discussed in later chapters, particularly in Chapter 6, ''The Interest Rate and International Finance Environments,'' and Chapter 14, ''Managing Financial Risk.''

price on the contract maturity date. A futures contract has the same kind of two-sided risk illustrated by the wheat example for the forward contract. By institutional practice futures contracts seek to reduce default risk by the traders through two requirements. The gain or loss on a futures contract is calculated daily (it is "marked to market" at the end of each day) and cash settled daily. In addition, participants in futures markets are required to post a bond as a form of guarantee. Empirical studies indicate no statistically significant differences in the price behavior of forward contracts as compared with futures contracts.

A swap contract obligates two parties to exchange specified cash flows at designated intervals. An example would be to exchange a five-year fixed rate bond for a five-year floating rate bond. Many circumstances might stimulate swaps. For example, a business firm may enter into a contract in a country that does not permit floating rate contracts. Or a firm's assessment of the future results in the decision to prefer a floating rate debt obligation rather than a fixed rate obligation. The other end of the swap contract may represent a financial institution that is entering into many such transactions so that its position in fixed rate versus floating rate obligations might be closely balanced so that risk is thereby reduced.

Options

An option gives the owner the right (but not a requirement or obligation) to buy (a call) or sell (a put) an asset by the end of a specified period.[6] For example, a 90-day call on the common stock of the Alcoa Corporation with an exercise price of $65 would enable the owner to buy Alcoa common stock at a $65 price any time during that 90-day period. For example, if during the 90-day period the call were exercised at a price of $75 the owner of the call would have a $10 gain per share less what the owner paid for the calls. If a put contract is bought, it gives the owner the right to sell the stock to the seller of the put at a specified price during a specified period. The buyer of the put expects a price decline in which case the stock can be sold to the seller of the put at the higher price specified in the put contract.

Options as well as forward or futures contracts are called derivative securities. They are created by those who trade in them. They usually do not represent claims on business assets as do debt and equity securities.

Ownership Position

Finally, we consider ownership positions. A long position means that you will gain if the price goes up; typically this means that you are in an ownership position. Owning a call represents a long position; the difference is that the call only gives the owner of the call contract the ability to take an ownership position. To be short means that you will gain if the price goes down. Thus selling short means that you might sell stock you do not own. There are institutional arrangements that make this possible. If you sell a stock for $100 and then later the stock goes down to $60, you "cover your position" by buying the stock at $60 and have gained $40 per share. Or you might own 100 shares of stock (a long

---

[6]Options are discussed in Chapter 12, "Options on Risky Assets."

position) at a price of $100 and you wish to protect yourself from a future price decline. You may buy a put, which obligates the seller of the put to pay you $100 per share for your 100 shares. If the price goes down to $60 you will then put the stock to the seller of the put at $100 a share avoiding a loss of $40 per share less what you paid for the 100 put contracts that you bought. In concept, it is also possible to be long or short in call options or long or short in put options.

Many of these relations will be developed in greater detail in subsequent chapters. However, from this brief overview it is clear that the eleven forms of contracts covered in Table 4.3 could have different payment patterns, different settlement conventions, different maturities as well as be put together in different combinations. Hence, the number of different contracts that can be formed is limited only by the imagination of the participants to the contracts. The innovations in types of contracts in recent years have resulted in literally hundreds of new forms of financial instruments or securities. It is likely that financial engineering will continue to produce new forms of financial instruments in future years as well.

FINANCIAL MARKET INSTITUTIONS

Within the framework of the broad functions of financial intermediation and the monetary and fiscal policies briefly summarized in the preceding sections is another important set of financial market institutions in the operation of the financial system. One basis for classifying securities markets is the distinction between *primary markets*, in which stocks and bonds are initially sold, and *secondary markets*, in which they are subsequently traded. Initial sales of securities are made by investment banking firms that purchase the securities from the issuing firm and sell them through an underwriting syndicate or group. Subsequent transactions take place in organized securities or less formal markets.

The Exchanges

The major stock exchange is the New York Stock Exchange (NYSE), with more than 1,700 common stocks listed. In 1989, the New York Stock Exchange alone accounted for 67 percent of the dollar volume and 48 percent of the share volume of trading in U.S. equities. This represented trading of over $1.5 trillion on a volume of over 41 billion shares. The second largest exchange is the American Stock Exchange (AMEX), with over 850 listed issues accounting for about 3 percent of the dollar volume. A further 7.7 percent of the share volume of trading in U.S. equities takes place on five registered regional exchanges.

The larger of the organized stock exchanges around the world occupy their own buildings and have an elected executive body, their board of governors. Members may buy seats, which represent the right to trade on the exchange. Most of the larger stock brokerage firms own seats on the exchange and designate one or more of their officers as members of the exchange.

The role of stock markets varies considerably around the world. In planned economies, like the USSR, no stock exchange exists at all, hence no prices exist to indicate the relative performance of companies. In October 1990, the USSR took steps to develop a stock exchange as it moved toward the introduction of a market economy. Many countries have decided that the government should sell its ownership of companies. This is called *privatization;* when it happens, the direct public ownership of companies grows. In the early 1980s the London Stock Exchange and the Paris Bourse grew rapidly as the English and French governments privatized many companies. Now privatization is spreading around the world with Mexico, Indonesia, and Brazil rapidly changing from government to public ownership of companies. Eastern Europe promises to be close behind.

Traditional commodity markets such as the Chicago Board of Trade (CBOT) and the Chicago Mercantile Exchange (CME) have expanded their operations to include the derivative securities such as futures contracts and options. The stock exchanges have also been adding trading in derivative securities as a part of their activities.

Over-the-Counter (OTC) Security Markets

Over-the-counter security markets is the term used for all the buying and selling activity in securities that does not take place on a stock exchange. In the United States, the OTC market handles transactions in (1) almost all bonds of U.S. corporations; (2) almost all bonds of federal, state, and local governments; (3) open-end investment company shares of mutual funds; (4) new issues of securities; and (5) most secondary distributions of large blocks of stock, regardless of whether they are listed on an exchange.

The exchanges operate as auction markets; the trading process is achieved through agents making transactions at one geographically centralized exchange location. On an exchange, firms known as "specialists" are responsible for matching buy and sell orders and for maintaining an orderly market in a particular security. In contrast, the OTC market is a dealer market; that is, business is conducted across the country by broker/dealers known as *market makers,* who stand ready to buy and sell securities in a manner similar to wholesale suppliers of goods or merchandise. The exchanges are used to match buy and sell orders that come in more or less simultaneously. But if a stock is traded less frequently (perhaps because it is a new or a small firm), matching buy and sell orders might require an extended period of time. To avoid this problem, some broker/dealer firms maintain an inventory of stocks. They buy when individual investors want to sell and sell when investors want to buy. At one time, these securities were kept in a safe; when they were bought and sold, they were literally passed over the counter.

The National Association of Securities Dealers, Inc., is the self-regulatory organization of the OTC markets in the United States. The brokers and dealers in the OTC markets communicate primarily through a computerized quotation system called NASDAQ, which presently enables current price quotations for over 4,900 actively traded OTC securities to be displayed on terminals in subscribers' offices. In 1982, the National Market System (NMS) was introduced. The National Market System gives price quotations and volume figures for NASDAQ securities throughout the trading day. By 1990, 2,610 securities were included in the NMS. The NMS is based on a computerized quotation system in 48 countries with an average of 11.5 competing market makers for each security. The *third market* refers to these transactions from dealer accounts in the OTC market. Unlisted stocks will be handled only in the OTC market, but listed stocks may also be involved in these transactions. They can also include trades of large blocks of listed stocks off the floor of the exchange, with a brokerage house acting as intermediary between two institutional investors.

The Fourth Market

The *fourth market* refers to direct transfers of blocks of stock among institutional investors without an intermediary broker. A well-known example is the arrangement between the Ford Foundation and the Rockefeller Foundation to exchange the common stocks of the Ford Motor Company and Standard Oil of New Jersey. Such transactions have led to the development of Instinet, a computerized quotation system with display terminals to provide communications among major institutional investors. Other automated transaction systems are the Crossing Network and POSIT. Increasingly, computers are used to evaluate companies by investors and traders who then use the fourth market for their transactions. These developments were described in detail by *Business Week*, which referred to them as "a trading floor on every screen."[7] In the same article, *Business Week* estimated that only 60 percent of the trading in NYSE-listed stocks was taking place on the exchange. Also, international activity is accelerating these developments.

The International Dimensions

The international debt market consists of three major components—foreign bonds, Eurobonds, and Euro-commercial paper. Foreign bonds are issued in a foreign country and denominated in that country's currency. Eurobonds are long-term instruments issued and traded outside the country of the currency in which they are denominated. Euro-commercial paper is the short-term debt version of Eurobonds. Japan is the largest source of Eurobonds because they can be issued more cheaply than corporate bonds in Japan. Japanese companies were the source of 21 percent of all Eurobond issues in 1988 [Pavel and McElravey, 1990, pp. 9–10].

The value of world equities was also just under $10 trillion in 1988 — about the same size as the value of publicly issued bonds in the world. Three countries — the United States, Japan, and the United Kingdom — accounted for three-fourths of the total capitalization on world equity markets and almost one-half of the 15 percent equity issues listed on the world stock exchanges [Idem, p. 10].

Globalization has resulted in the rapid growth of derivative international financial products such as Eurodollar futures and options as well as futures and options on foreign currencies and domestic securities that trade globally (for example, U.S. Treasury securities). Futures and options exchanges have been established worldwide, with 72 exchanges by the end of 1988. The strongest competitors to the U.S. exchanges are the London International Financial Futures Exchange (LIFFE) and the Singapore International Monetary Exchange (SIMEX).

During the first quarter of 1989, two foreign-based investment banking companies ranked sixth and seventh based on the value of mergers and acquisitions (Kleinwort

---

[7]"The Future of Wall Street," *Business Week*, November 5, 1990, p. 128.

Benson and S. G. Warburg, respectively). The "Big Four" Japanese investment banking firms — Nomura Securities, Daiwa Securities, Nikko Securities, and Yamaichi Securities Company — have been making efforts to penetrate the U.S. investment banking markets. They have also been active in U.S. derivative markets for options and futures.

To List or Not to List

In order to list their stock, firms must meet exchange requirements relating to such factors as size of company, number of years in business, earnings record, the number of shares outstanding and their market value. In the United States, requirements become more stringent as viewed on a spectrum ranging from the regional exchanges toward the NYSE.

The firm itself makes the decision whether to seek to list its securities on an exchange. Typically, the stock of a new and small company is traded over the counter; there is simply not enough activity to justify the use of an auction market for such stocks. As the company grows and establishes an earnings record, expands its number of shares outstanding, and increases its list of stockholders, it may decide to apply for listing on one of the regional exchanges. For example, a West Coast company may list on the Pacific Stock Exchange. As the company grows still more, and its stock becomes distributed throughout the country, it may seek a listing on the American Stock Exchange, the smaller of the two national exchanges. Finally, if it becomes one of the nation's leading firms, it may, if it qualifies, switch to the Big Board, the New York Stock Exchange.

Some multinationals issue equity in several stock markets. The benefits of international stock listing include greater share liquidity, firm publicity, and prestige. On the other hand, the costs of listing on additional exchanges may not be worth the greater liquidity. In addition, reporting requirements in other countries may increase the costs of overseas listing.

Some believe that listing is beneficial to both the company and its stockholders. Listed companies receive a certain amount of free advertising and publicity, and the status of being listed enhances their prestige and reputation. The exchanges maintain that listing is advantageous in terms of lowering the required rate of return on a firm's common stock. Investors, of course, respond favorably to increased information, liquidity, and prestige. By providing investors with these benefits by listing their company's stocks, financial managers may lower their firms' cost of capital. There may also be costs of obtaining wider ownership of a firm's stocks. These include the risk of attracting possibly unwanted takeover attempts and the cost of disclosing financials due to Securities and Exchange Commission requirements [DeAngelo and DeAngelo, 1987].

With increased computerization and electronic communication, the information gap between listed and unlisted stocks appears to be narrowing. For example, the National Association of Securities Dealers in 1990 introduced the PORTAL market, which allows computerized transactions in the multi-billion-dollar private placement market worldwide under SEC Rule 144A. In private placements, firms are restricted in the number of investors that can hold their securities, but are also exempt from Security and Exchange Commission disclosure requirements.

Some studies have concluded that listing on the NYSE does not affect the cost of capital for comparable companies [Baker and Spitzfaden, 1981; Phillips and Zecher,

1982]. Information availability, at least in terms of newspaper coverage, appears to be related more to firm size and trading volume than to listing status. Other empirical studies appear to indicate that there is some value to listing [Cary and Copeland, 1984; Dhaliwal, 1983]. However, there has been little evidence developed on the causes of this value increase.

Margin Trading and Short Selling

Margin trading and short selling are two practices said to contribute to the securities markets' efficiency. *Margin trading* involves the buying of securities on credit. For example, when margin requirements are 60 percent, 100 shares of a stock selling for $100 a share can be bought by putting up, in cash, only $6,000, or 60 percent of the purchase price, and borrowing the remaining $4,000. The stockbroker lends the margin purchaser the funds, retaining custody of the stock as collateral. Margin requirements are determined by the Federal Reserve Board. When the Fed judges that stock market activity and prices are unduly stimulated by easy credit, it raises margin requirements and thus reduces the amount of credit available for the purchase of stocks. On the other hand, if the Fed wants to stimulate the market as part of its overall monetary policy, it reduces margin requirements.

Margin trading is a form of leverage that magnifies the percentage gain (or the loss) from a given swing in security prices. An oversimplified example (disregarding dividends or transaction costs) will suffice to demonstrate the impact of margin trading.

Walter Smith buys 100 shares of Provo Company's stock at $20 per share. He holds the stock for one year and sells when the price is $25 per share. His initial cash outlay is $2,000, and his cash inflow one year later is $2,500. We can thus calculate Smith's return on investment:

$$\text{Return on investment} = \text{Net cash inflow/Initial cash outflow}$$
$$= (\$2,500 - \$2,000)/\$2,000$$
$$= \$500/\$2,000$$
$$= 25\%.$$

Now suppose that instead of investing the entire $2,000, Smith bought the Provo Company stock on the margin when the margin requirement was 60 percent. Smith's initial investment is reduced to $1,200 (that is, 60 percent of $2,000), and he borrows the remaining $800 from his broker (assume that the broker charges 10 percent annual interest on the loan). As before, Smith sells his stock after one year at $25 per share, for a cash inflow of $2,500. To calculate Smith's return on investment in this case, we must reduce his gross cash inflow by the initial $1,200 investment, by the repayment of the $800 loan, and by the $80 interest due on the loan.

$$\text{Net cash inflow} = \$2,500 - \$1,200 - \$800 - \$80 = \$420$$
$$\text{Return on investment} = \$420/\$1,200$$
$$= 35\%$$

Although the dollar amount of net cash inflow is less, the investment required to initiate the transaction is also less, and the percentage return on investment rises from 25 to 35 percent.

On the other hand, if the price of Provo Company stock fell to $15 by the end of the year, Smith would experience a loss by selling. The cash inflow at year end would be only $1,500, for a $500 loss, and the percentage return on investment for the nonmargin case would be $-\$500/\$2,000 = -25\%$.

For the 60 percent margin example, net cash inflows would be $\$1,500 - \$1,200 - \$800 - \$80 = -\$580$, and the percentage return on investment would be $-\$580/\$1,200 = -48\%$. Thus, we have illustrated how both gains and losses are magnified by margin trading. The use of debt makes investment returns riskier, since the range of probable returns is extended in both the positive and negative directions. This applies not only to individual transactions but to investments by business firms as well. Leverage decisions by business firms will be one of the central issues of financing to be discussed in subsequent chapters.

Short selling means selling a security that is not owned by the seller. Suppose you own 100 shares of ZN, which is currently selling for $80 a share. If you become convinced that ZN is overpriced and that it is going to fall to $40 within the next year, you will probably sell your stock. Now suppose you do not own any ZN, but you still think the price will fall from $80 to $40. You can, through a lending arrangement with a broker, *go short* in ZN, or *sell ZN short*.

Instead of borrowing cash from the broker as in margin trading, the investor borrows shares of street-name stock (that is, shares registered in the broker's name although they may in fact belong to another investor, who, for example, purchased them on the margin, and thus held by the broker as collateral). The borrowed shares are then sold at the current market price. The short seller anticipates that by the time he must return the borrowed shares, the price will have fallen; he will then purchase the shares on the open market to repay the broker. Thus, his upside gain will be the difference between the (higher) price at which he sells the borrowed shares and the (lower) price at which he later buys shares to substitute for those borrowed. Of course, if the investor is wrong, and the stock price rises rather than falls, he will suffer a loss. Brokerage houses recognize this possibility by establishing *maintenance requirements*. For example, they may stipulate a 50 percent margin on the proceeds of the short sale, with additional cash deposits for each 2.5 point rise in the price of the stock sold short. These requirements vary from firm to firm.

Short selling involves such other problems as the need for double coverage of any dividends paid—one for the individual whose stock was borrowed to make the short sale and one for the purchaser of the stock. One dividend will be paid by the company, and the other will have to be paid by the short seller, reducing his gain.

Margin trading and short selling contribute to the making of a continuous market. They broaden ownership of securities by increasing the ability of people to buy them and provide for a more active market, effecting narrower price fluctuations. However, when a strong speculative psychology grips the market, margin trading can be a fuel that feeds the speculative fervor. Short selling, on the other hand, can aggravate pessimism on the downside. The downside effects of short selling are somewhat restricted, however, since the SEC has ruled that a short sale cannot be made at a price lower than that of the last previously recorded sale. If a stock is in a continuous decline, short selling cannot occur; hence, it cannot be used to push the stock down. In the 1920s, before this rule was put into effect, market manipulators could and did use short sales to drive prices down.

Benefits Provided by Securities Markets

Securities markets are said to provide at least four economic functions.

1. Security exchanges facilitate the investment process by providing a marketplace to conduct efficient and relatively inexpensive transactions. Investors are thus assured that they will have a place to sell their securities if they decide to do so. Increased liquidity is provided by the securities markets investors who are willing to accept a lower rate of return on securities than they would otherwise require.

2. They are capable of handling continuous transactions, testing the values of securities. The purchases and sales of securities record judgments on the values and prospects of companies. Those whose prospects are judged favorably by the investment community have higher values, which facilitate new financing and growth.

3. Security prices are relatively more stable because of the operation of the security markets. Securities markets improve liquidity by providing continuous markets that make for more frequent but smaller price changes. In the absence of active markets, price changes are less frequent but more violent.

4. The securities markets aid in the digestion of new security issues and facilitate their successful flotation.

THE ROLE OF THE FINANCIAL MANAGER

In Figure 4.1, the financial manager is shown linking the financing of an organization to its financing sources via the financial markets.

In the aggregate, business firms are savings deficit units that obtain funds to make investments to produce more goods and services. As part of the process by which funds are allocated to their most productive uses, financial managers have two important areas of responsibility:

To obtain external funds through the financial markets.

- What financing forms and sources are available?
- How can the funds be acquired efficiently?
- What is the most economical mix of financing?
- What will be the timing and form of returns and repayments to financing sources?

To see that the funds obtained are used effectively.

- To what projects and products should funds be allocated?
- What assets and resources must be acquired in order to produce the product or service?

FIGURE 4.1   Financial Markets, the Financial Manager, and the Firm

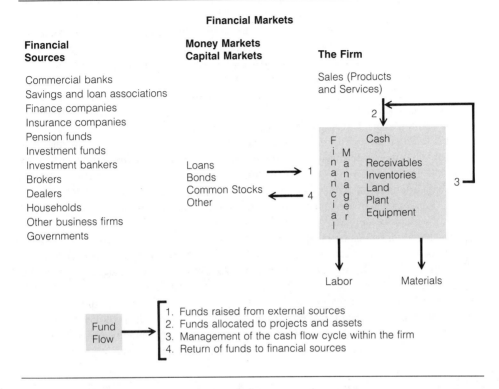

1. Funds raised from external sources
2. Funds allocated to projects and assets
3. Management of the cash flow cycle within the firm
4. Return of funds to financial sources

- How should the use of funds be monitored so that they are most effectively distributed among the various operating activities?

It is the financial manager's responsibility to implement these choices in the various financial markets to meet the firm's capital requirements.

MARKET EFFICIENCY

To allocate capital effectively, the financial markets should price securities solely by economic considerations based on publicly available information. In such a market, the prices for a company's securities reflect investors' estimates of the level and riskiness of future cash flows. Since higher stock prices reflect investors' positive assessments of the future, companies with higher expected cash flows will find it easier to raise additional capital. On the other hand, companies with lower expected cash flows will find less favorable terms when they try to raise additional capital. Securities that are priced efficiently guide the financial market in allocating funds to their most productive use.

Efficiency in the stock market implies that all relevant, available information regarding a given stock is instantaneously reflected in its price. Stated another way, an efficient market is one where a security's current price gives the best estimate of its true worth. In an efficient market there are neither free lunches nor expensive dinners. It is not possible to systematically gain or lose abnormal profits from trading on the basis of available public information.

Some related important concepts will help sharpen the meaning of market efficiency. A market is *allocationally efficient* when rates of return adjusted for risk are equated at the margin for all investments. A market is *operationally efficient* when investment funds can be transferred (shifted) at minimum cost. *Capital market efficiency* exists when prices reflect all available information. In a *fair game* the expected return on an asset equals its actual return. For example, in a gambling game at Las Vegas if the house takes an 8 percent cut, a player of average ability over the long run will lose 8 percent. The stock market is said to represent a *submartingale* because a positive expected return is earned. A market that has the properties of a *martingale* is one in which the expected return is zero.

Finally, a *random walk* says that there is no difference between the distribution of returns conditional on a given information structure and the unconditional distribution of returns. Random walks are much stronger conditions than fair games or martingales. A statistical difference between fair games and random walks is that the latter hypothesis requires that all drawings be independently taken from the same distribution, whereas the former does not. This means that the random walk requires that serial covariances between returns for any lag must be zero. Fama [1965] has presented evidence to show that the serial correlations of one-day changes in the natural logarithm of price are significantly different from zero for 11 out of 30 of the Dow Jones Industrials.[8] Furthermore, 22 of the 30 estimated serial correlations are positive. This, as well as evidence collected by other authors, shows that security returns are not, strictly speaking, random walks. However, the evidence is not inconsistent with fair game models or, in particular, the submartingale.

Informational Efficiency of the Stock Market

One set of tests of market efficiency examines the informational efficiency of security prices. Existing models of efficient stock markets imply that all relevant information regarding a given stock is reflected in its current market price. This notion of market efficiency can be divided into three categories based on the type of information used in making market decisions:

1. *Weak-form* market efficiency hypothesizes that today's security prices fully reflect all information contained in historical security prices. This implies that no investor can earn excess returns by developing trading rules based on historical price or return information.

2. *Semi-strong-form* market efficiency says that security prices fully reflect all publicly available information. Thus, no investor could earn excess returns using publicly

---

[8]To show that the logarithm of successive price changes is a good approximation of returns, assume one-period continuous compounding:

$$P_{t+1} = P_t e^{rt}, \text{ where } t = 1$$

$$ln\ P_{t+1} - ln\ P_t = \frac{P_{t+1} - P_t}{P_t}, \text{ where } r = \frac{P_{t+1} - P_t}{P_t}$$

available sources such as corporate annual reports, NYSE price information, or published investment advisory reports.

3.   *Strong-form* market efficiency hypothesizes that security prices fully reflect all information whether it is publicly available or not.

A rich set of empirical evidence helps to address the question: Do prices instantaneously and fully reflect all publicly available information?

Evidence on Weak-Form Efficiency

Technical trading rules are a common form of investment strategy. Advocates claim that the pattern of past prices can be used to predict future price movements and thereby make trading profits. The weak form of market efficiency claims the opposite, namely, that *it is impossible to use technical trading rules to earn excess returns because current prices already reflect all information in past price patterns*. Tests of trading rules were first provided by Alexander [1961] and Fama and Blume [1966]. They tested a technical filter rule which used past price movements to predict those in the future in an effort to earn excess returns. Fama and Blume showed that filter rules earned small abnormal returns but required frequent trading. After subtracting transactions costs they concluded that a higher return would have been earned with the same risk by using a strategy of buying and holding stocks for an extended period. Technical trading does not work.

Weak-form market efficiency means that security prices have no memory. Historical patterns in stock prices are of little use in predicting future price movements. A chief financial officer who claims to have no inside information and who refuses to issue new equity simply because the company's price has fallen is using bad logic. A recent price decline does not mean a price rise can be predicted, and it does not mean that a further decline can be predicted either.

Evidence on Semi-Strong-Form Efficiency

The semi-strong form of the market efficiency hypothesis says that current security prices reflect all publicly available information. There is an infinite variety of different types of publicly available information, and hundreds of empirical tests of the semi-strong-form efficiency hypothesis have been published. The preponderance of this evidence supports the conclusion that capital markets are indeed efficient in their semi-strong form, although some anomalies have been reported.

If financial markets are semi-strong-form efficient, then when new information becomes public, security prices should respond quickly by adjusting to a new level. Anyone attempting to use public information in a trading strategy will fail to earn excess returns because security prices will have already adjusted, and no further predictable price changes can be expected.

Annual and quarterly earnings reports are obvious examples of information that is made publicly available. Semi-strong-form efficiency can be tested by measuring security price responses when these reports are released. Ball and Brown [1968] were the first to study market responses to the release of accounting information. They used monthly returns data for a sample of 261 firms to determine whether returns prior to the annual report month were abnormally high. They found that returns appear to move upward gradually, until, by the time of the annual report, almost all of the adjustment has occurred. Most of the information contained in the annual report is anticipated by the market *before* the annual report is released. In fact, anticipation is so accurate that the actual income number does not appear to cause any unusual abnormal stock performance in the annual report month. Apparently, market prices adjust continuously to new information as it becomes publicly available throughout the year. The annual report has little new information to add.

The Ball and Brown study suggests that prices in the marketplace continuously adjust in an unbiased manner to new information. Two implications for corporate treasurers are (1) significant new information, which will affect the future cash flows of the firm, should be announced as soon as it becomes available so that shareholders can use it without the expense of discovering it from alternate sources, and (2) it probably does not make any difference whether the cash flow effects are reported in the balance sheet, the income statement, or footnotes — the market can evaluate the news as long as it is publicly available, whatever form it may take.

Others have argued that stock prices can be predicted using past information on macroeconomic variables such as the dividend yield, interest rates, and inflation rates. Fama and French [1989] show that the dividend yield (a high yield will produce higher prices to move yields toward more "normal levels") and the spread between risk-free and risky bonds (a large spread indicates excessive pessimism) can be used to predict much of the future movement in stocks. Pesaran and Timmerman [1990] show that a market timing strategy of entering and exiting the markets using macroeconomic indicators brings a return above a buy-and-hold-the-market strategy with less risk. However, such market timing strategies have been selected with the benefit of hindsight. Fuller and Kling [1990] show that strategies chosen without the benefit of hindsight based on variables other than the dividend yield would not have provided investors with returns greater than a buy-and-hold strategy. However, they found that a dividend yield strategy would have earned returns above buy-and-hold of approximately one percent per year. Nonetheless, they show that the dividend yield model makes predictions that are highly unstable over time, thus making for a very erratic market timing strategy.

Evidence on Strong-Form Efficiency

In order for markets to be strong-form efficient, prices must fully and instantaneously reflect all information whether it is publicly available or not. This is a difficult hypothesis to test because observations of trading behavior based on privately available information are difficult to obtain.

A direct test of strong-form efficiency is whether or not insiders with access to information that is not publicly available earn abnormal returns. Jaffe [1974] found that stock returns following periods of insider trading rose by more than three percent. These returns are statistically significant and suggest that insiders earn abnormal returns and that the strong-form hypothesis of market efficiency should be rejected.

Market Efficiency and Investment Decisions

We have emphasized that the market is an important guide with which to evaluate corporate decisions. At the same time we also emphasize that the stock market should not be the only guide used in making corporate decisions. Financial managers may be in a superior position to judge their own firms, or even other firms in the industry. They may recognize that the market does not fully value their firm's future opportunities, or conversely, has an overly optimistic assessment of their firm's prospects. In such conditions, managers should also study economic forces in their firm's markets. Information from market research, laboratory reports, and opinions about sales potential should also be considered when making investment decisions. No manager should ignore the stock market response to decisions. The market efficiently incorporates publicly available information into security prices. At the same time, no manager should ignore information about the economics of the firm's markets and strength of its products when making decisions.

Market Efficiency and Arbitrage

While markets may not perfectly incorporate all relevant information into security prices, there are powerful forces that operate to correct pricing errors. Pricing errors create opportunities for investors to profit without assuming additional risk, by *arbitrage*. For example, it is possible to purchase the stocks in the Standard & Poor's 500 (S&P 500) stock index on the stock exchanges. It is also possible to purchase them on the Chicago Mercantile Exchange in the form of a financial futures contract. To the extent that the futures contract is priced differently than the price of the stocks on the exchanges after a small adjustment for the cost of funds, it would be profitable to buy the S&P 500 in one market and sell it to the other without risk.

To the extent that similar profit opportunities arise when securities are mispriced, incentives will exist for investors to arbitrage. Arbitrage is the key force that serves to keep markets efficient.

Arbitrage and Economic Fundamentals

Arbitrage should operate to eliminate profit opportunities in stock and bond trading. Investors can take advantage of pricing mistakes by observing that security prices do not match the expected risk-adjusted profitability in the future. By doing so they observe that prices are "out of line" with fundamentals and attempt to profit as a result. Some people have argued that arbitrage does not always work over the long term to keep stock prices in line with fundamentals [Brennan, 1990; Shleifer and Vishny, 1990]. They argue that profit opportunities may take many years to realize. To illustrate their reasoning, a computer chip manufacturer may make an investment, say, in a project to automate and revolutionize chip design that is understood by only a few who appreciate its potential. Most investors do not understand that the investment promises high expected risk-adjusted profits in the long run, so the firm's stock price does not fully capitalize the expected cash flows. This creates an opportunity for the few observers who do appreciate the importance of the investment to profit handsomely if they buy the firm's stock and wait for the investment to pay off.[9] However, the cost of tying up capital in such a project may be excessive for these investors, and the uncertainty about the company's future cash flows may be too great, leading them to forego the profit opportunity.

While it is possible that security pricing mistakes persist over time, there is also ample evidence that stock prices rapidly incorporate news about changes in cash flows. The empirical evidence on the persistence of security pricing mistakes can be divided into two classes. The first class has attempted to relate movements in stock price indices to economic fundamentals to determine how well the stock market tracks economic movements. The second class has studied the informational efficiency of stock markets by investigating whether profits can be made by exploiting publicly available information. In the next two sections we examine the evidence on market efficiency in these two forms.

Fads and Fundamentals

The issue of whether stock markets reflect economic fundamentals is one with a rich history. In a famous chapter of the *General Theory of Employment, Interest and Money*, John Maynard Keynes voiced the opinion that investment based on perceptions of long-term fundamentals was unlikely to pay off.[10] This issue has been addressed more recently by Fischer Black [1986], who argues that financial markets reflect economic fundamentals only in the long run.[11] In the short run, Black argues, security prices are liable to wander far from their "fundamental" values because of the random acts of investors who pay little attention to economic factors.

The empirical evidence on the relation between stock prices and economic fundamentals remains inconclusive. Cutler, Poterba, and Summers [1989] argue that important economic and political news has little predictable influence on stock prices and that the influence of economic forces on stock prices leaves ample room in which to argue that "fads" unrelated to fundamentals drive stock prices. On the other hand, Barsky and De Long [1989] note that expectations of future dividends, which seem to have supported "faddish" stock price movements in the past century, have been based on reasonable expectations of economic performance. Similarly, Fama [1990] has shown that well over 50 percent and possibly much more of the movement in a broad index of stock prices can be rationalized as a response to present and future changes in industrial production — a

---

[9]In the mid-1980s Gordon Campbell, the founder of Chips and Technologies, sought to obtain financing from venture capitalists, commercial banks, and investment banks for a business plan to create customized chips using then little understood "silicon compiler" technology to make clones of IBM personal computers without success. After Campbell obtained financing from a friend, his financial officer, and some Japanese companies, Chips and Technologies proceeded to become the fastest growing chip firm in history with more than $200 million in sales in 1989 [Gilder, 1990].

[10]Keynes [1936, p. 157] wrote, "Investment based on long-term expectation is so difficult to-day as to be scarcely practicable. He who attempts it must surely lead much more laborious days and run greater risks than he who tries to guess better than the crowd how the crowd will behave; and, given equal intelligence, he may make disastrous mistakes."

[11]Other authors who make similar arguments include Shiller [1990] and Shleifer and Summers [1990].

key fundamental.[12] This evidence suggests that there is relatively little room in which to argue that the market is driven by irrational fads.

Another dimension is the process by which new information becomes reflected in security prices. When a group of investors becomes informed about a change in expected cash flows, how is their information passed on? One hypothesis that seems to be consistent with some experimental economics research is that uninformed investors attempt to infer information held by informed investors by observing their trading behavior as it affects market prices and trading volume. This type of rational behavior can result in "information mirages" where market prices are too high or too low relative to the fundamentals because uninformed traders believe that observed price changes contain information when, in fact, they do not. The result is that the variability of security prices will be higher than it would be if all individuals had the same information at the same time. Empirical tests of the "information mirage" hypothesis are impossible because no one can observe when information reaches the market, who receives it, or how it is incorporated in market prices. Experimental research in controlled (but artificial) market environments seems to offer a promising avenue of research.

Costly Information

If capital markets are efficient, then no one can earn abnormal returns because prices reflect all available information. But without the hope of abnormal returns, investors have no strong incentive to acquire information. Why bother to try to beat the market by doing securities analysis when one can do equally well by simply randomly choosing stocks from *The Wall Street Journal*? This is an argument that one often hears from critics of the efficient markets hypothesis. They ignore two things — private information is valuable and it is costly to obtain.

The above argument may have some merit in a world with costless information because all investors would have zero abnormal returns. However, it is probably premature to predict the demise of the security analysis industry or to argue that prices are uninformative. Grossman and Stiglitz [1976, 1980] and Cornell and Roll [1981] have shown that a sensible efficient market equilibrium must leave some room for security analysis. The basic argument is simple. If good information is costly to obtain, then investors who bear the expense of seeking it out must earn abnormal rates of return large enough to cover their expenses. However, when we net out their costs, then their net return is the same as the net return for investors who randomly selected their portfolios.

Because we cannot have an equilibrium with 100 percent informed traders or with 100 percent uninformed traders, there must be a stable equilibrium where the two strategies coexist — a mixed strategy stable equilibrium. This equilibrium will occur when the expected net payoff to both strategies is equal. Furthermore, the net profit to both kinds of traders is zero, which is the standard equilibrium condition for competitive markets. In equilibrium, more and more investors will seek out costly information until their net

---

[12]Similar studies looking at other fundamentals, time periods, and countries include Barro [1990], Cochrane [1989], Harris and Opler [1990], and Schwert [1990].

returns are the same as the returns earned by investors who use no information at all. But most important of all, market prices will reflect the information of informed traders.

Implications for Managerial Decision Making

The existence of efficient markets has important implications for financial managers. Market efficiency means that a firm's share price is the best available estimate of its future cash flows. Despite the sometimes speculative nature of security markets, share prices give the best benchmark for corporate financial choices. Thus decisions should be oriented towards maximizing the market value of the firm. If security prices reflect all publicly available information, then managers can watch their company stock price to find out what the market thinks of recently announced decisions. For example, Ruback [1982] analyzed the takeover of Conoco by du Pont in 1981, when du Pont offered to pay a total of $7.54 billion for Conoco. It was the largest merger up to that time. On July 6, 1981, the day the du Pont bid was announced, du Pont shares fell in value by 8.05 percent and Conoco shares rose by 11.87 percent.[13] The wealth of du Pont shareholders fell by approximately $642 million in a single day. The message to du Pont managers was unavoidable. The market felt they had made a mistake. The moral of the story is simple — trust market prices.[14]

Market efficiency is one of the most important themes in finance. The rapid adjustment of securities prices to new information has many implications for managers. Among them are the following:

1. All securities are perfect substitutes (at least before taxes). The implication is that *the net present value of any securities investment is zero*. For example, if you pay $850 for a bond with a promised yield of 8 percent, you expect to receive cash flows whose present value is exactly $850. The NPV is zero because your investment outlay (the $850 you pay out) is exactly equal to the discounted cash inflows (also $850). This is true for all securities. A common stock that costs $35 per share has discounted cash flows of $35 and a zero NPV. The expected yield on the stock will be higher than the bond because the stock is riskier. But its higher promised cash flows (dividends and capital gains) exactly offset its higher risk.

2. If securities are perfect substitutes, then investors can effortlessly duplicate a wide variety of management decisions. They can either undo management errors or can manufacture results left undone by management. *Homemade financial decision making is a low-cost alternative to corporate financial decision making*. In 1984, when Bell Telephone was split into many geographically different operating companies, it was possible to buy a mutual fund (called a Humpty Dumpty fund), which consisted of a portfolio recombining the split-up companies, thus undoing the split-up — at least from a financial point of view.

---

[13]These are "abnormal" returns that have removed general stock market movement on the announcement date.

[14]A related study [Healy, Palepu, and Ruback, 1990] reinforces this message. The study found that the stock market reaction to takeover announcements provides a good forecast of operating performance after takeovers take place.

3. *There are no illusions in securities markets.* Securities prices are based on discounted expected cash flows. Cosmetic changes that have no effect on the perceived risk of a firm or on its expected cash flows will have no effect on its security prices in an efficient market. Moving publicly available information (such as lease commitments or pension fund liabilities) from the footnotes of your accounting statement onto the balance sheet will have no effect.

4. *Today's securities prices are the best estimate of future prices.* Why? Because thousands of investors are continuously gathering information in order to evaluate prices. If you think you can beat the market by predicting market interest rates or future stock price movements, you should consider the lesson of market efficiency. What do you know that thousands of other investors do not?

SUMMARY

The financial sector of the economy, an important part of the financial manager's environment, is comprised of financial markets, financial institutions, and financial instruments.

Financial markets involve the creation and transfer of financial assets and liabilities. The financial manager uses these markets to obtain needed funds for the operation and growth of the business and to employ funds temporarily not needed by the business. Funds are provided by savings surplus units to be used by savings deficit units. This transfer of funds creates a financial asset for the surplus unit and a financial liability for the deficit unit. Transfers can be made directly between a surplus and a deficit unit or can involve a financial intermediary, such as a bank. Intermediaries take on financial liabilities in order to create financial assets, typically profiting from their expertise in packaging these assets and liabilities. The operations of intermediaries, and financial markets in general, bring about a more efficient allocation of real resources.

The money markets involve financial assets and liabilities with maturities of less than one year, and the capital markets involve transfers for longer periods. Since most businesses are savings deficit units, the financial manager is concerned with the choice of financial markets, intermediaries, and instruments best suited to the financing needs of the firm and with the decision of how best to employ excess funds for short periods.

Two major forms of financing are used by business firms: equity financing through common stock and various forms of debt financing. Numerous alternative types of debt instruments exist; they differ in maturity, in terms, and in the degree of risk that the borrower (the issuer of the debt) will become unable to meet the obligation. Other forms of financial contracts include forward and futures contracts, swaps, options, and combinations thereof.

The initial sale of stocks and bonds is known as the primary market. Subsequent trading takes place in the secondary market, the organized exchanges. The over-the-counter market, the third market, is a dealer market, where broker-dealers throughout the country act as market makers. Sometimes large blocks of stock are traded directly among institutional investors, constituting the fourth market.

In addition to the cash purchase or sale of stocks or bonds, margin trading involves borrowing. Margin requirements, set by the Fed, change from time to time. Short selling is the practice of selling securities that are not presently owned, anticipating an opportunity to repurchase them later at a lower price. (That is, the short seller benefits if the price falls.) Short selling and margin trading make markets more active and may contribute to the ability to buy or sell securities with smaller price swings than otherwise would occur.

The financial markets have increasingly become international in scope as will be discussed in subsequent chapters.

Most of the research on capital markets supports the conclusion that they are weak-form and semi-strong-form efficient but are probably not strong-form efficient. A semi-strong-form efficient market is one where prices instantaneously and fully reflect all publicly available information. In order for a message to contain relevant information, there must be a security price change when the news is released. This test allows us to separate meaningful information (for example, quarterly earnings reports) from immaterial information such as corporate name changes. The evidence on block trading shows that block sales contain negative information but, even more important, that prices fully adjust to their new permanent level within 15 minutes after the block transaction becomes publicly available information. Perhaps prices do not react instantaneously, but they certainly adjust very rapidly. When we say that prices "fully reflect" information, we mean that they reflect an average of investor expectations. The fact that the market is not strong-form efficient implies that prices are not fully aggregating. Finally, we saw that if information is costly, then there is every reason to believe that costly securities analysis pays off well enough to recover its expense.

QUESTIONS

4.1   What are financial intermediaries, and what economic functions do they perform?

4.2   How could each tool of the Fed be used to slow down expansion?

4.3   Evaluate each of the arguments in favor of today's organized securities exchanges relative to OTC markets of 100 years ago.

4.4   One day, the New York Stock Exchange composite transactions reported in *The Wall Street Journal* showed XYZ Corporation as follows:

49   27   XYZ   1.20   3.8   8   60   33   30   32   +1

   a.   Is XYZ trading near its high or its low for the year?
   b.   What was yesterday's closing price?
   c.   In terms of closing price, what is the expected dividend yield on XYZ stock?
   d.   Based on the information given in the report, what would you estimate XYZ's annual earnings per share to be?

4.5   Why might an investor want to sell short?

4.6   You are approached by salespersons from two competing mutual funds. The first fund earned an 18 percent rate of return last year while the second earned only 14 percent.

    a. What questions do you need to ask the salespersons to determine which fund really did better?

    b. What can be said about the expected future performance of the two funds?

4.7 You are told that the market for options is a fair game but that four out of five options expire worthless. How can these two statements be true?

4.8 If the stock market is semi-strong-form efficient, then you cannot hope to earn abnormal profits; consequently, it does not pay to try. True or false? Why?

PROBLEMS

4.1 Select a recent issue of the *Federal Reserve Bulletin* and locate the table giving information on margin requirements for margin stocks, convertible bonds, and short sales.

    a. Do *margin requirements* refer to the percentage of borrowing to market value of the collateral or to the percentage of funds provided by the investor?

    b. Are the requirements always the same for the three types of securities?

    c. What has been the trend in margin requirements since June 8, 1968?

    d. What are current margin requirements?

4.2 Using a recent issue of *The Wall Street Journal,* answer the following questions with respect to General Electric Company common stock:

    a. On what exchange is it listed?

    b. What is the annual dollar amount of dividends based on the last quarterly or semiannual distribution?

    c. What percentage yield is represented by this dollar amount of dividends based on the closing price of the stock?

    d. How does this compare with the rate of interest the same funds could earn in a savings account?

    e. What is the indicated price-earnings ratio of the stock based on the closing price and the most recent 12 months' earnings?

    f. By what percentage is the closing price below the high price for the previous 52 weeks?

    g. By what percentage is the closing price above the low price for the previous 52 weeks?

    h. Would you say that the common stock of General Electric has experienced high, low, or moderate volatility during the previous 52 weeks?

4.3 Using a recent issue of *The Wall Street Journal,* answer the following questions about the $8\frac{7}{8}$ percent bonds of the Dow Chemical Company maturing 2000. (You may have to check more than one issue to find a trade for this particular bond.)

    a. On what exchange are they listed?

    b. What is their current yield?

    c. What was their closing price?

    d. Was their closing price below or above their par value of 100?

SELECTED REFERENCES

Alexander, S. S., "Price Movements in Speculative Markets: Trends or Random Walks," *Industrial Management Review,* (May 1961), pp. 7–26.

Baker, H. Kent, and Spitzfaden, J., "The Impact of Exchange Listing on the Cost of Equity Capital," Washington, D. C.: American University, Kogod College of Business Administration, 1981.

Ball, R., and Brown, P., "An Empirical Evaluation of Accounting Income Numbers," *Journal of Accounting Research,* (Autumn 1968), pp. 159–178.

Barsky, Robert B., and De Long, J. Bradford, "Bull and Bear Markets in the Twentieth Century," National Bureau of Economic Research, Working Paper No. 3171, (1989).

Black, Fischer, "Noise," *Journal of Finance,* 41 (July 1986), pp. 529–543.

Brennan, Michael J., "Latent Assets," *Journal of Finance,* 45 (July 1990), pp. 709–730.

Cary, David, and Copeland, Thomas E., "Listing on the New York Stock Exchange, Prediction and Changes in Value: An Empirical Study," Los Angeles: University of California, Working Paper, 1984.

Cornell, B., and Roll, R., "Strategies for Pairwise Competitions in Markets and Organizations," *Bell Journal of Economics,* (Spring 1981), pp. 201–213.

Cutler, David; Poterba, James; and Summers, Lawrence, "What Moves Stock Prices?," *Journal of Portfolio Management,* (1989), pp. 4–12, 15.

DeAngelo, Harry, and DeAngelo, Linda, "Management Buyouts of Publicly Traded Corporations," in Thomas E. Copeland, ed., *Modern Finance and Industrial Economics,* New York: Basil Blackwell, 1987, pp. 92–113.

Dhaliwal, Dan S., "Exchange-Lister Effects on a Firm's Cost of Equity Capital," *Journal of Business Research,* 11 (1983), pp. 139–151.

Fama, Eugene, "Stock Returns, Expected Returns, and Real Activity," *Journal of Finance,* 45 (September 1990), pp. 1089–1108.

———, "The Behavior of Stock Market Prices," *Journal of Business,* (January 1965), pp. 34–105.

———, and Blume, M., "Filter Rules and Stock Market Trading Profits," *Journal of Business,* (January 1966, spec. supp.), pp. 226–241.

Fama, Eugene F., and French, Kenneth R., "Business Conditions and Expected Returns on Stocks and Bonds," *Journal of Financial Economics,* (November 1989), pp. 23–49.

Fuller, Russell J., and Kling, John L., "An Investigation into the Predictability of Stock Market Returns Using Regression-Based Models," ms., Washington State University, (1990).

Grossman, S. J., and Stiglitz, J., "The Impossibility of Informationally Efficient Markets," *American Economic Review,* (June 1980), pp. 393–408.

———, "Information and Competitive Price Systems," *American Economic Review,* (May 1976), pp. 246–253.

Healey, Paul M.; Palepu, Krishna G.; and Ruback, Richard S., "Does Corporate Performance Improve after Mergers?" National Bureau of Economic Research, Working Paper No. 3348, May 1990.

Jaffe, Jeffrey F., "Special Information and Insider Trading," *Journal of Business,* 47 (July 1974), pp. 410–428.

Pavel, Christine, and McElravey, John N., "Globalization in the Financial Services Industry," *Economic Perspectives,* Federal Reserve Bank of Chicago, (May/June 1990), pp. 3–18.

Pesaran, M. Hashem, and Timmerman, Allan, "The Statistical and Economic Significance of the Predictability of Stock Returns," ms., UCLA, (1990).

Phillips, Susan M., and Zecher, J. Richard, "Exchange Listing and the Cost of Equity Capital," U.S. Securities and Exchange Commission, Directorate of Economic and Policy Analysis, Capital Marketing Working Paper No. 8, (1982).

Ruback, R., "The Conoco Takeover and Stockholder Returns," *Sloan Management Review,* (Winter 1982), pp. 13–32.

Shleifer, Andrei, and Vishny, Robert W., "Equilibrium Short Horizons of Investors and Firms," *American Economic Review,* (May 1990), pp. 148–153.

CHAPTER 5

Business Organization and Taxes*

The federal government is often called the most important shareholder in the U.S. economy. While this is not literally true, since the government does not own corporate shares in the strict sense of the word, the government receives a significant percentage of business profits in the form of taxes. The form of business organization affects the taxes paid; income of unincorporated businesses is taxed at personal income tax rates, to a maximum rate of 31 percent; corporate income above $335,000 is taxed at a rate of 34 percent. Furthermore, dividends received by stockholders are subject to personal income taxes at the stockholders' individual tax rates. State and local taxes are added to the federal taxes.

With such a large percentage of business income going to the government, it is not surprising that taxes play an important role in financial decisions. To incorporate or to conduct business as a partnership or proprietorship, to lease or to buy, to issue common stock or debt, to make or not to make a particular investment, to merge or not to merge — all these decisions are influenced by tax factors.

Tax laws are constantly changing in response to different political and public policy goals. Complex rules of taxation cannot be treated in a book of this type. Nevertheless, this chapter summarizes certain basic elements of the tax structure important for financial decisions.

INTRODUCTION

Tax laws are constantly revised to achieve both revenue-raising and public policy goals. Since 1980, we have had the Economic Recovery Tax Act of 1981 (ERTA), the Tax Equity and Fiscal Responsibility Act of 1982 (TEFRA), the Deficit Reduction Act of

---

*For counsel on this chapter we thank Lamb & Fleming, a tax accounting firm in West Los Angeles, California.

1984, the Tax Reform Act of 1986 (TRA86), the Revenue Act of 1987, and the Revenue Reconciliation Acts of 1989 and 1990 among others. These laws have made numerous changes in the Internal Revenue Code. Most major acts generate a trailer act of "corrections," for example, the Technical and Miscellaneous Revenue Act of 1988. The Tax Reform Act of 1986 was the most far-reaching in recent years with its much publicized goals of simplification and fairness. Yet some basic patterns of relations important for financial decisions remain basically unchanged. These basic relations are the emphasis of this brief summary of the key aspects of the tax laws and regulations. It is not intended to substitute for the need to use tax accountants and tax lawyers on real-life matters of complexity.

CORPORATE INCOME TAX

The Tax Reform Act of 1986 adopted a new rate structure, effective July 1, 1987, for the corporate income tax.

Rate Structure

- First $50,000 of income taxed at 15%.
- Next $25,000 of income taxed at 25%.
- Over $75,000 of income taxed at 34%.
- A 5% surtax is assessed on income between $100,000 and $335,000.

For example, if in 1991 a corporation has taxable net income of $110,000, its tax will be computed as follows:

```
.15($50,000) = $ 7,500
.25($25,000) =   6,250
.34($35,000) =  11,900
.05($10,000) =     500
Total tax       $26,150
```

Thus, the corporation's average tax rate will be $26,150/$110,000 = 23.8 percent. However, even though the nominal maximum corporate rate is 34 percent, the *marginal* tax rate on incremental income between $100,000 and $335,000 is 39 percent, because of the 5 percent surtax. The purpose of the surtax is to offset the benefits of low tax rates on low levels of corporate taxable income for high-income corporations. For any corporation fully subject to the surtax, the marginal and average tax rates are the same, 34 percent, as illustrated in Table 5.1 and Figure 5.1. The effect is that all income (including the first $50,000, income between $100,000 and $335,000, and any income beyond $335,000) is taxed at not more than the maximum 34 percent rate.

Prior to TRA 86, the maximum corporate rate was 46 percent. Because of the sharp increase in tax rates on corporate taxable income over $100,000, many moderate-sized companies were organized in the form of two or more separate corporations to keep the taxable income of each at a level where lower corporate tax rates were applicable. Before

FIGURE 5.1 Marginal and Average Corporate Tax Rates

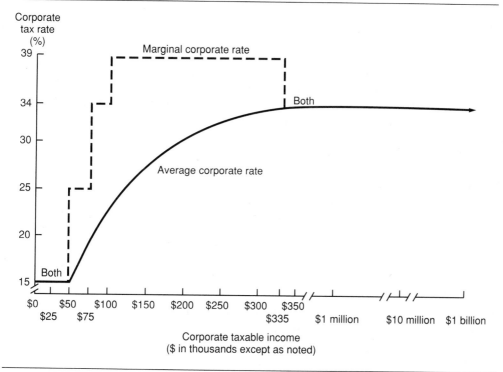

the Tax Reform Act of 1969 substantially eliminated the advantages of multiple corporations, some retail chains and small loan companies consisted of literally thousands of separate corporations.

TABLE 5.1 Marginal and Average Corporate Tax Rates

Taxable Corporate Income (in dollars) (1)	Marginal Tax Rate (Percent) (2)	Incremental Taxes Paid (3)	Total Taxes Paid* (4)	Average Tax Rate (Percent)* (5)
0–50,000	15	7,500	7,500	15.00
50,001–75,000	25	6,250	13,750	18.33
75,001–100,000	34	8,500	22,250	22.25
100,001–200,000	39	39,000	61,250	30.63
200,001–335,000	39	52,650	113,900	34.00
335,001–1,000,000	34	226,100	340,000	34.00

*Columns (4) and (5) are based on upper limit of income range.

Tax Credits

Tax credits are deductions from the tax bill itself, rather than deductions from taxable income, and thus are potentially very valuable. The investment tax credit program was typical. It was first incorporated into the federal income tax laws in 1962 as an incentive for investment. Under the program, business firms could deduct from their income tax liability a specified percentage of the dollar amount of new investment in each of certain categories of capital assets. Tax credits, like tax rates and depreciation methods, are subject to congressional changes reflecting public policy considerations. During the economic boom in the early part of 1966, for example, the investment tax credit was suspended in an effort to reduce investment; it was reinstated later that year, suspended again in 1969, reinstated in 1971, and modified by almost every tax bill since. The Tax Reform Act of 1986 largely eliminated the investment tax credit on capital assets. The tax credits that remain (extended through 1991 by the Revenue Reconciliation Act of 1990) include those for investment in targeted jobs (employers may deduct a percentage of first year wages paid to "disadvantaged" individuals), incremental research and development, alternative sources of business energy (including solar, geothermal and ocean thermal), and low-income housing.

Corporate Capital Gains and Losses

Corporate taxable income consists of two kinds: profits from the sale of capital assets (capital gains and losses) and all other income (*ordinary income*). *Capital assets* (for example, buildings or security investments) are defined as assets not bought or sold in the ordinary course of a firm's business. Gains and losses on the sale of capital assets are defined as capital gains and losses. Tax laws distinguish between *long-term* versus *short-term* capital gains, based on the length of time the asset is held (six months, nine months, or one year under various tax laws). Previous tax laws gave preferential tax treatment to long-term capital gains in that 60 percent of long-term capital gains could be excluded from taxable income, resulting in a lower effective tax rate. Short-term capital gains have always been taxed at the same rates as ordinary income. While retaining the concept of long- and short-term capital gains (and losses), the Tax Reform Act of 1986 eliminated the preferential treatment of corporate long-term gains. Long-term capital gains and losses are netted out separately from short-term capital gains and losses. *All* net gains are taxed as ordinary income. Net losses, however, cannot be used to offset ordinary income; however, they can be carried over to offset previous or future capital gains.

Dividend Income

Another important rule for corporate taxation is that various percentages of dividends received by one corporation from another are exempt from taxation. If a corporation owns up to 20 percent of the stock of another, 70 percent of the dividends received may be excluded from taxable income. If the corporation owns at least 20 percent, but less than 80 percent, of another, it may exclude 80 percent of dividends received. If the corporation owns 80 percent or more of the stock of another firm, it can file a consolidated tax return.

In this situation, there are no dividends as far as the Internal Revenue Service is concerned, so there is obviously no tax on fund transfers between the two entities. For example, Corporation H owns 40 percent of the stock of Corporation J and receives $100,000 in dividends from that corporation. It pays taxes on only $20,000 of the $100,000. Assuming H is in the 34 percent tax bracket, the tax is $6,800 or 6.8 percent of the dividends received. The reason for this reduced tax is that subjecting intercorporate dividends to the full corporate tax rate would be triple taxation. First, Corporation J would pay its regular taxes. Then Corporation H would pay a second tax on the dividends received from Corporation J. Finally, H's own stockholders would be subject to taxes on their dividends. The dividend exclusion thus reduces the multiple taxation of corporate income.

Deductibility of Interest and Dividends

Interest payments made by a corporation are a deductible expense to the firm, but dividends paid on its common stock are not. Thus, if a firm raises (through debt) $100,000 and contracts to pay the suppliers of this money 10 percent, or $10,000 a year, the $10,000 is deductible.[1] It is not deductible if the $100,000 is raised by selling stock and the $10,000 is paid as dividends. This differential treatment of dividends and interest payments has an important effect on the methods by which firms raise capital.

Payment of Tax in Installments

Firms must estimate their taxable income for the current year and, if reporting on a calendar year basis, pay one-fourth of the estimated tax on April 15, June 15, September 15, and December 15 of that year. The estimated taxes must be identical to those of the previous year or at least 90 percent of actual tax liability for the current year, or the firm will be subject to penalties. Any differences between estimated and actual taxes are payable by March 15 of the following year. For example, if a firm expected to earn $100,000 in 1990 and to owe a tax of $22,250 on the income, then it must file an estimated income statement and pay $5,563 on the 15th of April, June, September, and December of 1990. By March 15, 1991, it must file a final income statement and pay any shortfall (or receive a refund for overages) between estimated and actual taxes.

Net Operating Losses Carryover

For most businesses, net operating losses (NOLs) incurred in taxable years ending after 1975 can now be carried forward for 15 years. The allowable carryback period for net operating losses is 3 years, thereby giving firms an 18-year period in which to absorb losses against future profits or to recoup taxes paid on past profits. The purpose of permitting this loss averaging is to avoid penalizing firms whose incomes fluctuate widely. To illustrate: The Ritz Hotel made $100,000 before taxes in all years except 1983, when it

---

[1]Limits have been placed on the deductibility of interest payments on some forms of securities issued in connection with mergers.

suffered a $600,000 operating loss. The Ritz could utilize the carryback feature to recompute its taxes for 1980, using $100,000 of its operating loss to reduce 1980 profit to zero, and recovering the taxes it paid in that year. Since $500,000 of losses remain, taxable income for 1981 and 1982 could also be offset to recover the taxes paid in those years. The remaining $300,000 of loss could be carried forward to reduce taxable income to zero in 1984, 1985 and 1986. Alternatively, the Ritz could have carried forward the entire amount to offset income in 1984 through 1989.

The Tax Reform Acts of 1976 and 1986 limit the use of a company's net operating losses in periods following a change in ownership. The carryover is disallowed if the following conditions exist: (1) 50 percent or more of the corporation's stock changes hands during a two-year period as a result of purchase or redemption of stock, and (2) the corporation changes its trade or business. (There are other important restrictions on the acquisition of a loss company, but they are too complex to be covered in this brief summary.)

Net operating loss carryovers also figure prominently in the calculation of the Alternative Minimum Tax, which was strengthened by the Tax Reform Act of 1986 to assure that all profitable corporations pay some taxes.

Improper Accumulation

A special surtax on improperly accumulated income is provided for by Section 531 of the Internal Revenue Code, which states that earnings accumulated by a corporation are subject to penalty rates *if the purpose of the accumulation is to enable the stockholders to avoid the personal tax*. The penalty rate is 28 percent on the first $100,000 of improperly accumulated income for the current year and 38.5 percent on all amounts over $100,000. Of income not paid out in dividends, a cumulative total of $250,000 in retained earnings is prima facie justified for the reasonable needs of the business; this benefits small corporations. Of course, when large corporations have legitimate reasons for retaining earnings well over $250,000, they are not subject to the penalty.

Earnings retention can be justified if the firm is paying off debt, financing growth, or increasing marketable securities to provide the corporation with a cushion against possible cash drains caused by losses. How much a firm should properly accumulate for uncertain contingencies is a matter of judgment. Fear of the penalty taxes that can be imposed under Section 531 may cause a firm to pay out a higher rate of dividends than it otherwise would.

It is important to remember the distinction between retained earnings and cash. The balance sheet account, retained earnings, simply represents cumulated earnings after dividend payments since the firm's founding. These earnings could have been invested in any of the asset accounts. It is not a piggy bank full of cash; the cash account usually represents only a fraction of retained earnings. Note that the retained earnings account is included in the stockholders' equity section, representing further investment in the corporation by the stockholders.

In the past, Section 531 has sometimes stimulated mergers. A clear illustration is provided by the purchase of the Toni Company (home permanents) by the Gillette Safety

Razor Company.[2] The sale was made at a time when Toni's sales volume had begun to level off. Since earnings retention might have been difficult to justify, Toni's owners, the Harris brothers, were faced with the alternatives of paying penalty rates for improper accumulation of earnings or of paying out the income as dividends. Toni's income after corporate taxes was $4 million per year; with the Harris brothers' average personal income tax rate of 75 percent, only $1 million per year would have been left after they had paid personal taxes on the dividends. By selling Toni for $13 million, they realized a $12 million capital gain because their book value was $1 million. After paying the 25 percent capital gains tax (then in effect) on the $12 million, or $3 million, the Harrises realized $10 million after taxes ($13 million sale price minus $3 million tax). Thus, Gillette paid the equivalent of three and one-quarter years' after-corporate-tax earnings for Toni, while the Harris brothers received ten years' after-personal-tax net income for it. The tax factor made the transaction advantageous to both parties. The Tax Reform Act of 1986 weakened Section 531 as a stimulus of mergers by reducing personal tax rates and eliminating preferential tax treatment of capital gains.

DEPRECIATION

Depreciation refers to allocating the cost of an asset over its life. Suppose a business firm buys a piece of equipment that costs $200,000 and is expected to last five years. The equipment will increase gross profits (earnings before depreciation, interest and taxes, or EBDIT) to $500,000 per year. Without depreciation, the entire cost of the equipment would be a business expense against the first year's income alone; this is equivalent to depreciating the asset over one year. The pattern of accounting net income would be as indicated below (we assume interest costs are zero to focus on depreciation):

Case 1: Immediate Write-off

	Year 1	Years 2–5
EBDIT	$500,000	$500,000
Depreciation	200,000	—
EBIT	300,000	500,000
Taxes (34%)	102,000	170,000
Net income	$198,000	$330,000

The cardinal assumption of depreciation is that because the equipment contributes revenues over the entire five-year period, its cost should be allocated over the same period. If we accept this assumption, then the immediate write-off illustrated understates net income for year 1 and overstates net income for years 2 through 5.

---

[2]See Butters, Lintner and Cary [1951]. The lucid presentation by these authors has been drawn on for the general background, but the data have been approximated to simplify the illustration. The principle involved is not affected by the modifications of the facts.

Now assume that the firm uses straight-line depreciation, so that one-fifth of the cost of the equipment is allocated against each year's revenues. Accounting net income is now the same for each of the five years as illustrated:

Case 2: Straight-Line Depreciation — Accounting Net Income

	Years 1–5
EBDIT	$500,000
Depreciation	40,000
EBIT	460,000
Taxes (34%)	156,400
Net income	$303,600

Depreciation and Cash Flows

We have illustrated the effect of depreciation on accounting earnings. However, depreciation is a special kind of tax-deductible expense in that it is *not* a cash outlay. Whether we consider depreciation or not, the only cash outflow in our example occurs in year 1 when the equipment is initially purchased. For Case 1, therefore, cash flows and accounting net income are the same, but for Case 2, the noncash nature of depreciation expense causes cash flows to be different from accounting income. Now, we calculate the cash flows for Case 2:

Case 2: Straight-Line Depreciation — Cash Flows

	Year 1	Years 2–5
EBDIT	$500,000	$500,000
Depreciation	40,000	40,000
EBIT	460,000	460,000
Taxes (34%)	156,400	156,400
Net income	$303,600	$303,600
Add back depreciation	+40,000	+40,000
Less cost of equipment	−200,000	—
Cash flow	$143,600	$343,600

Because depreciation is not a cash charge, it is added back to net income to determine cash flows. Cash flows must also be adjusted in year 1 to reflect the cash outlay that took place when the equipment was purchased. The effect of depreciation is to reduce the cash outflow on income taxes. Recall that in Case 1, the cash outflow for taxes in years 2–5 (the years for which we have no depreciation expense) is $170,000, while in Case 2, cash outflows for taxes are the same every year at $156,400.

Without for the moment considering the time value of money, the sum of net income (equal to cash flows) for Case 1 is $1,518,000. This is the same as the sum of accounting net income for Case 2; and it is the same as the sum of cash flows for Case 2. Also, in each case, the total dollar amount of cash outlay for income taxes is identical at $782,000. So what is the point of depreciation? The only effect is on the *timing of cash flows.*

Using a 10 percent discount rate, we calculate the present value of cash flows for Case 1 and Case 2:

Year	PV Factor	Case 1		Case 2	
		Cash Flow	Present Value	Cash Flow	Present Value
1	.9091	$ 198,000	$ 180,002	$ 143,600	$ 130,547
2	.8264	330,000	272,712	343,600	283,951
3	.7513	330,000	247,929	343,600	258,147
4	.6830	330,000	225,390	343,600	234,679
5	.6209	330,000	204,897	343,600	213,341
		$1,518,000	$1,130,930	$1,518,000	$1,120,665

The present value of cash flows is $10,265 greater for Case 1 (immediate write-off) than for Case 2. (If we calculated the present value of cash outlays for taxes, that would explain the difference.)

Thus, if businesses value cash flow over accounting income, firms would prefer to write off assets as they are purchased, rather than depreciating them over their useful lives. This is not permitted, however, by either accounting conventions or tax laws. Given that assets must be depreciated, firms will generally want to depreciate them as quickly as possible.

Accelerated Depreciation

There are two ways for a firm to write off assets more quickly. One is to shorten the period over which the asset is depreciated. The other is to use an accelerated depreciation method (such as sum-of-the-years'-digits or double declining balance method). U.S. tax laws permit firms to do both, most recently via a procedure known as the Modified Accelerated Cost Recovery System (or MACRS, pronounced "makers"). The initial Accelerated Cost Recovery System (ACRS or "acres") was incorporated into the Tax Reform Act of 1986; the modified system applies to assets placed in service after 1986.

Under MACRS, there is no need to estimate the expected useful economic life of an asset. Instead, assets are categorized into several classes, each with its own *class life* and *recovery period* over which the asset is to be depreciated. The asset classes and types of property included in each are listed in Table 5.2. These statutory lives are generally shorter than the economic lives of the assets; furthermore, MACRS allows an accelerated depreciation method, specifically, 200 percent (or double-declining balance) depreciation for most classes of assets. (Fifteen-year and 20-year assets are depreciated using the 150 percent declining balance method, and real property must be depreciated over 27.5 or 31.5 years using the straight-line method.) The effect of MACRS is to accelerate depreciation, increasing the depreciation tax shelter and thus increasing cash flows.

The recovery allowance percentages in Table 5.3 use the 200 percent declining balance method for the 3-, 5-, 7-, and 10-year asset classes, and the 150-percent declining balance method for 15- and 20-year assets. The percentages are applied to the cost of the asset, without consideration of salvage value, and use a half-year convention for the initial and final year. For example, consider the 10-year recovery allowance percentages. Annual straight-line depreciation would have been 10 percent per year, so with 200-percent

TABLE 5.2   Recovery Periods for MACRS under TRA 86

Class	Type of Property
3-year	Includes short-lived property, such as tractor units, race horses over two years old, and other horses over 12 years old
5-year	Includes cars and trucks, computers and peripherals, calculators, copiers and typewriters, and specific items used in research
7-year	Includes office furniture and fixtures, plus any asset not designated to be in another class; most industrial equipment
10-year	Includes vessels, barges, tugs and similar equipment related to water transportation, and single-purpose agricultural structures
15-year	Includes roads, shrubbery, wharves, and sewage treatment plants
20-year	Includes farm buildings, sewer pipe, and other long-lived equipment
27.5-year[a]	Includes residential rental real property
31.5-year[a]	Includes nonresidential real property

[a]Depreciated using the straight-line method

TABLE 5.3   Recovery Allowance Percentages for Personal Property under MACRS (half-year convention)

Ownership Year	Class Life					
	3-Year[a]	5-Year[a]	7-Year[a]	10-Year[a]	15-Year[b]	20-Year[b]
1	33.33%	20.00%	14.29%	10.00%	5.00%	3.750%
2	44.45	32.00	24.49	18.00	9.50	7.219
3	14.81	19.20	17.49	14.40	8.55	6.677
4	7.41	11.52*	12.49	11.52	7.70	6.177
5	100.00	11.52	8.93*	9.22	6.93	5.713
6		5.76	8.92	7.37	6.23	5.285
7		100.00	8.93	6.55*	5.90*	4.888
8			4.46	6.55	5.90	4.522
9			100.00	6.56	5.91	4.462*
10				6.55	5.90	4.461
11				3.28	5.91	4.462
12				100.00	5.90	4.461
13					5.91	4.462
14					5.90	4.461
15					5.91	4.462
16					2.95	4.461
17					100.00	4.462
18						4.461
19						4.462
20						4.461
21						2.231
						100.00

[a]Depreciated using 200-percent declining balance method, with a switch to straight-line as indicated
[b]Depreciated using 150-percent declining balance method, with a switch to straight-line depreciation as indicated
*Switch to straight-line depreciation
Source: IRS Publication 534, *Depreciation*, Table 1, p. 28.

declining balance, the percentage would be 2 times 10 percent, or 20 percent for year 1. The half-year convention applies in year 1, however, so the recovery allowance percentage for year 1 is only half, or 10 percent. At the start of year 2, 90 percent of the asset's value remains to be depreciated; applying the 20 percent rate, the recovery allowance for year 2 is .2(90%) = 18%. In year 3, 28 percent of the asset has been written off, leaving 72 percent; the recovery allowance percentage for year 3 is .2(72%) = 14.4%. In year 4, the remaining basis to be depreciated is 57.6 percent, so the percentage to apply is .2(57.6%) = 11.52%. The calculations for years 5 and 6 are analogous. However, at the start of year 7, 4 years of depreciable life remain, with only 29.49 percent of the basis left to be depreciated. The switch is made to straight-line depreciation because it exceeds the double declining balance amount. Straight-line depreciation of 6.55 percent of the asset's cost is taken over years 7 through 9. (In some years 6.56 percent is taken to account for rounding differences.) In year 10, 9.83 percent of the depreciable basis remains to be written off over 1.5 years; recall the half-year convention in year 1 — the remaining half-year is applied in year 11. The percentage applied in year 10 is 9.83%/1.5 = 6.55%, with the remaining 3.28 percent taken in year 11. Firms generally apply these percentages to the depreciable basis of assets by computer programs.

Present Value of Accelerated Depreciation

Straight-line depreciation results in a uniform stream of cash flows over the life of an investment, other factors being equal. Thus, we are able to use the interest factors for the present value of an annuity (PVIFA) to find the present value of the investment. Realistically, however, firms use accelerated depreciation methods in which the annual deduction for depreciation expense is not a constant amount, so we cannot apply the PVIFA to a constant stream of cash flows. We can, however, calculate the present value of the accelerated depreciation as a whole separately from the other (constant) cash flows.

Appendix C (at the end of the book) contains present value factors for accelerated depreciation based on MACRS rules for a range of discount rates. The factors in Appendix C are developed as shown in the example in Table 5.4. In this example we are interested in the present value of depreciation for a 5-year asset when the interest rate (or cost of capital) is 10 percent. The recovery allowance percentage for each year (from

TABLE 5.4   Calculation of Accelerated Depreciation Factor

Year	Recovery Allowance Percentage	10% Discount Factor	Product
1	.2000	.9091	.1818
2	.3200	.8264	.2644
3	.1920	.7513	.1442
4	.1152	.6830	.0787
5	.1152	.6209	.0715
6	.0576	.5645	.0325
		Factor =	.7731

Table 5.3) is multiplied by the present value interest factor (PVIF) at 10 percent for that year. These products are summed to arrive at the accelerated depreciation factor, in this case, .7731. But for rounding, this is the same as the factor in Appendix C in the 5-year column at a 10 percent interest rate.

To find the present value of the depreciation tax savings to use in capital budgeting (discussed in Chapter 9) when an investment is depreciated by an accelerated method, we multiply the tax rate (T) by the accelerated depreciation factor by the amount of the investment (I). For a $200,000 investment:

$$PV = T(\text{Accelerated depreciation factor})I$$
$$= .34(.7731)\ (\$200,000)$$
$$= \$52,571.$$

Sale of Depreciable Assets

If a depreciable asset is sold, then the sale price (actual salvage value) minus the then-existing book value, which reflects the depreciation taken up to the sale, is added to operating income and taxed at the firm's marginal rate.

Benefit for Small Companies

Under Section 179 of the Tax Code, companies are allowed to expense up to $10,000 worth of equipment per year. For small businesses, this is equivalent to depreciating some equipment over a single year.

Tax Purposes Versus Reporting Purposes

Firms are required to depreciate assets. For purposes of income tax reporting, they must use either the MACRS method or the straight-line method; for reasons we have illustrated, virtually all firms will choose the method which provides the faster write-off. Accelerated depreciation reduces the cash outlay for taxes early in the asset's life, giving the firm the use of that cash for other purposes.

The use of accelerated depreciation increases cash flows (over straight-line depreciation), while reducing accounting net income. Firms are allowed by law to keep two sets of books — one for taxes and one for reporting to investors. If stockholders of business firms value cash flows over net income, they will support the use of accelerated depreciation methods. Considerable evidence shows that stockholders *do* value cash flows, and that they are not misled by accounting techniques that affect only reported net income rather than underlying cash flows. Nevertheless, most firms use accelerated depreciation for tax purposes, but straight-line depreciation (with its higher reported net income) for stock-holder reporting purposes. The use of straight-line depreciation minimizes the negative effect on accounting net income and is said to "normalize" or stabilize reported income, especially when asset purchases are "lumpy."

Effects of Depreciation on Taxes and Net Income

Table 5.5 shows the pre-tax income, taxes, and net income for a firm that has sales of $1 million per year, costs of $500,000 per year, a single asset with a cost of $200,000, and 1,000 shares of common stock. This asset has a five-year economic life, and it will have zero salvage value at the end of the five years. However, the asset class life under MACRS is only 3 years. Straight-line depreciation charges would be $200,000/5 = $40,000 per year (ignoring the half-year convention). For the asset's 3-year MACRS class, the depreciation is calculated below:

Year	MACRS Rate	Depreciation
1	.33	$ 66,000
2	.45	90,000
3	.15	30,000
4	.07	14,000
		$200,000

Section I of Table 5.5 shows the calculation of actual taxes owed using MACRS; Section II shows income and taxes reported to shareholders using straight-line depreciation; and Section III shows the effect of using MACRS for both tax and reporting purposes.[3]

Note that in Year 1 the firm reports to the Internal Revenue Service $66,000 in depreciation and $434,000 of taxable income, and it pays $147,560 in taxes. If it uses MACRS depreciation for stockholder reporting as well, as shown in Section III, it reports net income of $286,440. However, if it uses straight-line depreciation for stockholder reporting, as shown in Section II, it reports $40,000 in depreciation, $147,560 + $8,840 = $156,400 in taxes, and a net income of $303,600, even though its actual tax bill is only $147,560. The difference of $156,400 − $147,560 = $8,840 in reported versus paid taxes is shown on the income statement as *deferred taxes* — that is, the firm has been able to defer paying these taxes until a later date because it used an accelerated depreciation method for calculating taxable income. Deferred taxes are equal to 34 percent of the difference between the constant earnings before tax (EBT) under straight-line depreciation and the varying EBT calculated using MACRS.

Section III shows that net income and EPS fluctuate if the firm uses MACRS for both tax and reporting purposes, whereas the numbers reported to stockholders using straight-line depreciation are stable over the entire period. Thus, firms that use deferred tax accounting (as in Section II) are said to be *normalizing* income.

In Table 5.6 we assume that the normalizing firm had Year 1 costs of $934,000 instead of $500,000. Its taxable income and actual taxes paid would have been zero (MACRS Dep. = $66), yet it would still be able to report a net income to stockholders of $17.2 with deferred taxes of $8.8. A number of very successful companies have been in this position — reported high profits yet no cash outflow for federal income taxes. This

---

[3]If the straight-line method had been used for both reporting and tax purposes, pre-tax income would have been $460,000 each year (disregarding the half-year convention), so taxes would have been 0.34 × $460,000 = $156,400 each year, or 5 × $156,400 = $782,000 in total. This is exactly the same total as when the MACRS method is used for tax purposes, but the timing of tax payments differs.

TABLE 5.5   Effects of Depreciation on Taxes and Profits
(in thousands except EPS)

Section I.   Tax Calculations Using MACRS

Year	1	2	3	4	5
Sales	$1,000	$1,000	$1,000	$1,000	$1,000
Costs	500	500	500	500	500
EBDIT	500	500	500	500	500
Dep.	66	90	30	14	0
EBT	434	410	470	486	500
Tax (34%)	$147.6	$139.4	$159.8	$165.2	$ 170

Section II.   Income Statements Reported to Stockholders Using Straight-Line Depreciation with Deferred Taxes for Reporting Purposes (Normalizing)

Year	1	2	3	4	5
Sales	$1,000	$1,000	$1,000	$1,000	$1,000
Costs	500	500	500	500	500
EBDIT	500	500	500	500	500
Dep.	40	40	40	40	40
EBT	460	460	460	460	460
Actual taxes paid	$147.6	$139.4	$159.8	$165.2	$ 170
Deferred taxes	8.8	17.0	(3.4)	(8.8)	(13.6)
Total taxes	$156.4	$156.4	$156.4	$156.4	$156.4
Net income	$303.6	$303.6	$303.6	$303.6	$303.6
EPS	$ 0.30	$ 0.30	$ 0.30	$ 0.30	$ 0.30

Section III.   Income Statements Reported to Stockholders Using MACRS Depreciation for Both Tax and Reporting Purposes

Year	1	2	3	4	5
Sales	$1,000	$1,000	$1,000	$1,000	$1,000
Costs	500	500	500	500	500
EBDIT	500	500	500	500	500
Dep.	66	90	30	14	0
EBT	434	410	470	486	500
Taxes paid	$147.6	$139.4	$159.8	$165.2	$ 170
Net income	$286.4	$270.6	$310.2	$320.8	$ 330
EPS	$ 0.29	$ 0.27	$ 0.31	$ 0.32	$ 0.33

situation helped create the political climate that led to TRA 86, in particular that part of TRA 86 which imposes the *alternative minimum tax*. The purpose of the alternative minimum tax is to insure that any company that reports profits to stockholders will pay at least some tax.

TABLE 5.6 Income Statements Reported to Stockholders Using Straight-Line Depreciation with Deferred Taxes for Reporting Purposes (Normalizing)

	Year				
	1	2	3	4	5
Sales	$1,000	$1,000	$1,000	$1,000	$1,000
Costs	934.0	500	500	500	500
EBDIT	66	500	500	500	500
Dep.	40	40	40	40	40
EBT	26	460	460	460	460
Actual taxes paid	$ 0	$139.4	$159.8	$165.2	$ 170
Deferred taxes	8.8	17.0	(3.4)	(8.8)	(13.6)
Total taxes	$ 8.8	$156.4	$156.4	$156.4	$156.4
Net income	$ 17.2	$303.6	$303.6	$303.6	$303.6
EPS	$ 0.17	$ 0.30	$ 0.30	$ 0.30	$ 0.30

Effects of Depreciation on the Balance Sheet

The cumulative deferred taxes for each year are reported on the balance sheet under an account titled "deferred taxes." Deferred taxes constitute a liability — in effect, they represent a loan from the federal government. Our normalizing company in Section II of Table 5.5 above, would show deferred taxes on its End-of-Year 1 balance sheet of $8,840. The amount shown at the end of Year 2 would be $8,840 + $17,000 = $25,840; and so on. By the end of Year 5, however, the negative deferred taxes in Years 3, 4, and 5 would bring the balance sheet account of deferred taxes to a zero balance. However, for growing firms, assets and their depreciation are growing over time, so the deferred taxes account is never reduced to zero. For a growing firm, the deferred taxes account is likely to grow while the deferred taxes for individual older assets decline to zero.

PERSONAL INCOME TAX

Of some 16 million business firms filing tax returns in the United States, about 13 million are organized as sole proprietorships or partnerships. The income of these firms is taxed as personal income to the owners or the partners. The net income of a proprietorship or partnership provides a basis for determining the individual's income tax liability. Thus, as a business tax, the individual income tax can be as important as the corporate income tax.

The personal income tax is conceptually straightforward, although many taxpayers find it confusing. Virtually all the income a person or family receives goes into determining the tax liability.

Total income from all sources is called gross income. All taxpayers are permitted to make deductions from their gross income before computing any tax. These deductions are of two types: deductions and personal exemptions.

Deductions. Taxpayers may choose to itemize deductions, such as state and local taxes, mortgage interest, and charitable contributions, or claim the standard deduction, whichever is higher. Under the Tax Reform Act of 1986, the standard deduction was changed from a constant amount to a deduction indexed to inflation. For 1990, the standard deduction was $5,450 for the joint returns of married couples and $3,250 for single taxpayers (up from $5,200 and $3,100 respectively in 1989). The standard deduction is increased for blind and/or elderly taxpayers.

Personal Exemptions. A personal exemption is allowed for the taxpayer and each of the taxpayer's dependents. The apparent intent of the personal exemption is to exempt the first part of income from taxation, enabling individuals to obtain the basic necessities of life, such as food, clothing, and shelter. Consistent with this intent, the personal exemption is phased out for very high-income taxpayers. As with the standard deduction, the personal exemption (and the threshold income level at which the phase-out mechanism to eliminate it kicks in) are now indexed for inflation. The personal exemption was $2,050 in 1990 (up from $2,000 in 1989). (Because of inflation indexing, the standard deductions, personal exemptions, and threshold income levels for 1991 will not be known until the end of 1991.)

A number of classifications are used in connection with calculating personal income tax liability.

Gross Income. Gross income includes wages, salaries, tips; dividend and interest income; business income; applicable capital gains and losses; pensions, annuities, rents, royalties, partnership, income; alimony received; plus other categories.

Adjusted Gross Income. Gross income is reduced by the so-called "above-the-line" deductions to arrive at adjusted gross income (AGI), which is used as a benchmark for the deductibility of miscellaneous itemized deductions, including the deduction for medical expenses. The Tax Reform Act of 1986 eliminated most of these adjustments to income, severely limited others, and moved the rest to "below-the-line" so that they are available only to taxpayers who itemize deductions. The two-earner deduction has been eliminated; the deductions for charitable contributions, job-related moving expenses, and employee business expenses have been changed to itemized deductions; and the deduction for contributions to individual retirement accounts (IRAs) has been severely curtailed for individuals who are covered by another retirement plan. The adjustment for alimony paid remains intact.

Less: Personal Exemptions. Subtract the number of personal exemptions times $2,050 (for 1990). Starting in 1991, total personal exemptions are reduced by 2 percent for each $2,500 (or fraction thereof) by which adjusted gross income exceeds a threshold amount ($150,000 for married couples filing joint returns, $100,000 for single taxpayers). For example, suppose a married couple (with no dependents) has adjusted gross income in 1991 of $200,000, or $50,000 in excess AGI. Because $2,500 goes into $50,000 20 times, the personal exemption is reduced by 20 × 2% = 40%. Assuming a personal exemption in 1991 of $2,100 for a total of $4,200, the reduction would be .40 × $4,200 or $1,680 for a remaining combined personal exemption of $2,520. The phase-out cannot eliminate more than 100 percent of the personal exemption; once AGI exceeds the threshold amount by more than $122,500, the personal exemption is fully extinguished ($122,500 is divisible by $2,500 49 times; any excess over $122,500 would be a fraction of $2,500, and would create the 50th two-percent reduction).

Less: Deductions.   Subtract the greater of itemized deductions or the standard deduction.

Itemized Deductions.   Itemized deductions include such items as state and local income and property taxes (but not sales tax); mortgage interest on first and qualifying second homes (all other personal interest expense deductions have been phased out under TRA 86); job-related moving expenses; casualty losses; and charitable contributions. Some itemized deductions are deductible only to the extent that they exceed two percent of Adjusted Gross Income (AGI); these include employee business expenses, investment expenses, tax counsel and preparation fees, continuing education, job-hunting expenses, subscriptions to professional journals, and travel, meals, and entertainment expenses (limited to 80 percent of the amount incurred). Medical expenses are deductible to the extent that they exceed 7.5 percent of AGI (although the 1990 tax act disallowed the deductions for medical expenses for most cosmetic surgery). The 1990 act also added a temporary provision to reduce itemized deductions for high income taxpayers. (The provision is due to terminate after 1995, but recall that the income tax itself was initially introduced as a temporary measure.) For tax years beginning in 1991, itemized deductions are reduced by 3 percent of the amount of adjusted gross income over $100,000. However, itemized deductions cannot be reduced by more than 80 percent, and certain categories of deductions are exempted, for example, medical expenses, casualty and theft loss, and investment interest. The $100,000 threshold is to be adjusted for inflation in years 1992 through 1995.

The result of these calculations is *taxable income* to which the personal tax rates are applied.

Tax Rates for the Personal Income Tax.   Effective 1991, there are only three tax brackets for the personal income tax — 15, 28, and 31 percent. The rates and income ranges for 1991 are:

	Taxable Income	
	Married Filing Joint Returns	**Single Taxpayers**
15%	0–$34,000	0–$20,350
28%	$34,001–$82,150	$20,351–$49,300
31%	Over $82,150	Over $49,300

TABLE 5.7   Personal Taxes*

AGI	Taxable Income	Adjusted Taxable Income	Tax	Marginal Rate**	Average Rate**
$48,400	$20,000	$20,000	$3,000	15.0%	15.0%
68,400	40,000	40,000	6,982	28.0	17.5
88,400	60,000	60,000	12,582	31.0	21.0
108,400	80,000	80,252	18,308	31.9	22.9
128,400	100,000	100,852	24,694	31.9	24.7
228,400	200,000	209,120	58,257	33.6	29.1
428,400	400,000	420,952	123,925	32.8	31.0
628,000	600,000	624,252	186,948	31.5	31.2
828,000	800,000	824,400	248,994	31.0	31.1
1,028,400	1,000,000	1,024,400	310,870	30.9	31.1

*1991 tax rates, married filing joint return, four personal exemptions at $2,100 each (assuming a $50 increase over the 1990 personal exemption). Itemized deductions are assumed to be $20,000, with none exempt from the reduction provision.
**Marginal and average tax rates are based on unadjusted taxable income. The marginal rate on $80,000 taxable income is based on excess over $78,400 taxable income.
AGI threshold for itemized deduction reduction = $100,000.
AGI threshold for personal exemption phaseout = $150,000.

Although the maximum stated rate on taxable income is 31 percent, the effective rate on higher gross income levels will be greater due to the standard deduction and personal exemption phase-outs.

Table 5.7 lists the average and marginal personal tax rates for a range of taxable income from $20,000 to $1,000,000. Thus, pre–TRA 86, the top marginal corporate tax rate was 46 percent and the top marginal personal rate was 50 percent. Effective 1991, these rates became 34 percent and 31 percent, respectively.

Of all the recent tax acts, TRA 86 made the most drastic changes in the tax structure; the prior personal income tax structure included 14 tax brackets up to a maximum rate of 50 percent. TRA 86 was phased in over a period of years. Figure 5.2 illustrates the effects of these changes on marginal and average personal tax rates.

Other Changes in the 1986 Tax Reform Act

The holding period for short-term gains or losses on the sale of property is six months or less. Long-term gains result from a holding period greater than six months. Before 1987, net long-term capital gains could be reduced by 60 percent before application of tax. Thus an individual in the 50 percent tax bracket would have an effective tax rate on net long-term capital gains of 20 percent (40 percent times 50 percent). In 1987, the 60 percent deduction was eliminated, but the maximum rate on long-term capital gains was 28 percent, although net short-term gains were fully taxable at ordinary income tax rates. Short-term and long-term capital gains can be offset against each other. If capital losses exceed capital gains, the net capital loss is deductible up to $3,000 per year against ordinary income.

IRA deductions are phased out for moderate to high income taxpayers who are ''active participants'' in an employer retirement plan. Self-employed taxpayers may continue

FIGURE 5.2   Marginal and Average Personal Tax Rates

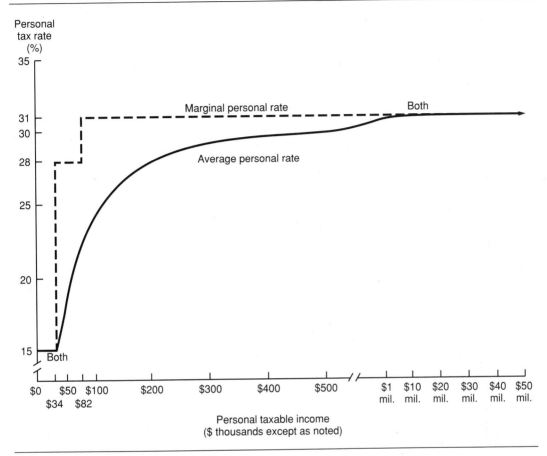

to set up retirement plans called Keogh plans. Deductible contributions may be made up to the lower of 25 percent of earned income or $30,000. Because of technicalities in computing the deduction, the taxpayer will have to use at least two plans such as a money-purchase pension plan and a profit-sharing plan. The financial institution handling the Keogh plan for the taxpayer can take care of the technicalities that must be satisfied to obtain the maximum deduction of 25 percent of earned income.

CHOICES AMONG ALTERNATIVE FORMS OF BUSINESS ORGANIZATION

Taxes are an important influence in choosing among alternative forms of business organization. In the following sections, the nature of the various alternatives and their advantages and disadvantages will be described. Then the tax aspects will be considered.

From a technical and legal standpoint, there are three major forms of business organization: the sole proprietorship, the partnership, and the corporation.[4] In terms of numbers, 70 percent of business firms are operated as sole proprietorships, 8 percent are partnerships, and 14 percent are corporations. By dollar value of sales, however, about 80 percent of business is conducted by corporations, about 13 percent by sole proprietorships, and about 7 percent by partnerships. The remainder of this section describes and compares the characteristics of these alternative forms of business organization.

Sole Proprietorship

A sole proprietorship is a business owned by one individual. Going into business as a sole proprietor is very simple; a person merely begins business operations. However, cities or counties may require even the smallest establishments to be licensed or registered. State licenses may also be required.

The proprietorship has key advantages for small operations. It is easily and inexpensively formed, requires no formal charter for operations, and is subject to few government regulations. Further, it pays no corporate income taxes, although all earnings of the firm are subject to personal income taxes, regardless of whether the owner withdraws the funds for personal use.

The proprietorship also has important limitations. Most significant is its inability to obtain large sums of capital. Further, the proprietor has unlimited personal liability for business debts; creditors can look to both business assets and personal assets to satisfy their claims. Finally, the proprietorship is limited to the life of the individual who creates it. For all these reasons, the sole proprietorship is limited primarily to small business operations. However, businesses frequently are started as proprietorships and then converted to corporations when their growth causes the disadvantages of the proprietorship form to outweigh its advantages.

Partnership

A partnership is the association of two or more persons to conduct a business enterprise. Partnerships can operate under different degrees of formality, ranging from an informal oral understanding to a written partnership agreement to a formal agreement filed with the state government. Like the proprietorship, the partnership has the advantages of ease and economy of formation as well as freedom from special government regulations. Partnership profits are taxed as personal income in proportion to the partners' claims, whether or not they are distributed to them.

One of the advantages of the partnership over the proprietorship is that it makes possible a pooling of various types of resources. Some partners contribute particular skills or contacts, while others contribute funds. However, there are practical limits to the number of co-owners who can join in an enterprise without destructive conflict, so most partnership agreements provide that the individual partners cannot sell their share of the business unless all the partners agree to accept the new partner (or partners).

---

[4]Other less common forms of organization include business trusts, joint stock companies, and cooperatives.

If a new partner comes into the business, the old partnership ceases to exist and a new one is created. The withdrawal or death of any of the partners also dissolves the partnership. To prevent disputes under such circumstances, the articles of the partnership agreement should include terms and conditions under which assets are to be distributed upon dissolution. Of course, dissolution of the partnership does not necessarily mean the end of the business; the remaining partners may simply buy out the one who left the firm. To avoid financial pressures caused by the death of one of the partners, it is a common practice for each partner to carry life insurance naming the remaining partners as beneficiaries. The proceeds of such policies can be used to buy out the investment of the deceased partner.

A number of drawbacks stemming from the characteristics of the partnership limit its use. They include impermanence, difficulty of transferring ownership, and unlimited liability (except for limited partners). Partners risk their personal assets as well as their investments in the business. Further, under partnership law, the partners are jointly and separately liable for business debts. This means that if any partner is unable to meet the claims resulting from the liquidation of the partnership, the remaining partners must take over the unsatisfied claims, drawing on their personal assets if necessary.[5]

Corporation

A corporation is a legal entity created by a governmental unit — mostly states in the United States.[6] It is a separate entity, distinct from its owners and managers. This separateness gives the corporation four major advantages: (1) it has an unlimited life — changes of owners and managers do not affect its continuity; (2) it permits limited liability — stockholders are not personally liable for the debts of the firm;[7] (3) the residual risk of the owners is divided into many units so that the risk exposure in any one firm can be small and diversification by investors across many firms is facilitated; and (4) it permits easy transferability of ownership interest in the firm — the divided ownership interests can be transferred far more easily than partnership interests.

While a proprietorship or a partnership can commence operations without much paperwork, the chartering of a corporation involves more legal formalities. First, a certificate of incorporation is drawn up; in most states, it includes the following information: (1) name of proposed corporation, (2) purposes, (3) amount of capital stock, (4) number of directors, (5) names and addresses of directors, and (6) duration (if limited). The certificate is notarized and sent to the secretary of the state in which the business seeks incorporation. If approved, the corporation officially comes into being.

The actual operations of the firm are governed by two documents, the charter and the bylaws. The corporate charter technically consists of a certificate of incorporation and, by reference, the general corporation laws of the state. Thus, the corporation is bound by the

---

[5]It is possible to limit the liabilities of some partners by establishing a limited partnership, wherein certain partners are designated general partners and others limited partners. Limited partnerships are quite common in the area of real estate and oil exploration investments.

[6]Certain types of firms (for example, banks) are also chartered by the federal government.

[7]In the case of small corporations, the limited liability feature is often a fiction, since bankers and credit managers frequently require personal guarantees from the stockholders of small, weak businesses.

general corporation laws of the state as well as by the unique provisions of its certificate of incorporation. The bylaws are a set of rules drawn up by the founders of the corporation to aid in governing the internal management of the company. Included are such points as (1) how directors are to be elected (all elected each year or, say, one-third each year, and whether cumulative voting will be used), (2) whether the preemptive first right of purchase is granted to existing stockholders in the event new securities are sold, and (3) provisions for management committees, such as an executive committee or a finance committee, and their duties. Also included is the procedure for changing the bylaws themselves if necessary.

Master Limited Partnerships

In recent years the master limited partnership (MLP) has increased in importance. The MLP is similar to an ordinary limited partnership except that its shares are freely traded. The MLP has tax advantages over the corporation in that the MLP is not taxed as an entity. Thus the MLP avoids double taxation of corporate earnings. Because of the tax advantages, the Internal Revenue Service (IRS) has developed guidelines for distinguishing between a corporation and MLP. Four factors are used in distinguishing between a corporation and MLP: (1) unlimited life, (2) limited liability, (3) centralized management, and (4) transferability. An MLP may have only two and no more of the four corporate characteristics. The MLP usually has centralized management and transferability, but MLPs typically specify a limited life and the general manager of the partnership has unlimited liability.

A number of different types of MLPs have been distinguished. Roll-up MLPs combine existing mature limited partnerships offered by a general partner. These provide liquidity for nontraded limited partnerships. A larger proportion of MLPs are roll-outs. One type of roll-out is the MLP spin-off in which units in the MLP are distributed to corporate shareholders in exchange for a subset of existing shares. In a public issue roll-out, the corporation transfers a subset of its assets to an MLP selling depository units to the public for cash — analogous to equity carve-outs. In total conversions, the corporation transfers all of its assets to the MLP in exchange for all of the depository units. New issue MLPs are public offerings of a new form of ownerships such as the conversion of the Boston Celtics basketball team to a master limited partnership.

The Omnibus Budget Reconciliation Act of December 1987 eliminated some tax advantages of MLPs but not the critical advantage of being taxed as a partnership. Nevertheless, the administrative costs of maintaining tax records and tracking changes in ownership can be burdensome. For example, MLPs were first developed in the oil and gas industry with the formation of an MLP by Apache Petroleum in 1981. In August 1988, Apache Petroleum restructured as a corporation that was said to have saved Apache $4 million per year.

Muscarella [1988] analyzed the initial pricing of MLPs, covering the period January 1983 to July 1987. He found no significant underpricing or overpricing except for a slight overpricing of oil and gas and hotel/motel MLPs. This contrasts with substantial underpricing of initial public offerings (IPOs) of corporate securities. Moore, Christensen, and Roenfeldt [1989] studied the effects on corporations announcing MLP formations during the period 1982–1987. They observed significant positive equity valuation announcement effects. For MLP spin-offs, 6.41 percent; for public issue roll-outs, 2.41 percent; and for total conversions, 4.61 percent. They discuss several possible explanations of these positive valuation effects including tax effects, free cash flow effects, signaling of private information, improved information flow, and improved asset management.

The general partner of the MLP has unlimited liability but also complete control of the information flow and decision making. The general partner is in an autocratic position, which makes it extremely difficult for the limited partners to exercise influence over the decisions of the general partner. For this reason, in public issues of MLP, cash distributions of specified amounts are usually promised. As a result, MLPs typically sell on an expected yield basis similar to preferred stocks purchased by individuals.

Joint Ventures

Joint ventures (JV) are enterprises owned by two or more participants. They are typically formed for special purposes for a limited duration. The participants enter into a contract to work together for a period of time. Each participant expects to gain from the activity but also must make a contribution. For example, in the GM-Toyota joint venture, GM hoped to gain new experience in the management techniques of the Japanese in building high-quality, low-cost compact and subcompact cars. Toyota was seeking to learn from the management traditions that had made GM the number one auto producer in the world and in addition to learn how to operate an auto company under the conditions in the United States, dealing with contractors, suppliers, and workers.

To some degree the joint venture represents a relatively new thrust by each participant, so it is often called a strategic alliance. Probably, the main motive for joint ventures is to share risks. This explains why joint ventures are frequently found in bidding on oil contracts and in drilling oil wells, in large real estate ventures, in movies, plays, and in television productions. The second most frequently cited aim in joint ventures is knowledge acquisition. One or more participants is seeking to learn more about a relatively new product-market activity. This may be all aspects of the activity, or a limited segment such as R&D, production, marketing, or servicing products.

Other reasons for joint ventures are numerous. One frequently encountered is the small firm with a new product idea that involves high risk and requires relatively large amounts of investment capital. A larger firm may be able to carry the financial risk and be interested in becoming involved in a new business activity that promises growth and profitability. By investing in a large number of such ventures, the larger firm has limited risk in any one and the possibility of very high financial payoffs. In addition, the larger firm may thereby gain experience in a new area of activity that may represent the opportunity for a major new business thrust in the future.

A basic tension is often found in joint ventures. Each participant hopes to gain as much as possible from the interaction, but would like to limit the gains to the other participants. This is particularly true when the firms are competitors in other areas of their activities.

Antitrust authorities often view joint ventures with suspicion. One concern is that each of the participants might have entered the new area independently. Hence, they reason that absent the joint venture, multiple new competitors might have emerged. But it is also possible that the risk to reward outlook is so uncertain that absent the joint venture, no additional competitors would have emerged. In areas of research and development activities, the antitrust authorities are more favorably disposed. For one reason, R&D activity is recognized to be inherently risky. For another, if the R&D joint venture effort turns out to be successful, it may contribute to the economic and competitive strength of the nation as a whole in the world economy.

The most thorough study of the value effects of joint ventures finds that positive returns are achieved [McConnell and Nantell, 1985]. When scaled to the size of investments, joint ventures appear to achieve about a 23 percent return higher than predicted by general capital market return-risk relationships. Overall joint ventures appear on average to make important contributions to the well-being of business firms and to the economy as a whole.

Employee Stock Ownership Plans (ESOPs)

Another new organizational form that has been growing in importance in recent years is the Employee Stock Ownership Plan (ESOP). An ESOP is a type of employee pension plan. Since 1974 employee pension plans have been regulated by the Employee Retirement Income Security Act (ERISA). ERISA divides employee pension plans into two major types: (1) defined benefit plans, and (2) defined contribution plans. The defined benefit plan specifies the amounts that participants will receive in retirement according to a formula set in advance. Defined contribution plans make no fixed commitment to a pension level. Only the contributions into the plan are specified, and participants receive what is in their accounts when they retire. ESOPs represent a form of a defined contribution plan. ERISA regulations permit ESOP contributions to be invested primarily in the securities of the employer.

There are tax benefits involved in ESOPs. Tax deductions for corporate contributions to ESOPs can be made up to 15 percent of employee compensation. There are tax deductions for the organization and administrative costs of the ESOP. In leveraged ESOPs, the ESOP borrows funds to purchase employer securities with the loan guaranteed by the employer. The employer makes tax deductible contributions to the ESOPs sufficient to repay both principal and interest on the loan. Thus the repayment of principal becomes tax deductible as well as the payment of interest. In addition, the financial intermediary who is the lender on the loan can exclude 50 percent of the interest received from taxable income.

By 1989 over 10,000 ESOPs had been established, with over 12 million employees as participants. ESOPs have been used as a method of raising funds by the firm. ESOPs have been used as an alternative to mergers. ESOPs have also been increasingly used as a takeover defense. For example, in response to a tender offer by Shamrock Holdings (the investment vehicle for the family of Roy E. Disney, nephew of the late Walt Disney), Polaroid established an ESOP holding 14 percent of Polaroid common stock. Like most large corporations, Polaroid is chartered in Delaware. The Delaware antitakeover statute forbids hostile acquirers from merging with a target for at least three years unless 85 percent of the company's voting shares are tendered. Thus, it is unlikely that Shamrock would be able to obtain 85 percent of Polaroid shares if the ESOP does not tender [Rice and Spring, 1989].

The argument for employee stock ownership holds that employees who own stock in their employer are more productive, since as part owners they have a greater stake in the firm's profitability. ESOPs, however, provide a good deal less than direct stock owner-ship. Participants typically do not receive any distribution of securities from the plan until they separate from service. Dividends and voting rights are passed through only with respect to shares actually allocated to participants' accounts. But most participants are not allowed to sell even those shares that have been allocated to them and thus cannot achieve a level of diversification in their benefit plans. (ERISA excludes ESOPs from the require-ment to diversify.) A 1987 report by the General Accounting Office (GAO) concluded that while ESOPs do broaden stock ownership within participating firms, given the lim-ited number of ESOPs within the economy as a whole, the effect is modest overall. Perhaps more important, it found little evidence of improved performance in terms of either profitability or productivity.

As a financing tool, ESOPs provide benefits midway between debt and equity financ-ing. They can bring additional debt capacity to highly leveraged firms or provide a market for equity financing for closely-held firms. They are very useful devices for transferring ownership. The same 1987 GAO report indicated that the use of ESOPs in corporate finance has not lived up to its potential—most leveraged ESOP funds are used to buy back stock from existing shareholders (for instance, retiring major shareholders) and not for capital expansion by the sponsoring firms. Thus ESOPs' contributions to corporate finance have been limited. However, the exploding events in connection with ESOPs during 1989 may substantially alter these earlier patterns. In mid-1989 the IRS ruled that the special tax benefits of ESOP debt would still be allowed even if the debt of the ESOP is traded publicly. Shortly thereafter, however, it was announced that the House Ways and Means Committee was considering a bill to repeal the exclusion [Birnbaum and Winkler, 1989]. On June 7, 1989, an IRS private ruling (8921101) held that dividends on ESOP stock were deductible if used to help retire the ESOP loan for leveraged ESOPs. The ruling indicated that companies might transfer stock to leveraged ESOPs from employee profit sharing or stock bonus plans and thereby deduct previously nondeductible divi-dends. The ruling would also require the ESOP to allocate added stock to employees based on the value of the dividends used for loan payments [Schmedel, 1989]. Thus the events of 1989 may have transformed the significance of ESOPs.

TAX ASPECTS OF THE FORMS OF ORGANIZATION

To a small, growing firm, there may be advantages in the corporate form of organization. There is ''double taxation'' of dividends, but salaries paid to principals in the corporation are a tax-deductible expense and so are not subject to double taxation. The tax advantages of incorporation were significantly reduced by TRA 86; the maximum personal rate is now 31 percent versus 34 percent for corporations. However, by splitting organizational earnings between the corporation and the individual, both may be put into a lower tax bracket. Also of importance is that all the earnings of partnerships and proprietorships are taxable at the personal income tax rate whether they are reinvested in the business or withdrawn from it. In the aftermath of TRA 86, considerations other than taxation become more important in the decision to incorporate.

A specific example will illustrate some of the tax aspects of the form of organization. Craig Vernon, a married man with two children, is the sole proprietor of a small business, CV Manufacturing. He is trying to decide whether to incorporate or to continue as a proprietorship. He currently owns 100 percent of the firm and would (at least initially) plan to own 100 percent of its stock if he decides on the corporate form. Tax considerations are important to him because he plans to finance the continued growth of the firm by plowing all profits back into the enterprise after drawing a salary sufficient for his living expenses, $150,000 per year. Vernon has no other source of income. He estimates that his personal exemptions plus itemized deductions will be $50,000.

Current business income before taxes is $300,000 per year, and Vernon is optimistic about the potential for growth. To determine from a tax standpoint whether Vernon should incorporate, we calculate total taxes under both the corporate form (in Table 5.8) and the proprietorship form (in Table 5.9) for a range of business incomes, starting with the current $300,000 to an estimated $1,000,000.

Comparing total taxes, except for the first year, total taxes will be lower for the proprietorship form. This is because the maximum personal rate is 31 percent, while the maximum corporate rate is 34 percent. Since we assumed a constant salary of $150,000 for Vernon as business income rose, this meant that a larger proportion of income was being taxed at the maximum corporate rate. The difference could have been mitigated somewhat if Vernon increased his salary as business income rose. Thus, we see that, in spite of the income splitting effect that would tend to keep both corporate and personal income in lower tax brackets, TRA 86 virtually eliminated the tax advantages of incorporation except for very small businesses. Marginal corporate tax rates exceed personal rates from an income level of above $75,000. Figure 5.3 shows that average corporate rates are higher than personal rates for income over $123,319.

Furthermore, the figures shown for the corporation deal with dollars that have not yet come into the hands of the stockholder/owner. If the earnings are distributed as dividends, there will be additional taxes to be borne by the stockholder. If a stockholder sells his or her stock, there is a further tax on the capital gain.

Foremost among the advantages favoring the corporate form in spite of the tax disadvantage is the corporation's effectiveness in raising large sums of capital from a large number of sources. While broad generalizations are not possible, these are factors that should at least be taken in account in making the decision about the form of organization for any business enterprise.

S Corporations

Subchapter S of the Internal Revenue Code provides that some small, incorporated businesses may still elect to be taxed as proprietorships or partnerships if some technical requirements are met, for example, a maximum of 35 shareholders. Thus, the firm may enjoy the protection of the limited liability provided by incorporation but still retain some tax advantages.

TABLE 5.8   Taxes as a Corporation

Corporate Form				
Business income	$300,000	$500,000	$800,000	$1,000,000
Less salary	150,000	150,000	150,000	150,000
Corporate taxable income	$150,000	$350,000	$650,000	$ 850,000
Corporate Tax Calculation				
$50,000 @ 15%	7,500	7,500	7,500	7,500
$50,000–$75,000 @ 25%	6,250	6,250	6,250	6,250
Over $75,000 @ 34%	25,500	93,500	195,500	263,500
$100,000–$335,000 @ 5%	2,500	11,750	11,750	11,750
Total corporate tax	$ 41,750	$119,000	$221,000	$ 289,000
Personal Taxes				
Salary = AGI	$150,000	$150,000	$150,000	$ 150,000
Personal taxable income	100,000	100,000	100,000	100,000
Personal Tax Calculation				
0–$34,000 @ 15%	$ 5,100	$ 5,100	$ 5,100	$ 5,100
$34,000–$82,150 @ 28%	13,482	13,482	13,482	13,482
$82,150–$100,000 @ 31%	5,534	5,534	5,534	5,534
Total personal tax	$ 24,116	$ 24,116	$ 24,116	$ 24,116
TOTAL TAXES	$ 65,866	$143,116	$245,116	$ 313,116

TABLE 5.9   Taxes as a Proprietorship

Proprietorship Form				
Business income = AGI	$300,000	$500,000	$800,000	$1,000,000
Personal taxable income	250,000	450,000	750,000	950,000
Personal Tax Calculation				
0–$34,000 @ 15%	$ 5,100	$ 5,100	$ 5,100	$ 5,100
$34,000–$82,150 @ 28%	13,482	13,482	13,482	13,482
Over $82,150 @ 31%	52,034	114,034	207,034	269,034
TOTAL TAXES	$ 70,616	$132,616	$225,616	$ 287,616

These benefits are particularly useful to a small new firm that may incur losses while it seeks to become established in its beginning years. Its operating losses may be used on a pro rata basis by its stockholders as deductions against their ordinary income. In the past, this stimulated persons in high marginal personal income tax brackets to invest in small, new, risky enterprises. Similarly, new firms making large capital investments were likely to generate more investment tax credits than they could use, even with carryforwards; these credits could also be passed through to high income stockholders. While the Tax Reform Act of 1986 has eliminated the investment tax credit, S corporations are

FIGURE 5.3 Comparison Between Average Corporate and Personal Tax Rates

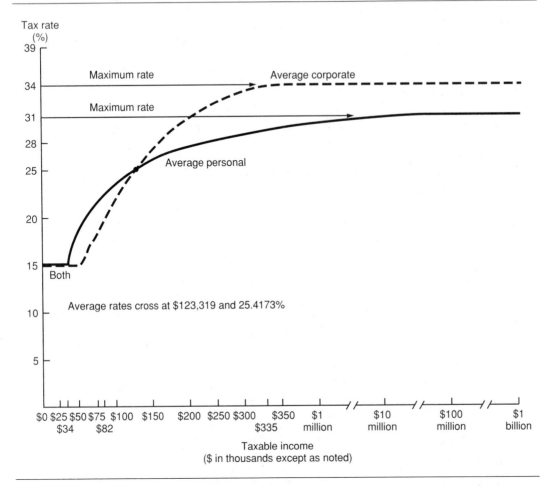

expected to remain popular, not on account of their losses, but for their profits. Even with the surtaxes on higher levels of income, the maximum personal income tax rate is now 31 percent; the maximum corporate rate is 34 percent. If other aspects of incorporation are attractive, especially the limited liability feature, then perhaps organizing as an S corporation is the preferred alternative.

SUMMARY

This chapter provides some basic background on the tax environment within which business firms operate. The corporate and personal tax rate structures have been simplified by the Tax Reform Act of 1986. For corporations, the tax rate is 15 percent on income up to $50,000, 25 percent on the next increment of $25,000, and 34 percent on all income over

$75,000. A five-percent surtax on taxable income between $100,000 and $335,000 effectively applies a 34 percent rate to all increments of income for high income corporations. Estimated taxes are paid in quarterly installments during the year in which the income is earned; when the returns are filed, the actual tax liability results either in additional payments or in a refund due. Any operating loss incurred by the corporation can be carried back 3 years and forward 15 years against income in those years. The firm can elect not to employ the carryback provision. There are strict limitations on the utilization of operating loss carryovers following a change in ownership.

Of the dividends received by a corporation owning stock in another firm, 70 to 80 percent may be excluded from the receiving firm's taxable income depending on how much stock is owned. Dividends paid are not a tax-deductible expense. Regardless of its profitability, a corporation does not have to pay dividends if it needs funds for expansion or other legitimate business purposes. If, however, earnings are retained merely to enable stockholders to avoid paying personal income taxes on dividends received, the firm is subject to an improper accumulations tax. Interest received is taxable as ordinary income; interest paid is a tax-deductible expense.

Depreciation is a special kind of tax-deductible business expense in that it does not represent a cash outflow, but reduces the cash outflow on taxes. Tax authorities allow specified accelerated depreciation methods under the Modified Accelerated Cost Recovery System of TRA 86 for purposes of tax reporting; the effect is to reduce taxable income, and thus the cash outflow on taxes. However, firms may use alternative methods to maximize reported net income for purposes of reporting to shareholders.

Unincorporated business income is taxed at the personal tax rates of the owners. There are three personal income tax rates — 15, 28, and 31 percent. The 1991 rates for married persons filing joint returns, the 15 percent rate applies to income up to $34,000, the 28 percent rate applies to income from $34,000 to $82,150, and the 31 percent rate applies to all income above $82,150. High income taxpayers face special provisions that reduce personal exemptions and itemized deductions for AGI over $150,000 and $100,000 respectively (for married persons filing joint returns), thus raising the effective marginal tax rate related to AGI.

Sole proprietorships and partnerships are easily formed. All earnings (losses) are taxed as regular income of the owner or partner. Owners and partners are also personally liable for the debts of the business. The corporation has the advantage of limiting the liability of the participants, but it is generally more expensive to organize. Once organized, a corporation provides an easy means to transfer ownership to others. Corporate earnings paid as dividends are subject to double taxation. The other tax differences between corporations and proprietorships or partnerships depend on the facts of individual cases. A number of other organizational forms have gained importance in recent years. Among these are master limited partnerships, joint ventures, and employee stock ownership plans.

The information presented here on the tax system is not designed to make a tax expert of the reader. It merely provides a few essentials for recognizing the tax aspects of business financial problems and for developing an awareness of the kinds of situations that should be dealt with by tax specialists. These basics are, however, referred to frequently throughout the text because income taxes are often an important factor in business financial decisions.

QUESTIONS

5.1   Compare the marginal and the average tax rates of corporations for taxable incomes of $5,000, $75,000, $500,000, and $50,000,000. Can you make such a comparison for sole proprietorships or for partnerships?

5.2   Which is the more relevant tax rate — the marginal or the average — in determining the form of organization for a new firm? Discuss aspects of the tax laws that make the form of organization less important.

5.3   For tax purposes, how does the treatment of interest expense compare with the treatment of common stock dividends from each of the following standpoints: a firm paying the interest or dividends, an individual recipient, and a corporate recipient?

5.4   What is the purpose of the Internal Revenue Code provision dealing with improper accumulation of corporate income?

5.5   Why is personal income tax information important to the study of business finance?

5.6   What are the advantages and disadvantages of the use of a sole proprietorship versus a partnership for conducting the operations of a small business firm?

5.7   Under what circumstances does it become advantageous for the small business to incorporate?

5.8   In what sense is a corporation a person?

5.9   Would it be practical for General Motors to be organized as a partnership?

PROBLEMS

5.1   A corporation had net taxable income of $60,000 in 1991.
   a.   How much income tax must the corporation pay?
   b.   What is the marginal tax rate?
   c.   What is the average tax rate?

5.2   The Dolmite Corporation had net operating income of $40,000. It also had $20,000 of interest expense and $35,000 of interest revenue during 1991.
   a.   How much income tax must the corporation pay?
   b.   What is the marginal tax rate?
   c.   What is the average tax rate?

5.3   The Triangle Corporation had net income from operations of $130,000 in 1991, including $30,000 in dividend income on small holdings of stocks of various major publicly held corporations.
   a.   How much tax must the corporation pay?
   b.   What is the average tax rate?
   c.   What is the marginal tax rate?

5.4   Determine the marginal and average income tax rates for a corporation earning (a) $10,000, (b) $100,000, (c) $1,000,000, and (d) $100,000,000.

5.5 The taxable income of the Pennock Corporation, formed in 19X0, is indicated below. (Losses are shown as minuses.)

Year	Taxable Income
19X0	−$80,000
19X1	60,000
19X2	50,000
19X3	70,000
19X4	−120,000

What is the corporate tax liability for each year? (Use 1991 tax rates.)

5.6 The Onwee Company has purchased a fleet of small trucks to deliver and service its products. The total cost of the vehicles was $150,000; they qualify as five-year assets for purposes of MACRS depreciation. Onwee uses straight-line depreciation for stockholder reporting. The applicable corporate tax rate is 34 percent. Onwee projects incremental earnings before depreciation, interest, and taxes (EBDIT) over the six-year tax life of the trucks as follows (in thousands of dollars):

Year	EBDIT
1	$400
2	400
3	400
4	400
5	400
6	400

a. Calculate Onwee's tax liability over the life of the truck fleet.

b. Prepare the income statements that will be reported to shareholders.

5.7 Victor Stone has operated his small machine shop as a sole proprietorship for several years, but on advice from his brother-in-law he is now considering incorporation. Stone is married and has two children. His only income, an annual salary of $40,000, is from operating the business. His applicable personal exemptions plus itemized deductions will total $20,000 per year. Stone estimates that his proprietorship earnings before salary and taxes for a three-year period will be:

Year	Income before Salary and Taxes
19X1	$50,000
19X2	70,000
19X3	90,000

a. What will his total taxes (use 1991 rates) be under:

   (1) A proprietorship?

   (2) A corporate form of organization?

b. Should Stone incorporate? Discuss.

SELECTED REFERENCES

Barro, Robert J., and Sahasakul, Chaipat, "Measuring the Average Marginal Tax Rate from the Individual Income Tax," *Journal of Business,* 56 (October 1983), pp. 419–452.

Birnbaum, Jeffrey H., and Winkler, Matthew, "Rostenkowski Acts to Repeal ESOP Provision," *The Wall Street Journal,* June 8, 1989, pp. C1, C17.

Butters, J. K.; Lintner, J.; and Cary, W. L., *Effects of Taxation on Corporate Mergers,* Boston, Mass.: Harvard Business School, 1951, pp. 96–111.

Caks, John, "Sense and Nonsense About Depreciation," *Financial Management,* 10 (Autumn 1981), pp. 80–86.

Comiskey, Eugene E., and Hasselback, James R., "Analyzing the Profit-Tax Relationship," *Financial Management,* 2 (Winter 1973), pp. 57–62.

Dyl, Edward A., "Capital Gains Taxation and Year-End Stock Market Behavior," *Journal of Finance,* 32 (March 1977), pp. 165–175.

Federal Tax Course, Englewood Cliffs, N. J.: Prentice-Hall, Annual.

Hall, J. K., *The Taxation of Corporate Surplus Accumulations,* Washington, D. C.: The Government Printing Office, 1952.

McCarty, Daniel E., and McDaniel, William R., "A Note on Expensing Versus Depreciating Under the Accelerated Cost Recovery System: Comment," *Financial Management,* 12 (Summer 1983), pp. 37–39.

McConnell, John J., and Nantell, Timothy J., "Corporate Combinations and Common Stock Returns: The Case of Joint Ventures," *Journal of Finance* (June 1985), pp. 519–536.

Moore, W. T.; Christensen, D. G.; and Roenfeldt, R. L., "Equity Valuation Effects of Forming Master Limited Partnerships," *Journal of Financial Economics,* 24 (1989), pp. 107–124.

Muscarella, C. J., "Price Performance of Initial Public Offerings of Master Limited Partnership Units," *The Financial Review,* 23 (November 1988), pp. 513–521.

Rice, B., and Spring R., "ESOP at the Barricades," *Barron's,* February 6, 1989, pp. 38–39.

Schmedel, Scott, "Tax Report," *The Wall Street Journal,* June 7, 1989, p. A1.

APPENDIX A TO CHAPTER 5

Depreciation Methods

The depreciation method a firm uses is largely determined by the method allowed by the Internal Revenue Service. However, since firms can use alternative depreciation methods for shareholder reporting, and since the tax laws can be and are frequently changed, it is useful to be aware of how depreciation is calculated under a variety of methods.

The four principal methods of depreciation — straight-line, sum-of-years'-digits, declining balance, and units of production — and their effects on a firm's taxes are illustrated in this appendix. We will begin by assuming that a machine is purchased for $1,100 and has an estimated useful life of 10 years or 10,000 hours, whichever comes first. It will have a scrap value of $100 at the end of its useful life. Table 5A.1 illustrates each of the

TABLE 5A.1   Comparison of Depreciation Methods for a 10-Year, $1,100 Asset with a $100 Salvage Value

Year	Straight Line	Sum-of-Years'-Digits	Units of Production[a]	Declining Balance (200%)
1	$ 100	$ 182	$ 200	$ 220
2	100	164	180	176
3	100	145	150	141
4	100	127	130	113
5	100	109	100	90
6	100	91	80	72
7	100	73	60	58
8	100	55	50	46
9	100	36	30	42
10	100	18	20	42
Total	$1,000	$1,000	$1,000	$1,000

Columns may not add to the total because of rounding.
[a]The assumption is made that the machine is used the following number of hours: first year, 2,000; second year, 1,800; third year, 1,500; fourth year, 1,300; fifth year, 1,000; sixth year, 800; seventh year, 600; eighth year, 500; ninth year, 300; tenth year, 200.

four depreciation methods and compares the depreciation charges of each method over the 10-year period.

Straight-Line

With the straight-line method, a uniform annual depreciation charge of $100 is provided. This figure is arrived at by simply dividing the economic life into the total cost of the machine minus the estimated salvage value.

$$\frac{(\$1,100 \text{ cost} - \$100 \text{ salvage value})}{10 \text{ years}} = \$100 \text{ a year depreciation charge}$$

If the estimated salvage value is not in excess of 10 percent of the original cost, it can be ignored, but we are leaving it in for illustrative purposes.

Sum-of-Years'-Digits

Under the sum-of-years'-digits method, the yearly depreciation allowance is determined as follows:

1. Calculate the sum of the years' digits; in our example, there is a total of 55 digits:

$$1 + 2 + 3 + 4 + 5 + 6 + 7 + 8 + 9 + 10 = 55.$$

This figure can also be arrived at by means of the sum of an algebraic progression equation where n is the life of the asset:

$$\text{Sum} = n\left(\frac{n + 1}{2}\right) = 10\left(\frac{10 + 1}{2}\right) = 55. \tag{5A.1}$$

2. Divide the number of remaining years by the sum-of-years'-digits, and multiply this fraction by the depreciable cost (total cost minus salvage value) of the asset:

Year 1:   (10/55)($1,000) = $182 depreciation
Year 2:   (9/55)($1,000) = $164 depreciation
  ⋮   ⋮   ⋮
Year 10:   (1/55)($1,000) = $18 depreciation.

It will be noted that in the above expressions, the numerator of each fraction can be written as $(n + 1 - t)$, where t is the number of years in use; the denominator, of course, is the sum of the digits expression set forth in Equation 5A.1. This fraction is multiplied times the original depreciable amount, which we will call I. Hence, the formula for the annual amount of the sum-of-years'-digits depreciation can be written as:

$$\text{Dep}_t = \frac{2(n + 1 - t)I}{n(n + 1)} \tag{5A.2}$$

Units of Production

Under the units of production method, the expected useful life of 10,000 hours is divided into the depreciable cost (purchase price minus salvage value) to arrive at an hourly depreciation rate of 10 cents. Since, in our example, the machine is run for 2,000 hours in the first year, the depreciation charge in that year is $200; in the second year, $180; and so on. With this method, depreciation charges cannot be estimated precisely ahead of time; the firm must wait until the end of the year to determine what usage has been made of the machine and hence its depreciation.

Declining Balance Methods

In the declining balance methods of accelerated depreciation, the annual depreciation charge is calculated by multiplying a fixed rate times the undepreciated balance, or net book value (that is, the cost less accumulated depreciation). Since the undepreciated balance becomes smaller in each successive period, the amount of depreciation declines during each successive period; the rate applied to the undepreciated balance is fixed.[1] In the 200 percent declining balance — also known as double declining balance — the rate

---

[1] In this Appendix we are discussing declining balance depreciation in general; the application of declining balance depreciation specified under the Modified Accelerated Cost Recovery System (MACRS) was discussed at length in the text of the chapter. One major difference to be distinguished at this point is that the annual depreciation percentages set out by the IRS for various asset lives are applied to the total purchase price of the asset, and not to the undepreciated balance as in the present discussion. The varying annual percentages are, however, derived from the application of the principles discussed in this section.

TABLE 5A.2   200% Declining Balance Method

Year (1)	Net Book Value (1,100 − Col. 4 of Previous Year) (2)	200% DB Deprec. (0.2 × Col. 2) (3)	Total Depreciation (Sum of Col. 3) (4)	Test of Straight-Line Method (5)	Adjusted Total Depreciation (6)
1	$1,100	$220	220		
2	880	176	396		
3	704	141	537		
4	563	113	650		
5	450	90	740		
6	360	72	812		
7	288	58	870		
8	230	46	916	43[a]	
9	184	37	953	42[b]	958
10	147	29	982	42	1,000

[a]$1,100 − 100 − 870 = 130 \div 3 = 43$
[b]$1,100 − 100 − 916 = 84 \div 2 = 42$

applied to the undepreciated balance is two times the straight-line rate. For example, on our asset, with a 10-year life, the straight-line depreciation rate would be 10 percent per year; for the 200 percent declining balance method, the fixed rate would be $2 \times 10\% = 20\%$ per year (applied to the undepreciated balance). For the 150 percent declining balance method, the rate would be $1.5 \times 10\% = 15\%$ per year; for 175 percent declining balance, the rate would be $1.75 \times 10\% = 17.5\%$ per year. (Suppose an asset has a 15-year life; the straight-line depreciation rate would be $1/15 = 6.67$ percent per year; the double declining balance rate would be $2 \times 6.67\% = 13.3\%$ per year and so on.)

In the declining balance methods, the estimated salvage value is typically not subtracted from the cost of the asset in making the depreciation calculation as is done in other depreciation methods. The 200 percent method is illustrated for the data of our example in Table 5A.2.

Column (2) is the net book value subject to depreciation. It is the purchase price of the asset less the depreciation already taken. For the second year, the depreciation rate is applied to $1,100 less $220, or $880; then, 20 percent of $880 is $176, the amount of depreciation for Year 2. This procedure continues for each successive year.

The company makes a switch from the declining balance method to straight line whenever straight-line depreciation on the remaining net book value of the asset exceeds the depreciation amount under the declining balance method. In switching from declining balance to straight-line depreciation, however, we must deduct the salvage value to obtain the depreciable amount of the asset. In Table 5A.2, we test for this in the eighth year, but declining balance depreciation is still somewhat higher. In the ninth year, the depreciable amount of $1,000 less accumulated depreciation of $916 equals $84, which is $42 per year for the remaining two years. The switch is made at this point so that the adjusted accumulated depreciation shown in Column (6) is the full $1,000 net depreciable value of the asset. Thus, although salvage is not initially taken into account in applying the declining balance method, it is brought in at the point where the switch to straight-line depreciation is made. A compact formula can be written for calculating the annual amount of depreciation under the 200 percent declining balance method. Using the symbols we have employed before, the formula can be written as:

$$Dep_t = \frac{2[1 - (2/n)]^{t-1}I}{n}.$$ (5A.3)

The logic of this formula is: The expression in the brackets in the numerator, when multiplied times I, gives us the undepreciated balance. We multiply this by 2 and divide by n to obtain the depreciation for the year.

Similarly, the formula for the annual amount of depreciation under the 150% declining balance method is the following:

$$Dep_t = \frac{1.5[1 - (1.5/n)]^{t-1}I}{n}.$$ (5A.4)

The logic of the formula is, of course, exactly the same as for the 200 percent declining balance except that 1.5 is substituted for the 2.

Above we have illustrated the basic principles of declining balance depreciation. In the text of the chapter we demonstrated the use of 200% and 150% declining balance depreciation as adapted for use in the Modified Accelerated Cost Recovery System (MACRS) specified in the tax law.

PROBLEMS

5A.1 The Altmont Corporation has purchased an asset for $5,200. It has an estimated salvage value of $200 at the end of its five-year life. Calculate the annual depreciation expense under each of the following methods:
  a. Straight-line method
  b. Declining balance method (use 200%)
  c. Sum-of-years'-digits method

5A.2 The Rudd Corporation has purchased a machine for $8,500 with an expected useful life of eight years or 6,000 hours. It has an expected salvage value of $500. The annual usage of the machine is estimated as follows:

Year	Hours of Usage
1	1,500
2	1,200
3	1,000
4	800
5	500
6	400
7	300
8	300
	6,000

a. Calculate the annual depreciation expense under each of the following methods:
   (1) Straight-line method
   (2) Sum-of-years'-digits method
   (3) Units of production method
   (4) Declining balance method (use 200%)
b. Add the depreciation expenses for the first two years and rank each method in descending order of the amount of tax deductible depreciation expenses.

5A.3 Assume the same facts as in the above problem except for a four-year life and hours of usage per year of:

Year	Hours of Usage
1	6,000
2	1,800
3	1,200
4	1,000
	10,000

Answer the same questions asked in Problem 5A.2, parts (a) and (b).

CHAPTER 6

The Interest Rate and the International Financial Environment

In this chapter we first explain how the marketplace determines interest rates and other rates of return. Interest rates and rates of return from assets and securities are a central part of financial management because they represent the opportunity cost of investment. We next provide an overview of the basic principles of international finance. The reasons for combining these two topics are that (1) international financial markets are now integrated, and (2) therefore, we cannot understand interest rates and their behavior without considering the international interactions.

HOW THE MARKET DETERMINES INTEREST RATES AND RATES OF RETURN

Interest rates and rate of return data provide information from which financial managers can determine the opportunity costs of investments. The return on investment must exceed the market rate on projects of equivalent risk. In this section, our objective is to explain the underlying factors that determine interest rates (e.g., the rate on U.S. government bonds) and rates of return (e.g., the rate of return on common stocks).

Why Interest Rates Differ

Different assets and securities may have different rates of return. For example, Ibbotson and Sinquefield [1990] compiled data on various types of securities over the time period

1926 to 1989 and found the following long-run pretax rates of return (compounded annually):

Common stocks	10.3%
Stocks of smaller companies	12.2%
Long-term corporate bonds	5.2%
Long-term U.S. government bonds	4.6%
Short-term U.S. Treasury bills	3.6%
Inflation	3.1%

Why have rates of return been different over a long period of time? As we shall see, the pretax nominal rate of return on any asset can be explained by four components: the expected real rate of return, expected inflation over the life of the asset, the liquidity of the asset, and the riskiness of the asset. For example, most of the difference between the rate of return on common stocks, 10.3 percent, and on long-term government bonds, 4.6 percent, can be explained by the extra risk of common stock. Equation 6.1 shows that interest rates are a function of four components:

$$\text{Nominal rate of return} = f[E(\text{real rate}), E(\text{inflation}), \qquad \textbf{(6.1)}$$
$$E(\text{liquidity premium}), E(\text{risk premium})].$$

Note that each term on the right-hand side is preceded by an expectations operator, E. For example, $E(\text{inflation})$ is the market's estimate of expected future inflation. Investors try to estimate what inflation will be, and, consequently, the market rates of return on securities with different lives will reflect the market's expectation of inflation over the life of the asset.

The remainder of this chapter will proceed by starting with the simplest possible type of market instrument, one which lasts only one time period in a world without any inflation and with no risk. This will help to explain the real rate of return. Then, we will complicate things step by step. First, we will add in the effect of expected inflation and liquidity in an effort to explain how rates of return on default-free U.S. government bonds depend on their maturity. Second, we will look at the effect of default risk in order to show why corporate bonds, which are subject to bankruptcy, have higher expected rates of return than U.S. government bonds of equal maturity. Finally, we will introduce return risk (later discussed in Chapters 10 and 11).

The Real Rate of Interest

The real rate of interest, in a world without inflation or uncertainty, is the rate that equates the demand for funds with supply. People demand funds in order to invest them in profitable projects. The demand schedule is downward sloping because we assume that as more money is invested investors begin to run out of profitable projects and as a result, the expected rate of return on marginal investments declines. The supply schedule is upward sloping because higher and higher rates of return are needed to induce people to lend greater amounts of money. The real rate of return equates supply and demand, as shown in Figure 6.1. Projects that earn more than the real rate will be undertaken and the borrowed funds will be used to finance them.

FIGURE 6.1   The Supply and Demand for Borrowed Funds

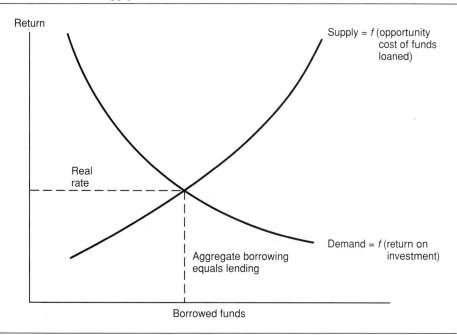

Note that all individuals in the economy will use the market equilibrium real rate of return in order to decide to accept or reject an investment opportunity. They will not use their private, subjective time value of money to make the decision. Hence the market rate, the market price of capital, is a useful piece of information for allocating capital. The fact that individuals will use the market real rate of interest and disregard their own subjective rates is called the *Fisher Separation Principle* and is a key concept for allocating capital in free economies.

THE TERM STRUCTURE OF INTEREST RATES

We now extend our understanding of equilibrium interest rates to incorporate expected inflation and liquidity while holding default risk and return risk constant. For example, all U.S. government debt, regardless of its maturity, may be assumed to have zero default risk. Yet, as shown in Figure 6.2, the yield changes with the term to maturity of the debt. The *term structure of interest rates* describes the relationship between interest rates and loan maturity.

The yield to maturity on a long-term bond is computed in exactly the same way one would solve for the internal rate of return on a security. For example, suppose a bond promises to pay a 14 percent coupon at the end of each year for three years and then pay a face value of $1,000. The current market price of the bond, B_0, is $1,099.47. The yield

FIGURE 6.2   Term Structure of Rates on U.S. Government
Securities, 1976, 1980, 1984, and 1990

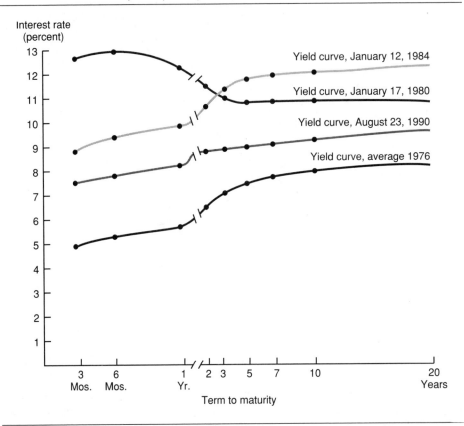

Sources: Curve for January 17, 1980, is from Salomon Brothers, *Bond Market Roundup*, week ending January 18, 1980; curve for 1976 is from *Federal Reserve Bulletin*, February 1978, p. A27; and the curves for January 12, 1984, and August 23, 1990, are from *The Wall Street Journal*.

to maturity on the bond, which we shall designate as $_0R_T$, may be computed (assuming annual compounding) by solving the following expression:

$$B_0 = \sum_{t=1}^{T} \frac{\text{coupon}_t}{(1 + {}_0R_T)^t} + \frac{\text{face value}}{(1 + {}_0R_T)^T} \tag{6.2}$$

$$\$1,099.47 = \sum_{t=1}^{3} \frac{\$140}{(1 + {}_0R_3)^t} + \frac{\$1,000}{(1 + {}_0R_3)^3}.$$

Solving, we find that the yield to maturity, $_0R_3$, is 10 percent.

One problem with this procedure is that it implicitly assumes that the annual interest rate is the same for each year of the bond's life. As we shall see, this is usually not true.

For example, an average return of 10 percent for three years can be earned by receiving 8 percent in the first year, 10.5 percent in the second, and 11.53 percent in the third year.[1] Later on, we will show how it is possible to use the observed term structure in order to estimate the market's prediction of future one-period interest rates.

Figure 6.2 shows the term structure of rates in four years, 1976, 1980, 1984, and 1990. In the lowest curve, for 1976, we see a pattern of rising yields. The shorter-term maturities carry lower rates of interest than the longer-term maturities. This rising yield structure has been characteristic of most years since 1930. The yield curves for 1984 and 1990 had similar patterns but were shifted up from the 1976 curve. The curve for 1980 shows a pattern that starts high and then declines until the fifth year, becoming relatively flat thereafter. By May 1980, the yield curve had dropped and its slope became positive, rising from 10 percent on short-term issues to about 11 percent on 30-year maturities.

In addition to illustrating the changing term structure of interest rates, Figure 6.2 also reveals a shift in the *level of rates*. Between 1976 and 1980, the interest rate on all government securities — long-term and short-term — increased. Such movements represent changes in the general level of interest rates.[2] The historical pattern of the relationship between long- and short-term interest rates is shown for the period 1982 through 1990 in Figure 6.3. The long-term rate is represented by the Aaa bond rate — the rate on high-grade, long-term (25 years or more) corporate bonds. The short-term rate is represented by the rate on three-month U.S. Treasury bills. So differences reflect both maturity and risk.

Three points should be made about Figure 6.3:

1. Both long-term and short-term rates generally declined over the period.

2. Short-term rates were more volatile than long-term rates.

3. Long-term rates were generally above short-term rates.

Other data show that both short-term and long-term rates experienced considerable volatility from 1979 to 1984. Rates rose to historic highs several times. In 1980, the prime bank loan rate ranged from 19.8 percent in April to 11.1 percent in August and back up to over 20 percent by year-end.[3]

THEORETICAL EXPLANATIONS FOR THE TERM STRUCTURE OF INTEREST RATES

Three theories have been advanced to explain the term structure — the relationship between short-term and long-term interest rates: the expectations theory, the liquidity preference theory, and the market segmentation theory. We consider each in turn.

---

[1] In other words,

$$(1.10)^3 = (1.08)(1.105)(1.1153).$$

[2] In addition to the level and term structure of rates on a given class of securities (in this case, government securities) there is also the pattern of relationships among different classes of securities — for example, mortgages, government bonds, corporates, and bank business loans.

[3] Federal Reserve Bank of St. Louis, *U.S. Financial Data*, weekly issues, 1979–1982.

FIGURE 6.3   Long- and Short-Term Interest Rates

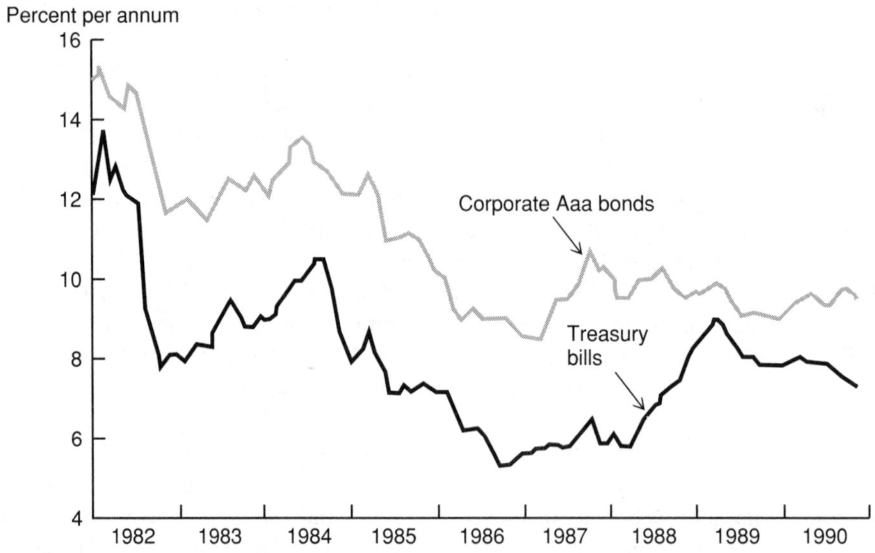

Percent per annum

Source: *Economic Indicators,* December, 1990, p. 30.

Expectations Theory

The unbiased *expectations theory* asserts that *expected future interest rates* are equal to *forward rates* computed from observed bond prices. The *n*-period forward rate is the yield to maturity which is fixed today on a *T*-year bond from Year $T - n$ to Year *T*. In order to keep things simple, we will stick to one-period forward rates. For example, in 1991 we can calculate the one-year forward rate for 1992 — a rate predicted by the current market prices of forward contracts. To illustrate, let us consider ourselves investors whose planning horizon is two years. Let $_0R_T$ be the yield to maturity for a *T*-year bond; let $_tf_{t+1}$ be the observed one-period forward rate from Year *t* to Year $(t + 1)$, which is computed from the market prices of bonds; and let $E(_tr_{t+1})$ be the expected one-period future rate of interest. Suppose we are considering two alternative investment strategies: (1) purchasing a two-year bond with a yield of 9 percent per year or (2) purchasing a one-year bond that yields 8 percent, and then reinvesting the $108 we will have at the end of the year in another one-year bond. If we choose Strategy 1, at the end of two years, we will have

$$\text{Ending value} = \$100(1.09)(1.09) = \$118.81.$$

If we follow Strategy 2, our expected value at the end of two years will depend upon our expected future rate on the one-year bond during the second year $[E(_1r_2)]$:

$$\text{Ending value} = \$100(1.08)[1 + E(_1r_2)] = \$108[1 + E(_1r_2)].$$

Under the expectations theory, the expected value of $E({_1}r_2)$ will be 10.01 percent, found as follows:

$$\$118.81 = \$108[1 + E({_1}r_2)]$$
$$1 + E({_1}r_2) = 1.1001$$
$$E({_1}r_2) = 0.1001 = 10.01\%.$$

Now, suppose that actual market prices showed the observed one-period forward rate in the second year $({_1}f_2)$ to be greater than 10.01 percent, say 10.5 percent. In that case, if we are maximizing our expected payoff, we would be better off investing short term, because we would end up with \$119.34, which is greater than \$118.81.[4] Just the reverse would hold if ${_1}f_2$ is less than 10.01 percent. Thus, according to the expectations theory, capital market competition forces forward rates to be equal to expected future rates over the holding period.

$$_tf_{t+1} = E({_t}r_{t+1}) \qquad (6.3)$$

Observed forward rates of interest are easy to measure because we can use observed yields to maturity. The T-year yield to maturity on a bond must be equal to the geometric average of the forward rates over its life. In general,

$$(1 + {_0}R_T)^T = (1 + {_0}r_1)(1 + {_1}f_2) \ldots (1 + {_{T-1}}f_T). \qquad (6.4)$$

Note that in the first time period (that is, for the shortest bond), the observed spot rate $({_0}r_1)$ is equal to the forward rate, by definition.

To illustrate the computation of forward rates, suppose that we have three default-free bonds, each paying \$140 (at the end of each year) and having a face value of \$1,000 at maturity. They mature one, two, and three years hence and are observed to have current market prices of \$1,036.36, \$1,016.68, and \$1,000.00 respectively. Using Equation 6.4, their computed yields to maturity are 10 percent, 13 percent, and 14 percent. The term structure for this example is shown in Figure 6.4. Suppose we want to know the forward rate implied for the third time period. It can be computed by taking the ratio of the (geometric product of the) yields to maturity on the three- and two-period bonds as shown below:

$$1 + {_2}f_3 = \frac{(1 + {_0}R_3)^3}{(1 + {_0}R_2)^2}$$
$$= \frac{(1 + {_0}r_1)(1 + {_1}f_2)(1 + {_2}f_3)}{(1 + {_0}r_1)(1 + {_1}f_2)}$$

---

[4] If we start with \$100 and invest it at 8 percent in the first year and 10.5 percent the second year, investing in this series of one-year bonds, we obtain

$$\$100(1.08)(1.105) = \$119.34.$$

This result is better than investing in a two-year bond. As more investors adopt the strategy of buying two one-year bonds, the prices of the bonds go up and their yield falls back into equilibrium.

FIGURE 6.4   A Simple Term Structure Example

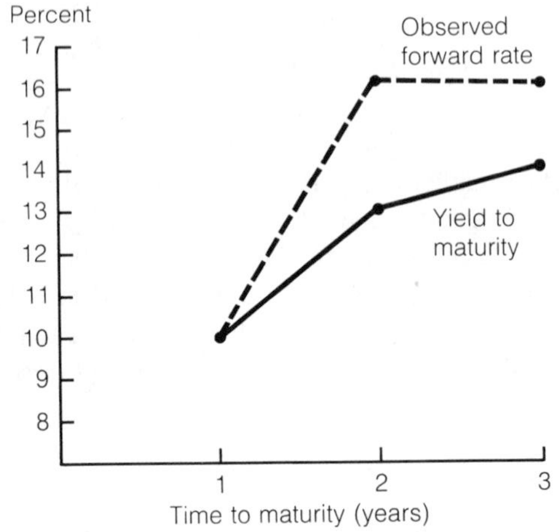

$$= \frac{(1.14)^3}{(1.13)^2} = \frac{(1.481544)}{1.2769} = 1.1603$$

$$_2f_3 = 16.03\%.$$

Similarly, one can compute the second-period forward rate as 16.08 percent, and, of course, the one-period rate is observed directly to be 10 percent.

By itself, the forward rate is merely an algebraic computation from observed bond data. The unbiased expectations theory attempts to explain observed forward rates by saying (as in Equation 6.3) that expected future rates $E(_tr_{t+1})$ will, on average, be equal to the forward rates. There are, however, reasons why this may not be true. First, the transactions costs of rolling over a one-year bond n times may be such that a series of one-year bonds is not a perfect substitute for an n-year bond. Second, there is uncertainty about future one-year rates of interest that cannot be immediately resolved. These issues lead to the possibility of a liquidity premium in the term structure.

Liquidity Preference Theory

The future is inherently uncertain, and when uncertainty is considered, the pure expectations theory must be modified. To illustrate, let us consider a situation where future short-term rates are expected to remain unchanged on average, but they may be higher or lower depending on changes in the money supply. In this case, the pure expectations theory predicts that short- and long-term bonds sell at equal yields. The *liquidity preference theory*, on the other hand, holds that long-term bonds must yield more than short-term bonds for two reasons. First, in a world of uncertainty, investors will, in general, prefer to hold short-term securities because they are more liquid; they can be converted to

FIGURE 6.5   Term Structure with and without a Liquidity Premium

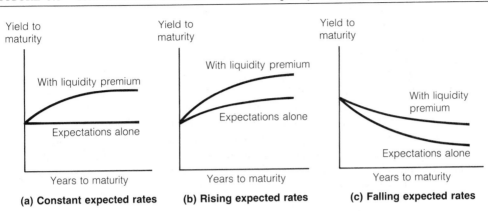

(a) Constant expected rates   (b) Rising expected rates   (c) Falling expected rates

cash without losing principal. Investors will, therefore, accept lower yields on short-term securities. Second, borrowers react exactly the opposite from investors—business borrowers generally prefer long-term debt because short-term debt subjects a firm to greater dangers of having to refund debt under adverse conditions. Accordingly, firms are willing to pay a higher rate, other things held constant, for long-term funds.

We see, then, that pressures on both the supply and demand sides—caused by liquidity preferences of both lenders and borrowers—will tend to make the yield curve slope upward. Figure 6.5 illustrates this effect for constant, rising, and falling term structures.

Market Segmentation Hypothesis

The expectations theory assumes that, in the aggregate, lenders and borrowers are indifferent between long- and short-term bonds except for any expected yield differentials based on maturity. The liquidity preference theory states that an upward bias exists—the yield curve slopes upward to a greater extent than is justified by expectations about future rates because investors prefer to lend short while borrowers prefer to borrow long.

The *market segmentation, institutional,* or *hedging-pressure theory* admits the liquidity preference argument as a good description of the behavior of investors with short horizons, such as commercial banks, which regard certainty of principal as more important than certainty of income because of the nature of their deposit liabilities. However, certain other investors with long-term liabilities, such as insurance companies, might prefer to buy long-term bonds because, given the nature of their liabilities, they find certainty of income highly desirable. On the other hand, borrowers relate the maturity of their debt to the maturity of their assets. Thus, the market segmentation theory characterizes market participants as having strong maturity preferences, then argues that interest rates are determined by supply and demand in each segmented market, with each maturity constituting a segment. In the strictest version of this theory, expectations play no role—bonds with different maturities are not substitutes for one another because of different demand preferences or the preferred habitat of both lenders and borrowers.

Empirical Evidence

Empirical studies suggest that there is some validity to each of these theories. Specifically, the recent work indicates that if lenders and borrowers have no reason for expecting a change in the general level of interest rates, the yield curve will be upward sloping because of liquidity preferences. (Under the expectations theory, the term structure of interest rates would be flat if there were no expectations of a change in the level of short-term rates.) However, it is a fact that during periods of extremely high short-term interest rates, the yield curve is downward sloping; this proves that the expectations theory also operates. At still other times, when supply and demand conditions in particular maturity sectors change, the term structure seems to be modified, thus confirming the market segmentation theory. In summary, each theory has an element of truth, and each must be taken into account in seeking to understand the changing patterns observed in the term structure of interest rates.

Inflation and the Term Structure

Anyone who has lived through an inflationary economy is well aware of the fact that there is an important difference between nominal and constant dollar prices and between nominal and real interest rates. What really counts is what you can consume, not the unit of exchange in which it is denominated. Suppose that you are indifferent between a loaf of bread today and 1.2 loaves at the end of one year. This implies a 20 percent real rate of interest. But suppose that a loaf costs $1.00 today and you expect that it will cost $1.80 at the year's end. This implies an inflation rate of 80 percent. What nominal rate of interest must you charge in order to maintain a real rate of 20 percent? The answer is that if you lend one loaf today, you must require that the borrower repay enough tomorrow so that you consume 1.2 loaves of bread, each costing $1.80. Your computation would be

$$\text{Loan repayment amount} = (1.2 \text{ loaves})(\$1.80/\text{loaf})$$
$$= \$2.16.$$

Thus, your nominal rate of interest is 116 percent. To generalize this example, we see that the nominal rate of interest, R, is the product of the real rate of interest, r, and expected inflation $E(i)$ as shown below:

$$1 + R = (1 + r)[1 + E(i)] \qquad (6.5)$$
$$1 + R = 1 + r + E(i) + rE(i).$$

Usually the cross product term $[rE(i)]$ is small and is ignored. This is why the nominal rate (assuming no liquidity premium and no default or rate of return risk) is often expressed as the sum of the real rate and the expected inflation rate, that is,

$$\text{Nominal rate} = E(\text{real rate}) + E(\text{inflation}).$$

If the real rate of return is relatively constant, then we can turn this equation around to say that expected inflation is the observed nominal rate minus the real rate, a constant.

$$E(\text{inflation}) = \text{Nominal rate} - \text{Real rate}$$

If the marketplace makes unbiased forecasts of inflation, then actual inflation should be equal to expected inflation plus a random error term.

$$\text{Actual inflation} = E(\text{inflation}) + \text{Error term} \qquad \textbf{(6.6)}$$
$$= \text{Nominal rate} - \text{Real rate} + \text{Error term}$$

This relationship has been studied by Fama [1975], by Nelson and Schwert [1977], and by Hess and Bicksler [1975] via regression equations similar to the following:

$$\text{Actual inflation} = a + b(\text{nominal rate}) + \text{Error term.} \qquad \textbf{(6.7)}$$

If the real rate is constant, the intercept (a) in Equation 6.7 will be equal to minus the real rate, and the slope term (b) should be close to 1.0. Fama [1975] fit the equation to data on U.S. Treasury bills between 1953 and 1971 and found that b was .98. This suggests that changes in current nominal rates are fairly good forecasts of inflation. Nelson and Schwert [1977] and Hess and Bicksler [1975] have pointed out that although the real rate appears to have been relatively constant during 1953–1971, in general it does vary across time and was much more variable after 1971.

These empirical results are useful because they imply that the term structure of interest rates contains useful information about expected inflation. If the term structure is downward sloping, as in Figure 6.5(c), the market is telling us that it expects near-term inflation to be higher than in the long run. An upward-sloping term structure, as in Figure 6.5(b), implies higher long-run inflation.

If one could estimate the expected real rate and the expected liquidity premium for a given maturity of riskless debt, then observed forward rates on U.S. government bonds could be used to forecast inflation as follows:

$$E(\text{inflation}) = \text{Nominal rate} - E(\text{real rate}) - E(\text{liquidity premium}).$$

RISK AND MARKET DISCOUNT RATES

So far, we have discussed three of the four components of a security's rate of return: the real rate, expected inflation over the life of the security, and the liquidity premium. The remaining element is risk and it can be broken down into two categories: default risk and covariance risk. *Default risk* is most relevant for corporate long-term debt where there is a chance of bankruptcy. We will discuss it first, and then move on to *covariance risk*, which has to do with the sensitivity of security prices to changes in general economic conditions.

The usual method for determining the default risk of corporate long-term debt is to refer to the *bond ratings* supplied by various agencies. Major bond rating agencies are Moody's Investors Service Inc., Standard & Poor's Corp., and Fitch Investor Service. Moody's bond rating has seven classifications ranging from Aaa, which is the highest quality bond, down to Caa. Table 6.1 shows the distribution by S&P's risk class. Between 1971 and 1986, the new bonds that qualified for the two highest quality ratings declined from over 50 percent to 41 percent. Table 6.2 shows the yields on bonds of different risk. Just as expected, the high-quality, low-risk bonds have lower yields than do the low-

TABLE 6.1   Corporate Bond Issuance by S&P Bond Rating for
Selected Years (in millions of dollars)

Bond Rating	1971 Amount	1971 Percent	1981 Amount	1981 Percent	1985 Amount	1985 Percent	1986 Amount	1986 Percent
AAA	$ 5,125	25.9%	$11,835	28.8%	$ 9,016	11.8%	$ 14,438	9.6%
AA	5,467	27.6	11,748	28.6	23,223	30.4	46,978	31.2
A	6,688	33.7	12,432	30.2	23,381	30.6	34,173	22.7
BBB	2,139	10.8	3,900	9.5	11,068	14.5	21,993	14.6
BB	292	1.5	290	0.7	2,041	2.7	7,098	4.7
B	112	0.6	894	2.2	5,945	7.8	21,260	14.1
CCC	0	0.0	0	0.0	1,668	2.2	4,668	3.1
Total	$19,823		$41,099		$76,342		$150,608	

Source: Edward I. Altman, "Measuring Corporate Bond Mortality and Performance," *Journal of Finance*, 64 (September 1989), pp. 909–922.

TABLE 6.2   Yield to Maturity on Various Bond Rating Categories: 1973–1987
(Yield is the Average for the Twelve Monthly Rates)

Year	Treasury Bond	AAA	AA	A	BBB	BB	B	CCC
1973	7.15	7.56	7.71	7.87	8.40	NR*	NR	NR
1974	8.13	8.33	8.56	8.65	9.37	NR	NR	NR
1975	8.28	8.64	8.89	9.31	10.12	NR	NR	NR
1976	7.88	8.36	8.37	8.81	9.45	NR	NR	NR
1977	7.76	8.12	8.34	8.48	8.87	NR	NR	NR
1978	8.57	8.74	8.93	9.05	9.53	NR	NR	NR
1979	9.27	9.53	9.80	10.01	10.62	11.66	13.16	NR
1980	11.22	11.66	12.02	12.31	13.09	14.15	14.98	NR
1981	13.20	13.91	14.32	14.60	15.50	16.54	17.33	NR
1982	12.51	13.32	13.73	14.19	15.45	16.32	17.76	21.86
1983	11.09	11.66	11.86	12.17	12.79	13.63	14.61	18.62
1984	12.34	12.43	12.94	13.25	13.97	14.99	15.53	17.71
1985	10.74	10.94	11.41	11.66	12.16	13.65	14.52	16.75
1986	8.16	9.02	9.40	9.64	10.19	11.79	12.82	15.98
1987	8.76	9.32	9.66	9.92	10.42	11.46	12.96	16.12

*NR = not relevant due to small samples and unreliable data.
Source: Edward I. Altman, "Measuring Corporate Bond Mortality and Performance," *Journal of Finance*, 64 (September 1989), p. 919.

quality, high-risk bonds. Of the roughly 2,000 major corporations that are evaluated by the agencies, approximately 500 are rerated quarterly because they issue commercial paper, another 500 are rerated annually (most of the utilities), and the remaining 1,000 have no established review date but are usually reviewed annually.

From an investor's point of view, one might ask the following question: Do the agencies determine the prices and interest rates paid for bonds or do investors in the capital markets? The evidence collected by Wakeman [1978] and Weinstein [1978] shows that changes in bond ratings are not treated as new information by capital markets. In fact, changes in ratings usually occur several months after the capital markets have already reacted to the fundamental change in the bond's quality. Changes in agency ratings do not cause changes in required yields to maturity. It is the other way around. However, this does not imply that bond ratings are without value. On average, the ratings provide unbiased estimates of bond risk and are therefore a useful source of information.

Promised vs. Expected Rates of Return

The yields to maturity in Table 6.2 are only *promised* yields. They are calculated by assuming that a bond, regardless of its rating, will pay off all cash flows as promised. For example, consider an 8 percent coupon bond with only one year to maturity that promises to pay a $1,000 face value and a coupon of $80 at maturity. If it was riskless and if the market risk-free rate was 8 percent, then the current price of the bond, B_0, would be

$$B_0 = \$1,000 = \frac{\$1,000 + \$80}{1.08}.$$

But suppose it has some probability of default, so that the market prices it at $939.13. Then, the yield to maturity would be calculated as follows:

$$B_0 = \$939.13 = \frac{\$1,000 + \$80}{1 + R}$$

$$R = \frac{\$1,080}{\$939.13} - 1 = 15\%.$$

But, 15 percent is actually only a promised yield. Assuming zero payoff in default, a measure of the probability of default can be calculated from the above data as shown in Equation 6.8.

$$\$939.13 = [p(0) + (1 - p)1,080]/(1.08) \tag{6.8}$$

Solving for p, we obtain

$$\$1,014.26 = 1,080 - 1,080\,p$$

$$p = .0609 = 6.09\%.$$

Thus, we see that for one-year instruments a yield spread of 7 percentage points (700 basis points) above a default-free yield implies a probability of default of slightly over 6 percent.

In order to compute the *expected rate of return* on the risky bond, it is necessary to use the expected cash flows in the numerator. Therefore, we must rewrite the bond valuation equation as follows:

$$B_0 = \frac{E(\text{coupon} + \text{face value})}{1 + E(\text{rate of return})}.$$

The expected, or average, cash flows are the promised cash flows, each multiplied by its respective probability. If we assume that no payment is in default and that the probability of default is 6.09 percent,

$$E(\text{coupon} + \text{face value}) = .0609 \ (\text{no payment}) + .9391(\$1,080)$$
$$= \$1,014.228.$$

The expected cash flow is what you would receive if you held a large well-diversified portfolio of bonds of similar default risk (but no market covariance risk). If the market value (B_0) of our bond is $939.13, then the expected return is

$$\$939.13 = \frac{\$1,014.228}{1 + E(\text{rate of return})}$$

$$E(\text{rate of return}) = 8\%.$$

This is the same return as expected on a completely default-free bond.

To this point we assumed a complete loss on default. Suppose that the recovery rate is 40 percent, the probability of default is again 6.09 percent, and the yield on the default-free bond is 8 percent. What is the required promised yield on the risky bond for it to have an expected return equal to the 8 percent return on the default-free bond? Thus, we see that in Equation 6.8a the term for the probability of default indicates a recovery of 40 percent.

$$939.13 = \frac{p(.4)(1,080) + (1 - p)1,080}{1 + r} \tag{6.8a}$$

$$r = 10.80\%$$

The 10.80 percent represents the required promised yield on the risky bond. Note that as compared with the previous zero recovery example, the yield spread drops to 2.80 percentage points as compared with the 7 percent yield spread with zero recovery.

We can now indicate the relationships for multiyear bonds.[5] To facilitate the computations we use pure discount or zero coupon bonds in the example. Bond f is risk free and sells for $422.41; the risky bond sells for $226.69. Both bonds pay $1,000 at maturity. First we calculate the yield to maturity on each of the bonds:

$$B_f = \$422.41 = \frac{\$1,000}{(1 + r_f)^{10}}$$

$$(1 + r_f)^{10} = \$1,000/\$422.41$$

$$= 2.3674$$

---

[5]Problem 6.7 also illustrates this procedure.

$$1 + r_f = 1.09$$

$$r_f = 9\% = \text{promised yield} = \text{expected yield}.$$

$$B = \$226.69 = \frac{\$1,000}{(1 + r)^{10}}$$

$$(1 + r)^{10} = \$1,000/\$226.69$$

$$= 4.4114$$

$$1 + r = 1.16$$

$$r = 16\% = \text{promised yield}.$$

We see that the risky bond has a yield of 16 percent as compared with the yield on the default-free bond of 9 percent. This represents a spread of 7 percentage points or 700 basis points.

Next we assume that the risk of default of the higher yielding bond is uncorrelated with the economy as a whole and that the expected yields on the two bonds will be the same. If the risky bond pays nothing in default, we can calculate the expected probability of default from the differences in the promised returns. Again, we use the relationship in Equation 6.8.

$$\$226.69 = \frac{p(0) + (1 - p)\$1,000}{(1 + .09)^{10}}$$

$$p = .4633 \text{ or } 46.33\%$$

Note that the probability of default on these multiple-year bonds has to be much higher than for the one-year bonds considered previously. The reason is that the yield spread in favor of the risky bond occurs for ten years so that a higher probability of default is required to bring about equality in expected returns.

Covariance Risk

We next consider *covariance risk*. It is so important that an entire chapter, Chapter 11, is dedicated to it. The variability of returns for every security can be separated into two parts:

$$\text{Variability of returns} = \text{diversifiable risk} + \text{covariance risk.} \qquad \textbf{(6.9)}$$

Risks that are not correlated with the economy as a whole can usually be eliminated simply by holding a diversified portfolio. Since diversification is virtually costless, investors will not pay a premium to avoid diversifiable risk. They will pay a premium, however, to avoid covariance risk (also called *systematic risk*), because it cannot be eliminated via diversification.

Figure 6.6 gives a rough idea of how differences in covariance risk affect the expected rates of return on different types of securities. Treasury bills are virtually risk free. Long-term corporate bonds are riskier because their probability of default depends in part on whether the economy is in a recession or recovery. Common stock is much more sensitive to the state of the economy and, consequently, has greater undiversifiable risk

---

FIGURE 6.6   The Risk-Return Trade-off

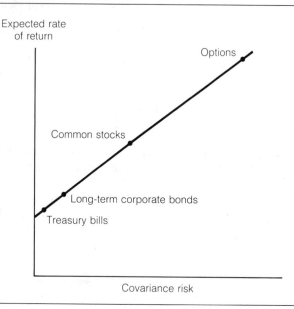

and a higher expected return. Finally, options are very risky and require among the highest expected rates of return. There is a linear trade-off between expected rates of return and covariance risk. Securities whose returns are more sensitive to the economic cycles in the economy must pay higher expected returns if investors are to hold them.

How the Market Determines Discount Rates

The observed nominal pretax rate of return on any asset can be explained by four factors: the real rate of return, expected inflation, liquidity, and covariance risk.

Nominal rate $= f[E(\text{real rate}), E(\text{inflation}), E(\text{liquidity premium}), E(\text{risk premium})]$

Assets can be grouped according to how they fit these characteristics. For example, one can collect all Aaa rated corporate bonds with ten years to maturity. Within this group, all four factors are held constant. Consequently, all securities within the group are close economic substitutes and will have the same nominal rate of return. Other characteristics, such as the name of the company issuing the bond, its date of issue, or the name of the investor currently holding it are irrelevant.

Understanding the economic determinants of nominal rates of return helps to sort out why rates of return differ from security to security. Common stocks have averaged 10.3 percent per year between 1926 and 1989 primarily because they are riskier than long-term corporate bonds, which have yielded 5.2 percent. On any given day, long-term bonds of a given default risk will have higher (or lower) promised yields than short-term bonds with the same default risk either because the long-term bonds are less liquid or because expected inflation is higher in the long run.

HIGH-YIELD DEBT

Outstanding high-yield or "junk" bonds increased to a market size of more than $200 billion by 1989. Junk bonds are defined as bonds with ratings of BBB or Baa. It is estimated that about 25 percent of the junk bond market is comprised of "fallen angels" — bonds originally issued as investment grade bonds but whose ratings were later reduced. Another 25 percent of the market represented bonds originally issued with below investment grade ratings for "normal business purposes" [Altman, 1990]. The remaining 50 percent of the market consists of high-yield (originally mainly B-rated) bonds issued to finance takeovers and leveraged buyouts [Altman, 1990].

A number of controversies have arisen in the literature over the performance of high-yield or junk bonds. One issue is how to measure default rates and interpret their significance. One measure is the ratio of annual defaults to the total dollar amount of all issues outstanding. By this measure default rates were around 2 percent per annum over the period 1978–1988, rising to 4 percent in 1989. This measure was criticized on grounds that the probability of junk bond defaults increases with the age of the bonds, which would be obscured by the rapid growth in the issuance of junk bonds. The par value of junk bonds outstanding grew from $9 billion in 1978 to $28 billion in 1983 — an annual compound growth rate during the five-year period of almost 25 percent. During the next five-year period beginning in 1984 and ending in 1989, the market grew from $42 billion to $201 billion, representing a compound growth rate of 37 percent per annum or a doubling of the market every two years.

The traditional method of calculating default rates was criticized by Asquith, Mullins, and Wolff [1989]. They interpreted their data as evidence that the probability of junk bond defaults increases with the age of the bond so that the traditional procedure understates the true default rate when the total outstandings are rapidly increasing as occurred during the second half of the 1980s. Their evidence is presented in Table 6.3. Altman [1990] observes that for the 1977 group the default rate does not rise through the seventh year and is lower in the eleventh year than in the tenth year. For the 1978 issue group, the highest default rate occurs in the second year after issue. Similar exceptions are noted in all of the issue years through 1983. Also if the cumulative default rates shown in the last column of the table are divided over the number of years covered, the resulting average per year default rates are mostly in the range of 2 to 4 percent, not greatly different from the results obtained by the traditional method. Another complication is that junk bonds issued during the years 1977 through 1982 were subject to a high rate of calls. Data presented by Asquith et al. (in their Table 9, p. 937), shows that cumulative calls through December 31, 1988, for junk bonds issued in 1977–1983 represented about one-third of the total amounts originally issued. Lower interest rates resulting from changes in the credit strength of the issuer or from a changed financial environment could stimulate junk bond calls as their market prices rose above their call prices.[6] Also Altman refers to

---

[6]See Chapter 25 for further discussion of the call provisions of bonds.

TABLE 6.3   Aged Defaults for High-Yield Bonds Grouped by Year of Issue

Issue Year	1st	2nd	3rd	4th	5th	6th	7th	8th	9th	10th	11th	12th	Total
Panel A: % of Par Amount Defaulted in *n*th Year After Issue													
1977	0.00	0.00	0.00	0.00	0.00	0.00	0.00	7.71	3.63	19.27	3.30	0.00[a]	33.92
1978	0.00	8.32	0.00	1.39	0.00	7.91	4.85	3.12	5.55	1.39	1.73[a]	—	34.26
1979	0.00	0.00	5.54	1.11	2.38	6.73	1.98	0.00	5.78	1.19[a]	—	—	24.70
1980	0.00	0.57	2.45	0.00	0.00	13.90	6.30	1.88	2.45[a]	—	—	—	27.56
1981	0.00	6.05	0.00	8.06	6.85	0.00	0.00	0.00[a]	—	—	—	—	20.97
1982	1.00	2.41	1.61	11.49	0.00	9.44	0.00[a]	—	—	—	—	—	25.94
1983	0.00	0.00	6.08	7.83	4.80	0.50[a]	—	—	—	—	—	—	19.21
1984	2.29	1.99	2.03	3.06	0.00[a]	—	—	—	—	—	—	—	9.38
1985	0.00	0.80	2.28	0.45[a]	—	—	—	—	—	—	—	—	3.53
1986	2.73	3.84	1.57[a]	—	—	—	—	—	—	—	—	—	8.14
Panel B: Cumulated % of Par Amount Defaulted for *x* Years After Issue													
1977	0.00	0.00	0.00	0.00	0.00	0.00	0.00	7.71	11.34	30.62	33.92	33.92[a]	33.92
1978	0.00	8.32	8.32	9.71	9.71	17.61	22.47	25.59	31.14	32.52	34.26[a]	—	34.26
1979	0.00	0.00	5.54	6.65	9.03	15.76	17.74	17.74	23.52	24.70[a]	—	—	24.70
1980	0.00	0.57	3.03	3.03	3.03	16.93	23.22	25.10	27.56[a]	—	—	—	27.56
1981	0.00	6.05	6.05	14.11	20.97	20.97	20.97	20.97[a]	—	—	—	—	20.97
1982	1.00	3.41	5.02	16.51	16.51	25.94	25.94[a]	—	—	—	—	—	25.94
1983	0.00	0.00	6.08	13.91	18.71	19.21[a]	—	—	—	—	—	—	19.21
1984	2.29	4.28	6.32	9.38	9.38[a]	—	—	—	—	—	—	—	9.38
1985	0.00	0.80	3.08	3.53[a]	—	—	—	—	—	—	—	—	3.53
1986	2.73	6.57	8.14[a]	—	—	—	—	—	—	—	—	—	8.14

[a]May be incomplete; i.e., entire sample may not have been outstanding for *x* years.
Source: Asquith et al., [1989].

studies by Blume, Keim, and Patel that found when default rates are adjusted for overall economic conditions, no aging effect is observed.[7]

Another issue is the performance of junk bonds relative to higher-rated securities. The issue is whether after consideration of default rates, recovery rates, and liquidity factors, the realized returns on junk bonds were higher or lower than the returns for U.S. Treasury bonds or investment grade (rating higher than BBB) corporate bonds. For much of the 1980s the realized returns on junk bonds were higher than the returns on treasuries or high-rated corporate bonds. In part at least, this reflected increasing optimism about the economic functions of junk bonds. With the stock market crash of October 1987, there was a ''flight to quality'' that caused declines in the prices of junk bonds. With the collapse of the Drexel Burnham Lambert company, the major originator and market maker for junk bonds, along with the failures of some highly leveraged transactions such as the takeover of a number of department stores by Robert Campeau, the prices of junk bonds dropped even further. Also, a 1989 law virtually required substantial sales of junk

---

[7]Marshall E. Blume, Donald B. Keim, and Sandeep Patel, ''Returns and Volatility of Low-Grade Bonds, 1977–1989,'' *Journal of Finance*, 46 (March 1991) pp. 49–74.

bonds by the S&Ls. In the heyday of the junk bonds the differential yield over treasuries was only two to three percentage points. By the 1990s, the differential (promised) spread had moved up to seven or eight percentage points and in some individual cases over ten points. By 1990, the yields on junk bonds had risen so greatly that investment companies were being formed on the expectation that the pendulum had swung too far in the negative direction with respect to junk bonds. The future of the high-risk bond market will undoubtedly provide more interesting stories that will unfold.

THE IMPORTANCE OF INTERNATIONAL FINANCE

International finance in recent years has taken on great significance. Widely fluctuating exchange rates have affected not only profits and losses from changes in foreign currency values but also the ability to sell abroad and to meet import competition. For example, suppose that a Japanese auto producer needs to receive 1.2 million yen per car to cover costs plus a required return on equity. At an exchange rate of 200 yen to the dollar, a rate which existed in the late 1970s, the Japanese producer would have to receive $6,000 for an automobile sold in the United States. When the exchange rate is 265 yen to the dollar, as existed in early 1985, dividing the 1.2 million yen by 265 tells us that the dollars required now are $4,528. Thus, the Japanese producer is in a position to either reduce its dollar price by approximately 25 percent and still receive the same number of yen or take higher profit margins on sales in the United States. In June 1990, the yen fluctuated in the region of 150 to the dollar. The U.S. wholesale price to yield 1.2 million yen to the Japanese auto company would be $8,000. Thus the competitive position of the Japanese producer in selling in the U.S. market is reduced by the stronger yen. Of course, the success of Japanese auto companies in the United States has not been completely due to changes in foreign exchange rates alone. Auto producers in Japan have achieved improved production processes that have resulted in greater productivity and high quality cars. But, exchange rate movements have also been a factor, as the above example illustrates.

From the standpoint of American companies selling products abroad, the rising value of the dollar in relation to foreign currencies has the opposite consequences. It is more difficult for U.S. firms to sell abroad, and it is much more attractive for foreign firms to sell in the United States. For example, suppose that an American producer is selling a product in the United Kingdom, and to meet competition, it has to be sold for 500 pounds. When the pound had a value of $2.25, as it did in the late 1970s, the dollar amount received by the U.S. seller would be $1,125. By March 1985, the value of the pound had fallen to $1.07. If the U.S. producer continued to sell the product for 500 pounds, it would now receive $535. If the original $1,125 represented a dollar price necessary to earn its cost of capital, the U.S. firm would find it difficult to survive with a price that had declined by more than 50 percent. Or alternatively, to continue to realize a dollar price of $1,125 at the exchange rate of $1.07 to the pound would require a new selling price of 1,051 pounds, a price increase of over 100 percent expressed in pounds. In June 1990, the British pound traded at $1.72. At this level, the price of 500 pounds would represent $860. A price of $1,125 would require 654 pounds, representing a price increase of "only" 31 percent in pounds.

TABLE 6.4   Number of Foreign Currency Units per U.S. Dollar

	1965	1970	1975	1980	March 27, 1985	June 21, 1990
Japan X	360.90	357.60	305.15	215.45	255.40	153.90
E	0.00277	0.00280	0.00328	0.00464	0.003915	0.006498
Index	100	101	118	168	141	235
W. Germany X	4.00	3.65	2.62	1.76	3.2090	1.6778
E	0.2500	0.2740	0.3817	0.5682	0.3116	.5960
Index	100	110	153	227	125	238
Mexico X	12.50	12.50	12.50	22.83	244.00	2,846.00
E	0.08	0.08	0.08	0.0438	.004098	.0003514
Index	100	100	100	55	5.1	0.44

X = Number of FC's (foreign currency units) per dollar.
E = Dollar value of one FC (foreign currency unit).
Index is of dollar value, with 1965 = 100.
Sources: International Monetary Fund, *International Financial Statistics,* monthly issues; and ''Foreign Exchange,'' *The Wall Street Journal,* June 21, 1984, p. 52; March 28, 1985, p. 49; June 22, 1990, p. C10.

These are not just hypothetical examples. They reflect the actual patterns of foreign exchange movements during recent years. There have been upward and downward fluctuations in the value of the dollar in relation to the currencies of developed countries such as Japan and West Germany. For less developed countries, the movements have represented a one-way street as shown in Table 6.4. From 1954 through 1970, the value of the Mexican peso was stable at 12.5 pesos to the U.S. dollar. Subsequent devaluations caused a continued erosion, so that by June 1990, 2,846 pesos were required for one dollar — the peso had declined from eight U.S. cents in value to a small fraction of one cent.

Thus, changes in foreign currency values in relation to the dollar have been both substantial and uncertain. Most business firms, as well as individuals, have experienced some of the effects of these changes in currency values that have taken place and are likely to continue — with magnitudes and directions of movements subject to considerable uncertainty. These changes have particularly severe effects on a manufacturing firm. Its inputs may include imported materials, and its products may be exported or become part of an exported product. Some large companies earn more than half their profits abroad. Even for smaller companies, it is not uncommon to find that, if international sales can be developed to about one-fourth of total sales, earnings from foreign sales or operations are likely to be as high as 40 to 50 percent of total earnings. International operations often enable the smaller firm to achieve better utilization of its investment in fixed plant and equipment.

SOME HISTORICAL BACKGROUND

To understand the forces behind the movements in U.S. foreign exchange rates with respect to other countries, a brief historical perspective is required. For many years the ruling mechanism governing the relationship between prices in different countries was the gold standard with fixed exchange rates. This is how the system at least in theory was supposed to work. Country A runs an export balance surplus, while country B runs a deficit. Hence gold flows into A while it flows out of B. Domestic prices rise in A, the prices fall in B. Country A is an attractive market for imports from other countries. Country A's goods are more expensive in the currency of other countries so its export sales decrease. Thus A's export surplus will be reduced while B's export deficit will be diminished until equilibrium between relative prices of the countries is restored. The flow of gold operated through prices to function as an adjustment mechanism for international balances of trade and payments as well as to regulate the price relationships between countries.

Under the gold standard, the exchange rates remain "fixed" through this entire adjustment process. Gold flow prevents exchange rates from moving beyond the costs of transportation and insurance for shipping gold between the countries, referred to as the "gold points."

The gold standard with fixed exchange rates worked because maintaining two-way convertibility between a nation's monetary unit and a fixed amount of gold was a policy goal that received great emphasis and high priority. As long as it was recognized that convertibility was a major policy goal, speculative capital movements were likely to be stabilizing rather than destabilizing. In other words, the general expectation that the convertibility of the currency would be maintained was so strong that when a gold standard currency did weaken almost to its gold export points, one could reasonably assume that it would not drop much lower and indeed would probably rise. Speculators would then take positions based on the expectations that a rise in the value of the currency was imminent, and this would, of course, strengthen the currency.

One difficulty with a strict gold standard was that the growth of the world economies was constrained by the growth rates in the production of gold. Another difficulty was that the rate of economic development in different countries could be so unequal that some countries were subject to substantial gold drains that were deflationary. As a consequence, individual countries would seek to protect their gold reserves by a wide variety of policies such as tariffs and various administrative restrictions against imports and subsidies to exports. These nationalistic economic policies restricted the growth of international trade and represented an economic drag on all nations. The result was to aggravate the worldwide recession that began in 1929.

At the end of World War II, the allied nations determined to avoid the "beggar-my-neighbor" policies that led to the economic chaos that some felt helped cause World War II. A United Nations monetary and financial conference was held in the United States at Bretton Woods in July 1944. The International Monetary Fund was established to promote monetary stability and to remove exchange restrictions that interfered with world trade. A gold exchange standard was established in which countries related their exchange rates to one of the "key" or "reserve" currencies, holding part of their official reserves in that currency. Dollars and sterling were key currencies immediately after the end of World War II. The International Bank for Reconstruction and Development (World Bank) was created to provide financing of reconstruction and particularly to provide investment aid to the less developed countries.

However, problems also developed with the gold exchange standard. Fundamental imbalances between countries put pressure on the fixed exchange rates. When the imbalances became too large, individual countries would have to either revalue their currency upward or engage in devaluation. Competitive devaluations began to take place. Another problem was the persistent balance of payments deficits of the United States. During the early 1950s the dollar was strong and the U.S. deficits increased the supply of international reserves. In 1970 and 1971, particularly, U.S. deficits reached unprecedented levels. On a Sunday night, August 15, 1971, President Nixon on television announced that the U.S. gold window was to be permanently closed and convertibility between gold and other currencies by the United States would no longer be maintained. The dollar would be allowed to float, following the example of other currencies, notably the German mark, which began to float in May 1971. In other words, the nations had moved from fixed exchange rates to flexible exchange rates.

An argument for the use of flexible exchange rates is that the relations between the prices of domestic and foreign goods adjust through exchange rates. The prices of internationally traded goods carry most of the adjustment process. It is argued that under the gold standard with fixed exchange rates, an incorrect exchange rate is adjusted not by changing exchange rates but by adjusting all other things. Under flexible exchange rates, when exchange rates are out of line the correction takes place in the exchange rates themselves. Since domestic wages and prices are relatively inflexible, they cannot in fact make the necessary adjustments. However, exchange rates do not have the same built-in institutional barriers to upward and downward flexibility and hence they are much more flexible tools of adjustment.

Unfortunately, flexible exchange rates have not solved the problem of achieving satisfactory adjustment processes in the international financial markets. Some writers have argued that the exchange values of currencies have fluctuated excessively under the regime of flexible exchange rates [Triffin, 1986]. Now, it is recognized that the economic policies of individual countries determine the variability in the exchange values of currencies; and the degree of coordination of economic policies among countries determines the degree of fluctuations in foreign exchange rates rather than a fixed rate versus a flexible exchange rate regime.

IMPACT OF EXCHANGE RATE FLUCTUATIONS

A difference between international business finance and domestic business finance is that international transactions and investments are conducted in more than one currency. For example, when a U.S. firm sells goods to a French firm, the U.S. firm usually wants to be paid in dollars and the French firm usually expects to pay in francs. Because of the existence of a foreign exchange market in which individual dealers and many banks trade, the buyer can pay in one currency and the seller can receive payment in another.

Since different currencies are involved, a rate of exchange must be established between them. The conversion relationship of the currencies is expressed in terms of their price relationship. If foreign exchange rates did not fluctuate, it would make no difference whether firms dealt in dollars or any other currency. However, since exchange rates do fluctuate, firms are subject to exchange rate fluctuation risks if they have a net asset or net liability position in a foreign currency. When net claims exceed liabilities in a foreign currency, the firm is said to be in a "long" position, because it will benefit if the value of the foreign currency rises. When net liabilities exceed claims in regard to foreign currencies, the firm is said to be in a "short" position, because it will gain if the foreign currency declines in value.

Expressing Foreign Exchange Rates

The foreign exchange rate represents the conversion relationship between currencies and depends on demand and supply relationships between the two currencies. The foreign exchange rate is the price of one currency in terms of another. Exchange rates may be expressed in dollars per foreign currency unit or units of foreign currency per dollar. An exchange rate of $0.50 to FC1 shows the value of one foreign currency unit in terms of the dollar. We shall use E_0 to indicate the spot rate, E_f to indicate the forward rate at the present time, and E_1 to indicate the actual future spot rate corresponding to E_f.[8] An exchange rate of FC2 to $1 shows the value of the dollar in terms of the number of foreign currency units it will purchase. We will use the symbol X with corresponding subscripts to refer to the exchange rate expressed as the number of foreign currency units per dollar.

Measuring the Percentage of Devaluation or Revaluation

Assume that there has been a devaluation of the French franc from 3 per U.S. dollar to 4 per U.S. dollar. This can be expressed as the percentage change in the number of French francs required to purchase 1 U.S. dollar ($= D_{fd}$).

For example, where $X_0 = 3$ and $X_1 = 4$,

$$\% \text{ change} = (X_1 - X_0)/X_0 = (4 - 3)/3 = \tfrac{1}{3}, \text{ or } 33\tfrac{1}{3}\% = D_{fd}.$$

There has been an increase of $33\tfrac{1}{3}$ percent in the number of French francs required to equal one U.S. dollar, which is a $33\tfrac{1}{3}$ percent appreciation in the franc value of the dollar.

To show the percentage change in the dollar value of the franc ($= D_{df}$),

$$E_0 = \frac{1}{X_0} = \frac{1}{3} \text{ and } E_1 = \frac{1}{X_1} = \frac{1}{4}.$$

Now the percentage change is given by

$$\% \text{ change} = (E_1 - E_0)/E_0 = \left(\frac{1}{X_1} - \frac{1}{X_0}\right) \Big/ \frac{1}{X_0}$$

$$= (\tfrac{1}{4} - \tfrac{1}{3})/(\tfrac{1}{3}) = [(3 - 4)/12]/(\tfrac{1}{3}) = -\tfrac{1}{4} = -25\% = D_{df}.$$

There has been a 25 percent decrease in the value of the franc in terms of the U.S. dollar, that is, there has been a 25 percent depreciation in the dollar value of the franc. These relations can be summarized in Equations 6.10a and 6.10b.

---

[8]Recall that a forward contract is a purchase or sale at a price specified now (the *forward rate*), with the transaction to take place at some future date.

D_{fd} is the change of value in terms of FC/$:

$$D_{fd} = \frac{X_1 - X_0}{X_0} = \frac{\frac{1}{E_1} - \frac{1}{E_0}}{\frac{1}{E_0}} = \frac{E_0}{E_1} - 1 = \frac{E_0 - E_1}{E_1}. \qquad \textbf{(6.10a)}$$

D_{df} is the change in value in terms of $/FC:

$$D_{df} = \frac{E_1 - E_0}{E_0} = \frac{\frac{1}{X_1} - \frac{1}{X_0}}{\frac{1}{X_0}} = \frac{X_0}{X_1} - \frac{X_0}{X_0} = \frac{X_0 - X_1}{X_1}. \qquad \textbf{(6.10b)}$$

Because of the risks of exchange rate fluctuations, transactions have developed in a forward, or futures, foreign exchange market. This market enables a firm to hedge in an attempt to reduce the risk. Individuals also may speculate by means of transactions in the forward market. Forward contracts are normally for a 30-, 60- or 90-day period, although special contracts for longer periods can be arranged by negotiation.

The cost of this protection is the premium or discount of the forward contract over the current spot rate, which varies from 0 to 2 or 3 percent per year for currencies that are considered reasonably stable. For currencies undergoing devaluation in excess of 4 to 5 percent per year, the required discounts may be as high as 15 to 20 percent per year. When it is probable that future devaluations may exceed 20 percent per year, forward contracts are usually unavailable.

The magnitude of the premium or discount required depends on the forward expectations of the financial communities of the two countries involved and on the supply and demand conditions in the foreign exchange market. Since members of the financial communities are usually well informed about the expected forward exchange values of their respective currencies, the premiums or discounts quoted are very closely related to the probable occurrence of changes in the exchange rates.

BASIC PARITY CONDITIONS

Four basic relationships will be treated:

1. Consistent foreign exchange rates
2. The Fisher effect
3. The interest rate parity theorem (IRPT)
4. The purchasing power parity theorem (PPPT).

Consistent Foreign Exchange Rates

Equilibrating transactions take place when exchange rates are not in proper relationship with one another. This will be illustrated by some examples with unrealistically rounded numbers that make the arithmetic of the calculations simple. The right direction of analysis will be obtained if the reader remembers the general maxim that arbitrageurs will seek to sell high and to buy low. First, we will indicate the consistency of spot rates. Suppose the dollar value of the pound is $2 in New York City and $1.90 in London. The following adjustment actions would take place: In New York City, sell £190 for $380. Pounds are sold in New York because the pound value is high there. In London, sell $380 for £200. In London, the dollar value is high in relation to the pound. Thus, £190 sold in New York City for $380 can be used to buy £200 in London, a gain of £10. The sale of pounds in New York causes their value to decline in New York, and the purchase of pounds in London causes their value in London to rise until no further arbitrage opportunities remain. The same foreign exchange prices, assuming minimal transportation costs, would have to prevail in all locations.

The relations between two individual localities can be generalized across all countries. This is referred to as "consistent cross rates." It works in the following fashion: Assume that the equilibrium relation between the dollar and the pound is $2 to £1 and that the dollar to franc rate is $.25 to Fr 1. Now, suppose that in New York City £.10 = Fr 1. The following adjustment process would take place. Sell $200 for £100 used to obtain Fr 1,000. The Fr 1,000 will buy $250. This is a $50 profit over the initial $200. Sell dollars for pounds and pounds for francs, since the pound is overvalued with respect to both the dollar to pound and dollar to franc relationships. Dollars will fall in relation to the pound, and the pound will fall in relation to the franc until consistent cross rates obtain. If the relation were Fr 1 = £.125, consistent cross rates would obtain. Check using the following relation:

$$\$1 = £.5$$
$$£1 = Fr\ 8.00$$
$$Fr\ 1 = \$.25.$$

The product of the right-hand sides of the three relationships must equal 1. Checking, we have $0.5 \times 8 \times 0.25 = 1$. We have thus established consistency between foreign exchange rates.

The Fisher Effect

The Fisher effect states the relationship between interest rates and the anticipated rate of inflation. While it can also be regarded as purely a relationship for a domestic economy (Equation 6.5), it is also utilized in developing some of the international relationships. The Fisher effect states that nominal interest rates rise to reflect the anticipated rate of inflation. The Fisher effect can be stated in a number of variations of Equation 6.11.

$$\frac{P_0}{P_1} = \frac{1 + r}{1 + R_n} \tag{6.11}$$

$$1 + r = (1 + R_n)\frac{P_0}{P_1}$$

$$r = \left[(1 + R_n)\frac{P_0}{P_1}\right] - 1 \tag{6.11a}$$

$$R_n = \left[(1 + r)\frac{P_1}{P_0}\right] - 1, \tag{6.11b}$$

where

P_0 = initial price level

P_1 = subsequent price level

$\dfrac{P_1}{P_0}$ = rate of inflation

$\dfrac{P_0}{P_1}$ = relative purchasing power of the currency unit

r = real rate of interest

R_n = nominal rate of interest.

While the Fisher effect can be stated in a number of forms, its basic idea can be conveyed by a simple numerical example. Over a given period of time, if the price index is expected to rise by 10 percent and the real rate of interest is 7 percent, then the current nominal rate of interest is

$$R_n = [(1.07)(1.10)] - 1$$
$$= 17.7 \text{ percent.}$$

Similarly, if the nominal rate of interest is 12 percent and the price index is expected to rise by 10 percent over a given time period, the current real rate of interest is

$$r = \left[1.12 \left(\frac{100}{110} \right) \right] - 1$$
$$= 1.018 - 1 = 0.018 = 1.8 \text{ percent.}$$

The Interest Rate Parity Theorem (IRPT)

The interest rate parity theorem is an extension of the Fisher effect to international markets. It holds that the ratio of the forward and spot exchange rates will equal the ratio of foreign and domestic gross interest rates.[9] The formal statement of the interest rate parity theorem can be expressed in Equation 6.12.

$$\frac{X_f}{X_0} = \frac{1 + R_{f0}}{1 + R_{d0}} = \frac{E_0}{E_f}, \qquad (6.12)$$

where

X_f = current forward exchange rate expressed as FC units per \$1

E_f = current forward exchange rate expressed as dollars per FC1

X_0 = current spot exchange rate expressed as FC units per \$1

E_0 = current spot exchange rate expressed as dollars per FC1

R_{f0} = current nominal foreign interest rate

R_{d0} = current nominal domestic interest rate.

---

[9]These relations are further clarified by Problem 6.13.

FIGURE 6.7 Illustration of the Interest Rate Parity Theorem

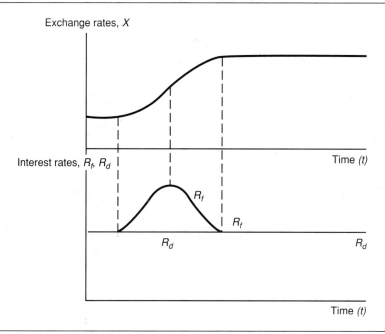

Thus, if the foreign interest rate is 15 percent while the domestic interest rate is 10 percent and the spot exchange rate is $X_0 = 10$, the predicted current forward exchange rate will be

Annual Basis	Quarterly Basis
$X_f = \dfrac{1 + R_{f0}}{1 + R_{d0}} (X_0)$	$X_f = \dfrac{1 + R_{f0}/4}{1 + R_{d0}/4} (X_0)$
$= \dfrac{1.15}{1.10} (10)$	$= \dfrac{1.0375}{1.025} (10)$
$= 10.45.$	$= 10.122.$

Thus, the indicated foreign forward rate is 10.45 units of foreign currency per $1, and the foreign forward rate is at a discount of 4.5 percent on an annual basis. If the time period of a transaction is 90 days, we have to rework the problem, first changing the interest rates to a quarterly basis. The discount on the 90-day forward rate would now be 1.22 percent on the quarterly basis, since the 90-day forward rate would be 10.122.

Alternatively, the example could be formulated for the effect on interest rates of expected changes in future foreign exchange rates. Here is a dynamic relationship that needs to be recognized: If the foreign exchange rate is expected to rise over a period of time, relative interest rates will reflect the rate of change expected in the foreign exchange rates. This is illustrated in Figure 6.7.

FIGURE 6.8   Covered Interest Arbitrage with Investment Outflows

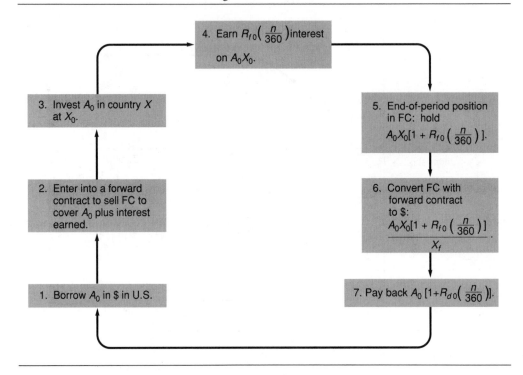

The figure shows that as the value of the foreign currency falls (the exchange rate expressed in the number of foreign currency units per dollar rises), the ratio of foreign interest rates to domestic interest rates rises. At the inflection point of the rise in the expected number of foreign currency units per dollar, the ratio of foreign interest rates to domestic interest rates peaks. When the expected ratio of the number of foreign currency units per domestic currency unit levels off, the former ratio of foreign interest rates to domestic interest rates is reestablished.

The approximation for the IRPT is

$$R_{fi} - R_{di} \cong \frac{X_f - X_0}{X_0}.$$

The data for the annual example are used to illustrate the approximation:

$$.15 - .10 \cong \frac{10.45 - 10}{10},$$

$$0.05 \cong .045.$$

The IRPT can also be used to illustrate another general proposition for international finance. In the absence of market imperfections, risk-adjusted expected real returns on financial assets will be the same in foreign markets as in domestic markets. Equilibrium

FIGURE 6.9   Covered Interest Arbitrage with Investment Inflows

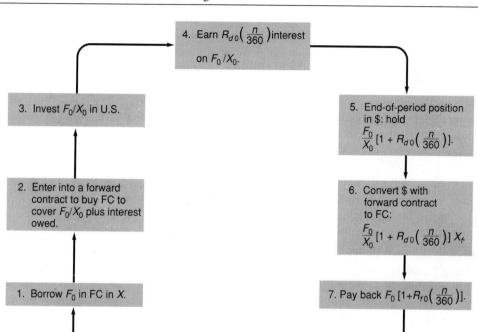

among the current exchange rate, the forward exchange rate, the domestic interest rate, and the foreign interest rate is achieved through covered interest arbitrage. Assume that the forward contract is for n days and that R_{f0} and R_{d0} are annual rates. A sequence of seven transactions takes place when the interest rate differential in X exceeds the forward exchange discount on the currency of X (see Figure 6.8).

Equilibrium occurs when the principal plus interest earned in country X equals the principal plus interest paid in the United States, or when

$$\frac{A_0 X_0 [1 + R_{f0}(n/360)]}{X_f} = A_0 \left[1 + R_{d0}\left(\frac{n}{360}\right)\right], \text{ or } \frac{X_f}{X_0} = \frac{1 + (n/360)R_{f0}}{1 + (n/360)R_{d0}}.$$

Alternatively, we would obtain the same equilibrium requirement if the interest rate differential in X were less than the forward exchange discount in the currency of X, by borrowing in the foreign country and buying FC to cover the amount borrowed plus interest owed (see Figure 6.9).

Equilibrium occurs when the principal plus interest earned in the United States equals the principal plus interest paid in country X, or when

$$\left\{\frac{F_0}{X_0}\left[1 + R_{d0}\left(\frac{n}{360}\right)\right]\right\}X_f = F_0\left[1 + R_{f0}\left(\frac{n}{360}\right)\right], \text{ or } \frac{X_f}{X_0} = \frac{1 + R_{f0}(n/360)}{1 + R_{d0}(n/360)}.$$

FIGURE 6.10   Covered Interest Arbitrage

		Interest Rate Differential (foreign currency less U.S. $)	
		Plus	**Minus**
Forward market rates (in foreign currency units, X_f)	Discount	−1%, +2% IF −2%, +1%, IH	
	Premium		+1%, −2% IH +2%, −1% IF

If the interest differentials are positive in the foreign country, the forward rate on the foreign currency will be at a discount. If negative, the forward rate on the foreign currency will be at a premium, as shown in Figure 6.10. The pair of relations followed by "IF" indicate foreign investment in the covered interest arbitrage operation. The pair of relations followed by "IH" leads to investment in the United States in the covered interest arbitrage operation.

As we have demonstrated, whether or not the covered interest arbitrage operation results in investment in a foreign country in preference to investment in the United States, the resulting equilibrium interest and forward exchange parity relationship is the same.

The transactions that result in interest rate parity are referred to as *covered interest arbitrage*. The basic facts of an *arbitrage outflow* situation are:

$$\text{U.S. interest rate} = 8\%$$

$$\text{French interest rate} = 10\%$$

$$\text{Spot exchange rate } \$1 = \text{Fr}5$$

$$\text{Forward exchange rate discount} = 1\%.$$

The following arbitrage transaction will take place. In New York, borrow $100,000 for 90 days (one-fourth year) at 8 percent. The loan repayment at the end of 90 days is $100,000 [1 + (0.08/4)] = $102,000. At the spot exchange rate, convert the $100,000 loan into Fr500,000. In France, invest the Fr500,000 for 90 days at 10 percent. Receive at the end of 90 days Fr500,000 [1 + (0.10/4)] = Fr512,500.

A covering transaction is also made. To insure against adverse changes in the spot rate during the 90-day investment period, sell investment proceeds forward. Since the forward exchange rate discount is 1 percent, then 5[1 + (0.01/4)] = Fr5.0125 is required to exchange for $1, in 90 days (forward). Sell investment proceeds forward; that is, contract to receive Fr512,500/5.0125 = $102,244.

$$\text{Arbitrage profits} = \text{Investment receipts} - \text{Loan payments}$$

$$= \$102,244 - \$102,000$$

$$= \$244$$

The arbitrage transaction increases the *demand* for currency in New York and increases the *supply* of funds in France. This raises the interest rate in New York and lowers it in

France, thus narrowing the differential. The covering transaction increases the supply of French forward exchange, while the arbitrage investment action increases the demand for spot funds. Both forces tend to increase the forward exchange discount. The interest rate differential decreases and the forward rate discount increases until both are equalized, and arbitrage profits are eliminated.

An *arbitrage inflow* takes place when the forward exchange rate discount exceeds the interest rate differential. The basic facts are now:

$$\text{U.S. interest rate} = 8\%$$

$$\text{French interest rate} = 9\%$$

$$\text{Spot exchange rate Fr5} = \$1$$

$$\text{Forward exchange rate discount} = 2\%.$$

The arbitrage transaction involves borrowing in the foreign country. In France, borrow Fr500,000 for 90 days at 9 percent. The loan repayment at the end of 90 days is Fr500,000 $[1 + (0.09/4)]$ = Fr511,250. At the spot exchange rate, convert the Fr500,000 loan into $100,000. In New York, invest the $100,000 for 90 days at 8 percent. Receive at the end of 90 days $100,000 $[1 + (0.08/4)]$ = $102,000.

Again, a covering transaction would be made. To insure coverage for the loan repayment, buy Fr511,250 forward. At a 2 percent forward exchange rate discount, it costs Fr5$[1 + (0.02/4)]$ = Fr5.02 to buy $1 forward. Thus, to repay the Fr511,250 with a certain amount of dollars requires Fr511,250/5.02 = $101,843.

$$\text{Arbitrage profits} = \text{Investment receipts} - \text{Loan repayments}$$
$$= \$102,000 - \$101,843$$
$$= \$157$$

The arbitrage transaction increases the *demand* for francs and increases the *supply* of dollars. The U.S. interest rate decreases and the rate in France rises; thus, the differential increases. Covering transactions increase the spot supply of francs, thus decreasing the premium on forward francs. The interest rate differential increases and the forward exchange rate discount decreases until both rates are equalized.

As a result of the covered interest arbitrage transactions of the types described, the relationships depicted by the interest rate parity theorem would obtain. This relationship determines the home-currency cost that would be involved when a purchase or sale is made and a future payment or receipt is involved.

The Purchasing Power Parity Theorem (PPPT)

The purchasing power parity doctrine states that currencies will be valued for what they will buy. If an American dollar buys the same basket of goods and services as five units of a foreign currency, we have an exchange rate of five foreign currency units to the dollar or 20 cents per foreign currency unit. An attempt to compare price indexes to computed purchasing power parity assumes that it is possible to compile comparable baskets of goods in different countries. As a practical matter, the parity rate is, in general, estimated from changes in the purchasing power of two currencies with reference to some past base period when the exchange rate was theoretically in equilibrium. In formal terms, the PPPT may be stated as in Equation 6.13.

$$CX = \frac{X_1}{X_0} = \frac{P_{f1}/P_{f0}}{P_{d1}/P_{d0}} = RPC \qquad (6.13)$$

where

$$\frac{X_1}{X_0} = \frac{E_0}{E_1}, \quad X_0 = \text{FC units per dollar now,}$$

$$X_1 = \text{FC units per dollar one period later,}$$

$$E_0 = \frac{1}{X_0} = \text{dollars per FC unit now,}$$

$$E_1 = \frac{1}{X_1} = \text{dollars per FC unit one period later,}$$

$$CX = \frac{X_1}{X_0} = \text{change in exchange rate,}$$

P_{f0} = initial price level in the foreign country,

P_{f1} = foreign country price level one period later,

P_{d0} = initial domestic price level,

P_{d1} = domestic price level one period later,

$$RPC = \frac{P_{f1}/P_{f0}}{P_{d1}/P_{d0}} = \text{change in relative prices} = \text{ratio of inflation rates.}$$

A few numerical examples will illustrate some of the implications of the purchasing power parity doctrine. Let us assume that for a given period, foreign price levels have risen by 32 percent while domestic price levels have risen by 20 percent. If the initial exchange rate is FC 10 to $1, the subsequent new exchange rate will be

$$\frac{1.32}{1.20} = \frac{X_1}{10}, \quad X_1 = 1.1(10) = 11.$$

It will now take 10 percent more foreign currency units to equal $1, because the relative inflation rate has been higher in the foreign country. Alternatively, with an exchange rate of FC 10 to $1, let us assume that foreign prices have risen by 17 percent while domestic prices have risen by 30 percent. The new expected exchange rate would be

$$\frac{1.17}{1.30} = \frac{X_1}{10}, \quad X_1 = .9(10) = 9.$$

In the present instance, the number of foreign currency units needed to buy $1 would drop by 10 percent. Thus, the value of the foreign currency has increased by 10 percent due to the differential rates of inflation in domestic versus foreign prices.

Empirical studies indicate that while the purchasing power parity relationship does not hold perfectly, it tends to hold in the long run. More fundamentally, the doctrine predicts that an equilibrium rate between two currencies will reflect market forces and that random deviations from the central tendency will tend to be self-correcting; that is, it suggests the existence of some strong equilibrating forces. Furthermore, it argues that the relations between exchange rates will not be haphazard but will reflect underlying economic conditions and changes in these conditions. The relationships are not precise because of a number of factors. These include (1) differences in incomes or other endowments between the two countries, (2) differences in government monetary and fiscal policies, (3) large capital movements motivated by changes in relative political risks or differences in prospective economic opportunities, (4) transportation costs, (5) lags in market responses, (6) differences between the two countries in the price ratios of internationally traded goods to domestically traded goods, (7) the impact of risk premium influences, and (8) differences in rates of productivity growth.

An interesting application of PPPT is the Big Mac index developed by the London *Economist* [*The Economist*, May 5, 1990, p. 92]. In this case the "identical basket of goods and services" to be compared across countries is a Big Mac, which is made in more than 50 countries. In the United States the average price of a Big Mac is about $2.20 compared with 370 yen in Tokyo. The implied PPP for the dollar is a yen to dollar ratio of 168. Similarly, the Mac-PPP for the deutsche mark is 1.95. The dollar's rate against the pound in the spring of 1990 was $0.61, very close to its Mac-PPP of $0.64. All of these Mac rates were fairly close to the estimates of PPP parities published by a number of distinguished economists during the winter and spring of 1990. The opening of McDonald's in Moscow enabled *The Economist* to establish a Mac-PPP for the rouble (the English spelling). At the official exchange rate, the price of the Big Mac in Moscow was $6.25. This implied a PPP ratio of $1.70 roubles to the dollar, compared with an official rate against the dollar of 0.60 roubles. *The Economist* observes that if the two- to three-hour waiting time is valued at average Soviet hourly wages, then the "queue-adjusted" Mac-PPP is 3.40 roubles.

Risk Position of the Firm in Foreign Currency Units

The risk position of a firm in relation to possible fluctuations in foreign exchange rates can be clarified by referring to expected receipts or obligations in foreign currency units. If a firm is expecting receipts in foreign currency units (if it is "long" in the foreign currency units), its risk is that the value of the foreign currency units will fall (devaluing the foreign currency in relation to the dollar). If a firm has obligations in foreign currency units (if it is "short" in the foreign currency units), its risk is that the value of the foreign currency will rise and it will have to buy the currency to repay the obligations at a higher price.

Subsequent chapters will discuss policies and procedures for managing the risks resulting from fluctuations in foreign exchange rates.

SUMMARY

In this chapter we analyze how interest rates are determined, taking into account international influences. The globalization of international financial markets makes it impossible to understand interest rate determination without taking international exchange rate influences into account. We begin with the observed nominal pre-tax rates of return. Four influences are operating:

$$\text{Nominal rate of return} = f[E(\text{real rate}), E(\text{inflation}),$$
$$E(\text{liquidity premium}), E(\text{risk premium})].$$

The risk premium includes the risk of exchange rate fluctuations. Assets can be grouped according to how they fit these characteristics. For example, one can collect all Aaa rated corporate bonds with ten years to maturity. Within this group, all four factors are held constant. Consequently, all securities within the group are close economic substitutes and will have the same nominal rate of return.

Some fundamental exchange rate relationships provide a basis for understanding interest rates in an international setting. Because a different set of relationships is involved, the following key symbols have been used: D = devaluation, E = dollars per foreign currency (FC) unit, X = FC units per dollar, P = price level, R = the nominal interest rate, and r = the real rate of interest. D_{fd} is the change in the number of FC units per dollar:

$$D_{fd} = \frac{X_1 - X_0}{X_0} = \frac{E_0 - E_1}{E_1}. \tag{6.10a}$$

Alternatively, D_{df} is the change in the dollar value of a foreign currency unit:

$$D_{df} = \frac{E_1 - E_0}{E_0} = \frac{X_0 - X_1}{X_1}. \tag{6.10b}$$

In addition to presenting the requirements for consistent foreign exchange rates, three fundamental exchange rate relationships were explained.

1. Fisher Effect (FE)

$$R_n = \left[(1 + r)\left(\frac{P_1}{P_0}\right) \right] - 1 \tag{6.11b}$$

2. Interest Rate Parity Theorem (IRPT)

$$\frac{X_f}{X_0} = \frac{1 + R_{f0}}{1 + R_{d0}} = \frac{E_0}{E_f} \tag{6.12}$$

3. Purchasing Power Parity Theorem (PPPT)

$$\frac{X_1}{X_0} = \frac{P_{f1}/P_{f0}}{P_{d1}/P_{d0}} \tag{6.13}$$

For an understanding of interest rate relationships, these three fundamental parity conditions need to be taken into account. PPPT relates relative inflation rates to exchange rate movements. The Fisher effect relates nominal interest rates and real interest rates through the influence of inflation. Differences in interest rates between different countries are linked to movements between current spot exchange rates and future exchange rates.

International business transactions are conducted in more than one currency. If a firm is expecting receipts in foreign currency units, its risk is that the value of the foreign currency units will fall. If it has obligations to be paid in foreign currency units, its risk is that the value of the foreign currency will rise. To reduce foreign exchange risk, firms can engage in transactions in the forward foreign exchange market. They can also borrow at current spot exchange rates the amount of foreign currency needed for future transactions. These two forms of hedging are essentially insurance and, therefore, involve costs. Firms also take protective action against long or short positions in foreign currencies resulting from the balance sheet position of their foreign subsidiaries.

QUESTIONS

6.1 What happens to the real rate of interest when the demand for capital increases because technological innovations have caused the aggregate investment opportunity set to increase?

6.2 Why is the long-run rate of return on long-term corporate bonds (5.2 percent) higher than the long-run rate of return on long-term U.S. government debt (4.6 percent)?

6.3 If the rate of return on long-term U.S. government bonds has been 4.6 percent, the long-run rate of inflation (1926–1989) has been 3.1 percent, and the rate of return on U.S. Treasury bills (that is, short-term U.S. government bonds) has been 3.6 percent, what does this suggest about the liquidity premium on long-term bonds?

6.4 Given that the liquidity premium is positive, how can you explain a downward-sloping term structure?

6.5 What is the major implication of Fisher separation?

6.6 There have been times when the term structure of interest rates has been such that short-term rates were higher than long-term rates. Does this necessarily imply that the best financial policy for a firm is to use all long-term debt and no short-term debt? Explain.

6.7 How would you use term structure to predict inflation?

6.8 What is the difference between the promised return and the expected return on risky long-term bonds?

6.9 Why is the historical rate of return on common stock (10.3 percent) higher than the rate on long-term corporate bonds (5.2 percent)?

6.10 What has been the impact of advances in the technology of transportation and communication on international trade and finance?

6.11 Why is the ratio of foreign earnings to a firm's total earnings likely to be greater than the ratio of its foreign sales to total sales?

6.12 If a firm has difficulty developing a product that will sell in the local domestic market, is it likely to have greater success in a foreign market? Explain.

PROBLEMS

6.1   From a recent issue of the *Federal Reserve Bulletin* or from another convenient source:
   a.   Construct a yield curve for recent monthly data for U.S. government securities, using market yields for maturities of one year or less and the capital market rates for constant maturities for the maturities from 2 to 30 years.
   b.   Why does the yield curve show only U.S government security yields instead of including yields on commercial paper and corporate bonds?

6.2   Suppose that expected future short-term interest rates have the following alternative patterns:

Year	A	B	C	D
1	4%	8%	4%	8%
2	5	7	6	7
3	6	6	15	5
4	7	5	6	7
5	8	4	4	8

   a.   Using a simple arithmetic average, what is the current rate on a five-year note for each of the four patterns?
   b.   Using a geometric average, answer the same question as for Part (a). (Hint: Add 1 to each percentage — for example, 1.04 — then multiply the five numbers, and then take their fifth root. Subtract 1 from the result. On a hand calculator, use the y^x or x^x button with 0.2, which equals 1/5. For example, for interest rate A, the product is 1.3376, and the fifth root minus 1 is 5.991 percent.)
   c.   Optional:
      (1)   Calculate the current two-, three-, and four-year note yields using both the arithmetic and geometric averages and then graph the resulting yield curves in four graphs of two curves each.
      (2)   Is the height of the yield curve based on the arithmetic averages higher or lower than that based on the geometric averages?

6.3   Given below are the yields to maturity on a five-year bond:

Years to Maturity	Yield to Maturity
1	8.0
2	9.0
3	10.0
4	10.5
5	10.8

   a.   What is the implied forward rate of interest for the third year?
   b.   What (geometric) average annual rate of interest would you receive if you bought a bond at the beginning of the third year and sold it at the beginning of the fifth year?

6.4   The Comex Company is considering investing in a machine that produces Frisbees. The cost of the machine is $40,000. Production by year during the four-year life of the machine is expected to be as follows: 12,000 units, 16,000 units, 20,000 units, and 18,000 units. The market for Frisbees is increasing; hence, management believes that the price of

Frisbees will increase at about 10 percent annually, compared to the general rate of inflation of 9 percent. The price of Frisbees in the first year will be $2, but plastic used to produce Frisbees is rapidly becoming more expensive. Because of this, production cash outflows are expected to grow at 15 percent per year. First-year production cost will be $1 per unit.

The company will use sum-of-years'-digits depreciation on the new machine. There will be no salvage value at the end of the fourth year. The company's tax rate is 40 percent, and its cost of capital is 18 percent, based on the existing rate of inflation. Should the project be undertaken?

6.5 The table below gives the yields to maturity and implied forward rates on bonds that are expected to have about the same risk as two projects your firm is considering (Projects A and B). Cash flows are also given in the table.

Year	Yield to Maturity	Forward Rate	Cash Flow for A	Cash Flow for B
0	—	—	$-100	$-100
1	21%	21.00%	62	48
2	18	15.07	50	52
3	16	12.10	28	44

You have been asked to answer the following questions.

a. Common practice is to use the yield to maturity on three-year bonds as the appropriate discount rate for the project's cash flows. What is the NPV of the two projects if you use this rate?

b. An alternative is to use the annual forward rates to discount the cash flows. What is the NPV of each project if you use this procedure?

c. Which procedure is correct? Why?

6.6 The table below gives the yields to maturity for bonds with approximately the same risk as Project X and Project Y, for which cash flows are also given.

Year	Yield to Maturity	Cash Flows X	Y
0	—	−1,000	−1,000
1	14.00%	300	600
2	15.00	400	500
3	15.99	600	200

a. Find the NPV of each project using the three-year yield to maturity.

b. Find the NPV of each project using the annual forward rates to discount cash flows.

6.7 You have priced two pure discount bonds, each with five years to maturity and with a face value of $1,000. They pay no coupons. The first bond sells for $780.58 and the second sells for $667.43.

a. What are their yields to maturity?

b. Why does the second bond sell for less than the first?

c. If their default risk is uncorrelated with the rest of the economy, then their expected cash flows can be discounted at the riskless rate, which is 5 percent. If they have the same expected yield, what is the probability of default for the second bond? (Assume that if the bond defaults, you receive nothing, but if it does not default, you receive the full face value.)

6.8 In 1980, the number of Japanese yen required to equal one U.S. dollar was 226.63. In March 1991, the U.S. dollar was worth 137.39 yen.
    a. What is X_0 (1980)? What is X_1 (1991)?
    b. What is E_0 (1980)? What is E_1 (1991)?
    c. What was the percentage devaluation or revaluation of the yen in terms of the U.S. dollar?
    d. What was the percentage devaluation or revaluation of the dollar in terms of the yen?

6.9 If the exchange rate between dollars and francs is Fr 5 = $1.00, and between dollars and pounds is £1 = $1.60, what is the exchange rate between francs and pounds?

6.10 *The Wall Street Journal*, on March 5, 1981, listed the following information on the exchange rates between the dollar and the German mark:

$$X_0 = 2.1436 \text{ DM/\$}$$
$$E_0 = \$0.4665/\text{DM}$$
$$X_f(90 \text{ days}) = 2.1304 \text{ DM/\$}$$
$$E_f(90 \text{ days}) = \$0.4694/\text{DM}.$$

The U.S. prime interest rate on that day was 18.5 percent.
    a. What is implied about the German interest rate?
    b. If the forward exchange rate was $0.45/DM, what would be the German interest rate?
    c. If the German interest rate was 12 percent, what would be the 90-day forward rate on deutsche marks per dollar?

6.11 The treasurer of a company in Mexico borrowed $10,000 in dollars at a 15 percent interest rate when the exchange rate was 22 pesos to the dollar. His company paid the loan plus interest one year later, when the exchange rate was 25 pesos to the dollar.
    a. What rate of interest was paid, based on the pesos received and paid by the treasurer?
    b. Show how your result illustrates the interest rate parity theorem.

6.12 The treasurer of a company in Mexico is comparing two borrowing alternatives for a 180-day loan. He can borrow in U.S. dollars from a U.S. bank at a 15 percent interest rate or from a Mexican bank in pesos at a 25 percent interest rate. The spot exchange rate is 23.5 pesos to the dollar. The 180-day forward exchange rate is 25 pesos to the dollar.
    a. What is the effective interest rate in pesos on the U.S. loan?
    b. Verify your answer by use of the interest rate parity relationship.

6.13 In January 1977 (when DM 3 = $1), it was expected that by the end of 1977, the price level in the United States would have risen by 10 percent and in West Germany by 5 percent. Assume that the real rate of interest in both countries is 4 percent.
    a. Use the purchasing power parity theorem (PPPT) to project the expected DMs per $1 at the end of 1977 (the expected future spot rate of DMs per $1).
    b. Use the Fisher relation to estimate the nominal interest rates in each country that make it possible for investments in each country to earn its real rate of interest.
    c. Use the interest rate parity theorem (IRPT) to estimate the current one-year forward rate of DMs per $1.

   d. Compare your estimate of the current forward rate in (c) with your estimate of the expected future spot rate in (a).
   e. Prove analytically that the Fisher effect and the IRPT guarantee consistency with the PPPT relation when real interest rates in the different countries are equal. (Assume that all the fundamental relations hold.)

6.14 *(Use the computer diskette, File name: 06INT, How the Market Determines Interest Rates.)*
   a. Given two individuals, *A* and *B*, with different subjective rates of return and different investment opportunities, how much does each invest?
   b. What are the individual demands for borrowed funds of *A* and *B*, respectively?
   c. View the schedule of different levels of market rate of interest of the demand and supply for borrowing by *A* and *B*, respectively.
      (1) At what market rate of interest is the total demand for funds equal to the total supply of funds?
      (2) What is the excess demand for borrowing at the interest rate just determined?
   d. If individual *A*'s investment opportunity schedule is improved by changing the intercept of his demand for funds schedule from 15 to 25 (for example) or reducing the slope from 3 to 2 (for example) how does this affect each individual's demand for borrowed funds and the market rate of interest?
   e. Do a similar analysis by improving or making less favorable the investment opportunity schedule for individual *B*.
   f. Go back to the original conditions and increase individual *B*'s subjective required rate of return from 5 percent to 8 percent. How will this affect the demand by each individual for borrowed funds and the market clearing rate of interest?
   g. You can now gain some further insights on the fundamental economic factors that determine interest rate levels by making alternative assumptions about different subjective required rates of return and investment opportunities available.

6.15 *(Use the computer diskette, File name: 06IRPT, Interest Rate Parity Theorem.)*
   a. The treasurer of a Mexican firm needs to borrow $100,000 for 1 year. He can borrow in dollars from a U.S. bank at 10 percent interest. The current exchange rate is 690 pesos for each U.S. dollar; the 1-year forward rate is 725 pesos per dollar. Given the assumptions in Screen #3, what interest rate on a peso loan would make the treasurer indifferent between borrowing in pesos or dollars?
      (1) If the 1-year forward rate were 780 pesos per dollar, what interest rate would you expect to find on a 1-year loan in pesos?
      (2) If the interest rate in Mexico were 26 percent, what would this imply for the 1-year forward exchange rate? (Hint: Substitute alternative forward exchange rates until you find the one which results in R_{f0} of 26 percent.)
   b. What is the relationship between *X* and *E*?
      (1) If *X* is 4 FC units per dollar, what is *E*?
      (2) What would *X* have to be for *E* to equal 2 dollars per FC unit?
   c. A U.S. firm operating in Europe can borrow in Swiss francs for 6 months (.5 years) at 8 percent interest or in U.S. dollars at 10 percent. The current exchange rate is 1.69 Swiss francs per dollar; the 6-month forward rate is 1.65 Swiss francs per dollar.

Which loan should be chosen? (Hint: Calculate the foreign interest rate implicit in the exchange rate relationship and compare this to the quoted interest rate of the Swiss franc loan. If the implicit rate is higher than the quoted rate, the firm should borrow in Swiss francs.)

d. Feel free to change any of the initial assumptions.

SELECTED REFERENCES

Altman, Edward I., "Setting the Record Straight on Junk Bonds: A Review of the Research on Default Rates and Returns," *Journal of Applied Corporate Finance,* 3, no. 2, (Summer 1990), pp. 82–95.

———, "Measuring Corporate Bond Mortality and Performance," *Journal of Finance,* 44, no. 4, (September 1989), pp. 909–922.

Asquith, Paul; Mullins, David W.; and Wolff, Eric D., "Original Issue High Yield Bonds: Aging Analyses of Defaults, Exchanges, and Calls," *Journal of Finance*, 44, no. 4 (September 1989), pp. 923–952.

Blume, Marshall E., and Keim, Donald B., "Realized Rates and Defaults on Low-Grade Bonds: The Cohorts of 1977 and 1978," University of Pennsylvania Working Paper, 1989.

Fama, Eugene F., "Short-term Interest Rates as Predictors of Inflation," *American Economic Review,* (June 1975), pp. 269–282.

Hess, P., and Bicksler, J., "Capital Asset Prices versus Time Series Models as Predictors of Inflation," *Journal of Financial Economics*, (December 1975), pp. 341–360.

Ibbotson Associates, Inc., *Stocks, Bonds, Bills and Inflation 1990 Yearbook: Market Results for 1926–1989*, Chicago: Ibbotson Associates, Inc., 1990.

Nelson, C., and Schwert, G. William, "Short-term Interest Rates as Predictors of Inflation: On Testing the Hypothesis that the Real Rate is Constant," *American Economic Review,* (June 1977), pp. 478–486.

Triffin, R., "Correcting the World Monetary Scandal," *Challenge,* (January-February 1986), pp. 4–14.

Wakeman, Lee, "Bond Rating Agencies and Capital Markets," Working Paper, Graduate School of Management, University of Rochester, Rochester, New York, 1978.

Weinstein, Mark, "The Seasoning Process of New Corporate Bond Issues," *Journal of Finance*, (December 1978), pp. 1343–1354.

———, "The Effect of a Rating Change Announcement on Bond Price," *Journal of Financial Economics,* (December 1977), pp. 329–350.

Basic Financial Planning and Investment

The chapters of Part Three discuss financial planning and control systems in firms. They provide the framework for planning the firm's growth and development of financial controls for efficiency. Although these areas of finance do not have the sophistication of the formal models developed in other parts of the book, they are vital to the firm's healthy profitability. Chapter 7 examines the construction and use of the basic ratios of financial analysis; through this ratio analysis, we can pinpoint a firm's strengths and weaknesses.

Chapter 8 begins with the broad planning framework of the relations among revenues, volume, and profits in a breakeven analysis. The chapter then continues with a more detailed consideration of budget systems and controls for decentralized operations. Chapter 8 also covers financial forecasting: Given a projected increase in sales, how much money must the financial manager raise to support this level of sales?

Chapter 9 discusses capital budgeting under certainty. Capital budgeting involves all aspects of planning expenditures with returns that are expected to continue over a period of years. In Chapter 9, we postulate a world with certainty and supply the discount rates required for the analysis. We have previously discussed how discount factors are determined in Chapter 6. We revisit these topics in Part Four, which deals with decision making under uncertainty.

CHAPTER 7

Financial Analysis

Effective planning and control are central to enhancing enterprise value. Financial plans may take many forms, but any good plan must be related to the firm's existing strengths and weaknesses. The strengths must be understood if they are to be used to proper advantage, and the weaknesses must be recognized if corrective action is to be taken. For example, are inventories adequate to support the projected level of sales? Does the firm have too heavy an investment in accounts receivable, and does this condition reflect a lax collection policy? For efficient operations, does the firm have too much or too little invested in plant and equipment? The financial manager can plan future financial requirements in accordance with the forecasting and budgeting procedures we will present in later chapters, but the plan must begin with the type of financial analysis developed in this chapter.

INTRODUCTION

Traditional financial ratio analysis has focused on the numbers. The value of this approach is that quantitative relations can be used to diagnose strengths and weaknesses in a firm's performance. But the world is becoming more dynamic and subject to rapid changes. It is not enough to analyze operating performance. Financial analysis must also include consideration of the strategic and economic developments to which the firm must relate for its long-run success. In addition, the categories of stakeholders must be broadened. Formerly ratio analysis was performed from the point of view of the firm's owners and creditors. In the present political and social environment, the stakeholders must be expanded to include employees, consumers, social and environmental considerations, and other government regulatory interests. We shall begin with the traditional financial statements, but broaden the analysis to consider the wider range of variables and influences.

Different sources and different analysts use different lists or combinations of financial ratios for analysis. The list provided in this chapter is intended to be suggestive only. For some situations, even more elaborate lists of financial ratios might be useful, and for other decisions, only a few ratios would be sufficient. In the end-of-chapter problems we illustrate different combinations of ratios ending with a pattern that matches the chapter discussion. There is no one set of ratios that needs to be used all the time — only those ratios required for the decision at hand.

Financial analysis is a science *and* an art. This chapter seeks to cover the science part; the art comes with practice and experience — from many hours of number crunching and use of the numbers to make decisions on the firing line. Good finance managers are made not born — they are developed from the crucible of experience. Wisdom comes from experience and from mistakes made along the way.

We have tried in this chapter to help make the material come alive by applications with the data for actual companies in industries with which the authors have had experience. We start with annual reports to demonstrate the kinds of information that can be developed from this easily available source. To perform trend analysis, it is convenient to draw on sources such as Standard & Poor's Compustat Services which provide an abundance of data in computer-accessible form. In using data from multiple sources the problem of data consistency is aggravated. Even if data comes from a single source such as company annual reports we encounter many instances of restatements of financial reports. In addition, within the application of generally accepted accounting and financial principles, the formats of balance sheets and income statements will vary across individual companies. To make comparisons it is sometimes necessary to recast financial statements as presented by the companies themselves. For such reasons the careful reader may find discrepancies and inconsistencies between numbers, but they will not be large and will not have a material influence on the interpretations or implications of the data. Furthermore, the numbers are not an end in themselves — they are aids to stimulate questions, further investigation, and analysis relating the numbers to a business economic analysis of the industry and firms.

Company and Industry Background

To illustrate a modern approach to financial analysis, we shall use an actual company, Kellogg Co. Kellogg is the world's largest manufacturer of ready-to-eat cereals. Its well-known ready-to-eat cereals include Corn Flakes, Rice Krispies, Special K, Froot Loops, and Nutri-Grain. It also produces Eggo mayonnaise, sauces, pancakes, waffles; has a line of LeGout desserts, drink mixes, pudding and pie fillings, soups; and produces Mrs. Smith's pies and Whitney's yogurt. In ready-to-eat cereals, Kellogg accounted for about 40 percent of the U.S. market and about 52 percent of non-U.S. markets in 1990.

In the United States, Kellogg competes most directly with General Mills, Quaker Oats, Ralston Purina, General Foods (acquired by Philip Morris), and Nabisco (a part of RJR Nabisco). Other competitors to Kellogg include Borden, CPC International, Campbell Soup, ConAgra, H. J. Heinz, Hershey Foods, McDonald's, and Sara Lee. In recent years, Kellogg has lost some U.S. market share in oat-based products to General Mills and Quaker Oats as well as to private label products. Private label products are often the same as brand name products, but the packages carry the name of a large retail operation such as a supermarket chain and typically sell at a price lower than their related brand name counterparts.

The foregoing description of the products and competitors of Kellogg is to provide a business setting to help interpret the financial analysis that will be made. Financial ratios cannot be interpreted without comparing them to some standards, such as the historical data of the individual company and "the industry" as a whole. While Kellogg's products overlap those of the 13 other companies listed above, Kellogg is still primarily a ready-to-eat cereal manufacturer. Therefore, our comparisons will be with the companies whose product lines most completely overlap those of Kellogg, namely General Mills, Quaker Oats, and Ralston Purina.

BASIC FINANCIAL STATEMENTS

In Chapter 2 we describe the characteristics of three key financial statements: the balance sheet, the income statement, and the statement of cash flows. Kellogg's 1988 and 1989 balance sheets are presented in Table 7.1. The first thing we can do with the balance sheet is to perform a common size analysis by relating each item to total assets. We note that current assets are less than one-third of total assets while net property is more than two-thirds. Shareholders' equity is just under 50 percent of total assets. We would also want to make the balance sheet common size analysis in relationship to the comparable companies but shall not do so to save space since we perform similar comparisons in detail.

The income statements for Kellogg for 1988 and 1989 are presented in Table 7.2. Again, we start with a common size analysis relating all items to net revenues. The gross margin is just under 50 percent of net revenues. Selling and administrative expense represents about one-third of net revenues. Since general and administrative expenses usually run about 7 or 8 percent of sales, selling expense is probably in the range of 25 percent of sales. The net operating income for 1989 is down somewhat from 1988. Also, except for the accounting adjustment placed in other income and expense for 1989, the difference between net operating income (NOI) and earnings before interest and taxes (EBIT) is not substantial.

The third basic financial statement is the statement of cash flows. For Kellogg this statement is presented in Table 7.3. Note that Kellogg uses the indirect method of presenting cash flows from operating activities. As set forth in Chapter 2, this method starts with net income and makes the necessary adjustments to arrive at cash provided by operating activities. Although cash provided by operations increased in 1989, the increase in the reduction in notes payable as well as the increase in the reduction in long-term debt resulted in a negative amount of cash provided by financing activities. Hence the increase in cash and temporary investments in 1988 was a positive $59 million, but in 1989 was a negative $105 million.

TABLE 7.1 Kellogg Company and Subsidiaries Consolidated
Balance Sheet December 31 ($ millions)

	1989 Amount	1989 %	1988 Amount	1988 %
Current assets				
Cash and temporary investments	$ 80.3	2.4	$ 185.0	5.6
Accounts receivable, net	355.2	10.5	404.6	12.3
Inventories	394.0	11.6	362.2	11.0
Prepaid expenses	76.6	2.3	111.4	3.4
Total current assets	$ 906.1	26.7	$1,063.2	32.3
Property, gross	3,302.4		2,916.4	
Accumulated depreciation	(896.1)		(784.5)	
Property, net	$2,406.3	71.0	$2,131.9	64.6
Intangible assets	34.9	1.0	53.4	1.6
Other assets	43.1	1.3	49.4	1.5
Total assets*	$3,390.4	100.0	$3,297.9	100.0
Current liabilities				
Current maturities of long-term debt	$ 102.1	3.0	$ 133.1	4.0
Notes payable	376.1	11.1	307.1	9.3
Accounts payable	250.9	7.4	365.3	11.1
Accrued liabilities	308.1	9.1	378.0	11.5
Total current liabilities	$1,037.2	30.6	$1,183.5	35.9
Long-term debt	371.4	11.0	272.1	8.2
Other liabilities	58.6	1.7	66.9	2.0
Deferred income taxes	288.8	8.5	292.2	8.9
Shareholders' equity				
Common stock, $0.25 par	$ 38.6		$ 38.5	
Capital in excess of par	72.8		63.3	
Retained earnings	2,271.4		2,011.1	
Treasury stock	(710.4)		(631.8)	
Currency translation adjustment	(38.0)		2.1	
Total shareholders' equity	$1,634.4	48.2	$1,483.2	45.0
Total liabilities and shareholders' equity*	$3,390.4	100.0	$3,297.9	100.0

*Columns may not add to totals due to rounding.

We have provided an overview of the three main types of financial statements generated by business firms. From these and information provided in footnotes to financial statements, a penetrating financial analysis can be performed. This is our next task.

TABLE 7.2   Kellogg Company and Subsidiaries Consolidated Earnings
Year Ended December 31 ($ millions)

	1989 Amount	1989 %	1988 Amount	1988 %
Net revenues	$4,620.0	100.0	$4,354.4	100.0
Cost of goods sold	2,413.8	52.2	2,233.4	51.3
Gross profit	$2,206.2	47.8	$2,121.0	48.7
Selling and administrative expense	1,505.4	32.6	1,321.3	30.3
Net operating income	$ 700.8	15.2	$ 799.7	18.4
Other income and expense, net	62.6*	1.3	13.8	0.3
Earnings before interest and taxes	$ 763.4	16.5	$ 813.5	18.7
Less: Interest expense	48.3	1.0	38.8	0.9
Income before tax	$ 715.1	15.5	$ 774.7	17.8
Less: Income taxes	244.9	5.3	294.3	6.8
Net income	$ 470.2	10.2	$ 480.4	11.0

*Includes interest revenue of $14.5 million and accounting adjustment of $48.1 million.

TABLE 7.3   Kellogg Company and Subsidiaries Consolidated
Statement of Cash Flows Year Ended
December 31 ($ millions)

	1989	1988
Operating activities		
Net earnings	$ 470.2	$ 480.4
Items in net earnings not requiring (providing) cash:		
Depreciation	167.6	139.7
Cumulative effect of change in method of accounting for income taxes	(48.1)	
Deferred income taxes	32.0	34.8
Other	25.1	(1.4)
Change in operating assets and liabilities:		
Accounts receivable	49.4	(129.5)
Inventories	(31.8)	(51.3)
Prepaid expenses	34.8	(21.7)
Accounts payable	(114.4)	53.4
Accrued liabilities	(51.3)	(12.1)
Cash provided by operations	533.5	492.3
Investing activities		
Additions to properties	(508.7)	(538.1)
Property disposals	15.0	45.6
Other	(1.5)	5.0
Cash used by investing activities	(495.2)	(487.5)
Financing activities		
Borrowings of notes payable	268.9	240.4
Reduction of notes payable	(199.9)	(60.7)

(continued)

TABLE 7.3   *(continued)*

	1989	1988
Issuance of long-term debt	202.5	111.1
Reduction in long-term debt	(135.2)	(23.5)
Issuance of common stock	9.5	5.2
Purchase of treasury stock	(78.6)	(33.6)
Cash dividends	(209.9)	(187.2)
Other	(0.5)	0.4
Cash provided (used) by financing activities	(143.2)	52.1
Effect of exchange rate changes on cash	0.2	1.9
Increase (decrease) in cash and temporary investments	(104.7)	58.8
Cash and temporary investments at beginning of year	185.0	126.2
Cash and temporary investments at end of year	$ 80.3	$ 185.0

FINANCIAL RATIO ANALYSIS

As we have indicated, financial ratio analysis will be of interest to a wide range of stakeholders. In the analysis that follows, we cover a wide range of factors that will be of use to the many different kinds of stakeholders in the firm.

Financial Ratio Standards

To make use of financial ratios we need standards for comparison. One approach is to compare the ratios for the firm with the patterns for the industry or line of business in which the firm predominantly operates. This approach is based on the premise that some underlying economic and business forces compel all firms in an industry to behave similarly. Even if this were true, it is still likely that the financial ratios of small firms might be different from those for large firms. For example, a large firm is more likely to be vertically integrated or more capital intensive. If so, the turnover of its assets into sales would be lower than for small firms. It is sometimes difficult to place an individual firm cleanly in a designated industry. For example, Occidental Petroleum is generally regarded as an oil company, but has been classified by some agencies as a food processor because of a major acquisition of a beef processing company.

Another approach for developing standards is sometimes called "the investment banker's spreadsheet." This involves listing the data for an individual company alongside data for a selected number of other "comparable" firms. Differences will likely be exhibited in the patterns among the individual firms. In this approach, when ratios vary widely the analysts should find out the reasons. Analyzing groups of comparable companies may provide insights about the broader strategic and economic factors affecting the group.

Whether industry standards compiled by various sources or "comparable groups" are employed, analysis is a kind of detective work used to evaluate how a firm is performing and how it is positioned for the future. Financial ratio analysis should not be done mechanically. Broader economic and strategic considerations must be included to assess the probable future performance of the company. In the analysis of Kellogg, we shall use the comparable group approach and include consideration of economic and strategic factors where feasible.

Overview of Financial Relations

An overview of financial analysis relations is presented in Table 7.4. We first make three broad groupings: Performance Measures, Operating Efficiency Measures, and Financial Policy Measures. The logic of the sequence is to start with overall results and then analyze their determinants.

Performance measures are analyzed in three groups:

- A. *Profitability ratios* measure management's effectiveness by the returns generated on sales and investment.

- B. *Growth ratios* measure the firm's ability to maintain its economic position in the growth of the economy and the industries or product-markets in which it operates.

- C. *Valuation measures* measure the ability of management to achieve market values in excess of cost outlays.

Performance measures reflect strategic, operating, and financing decisions. Strategies involve critically important decision areas such as choice of product-market areas in which the firm conducts its operations, whether to emphasize cost reduction or product differentiation, whether to focus on selected product areas or seek to cover a broad range of potential buyers, etc.[1] Characterizations of strategy are not amenable to financial measures directly but have an overriding impact on performance results. To continue the quantitative analysis, we next consider the second major category covered in Table 7.4, the operating efficiency measures. Here two sets of ratios are involved:

- A. *Asset and investment management* measures the effectiveness of the firm's investment decisions and the utilization of its resources.

- B. *Cost management* measures how individual elements of costs are controlled.

The third group of financial relations represents financial policy decisions. These must necessarily relate to strategic decisions as well as to investment management and cost management. Financial policy measures are of two major types:

- A. *Leverage ratios* measure the degree to which the assets of the firm have been financed by the use of debt.

- B. *Liquidity ratios* measure the firm's ability to meet its maturing obligations.

---

[1]For a more extended discussion of the nature of strategy, see Chapter 3 in Weston, Chung, and Hoag, 1990.

TABLE 7.4 Overview of Financial Analysis Relations

I. Performance Measures
    A. Profitability Ratios
        1. Net Operating Income (NOI)/Sales
        2. NOI/Total Assets
        3. NOI/Total Capital
        4. Net Income (NI)/Sales
        5. NI/Equity or (ROE)
        6. Change in NOI/Change in Total Capital
        7. Change in NI/Change in Equity
    B. Growth Ratios
        1. Sales
        2. NOI
        3. Net Income
        4. Earnings per Share
        5. Dividends per Share
    C. Valuation Measures
        1. Price/Earnings
        2. Market Value of Equity/Book Value of Equity
        3. Dividend Yield + Capital Gain (or Shareholder Returns), 5-Year, 8-Year
II. Operating Efficiency Measures
    A. Asset and Investment Management
        1. Cost of Goods Sold/Inventories
        2. Average Collection Period
        3. Sales/Fixed Assets
        4. Sales/Total Capital
        5. Sales/Total Assets
        6. Change in Total Capital/Total Capital
    B. Cost Management
        1. Gross Profit/Sales (or Gross Margin)
        2. Marketing and Administrative Expense/Sales
        3. Labor Costs/Sales
        4. Employee Growth Rate
        5. Pension Expense per Employee
        6. Research and Development Expense (R&D)/Sales
III. Financial Policy Measures
    A. Leverage Ratios
        1. Total Assets/Book Value of Equity
        2. Interest-Bearing Debt (IBD)/Total Capital
        3. IBD/Total Capital, Market
        4. Earnings before Interest and Taxes (EBIT)/Interest Expense
        5. EBIT + Lease Expense/Fixed Charges
        6. IBD/Funds from Operations
    B. Liquidity Ratios
        1. Current Assets/Current Liabilities (or Current Ratio)
        2. Current Assets − Inventories/Current Liabilities (or Quick Ratio)
        3. (Increase in Retained Earnings + Depreciation)/Investment

With this overview of the three major categories of financial analysis, we next consider the individual ratios. We shall discuss the nature of each ratio indicating the information conveyed and its limitations.

PERFORMANCE MEASURES

The central theme of this book is enhancing the value of the organization. In quantitative terms, this involves estimating a future stream of cash flows and discounting by an appropriate capitalization factor. Traditionally, the analysis of the expected future cash flow streams begins with profitability analysis, the first category of *performance measures*.

Profitability Ratios

The future stream of cash flows is the result of a large number of policies and decisions. We start with historical data about cash flow and profitability but emphasize that these represent only the starting point. Further strategic and operating analysis is required to make meaningful projections for the future.

Net Operating Income to Sales. The ratio of net operating income to sales is widely used by financial practitioners as a key "value driver" influencing the valuation of a firm. As we shall discuss in Chapter 17 on value-based management, the general practice is to analyze cash flows net of depreciation expense. We shall demonstrate that the free cash flow measure used in valuation analysis is the same whether investment is measured on a gross basis and depreciation expense is included in the cash flow measure or on a net basis and the related cash flows exclude depreciation. Net operating income focuses on the results of operations and measures cash flows before deduction of interest expense and income taxes.

$$\text{Net operating income/Sales} = \$700.8/\$4,620.0 = 15.2\%$$

$$\text{Comparable companies} = 10.3\%$$

Although some financial commentators observed during 1989 that Kellogg's profit margins were under pressure in relation to comparable companies, Kellogg has a relatively favorable operating profit performance.

Net Operating Income to Total Assets. This ratio is usually referred to as "the return on total assets." It seeks to measure the effectiveness with which the firm has employed its total resources. Sometimes this ratio is called the return on investment or ROI. This description is particularly applicable in measuring the performance of individual segments or divisions of a company. Management needs to know the operating returns on the resources used by an individual segment.

$$\text{Return on total assets} = \text{Net operating income/Total assets}$$

$$= \$700.8/\$3,390.4 = 20.7\%$$

$$\text{Comparable companies} = 18.0\%$$

Again, we see that by this second measure of profitability Kellogg is strong relative to comparable companies. We should note also that this ROI measure plays a key role in a method of analysis pioneered by the du Pont company. The basic relationship is:

$$\text{ROI} = \text{Profit margin} \times \text{Turnover}$$
$$\text{ROI} = \text{NOI/Total assets} = \text{NOI/Sales} \times \text{Sales/Total assets}$$
$$.2067 = .1517 \times 1.3627.$$

This so-called du Pont method emphasizes that the return on investment is the result of the interaction of the profit margin on sales and the effectiveness with which total assets are utilized in producing sales—the turnover of total assets discussed below.

Net Operating Income to Total Capital. Total assets measure the total economic resources used by the firm. However, the firm finances its total assets in part from sources of financing that do not have an explicit cost, such as accounts payable and accruals for wages and other expenses. We refer to such sources of financing as Non-Interest-Bearing Debt (NIBD). Total assets less non-interest-bearing debt = total capital.

Total capital can also be measured by the sum of shareholders' equity plus interest-bearing debt. A further refinement is to deduct marketable securities (sometimes referred to as short-term investments) from interest-bearing debt so that the resulting net total capital figure provides a measure of required operating assets. Some firms show cash and marketable securities as separate items; others combine the two. The separate figures can be obtained from the 10K report if they are not provided in the firm's annual report. Because of the inconvenience of obtaining the marketable securities figure and because marketable securities may be related to the firm's broader strategies and in this sense is an operating asset, we do not make this further refinement in the measurement of total capital. The measurement of this version of return on investment is:

$$\text{Return on total capital} = \text{Net operating income/(Interest-bearing}$$
$$\text{debt} + \text{Shareholders' equity)}$$
$$= \$700.8/\$2,484.0 = 28.2\%$$
$$\text{Comparable companies} = 30.6\%.$$

On this measure of profitability, Kellogg is slightly below the comparable companies.

Net Income to Sales. This ratio is usually referred to as the profit margin on sales. Like the ratio of net operating income to sales, this ratio can be influenced by the capital intensity of the industry of the firm. Firms in highly capital-intensive industries such as steel, automobiles, and chemicals are likely to have lower sales to asset turnovers. To produce the same return on capital or equity, a higher return on sales is required.

$$\text{Profit margin} = \text{Net income/Sales}$$
$$= \$470.2/\$4,620.0 = 10.2\%$$
$$\text{Comparable companies} = 5.7\%$$

Since the comparable companies by definition are in similar product market areas, Kellogg's profit margin appears very strong.

Return on Equity. The return on equity measures the book return to the owners of the firm. It is a "bottom line ratio" in that sense. The calculation is:

$$\text{Return on equity} = \text{Net income/Shareholders' equity}$$
$$= \$470.2/\$1,634.4 = 28.8\%$$
$$\text{Comparable companies} = 41.3\%.$$

We see that ROE is much lower for Kellogg than for the comparable companies. However, the results for both are very impressive. The return on equity for all manufacturing corporations during 1988 and 1989 was in the range of 15 to 16 percent, so the performance for Kellogg and comparable food companies is quite impressive. The return on equity is sensitive to cyclical changes in the economy as a whole. For example, during the recession of 1982, the return on equity for all manufacturing corporations was 9.2 percent. By the end of the 1980s, this measure of return had risen to the 15 to 16 percent range. Part of this rise in the return on equity is attributable to restructuring activities during the 1980s. Many firms had common stock repurchase programs. The funds for equity share repurchase came from cash invested in marketable securities or from the disposition of assets with low earning power. Thus net income would not be reduced by share repurchases, but the book amount of equity would shrink. As a result, where share repurchase programs were substantial, the return on equity (as well as earnings per share) could be elevated.

Marginal Profitability Rate. The previous five ratios represent average relationships. When assets or measures related to assets are in the denominator, they reflect the traditional accounting practice of measurements at historical costs. Especially in the food industry, relatively old equipment can sometimes be economically reconditioned and be as productive as new machinery would be. But such reconditioned equipment is carried on the balance sheet at costs that are relatively low on a net depreciated basis. This can artificially inflate profitability measures that represent average relationships. Therefore, in the final two profitability ratios, we consider marginal or incremental relationships. The use of incremental changes will mitigate some of the infirmities, but a problem still remains. Both the measure of total capital and the measure of equity have been reduced during the restructuring and share repurchase activities in the 1980s.

$$\text{Marginal profitability rate} = \text{Change in NOI/Change in total capital}$$
$$= \$237.6/\$1,292.1 = 18.4\% \text{ (for 1984–1989)}$$
$$\text{Comparable companies} = 21.6\%$$

We observe that the marginal profitability ratio is substantially lower than the average profitability ratio found earlier. When marginal profitability is lower than average profitability, new investments are earning lower rates of return or the average reflects understated values in the denominator.

Marginal Return to Equity. The same ideas are involved in the measurement of incremental returns to incremental equity.

$$\text{Marginal return to equity} = \text{Change in NI/Change in equity}$$
$$= \$219.7/\$1,147.2 = 19.2\% \text{ (for 1984–1989)}$$
$$\text{Comparable companies} = 15.3\%$$

The marginal return on equity is somewhat higher than the marginal return on total capital for Kellogg. The reverse is true for the comparable companies, but share repurchase programs for some companies resulted in meaningless negative ratios using incremental data.

Overall, we see that Kellogg has profitability ratios that are strong in an absolute sense and in relation to comparable companies in the food industry. We next turn to another set of performance ratios.

Growth Ratios

Growth ratios measure how well the firm is maintaining its economic position in its industry. The reported data are in nominal terms so that growth rates as calculated represent the sum of real growth plus a price level increase factor. For economy of presentation, we shall use nominal growth rates. However, as a part of the further internal analysis by business firms, a separation should be made between real growth and the price level change factor. Growth rate comparisons are made in Table 7.5. We have calculated growth by dividing the last period figure by the first period figure, which gives a compound sum interest factor. From this we calculate growth rates by the endpoints method discussed in Chapter 3 on decisions across time. In general, Kellogg outstripped the comparable companies both in the most recent five-year period as well as in the longer ten-year period. For net operating income, however, the growth rate of Kellogg was somewhat lower than that of the comparable companies during the most recent five-year period but higher during the longer period.

We make comparisons with growth rates for the economy as a whole. The growth rate in gross national product for the 1984–1989 period was 6.8 percent and for the longer 1979–1989 period was 7.6 percent. The growth rate of corporate profits after tax was zero for the 1984–1989 period and 4.2 percent for the 1979–1989 period. Total dividends for the corporate sector grew at a 9.1 percent rate for the 1984–1989 period and at a 9.3 percent rate for the longer 1979–1989 period.

Interestingly, net income growth is slightly lower for Kellogg for both growth periods. However, its earnings per share are higher during the most recent five-year growth

TABLE 7.5   Growth Rate Data

	Five Years 1984–1989		Ten Years 1979–1989	
	Kellogg	Comparable Companies	Kellogg	Comparable Companies
Sales	12.3%	6.1%	9.7%	6.8%
Net operating income	8.6	10.3	9.6	8.5
Net income	13.4	16.2	11.3	12.6
Earnings per share	18.0	14.3	13.8	13.9
Dividends per share	15.1	13.9	10.2	12.9

Source: Company Annual Reports.

period and about the same for the longer period. Dividends per share growth is somewhat higher for Kellogg for the most recent five-year period, but somewhat lower for the longer period.

As shown in the growth rate data, Kellogg exhibits particularly strong growth in sales. The data suggest that Kellogg may have been emphasizing market share more than profitability since its net operating income and net income growth rates are lower than for the comparable companies during the most recent years. However, the performance of both Kellogg and the comparable companies is strong on all of the growth measures.

Valuation Ratios

Valuation ratios are the most comprehensive measures of performance for the firm in that they reflect the combined influence of return and risk ratios.

Price/Earnings Ratios.   The market price per share to earnings per share (also called the price/earnings or P/E ratio) is a widely used measure.

$$\text{P/E Ratio} = \text{Market price per share/Earnings per share}$$
$$= \$69.69/\$3.85 = 18.1 \text{ times}$$
$$\text{Comparable companies} = 15.9 \text{ times}$$

P/E ratios reflect many and sometimes offsetting influences that make their interpretation difficult. The higher the risk, the higher the discount factor and the lower the P/E ratio. The higher the growth rate of the firm, the higher the price/earnings ratio. Some regard high rates of growth as difficult to sustain so that the risk element of high growth rates would tend to pull down the P/E ratio. For 1989, the price/earnings ratio was higher for Kellogg than for the comparable companies.

The P/E ratio of a given firm is often compared to market averages such as the Dow Jones or the Standard and Poor's composites. Financial analysts often seek to establish a consistent relationship measured by a premium or discount for a particular stock in relation to the Dow or the S&P. One would expect Kellogg to sell at a premium over the price/earnings ratio for broader stock market averages, and it does.

Market-to-Book Ratio.   This ratio measures the value that the financial markets attach to the management and organization of the firm as a growing concern.

$$\text{Market-to-book ratio} = \text{Market price per share/Book value of equity per share}$$
$$= \$69.69/\$13.41 = 5.2 \text{ times}$$
$$\text{Comparable companies} = 4.8 \text{ times}$$

The book value of equity reflects the historical costs of brick-and-mortar — the physical assets of the company. A well-run company with strong management and an organization that functions efficiently should have a market value greater than the historical book value of its physical assets. Kellogg sells at a substantial multiple. The market price of Kellogg is over five times its book value per share. The market-to-book ratio of the comparable companies is relatively close.

Tobin's q-Ratio.   The q-ratio is defined as the market value of all securities divided by the replacement costs of assets. The q-ratio differs in two respects from the market-to-book ratio. All securities, not just shareholders' equity, are covered in the numerator. The denominator is not just the book value of equity but the replacement cost of all assets. The q-ratio was developed by Professor James Tobin, who used it in macroeconomic analysis as a predictor of future investment activity. The q-ratio is a valuable concept since it represents the prevailing financial market estimate of the value of the returns per dollar of incremental investment. When the q-ratio is above one, this indicates that investments in assets have earnings that produce values greater than investment outlays. This should stimulate new investment. When the q-ratio is below one, investments in assets are not attractive.

Thus the q-ratio is a more rigorous measure of how effectively management is utilizing the economic resources at its command. In a pathbreaking study, Lindenberg and Ross [1981] showed how the q-ratio could be applied to individual companies. They found that some firms were able to maintain q-ratios greater than one. Economic theory suggests that q-ratios greater than one would attract the flow of new resources and competition until the q-ratio approached one. It is often difficult to determine whether high q-ratios reflect management superiority or the benefits of patents or strong brand positions. Of course, it is management excellence that produces a strong competitive position resulting from patents, superior products, strong brand positions, etc. This is an area for continued research.

The calculation of the q-ratio is not easy. In earlier years, the Financial Accounting Standards Board (FASB) required large firms to report current replacement cost data. However, this is no longer a requirement. At the macroeconomic level the annual *Economic Report of the President* formerly presented q-ratio data, but has not done so for several years.

Returns to Shareholders.   The return to shareholders has become the touchstone of much financial analysis. The theme of enhancing shareholder value is the subject of many books, articles, and is highlighted in the annual reports of many individual companies. The return to shareholders measures what shareholders actually earn over a period of time. This is a widely used measure in making comparisons between the market returns among a wide range of financial instruments.

The return to shareholders is defined as the average of the sums of the dividend yield plus capital gains per year over the measurement period. The return to shareholders for the 1981–1989 period for Kellogg was 30.1 percent. This compares with 24.8 percent for General Mills, with 29.5 percent for Quaker, and with 17.0 percent for Ralston. In relation to the stock market as a whole as measured by the Standard & Poor's 500 Stock Composite Index, the return for the 1981–1989 period was 16.9 percent. Thus returns to shareholders for Kellogg outpaced two of the three comparable companies. In addition, they were substantially higher for Kellogg than for the market as a whole. These superior results reflect continued improvements by Kellogg, General Mills, and Quaker over year-to-year market expectations. On average, over the last decade, Kellogg has continued to make unanticipated improvements that later become reflected in increases in its stock price on a year-to-year basis.

Overall, with respect to valuation ratios, Kellogg and its comparable competitive companies have performed superbly during the most recent decade.

OPERATING EFFICIENCY MEASURES

The first group of ratios analyzes performance. In the case of Kellogg, performance is superior by any and all criteria. If Kellogg's performance had been clearly deficient, the natural reaction would be to find out the source of the problems. But it is equally important to analyze the sources of superior performance as well, in order to maintain checks on the important factors that contribute to success. In this section we deal with operating efficiency measures.

Asset and Investment Management

Traditionally, asset and investment management ratios have been called activity ratios or turnover ratios. Whatever the designation, the idea is to measure how effectively the firm utilizes the investments and the economic resources at its command. Investments are made in order to produce profitable sales. Achieving profitable sales, therefore, involves making sound investments. At the practical level, this involves comparisons between the level of sales and the investment in various asset accounts. The methodology postulates an optimal relationship between sales and the various types of asset investments.

Inventory Turnover.   The inventory turnover is defined as the cost of goods sold divided by inventory.

$$\text{Inventory turnover} = \text{CGS/Inventory}$$
$$= \$2{,}413.8/\$394.0 = 6.1 \text{ times}$$
$$\text{Comparable companies} = 6.4 \text{ times}$$

Kellogg's inventory turnover is slightly below that of the comparable companies but could readily be explained by differences in product mix or other factors not related to management efficiency. Some companies that provide industry composite ratios use sales in the numerator of the ratio. However, since inventories are carried at cost it is more logical to relate them to a cost figure rather than sales.

Also, some analysts use different measures to test for activity, but it can be readily shown that they are equivalent to the turnover measure. For example, using Kellogg's turnover to the nearest round number, we would have a turnover of 6. This is equivalent to 60 days (360/6) of cost of goods sold in inventories or 16.7 percent (1/6) of CGS. So it should be recognized that turnover, number of days sales in, and percentage of sales or of CGS are all equivalent activity measures.

Average Collection Period.   The average collection period is calculated in two steps: (1) annual sales are divided by 365 to determine average daily sales, and (2) daily sales are divided into accounts receivable to find the number of days' sales tied up in receivables. Sales per day = $4,620.0/365 = $12.7.

$$\text{Average collection period} = \text{Receivables/Sales per day}$$
$$= \$355.2/12.7 = 28 \text{ days}$$
$$\text{Comparable companies} = 36 \text{ days}$$

We see that Kellogg has a shorter average collection period than the comparable companies. The difference is not great. The critical test is to compare the average collection period with the terms of sale. For example, if Kellogg's sales terms call for payment within 20 days, the actual average collection period of 28 days would represent only moderate slippage. Since the companies compared have somewhat different product mixes, differences in customary terms of sale could account for the observed difference between Kellogg and the other companies.

The average collection period is a measure of the average period of time between the dates of sales and the dates payments are received. Again, the activity measure of receivables could be expressed as a turnover or as a percentage of sales. The average collection period for Kellogg is 28 days. This represents a turnover of slightly over 13 times during the year. We can obtain this result by dividing sales by receivables: $4,620.0/$355.2 = 13.01. Alternatively, we can divide 365 by 28 to obtain approximately the same result. Also, a turnover of accounts receivable of 13 times per year is equivalent to stating that receivables are 7.69 percent of sales. We can obtain this result by dividing receivables by sales or taking the reciprocal of 13. Other tests of the efficiency of receivables and inventory management are discussed in Chapter 19.

Fixed Asset Turnover. The rate of utilization of fixed assets is critical because investments in plant and equipment are both large and of long duration. A mistake in fixed asset investments may be reversed, but the consequences are likely to be long-lasting.

$$\text{Fixed assets turnover} = \text{Sales/Net fixed assets}$$
$$= \$4,620.0/\$2,406.3 = 1.9 \text{ times}$$
$$\text{Comparable companies} = 4.2 \text{ times}$$

The turnover of net fixed assets is lower for Kellogg than for the comparable companies. This raises some questions. The difference could be due to differences in product mix and the related equipment required. Or if Kellogg's plant and equipment are newer, the ratio would be lower because the denominator is net of the reserve for depreciation, which is smaller for recent purchases and larger for older equipment. Or Kellogg might not be using its fixed assets as efficiently as the comparable companies. But further analysis would be required before reaching a conclusion.

Total Assets Turnover. The total asset turnover reflects the efficiency of management of investments in each of the individual asset items. It is calculated as follows:

$$\text{Total assets turnover} = \text{Sales/Total assets}$$
$$= \$4,620.0/\$3,390.4 = 1.4 \text{ times}$$
$$\text{Comparable companies} = 1.8 \text{ times}$$

Again, Kellogg has a relatively low fixed assets turnover. The total asset turnover is a good summary measure of the efficiency of investments in all categories of assets. It is a key ratio, because as observed above in the du Pont analysis, turnover times profit margin equals ROI or return on total investment.

Total Capital Turnover. The total capital turnover is of interest because total capital represents the portion of total assets that is financed by sources carrying explicit costs. Its calculation:

$$\text{Total capital turnover} = \text{Sales/Total capital}$$
$$= \$4,620.0/\$2,484.0 = 1.9 \text{ times}$$
$$\text{Comparable companies} = 3.0 \text{ times.}$$

Again, this ratio is somewhat low for Kellogg, but further investigation would be required before drawing any conclusions.

Investment Rate. The investment rate is calculated as the percentage by which the total capital in a given year has increased over total capital of the previous year. Investment is defined as the change in total capital between two time periods.

$$\frac{\text{Investment}}{\text{rate (1989)}} = \frac{\text{Total capital (1989)} - \text{Total capital (1988)}}{\text{Total capital (1988)}}$$
$$= \text{Investment/Total capital}$$
$$= \$288.5/\$2,195.5 = 13.1\%$$
$$\text{Comparable companies} = 5.3\%$$

The investment rate for Kellogg for 1989 was more than double that of the comparable companies. This suggests that Kellogg is expanding its investments to produce greater sales. If these investments are wisely made and well-managed, this is a plus for Kellogg. This could also help explain Kellogg's somewhat lower investment turnover ratios.

Cost Management

The two main areas critical for efficient operations are to manage investments well and to control costs effectively. The subject of cost management is relatively neglected in financial writings because business firms do not provide much cost detail in their annual reports. Details on cost are considered important competitive information among firms. From the cost data provided, we make the best inferences we can.

Gross Profit Margin. The gross profit margin is a critical measure. It influences cost policies further down the line. It tells how much can be spent for general and administrative expenses, advertising and marketing, research and development, and still achieve satisfactory bottom-line profitability. Its calculation:

$$\text{Gross margin} = (\text{Sales} - \text{Cost of goods sold})/\text{Sales}$$
$$= \$4,620.0 - \$2,413.8/\$4,620.0 = 47.8\%$$
$$\text{Comparable companies} = 44.7\%.$$

Kellogg's gross margin is above that of the other companies. For comparable product mixes, this would suggest superior manufacturing cost control for Kellogg.

Marketing and Administrative Expense to Sales. Here is an example where many different kinds of costs are combined. The data:

$$\text{Marketing and administrative costs/Sales} = \$1,505.4/\$4,620.0 = 32.6\%$$

$$\text{Comparable companies} = 33.3\%.$$

The ratio for Kellogg is slightly below that for the other companies. At least three major elements of costs are involved in the ratio. General and administrative expense generally runs from 5 to 7 percent of sales. Efficient distribution for the type of food products involved would run 10 to 15 percent of sales. The third category would be advertising and other promotion expenses. These are likely to be relatively high for companies in the food product industries where a high rate of introduction of new products, essential for maintaining a high growth rate of sales, requires high promotion expenses.

Labor Cost Ratio. The ratio of labor cost to sales is important because employee costs can critically affect profitability.

$$\text{Kellogg} = 18.0\%$$

$$\text{Comparable companies}[2] = 20.0\%$$

From the data available, Kellogg appears to be efficient in managing labor costs.

Employment Growth Rate. The percentage change in the number of employees on a year-to-year basis is one measure of growth in operations. Comparing it with the investment rate may provide insights on the substitution of capital for labor or vice versa. Also, after mergers or takeovers, it is of interest to determine whether changes in profitability are produced by reducing employment as measured by this ratio or employee compensation as measured by the previous ratio. The data:

$$\text{Kellogg employment growth rate} = -11.1\%$$

$$\text{Comparable companies} = +4.3\%.$$

We observe that during 1989 Kellogg has reduced employment while other companies in the industry have increased employment. This ratio should be examined over a longer time period. A full evaluation cannot be made without additional information on company strategies, policies, and practices in these areas.

Pension Expense per Employee. This is measured as total pension expense divided by the number of employees. This ratio is of interest to determine company policies in another important aspect of managing a company's labor relationships. The data:

$$\text{Kellogg pension expense per employee} = \$1,372$$

$$\text{Comparable companies} = \$348.$$

It is difficult to interpret these figures without additional information. Pension expense per employee in the comparable firms ranges from a negative $425 for General Mills (net pension credit per employee) to $1,304 for Ralston Purina.

---

[2]Quaker only. Data not available for General Mills and Ralston Purina.

R&D Expenditures. Research and development expenditures may be critical to the future of a company. R&D activity is sometimes related to total assets but more generally to sales. In research intensive industries such as the pharmaceutical industry, R&D expenses to sales will be somewhat over 10 percent for most companies. The food industry is not generally regarded as R&D intensive. The data:

Kellogg R&D expenditures/sales = 0.9%

Comparable companies[3] = 0.7%.

We see that R&D expenditures are about one percent of sales in this industry. There are opportunities for innovation in production methods, distribution methods, developing new product varieties, and determining the nutritional impact of both old and new products.

We have completed our review of the operating efficiency ratios for Kellogg. A question is raised about Kellogg's low turnover of fixed assets. On the cost management side, Kellogg appears to be highly effective. We next turn to the area of financial policy measures.

FINANCIAL POLICY MEASURES

Two major types of financial policy ratios are considered. Leverage ratios measure the degree to which total assets are financed by owners compared with financing provided by creditors. Liquidity ratios measure the ability of the firm to meet its maturing obligations.

Leverage Ratios

Leverage ratios have a number of implications. First, creditors look at equity, or owner-supplied funds, as a cushion or base for the use of debt. If owners provide only a small proportion of total financing, the risks of the enterprise are borne mainly by the creditors. Second, by raising funds through debt the owners gain the benefits of achieving control of the firm with a limited commitment. Third, the use of debt with a fixed interest rate magnifies both the gains and losses to the owners. Fourth, the use of debt with a fixed interest cost and with a specified maturity increases the risks that the firm may not be able to meet its obligations. Dramatic practical illustrations of this point are provided by the difficulties of the Campeau group with suppliers in 1989 and the pressures on Donald Trump when he had problems in meeting interest and maturities beginning in 1990. Decisions about the use of leverage must balance hoped-for higher returns against the increased risk of the consequences firms face when they are unable to meet interest payments or maturing obligations.

In practice, leverage is approached in two ways. One approach examines balance sheet ratios and determines the extent to which borrowed funds have been used to finance the firm. The other approach measures the risks of debt by income statement ratios designed to determine the number of times fixed charges are covered by operating profits. These sets of ratios are complementary, and most analysts examine both.

---

[3]General Mills only. Data not available for Quaker and Ralston Purina.

The Leverage Factor. The ratio of total assets to shareholders' equity is frequently referred to as "the leverage factor," because it measures the extent to which the shareholders' equity investment is magnified by the use of debt in financing total assets. It is one of the key factors in analyzing ROE (return on equity). The following relationship is used:

$$\frac{\text{Net income}}{\text{Sales}} \times \frac{\text{Sales}}{\text{Total assets}} \times \frac{\text{Total assets}}{\text{Equity}} = \frac{\text{Net income}}{\text{Equity}} = \text{ROE}.$$

The difference between total assets and shareholders' equity represents a wide range of debt forms and other liabilities. It includes accounts payable, which represents financing by suppliers. It includes various types of accruals including accrued wages and accrued taxes payable. It is useful to distinguish between interest-bearing debt, such as notes payable to commercial banks carried in the current liabilities section, as well as long-term debt, and forms of financing that do not carry explicit interest costs such as accounts payable. Thus the three major sources of financing total assets are shareholders' equity, interest-bearing debt, and non-interest-bearing debt. These are important distinctions to which we shall refer in the subsequent analysis. The calculation:

$$\text{Leverage factor} = \text{Total assets/Equity}$$
$$= \$3,390.4/\$1,634.4 = 2.07$$
$$\text{Comparable companies} = 4.02.$$

The leverage factor is about 2 for Kellogg and about 4 for the other companies. For Kellogg, this means that slightly more than half of the financing of total assets comes from other sources than the owners of the company. For comparable companies, about three-quarters of the financing comes from sources other than owners' capital. These relations are placed in a broader perspective by a consideration of other measures of leverage.

Interest-Bearing Debt Ratio. Here we use the distinction between non-interest-bearing debt and interest-bearing debt. Total assets less non-interest-bearing debt may be defined as the total capital representing that portion of total assets financed from sources that carry explicit costs. An equivalent definition of total capital is the sum of shareholders' equity plus interest-bearing debt. The data:

$$\text{Interest-bearing debt/Total capital} = \$849.6/\$2,484.0 = 34.2\%$$
$$\text{Comparable companies} = 54.7\%.$$

Thus we see that of the financing that carries explicit financial costs, interest-bearing debt is about one-third for Kellogg and about one-half for the other companies.

Interest-Bearing Debt Ratio (At Market Value). Much research argues that leverage ratios should use market values rather than book values. In addition, articles in the financial press frequently observe that a decline in the market value of a company's equity limits its ability to obtain external debt financing. Ideally, we would measure both debt and equity at their market values. As a practical matter, much debt is obtained directly from financial institutions such as commercial banks and insurance companies with no current market quotations for the value of the debt. However, the market value of equity is readily obtainable for companies that have gone public. Therefore, in calculating the ratio, it is customary to calculate the debt at book values and to calculate equity at market value. We have:

$$\text{Interest-bearing debt/Total capital at market value}$$
$$= \$849.6/\$8,509.1 = 10.0\%$$
$$\text{Comparable companies} = 23.9\%.$$

When equity is valued at market, the debt ratios for Kellogg and similar companies drop substantially. We next turn to income statement measures of leverage.

Interest Coverage Ratio. The interest coverage ratio (also called the "times interest earned" ratio) is determined by dividing earnings before interest and taxes (EBIT) by the interest charges. The ratio measures the extent to which the firm's earnings can decline without inability to meet annual interest costs. Failure to meet such obligations can bring legal action by the creditors, possibly resulting in bankruptcy. Note that the before-tax income figure is used in the numerator. Because income taxes are computed after interest expense is deducted, the ability to pay current interest is not affected by income taxes.

$$\text{Interest coverage} = \text{EBIT/Interest charges}$$
$$= \$763.4/\$48.3 = 15.8 \text{ times}$$
$$\text{Comparable companies} = 5.8 \text{ times}$$

Fixed Charge Coverage Ratio. The fixed charge coverage ratio is similar to the interest coverage ratio, but it is somewhat more inclusive in that it recognizes a firm's long-term obligations under lease contracts. Leasing has become widespread in recent years, making this ratio preferable to the interest coverage ratio for most financial analyses. Fixed charges are defined as interest plus annual long-term lease obligations. The fixed charge coverage ratio is defined as follows:

$$\text{Fixed charge coverage} = \frac{\text{EBIT} + \text{Lease obligations}}{\text{Interest charges} + \text{Lease obligations}}$$
$$= (\$763.4 + \$38.7)/(\$48.3 + \$38.7) = 9.2 \text{ times}$$
$$\text{Comparable companies} = 4.2 \text{ times}.$$

Interest-Bearing Debt/Funds from Operations. With the greater emphasis on the use of the cash flow statement, a relatively new leverage ratio is the ratio of interest-bearing debt to funds from operations from the cash flow statement. This is a measure of how many years would be required to pay off interest-bearing debt from cash provided by operations. The data:

$$\text{Interest-bearing debt/Funds from operations} = \$849.6/\$533.5$$
$$= 1.6 \text{ times}$$
$$\text{Comparable companies} = 2.8 \text{ times}.$$

All coverage ratios have declined in recent years. Standards for industrial companies have dropped from 4–5 to 1.5–3.0; in leveraged buyouts, 1 was sometimes observed initially.

Liquidity Ratios

Current Ratio. The current ratio is computed by dividing current assets by current liabilities. Current assets normally include cash, marketable securities, accounts receivable, and inventories; current liabilities consist of accounts payable, short-term notes payable, current maturities of long-term debt, accrued income taxes, and other accrued expenses (typically wages). The current ratio is the most commonly used measure of short-term solvency, since it indicates the extent to which the claims of short-term creditors are covered by assets that are expected to be converted to cash in a period roughly corresponding to the maturity of the claims.

$$\text{Current ratio} = \text{Current assets/Current liabilities}$$
$$= \$906.1/\$1,037.2 = .87$$
$$\text{Comparable companies} = 1.34$$

A longtime standard was 2 to 1, but it declined during the 1980s.

Quick Ratio. The quick ratio, or acid test, is calculated by deducting inventories from current assets and dividing the remainder by current liabilities. Inventories are typically the least liquid of a firm's current assets and the assets on which losses are most likely to occur in the event of liquidation. Therefore, this measure of the firm's ability to pay off short-term obligations without relying on the sale of inventories is important.

$$\text{Quick ratio or acid test} = \frac{\text{Current assets} - \text{Inventories}}{\text{Current liabilities}}$$
$$= (\$906.1 - \$394.0)/\$1,037.2 = .49$$
$$\text{Comparable companies} = .81$$

The traditional standard was 1 to 1.

Investment Financing. Widely used in the financial press is a measure of the extent to which cash flow, in this case defined as the increase in retained earnings plus depreciation, is available for financing current investment. When this ratio is low, analysts consider some pressure on the vigor of investment programs. The data here are:

$$(\text{Increase in retained earnings} + \text{Depreciation})/\text{Investment}$$
$$= (\$260.3 + \$167.6)/\$288.5 = 148.3\%$$
$$\text{Comparable companies} = 862.8\%.$$

Kellogg has sufficient cash flow to finance its current investments. The comparable companies have cash flow that is a substantial multiple of their current investment requirements. The data suggest that Kellogg has a larger investment program than do the other companies. This is supported by the previous data on the rate of investment at Kellogg versus the comparable companies.

Review of the Financial Ratio Analysis

Clearly Kellogg has achieved excellent performance in both absolute terms and by reference to comparable companies. The only area where questions might be raised is in the ratio of sales to fixed assets, which is somewhat low in relation to comparable companies and has the effect of pulling down the sales-to-total-assets ratio. This could be explained by the higher rate of new investments in plant and equipment by Kellogg. This can be checked by looking at the extent to which gross plant and equipment has been written off. This ratio is 27.1 percent for Kellogg as compared with an average of 35.2 percent for the three other companies. This indicates that Kellogg's assets are newer and have been written off to a lesser degree than for the other companies. The consequence is a lower sales-to-net-fixed-assets turnover for Kellogg, compared with the other companies. This might well be an indication of strength rather than weakness on the part of Kellogg. Its newer assets may reflect modernization and productivity improvements. Such an interpretation would be consistent with Kellogg's outstanding performance in all of the areas of financial ratio analysis covered.

While the ratio analysis for Kellogg deals with a company with outstanding performance, we can also consider what the effects would be if we were dealing with a company that had weaknesses. For example, if assets were managed inefficiently, this could show up in a number of possible areas. If the inventory turnover were low and the average collection period long in relation to terms of sale, such excessive investments would show up in a lower sales-to-total-assets turnover. In addition, it would have a negative impact on profit margins. Excessive inventories might also mean obsolete inventories and a need to dispose of them at reduced prices. A high average collection period could mean that customers were slow in paying their accounts and that at some point bad receivables would have to be written off. The combination of a lower turnover and a lower profit margin would result in low returns on investment. Similarly, if costs are not managed effectively, profit margins will suffer.

In the area of financial policy, if a firm loads up with debt to the point where the interest on its debt obligations becomes excessively high, the firm may report high operating profit but net income after debt servicing that is low or negative. Notable examples are found in the leveraged buy-out of RJR Nabisco and in the Time/Warner merger. Both companies reported negative net income in several quarters immediately following the completion of their restructuring activity. Thus financial ratios can show up a good performance or bad performance. Financial ratios can be used to make clear the sources of either excellent or deficient performance.

FINANCIAL RATIOS OVER TIME

As a further check on financial ratio analysis for a particular year, it is useful to look at the pattern of the financial ratios over time. Such analysis may point to the erosion of a strong position or improvements in a relatively weak situation.

TABLE 7.6   Financial Ratio Comparisons over Time

I. Performance Measures	Kellogg		Comparable Companies	
	1989	1988	1989	1988
A. *Profitability Ratios*				
1. NOI/Sales	15.2%	18.4%	10.3%	11.2%
2. NOI/Total Assets	20.7%	24.2%	18.0%	18.7%
3. NOI/Total Capital	28.2%	36.4%	30.6%	31.0%
4. NI/Sales	10.2%	11.0%	5.7%	6.0%
5. NI/Equity	28.8%	32.4%	41.8%	33.2%
B. *Valuation Measures*				
1. Price/Earnings	18.1 times	15.1 times	15.9 times	8.7 times
2. Market/Book	5.2 times	4.9 times	4.8 times	4.8 times
	Five-Year	**Ten-Year**	**Five-Year**	**Ten-Year**
C. *Growth Measures*	**(1984–1989)**	**(1979–1989)**	**(1984–1989)**	**(1979–1989)**
1. Sales	12.3%	9.7%	6.1%	6.8%
2. Net Operating Income	8.6%	9.6%	10.3%	8.5%
3. Net Income	13.4%	11.3%	16.2%	12.6%
4. Earnings per share	18.0%	13.8%	14.3%	13.9%
5. Dividends per share	15.1%	10.2%	13.9%	12.9%
6. Change in NOI/Change in Total Capital[a]	18.4%	24.6%	21.6%	26.2%
7. Change in NI/Change in Equity[b]	19.2%	31.5%	15.3%	16.6%
8. Shareholder Returns	34.1%	30.1%	23.7%	23.8%

Some Time Patterns

Table 7.6 covers one-year, five-year, and ten-year changes. Table 7.6 serves to summarize the ratios employed as well as to delineate changes over time. The profitability ratios show a somewhat downward trend from a very high level for Kellogg as well as for the comparable companies. The return on equity measure for the comparable companies, however, is the exception in showing strong improvement between 1988 and 1989. A better picture of changes in profitability is provided by consideration of the marginal net operating income profitability rate as well as the marginal return on equity rate. Over the previous ten-year period, these marginal returns were very strong; the marginal return on equity was superior for Kellogg as compared with the other companies. However, in the most recent five-year period, these marginal rates of profitability have declined. This is consistent with the *Value Line* analysis, which indicates pressure on profit margins for Kellogg and its competitors.

TABLE 7.6   *(continued)*

	Kellogg		Comparable Companies	
II. Operating Efficiency Measures	**1989**	**1988**	**1989**	**1988**
A. Asset Management				
1. Cost of Goods Sold/Inventory	6.1 times	6.2 times	6.4 times	5.8 times
2. Average Collection Period (days)	28	34	36	35
3. Sales/Fixed Assets	1.9 times	2.0 times	4.2 times	4.1 times
4. Sales/Total Assets	1.4 times	1.3 times	1.8 times	1.7 times
5. Sales/Total Capital	1.9 times	2.0 times	3.0 times	2.8 times
6. Change in Total Capital/Total Capital	13.1%		5.3%	
B. Cost Management				
1. Gross Profit/Sales	47.8%	48.7%	44.7%	46.0%
2. Marketing and Admin. Expense/ Sales	32.6%	30.4%	33.3%	34.0%
3. Labor Costs/Sales	18.0%		20.0%[c]	
4. Employee Growth Rate	−11.1%	−1.7%	+4.3%	+4.1%
5. Pension Expense per Employee	$1,372	$1,243	$348	$198
6. R&D Expense/Sales	0.9%	1.0%	0.7%[d]	0.8%[d]
III. Financial Policy Measures				
A. Leverage Ratios				
1. Total Assets/Equity	2.07	2.22	4.02	3.40
2. IBD/Total Capital	34.2%	32.4%	54.7%	49.3%
3. IBD/Total Capital, Market	10.0%	9.0%	23.9%	18.0%
4. EBIT/Interest Expense	15.8 times	21.0 times	5.8 times	6.9 times
5. (EBIT + Lease Exp.) Fixed Charges	9.2 times	10.4 times	4.2 times	4.9 times
6. IBD/Funds from Operations	1.6 times	1.5 times	2.8 times	2.5 times
B. Liquidity Ratios				
1. Current Ratio	.87	.90	1.34	1.28
2. Quick Ratio	.49	.59	.81	.79
3. Cash Flow/Investment	148.3%		862.8%	

[a]Quaker and Ralston Purina only. General Mills had a meaningless negative ratio.
[b]Quaker only. Ralston Purina and General Mills both had meaningless negative ratios.
[c]Quaker only. Data not available for General Mills and Ralston Purina.
[d]General Mills only. Data not available for Ralston Purina.

In Table 7.6, the section on growth rates also provides insights on trend analysis. Comparing ten-year growth patterns with those in the most recent five years is a quick way of detecting changes in trends. For Kellogg, we see an improvement in sales growth in the most recent five-year period as compared with the longer ten-year period, but a small decline in the growth of net operating income. Net income, however, improves in the most recent period. For the comparable companies, the growth of sales appears to be declining somewhat, but profitability margins are improving.

Another critical test is in the pattern of shareholder returns over the five-year and eight-year periods shown in Table 7.6. Since an important component of this measure is changes in the market price of the firm's stock, the capital gains measure, there is some subtlety involved. Stock market prices reflect expectations over a future time period. If in a given year all future improvements were correctly anticipated, stock prices would increase in that year but then remain flat because future improvements had already been captured by the stock price data. Therefore continued capital gains reflect, at least in part, unanticipated improvements in underlying profitability. Thus the higher level of shareholder returns for Kellogg in the most recent five-year period is an indication of continued strength in performance. For the comparable companies, shareholder returns during the most recent five-year period were about the same as for measurements over longer periods of time. But as emphasized before, shareholder returns for Kellogg and the other companies were well above the market as a whole for the periods measured.

Without pursuing the data in Table 7.6 in detail, the methodology of analyzing year-to-year changes is illustrated. By all the criteria discussed, we see no indication of deterioration for Kellogg or the other companies. There is a possibility of some pressure on profit margins, but this factor represents only some moderating of continued outstanding improvements rather than any serious management or profitability problems.

Trends — Chart Portrayal

An even more extended time analysis can be performed. We shall illustrate this for selected ratios. Recall that we have three main types of ratios: performance ratios, operating efficiency ratios, and financial policy ratios. We illustrate each type.

Figure 7.1 presents the profitability ratio, which measures net operating income to sales. Kellogg has been clearly superior for some time. Kellogg peaked in 1986, while the other companies peaked in 1988. Kellogg experienced a sharp decline in 1989 but is still far above the others.

In one sense the bottom-line profitability ratio is net income to equity (ROE), shown in Figure 7.2. Kellogg has long had a strong comparative return on equity, earning 25 percent compared to about 15 percent for the other companies. Kellogg peaked at a high over 50 percent in 1984 and subsequently returned to a more sustainable 30 percent range. The other companies improved their ROE to over 40 percent by 1989. Given the competitive nature of the food industry one would predict that the marginal ROE measures of the other companies will return to levels at or below Kellogg's during the next few years.

Among the operating efficiency ratios a summary measurement of asset management is the sales-to-total-assets ratio. Figure 7.3 shows that the other companies have had superior turnover of total assets during the past decade. The higher turnover may reflect differences in the capital intensity of the product activities of Kellogg, which is more specialized in ready-to-eat cereals. Also as indicated earlier, in recent years Kellogg has had a more active investment program, making the ratio of its net assets to gross assets higher.

The third major category of ratios is concerned with financial policies: leverage and liquidity. The most comprehensive leverage measure is the ratio of total assets to equity.

FIGURE 7.1 Net Operating Income to Sales

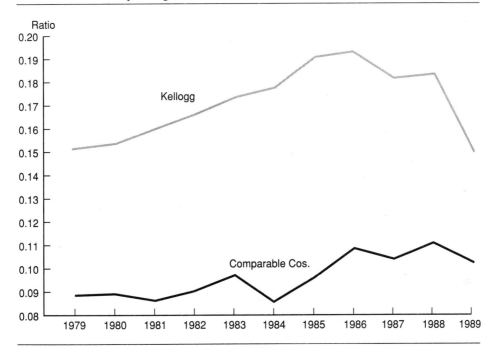

FIGURE 7.2 Return on Equity

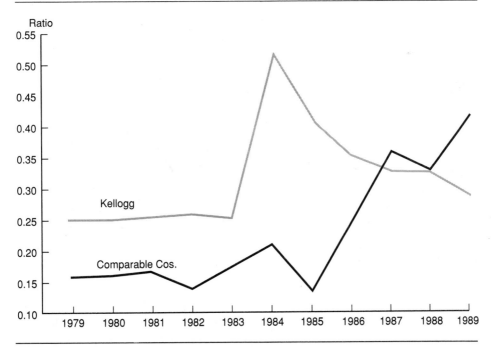

FIGURE 7.3 Sales to Total Assets

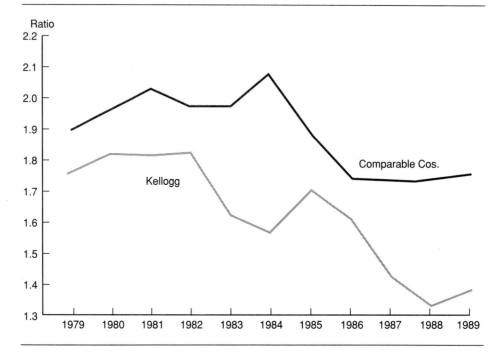

FIGURE 7.4 Total Assets to Equity

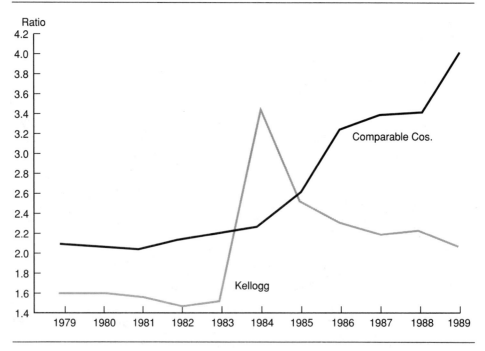

FIGURE 7.5   Current Ratio

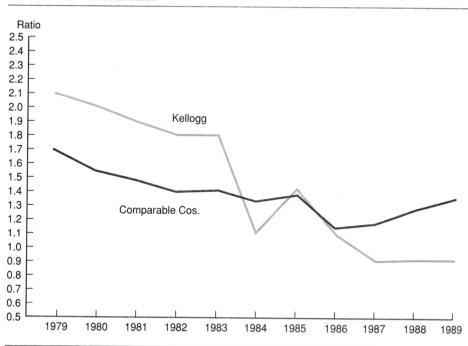

Figure 7.4 shows that the other companies have generally used much more leverage than Kellogg. The leverage ratio of the other companies rose during the second half of the 1980s when equity was measured at book values.

The basic liquidity ratio is the current ratio. A long-term standard has been a ratio of two. Figure 7.5 shows that Kellogg started out at a current ratio above two but its ratio has declined to about one in recent years. The ratios for the other companies started somewhat lower but by 1989 were somewhat higher than Kellogg's. Decreased liquidity appears to have developed along with higher leverage in recent years, particularly for nondurable goods industries such as food.

Trend analysis is highly useful because the ability to analyze patterns visually over time raises many questions about company policies. We reemphasize that financial ratios represent the start of the analysis and usually raise important issues for further study and inquiry.

SOURCES OF COMPARATIVE RATIOS

A wide variety of sources can be used to obtain standards for evaluating the ratios that have been calculated for an individual company. We shall describe many specialized producers of industry data, both private and governmental sources. A problem that may be encountered is that many diverse firms may be included in the industry category. Some compilers group the firms by size when it is helpful. But with the considerable diversification by firms, selected firms may be more comparable than an industry grouping containing firms with highly diverse product-market activities. In this chapter we illustrated the use of selected comparable companies. We shall now describe a number of sources of industry composite financial data that may be used for standards to evaluate and raise questions about the ratios calculated for an individual company.

Dun & Bradstreet

Dun & Bradstreet (D&B) provides ratios calculated for a large number of industries. The data give industry norms (common-size financial statements) and 14 ratios, with the median, lower, and upper quartiles, for over 800 types of business activity based on their financial statements.[4] The compilations include over 1,000,000 companies. More detailed asset and geographical breakdowns of the data are available for five industry segments:

1. Agriculture/Mining/Construction/Transportation/Communication/Utilities
2. Manufacturing
3. Wholesaling
4. Retailing
5. Finance/Real Estate/Services

Data are generally available in the form of directories and diskettes.

Robert Morris Associates

Another group of useful ratios can be found in the annual *Statement Studies*, compiled and published by Robert Morris Associates, the national association of bank loan officers. These are representative averages based on 80,000 financial statements of commercial borrowers. Average balance sheet and income statement data and 17 ratios are calculated for 341 industries. Balance sheet accounts are all expressed as a percent of total assets. Income statement data are expressed as a percent of net sales. Data are presented for four size categories as well as for all of the firms in the industry. Industry trend data are presented for a five-year period. The industry names are related to the Standard Industrial Classification (SIC) codes of the U.S. Bureau of the Census.

Quarterly Financial Report for Manufacturing Corporations

The Bureau of the Census in the U.S. Department of Commerce publishes quarterly financial data on manufacturing companies. Both balance sheet and income statement data are developed from a systematic sample of corporations. The reports are published about

---

[4]The median and quartile ratios can be illustrated by an example. The median ratio of current assets to current debt of manufacturers of airplane parts and accessories in a recent year was 2.30. To obtain this figure, the ratios of current assets to current debt for each of some 41 firms were arranged in a graduated series, with the largest ratio at the top and the smallest at the bottom. The median ratio of 2.30 is the ratio halfway between the top and the bottom. The ratio of 4.40, representing the upper quartile, is one-quarter of the way down from the top (or halfway between the top and the median). The ratio 1.50, representing the lower quartile, is one-quarter of the way up from the bottom (or halfway between the median and the bottom).

six months after the financial data have been made available by the companies. They include an analysis by industry groups and by asset size, and financial statements in ratio form (or common-size analysis) as well. These data are also available on tapes and diskettes.

Trade Associations and Public Accountants

Financial ratios for many industries, compiled by trade associations and public accountants, constitute an important source to be checked by a financial manager seeking comparative data. These averages are usually the best obtainable. In addition to balance sheet data, they provide detailed information on operating expenses, making an informed analysis of the firms' efficiency possible. Credit departments of individual firms also compile financial ratios and averages on their customers in order to judge their ability to meet obligations and on their suppliers in order to evaluate their financial ability to fulfill contracts.

Financial Services

Specialist firms that compile and publish financial data, such as Standard & Poor's and Moody's, develop industry composites. Brokerage firms such as Merrill Lynch, Kidder Peabody, Dean Witter, Paine Webber, etc., periodically publish industry studies with financial data in various forms.

Computer Accessible Data Sources

A number of computer accessible data sources are available. The Standard & Poor's *Compustat* datasets provide a wide range of financial data for almost 2,500 surviving New York and American stock exchange firms, over 4,600 surviving NASDAQ firms, and for almost 5,900 firms for historical segments. The *Disclosure Database* is accessed from a compact disk. It includes financial statements for all companies that file 10-K reports to the Securities and Exchange Commission. Twenty-nine financial ratios are calculated for the most recent three years. The CRSP datasets (from the Center for Research on Security Prices at the University of Chicago) cover NYSE, AMEX, and NASDAQ companies providing daily and monthly data on stock prices, dividends, stock splits, return data, delistings, CUSIP numbers, etc. The data begin with July 2, 1962 running to the most recent periods with an average lag of about one year.

USERS OF FINANCIAL RATIOS

Financial ratios have diverse kinds of users. User interests vary from a very broad set of items to a limited number. Our present coverage has been expanded beyond the traditional textbook patterns and can be summarized as follows:

I. Performance Measures
    A. Profitability Ratios
    B. Growth Ratios
    C. Valuation Measures

II. Operating Efficiency Measures
  A. Asset Management
  B. Cost Management
III. Financial Policy Measures
  A. Leverage Ratios
  B. Liquidity Ratios

Our new and expanded treatment now covers three major categories of ratios with seven sub-groupings, with a total of 36 ratios. This is a large number of ratios, but each has some useful information to convey. As we describe the types of users of financial information, it will be seen that some users will require even more items while others need only a small number of ratios.

Internal Users

For an effective management information system, a large number of ratios may be calculated. Particularly, the number of operating efficiency ratios are likely to be expanded. In the cost management area, published data cover only a small number of aggregated cost items since more detail is regarded as sensitive, competitive information. But for management's internal control purposes, much more detail would be provided on R&D outlays and the elements of the cost of goods sold; marketing expense would be separated from general and administrative expenses.

The credit department of a business firm will generally use a broad range of ratios. However, when a credit department must deal with a large number of customers, such as a food wholesaler selling to many retail outlets, a large number of accounts may be involved. For a first screening, the analysis could be limited to three ratios to help predict whether the prospective buyer of merchandise is a good credit risk.

1. The total assets to shareholders' equity ratio to determine the extent to which the prospective customer's own funds are invested in the business.

2. The current and/or quick ratio to measure the ability of the prospective buyer to meet its maturing obligations.

3. The return on equity compared with the firm's cost of equity capital or some broad norm for the cost of equity capital as a test of the firm's profitability.

Logical relationships can be discerned among these three key ratios. If the leverage factor is high, the owners may have insufficient funds in the business and are likely to use supplier financing, which increases current liabilities and reduces the current ratio. So high leverage ratios are likely to cause low liquidity ratios and the customer is likely to be slow in paying its bills. The account can still be profitable depending upon how slowly payments are made and whether the profitability level of the customer is sufficient to make ultimate payments possible. A high leverage ratio coupled with low liquidity and weak profitability is likely to lead the credit manager to withhold approval of a sale on credit.

Of necessity, the credit manager is more than a calculator and reader of financial ratios. Qualitative factors may override quantitative analysis. For instance, in selling to truckers, oil companies often find that the financial ratios are adverse and that if they based their decisions solely on financial ratios, they would never make sales. Or, to take another example, profits may have been low for a period, but if the customer understands why and can remove the cause of the difficulty, a credit manager may be willing to approve a sale to that customer. This decision is also influenced by the profit margin of the selling firm. If it is making a large profit on sales, it is in a better position to take credit risks than if its own margin is low. Ultimately, the credit manager must judge each customer on character and management ability, and intelligent credit decisions must be based on careful consideration of conditions in the selling firm as well as in the buying firm. A more detailed discussion of credit management is provided in Chapter 19.

Financial Ratios and Security Analysis

Security analysts take a longer-term view. They are or should be interested in return-risk relationships. Their emphasis is on long-term profitability in conjunction with applicable capitalization or discount rates.

Other Stakeholders

Increasingly we recognize that the firm is responsible to a broad list of stakeholders. Customers are concerned that the firm has sufficient strength to maintain the quality of its products. When durable goods are involved, the customer must have confidence that the firm will remain a viable source of replacement parts and sometimes maintenance services as well. Employees are interested in healthy firms that can pay competitive wages including fringe benefits. They want to be assured that pension funds are managed reliably by the firm. Suppliers to the firm seek a good long-term relationship to support long-term investments to produce the products supplied. The government is interested in having the firm be a good economic citizen, meaning that the firm does not engage in price fixing, that it does not adulterate its products, that it does not mislead in advertising, and that it realizes its potential contribution to employment and growth in the economy. Thus the evaluation of the performance of the firm in our present social and political environment realizes a broader range of considerations than historically conveyed by traditional financial ratio analysis.

SOME LIMITATIONS OF RATIO ANALYSIS

Although ratios are exceptionally useful tools, they should be used with judgment. Ratios are constructed from accounting data, and these data are subject to different interpretations and even to manipulation. For example, two firms may use different depreciation methods or inventory valuation methods; depending on the procedures followed, reported profits can be raised or lowered. Similar differences can be encountered in the treatment of research and development expenditures, pension plan costs, mergers, product warranties, and bad-debt reserves. Further, if firms use different fiscal years, and if seasonal factors are important, this can influence the comparative ratios. Thus, if the ratios of two firms are to be compared, it is important to analyze the basic accounting data upon which the ratios were based and to reconcile any major differences.

A financial manager must also be cautious in judging whether a particular ratio is "good" or "bad" and in forming a composite judgment about a firm on the basis of a set of ratios. For example, a high inventory turnover ratio could indicate efficient inventory management, but it could also indicate a serious shortage of inventories and suggest the likelihood of stock-outs. When financial ratio analysis indicates that the patterns of a firm depart from industry norms, a basis for questions and further investigation and analysis is formed. Additional information and discussions may establish sound explanations for the difference between the pattern for the individual firm and industry composite ratios. Or the differences may identify poor management or superior management.

Conversely, conformance to industry composite ratios does not establish with certainty that the firm is performing normally and is managed well. In the short run, many tricks can be used to make a firm look good in relation to industry standards. The analyst must develop firsthand knowledge of the operations and management of the firm to provide a check on the financial ratios. In addition, the analyst must develop a sixth sense — a touch, a smell, a feel — for what is going on in the firm. Sometimes it is this kind of business judgment that uncovers weaknesses in the firm. The analyst should not be anesthetized by financial ratios that appear to conform with normality.

Ratios, then, are extremely useful tools. But as with other analytical methods, they must be used with judgment and caution, not in an unthinking, mechanical manner. Financial ratio analysis is a useful part of an investigation process. But financial ratios alone are not the complete answer to questions about the performance of a firm. Increasingly, it is recognized that the financial ratios of the firm should be related to trends in the strategic and economic factors that will impact the firm over time.

SUMMARY

Ratio analysis starts with the fundamental financial statements of the firm: balance sheets, income statements, and cash flow statements. Ratios are classified into three broad types: performance measures, operating efficiency measures, and financial policy measures. Performance measures include profitability ratios, growth ratios, and valuation measures. Operating efficiency involves asset management and cost management. Financial policy deals with leverage ratios and liquidity ratios.

To be useful, ratios must be related to some standards. One approach is to use the firm's own historical patterns, which involves computing its ratios for a number of years to determine whether it is improving or deteriorating. A second approach is to make comparisons with other firms in the same industry. Sometimes industry composite data supplied from outside sources will be useful. Sometimes it is necessary to select more directly comparable firms as a basis for relating the ratios of a given firm to those of comparable companies.

QUESTIONS

7.1 "A uniform system of accounts, including identical forms for balance sheets and income statements, would be a most reasonable requirement for the SEC to impose on all publicly owned firms." Discuss this statement.

7.2 We have divided financial ratios into seven groups: (1) Profitability, (2) Growth, (3) Valuation, (4) Asset management, (5) Cost management, (6) Leverage ratios, and (7) Liquidity ratios. We could also consider financial analysis as being conducted by four groups of analysts: management, equity investors, long-term creditors, and short-term creditors.
  a. Explain the nature of each type of ratio.
  b. Explain the emphasis of each type of analyst in dealing with the ratios.

7.3 Why can norms with relatively well-defined limits be stated in advance for some financial ratios but not for others?

7.4 How does trend analysis supplement the basic financial ratio calculations and their interpretation?

7.5 Why should the inventory turnover figure be more important to a grocery store than to a shoe repair store?

7.6 How can a firm have a high current ratio and still be unable to pay its bills?

7.7 "The higher the rate of return on investment (ROI), the better the firm's management." Is this statement true for all firms? Explain. If you disagree with the statement, give examples of cases in which it might not be true.

7.8 What factors would you, as a financial manager, want to examine if a firm's rate of return (a) on assets or (b) on net worth was too low?

7.9 Profit margins and turnover rates vary from industry to industry. What industry characteristics account for these variations? Give some contrasting examples to illustrate your answer.

7.10 Which relation would you, as a financial manager, prefer: (a) a profit margin of 10 percent and a capital turnover of 2 or (b) a profit margin of 20 percent and a capital turnover of 1? Can you think of any firm with a relationship similar to (b)?

PROBLEMS

7.1 The Wagner Company has $2,400,000 in current assets and $950,000 in current liabilities. How much can its short-term debt (notes payable) increase without violating a current ratio of 2 to 1? (The funds from the additional notes payable will be used to increase inventory.)

7.2 Complete the balance sheet and sales information (fill in the blanks) for the Goodrich Company using the following financial data:

Debt/net worth: 1.5
Acid test ratio: 0.40

Total asset turnover: 1.5 times
Days' sales outstanding in accounts receivable: 20
Gross profit margin: 25%
Sales to inventory turnover: 5 times

Balance Sheet

Cash	_____	Accounts payable	_____
Accounts receivable	_____	Common stock	$10,000
Inventories	_____	Retained earnings	$20,000
Plant and equipment	_____	Total liabilities and capital	_____
Total assets	_____		
Sales	_____	Cost of goods sold	_____

7.3 The following data were taken from the financial statements of the Wisconsin Furniture Company for the calendar year 19X0. The norms given below are composite industry averages for the wood and upholstered furniture industry based on various sources for industry composite data.

a. Fill in the ratios for the Wisconsin Furniture Company.

b. Indicate by comparison with industry norms the possible errors in management policies reflected in these financial statements.

Wisconsin Furniture Company
Balance Sheet as of December 31, 19X0

Assets		Liabilities	
Cash	$ 19,000	Accounts payable	$ 77,500
Receivables	180,000	Notes payable (@ 9%)	36,000
Inventory	433,000	Other current liabilities	67,000
Total current assets	$632,000	Total current liabilities	$180,500
Net fixed assets	190,500	Long-term debt (@ 10%)	200,000
		Net worth	442,000
Total assets	$822,500	Total claims on assets	$822,500

Wisconsin Furniture Company
Income Statement for Year Ended December 31, 19X0

Sales		$1,315,000
Cost of goods sold		
Material	$415,000	
Labor	360,000	
Heat, light, and power	45,000	
Indirect labor	52,000	
Depreciation	40,000	912,000
Gross profit		$ 403,000
Selling expense	$137,500	
General and administrative expense	195,000	332,500
Net operating profit (EBIT)		$ 70,500
Less interest expense		23,000
Net income before tax		$ 47,500
Less federal income tax (@ 40%)		19,000
Net income		$ 28,500

Wisconsin Furniture Company

Ratio	Ratio	Industry Norm
$\dfrac{\text{Current assets}}{\text{Current liabilities}}$	————	3.1 times
$\dfrac{\text{Debt}}{\text{Total assets}}$	————	45%
Times interest earned	————	5.8 times
$\dfrac{\text{Cost of goods sold}}{\text{Inventory}}$	————	5.2 times
Average collection period	————	46 days
$\dfrac{\text{Sales}}{\text{Total assets}}$	————	2.0 times
$\dfrac{\text{Net income}}{\text{Sales}}$	————	2.8%
$\dfrac{\text{EBIT}(1 - T)}{\text{Total assets}}$	————	8.6%
$\dfrac{\text{Net income}}{\text{Net worth}}$	————	10.2%

7.4 The following data were taken from the financial statements of Wheatland Pharmaceuticals Company, a wholesaler of drugs, drug proprietaries, and sundries, for the calendar year 19X0. The norms given below are the industry averages for wholesale drugs, drug proprietaries, and sundries.

a. Fill in the ratios for Wheatland Pharmaceuticals Company.

b. Indicate by comparison with the industry norms the possible errors in management policies reflected in these financial statements.

Wheatland Pharmaceuticals Company Balance Sheet as of December 31, 19X0 (Thousands of Dollars)

Assets		Liabilities	
Cash	$ 155	Accounts payable	$ 258
Receivables	672	Notes payable (@ 10%)	168
Inventory	483	Other current liabilities	234
Total current assets	$1,310	Total current liabilities	$ 660
Net fixed assets	585	Long-term debt (@ 12%)	513
		Net worth	722
Total assets	$1,895	Total claims on assets	$1,895

Wheatland Pharmaceuticals Company Income Statement for Year Ended December 31, 19X0 (Thousands of Dollars)

Sales	$3,244
Cost of goods sold	2,845
Gross profit	$ 399
Operating expenses	230
EBIT	$ 169
Interest expense	78
Net income before tax	$ 91
Taxes (@ 40%)	36
Net income	$ 55

Wheatland Pharmaceuticals Company

Ratio	Ratio	Industry Norm
$\dfrac{\text{Current assets}}{\text{Current liabilities}}$	_____	2.0 times
$\dfrac{\text{Debt}}{\text{Total assets}}$	_____	60%
Times interest earned	_____	3.8 times
$\dfrac{\text{Cost of goods sold}}{\text{Inventory}}$	_____	5.9 times
Average collection period	_____	35 days
$\dfrac{\text{Sales}}{\text{Total assets}}$	_____	2.9 times
$\dfrac{\text{Net income}}{\text{Sales}}$	_____	1.2%
$\dfrac{\text{EBIT}(1 - T)}{\text{Total assets}}$	_____	7.4%
$\dfrac{\text{Net income}}{\text{Net worth}}$	_____	8.3%

7.5 Richard Rutledge, a retired schoolteacher, holds a large number of shares of stock in the Bangor Corporation. The dividend payments from this stock make up a significant portion of Mr. Rutledge's income, so he was concerned when Bangor dropped its 19X2 dividend to $1.25 per share from the $1.75 per share it had paid for the previous two years.

Mr. Rutledge gathered the information below for analysis to determine whether the financial condition of Bangor was indeed deteriorating.

Bangor Corporation Balance Sheets as of December 31

	19X0	19X1	19X2
Cash	$ 76,250	$ 72,000	$ 40,000
Accounts receivable	401,600	439,000	672,000
Inventory	493,000	794,000	1,270,000
Total current assets	$ 970,850	$1,305,000	$1,982,000
Land and building, net	126,150	138,000	125,000
Machinery, net	169,000	182,000	153,000
Other fixed assets, net	74,600	91,000	82,000
Total assets	$1,340,600	$1,716,000	$2,342,000
Accounts and notes payable	$ 171,100	$ 368,800	$ 679,240
Accruals	78,500	170,000	335,000
Total current liabilities	$ 249,600	$ 538,800	$1,014,240
Long-term debt	304,250	304,290	408,600
Common stock	575,000	575,000	575,000
Retained earnings	211,750	297,910	344,160
Total liabilities and equity	$1,340,600	$1,716,000	$2,342,000

Bangor Corporation Yearly Income Statements for the Year Ending December 31

	19X0	19X1	19X2
Sales	$4,135,000	$4,290,000	$4,450,000
Cost of goods sold	3,308,000	3,550,000	3,560,000
Gross operating profit	$ 827,000	$ 740,000	$ 890,000
Gen. admin. & selling expense	318,000	236,320	256,000
Other operating expenses	127,000	159,000	191,000
EBIT	$ 382,000	$ 344,680	$ 443,000
Interest expense	64,000	134,000	318,000
Net income before taxes	$ 318,000	$ 210,680	$ 125,000
Taxes (40%)	127,000	84,270	50,000
Net income	$ 191,000	$ 126,410	$ 75,000
Number of shares outstanding	23,000	23,000	23,000
Per share data			
EPS	$8.30	$5.50	$3.26
Cash dividend per share	$1.75	$1.75	$1.25
Market price (average)	48 7/8	25 1/2	13 1/4

	Industry Financial Ratios (19X2)[a]
1. Quick ratio	1.0
2. Current ratio	2.7
3. Inventory turnover	7 times
4. Average collection period	32 days
5. Fixed asset turnover	13.0 times
6. Total asset turnover	2.6 times
7. EBIT$(1 - T)$ to total assets	14%
8. Net income to net worth	18%
9. Equity ratio	50%
10. Profit margin on sales	3.5%
11. P/E ratio	6 times

[a] Industry average ratios have been roughly constant for the past three years and are based on year-end balance sheet figures.

a. Calculate the key financial ratios for Bangor Corporation, graph them, and analyze the trends in the firm's ratios in relation to the industry averages.

b. What strengths and weaknesses are revealed by the ratio analysis?

7.6 You are presented with balance sheets, income statements, and cash flow statements for the years 1988 and 1989 for Quaker Oats and Ralston Purina. Using the seven categories with their 36 financial ratios, make a comparison between the two companies. A brief summary of the product characteristics of the firms is first provided.

Quaker Oats is a diversified food processor operating in three business segments. U.S. and Canadian Grocery Products, which accounted for 63 percent of sales (57 percent of operating profit) in 1989, produces ready-to-eat and hot cereals, grain-based snacks, mixes, syrups, frozen breakfast products; pet food; beverages, rice and pasta products, and institutional and food service products. International Grocery Products, 22 percent (21 percent), produces food and pet food products in Europe, Latin America, and the Pacific. Fisher-Price (discontinued), 15 percent (22 percent), produces infant and pre-school toys, playsets, riding toys, educational toys, audio-visual products, and juvenile furnishings.

Ralston Purina is the world's largest producer of dry dog foods and dry and soft-moist cat foods. The Company, through Continental Baking, is the largest wholesale baker of fresh bakery products in the United States. RAL is the world's largest manufacturer of dry cell battery products. Other consumer products include cereals, cookies, crackers, and snack foods. The Company is also a major producer of isolated soy protein and, outside the United States, of feeds for livestock and poultry. Trademarks include Purina, Ralston, The Checkerboard logo, Chow, Chex, Energizer, Eveready, Wonder, and Hostess. At September 30, 1989, sales were derived: Human and Pet Foods, 62 percent; Agricultural Products, 14 percent; and Other Consumer Products, 24 percent. Dividend payments have increased 18 consecutive years. (Source: *Moody's Handbook of Common Stock*.) The financial data that follow are generally in millions of dollars.

Quaker Oats Income Statement

	1989	1988
Net sales	$5,724.2	$5,329.8
Cost of goods sold	3,188.7	2,906.7
Gross profit	$2,535.5	$2,423.1
Selling & G&A expense	1,860.7	1,783.5
EBDIT	$ 674.8	$ 639.6
Depreciation	135.5	121.9
Net operating income	$ 539.3	$ 517.7
Other income (expense)	(134.7)	(41.2)
EBIT	$ 404.6	$ 476.5
Interest expense	75.9	62.9
Earnings before tax	$ 328.7	$ 413.6
Taxes	125.7	157.9
Net income	$ 203.0	$ 255.7

Quaker Oats Balance Sheet

	1989		1988	
Cash & equivalents		$ 21.0		$ 55.6
Marketable secs.		2.7		35.6
Accts. receivable		872.1		826.0
Inventories		589.4		539.8
Other current assets		113.0		33.3
Total current assets		$1,598.2		$1,490.3
Other investments		26.4		20.7
Prop., plant, & equip.	$1,725.2		$1,628.6	
Accum. depreciation	633.3		600.2	
Net fixed assets		1,091.9		1,028.4
Intangibles, net		505.4		435.2
TOTAL ASSETS**		$3,221.9		$2,974.6
Short-term debt		$ 104.0		$ 312.7
Current portion long-term debt		30.0		29.2
Accounts payable		363.2		295.4
Accruals		397.2		407.4
Income taxes payable		8.0		28.1
Total current liabilities		$ 902.4		$1,072.8
Long-term debt		766.8		299.1
Other liabilities		89.5		101.0
Deferred income taxes		326.1		250.6
Preferred stock		100.0		—
Deferred compensation		(100.0)		—
Shareholders' equity*		1,137.1		1,251.1
TOTAL LIABILITIES & SHAREHOLDERS' EQUITY**		$3,221.9		$2,974.6

*1989: 79.3 million shares; 1988: 79.8 million shares.
**Totals may not add because of rounding.
Source: Annual Report.

Quaker Oats Statement of Cash Flows

	1989	1988
Cash Flows from Operations:		
Net income	$ 203.0	$ 255.7
Adjustments to reconcile net income to net cash flows (used in) provided by operations:		
Depreciation and amortization	135.5	121.9
Deferred income taxes and other items	79.9	(20.5)
Provision for restructuring charges	124.3	29.9
Changes in operating assets and liabilities (used in) provided by continuing operations:		
(Increase) in receivables	(84.8)	(89.3)
(Increase) in inventories	(76.6)	(60.5)
(Increase) decrease in other current assets	(64.1)	21.4
Increase in trade accounts payable	98.7	31.6
(Decrease) in other current liabilities	(37.1)	(11.9)
Other — net	(8.8)	23.3
NET CASH FLOWS PROVIDED FROM OPERATIONS	$ 370.0	$ 301.6
Cash Flows from Investing Activities:		
Additions to property, plant, and equipment	$(271.8)	$(207.2)
Cost of acquisitions, excluding working capital	(112.9)	—
(Increase) in long-term receivables & investments	(5.7)	(5.9)
Proceeds (net assets) of businesses to be sold	—	191.6
Disposals of property, plant, & equipment	27.5	18.0
CASH (USED IN) INVESTING ACTIVITIES	$(362.9)	$ (3.5)
Cash Flows from Financing Activities:		
Cash dividends	$ (95.2)	$ (79.9)
Change in deferred compensation	(248.4)	1.5
Net increase (decrease) in short-term debt	42.1	(226.8)
Proceeds from long-term debt	251.2	25.3
Reduction of long-term debt	(30.1)	(257.4)
Issuance of common treasury stock	10.1	33.4
Purchase of common stock	(68.5)	(53.6)
Issuance of preferred stock	100.0	—
NET CASH (USED) BY FINANCING ACTIVITIES	$ (38.8)	$(557.5)
Effect of exchange rate changes on cash equivalents	$ (2.9)	$ 3.5
Net (Decrease) in Cash and Cash Equivalents	(34.6)	(255.9)
Cash and Cash Equivalents — Beginning of Year	55.6	311.5
Cash and Cash Equivalents — End of Year	$ 21.0	$ 55.6

Source: Annual Report.

Ralston Purina Income Statement

	1989	1988
Net sales	$6,658.3	$5,875.9
Cost of goods sold	3,653.2	3,114.7
Gross profit	$3,005.1	$2,761.2
Selling & G&A expense	1,990.7	1,740.5
EBDIT	$1,014.4	$1,020.7
Depreciation	223.1	214.6
Net operating income	$ 791.3	$ 806.1
Other income, net	2.1	18.2
EBIT	$ 793.4	$ 824.3
Interest expense	217.7	218.5
Earnings before tax	$ 575.7	$ 605.8
Taxes	224.5	242.4
Net income	$ 351.2	$ 363.4
Extraordinary items, net	71.3	24.4
Preferred stock dividend	(13.7)	—
Net income to common	$ 408.8	$ 387.8

Ralston Purina Balance Sheet

	1989		1988
Cash & equivalents		$ 28.6	$ 23.8
Marketable secs.		352.0	337.1
Accts. receivable		636.3	526.9
Inventories		677.8	559.9
Other current assets		126.3	246.8
Total current assets		$1,821.0	$1,694.5
Other investments		795.1	638.0
Prop., plant, & equip.	$2,718.3		$2,531.7
Accum. depreciation	952.7		819.8
Net fixed assets		1,765.6	1,711.9
TOTAL ASSETS**		$4,381.7	$4,044.4
Notes payable		$ 142.0	$ 150.2
Current maturity long-term debt		225.6	60.3
Accts. payable & accruals		824.9	753.1
Dividends payable		33.8	25.6
Income taxes payable		89.5	92.6
Total current liabilities		$1,315.8	$1,081.8
Long-term debt		1,790.7	1,486.5
Other liabilities		242.0	243.6
Deferred income taxes		172.9	142.6
Preferred stock		500.0	—
Unearned ESOP compensation		(471.4)	—
Shareholders' equity*		831.7	1,089.9
TOTAL LIABILITIES & SHAREHOLDERS' EQUITY**		$4,381.7	$4,044.4

*1989: 61.6 million shares; 1988: 68.2 million shares.
**Totals may not add because of rounding.
Source: Annual Report.

Ralston Purina Statement of Cash Flows

	1989	1988
Cash Flows from Operations:		
Earnings from continuing operations	$ 351.2	$ 363.4
Adjustments to reconcile net earnings to net cash flows provided by continuing operations:		
Depreciation and amortization	223.1	214.6
Deferred income taxes	18.4	32.7
Provision for restructuring	31.4	—
Changes in operating assets and liabilities used in continuing operations:		
(Increase) in receivables	(60.5)	(57.3)
(Increase) in inventories	(86.2)	(64.1)
(Increase) in other current assets	(36.7)	(11.0)
Increase in accts. payable & accruals	16.9	17.3
(Decrease) or increase in other current liabs.	(34.4)	35.5
Other — net	22.8	22.5
NET CASH FLOWS FROM CONTINUING OPERATIONS	$ 446.0	$ 553.6
Earnings from discontinued operations	$ 71.3	$ 24.4
Adjustments to reconcile earnings to net cash flows provided by discontinued operations		
Gain on sale of discontinued operations	(70.2)	—
Depreciation	.5	7.7
Deferred income taxes	—	(4.7)
Changes in operating assets and liabilities used in discontinued operations	12.9	(24.5)
NET CASH FLOWS FROM DISCONTINUED OPERATIONS	$ 14.5	$ 2.9
NET CASH FLOWS FROM OPERATIONS	$ 460.5	$ 556.5
Cash Flows from Investing Activities:		
Proceeds from sale of discontinued operations	$ 260.0	
Acquisition of battery products business	(124.0)	
Property additions	(221.6)	$(224.4)
Property disposals	16.3	36.6
Other, net	(99.6)	(17.6)
NET CASH USED BY INVESTING ACTIVITIES	$(168.9)	$(205.4)
Cash Flows from Financing Activities:		
Proceeds from sale of long-term debt	$ 39.6	$ 149.4
Principal payments on long-term debt	(78.5)	(216.7)
Net increase in notes payable	4.4	86.1
Proceeds from sale of preferred stock	500.0	—
Proceeds from sale of common stock	—	8.6
Treasury stock purchases	(578.1)	(178.7)
Dividends paid	(114.8)	(99.2)
NET CASH (USED) BY FINANCING ACTIVITIES	$(227.4)	$(250.5)
Effect of exchange rate changes on cash	$ (44.5)	$ (11.1)
Net Increase in Cash and Cash Equivalents	19.7	89.5
Cash and Cash Equivalents — Beginning of Year	360.9	271.4
Cash and Cash Equivalents — End of Year	$ 380.6	$ 360.9

	Quaker		Ralston Purina	
	1989	**1988**	**1989**	**1988**
Number of employees	31,700	31,300	56,219	56,734
Pension costs	$ 5.2	$ 3.3	$ 73.3	$ 53.6
R&D expense	$ 61.2	$ 54.6	$ 67.5	$ 65.5
Lease expense	$ 46.9	$ 44.2	$ 56.0	$ 58.2
Retained earnings	$1,106.2	$998.4	$2,919.7	$2,612.9

Data for 1989	Quaker	Ralston Purina
Net income	$ 79.7	$ 128.1
Net operating income	$175.9	$ 317.4
Interest-bearing debt	$250.2	$ 536.5
Shareholders' equity	$563.6	$1,038.5
Total capital	$813.8	$1,575.0

Data for Trend Analysis

	Sales		NOI		Net Income	
	Quaker	**Ralston**	**Quaker**	**Ralston**	**Quaker**	**Ralston**
1989	$5,724.2	$6,658.3	$539.3	$791.3	$203.0	$408.8
1988	5,329.8	5,875.9	517.7	806.1	255.7	387.8
1987	4,420.6	5,868.0	436.8	698.7	185.7	523.1
1986	3,670.7	5,514.6	355.2	657.9	174.2	388.7
1985	3,520.1	5,863.9	342.7	594.2	156.6	256.4
1984	3,344.1	4,980.1	313.9	512.7	138.7	242.7

	EPS		Dividends per Share	
	Quaker	**Ralston**	**Quaker**	**Ralston**
1989	$2.56	$6.44	$1.25	$1.65
1988	3.20	5.63	1.05	1.50
1987	2.36	7.23	.85	1.24
1986	2.18	3.43	.73	1.10
1985	1.88	3.15	.64	1.00
1984	1.68	2.68	.57	.92

	Average Share Price		Dividend Yield	
	Quaker	**Ralston**	**Quaker**	**Ralston**
1989	$59.25	$44.48	2.1%	1.8%
1988	50.00	76.06	2.1	2.0
1987	44.69	75.81	1.9	1.6
1986	36.13	61.25	2.0	1.8
1985	24.00	42.19	2.7	2.4
1984	16.38	30.56	3.5	3.0
1983	13.13	23.56	3.9	3.6
1982	10.06	14.38	4.6	5.4
1981	8.44	12.31	4.9	5.8
1980	7.50	11.31	4.8	5.7

	Quaker	Ralston Purina
Labor costs as a percent of sales	20%	NA

Sources: Standard and Poor's; Annual Report; Compustat.

7.7   *(Use the computer diskette, File name: 07GRATIO, Financial Ratio Analysis.)*

   a.   Based on the balance sheet and income statement in Screen 3, test yourself on the calculation of a firm's financial ratios.

   Compare the firm's ratios with the industry average ratios in Screen 6. View this comparison graphically.

   b.   Suppose poor management leads to inventory build-up and obsolescence resulting in lower sales. Increase inventory to $2,500; finance the increase by raising notes payable; reduce sales to $5,500.

   Which ratios are affected? Do any show apparent improvement?

   c.   Management decides to loosen its credit standards. Sales increase by $1,000 and accounts receivable rise to $2,000. The increase is financed by increasing notes payable.

   Which ratios are affected?

   d.   Suppose that a build-up of fixed assets is financed with a combination of short-term and long-term debt. Sales are initially unchanged by the increase in net fixed assets to $1,600, but cost of goods sold rises to $5,000. Notes payable increase by $300, and the remainder of financing is by long-term debt.

   Which ratios are affected?

   e.   Make whatever changes you like. (The number of data inputs necessitates a new method of making changes. Press the "Esc" button to leave the Menu mode; use the arrows to the right of the keyboard to move the cursor to the input you wish to change. After making the change, hold down the "Alt" key and press "S" to return to the list of screens.)

   NOTE: The balance sheet must balance. Also, consider the logical repercussions of any changes. Finally, comparison to the industry average ratios in Screen 6 will no longer be meaningful.

SELECTED REFERENCES

Altman, Edward I., "Financial Ratios, Discriminant Analysis, and the Prediction of Corporate Bankruptcy," *Journal of Finance*, 23 (September 1968), pp. 589–609.

———; Haldeman, Robert G.; and Narayanan, P., "ZETA Analysis: A New Model to Identify Bankruptcy Risk of Corporations," *Journal of Banking and Finance*, 1 (June 1977), pp. 29–54.

Barnes, Paul, "Methodological Implications of Non-Normally Distributed Financial Ratios: A Reply," *Journal of Business Finance & Accounting*, 10 (Winter 1983), pp. 691–693.

———, "Methodological Implications of Non-Normally Distributed Financial Ratios," *Journal of Business Finance & Accounting*, 9 (Spring 1982), pp. 51–62.

Beaver, William H., "Financial Ratios as Predictors of Failure," in *Empirical Research in Accounting: Selected Studies in Journal of Accounting Research*, (1966), pp. 71–111.

Branch, Ben, "The Impact of Operating Decisions on ROI Dynamics," *Financial Management*, 7 (Winter 1978), pp. 54–60.

Chen, Kung H., and Shimerda, Thomas A., "An Empirical Analysis of Useful Financial Ratios," *Financial Management*, 10 (Spring 1981), pp. 51–60.

Gombola, Michael J., and Ketz, J. Edward, "Financial Ratio Patterns in Retail and Manufacturing Organizations," *Financial Management*, 12 (Summer 1983), pp. 45–56.

Horrigan, James O., "Methodological Implications of Non-Normally Distributed Financial

Ratios: A Comment," *Journal of Business Finance & Accounting,* 10 (Winter 1983), pp. 683–689.

———, "A Short History of Financial Ratio Analysis," *Accounting Review,* 43 (April 1968), pp. 284–294.

Johnson, W. Bruce, "The Cross-sectional Stability of Financial Ratio Patterns," *Journal of Financial and Quantitative Analysis,* 14 (December 1979), pp. 1035–1048.

Lindenberg, E. B., and Ross, S. A., "Tobin's q-Ratio and Industrial Organization," *Journal of Business,* (January 1981), pp. 1–33.

Weston, J. Fred; Chung, Kwang S.; and Hoag, Susan E., *Mergers, Restructuring, and Corporate Control,* Englewood Cliffs, N.J.: Prentice Hall, 1990.

APPENDIX A TO CHAPTER 7

Effects of Changing Price Levels

Immediately after World War II, with the removal of price controls that had held prices to arbitrary levels, there was a burst of inflation. Thereafter, prices increased at a rate of 2 to 3 percent per year until the escalation of hostilities in Southeast Asia in 1966, when inflation again erupted in the United States. In 1971, the United States departed from the convertibility of the dollar into gold, and the major nations adopted floating exchange rates in place of nominally fixed exchange rates. Double-digit inflation (as measured by the wholesale price index or consumer price index) has been a reality or a threat in the United States for more than two decades.

INFLATION AND THE MEASUREMENT OF PROFITABILITY

In an economy experiencing a high rate of price increases, the measurement of profitability becomes complicated. The times at which assets are purchased have a great impact on accounting profitability measures and on taxation. For example, Firm A purchased its assets in Year 1, when their cost was $20 million, while Firm B purchased virtually identical assets five years later at a cost of $40 million. Let us assume that the assets will have an average 20-year life, that both firms use straight line depreciation, that the income before taxes and depreciation for both firms is $5 million per year over the life of the assets, and that their tax rate is 40 percent. Let us compare the financial profiles of the two companies:

	Firm A	Firm B
Income before taxes and depreciation	$5,000,000	$5,000,000
Less depreciation expense	−1,000,000	−2,000,000
Income before taxes	$4,000,000	$3,000,000
Taxes (@ 40%)	1,600,000	1,200,000
Net income after taxes	$2,400,000	$1,800,000
Average return on investment	24%	9%

Since the cost of the assets will be depreciated down to zero over their 20-year lives, their average value is half the original cost. The net income after taxes is assumed to be constant for each year so that the average annual returns are 24 percent for Firm A and 9 percent for Firm B. But does Firm A really have a return almost three times greater than Firm B's? The replacement value of Firm A's assets is $40 million, on which the current depreciation expense would be $2 million per year, not $1 million. Is it correct for an investor to project Firm A's earning power into the future at 20 percent, or should the higher replacement cost of Firm A's assets that are being used up be taken into account? Should the tax-deductible depreciation expense for Firm A be $2 million per year rather than $1 million?

There are no easy answers to these questions, which arise because of the changing values of assets. Some feel that Firm A is gaining windfall profits because it is using assets that it was able to purchase at lower than current costs. It could also be argued that Firm A is paying excessive taxes because the real depreciation expense should be doubled.

INFLATION AND INVENTORY VALUATION METHODS

The divergence between economic and accounting measures of profitability results from the valuation of both fixed assets and inventories. During periods of inflation, the method of inventory valuation for income statements and balance sheets has a major impact on profitability measurement.

By comparing FIFO (first-in-first-out) and LIFO (last-in-first-out) inventory costing and valuation methods, Table 7A.1 illustrates the difficulty of obtaining a meaningful economic measure of profitability during a period of unstable prices. During such a period, Firms C and D each have two batches of inventory. The first batch of 100 units

TABLE 7A.1   Effects of FIFO and LIFO Inventory Costing and Valuation

Firm C (FIFO)			Firm D (LIFO)		
Income statement			**Income statement**		
Sales (100 at $5)		$ 500	Sales (100 at $5)		$500
Inventories used	$100		Inventories used	$150	
Other costs	300		Other costs	300	
Total costs		400	Total costs		450
Net income		$ 100	Net income		$ 50
Balance sheet			**Balance sheet**		
Inventories on hand		$ 150	Inventories on hand		$100
Other assets		850	Other assets		850
Total assets		$1,000	Total assets		$950
Return on assets		10%	Return on assets		5.3%

Note: Inventories for both companies: Batch 1 is 100 units at $1.00 per unit, for a total of $100; Batch 2 is 100 units at $1.50 per unit, for a total of $150.

was acquired at a cost of $1.00 per unit; the second was acquired later at $1.50 per unit. Firm C uses the FIFO method, and Firm D uses the LIFO method. The income statement for each firm shows that it sold 100 units at $5.00 apiece. Since Firm C uses the FIFO method, it has figured the cost of goods sold (inventories used) as $100 (the cost of Batch 1). Since Firm D uses the LIFO method, it has figured the cost of goods sold as $150 (the cost of Batch 2). As a consequence, Firm C reports a net income of $100 and Firm D a net income of only $50.

However, the effects are reversed on the balance sheet, where Firm C carries inventories at $150 and Firm D at $100. On this basis, Firm C reports total assets of $1,000 and Firm D $950. The return on assets is thus 10 percent for Firm C and 5.3 percent for Firm D.

During a period of rising price levels, the use of LIFO results in an expense item on the income statement that is closer to the current replacement cost of items used from inventories. However, using LIFO also means that the balance sheet amount of inventory investment is carried at historical costs rather than current costs. Thus, although LIFO comes closer to a correct measure of *expenses* for the income statement, it results in an understatement of *investment* on the balance sheet. Conversely, if FIFO is used, the expense item on the income statement is understated and the balance sheet valuation of inventories is closer to current costs. The consequences are similar to those for depreciation based on historical acquisition costs versus current replacement costs.

Thus, in a period of inflation, distortions will result from the use of the historical cost postulate. Assets are recorded at cost, but revenue and other expense flows are in dollars of different purchasing power. The amortization of fixed costs does not reflect the current cost of these assets. Furthermore, net income during periods when assets are held does not reflect the effects of management's decision to hold the assets rather than sell them. Assets are not stated on the balance sheet at their current values, so the firm's financial position cannot be accurately evaluated. When assets are sold, gains or losses are reported during that period even though these results reflect decisions in prior periods to hold the assets.

PROPOSALS FOR ACCOUNTING POLICIES TO ADJUST FOR INFLATION

As a consequence of a continued high rate of inflation, proposals have been made to modify accounting procedures to recognize that the traditional postulate of a stable measuring unit is no longer valid. In December 1974, the Financial Accounting Standards Board issued a proposed statement entitled "Financial Reporting in Units of General Purchasing Power." On March 23, 1976, the Securities and Exchange Commission issued Accounting Series Release No. 190. SEC Release 190 requires disclosure of replacement costs for inventory items and depreciable plant from registrants with $100 million or more (at historical cost) of gross plant assets and inventories constituting 10 percent or more of total assets.

In September 1979, the Financial Accounting Standards Board (FASB) issued Statement No. 33, *Financial Reporting and Changing Prices*. A related publication, *Illustra-*

tions of Financial Reporting and Changing Prices, was issued in December 1979. FASB 33 requires major companies to disclose the effects of both general inflation (purchasing power) and specific price changes (current costs) as supplementary information in their published annual reports. FASB No. 33 applies to public enterprises having either (1) inventories and property, plant, and equipment (before deducting accumulated depreciation) amounting to more than $125 million or (2) total assets amounting to more than $1 billion (after deducting accumulated depreciation). Statement No. 33 is effective for fiscal years ended on or after December 22, 1979.[1]

Financial statements and financial ratio analysis are used to understand the past performance of a business firm as well as to lay a foundation for future projections. Traditional accounting methods assumed that the general price level was relatively stable. In addition, traditional accounting assumed that no major structural changes were taking place that caused the relative values of individual assets to change greatly. These assumptions were severely violated in the 1970s. It is, therefore, particularly important that methods be developed to make the appropriate adjustments in accounting data if they are to be used effectively in financial decision making.

---

[1] In its Accounting Series Release No. 271, issued shortly after the publication of FASB No. 33, the Securities and Exchange Commission ruled that companies giving supplemental current-cost information in accordance with FASB No. 33 need not provide the SEC with replacement-cost information.

SELECTED REFERENCES

Davidson, S., and Weil, R. L., "Replacement Cost Disclosure," *Financial Analysts Journal,* 32 (March-April 1976), pp. 57–66.

———, "Inflation Accounting and 1974 Earnings," *Financial Analysts Journal,* 31 (September-October 1975), pp. 42–54.

———, "Predicting Inflation-Adjusted Results," *Financial Analysts Journal,* 31 (January-February 1975), pp. 27–31.

Dhavale, Dileep G., and Wilson, Hoyt G., "Breakeven Analysis with Inflationary Cost and Prices," *Engineering Economist,* 25 (Winter 1980), pp. 107–122.

Financial Accounting Standards Board, *Illustrations of Financial Reporting and Changing Prices: Statement of Financial Accounting Standards No. 33,* Stamford, Conn.: Financial Accounting Standards Board, December 1979.

———, *Statement of Financial Accounting Standards No. 33: Financial Reporting and Changing Prices,* Stamford, Conn.: Financial Accounting Standards Board, September 1979.

———, *Summary Statement of Financial Accounting Standards No. 33: Financial Reporting and Changing Prices,* Stamford, Conn.: Financial Accounting Standards Board, September 1979.

Hong, Hai, "Inflationary Tax Effects on the Assets of Business Corporations," *Financial Management,* 6 (Fall 1977), pp. 51–59.

Weston, J. Fred, and Goudzwaard, Maurice B., "Financial Policies in an Inflationary Environment," in *The Treasurer's Handbook,* edited by J. Fred Weston and Maurice B. Goudzwaard, Homewood, Ill.: Dow Jones-Irwin, 1976, pp. 20–42.

APPENDIX B TO CHAPTER 7

Financial Ratios in Discriminant Analysis

Financial ratios give an indication of the financial strength of a company. The limitations of ratio analysis arise from the fact that the methodology is basically *univariate;* that is, each ratio is examined in isolation. The combined effects of several ratios are based solely on the judgment of the financial analyst. Therefore, to overcome these shortcomings of ratio analysis, it is necessary to combine different ratios into a meaningful predictive model. Two statistical techniques, namely, regression analysis and discriminant analysis, have been used for this purpose. *Regression analysis* uses past data to predict future values of a dependent variable, while *discriminant analysis* results in an index that allows classification of an observation into one of several *a priori* groupings.

CLASSIFICATION OF OBSERVATIONS BY DISCRIMINANT ANALYSIS

The general problem of classification arises when an analyst has certain characteristics of an observation and wishes to classify that observation into one of several predetermined categories on the basis of these characteristics. For example, a financial analyst has on hand various financial ratios of a business enterprise and wishes to use these ratios to classify it as either a bankrupt firm or a nonbankrupt firm. Discriminant analysis is one statistical technique that allows such classification.

Basically, discriminant analysis consists of three steps:

1. Establish mutually exclusive group classifications. Each group is distinguished by a probability distribution of the characteristics.

2. Collect data for observations in the groups.

3. Derive linear combinations of these characteristics which ''best'' discriminate between the groups. (By ''best,'' we mean the ones that minimize the probability of misclassification.)

Altman's Applications of Discriminant Analysis

Altman [1968] used discriminant analysis to establish a model for predicting bankruptcy of firms. His sample was composed of 66 manufacturing firms, half of which went bankrupt. From their financial statements one period prior to bankruptcy, Altman obtained 22 financial ratios, of which 5 were found to contribute most to the prediction model. The discriminant function Z was found to be

$$Z = .012X_1 + .014X_2 + .033X_3 + .006X_4 + .999X_5, \qquad \text{(7B.1)}$$

where

$$X_1 = \text{Working capital/Total assets (in \%)}$$
$$X_2 = \text{Retained earnings/Total assets (in \%)}$$
$$X_3 = \text{EBIT/Total assets (in \%)}$$
$$X_4 = \text{Market value of equity/Book value of debt (in \%)}$$
$$X_5 = \text{Sales/Total assets (times).}$$

Applications to Groups of Firms

We can illustrate how this discriminant function can be used by applying it to the group means reported by Altman for his groups of bankrupt and nonbankrupt firms.

	Group Means[a]	
	Bankrupt	**Nonbankrupt**
X_1	−6.1%	41.4%
X_2	−62.6%	35.5%
X_3	−31.8%	15.4%
X_4	40.1%	247.7%
X_5	1.5 times	1.9 times

[a]E. I. Altman, *Corporate Bankruptcy in America* (Lexington, Mass.: Heath-Lexington Books, 1971), p. 65.

The resulting Z values are as follows:

	X_1	X_2	X_3	X_4	X_5	Z
$Z_{br} =$	−.0732 −	.8764 −	1.0494 +	.2406 +	1.4985 =	−0.2599.
$Z_{nbr} =$	+.4968 +	.4970 +	.5082 +	1.4862 +	1.8981 =	+4.8863.

We observe that the group means for bankrupt firms produced a Z value of -0.2599, while the group means for nonbankrupt firms produced a Z value of 4.8863. To establish a guideline for classifying firms, a cutoff value for Z is chosen to be 2.675, the midpoint of the range of values of Z that results in minimal misclassifications. Thus, a firm with a Z score of greater (less) than 2.675 is classified as a nonbankrupt (bankrupt) firm. The largest contributor to group separation of the discriminant function was found to be the profitability ratio X_3, followed by X_5, X_4, X_2, and X_1, in that order. The model correctly classifies 95 percent of the total sample, as indicated by the following matrix:

	Predicted Group Membership	
Actual Group Membership	**Bankrupt**	**Nonbankrupt**
Bankrupt	31	2
Nonbankrupt	1	32

By applying the above discriminant function to data obtained two to five years prior to bankruptcy, it was found that the model correctly classified 72 percent of the initial sample two years prior to failure. A trend analysis shows that all five observed ratios X_1, . . . ,X_5 deteriorated as bankruptcy approached and that the most serious change in the majority of these ratios occurred between the third and second years prior to failure.

Application to an Individual Firm

The Altman model can also be applied to individual companies. For example, in Table 7B.1, the income statement and balance sheet for Chrysler Corporation are presented for the year ending December 31, 1979. These abbreviated financial statements provide the data needed to utilize the discriminant Z function presented in Equation 7B.1.

Using the data on Chrysler, we can make calculations of the five key financial ratios as presented in Table 7B.2. The data required for each ratio can be taken from the information in Table 7B.1. With the X values calculated in Table 7B.2, we can utilize Equation 7B.1 to calculate the Z value for Chrysler as of the end of 1979. This is done in Equation 7B.2.

$$Z = .012(-1.67) + .014(7.46) + .033(-13.33) + .006(11.74) + .999(1.8) \quad \textbf{(7B.2)}$$
$$= -.020 + .104 - .440 + .070 + 1.798$$
$$= 1.512.$$

The resulting Z value is 1.512. Recall that the critical Z value that appeared to discriminate between bankrupt and nonbankrupt firms was 2.675. Chrysler's Z value of 1.512 is below the critical value and places it in the category of firms likely to go bankrupt. However, Chrysler's situation was not as bad as the group of bankrupt firms whose Z value was $-.26$. The intermediate result for Chrysler suggests that it was indeed in

---

TABLE 7B.1   Chrysler Corporation Financial Statements

A. Chrysler Corporation Income Statement for Year Ended December 31, 1979 (in millions)

Revenues	$12,004
Costs (except depreciation and interest)	12,710
Depreciation	181
Interest expense, net	215
Income taxes (credit)	5
Net income	($1,097)

B. Chrysler Corporation Balance Sheet as of December 31, 1979

Current assets	$3,121	Current liabilities	$3,232	
Other assets	3,532	Long-term debt	1,597	
		Total debt		$4,829
		Preferred stock		219
		Common stock[a]	417	
		(66.7 million shares)		
		Paid-in capital	692	
		Retained earnings	496	
		Shareholders' equity		$1,605
Total assets	$6,653	Total claims		$6,653

[a] Average price per share in 1979 was approximately $8.50.

TABLE 7B.2   Use of Chrysler Data in the Z Equation

$$X_1 = \frac{\text{Current assets less Current liabilities}}{\text{Total assets}} = \frac{3,121 - 3,232}{6,653} = -1.67\%.$$

$$X_2 = \frac{\text{Retained earnings}}{\text{Total assets}} = \frac{496}{6,653} = 7.46\%.$$

$$X_3 = \frac{\text{Earnings before interest and taxes}}{\text{Total assets}} = \frac{(887)}{6,653} = -13.33\%.$$

$$X_4 = \frac{\text{Market value of equity}}{\text{Book value of debt}} = \frac{66.7 \times 8.50}{4,829} = \frac{567}{4,829} = 11.74\%.$$

$$X_5 = \frac{\text{Sales}}{\text{Total assets}} = \frac{12,004}{6,653} = 1.8 \text{ times}$$

difficulty but that even on a purely mechanical basis the loan guarantee might rescue Chrysler. Obviously, fundamental analysis of Chrysler's place in the dynamically changing automobile industry was required for a final decision. However, it is interesting to note that the discriminant analysis of Chrysler's position was consistent with the judgment that Chrysler was having problems but had some possibility of rescue in one form or another.

SELECTED REFERENCES

Altman, Edward I., "Examining Moyer's Re-examination of Forecasting Financial Failure," *Financial Management*, 7 (Winter 1978), pp. 76–79.

————, "Financial Ratios, Discriminant Analysis and the Prediction of Corporate Bankruptcy," *Journal of Finance*, 23 (September 1968), pp. 589–609.

————, and Eisenbeis, Robert A., "Financial Applications of Discriminant Analysis: A Clarification," *Journal of Financial and Quantitative Analysis*, 13 (March 1978), pp. 185–195.

Altman, Edward I.; Haldeman, Robert G.; and Narayanan, P., "ZETA Analysis: A New Model to Identify Bankruptcy Risk," *Journal of Banking and Finance*, 1 (June 1977), pp. 29–54.

Eisenbeis, Robert A., "Pitfalls in the Application of Discriminant Analysis in Business, Finance, and Economics," *Journal of Finance*, 32 (June 1977), pp. 875–900.

————, and Avery, Robert B., *Discriminant Analysis and Classification Procedures: Theory and Applications*, Lexington, Mass.: D. C. Heath, 1972.

Joy, O. Maurice, and Tollefson, John O., "On the Financial Applications of Discriminant Analysis," *Journal of Financial and Quantitative Analysis*, 10 (December 1975), pp. 723–739.

Moyer, R. Charles, "Reply to 'Examining Moyer's Re-examination of Forecasting Failure,'" *Financial Management*, 7 (Winter 1978), pp. 80–81.

————, "Forecasting Financial Failure: A Re-examination," *Financial Management*, 6 (Spring 1977), pp. 11–17.

Tollefson, John O., and Joy, O. Maurice, "Some Clarifying Comments on Discriminant Analysis," *Journal of Financial and Quantitative Analysis*, 13 (March 1978), pp. 197–200.

CHAPTER 8

Financial Planning and Control

It is not enough for a firm to perform well in the current quarter of the year. The firm must always be looking ahead. Hence it must always engage in long-range planning as well as operate efficiently in the present. This is especially true as markets become increasingly international in scope and the economies of the world increasingly interlinked. As a consequence, more variables affect the national economy and the industries within it. The resulting increased turbulence in the economic and political environments makes it necessary for business firms to engage in forward planning.

STRATEGY AND FINANCIAL MANAGEMENT

Because the functions performed by financial managers inherently involve looking ahead, finance is intertwined with strategic long-range planning. Alfred P. Sloan recognized these relationships when he became the chief executive of General Motors during a financial crisis aggravated by the recession of 1921. External financing was not feasible. As a last resort, General Motors obtained a cash infusion from the du Pont Corporation by selling du Pont 23 percent of the common stock of General Motors. Donaldson Brown, who had been the vice president of finance at du Pont, was moved to General Motors as the top finance person to watch over du Pont's large investment. Donaldson Brown brought with him the du Pont system of financial planning and control that provided for both financial planning and a close monitoring of performance.

Alfred Sloan describes in his book, *My Years With General Motors* [1963], how the institution of the du Pont planning and control system provided a framework within which the top management of General Motors could work out a strategy for improving its market position. At that point in time, Ford had almost 60 percent of the U.S. automobile market, while General Motors had only 17 percent. The joining of strategy and finance was an important innovation by Alfred Sloan that helped General Motors become the number one automobile producer in the world. Only in recent years has the close relation between strategy and finance been rediscovered and broadly implemented across industries and companies.

The Nature of Strategy

What is strategy? Many different theories and approaches to strategy are found in the literature.[1] Some equate strategy to long-range planning. Others draw distinctions. However defined, strategy is planning for the future of the enterprise. Although the emphasis of strategy is on the long view, to be implemented properly strategy also takes into account shorter-term decisions and actions. Strategy is not static. Individual strategies, plans, or policies may be utilized in a set of formal procedures. Strategy is a way of thinking requiring diverse inputs. In these continuing interactive processes, financial management is key.

The nature of strategies can be illustrated by some examples. Should a firm seek to produce products in all segments of the market? Or should it seek out a particular niche? For example, should an automobile producer emphasize low-cost basic transportation like the subcompacts, or the high end of the market alone like the Jaguar, or across-the-board transportation like GM? Should a firm start in a niche area, as the Japanese auto producers did, and then broaden into the other segments of the market?

Another good industry to consider is computers. IBM, of course, has covered a broad spectrum, but has left plenty of niches for hundreds of other companies, which together have eroded IBM's market share. How should a firm like IBM adjust to the increased computing power of the personal computers? A further illustration is represented by the strategic questions facing the regional telephone operating companies that AT&T was required to spin off. Some have stuck closely to the telephone business. Other "baby bells" have sought to diversify widely. These are illustrations of broad strategic considerations. Many other examples are found in the literature.

Approaches to Strategy

While diverse approaches to strategic planning are observed, the critical activities involved in strategic planning processes are encompassed by Table 8.1. Whether these represent formal or informal procedures, they are important areas to be covered. The nature and implementation of these procedures are described at length in the literature on strategy.[2]

Many alternative approaches to strategy formulation are found in the literature and practice of strategic planning as shown in Table 8.2.

---

[1]For a survey on the nature of strategy and its implementation, see J. Fred Weston, "Strategy and Business Economics," *Business Economics,* April 1989, pp. 5–12.

[2]See references in Weston [1989].

TABLE 8.1   Essential Elements in Strategic Planning Processes

---

1. Assessment of changes in the environments.
2. Evaluation of company capabilities and limitations.
3. Assessment of expectations of stakeholders (shareholders, workers, consumers, etc.).
4. Analysis of company, competitors, industry, domestic economy, and international economies.
5. Formulation of the missions, goals, and policies for the master strategy.
6. Development of sensitivity to critical external environmental changes.
7. Formulation of internal organization performance measurements.
8. Formulation of long-range strategy programs.
9. Formulation of mid-range programs and short-run plans.
10. Organization, funding, and other methods to implement all of the above.
11. Information flow and feedback system for continued repetition of above and for adjustments and changes at each stage.
12. Review and evaluation of above processes.

In addition to a profusion of methodologies, many different analytical frameworks can be used in strategic planning. Table 8.3 lists these frameworks and gives a brief description of the nature of each.

Leading practitioners in strategy consulting and implementation have emphasized particular methodologies and alternative analytical frameworks. In addition, considerable

---

TABLE 8.2   Alternative Approaches to Strategy

---

1. SWOT or WOTS UP—inventory and analysis of organizational strengths, weaknesses, environmental opportunities, and threats
2. Environmental Scanning—continuous analysis of all relevant environments
3. Gap Analysis—assessment of goals compared to forecasts or projections
4. Competitive Analysis—assessment of customers, suppliers, new entrants, products, and product substitutability
5. Top-Down or/and Bottom-Up—company forecasts compared to aggregation of segments
6. Computer Models—opportunity for detail and complexity
7. Intuition—insights of brilliant managers
8. Synergy—look for complementarities
9. Entrepreneurship—creative leadership
10. Delphi Technique—iterated opinion reactions
11. Logical Incrementalism—well-supported moves from current bases
12. Muddling Through—incremental changes selected from a small number of policy alternatives
13. Discontinuities—crafting strategy from recognition of trend shifts
14. Brainstorming—free-form repeated exchange of ideas
15. Game Theory—logical assessments of competitor actions and reactions
16. Game Playing—role assignment and simulation of alternative scenarios
17. Comparative Histories—learning from the experiences of others
18. Adaptive Processes—periodic reassessment of environmental opportunities and organization capability adjustments required

---

TABLE 8.3   Alternative Analytical Frameworks

1. Product Life Cycles—assess changing opportunities and threats in introduction, growth, maturity, and decline stages
2. Learning Curve—costs decline with cumulative volume experience resulting in first mover competitive advantages
3. Competitive Analysis—industry structure, rivals' reactions, supplier and customer relations, product positioning
4. Cost Leadership—low cost advantages
5. Product Differentiation—develop product configurations that achieve customer preference
6. Value Chain Analysis—control cost outlays to add product characteristics valued by customers
7. Niche Opportunities—specialize to needs or interests of customer groups
8. Product Breadth—carryover of organizational capabilities
9. Correlations with Profitability—statistical studies of factors associated with high profitability measures
10. Market Share—high market share associated with competitive superiority
11. Product Quality—customer allegiance and price differentials for higher quality
12. Technological Leadership—keep at frontiers of knowledge
13. Relatedness Matrix—unfamiliar markets and products involve greatest risk
14. Focus Matrix—narrow versus broad product families
15. Growth/Share Matrix—aim for high market share in high growth markets
16. Attractiveness Matrix—aim to be strong in attractive industries
17. Global Matrix—aim for competitive strength in attractive countries

---

use is made of checklist and checklist-like diagrams. The leading books on strategy contain a checklist or diagram about every two to three pages.

With a greater use of computers in strategic planning, more and more items are covered and the different schools of strategy have adopted more and more elements in common. Particularly in recent years, expert systems and other decision support systems have been emerging. Expert systems represent a disciplined approach to strategic planning in which computer packages provide rules to guide implementation by reference to numerous checklists provided. Finance has increasingly related to this expert systems approach.[3]

Financial Planning and Control Processes

Financial planning and control processes are closely tied to strategic planning. The nature of these relations is sketched in Figure 8.1, which fills in some specifics for the general framework given in Table 8.1. In Figure 8.1, we begin with the enterprise statement of missions, goals, or objectives. What is the basic character and scope of a particular organization? In the framework of missions and goals, business strategies may be formulated. Key decisions involve the choice of products and markets. These decisions result in a product mix strategy. This, in turn, provides a basis for long-range sales forecasts from

---

[3]For example, *Financial Management*, the official publication of the Financial Management Association, has carried a number of articles on this subject and is planning a special issue in the future [Cf. *Financial Management*, Autumn 1988].

FIGURE 8.1   Strategy and Financial Planning

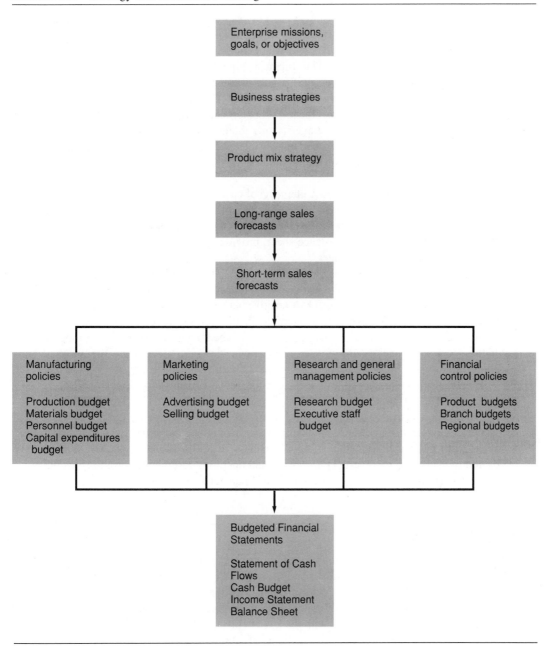

which shorter-term projections can be derived. Sales forecasts are the basis for modeling all of the other activities of the firm.

At this point, financial management has key responsibilities to perform, particularly in the areas of financial planning and control. Financial planning and control involve the use of projections based on standards and the development of a feedback and adjustment process to improve performance. This financial planning and control process involves forecasts and the use of several types of budgets. Budget systems are developed for every significant area of the firm's activities, as shown by Figure 8.1.

The production budget analyzes the use of materials, parts, labor, and facilities. Each of its major elements is likely to have its own budget as well: a materials budget, a personnel budget, and a facilities budget. To achieve sales of the products produced requires the use of a marketing budget. A budget is also developed to cover general office and executive requirements.

The results of projecting all these elements of cost are reflected in the budgeted (also called "pro forma" or "projected") income statement. Anticipated sales give rise to consideration of the various types of investments needed to produce the products. These investments, plus the beginning balance sheet, provide the necessary data for developing the assets side of the balance sheet.

Assets must be financed, but a cash flow analysis is needed. The cash budget indicates the combined effects of the budgeted operations on the firm's cash flows. The Statement of Cash Flows is also useful. A positive net cash flow indicates that the firm has sufficient financing. However, if an increase in the volume of operations leads to a negative cash flow, additional financing is required. The longer the lead time in arranging for the required financing, the greater is the opportunity for developing the required documentation and for working out arrangements with financing sources.

Financial planning and control seek to improve profitability, avoid cash squeezes, and improve the performance of individual divisions of a company. These responsibilities involve the topics covered in this chapter. Also, the literature of finance has developed a number of models that are useful inputs into strategic planning activities. In the remainder of this chapter, finance models that are particularly useful in strategic planning will be covered in the following order: (1) breakeven and operating leverage analysis, (2) overall financial planning models, and (3) forecasting financial statements.

BREAKEVEN ANALYSIS

Breakeven analysis is a basic financial planning and control model. The relationships between the size of investment outlays and the required volume to achieve profitability are referred to as breakeven analysis or profit planning. Breakeven analysis is a device for determining the point at which sales will just cover costs. If all of a firm's costs were variable — those that vary directly with the level of production — the subject of breakeven volume would not come up. But since the level of total costs can be greatly influenced by the size of the fixed investments the firm makes, the resulting fixed costs will put the firm in a loss position unless a sufficient volume of sales is achieved. Costs that fall into each of these categories are outlined in Table 8.4.

FIGURE 8.2   Breakeven Chart

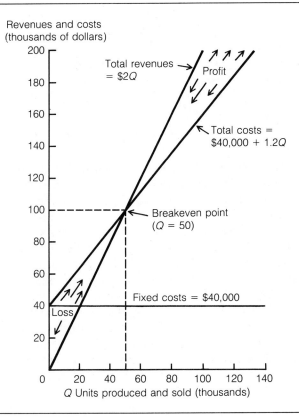

TABLE 8.4   Fixed and Variable Costs

Fixed Costs*	Direct or Variable Costs
Depreciation on plant and equipment	Factory labor
Rentals	Materials
Salaries of research staff	Sales commissions
Salaries of executive staff	
General office expenses	

*Some of these costs (for example, salaries and office expenses) can be varied to some degree; however, firms are reluctant to reduce these expenditures in response to temporary fluctuations in sales. Such costs are often called *semivariable* costs.

TABLE 8.5   Contribution Income Statement at Various Quantities of Units Sold

Units sold (Q)	20,000	40,000	50,000	80,000	100,000	200,000
Sales revenues (TR)	$40,000	$80,000	$100,000	$160,000	$200,000	$400,000
Total variable expenses (V)	24,000	48,000	60,000	96,000	120,000	240,000
Contribution margin (C)	$16,000	$32,000	$ 40,000	$ 64,000	$ 80,000	$160,000
Fixed operating expenses (F)	40,000	40,000	40,000	40,000	40,000	40,000
Net operating income (X)	($24,000)	($ 8,000)	—	$ 24,000	$ 40,000	$120,000

Note: $C = cQ$ and $X = cQ - F = C - F$

The nature of breakeven analysis is depicted in Figure 8.2, the basic breakeven chart. The chart is presented on a unit basis, with units produced shown on the horizontal axis and income and costs measured on the vertical axis. Fixed costs of $40,000 are represented by a horizontal line; they are the same (fixed) regardless of the number of units produced. Variable costs are assumed to be $1.20 a unit. Units are assumed to be sold at $2.00 each, so the total revenue is pictured as a straight line, which increases with production. The slope (or rate of ascent) of the total revenue line is steeper than that of the total cost line. This must be true, because the firm is gaining $2.00 of revenue for every $1.20 paid out for labor and materials — the variable costs. Until the breakeven point (found at the intersection of the total income and total cost lines), the firm suffers losses. After that point, it begins to make profits. Figure 8.2 indicates a breakeven point at a sales and cost level of $100,000 and a production level of 50,000 units.

Calculations of the breakeven point can also be carried out algebraically. From the data given, the firm's total revenue or sales function, TR, is

$$TR = \$2Q,$$

where Q is the number of units of production per period. The total cost function is

$$TC = \$40,000 + \$1.20Q.$$

At the breakeven quantity, Q^*, total revenues and total costs are equal. So equating the sales and total cost functions,

$$\$2Q = \$40,000 + \$1.20Q$$
$$Q^* = 50,000.$$

The relationships are clarified further by use of a contribution income statement for various levels of units sold, as shown by Table 8.5. From Table 8.5, we can readily observe that the breakeven quantity is 50,000 units sold. The breakeven level of sales is $100,000. To develop these relationships algebraically, we define them as follows:

$$TR^* = \text{breakeven revenues} = PQ^*$$
$$Q^* = \text{the breakeven quantity of units sold}$$
$$P = \text{selling price per unit}$$
$$F = \text{fixed costs}$$

v = variable cost per unit

V = total variable costs = vQ

c = contribution margin per unit = $(P - v)$

C = total contribution margin = $cQ = (P - v)Q$

CR = contribution ratio = $\left(1 - \dfrac{vQ}{PQ}\right) = \left(1 - \dfrac{v}{P}\right).$

We can then readily develop the breakeven quantity and the breakeven dollar volume of sales by beginning with the relationship that total revenues or sales equal total costs at breakeven. We then have the following:

Breakeven quantity = Q^*.

$$PQ^* = vQ^* + F$$

$$PQ^* - vQ^* = F$$

$$Q^* = \frac{F}{P - v}$$

$$= \frac{F}{c}. \quad \textbf{(8.1a)}$$

Breakeven revenues = TR^*.

$$TR^* = F + V$$

$$= F + \frac{V \times TR^*}{TR^*}$$

$$= PQ$$

$$TR^* - \frac{V}{PQ}TR^* = F$$

$$TR^* = \frac{F}{1 - \dfrac{V}{PQ}}$$

$$= \frac{F}{CR}. \quad \textbf{(8.1b)}$$

We can illustrate the calculation of both Q^* and TR^* from the data of our numerical example.

$$Q^* = \frac{F}{c}$$

$$= \frac{\$40,000}{\$.80}$$

$$= 50,000 \text{ units.}$$

$$TR^* = \frac{F}{CR}$$

$$\frac{V}{PQ} = .6 \text{ at all quantities sold;}$$

therefore,

$$CR = \left(1 - \frac{V}{PQ}\right) = .4.$$

Hence,

$$TR^* = \frac{\$40,000}{.4} = \$100,000.$$

Thus, the breakeven quantity or breakeven sales volume can readily be calculated by use of the total fixed costs and a contribution margin relationship.

Limitations of Breakeven Analysis

Breakeven analysis is useful in studying the relations among volume, prices, and costs; it is thus helpful in pricing, cost control, and decisions about expansion programs. It has limitations, however, as a guide to managerial actions.

Linear breakeven analysis is especially weak in what it implies about the sales possibilities for the firm. Any linear breakeven chart is based on a constant sales price. Therefore, in order to study profit possibilities under different prices, a whole series of charts is necessary—one for each price.

Breakeven analysis may also be deficient with regard to costs. If sales increase to levels at which the existing plant and equipment are worked to capacity, additional workers are hired and overtime pay increases. All this causes variable costs to rise sharply. If additional equipment and plant are required, fixed costs are also increased. Finally, the products sold by the firm may change in quality and quantity. Such changes in product mix influence the level and slope of the cost function. Breakeven analysis is useful as a first step in developing the basic data required for pricing and for financial decisions. But more detailed analysis is required before final judgments can be made.

Nonlinear Breakeven Analysis

Some of the deficiencies in traditional breakeven analysis are avoided by recognizing that the relationships are likely to be nonlinear. For example, it is reasonable to think that increased sales can be obtained only by successively reducing prices. Similarly, empirical studies suggest that average variable cost per unit falls over some range of output and then begins to rise. These assumptions are illustrated in Figure 8.3, which reflects the usual assumptions of economists about the shapes of the curves that depict total revenues and total costs.

Because of the role of fixed costs, there is an initial region where losses are incurred when sales are relatively low. This is followed by an area in which there is a positive profit. Subsequently, an upper breakeven point is reached beyond which losses are again incurred. Figure 8.3 illustrates that output in the profit region at which maximum profit is achieved. This is shown graphically as the point at which the slope of the total revenue curve is equal to the slope of the total cost curve. In economic terms, the slopes of these two curves are respectively marginal revenue and marginal cost. Hence, maximum profit is achieved when, in economic terms, marginal revenue equals marginal cost. Figure 8.3 illustrates that at that output, the amount by which total revenue exceeds total cost is the largest. Thus, traditional economic principles represent a form of breakeven analysis. Alternatively, we may say that breakeven analysis can be made more useful by putting it in the framework of less restrictive assumptions about the shapes of the total revenue and total cost functions.

Applications of Breakeven Analysis

Used appropriately, breakeven analysis can shed light on a number of important business decisions. In general, breakeven analysis can be used by the firm in three separate but related ways. In new-product decisions, breakeven analysis helps determine how large

FIGURE 8.3 Nonlinear Breakeven Chart

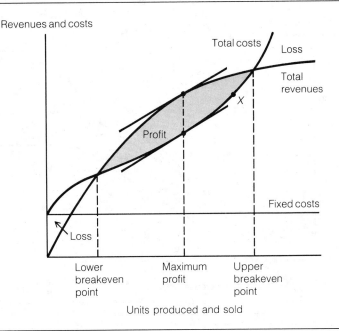

sales of a new product must be for the firm to achieve profitability. Breakeven analysis can also be used as a broad framework for studying the effects of a general expansion in the level of operations. Finally, in analyzing programs to modernize and automate, where the firm would be operating in a more mechanized, automated manner and thus substituting fixed costs for variable costs, breakeven analysis helps analyze the consequences of shifting from variable costs to fixed costs. The key factor is the influence of volume changes on profitability when firms have different relationships between fixed and variable costs.

CASH BREAKEVEN ANALYSIS

Some of the firm's fixed costs are noncash outlays, and, for a period, some of its revenues may be in receivables. The cash breakeven chart for Firm B, constructed on the assumption that $30,000 of the fixed costs from the previous illustration are depreciation charges and, therefore, a noncash outlay, is shown in Figure 8.4. Because fixed cash outlays are only $10,000, the cash breakeven point is at 12,500 units rather than 50,000 units, which is the profit breakeven point.

An equation for the cash breakeven point based on sales revenues can be derived from the equation for the profit breakeven point. The only change is to reduce fixed costs by the amount of noncash outlays:

FIGURE 8.4   Cash Breakeven Analysis for Firm B

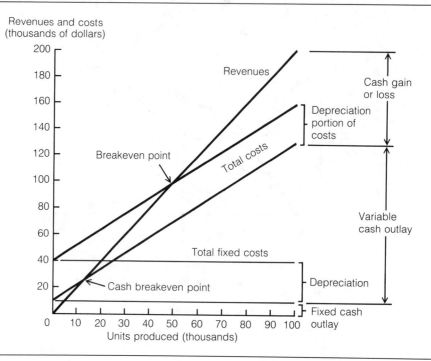

$$TR^* = \frac{F - \text{Noncash outlays}}{CR}.$$

If noncash outlays are very close to total fixed costs, the cash breakeven point approaches zero. The cash breakeven point based on units of output is comparable to the profit breakeven quantity, except that fixed costs must be adjusted for noncash outlays:

$$Q^* = \frac{F - \text{Noncash outlays}}{c}.$$

Here again, if noncash outlays are very large, the cash breakeven point may be low, despite a large amount of fixed charges.

Cash breakeven analysis does not fully represent cash flows; for this, a cash budget is required. But it is useful because it provides a picture of the flow of funds from operations. A firm may incur a level of fixed costs that will result in losses during business downswings but large profits during upswings. If cash outlays are small, the firm may be able to operate above the cash breakeven point even during periods of loss. Thus, the risk of insolvency (in the sense of being unable to meet cash obligations) is small. This allows a firm to reach out for higher profits through automation and operating leverage.

OPERATING LEVERAGE

To a physicist, *leverage* implies the use of a lever to raise a heavy object with a small force. In business terminology, a high degree of operating leverage implies that a relatively small change in sales results in a large change in net operating income.

Patterns of Operating Leverage

The significance of the degree of operating leverage is illustrated by Figure 8.5. Three firms — A, B, and C — with differing degrees of leverage are contrasted. Firm A has a relatively small amount of fixed charges; it does not have much automated equipment, so its depreciation cost is low. However, its variable cost line has a relatively steep slope, denoting that its variable costs per unit are higher than those of the other firms.

Firm B is considered to have a normal amount of fixed costs in its operations. It uses automated equipment (with which one operator can turn out a few or many units at the same labor cost) to about the same extent as the average firm in the industry. Firm B breaks even at a higher level of operations than does Firm A. At a production level of 40,000 units, B loses $8,000 but A breaks even.

Firm C has the highest fixed costs. It is highly automated, using expensive, high-speed machines that require very little labor per unit produced. With such an operation, its variable costs rise slowly. Because of the high overhead resulting from charges associated with the expensive machinery, Firm C's breakeven point is higher than that for either Firm A or Firm B. Once Firm C reaches its breakeven point, however, its profits rise faster than do those of the other firms.

Alternative operating leverage decisions can have a great impact on the unit cost position of each firm. When 200,000 units are sold, the average per unit cost of production for each firm, calculated by dividing total costs by the 200,000 units sold, is as shown:

	Average Cost per Unit at 200,000 Units
Firm A	$1.60
Firm B	$1.40
Firm C	$1.30

These results have important implications. At a high volume of operations of 200,000 units per period, Firm C has a substantial cost superiority over the other two firms and particularly over Firm A. Firm C could cut the price of its product to $1.50 per unit, which represents a level that would be unprofitable for Firm A, and still have more than a 13 percent ($.20/$1.50) return on sales. (The average pretax margin on sales for manufacturing firms is about 9 to 11 percent.) Another illustration of this idea is the difference in unit costs for Japanese versus U.S. steel companies. Most Japanese steel companies can produce 10 million tons or more per year, while only one or two U.S. steel companies can produce as much as 5 million tons per year. Operating at such a high capacity (in part due to the benefit of growth through export sales), the Japanese companies have been able to

FIGURE 8.5   Operating Leverage

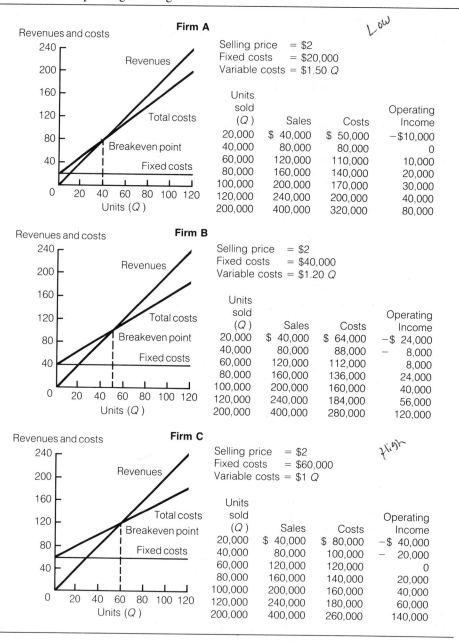

Firm A   *Low*

Selling price = $2
Fixed costs   = $20,000
Variable costs = $1.50 Q

Units sold (Q)	Sales	Costs	Operating Income
20,000	$ 40,000	$ 50,000	−$10,000
40,000	80,000	80,000	0
60,000	120,000	110,000	10,000
80,000	160,000	140,000	20,000
100,000	200,000	170,000	30,000
120,000	240,000	200,000	40,000
200,000	400,000	320,000	80,000

Firm B

Selling price = $2
Fixed costs   = $40,000
Variable costs = $1.20 Q

Units sold (Q)	Sales	Costs	Operating Income
20,000	$ 40,000	$ 64,000	−$ 24,000
40,000	80,000	88,000	− 8,000
60,000	120,000	112,000	8,000
80,000	160,000	136,000	24,000
100,000	200,000	160,000	40,000
120,000	240,000	184,000	56,000
200,000	400,000	280,000	120,000

Firm C

Selling price = $2
Fixed costs   = $60,000
Variable costs = $1 Q

High

Units sold (Q)	Sales	Costs	Operating Income
20,000	$ 40,000	$ 80,000	−$ 40,000
40,000	80,000	100,000	− 20,000
60,000	120,000	120,000	0
80,000	160,000	140,000	20,000
100,000	200,000	160,000	40,000
120,000	240,000	180,000	60,000
200,000	400,000	260,000	140,000

sell steel in the United States at prices below the costs of the U.S. steel companies. While the total story is complex, the firms' operating leverage factor is an important influence on their relative costs per unit.

Degree of Operating Leverage

Operating leverage can be defined more precisely in terms of the way a given change in sales volume affects net operating income (NOI). To measure the effect on profitability of a change in volume, we calculate the *degree of operating leverage,* the ratio of the percentage change in operating income to the percentage change in units sold or in total revenues. Algebraically,

$$\text{Degree of operating leverage} = \frac{\text{Percentage change in operating income}}{\text{Percentage change in units sold or in total revenues}}.$$

For Firm B in Figure 8.5, the degree of operating leverage (DOL_B) for a change in units of output from 100,000 to 120,000 is

$$\text{DOL}_B = \frac{\dfrac{\Delta\text{Income}}{\text{Income}}}{\dfrac{\Delta Q}{Q}} = \frac{\dfrac{\Delta X}{X}}{\dfrac{\Delta Q}{Q}}$$

$$= \frac{\dfrac{\$56{,}000 - \$40{,}000}{\$40{,}000}}{\dfrac{120{,}000 - 100{,}000}{100{,}000}} = \frac{\dfrac{\$16{,}000}{\$40{,}000}}{\dfrac{20{,}000}{100{,}000}}$$

$$= \frac{40\%}{20\%} = 2.0.$$

Here, ΔX is the increase in net operating income, Q is the quantity of output in units, and ΔQ is the increase in output.[4]

Using the same equation, the degree of operating leverage at 100,000 units is 1.67 for Firm A and 2.5 for Firm C. Thus, for a 10 percent change in volume, Firm C, the

---

[4]Note that an alternative formulation for calculating DOL at any level of output Q can be derived:

$$\text{DOL} = \frac{\dfrac{\Delta X}{X}}{\dfrac{\Delta Q}{Q}}$$

$$= \frac{\dfrac{c\Delta Q}{cQ - F}}{\dfrac{\Delta Q}{Q}}$$

$$= \frac{Qc\Delta Q}{\Delta Q(cQ - F)}$$

$$= \frac{cQ}{X}$$

$$= \frac{C}{X}.$$

company with the most operating leverage, will experience a profit gain of 25 percent, while Firm A, the one with the least leverage, will have only a 16.7 percent profit gain. The profits of Firm C are more sensitive to changes in sales volume than those of Firm A. Thus, the higher the degree of operating leverage, the more profits will fluctuate, both in an upward and downward direction, in response to changes in volume.

The degree of operating leverage of a firm has important implications for a number of areas of business and financial policy.[5] Firm C's high degree of operating leverage suggests gains from increasing volume. Suppose Firm C could increase its quantity sold from 100,000 units to 120,000 units by cutting the price per unit to $1.90. The equation for net operating income is

$$\text{Net operating income } (X) = PQ - vQ - F$$
$$= \$1.90(120,000) - (\$1)120,000 - \$60,000$$
$$= \$228,000 - \$120,000 - \$60,000$$
$$= \$48,000.$$

The equation shows that Firm C could increase its profits from $40,000 at a volume of 100,000 to $48,000 at a volume of 120,000. Thus, a high degree of operating leverage suggests that an aggressive price policy may increase profits, particularly if the market is responsive to small price cuts.

On the other hand, Firm C's high degree of operating leverage tells us that the company is subject to large swings in profits as its volume fluctuates. Thus, if Firm C's industry is one whose sales are greatly affected by changes in the overall level of economic activity (as are, for example, the durable goods industries, such as machine tools, steel, and autos), its profits are subject to large fluctuations. Hence, the degree of financial leverage appropriate for Firm C to take on is lower than that for a firm with a lower degree of operating leverage and for industries whose sales are less sensitive to fluctuations in the level of the economy. (Financial leverage is discussed in Chapter 15.)

OVERALL FINANCIAL PLANNING MODELS

Overall planning models provide a broad framework for understanding fundamental financial planning and control relationships. Since they generally emphasize the point of view of the firm as a whole, the focus is on the return on equity after the influence of financial leverage and taxes is taken into account. To illustrate these fundamental planning and control relationships, the following factors will be employed with numerical values that correspond to the average for all manufacturing firms in the United States in recent years. The notation will follow the literature on the subject.[6]

---

[5]The degree of operating leverage is a form of *elasticity concept* and thus is akin to the familiar price elasticity developed in economics. Since operating leverage is an elasticity, it varies depending on the particular part of the breakeven graph that is being considered. For example, in terms of our illustrative firms, the degree of operating leverage is greatest close to the breakeven point, where a very small change in volume can produce a very large percentage increase in profits simply because the base profits are close to zero near the breakeven point.

[6]See Higgins [1981], Babcock [1970, 1980], and Zakon [1976].

Symbol		Relationship	Numerical Value
T	=	asset turnover	2 times
m	=	margin on sales	5%
L	=	financial leverage	2 times
b	=	retention rate	.6
BV	=	book value	
BVS	=	book value per share	
EPS	=	earnings per share	
DPS	=	dividends per share	
G	=	sustainable growth rate	

The return on equity (ROE) involves the three fundamental factors of turnover, margin, and leverage:

Asset turnover × Margin on sales × Financial leverage = Return on equity.

These three fundamental factors are also expressed in terms of ratios.

$$\frac{\text{Sales}}{\text{Total assets}} \times \frac{\text{Net income}}{\text{Sales}} \times \frac{\text{Total assets}}{\text{Equity}} = \frac{\text{Net income}}{\text{Equity}}$$

In symbols, we have $TmL = \text{ROE}$. With the numerical values suggested above, ROE equals

$$2(.05)(2) = .20 = 20\%.$$

With the knowledge of return on equity, we can then calculate earnings per share (*EPS*).

Return on equity × Book value per share = Earnings per share (*EPS*)

$$\frac{\text{Net income}}{\text{Equity}} \times \frac{\text{Equity}}{\text{No. of shares}} = \frac{\text{Net income}}{\text{No. of shares}} = EPS$$

The earnings per share figure is widely used but reflects such arbitrary elements as the number of shares outstanding. In order to provide a numerical illustration, we therefore need two additional items of information. One is the size of the firm. The other is the number of equity shares outstanding. It will be noted that the return on equity measure above could be calculated independent of these two additional pieces of information. Let us assume a firm with total assets of $100 million and 1 million shares of equity stock outstanding. The earnings per share would therefore be

$$\frac{\$10 \text{ million}}{\$50 \text{ million}} \times \frac{\$50 \text{ million}}{1 \text{ million}} = \$10 \text{ per share.}$$

Having earnings per share, it is a short step to obtain dividends per share. The additional item needed is the dividend payout. The dividend payout is 1 minus the retention rate or is equal to

$$(1 - b) = (1 - .6) = .4.$$

For dividends per share we therefore have

Earnings per share × Dividend payout = Dividends per share.

$$\frac{\text{Net income}}{\text{No. of shares}} \times \frac{\text{Dividends}}{\text{Net income}} = \frac{\text{Dividends}}{\text{No. of shares}}.$$

We already have all of the numerical values for making the calculation. It is simply

$$\$10(.4) = \$4.$$

Much has been written on the concept of *sustainable dividends*. This can be expressed as the dollar amount of total dividends or the dollar amount of dividends per share. The concept involves nothing more than bringing together all of the factors for each of the target measures discussed to this point. The full set of factors for calculating dividends per share is now exhibited.

$$\frac{\text{Sales}}{\text{Total assets}} \times \frac{\text{Net income}}{\text{Sales}} \times \frac{\text{Total assets}}{\text{Equity}} \times \frac{\text{Equity}}{\text{No. of shares}}$$

$$\times \frac{\text{Dividends paid}}{\text{Net income}} = \text{Dividends per share}$$

In symbols and numbers, we have

$$T \times m \times L \times BVS \times (1 - b) = DPS \text{ (sustainable)}$$

$$2 \times .05 \times 2 \times \$50 \times .4 = \$4 \text{ per share.}$$

To obtain the total amount of dividends, we would use total book value rather than book value per share. In symbols,

$$T \times m \times L \times BV \times (1 - b) = \text{Dividends.}$$

The $50 would now represent $50 million, and the total amount of dividends would be $4 million.

Related to the idea of sustainable dividends is the concept of sustainable growth rate. It again involves the use of factors we have already discussed arranged in a slightly different manner. (See Babcock [1970].) The sustainable growth rate is simply the return on equity times the retention rate. Hence, we have

$$T \times m \times L \times b = \text{Sustainable growth rate.}$$

For our example, we would have

$$2 \times .05 \times 2 \times .6 = 12\% = \text{Sustainable growth rate.}$$

While the relationship appears to be simple, there is much business and financial analysis involved in the concept of sustainable growth rate. Each of the factors in the equation represents an important aspect of business decision making. Turnover refers to the effectiveness with which the firm's assets or resources are utilized. The profit margin on sales is an important measure of how well the firm has managed its costs in relationship to the prices received for its products. Financial leverage is one of the key aspects of financial decision making. The retention rate reflects investment requirements in relation to an important component of the firm's free cash flows.

While the above relationships are relatively simple, they provide the basic framework for highly sophisticated computerized business and financial planning models. No matter how bulky the computer output analysis may appear, the underlying relationships involved are the patterns which have been discussed in this section. These relationships can be calculated for business firms or segments of an operation with the use of hand calculators. They provide important insights for financial planning and control. Additional refinements and details may then be explored with the use of more elaborate computerized models.

THE DU PONT SYSTEM OF FINANCIAL PLANNING AND CONTROL

The system of financial planning and control that has come to be referred to as the "du Pont system" is another comprehensive approach with applications at both the firm level and division or segment level. It can be a vehicle for longer-term (5–10 year) forecasts or annual and even monthly projections. The nature of the du Pont system is conveyed by Figure 8.6. The upper part of the figure focuses on management of each important element of cost. Sales less all costs of sales gives a net operating income measure. The lower part of the chart emphasizes asset management. It analyzes investment in each type of asset. Total investment in relation to sales yields turnover.

When the asset turnover ratio is multiplied by this margin on sales, the product is the before-tax return on total investment (ROI) in the firm. This can be seen from the following formula:

$$\frac{NOI}{Sales} \times \frac{Sales}{Investment} = ROI.$$

Would it be better to have a 10 percent margin on sales and a total asset turnover of two times or a 5 percent sales margin and a turnover of four times? It makes no difference; in either case, the firm has a 20 percent return on investment. Actually, most firms are not free to make the kind of choice posed in this question. Depending on the nature of its industry, the firm *must* operate with more or fewer assets, and its turnover will depend on the characteristics of its particular line of business. In the case of a dealer in fresh fruits and vegetables, fish, or other perishable items, the turnover should be high — every day or two is most desirable. In contrast, some lines of business require heavy fixed investment or long production periods. A hydroelectric utility company, with its heavy investment in dams and transmission lines, requires heavy fixed investment; a shipbuilder or an aircraft producer needs a long production period. Such companies necessarily have a low asset turnover rate but a correspondingly higher profit margin on sales.

The logic of the du Pont system is also employed in formulating the determinants of the return on equity (ROE). This relationship was discussed in the previous section:

$$\frac{Sales}{Total\ assets} \times \frac{Net\ income}{Sales} \times \frac{Total\ assets}{Equity} = \frac{Net\ income}{Equity}.$$

This modified formulation of the du Pont system is widely used. It can be applied at the level of the firm from information readily available in annual reports, as illustrated by Problem 8.4.

FIGURE 8.6 The du Pont Chart System

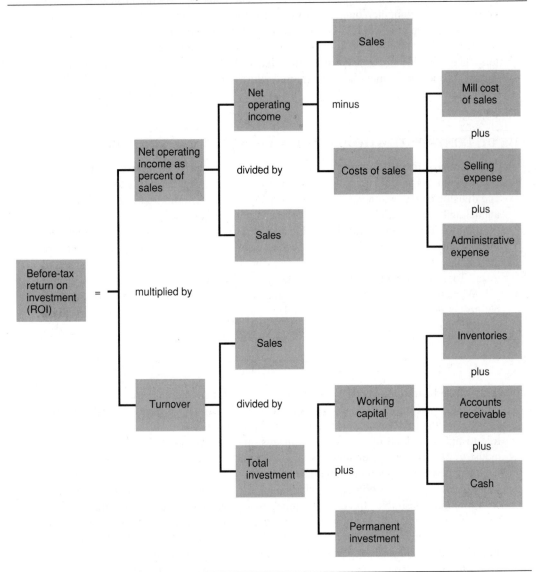

Control in Multidivision Companies

The du Pont system is particularly useful in control of divisions. For organizational reasons, large firms are generally set up on a decentralized basis. For example, General Electric establishes separate divisions for heavy appliances, light appliances, power transformers, fossil fuel generating equipment, nuclear generating equipment, and so on. Each division is defined as a *profit center,* and each has its own investments — fixed and current assets, together with a share of such general corporate assets as research labs and headquarters buildings — and is expected to earn an appropriate return on them. The corporate headquarters, or central staff, typically controls the various divisions by a form of the du Pont system.

When the du Pont system is used for divisional control, the process is often called return on investment (ROI) control. Return is measured by operating earnings — income before interest and taxes — as shown in Figure 8.6. Sometimes the earnings figure is calculated before depreciation, and total gross assets are measured before deduction of the depreciation reserve. Measurement on gross assets has the advantage of avoiding differences in ROI due to differences in the average age of the fixed assets. Older assets are more fully depreciated and have a higher depreciation reserve and lower net fixed asset amount. This causes the ROI on net total assets to be higher when fixed assets are older.

If a particular division's ROI falls below a target figure, then the centralized corporate staff helps the division's own financial staff trace back through the du Pont system to determine the cause of the substandard ROI. Each division manager is judged by the division's ROI and rewarded or penalized accordingly. Division managers are thus motivated to keep their ROI up to the target level. Their individual actions should in turn maintain the firm's ROI at an appropriate level.

In addition to its use in managerial control, ROI can be used to allocate funds to the various divisions. The firm as a whole has financial resources — retained earnings, cash flow from depreciation, and the ability to obtain additional debt and equity funds from capital markets. These funds can be allocated on the basis of the divisional ROIs, with divisions having high ROIs receiving more funds than those with low ones.

Pitfalls in the Use of ROI Control

Any system of divisional control runs the risk that executives will devise methods for "beating the system." Hence, a number of problems can arise if ROI control is used without proper safeguards.[7]

Since the divisional managers are rewarded on the basis of their ROI performance, it is absolutely essential for their morale that they feel their divisional ROI does indeed provide an accurate measure of relative performance. But ROI is dependent on a number of factors in addition to managerial competence:

1. *Depreciation.* ROI is very sensitive to depreciation policy. If one division is writing off assets at a relatively rapid rate, its annual profits — and hence its ROI — will be reduced.

2. *Book value of assets.* If an older division is using assets that have been largely written off, both its current depreciation charges and its investment base will be low. This will make its ROI high in relation to newer divisions.

---

[7]For a discussion of how to avoid the pitfalls of a static approach to ROI control and an emphasis on its use as a dynamic information feedback control process, see Weston [1972]. J. Fred Weston, "Return on Investment as a Dynamic Management Process," Section 4 in *Handbook of Corporate Finance,* E. I. Altman, ed., New York: John Wiley and Sons, 1986.

3. *Transfer pricing*. In most corporations, some divisions sell to other divisions. At General Motors, for example, the Fisher Body division sells to the Chevrolet division. In such cases, the price at which goods are transferred between divisions has a fundamental effect on divisional profits. If the transfer price of auto bodies is set relatively high, then Fisher Body will have a relatively high ROI and Chevrolet a relatively low one.

4. *Time periods*. Many projects have long gestation periods, during which expenditures must be made for research and development, plant construction, market development, and the like. Such expenditures add to the investment base without a commensurate increase in profits for several years. During this period, a division's ROI can be seriously reduced; and without proper constraints, its manager may be improperly penalized. Given the frequency of personnel transfers in larger corporations, it is easy to see how the timing problem can keep managers from making long-term investments that are in the best interests of the firm.

5. *Industry conditions*. If one division is operating in an industry where conditions are favorable and rates of return are high, while another is in an industry suffering from excessive competition, these differences may cause the favored division to look good and the unfavored one to look bad, quite apart from any differences in their managers. For example, Signal Companies' aerospace division could hardly have been expected to perform as well as their truck division did in 1973, when the entire aerospace industry suffered severe problems and truck sales soared. External conditions must be taken into account when appraising ROI performance.

Because of these factors, a division's ROI must be supplemented with other criteria for evaluating performance. For example, its growth rate in sales, profits, and market share (as well as its ROI) in comparison with other firms in its own industry has been used in such evaluations. Although ROI control has been used with great success in U.S. industry, the system cannot be used in a mechanical sense by inexperienced personnel. As with most other tools, it is helpful if used properly but destructive if misused.

FORECASTING FINANCIAL STATEMENTS

Beginning in Chapter 2 we have emphasized that a good picture of the firm's operations is provided by three key financial statements: balance sheet, income statement, and statement of cash flows. We also showed in Chapter 2 how the statement of cash flows can be derived from information provided by the previous two statements. For overall financial planning, elaborate management information systems (MISs) and more elaborate computer programs referred to as "expert systems" have been utilized. The logic behind these overall planning models can be conveyed by the methodologies involved in forecasting the firm's financial statements. Two basic approaches are employed — the percent of sales method and the regression method. Each will be discussed in turn.

PERCENT OF SALES METHOD

We have seen that the sales-to-assets turnover is an important control variable and reflects a fundamentally important proposition in managerial finance — that the volume of a firm's sales is a good predictor of the required investment in assets. Sales forecasts are, therefore, the first step in forecasting financial requirements.

Forecasting Sales

Sales forecasting is a science and art unto itself. Sales forecasting is not the primary domain of financial managers, but they are likely to interact with the managers in the firm that have primary responsibility such as the marketing and/or planning officers. Other top executives are likely to be involved as well.

The basic methodology of sales forecasting involves the following:

Top-Down Approach

1. Forecast the world economy.
2. Forecast the national economy.
3. Forecast sales volume in each of the industries in which the firm sells products.
4. Forecast the firm's share of the market in each of the industries in which it participates.
5. Translate market share forecasts into a sales forecast for the firm.

Bottom-Up Approach

1. Have each segment of the firm analyze trends in sales patterns.
2. Consider advertising and other promotional programs that may affect the level of sales.
3. Each segment of the firm makes forecasts for its product-market area.
4. The segment forecasts are aggregated into an overall forecast for the firm.

We now have two sales forecasts, one based on overall economy and industry trends, the other based on the forecasts of managers "close to the market." Repeated interactions and discussions between managers responsible for the top-down forecasts and those responsible for the bottom-up forecasts result in a consensus forecast. This consensus forecast and subsequent consensus sales forecasts become the basic planning premise for the firm and many of its activities, including the responsibilities of financial managers.[8]

The Logic of the Percent of Sales Method

The percent of sales method provides a practical method of forecasting financial statements. There is a basic logic behind sales and the behavior of individual asset items. For example, in order to make sales, a firm must have an investment in plant and equipment to

---

[8]More detailed discussions of sales forecasting are found in books on macroeconomics, business economics, and marketing.

TABLE 8.6   The Moore Company Balance Sheet as of December 31, 19X1

Assets		Liabilities	
Cash	$ 10,000	Accounts payable	$ 50,000
Receivables	85,000	Accrued taxes and wages	25,000
Inventories	100,000	Mortgage bonds	70,000
Fixed assets (net)	150,000	Common stocks	100,000
		Retained earnings	100,000
Total assets	$345,000	Total liabilities and net worth	$345,000

produce goods. Inventories of work in progress and finished goods are needed to make sales. When sales are made, there is usually an interval before payments are received. This results in the generation of accounts receivable. Note that investments in fixed assets and inventories lead sales, while investment in receivables lags sales. With sales fluctuations, these lead and lag relationships result in complex patterns that are understood only when the underlying logic of the relationships is kept in mind.

Another consideration to take into account is whether the relationship between sales and the balance sheet item represents good management or is optimal in some sense. The processes of financial analysis discussed in the previous chapter help improve the efficiency of asset and liability management.

Implementing the Percent of Sales Method

The percent of sales method begins by expressing each individual balance sheet item as a percentage of sales. As an example, consider the Moore Company, whose balance sheet as of December 31, 19X1, is shown in Table 8.6. The company's sales are running at $500,000 a year, its capacity limit; the profit margin after tax on sales is 4 percent. During 19X1, the company earned $20,000 after taxes and paid out $10,000 in dividends, and it plans to continue paying out half of net profits as dividends. How much additional financing will be needed if sales expand to $800,000 during 19X2? To determine this amount, we will use the percent of sales method.[9]

First, isolate those balance sheet items that can be expected to vary directly with sales. In the case of the Moore Company, this step applies to each category of assets — a higher level of sales necessitates more cash for transactions, more receivables, higher inventory levels, and additional fixed plant capacity. On the liability side, accounts payable as well as accruals may be expected to increase as sales do. Retained earnings will go up as long as the company is profitable and does not pay out 100 percent of earnings, but

---

[9]We recognize, of course, that as a practical matter, business firms plan their needs in terms of specific items of equipment, square feet of floor space, and other factors, and not as a percentage of sales. However, the outside analyst does not have access to this information. Also, even though the information on specific items is available, a manager needs to check forecasts in aggregate terms. The percent of sales method serves both these needs well.

TABLE 8.7   The Moore Company Balance Sheet as of
December 31, 19X1 (Percent of Sales)

Assets (%)		Liabilities (%)	
Cash	$ 2.0	Accounts payable	$10.0
Receivables	17.0	Accrued taxes and wages	5.0
Inventories	20.0	Mortgage bonds[a]	—
Fixed assets (net)	30.0	Common stock[a]	—
		Retained earnings[a]	—
Total assets	$69.0	Total liabilities and net worth	$15.0

Assets as percent of sales	$69.0
Less: Spontaneous increase in liabilities	$15.0
Percent of each additional dollar of sales that must be financed	$54.0

[a]Not applicable.

---

the percentage increase is not constant. In addition, neither common stock nor mortgage bonds will increase spontaneously with an increase in sales.

The items that can be expected to vary directly with sales are tabulated as a percentage of sales in Table 8.7. For every $1.00 increase in sales, assets must increase by $.69; this $.69 must be financed in some manner. Accounts payable will increase "spontaneously" with sales, as will accruals; these two items will supply $.15 of new funds for each $1.00 increase in sales. Subtracting the 15 percent for spontaneously generated funds from the 69 percent funds requirement leaves 54 percent. Thus, for each $1.00 increase in sales, the Moore Company must obtain $.54 of financing either from internally generated funds or from external sources.

In the case at hand, sales are scheduled to increase from $500,000 to $800,000, or by $300,000. Applying the 54 percent developed in the table to the expected increase in sales leads to the conclusion that $162,000 will be needed.

Analyzing External Funds Needed

Some of that need will be met by retained earnings. Total revenues during 19X2 will be $800,000; if the company earns 4 percent after taxes on this volume, profits will amount to $32,000. Assuming that the 50 percent dividend payout ratio is maintained, dividends will be $16,000 and $16,000 will be retained. Subtracting the retained earnings from the $162,000 that was needed leaves a figure of $146,000 — the amount of funds that must be obtained through borrowing or by selling new common stock.

This process may be expressed in equation form:

$$\text{External funds needed} = \frac{A}{TR}(\Delta TR) - \frac{L}{TR}(\Delta TR) - bc(TR_2). \qquad \textbf{(8.2)}$$

Here:

$\dfrac{A}{TR}$ = assets that increase spontaneously with total revenues or sales as a percent of total revenues or sales = .69

$\dfrac{L}{TR}$ = those liabilities that increase spontaneously with total revenues or sales as a percent of total revenues or sales = .15

ΔTR = change in total revenues or sales = \$300,000

c = profit margin on sales = .04

TR_2 = total revenues projected for the year = \$800,000

b = earnings retention ratio = .5.

For the Moore Company, then,

$$\text{External funds needed} = 0.69(\$300,000) - 0.15(\$300,000)$$
$$- 0.5(0.04)(\$800,000)$$
$$= 0.54(\$300,000) - 0.02(\$800,000)$$
$$= \$146,000.$$

The \$146,000 found by the formula method must, of course, equal the amount derived previously.

Notice what would have occurred if the Moore Company's sales forecast for 19X2 had been only \$515,000, or a 3 percent increase. Applying the formula, we find the external funds requirement as follows:

$$\text{External funds needed} = 0.54(\$15,000) - 0.02(\$515,000)$$
$$= \$8,100 - \$10,300$$
$$= (\$2,200).$$

In this case, no external funds are required. In fact, the company will have \$2,200 in excess of its requirements; it, therefore, could plan to increase dividends, retire debt, or seek additional investment opportunities. The example shows that while small percentage increases in sales can be financed through internally generated funds, larger percentage increases cause the firm to go into the market for outside capital. In other words, small rates of sales growth for profitable companies can be financed from internal sources, but higher rates of sales growth require external financing.[10]

Note that the sales level equals $(1 + g)TR_1$, where g equals the growth rate in sales. The increase in sales, therefore, can be written:

$$\Delta TR = (1 + g)TR_1 - TR_1 = TR_1(1 + g - 1) = gTR_1.$$

---

[10]At this point, one might ask two questions: ''Shouldn't depreciation be considered as a source of funds, and won't this reduce the amount of external funds needed?'' The answer to both questions is no. In the percent of sales method, we are relating fixed assets, net of the reserve for depreciation, to sales. This process implicitly assumes that funds related to the depreciation policies are used to replace assets to which the depreciation is applicable and are, therefore, not available for further asset investment. Gross fixed assets less the cumulative reserve for depreciation equals net fixed assets, as used in the forecast model.

Let us next take the expression for external funds needed, Equation 8.2, and use it to derive the percentage of the increase in sales that will have to be financed externally (percentage of external funds required, or PEFR) as a function of the critical variables involved. In Equation 8.2, let $\left(\dfrac{A}{TR} - \dfrac{L}{TR}\right) = I$, substitute for ΔTR and TR_2, and divide both sides by $\Delta TR = gTR_1$.

$$\text{PEFR} = I - \frac{c}{g}(1 + g)b = I - cb\left(\frac{1 + g}{g}\right) \tag{8.3}$$

Using Equation 8.3, we can now investigate the influence of factors such as an increased rate of inflation on the percentage of sales growth that must be financed externally. Based on the relationships for all manufacturing industries, some representative values of the terms on the right-hand side of the equation are $I = 0.5$, $c = 0.05$, and $b = 0.60$.

Impact of Inflation

During the period that preceded the onset of inflation in the United States after 1966, the economy was growing at about 6 to 7 percent per annum. If a firm was in an industry that grew at the same rate as the economy as a whole and if a firm maintained its market share position in its industry, the firm grew at 6 to 7 percent per annum as well. Let us see what the implications for external financing requirements would be. With a growth rate of 6 percent, the percentage of an increase in sales that would have to be financed externally would be as follows:

$$\text{PEFR} = 0.5 - \frac{0.05}{0.06}(1.06)(0.6)$$

$$= 0.50 - 0.53 = -0.03 = -3\%.$$

At 7 percent growth, the PEFR would be

$$\text{PEFR} = 0.5 - \frac{0.05}{0.07}(1.07)(0.6)$$

$$= 0.50 - 0.46 = 0.04 = 4\%.$$

Thus, at a growth rate of 6 percent, the percentage of external financing to sales growth would be a negative 3 percent. In other words, the firm would have excess funds which it could use to increase dividends or increase its investment in marketable securities. With a growth rate of 7 percent, the firm would have a requirement of external financing of 4 percent of the sales increase.

During the 1970s, the inflation rate in some years was in the two-digit range; that is, 10 percent or more. Suppose we add sufficient percentage points per annum of an inflation rate to the previous 6 to 7 percent growth rate to obtain a growth rate of 15 or 20 percent for a firm. Then, the external financing requirements will be as follows:

$$\text{PEFR} = 0.5 - \frac{0.05}{0.15}(1.15)(0.6)$$

$$= 0.50 - 0.23 = 0.27 = 27\%.$$

$$\text{PEFR} = 0.5 - \frac{0.05}{0.20}(1.20)(0.6)$$

$$= 0.50 - 0.18 = 0.32 = 32\%.$$

With a growth rate in sales of 15 percent, external financing rises to 27 percent of the firm's sales growth. If inflation caused the growth rate of the firm to rise to 20 percent, then the external financing percentage would rise to 32 percent. The substantial increase in the growth rate of sales of firms measured in inflated dollars in recent years points up why external financing has become more important for firms.[11] It underscores also why the finance function in firms has taken on increased importance. There is just a much bigger job to be done, particularly in requirements for using external financing sources to maintain the sales growth of a firm. Even if the firm were not growing in real terms, an inflation rate of 10 percent, for example, would make it necessary for the firm to raise external financing of 17 percent of its growth in sales of inflated dollars — even though the real growth of the firm was zero.

The percent of sales method of forecasting financial requirements is neither simple nor mechanical, although the ideas can be explained with simple illustrations. Applying the technique in practice suggests the importance of understanding (1) the basic technology of the firm and (2) the logic of the relation between sales and assets for the particular firm in question. Experience and good judgment are required to apply the technique effectively in actual practice.

FINANCIAL FORECASTING USING REGRESSION METHODS

Regression analysis represents a more general method of forecasting financial requirements and is less subject to the potential pitfalls of the percent of sales method. Regression methods are widely used by other managers in addition to financial managers, who need to be familiar with the techniques in order to communicate successfully with others. To convey the basic ideas we will limit ourselves in this presentation to linear regression with two variables. This simplifies the exposition, and the basic principles can be readily generalized to other types of regression methods.

Superiority of the Linear Regression Method

Figure 8.7 illustrates the difference between the percent of sales method and linear regression for the data in Table 8.8, which shows the sales and inventory levels for a major integrated oil company in recent years. The percent of sales method uses the average of the inventory to sales ratios in order to predict inventories. For example, the ten-year average shows inventories to be 7.31 percent of sales. Using the percent of sales method,

---

[11]Note, however, that PEFR has an upper limit, even when the growth in sales becomes very high. From Equation 8.3, it can be seen that as g becomes very large, $\left(\dfrac{1+g}{g}\right)$ approaches 1 so that the upper limit for PEFR is $(I - cb)$.

FIGURE 8.7   Comparing the Percent of Sales Method with Simple Linear Regression

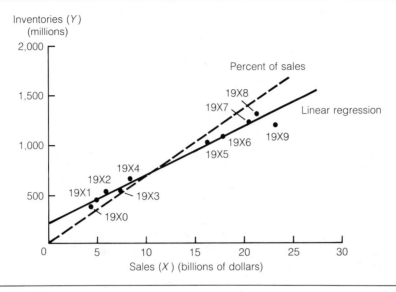

we would predict 19X9 inventory to be $1,762 million when it was actually $1,216 million, an error of $546 million. In Figure 8.7, the percent of sales method is illustrated by the dashed line. It is a ray from the origin with a slope of 7.31 percent. Its equation is

$$\text{Inventory} = .0731 \text{ Sales}$$

or

$$Y = bX,$$

where b is the slope of the line.

TABLE 8.8   Inventory to Sales Relationships for a Major Integrated Oil Company for a Ten-Year Period (Billions of Dollars)

	Inventory (Y)	Sales (X)	Inventory to Sales Ratio (Y/X)
19X0	$ .403	$ 4.560	0.088
19X1	.461	4.962	0.093
19X2	.506	5.728	0.088
19X3	.507	6.477	0.078
19X4	.665	8.480	0.078
19X5	1.087	17.924	0.061
19X6	1.165	17.524	0.066
19X7	1.278	20.181	0.063
19X8	1.438	21.752	0.066
19X9	1.216	24.106	0.050

The regression method is better because it does not assume the line that best fits the data automatically goes through the origin. Instead, it allows us to find the relationship that best fits the data. As shown in Figure 8.7, the solid linear regression line is an improvement over the percent of sales (dashed) line because it fits the data much better. The equation for the linear regression is

$$\text{Inventory} = \$.216 \text{ billion} + .04987 \text{ Sales} \tag{8.4}$$

or

$$Y = a + bX,$$

where a is the intercept where the regression line meets the Y-axis and b is the slope of the line. If we use the regression line to predict 19X9 inventory, given 19X9 sales, we have:

$$\text{Inventory} = \$.216 \text{ billion} + .04987(\$24.106 \text{ billion})$$
$$= \$1.418 \text{ billion}.$$

Actual inventory was \$1.216 billion; hence, the linear regression was off by \$.202 billion, a much smaller error than the percent of sales method, which was off by \$.546 billion.[12] This example demonstrates the value of the regression method. We next explain the calculation methods.

CALCULATION OF REGRESSION RELATIONSHIPS

We illustrate the procedures by a simple numerical example utilizing the data in Table 8.9. Table 8.9 has only five observations. In most practical situations we would want to have 10 or more observations. The numbers in Table 8.7 are purely hypothetical and small to facilitate easy computation. The spirit of the table is that Y might represent all assets that have to be financed and X represents the sales of the company. The remaining five columns in the table represent computations that will be used in the subsequent calculations.

We first define and calculate some basic measures: the mean, the variance, and the standard deviation.

$$\text{Mean} = \frac{\Sigma X}{n} = \frac{30}{5} = 6 = \bar{X} \qquad \frac{\Sigma Y}{n} = \frac{20}{5} = 4 = \bar{Y} \tag{8.5}$$

$$\text{Variance} = \sigma_X^2 = \frac{\Sigma (X - \bar{X})^2}{n - 1} = \frac{40}{4} = 10$$

$$\sigma_Y^2 = \frac{\Sigma (Y - \bar{Y})^2}{n - 1} = \frac{22}{4} = 5.5 \tag{8.6}$$

---

[12]An even better forecast can be attained by regressing inventory against the square root of sales. See Chapter 19 for an explanation of why inventory is usually a function of the square root of sales.

TABLE 8.9   Data for Regression Computations

	(1) Year	(2) Y	(3) X	(4) XY	(5) Y²	(6) X²	(7) $(X - \bar{X})$	(8) $(X - \bar{X})^2$	(9) $(Y - \bar{Y})$	$(Y - \bar{Y})^2$
	1	1	2	2	1	4	−4	16	−3	9
	2	2	4	8	4	16	−2	4	−2	4
	3	5	6	30	25	36	0	0	1	1
	4	6	8	48	36	64	2	4	2	4
	5	6	10	60	36	100	4	16	2	4
Sum		20	30	148	102	220	0	40	0	22

$\bar{Y} = 4 \quad \bar{X} = 6$

$$b = \frac{n\Sigma\,XY - \Sigma\,X\Sigma\,Y}{n\Sigma\,X^2 - (\Sigma\,X)^2} = \frac{5(148) - 30(20)}{5(220) - (30)^2} = \frac{140}{200} = 0.7$$

$a = \bar{Y} - b\bar{X} = 4 - .7(6) = 4 - 4.2 = -.2$

$Y_c = -.2 + .7X$

$$S_Y = \sqrt{\frac{\Sigma\,(Y^2) - [a\Sigma\,(Y) + b\Sigma\,(XY)]}{n - 2}} = \sqrt{\frac{102 - [-.2(20) + .7(148)]}{3}}$$

$$= \sqrt{\frac{102 - 99.6}{3}} = \sqrt{\frac{2.4}{3}} = \sqrt{.80} = .8944$$

$$S_b = \frac{S_Y}{\sqrt{\Sigma\,(X - \bar{X})^2}} = \frac{.8944}{\sqrt{40}} = \frac{.8944}{6.3246} = .1414$$

$$t_b = \frac{b}{S_b} = \frac{.7}{.1414} = 4.9505 \qquad R^2 = .8909$$

$$r = \frac{140}{\sqrt{200}\sqrt{5(102) - (20)^2}} = \frac{140}{14.1421\sqrt{510 - 400}} = \frac{140}{(14.14)(10.4881)}$$

$$= \frac{140}{148.3236} = .9439$$

$$\text{Standard deviation} = \sigma_X = \sqrt{\frac{\Sigma\,(X - \bar{X})^2}{n - 1}} = \sqrt{10} = 3.1623$$

$$\sigma_Y = \sqrt{\frac{\Sigma\,(Y - \bar{Y})^2}{n - 1}} = \sqrt{5.5} = 2.3452 \qquad \textbf{(8.7)}$$

In words, the arithmetic mean in Equation 8.5 is the sum divided by the number of observations — the average value. The variance in Equation 8.6 is a measure of the dispersion from the average value. It is the squared deviations from the mean divided by the number of observations less 1. We divided by $(n - 1)$ since the deviations are measured from the mean, so one degree of freedom is lost. The standard deviation in Equation 8.7 is the square root of the variance. As we shall see in this and subsequent chapters, each of these basic measures has important statistical properties.

FIGURE 8.8   Scatter Diagram of Years 1 to 5 Assets to Sales

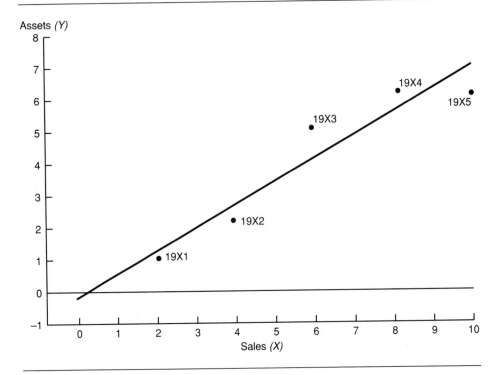

We next calculate the regression equation in the form of $Y = a + bX$. To do so, we need to calculate the parameters a and b. We start with the formula and computations for b:

$$b = \frac{N\Sigma\, XY - \Sigma X \Sigma Y}{N\Sigma\, X^2 - (\Sigma\, X)^2} = \frac{5(148) - 30(20)}{5(220) - (30)^2} = \frac{140}{200} = 0.7.$$

The formula we employ is a relatively simple expression that can be readily calculated from the data in Table 8.7. However, actual calculations would use more compact expressions such as deviations from the mean or matrix methods. From a practical standpoint, in solving actual problems we would undoubtedly use one of the many statistical packages available for use on personal computers.

The slope of the regression line that we have calculated is 0.7. Since the regression line goes through the means of the two variables, we can readily calculate the intercept term, a. We use the expression:

$$a = \bar{Y} - b\bar{X}.$$

Since we have calculated the mean of Y as 4 and the mean of X as 6 and have determined b to be .7, we have:

$$a = 4 - .7(6) = -.2.$$

We now have the parameters we need and can write the regression line:

$$Y_c = -.2 + .7X.$$

Our calculations to this point can be expressed in graphic form as shown in Figure 8.8. In Figure 8.8 we see that the regression line has a negative intercept and a positive slope. We have portrayed this relationship as between assets, for which the Y variable stands, and sales, represented by the X variable.

We next consider how good a forecasting tool the regression equation we have calculated represents. A commonly used regression model in Lotus 1-2-3 provides us with a measure of the statistical significance of the slope of the line we have calculated. This is useful because the slope of the line measures how strong an influence the independent variable (X, in this case) exerts on the dependent variable (Y, in our example). This measure is S_b, the standard error of estimate of b, the slope of the line.

The other information usually provided in the basic statistical package referred to is the correlation coefficient. The correlation coefficient measures how close the observations are to the regression line fitted through them. It represents how far from the regression line the individual points that are plotted fall. We can see visually in Figure 8.8 that the observations fall very close to the regression line and can judge that the correlation coefficient will be high. We shall illustrate the calculation of S_b and of r from our simple example. To calculate S_b we need first to calculate the standard error of the Y values that we have computed. We use the following expression:

$$S_Y = \sqrt{\frac{\Sigma (Y^2) - a\Sigma (Y) - b\Sigma (XY)}{N - 2}} = \sqrt{\frac{102 + .2(20) - .7(148)}{3}}$$

$$= \sqrt{.80} = .8944.$$

We use this value in calculating the standard error of estimate of the slope of the line:

$$S_b = \frac{S_Y}{\sqrt{\Sigma (X - \overline{X})^2}} = \frac{.8944}{\sqrt{40}} = .1414.$$

We can use the value we have calculated for S_b to determine whether the slope of the line is statistically significant. Since our null hypothesis is that the slope of the line is zero, we can write the expression for the t value of b.

$$t_b = \frac{b - 0}{S_b} = \frac{0.7}{.1414} = 4.95$$

The t value, calculated to be 4.95, is clearly significant. A rough rule of thumb would be that a t value of 3 would be significant at the 1 percent level and a t value of 2 would be significant at the 10 percent level. A more detailed explanation of the interpretation of t values and the use of the normal curve is provided in Appendix A to this chapter. We next calculate r, the correlation coefficient:

$$r = \frac{N\Sigma XY - \Sigma X\Sigma Y}{\sqrt{N\Sigma X^2 - (\Sigma X)^2}\sqrt{N\Sigma Y^2 - (\Sigma Y)^2}} = \frac{140}{\sqrt{200}\sqrt{5(102) - (20)^2}} = .9439.$$

The calculation is facilitated because the numerator of the formula for r and the first term of the denominator both are the formula for the calculation of b that we have already made.

TABLE 8.10 Data Inputs for a Judgment Forecast

	(1) State	(2) P_s	(3) Rev	(4) Y = GNP
	Bad	.2	8	90
	Average	.5	9	100
	Good	.3	13	110

Another statistical relationship is found by squaring the correlation coefficient, r. The squared term is usually expressed in capital letters as R^2 and has the statistical property of conveying the percentage of the total variation between the two variables explained by the regression line. R^2 in our example is .89. Thus 89 percent of the variation between the two variables is explained by the regression line, which tells us that the relationship is, indeed, statistically significant. R^2 is also called the "coefficient of determination."

We have now calculated the regression line and developed measures for determining whether the regression line relationships are statistically significant. We could use these relations to develop ranges of the dependent variable assets in this example, giving us a high degree of confidence based on our forecasts of the independent variable of sales. How to do this is illustrated in some detail in Appendix A to this chapter.

This is a useful starting point for the financial manager to obtain a sense of how stable the relationships have been in the past. However, our world is highly dynamic. We have experienced oil shocks, the S&L debacle, international political instabilities, etc. Computed historical relationships are not likely to be stable in the future. Thus the formal regression analysis is only a starting point. Projections or forecasts by the financial manager are likely to include an element of judgment as well. In addition, flexibility and a fast reaction time are required. This means there must be continuous monitoring of forecasts and rapid feedback in an effective information system.[13]

The Use of Judgmental Approaches

Since the financial manager is likely to exercise some judgment in making the forecast relationships, he or she may employ a subjective probability distribution. This is illustrated by Table 8.10. Column (1) represents the alternative possible future states-of-the-world — good, average, or bad. Column (2) lists the associated probabilities of the alternative states. Column (3) lists the firm's revenues or sales under the alternative states-of-the-world as influenced by the data in Column (4), which represents gross national product under the alternative states-of-the-world. We have employed index numbers for gross national product to simplify the calculations. Thus for average business conditions, we show gross national product as 100. For the good state-of-the-

[13]For more detail on the information system requirement, see J. Fred Weston, "ROI Planning and Control," *Business Horizons*, 15, (August 1972), pp. 35–42.

TABLE 8.11   Calculation of Estimates Based on
                 Alternative Future States-of-the-World

(1) $P_s\mathrm{Rev}$	(2) $\mathrm{Rev} - \overline{\mathrm{Rev}}$	(3) $(\mathrm{Rev} - \overline{\mathrm{Rev}})^2$	(4) $P_s(\mathrm{Rev} - \overline{\mathrm{Rev}})^2$
1.6	−2	4	.8
4.5	−1	1	.5
3.9	3	9	2.7
$\overline{\mathrm{Rev}} = 10$			$\sigma^2_{\mathrm{Rev}} = 4.0$
			$\sigma_{\mathrm{Rev}} = 2.0$

(5) P_sY	(6) $(Y - \overline{Y})$	(7) $(Y - \overline{Y})^2$	(8) $P_s(Y - \overline{Y})^2$
18	−11	121	24.2
50	−1	1	.5
33	9	81	24.3
$\overline{Y} = 101$			$\sigma^2_Y = 49$

(9) $(\mathrm{Rev} - \overline{\mathrm{Rev}})(Y - \overline{Y})$	(10) $P_s(\mathrm{Rev} - \overline{\mathrm{Rev}})(Y - \overline{Y})$
22	4.4
1	.5
27	8.1
	$\mathrm{Cov}(\mathrm{Rev}, Y) = 13$
$r = \mathrm{Cov}(\mathrm{Rev}, Y)/\sigma_{\mathrm{Rev}}\sigma_Y$	

world, gross national product increases by 10 percent. For the bad state-of-the-world, it drops by 10 percent. We note that for the firm, sales dropped slightly more than 10 percent under the bad state-of-the-world, but increased by 44 percent under the good state-of-the-world. Given these basic facts, we calculate some statistical results similar to those we developed under regression analysis. This is performed in Table 8.11.

Column (1) multiplies the alternative revenues by their probabilities to obtain the average or expected value. This represents the alternative values multiplied by their "frequencies" in the sense of their probabilities. In general, an average is the sum of the observations divided by the number of observations. Since the probabilities sum to 1, it is not necessary to divide by n in this type of calculation to obtain the mean. Column (2) measures the deviations of the firm's alternative sales levels from their mean or expected value. Column (3) squares these deviations. Column (4) multiplies the squared deviations by their associated probabilities. From this we obtain the variance and the standard deviation of the sales or revenues of the firm, dependent on alternative levels of GNP under alternative states-of-the-world. Columns (5) through (8) make similar computations for gross national product. GNP has an expected value of 101 with a variance of 49 and a standard deviation of 7. The final two columns analyze how the sales or revenues of the firm covary with fluctuations in GNP. In Column (9) we multiply the deviations that had been calculated in Columns (2) and (6). In Column (10) the product of the deviation is multiplied by the associated probabilities. We obtain a covariance (Cov) between the sales of the firm and gross national product of 13. From these calculations, we can also develop some other statistical properties. For example, the correlation coefficient between the firm's sales and GNP can be calculated by the following expression:

$$r = \text{Cov}(\text{Rev}, Y)/\sigma_{\text{Rev}}\sigma_Y.$$

Since we have already calculated the terms required, we can readily determine that the correlation coefficient is .9286. Another statistical relationship calculates the degree to which the total variation is explained by the regression line. This is the square of the correlation coefficient and is usually written as a capital letter, R^2. R^2 is the ratio of explained variance to total variance. In our example its numerical value would be $(.9286)^2 = .8623$.

The methodology reflected in Table 8.11 is also used in Chapter 10 when we develop some of the formal relations between risk and return.

From the expressions we have already calculated, we can readily obtain the regression line. The value of the slope, b, is equal to:

$$\text{Cov}(\text{Rev}, Y)/\text{Var } Y = 13/49 = .2653.$$

Since the regression line goes through the means, we have:

$$10 = a + .2653(101).$$

Solving, we find that a, the intercept term, is equal to -16.8.

Alternative Patterns of Regression Relationships

Regression relationships can take a number of forms. These different patterns follow from the logic of the relationship between sales and the individual asset or income statement accounts. Four different patterns may be encountered. These are shown in Figure 8.9. Panel (a) shows the relationship between receivables and sales. Receivables are not generated until sales on credit are made. With zero credit sales, there would be zero receivables. Hence the receivables to sales ratio is likely to be constant. In our example, the ratio is shown to be 10 percent, a constant 10 percent of sales or an average collection period of 36 days based on a 360-day year.

Work-in-process inventories and finished goods inventories must necessarily precede sales. There may be a "base stock" inventory even before sales are made. In Panel (b), a base stock inventory of $10 is shown. The regression line is:

$$\text{Inventories} = \$10 + .10 \text{ of Sales.}$$

For this regression line, the ratio of inventory to sales is 20 percent at $100 of sales, but only 15 percent at $200 of sales.

A third pattern is illustrated by the net income to sales ratio. Because fixed costs have to be incurred to start a business at a zero level of sales, we postulate a loss of $5. We have indicated the following regression relationship:

$$\text{Net income} = -\$5 + .10 \text{ Sales.}$$

FIGURE 8.9   Types of Regression Relationships

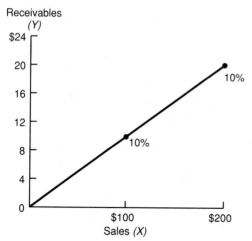

(a) Constant ratio
Receivables = .10 Sales

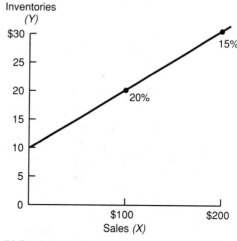

(b) Declining ratio
Inventories = $10 + .10 Sales

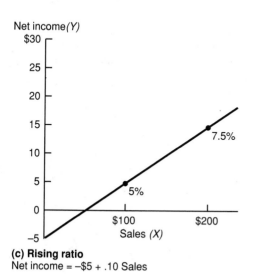

(c) Rising ratio
Net income = −$5 + .10 Sales

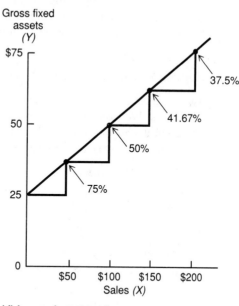

(d) Lumpy investments
Fixed assets = $25 + .25 Sales

At sales of $100, net income would be $5. At sales of $200, net income would be $15. The net income for sales of $100 is 5 percent. For sales of $200 the net income to sales ratio is 7.5 percent. People sometimes say: "With greater volume a firm should be able to cut its profit margin on sales." But it seems more logical to expect a regression relationship as depicted in Panel (c) of Figure 8.9. If so, the profit margin should rise with sales increases rather than decline. This logic is supported by breakeven analysis as well. Once the breakeven point (which is sales of $50 in our example) is reached, the ratio of profit or net income to sales rises because fixed costs are spread over a larger number of units.

Panel (d) in Figure 8.9 depicts the pattern for fixed assets. Investments for fixed assets are likely to be "lumpy" because capacity is added to take into account expected sales increases. The firm starts with an investment of $25 (thousands or millions) to support sales of up to $50 (thousands or millions). When factory capacity is reached, at the sales of $50, an additional investment of $12.5 is postulated to provide sufficient additional capacity to support a sales level of $100. We have drawn the regression line based on the beginning capacity for the subsequent sales increases. The resulting regression relationship is:

$$\text{Fixed assets} = \$25 + .25 \text{ Sales.}$$

Alternatively, if the empirical observations are consistent when full capacity is reached, the regression line will have the same slope but a lower intercept. Similarly, for intermediate points between beginning and full capacity, if we consistently hit the same degree of "temporary excess capacity" we will have a regression line with the same slope as depicted but an intercept somewhat lower than $25.

Application of the Regression Method

We now illustrate the application of the regression method for forecasting financial requirements. We assume that we have had at least 10 years of historical data. Using the regression methodology we have described, we have found significant and meaningful relationships that may be summarized as follows:

- Cash $= .02S$, where $S =$ Sales
- Receivables $= .17S$
- Inventories $= \$10,000 + .18S$
- Net fixed assets $= \$25,000 + .25S$
- Accounts payable $= .10S$
- Accruals $= .05S$
- Total operating costs $= \$25,000 + .80S$
- Net income $= -\$25,000 + .12S$

With these relationships, we can project the balance sheet and income statement for the Moore Company based on a sales forecast of $800,000. When we used the percent of sales method, we could express the new balance sheet in terms of percents for each item that is related to sales as we did in Table 8.7. With the regression method, we use actual dollar amounts as shown in Table 8.12. We have used the regression method to project the

TABLE 8.12   Moore Company Balance Sheet and Income Statement
as of December 31, 19X2 (Sales $800,000)

Assets		Liabilities	
Cash	$ 16,000	Accounts payable	$ 80,000
Receivables	136,000	Accruals	40,000
Inventories	154,000	Total current liabilities	120,000
Net fixed assets	225,000	Mortgage bonds	70,000
Total assets	$531,000	Common stock	100,000
		Retained earnings	142,600
		Subtotal	$432,600
		Additional financing required	98,400
		Total liabilities & net worth	$531,000

**Moore Company Income Statement for Year
Ended December 31, 19X2**

Sales	$800,000
Total operating costs	665,000
Net operating income	$135,000
Net income	71,000
Dividends @ 40%	28,400
Addition to retained earnings	$ 42,600

balance sheet and income statement of the Moore Company as sales increase from
$500,000 to $800,000. The additional financing required is $98,400, which is lower than
the $146,000 under the percent of sales method by $47,600. The reconciliation consists of
$6,000 less inventories and $15,000 less net fixed assets under the regression method.
The net income relation and new assumed payout ratio of 40 percent account for the
remaining $26,600 difference.

Under both the percent of sales method and the regression method an interdepend-
ency relationship exists. The additional financing required will cause additional financing
costs to be incurred. This will cause interest costs and possibly dividends to increase so
that net income and the addition to retained earnings are likely to be reduced, causing the
additional financing required to increase. We finessed this problem by assuming an independent regression relationship for net income. These feedback relationships are cumbersome to calculate by hand, but computerized financial models have built-in programs to
provide the required outputs.

COMPUTER-BASED FINANCIAL PLANNING MODELS

Computer-based financial planning models are now widely used by business managers
and by academics. But they are used with better understanding if the basic principles
developed in this chapter are understood. It is generally useful to start with relatively
simple models to illustrate the basic relations. Then the models can be complicated to
handle a wide variety of assumptions and alternative scenarios.

Computer-based financial planning models can be developed to handle a wide range of possibilities. Most important is a consideration of alternative sales forecasts since these provide the foundation for all financial planning. The structure of costs related to our previous discussion of cost management is especially critical. Also various aspects of investment and asset management are important since the resources tied up in individual assets will be affected, as well as capital intensity relationships. From the investigation of such relationships, management may be guided to change fundamental strategies, to change the firm's products or markets, to lease rather than own assets, to alter the extent of automated operations, or to reevaluate and even change key financial policy decisions.

Computerized financial planning models may give the firm perspective to improve decision making in many areas. But these good results do not come automatically. Careful analysis is required, coupled with substantial quantities of experience and good judgment. But computerized financial planning models provide a perspective to better decision making, so a working knowledge of how to utilize them is strongly recommended.

SUMMARY

The general theme of this chapter is the financial planning and control process. A number of analytical approaches are set forth to help implement financial planning and control. The relationship between investment outlays and the volume required to achieve profitability is referred to as breakeven analysis. Breakeven analysis focuses on the pattern of relations between total revenues and total costs. It is a method of relating fixed costs, variable costs, and total revenues to show the level of sales that must be attained if the firm is to operate at a profit. The analysis can be based on the number of units produced or on total dollar sales. It can be used for the entire company or for a particular product or division. With minor modifications, it can be put on a cash basis instead of a profit basis.

Operating leverage is defined as the extent to which fixed costs are used in operations. The degree of operating leverage (DOL) is the ratio of the percentage change in operating income to the percentage change in units sold or in sales. A firm's DOL is a precise measure of how much operating leverage the firm is employing. Breakeven analysis emphasizes the volume of sales the firm needs to be profitable. The degree of operating leverage measures how sensitive the firm's operating income is to changes in the volume of sales. Both concepts measure the effects of the relative proportion of fixed costs in the total cost function of the firm.

The budgeting process provides detailed analysis for the control of revenues and costs. Its overall purpose is to improve internal operations, thereby reducing costs and raising profitability. A budgeting system starts with a set of performance standards, or targets. The targets represent the firm's financial plan. The budgeted amounts are compared with the actual results. If there are differences, the reasons should be identified and appropriate adjustments in the firm's policies should be made. These changes include the correction of deficiencies and more aggressive pursuit of opportunities. This is the feedback and control part of the budget process. It is critical to achieving a high level of managerial performance.

As a firm becomes larger, it is necessary for it to decentralize operations to some extent. But decentralized operations still require some centralized control. The principal tool used for such control is the return on investment (ROI) method. There are problems with ROI control; but if budgeting and ROI control are viewed as a communication system that aids the flow of information among managers of the firm, a dynamic interaction among managers can be developed. If the emphasis is on an informed interaction process, the results of operations as measured by ROI will be improved. Communication and motivation, the behavioral aspects of the budgeting process, cannot be overemphasized.

Financial forecasting is one of the most important tools for planning. The cash flow necessary for paying expenses, for working capital, and for long-term investment can be forecast from pro forma income statements and balance sheets. The most important variable that influences financing requirements for most firms is the projected dollar volume of sales.

We have reviewed two different procedures for financial forecasting. The percent of sales method is the simplest but also the most restrictive because it implicitly assumes a linear relationship that is forced to pass through the origin. Simple linear regression differs because it does not assume that the line passes through the origin. Linear regression finds the slope and intercept in order to minimize the ''sum of squared'' errors from the line. We showed how to compute the least squares estimates of the intercept and slope, and we discussed the meaning of statistical significance tests. These forecasting techniques can be used to estimate the seasonal and cyclical fluctuations in the firm's financial statements. These forecasts are then used to plan to meet the financial needs of the company.

QUESTIONS

8.1   What benefits can be derived from breakeven analysis?

8.2   What is operating leverage? Explain how profits or losses can be magnified in a firm with high operating leverage as opposed to a firm without this characteristic.

8.3   What data are necessary to construct a breakeven chart?

8.4   What is the general effect of each of the following changes on a firm's breakeven point?
   a.   An increase in selling price with no change in units sold.
   b.   A change from the leasing of a machine for $5,000 a year to the purchase of the machine for $100,000. The useful life of this machine will be 20 years, with no salvage value. Assume straight line depreciation.
   c.   A reduction in variable labor costs.

8.5   In what sense can depreciation be considered a source of funds?

8.6   Assume that a firm is making up its long-run financial budget. What period should this budget cover—one month, six months, one year, three years, five years, or some other period? Justify your answer.

8.7   Is a detailed budget more important to a large, multidivisional firm than to a small, single-product firm?

8.8 Assume that your uncle is a major stockholder in a multidivisional firm that uses a naive ROI criterion for evaluating divisional managers and that bases managers' salaries in large part on this evaluation. You can have the job of division manager in any division you choose. If you are a salary maximizer, what divisional characteristics will you seek? If, because of your good performance, you become president of the firm, what changes will you make?

8.9 What should be the approximate point of intersection between the sales-to-asset regression line and the vertical axis (Y-axis intercept) for the following: inventory, accounts receivable, fixed assets? State your answer in terms of positive, zero, or negative intercept. Can you think of any accounts that might have a negative intercept?

8.10 How does forecasting financial requirements in advance of needs help financial managers perform their responsibilities more effectively?

8.11 What is the difference between the long-range financial forecasting concept (for example, the percent-of-sales method) and the budgeting concept? How might they be used together?

8.12 Explain this statement: To a considerable extent, current assets represent permanent assets.

8.13 What advantages does a simple linear regression have over the percent of sales method for financial forecasting?

8.14 Define the slope of a linear regression. What equation do you use? What does the slope mean?

PROBLEMS

8.1 The Bentley Corporation produces tea kettles, which it sells for $10. Fixed costs are $600,000 for up to 400,000 units of output. Variable costs are $7 per unit.
   a. What is the firm's gain or loss at sales of 175,000 units? Of 300,000 units?
   b. What is the breakeven point? Illustrate by means of a chart.
   c. What is Bentley's degree of operating leverage at sales of 225,000 units? Of 300,000 units?

8.2 For Pratt Industries, the following relationships exist: Each unit of output is sold for $35; the fixed costs are $160,000; variable costs are $15 per unit.
   a. What is the firm's gain or loss at sales of 6,000 units? Of 9,000 units?
   b. What is the breakeven point? Illustrate by means of a chart.
   c. What is Pratt's degree of operating leverage at sales of 6,000 units? Of 9,000 units?
   d. What happens to the breakeven point if the selling price rises to $40? What is the significance of the change to financial management? Illustrate by means of a chart.
   e. What happens to the breakeven point if the selling price rises to $40 but variable costs rise to $20 a unit? Illustrate by means of a chart.

8.3 For Ardell Industries, the following relations exist: Each unit of output is sold for $100; the fixed costs are $312,500, of which $250,000 are annual depreciation charges; variable costs are $37.50 per unit.

a. What is the firm's gain or loss at sales of 4,000 units? Of 7,000 units?

b. What is the profit breakeven point? Illustrate by means of a chart.

c. What is the cash breakeven point? Illustrate by means of a chart.

d. Assume Ardell is operating at a level of 3,500 units. Are creditors likely to seek the liquidation of the company if it is slow in paying its bills?

8.4 The board of directors of the San Jose Microprocessor Company has received numerous complaints from shareholders regarding the performance of the firm's management. In an effort to verify the validity of these complaints, the board has collected the information below.

a. Calculate the relevant financial ratios for San Jose Microprocessor.

b. Apply a du Pont chart analysis on San Jose and compare it to the du Pont chart analysis based on composite ratios for the industry as a whole.

c. Evaluate management's performance and list specific areas where improvement is needed.

San Jose Microprocessor Company
Balance Sheet as of December 31, 19X0 (Thousands of Dollars)

Assets		Liabilities	
Cash	$ 90	Accounts payable	$450
Marketable securities	40	Notes payable (@ 11%)	380
Receivables	1,550	Other current liabilities	280
Inventory	1,190	Total current liabilities	$1,110
Total current assets	$2,870	Long-term debt (@ 9%)	880
Net fixed assets	1,130	Total liabilities	$1,990
		Net worth	2,010
Total assets	$4,000	Total claims on assets	$4,000

San Jose Microprocessor Company
Income Statement for Year Ended December 31, 19X0
(Thousands of Dollars)

Sales		$6,200
Cost of goods sold		
Materials	$2,440	
Labor	1,540	
Heat, light, and power	230	
Indirect labor	370	
Depreciation	140	4,720
Gross profit		$1,480
Selling expenses	$ 490	
General and administrative expenses	530	1,020
Net operating income (NOI)(EBIT)		$ 460
Less interest expense		121

8.5 Gulf and Eastern, Inc., is a diversified multinational corporation that produces a wide variety of goods and services, including chemicals, soaps, tobacco products, toys, plastics, pollution control equipment, canned food, sugar, motion pictures, and computer software. The corporation's major divisions were brought together in the early 1960s under a decentralized form of management; each division was evaluated in terms of its profitability, efficiency, and return on investments. This decentralized organization persisted through most of the decade, during which Gulf and Eastern experienced a high average growth rate in total assets, earnings, and stock prices.

Toward the end of 1975, however, those trends were reversed. The organization was faced with declining earnings, unstable stock prices, and a generally uncertain future. This situation persisted into 1976, but during that year, a new president, Lynn Thompson, was appointed by the board of directors. Thompson, who had served for a time on the financial staff of I. E. du Pont, used the du Pont system to evaluate the various divisions. All showed definite weaknesses.

Thompson reported to the board that a principal reason for the poor overall performance was a lack of control by central management over each division's activities. She was particularly disturbed by the consistently poor results of the corporation's budgeting procedures. Under that system, each division manager drew up a projected budget for the next quarter, along with estimated sales, revenue, and profit; funds were then allocated to the divisions, basically in proportion to their budget requests. However, actual budgets seldom matched the projections; wide discrepancies occurred; and this, of course, resulted in a highly inefficient use of capital.

In an attempt to correct the situation, Thompson asked the firm's chief financial officer to draw up a plan to improve the budgeting, planning, and control processes. When the plan was submitted, its basic provisions included the following:

1. To improve the quality of the divisional budgets, the division managers should be informed that the continuance of wide variation between their projected and actual budgets would result in dismissal.

2. A system should be instituted under which funds would be allocated to divisions on the basis of their average return on investment (ROI) during the last four quarters. Since funds were short, divisions with high ROIs would get most of the available money.

3. Only about half of each division manager's present compensation should be received as salary; the rest should be in the form of a bonus related to the division's average ROI for the quarter.

4. Each division should submit to the central office for approval all capital expenditure requests, production schedules, and price changes. Thus, the company would be recentralized.

   a. (1) Is it reasonable to expect the new procedures to improve the accuracy of budget forecasts?

   (2) Should all divisions be expected to maintain the same degree of accuracy?

   (3) In what other ways might the budgets be made?

   b. (1) What problems would be associated with the use of the ROI criterion in allocating funds among the divisions?

   (2) What effect would the period used in computing ROI (that is, four quarters, one quarter, two years, and so on) have on the effectiveness of this method?

   (3) What problems might occur in evaluating the ROI in the crude rubber and auto tires divisions? Between the sugar products and pollution control equipment divisions?

c. What problems would be associated with rewarding each manager on the basis of the division's ROI?

d. How well would the policy of recentralization work in this highly diversified corporation, particularly in light of the financial officer's three other proposals?

8.6 The Burwick Company's 19X0 balance sheet is given below. Sales in 19X0 totaled $2 million. The ratio of net profit to sales was 5 percent, with a dividend payout ratio of 40 percent of net income. Sales are expected to increase by 30 percent during 19X1. No long-term debt will be retired. Using the percentage of sales method, determine how much outside financing is required in 19X1.

Burwick Company Balance Sheet as of December 31, 19X0

Assets		Liabilities	
Cash	$ 75,000	Accounts payable	$ 40,000
Accounts receivable	150,000	Accruals	25,000
Inventory	240,000	Notes payable	85,000
Current assets	$ 465,000	Total current liabilities	$ 150,000
Net fixed assets	735,000	Long-term debt	250,000
		Total debt	$ 400,000
		Capital stock	450,000
		Retained earnings	350,000
Total assets	$1,200,000	Total liabilities and net worth	$1,200,000

8.7 Given the following data on Hanes Corporation, predict next year's balance sheet:

This year's sales: $80,000,000
Next year's sales: $100,000,000
After-tax profits: 6% of sales
Dividend payout: 40%
Retained earnings at the end of this year: $21,500,000
Cash as percent of sales: 3%
Receivables as percent of sales: 12%
Inventory as percent of sales: 25%
Net fixed assets as percent of sales: 40%
Accounts payable as percent of sales: 8%
Accruals as percent of sales: 20%
Next year's common stock: $20,000,000.

Hanes Corporation Balance Sheet as of December 31, 19X0

Assets		Liabilities	
Cash	_____	Accounts payable	_____
Accounts receivable	_____	Notes payable	_____
Inventory	_____	Accruals	_____
Total current assets	_____	Total current liabilities	_____
Fixed assets	_____	Common stock	_____
		Retained earnings	_____
Total assets	_____	Total liabilities	_____

8.8 One useful method of evaluating a firm's financial structure in relation to its industry is to compare it with financial ratio composites for the industry. A new firm, or an established firm contemplating entry into a new industry, may use such composites as a guide to its likely approximate financial position after the initial settling-down period.

The following data represent ratios for the publishing and printing industry for 19X0.

Sales to net worth: 2.2 times
Current debt to net worth: 45%
Total debt to net worth: 80%
Current ratio: 2.4 times
Net sales to inventory: 5.1 times
Average collection period: 60 days
Net fixed assets to net worth: 72%.

a. Complete the pro forma balance sheet (round to nearest thousand) for Original Printers, whose 19X0 sales are $5 million.
b. What does the use of the financial ratio composites accomplish?
c. What other factors will influence the financial structure of the firm?

Original Printers, Inc. Pro Forma Balance Sheet as of December 31, 19X0

Assets		Liabilities	
Cash	_____	Current debt	_____
Accounts receivable	_____	Long-term debt	_____
Inventory	_____	Total debt	_____
Current assets	_____	Net worth	_____
Fixed assets	_____		
Total assets	_____	Total liabilities and net worth	_____

8.9 The Kolton Supply Company is a wholesale steel distributor. It purchases steel in carload lots from more than 20 producing mills and sells to several thousand steel users. The items carried include sheets, plates, wire products, bolts, windows, pipe, and tubing.

The company owns two warehouses of 25,000 square feet each and is contemplating the erection of another warehouse of 30,000 square feet. The nature of a steel supply business requires that the company maintain large inventories to take care of customer requirements in the event of mill strikes or other delays.

In examining historical patterns, the company found consistent relationships among the following accounts as a percent of sales.

Current assets: 65%
Net fixed assets: 25%
Accounts payable: 10%
Other current liabilities, including accruals and provision for income taxes but not bank loans: 12%
Net profit after taxes: 5%.

The company's sales for 19X0 were $10 million, and its balance sheet on December 31, 19X0, is shown below. The company expects its sales to increase by $1 million each year. If this level is achieved, what will the company's financial requirements be at the end of the five-year period? Assume that accounts not tied directly to sales (for example, notes payable) remain constant and that the company pays no dividends.

a. Construct a pro forma balance sheet for the end of 19X5, using "additional financing needed" as the balancing item.

b. What are the crucial assumptions you made in your projection method?

Kolton Supply Company Balance Sheet as of December 31, 19X0

Assets		Liabilities	
Current assets	$6,500,000	Accounts payable	$1,000,000
Fixed assets	2,500,000	Notes payable	1,200,000
		Other current liabilities	1,200,000
		Total current liabilities	$3,400,000
		Mortgage loan	1,000,000
		Common stock	2,000,000
		Retained earnings	2,600,000
Total assets	$9,000,000	Total liabilities and net worth	$9,000,000

8.10 The 19X1 sales of Ultrasonics, Inc., were $12 million. Common stock and notes payable are constant. The dividend payout ratio is 40 percent. Retained earnings shown on the December 31, 19X0, balance sheet were $80,000. The percent of sales in each balance sheet item that varies directly with sales is expected to be

	Percent
Cash	5
Receivables	15
Inventories	20
Net fixed assets	40
Accounts payable	10
Accruals	5
Profit rate (after taxes) on sales	4

a. Complete the balance sheet given below.
b. Suppose that in 19X2, sales will increase by 20 percent over 19X1 sales. How much additional (external) capital will be required?
c. Construct the year-end 19X2 balance sheet. Set up an account for "financing needed" or "funds available."
d. What would happen to capital requirements under each of the following conditions?
  (1) The profit margin went from 4 percent to 6 percent; from 4 percent to 2 percent. Set up an equation to illustrate your answers.
  (2) The dividend payout rate was raised from 40 percent to 80 percent; was lowered from 40 percent to 20 percent. Set up an equation to illustrate your answers.
  (3) Slower collections caused receivables to rise to 72 days of sales.

Ultrasonics, Inc., Balance Sheet as of December 31, 19X1

Assets		Liabilities	
Cash	_____	Accounts payable	_____
Receivables	_____	Notes payable	$ 900,000
Inventory	_____	Accruals	_____
Total current assets	_____	Total current liabilities	_____
Fixed assets	_____	Common stock	$6,532,000
		Retained earnings	_____
Total assets	_____	Total liabilities and net worth	_____

8.11 A firm has the following relationships. The ratio of assets to sales is 55 percent. Liabilities that increase spontaneously with sales are 15 percent. The profit margin on sales after taxes is 6 percent. The firm's dividend payout ratio is 40 percent.

    a. If the firm's growth rate on sales is 15 percent per annum, what percentage of the sales increase in any year must be financed externally?

    b. If the firm's growth rate on sales increases to 25 percent per annum, what percentage of the sales increase in any year must be financed externally?

    c. How will your answer to Part (a) change if the profit margin increases to 8 percent?

    d. How will your answer to Part (b) change if the firm's dividend payout is reduced to 10 percent?

    e. If the profit margin increases from 6 percent to 8 percent and the dividend payout ratio is 20 percent, at what growth rate in sales will the external financing requirement percentage be exactly zero?

8.12 You are starting a new business. You know only two things: (1) the business you are planning to enter and (2) an estimated volume of sales. With the use of industry financial composites, you can project the balance sheet and income statement you are likely to have. Departures from this projection will provide a basis for analyzing causes of the deviations.

    To illustrate: You plan to enter the manufacturing of industrial electrical instruments. Sales in your first full year of operation are expected to be $14 million. Based on the following industry composites for 19X8, write the pro forma balance sheet and income statement for your company for 19X9.

Current ratio: 2.4 times
Net income to sales: 5%
Sales to net worth: 3.5 times
Average collection period: 50 days
Sales to inventory: 5.5 times
Fixed assets on net worth: 60%
Current debt to net worth: 50%
Total debt to net worth: 80%
Cost of sales to sales: 60%
Operating expenses to sales: 30%
Profit before taxes to sales: 10%.

8.13 Using the following data, calculate the mean, variance, and standard deviation for sales.

Year	Sales	GNP
19X8	$721.3	$3998.9
19X7	525.1	3513.6
19X6	462.3	3172.5
19X5	315.7	2937.7
19X4	256.8	2633.1
19X3	111.5	2417.8
19X2	82.9	2163.9

8.14 Using the data given in Problem 8.13, estimate the intercept and slope of the regression line:

$$\text{Sales} = \hat{a} + \hat{b} \text{ GNP}.$$

Next, estimate the coefficient of determination for the above regression.

8.15 Compare the return on equity for Quaker Oats and Ralston Purina from the data provided in Problem 7.6 of the previous chapter using the modified du Pont system:

$$\text{Asset turnover} \times \text{Profit margin on sales}$$
$$\times \text{ Leverage factor} = \text{Return on equity}.$$

8.16 *(Use the computer diskette, File name: 08FINPLN, Financial Planning and Control.)*

   a. Compare breakeven units and breakeven revenues for two firms: McElroy Chocolates and Hoag Roller Skates. Which has the lowest breakeven units? Which has the lowest breakeven revenues? Why isn't one firm lowest in both ways?

   b. McElroy Chocolates is considering buying a new Switzka chocolate dipping machine, which will increase fixed cost from $50,000 to $75,000 and reduce variable cost from $1.00 to $.80. Will this machine have a positive or negative effect on the breakeven point?

   c. McElroy Chocolates is now offered a choice between a Switzka and a Dutchka, which costs $10,000 more, but reduces variable cost by an additional $.10 per unit. Which has the most beneficial effect on breakeven point?

   d. Make up your own questions. Vary fixed cost, variable cost, price.

8.17 *(Use the computer diskette, File name: 08FNFOR, Financial Forecasting.)*

You are the owner of Birds-R-Us, which manufactures decorative pink flamingos. Sales revenues have grown rapidly over the past two years and you would like to know why, so you can better predict future sales revenues.

   You speculate that one of three factors may be responsible: increased ratings for the Miami Spice television program; expanded household lawn area; or, higher attendance at local zoos.

   a. Examine linear regression data and the accompanying graph for each of these factors. Which factor seems most responsible for improving flamingo revenues?

   (1) How does the coefficient of determination (i.e., r^2) vary for each case (see third panel of Screen #4)? What effect does this have on the graph?

   (2) How does the regression coefficient for each of the factors vary? What does this imply for the slope of the line which measures the strength of the influence of each of the independent variables, respectively, on the dependent variable (sales of pink flamingos)? Are these regression coefficients statistically significant for each of the (independent) variables influencing the sales of pink flamingos? (For our rough purposes a *T*-value of over 2 for our sample size would probably be statistically significant. Under 2 we would have to check it in a table of *T*-values.)

   b. How do forecasted sales revenues for 1986 differ for each of these factors? What accounts for this difference?

c. For which factor is the standard deviation of values the largest (see Summary of Regression Statistics in Screen #4)? For which factor is it the smallest? How does this affect the coefficient of determination?

Industry duPont Analysis

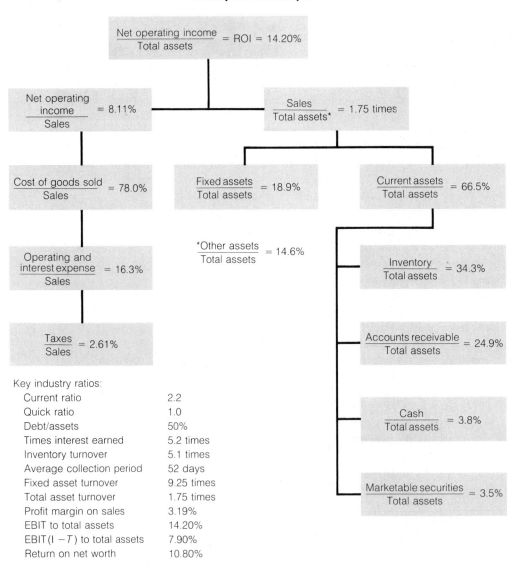

Key industry ratios:

Current ratio	2.2
Quick ratio	1.0
Debt/assets	50%
Times interest earned	5.2 times
Inventory turnover	5.1 times
Average collection period	52 days
Fixed asset turnover	9.25 times
Total asset turnover	1.75 times
Profit margin on sales	3.19%
EBIT to total assets	14.20%
EBIT $(1 - T)$ to total assets	7.90%
Return on net worth	10.80%

SELECTED REFERENCES

Babcock, G. C., "The Roots of Risk and Return," *Financial Analysts Journal*, 36 (January-February 1980), pp. 56–63.

————, "The Concept of Sustainable Growth," *Financial Analysts Journal*, 26 (May-June 1970), pp. 108–114.

Chambers, John, C.; Mullick, Satinder K.; and Smith, Donald D., "How to Choose the Right Forecasting Technique," *Harvard Business Review*, 49 (July-August 1971), pp. 45–74.

Christ, C. G., *Econometric Models and Methods*, New York: Wiley, 1966.

Dearden, John, "The Case Against ROI Control," *Harvard Business Review*, 47 (May-June 1969), pp. 124–135.

Dhavale, Dileep G., and Wilson, Hoyt G., "Breakeven Analysis with Inflationary Cost and Prices," *Engineering Economist*, 25 (Winter 1980), pp. 107–121.

Dhrymes, P. J., *Econometrics: Statistical Foundations and Applications*, New York: Harper and Row, 1970.

Francis, Jack Clark, and Rowell, Dexter R., "A Simultaneous Equation Model of the Firm for Financial Analysis and Planning," *Financial Management*, 7 (Spring 1978), pp. 29–44.

Gershefski, George W., "Building a Corporate Financial Model," *Harvard Business Review*, 47 (July-August 1969), pp. 61–72.

Goldberger, A. S., *Econometric Theory*, New York: Wiley, 1964.

Gup, Benton E., "The Financial Consequences of Corporate Growth," *Journal of Finance*, 35 (December 1980), pp. 1257–1265.

Higgins, Robert C., "Sustainable Growth Under Inflation," *Financial Management*, 10 (Autumn 1981), pp. 36–40.

Hoel, P. G., *Introduction to Mathematical Statistics*, 3rd ed., New York: Wiley, 1954.

Johnston, J., *Econometric Methods*, New York: McGraw-Hill, 1963.

Lee, Cheng F., and Junkus, Joan C., "Financing Analysis and Planning: An Overview," *Journal of Economics and Business*, 35 (August 1983), pp. 259–284.

Rao, P., and Miller, L., *Applied Econometrics*, Belmont, Calif.: Wadsworth, 1971.

Rappaport, Alfred, "Measuring Company Growth Capacity during Inflation," *Harvard Business Review*, 57 (January-February 1979), pp. 91–100.

————, "A Capital Budgeting Approach to Divisional Planning and Control," *Financial Executive*, 36 (October 1968), pp. 47–63.

Reinhardt, U. E., "Breakeven Analysis for Lockheed's Tri Star: An Application of Financial Theory," *Journal of Finance*, 28 (September 1973), pp. 821–838.

Searby, Frederick W., "Return to Return on Investment," *Harvard Business Review*, 53 (March-April 1975), pp. 113–119.

Sloan, Alfred P., Jr., *My Years with General Motors*, New York: Doubleday & Company, Inc., 1963.

Soldofsky, R. M., "Accountant's versus Economist's Concepts of Breakeven Analysis," *N.A.A. Bulletin*, 41 (December 1959), pp. 5–18.

Stone, Bernell K., and Miller, T. W., "Daily Cash Forecasting: A Structuring Framework," *Journal of Cash Management*, 1 (October 1981), pp. 35–50.

Stone, Bernell K.; Downes, David H.; and Magee, Robert P., "Computer-Assisted Financial Planning: The Planner-Model Interface," *Journal of Business Research*, 5 (September 1977), pp. 215–233.

Weston, J. Fred, "Strategy and Business Economics," *Business Economics*, (April 1989), pp. 5–12.

————, "Return on Investment as a Dynamic Management Process," Section 4 in *Handbook of Corporate Finance*, E. I. Altman, ed., New York: John Wiley and Sons, 1986.

————, "ROI Planning and Control: A Dynamic Management System," *Business Horizons*, (August 1972), pp. 35–42.

Wonnacott, R. J., and Wonnacott, T. H., *Econometrics*, New York: Wiley, 1970.

Zakon, Alan J., "Capital Structure Organization," Chapter 30 in *The Treasurer's Handbook*, eds., J. Fred Weston and Maurice B. Goudzwaard, Homewood, Ill.: Dow Jones-Irwin, 1976, pp. 641–668.

APPENDIX A TO CHAPTER 8

The Normal Distribution

One of the assumptions made in the development of linear regression is that the distribution of returns is approximately normal. The mean and variance (or standard deviation) can then be used to compare entire probability distributions. Because the normal distribution plays such an important role in financial economics, it is useful to know more about it.

Suppose that we have the continuous probability distribution shown in Figure 8A.1. This is a normal curve with a mean of 20 and a standard deviation of 5; X could be dollars, percentage rates of return, or any other units. If we want to know the probability that an outcome will fall between 15 and 30, we must calculate the area beneath the curve between these points, the shaded area in the diagram.

The area under the curve between 15 and 30 can be determined by integrating the curve over this interval, or, since the distribution is normal, by reference to statistical tables of the area under the normal curve, such as Appendix D.[1] To use these tables, it is necessary only to know the mean and standard deviation of the distribution. The distribution to be investigated must first be standardized by using the following formula:

$$z = \frac{X - \mu}{\sigma}, \tag{8A.1}$$

where z is the standardized variable, or the number of standard deviations from the mean;[2] X is the outcome of interest; and μ and σ are the mean and standard deviation of the distribution, respectively. For our example, where we are interested in the probability that an outcome will fall between 15 and 30, we first normalize these points of interest using Equation 8A.1:

$$z_1 = \frac{15 - 20}{5} = -1.0; \; z_2 = \frac{30 - 20}{5} = 2.0.$$

The areas associated with these z values are found in Table 8A.1 to be 0.3413 and 0.4773.[3] This means that the probability is 0.3413 that the actual outcome will fall be-

---

[1] The equation for the normal curve is tedious to integrate, thus making the use of tables much more convenient. The equation for the normal curve is:

$$f(X) = \frac{1}{\sqrt{2\pi\sigma^2}} e^{-(X - \mu)^2/2\sigma^2},$$

where $f(X)$ is the frequency of a given value of X, π is the ratio of the circumference to the diameter of a circle, and e is the base of natural logarithms; μ and σ denote the mean and standard deviation of the probability distribution, and X is any possible outcome.

[2] Note that if the point of interest is 1σ away from the mean, then $X - \mu = \sigma$, so $z = \sigma/\sigma = 1.0$. Thus, when $z = 1.0$, the point of interest is 1σ away from the mean; when $z = 2$, the value is 2σ, and so forth.

[3] Note that the negative sign on z_1 is ignored, since the normal curve is symmetrical around the mean; the minus sign merely indicates that the point lies to the left of the mean.

FIGURE 8A.1   Continuous Probability Distribution

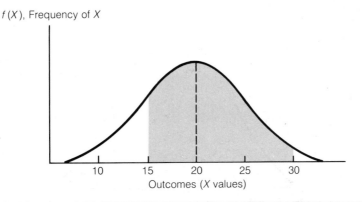

tween 15 and 20, and 0.4773 that it will fall between 20 and 30. Summing these probabilities shows that the probability of an outcome falling between 15 and 30 is 0.8186, or 81.86 percent.

Suppose we had been interested in determining the probability that the actual outcome would be greater than 15. Here, we would first note that the probability that the outcome will be between 15 and 20 is 0.3413. Then, we would observe that the probability of an outcome greater than the mean, 20, is 0.5000. Thus, the probability is 0.3413 + 0.5000 = 0.8413, or 84.13 percent, that the outcome will exceed 15.

Some interesting properties of normal probability distributions can be seen by examining Table 8A.1 and Figure 8A.2, which is a graph of the normal curve. For any normal distribution, the probability of an outcome falling within plus or minus one standard deviation from the mean is 0.6826, or 68.26 percent; 34.13 percent $\times$ 2.0. If we take the range within two standard deviations of the mean, the probability of an occurrence within this range is 95.46 percent; and 99.74 percent of all outcomes will fall within three

TABLE 8A.1   Area under the Normal Curve of Error

z	Area from the Mean to the Point of Interest	f(z) Ordinate
0.0	0.0000	0.3989
0.5	0.1915	0.3521
1.0	0.3413	0.2420
1.5	0.4332	0.1295
2.0	0.4773	0.0540
2.5	0.4938	0.0175
3.0	0.4987	0.0044

z = number of standard deviations from the mean. Some area tables are set up to indicate the area to the left or right of the point of interest; in this book, we indicate the area between the mean and the point of interest.

FIGURE 8A.2　The Normal Curve

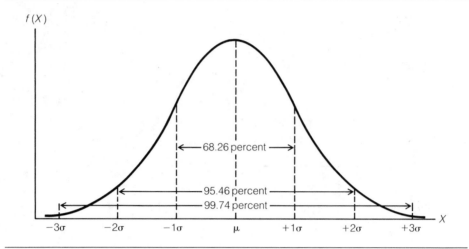

standard deviations of the mean. Although the distribution theoretically runs from minus infinity to plus infinity, the probability of occurrences beyond about three standard deviations is very near zero.

ILLUSTRATING THE USE OF PROBABILITY CONCEPTS

The concepts discussed in the preceding section of this appendix can be clarified by a numerical example. Consider three states of the economy; boom, normal, and recession. Next, assume that we can attach a probability of occurrence to each state of the economy and, further, that we can estimate the dollar returns that will occur on each of two projects under each possible state. With this information, we construct Table 8A.2.

The expected values of Projects A and B are calculated by Equation 8A.2,

$$E(X) = \sum_{i=1}^{S} p_i X_i,$$ (8A.2)

and the standard deviations of their respective returns are found by Equation 8A.3.

$$\sigma = \sqrt{\sum_{i=1}^{S} p_i [X_i - E(X)]^2}$$ (8A.3)

Note that since the probabilities of events are subjectively estimated, and are not sampling statistics, we multiply each event by its probability, p_i, instead of dividing by the number

TABLE 8A.2   Means and Standard Deviations of Projects A and B

State of the Economy (S)	Probability of Its Occurring p_i	Return X_i	p_iX_i
Project A			
1. Recession	0.2	$400	$ 80
2. Normal	0.6	500	300
3. Boom	0.2	600	120
			Expected
	1.0		value = $500
Standard deviation = σ_A = $63.25.			
Project B			
1. Recession	0.2	$300	$ 60
2. Normal	0.6	500	300
3. Boom	0.2	700	140
			Expected
	1.0		value = $500
Standard deviation = σ_B = $126.49.			

of observations. On the assumption that the returns from Projects A and B are normally distributed, knowing the mean and the standard deviation as calculated in Table 8A.2 permits us to graph probability distributions for Projects A and B; these distributions are

FIGURE 8A.3   Probability Distributions for Projects A and B

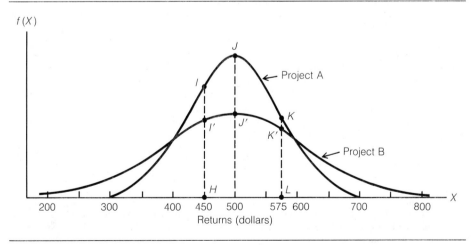

Returns (dollars)

shown in Figure 8A.3[4] The expected value of each project's cash flow is seen to be $500; however, the flatter graph of B indicates that this is the riskier project.

Suppose we want to determine the probabilities that the actual returns of Projects A and B will be in the interval $450 to $575. Using Equation 8A.1 and Figure 8A.3, we can calculate the respective probability distributions. The first step is to calculate the z values of the interval limits for the two projects:

Project A

$$\text{lower } z_1 = \frac{\$450 - \$500}{\$63.25} = -0.79.$$

$$\text{upper } z_2 = \frac{\$575 - \$500}{\$63.25} = 1.19.$$

Project B

$$\text{lower } z_1 = \frac{\$450 - \$500}{\$126.49} = -0.40.$$

$$\text{upper } z_2 = \frac{\$575 - \$500}{\$126.49} = 0.59.$$

In Appendix D, which is a more complete table of z values, we find the areas under a normal curve for each of these four z values:

---

[4]Normal probability distributions can be constructed once the mean and standard deviation are known, using a table of *ordinates* of the normal curve. (See Column 3 of Table 8A.1.) This table is similar to the table of areas used above, except that the ordinate table gives relative *heights* of probability curve $f(X)$ at various z values rather than areas beneath the curve. Figure 8A.3 was constructed by plotting points at various z values according to the following formula:

$$f(X) = \frac{1}{\sigma} \times (\text{Ordinate for } z \text{ value}),$$

where the ordinate value is read from a table of ordinates.

For example, the points corresponding to the mean and +1 and +2 standard deviations for Projects A and B were calculated as follows:

Project A (1)	z (2)	Ordinate at z (3)	1/σ (4)	f(X): (3) × (4) = (5)
Mean = 500.00	0	0.3989	1/63.25	0.0063
+1σ = 563.25	1	0.2420	1/63.25	0.0038
+2σ = 626.50	2	0.0540	1/63.25	0.0009
Project B				
Mean = 500.00	0	0.3989	1/126.49	0.0032
+1σ = 626.49	1	0.2420	1/126.49	0.0019
+2σ = 752.98	2	0.0540	1/126.49	0.0004

Column 5 above gives the relative heights of the two distributions: Thus, if we decide (for pictorial convenience) to let the curve for Project B be 3.2 inches high at the mean, then the curve should be 1.9 inches high at $\mu \pm 1\sigma$, and the curve for Project A should be 6.3 inches at the mean and 3.8 inches at $\pm 1\sigma$. Other points in Figure 8A.3 were determined in like manner.

Project A	z Value	Area
lower z:	−.79	0.2852
upper z:	1.19	0.3830

Total area = 0.6682, or 66.82 percent.

Project B	z Value	Area
lower z:	−0.40	0.1554
upper z:	0.59	0.2224

Total area = 0.3778, or 37.78 percent.

Thus, there is about a 67 percent chance that the actual cash flow from Project A will lie in the interval $450 to $575 and about a 38 percent probability that B's cash flow will fall in this interval.

Now look at Figure 8A.3 and observe the two areas that were just calculated. For Project A, the area bounded by *HIJKL* represents about 67 percent of the area under A's curve. For Project B, that area bounded by *HI'J'K'L* includes about 38 percent of the total area.

CUMULATIVE PROBABILITY

Suppose we ask these questions: What is the probability that the cash flows from Project A will be at least $100? $150? $200? and so on. Obviously, there is a higher probability of their being at least $100 rather than $150, at least $150 rather than $200, and so on. In general, the most convenient way of expressing the answer to such "at least" questions is through the use of *cumulative probability distributions;* these distributions for Projects A and B are calculated in Table 8A.3 and are plotted in Figure 8A.4.

Suppose Projects A and B each cost $450; then, if each project returns at least $450, they will both break even. What is the probability of breaking even on each project? From Figure 8A.4, we see that the probability is 78 percent that Project A will break even, while the breakeven probability is only 65 percent for the riskier Project B. However, there is virtually no chance that A will yield more than $650, while B has a 5 percent chance of returning $700 or more.

OTHER DISTRIBUTIONS

Thus far, we have assumed that project returns fit a probability distribution that is approximately normal. Many distributions do fit this pattern, and normal distributions are relatively easy to work with. Therefore, much of the work done on risk measurement assumes a normal distribution. However, other distributions are certainly possible; Figure 8A.5 shows distributions skewed to the right and left, respectively. For two possible investments with equal expected returns, *F*, would an investor prefer a normal, a left-skewed, or a right-skewed distribution? A distribution skewed to the right, such as the one in Figure 8A.5(a), would probably be chosen because the odds on a very low return are small, while

TABLE 8A.3 Cumulative Probability Distributions
for Projects A and B

	Expected Return	z Value	Cumulative Probability
Project A			
	$300	−3.16	0.9992[a]
	400	−1.58	0.9429[b]
	450	−0.79	0.7852
	500	0.00	0.5000[c]
	575	1.19	0.1170[d]
	600	1.58	0.0571
	700	3.16	0.0008[a]
Project B			
	$200	−2.37	0.9911[b]
	300	−1.58	0.9429
	400	−0.79	0.7852
	450	−0.40	0.6554
	500	0.00	0.5000[c]
	575	0.59	0.2776[d]
	600	0.79	0.2148
	700	1.58	0.0571
	800	2.37	0.0089

[a]Not shown in Appendix D.
[b]0.5000 plus area under left tail of the normal curve; for example, for Project A, 0.5000 + 0.4429 = 0.9429 = 94.3 percent for z = −1.58.
[c]The mean has a cumulative probability of 0.5000 = 50 percent.
[d]0.5000 less area under right tail of the normal curve; for example, for Project A, 0.5000 − 0.3830 = 0.1170 = 11.7 percent for z = 1.19.

FIGURE 8A.4 Cumulative Probability Distributions for Projects A and B

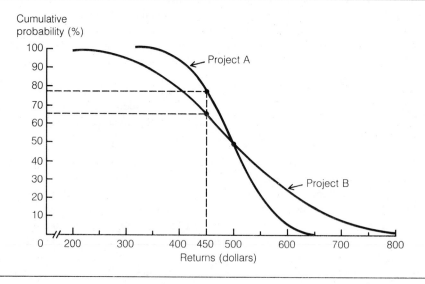

FIGURE 8A.5   Skewed Distributions

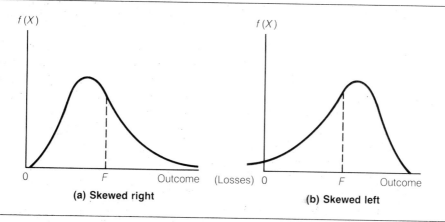

(a) Skewed right   **(b) Skewed left**

there is some chance of very high returns. For the left-skewed distributions, there is little likelihood of large gains but a large cumulative probability of losses. Skewness is in the direction of the "long tail" of the probability distribution.

PROBLEMS

8A.1 The sales of the Cleveland Company for next year have the following probability distribution:

Probability	Sales (Millions of Dollars)
0.1	$10
0.2	12
0.4	15
0.2	18
0.1	20

a. On graph paper, plot sales on the horizontal axis and probability of sales on the vertical axis, using the points given above. Draw a smooth curve connecting your plotted points. What can you say about this curve?
b. Compute the mean of the probability distribution.
c. Compute the standard deviation of the probability distribution.
d. Compute the coefficient of variation of the probability distribution.
e. What is the probability that sales will exceed $16 million?
f. What is the probability that sales will fall below $13 million?
g. What is the probability that sales will be between $13 and $16 million?
h. What is the probability that sales will exceed $17 million?

8A.2 Mutual of Poughkeepsie offers to sell your firm a $1 million, one-year term insurance policy on your corporate jet for a premium of $7,500. The probability that the plane will be lost or incur damages in that amount in any 12-month period is 0.001.
- **a.** What is the insurance company's expected gain from sale of the policy?
- **b.** What is the insurance company's expected gain or loss if the probability of a $1 million fire loss is 0.01? Would the insurance company still offer your firm the same policy for the same premium? Explain.

CHAPTER 9

Capital Budgeting under Certainty

Capital budgeting involves the entire process of planning expenditures with returns that are expected to extend beyond one year. The choice of one year is arbitrary, of course, but it is a convenient cutoff point for distinguishing between kinds of expenditures. Obvious examples of capital outlays are expenditures for land, buildings, and equipment, and for permanent additions to working capital associated with sales growth. An advertising or promotion campaign or a research and development program is also likely to have an impact beyond one year, so they too can be classified as capital budgeting expenditures.

THE COMPLEXITY OF CAPITAL BUDGETING

To facilitate an exposition of the investment decision process, we have broken the topic down into its major components. In this chapter, we consider the capital budgeting process and the techniques generally employed by reasonably sophisticated business firms. The compound interest concepts covered in Chapter 3 are used extensively. Uncertainty is explicitly considered in Chapter 13, the cost of capital concept is developed and related to capital budgeting in Chapter 15.

Analysis of major new projects is not easy. In the 1970s, a joint venture between British and French companies invested $2 billion to produce the Concorde, a plane with supersonic speed. They hoped to sell 300 but sold only 13. Higher than expected fuel prices required high fares. Because of its noise, coast-to-coast flights across the United States were prohibited. Its range was too short to provide service between Asia and other continents. In the spring of 1990 it was announced that a joint venture would try to develop a Super-Concorde with a range twice as far as the original. It was expected that 5 years would be required for research, 8 for production, and 2 to 3 for testing, a total of possibly 15 years involving an investment of an amount estimated between $9 billion and $14 billion. Such a risky venture cannot be completely quantified, but careful analysis provides an improved basis for judgments and decisions.

Another challenging investment area is nuclear energy. For example, the Seabrook, New Hampshire, nuclear power plant took 10 years to construct and received a full power license from the Nuclear Regulatory Commission not until four years after completion of construction. The project's cost was initially estimated at less than $2 billion for two reactors, but became more than $6 billion for one reactor because of delays and overruns. These heavy costs caused the Public Service Company of New Hampshire to file for bankruptcy in 1988 because it was unable to pay interest on the debt it incurred to finance its 35.6 percent stake in Seabrook. Nuclear energy could potentially lessen the U.S. dependency on Mideast oil, but its costs in practice have been far in excess of estimates. In addition, safety problems associated with operations and disposal of nuclear wastes have not been resolved.

The previous two examples are extreme cases, but for some industries the complexity of investment decisions must be successfully managed for profitable operations. A description of the nature of new product development and research and development efforts in the pharmaceutical industry illustrates the challenging nature of capital budgeting decisions.

The pharmaceutical industry screens some 10,000 compounds to find one that results in a product that receives approval from the Food and Drug Administration (FDA) so that it may legally be marketed. The new product process takes 10 to 15 years with an investment cost (including the opportunity cost of funds used in investment outlays) of some $200 million. Most products do not generate sufficient sales to earn their cost of capital; only the few "blockbuster" drugs generate earnings to cover their cost of capital [Virts and Weston, 1980].

With such great uncertainty involved in capital budgeting for new products, it is not possible to claim that this chapter will provide a simple cookbook recipe that will be an infallible guide. In addition to the guidelines that we shall explain, experience, intuition, good judgment, and good luck are often needed to make profitable investments. But the principles and procedures we describe will provide a useful roadmap through the complexity. This will discipline the analysis and free the decision maker to add judgment to the formal quantitative analysis. We now develop some systematic procedures for dealing with the challenges of capital budgeting.

THE STRATEGIC FRAMEWORK FOR CAPITAL BUDGETING DECISIONS

Although most capital budgeting decisions do not involve risks of the magnitude as those of building a Concorde or nuclear plants, capital budgeting decisions must be related to the firm's overall strategic planning. Strategy involves planning for the future of the firm. Capital budgeting inherently requires a commitment into the future. The purchase of an asset with an economic life of 10 years involves a long period of waiting before the final results of such actions can be known. During a 10-year period, a turbulent economic and financial environment can cause great uncertainty.

Consulting with the principal owner of a small chain of supermarkets underscored the complexity of long-term decisions. The owner stated that he preferred to avoid buying the stores and to use 20-year leases instead. His reason was that economic and financial changes made him unwilling to make an ownership commitment, but still he was making a contract for 20 years. Implicitly he was saying that a 20-year contract to rent was less risky and would produce more profits than ownership of his store outlets. Yet one of McDonald's major sources of profitability is probably their ownership of many prime locations for their restaurants. Without thinking through the advantages and disadvantages, the owner of the supermarkets had arrived at a judgment that one type of contract involved less risk than another.

Capital budgeting must be integrated with strategic planning because excessive investments or inadequate investments will have serious consequences for the future of the firm. If the firm has invested too much in fixed assets, it will incur unnecessarily heavy expenses. If it has not spent enough, it will have inadequate capacity and may lose a portion of its share of the market to rival firms. To regain lost customers is difficult and expensive.

A related problem is how to properly phase the availability of capital assets in order to have them come "on stream" at the correct time. For example, the executive vice president of a decorative tile company gave the authors an illustration of the importance of capital budgeting. His firm tried to operate near capacity most of the time. For about four years, there had been intermittent surges in the demand for its product; when these surges occurred, the firm had to turn away orders. After a sharp increase in demand, the firm would add capacity by renting an additional building and then purchasing and installing the appropriate equipment. It would take six to eight months to have the additional capacity ready. At this point, the company frequently found that there was no demand for its increased output—other firms had already expanded their operations and had taken an increased share of the market, with the result that demand for this firm had leveled off. If the firm had properly forecast demand and had planned its increase in capacity six months or one year in advance, it would have been able to maintain its market—indeed, to obtain a larger share of the market.

Good capital budgeting will improve the timing of asset acquisitions and the quality of assets purchased. This result follows from the nature of capital goods and their producers. Capital goods are not ordered by firms until sales are beginning to press on capacity. Such occasions occur simultaneously for many firms. When the heavy orders come in, the producers of capital goods go from a situation of idle capacity to one where they cannot meet all the orders that have been placed. Consequently, large backlogs accumulate. Since the production of capital goods involves a relatively long work-in-process period, a year or more of waiting may be involved before the additional modern capital goods are available. Furthermore, the quality of the capital goods, produced on rush order, may deteriorate. These factors have obvious implications for purchasing agents and plant managers.

Another reason for the importance of capital budgeting is that asset expansion typically involves substantial expenditures. Before a firm spends a large amount of money, it must make the proper plans—large amounts of funds are not available automatically. A firm contemplating a major capital expenditure program may need to plan its financing several years in advance to be sure of having the funds required for the expansion.

A number of factors combine to make capital budgeting perhaps the most important financial management decision. Further, all departments of a firm — production, marketing, and so on — are vitally affected by the capital budgeting decisions; so all executives, no matter what their primary responsibility, must be aware of how capital budgeting decisions are made and how to interact effectively in the processes.

CATEGORIES OF CAPITAL BUDGETING DECISIONS

The classification of capital investments is made in order to improve decision making. The administrative processes for approving and post-auditing capital investment decisions will differ for different kinds of projects. Thus by classifying investments a firm may be able to develop standardized administrative procedures for handling classes of proposals. Many different bases for classification exist, and they are not necessarily mutually exclusive.

Project Size

The size of a proposal clearly matters. Size may be measured by funds required or other types of scarce resources required such as land, floor space for equipment, and kinds of managerial personnel required. Most firms permit business segments to make capital outlays below some dollar amount without further review. The degree of formal review procedures is likely to increase as the size of the project increases. Major projects may be defined by an outlay of $10,000 in one company but be $1 million in another. Standardized procedures may be used for small projects, but more levels of review are likely to be required for larger outlays. Proposals involving significant changes in corporate strategy are likely to require approval of the board of directors.

Effect on Business Risk

Of considerable analytical importance is whether the risk of the portfolio of a firm's activities is changed by new investments. One way to analyze effects on risks is to distinguish between internal investments and external investments represented by mergers or takeovers. Internal investments are likely to represent areas with which the firm already has considerable familiarity. External acquisition activity may appear to be highly attractive but is also likely to carry considerable risk. An issue here is the degree to which the new investment is *related* to the firm's existing activities. In general, related projects involve less risk but are less likely to open up new important areas of activity for the firm. Differences in perceived risk may be a matter of judgment. Conflicting generalizations are made: ''Stay with what you know how to do best,'' ''Stick to your knitting and you will die on the vine,'' and ''Keep alert to the need for new products and new markets required by the changing economic environment.'' In the face of conflicting advice, careful balancing of different types of considerations is required.

Cost Reduction and Revenue Increase

Another approach to risk is to distinguish between three categories of investment: replacements, expansion, and growth.

Replacements. Ordinarily, replacement decisions are the simplest to make. Assets wear out or become obsolete, and they must be replaced if production efficiency is to be maintained. The firm has a very good idea of the cost savings to be obtained by replacing an old asset, and it knows the consequences of nonreplacement. The outcomes of most replacement decisions can be predicted with a high degree of confidence.

Expansion. Additional capacity in existing product lines has been defined as expansion. Examples are proposals for adding more machines of the type already in use or the opening of new branches in a chain of food stores. Expansion investments are frequently incorporated in replacement decisions. To illustrate, an old, inefficient machine may be replaced by a larger and more efficient one. A degree of uncertainty — sometimes extremely high — is clearly involved in expansion, but the firm at least has the advantage of examining past production and sales experience with similar machines or stores.

Growth. New product lines or new geographic markets, such as foreign investments, are examples of growth investments. The degree of experience available on which to base decisions may vary with the degree of relatedness of the new areas. Often decisions depend heavily on heroic judgments and vision. Lee Iacocca, in his speeches and writings, has often criticized financial managers for their lack of entrepreneurship. He complains that financial managers are often merely "bean pushers." In our preoccupation with counting the beans or manipulating the numbers, Iacocca states that "financial types" cause the firm to miss attractive opportunities because important dimensions cannot be quantified. Mr. Iacocca recommends that bold entrepreneurship override a preoccupation with looking at only what can be quantified.

Mandatory and Intangible Investments

Investments required by government regulations represent another category. The firm has little discretion on such matters. For example, pollution control devices may be required even though they produce no direct revenues. Related investments may represent intangibles such as proposals to boost employee morale and productivity by installing a music system.

Degree of Dependence

Independent projects have no interrelationships. An example would be installing new equipment to produce product A and installing equipment to produce product B where products A and B are completely different. In contrast, some investments may be mutually exclusive. An example would be whether to buy forklift trucks propelled by gas engines versus electrical engines.

Projects may be complements. The introduction of better lighting may improve all other operations. Projects may be substitutes. The introduction of a new ready-to-eat cereal may cause the sales of existing cereals to decline to some degree. The distinctions between independent projects and mutually exclusive projects are particularly important because ranking procedures may be affected.

Administrative Aspects

In most firms, there are more proposals for projects than the firm is able or willing to finance. Some proposals are good, others are poor, and methods must be developed for distinguishing between the good and the bad. Essentially, the end product is a ranking of the proposals and a cutoff point for determining how far down the ranked list to go.

Approvals are typically required at higher levels within the organization as we move away from replacement decisions and as the sums involved increase. One of the most important functions of the board of directors is to approve the major outlays in a capital budgeting program as well as the total capital budget for each planning period. Such decisions are crucial for the future well-being of the firm.

The planning horizon for capital budgeting programs varies with the nature of the industry. When sales can be forecast with a high degree of reliability for 10 to 20 years, the planning period is likely to be correspondingly long; electric utilities are an example of such an industry. Also, when the product-technology developments in the industry require an 8- to 10-year cycle to develop a new major product, as in certain segments of the aerospace industry, a correspondingly long planning period is necessary.

After a capital budget has been adopted, funding must be scheduled. Characteristically, finance is responsible for the acquisition of funds to meet budgeted requirements. The finance department is also primarily responsible for cooperating with the operating divisions to compile systematic records on the uses of funds and the installation of equipment purchased. Effective capital budgeting programs require such information as the basis for periodic review and evaluation of capital expenditure decisions—the feedback and control phase of capital budgeting, often called the *post-audit review*.

The foregoing represents a brief overview of the administrative aspects of capital budgeting; the analytical problems involved are considered next.

EVALUATION OF ALTERNATIVE RANKING METHODS

The point of capital budgeting—indeed, the point of all financial analysis—is to make decisions that will maximize the value of the firm. The capital budgeting process is designed to answer two questions: (1) Which among mutually exclusive investments should be selected? (2) How many projects, in total, should be accepted?

Alternative Ranking Criteria—An Overview

Nine major ranking criteria are found in the literature and in practice. We shall first present an overview of them to demonstrate their interrelatedness. The nine criteria are:

1. Cash Payback (PB)
2. Discounted Cash Payback (DPB)
3. Accounting Rate of Return (ARR)
4. Net Present Value (NPV)
5. Internal Rate of Return (IRR)

6. Net Terminal Value (NTV)
7. Opportunity Cost Return (OCR)
8. Profitability Index (PI)
9. Perpetuity Rate of Return (PRR)

General Principles

When comparing various capital budgeting criteria, it is useful to establish some guidelines. The optimal decision rule will have four characteristics:

1. It will appropriately consider all cash flows.
2. It will discount the cash flows at the appropriate market-determined opportunity cost of capital.
3. It will select from a group of mutually exclusive projects the one that maximizes shareholders' wealth.
4. It will allow managers to consider each project independently from all others. This has come to be known as the *value additivity principle*.

The value additivity principle implies that if we know the value of separate projects accepted by management, then simply adding their values, V_j, will give us the value of the firm. If there are N projects, then the value of the firm will be:[1]

$$V = \sum_{j=1}^{N} V_j, j = 1, \ldots N.$$

This is a particularly important point because it means that projects can be considered on their own merit without the necessity of looking at them in an infinite variety of combinations with other projects.

We now perform the actual implementation of the alternative capital budgeting techniques. We shall see that only one technique — the net present value method — satisfies all four of the desirable properties for capital budgeting criteria.

Data for the Evaluation

Some illustrative data provide a basis for the evaluation of the alternative criteria. Table 9.1 gives the cash flows for four mutually exclusive projects. They all have the same life, five years, and they all require the same investment outlay, $1,500. Once accepted, no project can be abandoned without incurring the outflows indicated. For example, Project A has negative cash flows during its fourth and fifth years. Once the project is

---

[1] The summation sign, Σ, simply means that we add up the present values of the projects. For example, if there are three projects, then $N = 3$ and

$$\sum_{j=1}^{N} V_j = \sum_{j=1}^{3} V_j = V_1 + V_2 + V_3.$$

TABLE 9.1   Cash Flows of Four Mutually Exclusive Projects

Year	A	B	C	D	PVIF @10%
		Cash Flows			
0	$-1,500	$-1,500	$-1,500	$-1,500	1.000
1	150	0	150	300	.909
2	1,350	0	300	450	.826
3	150	450	450	750	.751
4	-150	1,050	600	750	.683
5	-600	1,950	1,875	900	.621

accepted these expected cash outflows must be incurred. An example of a project of this type is a nuclear power plant. Decommissioning costs at the end of the economic life of the facility can be as large as the initial construction costs, and they must be taken into account.

The last column of Table 9.1 shows the appropriate discount factors for the present value of cash flows, assuming that the applicable opportunity cost of capital is 10 percent.[2] Since all four projects are assumed to have the same risk, they can be discounted at the same interest rate.

Cash Payback (PB)

The payback period is the number of years required to recover the initial capital outlay on a project. The payback periods for the four projects in Table 9.1 are as listed here:

- Project A, 2-year payback
- Project B, 4-year payback
- Project C, 4-year payback
- Project D, 3-year payback

If management were adhering strictly to the payback method, then Project A would be chosen as the best among the four mutually exclusive alternatives. Even a casual look at the numbers indicates that this would be a bad decision. The difficulty with the payback method is that it does not consider all cash flows and it fails to discount them. Failure to consider all cash flows results in ignoring the large negative cash flows that occur in the last two years of Project A. Failure to discount them means that management would be indifferent between the following two cash flow patterns:

---

[2]A discussion of how the cost of capital is calculated is presented in Chapter 15. For now, the cost of capital should be considered as the firm's opportunity cost of making a particular investment. That is, if the firm does not make a particular investment, it saves the cost of this investment; and if it can invest these funds in another project of equivalent risk that provides a return of 10 percent, then its opportunity cost of making the first investment is 10 percent.

TABLE 9.2   Cash Flows for Three Projects and Their Payback Period

	Cash Flows				
Year	1	2	3	1 and 3	2 and 3
0	$-1	$-1	$-1	$-2	$-2
1	0	1	0	0	1
2	2	0	0	2	0
3	-1	1	3	2	4
Payback in years	2	1	3	2	3

	Cash Flows	
Year	G	G*
0	$-1,000	$-1,000
1	100	900
2	900	100

Projects G and G* have the same payback period. Yet no one with a positive opportunity cost of funds would choose Project G because Project G* returns cash much faster.

The payback method also violates the value additivity principle. Consider the example in Table 9.2. The outlay in each case is $1 (billion, million, or thousand). Projects 1 and 2 are mutually exclusive but Project 3 is independent. Hence, it is possible to undertake Projects 1 and 3 in combination, 2 and 3 in combination, or any of the projects in isolation. Table 9.2 shows the alternatives and their cash flows.

If projects are considered separately, then Project 2 looks best, with a one-year payback. But if combinations of projects are considered, now Projects 1 and 3 look better than Projects 2 and 3. This is a clear violation of the value additivity principle because the decision we reach by studying mutually exclusive alternatives (for example, Project 2 is best) is different from the decision reached when projects are considered as combinations (for example, 1 and 3 are best). Shortly, we shall show that the internal rate of return method also violates the value additivity principle, but the net present value method does not.

Two arguments can be given for the use of the payback method. One, it is easy to use. Two, for a company in a tight cash position, it may be of great interest to know how soon it gets back the dollars it has invested.

Discounted Cash Payback (DPB)

The DPB is the number of years required for the sum of the cash flows discounted at k, the cost of capital, to equal the present value of the initial outlay. We can use the data for Project D to illustrate its computation:

Year	Cash Flows D	PVIF @ 10%	Present Value	Cumulative Present Value
0	$-1,500	1.000	$-1,500	$-1,500
1	300	.909	273	-1,227
2	450	.826	372	-855
3	750	.751	563	-292
4	750	.683	512	+220
5	900	.621	559	+779

The discounted cash inflows equal the initial investment outlay during the fourth year so the DPB period is between three and four years.

The discounted cash payback method does take the time value of money into account. However, it still suffers from the weakness that it does not consider all cash flows. In our example, the largest cash inflow occurs after the DPB period.

Accounting Rate of Return (ARR)

The accounting rate of return is the ratio of net income (NI) to the average investment outlay. Net income is equal to $(CF_t - Dep)$ where Dep is depreciation. The average investment is the arithmetic average of the beginning and ending investment values. In practice, the ARR is the ratio of NI to the depreciated value of fixed assets. We use Project D to illustrate the ARR computation, assuming straight-line depreciation of $300 per year.

Year	Cash Flows D	Net Income	Depreciated Value of Investment	ARR
0	$-1,500	—	$1,500	—
1	300	$ 0	1,200	0
2	450	150	900	16.67%
3	750	450	600	75.00%
4	750	450	300	150.00%
5	900	600	0	∞

The ARR does not take the time value of money into account. Also, the ARR rises with the age of assets even if the NI measure is constant, since the depreciated value of the investment declines. However, for a firm with a large portfolio of assets, the depreciated book value of fixed assets will approximate 50 percent of their original value. For example, for all U.S. manufacturing corporations the ratio of net to gross fixed assets is 51 percent.[3] We could apply this to our examples. The average value of fixed assets during the life of the project is ($1,500 + 0)/2 = $750. If net income were related to this figure, it would fluctuate less, but a summary measure for the life of the project would not be meaningful.

The ARR measure is related to the return on equity measure widely reported in business and government publications. But the book value of equity is a part of an accounting identity in which equity plus all other liabilities equals total assets, valuing fixed assets at their net value after deducting the reserve for depreciation. Hence the widely

---

[3]*Quarterly Financial Report for Manufacturing, Mining, and Trade Corporations,* Bureau of the Census, U.S. Department of Commerce, various issues.

used return on equity, which reflects the philosophy of the ARR, is based on the net or depreciated values of fixed assets. For the all manufacturing universe, the assumption of the ARR that assets are about 50 percent depreciated turns out to be factually correct. However, for individual companies and even industries, this assumption that fixed assets are about one-half depreciated may not be correct. For new and growing companies where large outlays are being made for new plant and equipment, the ratio of net to gross fixed assets would be much higher than 50 percent. This would bias the measured return on equity downward because the denominator would be higher than for the average corporation. Conversely, with old, mature companies, the ratio of net to gross fixed assets could be well below 50 percent. Hence the return on equity would be higher than otherwise. To the degree that return on equity guides the flow of economic resources, ARR sends undesirable information. It understates the return to growing sectors to which resources should flow. It overstates the return on equity for sectors from which resources should exit. Another definition of ARR calculates a single average return for projects. It is computed by averaging the expected cash flows over the life of a project and then dividing the average annual cash flow by the initial investment outlay. For example, this ARR for Project B in Table 9.1 is computed from the following definition:

$$\text{ARR} = \left(\sum_{t=0}^{n} \text{Cash flow}_t / n \right) \div I_0$$

where

$$I_0 = \text{Initial cash outlay} = \$1,500$$
$$n = \text{Life of the project} = 5 \text{ years.}$$

Using the applicable numbers from Table 9.1, we have

$$\text{ARR} = \left(\frac{-\$1,500 + \$0 + \$0 + \$450 + \$1,050 + \$1,950}{5} \right) \div \$1,500$$

$$= \frac{\$1,950}{5} \div \$1,500$$

$$= \frac{\$390}{\$1,500} = 26\%.$$

The ARRs for the four projects are: Project A, -8%; Project B, 26%; Project C, 25%; Project D, 22%. The ARR criterion chooses Project B as best. A major problem with ARR is that it does not take the time value of money into account. We would have obtained exactly the same ARR for Project B, even if the order of cash flows had been reversed with $1,950 received now, $1,050 at the end of Year 1, $450 at the end of Year 2, and $-\$1,500$ at the end of Year 5. But no one with a positive opportunity cost of capital would be indifferent between the alternatives. The opposite ordering of cash flows would always be preferred.

Net Present Value (NPV)

As the flaws in the payback and ARR methods were recognized, people began to search for methods of evaluating projects that would recognize that a dollar received immediately is preferable to a dollar received at some future date. This recognition led to the develop-

TABLE 9.3 Procedure for Calculating NPV

Year	Cash Flow	× PVIF =	PV
0	$-1,500	1.000	$-1,500.00
1	150	.909	136.35
2	300	.826	247.80
3	450	.751	337.95
4	600	.683	409.80
5	1,875	.621	1,164.38
		NPV = $	796.28

ment of *discounted cash flow (DCF) techniques* to take account of the time value of money. One such discounted cash flow technique is called the net present value method. *To implement this approach, find the present value of the expected net cash flows of an investment, discounted at the cost of capital, and subtract from it the initial cost outlay of the project.*[4] If the net present value is positive, the project should be accepted; if negative, it should be rejected. If two projects are mutually exclusive, the one with the higher net present value should be chosen.

The equation for the net present value (NPV) is[5]

$$\text{NPV} = \left[\frac{\text{CF}_1}{(1 + k)^1} + \frac{\text{CF}_2}{(1 + k)^2} + \cdots + \frac{\text{CF}_n}{(1 + k)^n} \right] - I_0 \qquad (9.1)$$

$$= \sum_{t=1}^{n} \frac{\text{CF}_t}{(1 + k)^t} - I_0.$$

Here CF_1, CF_2, and so forth represent the net cash flows; k is the firm's opportunity cost of capital; I_0 is the initial cost of the project; and n is the project's expected life. The examples based on the data in Table 9.1 assume the same initial outlays (scale of investment), the same lives, and the same cost of capital. We will relax these variables in subsequent sections.

To illustrate the procedures in calculating the net present value we use the data for Project C. We multiply the cash flow for each year by the appropriate discount factor (PVIF), assuming that the cost of capital, k, is 10 percent. The procedures are illustrated in Table 9.3.

---

[4]If costs are spread over several years, the present value of capital outlays must be taken into account. Suppose, for example, that a firm bought land in 1978, erected a building in 1979, installed equipment in 1980, and started production in 1981. One could treat 1978 as the base year, comparing the present value of the costs as of 1978 to the present value of the benefit stream as of that date.

[5]The second equation is simply a shorthand expression in which sigma (Σ) signifies "sum up" or add the present values of n cash flow terms. If $t = 1$, then $\text{CF}_t = \text{CF}_1$ and $1/(1 + k)^t = 1/(1 + k)^1$; if $t = 2$, then $\text{CF}_t = \text{CF}_2$ and $1/(1 + k)^t = 1/(1 + k)^2$; and so on, until $t = n$, the last year the project provides any cash flows. The symbol $\sum_{t=1}^{n}$ simply says, "Go through the following process: Let $t = 1$ and find the *PV* of CF_1; then let $t = 2$ and find the *PV* of CF_2. Continue until the *PV* of each individual cash flow has been found and then add the *PVs* of these individual cash flows to find the *PV* of the asset."

The net present values of all projects for which data were presented in Table 9.1 could be calculated as illustrated by Table 9.3. The results:

- Project A   NPV = $-610.95.
- Project B   NPV = $ 766.05.
- Project C   NPV = $ 796.28.
- Project D   NPV = $ 778.80.

If these projects were independent instead of mutually exclusive, we would reject A and accept B, C, and D. Why? Since they are mutually exclusive, we select the project with the greatest NPV, Project C. The NPV of the project is exactly the same as the increase in shareholders' wealth. This fact makes it the correct decision rule for capital budgeting purposes. The NPV rule also meets the other three general principles required for an optimal capital budgeting criterion. It takes all cash flows into account. All cash flows are discounted at the appropriate market-determined opportunity cost of capital in order to determine their present values. Also, the NPV rule obeys the value additivity principle.

The net present value of a project is exactly the same as the increase in shareholders' wealth. To see why, start by assuming a project has zero net present value. In this case, the project returns enough cash flow to do three things:

1. To pay off all interest payments to creditors who have lent money to finance the project

2. To pay all expected returns (dividends and capital gains) to shareholders who have put up equity for the project

3. To pay off the original principal, I_0, which was invested in the project

Thus, a zero net present value project is one which earns a fair return to compensate both debt holders and equity holders, each according to the returns they expect for the risk they take. A positive NPV project earns more than the required rate of return, and equity holders receive all excess cash flows because debt holders have a fixed claim on the firm. Consequently, equity holders' wealth increases by exactly the NPV of the project. It is this direct link between shareholders' wealth and the NPV definition that makes the net present value criterion so important in decision making.

Internal Rate of Return (IRR)

The internal rate of return (IRR) is defined as the *interest rate that equates the present value of the expected future cash flows, or receipts, to the initial cost outlay*. The equation for calculating the internal rate of return is

$$\frac{CF_1}{(1 + IRR)^1} + \frac{CF_2}{(1 + IRR)^2} + \cdots + \frac{CF_n}{(1 + IRR)^n} - I_0 = 0 \qquad (9.2)$$

$$\sum_{t=1}^{n} \frac{CF_t}{(1 + IRR)^t} - I_0 = 0.$$

Here we know the value of I_0 and also the values of CF_1, CF_2, . . . , CF_n, but we do not know the value of IRR. Thus, we have an equation with one unknown, and we can solve

TABLE 9.4   IRR for Project D

Year	Cash Flow	PV @10%		PV @20%		PV @25%		PV @25.4%	
0	$-1,500	1.000	$-1,500.00	1.000	$-1,500.00	1.000	$-1,500.00	1.000	$-1,500.00
1	300	.909	272.70	.833	249.90	.800	240.00	.797	239.10
2	450	.826	371.70	.694	312.30	.640	288.00	.636	286.20
3	750	.751	563.25	.579	434.25	.512	384.00	.507	380.25
4	750	.683	512.25	.482	361.50	.410	307.50	.404	303.00
5	900	.621	558.90	.402	361.80	.328	295.20	.322	289.80
	$ 1,650		$ 778.80		$ 219.75		$ 14.70		$ -1.65

for the value of IRR. Some value of IRR will cause the sum of the discounted receipts to equal the initial cost of the project, making the equation equal to zero, and that value of IRR is the internal rate of return.

Notice that the internal rate of return formula, Equation 9.2, is simply the NPV formula, Equation 9.1, solved for that particular value of k that causes the NPV to equal zero. In other words, the same basic equation is used for both methods, but in the NPV method, the discount rate (k) is specified as the market-determined opportunity cost of capital, while in the IRR method, the NPV is set equal to zero and the value of IRR that forces the NPV to equal zero is found.

The internal rate of return can readily be calculated by programs found in financial calculators or personal computers. With an ordinary calculator, the internal rate of return can also be found by trial and error. First, compute the present value of the cash flows from an investment, using an arbitrarily selected interest rate — for example, 10 percent. Then compare the present value so obtained with the investment's cost. If the present value is higher than the cost figure, try a higher interest rate and go through the procedure again. Conversely, if the present value is lower than the cost, lower the interest rate and repeat the process. Continue until the present value of the flows from the investment is approximately equal to its cost. *The interest rate that brings about this equality is defined as the internal rate of return.*[6]

Table 9.4 shows computations for the IRR of Project D in Table 9.1, and Figure 9.1 graphs the relationship between the discount rate and the NPV of the project.

In Figure 9.1, the NPV of Project D's cash flows decreases as the discount rate is increased. If the discount rate is zero, there is no time value of money and the NPV of a project is simply the sum of its cash flows. For Project D, the NPV equals $1,650 when the discount rate is zero. At the opposite extreme, if the discount rate is infinite, then the future cash flows are valueless and the NPV of Project D is its current cash flow, −$1,500. Somewhere between these two extremes is a discount rate which makes the

---

[6]In order to reduce the number of trials required to find the internal rate of return, make as good a first approximation as possible and "straddle" the internal rate of return by making fairly large changes in the interest rate estimates early in the iterative process.

FIGURE 9.1   NPV of Project D at Different Discount Rates

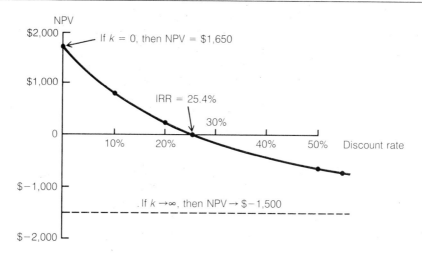

NPV equal to zero. In Figure 9.1, we see that the IRR for Project D is 25.4 percent. The IRRs for each of the four projects in Table 9.1 are given below.

- Project A   IRR = −200%.
- Project B   IRR =   20.9%.
- Project C   IRR =   22.8%.
- Project D   IRR =   25.4%.

If we use the IRR criterion and the projects are independent, we accept any project which has an IRR greater than the opportunity cost of capital, which is 10 percent. Therefore, we would accept Projects B, C, and D. However, since these projects are mutually exclusive, the IRR rule leads us to accept Project D as best.

Comparison of the NPV and IRR Methods

The numerical example given in Table 9.1 illustrates that each of the four capital budgeting criteria favors a different project. The results are summarized in Table 9.5, where the "best" project for each criterion is shown in a box.

We have already rejected the payback and ARR techniques because they fail to discount cash flows, but what about the NPV and IRR criteria? They both are discounted cash flow techniques, yet they select different mutually exclusive projects as optimal. Which technique is best? We shall see that *the NPV criterion is the only capital budgeting method that is always consistent with shareholder wealth maximization*. The material in this section shows why.

TABLE 9.5   Mutually Exclusive Projects Selected by Different
            Capital Budgeting Criteria

Criterion	Project A	Project B	Project C	Project D
Payback	2 years	4 years	4 years	3 years
ARR	−8%	26%	25%	22%
NPV	$−610.95	$766.05	$796.28	$778.80
IRR	−200%	20.9%	22.8%	25.4%

As noted above, the NPV method (1) accepts all independent projects whose NPVs are greater than zero and (2) ranks mutually exclusive projects by their NPVs, selecting the project with the higher NPV according to Equation 9.3:

$$NPV = \sum_{t=1}^{n} \frac{CF_t}{(1+k)^t} - I_0. \tag{9.3}$$

The IRR method, on the other hand, finds the value of IRR that forces the NPV to equal zero in Equation 9.4:

$$NPV = \sum_{t=1}^{n} \frac{CF_t}{(1+IRR)^t} - I_0 = 0. \tag{9.4}$$

The IRR method calls for accepting independent projects where IRR, the internal rate of return, is greater than k, the cost of capital, and for selecting among mutually exclusive projects depending on which has the highest IRR.

It is apparent that the only structural difference between the NPV and IRR methods lies in the discount rates used in the two equations — all the values in the equations are identical except for IRR and k. Further, we can see that if $IRR > k$, then $NPV > 0$.[7] Accordingly, it would appear that the two methods give the same accept/reject decisions for specific projects — if a project is acceptable under the NPV criterion, it is also acceptable if the IRR method is used. However, the following example illustrates that this statement is incorrect. Consider the pattern of cash flows in Table 9.6. Figure 9.2 illustrates the NPV for the cash flows in Table 9.6 for different discount rates. The internal rate of return is 15.8 percent. If the appropriate opportunity cost of capital is $k = 10\%$, then strict adherence to the IRR rule would lead us to accept the project since $IRR > k$. However, when we discount the cash flows at 10 percent, we discover that the NPV is

[7]This can be seen by noting that NPV = 0 only when IRR = k:

$$NPV = \sum_{t=1}^{n} \frac{CF_t}{(1+k)^t} - I_0 = \sum_{t=1}^{n} \frac{CF_t}{(1+IRR)^t} - I_0 = 0,$$

if and only if IRR = k. If $IRR > k$, then $NPV > 0$, and if $IRR < k$, then $NPV < 0$.

TABLE 9.6   PV at a 10 Percent Discount Rate

Year	Cash Flow	PV @ 10%
1	$ 400	$ 363.60
2	400	330.40
3	−1,000	−751.00
		$− 57.00

$−57.00. According to the NPV rule, the project should be rejected. Once again, the NPV and IRR rules give different answers.

Upon careful examination, we shall see that there are (at least) three reasons why the IRR rule is an inferior capital budgeting criterion: (1) it makes a bad reinvestment rate assumption; (2) it violates the value additivity principle; and (3) it can result in multiple IRRs for the same project. We shall examine each of these problems in turn.

First, the *reinvestment rate assumption* is actually an inaccurate use of terminology for what should be called the *opportunity cost assumption*.[8] All investment projects of equal risk will have the same opportunity cost from the point of view of all investors. We have assumed that all four projects in Table 9.1 are equally risky and that all investors require at least a 10 percent rate of return in order to invest in the projects. The rate of 10 percent is the appropriate opportunity cost of capital for the assumed level of risk of the project. That is why we discount the cash flows at a 10 percent rate. It would not be

FIGURE 9.2   The IRR versus the NPV

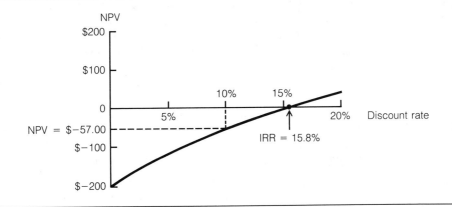

----

[8]The phrase ''reinvestment rate'' is misleading because it causes people to become involved in a debate about whether or not cash flows from the project can be reinvested at the IRR of the project. The real issue is, given the risk of the project, then at what rate can funds be invested (or reinvested) *somewhere else* for the same level of risk? Thus the appropriate ''reinvestment rate'' is the opportunity cost of capital.

FIGURE 9.3 Comparison of Two Mutually Exclusive Projects

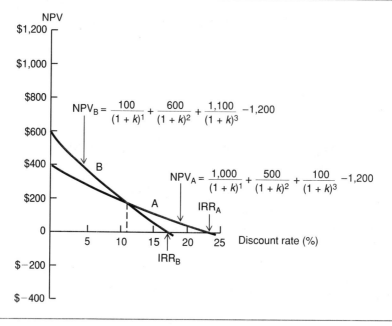

appropriate to discount the cash flows at a higher rate unless they had higher risk. But this is exactly what the IRR method does. The cash flows for Project C are discounted at a 22.8 percent rate (the IRR for Project C), and for Project D, they are discounted at 25.4 percent (the IRR for Project D). Although the projects have the same risk, they are discounted at different rates, neither of which is the correct opportunity cost of capital given the risk of the projects. The major difficulty with the IRR method is that it makes an inappropriate opportunity cost assumption. Projects of equal risk do not have different opportunity costs of capital.

TABLE 9.7 Present Values for Different Cash Flow Patterns

Year	Cash Flow from Project A	Cash Flow from Project B	Interest Factor PVIF @10%	Present Values A	Present Values B
0	$-1,200	$-1,200	1.000	$-1,200.00	$-1,200.00
1	1,000	100	.909	909.00	90.90
2	500	600	.826	413.00	495.60
3	100	1,100	.751	75.10	826.10
				$ 197.10	$ 212.60

The NPV rule, on the other hand, makes the correct assumption that the cash flows for all projects of equal risk must be discounted at the same rate. Figure 9.3 illustrates this point by graphing the relationship between the NPV and various discount rates for the two projects whose cash flows are given in Table 9.7. Notice that the IRR is the rate that causes the NPV to be equal to zero. As illustrated, the IRR for Project A (that is, 23 percent) is greater than for Project B (17 percent). Yet, given that these two projects have equivalent risk, every investor would discount their cash flows at, let's say, a 10 percent opportunity cost of capital.[9] And at a 10 percent discount rate, Project B has the highest NPV (NPV for A = $197 and NPV for B = $213) as shown in Table 9.7.

We have calculated that at a discount factor of 11.15 percent, the net present values of Projects A and B are equal at $176.69. This is shown as the crossover point in Figure 9.3. If the opportunity cost of capital is higher than the 11.15 percent crossover point, Project A will have a higher NPV than Project B. The logic is that the higher cash flows from Project A come in early, but the high cash flows from Project B come in later. The higher discount rates will, therefore, impact the later high cash flows of Project B more severely.

Second, the *value additivity principle* demands that managers be able to consider one project independently of all others. In order to demonstrate that the IRR criterion can violate the value additivity principle, consider the three projects whose cash flows are given in Table 9.8.[10]

Projects 1 and 2 are mutually exclusive, and Project 3 is independent of them. If the value additivity principle holds, we should be able to choose the better of the two mutually exclusive projects without having to consider the independent project. The NPVs of the three projects as well as their IRRs are also given in Table 9.8. If we use the IRR rule to choose between Projects 1 and 2, we would select Project 1. But if we consider combinations of projects, then the IRR rule would prefer Projects 2 and 3 to Projects 1 and 3. The

TABLE 9.8   The IRR Rule Violates Value Additivity

Year	Project 1	Project 2	Project 3	PV Factor @10%	1 + 3	2 + 3
0	$-100	$-100	$-100	1.000	$-200	$-200
1	0	225	450	.909	450	675
2	550	0	0	.826	550	0

	Project	NPV @10%	IRR
	1	$354.30	134.5%
	2	104.53	125.0%
	3	309.05	350.0%
	1 + 3	663.35	212.8%
	2 + 3	413.58	237.5%

---

[9]We have to wait until Chapters 10 and 11 to learn how to actually estimate the riskiness of different projects and how to modify our capital budgeting procedures to evaluate projects of different risk.

[10]This example is taken from Copeland and Weston [1983, p. 32].

IRR rule prefers Project 1 in isolation but Project 2 in combination with the independent project. In this example, the IRR rule does not obey the value additivity principle. The implication for management is that it would have to consider all possible combinations of projects and choose the combination which has the greatest internal rate of return. If, for example, a firm had only five projects, it would need to consider 32 different combinations.

The NPV rule always obeys the value additivity principle. Given that the opportunity cost of capital is 10 percent, we would choose Project 1 as being the best either by itself or in combination with Project 3. Note that the combinations of 1 and 3 or 2 and 3 are simply the sums of the NPVs of the projects considered separately. Consequently, if we adopt the NPV rule, the value of the firm is the sum of the values of the separate projects. Later (in Chapter 13) we shall see that this result holds even in a world with uncertainty where the firm may be viewed as a portfolio of risky projects.

Third, *multiple rates of return* are another difficulty with the IRR rule. A classic example of this situation has come to be known as the oil-well pump problem. An oil company is trying to decide whether or not to install a high-speed pump on a well that is already in operation. The estimated incremental cash flows are given in Table 9.9. The pump will cost $1,600 to install. During its first year of operation, it will produce $10,000 more oil than the pump that is currently in place. But during the second year, the high-speed pump produces $10,000 less oil because the well has been depleted. The question is whether to accept the rapid pumping technique, which speeds up cash flows in the near term at the expense of cash flows in the long term. Figure 9.4 shows the NPV of the project for different discount rates. If the opportunity cost of capital is 10 percent, the NPV rule would reject the project because it has negative NPV at that rate. If we are using the IRR rule, the project has two IRRs, 25 percent and 400 percent. Since both exceed the opportunity cost of capital, the project would probably be accepted.

Mathematically, the multiple IRRs are a result of Descartes' rule of signs, which implies that every time the cash flows change signs, there may be a new (positive, real) root to the problem. For the above example, the signs of cash flows change twice. There are two roots, that is, two IRRs, and neither of them has any economic meaning.

NPV, the IRR, and Terminal Value. The correct interpretation of the reinvestment rate is that it is the opportunity cost of capital. The reinvestment rate refers to investing funds elsewhere, in projects of equivalent risk. It does not refer to the rate at which funds can be put back into a given project. Consider the two projects whose cash flows are provided in

TABLE 9.9 Oil-Well Pump Incremental Cash Flows

Year	Estimated Cash Flow
0	$− 1,600
1	10,000
2	−10,000

FIGURE 9.4 Multiple Internal Rates of Return

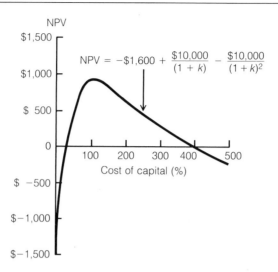

$$NPV = -\$1,600 + \frac{\$10,000}{(1 + k)} - \frac{\$10,000}{(1 + k)^2}$$

Table 9.10. The NPV rule is unambiguous. Project Y should be chosen, if they are mutually exclusive, because it has the greater NPV at a discount rate of 10 percent.

There is the temptation, however, to argue that Project X is superior because its cash flows can be reinvested each year at its IRR, which is 23.4 percent. Project Y, on the other hand, has no intermediate cash flows to be reinvested. In fact, the cash inflows from X will have a terminal value of $18,783 if reinvested at 23.4 percent. Project Y's terminal value remains at $17,280. On this basis, Project X seems better because it has a higher terminal value. The fallacy with this line of reasoning is that the cash inflows from Project X cannot be reinvested back into Project X. It required only a $10,000 initial outlay. Additional investments of $5,000 in years 2 and 3 are impossible. The only reasonable assumption is that the cash flows from either project can be reinvested somewhere else at the fair rate of return for projects of equivalent risk. This rate is the opportunity cost of capital, 10 percent, which is used to determine the project NPVs in the first place.

Terminal values, when correctly calculated, always provide the same capital budgeting decision as net present values. The correct reinvestment rate is the project's opportunity cost of capital, not its IRR.

TABLE 9.10 Comparison of Two Projects with Different Cash Flows Patterns

Project	Year 0	Year 1	Year 2	Year 3	Cost of Capital	NPV	IRR
X	$-10,000	$5,000	$5,000	$ 5,000	10%	$2,430	23.4%
Y	-10,000	0	0	17,280	10	2,977	20.0

Summarizing the comparison between the NPV and IRR criteria, we see that the IRR has many difficulties that invalidate it as a generally acceptable capital budgeting rule. First, the IRR method assumes that funds invested in projects have opportunity costs equal to the IRR for the project. This implicit reinvestment rate assumption violates the requirement that cash flows be discounted at the market-determined opportunity cost of capital that is appropriate for their risk. Second, the IRR does not obey the value additivity principle, and, consequently, managers who use the IRR cannot consider projects independently of each other. Finally, the IRR rule can lead to multiple rates of return whenever the sign of cash flows changes more than once. The NPV rule avoids all the problems of the IRR.

The two main competing ranking methods are the NPV and IRR. The NPV method is superior on analytical grounds. Surveys [Gitman and Forrester, 1977; Kim, Crick, and Kim, 1986] establish that in practice the IRR method is used by firms with higher frequency than the NPV. The IRR is attractive because it is expressed as a percentage return that can be directly compared with financing costs. This suggests the use of the IRR as an initial screening device with final reliance on the NPV analysis.

We next turn to a review of the four remaining methods of ranking projects. We shall briefly indicate the nature of each of these ranking criteria by means of a simplified example. The facts of the case example and the abbreviations we will use are as follows:

$$\text{Investment Outlay at Time 0 (The Present)} = I_0 = \$600{,}000$$

$$\text{Annual Cash Flows from the Project} = CF_t = \$200{,}000$$

$$\text{Life of the Project} = n = 5$$

$$\text{Applicable Cost of Capital} = k = 12\%$$

For this simplified example we assume no salvage value and no taxes. These are considered in later applications. For future comparisons we note that the NPV of this project is $120,960 and its IRR is 19.85 (or 20) percent.

Net Terminal Value (NTV)

The net terminal value expresses the comparison between the cash inflows and the investment outlay as of their future values at the termination of the project. The net terminal value grows the cash flows to the future terminal date at the opportunity cost of capital. For our example, the results are:

$$\begin{aligned}
\text{NTV} &= \sum_{t=1}^{n} CF_t(1 + k)^{n-t} - I(1 + k)^n \\
&= \$200{,}000(6.353) - \$600{,}000(1.762) \\
&= \$213{,}400.
\end{aligned}$$

When the net terminal value of $213,400 is discounted back to the present at $k = 12\%$, the applicable cost of capital, we obtain the net present value figure of $120,997 ($\cong$$121,000) for this example. Thus we are assured that for projects of the same life, the net terminal value will give us the same ranking as the net present value.

Opportunity Cost Return (OCR)

The opportunity cost rate of return is another variant of using terminal values. The relationships are:

$$I_0 = \frac{GTV}{(1 + k)^n} \quad \text{or} \quad \frac{GTV}{I_0} = (1 + k)^n$$

$$\frac{\sum\limits_{t=1}^{n} CF_t(1 + k)^{n-t}}{I_0} = 2.1177 \text{ or } k \approx 16.2\%.$$

This measure equates the gross terminal value to the present value of investment outlays. It expresses the relationships as a percentage as does the IRR. Note, however, that for our example the OCR is lower than the IRR of 20 percent. For these two measures using net terminal values, when the lives of the projects are the same and the applicable cost of capital is the same, we are assured that the results will be consistent with NPV calculations.

Profitability Index (PI)

The profitability index is the gross present value per dollar of investment outlay.

$$GPV/I_0 = \$721{,}000/\$600{,}000 = 1.20$$

A basic difficulty with the profitability index is indicated by an example. Suppose one investment involves an outlay of $1 and returns $2. Its profitability index is 2.0. Another investment requires an outlay of $1 million and at the end of the year has a return of $1.5 million. Its profitability index is 1.5. Under the NPV rule, the larger investment is clearly superior. If the firm can finance all available investments, the profitability index would not provide a ranking that the firm would want to follow.

Perpetuity Rate of Return (PRR)

The perpetuity rate of return converts the profitability index into a perpetuity percentage rate of return.

$$(PI)k = 1.2(.12) = .144 = 14.4\%$$

The value of the perpetuity rate of return is that it enables the business manager to make comparisons among projects in percentage terms as does the IRR, but avoids the weaknesses of the IRR. For projects of the same scale, same lives, and same risks, the PRR provides another useful ranking method. It fails, however, when mutually exclusive projects have differing risk.

Advantages of the NPV Method

We have established that the NPV rule is the correct economic criterion for ranking investment projects. It avoids the deficiencies of the alternative methods. It discounts cash flows at the appropriate opportunity cost of funds. It obeys the value additivity principle.

Following the NPV rule maximizes the value of the firm. Indeed, the value of the firm is the sum of the NPVs of the total portfolio of projects represented by the firm's assets. From the basic net present value expression, general and valid valuation measures can be derived. Thus the NPV rule is consistent with fundamental valuation principles.

CAPITAL BUDGETING: THE BASIC REPLACEMENT DECISION

From this point forward, we shall use the net present value method for all capital budgeting decisions. The following replacement decision is an example of a typical problem. It illustrates the use of cash flows for capital budgeting decisions. It emphasizes that all project cash flows must be represented as *changes* in the firm's cash flows. And it demonstrates the NPV method of discounted cash flows.

Straight-Line Depreciation Example

The Widget Division of the Culver Company, a profitable, diversified manufacturing firm, purchased a machine five years ago at a cost of $7,500. The machine had an expected life of 15 years at time of purchase and a zero estimated salvage value at the end of the 15 years. It is being depreciated on a straight-line basis and has a book value of $5,000 at present. The division manager reports that, for $12,000 (including installation), a new machine can be bought which, over its 10-year life, will expand sales from $10,000 to $11,000 a year. Further, it will reduce labor and raw materials usage sufficiently to cut operating costs from $7,000 to $5,000. The new machine has an estimated salvage value of $2,000 at the end of 10 years. The old machine's current market value is $1,000. Taxes are at a 40 percent rate and are paid quarterly, and the firm's cost of capital is 10 percent. Should Culver buy the new machine?

The decision calls for five steps: (1) estimating the actual cash outlay attributable to the new investment, (2) determining the incremental cash flows, (3) finding the present value of the incremental cash flows, (4) adding the present value of the expected salvage value to the present value of the total cash flows, and (5) determining whether the NPV is positive. These steps are explained further in the following sections.

Step 1: Estimated Cash Outlay. The net initial cash outlay consists of these items: (1) payment to the manufacturer, (2) tax effects, and (3) proceeds from the sale of the old machine. Culver must make a $12,000 payment to the manufacturer of the machine, but its next quarterly tax bill will be reduced because of the loss it will incur when it sells the old machine: Tax saving = (Loss)(Tax rate) = ($4,000)(0.4) = $1,600. The tax reduction will occur because the old machine, which is carried at $5,000, will be written down by $4,000 ($5,000 less $1,000 salvage value) immediately upon the purchase of the new one.

To illustrate, suppose the Culver Company's taxable income in the quarter in which the new machine is to be purchased would have been $100,000 without the purchase of the new machine and the consequent write-off of the old machine. With a 40 percent tax rate, Culver would have had to write a check for $40,000 to pay its tax bill. However, if it bought the new machine and sold the old one, it would take an operating loss of $4,000 — the

TABLE 9.11   Comparative Accounting Income Statement
Framework for Considering Cash Flows

	Without New Investment (1)		With New Investment (2)		Difference: (2) − (1) (3)
Sales		$10,000		$11,000		$1,000
Operating costs	$7,000		$5,000		($2,000)	
Depreciation	500		1,000		500	
Interest charges	500		1,000		500	
Income before taxes		$ 2,000		$ 4,000		$2,000
Taxes (T = 0.4)		800		1,600		800
Income after taxes		$ 1,200		$ 2,400		$1,200
Dividends paid		600		1,200		600
Additions to retained earnings		$ 600		$ 1,200		$ 600

$5,000 book value on the old machine less the salvage value of $1,000. (The loss is an operating loss, not a capital loss, because it is simply recognizing that depreciation charges, an operating cost, were too low during the old machine's five-year life.)[11] With this $4,000 additional operating cost, the next quarter's taxable income would be reduced from $100,000 to $96,000, and the tax bill from $40,000 to $38,400. This means, of course, that the firm's cash outflow for taxes would be $1,600 less *because* of the purchase of the new machine.

In addition, there would be a cash inflow of $1,000 from the sale of the old machine. The net result is that the purchase of the new machine would involve an immediate net cash outlay of $9,400, the cost used for capital budgeting purposes:

Invoice price of new machine	$12,000
Less: Tax savings	−1,600
Salvage of old machine	−1,000
Net cash outflow (cost)	$ 9,400

If additional working capital is required as a result of a capital budgeting decision, as would generally be true for sales expansion investments (as opposed to cost-reducing replacement investments), this factor must be taken into account. The amount of *net* working capital (additional current assets required as a result of the expansion minus any spontaneous funds generated by the expansion) is estimated and added to the initial cost outlay. We assume that Culver will not need any additional working capital, so this factor is ignored in the example.

Step 2: Annual Benefits.   Column (1) in Table 9.11 shows the Widget Division's estimated income statement as it would be without the new machine; Column (2) shows the statement as it would look if the new investment were made. (It is assumed that these

---

[11]If Culver traded in the old machine as partial payment for the new one, the loss would be added to the depreciable cost of the new machine, and there would be no immediate tax saving.

TABLE 9.12 Net Operating Cash Flow Statement

	Without New Investment (1)	With New Investment (2)	Difference or Incremental Flows: (2) − (1) (3)
Sales	$10,000	$11,000	$1,000
Operating cash costs (O)[a]	7,000	5,000	(2,000)
Net operating cash income (NOI)[a]	$ 3,000	$ 6,000	$3,000
Taxes (T = 0.4)	1,200	2,400	1,200
After-tax operating income: NOI (1 − T)	$ 1,800	$ 3,600	$1,800
Depreciation tax benefit (T × Dep)	200	400	200
Net cash flows (CF)	$ 2,000	$ 4,000	$2,000

[a]Does not include depreciation as a cash cost, since this is a cash flow statement and depreciation is not a cash cost.

figures are applicable for each of the next ten years; if this is not the case, then cash flow estimates must be made for each year.) Column (3) shows the differences between the first two columns.

For capital budgeting analysis, the cash flows that are discounted are the net after-tax operating cash flows. The data in Table 9.11 represent accounting income and must be adjusted in order to be on a cash rather than accrual basis and also to exclude all payments to the sources of financing. In Table 9.11 depreciation is a noncash charge; interest charges and dividends paid are cash flows to the financing sources.

While depreciation is a noncash charge, it is deductible for computing income tax, and income tax payments are cash flows. The cash flows must include the depreciation tax benefits.

Table 9.12 shows the operating cash flows without the new investment, with the new investment, and the difference, or incremental flows.

Step 3: Finding the PV of the Benefits. We have explained in detail how to measure the annual benefits. The next step is to determine the present value of the benefit stream. The interest factor for a ten-year, 10 percent annuity is found to be 6.1446 from Table A.4. This factor, when multiplied by the $2,000 incremental cash flow, results in a present value of $12,289.

Step 4: Salvage Value. The new machine has an estimated salvage value of $2,000; that is, Culver expects to be able to sell the machine for $2,000 after ten years of use. The present value of an inflow of $2,000 due in ten years is $771, found as $2,000 × 0.3855. If additional working capital had been required and included in the initial cash outlay, this amount would be added to the salvage value of the machine because the working capital would be recovered if and when the project is abandoned.

Notice that the salvage value is a return of capital, not taxable income, so it is *not* subject to income taxes. Of course, when the new machine is actually retired ten years hence, it might be sold for more or less than the expected $2,000, so either taxable income or a deductible operating loss could arise, but $2,000 is the best present estimate of the new machine's salvage value.

Step 5: Determining the Net Present Value. The project's net present value is found as the sum of the present values of the inflows, or benefits, less the outflows, or costs:

Inflows: PV of annual benefits	$12,289
PV of salvage value, new machine	771
Less: Net cash outflow, or cost	(9,400)
Net present value (NPV)	$ 3,660

Since the NPV is positive, the project should be accepted.

Capital Budgeting Worksheet

Table 9.13 presents a worksheet for evaluating capital projects. The top section shows net cash flows at the time of investment; since all these flows occur immediately, no discounting is required and the interest factor is 1.0. The lower section of the table shows future cash flows — benefits from increased sales and/or reduced costs, depreciation, and salvage value. These flows occur over time, so it is necessary to convert them to present values. The NPV as determined in the alternative format, $3,660, agrees with the figure calculated earlier.

TABLE 9.13   Worksheet for Replacement Analysis

	Amount before Tax	Amount after Tax[a]	Year Event Occurs	PV Factor @10%	PV
Outflows at time investment is made					
Investment in new equipment	$12,000	$12,000	0	1.0000	$12,000
Salvage value of old	(1,000)	(1,000)	0	1.0000	(1,000)
Tax effect of the sale[b]	(4,000)	(1,600)	0	1.0000	(1,600)
Increased working capital (if necessary)	0	0	0	1.0000	0
Total initial outflows (PV of costs)					$ 9,400
Inflows, or annual returns					
Benefits[c] (NOI)	$ 3,000	$ 1,800	1-10	6.1446	$11,060
Depreciation on new (annual)[b]	1,000	400	1-10	6.1446	2,458
Depreciation on old (annual)[b]	(500)	(200)	1-10	6.1446	(1,229)
Salvage value on new	2,000	2,000	10	0.3855	771
Return of working capital (if necessary)	0	0	10	0.3855	0
Total periodic inflows (PV of benefits)					$13,060

NPV = PV of benefits less PV of cost = $13,060 − $9,400 = $3,660.

[a]Amount after tax equals amount before tax times T or $(1 − T)$, where T = Tax rate.
[b]Deductions (tax loss and depreciation) are multiplied by T.
[c]Benefits are multiplied by $(1 − T)$.

TABLE 9.14   MACRS for 15-Year Class Life

Year	Depreciation Percentage	Remaining Book Value
1	5.0% (1/2 year)	$7,125.00
2	9.5%	6,412.50
3	8.6%	5,767.50
4	7.7%	5,190.00
5	6.9%	4,672.50
6	6.2%	4,207,50
7–15	5.9% (straight-line)	225.00
16	3.0% (1/2 year)	0.00

Replacement Analysis with Accelerated Depreciation

Next we consider the effect of MACRS depreciation on the replacement analysis. Accelerated depreciation, on both the old and the new equipment, complicates the computations somewhat, but the logic is the same.

Step 1: Estimated Cash Outlay. The old machine had an initial cost of $7,500 and a 15-year life. Using straight-line depreciation, its book value was $5,000 after five years. With a 15-year class life under MACRS, 150 percent declining balance depreciation is applied to the original $7,500 resulting in a book value of $4,673 after five years. This is less than the book value under straight-line depreciation because MACRS results in higher depreciation earlier in the life of the asset. The depreciation schedule is illustrated in Table 9.14.

The current market value of the old machine is assumed to be $1,000, as before. Selling the machine for $1,000 will result in a loss of $3,673 — the difference between its book and market value. This loss results in tax savings equal to (Loss)(Tax rate) = ($3,673)(.4) = $1,469.

The data given previously for the new machine are unchanged from above, except that the machine will be depreciated over a 10-year class life using MACRS depreciation (200 percent declining balance). This does not affect the initial cash outflow calculated below:

Invoice price of new machine	$12,000
Less: Tax savings	−1,469
Salvage of old machine	−1,000
Net cash outflow for capital budgeting	$ 9,531

Step 2: Annual Benefits. For capital budgeting analysis, the cash flows that are discounted are net after-tax operating cash flows. Depreciation is not a cash charge, so *operating* cash flows are not affected by the switch to MACRS; however, *after-tax* cash flows are affected because of the change in the tax shelter resulting from the use of accelerated depreciation. Furthermore, because the depreciation expense is not constant

TABLE 9.15   Worksheet for Replacement Analysis with MACRS

	Amount Before Tax	Amount After Tax	Year Event Occurs	PV Factor @ 10%	Present Value
OUTFLOWS					
Investment in new	$12,000	$12,000	0	1.0000	$12,000
Salvage value of old	(1,000)	(1,000)	0	1.0000	(1,000)
Tax effect of sale	(3,673)	(1,469)	0	1.0000	(1,469)
PV of costs					$ 9,531
INFLOWS					
Benefits (NOI)	$ 3,000	$ 1,800	1-10	6.1446	$11,060
Depreciation on new (T)	12,000	4,800	1-10	.6541*	3,140
Depreciation foregone on old (T)					
Year 6	(465)	(186)	1	.9091	(169)
Years 7–15	(443)	(177)	2-10	5.2355	(927)
Year 16	(225)	(90)	11	.3505	(32)
Salvage value of new	2,000	2,000	10	.3855	771
PV of benefits					$13,843

Net present value = PV of benefits less PV of costs
$$= \$13,843 - \$9,531$$
$$= \$4,312$$

*Interest factor at 10 percent for PV of 200% declining balance depreciation.

from year to year under accelerated depreciation as it is under straight-line depreciation, annual benefits will vary. The worksheet method illustrated in Table 9.15 captures the effect of depreciation on after-tax cash flows.

Step 3: Finding the PV of the Benefits.   Because annual cash flows were constant under straight-line depreciation, the present value interest factor for an annuity (PVIFA) was applicable. With MACRS, there are two alternatives: (1) calculate the present value of each year's after-tax net cash flows using the appropriate present value interest factor (PVIF) or (2) solve the problem using the worksheet method that separately discounts (constant) operating cash flows and the tax effects of accelerated depreciation, using the present value factors for accelerated depreciation in Appendix C at the back of this book.

Step 4: Salvage Value.   As in the original analysis, the new machine has an estimated salvage value of $2,000. Even though MACRS does not consider salvage value in depreciation calculations, the machine may have some economic value at the end of its 10-year life. The best current estimate of its after-tax salvage value after 10 years is $2,000, which is discounted to a present value of $771 as before.

Step 5: Determining the Net Present Value.   The net present value is the sum of the present value of the inflows or benefits, less the present value of the outflows, or costs. Using the figures obtained from the worksheet in Table 9.15 we have:

Inflows: PV of benefits	$13,843
Outflows: Net cash outflow, or cost	(9,531)
Net present value	$ 4,312

As before, the net present value is positive, indicating that the replacement project should be accepted. However, the NPV using accelerated depreciation is higher than that using straight-line depreciation by $652 or 18 percent. This is caused by the higher depreciation deductions (and resulting lower taxes) earlier in the life of the new equipment. These are not offset by the higher net cash outflow initially, nor by the use of accelerated depreciation (and its benefits foregone) on the old machine for two reasons: (1) the old machine cost less than the new machine for lower depreciation overall regardless of the method and (2) the old machine had almost reached that point in its life when the switch was made to straight-line depreciation — its benefits from accelerated depreciation had already been captured.

Calculation of Depreciation Amounts

In Table 9.15 the accelerated depreciation on the new machine is not constant, so we are unable to use the present value interest factor for an annuity to discount a constant annual flow. However, as we discussed in Chapter 5, tables of interest factors have been developed to reflect the present value of accelerated depreciation (see Appendix C). In this case, the interest factor is .6541 for a 10 percent cost of capital with 200 percent declining balance depreciation over 10 years. This factor is multiplied by the total asset cost times the tax rate to calculate the present value of the depreciation tax shelter on the new machine.

The depreciation tax shelter foregone on the old machine starts at a point one-third of the way through the asset's life. Year 6 in the life of the old machine is equivalent to year 1 in the current capital budgeting analysis. We use the MACRS for a 15-year class life shown in Table 9.14 to apply the 6.2 percent depreciation factor to the original purchase price of $7,500 to obtain $465 for the depreciation before tax for year 6. The PV factor for one year is applied to .4($465) to obtain $169. For years 7–15, the straight-line factor of 5.9 percent from Table 9.14 is applicable to the $7,500. Year 16 represents the depreciation factor reflecting the half-year convention for the 15-year MACRS.

CAPITAL BUDGETING: AN EXPANSION PROJECT

The Gomez Co. is considering an investment project. Gomez has sufficient excess capacity in its plant to take on the project by making an investment in additional new equipment. The investment in land is $2 million; in plant is $8 million, subject to MACRS depreciation at 3 percent per year. The equipment cost is $10 million, and it qualifies in the five-year asset class under MACRS depreciation. The project life is six years over the years 19X1 through 19X6. The investments take place in 19X0.

TABLE 9.16   Worksheet for an Expansion Project, without Inflation

	19X1	19X2	19X3	19X4	19X5	19X6
(1) Unit sales	10,000	14,000	20,000	25,000	28,000	30,000
(2) Sales price	$ 1,000	$ 1,000	$ 1,000	$ 1,000	$ 1,000	$ 1,000
(3) Net sales	10,000,000	14,000,000	20,000,000	25,000,000	28,000,000	30,000,000
(4) Cash op. costs (.75 Sales)	7,500,000	10,500,000	15,000,000	18,750,000	21,000,000	22,500,000
(5) EBDIT	2,500,000	3,500,000	5,000,000	6,250,000	7,000,000	7,500,000
(6) Dep. on equipment	2,000,000	3,200,000	1,900,000	1,200,000	1,100,000	600,000
(7) Dep. on building	120,000	240,000	240,000	240,000	240,000	240,000
(8) Income before taxes	380,000	60,000	2,860,000	4,810,000	5,660,000	6,660,000
(9) Tax @ 34%	129,200	20,400	972,400	1,635,400	1,924,400	2,264,400
(10) Net income	250,800	39,600	1,887,600	3,174,600	3,735,600	4,395,600
(11) Add back dep.	2,120,000	3,440,000	2,140,000	1,440,000	1,340,000	840,000
(12) Cash flow from ops.	2,370,800	3,479,600	4,027,600	4,614,600	5,075,600	5,235,600
(13) Inv. in NWC (.1Δ Sales)	(1,000,000)	(400,000)	(600,000)	(500,000)	(300,000)	(2,800,000)
(14) Net salvage values	0	0	0	0	0	9,340,000
(15) Total cash flows	$ 1,370,800	$ 3,079,600	$ 3,427,600	$ 4,114,600	$ 4,775,600	$17,375,600
(16) PVIF	0.9346	0.8734	0.8163	0.7629	0.7130	0.6663
(17) Present values	$ 1,281,121	$ 2,689,842	$ 2,797,943	$ 3,139,009	$ 3,404,937	$11,578,096

NPV $24,890,947 − $20,000,000 = $4,890,947
IRR   12.31%

The unit sales volumes for the new project over the years 19X1 through 19X6 is set forth in Table 9.16. The sales price per unit under the assumption of no inflation is $1,000 for each of the years. Cash operating costs are projected at 75 percent of sales. The applicable tax rate for Gomez is the corporate 34 percent rate. The project will require an investment in net working capital which in each year represents 10 percent of sales. Thus the incremental investment in net working capital each year will be 10 percent of the sales increase. The total net working capital investment will be recovered at the end of the sixth year. Although no salvage value is taken into account in calculating MACRS depreciation, Gomez forecasts that the equipment will have an after-tax salvage value of $1 million at the end of 19X6. The applicable cost of capital in real terms without inflation is 7 percent. The applicable depreciation schedule for the equipment as indicated in our discussion of the MACRS rules in Chapter 5 is the following:

Depreciation Schedule — Five-Year MACRS (200% Declining Balance)

19X1	19X2	19X3	19X4	19X5	19X6
20%	32%	19%	12%	11%	6%

Analysis of Expansion Project

The basic difference between the expansion project analysis presented in Table 9.16 and the replacement analysis is that various aspects of the equipment to be replaced are not involved in the expansion project analysis. However, the expansion of sales will require additional investments of working capital.

In Table 9.16, line (1) is the forecast of unit sales for the years 19X1 through 19X6. In line (2) the sales price is assumed to be constant at $1,000. (In a later section we shall discuss the impact of inflation. We will repeat this example with inflation built into the sales price. The cost of capital will also have to be adjusted to reflect the impact of inflation.) Line (3) is the product of the first two lines — net sales in dollars. In line (4) cash operating costs, assumed to be 75 percent of sales, are presented. Line (3) less line (4) is earnings before depreciation, interest, and taxes (EBDIT), shown in line (5). Line (6) is the depreciation on equipment developed from the MACRS five-year depreciation schedule using the double declining balance method, which would be applicable. Line (7) is depreciation on the building at 3 percent per year. Line (8) is line (5) minus lines (6) and (7), which gives us income before taxes. Line (9) applies the corporate income tax rate of 34 percent. Line (10) is net income after subtracting line (9) taxes from line (8). In line (11) we add back depreciation expenses to obtain line (12), cash flow from operations. Line (13) is the investment in net working capital, postulated to be 10 percent of the increase in sales. This is 10 percent of total sales in 19X1 and then in subsequent years it is 10 percent only of the sales increase. In 19X6, the project is assumed to end so that the net working capital is recovered as a positive inflow. In this analysis, all cash flows are assumed to occur at the end of the period. The sales increase during 19X6 was $2 million, requiring $200,000 additional working capital that is also recovered in 19X6. Hence this element cancels. The recovery of net working capital shown in 19X6 is the sum of the investments in net working capital for 19X1 through 19X5.

Line (14) presents the after-tax salvage values realizable in year 19X6. The backup for this amount is shown in Table 9.17. Line (a) represents the salvage values estimated for 19X6 for land, building, and equipment (PPE).

In this no-inflation case, the value of the land is assumed to be unchanged at $2,000,000. The value of the building is assumed to be its book value. The value of the

---

TABLE 9.17   Net Salvage Values, 19X6

	Land	Building	Equipment
(a) Salvage values, 19X6	$2,000,000	$6,680,000	$ 1,000,000
(b) Initial cost	2,000,000	8,000,000	10,000,000
(c) Depreciable basis 19X0	0	8,000,000	10,000,000
(d) Book value, 19X6	2,000,000	6,680,000	0
(e) Gain (loss)	0	0	1,000,000
(f) Taxes	0	0	340,000
(g) Net salvage values	2,000,000	6,680,000	660,000

equipment is placed at $1,000,000. Note that under MACRS depreciation, the equipment has been fully depreciated without consideration of a possible salvage value. This provides some advantage to the taxpayer and in a sense compensates for the lack of indexing for inflation. Line (b) lists the initial costs previously discussed. Line (c) indicates that only the building and equipment are depreciable. Line (d) is the book value of each category of PPE in 19X6. It represents line (c) plus cumulated depreciation for years 19X1 through 19X6. The salvage values in line (a) less the 19X6 book value of each category of PPE in line (d) gives the gain (loss) in line (e). Line (f) lists the dollar amount of applicable taxes calculated by multiplying line (e) by 34 percent. The net salvage values shown in line (g) represent the salvage values in line (a) less the taxes in line (f). Line (g) is summed to obtain the total net salvage values of $9,340,000 shown in Table 9.16 in line (14) in the 19X6 column.

Back to Table 9.16, line (15) is total cash flows representing the sum of lines (12) through (14). Line (16) is the present value interest factor for each year. Line (17) represents line (15) multiplied by line (16) to give the present values of cash flows for each year. When the items in line (17) are summed for the years 19X1 through 19X6, we obtain the gross present value for the project of $24,890,947. When the initial outlay of $20,000,000 is subtracted, the NPV is $4,890,947. This represents an internal rate of return of 12.31 percent.

Evaluation of the Project

This is a positive NPV project. In this example, the internal rate of return also indicates accepting this independent project since the applicable real cost of capital is 7 percent.

At this point some writers state that other factors should be taken into account. These include the effects on the firm's sales of other products (cannibalization), the reactions of rival firms, and the relation of this project to the firm's long-range strategies. However, these and related factors should already be reflected in the best estimate projections used in the analysis. Therefore, when the worksheet analysis has been completed, we have the best estimate results. Given that projections into the future are always uncertain, it would make sense to perform various types of sensitivity analysis based on reasonable alternative scenarios. (See use of diskette in Problem 9.18.) Since the studies to this point were in real terms without consideration of inflation, an alternative scenario with inflation would be useful.

THE IMPACT OF INFLATION

The impact of inflation requires at least two levels of consideration: neutral inflation and nonneutral inflation. Neutral inflation means that all prices and costs rise proportionately so that the general structure of prices and costs remains the same. Nonneutral inflation means that prices and costs may rise by different degrees so that some stakeholders gain and some lose by inflation. We first consider neutral inflation to convey the basic theory.

Neutral Inflation

Under neutral inflation some basic interest rate relations obtain. Consider the following: the applicable real cost of capital, k_r, is 7 percent; the investment outlay, I_0, is $100; the cash flow received at the end of one period is $128.4 so that the calculation of the net present value of the project in real terms is:

$$\text{NPV} = \frac{\$128.4}{1.07} - \$100 = \$20.$$

Next we assume a neutral inflation rate of 5 percent so that we need to multiply both the cost of capital and the end of period cash flow by 1.05 to place the analysis in nominal terms.

$$k_n = (1.07)(1.05) = 1.1235 \qquad CF_1 = \$128.4(1.05) = \$134.82$$

So the net present value in nominal analysis is:

$$\text{NPV} = \frac{\$134.82}{1.1235} - \$100 = \$20.$$

Note that $k_n = (1 + k_r)(1 + i) - 1 = 1 + k_r + i + ik_r - 1$.

In practice, the cross product term ik_r is often dropped when it is small. We then have $k_n = k_r + i$. This relation is referred to as the Fisher Equation after Irving Fisher, the financial economist of the first part of the 1900s who first set forth the relationship.[12]

Thus under neutral inflation we obtain the same result whether the analysis is performed in real terms or in nominal terms. Remember that the NPV of $20 is a present value before the impact of inflation. Under nonneutral inflation the results depend on the relative flexibility of revenues and costs.

Nonneutral Inflation

Under nonneutral inflation, selling prices might rise faster than wage costs, for example. If so, the revenues and income of the firm might benefit at the expense of wage income. Or wages may rise in anticipation of the inflation so that revenues and income of the firm may be squeezed. The coupon interest rates on bonds are likely to include an additional interest cost to reflect anticipated inflation and to some degree the risk of uncertain inflation. If actual inflation exceeds the inflation premium in the bond coupon, bondholders are hurt. Conversely if inflation is less than expected, they gain.

Inflation is likely to depress after-tax income because the current U.S. tax system taxes nominal income rather than real income. Thus the tax shield provided by the depreciation charge is fixed in nominal terms. Hence with higher inflation, the real value of the depreciation tax shield declines. With respect to salvage values that rise because of inflation, the gain is taxed even though in real terms there may have been no increase in

---

[12]We are using an after-tax cost of capital, k. The development of the relationship between the before-tax and after-tax measures requires careful procedures. For the caveats, see Keith Howe [1987a, 1987b, 1990].

TABLE 9.18 Worksheet for an Expansion Project, with Inflation

	19X1	19X2	19X3	19X4	19X5	19X6
(1) Unit sales	10,000	14,000	20,000	25,000	28,000	30,000
(2) Sales price	$ 1,000	$ 1,050	$ 1,103	$ 1,158	$ 1,216	$ 1,276
(3) Net sales	10,000,000	14,700,000	22,050,000	28,940,625	34,034,175	38,288,447
(4) Cash op. costs (.75 Sales)	7,500,000	11,025,000	16,537,500	21,705,469	25,525,631	28,716,335
(5) EBDIT	2,500,000	3,675,000	5,512,500	7,235,156	8,508,544	9,572,112
(6) Dep. on equipment	2,000,000	3,200,000	1,900,000	1,200,000	1,100,000	600,000
(7) Dep. on building	120,000	240,000	240,000	240,000	240,000	240,000
(8) Income before taxes	380,000	235,000	3,372,500	5,795,156	7,168,544	8,732,112
(9) Tax @ 34%	129,200	79,900	1,146,650	1,970,353	2,437,305	2,968,918
(10) Net income	250,800	155,100	2,225,850	3,824,803	4,731,239	5,763,194
(11) Add back dep.	2,120,000	3,440,000	2,140,000	1,440,000	1,340,000	840,000
(12) Cash flow from ops.	2,370,800	3,595,100	4,365,850	5,264,803	6,071,239	6,603,194
(13) Inv. in NWC (.1Δ Sales)	(1,000,000)	(470,000)	(735,000)	(689,063)	(509,355)	(3,403,418)
(14) Net salvage values	0	0	0	0	0	$11,838,541
(15) Total cash flows	$ 1,370,800	$ 3,125,100	$ 3,630,850	$ 4,575,741	$ 5,561,884	$21,845,152
(16) PVIF	0.8929	0.7972	0.7118	0.6355	0.5674	0.5066
(17) Present values	$ 1,223,929	$ 2,491,311	$ 2,584,367	$ 2,907,966	$ 3,155,962	$11,067,434

NPV $23,430,969 − $20,000,000 = $3,430,969
IRR   15.96%

salvage value. Without indexing for inflation, the tax system will decrease the real value of tax shields and tax phantom increases in salvage value. These effects are illustrated in the analysis of the Gomez Co. expansion project under inflation.

Worksheet Analysis of Expansion Project with Inflation

We have already analyzed an expansion project for the Gomez Co. under the assumption of no inflation. We have sought to follow the basic principles involved. The analysis can be made in either real terms or in nominal terms. Just keep the procedures consistent. When the analysis is in real terms, the cash flows are in real terms as are the applicable discount factors or cost of capital. When the analysis is in nominal terms, the cash flows are in nominal terms and the discount factors or applicable cost of capital rates are in nominal terms reflecting the influence of inflation.

Accordingly, Table 9.18 is a worksheet for an expansion project for the Gomez Co. under the assumption of inflation. Hence the cash flows and the cost of capital will be in

TABLE 9.19   Net Salvage Values with Inflation, 19X6

	Land	Building	Equipment
(a) Salvage values, 19X6	$3,173,800	$8,951,868	$ 1,340,000
(b) Initial cost	2,000,000	8,000,000	10,000,000
(c) Depreciable basis 19X0	0	8,000,000	10,000,000
(d) Book value, 19X6	2,000,000	6,680,000	0
(e) Gain (loss)	1,173,800	2,271,868	1,340,000
(f) Taxes @ 34%	399,092	772,435	455,600
(g) Net salvage values	2,774,708	8,179,433	884,400

nominal terms. Since we had covered the worksheet in Table 9.16 in real terms line by line, we will only note the changes in the present analysis. Line (2) converts the sales price to nominal terms by increasing prices after 19X1 at the rate of 5 percent per year compounded. Cash operating costs in line (4) are assumed to remain at 75 percent of sales. Lines (6) and (7) cover depreciation on equipment and on the building respectively. Despite inflation the dollar amounts for depreciation continue to be based on the original costs, which are not influenced by inflation. Since the tax regulations do not permit indexing, the actual depreciation in nominal terms is higher than the permitted deductions shown in lines (6) and (7). This is one respect in which inflation is nonneutral and is caused by tax regulations.

The other lines follow the logic described in our discussion of Table 9.16 until we come to line (14), net salvage values. The backup for this line is in Table 9.19. Line (a) represents the projected salvage values in 19X6. Land is assumed to increase in value at a rate higher than the generally assumed inflation rate of 5 percent. The expected rate at which the land increases in value is postulated to be 8 percent on the assumption that land is fixed in supply and will tend to have a higher inflation rate than the general price level change on average. A number of alternative assumptions could be made about the rate at which the value of the building is influenced by inflation. Certainly the location and use of the building would influence its value over time. We adopt the most neutral assumption that the salvage value of the building will be its tax basis or book value in 19X6 augmented by the general inflation rate of 5 percent for the six years. Thus the salvage value of the building is estimated to be its book value multiplied by the compound interest factor for the general inflation rate of 5 percent.

The impact of the general inflation on the salvage value of the equipment is another puzzler. Under MACRS, the equipment has been fully depreciated. However, economic value may remain. Its value is uncertain since equipment is more likely to be subject to obsolescence factors than is the building. Again, we make the simplifying assumption of applying the general inflation rate of 5 percent to the estimated salvage value of $1 million under the no-inflation case. The analysis in Table 9.19 then proceeds as in Table 9.17. In line (f) the dollar amount of taxes paid is the 34 percent tax rate applied to the salvage value in line (a) less the book value in line (d). The taxes paid in line (f) of Table 9.19 are in every case higher than the taxes paid under the no-inflation case in Table 9.17. To the extent that the real values of property, plant, and equipment are unchanged, the increase in taxes represents a levy on a phantom, not a real gain. The exception is the differential between the 8 percent increase in value of the land compared with the general inflation rate of 5 percent. The difference of 3 percent represents a differential gain in the real value of the land. But for buildings and equipment, it is likely that the increased taxes result from levying taxes on a phantom increase in value.

The net salvage values in line (g) of Table 9.19 are summed to total the amount of $11,838,541 that appears in line (14) of Table 9.18 for the year 19X6. The analysis then proceeds as before. We obtain a net present value of $3,430,969 for this inflation case. This is less than the NPV obtained in the no-inflation case covered by Table 9.16. Similarly, the internal rate of return calculated is 15.96 percent. If the inflation rate of 5 percent were added to the IRR of 12.31 percent obtained in the no-inflation case, we would have obtained an IRR of 17.31 percent for the inflation case. However, the actual IRR of 15.96 percent is lower. Hence inflation is not completely neutral for the Gomez Co. The profitability resulting from the patterns of revenues and costs in Table 9.18 shows that the real NPV and IRR have not been maintained by the Gomez Co. under inflation. The lag in profitability and in stock prices during the 1970s, a period characterized by an inflation rate at or near the two-digit level, appears to make our illustrative example quite realistic.

Even though profitability is somewhat reduced under the inflation case, the Gomez Co. still has a strongly positive NPV project. We may now turn to other topics in capital budgeting.

DEFINITION AND MEASUREMENT OF CASH FLOWS

The critical variables in the expressions for calculating the NPV and the IRR are the cash flows (CF_t) and the cost of capital (k). We have explained the cost of capital as the relevant marginal (opportunity) cost of capital commensurate with the risk of the project. We now seek to make clear the nature of the annual cash flows (CF_t). We do this at the level of the firm as a basis for discussing valuation in later chapters.

One of the elements of superiority of the NPV approach is that the value of the firm represents the sum of all of the NPVs of the portfolio of projects taken on by the firm. We need to emphasize that the cash flows that we are analyzing represent the incremental cash flows resulting from taking on new projects. From a capital budgeting standpoint, the financial statements that we utilize represent the incremental cash flows associated with an individual project. We also express the data in terms of annual figures to simplify the exposition.

We begin with an illustrative income statement, as shown in Table 9.20. In the illustrative income statement, the focus is on the elements below "Earnings before depreciation, interest, and taxes (EBDIT)." These are the components to be considered in defining the relevant cash flows. It is assumed that the project or segment or firm does not have any nonoperating income or expenses that would cause net operating income (NOI) to differ from earnings before interest and taxes (EBIT). Note that the abbreviations we use in the following models are defined in the illustrative income statement.

TABLE 9.20 Financial Statements

Illustrative Income Statement	Year 2
Sales	$145,000
Operating costs excluding depreciation	95,000
Earnings before depreciation, interest, and taxes (EBDIT)	$ 50,000
Depreciation expense (Dep.)	20,000
Earnings before interest and taxes (EBIT = NOI = X)	$ 30,000
Interest expense (f)	5,000
Earnings before taxes (EBT)	$ 25,000
Taxes @ 40 percent (T = tax rate)	10,000
Net income (Y = NI)	$ 15,000

Related Balance Sheets (in thousands, end-of-year amounts)

	Year 1	Year 2		Year 1	Year 2
Current assets	$ 40	$ 70	Interest-bearing debt	$ 30	$ 45
Gross fixed assets	70	100	Noninterest-bearing debt	20	30
Reserve for Dep.	10	30	Shareholders' equity	50	65
Net fixed assets	60	70			
Total assets (net)	$100	$140	Claims on assets	$100	$140

In the related balance sheets, the project or segment or firm is assumed to have no plant and equipment retirements during the two years so that the reserve for depreciation between Year 1 and Year 2 is the $20,000 amount in the income statement.

Also, gross fixed assets increase by $30,000, representing the amount of gross investment made by the firm during Year 2. It is further assumed that the segment pays no dividends, so that shareholders' equity in Year 2 increases by $15,000, the net income shown in the income statement.

Utilizing the information in the income statement and related balance sheets, we can measure key components of the segment's cash flows. These are first defined on a gross basis as follows:

Free Cash Flow (FCF) — Gross Basis

	Year 2
Net income	$15,000
+ Depreciation	20,000
= Cash flow from operations	$35,000
+ After-tax interest [f(1 − T)]	3,000
= Cash operating income (gross)	$38,000
− Investment (G)	30,000
= Free cash flow (FCF)	$ 8,000

On a gross basis, depreciation is added to net income to obtain *cash flow from operations*. This is consistent with the writings of financial analysts who, in evaluating common stock, measure cash flow in this same way. After-tax interest expenses (or more generally, financial charges) are added to cash flow from operations to obtain *cash operating income*. The segment pays $5,000 interest expense, but with a 40 percent tax rate, this saves $2,000 in taxes. Hence, the cash operating income (the cash flow, CF_t, used in evaluating investment projects) would include only the after-tax interest expenses. This item is used in the basic capital budgeting equation to calculate the NPV or IRR on a gross basis.

Cash flows (CF_t) or cash operating income can be calculated either on a top-down or a bottom-up basis, as follows:

Return to Capital Investments (Cash Operating Income)

1   EBDIT $(1 - T) + T$(Dep.) $= 50,000(.6) + .4(20,000) = $38,000$
1a $(X + $ Dep.$)(1 - T) + T$(Dep.) $= $38,000$
2 $X(1 - T) + $ Dep. $= 30,000(.6) + 20,000 = $38,000$
2a (EBT $+ f)(1 - T) + $ Dep. $= $38,000$
3   NI $+$ Dep. $+ f(1 - T) = 15,000 + 20,000 + 5,000(.6) = $38,000$

Measuring from the top down, the relevant cash flows on a gross basis for capital budgeting in line 1 start with earnings before depreciation, interest, and taxes (EBDIT) on an after-tax basis to which is added the tax shelter from depreciation [T(Dep.)]. Line 1a is the same except that EBDIT is broken into its component parts of NOI and Dep. In line 2, the same result of $38,000 is obtained by adding after-tax NOI to the full amount of depreciation. Line 2a breaks NOI into earnings before tax (EBT) and financial charges (f). Line 3 (a bottom-up method) begins with the financial analysts' measure of cash flow consisting of net income (NI) plus depreciation (Dep.) to which is added after-tax financial charges [$f(1 - T)$]. Thus, we can obtain cash operating income (CF_t) by a number of alternative methods that are equivalent and give the same numerical result, in this case — $38,000. Note that in lines 1 and 2, we do not need the data for interest expenses. This implies that in measuring the free cash flow, financial leverage need not be considered.

As in our simple example of capital budgeting for a project, we next deduct the amount of investment required for the period to finally arrive at the free cash flow (FCF) of the firm. Since we are measuring cash operating income gross of (adding back) depreciation, the investment figure that is deducted is also on a gross basis (before deducting depreciation). The result is a free cash flow (FCF) of $8,000.

We next set forth the calculation of the free cash flow on a net basis:

Free Cash Flow (FCF) — Net Basis

	Year 2
Net income (NI)	$15,000
+ After-tax interest [$f(1 - T)$]	3,000
= *Cash operating income* [$X(1 - T)$]	$18,000
− Investment (*I*)	10,000
= *Free cash flow (FCF)*	$ 8,000

On a net basis, we simply omit the same depreciation figure in the cash operating income item and in the investment measure. Both are net of depreciation. Cash operating income is now [$X(1 - T)$], which is net operating income after taxes, or $18,000 in our example. The same result is obtained by adding $NI + f(1 - T)$ which is $15,000 + $3,000 = $18,000. It is more convenient in practice and simpler from an analytical standpoint to do the analysis on a net basis. Hence, we use this procedure in subsequent chapters on valuation.

PROJECTS WITH DIFFERENT LIVES

All of the previous numerical examples in this chapter have compared mutually exclusive projects with the same economic life and the same initial capital outlay, that is, the same scale. We now turn our attention to capital budgeting techniques that handle the more realistic problem of projects with different lives and different scale.

Projects A and B in Table 9.21 are mutually exclusive and have different lives. If the opportunity cost of capital is 10 percent, the (simple) NPVs of the projects are

- NPV(A) = $723.14.
- NPV(B) = $894.44.

However, if these projects can be replicated at constant scale, then Project A should be superior to Project B because it recovers cash flow faster. As long as a project is not unique, we can reasonably assume that it can be repeated.

One way to put the two projects onto an equal footing is to string them together until the series of Project A repetitions lasts just as long as the series for Project B. An example which repeats Project A three times and Project B twice is illustrated in Figure 9.5. If Project A is repeated three times, it is equivalent to receiving an NPV of $723.14 now, at the end of Year 2, and at the end of Year 4. This is really an annuity (paid in advance) with payments every two years. Its net present value is

$$\text{NPV}(2,3) = \$723.14 + \frac{\$723.14}{(1.1)^2} + \frac{\$723.14}{(1.1)^4} = \$1,814.69.$$

The notation NPV(2,3) means that we are finding the NPV of a two-year project which is replicated three times. A similar calculation for Project B shows that NPV(3,2) = $1,566.45. Consequently, if the projects are repeated so that they both have a six-year cycle, we see that Project A is really superior.

The procedure we have just described is very cumbersome. What would we do, for example, if we were comparing five projects whose expected lives were 3, 5, 7, 11, and

TABLE 9.21   Mutually Exclusive Projects with Different Lives

Year	Project A	Project B
0	$-17,500	$-17,500
1	10,500	7,000
2	10,500	7,000
3		8,313

FIGURE 9.5   An Ad Hoc Procedure for Comparing Projects with Different Lives

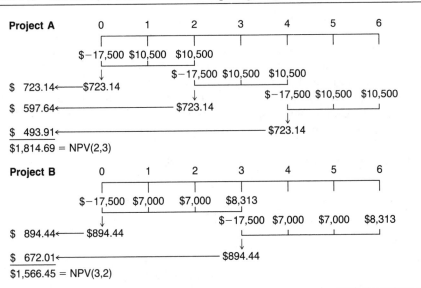

13 years? Each project would have to be replicated for $3 \times 5 \times 7 \times 11 \times 13 = 1{,}155$ years, a tedious task. The easiest thing to do (believe it or not) is to assume that each project is replicated at constant scale forever. Not only does every project have the same (infinite) life with this procedure, but also it is equivalent to maximizing shareholders' wealth. The NPV of an infinite stream of projects that are replicated every n years is really the same thing as the present value of a long-run strategy of investing in the n-year project.

In order to compute NPV(n,∞), the net present value of an n-year project that is replicated at constant scale forever, we start by using the concept of an equivalent annual annuity series (EAS) or uniform annuity series, defined by Equation 9.5.

$$\text{EAS} = \frac{\text{NPV}(n)}{\text{PVIFA}(k,t)} \tag{9.5}$$

In Chapter 3 we saw that:

$$\text{PVIFA}(k,t) = \frac{1 - \dfrac{1}{(1 + k)^n}}{k} = \frac{(1 + k)^n - 1}{k(1 + k)^n}$$

Substituting in Equation 9.5 we obtain:

$$\text{EAS} = \text{NPV}(n)\left[\frac{k(1 + k)^n}{(1 + k)^n - 1}\right]. \tag{9.6}$$

To express this result in value terms, we divide by the applicable k to get:

$$\text{NPV}(n,\infty) = \text{NPV}(n)\left[\frac{(1 + k)^n}{(1 + k)^n - 1}\right]. \tag{9.7}$$

Since we have treated the EAS as a perpetuity in dividing by k, Equation 9.7 is the NPV of an n-year project replicated at constant scale an infinite number of times. We can use it to compare replicable projects with different lives because when their cash flow streams are replicated forever, it is as if they had the same (infinite) life. It is not sufficient to stop with the EAS because projects may have different risks. Therefore, the NPV(n,∞) should be calculated by dividing the EAS by k, consistent with using the general NPV rule.

If we apply Equation 9.7 to the projects in Table 9.21, we see that for the two-year project,

$$\text{NPV}(2,\infty) = \text{NPV}(2)\left[\frac{(1 + .1)^2}{(1 + .1)^2 - 1}\right]$$

$$= \$723.14\left[\frac{1.21}{1.21 - 1}\right]$$

$$= \$723.14(5.76) = \$4,165.29,$$

and for the three-year project,

$$\text{NPV}(3,\infty) = \$894.44\left[\frac{(1.1)^3}{(1.1)^3 - 1}\right]$$

$$= \$894.44(4.02) = \$3,595.65.$$

If you had the opportunity to purchase the right to own Project A and repeat it forever, you would pay up to \$4,165.29 for it. Thus, NPV(n,∞) is exactly the same thing as the increase in shareholders' wealth if Project A is replicable (not unique).

A good example of choosing among mutually exclusive projects with different lives is the decision of when to harvest an area of growing trees or when to bottle and sell aging whiskey. For example, we could harvest trees after four years, five years, or nine years. Example cash flows are given in Table 9.22.[13] Each harvesting date is a mutually exclusive alternative. In fact, there are an infinite number of mutually exclusive harvesting decisions, and only the optimal harvest time will maximize shareholders' wealth.

TABLE 9.22 Cash Flows for Three Different Tree-Harvesting Strategies, $k = 5\%$

Strategy	I_0 = Initial Outlay	CF = Revenue at Harvest	NPV(n)	IRR	NPV(n,∞)
Harvest every 4 years	\$−15,000	\$22,361	\$3,396	10.50%	\$19,154
Harvest every 5 years	\$−15,000	\$24,494	\$4,192	10.31%	\$19,365
Harvest every 9 years	\$−15,000	\$31,664	\$5,411	8.64%	\$15,225

[13]This example is taken from Copeland and Weston [1983, p. 54].

One of the important aspects of the tree-harvesting problem is that the project can be repeated indefinitely. If we decide to harvest after five years, we will replicate the project by replanting the same acreage and then waiting five years before we harvest again. Consequently, the decision to harvest after five years is really a long-run strategy which goes on indefinitely. We can think of an infinite series of five-year projects that are replicated at constant scale, and $NPV(5, \infty)$ is the current value of the strategy.

If we were to employ the simple net present value technique (without replicating the project), and if the opportunity cost of capital is $k = 5\%$, we would discover that a strategy of harvesting every nine years yields the highest $NPV(n)$. The results for all three mutually exclusive alternatives are shown in Table 9.22. The calculation for the nine-year strategy is

$$
NPV(9) = \frac{CF_9}{(1 + k)^9} - I_0
$$

$$
= \frac{\$31{,}664}{(1.05)^9} - \$15{,}000
$$

$$
= \$31{,}664(.6446) - \$15{,}000 = \$5{,}411.
$$

Unfortunately, the nine-year harvesting strategy does not maximize shareholders' wealth. Because the projects can be replicated, shareholders' wealth is the NPV of a harvesting strategy repeated forever; that is, it is $NPV(n, \infty)$. The calculation for the five-year strategy uses Equation 9.7:

$$
NPV(5, \infty) = NPV(5) \left[\frac{(1 + .05)^5}{(1.05)^5 - 1} \right]
$$

$$
= \$4{,}192 \left[\frac{1.27628}{1.27628 - 1} \right]
$$

$$
= \$4{,}192(4.6195) = \$19{,}365.
$$

Since $NPV(n, \infty)$ is largest for the five-year strategy, it is the best choice among the mutually exclusive alternatives given in Table 9.22. It is the strategy which maximizes shareholders' wealth.[14]

Generally speaking, most projects are replicable in an approximate way. Even though technology may change, it is usually reasonable to assume that projects are replicable. Consequently, we recommend using the $NPV(n, \infty)$ procedure for comparing projects of different lives.

CAPITAL RATIONING

The previous topics in this chapter have generally assumed that the funds necessary to finance a given investment project are always available to the firm at some appropriate cost of capital. Surveys [Gitman and Forrester, 1977] indicate that for some firms the

---

[14]Note that the IRR for each project is also given in Table 9.21. Once again, the IRR gives the incorrect answer. It chooses a four-year harvest cycle, when five years is the best.

amount of funds available for investment in some time period is relatively fixed, independent of the capital market. Thus some positive NPV projects may be available but cannot be funded due to a capital constraint. If so, the firm faces the problem of *capital rationing*.

Capital rationing can arise for a number of reasons. A common situation is that the firm is reluctant to issue stock because it feels that it is undervalued by the market or because the firm seeks to avoid dilution of ownership control. This constraint on equity financing may impose similar restraints on borrowing to avoid exceeding what management regards as a desirable debt-to-equity ratio. Or there may be a debt limit imposed by existing loan agreements.

Another important reason why a firm may place a limit on the amount of funds it uses for investment is that top management feels it does not have time to carefully analyze the investment of more than a specified dollar amount of funds. Another strong influence is that an expansion rate beyond some percentage may involve difficulties of finding the requisite managers and workers and organization experience and effectiveness to utilize the funds efficiently. Examples abound of companies that expanded so rapidly that the quality of personnel deteriorated with resulting inefficiencies and severe declines in profitability. To avoid such organization problems the firm may impose limits on the amount of funds it will invest each year. We consider three approaches to dealing with the capital rationing problem.

Capital Rationing for Projects with Different Scale

Even if projects are independent, under capital rationing we have to choose between projects because taking all of them would exceed our capital constraint. The problem is complicated by the fact that the projects have different initial investment outlays. An example will illustrate one method of dealing with this situation.

Table 9.23 provides data for five independent projects. All projects are assumed to have the same economic life of five years; hence, using the simple NPV criterion will give the same accept/reject decision as using $NPV(n,\infty)$. If there are no capital constraints, then the first four projects should be accepted because they all have a positive NPV. The total outlay would be $1,300,000.

Suppose that there is a capital rationing situation where our budget is restricted to $600,000. How shall we choose projects? First, note that under conditions of true capital rationing, the firm's value is not being maximized. If management were maximizing

TABLE 9.23 Four Projects with Different Scale (Five-year lives, $k = 10\%$)

Project	Outlay = I_0	Annual CF	PV of CF	NPV	IRR	PI
A	$400,000	$121,347	$460,000	$60,000	15.7%	1.15
B	250,000	74,523	282,500	32,500	14.9	1.13
C	350,000	102,485	388,500	38,500	14.2	1.11
D	300,000	85,470	324,000	24,000	13.1	1.08
E	100,000	23,742	90,000	-10,000	6.0	.90

shareholders' wealth, it would accept all positive NPV projects and make an outlay of the full $1,300,000. If a financial manager does face strict capital rationing and cannot get the constraint lifted, the objective should be to maximize value subject to the constraint of not exceeding the capital budget. This amounts to a linear (or integer) programming problem. If we designate V_j as the net present value of each project, w_j as the fraction of each project accepted, and I_j as the initial cash outlay, then the linear programming problem may be written[15]

$$\text{MAX} \sum_j w_j V_j \qquad (9.8)$$

subject to:

$$\sum_j w_j I_j \leq \text{Budget},$$
$$w_j \leq 1.0.$$

The *profitability index* is an equivalent procedure for solving a one-period capital constraint problem. It has also often been proposed for dealing with the issue of projects of different scale. As we shall see, when correctly implemented, it is exactly the same as the NPV technique. We discuss it here because it is often misused. The profitability index (PI), or the benefit/cost ratio, as it is sometimes called, is defined as

$$\text{PI} = \frac{\text{PV Benefits}}{\text{Cost}} = \left[\sum_{t=1}^{n} \frac{CF_t}{(1+k)^t} \right] \div I_0. \qquad (9.9)$$

The PI shows the *relative* profitability of any project, or the PV of benefits per dollar cost.[16]

Looking at the last column of Table 9.23, it is tempting to meet our assumed $600,000 budget by accepting only Project A, which costs $400,000 and has the highest profitability index (PI = 1.15). However, this would be incorrect because there is $200,000 left over, which must be invested in cash or marketable securities with a profitability index of 1.0. At best, the unused budget can earn only the opportunity cost of capital; therefore, the PV of the inflows will just equal the $200,000, leaving us with a PI of 1.0 for the excess funds.

Correct use of the PI requires that we find the combination of projects and excess funds that maximizes a weighted average profitability index. For example, if Projects B and C are selected, the weighted average PI is

$$\text{PI} = \frac{250,000}{600,000}(1.13) + \frac{350,000}{600,000}(1.11) = 1.1183.$$

---

[15]For further readings on this topic, refer to articles by Lorie and Savage [1955], Weingartner [1963], Baumol and Quandt [1965], Carleton [1969], Bernhard [1969], and Myers [1972].

[16]If costs are incurred in more than one year, they should be netted against cash inflows in the corresponding years; if costs exceed cash inflows in some years, the denominator must be the PV of the costs.

It is computed by multiplying the PI of each project by the percentage of the total budget allocated to it. If Project A is selected, two-thirds of the total budget will be invested in the project, but the remaining one-third will be invested in cash and marketable securities which have a profitability index of only 1.0; hence, the weighted average profitability index will be

$$PI = \frac{400,000}{600,000}(1.15) + \frac{200,000}{600,000}(1.00) = 1.1000.$$

This example shows that, given a $600,000 budget, and the characteristics of the projects available, it is better to choose Projects B and C rather than Project A and excess cash. Note that this decision is exactly the same as maximizing the NPV of the firm subject to a budget constraint. The NPV of Projects B and C is $71,000 while Project A is worth only $60,000. Our advice to the reader is to stick with the NPV maximization principle and ignore the PI because, at best, it provides exactly the same results.

Mathematical Programming Approaches

Another approach is to use mathematical programming methods. These represent applications of linear programming or integer programming and can be employed efficiently with the use of computer programs. The reader may investigate this approach by reference to the available literature on the subject. The classical treatment of the subject may be found in Weingartner [1963, 1977].

AN INFORMATION FEEDBACK SYSTEM

It is essential that there be a continuous review of all aspects of making investment decisions. This is referred to by some writers as the post-audit. This term is somewhat misleading because what is called for is a continuous review of investments and a comparison of actual results with predictions as well as other ongoing opportunities and potentials. In effective planning and control systems, performance will be reviewed at least monthly and even more frequently if considerable uncertainty is associated with the project. However, the review and evaluation of investment decisions cannot be performed mechanically. An information feedback system must be developed to provide rapid feedback with provisions for modifying decisions previously made. The evaluation of capital budgeting processes must fit into the larger strategic planning and management control systems of the firm. (For further details see Weston [1972, 1986].)

FOREIGN INVESTMENT

Foreign investment should not be taken out of its realistic context for business firms. Two important points should be recognized. One, to be successful abroad, the firm must first be successful at home. Firms that seek to deal with failure in the domestic market by trying foreign markets will find their difficulties compounded.

A second important observation is that the movement of a firm into foreign operations is evolutionary in nature. If the firm is successful in its domestic market, the price and quality characteristics of its products may enable it to develop export sales. After building up a volume of sales abroad, the firm may then wish to consider manufacturing operations abroad. The main pressure for this is to manufacture to local needs and tastes as well as to provide prompt repair and service facilities. Successful manufacturing operations abroad require a carryover of capabilities that have been efficient from an economic standpoint in domestic operations. Because of different environmental conditions, the firm may conduct its foreign manufacturing operations jointly with a foreign firm, but often the need for dealing with local conditions can be met by hiring managers from the foreign countries in which the firm is operating.

Advantages of Foreign Operations

Foreign operations enable the domestic firm to utilize efficient capabilities in larger markets. In addition, foreign operations may enable the firm to utilize some fixed factors of production. As a result, often a firm with 20–30 percent of its sales or operations abroad will generate 50–60 percent of its net income from foreign operations. In addition, if changes in economic conditions abroad are not perfectly correlated with changes in economic conditions domestically, both total risk and systematic risk can be reduced. Total risk will be reduced by the benefits of diversification. Systematic risk is defined as the behavior of the firm's sales or net income or security returns in relation to "the market." The behavior of the firm's variables may be less sensitive to the world market than to the domestic market, because a different set of factors may be impacting the broader markets.

Possible Disadvantages of Foreign Investment

The firm may encounter a host of difficult conditions abroad. Government regulations may be different and complex. Worker attitudes and sensitivities may differ and require different management systems. The needs and tastes of consumers may be different. The firm may have a new set of market conditions to which it must adjust.

In addition, government laws and regulations may be different and even discriminatory toward foreign firms. Political conditions may be unstable and the firm may have to adjust to a succession of different governments with different attitudes and requirements. Some government regimes may actually be hostile to the point of imposing discriminatory taxation against foreign firms and, in the extreme, engaging in appropriation without adequate compensation.

On balance, foreign investment operations have become a fact of life for most large firms in the United States and many smaller firms as well. The world has, for some years, moved to global financial markets. In addition, the business operations of individual firms are becoming increasingly global in scope both on the production side and in sales policies. Increasingly, the world is viewed as one large market, and multinational firms source production inputs and products from the location where the operations can be conducted most effectively from the standpoint of the firms' overall performance.

SUMMARY

Capital budgeting, which involves commitments for large outlays whose benefits (or drawbacks) extend well into the future, is of the greatest significance to a firm. Decisions in these areas, therefore, will have a major impact on the future well-being of the firm. This chapter focused on how capital budgeting decisions can be made more effective in contributing to the health and growth of a firm. The discussion stressed the development of systematic procedures and rules for preparing a list of investment proposals, for evaluating them, and for selecting a cutoff point.

The chapter emphasized that one of the most crucial phases in the process of evaluating capital budget proposals is obtaining a dependable estimate of the benefits that will be obtained from undertaking the project. It cannot be overemphasized that the firm must allocate to competent and experienced personnel the making of these judgments.

Determining Cash Flows. The cash inflows from an investment are the incremental change in after-tax net operating cash income plus the incremental depreciation tax benefit; the cash outflow is the cost of the investment less the salvage value received on an old machine plus any tax loss (or less any tax savings) when the machine is sold.

Ranking Investment Proposals. Four commonly used procedures for ranking investment proposals were discussed in the chapter: payback, return on assets, net present value, and internal rate of return.

Payback is defined as the number of years required to return the original investment. Although the payback method is used frequently, it has serious conceptual weaknesses, because it ignores the facts that (1) some receipts come in beyond the payback period and (2) a dollar received today is more valuable than a dollar received in the future.

Return on assets is the average annual cash inflow divided by the original capital outlay. Like the payback method, its major conceptual problem is that it does not discount cash flows.

Net present value is defined as the present value of future returns, discounted at the cost of capital, minus the cost of the investment. The NPV method overcomes the conceptual flaws noted in the use of the payback method and ROA.

Internal rate of return is defined as the interest rate that equates the present value of future returns to the investment outlay. The internal rate of return method, like the NPV method, discounts cash flows.

In most cases, the two discounted cash flow methods give identical answers to these questions: Which of two mutually exclusive projects should be selected? How large should the total capital budget be? However, under certain circumstances, conflicts may arise. Such conflicts are caused primarily by the fact that the NPV and IRR methods make different assumptions about the rate at which cash flows may be reinvested, or the opportunity cost of cash flows. The assumption of the NPV method (that the opportunity cost is the cost of capital) is the correct one. Accordingly, our preference is for using the NPV method to make capital budgeting decisions.

Some principles related to foreign investment were also developed. First, the firm must be successful at home. Second, moving into foreign operations is evolutionary in nature. Third, the firm should be prepared to adjust to different government regulations, to different managerial and worker sensitivities, and to different consumer needs and tastes. Foreign operations enable a firm to utilize strong capabilities in larger markets. In addition, total and systematic risks may be reduced.

QUESTIONS

9.1 A firm has $100 million available for capital expenditures. Suppose Project A involves purchasing $100 million of grain, shipping it overseas, and selling it within a year at a profit of $20 million. The project has an IRR of 20 percent and an NPV of $20 million, and it will cause earnings per share (EPS) to rise within one year. Project B calls for the use of the $100 million to develop a new process, acquire land, build a plant, and begin processing. Project B, which, if chosen, cannot be postponed, has an NPV of $50 million and an IRR of 30 percent. But the fact that some of the plant costs will be written off immediately, combined with the fact that no revenues will be generated for several years, means that accepting Project B will reduce short-run earnings per share (EPS).
  a. Should the short-run effects on EPS influence the choice between the two projects?
  b. How might situations such as the one described here influence a firm's decision to use payback as a screening criterion?

9.2 Are there conditions under which a firm might be better off if it chose a machine with a rapid payback rather than one with the largest rate of return?

9.3 Company X uses the payback method in evaluating investment proposals and is considering new equipment whose additional net after-tax earnings will be $150 a year. The equipment costs $500, and its expected life is ten years (straight-line depreciation). The company uses a three-year payback as its criterion. Should the equipment be purchased under the above assumptions?

9.4 What are the most critical problems that arise in calculating a rate of return for a prospective investment?

9.5 What other factors in addition to rate of return analysis should be considered in determining capital expenditures?

9.6 Would it be beneficial for a firm to review its past capital expenditures and capital budgeting procedures? Explain.

9.7 Fiscal and monetary policies are tools used by the government to stimulate the economy. Using the analytical devices developed in this chapter, explain how each of the following might be expected to stimulate the economy by encouraging investment.
  a. A speedup of tax-allowable depreciation
  b. An easing of interest rates
  c. Passage of a new federal program giving more aid to the poor
  d. An investment tax credit

PROBLEMS

(*Note:* In some problem statements we will use pre-MACRS depreciation assumptions so that comparisons can be made with earlier tax rules to evaluate the effects of tax changes.)

9.1   A firm has an opportunity to invest in a machine at a cost of $656,670. The net cash flows after taxes from the machine would be $210,000 per year and would continue for five years. The applicable cost of capital for this project is 12 percent.
   a.   Calculate the net present value for the investment.
   b.   What is the internal rate of return for the investment?
   c.   Should the investment be made?

9.2   The MACRS (pronounced "makers") class life method of depreciation was introduced by the Tax Reform Act of 1986 as described in Chapter 5. A class life is designated by the IRS and a half-year convention is followed which assumes that the asset is purchased in the middle of the year acquired. In addition, MACRS provides that estimated salvage value need not be deducted from the original investment outlay.
   a.   Calculate the cumulative depreciation percentages under the MACRS declining balance methods and those for the MACRS straight-line method using Table P9.2.
   b.   Compare your results under MACRS DDB versus MACRS Straight Line.
   c.   Calculate the present value of using the MACRS DDB versus MACRS straight-line depreciation for a $10,000 asset for: (1) 3-year class life, (2) 5-year class life, and (3) 7-year class life.

TABLE P9.2   MACRS DDB versus MACRS Straight-Line Yearly Depreciation

Ownership Year	Class Life					
	3-Yr.		5-Yr.		7-Yr.	
	DDB	Straight Line	DDB	Straight Line	DDB	Straight Line
1	33.33%	16.667%	20.00%	10%	14.29%	7.142%
2	44.45	33.333	32.00	20	24.49	14.286
3	14.81	33.333	19.20	20	17.49	14.286
4	7.41	16.667	11.52	20	12.49	14.286
5	100.00	100.000	11.52	20	8.93	14.286
6			5.76	10	8.92	14.286
7			100.00	100	8.93	14.286
8					4.46	7.142
9					100.00	100.000

9.3   The Farlow Company is considering the replacement of a riveting machine with a new one that will increase the earnings before depreciation from $20,000 per year to $51,000 per year. The new machine will cost $100,000 and have an estimated life of eight years with no salvage value. The applicable corporate tax rate is 40 percent, and the firm's cost of capital is 12 percent. The old machine has been fully depreciated and has no salvage value.

a. Evaluate the replacement decision, using a MACRS 5-year class life.

b. Evaluate the replacement decision, using the pre-MACRS sum-of-years'-digits accelerated depreciation.

c. Compare the results.

9.4 The following facts are presented on an opportunity to invest in Machine A: Cost of equipment is $120,000. The economic life is ten years. The estimated after-tax salvage value at the end of ten years would be $20,000. The additional investment in working capital required would be $30,000. The applicable tax rate is 40 percent. The machine will qualify for the MACRS 7-year class life. The cost savings per year are estimated to be cash flows of $40,000 per year for ten years. The applicable cost of capital is 12 percent.

a. Use the worksheet method to calculate the NPV from the project.

b. Should the investment be made?

9.5 After using Machine A in Problem 9.4 for five years, the firm has an opportunity to invest in Machine B, which would replace Machine A. Machine B would have a five-year economic life, cost $80,000, have an after-tax salvage value of $20,000, generate sales of $150,000 per year, and reduce operating expenses by $10,000 per year. If the replacement were made by investing in Machine B, the amount realized on the sale of Machine A would be $10,000. Machine B would qualify for the MACRS 5-year class life.

a. What is the tax basis of Machine A at the end of 5 years?

b. What is the tax loss on the sale of Machine A?

c. Calculate what the effect of the purchase of Machine B would have on the depreciation tax shelter.

d. Calculate the NPV for the investment in Machine B using the worksheet method.

9.6 Natural Beverages is contemplating the replacement of one of its bottling machines with a newer and more efficient one. The old machine has a book value of $500,000 and a remaining useful life of five years. The firm does not expect to realize any return from scrapping the old machine in five years, but it can sell the machine now to another firm in the industry for $300,000. Pre-MACRS straight-line depreciation was used on the old machine.

The new machine has a purchase price of $1.1 million, an estimated useful life of five years, and an estimated salvage value of $200,000. It is expected to economize on electric power usage, labor, and repair costs and to reduce the number of defective bottles. In total, an annual saving of $250,000 will be realized if the new machine is installed. The company is in the 40 percent tax bracket, has a 10 percent cost of capital, and will use MACRS 5-year class life depreciation on the new machine.

a. What is the initial cash outlay required for the new machine?

b. Should Natural Beverages purchase the new machine? Support your answer.

9.7 The FM Company has cash inflows of $275,000 and cash outflows of $210,000 per year on Project A. The investment outlay is $144,000; its economic life is 10 years; the tax rate is 40 percent. The applicable cost of capital is 14 percent.

a. Calculate the net present value for Project A, using MACRS 7-year class life depreciation for tax purposes.

b. If the earnings before depreciation, interest, and taxes are $40,000 per year, what is the net present value for Project A, using MACRS 5-year class life?

9.8 The Starbuck Company is considering the purchase of a new machine tool to replace an obsolete one. The machine being used for the operation has both a tax book value and a market value of zero; it is in good working order and will last, physically, for at least an additional 5 years. The proposed machine will perform the operation so much more efficiently that Starbuck engineers estimate that labor, material, and other direct costs of the operation will be reduced $6,500 a year if it is installed. The proposed machine costs $30,000 delivered and installed, and its economic life is estimated to be 10 years, with zero salvage value. The company expects to earn 12 percent on its investment after taxes (12 percent is the firm's cost of capital). The tax rate is 40 percent, and the firm has been advised that the new equipment will qualify for a MACRS 7-year class life.

a. Should Starbuck buy the new machine?

b. Assume that the tax book value of the old machine is $6,000, that the annual depreciation charge is $400, and that the machine has no market value. How do these assumptions affect your answer?

c. Answer Part (b), assuming that the old machine has a market value of $4,000.

d. Answer Part (c), assuming that the annual savings will be $8,000.

9.9 Each of two mutually exclusive projects involves an investment of $120,000. Cash flows (after-tax profits plus depreciation) for the two projects have a different time pattern, although the totals are approximately the same. Project M will yield high returns early and lower returns in later years. (It is a mining type of investment, and the expense of removing the ore is lower at the entrance to the mine, where there is easier access.) Project O yields low returns in the early years and higher returns in the later years. (It is an orchard type of investment, and it takes a number of years for trees to mature and be fully bearing.) The cash flows from the two investments are as follows:

Year	Project M	Project O
1	$70,000	$10,000
2	40,000	20,000
3	30,000	30,000
4	10,000	50,000
5	10,000	80,000

a. Compute the present value of each project when the firm's cost of capital is 0 percent, 6 percent, 10 percent, and 20 percent.

b. Compute the internal rate of return (IRR) for each project.

c. Graph the present value of the two projects, putting net present value (NPV) on the Y-axis and the cost of capital on the X-axis.

d. Can you determine the IRR of the projects from your graph? Explain.

e. Which project would you select, assuming no capital rationing and a constant cost of capital of 8 percent? Of 10 percent? Of 12 percent? Explain.

9.10 Because of increasing energy prices, David Bradshaw, the chief financial officer of General Tools Company, is quite concerned about the gas bill of his firm. Also, Bradshaw is interested in the new tax benefits from installing energy conservation equipment. To encourage energy conservation and to promote industrial and agricultural conversions from oil and gas to alternative forms of energy, the Energy Tax Act of 1978 provided a 10 percent credit in addition to the regular investment credit for "alternative energy property," such as equipment that uses fuel other than oil or natural gas, and for "specially defined energy property" intended to reduce energy waste in existing facilities. The credit is not refundable, but it can be used to offset 100 percent of tax liability.

Bradshaw is considering the installation of new energy-saving solar equipment to replace the conventional boiler, which uses gas as the only energy source and can be used for another 15 years. The new solar system is estimated to have a lifetime of 15 years and requires a capital investment of $24,000. The net book value of the old boiler is $10,000. There is no salvage value for either equipment. However, the new system is expected to have an energy saving of 1 billion BTUs per year. The firm will have a combined 20 percent tax credit on the investment in the new solar system.

The current price is $2.04 for 1,000 cubic feet of natural gas, which contains 1 million BTUs. The required rate of return on investment is 15 percent after tax; the annual operating and maintenance expenses for the new solar system are estimated to be $400 less than for the conventional boiler; and the old boiler has a current market value of $8,000. The corporate tax rate is 40 percent, and the firm uses straight-line depreciation.

a. As a financial analyst, what is your recommendation to Bradshaw?

b. Suppose the annual growth rate of gas prices is expected to be 15 percent. How will this affect your evaluation?

9.11 The Grant Corporation is considering a project which has a five-year life and costs $25,000. It would save $4,100 per year in operating costs and increase revenue by $5,000 per year. It would be financed with a five-year loan with the following payment schedule (the annual rate of interest is 8 percent). No salvage value for the new purchased equipment is assumed at the end of the project.

Payment	Interest	Repayment of Principal	Balance
$626.14	$200.00	$ 426.14	$2,073.86
626.14	165.91	460.23	1,613.63
626.14	129.09	497.05	1,116.58
626.14	89.33	536.81	579.77
626.14	46.37	579.77	0
	$630.70	$2,500.00	

If the company has a 12 percent after-tax cost of capital and a 40 percent tax rate, what is the net present value of the project if the company uses MACRS 3-year class life depreciation?

9.12 You are considering the economic value of an MBA. Assuming that you can and do enroll in a business school, incremental expenses are $10,000 per year and foregone income is $28,000 per year for the required 2 years. Your expected yearly income for the following 18 years is increased by $28,404.

a. What is the return on investment earned? (Hint: It is more than 10 percent.)

b. What are some of the major complicating factors ignored in the information presented?

9.13 A firm is comparing the purchase of two mutually exclusive machine investments. Machine F involves an investment of $40,000 and would produce annual net cash flows after taxes of $12,000 for five years. Machine H would require an investment of $100,000 and would produce annual cash flows after taxes of $30,000 for seven years. Machine H is somewhat more risky and requires a cost of capital of 12 percent, compared to 10 percent for Machine F. Which machine should be selected?

9.14 The Longdon Company has two alternative investment projects, E and F. As a result of a capital rationing policy, the management is contemplating which project they should accept. The following table provides the management with all the related financial information:

	Project E	Project F
Cost	$15,000	$15,000
Cash flow per year (CF$_t$)	$ 5,500	$ 3,200
Life	4 years	8 years
Cost of capital	12%	12%

Calculate the NPV and IRR for each project and make your recommendation.

9.15 If the opportunity cost of capital is 15 percent, which of the following three projects has the highest PI? Which will increase shareholders' wealth the most?

Year	Project A	Project B	Project C
0	$-300	$-1,000	$-600
1	320	750	1,100
2	320	750	—
3	—	750	—

9.16 A coal mining firm is considering opening a strip mine, the cost of which is $4.4 million. Cash flows will be $27.7 million, all coming at the end of one year. The land must be returned to its natural state at a cost of $25 million, payable after two years. The IRR is found to be either 9.2 percent or 420 percent. Should the project be accepted (a) if $k = 8$ percent or (b) if $k = 14$ percent? Explain your reasoning.

9.17 *(Use the computer diskette, File name: 09CAPBUD, Capital Budgeting.)*

a. Project X and Project Y require the same investment outlay. The cash inflows to Project X are higher in the early years and for Project Y are higher in the later years. At a low discount rate which project would you expect to have the higher NPV?
  (1) At a zero discount rate which project has the higher NPV?
  (2) At what discount rate does the NPV of Project X become higher than the NPV of Project Y?

b. Looking at the graph, what is the NPV of each project at its calculated IRR?
  (1) Now change the discount rate until the calculated NPV for each project becomes zero. What does this discount rate represent?

c. If the total absolute amount of cash inflows of Project X and Project Y were equal but the returns to Project Y were somewhat later than for Project X (as illustrated) could Project Y ever have a higher NPV? Could it ever have a higher IRR?

d. For various reasons you could have the pattern exhibited in a graph of the product life cycle. One alternative is to spend $1,500 to modify a product which would continue its net cash inflows on a somewhat higher level for about five years and then very rapidly decline. This is compared with attempting to develop an entirely new product with low then high cash inflows. The analysis is performed over a ten-year time horizon.

(1) Would you modify the existing product or develop a new product if the discount rate is 10 percent? If the rate is 5 percent? What would the discount rate have to be before you would choose the alternative?

e. The apparatus available to you now is sufficiently flexible to consider a wide range of patterns of cash inflows. You can now investigate any pattern of assumptions that suggests itself to you on the basis of your experience or your curiosity.

9.18 *(Use the computer diskette, File name: 09CPLAN, Gomez Co.)*

Perform a sensitivity analysis for the capital budgeting problems analyzed in Tables 9.16 and 9.18. For example, you can investigate the effect of different assumptions about the tax rate, the amount of investment required, working capital requirements, impact of inflation on revenues and cost elements, etc.

SELECTED REFERENCES

Baumol, William J., and Quandt, Richard E., "Investment and Discount Rates under Capital Rationing — A Programming Approach," *Economic Journal,* 75 (June 1965), pp. 317–329.

Bernhard, Richard H., "Mathematical Programming Models for Capital Budgeting — A Survey, Generalization, and Critique," *Journal of Financial and Quantitative Analysis,* 4 (June 1969), pp. 111–158.

Bierman, Harold, Jr., and Smidt, Seymour, *The Capital Budgeting Decision,* 4th ed., New York: Macmillan, 1975.

Booth, Laurence D., "Correct Procedures for the Evaluation of Risky Cash Outflows," *Journal of Financial and Quantitative Analysis,* 17 (June 1982), pp. 287–300.

Carleton, W., "Linear Programming and Capital Budgeting Models: A New Interpretation," *Journal of Finance,* (December 1969), pp. 825–833.

Cooley, Philip L.; Roenfeldt, Rodney L.; and Chew, It-Keong, "Capital Budgeting Procedures under Inflation," *Financial Management,* 4 (Winter 1975), pp. 18–27.

Copeland, Thomas E., and Weston, J. Fred, *Financial Theory and Corporate Policy,* 2d ed., Reading, Mass.: Addison-Wesley, 1983.

Emery, Gary W., "Some Guidelines for Evaluating Capital Investment Alternatives with Unequal Lives," *Financial Management,* 11 (Spring 1982), pp. 14–19.

Findlay, M. Chapman, and Williams, Edward E., "The Problem of 'Unequal Lives' Reconsidered," *Journal of Business Finance & Accounting,* 8 (Summer 1981), pp. 161–164.

Gitman, Lawrence J., and Forrester, John R., Jr., "A Survey of Capital Budgeting Techniques Used by Major U.S. Firms," *Financial Management,* 6 (Fall 1977), pp. 66–71.

Howe, Keith M., "Perpetuity Rate of Return Analysis," *The Engineering Economist,* 36 (Spring 1991), pp. 248–257.

———, "Capital Budgeting Discount Rates Under Inflation: A Caveat," ms., DePaul University, Chicago, Illinois, (August 1990).

———, "Does Inflationary Change Affect Capital Asset Life?," *Financial Management,* (Summer 1987a), pp. 63–67.

———, and Lapan, H., "Inflation and Asset Life: The Darby Versus the Fisher Effect," *Journal of Financial and Quantitative Analysis,* (June 1987b), pp. 249–258.

Kim, Suk H.; Crick, Trevor; and Kim, Seung H., "Do Executives Practice What Academics

Preach?," *Management Accounting,* (November 1986), pp. 49–52.

Lorie, J. H., and Savage, L. J., "Three Problems in Capital Rationing," *Journal of Business* (October 1955), pp. 229–239.

Meyer, Richard L., "A Note on Capital Budgeting Techniques and the Reinvestment Rate," *Journal of Finance,* 34 (December 1979), pp. 1251–1254.

Myers, S. C., "A Note on Linear Programming and Capital Budgeting," *Journal of Finance,* (March 1972), pp. 89–92.

Rappaport, Alfred, and Taggart, Robert A., Jr., "Evaluation of Capital Expenditure Proposals Under Inflation," *Financial Management,* 11 (Spring 1982), pp. 5–13.

Sarnat, Marshall, and Levy, Haim, "The Relationship of Rules of Thumb to the Internal Rate of Return: A Restatement and Generalization," *Journal of Finance,* 24 (June 1969), pp. 479–489.

Schall, Lawrence D.; Sundem, Gary L.; and Geijsbeek, William R., "Survey and Analysis of Capital Budgeting Methods," *Journal of Finance,* 33 (March 1978), pp. 281–292.

Schwab, Bernhard, and Lusztig, Peter, "A Note on Abandonment Value and Capital Budgeting," *Journal of Financial and Quantitative Analysis,* 5 (September 1970), pp. 377–380.

Smidt, Seymour, "A Bayesian Analysis of Project Selection and of Post Audit Evaluations," *Journal of Finance,* 34 (June 1979), pp. 675–688.

Taggart, Robert A., Jr., "Capital Budgeting and the Financing Decision: An Exposition," *Financial Management,* 6 (Summer 1977), pp. 59–64.

Virts, John R., and Weston, J. Fred, "Returns to Research and Development in the U.S. Pharmaceutical Industry," *Managerial and Decision Economics,* 1 (1980), pp. 103–111.

Weingartner, H. M., "Capital Rationing: *n* Authors in Search of a Plot," *Journal of Finance,* 32 (December 1977), pp. 1403–1432.

———, *Mathematical Programming and the Analysis of Capital Budgeting Problems,* Englewood Cliffs, N. J.: Prentice-Hall, 1963.

Weston, J. Fred, "Return on Investment as a Dynamic Management Process," Section 4, *Handbook of Corporate Finance,* Edward I. Altman, ed., New York: John Wiley & Sons, 1986, pp. 4.1–4.20.

———, "ROI Planning and Control," *Business Horizons,* 15 (August 1972), pp. 35–42.

PART FOUR

Decision Making under Uncertainty

Part Four introduces more realism into our view of financial management by summarizing the ideas that have been developed to make decisions in the face of uncertainty. In Chapter 10 we view the firm as a portfolio of risky assets and develop some fundamental relationships regarding trade-offs between risk and return. These ideas are then extended in Chapter 11 to an equilibrium setting in the Capital Asset Pricing Model (CAPM) and the more generalized Arbitrage Pricing Model (APM). By providing a unique relationship between risk and required return, these models advance our thinking about the risk-adjusted cost of capital and capital budgeting under uncertainty.

Chapter 12 introduces contingent claims — assets whose payoff depends on the value of an underlying risky asset. The value of contingent claims is determined using the Option Pricing Model (OPM). Many financial securities, including the debt and equity in a levered firm, can be viewed as options.

Chapter 13 applies decision making under uncertainty to capital budgeting under uncertainty, to illustrate how the principles developed in Chapters 10 through 12 may be applied.

CHAPTER 10

Risk and Return: Theory

This chapter introduces the modern theory of decision making under uncertainty. The financial ratios discussed in Chapter 7 have been used for centuries as rules of thumb to aid in understanding trade-offs between risk and return, but they only scratch the surface. In this chapter, we view financial decision making in a portfolio context. Portfolio theory is necessary to understand corporate finance, because the firm is really a portfolio of risky assets and liabilities. The fundamental issue is, How can a manager select the best combination of risk and return to maximize the wealth of shareholders?

INTRODUCTION

The tough part of decision making under uncertainty is deciding how much extra return should be required to accept a measurable risk. We will start out by taking an individual's point of view. For example, the owner and operator of a ship at sea faces a small chance of disaster, namely that the ship will sink and that all will be lost. From the ship captain's point of view, the risk is large. To avoid it, he may be prepared to give up substantial returns. His is the demand side of risk avoidance. From the point of view of a marine property and casualty insurer who supplies insurance, the picture is quite different. Lloyds of London can diversify its policies across all shipping. It need know only the probability that a given tonnage will go down. Since it can achieve diversification at low cost it can supply insurance at a low rate. In the same way, capital markets facilitate risk sharing among those who demand risk avoidance and those who supply it.

In this chapter, we review the mean and variance as measures of risk and return for a single risky asset. Then, we explore the effects of portfolio diversification. Combinations of risky assets, in the form of portfolios, provide a set of investment opportunities for investors. Given these investment opportunities, we then look at how risk-averse investors choose among them. If we know the risk and return of the objects of choice (portfolios) and the way investors make their choices (the theory of choice), then we can describe optimal portfolio choices. This is the goal of this chapter.

In Chapter 11, we will turn to a market equilibrium context in order to show that there is a market price of risk just as there is a market price for anything else, apples and oranges, for example. If it is possible to meaningfully measure the risk of an investment project, and if we know what the price of risk is, then we can determine the risk-adjusted rate of return, which can be used for computing the project's net present value. The chapter will present two similar equilibrium theories of the measurement and pricing of risk — the Capital Asset Pricing Model (CAPM) and the Arbitrage Pricing Model (APM). But first, we begin with a discussion of how risk-averse investors choose between different combinations of risk and return.

RISK AND RETURN: AN INDIVIDUAL'S POINT OF VIEW

Chapter 8 already introduced the mean and variance of a probability distribution and illustrated how they can be estimated from a sample of data. In this chapter, we shall assume that all decision makers are risk averse and prefer higher mean return and lower variance of return. Furthermore, we assume that nothing other than the mean and variance of return matters to investors.[1] Thus, the mean and variance are objects of choice much in the same way that apples and oranges are objects of choice. What we need first is a theory of choice which will tell us exactly how individual investors will choose between alternatives that have different combinations of risk and return.

In theory, we can identify three possible attitudes toward risk: a desire for risk, an aversion to risk, and an indifference to risk. A *risk seeker* is one who prefers risk. Given a choice between more and less risky investments with identical expected monetary returns, this person would prefer the riskier investment. Faced with the same choice, the *risk averter* would select the less risky investment. The person who is indifferent to risk would not care which investment he or she received. *There undoubtedly are individuals who prefer risk and others who are indifferent to it, but both logic and observation suggest that business managers and stockholders are predominantly risk averters.*

The assumption of risk aversion is basic to many decision models used in finance. But why does risk aversion generally hold? Given two investments, each with the same expected dollar returns, why would most investors prefer the less risky one? Several theories have been advanced in answer to this question, but perhaps the most logically satisfying one involves *utility theory*.

At the heart of utility theory is the notion of *diminishing marginal utility for wealth*. If, for example, you had no wealth and then received $100, you could satisfy your most immediate needs. If you then received a second $100, you could utilize it, but the second

---

[1] For example, the skewness of returns is assumed to be irrelevant. This will be true if investors' utility is a function of only the mean and variance of returns or if returns are normally distributed such that they can be completely described by the mean and variance, that is, there is no skewness.

FIGURE 10.1   Relationship between Wealth and Its Utility

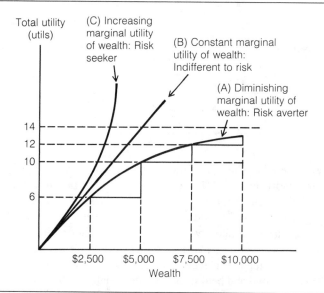

$100 would not be quite as necessary to you as the first $100. Thus, the "utility" of the second, or *marginal*, $100 is less than that of the first $100, and so on for additional increments of wealth. Therefore, we say that the marginal utility of wealth is diminishing.

Figure 10.1 graphs the relationship between wealth and its utility, where utility is measured in arbitrary units called *utils*. Curve A, the one of primary interest, is for someone with positive marginal utility for wealth, but this individual also has marginal utility which increases at a decreasing rate. The investor has diminishing marginal utility of wealth. An individual with $5,000 would have ten utils of "happiness" or satisfaction. With an additional $2,500, the individual's satisfaction would rise to twelve utils, an increase of two units. But with a loss of $2,500, the individual's satisfaction would fall to six utils, a loss of four units.

Most investors (as opposed to people who habitually gamble) appear to have a diminishing marginal utility for wealth, and this directly affects their attitude toward risk. Our measures of risk estimate the likelihood that a given return will turn out to be above or below the expected return. Someone who has a constant marginal utility for wealth will value each dollar of "extra" returns just as highly as each dollar of "lost" returns and will be indifferent to risk. On the other hand, someone with a diminishing marginal utility for wealth will get more "pain" from a dollar lost than "pleasure" from a dollar gained. Because of the diminishing utility of wealth, the second individual will be very much opposed to risk and will require a very high return on any investment that is subject to much risk. In Curve A of Figure 10.1, for example, a gain of $2,500 from a base of $5,000 would bring two utils of additional satisfaction, but a $2,500 loss would cause a four-util satisfaction loss. Therefore, a person with this utility function and $5,000 would

TABLE 10.1   Expected Returns from Two Projects

States of Nature	Probability (1)	Drilling Operation Outcome (2)	(1) × (2) (3)	Probability (1)	Government Bond Outcome (2)	(1) × (2) (3)
Oil	0.6	$7,500	$4,500	1.0	$5,250	$5,250
No oil	0.4	2,500	1,000			
		Expected value = $5,500				$5,250

be unwilling to make a bet with a 50-50 chance of winning or losing $2,500. However, the risk-indifferent individual with Utility Curve B would be indifferent to the bet, and the risk lover (with Utility Curve C) would be eager to make it. Why?

Diminishing marginal utility leads directly to risk aversion, and this risk aversion is reflected in the capitalization rate investors apply when determining the value of a firm. To make this clear, let us assume that government bonds are riskless securities and that such bonds currently offer a 5 percent rate of return.[2] Thus, someone who bought a $5,000 U.S. Treasury bond and held it for one year would end up with $5,250, a profit of $250. Suppose the same investor had an alternative investment opportunity that called for the $5,000 to be used to back a wildcat oil-drilling operation. If the drilling operation is successful, the investment will be worth $7,500 at the end of the year. If it is unsuccessful, the investor can liquidate the holdings and recover $2,500. There is a 60 percent chance that oil will be discovered and a 40 percent chance of a dry hole. If our investor has only $5,000 to invest, would the riskless government bond or the risky drilling operation be the wiser choice?

Let us first calculate, in Table 10.1, the expected monetary values of the two investments. The calculation for the oil venture shows that its expected value is $5,500, higher than that of the bond, which has an expected value of $5,250. [Also, the expected return on the oil venture is 10 percent (calculated as $500 expected profit/$5,000 cost) versus 5 percent for the bond.] Does this mean that our investor should put the $5,000 in the wildcat well? Not necessarily — it depends on the investor's utility function. If this individual's marginal utility for money is sharply diminishing, then the potential loss of utility that would result from a dry hole, or no oil, might not be fully offset by the potential gain in utility that would result from the development of a producing well. If the utility function that is shown in Curve A of Figure 10.1 is applicable, this is exactly the case. To show this, we modify the expected monetary value calculation to reflect utility considerations. Reading from Figure 10.1, Curve A, we see that this particular risk-averse investor would have approximately 12 utils if he or she invests in the wildcat venture and oil is found, 6 utils if this investment is made and no oil is found, and 10.5 utils with certainty if the investor chooses the government bond. This information is used in Table 10.2 to

---

[2]We shall not consider in this discussion any risk of declines in bond prices caused by increases in the level of interest rates. Thus, the risk with which we are concerned at this point is *default risk*, the risk that principal and interest payments will not be made as scheduled.

TABLE 10.2   Expected Utility of Oil Drilling Project

States of Nature	Probability (1)	Monetary Outcome (2)	Associated Utility (3)	(1) × (3) (4)
Oil	0.6	$7,500	12.0	7.2
No oil	0.4	2,500	6.0	2.4
			Expected utility = 9.6 utils	

calculate the *expected utility* for the oil investment. No calculation is needed for the government bond; we know its utility is 10.5 regardless of the outcome of the oil venture.

Since the *expected utility* from the wildcat venture is only 9.6 utils versus 10.5 from the government bond, we see that for this investor the government bond is the preferred investment. Thus, even though the *expected monetary value* for the oil venture is higher, *expected utility* is higher for the bond. Risk considerations, therefore, lead us to choose the safer government bond.

Mean-Variance Indifference Curves

Assuming that risk can be measured by the variance of return [or by the square root of the variance, which is called the standard deviation, $\sigma(R)$] and that return is measured by the expected return, $E(R)$, we can map out all combinations of mean and standard deviation which give a risk-averse investor the same total utility. For example, in Figure 10.2, Points A, B, and C all have the same total utility. They lie on an investor's *indifference curve*. The risk-averse investor is indifferent between Point A, which has no risk and low return, and Point C, which has high risk and return. The higher return offered by Point C is sufficient to compensate our investor for the extra risk. A risk-neutral investor would have a family of indifference curves like the horizontal lines in Figure 10.2. Point C would be preferred to Point A because it has higher return, regardless of its risk.

An infinite number of indifference curves (such as those in Figure 10.2) could be drawn to represent the risk-return trade-off for different levels of total utility for a given risk-averse individual. For a given level of σ, a greater $E(R)$ is received as the curves move farther out to the left. Each point on Curve V represents a higher level of satisfaction, or greater utility, than any point on IV, and III represents more utility than II. Also, different individuals are likely to have different sets of curves, or different risk-return trade-offs. This is illustrated in Figure 10.3. Since the curves of B start from the same point and have a greater slope in the risk-return plane than the curves of A, this indicates that Investor B requires a higher return for the same amount of risk. Then, similarly for Investor B, as the curves move to the left, they represent higher levels of satisfaction.

The sets of mean-variance indifference curves are literally a theory of choice. The only assumptions necessary to draw the indifference curves for risk-averse investors are (1) that people prefer more wealth to less (this was true for all utility functions in Figure 10.1) and (2) that they have diminishing marginal utility of wealth. These assumptions, if

FIGURE 10.2 Mean-Variance Indifference Curves

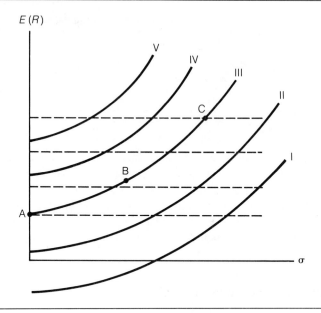

FIGURE 10.3 Family of Indifference Curves for Individuals A and B

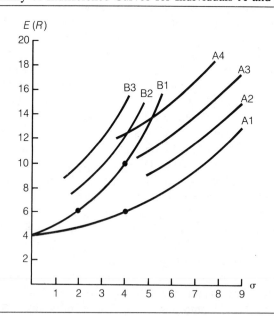

valid, imply that all decision makers are risk averse and will require higher return to accept greater risk.

As illustrated in Figures 10.2 and 10.3, investors' indifference curves represent a complete *theory of choice.* They tell us how risk-averse investors will behave when confronted with risk-return trade-offs. Next, we focus our attention on the *objects of choice:* risk and return. How are they measured, first for single risky assets and then for portfolios of risky assets?

RISK AND RETURN: OBJECTS OF CHOICE

Before turning to the risk and return for portfolios of assets, let us review measures of risk and return for single assets in isolation. Table 10.3 gives hypothetical expected rates of return for a steel company and a residential construction firm. Note that we are focusing on future rate of return projections. Hence, the data in Table 10.3 are not sample statistics. Rather, they are forecasts that are possibly subjectively determined. First, we will look at the mean and standard deviation of each firm separately. Then, we will study the effects of combining them into various portfolios.

The Mean and Variance of Single Assets

The mean, or average, return is defined as the probability of observing each rate of return, p_i, multiplied by the rate of return, R_i, and then summed across all possible returns. Mathematically, the mean return is defined as

$$E(R) = \sum_{i=1}^{N} p_i R_i. \tag{10.1}$$

Assuming that each economic condition in Table 10.3 is equally likely, the probability of each is $p_i = 1/5 = .2$ and the expected return computation for steel is

$$E(R) = .2(-.055) + .2(.005) + .2(.045) + .2(.095) + .2(.16)$$
$$= -.011 + .001 + .009 + .019 + .032$$
$$= .05, \text{ or } 5\%.$$

TABLE 10.3 Hypothetical Expected Rates of Return for Two Firms

	Economic Conditions	Probability	Steel	Construction	Combined (50% each)
I	Horrid	.2	−5.5%	35%	14.75%
II	Bad	.2	.5	23	11.75
III	Average	.2	4.5	15	9.75
IV	Good	.2	9.5	5	7.25
V	Great	.2	16.0	−8	4.00

Similar calculations for residential construction reveal a 14 percent expected return.[3]

The variance of return (given that we have subjective probability estimates and not sampling statistics) is defined as the average of the mean squared error terms. A mean squared error is simply the square of the difference between a given return, R_i, and the average of all returns, $E(R)$:

$$\text{Mean squared error} = [R_i - E(R)]^2.$$

The variance is the expectation (or average) of these terms; in other words, each mean squared error is multiplied by the probability, p_i, that it will occur and then all terms are summed. The mathematical expression for the variance of returns is

$$VAR(R) = E\{[R_i - E(R)]^2\}$$

$$= \sum_{i=1}^{N} p_i [R_i - E(R)]^2. \qquad \textbf{(10.2)}$$

Substituting in the numbers for the steel firm, we compute the variance of returns as follows:

$$\begin{aligned}
VAR(R) &= .2(-.055 - .05)^2 + .2(.005 - .05)^2 + .2(.045 - .05)^2 \\
&\quad + .2(.095 - .05)^2 + .2(.16 - .05)^2 \\
&= .2(.011025) + .2(.002025) + .2(.000025) + .2(.002025) \\
&\quad + .2(.0121) \\
&= .002205 + .000405 + .000005 + .000405 + .00242 \\
&= .00544.
\end{aligned}$$

Usually, we express risk in terms of the standard deviation, $\sigma(R)$, rather than the variance of returns. The standard deviation is just the square root of the variance.

$$\sigma(R) = \sqrt{VAR(R)}. \qquad \textbf{(10.3)}$$

For the steel firm, the standard deviation of returns is

$$\sigma(R) = \sqrt{.00544} = .0737564, \text{ or } 7.38\%.$$

Similar calculations will show that the variance of returns for the residential construction firm is $VAR(R) = .02176$ and that the standard deviation is $\sigma(R) = .1475127$, or 14.8 percent.[4]

Figure 10.4 plots the mean and standard deviation of returns for both firms. Because construction has a higher mean and standard deviation than steel it is possible for a risk-averse investor to be indifferent between the two alternatives, as shown by the indifference curve in Figure 10.4.

---

[3]Note that in Chapter 8, when we were using sampling statistics, it was always true that, given N observations, the probability of any observation was $p_i = 1/N$. With subjectively estimated forecasts, this is no longer necessarily true. Different events can have different probabilities.

[4]In Chapter 8, when we were using sampling statistics, the sum of the mean squared errors was divided by $(N - 1)$ in order to compute the variance. In this chapter, we are using the actual (subjectively estimated) universe. We are *not* using sample data to compute the variance; hence, we multiply each mean squared error term by its probability.

FIGURE 10.4   Risk and Return for Hypothetical Steel and
Residential Construction Firms

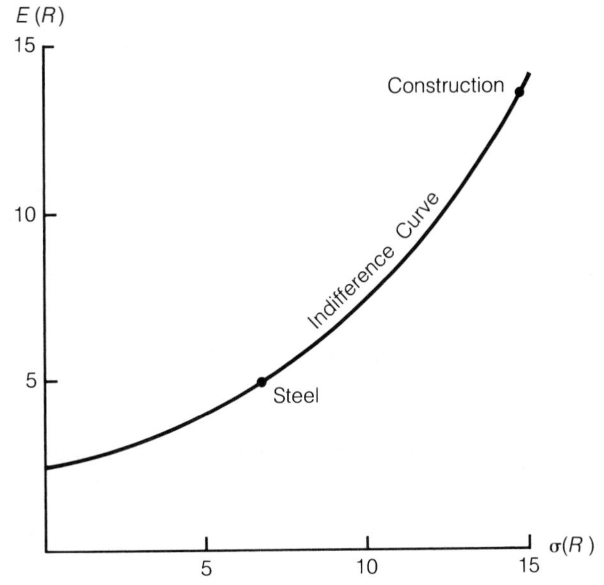

The Mean and Variance of Portfolios of Assets

Portfolios of assets usually offer the advantage of reducing risk through diversification. To illustrate, our steel company may decide to diversify into residential construction materials. We know that when the economy is booming, the demand for steel is high, and the returns from the steel mill are large. Residential construction, on the other hand, may be countercyclical: When the economy is strong, the demand for construction materials may be weak.[5] Because of these divergent cyclical patterns, a diversified firm with investments in both steel and construction could expect to have a more stable pattern of revenues than would a firm engaged exclusively in either steel or residential construction. In other words, the standard deviation of the returns on the *portfolio of assets,* $\sigma(R_p)$, may be less than the sum of the standard deviations of the returns from the individual assets.[6]

   This point is illustrated in Figure 10.5. Panel (a) of the figure shows the rate of return variations for the steel plant; Panel (b), the fluctuations for the residential construction

---

[5]The reason for the countercyclical behavior of the residential construction industry has to do with the availability of credit. When the economy is booming, interest rates are high. High interest rates seem to discourage potential home buyers more than they do other demanders of credit. As a result, the residential construction industry has historically shown countercyclical tendencies.

[6]These conclusions obviously hold also for portfolios of financial assets — stocks and bonds. In fact, the basic concepts of portfolio theory were developed specifically for common stocks by Markowitz [1952]. The logical extension of portfolio theory to capital budgeting calls for considering firms as having ''portfolios of tangible assets.''

FIGURE 10.5   Hypothetical Relationship between Steel and Residential
Construction Companies (Data from Table 10.3)

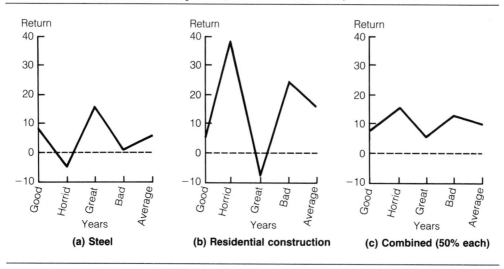

(a) Steel   (b) Residential construction   (c) Combined (50% each)

division; and Panel (c), the rate of return for the combined company, assuming that the separate firms are of equal size. When the returns from steel are large, those from residential construction are small, and vice versa. As a consequence, the combined rate of return is relatively stable. In fact, we shall show later on that there is one combination of steel and construction which results in no risk at all.

The Expected Return on a Portfolio of Assets

A portfolio is defined as a combination of assets. Portfolio theory deals with the selection of optimal portfolios; that is, portfolios that provide the highest possible return for any specified degree of risk or the lowest possible risk for any specified rate of return. Since portfolio theory has been developed most thoroughly for *financial assets* — stocks and bonds — we shall, for the most part, restrict our discussion to these assets.[7] However, extensions of financial asset portfolio theory to physical assets are readily made, and certainly the concepts are relevant in capital budgeting.

The rate of return on a portfolio is always a weighted average of the returns of the individual securities in the portfolio. Let us assume that instead of combining a steel firm and a residential construction firm, we invest in various combinations of their shares of stock. For example, suppose 50 percent of the portfolio is invested in a steel security with a 5 percent expected return (Security S), and 50 percent in a construction security with a

---

[7]Financial assets are easily divisible and available in large numbers, and a great deal of data is available on such assets. Capital assets such as plant and equipment, on the other hand, are "lumpy," and the data needed to apply portfolio theory to such assets are not readily available.

FIGURE 10.6   Rates of Return on a Two-Asset Portfolio

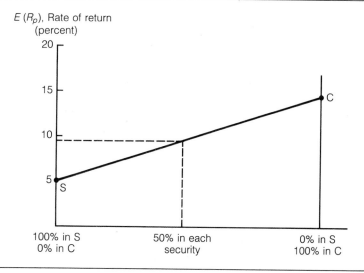

14 percent expected return (Security C). In general, we can write the return on a portfolio of two assets as

$$R_p = wR_S + (1 - w)R_C, \tag{10.4}$$

where w is the percentage invested in Security S and $(1 - w)$ is the remainder of the portfolio. The expected rate of return on the portfolio is

$$E(R_p) = wE(R_S) + (1 - w)E(R_C) \tag{10.5}$$
$$= w(5\%) + (1 - w)(14\%)$$
$$= 0.5(5\%) + 0.5(14\%) = 9.5\%.$$

Here, $E(R_p)$ is the *expected* return on the portfolio. If all of the portfolio is invested in S, the expected return is 5 percent. If all is invested in C, the expected return is 14 percent. If the portfolio contains some of each, the expected portfolio return is a linear combination of the two securities' expected returns — for example, 9.5 percent in our present case. Therefore, given the expected returns on the individual securities, the expected return on the portfolio depends upon the amount of funds invested in each security.

Figure 10.6 illustrates the possible returns for our two-asset portfolio. Line SC represents all possible expected returns when Securities S and C are combined in different proportions. Note that when 50 percent of the portfolio is invested in each asset, the expected return on the portfolio is seen to be 9.5 percent, just as we calculated above.

The Variance of a Portfolio

A fundamental aspect of portfolio theory is the idea that the riskiness inherent in any single asset held in a portfolio is different from the riskiness of that asset held in isolation. As we shall see, it is possible for a given asset to be quite risky when held in isolation, but not very risky if held in a portfolio. The impact of a single asset on a portfolio's riskiness — which is the riskiness of the asset when it is held in a portfolio — is discussed later in this chapter. But first, how shall we calculate the variance of a portfolio of assets?

According to Equation 10.2, the definition of variance is

$$\text{VAR}(R) = \sum_{i=1}^{N} p_i[R_i - E(R)]^2, \tag{10.2}$$

and the return and expected return on a two-asset portfolio are defined as

$$R_p = wR_S + (1 - w)R_C \tag{10.4}$$

$$E(R_p) = wE(R_S) + (1 - w)E(R_C). \tag{10.5}$$

By squaring the terms in brackets and rearranging terms, we have[8]

$$\text{VAR}(R_p) = \sum_{i=1}^{N} p_i w^2[R_S - E(R_S)]^2$$

$$+ \sum_{i=1}^{N} 2p_i w(1 - w)[R_S - E(R_S)][R_C - E(R_C)]$$

$$+ \sum_{i=1}^{N} p_i(1 - w)^2[R_C - E(R_C)]^2.$$

---

[8]In order to find the correct expression for the variance of a two-asset portfolio, we can substitute Equations 10.4 and 10.5 into the definition of variance, Equation 10.2:

$$\text{VAR}(R_p) = \sum_{i=1}^{N} p_i\{wR_S + (1 - w)R_C - [wE(R_S) + (1 - w)E(R_C)]\}^2.$$

In order to simplify this expression, we can rearrange terms as follows:

$$\text{VAR}(R_p) = \sum_{i=1}^{N} p_i\{[wR_S - wE(R_S)] + [(1 - w)R_C - (1 - w)E(R_C)]\}^2.$$

In order to simplify further, if we let

$$a = wR_S - wE(R_S)$$
$$b = (1 - w)R_C - (1 - w)E(R_C),$$

the expression is seen to be a binomial equation:

$$\text{VAR}(R_p) = \sum_{i=1}^{N} p_i(a + b)^2$$

$$= \sum_{i=1}^{N} p_i[a^2 + 2ab + b^2].$$

Finally, by substituting back the values of a and b, we have the expression for the variance of a portfolio of two risky assets.

The first term of this equation is w-squared times the variance of the first asset, S.

$$w^2\mathrm{VAR}(R_S) = w^2\sum_{i=1}^{N}p_i[R_S - E(R_S)]^2$$

The third term is $(1 - w)$-squared times the variance of the second asset, C.

$$(1 - w)^2\mathrm{VAR}(R_C) = (1 - w)^2\sum_{i=1}^{N}p_i[R_C - E(R_C)]^2$$

The middle term, the cross-product term, is defined as the product of the portfolio weights, $w(1 - w)$, times twice the covariance between the returns on the two assets,

$$2w(1 - w)\mathrm{COV}(R_S,R_C) = 2w(1 - w)\sum_{i=1}^{N}p_i[R_S - E(R_S)][R_C - E(R_C)],$$

and the definition of *covariance* is simply[9]

$$\mathrm{COV}(R_S,R_C) \equiv \sum_{i=1}^{N}p_i[R_S - E(R_S)][R_C - E(R_C)]. \qquad \textbf{(10.6)}$$

Thus, the variance of a portfolio of two risky assets is not merely the sum of their separate variances. It also includes the covariance between them. The expression for the variance of a portfolio of two risky assets is

$$\mathrm{VAR}(R_p) = w^2\mathrm{VAR}(R_S) + 2w(1 - w)\mathrm{COV}(R_S,R_C)$$
$$+ (1 - w)^2\,\mathrm{VAR}(R_C). \qquad \textbf{(10.7)}$$

In Figure 10.4, we illustrated the risk and return of a steel and a residential construction firm, and in Figure 10.5, we saw that by combining them, it was possible to reduce risk. Now, let us use the definitions of portfolio mean and variance to compute the return and risk of the merged firm. Since the firms were assumed to be the same size, they each will represent 50 percent of the merged firm; thus, our weights are $w = .5$ and $1 - w = .5$. Using the definition of the mean return of a two-asset portfolio, Equation 10.2, we have

$$E(R_p) = wE(R_S) + (1 - w)E(R_C)$$
$$= .5(.05) + (1 - .5)(.14)$$
$$= .025 + .07 = .095, \text{ or } 9.5\%.$$

Note that a return of 9.5 percent is halfway between the return on the steel firm (5 percent) and the construction firm (14 percent). In order to compute the portfolio variance, we need to know the variance of the steel firm (already calculated as [$\mathrm{VAR}(R_S) = .00544$]) and the variance of the construction firm [$\mathrm{VAR}(R_C) = .02176$] and the covariance be-

---

[9]The definition of covariance was also introduced in Chapter 8, where it was part of the definition of the slope in a linear regression. We shall use this fact later in this chapter.

TABLE 10.4   The Covariance between Two Risky Assets*

State of Nature	Probability	Return on Steel = R_S	Return on Construction = R_C	$R_S - E(R_S)$	$R_C - E(R_C)$	$p_i[R_S - E(R_S)][R_C - E(R_C)]$
Horrid	.2	−5.5%	35%	−.105	.210	$.2(-.105)(.210) = -.00441$
Bad	.2	.5	23	−.045	.090	$.2(-.045)(.090) = -.00081$
Average	.2	4.5	15	−.005	.010	$.2(-.005)(.010) = -.00001$
Good	.2	9.5	5	.045	−.090	$.2(.045)(-.090) = -.00081$
Great	.2	16.0	−8	.110	−.220	$.2(.110)(-.220) = -.00484$
Sum	1.0					$COV(R_S,R_C) = -.01088$

*We had already calculated that $E(R_S) = 5\%$ and $E(R_C) = 14\%$.

tween them. Table 10.4 uses the definition of covariance (Equation 10.6) to perform the necessary calculations. The sum of the numbers in the last column is the covariance between returns on the steel and construction companies. The negative covariance (−.01088) reflects the fact that the returns of the two companies are offsetting.

We can now calculate the portfolio variance assuming the two companies are merged. From Equation 10.7, the definition of portfolio variance is

$$VAR(R_p) = w^2 VAR(R_S) + 2w(1-w)COV(R_S,R_C) + (1-w)^2 VAR(R_C) \qquad (10.7)$$

$$= (.5)^2(.00544) + 2(.5)(1 - .5)(-.01088) + (1 - .5)^2(.02176)$$

$$= .25(.00544) + .5(-.01088) + .25(.02176)$$

$$= .00136 - .00544 + .00544$$

$$= .00136,$$

and the portfolio standard deviation is

$$\sigma(R_p) = \sqrt{VAR(R_p)} = \sqrt{.00136} = .036878, \text{ or } 3.69\%.$$

Note that the standard deviation of return for the merged companies is less than either of their separate standard deviations. This result is shown in Figure 10.7. Also illustrated are the indifference curves of a risk-averse investor, who would prefer the merged firm to the alternatives of owning each firm separately. Note that no risk-averse investor would prefer to invest 100 percent in the steel firm (Point S) because the merged firm (Point M) has higher return and lower risk. However, this does not mean that no one will hold shares of the steel firm. It only means that the steel firm will always be held as part of a diversified portfolio.

Although merger is one way of reducing risk, it is not necessarily the best way because the relative sizes of the merging firms determine their weight in the resulting portfolio. In our example, the steel and construction firms were of equal size, so that each contributed 50 percent to the new merged firm. Investors who purchase the common stock of steel and construction have an advantage because they can choose any portfolio weights they desire. Table 10.5 shows the expected returns and standard deviations of return for

FIGURE 10.7   The Risk of a Merged Firm

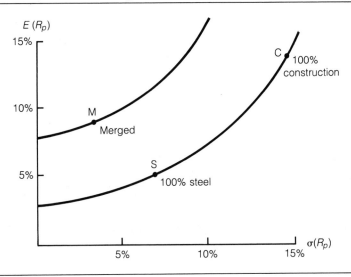

various portfolio combinations of steel and construction. The set of all mean-standard deviation choices is called the *portfolio opportunity set* because it is a list of all possible opportunities available to the investor. Notice that there is one special portfolio (with approximately two-thirds in steel and one-third in construction) where there is no risk at all. This possibility was not obtainable by simply merging the steel and construction firms. However, it becomes possible by holding a portfolio of their securities. Panel (a) of Figure 10.8 graphs the opportunity set of risk-return combinations for the portfolios in Table 10.5. Panel (b) shows the standard deviation as a function of the portfolio weights, and Panel (c) shows the expected return as a function of the portfolio weights.

The sample opportunity set shown in Figure 10.8 is unusual because the rates of return for steel and construction were chosen to be perfectly negatively correlated, some-

TABLE 10.5   The Portfolio Mean-Standard Deviation Opportunity Set

	Percent in Steel	Percent in Construction	$E(R_P)$	$\sigma(R_P)$
A	−50.0%	150.0%	18.50%	25.81%
C	0.0	100.0	14.00	14.75
D	25.0	75.0	11.75	9.22
M	50.0	50.0	9.50	3.69
E	66.7	33.3	8.00	0.00
S	100.0	0.0	5.00	7.38
G	150.0	−50.0	0.50	18.44

FIGURE 10.8 The Mean-Standard Deviation Opportunity Set
(Steel and Construction)

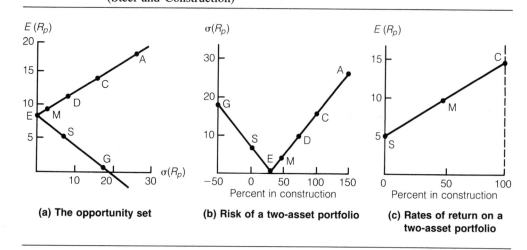

(a) The opportunity set

(b) Risk of a two-asset portfolio

(c) Rates of return on a two-asset portfolio

thing that almost never happens in the real world.[10] What we need to do now is generalize our understanding of the portfolio opportunity set to include all possible correlations between assets.

Correlation and Covariance

Chapter 8 introduced the coefficient of determination, r^2, for a linear regression. It measures the percentage of the variance of the dependent variable, which is explained by the independent variable. The square root of the coefficient of determination is called the *correlation coefficient, ρ*. It is defined as the covariance between the dependent and independent variables, divided by the product of their standard deviations,

$$\rho_{xy} = \frac{\text{COV}(x,y)}{\sigma_x \sigma_y}. \tag{10.8}$$

Figure 10.9 shows asset returns which are perfectly correlated, $\rho_{xy} = 1.0$; which are independent of each other, $\rho_{xy} = 0$; and which are perfectly inversely correlated, $\rho_{xy} = -1.0$. The returns on the steel and construction firms in our earlier example were perfectly inversely correlated and had a negative covariance. When assets have zero correlation with each other, they are unrelated in any way and have zero covariance. Positive correlation implies positive covariance.

We can use the relationship between correlation and covariance to rewrite the equation for the variance of a portfolio. From Equation 10.8, we see that

$$\text{COV}(x,y) = \rho_{xy}\sigma_x\sigma_y. \tag{10.9}$$

---

[10]The equation used was:

Return on construction = 24% − 2(Return on steel).

FIGURE 10.9 Examples of Different Correlation Coefficients

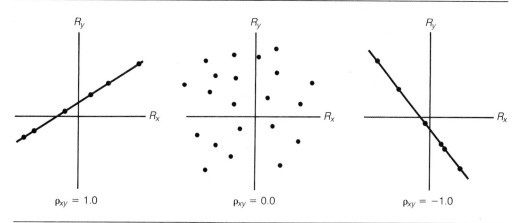

This relationship can be substituted into the expression for the variance of a portfolio of two assets, Equation 10.7, to give

$$VAR(R_p) = w^2 VAR(R_x) + 2w(1 - w)\rho_{xy}\sigma_x\sigma_y + (1 - w)^2 VAR(R_y). \quad \textbf{(10.10)}$$

In order to illustrate the usefulness of this new definition, suppose that we have two securities, X and Y. We can allocate our investment funds between the securities in any proportion. Security X has an expected rate of return $E(R_x) = 5\%$ and a standard deviation $\sigma_x = 4\%$. For Security Y, the expected return is $E(R_y) = 8\%$ and the standard deviation is $\sigma_y = 10\%$.

Our ultimate task is to determine the optimal portfolio, that is, the optimal percentage of our available funds to invest in each security. Intermediate steps include (1) determining the opportunity set of attainable portfolios, (2) determining the best or efficient set from among all those which are attainable, and (3) selecting the optimal portfolio from the efficient set.

There is not yet sufficient information to select the best portfolio—we need data on the correlation between the two securities' returns (ρ_{xy}) in order to construct the portfolio opportunity set. Let us examine three different degrees of correlation, $\rho_{xy} = +1.0$, $\rho_{xy} = 0$, and $\rho_{xy} = -1.0$, and then develop the portfolio's expected return, $E(R_p)$, and standard deviation of return, $\sigma(R_p)$, for each case.

Equation 10.5 gives the expected return and 10.10 gives the standard deviation for a portfolio of two risky assets. They are repeated below:[11]

$$E(R_p) = wE(R_x) + (1 - w)E(R_y) \quad \textbf{(10.5)}$$

$$\sigma(R_p) = \sqrt{w^2\sigma_x^2 + 2w(1 - w)\rho_{xy}\sigma_x\sigma_y + (1 - w)^2\sigma_y^2}. \quad \textbf{(10.10)}$$

We may now substitute in the given values of the asset mean and standard deviations for a given correlation and then observe how the portfolio mean and standard deviation

---

[11]We have written the portfolio variance as the square of the standard deviation, that is, $VAR(R_x) = \sigma_x^2$.

TABLE 10.6   Portfolio Mean-Standard Deviation Combinations for
Different Correlations between Two Risky Assets

Percent in X Value of w	Percent in Y Value of (1 − w)	$\rho_{xy} = +1.0$		$\rho_{xy} = 0$		$\rho_{xy} = -1.0$	
		$E(R_p)$	$\sigma(R_p)$	$E(R_p)$	$\sigma(R_p)$	$E(R_p)$	$\sigma(R_p)$
100%	0%	5.00%	4.00%	5.00%	4.00%	5.00%	4.00%
75	25	5.75	5.50	5.75	3.91	5.75	.50
50	50	6.50	7.00	6.50	5.39	6.50	3.00
25	75	7.25	8.50	7.25	7.57	7.25	6.50
0	100	8.00	10.00	8.00	10.00	8.00	10.00

(return and risk characteristics) are affected by changing the weights which we choose for each asset. For example, when the asset returns are independent, they have zero correlation, $\rho_{xy} = 0$. If we choose to put 75 percent of our wealth in Asset X (and the remainder in Asset Y), then $w = .75$ and $(1 - w) = .25$. The resulting portfolio mean and standard deviation are

$$E(R_p) = .75(5\%) + .25(8\%) = 5.75\%$$
$$\sigma(R_p) = \sqrt{.75^2(4\%)^2 + 2(.75)(.25)(0)(4\%)(10\%) + .25^2(10\%)^2}$$
$$= \sqrt{.5625(.0016) + 0 + .0625(.01)}$$
$$= \sqrt{.001525} = 3.9051\%.$$

Similar calculations can be made for any choice of portfolio weights. The results are shown in Table 10.6 and illustrated in Figure 10.10. In both the table and the graphs, note the following points:

1.   The portfolio mean return, $E(R_p)$, is a linear function of w, the percentage of wealth invested in Asset X. It is the same straight line in the left-most column of the graphs. This serves to illustrate that the relationship between $E(R_p)$ and w is unaffected by the degree of correlation between the two risky assets.

2.   The portfolio standard deviation, $\sigma(R_p)$, is a function of the correlation, ρ_{xy}, between the risky assets. In Case 1, where $\rho_{xy} = 1.0$, it is a straight line. There is a proportionate trade-off between risk and return. In Case 2, the assets are uncorrelated and the relationship between $\sigma(R_p)$ and w is nonlinear. Finally, when the assets are perfectly inversely correlated, $\rho_{xy} = -1.0$, risk can be completely diversified away.

3.   Panels (a.3), (b.3), and (c.3) show the attainable risk-return trade-offs for various portfolios. Panels (a.3) and (c.3) represent the most extreme possibilities when $\rho_{xy} = +1.0$ or $\rho_{xy} = -1.0$. Panel (b.3) is typical of the general shape of a portfolio opportunity set.

The Portfolio Opportunity Set and the Efficient Set

Figure 10.11 illustrates the general relationship between return and risk for portfolios of two risky assets. We know that the correlation coefficient can never be larger than $+1.0$ nor smaller than -1.0 ($-1.0 \leq \rho_{xy} \leq 1.0$). Line XY shows the return-risk combinations

FIGURE 10.10 Illustrations of Portfolio Returns, Risks, and
the Attainable Sets of Portfolios

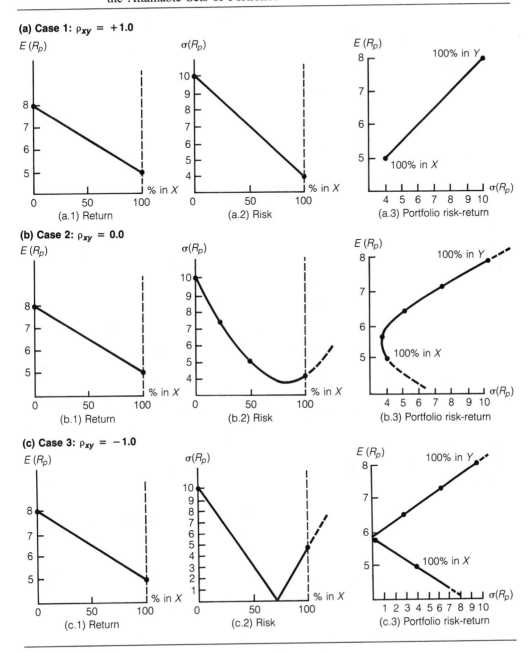

which are attainable if $\rho_{xy} = +1.0$. This was also illustrated in Figure 10.10, Panel (a.3).
At the other extreme, line XZY shows the return-risk trade-offs when $\rho_{xy} = -1.0$. This

FIGURE 10.11   The General Shape of the Portfolio Opportunity Set

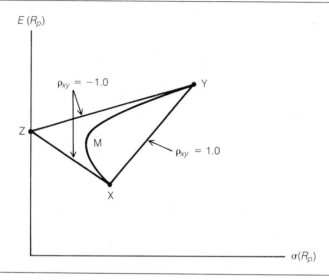

was illustrated in Figure 10.10, Panel (c.3). The triangle XYZ bounds the set of possibilities. It was also the shape of the opportunity set for our steel and construction example. The general case occurs when the risky assets are not perfectly correlated and is illustrated by the curved line XMY, which is called the *minimum variance portfolio opportunity set*. It is the combination of portfolios that provides the minimum variance (or standard deviation) for a given rate of return. It will always have a shape similar to line XMY.

FIGURE 10.12   The Portfolio Opportunity Set and the Efficient Set
with Many Risky Assets

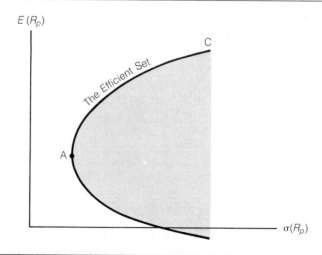

If there are many risky assets, instead of just two, the general shape of the portfolio opportunity set is unaltered; however, there are an infinite number of attainable points in the interior of the set. They are illustrated by the shaded region in Figure 10.12. The solid line, AC, which starts with the minimum variance portfolio at Point A, is called the *efficient set*. It represents the locus of all portfolios that has the highest return for a given level of risk. Risk-averse investors will choose only those portfolios that lie on the efficient set. Why? Assets that lie in the interior of the opportunity set are said to be inefficient and must be held as part of a diversified portfolio in market equilibrium.

Optimal Choice: The Individual's Point of View

Figure 10.13 illustrates portfolio choices for two individuals who have different indifference curves because they have differing attitudes toward risk. They face the same risk-return opportunity set, but choose different optimal portfolios. Individual A prefers lower risk and is consequently willing to accept lower return than individual B. Points A and B in Figure 10.13 represent the optimal (utility maximizing) portfolio choices for the two individuals.

Figure 10.13 summarizes portfolio selection from an individual's point of view, but ignores market equilibrium. When capital markets exist, individuals not only decide how much of their wealth to put into combinations of risky alternatives, they also have the opportunity to borrow or lend. The next section of this chapter shows that the portfolio choices made by individuals are fundamentally changed in a capital market equilibrium setting.

FIGURE 10.13   Optimal Portfolio Choices for Two Individuals
Who Have Different Risk Preferences

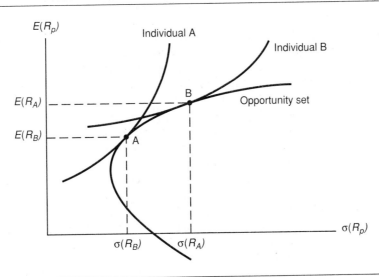

MARKET EQUILIBRIUM: THE CAPITAL MARKET LINE

So far, we have discussed the theory of choice (that is, indifference curves) and the objects of choice (that is, the portfolio opportunity set). Now we seek to put these concepts together in a market equilibrium setting. In order to do so, we must recognize that the opportunity set, up to this point, has been composed of only risky assets. We have not discussed what opportunity set might result if there is a riskless asset. There has been no opportunity for investors to trade among themselves by borrowing and lending. By introducing borrowing and lending at the risk-free rate of interest, we can characterize a market equilibrium with many market participants. First, we will look at the opportunity set that results from combining one risky asset (or portfolio) with one riskless asset. Then, we will extend the analysis to a full market equilibrium with one riskless and many risky assets.

The Opportunity Set with One Risky and One Riskless Asset

The return on a portfolio composed of $a\%$ of our wealth in a risky Asset X and $(1 - a)\%$ in a riskless asset with return R_F can be written as

$$R_p = aX + (1 - a)R_F. \tag{10.11}$$

The expected return on this portfolio is

$$E(R_p) = aE(X) + (1 - a)R_F. \tag{10.11a}$$

Note that it is unnecessary to calculate the mean (or expectation) for the riskless return because a risk-free asset has the same return in every state of nature. The standard deviation of return for this portfolio is

$$\sigma(R_p) = a\sigma_x. \tag{10.11b}$$

There is no covariance term because the covariance between a riskless asset and a risky asset is zero. Furthermore, the variance of a riskless asset is also zero.

Figure 10.14 shows the linear mean-standard deviation portfolio opportunity set that results from combinations of the risky and riskless assets. At Point X, you have 100 percent of your wealth in the risky asset. To the right of Point X (along XY), you have more than 100 percent of your wealth in X. This is accomplished by borrowing (sometimes called buying a stock on margin). In other words, you have a negative weight in the riskless asset. In effect, borrowing is the same thing as selling the riskless asset short. You are receiving cash now in return for issuing a certificate (a bond) which promises to pay back the loan plus interest at the end of the year. Between Points X and R_F, you have part of your wealth in the risky asset (that is, $0 < a < 1$), and the rest has been lent out at the riskless rate. At Point R_F, you have 100 percent of your wealth invested at the riskless rate. And finally, between R_F and Z, you have sold the risky asset short (that is, $a < 0$) in order to invest more than 100 percent of your wealth in the riskless asset. Note however, that no risk-averse investor would do this because points along R_FZ are dominated by any point along R_FXY. An investor can always achieve a higher return for the same risk (standard deviation) along R_FXY.

FIGURE 10.14   Opportunity Set for One Risky and One Riskless Asset

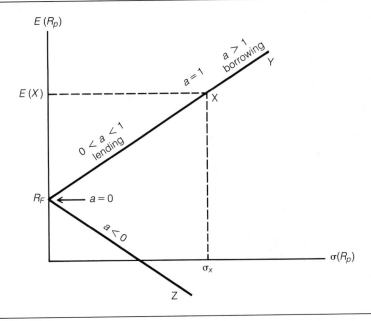

FIGURE 10.15   The Capital Market Line

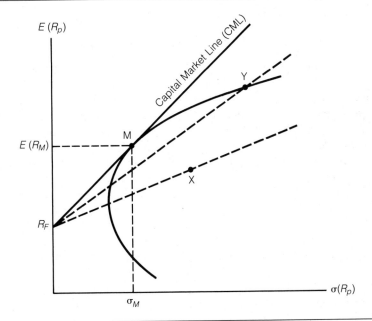

FIGURE 10.16   All Risk-Averse Investors Choose Optimal Portfolios
along the Capital Market Line

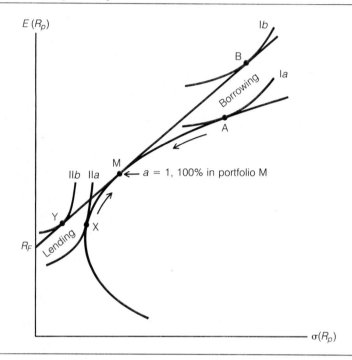

The Opportunity Set with One Riskless and Many Risky Assets

If we extend the analysis to a world with riskless borrowing and lending and N risky
assets, we can explain market equilibrium. Line $R_F X$ in Figure 10.15 shows all of the
feasible portfolios made up of the riskless asset, R_F, and risky asset (or portfolio), X.
Clearly, all risk-averse investors will prefer portfolios along line $R_F Y$ because they have
higher return for a given risk. But, best of all are portfolios along line $R_F M$. They provide
the highest expected return for each level of risk. Line $R_F M$ is given a special name. It is
called the *Capital Market Line (CML)* because it represents the market equilibrium trade-
off between risk and return. It exists because of opportunities for investors to borrow and
lend at the riskless rate, R_F. Thus, in equilibrium, all risk-averse investors will choose
their optimal portfolios from combinations of the riskless asset, R_F, and the risky Portfolio
M. This fact is illustrated in Figure 10.16. Here, for the first time, we combine the theory
of choice, as described by investor indifference curves, with the objects of choice, which
are represented by the portfolio combinations along the Capital Market Line. Investor I
would have chosen Point A as his or her optimal portfolio in a world without opportunities
to borrow or lend. This point represents the tangency between his or her indifference
curve and the opportunity set of risky assets only. Without a capital market and without
opportunities to borrow and lend, Point A would represent the utility maximizing portfolio
for Investor I. But if this investor moves to Point M and then borrows to reach Point B, it

is possible to reach a higher indifference curve (that is, curve I*b*). Hence, Investor I is better off if the capital market exists. Investor II is also better off in a world with opportunities to borrow and lend. If he or she were initially at Point X, it would be possible to achieve greater utility by moving along the opportunity set to Point M and then lending to reach Point Y, which is on a higher indifference curve.

In fact, almost every risk-averse investor is better off in a world where there are opportunities to exchange wealth by borrowing and lending. The only investor who would not have higher expected utility is the individual whose original tangency was at Point M, and he or she would be equally well off, holding Portfolio M in both worlds (with exchange and without). The important conclusion is that opportunities to freely exchange in capital markets by borrowing and lending increase welfare at the expense of no one. An economy with free exchange is better than one without.

Point M is a very special portfolio. It is the portfolio of risky assets held by all investors in equilibrium. By definition, it is the *market portfolio* of risky assets. The market portfolio is defined as a portfolio made up of all assets in the economy held according to their market value weights. The weight of the ith asset in the market portfolio is

$$w_i = \frac{\text{Market value of the } i^{th} \text{ asset}}{\text{Market value of all assets in the economy}}. \tag{10.12}$$

Point M in Figures 10.15 and 10.16 must be the market portfolio for two reasons. First, we assume that all investors have the same information about the risk-return characteristics of all assets and, therefore, perceive the same investment opportunity set. All investors will then seek to hold portfolios with the highest return for a given level of risk. In equilibrium, all assets will be held according to their market value weights because that is how equilibrium is defined. Therefore, the market portfolio must be one of those along the upper half of the minimum variance opportunity set. Second, the market Portfolio M must be the tangency portfolio in Figures 10.15 and 10.16 because all individuals will seek to hold the best efficient portfolio, that is, the one that maximizes their utility. The best portfolio is the tangency portfolio and it must be the market portfolio. To see why, suppose that Portfolio Y in Figure 10.15 was the market portfolio. Then it would be clearly dominated by Portfolio M because everyone could attain higher utility by choosing to hold combinations of M and the riskless asset, R_F. But the market portfolio cannot be dominated because all assets must be held according to their market value weights in equilibrium. Therefore, Portfolio M, the tangency portfolio, must also be the market portfolio.

The Equilibrium Price of Risk

Perhaps the most important aspect of the Capital Market Line (CML) is that it describes the market price of risk which will be used by all individuals who make decisions in the face of uncertainty. As shown in Figure 10.17 the intercept of the CML is R_F and its slope is $[E(R_M) - R_F]/\sigma_M$; therefore, the equation of the CML is

$$E(R_p) = R_F + \left[\frac{E(R_M) - R_F}{\sigma_M} \right] \sigma(R_p), \tag{10.13}$$

FIGURE 10.17   The CML and the Equilibrium Price of Risk

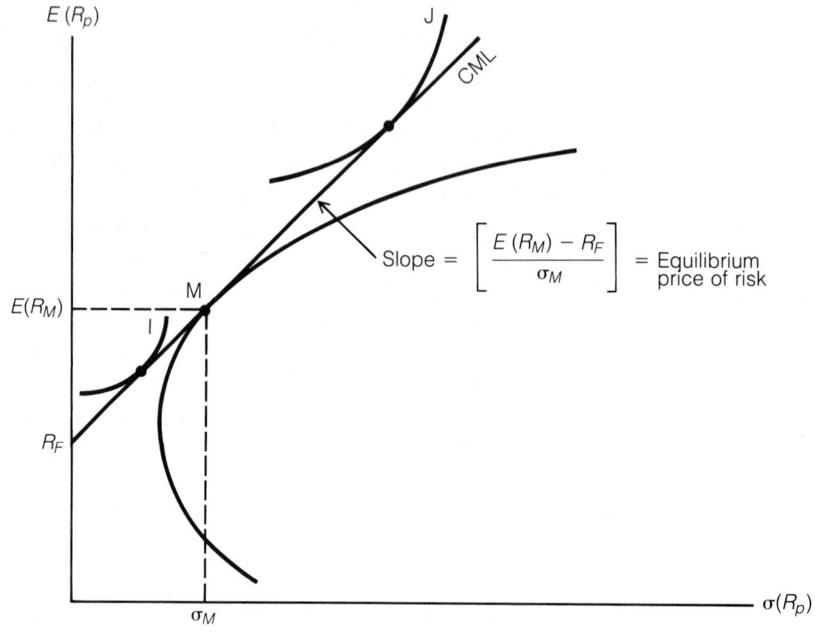

where

$E(R_p)$ = the expected rate of return for portfolios along the CML, that is, combinations of R_F and R_M

R_F = the riskless borrowing and lending rate

$E(R_M)$ = the expected rate of return on the market Portfolio M

σ_M = the standard deviation of return on the market Portfolio M

$\sigma(R_p)$ = the standard deviation of portfolios along the CML.

The term in brackets in Equation 10.13 measures the market rate of exchange between risk and return in equilibrium. It is the market equilibrium price of risk. The *marginal rate of substitution* for each investor is his or her rate of exchange between return and risk; in other words, it is the price of risk. The marginal rate of substitution for Investor I in Figure 10.17 is the slope of the line tangent to his or her indifference curve, but the tangent line is the CML. Therefore, Investor I will use the market price of risk (the slope of the CML) in making trade-offs between risk and return. The same thing can be said for Investor J. He or she will also use the market price of risk as the appropriate marginal rate of substitution. The CML is also tangent to the portfolio opportunity set; thus, the slope of the CML is equal to the objectively determined rate of exchange between risk and return in equilibrium. This is called the *marginal rate of transformation*. We have the result that, in equilibrium, the marginal rate of substitution for Individuals I and J is equal to the marginal rate of transformation, which, in turn, equals the slope of the CML.

$$\text{Slope of CML} = \text{Market price of risk} = \frac{E(R_M) - R_F}{\sigma_M} \qquad (10.14)$$

$$= \text{MRS}_I = \text{MRS}_J = \text{MRT}.$$

Equation 10.14 is the usual equilibrium result familiar to economics students. All individuals, regardless of the shape of their indifference curves, look to the market price in making decisions. Here, we look to the market price of risk in order to determine our optimal portfolios. An important implication for managers is that it is unnecessary to know the risk preferences of individual shareholders. They will unanimously agree that the market-determined price of risk is the correct rate of exchange between risk and return for decision making under uncertainty.

PRICING INEFFICIENT PORTFOLIOS

Unfortunately, the Capital Market Line tells us only how to evaluate the risk-return combinations of the market portfolio and the riskless asset. All points along the CML are combinations of two "mutual funds," namely, the market portfolio and the riskless asset. We would like to know more. For example, what is the equilibrium relationship between

FIGURE 10.18   Portfolios with Different Standard Deviations but Equal Expected Returns

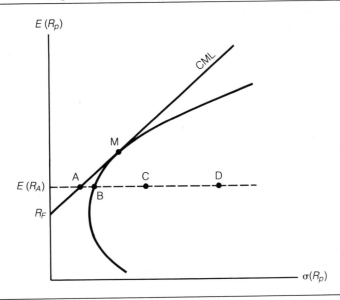

risk and return for inefficient assets and portfolios such as Points B, C, and D which do not lie on the CML in Figure 10.18? They all have the same expected return as Point A, which does lie on the CML, but they are inefficient because none are as well diversified as the market portfolio, which is used in combination with the riskless asset to form Portfolio A. In order to see how to price inefficient assets in equilibrium, we need to understand more about portfolio diversification. In particular, we shall see that the total risk (the variance) of any inefficient asset or portfolio can be partitioned into two parts: diversifiable and undiversifiable risk. Because diversifiable risk can be eliminated at virtually no cost, the market will not offer a risk premium to avoid it. Thus, we shall see that only undiversifiable risk is relevant in pricing inefficient assets. This fact shall lead to a theory which tells us how to price all risky securities in equilibrium — the subject of Chapter 12.

Diversification

An empirical study by Wagner and Lau [1971] can be used to demonstrate the effects of diversification. They divided a sample of 200 NYSE stocks into six subgroups based on the Standard and Poor's quality ratings as of June 1960. Then, they constructed portfolios from each of the subgroups, using 1 to 20 randomly selected securities and applying equal weights to each security. Table 10.7 can be used to summarize some effects of diversification for the first subgroup (A+ quality stocks). As the number of securities in the portfolio increases, the standard deviation of portfolio returns decreases, but at a decreasing rate, with further reductions in risk being relatively small after about 10 securities are included in the portfolio. More will be said about the third column of the table, correlation with the market, shortly.

These data indicate that even well-diversified portfolios possess some level of risk that cannot be diversified away. Indeed, this is exactly the case, and the general situation is illustrated graphically in Figure 10.19. The risk of the portfolio, σ_p, has been divided into two parts. The part that can be reduced through diversification is defined as *unsystem-*

TABLE 10.7   Reduction in Portfolio Risk through Diversification

Number of Securities in Portfolio	Standard Deviation of Portfolio Returns (σ_p) (Percent per Month)	Correlation with Return on Market Index[a]
1	7.0%	0.54
2	5.0	0.63
3	4.8	0.75
4	4.6	0.77
5	4.6	0.79
10	4.2	0.85
15	4.0	0.88
20	3.9	0.89

[a]The "market" here refers to an unweighted index of all NYSE stocks.

FIGURE 10.19   Reduction of Risk through Diversification

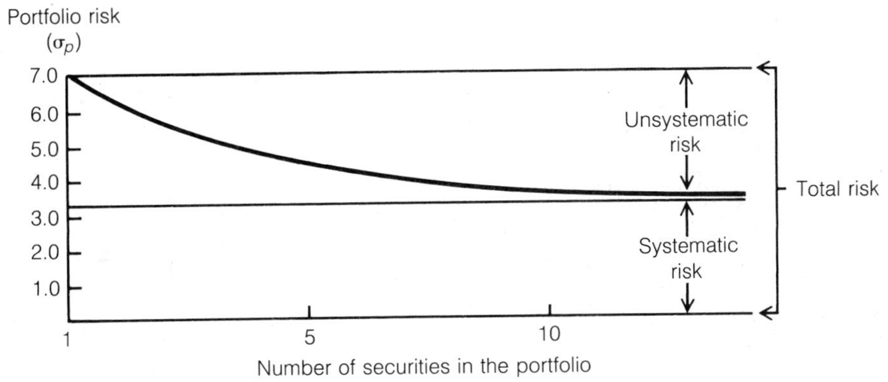

---

atic risk, while the part that cannot be eliminated is defined as *systematic*, or market-related, risk.

Now refer back to the third column of Table 10.7. Notice that as the number of securities in each portfolio increases, and as the standard deviation decreases, the correlation between the return on the portfolio and the return on the market index increases. Thus, a broadly diversified portfolio is highly correlated with the market, and its risk (1) is largely systematic and (2) arises because of general market movements. In fact, the portfolios along the Capital Market Line (*CML*) are all perfectly correlated with each other because they contain nothing more than different proportions of the market portfolio and the riskless asset. Furthermore, the market portfolio has the maximum possible diversification. Any combination of the market portfolio and the riskless asset will be perfectly correlated with the market portfolio and with each other.

We can summarize our analysis of risk to this point as follows:

1. The risk of a portfolio can be measured by the standard deviation of its rate of return, σ_p.

2. The risk of an individual security is its contribution to the portfolio's risk, namely, its covariance with the portfolio.

3. A stock's standard deviation reflects both unsystematic risk that can be eliminated by diversification and systematic, or market-related, risk; only the systematic component of security risk is relevant for the well-diversified investor, so only this element is priced in the marketplace.

4. A stock's systematic risk is measured by the covariance between its returns and the general market.

Table 10.8 provides 11 years of data for the Standard and Poor's 500 stock index, which is a value weighted index of 500 of the largest companies. We shall assume that this index is a good proxy for the true market portfolio. Table 10.8 also contains data for General

TABLE 10.8   Standard and Poor's Stock Index

Year	S&P 500 Price Index	S&P 500 Dividend Yield	S&P 500 Total Return	GM Price	GM Dividend Yield	GM Total Return
19X0	55.85	—	—	48	—	—
19X1	66.27	.0298	.2164	49	.05	.0708
19X2	62.38	.0337	−.0250	52	.06	.1212
19X3	69.87	.0317	.1518	74	.05	.4731
19X4	81.37	.0301	.1947	90	.05	.2662
19X5	88.17	.0300	.1136	102	.05	.1833
19X6	85.26	.0340	.0010	87	.05	−.0971
19X7	91.93	.0320	.1102	78	.05	−.0534
19X8	98.70	.0307	.1043	81	.05	.0885
19X9	97.84	.0324	.0237	74	.06	−.0264
19X0	83.22	.0383	−.1111	70	.05	−.0041

Motors stock. We would like to use these data for two purposes: (1) to find out how General Motors stock relates to the market index and (2) to partition the variance of General Motors returns into diversifiable and undiversifiable risk.

Suppose we assume that GM returns are linearly related to the market index. The linear regression equation would be[12]

$$\tilde{R}_{i,t} = a + b\,\tilde{R}_{M,t} + \tilde{\epsilon}_{i,t}, \tag{10.15}$$

where

$\tilde{R}_{i,t} = $ the return on GM in Year t

$a = $ the intercept term, a constant

$b = $ the slope term which measures the average relationship between GM and the market index. Recall (from Chapter 8) that $b = \text{COV}(R_i, R_M)/\text{VAR}(R_M)$

$\tilde{R}_{M,t} = $ the return on the market index in Time t

$\tilde{\epsilon}_{i,t} = $ a random error term, that is, the part of GM returns that is uncorrelated with the market index.

Figure 10.20 plots the relationship between GM and the market index. Note that each return is the sum of capital gains and dividends. For example, the return on General Motors for 19X1 was

$$R = \frac{P_t - P_{t-1} + d_t}{P_{t-1}} = \frac{49 - 48 + .05(48)}{48} = .0708.$$

Each point in Figure 10.20 represents a pair of returns, one for GM and one for the market, in the same year. Figure 10.20 makes it obvious that there is a positive covariance

---

[12]The reader is referred to Chapter 8 for a description of linear regression.

FIGURE 10.20   The Joint Distribution of GM and the S&P 500 Index

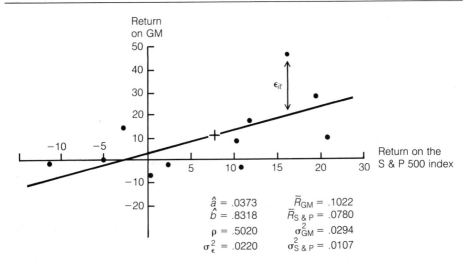

between General Motors stock and the market. Much of the total variance (about 25.2 percent) of GM returns is explained by the market.

Equation 10.15 gives the return on GM as a linear function of the market index. The general expression for the variance of $R_{i,t}$ is much like the variance of a portfolio of two risky assets,

$$VAR(R_{i,t}) = b^2 VAR(R_{M,t}) + 2b\ COV(R_{M,t}, \epsilon_{i,t}) + VAR(\epsilon_{i,t}).$$

But we know that the random error term, $\epsilon_{i,t}$, is independent of the market return, $R_{M,t}$. In other words $COV(\epsilon_{i,t}, R_{M,t}) = 0$. Therefore, the variance of $R_{i,t}$ is

$$VAR(R_{i,t}) = b^2 VAR(R_{M,t}) + VAR(\epsilon_{i,t}) \qquad \textbf{(10.16)}$$

Total risk = Undiversifiable risk + Diversifiable risk.

Equation 10.16 has partitioned the total variance of return on the ith security into two parts, undiversifiable risk and diversifiable risk.[13]

Diversifiable risk can, in principle, be completely eliminated simply through costless diversification. All we need to do is combine a large number of assets into a portfolio so that their independent error terms cancel each other out.[14] A good analogy is that the

---

[13]Later on, we shall refer to the slope coefficient, b, as "beta," a "measure of" undiversifiable risk. Although not exactly the same as $b^2 VAR(R_M)$, which is the exact definition of undiversifiable risk, beta is a measure of undiversifiable risk because, for a given $VAR(R_M)$, it provides a one-for-one correspondence.

[14]In fact, the error terms estimated from Equation 10.15 are not cross-sectionally independent. For this, and other reasons, one might suspect that the market index, by itself, does not provide a complete explanation of individual asset returns. In the next chapter, we shall see that a multi-factor model called the Arbitrage Pricing Model does better.

physicists tell us that every molecule in this page is in constant random motion, called Brownian motion. Yet, the page does not move. Why? The reason is that the molecules are all moving independently of each other. Consequently, their independent random movements cancel out and the page appears to be stationary. If all of the molecules were to move in the same direction at the same time, the page would move violently. There are, however, so many molecules that the probability of the page actually moving is lower than the probability of a nearby star going supernova.

The theoretically correct measure of risk for a single asset is its contribution to the market portfolio of all assets, that is, its covariance with the market portfolio. All other risk can be diversified away at no cost, at least in a world with no transactions costs. Equation 10.16 demonstrates that the total risk of an asset can be separated into two parts, undiversifiable, or systematic, risk and diversifiable, or unsystematic, risk.

$$\text{VAR}(R_{i,t}) = b^2 \text{VAR}(R_{M,t}) + \text{VAR}(\epsilon_{i,t}) \tag{10.16}$$

Total risk = Undiversifiable risk + Diversifiable risk.

Because of costless diversification, investors will only care about the undiversifiable risk of individual assets.

To add more substance to the argument, we note that the slope coefficient, b, in a linear regression is defined as[15]

$$b = \frac{\text{COV}(R_i, R_M)}{\text{VAR}(R_M)}.$$

In our General Motors example (Table 10.8), we suggested that General Motors stock returns could be regressed against a proxy for the market portfolio (the S&P 500 index). When this is done, we find the slope coefficient to be .8318. This is a measure of the undiversifiable risk of General Motors. It tells us that when the market rises (or falls) by 10 percent, General Motors will rise (or fall) by roughly 8.32 percent. In other words, General Motors is less volatile than the market portfolio when one considers only undiversifiable risk. Of course, the total risk of GM [$\text{VAR}(R_i) = .0294$] is greater than the total risk of the S&P 500 index [$\text{VAR}(R_M) = .0107$], but a great portion of GM's total risk is completely uncorrelated with the market. This uncorrelated, or idiosyncratic, risk may be diversified away (completely) at no cost. When applied to the GM example, Equation 10.16 becomes

Total risk = Undiversifiable risk + Diversifiable risk

$$\text{VAR}(R_i) = b^2 \text{VAR}(R_M) + \text{VAR}(\epsilon)$$

$$.0294 = (.8318)^2(.0107) + .0220$$

$$.0294 = .0074 + .0220.$$

The undiversifiable risk of General Motors is only 25.2 percent of its total risk. In the next chapter, we shall see that the slope coefficient, b, can be used as an equilibrium measure of risk for individual assets.

---

[15]Refer to Chapter 8 for the definition of the slope coefficient in a linear regression.

There are many synonyms for the two components of total risk. For example, diversifiable risk is variously referred to as idiosyncratic risk, unsystematic risk, or firm specific risk. However, no matter how you look at it, this risk is unrelated to whatever else is going on in the economy. That is why it can be diversified away. On the other hand, undiversifiable risk is often called systematic risk (or beta) to reflect the fact that it is related to general economic conditions.

Hedging: An Application of Portfolio Theory

Hedging is the practice of reducing the riskiness of your current portfolio position by taking an offsetting position in an asset (or portfolio of assets) that is correlated with it. For example, if a portfolio manager believes she can select securities that will outperform others in the same industry group, but fears general market fluctuations, she can hedge against market movements by selling short a position in stock index futures. For example, if her portfolio falls 8 percent while the industry group and the market fall 10 percent, she can net a positive 2 percent return by being short stock index futures because a positive 10 percent return on her futures position will offset the market decline of 10 percent.

Hedging for its own sake is not a free lunch. There must be a good business reason for undertaking a hedging program.[16] For example, an oil refinery may want to hedge in order to avoid the costs of business disruption associated with potential bankruptcy if operating margins fall because the cost of crude oil rises faster than the price of refined products. Or a commercial bank may be able to achieve a competitive advantage if sophisticated hedging practices allow it to profit from accepting risks anywhere along the risk spectrum. Or an aluminum fabricator may be able to capture greater market share if it accepts risk by writing long-term, fixed-price contracts that its customers want, but at the same time offsets the additional risk by taking positions in the aluminum futures market. In each of the aforementioned examples, there is a good business reason for hedging. Hedging for its own sake is not advisable because shareholders can always diversify or hedge their own accounts—there is no need for management to do it for them.

Building a Static Hedge: Perfectly Correlated Assets

A static hedge "locks in" a position in an effort to protect against downside losses. However, it also eliminates upside gains. The simplest type of hedge uses futures markets, when they exist, to take an offsetting position. For example, suppose an oil distributor has just written a contract to deliver 1 million barrels of oil at $28 a barrel to a refiner two months from now. If he does not already own the oil, he is exposed to considerable risk if prices should rise. To offset the risk and guarantee a locked in profit, he might take a long position of 1 million barrels in the oil commodity futures market at, let's say, $24 a barrel. The outcome is illustrated in Figure 10.21. His current position amounts to selling 1 million barrels short (because he doesn't own them) but covering this position by buying

---

[16]For example, see Smith and Stulz [1985], or Breeden [1990].

FIGURE 10.21   A Simple Hedge Using Oil Futures

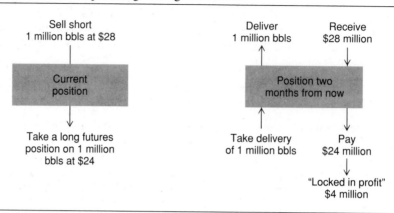

---

1 million barrels in the futures market for delivery two months from now at a fixed price of $24 per barrel. Two months later, he pays $24 million in the futures market to receive delivery of 1 million barrels, then delivers the oil at $28 per barrel. Once the futures position is taken, he will receive a $4 million profit on the deal no matter what happens to the market price of oil. This simple hedge works because his gains on his real position are exactly offset by his losses on his futures position and vice versa. The futures position is perfectly inversely correlated with his real position, therefore hedging was easy. His hedge ratio was one-for-one. He bought one barrel of oil in the futures market for each barrel he had sold short. Since the two positions were perfectly inversely correlated he could eliminate all risk.

Building a Static Hedge: Assets That Are Not Perfectly Correlated

In most hedging situations the risky asset and the futures position are not perfectly correlated, and the hedger needs to figure out an optimal hedge ratio to minimize her risk. The solution requires applying our knowledge of portfolio theory. Suppose she has a risky asset worth X dollars and wants to hedge its risk with N futures contracts whose price is $P. The correlation between the risky asset and the futures contracts is $\rho_{X,C}$ and their respective variances are σ_X^2 and σ_C^2.

The return on a portfolio of the asset and N futures contracts, R_P, measured in dollars, is

$$R_P = X(R_X) + (NP)R_C,\tag{10.17}$$

and, similar to Equation 10.10 the portfolio variance is

$$\text{VAR}(R_P) = X^2\sigma_X^2 + 2X(NP)\rho_{X,C}\sigma_X\sigma_C + (NP)^2\sigma_C^2.\tag{10.18}$$

To minimize risk, take the derivative of the variance with respect to N, the number of futures contracts, set the result equal to zero, and solve for the optimum number of contracts.[17] The result is

$$N = -\left(\frac{X}{P}\right)\left[\frac{\rho_{X,C}\sigma_X\sigma_C}{\sigma_C^2}\right]. \tag{10.19}$$

Thus, the optimal number of futures contracts depends on three things:

1. The value of the asset, X, and the price of the futures contract, P
2. The correlation between the futures contract and the risky asset, $\rho_{X,C}$
3. The standard deviations of the risky asset, σ_X, and the futures contract, σ_C

If the asset and the futures contract are uncorrelated ($\rho_{X,C} = 0$), then from Equation 10.19 we see that the optimal number of contracts is zero. In other words, the futures contract will not work as a hedge. At the opposite extreme, if the asset and the futures contract are perfectly correlated ($\rho_{X,C} = 1$), have the same standard deviations ($\sigma_X = \sigma_C$), and the same values ($X = P$), then one contract will be the best hedge against each asset. This is the result we had earlier when we covered the simple oil hedge.

Hedging is an important application of portfolio theory because all companies can be viewed as portfolios of risky assets and liabilities. If there are good business reasons for constructing a hedge, then portfolio theory can be used to do the job. Further aspects of managing risk are discussed in Chapters 13 and 14.

SUMMARY

We began with the theory of choice in the face of uncertainty. We saw that if investors have diminishing marginal utility of wealth, they will be risk averse. They will require higher returns to compensate them for increased risk. Next, we studied the objects of choice. Return and risk were measured by the mean and variance of security returns. When assets were combined into portfolios, their covariances were seen to be important for determining portfolio risk. We defined the portfolio minimum variance opportunity set as the portfolios of securities which have the lowest variance for a given rate of return.

Market equilibrium was introduced by allowing opportunities to borrow and lend at the riskless rate of return. The result was the Capital Market Line, which consisted of various combinations of riskless borrowing (and lending) and the market portfolio. The slope of the Capital Market Line was the equilibrium price of risk. All investors, regardless of their attitudes towards risk, will use this price of risk to determine the risk premia required to take on extra risk.

---

[17]Throughout the book we have maintained the assumption that calculus is not needed. If you have this skill, the derivative is

$$\frac{d\ \text{VAR}(R_P)}{dN} = 2XP\rho_{X,C}\sigma_X\sigma_C + 2NP^2\sigma_C^2.$$

Finally, by studying the effects of diversification, we saw that the total risk (or variance) of any asset can be separated into two parts: diversifiable and undiversifiable risk. Undiversifiable risk is a function of its covariance with the market portfolio of all assets, divided by the variance of the market portfolio.

In the next chapter, we shall see that in equilibrium, the only risk which counts is undiversifiable risk. This fact will allow us to develop a model (called the Capital Asset Pricing Model) which uniquely relates an asset's undiversifiable risk (or beta) to the rate of return which will be required of it in equilibrium.

QUESTIONS

10.1   Define the following terms, using graphs whenever feasible to illustrate your answer.
   a.   risk
   b.   expected value
   c.   standard deviation
   d.   marginal rate of substitution between return and risk
   e.   marginal rate of transformation between return and risk
   f.   the market price of risk

10.2   Assume that the residential construction industry is countercyclical to the economy in general and to steel in particular. Does this negative correlation between construction and steel necessarily mean that a savings and loan association, whose profitability tends to vary with residential construction levels, would be less risky if it diversified by acquiring a steel distributor?

10.3   If Firm A merges with Firm B, which is of equal size, and if there are no economic synergies,
   a.   how would you estimate the total risk of the merged Firm AB?
   b.   how would you estimate the undiversifiable risk of the merged Firm AB?

10.4   Define the minimum variance opportunity set and the efficient set in a world with only risky assets. How does your definition of the efficient set change if there are opportunities to borrow and lend at the riskless rate?

10.5   Define diversifiable and undiversifiable risk. How can you use linear regression to estimate the undiversifiable risk of an asset?

10.6   What are the advantages of diversification? What is the most diversified portfolio?

10.7   As you add more and more randomly selected securities to your portfolio,
   a.   what happens to the portfolio's variance?
   b.   what conditions are necessary for the variance to diminish to zero as the number of securities becomes very large?
   c.   what usually happens to the variance of the portfolio if the number of securities becomes very large?

10.8   Suppose you can choose a portfolio from among ten assets, all with the same expected return, $E(R)$, and the same standard deviation, $\sigma(R)$. Graph the opportunity set and the efficient set.

10.9   How would the Capital Market Line change if expected inflation suddenly increased by 10 percent?

10.10 Why don't all risky assets lie exactly on the Capital Market Line?

10.11 Why will all investors choose combinations of riskless borrowing and lending and the market portfolio, but not hold other risky assets (except according to their market values)?

10.12 What is the relationship between correlation and covariance?

10.13 Why is the market portfolio the tangency portfolio for the Capital Market Line?

10.14 Why does diminishing marginal utility imply risk aversion?

10.15 In Figure 10.7, why would no risk averse investor put 100 percent of his or her wealth into steel? How will steel be held in equilibrium?

PROBLEMS

10.1   Figure 10.1 shows the utility curve of a risk neutral investor. Graph the mean-standard deviation indifference curves for a risk neutral investor.

10.2   Figure P10.2 shows the indifference curves for a risk-averse investor.
   a.   Point A has a higher expected return than Point B. Is it preferred to Point B? Why or why not?
   b.   Point C has lower risk (standard deviation) than Point B. Is it preferred? Why or why not?

FIGURE P10.2   Indifference Curves for a Risk-Averse Investor

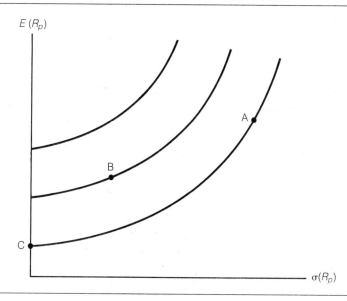

    c. Draw an indifference curve for a risk-averse investor who would be indifferent between Points B and C.

    d. Draw an indifference curve for a risk-averse investor who would be indifferent between Points A and C.

    e. Which of the two investors whose indifference curves you drew for Parts (c) and (d) is the more risk averse? Why?

10.3 Based on the following historical market data, calculate the expected return on the market, the variance of the returns on the market, the standard deviation of the returns on the market, and the expected risk-free returns.

Year	S&P 500 Price Index	Dividend Yield	R_F
1	55.85	—	0.035
2	66.27	0.0298	0.032
3	62.38	0.0337	0.035
4	69.87	0.0317	0.039
5	81.37	0.0301	0.042
6	88.17	0.0300	0.051
7	85.26	0.0340	0.049
8	91.93	0.0320	0.056
9	98.70	0.0307	0.068
10	97.84	0.0324	0.065
11	83.22	0.0383	0.064
12	98.29	0.0314	0.086
13	109.20	0.0284	0.099
14	107.43	0.0306	0.119

10.4 Assuming the following probability distribution of market returns, calculate the $E(R_M)$, $VAR(R_M)$, and σ_M.

State	Probability	Market Return (R_M)
1	0.12	−0.10
2	0.26	0.15
3	0.44	0.20
4	0.18	0.25

10.5 The Barfield Company has a new investment project. The project returns are estimated as follows:

Year	Project Return (R_j)
19X1	0.10
19X2	0.17
19X3	0.24
19X4	0.20
19X5	0.14

Calculate:

    a. The expected return on the investment.

    b. The variance of returns.

    c. The standard deviation of returns.

10.6 The McCoy Company has developed the following data regarding a project to add new production facilities.

State (s)	Probability (p_j)	Market Return (R_M)	Project Return (R_j)
1	0.05	−0.20	−0.30
2	0.25	0.10	0.05
3	0.35	0.15	0.20
4	0.20	0.20	0.25
5	0.15	0.25	0.30

Calculate:
a. The expected return on the project.
b. The variance of the project returns.
c. The standard deviation of project returns.
d. The covariance of the project returns with the market returns.
e. The correlation coefficient between the project returns and the market returns.

10.7 The expected returns for two firms, A and B, are as follows:

State of Nature	Probability = p_i	Return of Firm A	Return of Firm B
Great	.1	−.05	−.10
Good	.4	.10	.15
Average	.3	.25	.10
Bad	.2	.30	.18

Firm A has a total investment in assets of $75 million, three times the size of Firm B.
Assume that a new Firm, C, is formed through a merger between Firms A and B. The share of A and B in the portfolio represented by the new Firm C is based on the ratio of their total assets prior to merger. Calculate:
a. The expected return and standard deviation of Firms A and B before the merger.
b. The covariance and the correlation between the returns for Firms A and B before the merger.
c. The expected return of Firm C.
d. The standard deviation of return for Firm C.

10.8 You are planning to invest $100,000. Two securities, A and B, are available. The expected return for A is 9 percent and its standard deviation is 4 percent. For B, the expected return and standard deviations are 10 percent and 5 percent respectively. The correlation between the two assets is $\rho_{AB} = .5$.
a. Construct a table giving the portfolio expected return and standard deviation for 100 percent, 75 percent, 50 percent, 25 percent, and 0 percent in Security A.
b. Use your calculated values of $E(R_p)$ and $\sigma(R_p)$ to graph the minimum variance portfolio opportunity set and the efficient set.
c. Using hypothetical indifference curves, show how an investor might choose his or her optimal portfolio.

10.9 You are planning to invest $100,000. Two securities, I and J, are available, and you can invest in either of them or in a portfolio with some of each. You estimate that the following probability distributions of returns are applicable:

Probability	Security I	Security J
0.1	−5%	0%
0.2	0	5
0.4	11.25	8.75
0.2	15	10
0.1	20	15

The expected returns are 9 percent and 8 percent for I and J, respectively. Also, $\rho_{ij} = .96$, $\sigma_i = 7.56$ percent, and $\sigma_j = 3.76$ percent.

a. Graph the *opportunity* set of portfolios and identify the *efficient* section of the opportunity set.

b. Suppose your risk-return trade-off function, or indifference curve, is a linear family of lines with a slope of 0.40. Use this information, plus the graph constructed in Part (a), to locate (approximately) your optimal portfolio. Give the percentage of your funds invested in each security and the optimal portfolio's σ_p and $E(R_p)$. [Hint: Estimate σ_p and $E(R_p)$ graphically and then use the equation for $E(R_p)$ to determine w.] What is the probability that your optimal portfolio will, in fact, yield less than 4.15 percent?

c. Demonstrate why a graph of the efficient set such as the one you constructed in Part (a) above is always linear if portfolios are formed between a riskless security (a bond) and a risky asset (a stock or perhaps a portfolio of stocks).

10.10 You are planning to invest $200,000. Two securities, C and D, are available, and you can invest in either of them or in a portfolio with some of each. You estimate that the following probability distributions of returns are applicable:

Probability	Security C	Security D
0.2	−4%	2%
0.3	0	−2
0.3	12	−3
0.2	26	4

The expected returns are 8 percent and −.3 percent for C and D, respectively; that is, $E(R_c) = 8$ percent, and $E(R_d) = -.3$ percent; $\sigma_c = 10.84$ percent, and $\sigma_d = 2.795$ percent.

a. Calculate $E(R_p)$ and $\sigma(R_p)$ for portfolios having 150 percent, 100 percent, 50 percent, 0 percent, and −50 percent in Security C.

b. Graph the minimum variance opportunity set and the efficient set.

c. Suppose your indifference curves are a linear family of lines with a slope of .90. Use this information, plus the graph constructed in Part (b), to locate (approximately) your optimal portfolio. Give the percentage of your funds invested in each security and the mean and standard deviation for your optimal portfolio. [Hint: Estimate $E(R_p)$ and $\sigma(R_p)$ graphically and then use the equation for $E(R_p)$ to determine the optimal percent of your wealth in Security C.]

d. What is the probability that your optimal portfolio will yield less than 1.15 percent?

e. Demonstrate *why* a graph of the efficient set such as the one you constructed in Part (b) above is always linear if portfolios are formed from a riskless security and a risky security.

10.11 Given that the risk-free rate is 10 percent, the expected return on the market portfolio is 20 percent, and the standard deviation of returns on the market portfolio is $\sigma(R_M) = .2$,

a. What is the equilibrium price of risk?

b. What percentage of your wealth would you have to put into the riskless asset and into the market portfolio in order to have a 25 percent expected rate of return?

c. What would be the variance of the portfolio in Part (b)?

d. What is the correlation between the portfolio in Part (b) and the market portfolio?

10.12 The rates of return for Security J and the market portfolio are given here:

Probability	Return on Security J	Return on the Market Portfolio
1/7	15%	20%
1/7	22	16
1/7	−5	9
1/7	0	−6
1/7	2	−8
1/7	12	12
1/7	−8	−5

a. Estimate the undiversifiable risk of Security J using linear regression.

b. What is the correlation between Security J and the market portfolio?

c. What percentage of the total risk of Security J is undiversifiable?

10.13 (*Use the computer diskette, File name: 10PORTFO, Portfolio Theory.*)

a. Is it possible, through combining Security A and Security B into a portfolio, to reduce the standard deviation of the portfolio below the standard deviation of either of the individual securities?

    (1) When the standard deviation of the portfolio is below the standard deviation of Security A, is the expected return on the portfolio greater or less than the expected return on Security A?

b. How would your results change if the correlation between the assets was −1?

c. How would your results change if the correlation between the returns on these securities was +1?

d. Suppose instead of Security A, you had Security C, which had triple the expected return, or 15 percent, and triple the standard deviation, or 12 percent, and starting with zero correlation, what kind of portfolio performance would you be able to obtain now?

e. For the original Securities A and B, does the graph have a minimum standard deviation area? Is this minimum standard deviation below that of either of the securities?

f. Suppose you had Security D, with an expected return of 6 percent and a standard deviation of 9 percent and Security E with an expected return of 10 percent and a standard deviation of 30 percent.

    (1) If your objective is a 9 percent portfolio expected return, what would be your portfolio weights?

    (2) If the correlation between Securities D and E is minus 0.5, what is the standard deviation of this portfolio?

    g. Suppose it is possible to combine Security A, above, with riskless Security F. Security F has an expected return of 4 percent and a standard deviation of zero. (What is the correlation coefficient between any risky security and any risk-free security?)

      (1) What portfolio weights are necessary to achieve an expected return of 4 percent? What is the standard deviation of this portfolio? Are you borrowing or lending at the risk-free rate to achieve this return?

      (2) What portfolio weights are necessary to achieve an expected return of 8 percent? What is the portfolio standard deviation? Are you borrowing or lending at the risk-free rate to achieve this return?

      (3) What portfolio weights would result in an expected return of 3 percent? What does this result imply?

    h. You are free to "play" with the program in any way you choose, to see for yourself the effects of portfolio diversification. For example, you might see how high you could get expected return regardless of risk for a given pair of securities and correlation coefficient, etc.

SELECTED REFERENCES

Black, F., "Capital Market Equilibrium with Restricted Borrowing," *Journal of Business,* 45 (July 1972), pp. 444–454.

————; Jensen, M. C.; and Scholes, M., "The Capital Asset Pricing Model: Some Empirical Tests," in *Studies in the Theory of Capital Markets,* M. C. Jensen, ed., New York: Praeger, 1972.

Bowman, Robert G., "The Theoretical Relationship Between Systematic Risk and Financial (Accounting) Variables," *Journal of Finance,* 34 (June 1979), pp. 617–630.

Breeden, D., "Bank Risk Management," in *Handbook of Modern Finance,* 2d ed., D. Logve, ed., Boston, Mass.: Warren, Gorham & Lamont, 1990.

Brennan, M. J., "Capital Market Equilibrium with Divergent Borrowing and Lending Rates," *Journal of Financial and Quantitative Analysis,* 6 (December 1971), pp. 1197–1205.

Evans, J. L., and Archer, S. H., "Diversification and the Reduction of Dispersion: An Empirical Analysis," *Journal of Finance,* 23 (December 1968), pp. 761–767.

Fama, E. F., "Risk, Return, and Equilibrium," *Journal of Political Economy,* 79 (January-February 1971), pp. 30–55.

Fama, E. F., and MacBeth, J., "Risk, Return and Equilibrium: Empirical Tests," *Journal of Political Economy,* 81 (May-June 1973), pp. 607–636.

Fama, E. F., and Miller, M. H., *The Theory of Finance,* New York: Holt, Rinehart and Winston, 1972.

Ibbotson, Roger G., and Sinquefield, Rex A., "Stocks, Bonds, Bills, and Inflation: Simulations of the Future (1976-2000)," *Journal of Business,* 49 (July 1976), pp. 313–338.

Jacob, N., "The Measurement of Systematic Risk for Securities and Portfolios: Some Empirical Results," *Journal of Financial and Quantitative Analysis,* 6 (March 1971), pp. 815–834.

Jensen, M. C., "Capital Markets: Theory and Evidence," *Bell Journal of Economics and Management Science,* 3 (Autumn 1972), pp. 357–398.

————, ed., *Studies in the Theory of Capital Markets,* New York: Praeger, 1972.

————, "Risk, the Pricing of Capital Assets, and the Evaluation of Investment Portfolios," *Journal of Business,* 42 (April 1969), pp. 167–247.

Lintner, J., "The Valuation of Risk Assets and the Selection of Risky Investments in Stock Portfolios and Capital Budgets," *Review of Economics and Statistics,* 47 (February 1965), pp. 13–37.

———, "Security Prices, Risk, and Maximal Gains from Diversification," *Journal of Finance,* 20 (December 1965), pp. 587–616.

Markowitz, H. M., *Portfolio Selection: Efficient Diversification of Investments,* New York: Wiley, 1959.

———, "Portfolio Selection," *Journal of Finance,* 7 (March 1952), pp. 77–91.

Modigliani, Franco, and Pogue, Gerald A., "An Introduction to Risk and Return," *Financial Analysts Journal,* 30 (March-April 1974), pp. 68–80; 30 (May-June 1974), pp. 69–86.

Mossin, J., "Security Pricing and Investment Criteria in Competitive Markets," *American Economic Review,* 59 (December 1969), pp. 749–756.

———, "Equilibrium in a Capital Asset Market," *Econometrica,* 34 (October 1966), pp. 768–783.

Robichek, Alexander A., and Cohn, Richard A., "The Economic Determinants of Systematic Risk," *Journal of Finance,* 29 (May 1974), pp. 439–447.

Ross, Stephen A., "A Simple Approach to the Valuation of Risky Streams," *Journal of Business,* 51 (July 1978), pp. 453–475.

Schall, Lawrence D., "Asset Valuation, Firm Investment, and Firm Diversification," *Journal of Business,* 45 (January 1972), pp. 11–28.

Sharpe, W. F., *Portfolio Theory and Capital Markets,* New York: McGraw-Hill, 1970.

———, "Capital Asset Prices: A Theory of Market Equilibrium under Conditions of Risk," *Journal of Finance,* 19 (September 1964), pp. 425–442.

———, "A Simplified Model for Portfolio Analysis," *Management Science,* 9 (January 1963), pp. 277–293.

Smith, C., and Stulz, R., "The Determinants of a Firm's Hedging Policies," *Journal of Financial and Quantitative Analysis,* (December 1985), pp. 391–406.

Thompson, Donald J., II, "Sources of Systematic Risk in Common Stocks," *Journal of Business,* 49 (April 1976), pp. 173–188.

Tobin, J., "Liquidity Preference as Behavior toward Risk," *Review of Economic Studies,* 25 (February 1958), pp. 65–86.

Wagner, W. H., and Lau, S. C., "The Effect of Diversification on Risk," *Financial Analysts Journal,* 27 (November-December 1971), pp. 48–53.

CHAPTER 11

Risk and Return in Equilibrium: Evidence and Applications

The Capital Asset Pricing Model (CAPM) and the Arbitrage Pricing Theory (APT) are theories of how risky assets are priced in market equilibrium. They provide decision makers with useful estimates of the required rates of return on risky securities and on capital budgeting projects. This chapter introduces the theories and shows how they may be used in a variety of applications, such as capital budgeting, the cost of capital, and security valuation. Empirical tests of the validity of the CAPM and the APT are also discussed.

INTRODUCTION

In Chapter 10, we developed the basics of decision making under uncertainty in a portfolio theory context. Figure 11.1 summarizes market equilibrium as the Capital Market Line. Equation 11.1 is the algebraic expression for the CML.

$$E(R_p) = R_F + \left[\frac{E(R_M) - R_F}{\sigma_M} \right] \sigma(R_p) \qquad (11.1)$$

It allows us to predict the expected return for all portfolios along the Capital Market Line. Unfortunately, this result is of limited usefulness because points along the CML are various combinations of the riskless asset and the market portfolio, and, consequently, they are all perfectly correlated. The CML cannot be used to predict the return for ineffi-cient securities which lie in the interior of the portfolio opportunity set (these securities are

FIGURE 11.1   The Capital Market Line

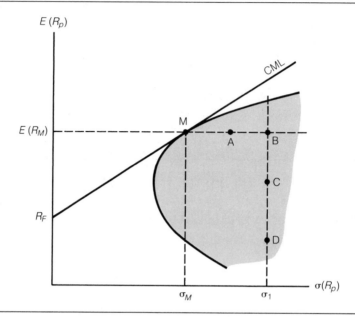

represented by dots in Figure 11.1). For example, if we learn that a security has a standard deviation of σ_1, we cannot predict the rate of return which the market will require. Points B, C, and D in Figure 11.1 all have a total risk of σ_1, but they have different expected returns. Thus, there is no unique relationship between the standard deviations of inefficient securities and their required rates of return. We have to find a better measure of risk.

Near the end of Chapter 10, we saw that the total risk of an asset can be separated into two parts: undiversifiable and diversifiable risk,

$$\text{Total risk} = \text{Undiversifiable risk} + \text{Diversifiable risk} \qquad \textbf{(11.2)}$$
$$\text{VAR}(R_j) = b^2\text{VAR}(R_M) + \text{VAR}(\epsilon),$$

where

$\text{VAR}(R_j) = $ the variance of return on the jth asset

$\quad\quad b = $ the slope from a linear regression of return on the jth asset against return on the market portfolio $= \text{COV}(R_j,R_M)/\text{VAR}(R_M)$

$\text{VAR}(\epsilon) = $ the variance of error terms from the linear regression. The error terms are uncorrelated with the market return.

This result is important because we know that the diversifiable risk is made up of error terms that are uncorrelated with the market portfolio. They are sometimes called the *idiosyncratic risk* of the asset. Since they have zero correlation with the market portfolio and with each other, the error terms can be completely eliminated through costless diversification. If diversifiable risk can be eliminated at zero cost, no risk premium will be associated with it, and it will be irrelevant in determining the risk-adjusted rate of return on individual assets. The only risk relevant for individual securities is their undiversifiable risk. This measure of risk, called beta, β, is at the heart of the Capital Asset Pricing Model, CAPM. It is the better measure of risk which we are seeking.

THE CAPM AND THE SECURITY MARKET LINE

The significant contribution of the Capital Asset Pricing Model (CAPM) is that it provides a measure of the risk of an individual security which is consistent with portfolio theory. It enables us to estimate the undiversifiable risk of a single asset and compare it with the undiversifiable risk of a well-diversified portfolio. Originally developed by Sharpe, Treynor, Mossin, and Lintner, the CAPM equation, or Security Market Line (SML), is usually written as[1]

$$E(R_j) = R_F + [E(R_M) - R_F]\beta_j, \tag{11.3}$$

where

$E(R_j)$ = the expected or *ex ante* return on the jth risky asset

R_F = the rate of return on a riskless asset

$E(R_M)$ = the expected or *ex ante* return on the market portfolio

β_j = COV(R_j, R_M)/VAR(R_M) = a measure of the undiversifiable risk of the jth security.[2]

The CAPM is graphed in Figure 11.2, Panel (b), where it is called the *Security Market Line (SML)*. In equilibrium, all securities must be priced so that they fall on the Security Market Line. Assets A, B, C, and D in Panel (a) all have different variances but the same expected return. In Panel (b), they all fall on the Security Market Line at Point X. They all have the same undiversifiable risk, that is, $\beta_A = \beta_B = \beta_C = \beta_D$, and the same expected return. The fact that they have different total risk (that is, different variances) is irrelevant for determining their expected return, because total risk contains a diversifiable component which is not priced in market equilibrium.

The Capital Market Line (CML) and the Security Market Line (SML) are merely different pictures of the same market equilibrium. The CML may be used for determining the required return only for those efficient portfolios that are perfectly correlated with the market portfolio because they fall on the CML, but the SML may be used to explain the required rate of return on all securities whether or not they are efficient. The SML provides a unique relationship between undiversifiable risk (measured by β) and expected return. Hence, if we can accurately measure the beta of a security, we can estimate its equilibrium risk-adjusted rate of return.

---

[1]See Copeland and Weston [1988], Chapter 7, for the derivation.

[2]Note that β_j, a measure of the undiversifiable risk of the jth security, is exactly the same as the slope, b, of a linear regression of the returns on the jth asset against the returns on the market portfolio. See Equation 11.2.

FIGURE 11.2   Comparison of the Capital Market Line (CML)
                   and the Security Market Line (SML)

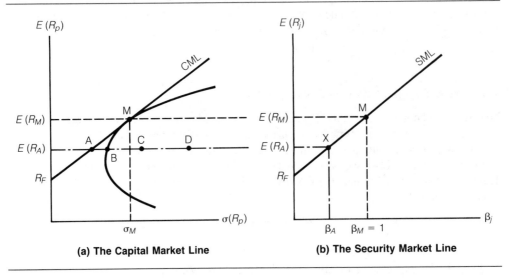

(a) The Capital Market Line   (b) The Security Market Line

The relationship between the CML and the SML can be seen by writing the two equations, one underneath the other.

$$\text{CML: } E(R_p) = R_F + \left[\frac{E(R_M) - R_F}{\sigma_M}\right]\sigma(R_p) \qquad (11.4)$$

$$\text{SML: } E(R_j) = R_F + [E(R_M) - R_F]\beta_j \qquad (11.5)$$

Rewriting the SML by using the definition of β_j, we have

$$\text{SML: } E(R_j) = R_F + [E(R_M) - R_F]\frac{\text{COV}(R_j,R_M)}{\text{VAR}(R_M)}. \qquad (11.6)$$

Note that the beta of the market portfolio is equal to one because the covariance of the market with itself, $\text{COV}(R_M,R_M)$ is the same as the variance of the market, $\text{VAR}(R_M)$, and $\text{VAR}(R_M)/\text{VAR}(R_M) = 1$. Furthermore, since $\text{VAR}(R_M) = \sigma_M^2$,

$$\text{SML: } E(R_j) = R_F + \left[\frac{E(R_M) - R_F}{\sigma_M}\right]\frac{\text{COV}(R_j,R_M)}{\sigma_M}. \qquad (11.7)$$

The above equation shows that the market price of risk per unit of risk is the same for the SML and for the CML.

$$\text{Market price of risk} = \frac{E(R_M) - R_F}{\sigma_M}$$

Also, if we recall that $COV(R_j, R_M) \equiv \rho_{jM}\sigma_j\sigma_M$, where ρ_{jM} is the correlation between the return on asset j and the market rate of return, we can rewrite the SML as

$$SML:\ E(R_j) = R_F + \left[\frac{E(R_M) - R_F}{\sigma_M}\right]\frac{\rho_{jM}\sigma_j\sigma_M}{\sigma_M} \tag{11.8}$$

$$= R_F + \left[\frac{E(R_M) - R_F}{\sigma_M}\right]\rho_{jM}\sigma_j.$$

This equation shows that the undiversifiable risk of each asset can be thought of as having two parts: the asset's standard deviation of returns, σ_j, and its correlation with the market portfolio, ρ_{jM}. If we recall that all points along the CML are perfectly correlated with the market portfolio, $\rho_{jM} = 1$, then Equation 11.8 for the SML reduces to be equal to Equation 11.4 for the CML. Hence, for portfolios that are made up of the riskless asset and the market portfolio, the CML and the SML are identical. Equations 11.8, 11.7, and 11.5 are merely different ways of writing the Security Market Line, but the reader should be familiar with all of them.

The Capital Asset Pricing Model (the SML) is an equilibrium theory of how to price and measure risk. As we shall soon see, it has many applications for decision making under uncertainty. We will show how to use it for (1) capital budgeting, (2) asset valuation, (3) determining the cost of equity capital, and (4) explaining risk in the structure of interest rates.

The logic of the Security Market Line equation is that the required return on any investment is the risk-free return plus a risk adjustment factor. The risk adjustment factor is obtained by multiplying the risk premium required for the market return by the riskiness of the individual investment. If the returns on the individual investment fluctuate by exactly the same degree as the returns on the market as a whole, the beta for the security is one. In this situation, the required return on the individual investment is the same as the required return on the total market. If the undiversifiable (or systematic) risk in the return of an individual investment is greater than for the market portfolio, then the beta of the individual investment is greater than one, and its risk adjustment factor is greater than the risk adjustment factor for the market as a whole. The relationship between the riskiness of an individual investment, as measured by its beta, and the risk adjustment factor is illustrated in Figure 11.3. The risk-free return is given as 5 percent. If we use 11 percent as the long-term average return on the market, the market risk premium is 11 percent minus 5 percent, which is 6 percent, the slope of the SML. If the risk-free return is 5 percent, the required return on the market is 5 percent plus a risk adjustment factor of 6 percent, totaling 11 percent.

The required return on an individual investment depends on the size of its beta, which measures the covariation of its returns in relation to the returns on the market. If the beta of an individual investment is 1.2, its risk adjustment factor is 1.2 times the market risk adjustment factor of 6 percent. The risk adjustment factor for the individual investment, therefore, is 7.2 percent, and its required return is 12.2 percent. If the beta measure of an investment is 1.4, its risk adjustment factor is 8.4 percent, and its required return is 13.4 percent.

FIGURE 11.3   Graph of the Security Market Line

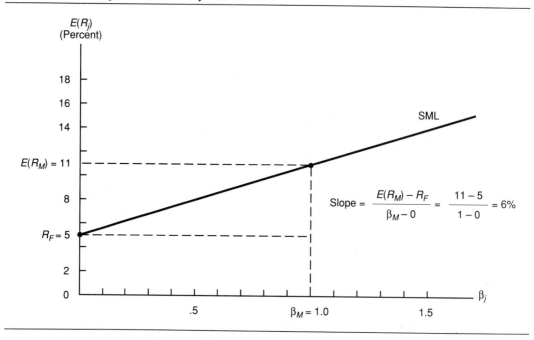

The advantages of the Security Market Line approach to measuring the risk adjust-ment factor and the required return on an investment are that the relationships can be quantified and that they have been subjected to considerable statistical testing. The empir-ical evidence on the validity of the CAPM will be reviewed later on in this chapter.

APPLICATIONS OF THE CAPM

One of the most useful properties of the CAPM is that the beta of a portfolio, β_p, of securities (or assets) is the weighted average of the betas of the individual securities, β_i. The weights, w_i, are the value of the ith security divided by the value of the portfolio.

$$\beta_p = \sum_{i=1}^{N} w_i \beta_i \qquad (11.9)$$

For example, if a steel company with total assets of $100 million and a β_s of 1.5 were to merge with a construction company worth $50 million and having a β_c of .7, then (in the absence of any synergy) the resulting firm would be worth $150 million and have a β of

$$\beta = w_s\beta_s + w_c\beta_c$$

$$= \frac{100,000,000}{150,000,000}(1.5) + \frac{50,000,000}{150,000,000}(.7)$$

$$= 1.00 + .23 = 1.23.$$

We can think of a firm as being nothing more than a portfolio of risky assets. The undiversifiable risk of the firm (its beta) is simply the weighted average of the betas of all of its projects.

Required Return on Securities

Equation 11.3 states that the expected return on an individual security or productive investment is represented by a risk-free rate of interest plus a risk premium. Earlier literature did not provide a theory for the determination of the risk premium. Capital market theory shows the risk premium to be equal to the market premium, $E(R_M) - R_F$, weighted by the index of the systematic risk, β, of the individual security or productive investment.

The β for an individual security reflects industry characteristics and management policies that determine how returns fluctuate in relation to variations in overall market returns. If the general economic environment is stable, if industry characteristics remain unchanged and management policies have continuity, the measure of β will be relatively stable when calculated for different time periods. However, if these conditions of stability do not exist, the value of β will vary.

The great advantage of Equation 11.3 is that all of its parameters other than β are marketwide constants. If β's are stationary across time, the measurement of expected returns is straightforward. For example, the returns on the market for long periods have been shown by the studies of Fisher and Lorie [1964] and Ibbotson and Sinquefield [1989] to be at the 9 to 11 percent level. The level of R_F has been characteristically at the 4 to 6 percent level. Thus, the expected return on an individual investment, using the lower of each of the two numbers and a β of 1.2, would be

$$E(R_j) = 4\% + (9\% - 4\%)1.2 = 10\%.$$

The higher of each of the two figures gives an $E(R_j)$ of 12%:

$$E(R_j) = 6\% + (11\% - 6\%)1.2 = 12\%.$$

Thus, we have numerical measures of the amount of the risk premium that is added to the risk-free return to obtain a risk-adjusted discount rate. The risk-free rate and the market risk premium (the excess of the market return over the risk-free rate) are economywide measures. They vary for different time periods but provide a basis for measurements that can be used in making judgmental decisions. In the numerical illustrations above, if a firm has a beta of 1.2 (and if the risk-free rate is currently in the 4 to 6 percent range), we would expect its required return, according to the Security Market Line, to be between 10 and 12 percent. This provides us with a relatively narrow boundary of returns within which managerial judgments may be exercised.

In Chapter 6 we discussed the issue of how the market determines interest rates. The nominal rate of return on any security was seen to be determined as a function of four variables: the expected real rate of return over the life of the security, expected inflation, a liquidity premium, and a risk premium. Earlier, we had to defer any discussion of the risk premium, but now we know that it is determined by the Capital Asset Pricing Model. From Equation 11.3 the CAPM is

$$E(R_j) = R_F + [E(R_M) - R_F]\beta_j. \tag{11.3}$$

The second term is the risk premium. The risk-free rate includes

$$R_F = f(\text{expected real rate, expected inflation, liquidity}).$$

In this way, we see that the CAPM includes all four elements of the nominal rate.

Figure 11.4 shows how expected inflation affects the CAPM. Both the risk-free rate and the expected return on the market portfolio include expected inflation, i. Suppose we write the real riskless rate as R_F^* and the real rate of return on the market portfolio as $E(R_M^*)$. Then, if we are specific, the CAPM can be written:

$$\begin{aligned} E(R_j) &= R_F^* + i + [E(R_M^*) + i - (R_F^* + i)]\beta_j \\ &= R_F^* + i + [E(R_M^*) - R_F^*]\beta_j. \end{aligned}$$

Note that changes in expected inflation do not change the slope of the Security Market Line (SML). Rather, they cause parallel shifts in the SML.[3]

The CAPM and the Market Return on Risky Debt

Usually, the yield to maturity on bonds is computed by finding the internal rate of return which equates the promised payments (coupons and face value) with the current market value of the bond. For example, suppose a bond is currently selling for $952. It promises to pay $100 at the end of each year for three years and a face value of $1,000 at the end of the third year. We would find its promised yield by solving for r in the following equation:

$$B_0 = \sum_{t=1}^{3} \frac{\text{Coupon}_t}{(1 + r)^t} + \frac{\text{Face value}}{(1 + r)^3}. \tag{11.10}$$

The promised yield is $r = 12\%$. But suppose the bond has some default risk, so that 8 percent of the time it goes into bankruptcy and only pays $700 instead of the promised face value of $1,000. There is a difference between its expected payments and its promised payments. The expected payment of the face value is

$$E(\text{face value}) = .92(\$1,000) + .08(\$700)$$

$$= \$976.$$

---

[3]Recent theoretical work has shown that if the uncertainty about inflation changes, then greater variability in the inflation rate may also cause an increase in the slope of the SML. More research needs to be done to determine whether this hypothesis is an empirical fact.

FIGURE 11.4   The CAPM and Expected Inflation

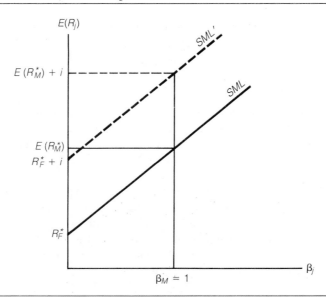

Given this fact, the logical thing to do is find the interest rate which discounts the *expected* payments so that they equal the present value of the bond. This rate is the market-determined, risk-adjusted rate, $E(R_j) = k_b$. Now Equation 11.11 becomes

$$B_0 = \sum_{t=1}^{N} \frac{E(\text{Coupon})_t}{(1 + k_b)^t} + \frac{E(\text{Face value})}{(1 + k_b)^N} \qquad \textbf{(11.11)}$$

$$\$952.00 = \sum_{t=1}^{3} \frac{\$100}{(1 + k_b)^t} + \frac{\$976}{(1 + k_b)^3}.$$

By trial and error, we find that $k_b = 11$ percent. But what is this rate? How can it be interpreted? Remember that the market prices only the undiversifiable risk of securities. If default risk is completely independent of the rest of the economy, then it will be uncorrelated with the market portfolio. Any investor or institution which holds well-diversified portfolios of risky bonds may find that default risk, being uncorrelated with the market, cancels out so that the portfolio earns the risk-free rate of return. Although any one firm may default on its debt in a given year, if we hold a well-diversified portfolio, in the long run the default rate will be within a narrow range. In this case, the 11 percent rate on our bond is the riskless rate. If the beta of risky bonds is positive because default risk is somewhat correlated with the economy, then 11 percent is above the riskless rate. Suppose we know that the risk-free rate is 10 percent and the expected return on the market portfolio is 17 percent. Then, we can use the CAPM to determine the beta of our risky bond.

$$E(R_j) = R_F + [E(R_M) - R_F]\beta_j$$
$$11\% = 10\% + [17\% - 10\%]\beta_j$$
$$\beta_j = \frac{11\% - 10\%}{7\%} = .14286$$

The purpose of this example is to illustrate that (1) the promised yield to maturity on risky bonds is biased upward from the market equilibrium rate, (2) the market equilibrium rate is calculated by discounting the *expected* cash flows on the bond until their discounted value equals their market price, and (3) a great deal of default risk is diversifiable. Risky bonds have low risk relative to common stock.

The market required rate of return on risky bonds is the before-tax cost of debt to corporations. The cost of debt is a necessary component of the weighted average cost of capital for levered firms. It can be estimated in one of two equivalent ways: Either (1) compute the beta (undiversifiable risk) of the risky bond and use the CAPM to estimate the cost of debt, or (2) use the *expected* cash payments and the current market value of the bond to compute its market yield to maturity.[4]

The CAPM and the Cost of Equity

Stock prices for publicly held firms are readily available, making it relatively easy to estimate the beta of a firm's equity. In fact, there are a large number of companies that are in the business of selling statistical estimates of beta for thousands of firms listed on the New York and American Stock exchanges. Once you have a good estimate of a firm's equity beta, β_s, you can use the CAPM (Equation 11.3) to estimate the cost of equity capital. This is illustrated in Figure 11.5.

Suppose that in 19X4, Spectra Physics, a manufacturer of laser instruments, had a β_s of 1.4. If the risk-free rate was 10 percent and the market risk premium, $[E(R_M) - R_F]$, was 6.1 percent, then using the CAPM, we would estimate the cost of equity as

$$E(R_j) = k_s = R_F + [E(R_M) - R_F]\beta_s \qquad (11.12)$$
$$= 10\% + [16.1\% - 10\%]1.4$$
$$= 18.54\%.$$

The cost of equity for Spectra Physics was approximately 18.5 percent. This estimate takes into account such company-specific information as business risk and financial risk, industrywide risk, and such conditions of the economy as expected inflation and the real rate of interest. If any of these factors should change, then the cost of equity for Spectra Physics will also change.

---

[4]Because quoted bond prices are infrequent and sometimes inaccurate, it is difficult to estimate the CAPM beta for corporate bonds. Hence, the second method, which requires an estimate of expected cash flows, is usually the preferred technique.

FIGURE 11.5   The CAPM and the Cost of Equity

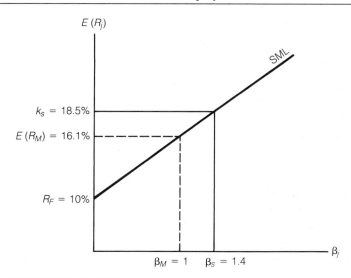

The CAPM and the Weighted Average Cost of Capital

Estimating the weighted average cost of capital (WACC) is a simple matter once the market required rates of return on a firm's debt and equity have been estimated as shown in the previous two sections. There are only two things to keep in mind. First, the market required rates of return, as estimated by the CAPM, are before-tax rates. Hence, the WACC must be written to reflect the fact that interest payments on debt are tax deductible, but payments to equity holders are not. The after-tax WACC is

$$\text{WACC} = k_b(1 - T)\frac{B}{B + S} + k_s\frac{S}{B + S}. \tag{11.13}$$

When k_b and k_s in Equation 11.13 are estimated using the CAPM, then the WACC is a risk-adjusted rate which takes into account the undiversifiable risk of debt and equity.

The second thing to remember is that the WACC uses the company's target capital structure, expressed in market value weights rather than book value weights.

$$\frac{B}{B + S} = \text{the target market value of debt divided by the}$$
market value of the firm

$$\frac{S}{B + S} = \text{the target market value of equity divided by the}$$
market value of the firm

Once the risk-adjusted WACC is known, the expected cash flows of the firm can be discounted at this rate in order to estimate the total value of the firm, V. We then get the consistent result that $V = B + S$, as found in the market. Also, note that the WACC is the opportunity cost of capital for the firm. It is the rate used to discount cash flows for capital budgeting purposes in order to determine the net present value of projects.

The CAPM and Capital Budgeting

The risk-return trade-off given by the Capital Asset Pricing Model requires that all capital budgeting projects earn at least the rate of return required by the market on projects of equivalent risk. The implication is that each project has its own WACC because each project has different risk. The corporate WACC is only an average cost of capital appropriate for the entire portfolio of corporate assets. It may not be (and usually is not) appropriate for an individual project.

In order to illustrate this important concept, let us consider the Morton Company case. The Morton Company is considering four projects in a capital expansion program. The economics staff has projected the future course of the market portfolio over the estimated life span of the projects under each of four states-of-the-world (Column 3 in Table 11.1). State 1 represents a relatively serious recession, State 2 is a mild recession, State 3 is a mild recovery, and State 4 is a strong recovery. The probabilities of these alternative future states-of-the-world are set forth in Column 2 of Table 11.1. Estimates of the project rates of return conditional on the state-of-the-world are set forth in Columns 4 through 7. It is recommended that a risk-free rate of 5 percent be used. Each project requires the same dollar amount of capital outlay. The Morton Company has a WACC of 10 percent and a corporate beta of 1.0. Assuming that the projects are independent (as opposed to mutually exclusive) and that the firm can raise sufficient funds to finance all four projects, which projects should be accepted?

In Table 11.2, the data provided by market relationships are utilized to calculate the expected return on the market along with its variance and standard deviation. The probabilities of the future states-of-the-world are multiplied by the associated market returns and their products are summed to obtain the expected market return $E(R_M)$ of 10 percent.

The expected market return, $E(R_M)$, is used in calculating the variance and standard deviation of the market returns. This is shown in columns 4 through 6 of Table 11.2. The expected return is deducted from the return under each state, and deviations from $E(R_M)$ in Column 4 are squared in Column 5. In Column 6, the squared deviations are multiplied by

TABLE 11.1   Summary of Information — Morton Case

State of World (s) (1)	Subjective Probability (p_s) (2)	Market Return (R_M) (3)	Project Rates of Return			
			Project 1 (4)	Project 2 (5)	Project 3 (6)	Project 4 (7)
1	0.1	−0.15	−0.30	−0.30	−0.09	−0.05
2	0.3	0.05	0.10	−0.10	0.01	0.05
3	0.4	0.15	0.30	0.30	0.05	0.10
4	0.2	0.20	0.40	0.40	0.08	0.15

TABLE 11.2   Calculation of Market Parameters

s	p_s (1)	R_M (2)	$p_s R_M$ (3)	$(R_M - \bar{R}_M)$ (4)	$(R_M - \bar{R}_M)^2$ (5)	$p_s(R_M - \bar{R}_M)^2$ (6)
1	0.1	−0.15	−0.015	−0.25	0.0625	0.00625
2	0.3	0.05	0.015	−0.05	0.0025	0.00075
3	0.4	0.15	0.060	0.05	0.0025	0.00100
4	0.2	0.20	0.040	0.10	0.0100	0.00200
		$E(R_M) = \bar{R}_M = 0.10$				$VAR(R_M) = 0.01$
						$\sigma_M = 0.1$

the probabilities of each expected future state (which appear in Column 1). These projects are summed to give the variance of the market return. The square root of the variance is its standard deviation.

A similar procedure is followed in Table 11.3 for calculating the expected return and the covariance for each of the four individual projects. The expected return is obtained by multiplying the probability of each state times the associated forecasted return. The deviations of the return under each state from the expected return are next calculated in Column 4. The deviations of the market returns from their mean are repeated for convenience in Column 5, and the products of these two are calculated in Column 6. Finally, these products are multiplied by the probability factors and summed to determine the covariance for each of the four projects (Column 7).

In Table 11.4, the beta for each project is calculated as the ratio of its covariance to the variance of the market return, and they are employed in Table 11.5 to estimate the required return on each project in terms of the market line relationship. The risk-free rate of return is assumed to be 5 percent; consequently, the market risk premium is $[E(R_M) - R_F] = 10\% - 5\% = 5\%$. Required returns, as shown in Column 2 of Table 11.5, are deducted from the estimated returns for each individual project to derive the "excess returns." These relations are depicted graphically in Figure 11.6.

Recall that the Morton Company had a WACC of 10 percent and a beta of 1.0. If it uses its WACC as the project hurdle rate, it will erroneously reject Project 4, which has an estimated return of 8 percent, and will erroneously accept Project 2, which has a 14 percent estimated return. These decisions are wrong because none of the four projects has the same risk (that is, the same β) as the firm. Projects 3 and 4 are less risky than the firm as a whole while Projects 1 and 2 are riskier.

The correct decision rule is to accept all projects that have positive excess rates of return — those projects that fall above the Security Market Line in Figure 11.6. Thus, Project 4 should be accepted even though it earns less than the firm's WACC of 10 percent. The reason is that Project 4 is less risky than the firm as a whole. Given the β of Project 4, the market requires a return of 7.75 percent for projects of equivalent risk, but Project 4 is estimated to earn 8 percent. Thus, it has an excess return of 0.25 percent and should be accepted. Project 2, on the other hand, is much riskier than the firm, and although it is estimated to earn more than the WACC, it does not earn enough to compen-

TABLE 11.3 Calculation of Expected Returns and Covariances for the Four Hypothetical Projects

s	p_s (1)	R_j (2)	$p_s R_j$ (3)	$(R_j - \bar{R}_j)(R_M - \bar{R}_M)$ (4) (5) (6)	$p_s(R_j - \bar{R}_j)(R_M - \bar{R}_M)$ (7)
1	0.1	−0.30	−0.03	(−0.50)(−0.25) = 0.125	0.0125
2	0.3	0.10	0.03	(−0.10)(−0.05) = 0.005	0.0015
3	0.4	0.30	0.12	(+0.10)(+0.05) = 0.005	0.0020
4	0.2	0.40	0.08	(+0.20)(+0.10) = 0.020	0.0040
		$\bar{R}_1 =$	0.20		$COV(R_1,R_M) = 0.0200$
1	0.1	−0.30	−0.03	(−0.44)(−0.25) = 0.110	0.0110
2	0.3	−0.10	−0.03	(−0.24)(−0.05) = 0.012	0.0036
3	0.4	0.30	0.12	(+0.16)(+0.05) = 0.008	0.0032
4	0.2	0.40	0.08	(+0.26)(+0.10) = 0.026	0.0052
		$\bar{R}_2 =$	0.14		$COV(R_2,R_M) = 0.0230$
1	0.1	−0.09	−0.009	(−0.12)(−0.25) = 0.030	0.0030
2	0.3	0.01	0.003	(−0.02)(−0.05) = 0.001	0.0003
3	0.4	0.05	0.020	(+0.02)(+0.05) = 0.001	0.0004
4	0.2	0.08	0.016	(+0.05)(+0.10) = 0.005	0.0010
		$\bar{R}_3 =$	0.030		$COV(R_3,R_M) = 0.0047$
1	0.1	−0.05	−0.005	(−0.13)(−0.25) = 0.0325	0.00325
2	0.3	0.05	0.015	(−0.03)(−0.05) = 0.0015	0.00045
3	0.4	0.10	0.040	(+0.02)(+0.05) = 0.0010	0.00040
4	0.2	0.15	0.030	(+0.07)(+0.10) = 0.0070	0.00140
		$\bar{R}_4 =$	0.080		$COV(R_4,R_M) = 0.00550$

TABLE 11.4 Calculation of the Betas

$$\beta_1 = 0.0200/0.01 = 2.00$$
$$\beta_2 = 0.0230/0.01 = 2.30$$
$$\beta_3 = 0.0047/0.01 = 0.47$$
$$\beta_4 = 0.0055/0.01 = 0.55$$

TABLE 11.5 Calculation of Excess Returns

Project Number (1)	$E(R_j)$ Measurement of Required Return (2)	$\bar{R}_j$ Estimated Return (3)	Excess Return (Percent) (4)
P1	$E(R_1) = 0.05 + 0.05(2.0)$ = 0.150	0.200	5.00
P2	$E(R_2) = 0.05 + 0.05(2.3)$ = 0.165	0.140	−2.50
P3	$E(R_3) = 0.05 + 0.05(0.47) = 0.0735$	0.030	−4.35
P4	$E(R_4) = 0.05 + 0.05(0.55) = 0.0775$	0.080	0.25

FIGURE 11.6 Application of the CAPM Investment Criterion

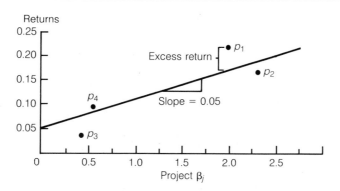

sate investors for the risk. With a negative excess return of -2.5 percent it should be rejected.

Discounting Project Cost Streams

Among the most common types of capital budgeting proposals are equipment replacement projects. The usual assumption is that revenues and output will be unaffected by the investment but that costs will be reduced. Cash flow data are usually limited to costs without any revenue projections. Should "riskier" cost streams be discounted at a higher or a lower rate?

Consider the data in Table 11.6. Projects A and B both have the same end-of-period revenues (assumed to be \$1,500), and they both cost \$1,000. Their end-of-period cash flows, however, are different. Although both projects have an expected end-of-period outflow of \$400, Project A has a low cost variance ($\sigma_A^2 = 81.65$) compared to Project B ($\sigma_B^2 = 163.30$). Which project has the greater NPV? What risk-adjusted discount rate should be used for the risky cost streams?

The CAPM requires that we compute the betas for each project in order to find the risk-adjusted discount rate. The one-period return for Project A in the "great" state is

$$1 + R_A = \frac{\$1,500 - \$500}{\$1,000} = 1$$

$$R_A = 0\%.$$

The project rates of return in each state of nature are given in Table 11.7. From the rates of return, R_i, and the probabilities, p_i, we can calculate, for each project, the expected rates of return,

$$\bar{R}_A = \Sigma \, p_i R_{Ai} = \frac{30}{3} = 10\%$$

$$\bar{R}_B = \Sigma \, p_i R_{Bi} = \frac{30}{3} = 10\%,$$

TABLE 11.6   Risky Cash Outflows for Mutually Exclusive Projects

| State of Nature | Probability | End-of-Period Outflows | | Market Return |
		Project A	Project B	
Great	1/3	$500	$600	20%
Average	1/3	400	400	10
Horrid	1/3	300	200	0

TABLE 11.7   Returns Data for Two Risky Projects

State of Nature	Probability	R_A	R_B	$R_A - \bar{R}_A$	$R_B - \bar{R}_B$	R_M	$R_M - \bar{R}_M$
Great	1/3	0%	−10%	−10%	−20%	20%	10%
Average	1/3	10	10	0	0	10	0
Horrid	1/3	20	30	10	20	0	−10

		$(R_A - \bar{R}_A)(R_M - \bar{R}_M)$	$(R_B - \bar{R}_B)(R_M - \bar{R}_M)$	$(R_M - \bar{R}_M)^2$
Great	1/3	−10(10) = −100	−20(10) = −200	10(10) = 100
Average	1/3	0(0) = 0	0(0) = 0	0(0) = 0
Horrid	1/3	10(−10) = −100	20(−10) = −200	−10(−10) = 100

the covariances with the market portfolio,

$$COV(R_A,R_M) = \Sigma\, p_i(R_{Ai} - \bar{R}_A)(R_{Mi} - \bar{R}_M) = \frac{-200}{3}$$

$$COV(R_B,R_M) = \Sigma\, p_i(R_{Bi} - \bar{R}_B)(R_{Mi} - \bar{R}_M) = \frac{-400}{3},$$

and the betas,

$$\beta_A = \frac{COV(R_A,R_M)}{VAR(R_M)} = \frac{-200/3}{200/3} = -1$$

$$\beta_B = \frac{COV(R_B,R_M)}{VAR(R_M)} = \frac{-400/3}{200/3} = -2.$$

Our results indicate that the project with greater variance in costs (Project B) has lower systematic risk for the project as a whole. The reason is that the absolute value of the cost stream is positively correlated with the market portfolio. This means that, in favorable states of the economy, the project rates of return will be lower than they might have been had costs been less correlated with the economy and that, in unfavorable states, the returns will be higher than otherwise. For example, if costs go up in a booming economy due to excessive amounts of overtime paid to labor, profits will be lower than they otherwise might have been. But in a slack economy, profits will be relatively higher because of layoffs. The overall effect is to reduce the variability of total returns on the project and to reduce the covariance between the project's total returns and the market portfolio returns. In our example, the more variable cost stream should be discounted at a lower rate (regardless of the variability of the revenue stream), because it reduces the project's beta.

Which project has the greater net present value? The risk-adjusted discount rate method for evaluating projects is

$$NPV = -I + \frac{E(CF)}{1 + E(R_j)},$$

where $E(R_j)$ is the risk-adjusted rate. Since Project B has the lower beta, it will also have the lower risk-adjusted rate. If the risk-free rate is 8 percent, then the risk-adjusted rates for the two projects are

$$E(R_A) = R_F + [E(R_M) - R_F]\beta_j$$
$$= 8\% + [10\% - 8\%](-1) = 6\%$$
$$E(R_B) = 8\% + [10\% - 8\%](-2) = 4\%,$$

and their net present values are

$$NPV(A) = -1,000 + \frac{1,500 - 400}{1.06} = 37.74$$

$$NPV(B) = -1,000 + \frac{1,500 - 400}{1.04} = 57.69.$$

As long as the absolute value of the cost stream is positively correlated with the economy, more variable costs will be discounted at a lower risk-adjusted rate.[5]

Factors Affecting Beta

Practical use of the CAPM requires that estimates of beta for stock, bonds, divisions of corporations, or even of individual projects be good enough to be reliable. If estimates of beta based on historical data are unrelated to actual risk, now or in the future, then the CAPM is not a good tool for decision making.

There are dozens of companies that currently estimate (with different levels of statistical sophistication) market betas for virtually every common stock listed on the New York or American Stock exchanges and many of the stocks on the over-the-counter or NAS-DAQ markets.[6] Those companies that use sophisticated econometrics techniques produce reliable estimates of beta. But what should you do if you are trying to come up with a ball park estimate of the risk of a division within your firm or if you want to know how a financial maneuver will change the beta of your equity? What are the underlying factors which affect beta?

---

[5] For more on this topic, see Booth [1982].

[6] When attempting to buy "better betas," the old rule of *caveat emptor* applies. The econometric difficulties of obtaining good beta estimates are many, and the quality of estimated betas differs greatly. The nonsynchronous trading problem is one of the most important issues. For example, see Scholes and Williams [1977], Dimson [1979], Fowler and Rorke [1983], and Cohen, Hawawini, Maier, Schwartz, and Whitcomb [1983].

TABLE 11.8   Representative Betas (March 1991)

Industry	Predicted Beta	Company	Predicted Beta
Thrift institutions	1.30	**Ten highest betas:**	
Forest products	1.30		
Construction	1.19	First City Bancorp Texas	2.46
Real property	1.19	Major Group, Inc.	2.38
Railroads	1.14	Far West Financial Corp.	2.30
Electronics	1.14	Security Cap Corp. Del	2.30
Retail (excluding food)	1.12	Ames Dept. Stores, Inc.	2.30
Consumer durables	1.11	Homefed Corp.	2.28
Chemicals	1.11	Carolyn Bean Pubg, Ltd.	2.28
Producers' goods	1.11	CM Communications, Inc.	2.27
Paper	1.11	Pope Evans & Robbins	2.27
Tire and rubber	1.10	LVI Group, Inc.	2.26
Apparel, textiles	1.10		
Health care	1.09	**Eleven lowest betas:**	
Publishing	1.07		
Life insurance	1.07	Unitil Corp.	0.18
Iron and steel	1.05	Calton Cons. Prin, Ltd.	0.18
Banks	1.04	Gold Express Corp.	0.22
Containers	1.03	Key Productions, Inc.	0.24
Media	1.03	Centurion Mines Corp.	0.26
Drugs, medicine	1.03	Marina Ltd. Partners	0.27
Trucking	1.03	Upper Peninsula Power Co.	0.31
Hotels, restaurants	1.02	St. Joseph Light & Power Co.	0.32
Business machines	1.01	Tide West Oil Co.	0.32
Coal and uranium	1.01	Kelley Oil & Gas Co.	0.32
Motor vehicles	1.01	Great Falls Gas Co.	0.32
Beverages	1.00		
Air transport	0.99		
Liquor	0.98		
Food	0.96		
Tobacco	0.95		
Gas utilities	0.93		
Aluminum	0.92		
Telephone, telegraph	0.89		
Electric utilities	0.84		
International oil	0.84		
Oil refining, distribution	0.82		
Precious metals	0.56		

Source: BARRA, *U.S. Equity Beta Book,* Berkeley, California, March 1991.

Perhaps the most fundamental factor determining a company's beta is its line of business. Its business risk includes both the cyclical nature of revenues and the firm's operating leverage. Table 11.8 shows the betas for various industry groups and for the highest and lowest beta stocks. Among the lowest beta industries are utilities, whose rates of return are regulated. Their profits depend on boards of commissioners and, conse-

FIGURE 11.7   Equity Betas Increase with Greater Financial Leverage

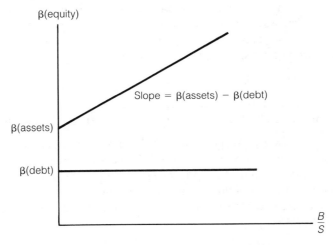

quently, are not as sensitive to general movements in the economy. On the other hand, the highest beta group was the thrift institutions with their well-known problems. Table 11.8 also shows that the ten lowest beta firms are mostly in regulated or natural resource industries.

Another strong factor is the amount of financial leverage undertaken by each firm. The beta of the firm's common stock will increase linearly as the firm's financial leverage increases. To prove that this is true, recall that earlier, we discussed the fact that the beta of a firm's portfolio of assets was equal to the weighted average of its liability betas.

$$\beta(\text{assets}) = \beta(\text{debt})\frac{B}{B + S} + \beta(\text{equity})\frac{S}{B + S} \tag{11.14}$$

Equation 11.14 can be rearranged to solve for the equity beta as a function of the firm's debt to equity ratio.

$$\beta(\text{equity}) = \beta(\text{assets}) + [\beta(\text{assets}) - \beta(\text{debt})]\frac{B}{S} \tag{11.15}$$

If we assume that the undiversifiable risk of the debt is invariant to the debt-equity ratio, then Equation 11.15 can be plotted in Figure 11.7 as a straight line. The equity beta increases with higher financial leverage because shareholders are residual claimants to the firm's cash flows. If the firm's use of debt increases, then more of its asset risk is shifted to the shareholders.

In addition to business risk and financial leverage, there are many other factors which may affect equity betas. Dividend payout, liquidity, firm size, and rate of growth have all been suggested as possibilities.[7] But suppose you are interested in estimating the risk of a

---

[7]For example, see Beaver, Kettler, and Scholes [1970] or Rosenberg and Marathe [1975].

new project rather than the beta for an entire firm. In this case, you have no way to statistically estimate the level of risk. What can you do? Our advice is that you try to compare your subjective estimate of the project's systematic risk with that of known entities such as the industries or firms mentioned in Table 11.8. Once you are satisfied you have a valid comparison, convert the equity betas to asset betas, which can then be used as a basis for estimating the risk of your project (see Chapter 15).

EMPIRICAL EVIDENCE ON THE CAPITAL ASSET PRICING MODEL

Any practitioner who wishes to employ the CAPM for managerial decision making naturally wants to know whether or not the CAPM theory is empirically valid. As we shall shortly see, the evidence on the CAPM is mixed. It fits the data fairly well, but there are some anomalies — phenomena that are not explained by the CAPM.

In order to test the CAPM, we need to know what predictions it makes. The empirical analog of the CAPM is

$$R_{jt} = R_{Ft} + (R_{Mt} - R_{Ft})\beta_j + \epsilon_{jt}. \qquad (11.16)$$

The three differences between Equation 11.16 and the theoretical CAPM (Equation 11.3) are that (1) time subscripts have been added to the variables, (2) the expectations operator, E, has been dropped because we use *ex post* data to test the *ex ante* CAPM, and (3) an error term, ϵ_{jt}, has been added. The model is usually tested in the following form:

$$R_{jt} - R_{Ft} = a + b\beta_j + \epsilon_{jt}. \qquad (11.17)$$

This is exactly the same as Equation 11.16 except that the risk-free rate has been subtracted from both sides and an intercept term, a, has been added. If the CAPM is true, then[8]

1. The intercept term, a, should not be significantly different from zero. If it is different from zero, then there may be something "left out" of the CAPM which is captured in the empirically estimated intercept term.

2. Beta should be the only factor which explains the rate of return on a risky asset. When other terms (such as residual variance, dividend yield, firm size, price-earnings ratios, or beta squared) are added to the regression, they should have no explanatory power.

3. The relationship should be linear in beta.

4. The coefficient of beta, b, should be equal to $R_{Mt} - R_{Ft}$.

5. When the equation is estimated over long time intervals, the rate of return on the market portfolio should be greater than the risk-free rate. Because the market portfolio is riskier, on average, it should have a higher rate of return.

---

[8]Any test of the CAPM is also a joint test of capital market efficiency because the CAPM is derived under the assumption that capital markets are efficient. For more on market efficiency, see Chapter 4.

There have been literally hundreds of published papers that test the CAPM.[9] Most of them use monthly total returns (dividends are reinvested) on listed common stocks as their data base. Some, such as Black, Jensen, and Scholes [1972] and Fama and MacBeth [1973], group individual stocks into portfolios chosen to provide the maximum dispersion in systematic risk. And others, such as Litzenberger and Ramaswamy [1979] and Gibbons [1982], use individual security regressions. With few exceptions, the empirical studies agree on the following conclusions:

1. The intercept term, a, is significantly different from zero, and the slope, b, is less than the difference between the return on the market portfolio and the risk-free rate. The implication is that low beta securities earn more than the CAPM predicts while high beta securities earn less.

2. Versions of the model which include a squared beta term or unsystematic risk find that at best these explanatory factors are useful only in a small number of the time periods sampled. Beta dominates them as a measure of risk.

3. The simple linear model (Equation 11.16) fits the data best. Returns are linear in beta. Also, over long periods of time, the rate of return on the market portfolio is greater than the risk-free rate (that is, $b > 0$).

4. Factors other than beta are successful in explaining that portion of security returns not captured by beta. Basu [1977] found that low price/earnings portfolios have rates of

---

FIGURE 11.8   The Empirical Market Line

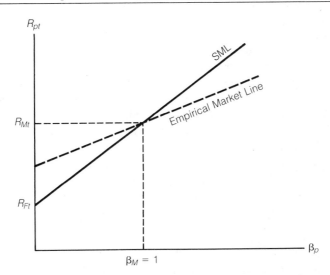

---

[9]A partial list of empirical tests of the CAPM includes Blume and Friend [1970, 1973], Black, Jensen, and Scholes [1972], Miller and Scholes [1972, 1982], Blume and Husick [1973], Fama and MacBeth [1973], Basu [1977], Reinganum [1981], Litzenberger and Ramaswamy [1979, 1982], Banz [1981], Stambaugh [1982], Gibbons [1982], and Keim [1983].

return higher than could be explained by the CAPM. Banz [1981] and Reinganum [1981] found that the size of a firm is important. Smaller firms tend to have higher rates of return. Litzenberger and Ramaswamy [1979, 1982] found that the market requires higher rates of return on equities with high dividend yields. Keim [1983] finds evidence that stock returns are seasonal.

In sum, the empirical evidence leads to the conclusion that the CAPM must be rejected. There are two primary reasons. First, the intercept term is significantly different from zero. Second, much of the returns unexplained by the CAPM can be explained by various anomalies such as firm size, dividend yield, price-earnings ratios, or seasonality.

Although the empirical evidence requires that we reject the CAPM as a theoretical construct, it does not mean that expected returns are unrelated to beta. As shown in Figure 11.8, the results show that the *empirical market line* (represented by the dashed line) is linear in beta. Hence, if you have an estimate of beta, you can predict its required return from the empirical market line. The primary difference between the Empirical Market Line (EML) and the theoretical CAPM is that the EML has a higher intercept and a lower slope.

THE ARBITRAGE PRICING THEORY (APT)

One of the problems with using the CAPM is that only a single factor, the market portfolio, is used to explain security returns. It is a little like flying a private plane and being lost in the clouds. When you call the airport tower to ask for your location, suppose they respond by saying, "You are 100 miles away." Such a message is not of much help. Obviously, you would like to have a little more information. Altitude, longitude, and latitude would also be useful.

The Arbitrage Pricing Theory allows us to use many factors, not just one, to explain security returns. For example, unexpected changes in interest rates are a logical candidate for being a common factor that affects all securities at once. When interest rates rise, the market value of bonds and stocks tends to fall. Fundamental factors have the property that they are not diversifiable, hence one must pay a risk premium to avoid them. First derived by Ross [1976], the APT starts out by assuming that the rate of return on any security is a linear function of the movement of a set of fundamental factors, $\tilde{F}_k$, common to all securities,

$$\tilde{R}_j = E(\tilde{R}_j) + b_{j1}\tilde{F}_1 + b_{j2}\tilde{F}_2 + \ldots + b_{jk}\tilde{F}_k + \tilde{\epsilon}_j, \qquad (11.18)$$

where

$\tilde{R}_j$ = the stochastic rate of return on the jth asset

$E(\tilde{R}_j)$ = the expected rate of return on the jth asset

b_{jk} = the sensitivity of the jth asset's returns to the kth factor

$\tilde{F}_k$ = the mean zero k^{th} factor common to the returns of all assets under consideration

$\tilde{\epsilon}_j$ = a random, mean zero, noise term for the jth asset.

TABLE 11.9 Macroeconomic Variables Related to the APT

1. Industrial production (or the market portfolio)
2. Changes in a default risk premium (measured by the differences in promised yields-to-maturity on AAA versus Baa corporate bonds)
3. Twists in the yield curve (measured by the differences in promised yields to maturity on long- and short-term government bonds)
4. Unanticipated inflation
5. Changes in the real rate (measured by the Treasury bill rate minus the consumer price index)

In the CAPM, the single factor underlying all asset returns is the rate of return on the market portfolio. Each asset's beta, or sensitivity, was estimated by regressing its return on the market portfolio rate of return. The Arbitrage Pricing Theory does not allow us to simply regress an asset's returns against arbitrarily determined factors. Instead, factor analysis must be employed to extract the fundamental factors underlying all security returns. Although it is mathematically impossible to use factor analysis to unambiguously identify the underlying factors, Chen, Roll, and Ross [1986] have correlated various macroeconomic variables with the returns on five portfolios which mimic the underlying factors. Their conclusions provide some insight into what the underlying factors might be. Five macroeconomic variables were significant[10] and are described in Table 11.9. The economic logic underlying these variables makes sense. Common stock prices are the present values of discounted cash flows. The industrial production index is obviously related to profitability. The remaining variables are related to the discount rate. Although more research remains to be done to understand the factors which underlie asset prices, the work of Chen, Roll, and Ross [1986] is a good start and provides intuition for what the common factors might be.

The logic behind the APT is much the same as that for the CAPM. Diversifiable, or idiosyncratic, risk is not priced by the marketplace because it can be eliminated at virtually no cost simply by spreading one's wealth among a large number of assets in a portfolio. All that counts is systematic risk. It cannot be diversified away. Consequently, a risk premium must be paid in order to compensate investors for bearing systematic risk. The measure of systematic risk is the sensitivity of an asset's returns to various factors which affect all assets. In the CAPM, the single underlying factor was the return on the market portfolio. In the APT, the underlying factors may be thought of as industrial production (or the market index), a default risk premium, twists in the yield curve, and unanticipated inflation. These are all economywide risks which cannot be diversified away. In order to show how these systematic risks are priced in equilibrium, Ross [1976] used the concept of arbitrage portfolios to derive market equilibrium.

An *arbitrage portfolio* is one that has no risk, requires no capital investment, and earns a positive return. Much like the mythical unicorn, an arbitrage portfolio is a nice

---

[10]It is also interesting to note some of the variables which were not significant — for example, oil price changes and changes in real per capita consumption.

idea, but it should not exist in equilibrium. No one should be able to earn arbitrage profits. In fact, we rely on the nonexistence of arbitrage opportunities to establish capital market equilibrium.[11]

Ross [1976] has shown that if no arbitrage opportunities exist, then the Arbitrage Pricing Theory (APT) can be written as

$$E(R_j) = R_F + [\bar{\delta}_1 - R_F]b_{j1} + \ldots + [\bar{\delta}_k - R_F]b_{jk}, \qquad (11.19)$$

where

$E(R_j) =$ the expected return on the jth asset

$R_F =$ the return on the riskless asset

$\bar{\delta}_k =$ the expected return on a mimicking portfolio which has unitary sensitivity to the kth factor and zero sensitivity to all other factors[12]

$b_{jk} =$ the sensitivity of the jth asset to the kth factor.

The APT is very similar to the CAPM. It says (in Equation 11.19) that the expected return on any security in equilibrium will be equal to the risk-free rate plus a set of risk premia. The risk premium for each asset is the market price of risk for the kth factor, $\bar{\delta}_k - R_F$, times the sensitivity of the jth asset to the kth factor, b_{jk}. Under some simplifying assumptions, the factor sensitivities may be interpreted in the same way as beta in the CAPM.[13]

$$b_{jk} = \frac{\text{COV}(\tilde{R}_j, \tilde{\delta}_k)}{\text{VAR}(\tilde{\delta}_k)} \qquad (11.20)$$

This implies that the CAPM is simply a special case of the APT where only one factor, the expected return on the market portfolio, is used to explain asset returns.

A numerical example will convey the way the APT works [Cf. Roll and Ross, 1983]. We begin with Equation 11.19a in which $E(R_j)$ and R_F have the same meaning as in Equation 11.19.

$$E(R_j) = R_F + k_1 b_1 + k_2 b_2 + k_3 b_3 + k_4 b_4 + k_5 b_5 \qquad (11.19a)$$

Five factors are indicated. The k's are the factor return premiums and the b's are the factor sensitivities. To illustrate the application of Equation 11.19a we assume the following numerical values:

- $R_F = 9\%$
- $k_1 = 2\%$ $b_1 = .6$
- $k_2 = 5\%$ $b_2 = .4$
- $k_3 = 8\%$ $b_3 = .2$

---

[11]See Copeland and Weston [1988], Chapter 7, for a derivation of the Arbitrage Pricing Theory.

[12]Think of the CAPM as a single factor APT and then recall that the beta of the market portfolio is one, $\beta_M = 1$. This is an example of unitary sensitivity. Just as the market portfolio in the CAPM has unitary sensitivity to itself, so too each APT factor (mimicking) portfolio has unitary sensitivity to itself and zero sensitivity to all other factor portfolios.

[13]Assuming that the vectors of asset returns have a joint normal distribution and that the factors have been linearly transformed so that their transformed vectors are orthonormal.

- $k_4 = 4\%$ $b_4 = .3$
- $k_5 = 2\%$ $b_5 = .5$

The five factors are described in Table 11.9. Applying the values given, we obtain Equation 11.19b.

$$E(R) = 9\% + (.6)(2\%) + (.4)(5\%) + (.2)(8\%) + (.3)(4\%) + (.5)(2\%) \quad \textbf{(11.19b)}$$
$$= 9\% + 1.2\% + 2.0\% + 1.6\% + 1.2\% + 1.0\%$$
$$= 15\%$$

Working through the numerical example we obtain 15 percent as the expected equity return based on the APT.

Table 11.10 compares estimates of the cost of equity capital using the Capital Asset Pricing Model (CAPM) and the Arbitrage Pricing Theory (APT). About half of the time, the differences are statistically significant and in two cases (oil companies and savings and loans) they are quite large.

The CAPM tends to provide inferior estimates of the cost of capital when the company or industry under investigation is sensitive to factors not well represented in the CAPM index — usually an index of common stocks like the S&P 500. The CAPM does not do well for oil companies with over 50 percent of their assets in the form of reserves in the ground because these companies are really large commodity portfolios. When commodity prices rise, their market values go up, but the stock market index tends to go down due to an unexpected increase in inflation. The poor correlation with the market index causes the CAPM to underestimate the cost of equity for commodity-linked companies. The CAPM does poorly for savings and loans and money center banks because their value is highly interest rate sensitive and the CAPM market index is much less so. Many of the anomalies of the CAPM can be explained by the APT because it is a more complete theory.

TABLE 11.10 CAPM and APT Estimates of the Cost of Equity (1989 data)

	Number of Companies	Cost of Equity		
		CAPM	APT	Difference
Brokerage	10	17.1%	17.4%	.3%
Electric Utilities	39	12.7	11.8	−.9*
Food and Beverage	11	14.1	14.3	.1
Forest Products	7	16.8	15.0	−1.8*
Large Savings and Loans	18	15.8	19.6	3.8*
Mining	15	14.7	14.2	−.5
Money Center Banks	12	15.9	16.9	1.0*
Oil Cos. with Large Reserves	12	14.4	19.1	4.7*
Property and Casualty Insurance	13	14.6	13.7	−.9

*Statistically significant at the 5 percent confidence level.
Source: ALCAR APT! and McKinsey analysis.

The APT: Applications and Empirical Evidence

A detailed discussion of APT applications would be redundant with the CAPM applications discussed earlier in this chapter. The APT can be used in exactly the same way as the CAPM for determining the cost of capital, for valuation, and for capital budgeting. The only difference between them is that the CAPM is a single-factor and the APT is a multiple-factor model.[14]

The question which everyone asks is how much of an improvement can be obtained if one uses the APT rather than the CAPM for various applications? Bower, Bower, and Logue [1984] and Roll and Ross [1983] find that the APT gives improved estimates for the cost of equity in the electric utilities industry. Chen [1983] finds that the CAPM anomaly known as the size effect is largely eliminated by the APT, and that the APT can explain CAPM residuals but not vice versa. These studies seem to suggest that the APT is an improvement over the CAPM, particularly when security returns contain some CAPM anomaly. On the other hand, portfolio performance studies by Brown and Weinstein [1983] and Chen, Copeland, and Mayers [1983] find no difference between the APT and the CAPM. However, the lack of difference is probably attributable to the fact that the portfolios they were studying contained no CAPM anomalies.

Finally, papers by Gehr [1975], Roll and Ross [1980], Reinganum [1981], Chen [1983], and Dhrymes, Friend, and Gultekin [1984] have tested the APT. In general, the findings indicate that there are at least three or four underlying factors that are important in explaining security returns. This is enough to encourage further research into the APT. Only time will tell whether the APT replaces the CAPM as a central paradigm for understanding risk and return in equilibrium.

SUMMARY

The APT and the CAPM are equilibrium models of asset pricing which focus on systematic or undiversifiable risk as the appropriate measures of risk. Total risk, as measured by the variance of an asset's returns, is not necessarily related to the equilibrium rate of return. In order to illustrate, consider the risk faced by an entrepreneur who owns and captains his own ship. If the ship goes down in a storm, the owner/captain loses everything. If he is risk averse, he will be willing to pay a relatively large fee for insurance. From his point of view, he is bearing a great deal of risk. If we look at the same problem from an insurance company's point of view, Lloyds of London, for example, the picture changes. Lloyds doesn't care about the specific risk faced by a single ship owner. It focuses on the riskiness of all shipping worldwide. If shipping mishaps are independent of each other and if there are many ships, then Lloyds can predict with relative certainty the total damage from sinkings each year. Consequently, Lloyds can charge the risk-free rate on its shipping insurance policies.[15] Individual ship owners will sensibly buy insurance

---

[14]For an interesting application of the APT to multiperiod capital budgeting, see Gehr [1981].

[15]This does not imply, however, that Lloyds' cost of equity is equal to the risk-free rate, because the volume of insurance written each year depends on the health of the economy. Hence, Lloyds' equity cash flow stream has a positive beta.

from Lloyds because the cost of insurance is well below what they would be willing to pay in order to avoid their specific risks. The point of this story is that the individual wealth variance faced by a sea captain is irrelevant in determining the market price of shipping insurance. All that counts is the covariance among shipping catastrophes. In our example, the covariance was implicitly assumed to be zero, and, therefore, the insurance companies could charge the risk-free rate.

Once we have estimated the covariance (or systematic) risk of an asset, either in the CAPM where the only factor is the market portfolio or in the APT where many factors may be relevant, then we can estimate the equilibrium risk-adjusted return required by the marketplace. This is a powerful and useful tool for decision making under uncertainty. The CAPM or the APT can be used for capital budgeting, for determining the cost of capital for debt and equity, and for valuation of securities. Empirical evidence indicates that although the CAPM must be rejected on statistical grounds, there does appear to be a linear relationship between beta and expected returns. The APT is an improvement over the CAPM because it appears to correct for some well-known CAPM anomalies, such as the firm size effect.

QUESTIONS

11.1   Why is the beta of the market portfolio equal to 1.0?

11.2   Suppose that expected inflation causes the nominal risk-free return and the market return to rise by an equal amount. How will the market risk premium be affected?

11.3   Why is total risk, as measured by the variance of returns, unrelated to the market required rate of return on a project?

11.4   Consider two firms which are alike in every way except that Firm A has fixed rate debt in its capital structure and Firm B has variable rate debt. Which firm has riskier equity? Why?

11.5   Firms X and Y have exactly the same ratio of debt to total assets. However, Firm X employs short-term debt and rolls it over each year at the existing interest rate while Firm Y has just issued fixed rate long-term debt. Which firm has riskier equity? Why?

11.6   Where do Points A, B, and C in Panel (a) of Figure Q11.6 plot in Panel (b) of Figure Q11.6? Why?

11.7   **a.**   Why do firms in the same industry tend to have similar betas?
    b.   Why is the average beta of brokerage firms high (that is, 1.55) and the beta of electric utilities low (that is, .84)?

11.8   What empirical facts have caused researchers to reject the Capital Asset Pricing Model?

11.9   What is the empirical market line, and how does it differ from the Security Market Line?

11.10   What are the five factors which Chen, Ross, and Roll have determined to be common to all asset returns?

11.11   What is an arbitrage portfolio? What role do arbitrage portfolios play in market equilibrium?

FIGURE Q11.6

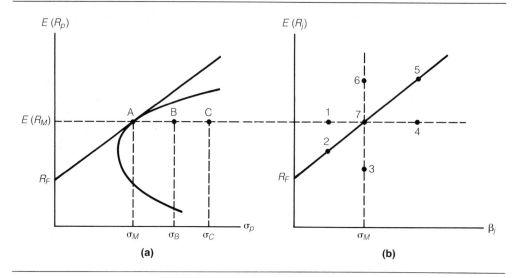

(a)   **(b)**

PROBLEMS

11.1 Prove that β_M (the beta of the market portfolio) equals 1.0.

11.2 Prove that

$$\beta_p = \sum_{i=1}^{N} w_i \beta_i$$

for a two asset case.

11.3 The Rowan Company is faced with two mutually exclusive investment projects. Each project costs $4,500, and each has an expected life of three years. Annual net cash flows from each project begin one year after the initial investment is made and have the probability distributions given.

Project A		Project B	
Probability	Cash Flow	Probability	Cash Flow
0.2	$4,000	0.2	$ 0
0.6	4,500	0.6	4,500
0.2	5,000	0.2	12,000

Rowan has decided to evaluate the riskier project at a 12 percent rate and the less risky project at a 10 percent rate.

a. What is the expected value of the annual net cash flows from each project?

b. What is the risk-adjusted NPV of each project?

c.   If it were known that Project B was negatively correlated with other cash flows of the firm while Project A was positively correlated, how should this knowledge affect the decision?

11.4   The risk-free rate is 4 percent, and the market risk premium is 5 percent. Under consideration for investment outlays are Projects A, B, and C, with estimated betas of 0.8, 1.2, and 2, respectively. What will be the required rates of return on these projects based on the Security Market Line approach?

11.5   The risk-free rate of return is 6 percent, and the market risk premium is 5 percent. The beta of the project under analysis is 1.8, with expected net cash flows after taxes estimated at $600 for five years. The required investment outlay on the project is $1,800.
   a.   What is the required risk-adjusted return on the project?
   b.   Should the project be accepted?

11.6   The McWilliams Company is considering two investment projects, A and B, for which the following information has been calculated.

	Investment A	Investment B
Investment outlay required (*I*)	$20,000	$20,000
Expected return [*E*(*R*)]	0.20	0.20
Standard deviation of returns (*σ*)	0.40	0.60
Coefficient of variation of returns (*CV*)	2.0	3.0
Beta of returns (*β*)	1.8	1.2

The vice president of finance has formulated a risk adjustment relationship based on the coefficient of variation, *CV*, which is defined as the standard deviation of return divided by the mean:

$$\text{Required return on a project} = \text{Risk-free return} + 0.04CV.$$

He also takes into consideration the Security Market Line relationship, using 6 percent as the estimate of the risk-free return and 5 percent as the market risk premium.
   a.   What is the required return on each project, using alternative methods of calculating the risk adjustment factor?
   b.   If the two projects are independent, should they both be accepted?
   c.   If the projects are mutually exclusive, which one should be accepted?
   d.   Depending upon the approach to risk measurement used, why might the two investments have different risks?
   e.   What additional analysis might be performed before a final decision is made?

11.7   You are given the following information for an investment project: $P = \$3$ per unit; $VC = \$2$ per unit; $FC = \$300$. The risk-free rate is 5 percent $= R_F$. (Use VAR $R_M = 0.01$.) Also,

Probability	R_M	Q
0.2	−0.05	0
0.5	0.10	600
0.3	0.20	1,000

where

$$P = \text{Selling price per unit sold}$$
$$VC = \text{Variable costs per unit sold}$$
$$c = (P - VC) = \text{Contribution margin per unit}$$
$$Q = \text{Units of output sold}$$
$$FC = \text{Total fixed costs.}$$

a. What is the price of risk, that is, $[E(R_M) - R_F]/\sigma_M^2$?
b. What is the value of the investment project?
c. What is the required return on the investment project?

11.8   Given the data here (the investment cost of each project is $1,000), calculate

S	Probability	R_M	Return to Project 1	Return to Project 2
1	0.1	−0.3	−0.4	−0.4
2	0.2	−0.1	−0.2	−0.2
3	0.3	0.1	0	0.6
4	0.4	0.3	0.7	0

a. The three means, the variances, the standard deviations, and the covariance of Project 1 with the market, covariance of Project 2 with the market, covariance of Project 1 with Project 2, the correlation coefficients ρ_{1M}, ρ_{2M}, and the correlation coefficient of Project 1 with Project 2.
b. If Projects 1 and 2 were to be combined into a portfolio with 40 percent in Project 1 and 60 percent in Project 2, what would be the expected return on that portfolio and its standard deviation?
c. $R_F = 0.04$. Calculate the Security Market Line. On a graph:
    (1) Plot the Security Market Line.
    (2) Plot points for Project 1 and for Project 2.
d. If you had to choose between the two projects, which would you select?

11.9   Consider two projects with different risk. The risky project has a risky rate of 12 percent. The riskless project has a riskless rate of 6 percent.
a. Calculate the certainty equivalent factor, $(cef)'$, for each project for Years 0, 1, 5, 10, 20, and 30.
b. What are the implications of your results?

11.10   We have the following data on market parameters. The risk-free rate is 6 percent, the expected return on the market is 11 percent, and the variance on the market is 1 percent. The covariance of the net operating income of the firm with the market returns is $40. The expected net operating income of the firm (X) is $320.
a. Calculate the value of the firm, using a certainty equivalent amount in the numerator and the risk-free rate in the denominator.
b. Calculate the value of the firm using risk-adjusted measures.
c. How do your results compare?

11.11   The Pierson Company is considering two mutually exclusive investment projects, P and Q. The risk and return estimates for these two investment projects are given here:

	Project P	Project Q
Expected return [$E(R)$]	0.15	0.18
Standard deviation (σ)	0.50	0.75
Beta (β)	1.80	1.40

Assume that the risk-free rate is 10 percent and the expected market return is 14 percent. What would be the firm's decision if the SML analysis is used?

11.12 The Magic Manufacturers Corporation has risky debt with a β_d of .2 and its stock has a beta of 1.6.

    a. If MMC has 60 percent debt to total assets, what is the beta of the firm as a whole?

    b. If MMC reduces its debt to total assets ratio to 40 percent debt, without changing the risk of debt, what will its equity beta become?

11.13 The expected return on the market portfolio is 16.2 percent and the risk-free rate is 10 percent. A risky bond is selling for $942.02. Its coupon rate is 10 percent and its face value is $1,000. It has three years to maturity. Although you expect all of its coupons to be paid with certainty, you believe that there is a 10 percent chance it will default on its face value and pay only $700. What is the beta of this bond?

11.14 Given the facts in this table:

Year	McNichols Corporation Equity Return	Market Return
19X9	2%	−12%
19X0	13	18
19X1	10	5
19X2	5	15
19X3	−8	10
19X4	−2	12
19X5	6	26

    a. Estimate the historical beta for the equity of McNichols Corporation.

    b. If the risk-free rate is currently 10 percent and the expected return on the market portfolio is 18 percent, what is the cost of equity for the McNichols Corporation?

    c. What assumption do you have to make in order to use a historical estimate of beta to compute a current cost of equity?

11.15 The Jacquier Company has three divisions, each of approximately the same size. The financial staff has estimated the rates of return for different states of nature as given.

State of World	Subjective Probability	Market Return	Division Rate of Return		
			Division 1	Division 2	Division 3
Great	.25	.35	.40	.60	.20
Good	.25	.20	.36	.30	.12
Average	.25	.13	.24	.16	.08
Horrible	.25	−.08	.00	−.26	−.02

    a. If the risk-free rate is 9 percent, what rate of return does the market require for each division?

    b. What is the beta of the entire company?

    c. If the company has 30 percent of its funds provided by riskless debt and the remainder by equity, what is the equity beta for the company?

d. Which of the divisions should be kept? Which should be spun off?

e. What will the company's beta be if the actions in Part (d) are undertaken?

11.16 Projects A and B are mutually exclusive equipment replacement proposals. Both require an immediate cash outlay of $1,000, both last one year, and both have end-of-year revenues of $3,000 with certainty. Cash outflows at the end of the year, however, are risky. They are given here along with the market rate of return, R_M.

State of Nature	Probability	End-of-Period Outflows Project A	Project B	R_M
Great	.333	$1,000	$1,200	30%
Average	.333	800	800	15
Horrid	.333	600	400	0

Since you are given the cash flows, there is no need to worry about taxes, depreciation, or salvage value. Note that the cash outflows of Project B have a higher variance than those of Project A. Which project has the higher net present value?

11.17 (*Use the computer diskette, File name: 11RSKRET, Risk & Return.*)

a. Given the assumptions in Screen 3, which project has the higher expected return? Which project is riskier?

(1) Which project has the higher excess return (that is, the difference between the expected return and the return required by the Security Market Line relationship)? View this graphically.

(2) Assume that each project requires a $1,000 investment, and all returns come at the end of Year 1. Which project has the higher NPV?

b. New engineering studies now cause the return estimates for Project 2 to be revised to $-.2$, $-.1$, $.5$, and $.1$ for the four alternative states of nature respectively. How does this affect the investment decision? Answer the same questions as in part (a) above.

c. Further engineering studies reveal that the return estimates for Project 1 should be $-.7$, $-.3$, 0, and $.7$. Answer the same questions as in part (a).

d. You are free to use the model to investigate alternative sets of possible project and market returns, alternative forecasts of future states of the world, or a different risk-free rate of return. Be mindful, however, that some substitutions may result in such anomalies as a negative market risk premium or a negative required return for a given project.

SELECTED REFERENCES

Aggarwal, Raj, "Corporate Use of Sophisticated Capital Budgeting Techniques: A Strategic Perspective and a Critique of Survey Results," *Interfaces*, 10 (April 1980), pp. 31–34.

Banz, Ralph, "The Relationship Between Return and the Market Value of Common Stocks," *Journal of Financial Economics*, (March 1981), pp. 3–18.

Bar-Yosef, Sasson, and Mesnick, Roger, "On Some Definitional Problems with the Method of Certainty Equivalents," *Journal of Finance*, 32 (December 1977), pp. 1729–1737.

Basu, S., "Investment Performance of Common Stocks in Relation to Their Price-Earnings Ratios: A Test of the Efficient Markets Hypothesis," *Journal of Finance*, (June 1977), pp. 663–682.

Beaver, W.; Kettler, P.; and Scholes, M., "The Association Between Market-Determined and Accounting-Determined Risk Measures," *Accounting Review*, (October 1970), pp. 654–682.

Black, Fisher; Jensen, Michael; and Scholes, Myron, "Capital Market Equilibrium with Restricted Borrowing," *Journal of Business*, (July 1972), pp. 444–455.

Blume, Marshall, "Portfolio Theory: A Step Toward Its Practical Application," *Journal of Business*, (April 1970), pp. 152–173.

———, and Friend, Irwin, "A New Look at the Capital Asset Pricing Model," *Journal of Finance*, (March 1973), pp. 19–34.

Blume, Marshall, and Husick, Frank, "Price, Beta and Exchange Listing," *Journal of Finance*, (May 1973), pp. 283–299.

Bogue, Marcus C., and Roll, Richard, "Capital Budgeting of Risky Projects with 'Imperfect' Markets for Physical Capital," *Journal of Finance*, 29 (May 1974), pp. 601–613.

Booth, L., "Correct Procedures for the Evaluation of Risky Cash Outflows," *Journal of Financial and Quantitative Analysis*, (June 1982), pp. 287–300.

Bower, D.; Bower, R.; and Logue, D., "Arbitrage Pricing Theory and Utility Stock Returns," *Journal of Finance*, (September 1984), pp. 1041–1054.

Chen, Nai-Fu, "Some Empirical Tests of the Theory of Arbitrage Pricing," *Journal of Finance*, (December 1983), pp. 1393–1414.

———; Copeland, T. E.; and Mayers, D., "A Comparison of Single and Multifactor Portfolio Performance Methodologies," *Journal of Financial and Quantitative Analysis*, 22, 4 (December 1987), pp. 401–417.

Chen, N. F.; Roll, R. W.; and Ross, S. A., "Economic Forces and the Stock Market: Testing the APT and Alternative Asset Pricing Theories," *Journal of Business*, 59, 3 (1986), pp. 383–403.

Cohen, K.; Hawawini, G.; Maier, S.; Schwartz, R.; and Whitcomb, D., "Friction in the Trading Process and the Estimation of Systematic Risk," *Journal of Financial Economics*, (August 1983), pp. 263–278.

Dhrymes, P.; Friend, I.; and Gultekin, B., "A Critical Reexamination of the Empirical Evidence on the Arbitrage Pricing Theory,"
Journal of Finance, (June 1984), pp. 323–346.

Dimson, E., "Risk Measurement When Shares are Subject to Infrequent Trading," *Journal of Financial Economics*, (June 1979), pp. 197–226.

Fama, Eugene F., "Risk-Adjusted Discount Rates and Capital Budgeting under Uncertainty," *Journal of Financial Economics*, 5 (August 1977), pp. 3–24.

———, and MacBeth, James, "Risk, Return and Equilibrium: Empirical Test," *Journal of Political Economy*, (May/June 1973), pp. 607–636.

Fisher, Lawrence, and Lorie, James, "Rate of Return on Investments in Common Stocks," *Journal of Business*, (January 1964), pp. 1–17.

Fowler, D., and Rorke, H., "Risk Measurement When Shares are Subject to Infrequent Trading: Comment," *Journal of Financial Economics*, (August 1983), pp. 279–283.

Gehr, Adam, "Risk-Adjusted Capital Budgeting Using Arbitrage," *Financial Management*, (Winter 1981), pp. 14–19.

———, "Some Tests of the Arbitrage Pricing Theory," *Journal of the Midwest Finance Association*, (1975), pp. 91–105.

Gibbons, Michael, "Multivariate Tests of Financial Models: A New Approach," *Journal of Financial Economics*, (March 1982), pp. 3–28.

Ibbotson, R., and Sinquefield, R., *Stocks, Bonds, Bills and Inflation*, Historical Returns Research Foundation of the Institute of Chartered Financial Analysts, Charlottesville, Virginia, 1990.

Keim, D., "Size-Related Anomalies and Stock Return Seasonality: Further Empirical Evidence," *Journal of Financial Economics*, (June 1983), pp. 13–32.

Litzenberger, Robert H., and Ramaswamy, Krishna, "The Effects of Dividends on Common Stock Prices: Tax Effects or Information Effects?" *Journal of Finance*, (May 1982), pp. 429–444.

———, "The Effect of Personal Taxes and Dividends on Capital Asset Prices: Theory and Empirical Evidence," *Journal of Financial Economics*, (June 1979), pp. 163–195.

Miller, Merton, and Scholes, Myron, "Rates of Return in Relation to Risk: A Re-examination of Some Recent Findings," in M. C. Jensen, ed., *Studies in the Theory of Capital Markets*, New York: Praeger, 1972, pp. 47–78.

Myers, Stewart C., "Procedures for Capital Budgeting under Uncertainty," *Industrial Management Review*, 9 (Spring 1968), pp. 1–15.

———, and Turnbull, Stuart M., "Capital Budgeting and the Capital Asset Pricing Model: Good News and Bad News," *Journal of Finance*, 32 (May 1977), pp. 321–332.

Reinganum, Mark, "The Arbitrage Pricing Theory: Some Empirical Results," *Journal of Finance*, (May 1981), pp. 313–321.

———, "Misspecification of Capital Asset Pricing: Empirical Anomalies Based on Earnings Yields and Market Values," *Journal of Financial Economics*, (March 1981), pp. 19–46.

Roll, R., and Ross, S., "A Critical Reexamination of the Empirical Evidence on the Arbitrage Pricing Theory: A Reply," *Journal of Finance*, (June 1984), pp. 347–350.

———, "Regulation, the Capital Asset Pricing Model, and the Arbitrage Pricing Theory," *Public Utilities Fortnightly*, (May 26, 1983), pp. 22–28.

———, "An Empirical Investigation of the Arbitrage Pricing Theory," *Journal of Finance*, (December 1980), pp. 1073–1103.

Rosenberg, B., and Marathe, V., "The Prediction of Investment Risk," Proceedings of the CRSP Seminar, University of Chicago, November 1975.

Ross, S., "Return, Risk and Arbitrage," in Friend, I. and Bicksler, I., eds., *Risk and Return in Finance*, Cambridge, Mass.: Ballinger Press, 1977.

———, "The Arbitrage Theory of Capital Asset Pricing," *Journal of Economic Theory*, (December 1976), pp. 341–361.

Scholes, M., and Williams, J., "Estimating Beta from Non-Synchronous Data," *Journal of Financial Economics*, (December 1977), pp. 309–327.

Stambaugh, Robert, "On the Exclusion of Assets from Tests of the Two-Parameter Model: A Sensitivity Analysis," *Journal of Financial Economics*, (November 1982), pp. 237–268.

Weston, J. Fred, "Investment Decisions Using the Capital Asset Pricing Model," *Financial Management*, 2 (Spring 1973), pp. 25–33.

———, and Chen, Nai-Fu, "A Note on Capital Budgeting and the Three Rs," *Financial Management*, 9 (Spring 1980), pp. 12–13.

CHAPTER 12

Options on Risky Assets

Options are contingent claim contracts that give their owner the right, but not the obligation, to buy or sell an asset at a predetermined price. An astonishing number of contracts fit this description. For example, the shareholders in a company that has issued debt have the right, but not the obligation, to pay off the debt and keep the remaining value of the company at the maturity date of the debt. Of course, they could also choose to accept bankruptcy. Thus, the equity in a levered firm is a call option. This chapter describes the generic varieties of option contracts, shows how to value them, and shows how they can be used to provide new insights into corporate finance issues, for example, the cost of capital and mergers.

INTRODUCTION TO OPTIONS

Options are contracts that give their holder the right (not the obligation) to buy (or sell) an asset at a predetermined price, called the *striking* or *exercise price,* for a given period of time. For example, on December 6, 19X6, a call option on Dow Chemical common stock gave its holder the right to buy one share of common at an exercise price of $45 until July 19X7. The price of a share of Dow was $39\frac{1}{2}$ and the call option sold for $1.75. This would be referred to as an *out-of-the-money option* — the exercise price was more than the current price of the common stock. An *in-the-money option* has an exercise price that is less than the current price of the common stock. An option to buy the Dow common stock at $35 when the common was selling at $39\frac{1}{2}$ would be an in-the-money option; it would sell for ($39\frac{1}{2}$ − $35) = $4\frac{1}{2}$ plus the aforementioned premium of about $1.75, or at about $6.25.

435

Option Pricing Models (OPMs) have been derived that enable us to predict the market prices of options with a great deal of accuracy.[1] These models are applicable to a wide range of option-type contracts, including the warrants and convertibles discussed in Chapter 25.

The considerable increase in interest in options and option pricing has been associated with the development of new options markets and important new theoretical developments. In April 1973 organized trading in standardized call options began on the Chicago Board Options Exchange (CBOE), followed by call option trading on the American Stock Exchange (AMEX options). The path-breaking paper by Black and Scholes [1973] appeared at about the same time. In addition to deriving the general equilibrium option pricing equation and conducting empirical tests, Black and Scholes suggested implications of option pricing that have significance for many other important aspects of business finance.

Black and Scholes observed that option pricing principles can be used to value other complex contingent claim assets, such as the equity of a levered firm. From this viewpoint, the shareholders of a firm have a call that gives them the right to buy back the firm from the bondholders by paying the face value of the bonds at maturity. A number of important applications of the Option Pricing Model were then made. As observed by Smith [1976] in his comprehensive review article, "the model is also applied by Merton [1974] to analyze the effects of risk on the value of corporate debt; by Galai and Masulis [1976] to examine the effect of mergers, acquisitions, scale expansions, and spin-offs on the relative values of the debt and equity claims of the firm; by Ingersoll [1976] to value the shares of dual purpose funds; and by Black [1976] to value commodity options, forward contracts, and future contracts."[2]

Because of the large number of additional areas on which the option pricing model provides new insights, it is useful to develop an understanding of the basic ideas involved. First, some of the fundamental characteristics of options contracts will be developed. Second, some of the basic relationships will be developed in an intuitive way as a background for the presentation and application of the binomial Option Pricing Model. Third, the relationship between the OPM and the CAPM will be developed. Fourth, empirical tests of the OPM will be reviewed. And, finally, applications of the OPM for corporate finance will be discussed.

Four Building Blocks of Financial Contracts

All financial contracts can be constructed with various combinations of only four basic building blocks: stocks, default-free bonds, call options, and put options. Figure 12.1 shows payoffs for put and call options. The vertical axis measures your change in wealth after T years at the time of the option's maturity. The horizontal axis measures the change in the price of the underlying asset (a share of common stock).

Suppose you buy a one-year call option on a share of du Pont stock. The stock sells for $S_0 = \$30$ and the exercise price is $X = \$30$. So, $S_0 = X$ and the option is said to be

---

[1]Black and Scholes [1973]; Merton [1973].

[2]Smith [1976], p. 5.

FIGURE 12.1   Payoffs from Put and Call Options where $S_0 = X$

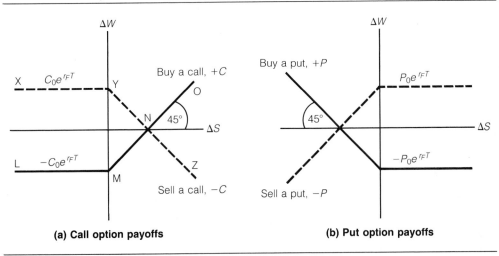

(a) Call option payoffs   (b) Put option payoffs

"at-the-money." A *call option* is a contract that pays its holder nothing if the option expires with the stock price less than the exercise price (if $S \leq X$), or the difference between the stock price and the exercise price if the option finishes in-the-money (that is, if $S > X$). Mathematically, we can write the option value at maturity as[3]

$$C_T = \text{MAX } [0, S_T - X]. \tag{12.1}$$

Suppose that the call option on du Pont stock costs \$3. If the change in the stock price, ΔS, in Figure 12.1(a), is negative, then the change in your wealth, ΔW, measured at the end of one year is[4]

$$\Delta W = -C_0 e^{r_F T}.$$

If the risk-free rate, r_F, is 10 percent and the time interval, T, is one year, then the change in your wealth is the loss of the future value of the \$3 which you paid for the call option.

$$\Delta W = -(\$3)e^{.1(1)} = -\$3(1.10517) = -\$3.32$$

In other words, if your option expires out-of-the-money, you will lose the future value of what you originally paid to buy the option. This is shown as line segment LM in Figure 12.1(a).

If the stock price rises, your wealth will rise \$1.00 for each dollar increase in the stock price, ΔS. For example, if the stock price rises \$3.32, then your end-of-period gain,

---

[3] Whenever we want to denote the current value of a security, we will use a subscript zero, S_0. The value at maturity will have a subscript T, S_T; and the value at intermediate dates (or the general value) will have no subscript, S.

[4] We are using continuous compounding. Therefore, the future value factor is $e^{r_F T}$ instead of $(1 + r_F)^T$. See Chapter 3 if you need to brush up on continuous compounding.

FIGURE 12.2   End-of-Period Payoffs for Common Stock and Riskless Bonds

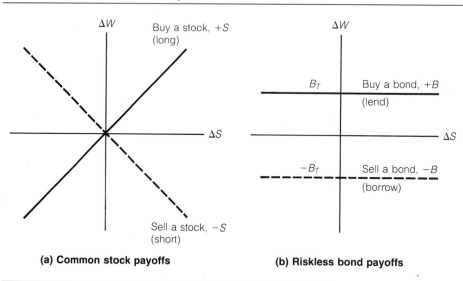

(a) Common stock payoffs   **(b) Riskless bond payoffs**

that is, $3.32, exactly equals the future value of the price you paid for the option, and your net change in wealth is zero. This is Point N in Figure 12.1(a). Line segment MNO has a slope of 45° because $\Delta W = \Delta S$ whenever $\Delta S > 0$. The entire line LMNO represents your end-of-period wealth if you buy one call option.

The line XYNZ in Figure 12.1(a) represents the payoffs from writing (that is, selling) a call option. These payoffs are exactly the opposite of those from buying a call.

A *put option* is the mirror image of a call. Buying a put option gives you the right to sell one share of stock at the exercise price. If the stock price falls (that is, if $\Delta S < 0$), a put option finishes in-the-money and your payoff is $X - S_T$. If the stock price rises, the put will expire worthless. Mathematically, the end-of-period payoffs for a put contract are

$$P_T = \text{MAX } [0, X - S_T]. \tag{12.2}$$

The end-of-period payoffs from buying a put are illustrated by the solid line in Figure 12.1(b), and the payoffs from selling a put are shown by the dotted line.

Put and call options are two of the building blocks from which all financial contracts are constructed. The other two are stocks and default-free bonds. Their end-of-period payoffs are illustrated in Figure 12.2. The solid line in Panel (a) shows that if you own the stock, your change in wealth increases dollar for dollar with the stock price change. If you go short (that is, sell) the stock, your wealth falls for each dollar increase in the stock price. Figure 12.2(b) illustrates the payoffs for a pure discount default-free bond. "Default-free" means that the bond pays off its face value in every state of nature, and "pure discount" implies that there are no interest payments during the life of the bond. If the face value of a pure discount risk-free bond is B_T, then its present value is

$$B_0 = B_T e^{-r_F T}. \tag{12.3}$$

FIGURE 12.3   Graphical Proof That $B = S + P - C$

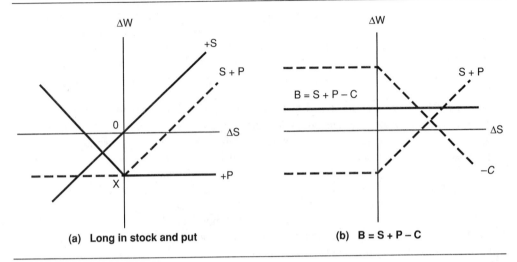

(a) Long in stock and put

(b) $B = S + P - C$

The solid line in Figure 12.2(b) gives your end-of-period payoff if you lend $\$B_0$ (that is, if you buy a default-free bond). The dashed line is your payoff if you sell a bond (that is, if you borrow). Note that these payoffs are represented by horizontal lines because the bond price is independent of changes in the stock price.

Now that we have covered the four basic building blocks, we can put them together according to the following relationship:

$$S + P = B + C. \qquad (12.4)$$

A long position in one share of stock and one put option (with an exercise price of X) written on that stock gives exactly the same payoff as a bond (with face value X) and a call option (with exercise price X) written on the same stock.

Equation 12.4 is valid no matter how it is rearranged. For example, suppose we wish to create a riskless position out of one share of stock, a call, and a put option. Rearranging Equation 12.4 we have

$$B = S + P - C.$$

We own one share of stock, one put option, and we have sold one call option. The resulting portfolio is shown in two steps in Figure 12.3. Panel (a) combines a long position in one share of stock and one put option, assuming that $S_0 = X$. The dashed line is the vertical sum of the two solid lines. For example, when the stock price change is zero, the change in wealth resulting from the stock is Point 0, and for the put option, it is Point X. The sum of the two is $0 + X = X$. Figure 12.3(b) combines the $S + P$ position with a short position in one call contract $(-C)$. The solid line is the vertical sum of the two, and we can see that the result is a constant payout no matter how the stock price changes. Hence, a perfectly riskless position can be obtained by buying a share of stock, buying a put, and selling a call.

PUT-CALL PARITY

If we restrict our analysis to *European* options, which may be exercised only at maturity, rather than *American* options, which may be exercised any time at all, then we can use Equation 12.4 to develop *put-call parity*. This relationship, derived by Stoll [1969], shows that for European options, there is a fixed relationship between the market price of put and call options written on the same security and with the same maturity date and exercise price.

As in the previous section of this chapter, suppose we have a portfolio where we purchase one share of stock and one put option and then sell one call option. Both options are written on a share of du Pont stock, which sells for $30. Also, they have the same maturity date, T, and the same exercise price, X, which is equal to the stock price, $30. We already know from Equation 12.4 that this portfolio is equivalent to a riskless bond. No matter what the stock price is at time T (maturity of the options), the portfolio will pay off $X (which is also equal to B_T, the face value of the bond).

At maturity, all states-of-the-world can be divided into those where the stock price is less than the exercise price, $S < X$, and those where it is greater than or equal to the exercise price, $S \geq X$. If the stock price is less than the exercise price, the portfolio payoff is:

		If S = $25
1. You hold the stock and, therefore, receive	S	$25.00
2. the call option is worthless and	0	0.00
3. the put option is worth	$X - S$	5.00
4. therefore, your net payoff is	X	$30.00

Alternatively, if $S \geq X$:

		If S = $35
1. You hold the stock and receive	S	$35.00
2. your short position in the call is worth	$-(S - X)$	−5.00
3. and the put option is worthless	0	0.00
4. therefore, your net payoff is	X	$30.00

No matter what state-of-the-world occurs at maturity, the portfolio will be worth $X. Consequently, the payoff from the portfolio is completely risk free, and we can discount its value at the risk-free rate. Using continuous discounting, this is

$$S_0 + P_0 - C_0 = Xe^{-r_F T} = B_0,$$

or

$$C_0 - P_0 = S_0 - Xe^{-r_F T}. \tag{12.5}$$

If $T = 1$ year and $r_F = 10\%$, then the current value of a pure discount bond with a $30 face value is

$$B_0 = Xe^{-r_F T}$$
$$= \$30.00 \, e^{-.1(1)}$$

$$= \$30.00(.9048)$$
$$= \$27.15.$$

But this is also equal to $S_0 + P_0 - C_0$. We can use the numbers in our example to solve for the difference between the call and put values:

$$C_0 - P_0 = S_0 - Xe^{-r_F T}$$
$$= \$30.00 - \$27.15$$
$$= \$2.85,$$

and if the call is worth \$3.00, the European put must be valued at \$3.00 − \$2.85 = \$.15.

Equation 12.5 is called the *put-call parity* relationship for European options. It is particularly useful because once we have derived an expression that allows us to price European calls, then we can use put-call parity to automatically price European puts as well. No separate derivation of a European put pricing formula is necessary.

A special case of the put-call parity relationship occurs when the exercise price is set equal to the stock price when the options are written. As long as $S_0 = X$, Equation 12.5 reduces to

$$C_0 - P_0 = S_0(1 - e^{-r_F T}) > 0.$$

Thus, when $S_0 = X$ (as was assumed when drawing Figure 12.3), the call price must be greater than the put price.

VALUING A CALL OPTION

A call option is a contingent claim security that depends on the value and riskiness of the underlying security on which it is written. We do not need an equilibrium theory of option pricing. All we need to know are the terms of the call contract and the stochastic process that describes the behavior of stock prices over time.

Intuition behind Five Factors Affecting a Call Option

Suppose that on October 4, 19X7, you bought a call option written on the common stock of Digital Equipment. The option was to expire on the third Friday in April 19X8 (199 days from the date of purchase).[5] Its exercise price was \$45.00 and the price of one share of Digital Equipment was \$46.75. What are the five factors that lead you to pay \$6.00 (the actual closing price) for the call option?

When you buy the call for \$6.00 on October 4, you are betting that the stock will be worth more than \$45.00 on the third Friday in April. The current stock price is \$46.75. If it were higher, say \$50.00, you would be willing to pay more for the call option. Clearly, the call value increases with the stock price. In fact, we can use this intuition to establish some boundaries for the value of a call option. If the option is still alive, it must have a

---

[5]All Chicago Board Options Exchange (CBOE) contracts expire on the third Friday of their month of maturity and may be exercised until noon on Saturday.

FIGURE 12.4   Simple Boundaries on the Value of a Call Option

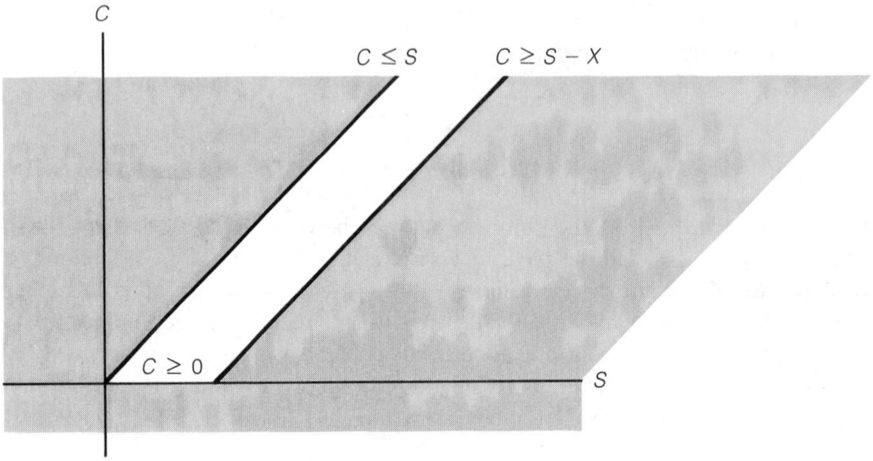

positive value because there is always some chance (however slim) that it will mature in-the-money. Therefore, one boundary is that the call must have a positive value,

$$C \geq 0. \tag{12.6a}$$

Next, the call price cannot exceed the value of the underlying stock.

$$C \leq S \tag{12.6b}$$

And finally, the call price can never be less than its value if exercised, that is, the difference between the stock price and the exercise price.

$$C \geq S - X \tag{12.6c}$$

These three boundaries are illustrated in Figure 12.4. The value of the call option must lie in the unshaded area. Note that the value of the call option is graphed on the vertical axis and the value of the underlying stock along the horizontal axis.

The next most obvious factor affecting the call value is the exercise price. The lower it is, the more valuable the call will be. In the most extreme case, the exercise price would be zero and the call would be worth as much as the stock because the boundaries represented by Equations 12.6b and 12.6c would collapse to a single line with $C = S$.

Investors always prefer longer-lived options. The reason is that with more time to maturity, there is a greater chance that the stock price will climb higher above the exercise price. In fact, a call option with an infinite maturity date will have the same value as the stock, regardless of the option's exercise price.

In addition to the stock price, the exercise price, and the time to maturity, there are two other important (but less obvious) factors which affect the option's value: the variance across time of the price of the underlying asset (the common stock) and the risk-free rate

TABLE 12.1   The Value of Higher Variance to a Call Option Holder

State of Nature	Probability	Low-Variance Stock	Payoff if X = $45	High-Variance Stock	Payoff if X = $45
Horrid	.2	$40	$ 0	$20	$ 0
Average	.6	50	5	50	5
Great	.2	60	15	80	35

of return. The holder of a call option will prefer more variance to less in the price of the stock. The greater the variance, the greater will be the probability that the stock price will exceed the exercise price on the upside while on the downside the minimum option (and stock) value is zero. Hence, a greater variance increases the probability of winning with a call option but does not affect the downside loss.

The value of a higher variance is illustrated in the example given in Table 12.1. Payoffs to the option on the low-variance stock are $0, $5, and $15 (if the exercise price is $45). Payoffs to the option on the high-variance stock are $0, $5, and $35. No matter what exercise price is given, the two options will be worthless when $S \leq X$, but the call option on the high-variance stock will be worth more when $S > X$. Even a risk-averse investor will prefer the option on the high-variance stock because its payoffs are always greater than or equal to the payoffs to the option on the low-variance stock.

The final factor determining the value of a European call is the risk-free rate of interest. Of all the factors, it is the least intuitive. It was not until Black and Scholes [1973] proved that it is possible to create a risk-free hedge portfolio consisting of a long position in the common stock and a short position in call options written on it that the role of the risk-free rate was fully understood.

Another way of understanding the effect of the risk-free rate on the value of a call option is to prove the following theorem.[6]

Theorem: An American call on a nondividend-paying stock will not be rationally exercised before the call expiration date.[7]

An *American call* may be exercised, at the discretion of its holder, at any time up to and including maturity.[8] It will, however, not be exercised until maturity because it is worth more in the marketplace than if it were exercised. Options on nondividend-paying stocks are always worth more alive than dead (exercised). To prove this, let us compare two

---

[6]This proof is attributable to Merton [1973].

[7]The theorem applies only to nondividend-paying stocks because American options on the CBOE are not dividend protected. A dividend payment represents a discrete jump in the stock price. When the stock goes ex-dividend, its price falls by (approximately) the value of the dividend, and, consequently, the value of a call option will also fall. If you know that your option will fall in price on the day the stock goes ex-dividend, your only protection is to exercise your option today. See Roll [1977] and Geske [1979b] for details on how to price options on dividend-paying stocks.

[8]We shall adopt the convention that European puts and calls are denoted with an uppercase P or C while American options are written with a lowercase p or c.

TABLE 12.2   Proof That an American Call Will Not Be Exercised Early

Portfolio	Current Value	Portfolio Value Given Stock Price at T	
		$S_T \leq X$	$S_T > X$
A	$C_0 + X\,B_0$	$0 + X$	$S_T - X + X$
B	S_0	S_T	S_T
Relationship between the terminal values of A and B		$V_A > V_B$	$V_A = V_B$

---

portfolios. As shown in Table 12.2, Portfolio A is composed of one European call option (written on one share of stock and having an exercise price X and a maturity date T) plus one zero coupon bond for each dollar of exercise price. For example, if the exercise price is \$45.00, then the portfolio will have 45 pure discount bonds. Each bond pays off \$1 with certainty at its maturity date, T. Portfolio B is simply one share of stock with a current value, S_0.

The third line in Table 12.2 shows that Portfolio A has a payout greater than or equal to Portfolio B in all states of nature. If the stock price is less than or equal to the exercise price ($S_T \leq X$) at maturity, the call is worthless and the bonds pay off \$X. Since $X \geq S_T$, Portfolio A is worth more than Portfolio B. Alternately, if the option finishes in-the-money (that is, $S_T > X$), then the option is worth $S_T - X$, the bonds are worth X, and adding these together, we see that Portfolio A is worth \$$S_T$. But Portfolio B is worth exactly the same amount; hence, whenever $S_T > X$, the two portfolios have the same value.

If Portfolio A has a future payoff that is always greater than or equal to that of Portfolio B, then the current value of A must be greater than the value of B.

$$C_0 + X\,B_0 \geq S_0$$

If we subtract $X\,B_0$ from both sides and recognize that a call option cannot have a negative value (see Equation 12.6a), then we can rewrite the above restriction as

$$C_0 \geq \text{MAX}\ [0,\ S_0 - X\,B_0]. \tag{12.7}$$

We also know, from Equation 12.3, that a bond which pays off a face value of ($B_T = \$1$) will have a present value which is

$$B_0 = B_T e^{-r_F T} = (\$1)e^{-r_F T}.$$

Substituting this into 12.7, we have

$$C_0 \geq \text{MAX}\ [0,\ S_0 - X e^{-r_F T}]. \tag{12.8}$$

Equation 12.8 says that the market value of a European call option must be no less than the current stock price minus the discounted value of the exercise price. An American call must be worth at least as much because it can be exercised anytime, not just at maturity.

FIGURE 12.5   Further Limitation of the Feasible Set of Call Option Prices

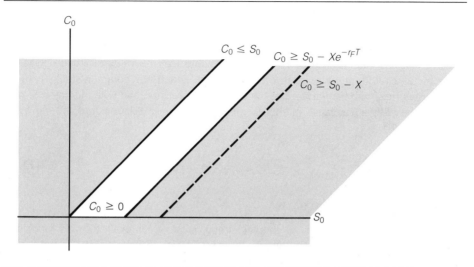

Consequently, if we designate an American call with a lowercase c_0 and a European call with an uppercase C_0, we can write

$$c_0 \geq C_0 \geq \text{MAX } [0, S_0 - Xe^{-r_F T}]. \tag{12.9}$$

There are three important conclusions to be drawn from Equation 12.9. First, an American option on a nondividend-paying stock will never be exercised early because its value if exercised is only $S_0 - X$ while its value if sold in the marketplace must be at least as great as $S_0 - Xe^{-r_F T}$. For example, using the numbers given earlier for the Digital Equipment stock, the value if exercised was

$$S_0 - X = \$46.75 - \$45.00 = \$1.75,$$

and the lower bound on the market value was[9]

$$S_0 - Xe^{-r_F T} = \$46.75 - \$45(.96676) = \$3.25.$$

Clearly, the option was worth more if not exercised — it was actually priced at $6.00.

The second important result from Equation 12.9 is that it shifts the lower bound on the value of a call option to the left, so that the value of a call option is higher for a given stock price, S. This is illustrated in Figure 12.5 by the solid line labeled $C_0 \geq S_0 - Xe^{-r_F T}$. If you ever find a call option on a nondividend-paying stock which is priced so that it violates one of these boundary conditions, then you have an opportunity to make an easy arbitrage profit.

[9]The risk-free interest rate was 6.2 percent, and 199 days to maturity translates into 199/365 = .5452 years.

Finally, the third result from Equation 12.9 is the relationship between the present value of a call option and the risk-free rate. The call must be worth more than the current stock price, S_0, minus the discounted value of the exercise price, $Xe^{-r_F T}$. If the risk-free rate increases (and nothing else changes), then the call must be worth more because the discounted present value of the exercise price declines.

We can now summarize the five factors which affect the value of a call option. Its value increases with an increase in the price of the underlying common stock, with the time to maturity, with the variance of the underlying security, and with the risk-free rate. It decreases with an increase in the exercise price. These relationships are shown in Equation 12.10:

$$C_0 = f(\overset{+}{S_0},\ \overset{-}{X},\ \overset{+}{T},\ \overset{+}{\sigma_S^2},\ \overset{+}{r_F}). \qquad (12.10)$$

A Simple Binomial Approach

We shall discuss two different but equivalent approaches to an exact formula for pricing call options. Historically, the first was derived by Black and Scholes [1973], but a more intuitive approach was later developed by Cox, Ross, and Rubinstein [1979] and Rendleman and Bartter [1979]. Besides being easier to understand, the binomial approach provides solutions not only for the European call option price but also for more difficult American put option prices, which (until recently) had to be solved by numerical approximation.

Before developing the analysis, it is useful to spell out in detail the assumptions which have been used while developing the option pricing model. As we shall point out later on, they are somewhat less restrictive than those used (in Chapter 11) to derive the CAPM. We assume

- Frictionless capital markets with no transactions costs or taxes and with information simultaneously and costlessly available to all individuals.
- No restrictions on short sales.
- Asset prices obey stationary stochastic processes across time.

FIGURE 12.6   A One-Period Binomial Stochastic Process

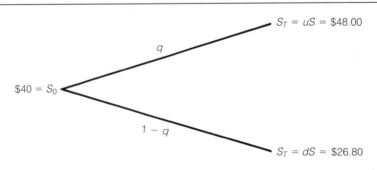

FIGURE 12.7   Payoffs for a One-Period Call Option

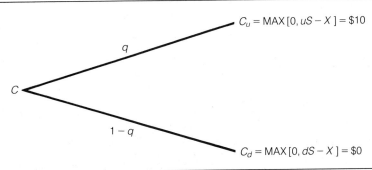

$$C_u = MAX[0, uS - X] = \$10$$

q

C

$1 - q$

$$C_d = MAX[0, dS - X] = \$0$$

- The risk-free rate is constant across time.
- Underlying assets pay no dividends (or cash disbursements of any kind).

Most of these assumptions can be relaxed without changing the basics of the Option Pricing Model (OPM).

In order to develop the binomial model, assume a one-period world where the stock price can move up or down from its current level. This is illustrated in Figure 12.6. In order to provide a concrete example, suppose that

$S_0 = \$40 =$ the current stock price

$q = .5 =$ the probability that the stock price will move up

$1 + r_F = 1.1 =$ one plus the risk-free rate of interest

$u = 1.2 =$ the multiplicative upward movement in the stock price
$\quad (u > 1 + r_F > 1)$

$d = .67 =$ the multiplicative downward movement in the stock price $(d < 1)$.

At the end of one time period, the stock price may increase to uS (that is, \$48.00) with probability $q = .5$ or decrease to dS (that is, \$26.80) with probability $1 - q = .5$. Note that the downward multiplier for the stock, d, must be less than one, and that it need not be related to the upward movement (that is, $d \neq 1/u$). The upward stock price movement, u, and the downward movement, d, are defined so that there is no upper limit to the stock price, but its lower limit is zero. This reflects the limited liability feature of common stock. If you buy a share of stock, you can lose what you paid but not more than that. If there are n periods, then

$$\underset{n \to \infty}{\text{Lim}}\ d^n = 0 \text{ if } 0 \leq d < 1$$

We also require that $u > (1 + r_F) \geq 1 > d$. If these inequalities did not hold, then riskless arbitrage opportunities would exist.

Now, imagine a call option, C, with an exercise price of $X = \$38$ which is written on the stock. The payoffs for the call are shown in Figure 12.7. There is a 50-50 chance of

FIGURE 12.8   The Payoffs for a Risk-Free Hedge

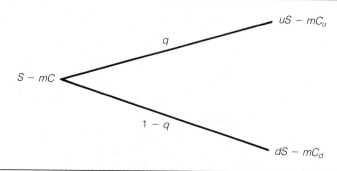

ending up with $10 or $0. The question is, how much would we pay for the call right now?

In order to answer this question, we begin by constructing a risk-free hedge portfolio composed of one share of stock, S_0, and m units of a call option written against the stock.[10] Figure 12.8 shows the payoffs for the hedge portfolio. We can find the correct hedge ratio, m, by equating the end-of-period payoffs,

$$uS - mC_u = dS - mC_d,$$

and then solving for m, the number of call options to be written against the share of stock.

$$m = \frac{S(u - d)}{C_u - C_d} \qquad (12.11)$$

Substituting the numbers from our example, we see that the proper *hedge ratio* is

$$m = \frac{\$40(1.2 - .67)}{\$10 - \$0} = 2.12.$$

Thus, the riskless hedge portfolio consists of buying one share of stock and writing 2.12 call options against it. Table 12.3 uses our numerical example to show that the hedge portfolio has the same payoff in either state of nature.

TABLE 12.3   Hedge Portfolio Payoffs

State of Nature	Portfolio	Payoff
Favorable	$uS - mC_u$	1.2($40) − 2.12($10) = $26.80.
Unfavorable	$dS - mC_d$	.67($40) − 2.12($0) = $26.80.

---

[10]The hedge portfolio could also consist of a long position in m units of the call and a short position in one share. The analytical results would not change.

Because the hedge portfolio is constructed to be riskless, we can multiply the current value of the portfolio by one plus the risk-free rate in order to obtain the end-of-period payoff. Mathematically, this is

$$(1 + r_F)(S - mC) = uS - mC_u.$$

Solving for C, the value of the call option, we have

$$C = \frac{S(1 + r_F - u) + mC_u}{m(1 + r_F)}.$$

Substituting the hedge ratio, m, into the equation and rearranging terms, we can rewrite the value of the call option as

$$C = \left[C_u\left(\frac{1 + r_F - d}{u - d}\right) + C_d\left(\frac{u - 1 - r_F}{u - d}\right) \right] \div (1 + r_F). \qquad \textbf{(12.12)}$$

If we let

$$p = \frac{1 + r_F - d}{u - d}, \qquad \text{and} \qquad 1 - p = \frac{u - 1 - r_F}{u - d},$$

Equation 12.12 can be simplified to be

$$C = [pC_u + (1 - p)C_d] \div (1 + r_F). \qquad \textbf{(12.13)}$$

We shall call p the *hedging probability*. It is always greater than or equal to zero and less than or equal to one, so it has all of the properties of a probability.[11]

Continuing with our numerical example, we can use Equation 12.13 to value the call option.

$$C = [pC_u + (1 - p)C_d] \div (1 + r_F)$$
$$= \left[\left(\frac{1 + .1 - .67}{1.2 - .67}\right) \$10 + \left(\frac{1.2 - 1 - .1}{1.2 - .67}\right) \$0 \right] \div (1 + .1)$$
$$= [(.8113)\$10 + (.1887)\$0] \div (1.1) = \$7.38$$

If the call is worth $7.38 and the hedge portfolio required that we buy one share of stock for $40 and sell 2.12 call options, our net investment was

$$S - mC = \$40 - 2.12(\$7.38) = \$24.35.$$

---

[11]In fact, p is the value that q would have if all investors were risk neutral. A risk-free investor would require only the risk-free rate on an investment in the common stock. Thus, the expected return would be $r_F S$, where

$$(1 + r_F)S = quS + (1 - q)dS.$$

Solving for q, we have

$$q = \frac{1 + r_F - d}{u - d}.$$

Thus, $p = q$ for a risk-neutral investor.

From Table 12.3, we know that the hedge portfolio earns $26.80 in either state of nature. Therefore, one plus the rate of return on our hedge portfolio is

$$1 + r_F = \frac{\$26.80}{\$24.35} = 1 + .1.$$

This confirms that the option is correctly priced and that the hedge portfolio earns the risk-free rate of 10 percent.

The preceding derivation of the value of a call option depends critically on the existence of a hedge portfolio and on the fact that the call must be priced so that the risk-free hedge earns exactly the risk-free rate of return. If the call had a higher (or lower) price, the hedge would earn more (or less) than the riskless rate and opportunities to earn risk-free arbitrage profits would exist. Arbitrage would force the call price back into line because traders can always form riskless hedges that will earn more than the riskless rate if prices are out of line.

The binomial OPM provides insight into three interesting features of option pricing.

1. The option price does not depend on knowing q, the probability of an upward movement in the stock price. Information about the market's expectation of future stock price movements is already captured in the current stock price, S_0. Consequently, even though investors may have heterogeneous expectations about future stock prices, they will still agree on the call value relative to its parameters, namely, S_0, u and d, X, r_F and T (where $T = 1$ in the one-period model).

2. Individuals' attitudes toward risk are irrelevant in deriving the call option formula. All that is required is that people prefer more wealth to less, so that arbitrage profits are eliminated.

FIGURE 12.9   The Unit Normal Distribution, Panel (a), and the
Cumulative Unit Normal Distribution, Panel (b)

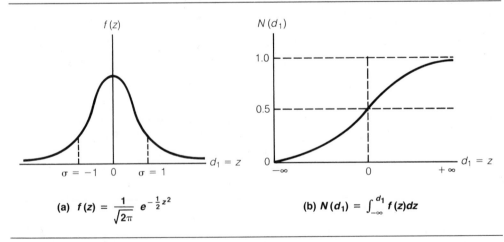

(a) $f(z) = \dfrac{1}{\sqrt{2\pi}} e^{-\frac{1}{2}z^2}$

(b) $N(d_1) = \int_{-\infty}^{d_1} f(z)dz$

3. The only random variable on which the call value depends is the stock price. The call value does not depend, for example, on the market portfolio of all securities.

These features serve to emphasize that the OPM is based on fewer assumptions than equilibrium models, for example, the CAPM. An option is merely a *contingent claim* on a risky asset. Once we observe the equilibrium value of the asset, we know that the option value must move in concert with it.

The binomial model can be extended into a multiperiod framework and used for solving such realistic problems as the value of an American call on a dividend-paying stock or the value of an American put.[12] In the limit, as the number of binomial jumps per unit of time becomes infinite, the binomial model approaches the Black-Scholes OPM. Therefore, we shall move on to discuss the Black-Scholes model, which assumes that stock prices follow a (geometric) Brownian motion process through time.

The Black-Scholes Model

The advantage of the Black-Scholes [1973] OPM over the binomial model is that it provides a closed-form solution for option prices. The Black-Scholes formula is given below:

$$C = S\,N(d_1) - Xe^{-r_F T}\,N(d_2), \tag{12.14}$$

where

$$d_1 = \frac{ln(S/X) + r_F T}{\sigma\sqrt{T}} + \frac{1}{2}\,\sigma\sqrt{T}$$

$$d_2 = d_1 - \sigma\sqrt{T}.$$

The terms $N(d_1)$ and $N(d_2)$ are the cumulative probabilities for a unit normal variable z. Recall that a unit normal variable has a mean of zero and a standard deviation of one.[13] The unit normal distribution and the cumulative unit normal distribution are illustrated in Figure 12.9, Panels (a) and (b) respectively.

A quick inspection of the Black-Scholes formula shows that the value of a call option is a function of the stock price, S, the exercise price, X, the time to maturity, T, the instantaneous variance, σ^2, and the risk-free rate, r_F. In order to show how to use the Black-Scholes formula, suppose we want to price an option written on Digital Equipment stock (which had a policy of paying no dividends in 19X7). Table 12.4 provides most of the information needed to value the call. The stock price, the exercise price, and the number of days to maturity are given for each option. The risk-free rate is estimated by using the average of the bid and ask quotes on U.S. Treasury bills of approximately the same maturity as the option. The only missing piece of information is the instantaneous variance of the stock price. Several different techniques have been suggested for estimating it (for example, see Latane and Rendleman [1976] or Parkinson [1977]).

---

[12]See Cox, Ross, and Rubinstein [1979] or Rendleman and Bartter [1979].

[13]Refer to Chapter 8, Appendix A, for a review of the unit normal distribution.

TABLE 12.4   Data Needed to Price Digital Equipment Calls

Exercise Price	Call Prices as of October 4, 19X7, for Calls Maturing in:			Closing Stock Price
	October	January	April	
$35	$11⅞	$12⅞	NA	$46¾
40	6⅞	8	NA	46¾
45	2¹⁵⁄₁₆	4¼	$6	46¾
50	¼	1¾	3	46¾
Maturity date	21 October	20 January	21 April	
Days to maturity	17	108	199	

Treasury Bill Rates on October 4, 19X7				
Maturity Date	Bid	Ask	Average	r_F
20 October 19X7	6.04%	5.70%	5.87%	5.9%
19 January 19X8	6.15	6.07	6.11	6.1
4 April 19X8	6.29	6.21	6.25 ⎱	
2 May 19X8	6.20	6.12	6.16 ⎰	6.2

The implicit variance is calculated by simply using the actual call price and the four known exogenous parameters (S, X, T, and r_F) in Equation 12.14 to solve for an estimate of the instantaneous variance. We did this, using the January 45's on Digital Equipment, which were priced at $4¼ on October 4.[14] The estimate of instantaneous variance was approximately 7.84 percent (which is a standard deviation of 28 percent).

We can now substitute our estimates of the five parameters into Equation 12.14 in order to estimate the value of any of the other 11 options on Digital Equipment. For example, let us value the April 45's. The parameters are

$$r_F = 6.2\%, \quad T = 199/365, \quad S = \$46.75, \quad X = \$45, \quad \text{and} \quad \sigma = .28.$$

First, we have to compute $N(d_1)$ and $N(d_2)$, which are the cumulative unit normal probabilities. The first unit normal probability is

$$d_1 = \frac{ln(S/X) + r_F T}{\sigma\sqrt{T}} + \frac{1}{2}\sigma\sqrt{T}$$

$$= \frac{ln(46.75/45) + .062(199/365)}{.28\sqrt{199/365}} + \frac{1}{2}(.28)\sqrt{199/365}$$

$$= \frac{ln(1.03889) + .062(.54521)}{.28\sqrt{.54521}} + .5(.28)\sqrt{.54521}$$

$$= \frac{.03815 + .03380}{.28(.73838)} + .5(.28)(.73838)$$

$$= .34801 + .10337 = .45138.$$

---

[14]It is necessary to use trial-and-error to converge on the estimate of the standard deviation which equate the right-hand side of Equation 12.14 with the observed call price.

FIGURE 12.10   Illustration of the Cumulative Normal Probability $N(d_1)$

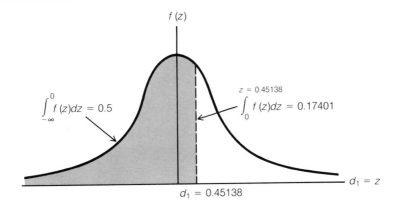

Given that $d_1 = .45138$, we can use Appendix D at the end of the book. It gives the areas under a unit normal curve, as shown in Figure 12.10. We know that when $d_1 = .45138$, the unit normal variable lies .45138 standard deviations above its mean (which is equal to zero). Hence, the cumulative probability is the sum of (1) the area from $(-\infty)$ to zero, which equals .5, plus (2) the area from zero to .45138, which equals .17401, when read from Appendix D.[15] Consequently,

$$N(d_1) = .5 + .17401 = .67401.$$

In a similar fashion, we can solve for $N(d_2)$. First, we solve for

$$d_2 = d_1 - \sigma\sqrt{T}$$
$$= .45138 - (.28)\sqrt{199/365}$$
$$= .24463.$$

From Appendix D, we see that

$$N(d_2) = .5 + .09661 = .59661.$$

Substituting the parameter values into Equation 12.14, we have

$$C = S\, N(d_1) - Xe^{-r_F T}N(d_2)$$
$$= \$46.75(.67401) - \$45\, e^{-.062(199/365)}(.59661)$$
$$= \$31.51 - \$45(.96676)(.59661)$$
$$= \$31.51 - \$25.96 = \$5.55.$$

The estimated call price turns out to be $5.55 while the actual call price is $6.00, an error of 7.5 percent. If we repeat the procedure for the October 45's (now $r_F = .059$ and

---

[15]The value of .17401 was attained via linear interpolation between the values given for $z = .45$ and $z = 46$ in the table. Linear interpolation is not exact in this case but is a close approximation.

$T = 17/365$), the estimated call price is \$2.28 while the actual price is \$2.94. Since both of the estimated prices are lower than the actual prices, our estimate of the instantaneous variance is probably too low.

The above examples show how the Black-Scholes valuation model may be used to price call options on nondividend-paying stocks. Roll [1977] and Geske [1979b] have solved the problem of valuing American calls when the common stock is assumed to make known dividend payments before the option matures. The binomial Option Pricing Model may be used for this purpose as well.

The Relationship Between the Binomial and Black-Scholes Models

The binomial Option Pricing Model is quite simple in concept. The up and down movements of the stock price (u and d) are analogous to the standard deviation in the Black-Scholes model, Equation 12.14. The exact correspondence between the two models was derived by Cox and Rubinstein [1979],

$$u = e^{\sigma \sqrt{T/n}}$$
$$d = e^{-\sigma \sqrt{T/n}}$$

where T is the fraction of a year left until expiration of the option, n is the number of branches in the binomial tree that is being used to estimate the option value, e is the base of natural logarithms, and σ is the annualized standard deviation of the stock. Using these facts and being careful to adjust the risk-free rate so that it corresponds to the time interval represented by one branch of a binomial tree, one can then use either Black-Scholes or a binomial tree to price an option. As the number of branches in the binomial tree becomes large, the option price estimated by the binomial tree approaches the Black-Scholes estimate very quickly.

Hedge Portfolios

In order to provide a little more intuition for the Black-Scholes formula, we have rewritten Equations 12.9 and 12.14 below. Recall that Equation 12.9 was a boundary condition derived earlier.

$$C_0 \geq \text{MAX } [0,\ S_0 - Xe^{-r_F T}]. \tag{12.9}$$
$$C = S\,N(d_1) - Xe^{-r_F T}N(d_2). \tag{12.14}$$

The two equations are very similar. The main difference is that in Equation 12.14, the stock price is multiplied by $N(d_1)$ and the discounted exercise price is multiplied by $N(d_2)$. Figure 12.11 shows the call price as a function of the stock price. As predicted earlier, the call value increases with the stock price until, when the call is deep in-the-money (that is, S is much greater than X), the call price is nearly equal to the stock price minus the discounted exercise price.

An intuitive explanation for $N(d_1)$ is provided by taking the partial derivative of the call price (Equation 12.14) with respect to the stock price.[16]

---

[16]Equation 12.15 is the exact solution even though the derivative is complicated by the fact that $N(d_1)$ is a function of S. The curious reader is referred to Galai and Masulis [1976] for the math.

FIGURE 12.11   The Call Pricing Function

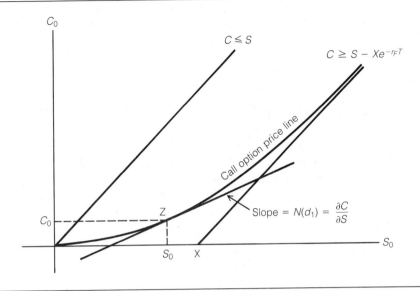

$$\frac{\delta C}{\delta S} = N(d_1) \qquad\qquad (12.15)$$

Thus, $N(d_1)$ is equal to the change in the call price with respect to a change in the stock price. It is the slope of a line drawn tangent to the call function (for example at Point Z) in Figure 12.11.

Given a stock price, S_0, we can construct a riskless hedge, long in stock and short in calls. Here we define the hedge ratio (h) as the ratio of the number of stock shares bought divided by the number of calls sold. Defining the hedge ratio in this way has properties directly related to terms in the Black-Scholes valuation formula for options. As defined here, h will always be one or less — like a probability measure that must lie between 0 and 1.0 for a call option and between 0 and -1.0 for a put option. The value of the hedge portfolio, V_h, is

$$V_h = hS - C,$$

whose change per unit of time is

$$\frac{dV_h}{dt} = h\frac{dS}{dt} - \frac{dC}{dt} = 0. \qquad\qquad (12.16)$$

Since the change in V_h for a small increment in time is zero, we can solve for h.

$$h\frac{dS}{dt} = \frac{dC}{dt} \text{ or } h = \frac{dC}{dS} = N(d_1)$$

Thus the hedge ratio, h, has the following properties:

1. It measures the change in the price of a call in response to a change in the price of the underlying security.
2. It is the ratio of the number of units of the underlying security to the number of calls.
3. It is equal to $N(d_1)$ in Black-Scholes.
4. It has the properties of a probability measure.
5. It measures the exposure of the price of the call to price changes in the underlying asset, generally called the *delta* risk of the call (or put).

To illustrate, the value of a deep out-of-the-money option will change only slightly for small variations in the price of the underlying assets since the probability that the option will be exercised is low — its delta measure will be very close to zero.

If we use the Digital Equipment April 45's to hedge against 100 shares of Digital Equipment common stock, then we would have to write 148.366 options. We earlier computed the value of $N(d_1)$ to be .67401. Therefore,

$$h = \frac{100.00}{148.366} = .67401 = N(d_1),$$

and we should write 148.37 call options in order to hedge against 100 shares.

It is important to bear in mind that this type of hedge is riskless only for small changes in the stock price. The hedge ratio must be adjusted whenever the stock price changes. For example, in Figure 12.11, if the stock price falls below S_0, then the slope of a line tangent to the call function decreases in value, that is, $N(d_1)$ decreases. And if $N(d_1)$ decreases, then the hedge ratio, which is $N(d_1)$, will decrease. Hence, it takes more out-of-the-money call options to hedge against one share of stock than in-the-money options because dC/dS is smaller.

$N(d_2)$, in Equation 12.14, also has an intuitive explanation, although it is difficult to show the logic without a much longer discourse on the binomial option pricing formula. We can interpret $N(d_2)$ as the probability that the option will finish in-the-money when it matures. Thus, for our Digital Equipment example, when the stock price is $46.75, the exercise price is $45.00, and 199 days are left until the option matures, we see that the probability of finishing in-the-money is $N(d_2) = .59661$.

APPLICATIONS OF THE OPM TO CORPORATE FINANCE

So far, the major application of the OPM model in this chapter has been an introduction to how option prices are predicted by the OPM. Now, we turn our focus to the financial management of a levered firm. Black and Scholes [1973] were the first to provide the insight that the equity in a firm which has debt in its capital structure (a levered firm) is really a call option on the value of the firm. Later articles by Galai and Masulis [1976], Myers [1977], Merton [1974], Shastri [1981], and others have further developed the implications of option pricing theory for corporate finance. Also, the option model has been applied to the pricing of convertible debt and warrants by Ingersoll [1977].

Equity as a Call Option

In order to keep the discussion as simple as possible, assume that the firm has only two sources of capital: equity and *risky* debt. The debt is a pure discount bond, which pays no coupons, has a face value D, and matures T years from now. It is secured by the assets of the firm, but bondholders may not force the firm into bankruptcy until the maturity date of the bond. In spite of these simplistic assumptions we can use the OPM to extend our understanding of corporate finance.

We saw, from Equation 12.4 (which is rewritten below), that any risky portfolio can be constructed from four basic building blocks.

$$S + P = B + C \qquad (12.4)$$

Earlier in the chapter, the underlying risky asset was a share of stock, S. Now it is the value of the firm, V. The equity in a levered firm, S, is really a call option on the value of the firm. If, on the maturity date, the value of the firm, V, exceeds the face value of the bonds, D, the shareholders will exercise their call option by paying off the bonds and keeping the excess. On the other hand, if the value of the firm is less than the face value of the bonds, the shareholders will default on the debt by failing to exercise their option. Therefore, at maturity, the shareholders' wealth, S, is

$$S = \text{MAX } [0, V - D]. \qquad (12.17)$$

If we substitute V for S and S for C in Equation 12.4, we have

$$V = (B - P) + S. \qquad (12.18)$$

Equation 12.18 tells us that the value of a risky asset, the levered firm, can be partitioned into two parts. The equity position, S, is a call option, and the risky debt position $(B - P)$, is equivalent to the present value of default-free debt, B, minus the value of a European put option, P. At maturity, the bondholders receive

$$B - P = \text{MIN } [V,D]. \qquad (12.19)$$

Table 12.5 shows how the payoffs to equity and risky debt add up to equal the value of the firm at maturity.[17] The table also illustrates the bondholders' position. If the firm is successful, that is, if $V > D$, the bondholders receive the face value of the riskless bond, D, and the put option is worthless. If the firm is bankrupt, they still receive the face value of the riskless bond, but a put option has, in effect, been exercised against them because they lose the difference between the face value of the riskless debt, D, and the market value of the firm, V. They gain D but lose $(D - V)$; therefore, their net position is V, the market value of the firm in bankruptcy.

Once we see that the market value of a levered firm is easily partitioned into equity and risky debt positions which can be formulated in an option-pricing framework, then we can use our understanding of the OPM to analyze such corporate finance decisions as risky investments, dividend policy, spinoffs, equity repurchases, subordinated debt, and mergers.

---

[17]We are implicitly assuming that there are no taxes and that there are no bankruptcy costs paid to third parties (for example, lawyers and the courts). The entire value of the firm at maturity goes to bondholders and shareholders.

TABLE 12.5   Stakeholders' Payoffs at Maturity

	Payoffs at Maturity	
	If $V \leq D$	If $V > D$
Shareholders' position: call option, S	0	$V - D$
Bondholders' position: risk-free bond, B put option, P	D $-(D - V)$	D 0
Total for bondholders	V	D
Sum of shareholders' and bondholders' positions	$0 + V = V$	$V - D + D = V$

The OPM and Investment Decisions

One of the surprising implications of considering equity in a levered firm as a call option is that investments which increase the idiosyncratic, or diversifiable, risk of a firm without changing its expected return will benefit shareholders at the expense of bondholders even though the value of the firm is unaffected. Because idiosyncratic risk is independent of the market portfolio, an increase in idiosyncratic risk will increase the variance of return for the firm without changing the firm's beta or its expected rate of return. Therefore, the value of the firm will not change. However, there will be a redistribution of wealth to shareholders away from bondholders. The reason is that higher variance will increase the value of the call option held by shareholders. Simultaneously, it will increase the value of the put written by bondholders so that their net position, $B - P$, will fall in value.

We can illustrate this result with an example. Assume the following: The current value of the firm, V, is \$3 million; the face value of debt, D, is \$1 million; and the debt will mature in $T = 4$ years. The variance of returns on the value of the firm, σ^2, is .01, and the riskless rate, r_F, is 5 percent. We can use the OPM, Equation 12.14, to calculate the value of the equity position, S_0. Substituting S for C, D for X, and V for S in Equation 12.14, we have

$$S = V N(d_1) - De^{-r_F T} N(d_2)$$

$$d_1 = \frac{ln(V/D) + r_F T}{\sigma \sqrt{T}} + \frac{1}{2} \sigma \sqrt{T}$$

$$d_2 = d_1 - \sigma \sqrt{T}.$$

First, solving for d_1 and $N(d_1)$, we have

$$d_1 = \frac{ln(3,000,000/1,000,000) + .05(4)}{.1\sqrt{4}} + .5(.1)\sqrt{4}$$

$$= 6.593,$$

and from Appendix D,

$$N(d_1) \cong 1.$$

The solution for d_2 is

$$d_2 = 6.593 - .1\sqrt{4} = 6.393,$$

and from Appendix D,

$$N(d_2) \cong 1.$$

Second, we calculate the value of the common stock,

$$S = \$3,000,000(1) - \$1,000,000e^{-.05(4)}(1)$$
$$= \$3,000,000 - \$818,731 = \$2,181,269.$$

The market value of debt is

$$(B - P) = V - S = \$3,000,000 - \$2,181,269 = \$818,731.$$

It is interesting to note that since $N(d_2) \cong 1$, the probability that the call option (that is, the equity position) will finish in-the-money is nearly 100 percent. This means that there is virtually no probability of default on the bond.[18]

Next, assume that the firm changes the idiosyncratic risk in its investment program so that the firm's variance rises from .01 to .16. Recalculating the market value of equity, we obtain

$$d_1 = \frac{ln(3/1) + .05(4)}{.4\sqrt{4}} + .5(.4)\sqrt{4} = 2.0233,$$

and

$$N(d_1) = .9785.$$

Also,

$$d_2 = 1.2233,$$

and

$$N(d_2) = .8894.$$

The revised market value of equity is

$$S = \$3,000,000(.9785) - \$1,000,000e^{-.05(4)}(.8894)$$
$$= \$2,935,500 - \$728,178 = \$2,207,322,$$

and the market value of debt becomes

$$(B - P) = V - S = \$3,000,000 - \$2,207,322$$
$$= \$792,678.$$

---

[18]In fact, $818,731 is just the present value of a risk-free pure discount bond which pays a face value of $1 million four years hence.

$$B_0 = De^{-r_F T}$$
$$= \$1,000,000e^{-.05(4)} = \$818,731.$$

In this case, $B - P = B$. The market value of the put is zero.

The increased risk of the investment program has raised the market value of equity by ($2,207,322 − $2,181,269 = $26,053). The market value of risky debt has fallen by an equal amount. The debt moves from being relatively default free [where $1 - N(d_2) = 0$] to an 11.06 percent chance of default [that is, $1 - N(d_2) = .1106$].

We can calculate the promised yield to maturity, k_b, that bondholders would require on the riskier debt by solving for the discount rate which equates the payoff four years hence with the current market value of the risky debt, $\tilde{B}_0$, which has been determined to be $792,678.[19]

$$\tilde{B}_0 = De^{-k_bT} \tag{12.20}$$

$$\$792,678 = \$1,000,000e^{-k_bT}$$

$$\frac{\$792,678}{\$1,000,000} = e^{-k_b(4)}$$

$$ln(.792678) = -k_b(4)$$

$$-.23234 = -4k_b$$

$$k_b = .05808.$$

In order to compensate them for their increased default risk, the bondholders would require a 5.808 percent yield to maturity instead of the 5 percent they require on a default-free bond.

Because increasing the riskiness of the firm's production operations increases the value of equity and decreases the value of debt, there is an inherent divergence of interests between shareholders and creditors of the firm. Since the shareholders possess voting control of the firm, they may take actions that may be adverse to the interests of the creditors. It is for this reason that various protective covenants are written into the bond indentures of most debt instruments. While actual restrictions on investment policy are relatively uncommon, one often finds restrictions on dividend policy, subordinated debt, and merger activity.

TABLE 12.6   The Promised Yield to Maturity on Risky Debt

Face Value of Debt	Firm Value	D/V	Market Value of Debt	Equity	B/V	Yield to Maturity = k_b
$ 0	$3,000,000	0	$ 0	$3,000,000	0	5.00%
500,000	3,000,000	.167	408,547	2,591,453	.136	5.05
1,000,000	3,000,000	.333	814,350	2,185,650	.271	5.13
1,500,000	3,000,000	.500	1,195,409	1,804,591	.398	5.67
2,000,000	3,000,000	.667	1,531,108	1,468,892	.510	6.68
2,500,000	3,000,000	.833	1,815,595	1,184,405	.605	8.00
3,000,000	3,000,000	1.000	2,054,483	945,517	.685	9.47

---

[19]We use the symbol tilde (˜) to differentiate between risky debt, $\tilde{B}$, and riskless debt, B.

FIGURE 12.12   The Relationship between the Yield to Maturity on
Risky Debt and Financial Leverage

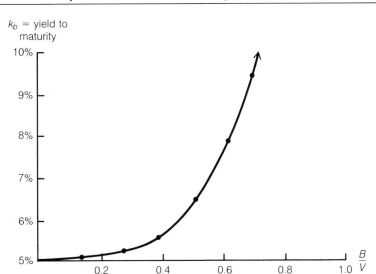

The Cost of Risky Debt

We can use the OPM to show the relationship between the yield to maturity, which bondholders will require for holding risky debt, and the amount of financial leverage employed by the firm. Using the same set of numbers as before, and assuming that the variance of returns on the value of the firm, σ^2, is .09, we can solve the OPM (repeatedly) for the market value of debt and equity implied by different ratios of the face value of debt to total assets. Then we can use Equation 12.20 to compute the required yield to maturity on the risky debt.[20] The results are shown in Table 12.6 and Figure 12.12. The yield to maturity required by bondholders who invest in risky debt rises quickly with financial leverage. We shall bear this result in mind, because later in the text (Chapter 15), we examine the cost of capital.

Mergers and Spinoffs

A conglomerate merger is defined as one where there is no economic synergy of any kind — no economies of scale; no increase in managerial effectiveness; no complementarities between research, marketing, and production; no tax advantages; and so on. In a pure conglomerate merger, the market value of the combined entities is the same as the

---

[20]Recall, from Chapter 6, that the yield to maturity is really the "promised" yield to maturity because it is the yield which discounts the face value of the bond rather than its expected value.

sum of their separate values. Thus, if two firms, A and B, propose to merge, the value of the merged firm, V_{AB} will be

$$V_{AB} = V_A + V_B.$$

No new value is created by a conglomerate merger as we have chosen to define it.

There will, however, be a portfolio diversification effect if the cash flows of the two levered firms are less than perfectly correlated. Because the cash flows of the two firms tend to offset each other, the effect of the merger will be to decrease the probability of bankruptcy. This benefits debtholders, and the market value of debt will rise due to lower risk. Conversely, shareholders' wealth will decline because they hold a call option on the merged firm, which has a lower variance.

The redistribution of wealth from shareholders to debtholders in a conglomerate merger occurs because *a call option written on a portfolio of assets is worth less than a portfolio of call options* (as long as the assets are less than perfectly correlated).

Because the option pricing approach to mergers and acquisitions is thoroughly discussed in Chapter 27, we shall not provide any numerical examples here. However, it is worth mentioning a few related issues in passing. For example, if conglomerate mergers can result in a decrease in shareholders' wealth, why do they take place at all? One possible explanation is that the greater debt capacity created in a conglomerate merger is utilized immediately. Greater financial leverage may raise the value of equity back to its premerger level by providing an additional tax shield due to increased interest payments.

It is often implicitly assumed that merging firms have equal return variances, equal amounts of debt outstanding, and that the debt issues of both firms have the same maturity. If these assumptions are relaxed, it is possible for a merger to be detrimental to the bondholders of one of the firms.[21] For example, suppose both firms have the same amount of debt outstanding, but the debt of Firm A matures in one year while the debt of Firm B matures in four years. These circumstances dictate that upon merger, the bonds of Firm B become subordinate to those of Firm A; hence, Firm B bonds will decrease in value and Firm A bonds will appreciate.[22] If both debt issues have the same maturity but Firm A has a larger amount of debt than Firm B, then A's bondholders experience a decrease in risk after the merger because they have equal claim on the combined assets of both firms. Firm A's debt will benefit while B's debt becomes riskier and declines in value. Finally, even though both debt issues may have the same size and maturity, it is possible for debtholders in Firm A to gain relative to those in Firm B if Firm A has a greater variance. After the merger, Firm A's bondholders are exposed to much less risk and Firm B's bondholders may even experience an increase in risk if Firm A had a high variance.

Debtholders can never be sure what effect a merger might have on their claim on the assets of the firm. They have no vote in whether a merger is consummated. And they have no way to be compensated for a loss in wealth after a merger takes place. Consequently,

---

[21]For a complete exposition of the effects of a conglomerate merger on all parties, see Shastri [1982].

[22]It is more accurate to say that Firm B's bonds decrease in value *relative* to Firm A's bonds. Because of the portfolio variance effect, which was discussed earlier, both bonds may increase in value, but Firm B's bonds will not increase as much as Firm A's bonds and may even decline in value.

one often finds bond indenture provisions that restrict merger in one way or another.[23] Smith and Warner [1979] examined a random sample of 87 public issues of debt registered with the Securities and Exchange Commission between January 1974 and December 1975. Merger activity was restricted by covenants in 39.1 percent of the bonds.

Spinoffs are the opposite of mergers. When a firm spins off a division, the result is a newly created, independent firm. If a spinoff divides a large firm into two smaller firms of equal size and with equal debt amounts and maturities, then the effect (in the absence of any negative synergies) should be to benefit shareholders at the expense of debtholders. Of course, the spinoff may not result in firms with equal size and financial structure. In the extreme, it is possible for shareholders to "strip" the parent firm by spinning off valuable assets paid in the form of shares in the spinoff firm. The parent firm becomes a shell and keeps all of the debt. In this way, shareholders can expropriate wealth from bondholders (but not without a lawsuit). Spinoffs of this type are analytically similar to dividend payments.

EMPIRICAL EVIDENCE ON THE OPM

It is important to understand that there are many different option pricing models. The Black-Scholes model was the first, but there are others better tailored to specific situations. For example, if the equity in a levered firm is a call option on the value of the firm's assets, then a CBOE call option written on the equity is really an option on an option. The model that solves this problem was derived by Geske [1977, 1979a]. He shows that a CBOE call written on a levered firm depends on the firm's financial leverage and the time to maturity of the firm's debt as well as the five parameters found in the Black-Scholes model (that is, the value of the underlying asset, the exercise price, the variance of return on the underlying asset, the time to maturity for the option, and the risk-free rate). Also, the Black-Scholes model makes no provision for dividend payments. This problem was solved by Roll [1977] and Geske [1978,1979b].

There have been many empirical tests of the Option Pricing Model since its publication in 1973. Studies which have used different versions of the Option Pricing Model to try to find economically exploitable biases have been unsuccessful in doing so when transactions costs were deducted from trading rule profits. From this, one can conclude that the Option Pricing Models fit observed prices well in an economic sense. Also, the results are consistent with semi-strong-form market efficiency (which is described in Chapter 4).

On the other hand, some studies have discovered statistically significant biases in the Black-Scholes model. Black and Scholes [1972] were the first to report that their model underpriced options on low-variance stocks and overpriced options on high-variance stocks. Black later [1975] reported that the model also underpriced out-of-the-money options and near-maturity options, while it overpriced in-the-money options. MacBeth

---

[23]For more on bond covenants, see the American Bar Association, *Commentaries on Model Debenture Indenture Provisions* [1971].

and Merville [1979] and Rubinstein [1981] found similar results but noted that the bias for in- and out-of-the-money options reversed itself around 1977.

The biases with respect to the time to maturity and the exercise price (that is, in- or out-of-the-money) have been explained by Whaley [1982] and Sterk [1982], who used the dividend-adjusted model of Roll [1977] and Geske [1979b]. The volatility bias has been explained by Geske and Roll [1984b], who use a superior variance estimator (called the ''Stein shrinker''). Of course, much work remains to be done before we can be sure which Option Pricing Model provides the best fit to the data.

THE RELATIONSHIP BETWEEN THE OPM AND THE CAPM

At first, it is easy to become confused when trying to compare the Option Pricing Model (OPM) with the Capital Asset Pricing Model (CAPM). The Option Pricing Model implies that option prices increase as the variance of the underlying asset increases. This does not mean that investors prefer greater risk. It only means that an option is a contingent claim on an underlying asset. To price the underlying asset, we need to use such equilibrium models as the CAPM or the APT (Arbitrage Pricing Theory). The OPM prices contingent claims while the CAPM prices the underlying assets. The two models are perfectly consistent with each other.

Figure 12.13 helps to give an intuitive feel for the relationship between the CAPM and the OPM. The horizontal axis represents the (lognormal) distribution of stock prices at the maturity of a European option. The CAPM exploits the covariance between the stock and the market portfolio to estimate the stock's systematic risk and its beta and to determine its equilibrium return. Hence, *the CAPM uses the entire distribution* in order to determine the equilibrium expected return on the stock. *The OPM, on the other hand, uses only a portion of the distribution.* Options are contingent claims. For example, a European

FIGURE 12.13   Lognormal Distribution of Stock Values

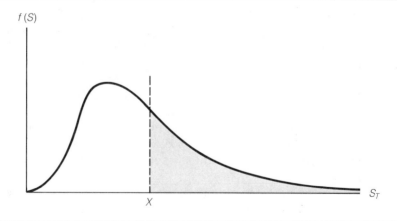

call option with an exercise price of X, pays off only when $S_T \geq X$. Hence, as illustrated in Figure 12.13, the OPM "prices" only the shaded region of the stock price distribution, the area to the right of the exercise price, X.

The relationship between the CAPM beta of a stock, β_S, and the beta of a European call option written on that stock, β_C, is given in Equation 12.21.

$$\beta_C = N(d_1) \frac{S}{C} \beta_S \qquad \qquad (12.21)$$

The beta of the call is a function of the common stock beta, β_S, the ratio of the stock price to the call price, S/C, and the inverse of the hedge ratio, $N(d_1)$. While common stock betas are relatively stationary through time, option betas change rapidly. For example, an out-of-the-money call option will have a high beta and a high expected return. If the stock price rises, the option beta will rapidly fall and so too will its expected return.

The partial derivatives of call option betas are[24]

$$\frac{\delta\beta_C}{\delta S} < 0, \ \frac{\delta\beta_C}{\delta X} > 0, \ \frac{\delta\beta_C}{\delta r_F} < 0, \ \frac{\delta\beta_C}{\delta\sigma^2} < 0, \ \frac{\delta\beta_C}{\delta T} < 0.$$

The call becomes less risky if the stock price goes up, if the riskless rate increases, if the variance of the underlying asset increases, or if the option has greater time to maturity. The option's risk rises when the exercise price rises, all other things being held constant.

The equilibrium rate of return, $E(r_C)$, which is expected on a call option can be found by using β_C and the Capital Asset Pricing Model.

$$E(r_C) = r_F + [E(r_M) - r_F]\beta_C$$

One of the most interesting things about a call option is that its systematic risk (and its expected rate of return) changes every day simply because it is closer to maturity.

SUMMARY

The Option Pricing Model is an extremely useful tool because so many financial assets are options. A partial list includes stocks, risky bonds, warrants, convertible debt, call options, and put options. We have discussed two types of option pricing formulae: the binomial model and the Black-Scholes model. There are, of course, many more. We have also shown that literally any risky asset can be replicated by some combination of the four basic building blocks of finance theory: stocks, riskless bonds, call options, and put options. For example, a risky bond can be thought of as a combination of a pure discount riskless bond and a put option.

The Option Pricing Model is perfectly consistent with the equilibrium theories of asset pricing which were discussed in Chapter 11, the Capital Asset Pricing Model, and the Arbitrage Pricing Theory. Empirical evidence indicates that the Black-Scholes OPM explains actual market prices of options so well that it is impossible to make an economic

---

[24]See Galai and Masulis [1976] for proof.

profit by trying to arbitrage when the model price is different from the observed market price. The statistically significant biases in the Black-Scholes model can be explained if one uses slightly more complicated option pricing models which were not discussed here.

In sum, the Option Pricing Model is a powerful and useful tool which provides great insight into an enormous variety of financial assets.

QUESTIONS

12.1 What are the five factors which affect the value of a call option? Describe how an increase in each one will affect the call option's price.

12.2 What is put-call parity? Why is it important?

12.3 Why will an American call option on a nondividend-paying stock never be exercised before its maturity date?

12.4 Why is it true that investors' subjective estimates of the probability of up or down movements in the value of a common stock are irrelevant for pricing a call option on that stock?

12.5 Why is the equity in a levered firm considered to be a call option on the value of the firm's assets?

12.6 Why is risky debt in a levered firm considered to be a combination of a risk-free bond and a put option on the value of the firm's assets?

12.7 How is the market value of equity affected by a conglomerate merger between two firms of equal size and identical financial leverage?

12.8 How is the market value of equity in a levered firm affected if the shareholders decide to take on riskier projects which increase the variance of the firm's assets? How is the market value of debt affected?

12.9 What is the relationship between the beta of a call option and the beta of the common stock on which it is written? What happens to the beta of the call option if the stock price goes up? What happens to the beta of the call option as it gets closer to its expiration date?

12.10 After a call contract is created, the outcome must be a zero-sum game; that is, the call writer may win or lose N, but the call buyer will experience an opposite return of exactly N, and, consequently, their aggregate payoff is zero. Given this fact, can you explain how they both could enter into the contract anticipating a positive return?

PROBLEMS

12.1 A straddle is a combination of a put and a call option in the same contract where both options are written on the same stock and where both have the same exercise price and maturity date. Graph the payoffs at maturity for a straddle.

12.2 Show graphically how one can use a riskless bond and a put and a call in order to duplicate the payoffs on a share of stock.

12.3 Using the simple one-period binomial OPM, determine the value of a call option which has an exercise price of $30, given that the stock price is $28, that $u = 1.4$, that $d = .8$, and that $r_F = 10\%$.

12.4 Given that the price of a nondividend-paying stock is $25, the instantaneous variance on the stock is 64 percent, and the risk-free rate is 20 percent, what is the value of a call option which has an exercise price of $23 and 160 days to maturity?

12.5 Using the facts for Problem 12.4, how many call options must you write (that is, sell short) in order to create a riskless hedge, given that you own 100 shares of stock?

12.6 Estimate the instantaneous variance for a common stock, given the following facts: a call written on the stock sells for $3.50, the stock price is $50.00, the call has an exercise price of $51.00 and has 120 days to maturity, and the risk-free rate is 12 percent.

12.7 The Monarch Company is currently valued at $500,000. Seventy percent of current value is the face value of pure discount debt, all of which will mature in four years. The variance of percentage returns is 56.25 percent. The risk-free rate is 10 percent.
  a. Determine the market value of the equity.
  b. Determine the market value of the debt.
  c. What is the yield to maturity on the debt?

12.8 Itex Distributing Company is currently valued at $4 million. Twenty percent of current value is the face value of pure discount debt, all of which matures in four years. The variance of percentage returns is 42.25 percent. The risk-free rate is 10 percent.
  a. Determine the value of the equity.
  b. Determine the value of the debt.
  c. What is the yield to maturity on the debt?

12.9 Stacy Johnston plans to invest in the newly issued call option of the Remington Corporation. The call option has an exercise price of $50 and a maturity date three months from now. The stock price is $32, the instantaneous variance of the stock price is 0.64, and the risk-free rate is 8 percent. Remington Corporation pays no dividends. What is the value of the call option?

12.10 The Perry Company has a market value of $25 million and outstanding debt of $16 million, which matures in nine years. The variance of the firm's rate of return is 0.49. The firm pays no cash dividends and pays out the interest at maturity only. If the rate of inflation is expected to rise by 4 percent (thus raising the riskless nominal interest rate from 6 percent to 10 percent), use what you know about the OPM to determine which class of Perry's security holders benefits from the rise in r_F. (No calculations are necessary.)

12.11 The Lansing Corporation has $30 million of pure discount debt, which will mature in one year. In the market, the firm has a current value of $100 million. The total risk of Lansing's assets is $\sigma = 1.44$. The expected market rate of return is 15 percent. The riskless rate is 10 percent. The beta of Lansing's equity is 1.4, and the beta of its debt is 0.3.
  a. Determine the market value of the firm's debt and equity.
  b. Determine the cost of debt and equity capital (assuming a world without taxes).
  c. If nothing else changes, what will the beta of Lansing's equity be six months from now?

12.12 The Sandvik Company and the Weller Corporation have the same market value of $75 million. Both firms have the following identical parameters:

$$D_S = D_W = \$25 \text{ million} \qquad \text{Face value of debt}$$
$$T_S = T_W = 4 \text{ years} \qquad \text{Maturity of debt}$$
$$\sigma_S = \sigma_W = 0.36 \qquad \text{Instantaneous standard deviation}$$
$$r_F = 0.11 \qquad \text{Risk-free rate.}$$

a. What is the initial market value of debt and equity for Sandvik and Weller?

b. The correlation between the two firms' cash flows is 0.5. If the two firms merge, the surviving firm will be worth $150 million. What will the market value of debt and equity in the merged firm be? If there were no other merger effects, would shareholders agree to the merger?

12.13 Suppose a firm has three classes of securities: senior debt, subordinated debt, and equity. Both debt issues are pure discount debt which mature at the same time, and the common stock pays no dividends. Use the OPM to write equations for the values of each of the three classes of securities. Use the following notation:

V = market value of the firm

S = market value of the stock

B_S = market value of the senior debt with face value D_S

B_J = market value of the junior (subordinated) debt which has face value D_J.

12.14 Suppose the government passes a usury law which prohibits lending at more than 8 percent interest, but normal market rates are much higher due to inflation. You have a customer who is willing to borrow at a 25 percent rate and can put up his business, which has been appraised at $100,000, for collateral. Rather than refusing to lend, you decide to create a ten-year contract with the following terms. You hold title to the business assets and receive the right to sell back the business for $X at the end of ten years. If you decide to sell, the borrower *must* buy. In return, you lend $80,000 in cash (the amount he wants to borrow), and you give the borrower the right to buy the store from you for $X at the end of ten years. What value must $X be in order to provide you with a riskless 25 percent annual rate of return?

12.15 *(Use the computer diskette, File name: 12OPTION, Options on Risky Assets.)*

a. Given the following key input parameter values for the Black-Scholes option pricing model, what would be the value of the call?

S (stock price)   = $25 I (instantaneous variance) = 0.09

X (exercise price) = $20 r_F (risk-free rate)   =   6%

T (time in years) =   4

(1) How does the value of the call change as you increase the stock price in increments of $5 to $50?

(2) If the premium on the call is defined as the value of the call minus the quantity $(S - X)$, what happens to the size of the premium as the stock price goes from $25 to $50, while the exercise price remains at $20?

(3) How would a graph of the call price look in relation to a line which simply represents $S - X$? View this graphically. What happens to the size of the distance between the call price line and the $(S - X)$ line?

b. Answer the same questions for a call whose maturity is 9 years rather than 4 years.

c. Going back to the original conditions in Part (a), does the value of the call increase or decrease as each of the key input parameters increases? For example, successively increase each of the variables by 50 percent and see whether the call price increases or decreases.

d. Go back to the original conditions in part (a) and think of S as being the market value of the firm of $25 million, and X as the face value of the debt at $20 million. The T in this case is interpreted as years to maturity of the debt. Now what corresponds to the value of the call is the market value of equity. What is the market value of equity under the original conditions? Also, what is the market value of the debt, as compared with its face value?

e. Assume that one firm is engaged in a merger with a firm of exactly equal size. Because the cash flow streams of the two firms are not perfectly correlated, the variance of the combined cash flow is reduced. What effect would this have on the value of the equity of the combined firm? To test this, go back to the initial conditions, double the value of the firm, double the face value of the debt, hold everything else the same, and decrease the variance to .06. Then, is the equity value more or less than doubled?

f. Continue to explore option pricing by changing any assumptions used in the Black-Scholes model.

SELECTED REFERENCES

Ball, Clifford A., and Torous, Walter N., "The Maximum Likelihood Estimation of Security Price Volatility: Theory, Evidence, and Application to Option Pricing," *Journal of Business,* 57 (January 1984), pp. 97–112.

Beckers, S., "The Constant Elasticity of Variance Model and Its Implications for Option Pricing," *Journal of Finance,* 35 (June 1980), pp. 661–673.

Black, Fisher, "The Pricing of Commodity Contracts," *Journal of Financial Economics,* 3 (January-March 1976), pp. 167–179.

———, "Fact and Fantasy in the Use of Options," *Financial Analysts Journal,* (July-August 1975), pp. 61–72.

———, and M. Scholes, "The Pricing of Options and Corporate Liabilities," *Journal of Political Economy,* 81 (May-June 1973), pp. 637–654.

Black, Fisher, and Scholes, Myron, "The Valuation of Option Contracts and a Test of Market Efficiency," *Journal of Finance,* (May 1972), pp. 399–418.

Bookstaber, Richard M., "Observed Option Mispricing and the Nonsimultaneity of Stock and Option Quotations," *Journal of Business,* 54 (January 1981), pp. 141–155.

Chiras, Donald P., and Manaster, Steven, "The Information Content of Option Prices and a Test of Market Efficiency," *Journal of Financial Economics,* 6 (June-September 1978), pp. 213–234.

Courtadon, Georges, "The Pricing of Options on Default-Free Bonds," *Journal of Financial and Quantitative Analysis,* 17 (March 1982), pp. 75–100.

Cox, John C., and Ross, Stephen A., "The Valuation of Options for Alternative Stochastic

Processes," *Journal of Financial Economics,* 3 (January-March 1976), pp. 145–166.

————; and Rubinstein, Mark, "Option Pricing: A Simplified Approach," *Journal of Financial Economics,* 7 (September 1979), pp. 229–263.

Emanuel, David D., and MacBeth, James D., "Further Results on the Constant Elasticity of Variance Call Option Pricing Model," *Journal of Financial and Quantitative Analysis,* 17 (November 1982), pp. 533–554.

Galai, Dan, "Tests of Market Efficiency of the Chicago Board Options Exchange," *Journal of Business,* 50 (April 1977), pp. 167–197.

————, and Masulis, R. W., "The Option Pricing Model and the Risk Factor of Stock," *Journal of Financial Economics,* 3 (January-March 1976), pp. 53–82.

Geske, Robert, "The Valuation of Compound Options," *Journal of Financial Economics,* 7 (March 1979a), pp. 63–81.

————, "A Note on the Analytical Valuation Formula for Unprotected American Call Options on Stocks with Known Dividends," *Journal of Financial Economics,* (December 1979b), pp. 375–380.

————, "The Pricing of Options with Stochastic Dividend Yield," *Journal of Finance,* 33 (May 1978), pp. 617–625.

————, "The Valuation of Corporate Liabilities as Compound Options," *Journal of Financial and Quantitative Analysis,* 12 (November 1977), pp. 541–552.

————, and Roll, R., "On Valuing American Call Options with the Black-Scholes European Formula," *Journal of Finance,* (June 1984a), pp. 443–455.

————, "Isolating the Observed Biases in American Call Option Pricing: An Alternative Variance Estimator," Working Paper #4-84, Graduate School of Management, UCLA, February 1984b.

Ingersoll, Jonathan E., Jr., "A Contingent-Claims Valuation of Convertible Securities," *Journal of Financial Economics,* 4 (May 1977), pp. 289–322.

————, "A Theoretical and Empirical Investigation of the Dual Purpose Funds: An Application of Contingent-Claims Analysis," *Journal*

of *Financial Economics,* 3 (January-March 1976), pp. 83–124.

Johnson, H. E., "An Analytic Approximation for the American Put Price," *Journal of Financial and Quantitative Analysis,* 18 (March 1983), pp. 141–148.

Latane, Henry A., and Rendleman, Richard J., Jr., "Standard Deviations of Stock Price Ratios Implied in Option Prices," *Journal of Finance,* 31 (May 1976), pp. 369–381.

MacBeth, James D., and Merville, Larry J., "Tests of the Black-Scholes and Cox Call Option Valuation Models," *Journal of Finance,* (May 1980), pp. 285–300.

————, "An Empirical Examination of the Black-Scholes Call Option Pricing Model," *Journal of Finance,* 34 (December 1979), pp. 1173–1186.

Margrabe, William, "The Value of an Option to Exchange One Asset for Another," *Journal of Finance,* 33 (March 1978), pp. 177–198.

Merton, Robert C., "On the Pricing of Corporate Debt: The Risk Structure of Interest Rates," *Journal of Finance,* 29 (May 1974), pp. 449–470.

————, "The Theory of Rational Option Pricing," *Bell Journal of Economics and Management Science,* 4 (Spring 1973), pp. 141–183.

Myers, S., "Determinants of Corporate Borrowing," *Journal of Financial Economics,* (November 1977), pp. 147–175.

Parkinson, M., "Option Pricing: The American Put," *Journal of Business,* (January 1977), pp. 21–36.

Phillips, Susan M., and Smith, Clifford W., Jr., "Trading Cost for Listed Options: The Implications for Market Efficiency," *Journal of Financial Economics,* 8 (June 1980), pp. 179–201.

Rendleman, Richard J., Jr., and Bartter, Brit J., "Two-State Option Pricing," *Journal of Finance,* 34 (December 1979), pp. 1093–1110.

Roll, Richard, "An Analytic Valuation Formula for Unprotected American Call Options on Stocks with Known Dividends," *Journal of Financial Economics,* 5 (November 1977), pp. 251–258.

Rubinstein, Mark, "Displaced Diffusion Option Pricing," *Journal of Finance,* 38 (March 1983), pp. 213–217.

———, "Nonparametric Tests of Alternative Option Pricing Models," Working Paper # 117, University of California at Berkeley, 1981.

———, "The Valuation of Uncertain Income Streams and the Pricing of Options," *Bell Journal of Economics and Management Science,* 7 (Autumn 1976), pp. 407–425.

Scholes, Myron, "Taxes and the Pricing of Options," *Journal of Finance,* 31 (May 1976), pp. 319–322.

Shastri, K., "Valuing Corporate Securities: Some Effects of Mergers by Exchange Offers," University of Pittsburgh, WP-517, revised January 1982.

———, "Two Essays Concerning the Effects of Firm Investment/Financing Decisions on Security Values: An Option Pricing Approach," unpublished Ph.D. thesis, UCLA, 1981.

Smith, C., Jr., "Option Pricing: A Review," *Journal of Financial Economics,* (January-March 1976), pp. 1–51.

———, and Warner, J. B., "On Financial Contracting: An Analysis of Bond Covenants," *Journal of Financial Economics,* (June 1979), pp. 117–161.

Sterk, W., "Comparative Performance of the Black-Scholes and the Roll-Geske-Whaley Option Pricing Models," *Journal of Financial and Quantitative Analysis,* (September 1983), pp. 345–354.

———, "Tests of Two Models for Valuing Call Options on Stocks with Dividends," *Journal of Finance,* 37 (December 1982), pp. 1229–1237.

Stoll, Hans R., "The Relationship Between Put and Call Option Prices," *Journal of Finance,* (December 1969), pp. 802–824.

Whaley, R., "Valuation of American Call Options on Dividend-Paying Stocks: Empirical Tests," *Journal of Financial Economics,* 10 (March 1982), pp. 29–58.

———, "On the Valuation of American Call Options on Stocks with Known Dividends," *Journal of Financial Economics,* 9 (June 1981), pp. 207–211.

CHAPTER 13

Capital Budgeting under Uncertainty

Chapter 9 introduced capital budgeting techniques in a world where future events were known with certainty. It was largely an exercise in decision making across time with known discount rates. Chapters 10 through 12 introduced decision making under uncertainty (e.g., the Capital Asset Pricing Model, the Arbitrage Pricing Theory, and the Option Pricing Model). This chapter revisits the investment decision in a world where cash flows and even discount rates are uncertain, and where management may or may not have flexibility in the decisions that can be made. We will cover three decision-making methodologies in increasing order of complexity: decision trees (with Monte Carlo analysis), CAPM-based approaches, and option pricing approaches to capital budgeting.

THE STRUCTURE OF DECISIONS

Every project may be described as a decision tree that requires information about five things:

- Cash flows along branches of the decision tree
- Timing of the cash flows
- Probabilities of the cash flows
- Types of decisions that can be made at nodes in the decision tree
- Comparable *priced* asset or its equivalent, a risk-adjusted discount rate

To illustrate what we mean, suppose that you are asked to evaluate the project illustrated in Figure 13.1. You are given the facts in the figure and are told that the project is unlike any other project in the company or the company as a whole. It is not an unusual set of

FIGURE 13.1   A Simple Project

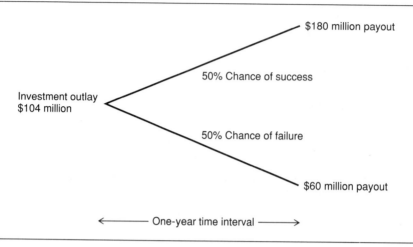

facts. You know the required investment outlay, the expected payouts, their probabilities, and when they are expected to occur (a year from now). But you cannot solve the problem without a discount rate. In Chapter 9 the discount rate was always given to you, but in real life it is not. What can you do? The ideal way to solve the problem is to find a *priced* and *perfectly correlated* security, like the one illustrated in Figure 13.2.

Note that it has exactly the same probability of success or failure, the same timing, and payouts that are perfectly correlated with the simple project that we are trying to evaluate (up 80 percent in the favorable state of nature and down 40 percent in the unfavorable state). Also, it has an observable, market-determined price, i.e., $20. The relationship between the current price and the expected future payouts allows us to determine a risk-adjusted discount rate, k.

$$S = \frac{E(CF)}{1 + k} = \frac{.5(\$36) + .5(\$12)}{1 + k} = \$20$$

$$k = 20\%$$

Since the project is perfectly correlated with the priced security, it has exactly the same risk. Knowing this, we can evaluate the project.

$$NPV = \frac{\text{Expected cash flows}}{1 + \text{risk-adjusted rate}} - \text{Investment outlay}$$

$$= \frac{.5(\$180 \text{ million}) + .5(\$60 \text{ million})}{1 + .2} - \$104 \text{ million}$$

$$= -\$4 \text{ million}$$

FIGURE 13.2   A Perfectly Correlated Security

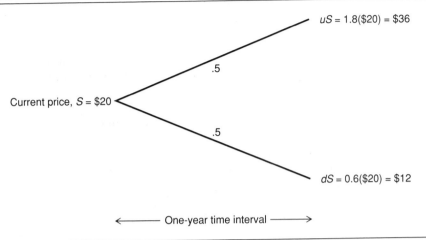

Alternately, if the risk-free rate is 8 percent, we can calculate the certainty-equivalent probabilities that give exactly the same net present value. If we designate p as the certainty-equivalent probability of success, then

$$NPV = \frac{p(\$180 \text{ million}) + (1 - p)(\$60 \text{ million})}{1 + r_f} - \$104 \text{ million}$$

$$-\$4 = \frac{p(\$180) + (1 - p)(\$60)}{1.08} - \$104$$

$$p = 0.4, \text{ and } 1 - p = 0.6.$$

In practice, the key role of the priced, perfectly correlated security is filled by using comparables that are surrogates for the risky project that is being analyzed. If we are using a CAPM (Capital Asset Pricing Model) approach, we try to find priced securities that have the same systematic risk (or beta) as the project being evaluated. If we are using the Option Pricing Model (OPM), we construct mimicking portfolios that are composed of priced, perfectly correlated securities. The price of the mimicking portfolio is equal to the price of the option.

Ross [1979] shows how the APT (Arbitrage Pricing Theory) can be used to value risky income streams, and Gehr [1981] shows how the idea can be applied specifically to the multiperiod capital budgeting problem. His approach is an extension of the simple example that we just finished. As before, it requires a priced, perfectly correlated security. It also assumes no flexibility in decision making. We shall see, later on, that many (but certainly not all) option-pricing applications work well in practice because good data about the underlying risky asset is available and because flexibility in the decision-making process can be modeled.

One-Period, Two-State Problem

To describe Gehr's approach, let's begin with a simple one-period, two-state problem. The facts are given in Table 13.1. The initial outlay is $8,000 and the project will return $8,000 if economic conditions are bad or $15,000 otherwise. If we can create a *cash-equivalent portfolio* from the risk-free asset and the comparison stock, then we can value the project. The cash-equivalent portfolio will have exactly the same payoffs as the project in each state of nature. Because we know the market prices of both the risk-free asset and the comparison stock, the price of the cash-equivalent portfolio will be the value of the project; otherwise, arbitrage opportunities would exist between the project and the cash-equivalent portfolio.

How much should we invest in the risk-free asset and in the comparison stock to obtain exactly the same payoffs as the project? Let Q_f be the dollars invested in the risk-free asset and Q_s the number of shares in the comparison stock. The two equations below show the payoffs of the cash-equivalent portfolio in each state of nature. Note that $1 invested in the riskless asset returns $1.10 at the end of the period.

$$\text{Bad economic conditions: } \$8.00 \; Q_s + \$1.10 \; Q_f = \$8,000$$
$$\text{Good economic conditions: } \$25.50 \; Q_s + \$1.10 \; Q_f = \$15,000$$

With two equations and two unknowns, we can solve to find that $Q_s = 400$ shares and $Q_f = \$4,363.64$. Since the current price of the stock is $9.00 per share and the price of the riskless bond is $1.00, the current value of the cash-equivalent portfolio must be

$$PV = (400 \text{ shares})(\$9.00/\text{share}) + (4,363.64 \text{ bonds})(\$1.00/\text{bond})$$
$$= \$3,600.00 + \$4,363.64 = \$7,963.64.$$

This is also the present value of the project because the cash-equivalent portfolio duplicates the project's payouts in each state of nature. The NPV of the project is its present value minus the cash outlay needed to acquire it:

$$NPV = PV - I$$
$$= \$7,963.64 - \$8,000.00 = -\$36.36.$$

Because the NPV is negative, the project should be rejected. Another way of saying the same thing is that an investor would be better off buying 400 shares of the comparison stock and $4,363.64 worth of bonds.

TABLE 13.1   One-Period APT Example

Period	Economic State	Subjective Probability	Project CF	Risk-Free Rate, r_f	Price of Comparison Stock, S
0	Current	1.0	−$8,000	N/A	$ 9.00
1	Bad	0.3	8,000	10%	8.00
1	Good	0.7	15,000	10%	25.50

Note that it was not necessary to directly estimate the probabilities of the states of nature, nor was it necessary to directly compute the risk-adjusted discount rate for the project. All this information is implicitly included in the relative prices (across time and across states of nature) of the risk-free asset and the risky comparison stock. As long as their prices are true equilibrium prices, then the market information tells us all that we need to know.

Two-Period APT Problem

Gehr's technique can readily be extended to a multiperiod economy, even one where the risk-free rate changes through time. Figure 13.3 gives data for a two-period example. The probabilities of states of nature are not given because they are not explicitly needed to solve the problem (they are implicit in the equilibrium prices of the comparison securities). Note that the risk-free rate is state-contingent. If a favorable state of the economy prevails in Period 1, then $r_f = 10$ percent; otherwise it is 8 percent. Note also that there is no flexibility in this decision tree. This is designated by a closed circle at each decision node in Period 2. For example, if State B occurs in Period 1 then the project will move to either State E or State F in Period 2 with no additional decision being made. If there were flexibility, the decision maker might be given the option to abandon the project if State B

FIGURE 13.3 Two-Period APT Example, First Stage (Period 2)

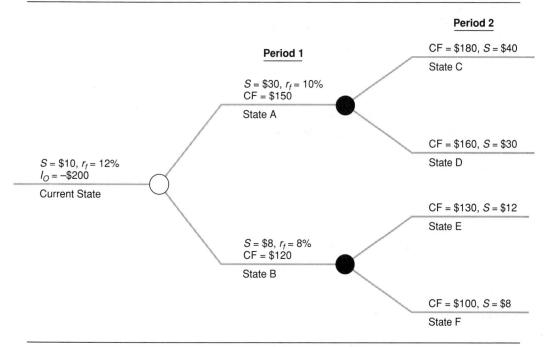

FIGURE 13.4   Two-Period APT Example, Second Stage (Period 1)

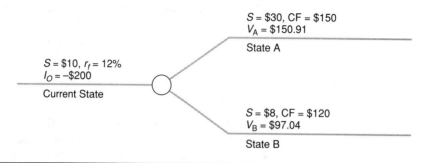

were to occur. Later on we will discuss the implications of flexibility. Some of the Period 2 decision nodes will be open.

As before, the project can be evaluated by finding the cash-equivalent portfolios between Periods 1 and 2, then using this information to find the Period 0 cash-equivalent portfolio. The two sets of simultaneous equations given below are used to determine the Period 1 cash-equivalent portfolios:

State C: $40 \, Q_s + \$1.10 \, Q_f = \$180$ $Q_s = 2, \, Q_f = 90.91$

State D: $30 \, Q_s + \$1.10 \, Q_f = \$160$ $V_A = \$150.91$

State E: $12 \, Q_s + \$1.08 \, Q_f = \$130$ $Q_s = 7.5, \, Q_f = 37.04$

State F: $\$8 \, Q_s + \$1.08 \, Q_f = \$100$ $V_B = \$97.04.$

The values of the cash-equivalent portfolios in States A and B are:

$$V_A = \$30(2) + \$1(90.91) = \$150.91$$
$$V_B = \$8(7.5) + \$1(37.04) = \$97.04.$$

As shown in Figure 13.4, the value of the project in each state is the cash flow that it provides in that state of nature, plus the cash-equivalent value (V_i) in that state. This information can be used to write the appropriate set of payoffs for the Period 1 cash-equivalent portfolio, as shown below:

State A: $\$30 \, Q_s + \$1.12 \, Q_f = \$150 + \$150.91$

State B: $\$8 \, Q_s + \$1.12 \, Q_f = \$120 + \$97.04.$

Solving, we find that $Q_s = 3.812$ shares and $Q_f = 166.56$ bonds. Thus, the value of the cash-equivalent portfolio for the two-year project is

$$PV = (3.812 \text{ shares})(\$10/\text{share}) + (166.56 \text{ bonds})(\$1/\text{bond})$$
$$= \$38.12 + \$166.56 = \$204.68$$

and the net present value of the project is

$$NPV = PV - I_o = \$204.68 - \$200.00 = \$4.68.$$

Therefore, the project should be accepted.

FIGURE 13.5   Two-Period OPM Example, First Stage (Period 2)

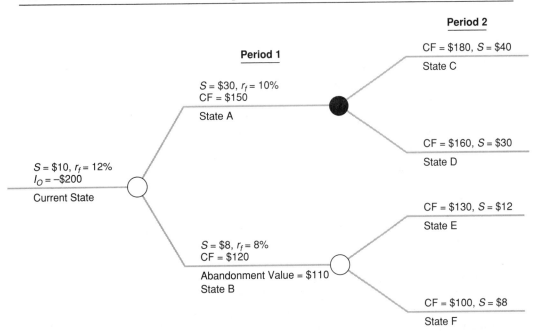

Two-Period OPM Problem

To show the value of flexibility, suppose that the two-period decision tree had looked like Figure 13.5. The big difference is that the decision tree now has two decision points, not just one. The decision maker must decide whether to undertake the project — a current decision. The decision maker must also decide whether to abandon the project for $110 if State B occurs. The State B abandonment decision is an option because the decision maker has the right to abandon the project but is not required to do so. To make his decision, he will compare the cash-equivalent value, $V_B = \$97.04$, with the abandonment cash flow, $110. His payoff in State B is

$$\text{State B:}\quad \text{payoff} = \$120 + \text{MAX } [\$97.04, \$110].$$

Since his payoff is higher if he abandons the project in State B, he will do so. Figure 13.6 illustrates the second-stage payoffs. If we use this information to find the cash-equivalent portfolio, we have

$$\text{State A:}\quad \$30\ Q_s + \$1.12\ Q_f = \$150 + \$150.91$$
$$\text{State B:}\quad \$8\ Q_s + \$1.12\ Q_f = \$120 + \$110.00.$$

Solving, we find that $Q_s = 3.223$ shares and $Q_f = 182.334$ bonds. Therefore, the value of the cash-equivalent portfolio for the two-year project increases to

$$PV = (3.223 \text{ shares})(\$10/\text{share}) + (182.334 \text{ bonds})(\$1/\text{bond})$$
$$= \$32.23 + \$182.33 = \$214.56$$

FIGURE 13.6   Two-Period OPM Example, Second Stage (Period 1)

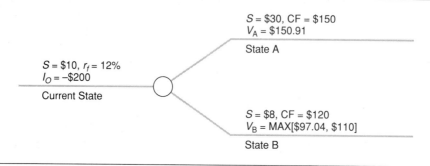

and the net present value is

$$\text{NPV} = PV - I_o = \$214.56 - \$200 = \$14.56.$$

The additional value that results from the option to abandon the project for $110 if State B occurs is worth $14.56 − $4.68 = $9.88. Additional flexibility, at any exercise price, cannot decrease the value of the project. In this simple example, the decision maker would be willing to pay up to $9.88 for the right to be able to abandon the project for $110 if State B occurs. Thus $9.88 is the value of a put option. Later on in the chapter, we shall explore other types of options that decision makers have.

What have we learned so far in this chapter? The first thing is that there are five pieces of information that are necessary to evaluate capital budgeting projects in the face of uncertainty:

- Cash flows along branches of the decision tree
- Timing of cash flows
- Probabilities of cash flows
- Types of decisions that can (or cannot) be made at nodes in the decision tree
- Comparable *priced* asset or its equivalent, a risk-adjusted discount rate

We have seen that the role of a comparable priced asset is crucial. Implicit in it is the correct risk-adjusted discount rate, or alternatively it can be used to form cash-equivalent portfolios that can be used to evaluate risky projects. It is also important to understand the role of decision nodes. Too often, projects are evaluated by making the implicit assumption that the only decision is whether to accept or reject a project at its outset. Not enough attention is given to the flexibility offered by future decision nodes.

The next three sections of the chapter describe three widely used approaches for decision making under uncertainty: decision trees (with Monte Carlo analysis), the Capital Asset Pricing Model (CAPM), and the Option Pricing Model (OPM). None is perfect or applicable in every situation.

DECISION TREES

The capital budgeting process requires estimates of expected cash flows over the life of a project and an accurate estimate of the appropriate risk-adjusted cost of capital. The expected cash flows are then discounted in order to compute the net present value of the project. It sounds simple — right? Actually, there is nothing simple about capital budgeting decisions. A major problem is that cash flows and costs of capital are estimated with error. Sometimes the errors are huge. Also, as we have just seen, it is no simple task to figure out the appropriate risk-adjusted discount rate. Consequently, it is wise to undertake a sensitivity analysis of project NPVs in order to gain a better appreciation of the potential errors involved in the decision-making process.

The NPV of a project will, in the final analysis, depend upon such factors as quantity of sales, sales prices, input costs, the opportunity cost of capital, and so on. If these values turn out to be favorable — that is, output and sales prices are high and costs are low — then profits, the realized rate of return, and the actual NPV will be high, and the converse if these values are unfavorable. Recognizing these causal relationships, managers often calculate project NPVs under alternative assumptions and then see just how sensitive NPV is to changing conditions. One recent example involves a chemical company that was comparing two alternative types of phosphate plants. Fuel represented a major cost, and one plant used coal, which may be obtained under a long-term, fixed-cost contract, while the other used oil, which must be purchased at current market prices. Considering present and projected future prices, the oil-fired plant looked better — it had a considerably higher NPV. However, oil prices are volatile, and if prices rose by more than the expected rate, this plant would have been unprofitable. The coal-fired plant, on the other hand, had a lower NPV under the expected conditions, but this NPV was not sensitive to changing conditions in the energy market. The company finally selected the coal plant because the sensitivity analysis indicated that there was less potential error in its NPV estimates.

Sensitivity analysis, as practiced by the chemical company described in the example, is informal in the sense that no probabilities are attached to the likelihood of various outcomes. *Monte Carlo simulation analysis* represents a refinement that does employ probability estimates. In this section, we first describe how *decision trees* can be used to attach probabilities to different outcomes, and then we illustrate how full-scale computer simulation can be employed to analyze major projects.

Most important decisions are not made once and for all at one point in time. Rather, decisions are made in stages. For example, a petroleum firm considering the possibility of expanding into agricultural chemicals might take the following steps:

1. Spend $100,000 for a survey of supply-demand conditions in the agricultural chemical industry.

2. If the survey results are favorable, spend $500,000 on a pilot plant to investigate production methods.

3. Depending on the costs estimated from the pilot study and the demand potential from the market study, either abandon the project, build a large plant, or build a small one.

Thus, the final decision actually is made in stages, with subsequent decisions depending on the results of previous decisions.

FIGURE 13.7 Illustrative Decision Tree

Action (1)	Demand Conditions (2)	Probability (3)	Present Value of Cash Flows (4)	Less Initial Cost (5)	Possible NPV (4) - (5) (6)	Probable NPV (3) × (6) (7)
Build big plant: Invest $5 million	High	0.5	$8,800,000	$5,000,000	$3,800,000	$1,900,000
	Medium	0.3	$3,500,000	$5,000,000	($1,500,000)	($450,000)
	Low	0.2	$1,400,000	$5,000,000	($3,600,000)	($720,000)
					Expected NPV	$730,000
	High	0.5	$2,600,000	$2,000,000	$600,000	$300,000
	Medium	0.3	$2,400,000	$2,000,000	$400,000	$120,000
Build small plant: Invest $2 million	Low	0.2	$1,400,000	$2,000,000	($600,000)	($120,000)
					Expected NPV	$300,000

The sequence of events can be mapped out like the branches of a tree, hence the name *decision tree*. As an example, consider Figure 13.7. There it is assumed that the petroleum company has completed its industry supply-demand analysis and pilot plant study and has determined that it should proceed to develop a full-scale production facility. The firm must decide whether to build a large plant or a small one. The estimated probabilities of demand levels for the plant's products are 50 percent for high demand, 30 percent for medium demand, and 20 percent for low demand. Depending on demand, net cash flows (sales revenues minus operating costs, all discounted to the present) will range from $8.8 million to $1.4 million if a large plant is built and from $2.6 million to $1.4 million if a small plant is built.

The initial costs of the large and small plants are shown in Column 5 of the figure; when these investment outlays are subtracted from the PV of cash flows, the result is the set of possible NPVs shown in Column 6. One, but only one, of these NPVs will actually occur. Finally, we multiply Column 6 by Column 3 to obtain Column 7, and the sums in Column 7 give the expected NPVs of the large and small plants.

Because the expected NPV of the larger plant ($730,000) is larger than that of the small plant ($300,000), should the decision be to build the large plant? Perhaps, but not necessarily. Notice that the range of outcomes is greater if the large plant is built, with the actual NPVs (Column 6 in Figure 13.7) varying from $3.8 million to *minus* $3.6 million. However, a range of only $600,000 to minus $600,000 exists for the small plant.

The decision tree illustrated in Figure 13.7 is quite simple; in actual use, the trees are frequently far more complex and involve a number of sequential decision points. As an example of a more complex tree, consider Figure 13.8. The boxes numbered 1, 2, and so on are *decision points,* that is, instances when the firm must choose between alternatives, while the circles represent the possible actual outcomes, one of which will follow these decisions. At Decision Point 1, the firm has three choices: to invest $3 million in a large plant, to invest $1.3 million in a small plant, or to spend $100,000 on market research. If the large plant is built, the firm follows the upper branch, and its position has been fixed — it can only hope that demand will be high. If it builds the small plant, then it follows the lower branch. If demand is low, no further action is required. If demand is high, Decision Point 2 is reached, and the firm must either do nothing or else expand the plant at a cost of another $2.2 million. (Thus, if it obtains a large plant through expansion, the cost is $500,000 greater than if it had built the large plant in the first place.)

If the decision at Point 1 is to pay $100,000 for more information, the firm moves to the center branch. The research modifies the firm's information about potential demand. Initially, the probabilities were 70 percent for high demand and 30 percent for low demand. The research survey will show either favorable (positive) or unfavorable (negative) demand prospects. If they are positive, we assume that the probability for high final demand will be 87 percent and that for low demand will be 13 percent; if the research yields negative results, the odds on high final demand are only 35 percent and those for low demand are 65 percent. These results will, of course, influence the firm's decision as to whether to build a large or a small plant.

If the firm builds a large plant and demand is high, then sales and profits will be large. However, if it builds a large plant and demand is weak, sales will be low, and losses, rather than profits, will be incurred. On the other hand, if it builds a small plant and demand is high, sales and profits will be lower than they could have been had a large plant been built, but the chances of losses in the event of low demand will be eliminated. Thus, the decision to build the large plant has greater variability than the one to build the small plant. The decision to commission the research is, in effect, an expenditure to reduce the degree of uncertainty in the decision on which plant to build; the research provides additional information on the probability of high versus low demand, thus lowering the level of uncertainty.

The decision tree in Figure 13.8 is incomplete in that no dollar outcomes are assigned to the various situations. If this step were taken, along the lines shown in the last two columns of Figure 13.7, then expected values could be obtained for each of the alternative actions. These expected values could then be used to aid the decision maker in choosing among the alternatives.

The good thing about decision trees and Monte Carlo analysis of them is that they are explicit in listing decision nodes and careful in the way they treat conditional probabilities. The major weakness in practice is finding the correct risk-adjusted discount rate. At best, it will be selected in an ad hoc manner because the approach outlined above makes no specific attempt to link cash flows along the decision tree with priced securities that have payouts that are correlated with the project in the enumerated states of nature.

The concepts embodied in decision tree analysis can be extended to computer simulation. To illustrate the technique, let us consider a proposal to build a new textile plant. The cost of the plant is not known for certain, although it is expected to run about $150 million. If no problems are encountered, the cost can be as low as $125 million, while an

Figure 13.8 Decision Tree with Multiple Decision Points

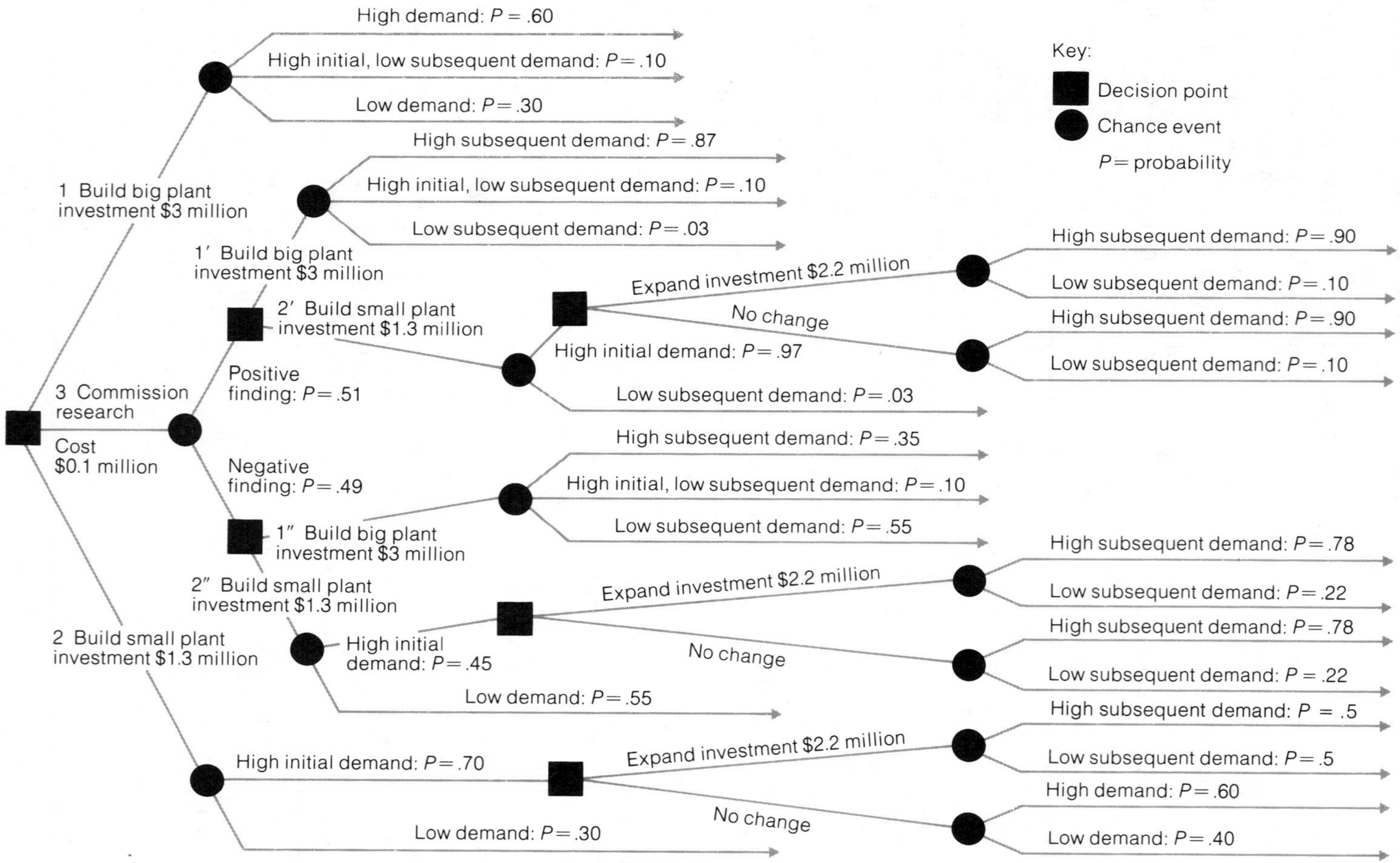

Key:

■ Decision point

● Chance event

P = probability

1 Build big plant investment $3 million

High demand: P = .60

High initial, low subsequent demand: P = .10

Low demand: P = .30

1′ Build big plant investment $3 million

High subsequent demand: P = .87

High initial, low subsequent demand: P = .10

Low subsequent demand: P = .03

Expand investment $2.2 million

No change

2′ Build small plant investment $1.3 million

High initial demand: P = .97

Low subsequent demand: P = .03

Positive finding: P = .51

3 Commission research

Cost $0.1 million

Negative finding: P = .49

1″ Build big plant investment $3 million

High subsequent demand: P = .35

High initial, low subsequent demand: P = .10

Low subsequent demand: P = .55

Expand investment $2.2 million

No change

2″ Build small plant investment $1.3 million

High initial demand: P = .45

Low demand: P = .55

2 Build small plant investment $1.3 million

High initial demand: P = .70

Expand investment $2.2 million

No change

Low demand: P = .30

High subsequent demand: P = .90

Low subsequent demand: P = .10

High subsequent demand: P = .90

Low subsequent demand: P = .10

High subsequent demand: P = .78

Low subsequent demand: P = .22

High subsequent demand: P = .78

Low subsequent demand: P = .22

High subsequent demand: P = .5

Low subsequent demand: P = .5

High demand: P = .60

Low demand: P = .40

unfortunate series of events—strikes, unprojected increases in materials costs, technical problems, and the like—could result in the investment outlay running as high as $225 million.

Revenues from the new facility, which will operate for many years, will depend on population growth and income in the region, competition, developments in synthetic fabrics research, and textile import quotas. Operating costs will depend on production efficiency, materials, labor cost trends, and the like. Since both sales revenues and operating costs are uncertain, annual profits are also uncertain.

Assuming that probability distributions can be assigned to each of the major cost and revenue determinants, a computer program can be constructed to simulate what is likely to happen. In effect, the computer selects one value at random from each of the relevant distributions, combines it with other values selected from the other distributions, and produces an estimated profit and net present value or rate of return on investment.[1] This particular profit and rate of return occur, of course, only for the particular combination of values selected during this trial. The computer goes on to select other sets of values and to compute other profits and rates of return repeatedly, for perhaps several hundred trials. A count is kept of the number of times each rate of return is computed, and when the computer runs are completed, the frequency with which the various rates of return occurred can be plotted as a frequency distribution.

The procedure is illustrated in Figures 13.9 and 13.10. Figure 13.9 is a flowchart outlining the simulation procedure described above, while Figure 13.10 illustrates the frequency distribution of rates of return generated by such a simulation for two alternative projects, X and Y, each with an expected cost of $20 million. The expected rate of return on Investment X is 15 percent and that of Investment Y is 20 percent. However, these are only the *average* rates of return generated by the computer; simulated rates range from −10 percent to +45 percent for Investment Y and from 5 to 25 percent for Investment X. The standard deviation generated for X is only 4 percentage points—68 percent of the computer runs had rates of return between 11 and 19 percent—while that for Y is 12 percentage points. Clearly, then, Investment Y has greater potential for estimation errors than Investment X.

The computer simulation has provided us with both an estimate of the expected internal rates of return on the two projects and an estimate of their relative estimation errors. A decision about which alternative should be chosen can now be made.

Very little literature has been written on how to adjust NPV calculations so that known estimation errors can be taken into account. However, the interested reader is referred to Smidt [1979] for an analysis of the issue. If the true cash flows and true risk-adjusted discount rate are known without error, then the NPV of the project is all that is needed to make a correct decision. However, if errors are made in estimating these inputs, then it is necessary to take any potential bias and error into account. Smidt [1979] gives an example where management believes that projects of a given type are drawn from a normal distribution where the mean is −$50 and the standard deviation is $33.33. This implies that 93.3 percent of the project proposals are considered to have negative NPVs.

---

[1] If the variables are not independent, then conditional probabilities must be employed. For example, if demand is weak, then both sales in units and sales prices are likely to be low, and these interrelationships must be taken into account in the simulation.

FIGURE 13.9 Simulation for Investment Planning

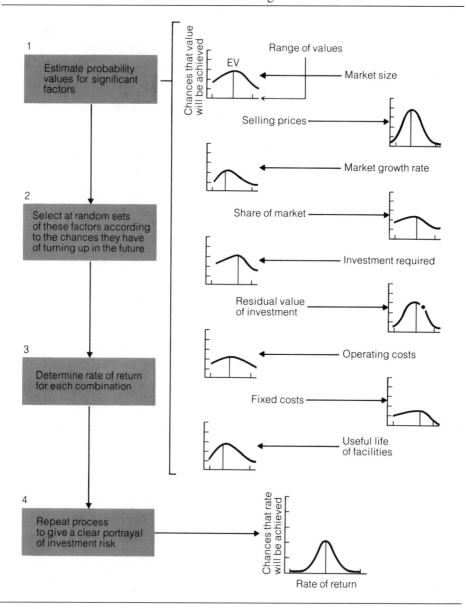

Source: Adapted from David B. Hertz, ''Uncertainty and Investment Selection,'' in J. Fred Weston and Maurice Goudzwaard, eds., *The Treasurer's Handbook* (Homewood, Ill.: Dow Jones-Irwin, 1976), p. 408. © 1976 by Dow Jones-Irwin.

FIGURE 13.10   Expected Rates of Return on Investments X and Y

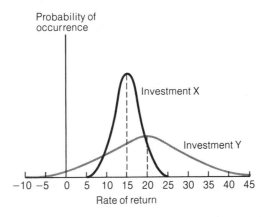

Management also believes that project analysts have a routine bias of +$25 in their forecasts of NPV and that the standard deviation of their forecasts is $25. Smidt then shows that the *minimum* acceptable NPV for projects under these circumstances is not $0, but rather is $53. Thus, in our example illustrated by Figure 13.10, it is not immediately obvious that Investment Y should be favored over Investment X. Although Investment Y has a higher expected internal rate of return, it also has higher estimation errors.

USING THE CAPITAL ASSET PRICING MODEL

The usual approach to investment decisions is to determine the net present value of a project by discounting its expected cash flows at the weighted average cost of capital, as shown in Equation 13.1

$$\text{NPV} = -I_0 + \sum_{t=1}^{N} \frac{E(\text{CF}_t)}{(1 + \text{WACC})^t}, \tag{13.1}$$

where:

$$\text{NPV} = \text{the net present value of the project}$$
$$-I_0 = \text{the initial outlay for investment}$$
$$E(\text{CF}_t) = \text{the expected free cash flows in period } t$$
$$\text{WACC} = \text{the weighted average cost of capital.}$$

Of course, the weighted average cost of capital depends on your estimate of the systematic risk, or beta, of the project, given the project's target capital structure.

$$\text{WACC} = k_b(1 - T)\frac{B}{B + S} + k_s\frac{S}{B + S} \tag{13.2}$$

where:

$$k_b = \text{the before-tax marginal cost of debt}$$
$$T = \text{the statutory marginal corporate tax rate}$$
$$B = \text{the market value of debt}$$
$$S = \text{the market value of equity}$$
$$k_s = \text{the marginal cost of equity}$$
$$B/(B + S) = \text{the project's long-term target capital structure.}$$

The marginal costs of debt and equity are both functions of their betas.

The Relationship Between Risk and Time

Earlier examples of capital budgeting using the CAPM were usually one-period situations. Now we want to look into the implications of using risk-adjusted rates for projects whose cash flows extend across multiple time periods. We will begin by showing how the CAPM can be used, in a one-period framework, to determine project net present values using either of two techniques: (a) the risk-adjusted discount rate or (b) the certainty-equivalent approach. Then we will discuss the multiperiod implications.

The present value, PV, of a one-period project can be found by discounting its expected cash flow, $E(CF)$, at a risk-adjusted rate, $E(R_j)$.

$$PV = \frac{E(CF)}{1 + E(R_j)} \tag{13.3}$$

If we assume an all-equity project, to keep things simple, the correct risk-adjusted rate is given by the CAPM as

$$k_s = E(R_j) = R_F + [E(R_M) - R_F]\beta_j. \tag{13.4}$$

Substituting the CAPM, Equation 13.4, into the risk-adjusted present value formula, we have

$$PV = \frac{E(CF)}{1 + R_F + [E(R_M) - R_F]\beta_j}. \tag{13.5}$$

If the project's expected cash flows are $1,000, the risk-free rate is 10 percent, the expected market return is 17 percent, and the project's beta is 1.5, then its present value is

$$PV = \frac{\$1,000}{1 + .10 + [.17 - .10]1.5}$$
$$= \frac{\$1,000}{1.205} = \$829.88.$$

If the investment outlay for the project, I, is $800, then its net present value is

$$NPV = PV - I = \$829.88 - \$800.00 = \$29.88,$$

and the project should be accepted.

The *certainty equivalent method* is an equivalent approach for a one-period project. Rather than adjusting for risk by raising the discount rate, the certainty equivalent method

(CEM) subtracts a risk premium from the expected cash flows and then discounts this certainty equivalent at the risk-free rate. The CEM can be derived from Equation 13.5. First note that the definition of β_j is

$$\beta_j = \frac{COV(R_j, R_M)}{\sigma_M^2},$$

where $COV(R_j, R_M)$ = the covariance between the return on the jth asset and the return on the market portfolio, and σ_M^2 = the variance of the market portfolio. The one-period return on the project is

$$R_j = \frac{CF - PV}{PV} = \frac{CF}{PV} - 1.$$

Substituting the project return definition into the definition of undiversifiable risk, we have

$$\beta_j = \frac{COV\left[\dfrac{CF}{PV} - 1, R_M\right]}{\sigma_M^2}.$$

Note that risky end-of-period cash flows are multiplied by $1/PV$, which is a constant that does not covary with the return on the market; therefore, it can be factored out. Also, the minus one which is subtracted from CF/PV has no effect on the covariance. Therefore, the beta becomes

$$\beta_j = \left(\frac{1}{PV}\right)\frac{COV(CF, R_M)}{\sigma_M^2}. \qquad (13.6)$$

Substituting Equation 13.6 into Equation 13.5, we have

$$PV = \frac{E(CF)}{1 + R_F + [E(R_M) - R_F](1/PV)\left[\dfrac{COV(CF, R_M)}{\sigma_M^2}\right]}.$$

Note that the expression $[E(R_M) - R_F]/\sigma_M^2$ is the market price of risk which we discussed in Chapter 10. If we let λ be the market price of risk and solve for PV, we get the certainty equivalent model (CEM),

$$PV = \frac{E(CF) - \lambda COV(CF, R_M)}{1 + R_F}, \qquad (13.7)$$

where

$$\lambda = [E(R_M) - R_F]/\sigma_M^2.$$

In Equation 13.7, the CEM adjusts for risk by subtracting a certainty equivalent risk premium from the expected cash flow and then discounts at the risk-free rate. It is the same as asking the question, what cash flow with no risk at all would make the market indifferent to the project's risky cash flows? Once the certainty equivalent cash flow has been found, we can then discount at the risk-free rate.

By equating (13.5) and (13.7), we can find the dollar amount of the certainty equivalent risk premium for our example.

$$PV = \frac{E(CF)}{1 + R_F + [E(R_M) - R_F]\beta_j} = \frac{E(CF) - \lambda COV(CF, R_M)}{1 + R_F}$$

$$\$829.88 = \frac{\$1,000}{1.205} = \frac{\$1,000 - \lambda COV(CF, R_M)}{1.100}.$$

Solving for the certainty equivalent risk premium, we see that it is

$$\lambda COV(CF, R_M) = \$87.13.$$

Thus, we are indifferent between $1,000 - $87.13 = $912.87 with no risk and a risky expected cash flow of $1,000 with a beta of 1.5.

The certainty equivalent method and the risk-adjusted return are equivalent for a one-period project. But how can they be compared for a multiple-period project? Suppose our example specified that the $1,000 cash flow was expected two years hence instead of just one. What are the consequences of using the two approaches?

By its nature, the risk-adjusted discount rate allows for both the time value of money and the relative riskiness of a project's returns. Both *time* and *risk* are accounted for by one adjustment process. Since time and risk are really separate variables, we must be very careful about how we combine them if the risk-adjusted discount rate is to be used for its intended purpose. If $E(R_j)$ is the one-period risk-adjusted discount rate and if the $1,000 cash flow is received two years hence, then the risk-adjusted discount rate method would compute its present value as

$$PV = \sum_{t=0}^{N} \frac{E(CF_t)}{[1 + E(R_j)]^t}$$

$$= \frac{\$1,000}{(1.205)^2} = \frac{\$1,000}{1.452} = \$688.70.$$

If the investment outlay is $800, the net present value of the project would be $688.70 − $800.00 = −$111.30, and it would be rejected.

If we use the certainty equivalent method on the same project, we can obtain the same answer only if we make a certainty equivalent adjustment that takes two periods of risk into account. Subtracting a one-period certainty equivalent risk premium of $87.13 will not do the trick. In order to make the two methods equivalent, we can *multiply* the expected cash flows in the certainty equivalent model by a certainty equivalent factor, cef, which is the ratio of the one-period certainty equivalent cash flow to the one-period expected cash flow.

$$cef = \frac{E(CF) - \lambda COV(CF, R_M)}{E(CF)} \tag{13.8}$$

$$= \frac{\$1,000 - \$87.13}{\$1,000} = .91287.$$

FIGURE 13.11   An Example with Risk Changing Over Time

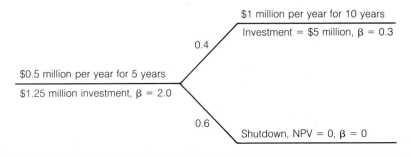

The multiperiod versions of the two models become

$$PV = \sum_{t=0}^{N} \frac{E(CF_t)}{[1 + E(R_j)]^t} = \sum_{t=0}^{N} \frac{(cef)^t E(CF_t)}{(1 + R_F)^t}.$$ **(13.9)**

Using the multiperiod certainty equivalent model and our numerical example, we have

$$PV = \frac{(.91287)^2 \$1,000}{(1.1)^2} = \frac{.8333(\$1,000)}{1.21} = \$688.70.$$

The fact that the two models can be made to give the same answer begs the fundamental question of how risk and time are interrelated. If we discount by using the same risk-adjusted discount rate over the life of a project, we are implicitly assuming that it has the same systematic risk (the same beta) each year of its life.[2] This may be an invalid assumption, particularly for new products, which tend to be highly sensitive to the health of the economy during their initial years and much less sensitive as they mature. For example, consider the 15-year oil shale project outlined in Figure 13.11.

The project has two phases. The five-year pilot study has expected net operating income of $0.5 million a year and an initial outlay of $1.25 million. After the pilot phase, uncertainty will be reduced and the project will either be shut down or continued with further investment of $5 million and expected net operating income of $1 million per year for ten years. The project has a beta of 2.0 during the pilot phase. If the risk-free rate is 10 percent and the expected return on the market portfolio is 20 percent, then the risk-adjusted rate of return on the project can be determined from the CAPM as

$$E(R_j) = R_F + [E(R_M) - R_F]\beta_j$$
$$= .10 + [.20 - .10]2.0 = 30\%.$$

---

[2]See Bogue and Roll [1974], Fama [1977], and Myers and Turnbull [1977] for more on the validity of the CAPM in a multiperiod framework.

If management uses 30 percent as the project hurdle rate for the entire life of the project, the NPV will be[3]

$$NPV = \sum_{t=0}^{15} \frac{E(CF_t)}{[1 + E(R_j)]^t}$$

$$= -1,250,000 + \sum_{t=1}^{5} \frac{500,000}{(1.3)^t} + \sum_{t=6}^{15} \frac{1,000,000}{(1.3)^t} - \frac{5,000,000}{(1.3)^5}$$

$$= -1,250,000 + 1,217,785 + 832,641 - 1,346,645$$

$$= -\$546,219.$$

The problem with this approach is that it falsely assumes the project is high risk over its entire life. The reason for the pilot project is to reduce uncertainty. There is a 40 percent chance that the project will be successful after the pilot and a 60 percent chance it will not. If the project is shut down, the cash flows are known with certainty to be zero and the NPV = 0. If the project is successful, the beta continues from years 6 through 15 at a level of .3. Therefore, the risk-adjusted discount rate is 13 percent and the NPV of the cash flows, if the project is successful, is:[4]

$$NPV \text{ (remainder)} = \sum_{t=6}^{15} \frac{1,000,000}{(1.13)^t} - \frac{5,000,000}{(1.13)^5}$$

$$= \$2,945,148 - \$2,713,800 = \$231,348.$$

Now the NPV of the project is the NPV of the pilot plus the expected NPV of the remainder of the project:

$$NPV \text{ (pilot)} = \$1,217,785 - \$1,250,000 = -\$32,215$$

$$NPV \text{ (remainder)} = .6 \text{ (NPV if shut down)} + .4 \text{ (NPV if successful)}$$

$$= .6(0) + .4(\$231,348)$$

$$= \$92,539$$

$$NPV \text{ (project)} = NPV \text{ (pilot)} + NPV \text{ (remainder)} = -\$32,215 + \$92,539$$

$$= \$60,324.$$

Now our analysis shows that the project should be accepted. The example illustrates that when the risk of a project changes during its life, it is necessary to discount the expected cash flows by a risk-adjusted rate which changes when the risk of the project does. The certainty equivalent method will provide equivalent results.

---

[3]Note that the pilot phase, when considered alone, has a negative NPV of $32,215. It is not unusual for pilot studies to lose money based on their operating income. The actual value of the pilot study is its NPV plus the value of information which it supplies. It provides the option of shutdown if the project fails or increased scale if it succeeds. This option is valuable. See Chapter 12 for the economics of option pricing.

[4]The discount rate is determined from the CAPM; given $R_F = 10\%$, $E(R_M) = 20\%$, and $\beta = .3$,

$$E(R_j) = R_F + [E(R_M) - R_F]\beta_j$$
$$= 10\% + [20\% - 10\%].3 = 13\%.$$

Managers often express the opinion that because distant cash flows are "riskier," they should be discounted at higher rates. They are forgetting that any risk-adjusted discount rate automatically recognizes that more distant cash flows have more risk. Higher discount rates should be applied to more distant cash flows only if there is good reason to believe that the project's beta will be higher in the distant future.

The Net Present Value Method and Flexibility

Perhaps the single most important criticism of the standard NPV methodology, even when the appropriate risk-adjusted rate is used to discount the expected cash flows, is that we often overlook the flexibility provided at decision nodes during the life of the project. For example, when evaluating oil field development projects, the standard procedure is to make an assumption about the growth rates of oil prices, extraction costs, etc.; to estimate the expected cash flows; to discount them at a constant risk-adjusted rate; and to compare the result with the capital outlay. The problem with this approach is that the variability of oil prices is high and management will be presented with future decision opportunities to accelerate, defer, shut down, or even abandon the development project. Any NPV procedure that simply assumes a growth rate in revenues and costs is inflexible because it implicitly ignores these opportunities.

Myers [1987] has pointed out, "Discounted cash flow analysis may have been misused, and consequently not accepted, in strategic applications," and ". . . may fail in strategic applications even if it is properly applied." Net present value methodologies are readily applied to relatively stable businesses and for standard capital budgeting decisions such as machine replacements, where the main benefit is reduced cost in a clearly defined activity. But NPV is less helpful for valuing investments that have substantial growth opportunities and is almost no help at all for pure research and development, where almost all of the value is an option value. To address this deficiency in the NPV method we discuss options on assets in the next section.

OPTIONS ON ASSETS

Option pricing approaches to valuation are the best way to think about capturing flexibility in the modeling process. As we shall see, they have been successfully applied whenever the market price of the underlying risky asset is known. From the introduction to the chapter, we saw that knowing the market price of a perfectly correlated asset is equivalent to knowing the risk-adjusted discount rate to apply to each stage of the decision tree. Option pricing has been successfully applied to investments in oil, natural gas, coal, gold, copper, silver, and aircraft. Its drawback is that it has not been more widely applied because the price and stochastic behavior of the underlying risky asset is usually not known. For example, how would you model the world commodity price of automobiles?

We will begin with the mechanics of valuing a simple deferral option, then provide a taxonomy of asset options with examples of the insights provided by valuing some of them. Asset options are one of the most promising areas of research in corporate finance because they show great promise in enabling managers to place numerical values on the flexibility offered by future decisions. We will conclude the discussion with a detailed example of an abandonment option.

Valuing a Simple Deferral Option

Go back and take a look at Figure 13.1. Suppose it is a representation of the cash flows of an oil development project and that the priced asset in Figure 13.2 is a barrel of oil that is worth $20 right now but has a 50-50 chance of being worth $36 or $12 within a year. We have already determined that the project, as diagrammed, has a negative NPV of −$4 million. Also, remember that we estimated the appropriate risk-adjusted discount rate to be 20 percent.

Suppose we complicate the picture by introducing a one-year license that allows management to wait one year, and then undertake the project if the good state of nature occurs or allow the license to expire if the bad state occurs. The license provides flexibility — the *option to defer*. Let us say the risk-free rate of interest is constant at 8 percent. Now the decision tree is more complex, as shown in Figure 13.12. Note that the option to defer (implied by the license) dramatically alters the shape of payouts. Instead of paying $104 now to receive either $180 or $60, we can wait to see if the state of nature is favorable, then go ahead and invest, for a net of $67.68; or we can decide to abandon the project in the bad state of nature. An analogous situation is an R&D project. We invest a

---

FIGURE 13.12 Decision Tree with an Option to Defer

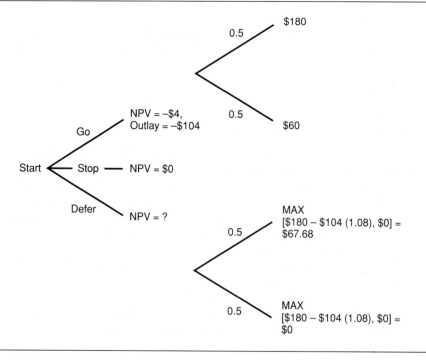

FIGURE 13.13   Payouts of a Mimicking Portfolio

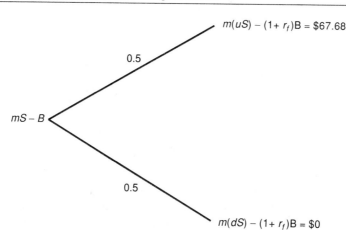

$m(uS) - (1 + r_f)B = \$67.68$

$mS - B$

0.5

0.5

$m(dS) - (1 + r_f)B = \$0$

small sum now to find out if a product or an idea is going to turn out to be good or bad. If it is good, we invest more and proceed. If it is bad, we stop. Without the license to defer, the optimal (inflexible) NPV decision was to stop, and its payout was $0.

How shall we value the license that provides a flexibility option to defer? We will illustrate both the decision tree and the option pricing approaches. The problem with the decision tree approach (DTA) is that we do not know the appropriate discount rate. The 20 percent rate derived from our NPV comparable is inappropriate, because the comparable security is not even approximately correlated with the payouts from the flexibility option. But let us use it anyway, just for the heck of it. The decision tree analysis would compute the NPV as

$$NPV = \frac{.5(\$67.68) + .5(\$0)}{1.20} = \$28.20.$$

Next, we turn to the option pricing approach. It combines the desirable features of both the NPV and DTA approaches. From the NPV approach, it borrows the idea that we must find a comparable (perfectly correlated security) to correctly evaluate risk, and from the DTA approach it uses decision nodes (not rigid event nodes) to model flexibility.

The option pricing approach proceeds to solve the problem by creating a portfolio of observable securities whose prices (and required rates of return) are known and whose payouts exactly mimic the payouts of our decision tree. Since the market prices of the comparable securities are known, we can value the option to defer. The mimicking portfolio whose payouts are diagrammed in Figure 13.13 consists of m shares of the comparable stock, S, and B borrowed dollars at the risk-free rate, r_f. The payouts in the good state ($67.68) and the bad state ($0) exactly replicate the payouts in the decision tree, given the option to defer (Figure 13.12). We can solve for the value of m and the number of units of the riskless bond, B, because we have two equations and two unknowns.

$$m(uS) - (1 + r_f)B = \$67.68$$
$$m(dS) - (1 + r_f)B = \$0$$

Given that $uS = \$36$, $dS = \$12$, and $r_f = .08$, we have

$$B = \$31.33 \text{ and } m = 2.82 \text{ shares.}$$

Thus, a mimicking portfolio with 2.82 shares of the comparable security and $31.33 in borrowed funds has exactly the same payouts as the flexible option to defer. Since the mimicking portfolio has the same payouts, it has the same value.

$$mS - B = 2.82 (\$20) - \$31.33$$
$$= \$25.07$$

Going back to Figure 13.12, this means that if the license to defer cost less than $25.07, we would purchase it. Then, if the favorable state of nature occurred, we would proceed with the project, paying $104(1.08) = $112.32 and receiving a cash flow stream worth $180. But if the unfavorable state turned up, we would simply decide not to go forward with the project.

If we compare the option pricing value of the option to defer, $25.07, with the DTA value, $28.20, we see that the DTA overvalued the option because it used the 20 percent discount rate taken from the NPV analysis—but the NPV payouts did not mimic the payouts on the flexibility option. Naively applied, the DTA was comparing apples and oranges. The DTA would have given the same answer as the option pricing approach had it used a discount rate of 35 percent:

$$\text{Value} = \frac{\text{Expected cash flow}}{1 + \text{Risk-adjusted rate}}$$

$$= \frac{.5(\$67.68) + .5(\$0)}{1.35}$$

$$= \$25.07.$$

Finally, the value of the flexibility provided by the option to defer is the difference between the NPV computed using only event nodes, and the value with the option to defer. Recall that the NPV was −$4 and the value with the option to defer was $25.07; therefore, the option to defer is worth $29.07.

To summarize this section, we have shown that the option pricing approach is superior to both the NPV technique and DTA. It combines the use of decision nodes with the concept of using risk-adjusted comparables to correctly evaluate decisions that involve flexibility. Next, we describe the broad categories of asset options and give real-world analogues for each.

A Taxonomy of Asset Options

Ordinary NPV analysis tends to understate a project's value because it fails to capture adequately the benefits of operating flexibility and other strategic factors such as follow-on investment. To identify potential operating flexibility and strategic factors, we will

FIGURE 13.14   Decision Tree with an Abandonment Option

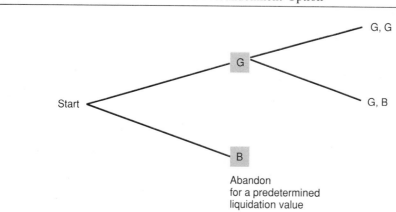

classify asset options into five mutually exclusive (but not exhaustive) categories and discuss some potential implications. The first part of using option pricing for investment decisions is simply recognizing when asset options are to be found in the decision tree for a project.

Abandonment Option.   The option to abandon (or sell) a project — for example, the right to abandon an open pit coal mine — is formally equivalent to an American put option on the stock. Figure 13.14 is a decision tree with an abandonment option attached to it. If the bad outcome turns up at the end of the first period, the decision maker may decide to abandon the project and realize the expected liquidation value. Then, the expected liquidation (or resale) value of the project may be thought of as the exercise price of the put. When the present value of the asset falls below the liquidation value, the act of abandoning (or selling) the project is equivalent to exercising the put. Because the liquidation value of the project sets a lower bound on the value of the project, the option to liquidate is valuable. A project that can be liquidated is therefore worth more than the same project without the possibility of abandonment. We shall go into a detailed example of an abandonment option later in this section of the chapter.

Most research and development projects are composed of a series of abandonment options. Figure 13.15 illustrates the decision tree for a pharmaceutical R&D project. Note that, depending on the success or failure of experiments at each phase of the project, it can be continued or abandoned (for zero value). Even though the discount rate was chosen in an ad hoc manner because there was no perfectly correlated underlying risky asset, fully 45 percent of the project's value resulted from the staged abandonment options. The remainder of its value was the NPV, without taking the abandonment options into account.

Option to Defer Development.   The option to defer an investment outlay to develop a property is formally equivalent to an American call option on the stock. (See Chapter 12.)

FIGURE 13.15   Analysis of a Multistaged Pharmaceutical R&D Project ($ Millions)

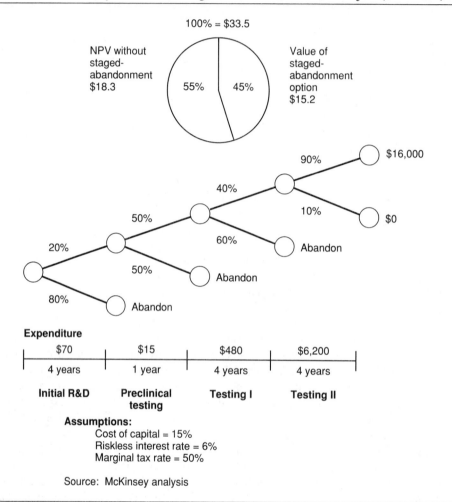

Assumptions:
Cost of capital = 15%
Riskless interest rate = 6%
Marginal tax rate = 50%

Source: McKinsey analysis

For example, the owner of a lease on an undeveloped oil reserve has the right to "acquire" a developed reserve by paying a lease-on-development cost. However, the owner can defer the development process until oil prices rise. In other words, the managerial option implicit in holding an undeveloped reserve is in fact a deferral option. The expected development cost may be thought of as the exercise price of the call. The net production revenue less depletion of the developed reserve is the opportunity cost incurred by deferring the investment. If this opportunity cost is too high, the decision maker may want to exercise the option (that is, develop the reserve) before its relinquishment date. Figure 13.16 illustrates this type of option.

FIGURE 13.16   Decision Tree with Option to Defer

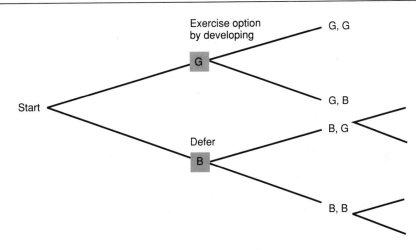

Because the deferrable investment option gives management the right, but not the obligation, to make the investment to develop the property, a project that can be deferred is worth more than the same project without the flexibility to defer development.

In one application, a mining company was deciding on the correct bid for a mineral property lease. A very careful NPV analysis that assumed a reasonable growth rate for the mineral price resulted in a value that was about 50 percent lower than what the company anticipated would be the winning bid. At the current price, the project would be only marginally profitable if developed immediately. However, the NPV analysis did not account for the value of an implicit option to defer development for up to five years — that is, to wait for better prices before making capital outlays to develop the project. Given the very high production rate that was anticipated once the site was developed, analysis showed that the deferral option increased the NPV estimate by up to 100 percent, depending on the variance of mineral prices and on whether they were assumed to be mean-reverting.

Mean reversion played an important role in developing a realistic model, because mineral prices tend to fluctuate around a long-term average. When prices rise rapidly, they are driven down as marginal suppliers open up production and users switch to substitutes. And when prices fall, producers shut down and users move away from alternate sources.

Option to Expand or Grow.   The option to expand the scale of a project's operation is formally equivalent to an American call option on the stock. For example, management may choose to build production capacity in excess of the expected level of output so that it can produce at a higher rate if the product is more successful than was originally antici-

FIGURE 13.17   Decision Tree with Option to Expand

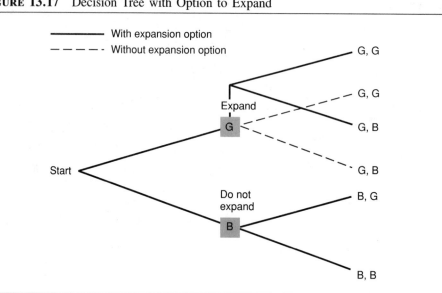

pated. Figure 13.17 illustrates this type of option. Because the expansion option gives management the right, but not the obligation, to make additional follow-on investment (for example, to increase the production rate) if project conditions turn out to be favorable, a project that can be expanded is worth more than the same project without the flexibility to expand.

The option to expand is difficult to evaluate in practice because its decision tree is complex. For example, the option to expand can be exercised today by building excess capacity or next year by building excess capacity then, and so it goes.

Option to Shrink. The option to shrink the scale of a project's operation is formally equivalent to an American put option on stock. Many projects can be engineered in such a way that output can be scaled back in the future. For example, a project can be modularized. Foregoing planned future expenditures on the project is equivalent to the exercise price of the put. Figure 13.18 illustrates this type of option. Because the shrinkage option gives management the right to reduce the operating scale if project conditions turn out to be unfavorable, a project that can be shrunk is worth more than the same project without the flexibility to scale back.

Switching Options. This is one of the most general classes of asset options. The option to switch project operations is in fact a portfolio of options that consists of both call and put options. For example, restarting operations when a project is currently shut down is equivalent to an American call option. Similarly, shutting down operations when unfavorable conditions arise is equivalent to an American put option. The cost of restarting (or

FIGURE 13.18   Decision Tree with an Option to Shrink

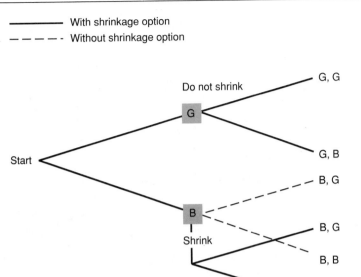

shutting down) operations may be thought of as the exercise price of the call (or put). A project whose operation can be dynamically turned on and off (or switched between two distinct locations, and so on) is worth more than the same project without the flexibility to switch. A flexible manufacturing system (FMS) with the ability to produce two products is a good example of this type of option. (See Figure 13.19.)

To illustrate the importance of switching options, we can discuss the results of a consulting assignment that applied option analysis to the valuation of a mineral extraction company. Let's call it Kryptonite. Kryptonite is a globally traded commodity product. Kryptonite Mining Limited was the world's leading producer of kryptonite, supplying over one-third of the free world's demand. It had four production sites, each with a different layout of operating mines and a different extraction technology. The random movement of spot kryptonite prices had been extremely volatile in the past four years. Our study focused on developing a valuation method for each site as well as providing some guidance regarding the shut-down/reopen decision — a switching option. Initial estimates of Kryptonite Mining's NPV based on analysts' forecasts of kryptonite prices measured only up to 45 percent of Kryptonite Mining's current market value of equity (see Figure 13.20). A scenario-based NPV analysis allowing for no explicit operational flexibilities increased this estimate to 71 percent of equity value. Finally, the option pricing valuation with shut-down/reopen and abandonment options gave us a valuation of Kryptonite Mining's equity of 116 percent of its current market value.

FIGURE 13.19   Decision Tree with Switching Options

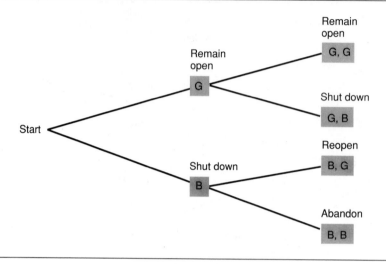

FIGURE 13.20   Valuation of Kryptonite Mining Corp. ($ Millions)

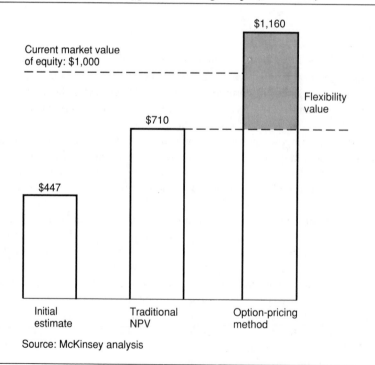

Source: McKinsey analysis

The shut-down, reopen, and abandonment option values as fractions of the corresponding site option pricing values ranged between 5 and 15 percent for a spot price range of $1.75/ounce to $2.25/ounce. These option values were much higher for lower spot prices and much lower for higher spot prices.

A major benefit of the analysis was that it provided insight into the economics of when to open up and shut down each site. Given that a mine was open, it was optimal to keep it open even when the marginal revenue from a ton of output was less than the marginal cost of extraction. The intuitive explanation is that the fixed cost of closing an operation might be incurred needlessly if the commodity price rose in the near future. The opposite result applies to a closed mine. Due to the cost of reopening it, the optimal decision might be to keep it closed until the commodity price rose substantially above the marginal cost of production.

Abandonment Option: Detailed Example

The following example shows how to analyze an abandonment decision in two ways: first, by using a decision tree with an ad hoc risk-adjusted discount rate, and second, by using option pricing with the NPV of the project without options taken as the price of the underlying risky asset.

The Palmer Corporation has invested $300 in new machinery with expected cash flows over two years. This is shown in Table 13.2. Two sets of probabilities are associated with the project. The initial probabilities should be interpreted as probabilities of particular cash flows from the first year only; the conditional probabilities are the probabilities of particular cash flows in the second year, given that a specific outcome has occurred in the first year. Thus, the results in the second year are *conditional* upon the results of the first year. If high profits occur in the first year, chances are that the second year will also bring high profits. To obtain the probability that a particular first-year outcome and a particular second-year outcome will both occur, we must multiply the initial probability by the conditional probability to obtain what is termed the *joint probability*.

TABLE 13.2   Expected Cash Flows

Year 1		Year 2	
Initial Probability P(1)	Cash Flow	Conditional Probability P(2|1)	Cash Flow
(0.3)	$200	(0.3)	$100
		(0.5)	200
		(0.2)	300
(0.4)	300	(0.3)	200
		(0.5)	300
		(0.2)	400
(0.3)	400	(0.3)	300
		(0.4)	400
		(0.3)	500

Table 13.3　Calculation of Expected Net Present Value

Year 1			Year 2			Probability Analysis				
Cash Flow (1)	PV Factor (2)	Present Value: (1) × (2) (3)	Cash Flow (4)	PV Factor (5)	Present Value: (4) × (5) (6)	Present Value of Total Cash Flow: (3) + (6) (7)	Initial Prob- ability (8)	Condi- tional Prob- ability (9)	Joint Prob- ability: (8) × (9) (10)	Expected Value: (7) × (10) (11)
			$100	0.7972	$ 80	$259		0.3	0.09	$ 23
$200	0.8929	$179	200	0.7972	159	338	0.3	0.5	0.15	51
			300	0.7972	239	418		0.2	0.06	25
			200	0.7972	159	427		0.3	0.12	51
300	0.8929	268	300	0.7972	239	507	0.4	0.5	0.20	101
			400	0.7972	319	587		0.2	0.08	47
			300	0.7972	239	596		0.3	0.09	54
400	0.8929	357	400	0.7972	319	676	0.3	0.4	0.12	81
			500	0.7972	399	756		0.3	0.09	68
									1.00	$501

Expected present value = $501

Expected net present value = $201

These concepts are applied to the data of Table 13.2 to construct Table 13.3. The project is not expected to have any returns after the second year. The cost of capital relevant to the project is assumed to be 12 percent.[5] To indicate the role of abandonment value, we first calculate the expected net present value of the investment and the expected standard deviation of the project's internal rate of return *without* considering abandonment value. In the calculation made in Table 13.3, we find the expected NPV to be $201.

In Table 13.4, we calculate the standard deviation of the project's rate of return, finding that $\sigma = 33.5\%$. Next, we can expand this analysis to take abandonment value into account. Suppose the abandonment value of the project at the end of the first year is estimated to be $250. This is the amount that can be obtained by liquidating the project after the first year, and the $250 is independent of actual first-year results.[6] If the project is abandoned after one year, then the $250 will replace any second-year returns. In other words, if the project is abandoned at the end of Year 1, then Year 1 returns will increase by $250 and Year 2 returns will be zero. The present value of this estimated $250 abandonment option is, therefore, compared with the expected present values of the cash flows that would occur during the second year if abandonment did not take place. To make the comparison valid, however, we must use the second-year flows based on the conditional

---

[5]This estimate may be obtained by using the CAPM and observing the required rates on projects or companies of similar risk.

[6]In other words, we assume that the exercise price of the put option at the end of the first year is known with certainty. It is not a random variable.

TABLE 13.4   Calculation of Rate of Return Standard Deviation

| Cash Flow | | | | | | | | |
Year 1	Year 2	IRR	$IRR - \overline{IRR}$	$(IRR - \overline{IRR})^2$	×	Joint Probability	=	$p_i(IRR - \overline{IRR})^2$
$200	$100	0.0%	−.594	.352		.09		.0318
200	200	21.5	−.379	.144		.15		.0215
200	300	38.7	−.207	.043		.06		.0026
300	200	45.7	−.137	.019		.12		.0023
300	300	61.8	.024	.001		.20		.0001
300	400	75.8	.164	.027		.08		.0022
400	300	86.9	.275	.076		.09		.0068
400	400	100.0	.406	.165		.12		.0198
400	500	112.0	.526	.277		.09		.0249
Sum						1.00	VAR(IRR) =	.1120

Note: $\overline{IRR} = \Sigma p_i IRR_i$, where p_i = joint probability, $\overline{IRR}$ = 59.4%
$[VAR(IRR)]^{1/2} = \sigma(IRR) = .3347$ or 33.47%.

probabilities only, rather than the joint probabilities that were used in the preceding analysis. This calculation is shown in Table 13.5.

We next compare the present value of the $250 abandonment value, $250 × 0.8929 = $223, with the branch expected present values for each of the three possible cash flow patterns (branches) depicted in Table 13.5. If the $223 present value of abandonment exceeds one or more of the expected present values of the possible branches of cash flows, taking abandonment value into account will improve the indicated returns from the project. The $223 does exceed the $152 expected PV shown in Table 13.5 for

TABLE 13.5   Expected Present Values of Cash Flow During the Second Year

Cash Flow	PV Factor	PV	Conditional Probability		Expected Present Value
$100	0.7972	$ 80	0.3		$ 24
200	0.7972	159	0.5		80
300	0.7972	239	0.2		48
				Branch total	$152
200	0.7972	159	0.3		$ 48
300	0.7972	239	0.5		120
400	0.7972	319	0.2		64
				Branch total	$232
300	0.7972	239	0.3		$ 72
400	0.7972	319	0.4		128
500	0.7972	399	0.3		120
				Branch total	$320

TABLE 13.6   Expected Net Present Value with Abandonment Value Included

Year 1 Cash Flow (1)	×	PV Factor (2)	=	PV (3)	Year 2 Cash Flow (4)	×	PV Factor (5)	=	PV (6)	Present Value of Total Cash Flow (7)	×	Joint Prob-ability (8)	=	Expected Value (9)
$450		0.8929		$402	$ 0		0.7972		$ 0	$402		0.30		$121
					⎰ 200		0.7972		159	427		0.12		51
300		0.8929		268	⎨ 300		0.7972		239	507		0.20		101
					⎱ 400		0.7972		319	587		0.08		47
					⎰ 300		0.7972		239	596		0.09		54
400		0.8929		357	⎨ 400		0.7972		319	676		0.12		81
					⎱ 500		0.7972		399	756		0.09		68
												1.00		

Expected present value = $523
Expected net present value = $223

second-year cash flows when the first-year cash flow is $200. In Table 13.6, therefore, abandonment after Year 1 is assumed for the $200 case and the new NPV is calculated; the $250 abandonment value is added to the $200 cash flow to obtain a $450 Year 1 cash flow, and the Year 2 cash flow becomes $0. The new calculation of the standard deviation of returns is shown in Table 13.7.

We may now compare the results when abandonment value is taken into account with the results when it is not considered. Including abandonment value in the calculations increases the expected net present value from $201 to $223, or by about 10 percent. It

TABLE 13.7   Calculation of Rate of Return Standard Deviation
with Abandonment Value Included

Cash Flow Year 1	Year 2	IRR	IRR − $\overline{\text{IRR}}$	(IRR − $\overline{\text{IRR}}$)²	×	Joint Probability	=	p_i(IRR − $\overline{\text{IRR}}$)²
$450	$ 0	50.0%	−.188	.035		.09		.0032
450	0	50.0	−.188	.035		.15		.0053
450	0	50.0	−.188	.035		.06		.0021
300	200	45.7	−.231	.053		.12		.0064
300	300	61.8	−.070	.005		.20		.0010
300	400	75.8	.070	.005		.08		.0004
400	300	86.9	.181	.033		.09		.0030
400	400	100.0	.312	.097		.12		.0116
400	500	112.0	.432	.187		.09		.0168
Sum						1.00		VAR(IRR) = .0498

Note: $\overline{\text{IRR}} = \sum_i p_i \text{IRR}_i$, where p_i = joint probability, $\overline{\text{IRR}}$ = 68.8%; [VAR(IRR)]$^{1/2}$ = σ(IRR) = .2232 or 22.32%.

TABLE 13.8   Calculation of Expected Net Cash Flow for Second Period
When $200 Was Earned During the First Year

Cash Flow	×	PV Factor	=	PV	×	Probability Factor	=	Discounted Expected Cash Flow
$100		0.8929		$ 89		0.3		$ 27
200		0.8929		179		0.5		90
300		0.8929		268		0.2		54
						Expected present value = $171		

reduces the expected standard deviation of returns from 33.5 percent to 22.3 percent. Thus, for this problem, abandonment value improves the attractiveness of the investment.

Abandonment value is important in another aspect of financial decision making: the reevaluation of projects in succeeding years after they have been undertaken. The decision to continue the project or to abandon it sometime during its life depends on which branch occurs during each time period. For example, suppose that during Year 1 the cash flow actually obtained was $200. Then the three possibilities associated with Year 2 are the three that were conditionally dependent upon a $200 outcome in Year 1. The other six probabilities for Year 2, which were considered in the initial evaluation, were conditional upon other first-year outcomes and are thus no longer relevant. A calculation (Table 13.8) is then made of the second-year net cash flows, discounted back one year.

At the end of the first year the abandonment value is $250. This is compared with the expected present value of the second-year net cash flow series discounted one year. This value is determined to be $171, so the abandonment value of $250 exceeds the net present value of returns for the second year. Therefore, the project should be abandoned at the end of the first year.

In summary, it is sometimes advantageous to abandon a project even though the net present value of continued operation is positive. The basic reason is that the present value of abandonment after a shorter time may actually be greater than the present value of continued operation.

Another, perhaps better way to analyze the abandonment decision is to compute the NPV of the project without the option to abandon, and then add to it the value of the abandonment put option. Thus, we have

NPV (with abandonment) = NPV (without abandonment)
+ Value of abandonment put option.

The greater the variance of returns on the project, the greater will be the value of the abandonment option. In Table 13.4 we saw that the standard deviation of returns was 33.5 percent for the project without the abandonment option. This is the correct standard deviation to use in the Black-Scholes formula because it is an estimate of the standard deviation of returns on the underlying asset. The way our example has been structured, we also know that the put option may be exercised only at the end of the first year. Therefore

TABLE 13.9 Present Value of the Project Excluding First-Year Cash Flows

Year 2 Cash Flow	Joint Probability	PV Factor	PV
$100	.09	.7972	$ 7.17
200	.15	.7972	23.92
300	.06	.7972	14.35
200	.12	.7972	19.13
300	.20	.7972	47.83
400	.08	.7972	25.51
300	.09	.7972	21.52
400	.12	.7972	38.27
500	.09	.7972	35.87
Sum	1.00		$233.57

it is a European put option with one year to maturity and an exercise price of $250. The present value of the underlying asset is the present value of the project without abandonment, that is, $501. We assume the risk-free rate is 5 percent.

Note that if the project is abandoned at the end of the first year, we will abandon it only after receiving the first year's cash flows. Therefore, we must compute the asset value *without* these cash flows in order to value the abandonment put option. The calculation is shown in Table 13.9.

The value of the abandonment put option can be found by using the Black-Scholes formula to value the corresponding call, then put-call parity to compute the put value. The Black-Scholes call value is

$$C = SN(d_1) - Xe^{-r_FT}N(d_2),$$

where

$$d_1 = \frac{ln(S/X) + r_FT}{\sigma\sqrt{T}} + \frac{1}{2}\sigma\sqrt{T}$$

$$d_2 = d_1 - \sigma\sqrt{T}.$$

Substituting in the numbers from our example we have

$$d_1 = \frac{ln(233.57/250) + .05(1)}{.335\sqrt{1}} + \frac{1}{2}(.335)\sqrt{1}$$

$$d_1 = \frac{ln(.9343) + .05}{.335} + .168$$

$$= \frac{-.068 + .05}{.335} + .168$$

$$= -.0537 + .168 = .1143$$

$$d_2 = .1143 - .335\sqrt{1} = -.2207.$$

Using Appendix D at the end of the book, we find that

$$N(d_1) = .5 + .0455 = .5455, \text{ and}$$
$$N(d_2) = .5 - .0874 = .4126.$$

Thus, the value of the call option is

$$C = 233.57(.5455) - 250(.4126)e^{-.05(1)}$$
$$= 127.41 - 250(.4126)(.9512)$$
$$= 127.41 - 98.12 = \$29.29.$$

Finally, from Chapter 12 we can use Equation 12.5, put-call parity, to find the value of the European put that is implied by the option to abandon.

$$C_0 - P_0 = S_0 - Xe^{-r_F T}$$
$$P_0 = C_0 - S_0 + Xe^{-r_F T}$$
$$= 29.29 - 233.57 + 250e^{-.05(1)}$$
$$= 29.29 - 233.57 + 250(.9512)$$
$$= 29.29 - 233.57 + 237.80$$
$$= \$33.52$$

The decision tree approach gave an abandonment value equal to $22 (that is, $223, the value with abandonment, minus $201, the value without abandonment). The option pricing approach gave an abandonment value of $33.52. We obtained different answers because the assumptions of the Black-Scholes OPM and the decision tree approach are different. For example, Black-Scholes assumes a lognormal distribution of outcomes whereas the decision tree only crudely approximates the continuum of possibilities.

FURTHER DEVELOPMENTS IN ABANDONMENT DECISION RULES

The traditional abandonment decision rule is that the project should be abandoned in the first year that abandonment value exceeds the present value of remaining expected cash flows from continued operation. More recently it has become evident that this decision rule may not result in the optimal abandonment decision.[7] Abandonment at a later date may result in an even greater net present value. For example, consider a truck with two years of remaining useful life. The present value of continued use is, say, $900, but the current market value of the truck is $1,000. Clearly, if the proceeds from the sale can be invested to earn at least the applicable cost of capital, the better decision would be to sell the truck now. However, there is one option that has not been considered, which is to operate the truck for another year and collect the cash flow from one year's operations (which has a present value of $500) and then abandon it (assuming the present value of abandonment in a year is $600). Thus, the present value of this alternative is $1,100. In this case, the truck should be used for one year and then sold.

---

[7]See Dyl and Long [1969]; Robichek and Van Horne [1967]; Joy [1976].

The optimal abandonment decision rule is to determine the combination of remaining operating cash flows and future abandonment that has the maximum expected net present value. This decision rule is, unfortunately, difficult to implement, especially when the project life is long and there are numerous opportunities for abandonment over time.[8] If a piece of equipment can be used for 20 years or abandoned at the end of any year, then 20 different net present value calculations might be required to determine the optimum pattern that will result in maximum expected net present value.

It is argued that this approach is too cumbersome and all that is required is to find at least one pattern of cash flows that yields an expected net present value greater than the value of abandonment. Thus the rule becomes an accept-reject decision: Continue to operate the project as long as expected present value of continued operation and abandonment at any later period is greater than the value of abandonment now. Under this system, there is no need ever to determine the maximum expected net present value. Furthermore, since it is impossible to predict accurately future abandonment value, whatever the expected net present value is, it will surely be inaccurate.

The accept-reject decision has one shortcoming, however. It does not provide a means of selecting between mutually exclusive investments or of making capital rationing decisions. To return to our truck example, we have shown that the present value is $1,100 when the truck is operated for another year. Using the accept-reject rule, we would continue to operate the truck. But suppose a truck could be leased for $1,000 for one year and would produce cash flows worth $1,200 at net present value. If only one truck is required (mutually exclusive choice decision), or if the only source of the $1,000 to lease the truck is the sale of the old truck (capital rationing), then the value to the firm is maximized if the truck is sold and the new truck leased.

It is evident that both rules (the maximum net present value rule and the accept-reject rule) have merit. Maximum net present value should be used whenever capital rationing or mutually exclusive choices are involved. Accept-reject can be used to reduce the cumbersomeness of the problem whenever one decision is independent of all others.

SUMMARY

We have discussed three approaches to capital budgeting under uncertainty and in a multiperiod setting. Each of them has its limitations. Decision trees explicitly recognize that there is flexibility that can be represented by future actions that are contingent on future states of nature, but provide no advice on which risk-adjusted discount rate should be used or how it may change through time. Net present value analysis is often used in a way that forgets to model the flexibility provided by decisions that can be made in the future and consequently often undervalues opportunities. Option pricing provides the most insights. It explicitly models flexibility and it uses the market price of the underlying risky asset to infer the correct risk-adjusted discount rates (which change over the life of

---

[8]If we were using an option pricing approach, we would have to value an American put option on a dividend paying stock. Although there are numerical solutions to this type of problem, they are beyond the scope of this text.

the project). The mere fact that decision makers should understand and recognize asset option opportunities such as deferral, expansion (growth), shrinkage, abandonment, or switching options is important. But our understanding of how to apply asset options in practice is limited. Sometimes there are too many important sources of uncertainty. Sometimes there are too many options involved. And all too often, there is no market price for the underlying risky asset.

As decision-making tools improve, the only limitation of analysis should be the ability of the decision maker to forecast cash flows and to capture the flexibility of future decisions in his or her decision-making model.

QUESTIONS

13.1 In evaluating risky projects that are not priced, we sometimes use a priced, perfectly correlated security in choosing comparables as surrogates for the risky project under analysis. Describe what is done under a CAPM approach versus the use of an option pricing model.

13.2 What is gained by the use of a sensitivity analysis?

13.3 What is the advantage of the use of a decision tree in analyzing a risky project?

13.4 Compare the use of a certainty equivalent method with a risk-adjusted return analysis for a one-period project.

13.5 What are the limits of conventional NPV analysis?

13.6 Why is a deferral option valuable?

13.7 The ability to defer an investment outlay is formally equivalent to what kind of option?

13.8 What is the benefit of switching options that enable the decision maker to exercise shutdown, reopen, and abandonment options?

PROBLEMS

13.1 In computer simulation, the computer makes a large number of trials to show what the various outcomes of a particular decision might be if the decision could be made many times under the same conditions. In practice, the decision will be made only once, so how can simulation results be useful to the decision maker?

13.2 Your firm is considering the purchase of a tractor. It has been established that this tractor will cost $32,000, will produce revenues in the neighborhood of $10,000 (before tax), and will be depreciated via straight line to zero in eight years. The board of directors, however, is having a heated debate as to whether the tractor can be expected to last eight years. Specifically, Wayne Brown insists that he knows of some that have lasted only five years. Tom Miller agrees with Brown but argues that it is more likely that the tractor will give eight years of service. Brown agrees. Finally, Laura Evans says she has seen some last as long as ten years. Given the discussion, the board asks you to prepare a sensitivity analysis to ascertain how important the uncertainty about the life of the tractor is. Assume a 40 percent tax rate on both income and capital loss, zero salvage value, and a cost of capital of 10 percent.

13.3 You have an investment opportunity for which the outlay and cash flows are uncertain. Analysis has produced the subjective probability assessments given in Table P13.3. Let the cost of capital be 12 percent, life expectancy be ten years, and salvage value be zero.

TABLE P13.3 Subjective Probability Estimates

Outlay		Annual Cash Flow	
Probability	Amount	Probability	Amount
0.4	$ 80,000	0.2	$14,000
0.3	100,000	0.5	16,000
0.2	120,000	0.3	18,000
0.1	140,000		

a. Construct a decision tree for this investment to show probabilities, payoffs, and expected NPV.
b. Calculate the expected NPV, again using expected cash flow and expected outlay.
c. What is the probability of and the NPV of the worst possible outcome?
d. What is the probability of and the NPV of the best possible outcome?
e. Compute the probability that this will be a good investment.

13.4 Given the facts in Table P13.4, calculate the NPV of the project to determine whether the project should be accepted.

TABLE P13.4

Period	Economic State	Subjective Probability	Project CF	Risk-Free Rate, r_f	Comparison Stock, S
0	Current	1.0	−$8,000	N/A	$ 9.00
1	Bad	0.3	8,000	10%	8.00
1	Good	0.7	25,000	10%	30.00

13.5. In this two-period APT example, we are given the data shown in Figure P13.5. Calculate the NPV to determine whether the project should be accepted.

13.6 In this two-period OPM example, to allow for the flexibility of abandonment we present the data as shown in Figure P13.6.
a. Calculate the NPV of the project to determine whether to accept it.
b. Why do the data in this problem result in a lower value for the implicit put option as compared with the example in the text?

FIGURE P13.5   Two-Period APT Problem

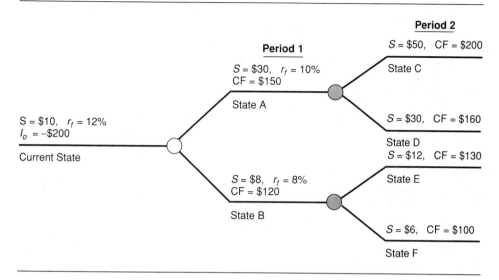

FIGURE P13.6   Two-Period OPM Problem

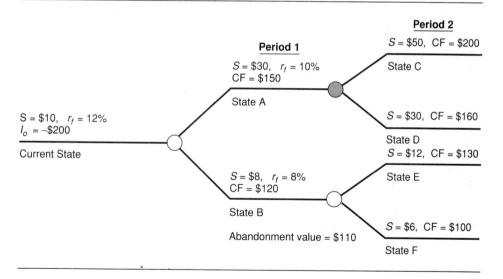

SELECTED REFERENCES

Bogue, M., and Roll, R., "Capital Budgeting of Risky Projects with 'Imperfect' Markets for Physical Capital," *Journal of Finance,* (May 1974), pp. 601–613.

Brennan, M., and Schwartz, E., "Evaluating Natural Resource Investments," *Journal of Business,* (April 1985), pp. 135–157.

Brumelle, Shelby L., and Schwab, Bernhard, "Capital Budgeting with Uncertain Future Opportunities: A Markovian Approach," *Journal of Financial and Quantitative Analysis,* 7 (January 1973), pp. 111–122.

Constantinides, G., "Admissible Uncertainty in the Intertemporal Asset Pricing Model," *Journal of Financial Economics,* (March 1980), pp. 71–86.

———, "Market Risk Adjustment in Project Valuation," *Journal of Finance,* (May 1978), pp. 603–616.

Copeland, T.E., and Weston, J.F., *Financial Theory and Corporate Policy,* 3rd ed., Reading, Mass.: Addison-Wesley Publishing Company, 1988.

———, "A Note on the Evaluation of Cancellable Operating Leases," *Financial Management,* 11 (Summer 1982), pp. 60–67.

Dyl, E.A., and Long, H.W., "Abandonment Value and Capital Budgeting: Comment," *Journal of Finance,* (March 1969), pp. 88–95.

Fama, E., "Risk-Adjusted Discount Rates and Capital Budgeting under Uncertainty," *Journal of Financial Economics,* (August 1977), pp. 3–24.

Gehr, A., "Risk-Adjusted Capital Budgeting Using Arbitrage," *Financial Management,* (Winter 1981), pp. 14–19.

Hillier, Frederick S., "The Derivation of Probabilistic Information for the Evaluation of Risky Investments," *Management Science,* 9 (April 1963), pp. 443–457.

Jacoby, H., and Laughton, D., "Project Evaluation Using a Probabilistic-Process Representation of Uncertainty," M.I.T. Energy Laboratory working paper 88-001WP, June 1988.

Joy, O. Maurice, "Abandonment Values and Abandonment Decisions: A Clarification," *Journal of Finance,* 31 (September 1976), pp. 1225–1228.

Kryzanowski, Lawrence; Lusztig, Peter; and Schwab, Bernhard, "Monte Carlo Simulation and Capital Expenditure Decisions—A Case Study," *Engineering Economist,* 18 (Fall 1972), pp. 31–48.

Lewellen, W., "Some Observations on Risk-Adjusted Discount Rates," *Journal of Finance,* (September 1977), pp. 1331–1337.

———, "Reply to Pettway and Celec," *Journal of Finance,* (September 1979), pp. 1065–1066.

Majd, S., and Pindyck, R., "Time to Build, Option Value, and Investment Decisions," *Journal of Financial Economics,* (March 1987), pp. 7–28.

Mason, S., and Merton, R., "The Role of Contingent Claims Analysis in Corporate Finance," in *Recent Advances in Corporate Finance,* E. Altman and M. Subrahmanyam, eds., Homewood, Ill.: Richard D. Irwin, 1985, pp. 7–54.

McDonald, R., and Siegel, D., "Investment and the Valuation of Firms When There is an Option to Shut Down," *International Economic Review,* 26 (June 1985), pp. 331–349.

Miller, M., and Upton, C., "A Test of the Hotelling Valuation Principle," *Journal of Political Economy,* 93 (February 1985), pp. 1–25.

Myers, S., "Financial Theory and Financial Strategy," *Midland Corporate Finance Journal,* (Spring 1987), pp. 6–13.

———, "Procedures for Capital Budgeting under Uncertainty," *Industrial Management Review,* (Spring 1968), pp. 1–20.

———, and Turnbull, S., "Capital Budgeting and the Capital Asset Pricing Model: Good News and Bad News," *Journal of Finance,* (May 1977), pp. 321–332.

Pappas, James L., "The Role of Abandonment Value in Capital Asset Management," *Engineering Economist,* 22 (Fall 1976), pp. 53–61.

Pindyck, R., "Irreversible Investment, Capacity Choice, and the Value of the Firm," *American Economic Review,* (December 1988), pp. 969–985.

————, and Siegel, D., "The Value of Working to Invest," *Quarterly Journal of Economics,* (November 1986), pp. 707–727.

————, "Abandonment Value and Capital Budgeting: Reply," *Journal of Finance,* 24 (March 1969), pp. 96–97.

Roberts, K., and Weitzman, M., "Funding Criteria for Research, Development and Exploration Projects," *Econometrica,* (September 1981), pp. 1261–1288.

Robichek, A.A., and Van Horne, J.C., "Abandonment Value and Capital Budgeting," *Journal of Finance,* 22 (December 1967), pp. 577–590.

Ross, S., "A Simple Approach to the Valuation of Risky Streams," *Journal of Business,* (July 1979), pp. 254–286.

————, "The Arbitrage Theory of Capital Asset Pricing," *Journal of Economic Theory,* (December 1976), pp. 341–361.

Smidt, Seymour, "A Bayesian Analysis of Project Selection and of Post Audit Evaluations," *Journal of Finance,* 34 (June 1979), pp. 675–688.

Stapleton, R., and Subrahmanyam, M., "A Multiperiod Equilibrium Asset Pricing Model," *Econometrica,* (September 1978), pp. 1077–1096.

Triantis, A., and Hodder, J., "Valuing Flexibility as a Complex Option," *Journal of Finance,* (June 1990), pp. 549–565.

Trigeorgis, L., and Mason, S., "Valuing Managerial Flexibility," *Midland Corporate Finance Journal,* 5 (Spring 1987), pp. 14–21.

Weitzman, M.; Newey, W.; and Rabin, M., "Sequential R&D Strategy for Synfuels," *Bell Journal of Economics,* (Autumn 1981), pp. 574–590.

CHAPTER 14

Managing Financial Risk

In the preceding chapter, we discuss decision-making methodologies for investment decisions under uncertainty. In the present chapter, we discuss more generally methods of dealing with all types of risks faced by business firms. We shall emphasize the need to look at risk management in a comprehensive manner. In particular, we shall describe methods by which all types of changes in costs or prices of all types of financial instruments as well as other assets and liabilities can be managed. We shall cover the following outline of topics.

I.   *Types of Risk*
   A.   *Market, systematic, or nondiversifiable risk*
   B.   *Nonmarket, unsystematic, or diversifiable risk*

II.   *Methods of Managing Risks*
   A.   *Static hedging methods*
   B.   *Dynamic hedging methods*

III.   *Applications*
   A.   *Portfolio insurance*
   B.   *Duration and immunization*
   C.   *Forward contracts*
   D.   *Futures markets*
   E.   *Interest rate swaps*

TYPES OF RISKS

In Chapters 10 and 11 on risk and return, we noted the distinction between market or systematic risk and nonmarket or unsystematic risk. Market risk can not be eliminated by diversification. Even the value of a portfolio that is well-diversified will fluctuate in response to variations in returns on the market. In addition, returns on assets will be sensitive to other market factors such as the rate of unexpected inflation, unexpected shifts in the yield curve, or unexpected shifts in risk differentials. The difficulty in practice of determining whether a risk is systematic or unsystematic can be seen in the case of unexpected changes in the prices of key commodities such as oil, aluminum, copper, or precious metals. For example, the oil supply shocks of the 1970s would represent a candidate for the systematic risk category because they appeared to trigger recession and hurt or helped firms in a wide range of industries. However, Chen, Roll, and Ross [1986] did not find oil to be a systematic factor.

Unsystematic or nonmarket risks are those specific to individual firms. They include strategic, operating, and financial policies and decisions of the firm. These will vary with firms and industries, so we focus on a discussion of systematic risks that generalizes across firms. The distinction between systematic and unsystematic risks is well-illustrated by the problems that developed in the savings and loan and commercial banking industries in the 1980s.

Since the use of a wide range of devices to manage risk is possible, why the difficulties of the savings and loan associations that emerged in the late 1980s and the difficulties of commercial banks that emerged in the early 1990s? The answer in part is that a relatively small fraction of financial institutions made use of hedging techniques available. A survey of banks and savings and loan associations for 1982 found that about 31 percent of S&Ls used interest rate futures compared with about 10 percent for banks [Booth, Smith, and Stolz, 1984]. Furthermore, it was difficult to manage fundamental unsystematic business and competitive risks. Some historical and legislative perspectives help explain what happened.[1]

In the 1970s, S&Ls were virtual "money machines." On average, they were investing in fixed rate 30-year mortgages paying 10 percent financed by deposits with six-month maturities paying about 6 percent. Low interest rates paid on their deposits were helped by the Federal Reserve Bank Regulation Q, which specified maximum interest that could be paid on savings deposits, giving S&Ls authority to pay 25 to 50 basis points (1 percentage point equals 100 basis points) higher than commercial banks. On October 6, 1979, the Federal Reserve announced it was shifting the target of monetary policy from interest rate stability to control over growth of the money supply permitting interest rates to find their market levels. These developments exposed a fundamental risk problem of the S&Ls. Their investments were long term, but financed from short-term sources. Their vulnerability to interest rate increases is illustrated by the nature of their basic risk profile as shown in Figure 14.1, where ΔV is the change in value of the S&L and Δr is the change in interest rate levels. With a rise in short-term interest rates, the value of S&Ls falls. In addition to their basic market risk, other competitive and managerial problems developed.

The growth of money market funds at brokerage firms and other financial institutions represented a new form of competition paying market rates of interest to savers. By the early 1980s, therefore, Regulation Q was inoperative and many existing S&Ls were in

---

[1]For an excellent analysis of the development of the problems see Norman Strunk and Fred Case, *Where Deregulation Went Wrong: A Look at the Causes Behind Savings and Loan Failures in the 1980s,* Chicago: United States League of Savings Institutions, 1988.

FIGURE 14.1 The Risk Profile for a U.S. S&L

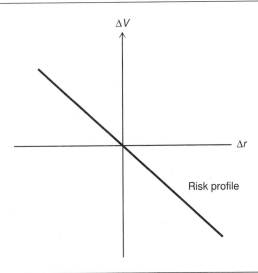

serious difficulty. In the attempt to help the S&Ls, deregulation of interest rates and loan practices took place. In addition, troubled S&Ls were permitted to borrow from their specialized central bank at low interest rates and to invest unregulated, which encouraged expansion, new S&Ls, and entry into new loan areas in which managers had no prior experience. The resulting overcapacity was aggravated by intense competition in unfamiliar areas. Deposit insurance provided a perverse incentive to speculate since it gave the financial institutions a mispriced put option to "put" the claims of depositors on the resources of the federal government under adverse outcomes.[2] Thus systematic risks were compounded by unsystematic risks.

Because of overcapacity, intense competition among lending institutions, including S&Ls and commercial banks, resulted in high ratios of loans to appraised values. The appraised values themselves were inflated by the speculative rises in both commercial and residential real estate. The equity base of both the S&Ls and commercial banks was quite low, at roughly a 3 percent level. With deposit insurance, the banks and S&Ls were able to attract deposits, but the pressure on the difference between the earning rate on assets and payment rates on deposits led to increasingly speculative investments in the attempt to develop a positive margin. As interest rates continued to fluctuate, some S&Ls in desperation bet on favorable interest rate movements. Various types of outright fraud aggravated the underlying problems. The development of holding company systems led some banks

[2]Robert Merton, "An Analytic Derivation of the Cost of Deposit Insurance and Loan Guarantees: An Application of Modern Option Pricing Theory," *Journal of Banking and Finance,* 1977, pp. 3–11; Roger C. Kormendi, Victor L. Bernard, S. Craig Pirrong, and Edward A. Snyder, "The Origins and Resolution of the Thrift Crisis," *Journal of Applied Corporate Finance,* 2 (Fall 1989), pp. 85–99.

and S&Ls to engage in transactions that generated paper profits. Real cash flows were funneled up to the holding company parent even though the business transactions of the operating subsidiaries were not generating genuine profits. All this came apart for the S&Ls during the 1980s.

Although the commercial banks were hurt by excessive lending to the less developed countries (LDCs), the commercial banks were able to take write-offs and still show profitability. But in part their profitability was maintained by expansion of loan volume at higher risk, particularly in commercial real estate. When the speculative boom in real estate subsided in the early 1980s, aggravated by regional problems in areas such as Texas and Oklahoma (later in New York and California), earnings and solvency problems began to affect commercial banks as well as the S&Ls.

The financial risks of banks and S&Ls could have been mitigated by controlling their systematic risk exposure better and by using hedges of the types described later in this chapter. Other fundamental business problems developed with excess capacity, competition that led to speculative lending and fluctuations in speculative markets. The use of hedging devices described in this chapter could have helped avoid the subsequent expansion of speculative investments. Thus the material of the present chapter has great significance not only for financial institutions, but also for corporate enterprise and the economy in general.

METHODS OF MANAGING RISKS

Since unsystematic risks vary across firms and industries, the methods of managing them can be described only in general terms. Strategic planning must be effective. Efficiency analysis for improvement of operations involves a wide variety of management methods. Diversification reduces unsystematic risks but may also move the firm into unfamiliar areas where the firm lacks managerial competence. Also investors can diversify on their own.

The management of systematic risks is the central focus of this chapter. In our presentation on options in Chapter 12, we explained how combining a position in risky assets with calls or puts enables the formation of a riskless hedge. Other methods of hedging systematic risks include the use of forward and futures contracts, swaps, and portfolio insurance. Before describing these in detail, we shall describe two alternative approaches: static hedges and dynamic hedges.

Static Hedging

A static hedge can be created by finding securities or contracts that are correlated with the risk that one is seeking to hedge. For example, in Chapter 12 we explained how call options could be combined with holdings of risky assets to form a riskless hedge. Recall that the required hedge ratio was determined by the slope of a line measuring the change in the price of a call in response to a change in the price of the risky security. Another example would be in relation to the risk profile of an S&L, depicted in Figure 14.1. Here the objective would be to enter into a contract whose value would rise with rising interest rates to neutralize the negative impact of investing long term and borrowing short term.

In a static hedge, one is "locked in" without changing hedge ratios over time. This may reduce transactions costs but creates other problems. Static hedges only work well when the hedge and the risk being hedged have the same time profile. For example, if a risk exposure has a three-year duration, a three-month forward or futures contract will be a poor hedge. A good hedge requires that the slope relationship determining the hedge ratio be stable — the correlation relationship should be high. Otherwise, the instability or nonstationarity of the relationship may signify that neither the correlation relationship nor the measured slope is statistically significant. Because of this, static hedges may not be optimal. Indeed, in seeking to form riskless hedges using options, the theory requires continuous adjustment of the hedge ratio as the price of the risky asset changes.

Dynamic Hedging

Dynamic hedging calls for continuously adjusting the hedge ratio. A number of techniques have been employed for developing hedging ratios and their adjustments. Some are regression models seeking to develop forecasting relationships measuring slopes and correlation coefficients. These are discussed at some length in writings on futures markets.[3]

Another approach to dynamic hedging is to make frequent adjustments on the basis of changes in the prices or returns of the risk-exposed assets in relation to the hedging assets. The quintessential example of this latter approach to dynamic hedging is portfolio insurance. We shall, therefore, begin our discussion of specific methodologies for hedging risks by describing portfolio insurance.

PORTFOLIO INSURANCE

The theory of dynamic trading strategies often called portfolio insurance was set forth by Leland and Rubinstein [1988] in the mid-1970s. The appearance of stock index futures in 1982 reduced the transactions costs of portfolio readjustments leading to considerable growth of portfolio insurance programs, approaching as much as $90 billion of equity assets by mid-1987. Although the stock market decline of October 1987 resulted in trading halts and reduced the popularity of traditional portfolio insurance, its fundamental methodology of option replication and related dynamic trading strategies is still sound. It continues to have an important impact on institutional portfolio management through the widespread use of its innovative concept that option strategy payoffs can be replicated without the actual use of options themselves.

Many forms of portfolio insurance have been developed. We shall limit ourselves to a description of the basic concepts from which other variations were developed. A manager responsible for a portfolio such as a company's pension fund would ideally like to participate in the upside potential of the stock market but be protected against a substantial decline in portfolio value. One way to do this would be to hold a portfolio of common stocks and then to buy protective puts against their decline in value. If perfectly hedged,

---

[3]See, for example, Thomas Schneeweis and Jot Yau, "Financial Futures Markets," Chapter 12 in *Handbook of Modern Finance*, 2d ed., Dennis E. Logue, ed., New York: Warren, Gorham & Lamont, 1990; Daniel R. Siegel and Diane F. Siegel, *Futures Markets*, Chicago: The Dryden Press, 1990.

FIGURE 14.2   Dynamic Asset Allocation, $u = 1.2$, $d = .9$

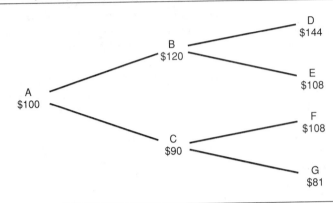

the portfolio could still participate in the rise of the price of stocks. If stock prices increased, the value of the portfolio would increase and the put options would go unused. If stock prices declined, a decline in the value of the portfolio would be avoided by exercising the put options. It is in this sense that the cost of the put options represents an insurance premium against the destruction of the values of the portfolio. Note that the use of listed puts represents a static hedge. The problem is that the puts must exist for exactly the time to exercise that the portfolio will be held. Such puts may not be available. Furthermore, transactions costs are a relatively high percentage of the value of the put.

An alternative to the use of puts is to engage in dynamic asset allocation. By frequent adjustments of the allocation of funds between the risky assets and a riskless security, results similar to that of a portfolio of risky assets plus protective puts can be achieved. Numerical examples will convey the underlying concepts involved.[4]

Case 1

This starts with risky stocks that have successive upward movements of 1.2 and downward movements of .9. An uninsured portfolio starting with an initial investment of $100 will have the binomial tree depicted in Figure 14.2. Figure 14.2 reflects the usual pattern of assumptions from the binomial option pricing model as discussed in Chapter 12. The portfolio manager does not want the pension fund to drop below 100 at node G, and therefore uses a dynamic hedging strategy, investing in risk-free bonds as well as the risky stocks.

Our first task is to determine the composition of the portfolio at node C, so that if the upbranch occurs, the expected value of F will be 108 and if the downbranch occurs, G will be 100. This is achieved by use of the following equation pattern:

$$1.2 \ S_C + 1.05 \ B_C = 108$$
$$.9 \ S_C + 1.05 \ B_C = 100$$

---

[4]These examples were developed by Daniel Asquith.

$$S_C = 26.67$$
$$1.05\ B_C = 76.00$$
$$B_C = 72.38.$$

So at node C the portfolio will be composed of risky stocks worth $26.67 and riskless bonds worth $72.38, for a total portfolio of $99.05. The next task is to choose a portfolio at node A, so that for the upside stock movement, the expected value of node B will be $120, and for the downside movement, the expected node portfolio total of $99.05 will result. Again, we set up an equation system and solution:

$$1.2\ S_A + 1.05\ B_A = 120.00$$
$$.9\ S_A + 1.05\ B_A = 99.05$$
$$S_A = 69.83$$
$$1.05\ B_A = 99.05 - 62.85$$
$$B_A = 34.48.$$

Thus to achieve the aims of the insured portfolio the composition at the start, node A will be risky stocks worth $69.83 and riskless bonds worth $34.48, totaling $104.31. Note that under the insurance program an additional investment of $4.31 is required at the starting point A. What is earned on this additional investment? The gain from the insured portfolio is the $19 additional amount earned at node G (the $100 versus $81). The implicit probability of this outcome is .25 so the expected value of the gain from the insured portfolio is $4.75. This represents exactly a 1.05 per period return from the additional $4.31 investment. Thus the additional investment earns the market rate of interest.

Case 2

Some further characteristics of portfolio insurance can be illustrated by specifying that the portfolio decision maker seeks to achieve a portfolio value of $108 at node G in Figure 14.2 rather than $100. The equation system for calculating the required portfolio composition at node C would therefore become:

$$1.2\ S_C + 1.05\ B_C = \$108$$
$$.9\ S_C + 1.05\ B_C = \$108$$
$$S_C = 0$$
$$1.05\ B_C = \$108$$
$$B_C = \$102.86.$$

Thus at node C there is no investment in stocks; the total investment of $102.86 is in the riskless bonds. We next determine the portfolio composition at starting node A. Another equation system is set up:

$$1.2\ S_A + 1.05\ B_A = \$120$$
$$.9\ S_A + 1.05\ B_A = \$102.86$$
$$S_A = \$57.13$$
$$1.05\ B_A = \$102.86 - \$51.42$$

FIGURE 14.3 Dynamic Asset Allocation, $u = 1.5$, $d = .9$

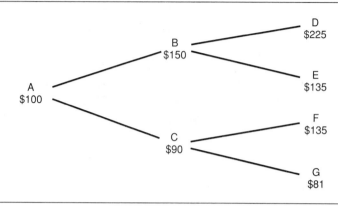

$$1.05\ B_A = \$51.44$$
$$B_A = \$48.99.$$

The starting portfolio is, therefore, $57.13 in stocks and $48.99 in riskless bonds for a total of $106.12. We thus invest an additional $6.12 to obtain the difference between $108 and the $81 at node G if uninsured. The implicit probability of obtaining the $27 differential is one-fourth, or $6.75, whose present value is $6.75/1.1025, which equals $6.12. This numerical example illustrates that to achieve more than the preservation of the $100 original portfolio value at node G required two changes. A larger additional initial investment is required. Also a larger proportion of the initial portfolio at node A is in the nonrisky asset.

Cases 1 and 2 were for zero NPV investments in stocks, which simply earn the market rate of interest. We now consider Case 3, which specifies stock movements resulting in positive NPV risky asset investments.

Case 3

In this example illustrated by Figure 14.3, the upside price movements in stocks are 1.5 while the downside movements are .9. The uninsured payoffs are shown in Figure 14.3. With the stock price movements specified, the expected return on stocks will be .5(1.5) plus .5(.9) equals 1.20. This result exceeds the 1.05 market rate of interest which we continue to assume. Our numerical example will illustrate the case where the objective for the portfolio is to achieve a return of $135 at node G. The equation system for determining the portfolio composition at node C is:

$$1.5\ S_C + 1.05\ B_C = \$135$$
$$.9\ S_C + 1.05\ B_C = \$135$$
$$.6\ S_C = 0$$
$$S_C = 0$$

$$1.05 \, B_C = \$135$$
$$B_C = \$128.57.$$

Hence the portfolio composition at node C is entirely in the riskless bonds. To determine the original portfolio at node A:

$$1.5 \, S_A + 1.05 \, B_A = \$150$$
$$.9 \, S_A + 1.05 \, B_A = \$128.57$$
$$.6 \, S_A = \$21.43$$
$$S_A = \$35.72$$
$$1.05 \, B_A = \$128.57 - \$32.145$$
$$1.05 \, B_A = \$96.425$$
$$B_A = \$91.83.$$

Thus the required initial investment is higher than in the previous two cases. The gain achieved by portfolio insurance is ($135 − $81).25, which equals $13.50. The additional insurance paid to achieve this gain is $27.55(1.1025), which equals $30.37. Thus under the conditions of the example, $30.37 is paid to gain an expected increase in value of $13.50. Thus portfolio insurance is not a "free lunch." If it had been assumed that the investment in risky assets had a negative NPV, the results would have shown a gain from the use of portfolio insurance. This case will be developed as an end-of-chapter problem.

We have described and illustrated the nature of dynamic hedging called portfolio insurance. We shall not seek to summarize the voluminous literature on a number of related controversial issues. One is whether portfolio insurance increases the volatility of stock price movements. Another is the extent to which the transactions costs involved in frequent portfolio adjustments erode the benefits.

The important theoretical contribution of portfolio insurance is unassailable. It demonstrates the general proposition that the number of securities (in relation to possible future states-of-the-world) can be increased and options strategy payoffs can be replicated without the actual use of options. In addition, we have illustrated the concept involved in dynamic hedging adjustments. We now turn to other methods of managing risk.

DURATION

Next we employ the concept of duration to explain how to hedge against interest rate risk. Duration is a measure of the sensitivity of bonds, or more generally any asset or portfolio of assets, to changes in interest rate levels or more generally to the opportunity cost of financing. Duration measures the percentage change in the value of the bond with respect to the percentage change in the level of interest rates. Thus in concept, it is an elasticity measure, with a negative sign. Since duration is also measured as the weighted average of the times at which the present value of cash inflows are received, we shall not use the negative sign. We shall follow the mainstream literature on the duration of bonds, but the concepts are applicable to any asset.

Calculation of Duration

Duration is generally not the same as the maturity of the payment stream on bonds. Only for zero coupon bonds is maturity equal to duration. Unlike maturity, duration considers all payments generated by a bond and weights them on the basis of the time at which each cash inflow occurs. The formula for duration can be expressed in several forms. A basic expression is shown in Equation 14.1:

$$D = \frac{\sum_{t=1}^{n} \dfrac{t(c_t)}{(1+r)^t} + \dfrac{nM}{(1+r)^n}}{\sum_{t=1}^{n} \dfrac{c_t}{(1+r)^t} + \dfrac{M}{(1+r)^n}}, \tag{14.1}$$

where:

D = duration in years (sign is understood to be negative)

c_t = dollar value of coupon payment in period t

M = dollar value of a maturity payment

n = maturity period

r = yield rate (later referred to as k_b); r_o = coupon rate

t = period in which payment is made.

The denominator represents the present value of the bond, which can be expressed as B_o. Hence we could also write the expression for duration as shown in Equation 14.1a.

$$\text{Duration} = \left[\frac{PV(c_1)}{B_o} \times 1\right] + \left[\frac{PV(c_2)}{B_o} \times 2\right] + \left[\frac{PV(c_3)}{B_o} \times 3\right] + \cdots$$
$$+ \left[\frac{PV(c_n)}{B_o} \times n\right] + \left[\frac{PV(M)}{B_o} \times n\right] \tag{14.1a}$$

Equation 14.1a shows explicitly that duration is the ratio of the present value of each cash inflow to the value of the bond times the number of time periods of waiting required to receive the cash inflow. We can also summarize the expression for duration as shown in Equation 14.1b.

$$D = \sum_{t=1}^{n} \frac{PV(c_t)t}{B_o} \tag{14.1b}$$

In addition to several formulas for the expression of duration, there are a variety of calculation methods. One straightforward procedure is illustrated in Table 14.1.

Table 14.1 assumes a five-year $1,000 bond has a coupon payment of $25 each six months (5 percent coupon rate), pays $1,000 at the end of the fifth year, and has a yield rate of 12 percent. In Table 14.1, each period in column (1) stands for each payment period of six months. Column (2) lists the cash flows received at the end of each payment period. In this case, $25 is received each six months as the coupon payment and a total of

TABLE 14.1 $1,000 Bond Issue, Five-Year with 12 Percent Yield Rate and 10 Percent Coupon Rate Paid Semiannually

Period (1)	Cash Payments (2)	Discount Factor at 6% (3)	Present Value of Cash Payments (2) × (3) (4)	Weighted Present Values (4) × (1) (5)
1	$ 25	.9434	$ 23.5850	$ 23.5850
2	25	.8900	22.2500	44.5000
3	25	.8396	20.9900	62.9700
4	25	.7921	19.8025	79.2100
5	25	.7473	18.6825	93.4125
6	25	.7050	17.6250	105.7500
7	25	.6651	16.6275	116.3925
8	25	.6274	15.6850	125.4800
9	25	.5919	14.7975	133.1775
10	1,025	.5584	572.3600	5,723.6000
		PV of bond =	$742.4050	$6,508.0775

$$D = \frac{\$6,508.0775}{\$742.405} = 8.7662 \text{ (semiannual)}$$
$$= 4.3831 \text{ years}$$

$1,025 is received at the end of the fifth year. The present value interest factors at a semiannual rate of 6 percent are shown in column (3). Multiplying columns (2) and (3), we get the present values of each payment in column (4). The total of $742.405 of all the present values in column (4) represents the current price of the bond. Column (5) is the present value of cash payments multiplied by the period number. We then divide the total of column (5) by the present value of the bond to obtain a duration of 8.7662 on a semiannual basis, which is equal to 4.3831 years on an annual basis. This means that for each 1 percent increase in interest rates there will be a 4.38 percent decrease in the value of the bond.

For a given par value of a bond, the higher the coupon payments and the higher the yield to maturity, the shorter is duration. This can readily be seen from the calculation method illustrated in Table 14.1. The higher the coupon payments or the higher the yield, the larger the proportion of cash inflows that is received before the repayment of the face value at the maturity of the bond. Since duration is a weighted average, the shorter duration payments will receive greater weight and the overall duration measure will be lower.

Duration as an Elasticity Measure

The duration measure is an elegant measure of bond price sensitivity in that it is exactly the same as the microeconomic concept of elasticity. Hence duration could also be expressed as shown in Equation 14.2.

$$D = \frac{dB_o/B_o}{d(1 + r)/(1 + r)} \qquad \textbf{(14.2)}$$

We shall now develop a numerical example and then more formally a demonstration of how the duration measure is, in fact, a measure of the elasticity of bond price change in relation to changes in interest rate levels. First, we postulate a bond with a coupon of 12 percent when the market yield for a bond of this type is 10 percent. We will further assume annual payments to simplify the calculations and a five-year maturity. The calculation of duration is shown in Table 14.2.

We observe from Table 14.2 that the duration is 4.074 years. We can use "years" to interpret duration because a zero coupon bond that matures in 4.074 years will have exactly the same duration (i.e., the same interest rate risk). We will next consider the effects of a yield change of plus/minus 1 percent and a yield change of plus/minus 0.5 percent. A yield rise of 1 percent would be 1.10 (.01) = .011. The new yield would, therefore, be 1.111. The new bond price would be $1,033.18. Similarly, a decline in the yield by 1 percent would be 1.10 − .011 = 1.089. The resulting price would be $1,120.89. Similarly, for a yield rise of 0.5 percent, the new yield would be 1.1055 and for a similar decline, 1.0945. Table 14.3 summarizes the results of our calculations.

From Table 14.3 we see that when we add the absolute values of the percentage price changes for the 1 percent price change, we obtain 8.15 percent. We obtain exactly the same result when we take the dollar amount of price change and divide it by the original price of $1,075.81. Since the 1 percent rise plus the 1 percent drop in interest rate levels represents a swing of 2 percentage points, we divide the 8.15 percent by 2 to obtain 4.075 as the measure of duration. The bottom part of Table 14.3 makes the same calculations for the yield rise and fall of 0.5 percent. Again, we obtain a duration measure of 4.075. In our original calculation of duration in Table 14.2, we obtained a measure of duration of 4.0740. The difference is due to rounding.

We have demonstrated that the calculation of duration as a time-weighted average of the present values of cash inflows received, as shown in Table 14.2, measures the elasticity of the bond value change in relation to percentage changes in interest rate levels. These data are for a bond that would sell at a premium since the coupon rate exceeds the required market yield rate.

TABLE 14.2   Calculation of Bond Duration for a Coupon of 12 Percent, Market Rate of 10 Percent, and Five-Year Life

Year (t)	Bond Coupon = 0.12 CF	PV	Yield = 0.1 Proportion	Proportion × t
1	$ 120	$ 109.09	0.1014	0.1014
2	120	99.17	0.0922	0.1844
3	120	90.16	0.0838	0.2514
4	120	81.96	0.0762	0.3048
5	1,120	695.43	0.6464	3.2320
		Price = $1,075.81		D = 4.0740

TABLE 14.3   Duration as a Measure of Bond Price Elasticity

	New Price	% Change
Yield falls 1% (1.089)	$1,120.89	4.19
Yield rises 1% (1.111)	1,033.18	−3.96
Price change $	87.71	8.15
Percent price change	8.15%	
		8.15/2 = 4.075
Yield falls 0.5%	$1,098.04	2.065
Yield rises 0.5%	1,054.20	−2.010
Price change $	43.84	4.075
Percent price change	4.075%	

Duration in a Continuous Time Framework

The above relationships hold only as an approximation for finite changes in interest rate levels. The theory calls for infinitely small changes. In this spirit we can demonstrate some of the more general properties of duration by assuming that time is a continuous variable at least twice differentiable and that the bond yields associated with time are defined as continuous compounding rates consistent with the continuity of the time variable. The present value of a bond using the same symbols as before can then be expressed in Equation 14.3.

$$B_o = \int_o^n r_o M e^{-rt} dt + M e^{-rn} \tag{14.3}$$

In a continuous time framework, bond duration can then be defined as shown in Equation 14.4.

$$D = \frac{\text{Percent change of } P}{\text{Changes of continuous compounding rate } r} = \frac{dP}{dr}\left(\frac{1}{P}\right) \tag{14.4}$$

The measure of duration shown in Equation 14.4 continues to be an elasticity measure because the differential dr of the continuous compounding rate is itself a percentage change. To evaluate the behavior of price elasticity or duration, we take the partial derivative of Equation 14.4 with respect to n. It can then be demonstrated that the measure of duration in continuous time can be expressed as shown in Equation 14.5.[5]

$$D = \frac{1}{r} + \frac{n(r - r_o)e^{-rn} - e^{-rn}}{r_o + (r - r_o)e^{-rn}} \tag{14.5}$$

Using Equation 14.5 we can illustrate the relation between duration and the length of the maturity of the bond for various types of bonds. For a perpetual bond where n is infinity, it can be shown that the second term goes to zero so that duration is equal to one

---

[5]See C. C. Hsia and J. F. Weston, "Price Behavior of Deep Discount Bonds," *Journal of Banking and Finance*, September 1981, pp. 357–361, and the associated manuscript dated March 1980 containing detailed proofs.

TABLE 14.4   Duration as a Function of Interest Rate Bond Maturity

n	(A) Zero Bond (10%)	(B) Perpetual Bond (10%)	(C) Discount Bond (5%)	(D) Par Bond (10%)	(E) Premium Bond (15%)
5	5	10	4.337	3.935	3.665
10	10	10	7.311	6.321	5.807
15	15	10	9.088	7.769	7.188
20	20	10	10.000	8.647	8.110
25	25	10	10.379	9.179	8.734
30	30	10	10.474	9.502	9.156
35	35	10	10.440	9.698	9.441
40	40	10	10.360	9.817	9.631
45	45	10	10.275	9.889	9.758
50	50	10	10.201	9.933	9.842

FIGURE 14.4   Duration as a Function of Maturity

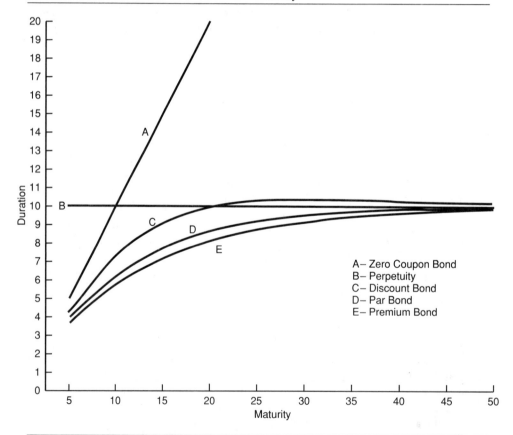

A– Zero Coupon Bond
B– Perpetuity
C– Discount Bond
D– Par Bond
E– Premium Bond

over the market yield (Bond B in Table 14.4). For a zero coupon bond, duration is equal to maturity (Bond A in Table 14.4). Assuming a market required yield of 10 percent we can calculate the duration pattern for a discount bond (C) with a coupon of 5 percent, a par bond (D) with a coupon of 10 percent, and a premium bond (E) with a coupon of 15 percent, again using Equation 14.5. The numerical results are shown in Table 14.4. The data in Table 14.4 are shown graphically in Figure 14.4, along with lines for a zero coupon bond and a perpetuity. It can be seen in Figure 14.4 and the related table that discount bonds have a somewhat unusual property. Table 14.4 and Figure 14.4 illustrate a point made earlier by Hsia and Weston [1981]—the curious nonintuitive price responsiveness (dP/dr) and the duration of discount bonds. For longer maturity discount bonds, both their price responsiveness and duration reach a maximum before starting to decline toward their asymptotic levels represented by the duration of a perpetuity. Having discussed some properties of duration, we next turn to its application.

Immunization

Immunization is a technique designed to achieve a specified return target in the face of changes in interest rates. The problem arises because with changing interest rates the reinvestment income will change. However, a bond or a bond portfolio can be immunized against interest rate risk if its holding period is set equal to the duration of the bond or portfolio [Bierwag, 1977; Bierwag and Khang, 1979; Leibowitz, 1981].

Another approach to immunization uses the total balance sheet position of a firm. The balance sheet for Bank A is shown in Table 14.5. Durations are shown in parentheses following the names of the individual accounts. Since duration has the property of additivity, we can use the duration procedure to illustrate the immunization of the total balance sheet position of a firm. For a portfolio of assets or claims, we can calculate the duration of the portfolio as shown in Equation 14.6.

$$D \text{ portfolio} = \frac{\sum\limits_{i=1}^{N} V_i D_i}{\sum\limits_{i=1}^{N} V_i} \tag{14.6}$$

TABLE 14.5 Bank A, Balance Sheet, December 31, 19X0

Item	Amount	Item	Amount
Cash (0)	$ 100	1-year CDs (1)	$ 800
		5-year CDs (5)	100
Investments (.5)	200		
Loans (1.75)	400	Equity	100
Mortgages (10)	300		
Total assets	$1,000	Total claims	$1,000

where:

$$V_i = \text{market values}$$
$$D_i = \text{their durations}$$
$$N = \text{number of assets or claims.}$$

First we calculate the duration of assets as shown in Equation 14.7.

$$D \text{ assets} = \frac{(100 \times 0) + (200 \times .5) + (400 \times 1.75) + 300(10)}{\$1,000} \tag{14.7}$$

$$= \frac{3,800}{1,000} = 3.8$$

Similarly, we can calculate the duration of *claims* on assets as shown in Equation 14.8.[6]

$$D \text{ claims} = \frac{(800 \times 1) + (100 \times 5)}{\$900} = \frac{1,300}{900} = 1.44 \tag{14.8}$$

With the above results we can next calculate the duration of the equity of the bank as the weighted average of the duration of the assets minus the duration of the claims. We utilize Equation 14.6 to perform the calculations in Equation 14.9.

$$D \text{ equity} = \frac{(1,000 \times 3.8) - (900 \times 1.44)}{100} = \frac{2,504}{100} = 25 \tag{14.9}$$

As shown in Equation 14.9 the elasticity of the value of the firm with respect to market yield levels is 25. Thus if market yields increase by 1 percent, the value of the equity of this bank would decline by 25 percent. If the firm is seriously concerned about the risks of rising interest rates, it should reduce the duration of its equity. It can achieve this by shortening the duration of its assets, by increasing the duration of the claims on assets, or by hedging with financial futures contracts. For example, if the bank were able to increase the average maturity of its claims to 4.222 years, then the duration of its equity would become zero, as shown in Equation 14.9a.

$$D \text{ equity} = \frac{(1,000 \times 3.8) - (900 \times 4.222)}{100} = \frac{0}{100} \tag{14.9a}$$

Then the bank would not be hurt by a rise in interest rates nor would it be helped by a decline in interest rates. The balance sheet of the bank would be completely immunized against the effects of interest rate changes.

The examples above illustrate the mechanics of immunization procedures. In actual application immunization involves a wide range of assumptions in connection with its use in immunizing bond portfolios. One assumption is parallel shifts in the yield curve (Yawitz and Marshall [1981]). The practical effects of this are small (Kolb and Gay [1982], p. 83).

---

[6]Note that (bank) liabilities exhibit quality risk in addition to interest rate risk.

Also, there may be multiple rate changes during the planning horizon. This problem is dealt with by rebalancing the portfolio to maintain a duration matching the remaining life of the planning period. In addition, more aggressive approaches to managing the bond portfolio have developed under the concept of contingent immunization (Leibowitz and Weinberger [1981], [1982]). Contingent immunization is a form of active portfolio management, and generally involves some degree of rate anticipation reflecting the portfolio manager's judgments about the future direction of interest rates. The procedures are too detailed to be covered in the present treatment.

Morris [1976a, 1976b] sought to apply the duration concept to the problem of corporate debt maturity strategies. Morris observes that when the covariance of interest costs with the firm's net operating income is high, a short-term borrowing policy will reduce the variation of net income even though it increases the uncertainty of interest costs in future periods. Thus for a weighted asset life with long duration, immunization through the choice of the duration of the debt structure is not necessarily the least risky maturity policy because of the variability of the income streams from the assets. A shorter debt maturity policy may decrease the uncertainty of net income derived from the assets when there is a high covariance between net operating income and interest costs. If the duration of the asset structure is short, immunization calls for a weighted maturity of short-duration debt. But if long-term debt with a longer duration were employed, and if interest rates were negatively correlated with the firm's net operating income, a long-term borrowing policy could reduce the variance of net income. In addition, the level of interest costs would be fixed over the life of the debt. Thus the concept of duration appears to have some potential for developing corporate debt maturity strategies.

FORWARD MARKETS AND FORWARD CONTRACTS

A forward rate is the marginal return gained from an investment by holding or committing the investment for one additional time period. Thus, the forward rate represents a return that will be realized over a future time period if the expectations implied by the current term structure of interest rates are realized. Forward rates can be computed by taking the ratio of yields to maturity for bonds of adjacent maturity. As developed in Chapter 6, the relation that would be employed is shown in Equation 14.10.

$$1 + {}_tf_{t+1} = \frac{(1 + {}_0R_{t+1})^{t+1}}{(1 + {}_0R_t)^t} \tag{14.10}$$

Another form of return from an investment held over a future time period is measured by the *futures rate*. Interest rate futures are contracts that call for transactions in specified financial instruments to take place on stated future dates. The yields on futures contracts for a series of years into the future would, in the absence of frictions or other types of market imperfections, be the same as the implied forward rates. Futures contracts differ from forward contracts in several respects. First, futures are "marked to the market" daily. The daily gain or loss from holding a futures contract is transferred between traders at the end of each day, while the profits and losses from holding a forward contract accumulate until the contract matures. Second, margins must be posted on futures contracts. Third, forward contracts are more individualized and customized than are futures contracts; futures contracts are standardized so that widely used common denominators of trading can be employed. Fourth, futures contracts usually have active secondary markets while forward contracts do not.

Forward contracts have a long history. They have been used most generally in connection with agricultural commodities. Some examples will illustrate their use.

Hedging Commodity Price Risks

A basic example involves the situation of a farmer. It is mid-summer and the price of wheat is quite favorable. The farmer is concerned that the price of wheat will be lower when he harvests it in the autumn. On 6/1, therefore, he sells 1,000 bushels of wheat for delivery on 9/1 at $3.30 per bushel. On 9/1 he delivers the wheat which he has harvested. Regardless of the spot or cash market price of wheat on 9/1, the farmer has received the $3.30 per bushel that he locked in by selling it at the forward market on 6/1.

The situation of a flour manufacturer illustrates the use of a long forward contract. Suppose that the flour manufacturer on 7/1 contracts with a cereal manufacturer for delivery of 100 bags of flour on 10/1 at $10 a bag. The flour manufacturer has in effect sold 100 bags of flour at a price of $10 per bag for delivery on 10/1. Assume that the flour manufacturer needs to have the delivery of the wheat on 9/15 in order to make delivery on 10/1. To protect against price fluctuations in wheat, the flour manufacturer buys (goes long) a forward contract in wheat for delivery on 9/15 at a price of $3.50 per bushel. Regardless of the price of wheat on 9/15, the flour manufacturer has locked in the cost of the raw material on the basis of the price flour was quoted for delivery on 10/1. If the price of wheat was lower on 9/15 when the flour manufacturer took delivery, a gain would have been made as compared with the $3.50 price contracted for in the forward market. But the whole point of hedging is not to speculate, rather to have profitability determined by the flour manufacturing activity. Nevertheless, it is often the case that both the farmers and grain mills will bet on the future price of wheat or other commodities. If so, they are acting as speculators, not as farmers or manufacturers.

Note that in the preceding example it was advantageous for the flour manufacturer to enter into the forward contract for the price of wheat because he had already contracted for the sale of the flour. In effect a short position had been taken which was protected by entering into a long position at the same time. If the flour manufacturer had not already locked in the price of flour, taking a long position in a wheat forward contract would have represented a speculative position rather than a hedge or risk reducing position. If the price of wheat was locked in at $3.50 a bushel for 9/15 and its actual price in the spot market on that date was $3.00 a bushel, our flour manufacturer would be at a competitive disadvantage. Other flour manufacturers free to buy $3.00 per bushel of wheat in the spot market would be in a position to bid a lower price for flour than the flour manufacturer who had committed to a price of $3.50 per bushel in the forward market. This illustrates that it is important to think through whether taking a position in a forward market represents a hedge or a speculative position.

Basis Risk

A significant part of the risk in a hedging operation depends on the relationship between the cash or spot market and the futures market over the life of the futures or forward contract. Basis is defined as the price in the cash market minus the price in the futures market. A wide range of factors can cause unpredictable movements in the size of the difference between spot and futures or forward prices. These include the cost of carry for commodities, opportunity costs for the use of funds when financial instruments are involved, the time until delivery, shifts in demand and supply conditions over the life of the forward or futures contract, the costs of delivery, the rate of convergence of future prices with the cash price, shifts in interest rate structures, and changes in expectations. Because of these many influences dynamic hedging policies will be required in the effort to deal with basis risk.

Hedging in Foreign Exchange Markets

Another arena in which the forward market is used is in connection with hedging against foreign exchange fluctuations. We shall first illustrate taking a short position in the forward market versus taking a long position. The foreign exchange examples illustrate that an equivalent hedge position can be achieved by simultaneously borrowing in one country and lending in the other.

We first illustrate the position of a firm that will receive foreign funds in the future. On 3/1 when $1 = 10 FC units the MNE Company makes a sale of equipment to a foreign firm and will receive FC 11,000,000 on 6/1. MNE has incurred all of its expenses in dollars and needs to know the dollar amounts it will receive on 6/1. The effective tax rate in both the domestic and foreign countries is 40 percent. MNE is considering two alternatives for managing the risk of foreign currency fluctuations.

Alternative 1: To use the forward market to sell (go short) FC 11,000,000 for dollars at the 90-day forward rate quoted on 3/1, which is 11 FC per dollar. Under this arrangement the MNE Company will receive a definite amount in dollars on 6/1 as determined by the forward rate on 3/1.

Alternative 2: MNE on 3/1 borrows from a foreign bank an amount in foreign currency that with interest will equal the amount the MNE Company will be receiving on 6/1. The interest rate on the loan will be 32 percent. By borrowing, the company will receive FCs and use the FCs received to immediately purchase dollars at the 3/1 spot rate, which is FC 10 per dollar. The dollars received can be invested in the United States at an interest rate of 12 percent. When MNE receives the FC 11,000,000 on 6/1, it can liquidate the local (foreign) currency loan plus interest. The results of the two transactions will be as follows.

Alternative 1:

$$\text{FC } 11,000,000 \div \text{ 90-day forward rate quoted on 3/1}$$
$$= \text{FC } 11,000,000 \div 11$$
$$= \$1,000,000.$$

Computation of loss for tax shelter:

$$FC\ 11,000,000 \div \text{spot rate on 3/1}$$
$$= FC\ 11,000,000 \div 10$$
$$= \$1,100,000$$
$$\$1,100,000 - \$1,000,000 = \$100,000\ \text{loss} \times \text{tax rate (40\%)}$$
$$= \text{tax shelter}$$
$$= \$40,000.$$
$$\text{Net proceeds with tax shelter} = \$1,040,000.$$

Alternative 2:
On 6/1 MNE will receive FC 11,000,000. Borrow FC for 90 days:

$$FC\ 11,000,000 = \text{Loan principal} \left[1 + \frac{R_f}{4}(1 - T_f) \right]$$
$$= \text{Loan principal} [1 + .08(.6)]$$
$$= \text{Loan principal} (1.048)$$
$$FC\ 10,496,183 = \text{Loan principal}.$$
$$\text{Interest expense} = FC\ 11,000,000 - 10,496,183 = FC\ 503,817.$$

Convert the FC loan to dollars at the 3/1 spot rate.

$$\text{Loan in } \$ = FC\ 10,496,183/FC\ 10\ \text{per}\ \$1$$
$$= \$1,049,618.$$

Invest proceeds in the United States.

$$\$1,049,618 \left[1 + \frac{R_{US}}{4}(1 - T_{US}) \right] = \$1,049,618\ [1 + .03(.6)]$$
$$= \$1,068,511.$$

Under the assumptions, MNE would receive $1,040,000 if the forward market was used. If it borrows foreign and invests domestic, the net proceeds would be $1,068,511, which is slightly higher. However, this would indicate arbitrage opportunities between the forward market and the borrow-invest market. The Interest Rate Parity Theorem discussed in Chapter 6 would cause forward market rates and/or interest rates in the two countries to adjust until both alternatives would yield the same result.

We next illustrate the use of the foreign exchange forward market by taking a long position or by transactions in the credit markets. On 3/1 the XYZ Company bought electronic equipment from a foreign firm that will require the payment of FC 900,000 on 6/1. The spot rate on 3/1 is FC 10 per dollar; the 90-day forward rate is FC 9 per dollar. The U.S. interest rate is 12 percent, the foreign interest rate is 8 percent, and the effective tax rates for both countries are 40 percent. XYZ is considering two alternatives to deal with the risk of exchange rate fluctuations.

Alternative 1: Enter the forward market to buy (go long) FC 900,000 at the 90-day forward rate in effect on 3/1.

Alternative 2: Borrow an amount in dollars to buy the FC at the current spot rate. These foreign currency units are invested in government securities of the foreign country; with the interest income, they will equal FC 900,000 on 7/1. The results of the use of the two alternatives are shown below.

Alternative 1:

$$\text{FC } 900,000 \div 90\text{-day forward rate effective on } 6/1$$
$$= \text{FC } 900,000 \div 9$$
$$= \$100,000.$$

Computation of loss for tax shelter:

$$\text{FC } 900,000 \div \text{spot rate on } 3/1$$
$$= \text{FC } 900,000 \div 10$$
$$= \$90,000.$$

Dollars required under forward rate	$100,000
Dollars required at current spot rate	$ 90,000
Loss	$ 10,000
× 40% tax rate = tax shelter	$ 4,000
After-tax cost using the forward contract	$ 96,000

Alternative 2:

$$\text{FC } 900,000 = (\text{Loan \$}) \left(\frac{\text{Current}}{\text{spot rate}}\right) \left[1 + \frac{R_f}{4}(1 - T_f)\right]$$

$$= \text{Loan \$ } (10) \left[1 + \frac{.08}{4}(1 - .4)\right]$$

$$= \text{Loan \$ } (10)(1.012)$$

$$= \text{Loan \$ } (10.12)$$

$$\text{Loan \$} = \$88,933.$$

Add interest expense:

$$\text{Total cost} = \$88,933 \left[1 + \frac{R_{US}}{4}(1 - T)\right]$$

$$= \$88,933 \left[1 + \frac{.12}{4}(1 - .4)\right]$$

$$= \$88,933 (1 + .018).$$

Cost of borrowing
domestic, investing foreign $= \$90,534.$

Thus we see that the cost of the purchase of the electronic equipment in dollars is slightly lower using the borrow and invest alternative versus the use of the forward market. Again, the Interest Rate Parity Theorem would cause arbitrage operations until the cost of the equipment under either of the alternatives would be equivalent.

The use of the forward market does, however, involve a premium or discount in the foreign currency value. In the above example, on 3/1, 10 foreign currency units are required per dollar (a dollar value of $.10). On 6/1 the number of foreign currency units per dollar has dropped to nine so that their dollar value is $.111. Thus the dollar value has increased. The use of the forward market, therefore, involves the payment of the premium in the foreign exchange value of the foreign currency. Thus the use of the forward market does not avoid the cost of the anticipated improvement in the exchange value of the foreign currency. The same must be true of the relative interest rate relationships between the two countries under interest rate parity. Thus the anticipated change in the forward rate reflected in the differences in current interest rate levels is a type of insurance premium paid to avoid the risk of unanticipated future changes in foreign exchange values and in interest rate relationships.

OTHER METHODS FOR DEALING WITH FOREIGN EXCHANGE RISKS

If a firm is expecting receipts in foreign currency units (if it is "long" in the foreign currency units), its risk is that the value of the foreign currency units will fall (devaluing the foreign currency in relation to the dollar). If a firm has obligations in foreign currency units (if it is "short" in the foreign currency units), its risk is that the value of the foreign currency will rise and it will have to buy the currency to repay the obligations at a higher price.

Transactions Balance

Forward markets for buying or selling foreign currencies or borrowing or lending in foreign currencies are not the only methods for managing foreign exchange risks. It is not appropriate to focus on individual transactions alone. A firm may seek to develop transactions across both strong and weak currency countries. A continued balance in the portfolios of transactions may provide a form of dynamic hedging of foreign exchange risks.

Monetary Balance

Firms must take protective actions not only in regard to future expected receipts or obligations but also against a long or short position in foreign currencies resulting from the balance sheet position of their foreign subsidiaries. For example, the sale of goods for FC 380,000 represents an account receivable for the three months until the obligation is paid. Suppose, however, that the number of FCs per $1 rises from 1.90 to 2.00. At 1.90 FCs per $1, the account receivable would be worth $200,000 in U.S. currency. But, at the lower value of the FCs, FC 2 = $1, the account receivable would be worth only $190,000. This represents a before-tax loss of $10,000 in the dollar value of the receivables.

Conversely, if a firm had an account payable of FC 380,000, an upward change in the FC value from FC 2.00 to FC 1.90 per $1 would result in a loss because the accounts payable expressed in dollars would have increased by $10,000. Hence, the concept of monetary balance comes into consideration. *Monetary balance* involves avoiding either a net receivable or a net payable position. Monetary assets and liabilities are those items whose value, expressed in local currency, does not change with devaluation or revaluation. To illustrate:

Monetary Assets	Monetary Liabilities
Cash	Accounts payable
Marketable securities	Notes payable
Accounts receivable	Tax liability reserve
Tax refunds receivable	Bonds
Notes receivable	Preferred stock
Prepaid insurance	

What is referred to as a firm's monetary position is another way of stating the firm's position with regard to real assets. For example, the basic balance sheet equation can be written as follows:

Monetary assets + Real assets = Monetary liabilities + Net worth.

Consider the following pattern of relationships:

	Monetary Assets	+	Real Assets	=	Monetary Liabilities	+	Net Worth
Firm A: Monetary creditor	$6,000		$4,000		$4,000		$6,000
Firm B: Monetary debtor	4,000		6,000		6,000		4,000

Firm A is a monetary creditor because its monetary assets exceed its monetary liabilities; its net worth position is negative with respect to its investment coverage of net worth by real assets. In contrast, Firm B is a monetary debtor because it has monetary liabilities that exceed its monetary assets; its net worth coverage by investment in real assets is positive. Thus, the monetary creditor can be referred to as a firm with a negative position in real assets and the monetary debtor as a firm with a positive position in real assets. From the foregoing, we can see that the following relationships are equivalent:

Firm A	(Long position in foreign currency)	≡	Monetary creditor	≡	Monetary assets exceed monetary liabilities	≡	Negative position in real assets	≡	Balance of receipts in foreign currency less obligations in foreign currency is *positive*
Firm B	(Short position in foreign currency)	≡	Monetary debtor	≡	Monetary liabilities exceed monetary assets	≡	Positive position in real assets	≡	Balance of receipts in foreign currency less obligations in foreign currency is *negative*

Thus, if Firm A has a long position in a foreign currency, on balance, it will be receiving more funds in foreign currency, or it will have a net monetary asset position that exceeds its monetary liabilities in that currency. The opposite holds for Firm B, which is in a short position with respect to a foreign currency.

Other Policies to Manage Foreign Exchange Risk

In addition to the specific actions of hedging in the forward market or borrowing and lending through the money markets, other business policies can help the firm achieve a balance sheet position that minimizes the foreign exchange rate risk exposure to either currency devaluation or currency revaluation upward. Specifically, in countries whose currency values are likely to fall, local management of subsidiaries should be encouraged to follow these policies:

1. Never have excessive idle cash on hand. If cash accumulates, it should be used to purchase inventory or other real assets.

2. Attempt to avoid granting excessive trade credit or trade credit for extended periods. If accounts receivable cannot be avoided, an attempt should be made to charge interest high enough to compensate for the loss of purchasing power.

3. Wherever possible, avoid giving advances in connection with purchase orders unless a rate of interest is paid by the seller on these advances from the time the subsidiary — the buyer — pays them until the time of delivery, at a rate sufficient to cover the loss of purchasing power.

4. Borrow local currency funds from banks or other sources whenever these funds can be obtained at a rate of interest no higher than U.S. rates adjusted for the anticipated rate of devaluation in the foreign country.

5. Make an effort to purchase materials and supplies on a trade credit basis in the country in which the foreign subsidiary is operating, extending the final date of payment as long as possible.

The opposite policies should be followed in a country where a revaluation upward in foreign currency values is likely to take place. All these policies are aimed at a monetary balance position in which the firm is neither a monetary debtor nor a monetary creditor. Some firms take a more aggressive position. They seek to have a net monetary debtor position in a country whose exchange rates are expected to fall and a net monetary creditor position in a country whose exchange rates are likely to rise.

Some writers have expressed reservations on whether a firm should try to hedge against foreign currency risk (Cornell and Shapiro [1983], p. 25). Several reasons have been given for this view. First, the real impact of nominal currency changes will be reduced by the offsetting effects of relative inflation. Second, shareholders can reduce foreign exchange risks by holding well-diversified portfolios. Third, shareholders may prefer that a portion of their returns be denominated in a foreign currency since their overall risk will be reduced by having foreign currency inflows to match their foreign currency outflows resulting from the purchase of foreign goods. Fourth, hedging is expensive since the simple strategy of forward hedging in the major currencies costs about 0.65 percent per year plus management time. Fifth, borrowing in local currencies is usually even more costly than forward hedging when points and other fees are taken into account. But, local borrowing often is the only alternative available, because active forward markets exist in fewer than a dozen currencies and many MNCs do business in more than 100 countries. Sixth, management cannot hedge against *anticipated* movements in exchange rates since they are already reflected in the forward premium and in the interest rate differentials. Hedging may provide partial protection against foreign exchange risks resulting from unanticipated fluctuations in foreign currency values.

FUTURES MARKETS

Interest rate futures are a relatively new development. In the fall of 1975, the Chicago Board of Trade (CBT) established a contract for GNMAs (Government National Mortgage Association Securities). In early 1976, the International Monetary Market (IMM) of the Chicago Mercantile Exchange introduced a contract for 90-day Treasury bills. In 1977, the Chicago Board of Trade extended trading to Treasury bond futures contracts. On August 7, 1980, the New York Stock Exchange, through its wholly owned subsidiary, the New York Futures Exchange, began trading in futures contracts for five major currencies plus 20-year Treasury bonds. The daily volume in interest rate futures trading is in billions.

The financial futures markets operate as do other futures markets. One of the most active futures markets is for three-month Treasury bills at the IMM. There are eight contract delivery months extending at quarterly intervals for about two years into the future. The contract price is quoted as the difference between $100 and the discount rate on the bill in question. Thus, a contract fixing a bill rate at 8.5 percent would be quoted at $91.50. Buyers and sellers contract not with one another but with the clearinghouse. For the financial liability of the clearinghouse, the clearing member firms must place margins on their contracts. For each purchase or sale of a three-month Treasury bill contract of $1 million on the IMM, the clearing member firm must post a small margin which can be in the form of cash or a bank letter of credit. The clearing member firm, in turn, imposes an initial margin of at least $1,500 on the individual trader.

While the position is outstanding, the contract will be "marked-to-market" by the clearinghouse at the end of each business day. Either profits or losses are recorded, based on the position and price movements. Profits in the margin account may be withdrawn. If losses reduce the firm's margin below $1,200, the firm must make up the difference to the clearinghouse in cash before the clearinghouse opens the next day. The customer's margin account may fall below the initial $1,500; but if it falls below the $1,200 maintenance margin, the account must be brought back up to $1,500. There are also daily limits on the degree of price fluctuations. At the IMM, for example, no futures trades in Treasury bills can involve prices more than 50 basis points above or below the final settlement price of the previous day, though these margins may be temporarily increased if the daily limit restricts trading for a few days. (One hundred basis points equal 1 percent. The number of basis points is a convenient way to describe interest rate changes of fractions of a percent.)

TABLE 14.6   U.S. Treasury Bond Futures Contract Traded
at the Chicago Board of Trade

Basic Trading Unit	U.S. Treasury bonds with $100,000 face value.
Deliverable Grade	U.S. Treasury bonds. Maturing at least 15 years from delivery day if not callable; and if callable are not so for at least 15 years from delivery day.
Delivery Method	Federal Reserve book entry wire transfer system. Invoice is adjusted for coupon rates and maturity or call dates.
Price Quotation	Percentage of par, e.g., 94-01 or 94 1/32.
Minimum Fluctuation	1/32 of a point or $31.25 per contract.
Daily Price Limit	64/32 ($2,000 per contract) above and below the previous day's settlement price.

Use of Futures Markets for Hedging

Daily newspapers provide tables of information on spot and future prices for a wide range of commodities (gold, silver, copper, aluminum, platinum, etc.) and financial instruments (Treasury bonds, Treasury bills, commercial paper, etc.). In this discussion we will focus on the use of financial futures contracts. We will begin with the discussion of U.S. Treasury bond futures contracts traded on the CBT. Their basic characteristics are summarized in Table 14.6. Although the CBT Treasury bond futures contract is based on an 8 percent coupon with at least 15 years to maturity or call, a wide variety of coupon values and maturities are available. These other deliverable bonds are priced in relation to the 8 percent, 15-year maturity via conversion factors. For any delivery month, each deliverable issue has a specific conversion factor based on its maturity and value at that particular time. With this background, we shall now explain the use of the futures contracts.

The financial manager faces the risk of either (1) a rise in interest rates or (2) a decline in interest rates. When the firm is *holding* bonds or other financial instruments, a rise in interest rates would lower their value; when funds are to be *raised* in the future, the risk is that higher interest rates would have to be paid on the financial instruments sold. When funds are to be *received* in the future, the risk is that they would have to be invested at lower interest rates.

We first discuss hedging against the risk of rising interest rates. This is hedged by *selling* futures contracts, which represents taking a *short* position in the futures market.

Example of a Short Hedge in the Futures Market.   A corporate treasurer is holding $1 million in 15-year Treasury bonds on 2/1. He could sell them today for $101-20 (20/32). He plans to sell the bonds to meet some cash flow requirements in six months. He fears a rise in interest rates, which will cause the bonds to be sold at a lower price. He sells (goes short) 10 July T-bond futures contracts on a 100-08 basis. On 8/1 interest rates have risen. He sells the $1 million in T-bonds at 100. He buys in the futures contract at 98-20.

His results are as follows:

Cash Market		Futures Market		Basis
2/1 Could sell	101-20	2/1 Sold 10 at	100-08	+ 1-12
8/1 Sells at	100-00	8/1 Buy at	98-20	+ 1-12
Loss	1-20	Gain	1-20	

1/32 of 1% of 100,000 = $31.25 per point.

Gained same $16,250 in the futures market.

$31.25 × (52) × 10 = $16,250 loss.

By using the futures market, the treasurer offsets the rise in interest rates that resulted in a decline in the value of his bonds. The results are the same as if he had sold the 15-year T-bonds at their 2/1 price of $101-20. The loss in the cash market was exactly offset by the gain in the futures market in this example because we assumed that the basis between the two markets remains constant.

Basis Risk

Basis is defined as the price in the cash market minus the price in the futures market.[7] Thus if cash prices are higher than prices in the futures market, the basis is positive, and conversely. The basis becomes more positive when futures prices decline more than cash prices or when cash prices rise more than futures prices. A short hedge of the type described benefits from a strengthening basis. Conversely the basis becomes more negative when futures prices increase more than cash prices. Or cash prices fall more than futures prices. A long hedge benefits from a weakening basis.

If in our example the future price at 8/1 had declined to $98, this would have represented the strengthening of the basis from 1-12 to 2-0. The gain in the futures market would have become 2-08 or 72 basis points. Hence the gain in the futures market would have become: 72 × 10 × $31.25 = $22,500. Compared with the loss in the cash market of $16,250 the hedge would have resulted in a net gain of $6,250 from the rise in interest rates.

On the other hand, if the basis had weakened, a net loss would have resulted. For example, suppose that the 8/1 price in the futures market had been $99-00. This would have represented a decline in the basis to 1-00. The gain in the futures market would have become 1-08, or, in dollars: 40 × 10 × $31.25 = $12,500, so that a net loss of $3,750 would have resulted.

Thus in addition to an interest rate risk, there could also be a basis risk. When a loss occurs because of the weakening basis, it can be mitigated to some degree by the use of a weighted hedge. The weighting would be based in part on the conversion factor required because the characteristics of the bonds involved differ from the standard bond contract plus other hedge factors as discussed above in connection with forward contracts and options.

Example of a Long Hedge in the Futures Market. When funds are to be received in the future, the risk is that the investor will receive lower interest rate returns by the time the

---

[7]Some writers define basis as futures price minus cash price. The definition is arbitrary.

funds are received. The risk is a decline in interest rates. The appropriate action is to buy futures contracts — to execute a long hedge. To illustrate, on 3/1 a pension fund manager expects to receive $1 million on 6/1 to invest. He fears a decline in interest rates. Fifteen-year, 8 percent T-bonds on 3/1 can be sold on a 101-24 basis. The treasurer buys (goes long) 10 September T-bond futures $100,000 each at 100-00.

On 6/1 he buys $1 million of 15-year, 8 percent T-bonds at 103 ($\equiv$ 102-32). He sells his 10 September future contracts at 101-08.

His results are as follows:

Cash Market		Futures Market		Basis
6/1 Bought at	102-32	6/1 Sold at	101-08	+ 1-24
3/1 Could buy		3/1 Buy at	100-00	+ 1-24
if had money	101-24			
Loss	1-08	Gain	1-08	

1/32 of 1% of 100,000 = $31.25 per point.
$31.25 × 40 × 10 = $12,500 loss.

Gained same $12,500 in the futures market.

The result of the long hedge is the same as if the pension fund manager had bought the T-bonds at their 3/1 price of $101-24 instead of at the 6/1 price of $102-32. Again, the losses and gains are exactly offset because of the unchanged basis assumed between 3/1 and 6/1, the action dates. If the bonds had been sold in the futures market at $102-00, the basis would have weakened to 1-00. The gain in the futures market would have become 2-00, with a dollar amount of: $64 \times 10 \times \$31.25 = \$20,000$. This would have represented a net gain of $7,500. On the other hand, if the basis had strengthened, a loss would have resulted. To illustrate, suppose that the selling price in the futures market on 6/1 had been $101-00; the basis would have increased to 2-00. The gain in the futures market would have dropped to 1-00, or, in dollars: $32 \times 10 \times \$31.25 = \$10,000$, resulting in a loss of $2,500. Gains or losses could be changed by the use of a weighted long hedge based on the use of a conversion factor or hedging ratio adjustment as discussed in connection with short hedges in the futures markets.

FORWARD VERSUS FUTURES RATES

In theory, in the absence of frictions and other market imperfections, a divergence between forward and futures rates could not persist. We shall illustrate how arbitrage operations under idealized conditions would prevent the persistence of a divergence. The basic data to be used in the analysis are set forth in Figure 14.5.

Arbitrage operations signify that transactions can be made to obtain a sure profit without any risk. This will be illustrated by the pattern of data assumed in Figure 14.5. In that figure, rates are presented for four categories of Treasury bills. Treasury bill A is a 182-day bill yielding 10.6 percent. T-bill B is a 91-day bill starting immediately and carrying a yield of 10 percent. T-bill C is a 91-day bill starting 91 days later and bearing a yield of 11.2 percent. Continuous compounding is assumed, so the yield on the 182-day bill is a simple average of the yields on the successive 91-day bills spanned by bill A. Finally, Item D is a 91-day futures contract covering the second 91-day period and carry-

FIGURE 14.5   Pattern of Rates to Illustrate Arbitrage Operations

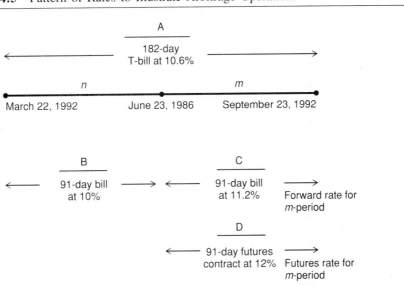

ing a yield of 12 percent. The 12 percent yield for the T-bill futures contract is chosen arbitrarily above bill C to illustrate the arbitrage transactions that would be stimulated.

The patterns imply a positive term structure with the rate on the futures contract assumed to be above the rate on the forward contract. In the example, the implied forward rate is the 11.2 percent on T-bill C. Under the relationships assumed, the following actions would be taken.

1. Buying the 91-day T-bill futures contract to run for the m period after the elapse of the n period.

2. Taking a long position in the 91-day T-bill B for the n period.

3. Selling short the 182-day T-bill A for the $(n + m)$ period.

The second and third transactions are equivalent to shorting a 91-day T-bill for the m period.

Thus, one earns 12 percent on the futures contract while paying only 11.2 percent in the short position in the 91-day T-bill for the m period. The results could also be expressed in terms of the lower price paid for the futures contract in which the buyer is taking a long position and the higher price on the forward contract that is sold short.

In expressing the results in the prices of the Treasury bills, we will follow the pattern laid out by Capozza and Cornell [1979]. Although the T-bill futures contracts are denominated in units of $1 million, for ease of encompassing the numbers, we will assume units of $1,000. The results are shown in Table 14.7.

Table 14.7   Gain from Arbitraging When the Futures Rate
Exceeds the Forward Rate

At time t:
Inflow from shorting 182-day bill $(n + m)$ = exp[−0.106(0.5)]($1,000)[a] = $ 948.38
Outflow for investment in n-day bills
(91 days) $ 948.38
Net   = $ 0
At time $t + n$ (end of 91 days):
Inflow from maturation of n-day bills   = (948.38/975.31)($1,000)[b]   = $ 972.39
Outflow from taking delivery of bills on
the futures contracts   = exp[−0.12(0.25)]($1,000)   = $ 970.45
Net gain   = $ 1.94 per bond
At time $t + n + m$:
Inflow from maturation of the m-day bill
bought through the futures market   = $1,000.00
Outflow from maturation of the shorted
$(n + m)$-day bill   = $1,000.00
Net   = $ 0

[a]Since continuous compounding of a discount bond is assumed, to have an annual yield of 10.6 percent requires that its price with six months to run is $e^{-0.106(0.5)}$ times the maturity value of the bond (here assumed to be $1,000). The "exp" is a generally used method of indicating the power to which e is raised.
[b]$975.31 represents the price of the n-day bill at t, so the fraction represents the portion of the $1,000 maturity value purchased from the proceeds of shorting the $(n + m)$-day bill at time t.

The net gain is thus $1.94 per $1,000 of bonds or $1,940 on the standard $1 million T-bill futures contract. In the illustration, the transactor is completely hedged, that is, he takes no risk, and no net investment is required to achieve the sure gain. The transactions would be expected to eliminate this arbitrage opportunity. Selling short the 182-day bill would tend to decrease its price, driving up its yield. Purchase of the futures contracts would tend to drive up their price and reduce their yield until profitable arbitrage opportunities no longer existed.

Empirical studies of opportunities for arbitrage profits in the relationship between forward and futures market rates have yielded different results through time. Both Puglisi [1978] and Branch [1978] found gains derived from hedged riding of the yield curve. Ederington [1979] found the results to be less consistent. Capozza and Cornell [1979] observed a substantial differential of futures rates above implied forward rates for contracts whose maturities extended beyond 17 to 18 weeks. A study of a later time period by Arak and McCurdy [1979] observed forward rates higher than futures rates on the June 1979 Treasury bills contracts over the period from November 1978 through April 1979. Arak and McCurdy also observed a substantial spread, with higher forward rates than futures rates in the September 1979 Treasury bill futures contracts traded on the International Monetary Market, particularly in June and July of 1979.

Most studies have found that the futures rates are below the forward rates near the maturity date of the futures contracts. The explanation generally given is the lower transactions costs in the futures contracts as compared with the spot or forward markets, in which transactions costs are generally greater.

For longer maturities, the persistently higher futures rates over forward rates that Capozza and Cornell observed are explained by the higher risk in futures contracts. Transactions in the Treasury bill cash and forward markets involve the creditworthiness of the instrument itself, and the T-bill presumably has no credit risk. The futures contracts, by contrast, involve the creditworthiness of the customers, of the trading firms, and of the clearinghouses. Therefore, futures contracts may involve some greater risks than do spot and forward contracts.

INTEREST RATE SWAPS

Another method of managing risk is the use of interest rate swaps. Their economic nature is quite close to short-term interest rate futures contracts and they are often used as an alternative to futures. Swaps may also be regarded as a series of forward contracts tied together. But, of course, this is the basic nature of a futures contract as well. The credit risk of a swap is somewhat smaller than a forward contract with the same maturity but greater than the credit risk of a comparable futures contract. The interest rate swap market has been a rapidly growing sector in the international capital markets in recent years, growing to hundreds of billions of dollars in value per year.

Basically an interest rate swap involves swapping fixed interest payments for another party's floating rate payments. But with use, the instruments have become increasingly sophisticated, including cross-country currency swaps. An example would be the swap of floating rate payments denominated in British pounds for fixed rate payments denominated in French francs. In this section we will describe only the simplest type of interest rate swap, usually referred to as a generic swap or a plain vanilla swap. We seek to cover only the basic concept so the relationship to other risk managing instruments can be demonstrated.

Two parties called counter parties (and usually an intermediary financial institution) are involved. One agrees to make periodic fixed payments to the other established at the time of the deal. The other party, the floating rate payer, agrees to make variable payments based on some short-term interest rate index. These payments are quoted at rates to be applied to a notational principal amount. No principal actually changes hands. The standard period for the generic swap is six months but annual payments are also used.

The commitment date between the counter parties is called the trade date. Interest begins to accrue on the effective date. Settlement dates are the times net cash payments are made between the two parties. The maturity date is the date payments have been completed.

Swap interest payments are made with a lag. The first payment would usually occur six months after the effective date based on the interest rate index on the effective date. The payment at the end of the second six months is based on the index six months earlier. Thus both parties know in advance what the next net settlement payment will be.

With these institutional arrangements as background we describe a basic interest rate swap. The AAA Company has a loan portfolio which earns the six-month London Inter-Bank Offer Rate (LIBOR) plus 2.00 percent. Its current financing is with a fixed rate Eurobond at 10.5 percent. It could also borrow at a floating LIBOR plus .50 percent. BBB

Company has a portfolio of fixed rate mortgages earning 13.00 percent. It is currently borrowing at the floating rate LIBOR plus 1.00 percent. It could borrow at a fixed rate of 12 percent. The quality spread differential (QSD) can be exploited to the benefit of each. AAA Company can obtain floating rate funds at 50 basis points less than BBB Company and can obtain fixed rate funds at a savings of 150 basis points. AAA Company's advantage in fixed rate funds less its advantage in floating rate funds is the QSD of 100 basis points.

An interest rate swap can provide benefits to each. AAA Company lends to BBB at a fixed rate of 11.5 percent. BBB Company lends to AAA Company at the LIBOR rate. AAA Company locks in a 200 basis point spread between the earnings of its loan portfolio and what it is paying to BBB Company. The BBB Company has locked in a 150 basis point spread by borrowing from AAA at the fixed 11.5 percent rate. Often a bank acts as the intermediary for the transaction, carrying the risk of nonperformance of the swap contract by either firm.

Another illustration of the QSD is based on the wider quality spread on long maturities compared with short maturity debt. The AAA Company might pay 50 basis points less for short-term funds but 150 basis points less for longer-term debt. Some literature, however, has questioned the reality of the QSD benefit. The argument is that the apparent gain to the higher-rated firm or to the financial intermediary simply constitutes compensation for the risk of nonperformance by the lower-rated party and that interest rate swaps are mainly "zero sum games" [Turnbull, 1987]. These issues have been examined extensively by Wall and Pringle [1989]. They set forth the theoretical arguments and then seek to test them empirically. At the theoretical level they argue that observed quality differentials may be explained by (1) differences in the risk borne by equity holders, (2) differences in the discounted value of expected bankruptcy costs, (3) differences in restrictive covenants and options, and (4) agency costs. Their analysis concludes that the first three cannot be exploited for economic gain and that only the fourth explanation provides real gains [pp. 63–64].

Other reasons for the use of swaps are also reviewed by Wall and Pringle. The level of debt in the form of long-term bonds can be adjusted downward only by the payment of a premium plus other transaction costs. Swaps may be "undone" with no call premium and lower transaction costs.

Another possible role for swaps may be due to information asymmetry. The firm's management may judge on the basis of their knowledge that the market is charging an excessive risk premium on the firm's debt. When this inside knowledge becomes publicly recognized, interest costs would decline. The firm could issue short-term debt in the interim but this would expose it to interest rate risk, which could be avoided by the use of an interest rate swap arrangement. A third possible role for swaps is tax and regulatory arbitrage. One example is based on the estimate that the regulatory costs of issuing bonds in the United States add as many as 80 basis points over the cost of a Eurodollar issue. Hence one firm might raise long-term funds in the Eurodollar market and swap with another firm using domestic short-term debt. A fourth potential benefit of swaps is to permit financial intermediaries to adjust repricing intervals. Savings and loan associations may have a comparative advantage in accruing short-term deposits and making long-term mortgage loans. Swaps may permit S&Ls to use their comparative advantage but to reduce their unfavorable risk profile.

Wall and Pringle seek to test the alternative explanations for interest rate swaps by analysis of 250 firms that reported the use of interest rate swaps in their 1986 annual reports. They suggest that bond rating patterns provide some support for the arbitrage and agency cost explanations of interest rate swaps. Of the fixed rate payers, 86 percent are rated A+ or lower while 50 percent of the floating rate payers are rated AA− or better. The debt adjustment motive was tested but appeared not to explain a large fraction of the activity of fixed-rate payers. They also test the information asymmetries by considering the hypothesis that among managers using swaps to postpone issuance of long-term debt, a higher proportion of upgrades should be observed among fixed rate payers as compared with the remainder of the sample. The data support the hypothesis. Wall and Pringle conclude that while the apparent benefits of QSD arbitrage are illusory, the other motives for the use of swaps receive at least limited empirical support. These other motives include ''reducing the agency costs of long-term debt, reducing the costs of shrinking the firm, exploiting information asymmetries, adjusting the repricing interval of outstanding debt, and tax and regulatory arbitrage'' [p. 69].

METHODS FOR MANAGING RISK

We have discussed alternative approaches to managing risk: forward, futures, swap, and options contracts along with portfolio insurance. Interest rate risk can be analyzed in terms of interest rate movements or their reciprocal, bond price movements. Figure 14.6 presents the pattern for interest rate exposure. The risk profile in Panel A shows that a long position in fixed rate bonds as a creditor or investor owner of bonds has a negatively sloped risk profile with respect to interest rate changes. A short position in fixed rate bonds as an issuer or seller-debtor in bonds has a positive risk profile with respect to interest rate changes.

Offsetting payoff profiles are shown in Panel B of Figure 14.6. To offset the negative risk profile for a long position in fixed rate bonds, a number of equivalent actions may be taken. These include buy a forward contract on interest rates; sell bond futures; take on more debt; or swap, i.e. pay fixed rates and receive floating rates. To avoid the risk of declines in value resulting from falling interest rates with a short position in fixed rate bonds, the opposite actions are taken. These include sell a forward contract on interest rates; buy bond futures; reduce debt; or swap: pay floating/receive fixed interest rate payments.

The literature demonstrates that forward, futures, and swap contracts are equivalent in their payoff profiles. Note also that borrowing and lending activities can achieve payoff profiles equivalent to those produced by forward, futures, and swap contracts.

Figure 14.7 analyzes the nature of risky asset price exposures. The risk profile is positively sloped for a long position in risky assets or risky securities. It is negatively sloped with respect to price changes for a short position. The offsetting risk profiles for a long position in risky assets are to sell forwards or futures contracts, increase short positions in assets, short a call plus long a put, or increase the ratio of riskless to risky assets. The offsetting payoff profiles for a short position in risky assets or risky securities is buy forwards or futures; increase long positions in assets; long a call plus short a put; or increase the ratio of risky assets to riskless assets.

FIGURE 14.6   Interest Rate Risk and Exposures

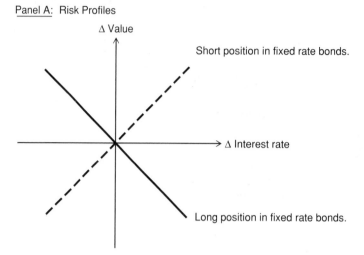

Panel A: Risk Profiles

Short position in fixed rate bonds.

Long position in fixed rate bonds.

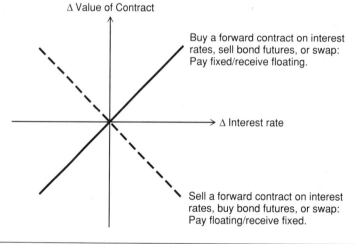

Panel B: Payoff Profiles for Forwards, Futures, and Swaps

Buy a forward contract on interest rates, sell bond futures, or swap: Pay fixed/receive floating.

Sell a forward contract on interest rates, buy bond futures, or swap: Pay floating/receive fixed.

Source: C. W. Smith, C. W. Smithson, and D. S. Wilford, *Managing Financial Risk,* Harper & Row, 1990, p. 246.

In Figure 14.7, call and put options are combined to achieve the same payoff profiles as forward or futures contracts. In Figure 14.8, the payoff profiles for individual options are analyzed further. Long a call is equivalent to holding a risky security with downside

FIGURE 14.7   Risky Asset Price Exposures

Panel A: Risk Profiles

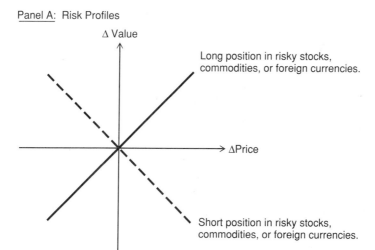

Panel B: Payoff Profiles for Forwards, Futures, and Swaps

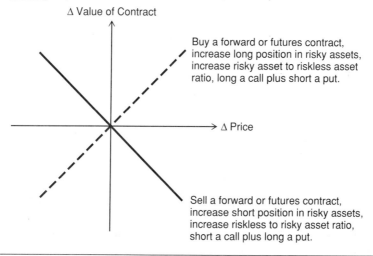

risk limited to the price of the call, as shown in Panel A. In Panel B, selling a naked call has a position that magnifies the risk of a short position in the risky security for a rise in prices, but for a fall in prices provides a buffer represented by the price for which the call was sold. In Panel C, a long position in a put yields gains with a decline in prices and thus

FIGURE 14.8   Payoff Profiles for Options

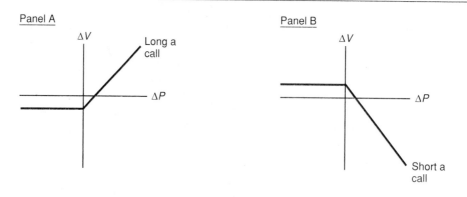

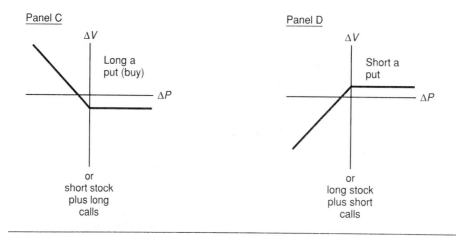

offsets the risks of a long position in risky securities. It is also equivalent to being short a stock plus long a call. In Panel D, writing a put (being short a put) has the same risk profile as a long position in risky securities for price declines. The position is also equivalent to being long a stock plus shorting a call.

A generalized pattern for the relationship between risky assets, riskless assets, and options is conveyed by the put–call parity relationship (discussed in Chapter 12), as shown in Equation 14.5.

$$S_o + P_o - C_o = B_o \qquad (14.5)$$

Equation 14.5 states that a riskless security can be created by long positions in a stock and in a put combined with a short position in a call. Equation 14.5 can be regrouped to

FIGURE 14.9 Put–Call Parity

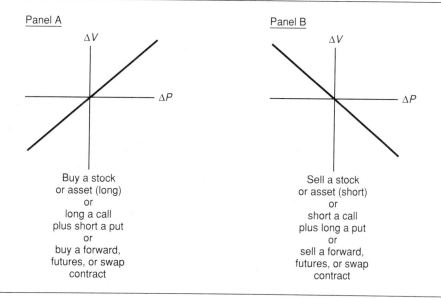

illuminate other groups of relationships. Equation 14.5a shows that a long position in a risky stock plus a short position in a riskless bond is equivalent to being long a call and short a put.

$$S_o - B_o = C_o - P_o \tag{14.5a}$$

This relationship is depicted in Panel A of Figure 14.9. This also represents the same risk or payoff profile as a long position in a risky asset or risky security or buying a forward or futures contract or swap. If we multiply both sides of Equation (14.5a) by -1, we obtain Equation (14.5b), which states that a long position in a riskless bond plus a short position in a risky stock is equivalent to being short a call plus long a put as depicted in Panel B of Figure 14.9.

$$B_o - S_o = P_o - C_o \tag{14.5b}$$

This is the payoff profile of a short position in a risky asset or stock or selling a forward, futures, or swap contract. Thus options can also be combined to create forwards, futures, and swap contracts [Black and Scholes, 1973; Black, 1976; Smithson, 1987]. The converse, of course, also holds. Forwards, futures, or swaps in combination can be used to create options. Black and Scholes [1973] also demonstrated that combinations of positions in risky stocks and in bonds can produce portfolios equivalent to options.[8]

With this ability to replicate any forms of derivative securities, a wide range of payoff patterns can be created. Starting from any specific underlying exposure faced, forwards,

---

[8]These relationships are nicely summarized in Cox and Rubinstein [1985, Table 2-4 on page 47]. See also our Problem 14.10.

futures, swaps, and options combinations can be used to create a new target exposure profile.[9] Increasingly, new security issues reflect a combination of forward-futures-swap plus options characteristics. Thus a wide variety of securities can be created in relation to underlying risk exposures and investment objectives. Creating innovative, new forms of financial products has been called financial engineering. Already literally hundreds of new financial products have been created by the use of the many new forms of building blocks that have become available. They increase the ability of firms and portfolios to alter underlying risk exposures in the direction of needs or objectives.

SUMMARY

In this chapter we began with the discussion of types of risks. We noted that systematic risks are related to the market or market factors. Managing unsystematic risks varies across firms and industries. Systematic risks can be managed by dynamic hedging methods.

We described a basic form of portfolio insurance in which risky stocks were combined with riskless bonds — a form of option replication. We developed the concept of duration, which measures interest rate risk and how these risks could be managed by the use of futures markets in financial instruments. Forward and futures contracts are also employed to manage the risks of commodity price fluctuations and fluctuations in foreign exchange values. We also described how combinations of monetary and nonmonetary assets and claims on assets could be used to manage foreign exchange risks. Borrowing and lending across financial currencies can also be used to hedge foreign exchange risks. The nature of swaps was also explained.

These applications of the use of forward markets, futures markets, and swaps provided a foundation for the insight that the payoff profiles of each are equivalent, and in addition, they can be used in combinations to create option contracts (and vice versa). Portfolios of risky and less risky assets can also be used to create synthetic options. These basic building blocks can be used in combination to alter a firm's or portfolio's underlying risk exposure into a wide range of any patterns of risk-return relationships.

QUESTIONS

14.1   Define and explain the following:
   a. Interest rate risk
   b. Forward contract
   c. Futures contract
   d. Cross-hedge
   e. Basis risk
   f. Notational principal

14.2   Explain the basic ideas of portfolio insurance.

---

[9]A clear illustration is provided in Smithson [1987], Figure 11 on page 26. See Problem 14.11.

14.3   Explain the concepts of duration and immunization.

14.4   Roger Bowman, a barley producer, is an excellent farmer. He has the latest equipment and knows the best techniques for improving crop yields. It is two months to harvest time and barley prices are favorable, but Roger hopes that barley prices will go even higher. However, he does not consider himself an expert on commodity price trends. Also, the current forward price for barley for October delivery would enable him to meet his mortgage interest payments comfortably; a lower barley price at harvest time would jeopardize his solvency. Should he enter into a forward contract to sell the barley for October delivery?

14.5   Do speculators perform any useful functions for the operation of futures markets?

14.6   What is the purpose of a selling or short hedge?

14.7   What is the purpose of a buying or long hedge?

14.8   With change in interest rates on the horizontal axis and change in value of a bond on the vertical axis, draw the payoff profile for selling a bond futures contract.

14.9   With the same axes as in Question 14.8, draw the payoff profile for buying a bond forward contract.

14.10   What are monetary assets and liabilities (as contrasted with "real" or nonmonetary assets and liabilities)?

PROBLEMS

14.1   You are given the following information on the returns from asset j (R_j) and the returns on the market (R_M):

Year	R_M	R_j
1	2%	1%
2	4	2
3	6	5
4	8	6
5	10	6

a.   Calculate:
   (1) The mean return of the market
   (2) The mean return of asset j
   (3) The variance of the market return
   (4) The variance of asset j's return
   (5) The covariance between the returns from asset j and the market return
   (6) The beta of asset j
   (7) The market or explained variance
   (8) The nonmarket or unexplained variance
   (9) R^2 — the portion of total variance explained by the market
   (10) The correlation coefficient, r, between the returns on asset j and the returns on the market

(11) The nonmarket or nonsystematic risk (the square root of nonmarket variance — the standard deviation).

(12) The regression equation $R_{je} = a + bR_M$

b. Discuss your results.

14.2 We have a five-year bond with a 6 percent annual coupon when the market yield is 10 percent.

a. Calculate its current price.

b. Calculate its duration.

c. Calculate the percentage change in the price of the bond for a plus or minus 0.5 percent change in the market yield rate.

d. Discuss your results.

14.3 On March 1 a pension fund manager knows she will receive $1 million on June 1 to invest. She fears a decline in interest rates. Fifteen-year, 8 percent T-bonds at that time sell at 102-20. She (buys/sells) 10 September T-bond futures contracts ($100,000 each) at 102-18. On June 1 she receives the funds expected and buys $1 million of 15-year, 8 percent T-bonds at 103-00. She covers her transaction in the futures market; she (buys/sells) at 102-30.

a. On March 1 does she buy or sell futures?

b. What are her gains and losses in the cash and futures markets?

14.4 A corporate treasurer on January 15 knows that on April 15 he will have to issue $10 million of commercial paper to finance inventory expansion. He fears a rise in interest rates. He (buys/sells) 10 June commercial paper loan futures contracts on a 9 percent basis. On April 15 interest rates have risen. He issues $10 million in commercial paper at 10 percent. He (buys/sells) in futures contracts at the same 10 percent. (Basis point = 1/100 of 1 percent of $1,000,000 = $100; for 1/4 year = $25/contract.)

a. On January 15 does he buy or sell futures?

b. What are his gains and losses in cash and futures markets?

14.5 In March, a film manufacturer estimates she'll need to purchase 10,000 troy ounces of silver in September. She fears a price rise from the current price of $3.70/ounce. On March 15, she establishes a hedge. At the time, CBOT's silver futures are trading at $3.90/ounce. (One CBOT silver futures contract equals 1,000 troy ounces.) On August 20, silver is selling for $4.10/ounce in the cash market and the September futures contract is trading at $4.50/ounce.

a. What action does the manufacturer take?

b. What is the net purchase price of the silver?

14.6 In April, a flour miller plans to buy 20,000 bushels of wheat in October, but fears that prices may rise. To protect himself, he establishes a hedge using CBOT May wheat futures. (One CBOT wheat futures contract equals 5,000 bushels.) In April, cash wheat is selling for $3.00/bushel and CBOT November wheat futures are trading at $3.20/bushel. On October 15, the miller purchases wheat at $3.65/bushel and offsets his futures position at $3.95/bushel.

a. What action does the miller take?

b. What is the net purchase price of the wheat?

c. How much did the miller save per bushel by using the futures market?

14.7 On January 1, a portfolio manager holds $1,000,000 of 8 percent U.S. T-bonds currently priced at 95-00. She needs to liquidate this Treasury portfolio by March 1. She fears that interest rates will increase. She decides to hedge her 8 percent bonds using the CBOT March T-bond futures contract, which is currently priced at 93-10. (One CBOT T-bond futures contract equals $100,000 face value U.S. Treasury bonds.) By February 20, interest rates have increased. The value of the manager's 8 percent bonds has decreased to 92-00, and the March T-bond contract has dropped to 91-20. She sells her 8 percent bonds and offsets her position in the CBOT March T-bond futures contract.

    a. What action does the portfolio manager take?

    b. What is the effective net sales price received for the T-bond portfolio?

14.8 An Aaa-rated firm can borrow 10-year fixed rate debt at 10 percent and floating rate debt at the T-bill rate plus 1 percent. At the same time, a Baa-rated firm can borrow 10-year fixed rate debt at 11.5 percent, and floating rate debt at the T-bill rate plus 1.5 percent. The short-term quality premium is only .5 percent, the long-term premium is 1.5 percent. The quality spread differential (QSD) is 100 basis points. The Aaa firm has borrowed $100 million at the 10 percent fixed rate. The Baa firm has borrowed $100 million at the T-bill rate plus 1.5 percent. Describe an interest rate swap arrangement in which the QSD is split equally.

14.9 A $100,000 portfolio will rise by 1.2 or fall to .8 of its original value over two successive periods; the riskless debt earns 5 percent. Fill in a binomial tree of the form in Figure P14.9, p. 558.

    a. For an uninsured portfolio (stock only).

    b. For an insured portfolio to obtain a value no less than the uninsured portfolio at nodes, D, E, and F and no less than $96,000 at node G.

14.10 Table P14.10 (p. 558) is from p. 47 of Cox and Rubinstein [1985]. For each of the eight innercells, explain how combinations of stock-bond portfolios replicates the options indicated.

14.11 Figure P14.11 (p. 559) is from p. 26 of Smithson [1987]. Explain how options or forward/future/swaps are used to alter the inherent exposure.

14.12 Figure P14.12 (p. 560) is taken from p. 24 of Smithson [1987].

    a. Explain how the use of calls and puts replicates a forward option.

    b. Since options can be used to replicate a forward contract, can forward contracts be used to replicate options? Explain.

FIGURE P14.9

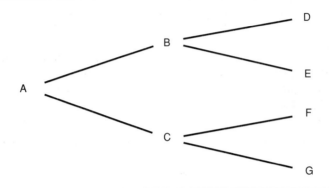

TABLE P14.10   Stock-Bond Portfolios Equivalent to Options

		Long Stock (less than one share)		Short Stock (less than one share)			
		+ Long Bonds (lending)	+ Short Bonds (borrowing)	+ Long Bonds (lending)	+ Short Bonds (borrowing)		
As Stock Price Rises	Buy stock and sell bonds	1. Long stock (one share) + Long one put	2. Long one call	3. Long one put	4. Short stock (one share) + Long one call	Sell stock and buy bonds	*As Stock Price Falls*
	Sell stock and buy bonds	5. Long stock (one share) + Short one call	6. Short one put	7. Short one call	8. Short stock (one share) + Short one put	Buy stock and sell bonds	

Source: John C. Cox and Mark Rubinstein, *Options Markets* (Englewood Cliffs, N.J.: Prentice-Hall, 1985).

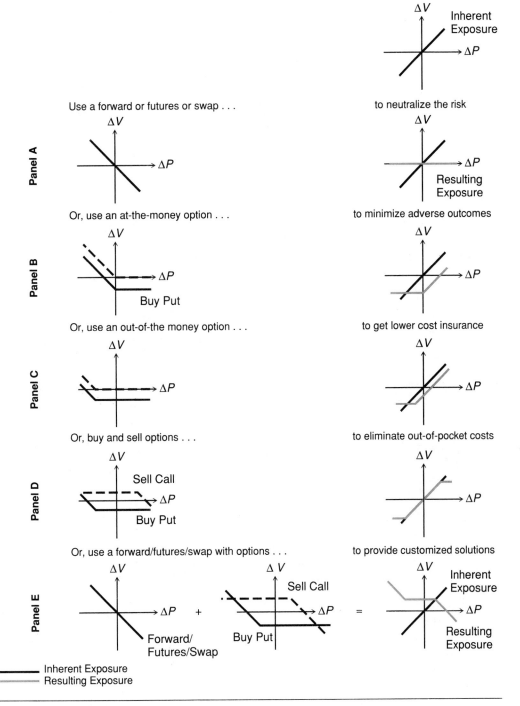

Use a forward or futures or swap . . . to neutralize the risk

Panel A

Or, use an at-the-money option . . . to minimize adverse outcomes

Panel B — Buy Put

Or, use an out-of-the money option . . . to get lower cost insurance

Panel C

Or, buy and sell options . . . to eliminate out-of-pocket costs

Panel D — Sell Call / Buy Put

Or, use a forward/futures/swap with options . . . to provide customized solutions

Panel E — Forward/Futures/Swap + Buy Put / Sell Call = Inherent Exposure / Resulting Exposure

—— Inherent Exposure
—— Resulting Exposure

Source: Charles W. Smithson, "A LEGO Approach to Financial Engineering: An Introduction to Forwards, Futures, Swaps, and Options," *Midland Corporate Finance Journal*, 4 (Winter 1987), pp. 16–28.

FIGURE P14.12

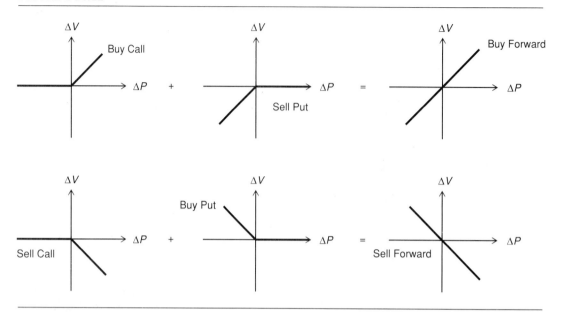

Source: Charles W. Smithson, "A LEGO Approach to Financial Engineering: An Introduction to Forwards, Futures, Swaps, and Options," *Midland Corporate Finance Journal*, 4 (Winter 1987), pp. 16–28.

SELECTED REFERENCES

Arak, Marcelle, and McCurdy, Christopher J., "Interest Rate Futures," *Quarterly Review, Federal Reserve Bank of New York*, 4 (Winter 1979-1980), pp. 33–46.

Bierwag, G. O., "Immunization, Duration, and the Term Structure of Interest Rates," *Journal of Financial and Quantitative Analysis*, 12 (December 1977), pp. 725–744.

———, and Khang C., "An Immunization Strategy is a Minimax Strategy," *Journal of Finance*, 34 (May 1979), pp. 389–399.

Black, Fischer, "The Pricing of Commodity Contracts," *Journal of Financial Economics*, 3 (January/March 1976), pp. 167–179.

———, and Scholes, Myron, "The Pricing of Options and Corporate Liabilities," *Journal of Political Economy*, 81 (1973), pp. 637–659.

Booth, J. R.; Smith, R. L.; and Stolz, R. W., "The Use of Interest Futures by Financial Institutions," *Journal of Bank Research*, (Spring 1984), pp. 15–20.

Branch, Ben, "Testing the Unbiased Expectations Theory of Interest Rates," *Financial Review*, (Fall 1978), pp. 51–66.

Capozza, Dennis R., and Cornell, Bradford, "Treasury Bill Pricing in the Spot and Futures Markets," *Review of Economics and Statistics*, 61 (November 1979), pp. 513–520.

Chen, N. F.; Roll, R. W.; and Ross, S. A., "Economic Forces and the Stock Market: Testing the APT and Alternative Asset Pricing Theories," *Journal of Business*, 59, 3 (1986), pp. 383–403.

Cornell, Bradford, and Shapiro, Alan C., "Managing Foreign Exchange Risk," *Midland Corporate Finance Journal*, 1 (Fall 1983), pp. 16–31.

Cox, John C., and Rubinstein, Mark, *Options Markets*, Englewood Cliffs, N.J.: Prentice-Hall, Inc., 1985.

Ederington, Louis H., "The Hedging Performance of the New Futures Market," *Journal of Finance*, 34 (March 1979), pp. 157–170.

Grove, M. A., "On 'Duration' and the Optimal Maturity Structure of the Balance Sheet," *Bell Journal,* (Autumn 1974), pp. 696–709.

Hsia, C. C., and Weston, J. F., "Price Behavior of Deep Discount Bonds," *Journal of Banking and Finance,* (September 1981), pp. 357–361.

Kolb, R. W., and Gay, G. D., "Immunizing Bond Portfolios with Interest Rate Futures," *Financial Management,* (Summer 1982), pp. 81–89.

Leibowitz, M. L., "Specialized Fixed Income Security Strategies," in Edward I. Altman, ed., *Financial Handbook,* 5th ed., New York: John Wiley & Sons, 1981, Section 19.

———, and Weinberger, A., *Contingent Immunization: A New Procedure for Structured Active Management,* New York: Salomon Brothers, 1981.

———, *Risk Control Procedures under Contingent Immunization,* New York: Salomon Brothers, 1982.

Leland, H., and Rubinstein, M., "The Evolution of Portfolio Insurance," in D. Luskin, ed., *Portfolio Insurance: A Guide to Dynamic Hedging,* John Wiley & Sons, 1988.

Morris, J. R., "On Corporate Debt Maturity Strategies," *Journal of Finance,* (March 1976a), pp. 29–37.

———, "A Model for Corporate Debt Maturity Decisions," *Journal of Financial and Quantitative Analysis,* (September 1976b), pp. 339–357.

Puglisi, Donald J., "Is the Futures Market for Treasury Bills Efficient?" *Journal of Portfolio Management,* 4 (Winter 1978), pp. 64–67.

Redington, F. M., "Review of the Principles of Life Office Valuations," *Journal of the Institute of Actuaries,* 78 (1952), pp. 286–340.

Smithson, Charles W., "A LEGO Approach to Financial Engineering: An Introduction to Forwards, Futures, Swaps, and Options," *Midland Corporate Finance Journal,* 4 (Winter 1987), pp. 16–28.

Turnbull, S. M., "Swaps: A Zero Sum Game?" *Financial Management,* (Spring 1987), pp. 15–21.

Wall, Larry D., and Pringle, John J., "Alternative Explanations of Interest Rate Swaps: A Theoretical and Empirical Analysis," *Financial Management,* 18 (Summer 1989), pp. 59–73.

Yawitz, J. B., and Marshall, W. J., "The Shortcomings of Duration as a Risk Measure for Bonds," *Journal of Financial Research,* (Summer 1981), pp. 91–101.

Risk and Valuation

Part Five provides the basis for determining the relevant cost of capital and how it is influenced by financial decisions. The chapters in this section examine financing decisions in the broad categories of debt versus equity, and attempt to determine the optimal financial structure — the financial structure that simultaneously minimizes the firm's cost of capital and maximizes its market value. Financing decisions and investment decisions are interdependent — the optimal financing plan and the optimal level of investment must be determined simultaneously. Therefore, Part Five also serves the important function of integrating the theory of capital budgeting with the theory of capital structure.

Chapter 15 analyzes the influence of capital structure decisions on the riskiness of the returns of a firm and hence on its required return. It then discusses how the firm may move toward its goals of minimizing its cost of capital and maximizing its value. Chapter 16 considers whether dividend policy influences the cost of capital and the value of the firm. Chapter 17, ''Value-Based Management,'' deals with factors and policies determining the value of the firm and how the patterns of future cash flow streams affect valuation.

CHAPTER 15

Financial Structure and the Cost of Capital

There are persistent differences across industries in the financial structure of the liabilities side of their balance sheets. Understanding these differences and why they persist is a central, and as yet unresolved, issue in financial economics. If there is an optimal capital structure for a company it will minimize the opportunity cost of capital and maximize shareholders' wealth. This chapter begins with a reminder that debt is a two-edged sword — it increases shareholder returns when the firm has high operating income, but makes them worse than they otherwise would be when the firm has low operating income. We then discuss the various theories of capital structure: tax effects, option and agency effects, signaling, the pecking order theory, and costs related to debt (bankruptcy and business disruption). Finally, we discuss the component costs of various sources of financing and an empirical procedure for estimating optimal capital structure.

FINANCIAL LEVERAGE

Some basic terms will be defined and will mean the same thing in all of the subsequent discussion. *Financial structure* refers to the way the firm's assets are financed. Financial structure is represented by the entire right-hand side of the balance sheet. It includes short-term debt and long-term debt as well as shareholders' equity. *Capital structure* or the *capitalization* of the firm is the permanent financing represented by long-term debt preferred stock, and shareholders' equity. Thus, a firm's capital structure is only part of its financial structure. The book value of shareholders' equity (E) includes common stock, paid-in or capital surplus, and the accumulated amount of retained earnings. The market value of common stock (S) is the price per share multiplied by the number of shares outstanding. If the firm has preferred stock (P) its market value is added to the shareholders' equity, and the two together may be termed the firm's *net worth*.

Leverage Concepts

The key concept for this chapter is financial leverage, or the leverage factor. The *leverage factor* is the ratio of the book value of total debt (D) to total assets (TA) in book value terminology or the market value of debt (B) to the total value (V) of the firm in market value terminology. When we refer to total assets (TA) we are referring to the total accounting book value of assets. Total value (V) refers to the total market value of all of the components of the firm's financial structure. While market values are used predominantly in developing financial theory, the leverage factor will also be defined with reference to accounting book values.

Financial Structure in Practice

Wide variations in asset structures and capital structure proportions are observed in practice. This generalization is supported by the book value data presented in Table 15.1. First, the patterns for wholesale trade, retail trade, and all manufacturing are compared. The ratio of shareholders' equity to total assets rises from 26 percent for retail trade to 33 percent for wholesale trade to 41 percent for all manufacturing. These variations reflect in part the differences in the nature of wholesaling, retailing, and manufacturing activities. Note the general rise in (book) debt ratios especially in manufacturing and retailing between 1984 and 1990. The sharp rise in debt in retail trade reflects some highly leveraged takeovers such as those by Robert Campeau of Allied and Federated Stores.

For example, among individual manufacturing industries depicted in the lower part of the table, the highest and lowest industries in the ratio of shareholders' equity to total assets are shown. The ratio of shareholders' equity to total assets ranges from 49 percent

TABLE 15.1 Capital Structure Proportions as a Percentage of Total Assets, 1984 and 1990

	Noninterest Bearing Debt		Interest Bearing Debt		Equity	
	1984	1990	1984	1990	1984	1990
Wholesale trade	31%	34%	33%	33%	36%	33%
Retail trade	32	30	27	44	41	26
All manufacturing	30	29	23	30	47	41
Individual manufacturing industries:						
Instruments	24%	25%	14%	27%	62%	48%
Drugs	21	28	20	23	59	49
Iron & steel	33	50	34	32	33	18
Aircraft & guided missiles	58	52	9	18	33	30

Source: Bureau of the Census, *Quarterly Financial Reports.*

TABLE 15.2   Capital Structures, Electric and Gas Utilities, 1991

| | Percent of Total Capitalization* | | | |
| | Electric Utilities** | | Gas Utilities** | |
	1985	1991	1985	1991
Long-term debt	49%	49%	41%	43%
Preferred stock	11	8	6	3
Common equity	39	43	53	54

* Defined as the sum of long-term debt, preferred stock, and common equity.
** Investor owned.
Source: Estimates by authors based on company financial data and industry composites.

for drugs down to 30 percent for aircraft and guided missiles and 18 percent for iron and steel. Variations in forms of debt are also observed. Noninterest bearing debt was at least 50 percent for iron and steel and for aircraft and guided missiles; the ratios were about 25 percent for the other two industries.

In Table 15.2, the capital structures of investor-owned electric and gas utilities are set forth. With the rise of debt ratios in manufacturing, the equity ratios of electric utilities are similar to those of manufacturing companies. The gas utilities, however, have a higher ratio of common equity to total capitalization.

Even lower ratios of equity to total assets are found among financial institutions. In recent years, commercial banks have had a ratio of common stock shareholders' equity to total assets of less than 5 percent. This ratio for savings and loans has been under 10 percent. For finance companies, it has averaged around 20 percent.

Thus, wide ranges in leverage ratios are observed among different industries and even among individual companies within a given industry. These large differences, in turn, reflect a wide range of historical, managerial, and other factors influencing financial leverage decisions. We shall analyze the major influences (such as relative costs, risk, and control) in determining a basis for choosing among alternative forms and sources of financing.

FINANCIAL LEVERAGE AND RISK

The payment of interest and principal on debt is an obligation of the firm that must be paid before any remaining profit (after taxes) is available for shareholders. The next subsection uses a numerical example to illustrate the general principle that greater financial leverage unambiguously increases the risk for shareholders. It does not make any difference whether risk is measured as the degree of financial leverage (DFL), the standard deviation of returns on equity, or the equity beta (systematic risk). When financial leverage increases, *ceteris paribus,* so does risk. The second subsection shows the relationship between operating leverage due to business risk and financial leverage.

TABLE 15.3 Hypothetical Company with Different Financial Structures

	State of Nature				
	Horrid	Bad	Average	Good	Great
Market return	−10%	0%	10%	20%	30%
Revenue @ $1.50 per unit	9,000	12,000	15,000	18,000	21,000
Minus COGS @ $0.70 per unit	−4,200	−5,600	−7,000	−8,400	−9,800
Minus Fixed costs	−6,000	−6,000	−6,000	−6,000	−6,000
EBIT	−1,200	400	2,000	3,600	5,200
Case 1: No Debt					
Minus Taxes @ 40%	480	−160	−800	−1,440	−2,080
NI	−720	240	1,200	2,160	3,120
Assets	10,000	10,000	10,000	10,000	10,000
ROA = ROE	−7.2%	2.4%	12.0%	21.6%	31.2%
Case 2: D/E = 0.25					
Minus Interest @ 10%	−200	−200	−200	−200	−200
EBT	−1,400	200	1,800	3,400	5,000
Minus Taxes @ 40%	560	−80	−720	−1,360	−2,000
NI	−840	120	1,080	2,040	3,000
Debt	2,000	2,000	2,000	2,000	2,000
Equity	8,000	8,000	8,000	8,000	8,000
ROE	−10.5%	1.5%	13.5%	25.5%	37.5%
Case 3: D/E = 1.0					
Minus Interest @ 14%	−700	−700	−700	−700	−700
EBT	−1,900	−300	1,300	2,900	4,500
Minus Taxes @ 40%	760	120	−520	−1,160	−1,800
NI	−1,140	−180	780	1,740	2,700
Debt	5,000	5,000	5,000	5,000	5,000
Equity	5,000	5,000	5,000	5,000	5,000
ROE	−22.8%	−3.6%	15.6%	34.8%	54.0%
Case 4: D/E = 4.0					
Minus Interest @ 20%	−1,600	−1,600	−1,600	−1,600	−1,600
EBT	−2,800	−1,200	400	2,000	3,600
Minus Taxes @ 40%	1,120	480	−160	−800	−1,440
NI	−1,680	−720	240	1,200	2,160
Debt	8,000	8,000	8,000	8,000	8,000
Equity	2,000	2,000	2,000	2,000	2,000
ROE	−84.0%	−36.0%	12.0%	60.0%	108.0%

Financial Leverage and Equity Risk

The first row of Table 15.3 shows the market rate of return in five equally likely states of nature ranging from horrid (a minus 10 percent return) to great (a plus 30 percent return). A hypothetical company, without any debt, will earn net income after taxes of −$720 in the horrid state up through $3,120 in the great state. Given that the company has $10,000 in assets, this translates into a return on assets ranging from −7.2 percent to 31.2 percent.

FIGURE 15.1   Financial Leverage Magnifies Variations in the Return on Equity

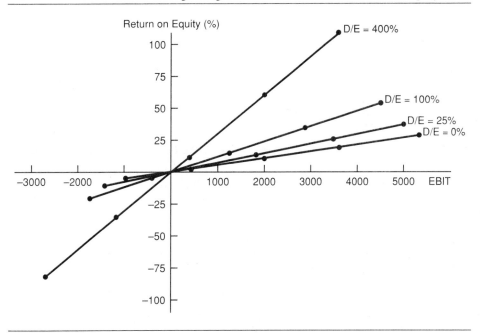

The company can change its financial structure by issuing debt and using the proceeds to buy back equity. This maneuver changes the ratio of debt and equity without changing total assets or the company's earnings before interest and taxes (EBIT). It does, however, have a significant impact on the return on equity. In the horrid state of nature the return on equity, given no debt, is −7.2 percent; but with a debt-to-equity ratio of 400 percent the return on equity is −84.0 percent; in fact, the company would probably be bankrupt. The return on equity is also magnified in the "great" state of nature. With no debt, it is 31.2 percent; with $D/E = 4.0$, it is 108 percent.

Figure 15.1 plots the return on equity against the company's earnings before interest and taxes for various leverage strategies. To add some realism to the example we have assumed that the interest rate charged by the debtholders increases as the ratio of debt to equity becomes more extreme. For modest debt ($D/E = 25\%$) the interest rate is assumed to be 10 percent, but when the debt-to-equity ratio is 400 percent, the risk-adjusted cost of debt is assumed to be 20 percent per annum. Figure 15.1 clearly illustrates that the variability of the return on equity is magnified by the amount of financial leverage that the company decides to use.

Table 15.4 measures the effect of leverage three ways: the degree of financial leverage (DFL), the standard deviation of returns on equity, and the levered equity beta. The degree of financial leverage is a point elasticity measure defined as the ratio of the percentage change in net income divided by the percentage change in earnings before interest and taxes.

TABLE 15.4   Measures of Risk for Different Financial Structures

State of Nature	Market Return	Return on Assets	ROE for Various D/E Ratios			
			0	0.25	1.0	4.0
Horrid	−10.0%	−7.2%	−7.2%	−10.5%	−22.8%	−84.0%
Bad	0	2.4	2.4	1.5	−3.6	−36.0
Average	10.0	12.0	12.0	13.5	15.6	12.0
Good	20.0	21.6	21.6	25.5	34.8	60.0
Great	30.0	31.2	31.2	37.5	54.0	108.0

State of Nature	$(R_M - \bar{R}_M)$	$(R_M - \bar{R}_M)^2$	Mean Differences for D/E Ratios				Mean Differences Squared			
			0	0.25	1.0	4.0	0	0.25	1.0	4.0
Horrid	−20.0%	.0400	−19.2%	−24.0%	−38.4%	−96.0%	.0369	.0576	.1475	.9216
Bad	−10.0	.0100	−9.6	−12.0	−19.2	−48.0	.0092	.0144	.0369	.2304
Average	0	.0000	0.0	0.0	0.0	0.0	.0000	.0000	.0000	.0000
Good	10.0	.0100	9.6	12.0	19.2	48.0	.0092	.0144	.0369	.2304
Great	20.0	.0400	19.2	24.0	38.4	96.0	.0369	.0576	.1475	.9216
		.1000					.0922	.1440	.3688	2.304

Covariance Calculations

State of Nature	D/E = 0	D/E = 0.25	D/E = 1.0	D/E = 4.0
Horrid	(−.200)(−.192) = .0384	(−.200)(−.240) = .0448	(−.200)(−.384) = .0768	(−.200)(−.960) = .1920
Bad	(−.100)(−.096) = .0096	(−.100)(−.120) = .0120	(−.100)(−.192) = .0192	(−.100)(−.480) = .0480
Average	(.000)(.000) = .0000	(.000)(.000) = .0000	(.000)(.000) = .0000	(.000)(.000) = .0000
Good	(.100)(.096) = .0096	(.100)(.120) = .0120	(.100)(.192) = .0192	(.100)(.480) = .0480
Great	(.200)(.192) = .0384	(.200)(.240) = .0448	(.200)(.384) = .0768	(.200)(.960) = .1920
	.0960	.1136	.1920	.4800

D/E Ratio	DFL in Average State	ROE Standard Deviation	Beta = COV(ROE, R_M)/VAR(R_M)
D/E = 0	1.00	$\sqrt{.0922/5}$ = 13.6%	.0960/.1000 = 0.96
D/E = 0.25	1.11	$\sqrt{.1440/5}$ = 17.0	.1136/.1000 = 1.14
D/E = 1.0	1.54	$\sqrt{.3688/5}$ = 27.2	.1920/.1000 = 1.92
D/E = 4.0	5.00	$\sqrt{2.304/5}$ = 67.9	.4800/.1000 = 4.80

$$\text{Degree of financial leverage (DFL)} = \frac{\%\ \text{change in net income}}{\%\ \text{change in EBIT}}. \tag{15.1}$$

We can develop this expression further by noting that net income is defined as:

$$NI = (EBIT − rD)(1 − T),$$

and that since interest expenses, rD, are a constant, the change in net income is

$$\Delta NI = \Delta EBIT(1 − T).$$

FIGURE 15.2   Financial Leverage and Risk

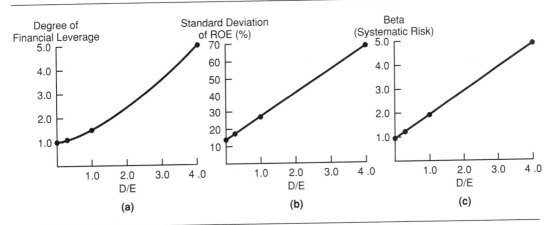

Therefore, the degree of financial leverage can be written as:

$$DFL = \frac{\dfrac{\Delta EBIT(1 - T)}{(EBIT - rD)(1 - T)}}{\dfrac{\Delta EBIT}{EBIT}} = \frac{EBIT}{EBIT - rD}. \tag{15.2}$$

When interest expenses are zero then DFL = 1.0, which makes sense because with no debt a 1 percent change in EBIT results in a 1 percent change in NI. At the other extreme, when the debt-to-equity ratio is 4.0, a 1 percent change in the DFL results in a 5 percent change in net income.

The standard deviation of the return on equity shows the same relationship between leverage and risk. The standard deviation is 13.6 percent with no debt but rises quickly to 67.9 percent when the debt-to-equity ratio is 4.0. Finally, the measure of systematic risk, beta, increases from 0.96 with no debt to 4.80 with $D/E = 4.0$. As illustrated in Figure 15.2, regardless of what measure of risk one uses, the conclusion is the same — *financial leverage increases risk.*

Financial Leverage and the Return on Equity

We learned in Chapter 11 that there is a unique relationship between systematic risk (e.g., beta in the Capital Asset Pricing Model) and the rate of return that the market requires on a security. One application of this concept was a procedure for estimating the cost of equity using the CAPM:

$$k_s = R_F + [E(R_M) - R_F]\beta_s. \tag{15.3}$$

For the purpose of illustration, assume that the risk-free rate of return, R_F, is 5 percent, and that the expected rate of return on the market portfolio is 10 percent. These assump-

TABLE 15.5   The Cost of Equity Increases with Increasing Financial Leverage

D/E Ratio	Actual Beta	Actual k_s	Theoretical Beta	Theoretical k_s
.00	0.96	9.8%	0.96	9.8%
.25	1.14	10.7	1.10	10.5
1.00	1.92	14.6	1.54	12.7
4.00	4.80	29.0	3.26	21.3

tions (Equation 15.3) and the actual betas computed in Table 15.4 allow us to compute the actual cost of equity (k_s) in Table 15.5. The undeniable conclusion is that, *ceteris paribus,* when the financial leverage of a company increases, so does the cost of equity.[1]

Table 15.5 also shows results derived from the theoretical relationship between the riskiness of the assets of a company, i.e., its beta if it has no debt (its unlevered beta, β_U) and the riskiness of its levered equity (β_L) when it does have debt. To obtain these results, we start with Figure 15.3, which shows the conservation of risk. The systematic risk of the firm's assets, β_U, must equal the systematic risk of the claims on assets, as shown in Equation 15.4:

$$\beta_U = W_B \beta_B + W_S \beta_S. \tag{15.4}$$

The market value weights for debt and equity are

$$W_B = \frac{B}{B + S} \text{ and } W_S = \frac{S}{B + S},$$

where B is the market value of debt (bonds) and S is the market value of equity (stocks). Substituting these weights into Equation 15.4 and solving for the levered equity beta, $\beta_L = \beta_S$, we have

FIGURE 15.3   The Asset Beta Equals the Weighted Average of the Liability Betas

Assets		Liabilities	
Asset 1	$W_1 \beta_1$		
Asset 2	$W_2 \beta_2$	Debt	$W_B \beta_B$
•			
•			
Asset N	$W_N \beta_N$	Equity	$W_S \beta_S$

$$\beta_U = \sum_{i=1}^{N} W_i \beta_i = W_B \beta_B + W_S \beta_S$$

---

[1]*Ceteris paribus* means "all other things being held constant." In the current context, it means that the company's investment decision, and therefore its return on assets, is invariant to its choice of financial structure.

$$\beta_L = \beta_S = \beta_U + (\beta_U - \beta_B)\frac{B}{S}.$$

When taxes are also taken into consideration the above equation is modified as follows:

$$\beta_L = \beta_U + (\beta_U - \beta_B)(1 - T)\frac{B}{S}. \qquad (15.5)$$

The usual assumption is that corporate debt has no systematic risk, i.e., $\beta_B = 0$. If so, Equation 15.5 reduces to[2]

$$\beta_L = \beta_U\left[1 + (1 - T)\frac{B}{S}\right]. \qquad (15.6)$$

Equation 15.6 was used to compute the theoretical levered equity betas in Table 15.5. The actual cost of equity and actual equity beta are higher than the theoretical values computed from Equation 15.6 because the theoretical solution assumes that debt is riskless. In our numerical example (Table 15.3), the interest rate on debt went up as the firm used more debt and became riskier.

Equation 15.6 is often used in practice as a way to unlever and relever betas. For example, you may want to know what your company's cost of equity would be if its financial leverage were to change. Table 15.6 shows the levered equity beta, β_L, the cost of equity, k_s, the statutory marginal tax rate (including state and local taxes), T, and the market value capital structure, B/S, for a group of publishing companies. As you can see, the unlevered betas are very similar. Their average, 1.01, reflects the average business risk in the industry. McGraw-Hill currently uses very little debt. Suppose it were to decide to increase its debt-to-equity ratio to 50 percent. What would its new cost of equity be?

The first step in the analysis is to use Equation 15.6 to estimate the unlevered beta, β_U, for each of the comparable companies in the same line of business. Their average, 1.01, is very close to the unlevered beta of 0.96 estimated for McGraw-Hill. Let's use 1.0 as the appropriate unlevered beta. With 50 percent debt to equity its new levered beta would be

$$\beta_L = 1.0[1 + (1 - .39).5] = 1.31.$$

TABLE 15.6   Observed Levered Betas for Publishing Companies

Company	β_L	k_s	T	B/S	β_U
McGraw-Hill	1.08	14.60%	39.0%	.212	0.96
Western Publishing	1.33	16.10	39.0	.209	1.18
Houghton Mifflin	1.17	15.14	39.0	.114	1.09
Wiley (John) & Sons	1.10	14.72	39.0	.510	0.84
Nelson (Thomas) Inc.	1.05	14.42	39.0	.088	1.00

Note: The cost of equity assumes a risk-free rate of 8.12 percent and a market risk premium of 6 percent.

---

[2]See Rubinstein [1973].

Using the Capital Asset Pricing Model and the assumptions of Table 15.6, its new cost of equity would be

$$k_s = R_F + (\bar{R}_M - R_F)\beta_L$$
$$k_s = 8.12\% + (6\%)1.31 = 15.98\%.$$

This example illustrates that the cost of equity increases as the firm uses more debt in its financial structure.

Financial and Operating Leverage

Operating leverage is a way of measuring the business risk of a company. Operating leverage causes a change in sales volume to have a magnified effect on EBIT. If financial leverage is superimposed on operating leverage, changes in EBIT have a magnified effect on NI, on ROE, and on EPS. Therefore, if a firm uses a considerable amount of both operating leverage and financial leverage, even small changes in the level of sales will produce wide fluctuations in NI, ROE, and EPS.

Recall that in Chapter 8 we defined the degree of operating leverage, DOL, as

$$\text{DOL} = \frac{\% \text{ change in EBIT}}{\% \text{ change in sales}} = \frac{(P - v)Q}{\text{EBIT}}, \qquad (15.7)$$

where as before:

$$P = \text{price per unit of quantity sold}$$
$$v = \text{variable costs per unit}$$
$$Q = \text{quantity of units sold.}$$

If we multiply this by the degree of financial leverage, DFL, we obtain the combined effect of both types of leverage, the degree of combined leverage, DCL:

$$\text{DCL} = \frac{\% \text{ change in EBIT}}{\% \text{ change in sales}} \times \frac{\% \text{ change in net income}}{\% \text{ change in EBIT}}. \qquad (15.8)$$

This can be rewritten as follows using Equations 15.2 and 15.7:

$$\text{DCL} = \frac{(P - v)Q}{\text{EBIT}} \times \frac{\text{EBIT}}{\text{EBIT} - rD} = \frac{(P - v)Q}{\text{EBIT} - rD}. \qquad (15.9)$$

Higher interest costs, rD, have the effect of raising the degree of combined leverage. This confirms Equation 15.6, which says that the business risk of a company is represented by its financial leverage.

A number of different combinations of operating and financial leverage could produce the same combined leverage factor. Hence, to some degree, firms can make trade-offs between operating and financial leverage. A firm with a high degree of operating leverage is likely to use financial leverage to a lesser extent. However, if its DOL is very high, the use of a lower DFL (or the use of no debt at all, which would produce a DFL of one) might not bring the firm's degree of combined leverage down as low as other firms' whose DOL was low to start with. Alternatively, a firm with a low degree of operating leverage might seek a high degree of financial leverage, but its degree of combined leverage might still be lower than that of other firms which started with a high DOL.

INVESTMENT AND LEVERAGE

Thus far in the chapter, we have varied leverage, holding constant the total amount of investment by the firm. In real-world decision making, it is often necessary to perform an analysis in which alternative leverage structures are considered along with financing that increases the firm's amount of investment and size of total assets. This aspect of combining the financing and leverage decisions will be developed with the Universal Machine Company example. Universal's latest balance sheet is set forth in Table 15.7. Universal manufactures equipment used in industrial manufacturing. Its major product is a lathe used to trim the rough edges off sheets of fabricated steel. As is typically the case for producers of durable capital assets, the company's sales fluctuate widely, far more than does the overall economy. For example, during 9 of the preceding 25 years, the company's sales have been below the breakeven point, so losses have been relatively frequent. Although future sales are uncertain, current demand is high and appears to be headed higher. Thus, if Universal is to continue its sales growth, it will have to increase capacity. A capacity increase involving $2 million of new capital is under consideration. James Watson, the financial vice president, learns that he can raise the $2 million by selling bonds with a 12 percent coupon or by selling 100,000 shares of common stock at a market price of $20 per share. Fixed costs after the planned expansion will be $6.4 million a year. Variable costs excluding interest on the debt will be 20 percent of sales.[3] The probability distribution for alternative future states-of-the-world is set forth in the first row of Table 15.8.

Although Watson's recommendation will be given much weight, the final decision for the method of financing rests with the company's board of directors. Procedurally, the financial vice president analyzes the situation, evaluates all reasonable alternatives, comes to a conclusion, and then presents the alternatives with his recommendations to the board.

TABLE 15.7 Universal Machine Company: Balance Sheet for Year Ended December 31, 19X4 (Thousands of Dollars)

Cash	$ 300	Total liabilities having an average cost of 10%	$ 5,000
Receivables (net)	1,200		
Inventories	1,400		
Plant (net)	3,000	Common stock ($10 par)	5,000
Equipment (net)	4,100		
Total assets	$10,000	Total claims on assets	$10,000

---

[3]The assumption that variable costs will be a constant percentage of sales over the entire range of output is not valid, but variable costs are relatively constant over the output range likely to be actually experienced.

TABLE 15.8 Profit Calculations at Various Sales Levels, Universal Machine Company (Thousands of Dollars)

Probability of indicated sales	0.2	0.5	0.3
Sales	$5,000	$12,000	$20,000
Costs:			
Fixed	6,400	6,400	6,400
Variable (0.2S)	1,000	2,400	4,000
Total costs	$7,400	$8,800	$10,400
Earnings before interest and taxes (EBIT)	−$2,400	$3,200	$9,600
Financing with bonds			
Earnings before interest and taxes	−$2,400	$3,200	$9,600
Less: interest (12% × $7,000)[a]	840	840	840
Earnings before taxes	−$3,240	$2,360	$8,760
Less: income taxes (40%)	−1,296	944	3,504
Net income (NI)	−$1,944	$1,416	$5,256
EPS on 500,000 shares[b]	−3.89	2.83	10.51
Return on equity	−38.9%	28.3%	105.1%
Expected EPS = $3.79			
Financing with stock			
Earnings before interest and taxes	−$2,400	$3,200	$9,600
Less: interest (10% × $5,000)	500	500	500
Earnings before taxes	−$2,900	$2,700	$9,100
Less: income taxes (40%)	−1,160	1,080	3,640
Net income (NI)	−$1,740	$1,620	$5,460
EPS on 600,000 shares[b]	−2.90	2.70	9.10
Return on equity	−24.8%	23.14%	78%
Expected EPS = $3.50			

[a]With higher financial leverage, the cost of debt rises to 12 percent on the new debt, and 12 percent represents the opportunity cost of the old debt as well. Some would argue for using 10 percent on the existing $5 million of debt, since this is the actual interest that would be paid until it matures. For cost of capital calculations or effects on earnings, we use the opportunity cost. For interest coverage, we will use actual interest outlays.

[b]The EPS figures can also be obtained using the following formula:

$$EPS = \frac{(Sales - Fixed\ costs - Variable\ costs - Interest)(1 - Tax\ rate)}{Shares\ outstanding}.$$

For example, at sales = $12 million:

$$EPS_{Bonds} = \frac{(12 - 6.4 - 2.4 - 0.84)(0.6)}{0.5} = \$2.83$$

$$EPS_{Stock} = \frac{(12 - 6.4 - 2.4 - 0.5)(0.6)}{0.6} = \$2.70.$$

For his own analysis, as well as for presentation to the board, Watson prepares the materials shown in Table 15.8.

The top third of the table calculates earnings before interest and taxes (EBIT) for different levels of sales ranging from $5 million to $20 million. The firm suffers an operating loss until sales are $8 million, but beyond that point, it enjoys a rapid rise in gross profit.[4]

---

[4]The breakeven sales are $S^* = \$6,400,000 + 0.2S^*$. Hence, $S^* = \$8,000,000$.

FIGURE 15.4 Probability Curves for Stock and Bond Financing

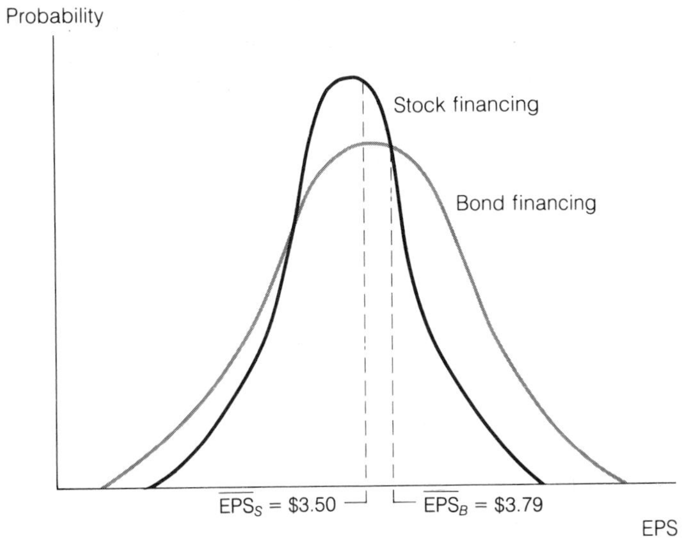

The middle third of the table shows the financial results that will occur at the various sales levels if bonds are used. First, the $840,000 annual interest charges ($600,000 on existing debt plus $240,000 on the new bonds) are deducted from the earnings before interest and taxes. Next, taxes are taken out; and if the sales level is so low that losses are incurred, the firm receives a tax credit. Then, net profits after taxes are divided by the 500,000 shares outstanding to obtain earnings per share (EPS) of common stock.[5] The various EPS figures are multiplied by the corresponding probability estimates to obtain an expected EPS of $3.79.

The bottom third of the table calculates the financial results that will occur with stock financing. Net profit after interest and taxes is divided by 600,000 — the original 500,000 shares plus the 100,000 new shares ($20 × 100,000 = $2,000,000) — to find earnings per share. Expected EPS is computed in the same way as for the bond financing.

Figure 15.4 shows the probability distribution of earnings per share. Stock financing has the tighter, more peaked distribution. Hence, stock financing is less risky than bond financing. However, the expected earnings per share are lower for stock financing than for bond financing, so we are faced with the kind of risk-return trade-off that characterizes most financial decisions. What choice should Watson recommend to the board? How much leverage should Universal Machine use? These questions cannot be answered at this point; the answers must be deferred until the effects of leverage on the cost of both debt and equity capital have been examined later on in this chapter.

---

[5]The number of shares initially outstanding can be calculated by dividing the $5 million common stock figure given on the balance sheet by the $10 par value.

FIGURE 15.5   Earnings per Share for Stock and Debt Financing

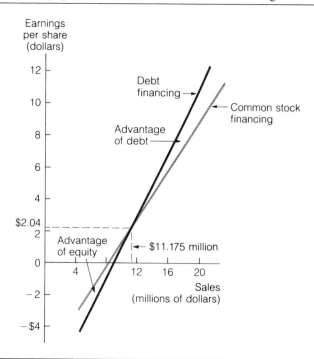

Figure 15.5 shows the relationship between the earnings per share and the level of sales for the two alternative types of financing. Above a breakeven point of $11.175 million of sales, highly leveraged financing is best for shareholders, while below that point, equity is best. If the board, based on its understanding of the business, believes that sales are very unlikely to fall below the breakeven point, then high leverage is advisable. Even a leveraged buyout or leveraged recapitalization of the company might make sense.

Effects of Fluctuating Interest Rates

Another aspect of leverage is the impact of fixed rate debt while general interest rates are fluctuating. In general, with fixed rate debt, rising interest rates will cause the market value of the firm's debt to decline. But with fixed rate debt, a rise or fall in interest rates may also have an impact on the firm's asset values. For example, if interest rates rise, for some firms, such as automobile manufacturers, the value of their assets may fall, other things being equal. This is because at higher interest rates, fewer automobiles may be sold because most automobiles are bought with credit, so that the monthly cost increases with higher interest rates. On the other hand, if the economy is stronger when interest rates are higher, the favorable income outlook for consumers may offset the negative impact of higher interest rates.

If the value of the firm's assets declines with higher interest rates, then a type of "immunization" has occurred. The values of the firm's assets have declined, but the market value of its debt has also decreased. Hence, these are offsetting changes.

On the other hand, if the values of the firm's assets are positively correlated with interest rate levels, a disparity is created. With high interest rates, the market value of liabilities falls and the market value of assets rises. With lower interest rates, the market value of liabilities rises and the market value of assets declines. Hence, if interest rate movements are positively correlated with asset values, this has a destabilizing impact on the firm. If interest rate levels are negatively correlated with asset values, this provides the firm with a form of "immunization" of the relationship between the value of its assets and the value of its liabilities.

The preceding analysis has been based on debt with a fixed interest rate coupon, or fixed rate debt. With increased economic uncertainty and interest rate volatility of recent years, both borrowers and lenders have agreed on using variable or floating rate debt. In some general sense, floating rate debt is fair to everybody. In effect, it says the borrower pays whatever current interest rate conditions call for, and similarly for the lender.

The effect on the borrower, whose viewpoint we are taking primarily here, depends upon the covariation of interest rates with general economic conditions, the revenues of the borrower, the costs of the borrower, and hence the level of the borrower's operating income. If interest rates are positively correlated with the borrower's net operating income, floating rate coupons will reduce financial risks to borrowers. This is because when interest rates are high, operating income is high. When interest rates are low, operating income is low. Hence, net income will tend to be relatively stable.

If interest rate levels are negatively correlated with the borrower's operating income, the opposite effects will occur. Fluctuating interest rates will increase the volatility of the borrower's net income and thereby increase the equity risk of the borrower.

But whether interest rates represent fixed coupons or fluctuating coupons, interest costs remain a fixed charge. They must be paid regardless of the level of the operating income of the firm. Hence, the increased use of floating rate debt does not fundamentally affect the general propositions developed in this chapter. If interest rates are positively correlated with operating income, the floating rate debt may mitigate to some degree the leverage effects. If interest rate levels are negatively correlated with the firm's net operating income, the leverage effects will be magnified.

FACTORS AFFECTING FINANCIAL STRUCTURE

Before beginning our theoretical discussion of factors that may affect the optimal capital structure of firms, we will take a few paragraphs to discuss some of the empirical factors related to the financial structure of the firm.

Growth Rate of Sales

The future growth rate of sales is a measure of the extent to which the earnings per share of a firm are likely to be magnified by leverage. If sales and earnings grow at a rate of 8 to 10 percent a year, for example, financing by debt with limited fixed charges should magnify the returns to owners of the stock.[6] This can be seen from Figure 15.1. However, the common stock of a firm whose sales and earnings are growing at a favorable rate commands a high price; this favors equity financing. The firm must weigh the benefits of using leverage against the opportunity of broadening its equity base when its common stock prices are high.

Cash Flow Stability

Cash flow stability and debt ratios are directly related. With greater stability in sales and operating earnings, a firm can incur the fixed charges of debt with less risk than when its sales and earnings are subject to substantial declines. When operating cash flow is low, the firm may have difficulty meeting its fixed interest obligations.

Industry Characteristics

Debt-servicing ability is dependent on the profitability, as well as the volume, of sales. Hence, the stability of profit margins is as important as the stability of sales. The ease with which new firms can enter the industry and the ability of competing firms to expand capacity both influence profit margins. A growth industry promises higher profit margins, but such margins are likely to narrow if the industry is one in which the number of firms can be easily increased through additional entry. For example, the franchised fast-service food companies were a very profitable industry in the early 1960s, but it was relatively easy for new firms to enter the business and compete with the older firms. As the industry matured during the late 1960s and early 1970s, the capacity of the old and the new firms grew at an increased rate. As a consequence, profit margins declined.

Asset Structure

Asset structure influences the sources of financing in several ways. Firms with long-lived fixed assets, especially when demand for their output is relatively assured (for example, public utilities), use long-term mortgage debt extensively.[7] Firms that have their assets mostly in receivables and in inventories whose value is dependent on the continued profitability of the individual firm (for example, those in wholesale and retail trade) rely less on long-term debt financing and more on short-term financing.

Management Attitudes

The management attitudes that most directly influence the choice of financing are those concerning control of the enterprise and risk. Large corporations whose stock is widely owned may choose additional sales of common stock because such sales will have little influence on the control of the company.

---

[6]Such a growth rate is also often associated with a high profit rate.

[7]But, the returns allowed on the assets by regulators of public utilities are also critical. In recent decades, the inadequate returns allowed caused the securities of many public utility companies to be considered to involve relatively high risks.

In contrast, the owners of small firms may prefer to avoid issuing common stock in order to be assured of continued control. Because they generally have confidence in the prospects of their companies and because they can see the large potential gains to themselves resulting from leverage, managers of such firms are often willing to incur high debt ratios.

The converse can, of course, also hold; the owner-manager of a small firm may be more conservative than the manager of a large company. If the net worth of the small firm is, say, $1 million, and if it all belongs to the owner-manager, that individual may well decide to limit the use of debt, which increases the risk of losing a substantial portion of his or her wealth.

Lender Attitudes

Regardless of managements' views, lenders' attitudes determine financial structures. The corporation discusses its financial structure with lenders and gives much weight to their advice. But, if management seeks to use leverage beyond norms for the industry, lenders may be unwilling to accept such debt increases. They emphasize that excessive debt reduces the credit standing of the borrower and the credit rating of the securities previously issued. The lenders' point of view has been expressed by a borrower (a financial vice president), who stated, ''Our policy is to determine how much debt we can carry and still maintain an Aa bond rating, then use that amount less a small margin for safety.''

CAPITAL STRUCTURE AND THE COST OF CAPITAL

The first part of this chapter introduced financial leverage and demonstrated that debt commitments increase the riskiness of the return to shareholders and often increase the expected level of returns as well. Without further analysis it is hard to say whether this risk-return trade-off is favorable from the shareholders' point of view. Stated another way, the problem that we seek to understand is this: Is there a value-maximizing capital structure?

We will address the capital structure puzzle in stages. First, we shall examine the effects of taxes on capital structure. We shall start with a world with no taxes, then move on to explain the effect of the tax deductibility of interest expenses (i.e., corporate taxes), and finally to analyze capital structure in a world with both personal and corporate taxes. After discussing tax effects, we will introduce the impact of bankruptcy costs. Next, we will discuss agency costs—the costs that govern the way principals and agents write contracts in order to organize ownership of the firm (e.g., the debt/equity mix). Then we will turn to the possibility that debt can be used as a signal to the marketplace regarding managers' information about the future of the firm. And last, but not least, we will discuss a pecking order theory of capital structure.

We are not covering all of these theories to frustrate the reader. We are including them all because each is an important part of the capital structure puzzle, and because the capital structure puzzle is unresolved. Each theory seems to have some validity but none has been accepted as a complete explanation.

Taxes, Capital Structure, and the Cost of Capital

The history of thinking about the effect of taxes on capital structure goes back to the seminal work of Modigliani and Miller in 1958 where they assume no taxes and conclude that the value of the firm is unaffected by capital structure. In a later article they introduce corporate taxes (but not bankruptcy costs) and show that the optimal capital structure is 100 percent debt. Finally, in 1977, Professor Miller argued that in a world with personal and corporate taxes, once again, capital structure is irrelevant. In the discussion that follows, we work through their derivations in detail because they are central to understanding the value of the firm.

The No-Tax Case. Initially, Modigliani and Miller (MM) discuss a no-growth firm with no net new investments in a world of no taxes. The value of such a firm (or project) would be its perpetual cash flows, $\overline{\text{NOI}}$ or $\overline{X}$, divided by its cost of capital, k:

$$V = \frac{\overline{\text{NOI}}}{k} = \frac{\overline{X}}{k}. \tag{15.10}$$

This is MM's Proposition I. It states that the market value of any firm (or project) "is given by capitalizing its expected return at the rate, k, appropriate to its class." This is what MM were referring to when they stated that firms in a given risk class would have the same applicable discount rate. In their discussions they stated that firms of different sizes would differ only by "scale factor" and pointed out that the expected cash flows from two firms of different size or scale (or projects) would be perfectly correlated.

The measurement of k depends upon the riskiness of the firm, project, or activity. Thus, if the expected net operating income, $\overline{\text{NOI}}$ or $\overline{X}$, in the numerator were \$200,000 and the activity were of relatively low risk, the discount factor, k, might be 10 percent. The value of the firm would then be \$2 million. If the activity of the firm was highly risky, the discount rate might be 20 percent. If so, the value of the firm would be \$1 million.

We now consider the influence of leverage. Under the assumptions to this point MM argue that the expression in Equation 15.10 would be unaffected by financial leverage. They obtain this result from an arbitrage process involving "homemade leverage," which can be formulated simply.[8] Consider two investment alternatives with the following patterns of investments and returns:

Decision	Investment	Dollar Return
A. Buy α of the equity of levered firm, L	αS_L	$\alpha(X - k_b B)$
B. Buy α of unlevered firm, U		
Borrow αB	$\alpha S_U - \alpha B$	$\alpha(X) - \alpha k_b B = \alpha(X - k_b B)$

In the above, the symbols have the following meanings:

L = levered

U = unlevered

S = market value of common stock (equity)

---

[8] Remember that $B = rD/k_b$ so that $k_b B = rD$. Recall that r is the coupon rate on debt and D is the book value of debt.

B = market value of debt (bonds)

k_b = marginal cost of debt

X = net operating income (also assumed to be equal to earnings before interest and taxes, EBIT)

α = a fraction, that is, $0 \le \alpha \le 1$.

Investment A is to buy a fraction of the common equity of a levered firm. Investment B is to buy the same fraction of the common equity of an unlevered firm and to create an amount of homemade leverage equivalent to that represented by the investment of the α fraction of equity of the levered firm. Since the returns from the two investments are equal, their investment market values will also be equal. Hence we set the two investment values equal to each other:

$\alpha S_L = \alpha S_U - \alpha B$ Divide by α.
$S_L = S_U - B$ Regroup terms.
$S_L + B = S_U$ Since $S_L + B = V_L$ and $S_U = V_U$, we have $V_L = V_U$.

Thus, under the conditions we have specified, the value of the levered firm is equal to the value of the unlevered firm.[9] This is the famous capital structure irrelevance or leverage irrelevance of Proposition I of Modigliani-Miller. We can also rewrite Equation 15.10 by solving for k to obtain Equation 15.11:

$$k = k_U = \frac{\overline{X}}{V}. \qquad (15.11)$$

This is a restatement of Proposition I in terms of the cost of capital (or return on assets). It states that the cost of capital to any firm is independent of its capital structure and is equal to the capitalization rate of a pure equity stream of its risk class, k_U.

Corporate Taxes Only.   Assume a proportional corporate tax rate that we will initially refer to as T. We will start with an unlevered firm. The net operating income available for distribution to claimants must now be expressed net of the corporate income tax. We, therefore, have Equation 15.12:

$$V_U = \frac{\overline{X}(1 - T)}{k_U}. \qquad (15.12)$$

A simple rearrangement gives us the cost of capital of an unlevered firm in Equation 15.13:

$$k_U = \frac{\overline{X}(1 - T)}{V_U}. \qquad (15.13)$$

We repeat the simple arbitrage process. Based on two decision alternatives described below, some associated investment and returns patterns follow:

---

[9]Note that the argument implicitly assumes that individuals can borrow at the same rate as the firm, k_b. This is a valid assumption in a world without transactions costs.

Decision	Investment	Dollar Return
A. Buy α of levered firm, L	αS_L	$\alpha(X - k_bB)(1 - T)$
B. Buy α of unlevered firm, U Borrow $\alpha(1 - T)B$	$\alpha S_U - \alpha(1 - T)B$	$\alpha(X)(1 - T) - \alpha(1 - T)k_bB = $ $\alpha(X - k_bB)(1 - T)$.

Decision A is to buy a fraction of the common equity of a levered firm. Decision B is to buy the same fraction of the common equity of an unlevered firm and to create an amount of homemade leverage equivalent to that represented by the investment in the equity of the levered firm by selling $\alpha(1 - T)B$ of debt. The return from the investment in the equity of the levered firm is the α percent of its income after deduction of debt interest, and taxes. For Decision B, the return is given as a fraction of the after-tax income of the unlevered firm less the interest (after taxes) paid on the homemade borrowings. The returns from the two investments are equal; consequently their market values will also be equal. It follows that

$\alpha S_L = \alpha S_U - \alpha(1 - T)B$ Divide through by α.
$S_L = S_U - (1 - T)B$ Expand the last term.
$S_L = S_U - B + TB$ Regroup terms.
$S_L + B = S_U + TB$.   Since $S_L + B = V_L$ and $S_U = V_U$,

then

$$V_L = V_U + TB. \tag{15.14}$$

Equation 15.14 conveys an important implication of the MM relations.[10] Because of the tax subsidy represented by the tax deductibility of interest on debt, the value of a levered firm will be greater than the value of an unlevered firm by the amount of debt multiplied by the applicable corporate tax rate. Myers has coined the term *adjusted present value* (*APV*) for Equation 15.14 to emphasize that the value of an all-equity firm can be adjusted upward by the present value of tax shields (*B*). Note that one of the implications of Equation 15.14 is that the value of the levered firm is maximized with 100 percent debt.

Since the value of the common equity, *S*, is equal to the value of a levered firm less the value of debt, the effects of leverage decisions on the market behavior of the common equity are predictable on the basis of Equation 15.14. This leads to MM's Proposition II, which deals with the cost of equity capital. We start with the definitions of the cost of equity and net income. For a perpetual income stream, we know that the stock value is

$$S = \frac{\overline{NI}}{k_s}.$$

Therefore the cost of equity is

$$k_s = \frac{\overline{NI}}{S}. \tag{15.16}$$

---

[10]For later use, note from Equations 15.13 and 15.14 that

$$k_U = \frac{\overline{X}(1 - T)}{V_L - TB}.$$

Hence

$$\overline{X}(1 - T) = k_UV_L - k_UTB. \tag{15.15}$$

FIGURE 15.6 Cost of Equity Capital as a Function of Leverage

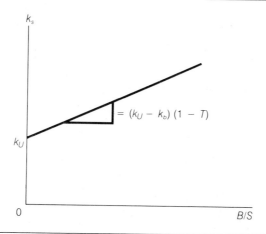

Next, the accounting definition of net income is

$$NI = (X - k_bB) - (X - k_bB)T$$

This is NOI after debt, interest, and taxes. We multiply through in the term with T. We then regroup terms.

$$= X - k_bB - XT + k_bBT$$
$$= X(1 - T) - k_bB(1 - T)$$

Use Equation 15.15 to substitute for $X(1 - T)$.

$$= k_UV_L - k_UBT - k_bB(1 - T).$$

Let $V_L = S + B$ and divide by S.

$$\frac{NI}{S} = k_s = \frac{k_US}{S} + \frac{k_UB}{S} - \frac{k_UBT}{S} - \frac{k_bB}{S}(1 - T)$$

Regroup terms.

$$k_s = k_U + k_U\frac{B}{S}(1 - T) - k_b\frac{B}{S}(1 - T)$$

Factor $B/S(1 - T)$ from last two terms.

$$k_s = k_U + (k_U - k_b)(1 - T)(B/S). \tag{15.17}$$

This is MM's Proposition II with corporate taxes, which states that the cost of equity is equal to the cost of capital of an unlevered firm plus the after-tax difference between the cost of capital of an unlevered firm and the cost of debt, weighted by the leverage ratio. Proposition II states that the cost of equity rises with the debt-to-equity ratio in a linear fashion, with the slope of the line equal to $(k_U - k_b)(1 - T)$, as shown in Figure 15.6. It makes sense that the cost of equity increases with greater financial leverage because shareholders are exposed to greater risk.

Next the weighted average (marginal) cost of capital (WACC) can be formulated in three versions. We start with the descriptive buildup of the cost of capital as the weighted costs of the market values of debt and equity. This traditional definition of the cost of capital is

$$k = WACC = k_b(1 - T)\frac{B}{V_L} + k_s\frac{S}{V_L}. \tag{15.18}$$

A major difficulty with this traditional definition is that although it can be used to compute the WACC given the currently observable costs of debt and equity, it cannot be used to tell us how the WACC changes as the financial leverage of the firm is changed. In order to see how the firm's WACC changes with leverage we will have to answer the basic question—How does the value of the firm change as a new investment is undertaken? The weighted average cost of capital is the return on assets that the firm must earn, given its leverage level, in order to increase shareholders' wealth.

If a new investment, ΔI, is undertaken, it will be financed with some combination of new debt, ΔB^n, and new equity, ΔS^n. Therefore, by definition,

$$\Delta I = \Delta B^n + \Delta S^n.$$

Furthermore, the accompanying change in the value of the levered firm, ΔV_L, must arise from one of four sources: original debt, ΔB^o, original shareholders' wealth, ΔS^o, new debt, or new equity. Hence, we know that

$$\Delta V_L = \Delta B^o + \Delta B^n + \Delta S^o + \Delta S^n.$$

Dividing through by the amount of new investment, ΔI, gives the change in the value of the firm with respect to new investment:

$$\frac{\Delta V_L}{\Delta I} = \frac{\Delta B^o}{\Delta I} + \frac{\Delta B^n}{\Delta I} + \frac{\Delta S^o}{\Delta I} + \frac{\Delta S^n}{\Delta I}.$$

If we assume that the new investment does not affect original bondholders' wealth so that

$$\frac{\Delta B^o}{\Delta I} = 0,$$

and if we rearrange terms, we have

$$\frac{\Delta V_L}{\Delta I} = \frac{\Delta S^o}{\Delta I} + \frac{\Delta B^n + \Delta S^n}{\Delta I}.$$

Finally, because $\Delta B^n + \Delta S^n = \Delta I$ (because all new investment dollars are provided by either new debt or new equity)

$$\frac{\Delta V_L}{\Delta I} = \frac{\Delta S^o}{\Delta I} + 1$$

$$\frac{\Delta S^o}{\Delta I} = \frac{\Delta V_L}{\Delta I} - 1. \tag{15.19}$$

We now have an expression for the change in original shareholders' wealth when new investment is undertaken. Since original shareholders completely control this decision, it is reasonable to make the behavioral assumption that the change in original shareholders' wealth must be positive, that is,

$$\frac{\Delta S^o}{\Delta I} = \frac{\Delta V_L}{\Delta I} - 1 > 0.$$

Another expression showing how the value of a levered firm changes with new investment is derived by substituting Equation 15.12 into Equation 15.14:

$$V_L = \frac{\overline{X}(1 - T)}{k_U} + TB.$$

Here the value of the levered firm is shown to be the sum of two parts. First is the discounted present value of the perpetual expected after-tax net operating income stream,

$$\frac{\overline{X}(1 - T)}{k_U},$$

and the second is the gain from leverage, TB. If the firm takes on a new investment with the same risk as the portfolio of projects already held by the firm, the change in the firm's value would be

$$\frac{\Delta V_L}{\Delta I} = \frac{\Delta X(1 - T)}{k_U \Delta I} + T\frac{\Delta B^n}{\Delta I}. \tag{15.20}$$

Substituting Equation 15.20 into 15.19, we have

$$\frac{\Delta S^o}{\Delta I} = \frac{\Delta \overline{X}(1 - T)}{k_U \Delta I} + T\frac{\Delta B^n}{\Delta I} - 1 > 0,$$

and rearranging terms gives,

$$\frac{\Delta \overline{X}(1 - T)}{\Delta I} > k_U\left(1 - T\frac{\Delta B^n}{\Delta I}\right). \tag{15.21}$$

The left-hand side of this expression is the change in the firm's after-tax operating income brought about by the new investment, ΔI. It is literally the after-tax return on assets that the firm would have if it had no debt. Remember that in Chapter 9 we carefully defined the cash flow for capital budgeting projects in exactly the same way. This definition appears again here in the derivation of the weighted average cost of capital because the expected cash flows for capital budgeting purposes are discounted by the weighted average cost of capital in order to determine the change in the value of shareholders' wealth. In other words,

$$V_L = \frac{\overline{X}(1 - T)}{k}.$$

Hence,

$$k = \text{WACC} = \frac{\overline{X}(1 - T)}{V_L}. \tag{15.22}$$

The right-hand side of Inequality 15.21 is the Modigliani-Miller definition of the weighted average cost of capital.

$$k = \text{WACC} = k_U\left(1 - T\frac{\Delta B^n}{\Delta I}\right)$$

We know that $\Delta I = \Delta B^n + \Delta S^n$. If we further assume that the firm issues new financing in proportion to its target capital structure, then the definition of WACC becomes

$$k = \text{WACC} = k_U\left(1 - T\frac{B}{B + S}\right). \tag{15.23}$$

The Modigliani-Miller definition of the weighted average cost of capital not only tells us how the WACC changes with increasing leverage, it also ties together other aspects of finance, namely

1. When firms undertake projects that earn more than their WACC, they must be increasing shareholders' wealth because $\Delta S^o/\Delta I > 0$.

2. All of the increase in the firm's value accrues to original shareholders. Bondholders merely maintain their original claim, that is, $\Delta B^o/\Delta I = 0$.[11]

3. When cash flows from new investment are discounted at the weighted average cost of capital, they are defined as the after-tax operating cash flows that the firm would have if it had no debt, that is, cash flows are $\text{CF} = \overline{X}(1 - T)$.

Three formulations of the WACC have been shown to be mathematically equivalent. For convenience, the three measures of the weighted cost of capital can be summarized as follows:

1. $k = k_b(1 - T)(B/V) + k_s(S/V)$ **(15.24 or 15.18)**

2. $k = \dfrac{\overline{X}(1 - T)}{V_L}$ **(15.25 or 15.22)**

3. $k = k_U(1 - TL)$, where $L = B/V$.   **(15.26 or 15.23)**

Figure 15.7 is a graphical representation of the cost of capital and its components as a function of the ratio of debt to equity. In a world without corporate taxes, the weighted average cost of capital is a constant. With taxes, the weighted average cost of capital declines as the ratio of debt to equity increases. In both panels of Figure 15.7, the cost of equity capital rises linearly with higher proportions of debt. The reason is that increasing financial leverage causes the residual claims of shareholders to become more variable, as described earlier in this chapter. Shareholders require a higher rate of return to compensate them for this additional risk. The cost of debt is assumed to be constant in both panels because the debt is assumed to be default free. In a world with taxes, the cost of debt remains constant, but at a lower level. (Note: From this point on, V is understood to be V_L, and the value of an unlevered firm will be designated as V_U.)

It will be useful to give content to the MM propositions with corporate taxes by the use of an illustrative case study for the Stevens Company. We consider two alternative capital structures for the Stevens Company:

---

[11]We obtain this result because debt is assumed to be default free. If debt is risky, then projects that earn more than WACC can, in principle, also raise the value of debt by decreasing its risk.

FIGURE 15.7   The Cost of Capital as a Function of the Ratio of Debt to Equity;
(a) Assuming $T = 0$; (b) Assuming $T > 0$

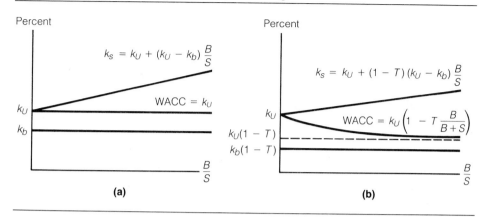

(a)

(b)

Stevens Company Balance Sheet, Unlevered

Total assets	$1,000,000	Stockholders' equity	$1,000,000

Stevens Company Balance Sheet, Levered

Total assets	$1,000,000	Debt at 10%	$ 500,000
		Stockholders' equity	500,000
		Total claims	$1,000,000

The applicable corporate tax rate is 40 percent. The income statements for Stevens would reflect the two different capital structures.[12]

Stevens Company Income Statements	Unlevered	Levered
Net operating income (X)	$200,000	$200,000
Interest on debt ($k_b B = rD$)	—	50,000
Income before taxes ($X - k_b B$)	$200,000	$150,000
Taxes at 40% $T(X - k_b B)$	80,000	60,000
Net income ($X - k_b B$)($1 - T$)	$120,000	$ 90,000

With the above accounting information, which represents data generally available in financial reports and financial manuals, we can apply the MM propositions. For an unlevered firm of similar characteristics to Stevens, we obtain a measure of the cost of capital for the unlevered cash flows, k_U, which we will assume to be 12 percent. All other relationships can now be computed.

---

[12]Recall that the firm pays rD, which we have shown is also equal to $k_b B$.

Stevens' value as an unlevered firm would be

$$V_U = \frac{\bar{X}(1 - T)}{k_U} = \frac{(\$200,000)0.6}{0.12} = \$1,000,000.$$

We find that without leverage, Stevens' market value is equal to the book value of its total assets. Next, consider Stevens as a levered firm. Its new value becomes

$$V_L = V_U + TB = \$1,000,000 + 0.4(\$500,000) = \$1,200,000.$$

Now the market value of Stevens exceeds the book value of its total assets. The market value of the equity, S, is

$$S = V_L - B = \$1,200,000 - \$500,000 = \$700,000.$$

The cost of equity capital of Stevens, unlevered, is equal to k_U, or 12 percent. The cost of equity capital for Stevens, as a levered firm, can be calculated by two relationships:

$$k_s = k_U + (k_U - k_b)(1 - T)B/S \quad \text{or} \quad k_s = NI/S.$$

The first formulation is MM's Proposition II (our Equation 15.17). The second can be calculated directly. We illustrate both:

$$k_s = 0.12 + (0.12 - 0.10)(0.6)(5/7) \qquad k_s = \$90,000/\$700,000$$
$$= 0.12 + 0.0086 \qquad\qquad\qquad = 12.86\%.$$
$$= 12.86\%.$$

Earlier in the chapter, we derived the relationship between the levered and unlevered betas in Equation 15.6.

$$\beta_L = \beta_U \left[1 + (1 - T)\frac{B}{S} \right]. \tag{15.6}$$

And in Chapter 11 we derived the Capital Asset Pricing Model and showed how it can be used to estimate the cost of equity

$$k_s = R_F + (\bar{R}_M - R_F)\beta_L.$$

Combining these results we have

$$k_s = R_F + (\bar{R}_M - R_F)\beta_U \left[1 + (1 - T)\frac{B}{S} \right].$$

For the Stevens example, let

$$R_F = 0.10, \bar{R}_M = 0.16, \text{ and } \beta_U = 0.333 \text{ and}$$
$$k_s = 0.10 + (0.16 - 0.10)0.333[1 + (5/7)(0.6)] = 0.1286 = 12.86\%.$$

With leverage, the cost of equity capital has risen from 12 percent to 12.86 percent. What happens to the weighted cost of capital? We can employ all three formulations:

1. $k = k_b(1 - T)(B/V) + k_s(S/V)$ \qquad\qquad $k = 0.10(0.6)(5/12) + 0.1286(7/12)$
$$= 0.025 + 0.075 = 10\%.$$

2. $k = \dfrac{\bar{X}(1 - T)}{V_L}$ $k = \dfrac{\$120,000}{\$1,200,000} = 10\%.$

3. $k = k_U(1 - TL)$ $k = 0.12[1 - 0.4(5/12)] = 0.12(5/6)$
                                             $= 10\%.$

Each formulation gives a weighted cost of capital of 10 percent. The example illustrates that the use of leverage has increased the value of the firm from $1,000,000 to $1,200,000. The weighted cost of capital has been reduced from 12 percent to 10 percent. Thus, under the MM propositions, with corporate taxes only, the influence of the tax subsidy on debt is to increase the value of the firm and decrease its weighted cost of capital.

Corporate and Personal Taxes. In our discussion of the cost of capital with corporate taxes, we obtain the result in Equation 15.14 that $V_L = V_U + TB$. A further implication of this result is that the weighted average cost of capital for a levered firm is below the cost of capital for an unlevered firm. This was most clearly seen in the expression for Equation 15.26:

$$k = k_U(1 - TL). \qquad (15.26)$$

An implication of these results is the more debt the better. Indeed it implies that firms would have 100 percent debt in their capital structures. We don't observe leverage ratios anywhere near this high, which suggests that the original MM model with taxes requires modification.

One possible extension is to consider personal taxes in addition to corporate taxes. We will use the following symbols:

T_c = corporate tax rate

T_{pb} = ordinary personal income tax rate (paid on debt interest)

T_{ps} = tax rate paid by persons who receive income or capital gains from stock. It is an "average" of the capital gains tax rate and the ordinary rate on dividends received, and is less than T_{pb}

We can analyze the effects of the two types of personal taxes by use of the simple arbitrage framework employed in our previous discussions of the MM models. We have the following:

Decision	Investment	Dollar Return
1. Buy α of the equity of levered firm L	$\alpha S_L = \alpha(V_L - B_L)$	$\alpha(X - R_F B)(1 - T_c)(1 - T_{ps})$
2. Buy α of the equity of unlevered firm V_U	$\alpha S_U - \alpha\left[\dfrac{(1 - T_c)(1 - T_{ps})}{(1 - T_{pb})}\right]B_L$	$\alpha X(1 - T_c)(1 - T_{ps})$
		$\quad - \alpha\left[\dfrac{(1 - T_c)(1 - T_{ps})}{(1 - T_{pb})}\right]$
Sell bonds	$\alpha\left[\dfrac{(1 - T_c)(1 - T_{ps})}{(1 - T_{pb})}\right]B_L$	$R_F B_L(1 - T_{pb}) =$
		$\alpha(X - R_F B_L)(1 - T_c)(1 - T_{ps})$

The analysis proceeds as before. The two alternatives are purchasing the equity of a levered firm versus purchasing the equity of an unlevered firm, and selling bonds in an amount such that the resulting dollar returns will be equal to the dollar returns when the alternative is the purchase of equity of a levered firm. The analysis proceeds as before with the result that since the dollar returns are equal, the investment values are equal. Therefore, we set the two investment values equal to each other. Hence we have

$$\alpha(V_L - B_L) = \alpha S_U - \alpha \left[\frac{(1 - T_c)(1 - T_{ps})}{(1 - T_{pb})} \right] B_L.$$

We cancel the α's and rearrange terms. We obtain

$$V_L = V_U + B_L - \left[\frac{(1 - T_c)(1 - T_{ps})}{(1 - T_{pb})} \right] B_L$$

$$= V_U + \left[1 - \frac{(1 - T_c)(1 - T_{ps})}{(1 - T_{pb})} \right] B_L. \qquad \textbf{(15.27)}$$

Suppose we designate G as the *gain from leverage* and use B for B_L,

$$G = \left[1 - \frac{(1 - T_c)(1 - T_{ps})}{(1 - T_{pb})} \right] B. \qquad \textbf{(15.28)}$$

The right-hand side of Equation 15.28 is the tax benefit of corporate debt with three types of taxes. This expression has also been referred to as the gain from leverage. Let us do some sensitivity analysis of this gain to understand better its properties and implications. If the tax on common stock income, T_{ps}, is the same as the tax on bond income, T_{pb}, we would have

$$V_L = V_U + (1 - 1 + T_c)B_L = V_U + T_c B.$$

This is the same as Equation 15.14, the expression that we had before for a world with corporate taxes alone. We obtain this result because the two types of personal taxes would cancel out. This indicates that the expression for the gain from corporate leverage is consistent with the previous analysis. Another way to analyze the implications of the gain term is to assume a tax rate on stock holdings of $T_{ps} = 20$ percent and investigate the effect of the level of the marginal ordinary personal income tax rate on the tax benefit of corporate debt. Assuming a corporate tax rate of 39 percent and a capital gains tax rate of 20 percent, we would have

$$G = \left[1 - \frac{(.61)(.8)}{(1 - T_{pb})} \right]$$

$$= \frac{1 - T_{pb} - .488}{1 - T_{pb}} = \frac{.512 - T_{pb}}{1 - T_{pb}}.$$

We can use this simple expression for the gain from corporate leverage factor to develop the data in Table 15.9. With a zero ordinary personal income tax rate, the tax benefit of corporate debt would be even greater than the corporate tax rate. At a personal income tax rate of roughly 50 percent, the tax benefit of corporate debt would be eliminated. This

TABLE 15.9   Tax Gain from Debt

T_{pb}	G = Tax Benefit of Corporate Debt
.0	.512
.2	.390
.3	.303
.4	.187
.5	.024
.6	−.220
.7	−.627

implies a corporate leverage clientele effect. Individual taxpayers in low tax brackets would benefit from investing in highly levered corporations. Investors in high tax brackets would benefit more from investing in corporations with low degrees of leverage. But this is not the end of the story. Let us consider some further possibilities.

Miller [1977] developed the framework of our Equation 15.28. Furthermore, in a later paper by Miller and Scholes [1978], procedures were described under which taxes on dividends received on common stock may be reduced to zero. The methods they describe are discussed in Chapter 16 on dividend policy. If the tax rate on dividends received on corporate stock or the capital gains from the sale of the stock of companies that retain earnings can be reduced to zero, the gain from leverage would become

$$G = \left[1 - \frac{(1 - T_c)}{(1 - T_{pb})} \right] B. \tag{15.29}$$

This expression was used by Miller to analyze the aggregate supply and demand for corporate debt as illustrated in Figure 15.8.

In Figure 15.8, the pretax rate of returns on bonds supplied by corporations is $r_b = r_o/(1 - T_c)$. This represents the aggregate supply of corporate bonds shown as the horizontal line in Figure 15.8. The supply curve is assumed to be horizontal because all corporations are assumed to have the same tax rate. The demand for corporate bonds starts with the intercept point r_o. This is the acceptable rate paid on the debt of tax-free institutions (municipal bonds, for example). If all corporate bonds paid only r_o, they would not be held by anyone except tax-free institutions. Other investors would require that their return be grossed up to $r_o/(1 - T_{pb})$. The personal income tax rate is progressive so that the demand curve for corporate bonds by taxable investors at some point begins to rise as shown in Figure 15.8. Where the demand and supply curves for corporate bonds intercept, we have

$$\text{Supply} = \text{Demand}$$

$$\frac{r_o}{1 - T_c} = \frac{r_o}{1 - T_{pb}}.$$

If corporations offered more than the equilibrium quantity of bonds (B^*), interest rates would be driven above their supply price and firms would find leverage unprofitable.

FIGURE 15.8   Aggregate Supply and Demand for Corporate
Bonds (Before-Tax Rates)

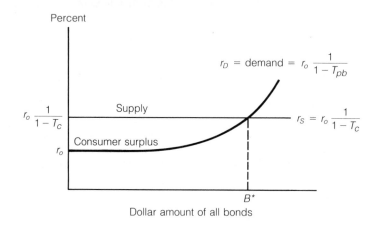

The supply of bonds would decline until the equilibrium quantity (B^*) was again reached.
If the volume initially supplied were below B^*, interest rates would be lower. Firms
would increase borrowing and this would proceed until the equilibrium quantity B^* was
again reached. Thus, we have an equilibrium where the gain from leverage is (once again)
zero. As long as all corporations have the same effective tax rate, the value of each firm
will be unaffected by its choice of financial leverage.

FIGURE 15.9   Possible Declining Benefit of Interest Tax Shields

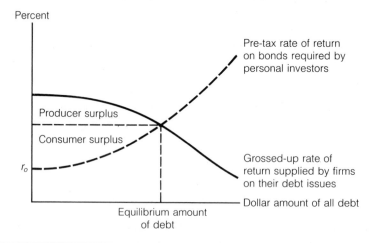

DeAngelo and Masulis [1980] further develop the analysis by considering the role of corporate tax shields in addition to interest payments on debt. Not all corporations pay the same effective tax rate. Corporate tax shields include investment tax credits, depreciation allowances, and oil depletion allowances. The DeAngelo and Masulis model predicts that firms will select a level of debt that is negatively related to the level of other tax shield substitutes such as investment tax credits, depreciation, or depletion. They also point out that as more and more debt is utilized the probability of having insufficient earnings to utilize fully all available interest tax shields will increase. Thus, the expected value of interest tax shields will decline. The supply curve for corporate debt would, therefore, have a downward slope as depicted in Figure 15.9. In these circumstances there would be an optimal amount of debt for the firm. Thus, the existence of multiple forms of tax shields may produce an optimal debt structure. In addition, if there are significant bankruptcy costs, this will reinforce conditions producing an optimal capital structure. The marginal expected benefit of interest tax shields will be related to the marginal expected cost of bankruptcy to produce an optimal degree of financial leverage.

THE EFFECTS OF BANKRUPTCY COSTS

To this point we have established that the cost of equity rises with financial leverage. The cost of debt may also rise with leverage. Even if the debt is risky, it has been established that the MM propositions still hold [Rubinstein, 1973] as long as there are no bankruptcy costs. But with bankruptcy costs, we have a further basis for arriving at an optimal degree of leverage for a firm.

Bankruptcy costs take several forms. The most obvious are the legal, accounting, and other administrative costs associated with financial readjustments and legal proceedings. In addition to these direct costs, some costs of bankruptcy arise before the actual legal procedures of bankruptcy take place. As the operating performance of the firm deteriorates in relation to its fixed contractual obligations, or as the amount of debt increases in relation to the firm's equity for a given level of operating performance, the financial markets may become increasingly reluctant to provide additional financing. A number of costs arise as a result of increased evidence of financial inadequacy or failure on the part of the firm. These costs, in order of seriousness, include the following:

1. Financing under increasingly onerous terms, conditions, and rates.

2. Loss of key employees. If the firm's prospects are unfavorable, able employees and executives will seek alternative employment.

3. Loss of suppliers of the most salable types of goods. The suppliers may fear that they will not be paid or that the customer will not achieve sales growth in the future.

4. Loss of sales due to lack of confidence on the part of customers that the firm will be around to stand behind the product.

5. Lack of financing under any terms, conditions, and rates to carry out favorable but risky investments because the overall prospects of the firm are not favorable in relation to its existing obligations.

6. Need to liquidate fixed assets to meet working capital requirements (forced reduction in the scale of operations).

7. Formal bankruptcy proceedings, with the incurrence of legal and administrative costs. In addition, a receiver will be appointed to conduct the firm's operations, and this may involve a disruption of operations.

The costs of building up new organizations after old ones have been broken up represent substantial transaction costs in the creation and destruction of organizations.

The inability to meet fixed charges may trigger a number of penalty clauses in the debt indentures (agreements) and lead to reorganization or bankruptcy (see Chapter 28), with attendant costs of attorneys and court proceedings. Even before such legal difficulties, the increasing risk of financial difficulties may result in the loss of key employees (who find positions with firms whose financial outlook is safer), in the reduced availability of goods from key suppliers, and in reduced financing.

Empirical studies suggest that the direct costs of bankruptcy such as attorney and court fees and lost management time are small but significant (Warner [1977]; Altman [1984]). However, when indirect costs like business disruption, loss in demand, and liquidation are taken into account, they may be substantial — as much as 20 percent of the value of the firm [Altman, 1984].

In Chapter 12 we discussed the fact that the equity in a levered firm is a call option on the value of the underlying assets. The payoff on this equity option is either zero or the difference between the market value of the firm, V, and the face value of the debt, D; i.e., $MAX[0, V - D]$. The return to debtholders was $MIN[V, D]$. Under the assumption that all firms draw from the same bankruptcy distribution *ex ante*, it can be argued that even with bankruptcy costs the outcome for the equity holders is unchanged. Because of limited liability they can lose nothing more than their original investment; this is not affected by bankruptcy costs. However, the outcome for the debtholders with bankruptcy costs becomes $MIN[V - \Theta V, D]$. The theta represents the magnitude of bankruptcy costs as some proportion of the value of the firm. Thus, the outcome for debtholders is diminished. The required return to debtholders will, therefore, increase as the probability of bankruptcy increases with increased leverage.

Thus, if firms go bankrupt in the same states of nature with or without bankruptcy costs, the required returns to equity holders would appear to be unaffected. But since the costs of bankruptcy are charged to debtholders, they will take this into account when debt is initially issued. So bondholders will require higher returns to compensate them for bearing the costs of bankruptcy. For the firm to receive the same dollars when selling debt now, they will have to promise a higher dollar amount of payment at maturity. Therefore, *the firm will go bankrupt in more states of nature* because the size of D is higher for a given V. Shareholders will, therefore, require compensation in the form of higher required returns to compensate them for the increased probability of bankruptcy. Hence the effect of bankruptcy will require higher rates of return both to debtholders and shareholders, as depicted in Figure 15.10.

In Figure 15.10 we have combined the tax benefit of leverage (if the firm is inframarginal and can earn a "producer's surplus") with the *ex ante* cost of bankruptcy. The trade-off between the expected tax benefit from carrying debt and the expected cost of

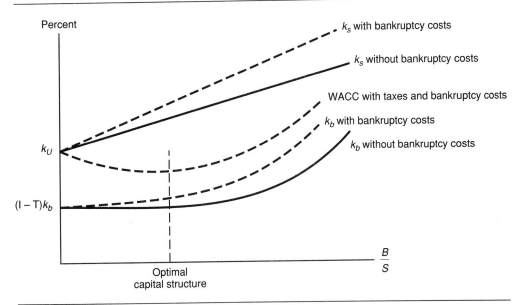

FIGURE 15.10 Effects of Bankruptcy Costs and Taxes on the Cost of Capital and Optimal Capital Structure

bankruptcy is a possible explanation for optimal capital structure. Furthermore, if the indirect costs of bankruptcy differ significantly across industries, then this approach can potentially explain why there are persistent differences among the capital structures adopted by various industries.

THE EFFECT OF AGENCY COSTS

The separation of ownership and control is often advisable in a world where specialized skills lead to more efficient production. A wealthy individual might want to own a company but to hire managers to operate it. Also, some investors may prefer a lower-risk debt position while others may prefer the higher-risk controlling equity position. In spite of the advantages of separating ownership from operating control and of having two classes of capital (debt and equity), there are associated agency costs that must be considered.

Jensen and Meckling [1976] discuss a number of ways agency problems of this kind may influence financial decisions. For example, equity holders can decide to change the firm's capital structure. If senior debtholders cannot protect themselves with perfect covenants, their wealth can be expropriated when more debt is added. Another way that equity holders can cause the position of bondholders to be affected adversely is to shift to more risky investment programs. Consider the two investment programs in Table 15.10. Pro-

TABLE 15.10   Investment Programs of Different Risks

	Probability	Program 1	Program 2
	.5	$40,000	$10,000
	.5	$60,000	$90,000

gram 1 has a 50/50 probability of achieving an end-of-period cash flow of $40,000 or $60,000. The second program has a 50/50 probability of returning $10,000 or $90,000. The expected value of each is $50,000, and the investment cost assumed is $40,000, so they are both positive NPV investments. If the firm borrows $20,000 to finance the investment, the lenders are assured of being repaid under Program 1, but only have a 50/50 probability of being paid under Program 2. Furthermore, they do not benefit if the $90,000 return is realized because they would still receive only $20,000, the face value of the bond, while the equity holders would receive the benefit of the difference.

The problem would be especially troublesome if bondholders had the expectation that the firm was going to follow Program 1, which is less risky, and then the firm actually follows Program 2, which involves greater risk. Such a shift would represent a transfer of wealth from bondholders to shareholders. This example illustrates another reason why bondholders require various types of agreements in the bond contract to protect their position. Agency costs refer to the costs of writing and enforcing such agreements. These expropriation costs are likely to increase with the percentage of financing provided by bondholders and the costs of protection against agency problems are likely to increase with leverage as well.

In addition agency problems are associated with the use of outside equity. Consider a firm initially owned entirely by one individual. All actions taken by the individual affect his position alone. If the original owner-manager sells a portion of the equity interest to outsiders, conflicts of interest arise. Extra consumption benefits paid to the original owner-manager by the firm are now entirely consumed by him, but paid for in part by the new outside owners. If the original owner-manager indulges in perquisites such as an expensive company car entirely for his own use, lavish furniture and rugs in his own spacious office, short working days to play more golf, etc., he doesn't bear the entire costs as he did when he was the sole owner. The new outside shareholders will have to incur monitoring costs of one kind or another to be sure that the original owner-manager acts fully in their interest.

As shown in Figure 15.11, agency costs increase with the use of higher proportions of outside equity as well as with higher proportions of debt. There is an optimum combination of outside equity and debt that may minimize total agency costs, which would result in a desired or optimum capital structure even in a world without taxes or bankruptcy costs.

Other considerations also may be regarded as agency costs with implications for capital structure. Titman [1981] points out that customers who buy durable products such as automobiles, washing machines, or refrigerators need to have future services such as

FIGURE 15.11   Optimal Capital Structure with Agency Costs of Equity and Debt

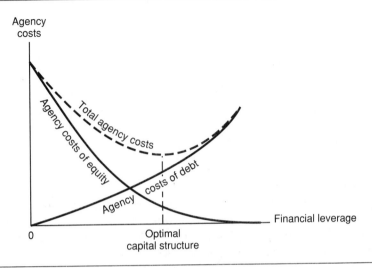

parts and repair. When a customer buys a durable good he is paying for the product itself, but also for the availability of follow-up parts and repair services. If a firm goes bankrupt and is liquidated, customers are unable to obtain the parts and services they had expected. The agency problem in this relationship is the assurance that the future required parts and services will be forthcoming. Consumers must judge the probability that a seller of durable goods may fail and be liquidated. Hence firms that produce and sell durable goods run the risk that if they use higher leverage, which will increase their probability of bankruptcy, it may reduce the demand for their products. Hence we would expect, other things being equal, that durable goods producers would carry less debt than producers of nondurable goods such as food.

Similarly agency factors are involved in labor contracts. Under competitive labor markets, workers will charge lower wages to work for firms that have a lower probability of bankruptcy. In some industries, a firm's labor force develops specialized skills that may not be used easily in other industries. For example, some aspects of producing steel might have little use in other industries. Another example would be the air traffic controllers who lost their jobs and found it difficult to use their skills in other work. Thus, firms and industries that involve the development of a considerable degree of job-specific human capital would tend to carry less debt than firms and industries in which workers can readily enter into and out of employment.

Still another related aspect is suggested by Scott [1976], who demonstrates that optimal leverage may be related to the collateral value of the firm's assets. If a firm fails and is liquidated, tangible nonspecific physical assets of the firm may have only a small decline in value, which should reduce losses upon bankruptcy. Collateral value also reduces the need for monitoring costs to protect the position of bondholders.

All of these aspects of agency considerations may have an influence on the degree of use of outside equity and the use of outside debt. All of these aspects are candidates for additional empirical research to test the propositions involved.

INFORMATION ASYMMETRY AND SIGNALING

Optimal capital structure can be explained either by a trade-off between tax benefits and bankruptcy costs or by a trade-off between the agency costs of debt and equity. However, other significant factors influence the debt-equity choice. One such factor is that changes in the firm's long-term mix of debt and equity can be interpreted as a signal by outsiders in the marketplace. In order to fully explain signaling we first need to establish that insiders and managers who are better informed than the public have correct incentives to send truthful signals to the marketplace.

Ross [1977] describes how signaling and manager compensation arrangements can be used to deal with information asymmetry and postulates that manager-insiders have information about their own firms not possessed by outsiders. He demonstrates that the capital structure decision is not irrelevant. In some cases a unique interior optimal capital structure exists if (1) the nature of the firm's investment policy is signaled to the market through its capital structure decision and (2) the manager's compensation is tied to the truth or falsity of the capital structure signal. In Ross's model a manager may not trade in the financial instruments of his own firm. This avoids the moral hazard problem as well as violation of the incentives structure that he develops. The essence of Ross's model can be expressed verbally.[13] Investors use the face amount of the debt or dividends the manager decides to issue as a signal of the firm's probable performance. Ross analyzes two types of firms. Type A is a firm that will be successful, whereas Type B is a firm that will be unsuccessful. With reference to a critical level of debt, D^*, the market perceives the firm to be Type A if it issues debt greater than this amount and Type B if it issues debt less than this amount. In order for the management of a Type B firm to have the incentive to signal that the firm will be unsuccessful, the payoff from telling the truth must be greater than that produced by telling lies. This is achieved by assessing a substantial penalty against the manager if his firm experiences bankruptcy.

A signaling equilibrium is achieved if "A" managers choose debt financing levels above the critical amount and "B" managers choose debt levels below that amount. An "A" manager will have no incentive to change because the compensation system maximizes his return under the true signal. The "B" manager will not have an incentive to signal falsely because the penalty built into the incentive structure would reduce his compensation.

Haugen and Senbet [1979] seek to implement Ross's penalty function through the use of contingent claims. They require that the manager simultaneously sell a combination of calls and puts so that the manager of an "A" firm is completely hedged, suffering no penalty if the firm turns out to be successful. If the firm turns out to be unsuccessful, prior

---

[13]See Chapter 16 for an algebraic development of the same issue in the context of dividend policy.

to the expiration of the contingent claims, the holders of the puts will exercise them with a consequent penalty for management compensation. This design also provides a control on agency problems. If the manager consumes an excessive amount of perquisites, the value of the firm will decline. In effect, he causes an "A" firm to become a "B" firm. If so, the puts will be exercised and the manager will suffer the consequences of his having caused a decline in the value of the firm.

Leland and Pyle [1977] use information asymmetry influences to rationalize the existence of financial intermediation institutions. They find informational asymmetries to be a primary explanation for the existence of intermediaries and rely on signaling as a significant aspect of the operations of financial intermediaries. For assets, particularly those related to individuals, such as mortgages or insurance, information is not publicly available and can be developed only at some cost. Since such information is valuable to potential lenders, if there are economies of scale, firms will be developed to assemble the information and to sell it.

Two problems would arise if such firms sought to sell the information directly to investors. One is the "public good" aspect of information. Individual purchasers of information could resell it to others without diminishing its usefulness to themselves. The second problem is the reliability of the information. It would be difficult for potential users to make a judgment of the likelihood that they are receiving good versus bad information. Thus, the price of information will reflect its average value and the average value of information offered for sale will be lower than what potentially could be available.

Both these problems in obtaining a return on information are overcome by a financial intermediary that buys and holds assets on the basis of accumulated information. The value of the firm's information is reflected in a private good, the returns from its portfolio. Potential buyers of the intermediary's claim can judge whether the intermediary has developed valuable information by observing the extent to which the entrepreneurs or organizers of the financial intermediary have been willing to invest in their own firm's equity shares. In general, the degree to which owners are willing to invest in their own projects will serve as a signal of project quality. Thus, a firm's value will be related positively to the fraction of its equity held by its organizers. This higher value will also give the firm greater debt capacity and lead it to use greater amounts of debt. While debt is not a signal in this model, its use will be correlated positively with the firm's value.

Once we have established that insiders/managers have the correct incentive to issue truthful signals, we can turn to the market's interpretation of them. Myers and Majluf [1984] present a signaling model that combines investment and financing decisions and is rich in empirical implications. For example, they establish a pecking order of financing where managers will prefer to use retained earnings first, then debt, and external equity as a last resort.

As before, managers, better than anyone else, are assumed to know the "true" future value of the firm and of any projects that it might undertake. Furthermore, they are assumed to act in the interest of "old" shareholders, i.e., those who hold shares in the firm at the time a decision is made. Finally, "old" shareholders are assumed to be passive in the sense that they do not actively change their personal portfolios to undo the decisions

TABLE 15.11   Issue Equity, No Positive NPV Projects

	Do Nothing		Issue Equity	
	Good	Bad	Good	Bad
Liquid assets, L_i	50	50	150	150
Assets in place, A_i	200	80	200	80
Value of firm, V_i	250	130	350	230

of management.[14] To keep things simple, assume that interest rates are zero and that there are no taxes, transactions costs, or other market imperfections.

To begin the analysis, consider a situation where there are two equally likely states of nature (good news and bad news). The firm has liquid assets, L_i, and tangible assets in place, A_i, that can take the values illustrated in Table 15.11. It has no positive net present value projects for the time being. (We shall examine the effect of positive NPV projects next.) Also, there is no debt (that will be the third case.) Information asymmetry is created by the fact that insiders are assumed to know which state, good or bad, will turn up for the firm. The market, however, knows nothing except what the value of the firm would be in each state of nature. If the firm does nothing, the market (i.e., outsiders) will compute the current value of the firm as the expected value of its payouts,

$$V_0 = \sum p_i(L_i + A_i) = .5(250) + .5(130) = 190.$$

This is equal to the value of the "old" shareholders' claim.

To establish a rational expectations signaling equilibrium let us look at the payoffs to "old" shareholders in each state of nature given each of two possible actions: (1) do nothing or (2) issue $100 of new equity to new shareholders. We will see that although "old" shareholders have the incentive to issue new shares when the firm is overvalued—i.e., when they know the bad news is coming—the very fact that they try to issue shares will signal their information to the market and consequently destroy their informational advantage. If "old" shareholders know good news (state 1) will occur, their wealth conditional on doing nothing is

$$(V_0 | \text{good news, do nothing}) = L_1 + A_1 = 250.$$

Alternately, they can issue $100 of new equity, E, and their value is

$$(V_0 | \text{good news, issue equity}) = \frac{V_0}{V_0 + E}(L_1 + A_1 + E)$$

$$= \frac{190}{290}(350) = 229.31.$$

---

[14]If shareholders systematically undertake personal portfolio changes to reverse management decisions, then managerial financial decisions become irrelevant. In many cases, however, managers *are* "old" shareholders.

Their fraction of the firm if they issue new equity is their current value, 190, divided by 190 plus the cash received from the new equity issue, 100. If "old" shareholders know bad news (state 2) will occur, their payoff from doing nothing is

$$(V_0|\text{bad news, do nothing}) = L_2 + A_2 = 130,$$

and if they issue new equity it is

$$(V_0|\text{bad news, issue equity}) = \frac{V_0}{V_0 + E}(L_2 + A_2 + E)$$

$$= \frac{190}{290}(230) = 150.69.$$

The payouts to original shareholders are summarized in Table 15.12. It seems that the optimal actions of the informed "old" shareholders (i.e., the payouts with asterisks) are to do nothing if they think the good news state will occur and to issue equity if the bad news state will occur, because the firm is currently overvalued. Outsiders, however, will not be fooled. When the firm issues new equity they know the firm believes the bad news state will occur, and they impute the bad news value, 130, to the firm. Therefore the expected payout to "old" shareholders, given that they issue new equity and that the outsiders infer bad news, is

$$(V_0|\text{issue equity}) = \frac{V_2}{V_2 + E}(V_2 + E) = V_2 = 130.$$

The upshot of this argument is that original shareholders cannot take advantage of their inside information because the very act of issuing new shares (when they think the firm is overvalued) will reveal their information to the market. Hence they are indifferent between doing nothing and issuing new equity, and the market will attach no significance to new equity issues.

Next, let us complicate the model slightly by assuming that the firm has a positive net present value project that requires an initial cash outlay of $100, and that has the state-dependent net present values, b_i, illustrated in Table 15.13. Going through the same type of computations as before, we first compute V_0, the unconditional value of original shareholders' wealth, assuming they do nothing.

$$V_0 = \sum p_i(L_i + A_i) = .5(250) + .5(130) = 190$$

TABLE 15.12   "Old" Shareholder Payoffs — Issue versus Do Nothing

	Do Nothing	Issue Equity
Good news	250.00*	229.31
Bad news	130.00	150.69*

TABLE 15.13   Positive NPV Project and New Equity

	Do Nothing		Invest and Issue Equity	
	Good	Bad	Good	Bad
Liquid assets, L_i	50	50	50	50
Assets in place, A_i	200	80	300	180
NPV of new project, b_i	0	0	20	10
Value of firm, V_i	250	130	370	240

Alternately, if they issue and invest, their unconditional expected wealth is

$$V_0' = \sum p_i(L_i + A_i + b_i) = .5(270) + .5(140) = 205.$$

Now let us examine their wealth, contingent on each state of nature. If they issue $100 of new equity and invest the proceeds in the new positive NPV project, their wealth in the good news state is

$$(V_0|\text{good news, invest and issue}) = \frac{V_0'}{V_0' + E}(L_1 + A_1 + b_1 + E)$$

$$= \frac{205}{205 + 100}(370) = 248.69,$$

and if they do nothing, given good news, their wealth is 250. Given bad news, their payout if they issue and invest is

$$(V_0|\text{bad news, invest and issue}) = \frac{V_0'}{V_0' + E}(L_2 + A_2 + b_2 + E)$$

$$= \frac{205}{205 + 100}(240) = 161.31,$$

and if they do nothing, given bad news, their wealth is 130. Table 15.14 summarizes the payoffs from the "old" shareholders' point of view. As before, original shareholders are better off doing nothing in the good state because the positive NPV of the project (given

TABLE 15.14   "Old" Shareholder Payoffs — Issue and Invest versus Do Nothing

	Do Nothing	Issue and Invest
Good news	250*	248.69
Bad news	130	161.31*

TABLE 15.15   Rational Expectations Equilibrium

	Do Nothing	Issue and Invest
Good news	250*	248.69
Bad news	130	140.00*

good news) is not large enough to offset the fraction of ownership that they must sacrifice by issuing new shares.[15] Hence they desire to issue new equity and invest only if they know the bad state will occur. As before, the market is not fooled. As soon as insiders announce their intention to issue and invest, the market learns that the bad state is forthcoming, and in the bad state the firm is worth only 240, with 100 going to outsiders and the remaining 140 going to original shareholders. The rational expectations equilibrium payoffs are illustrated in Table 15.15. In equilibrium, given the set of numbers we have chosen, the firm issues and invests in the bad news state but not in the good news state.[16] This surprising result implies that the value of the firm may fall when new equity issues are announced—an important empirical implication.

So far we have examined two cases. First, when the firm had no new projects and the market knew it, then issuing new equity was an unambiguous financial signal that the market could use to discover the inside information held by managers. Hence it was impossible for managers to benefit from issuing new equity when they knew the future prospects of the firm were dismal. Second, when positive NPV projects (good news) were financed with equity issues (bad news), the signal became mixed. The market could not separate information about new projects from information about whether the firm is under or overvalued. If there were some way to provide two separate signals—one for investment decisions and another for financing decisions—the problem would vanish. If project outcomes were uncorrelated with states of nature (e.g., if the project had the same NPV in both states of nature), the problem would vanish. Or if the firm were to use financing that is not subject to the information asymmetry problem, the problem would vanish.

Myers and Majluf point out that if the firm uses its available liquid assets, L_i, to finance positive NPV projects, then all positive NPV projects would be undertaken because no new equity is issued and the information asymmetry problem is thereby resolved. They suggest that this may be a good reason for carrying excess liquid assets. They also suggest that debt financing, which has payoffs less correlated with future states of nature than equity, will be preferred to new equity as a means of financing. Myers [1984] suggests a *pecking order theory* for capital structure. Firms are said to prefer retained earnings (available liquid assets) as their main source of funds for investment. Next in order of preference is debt, and last comes external equity financing. Firms wish to avoid

---

[15]It is important to realize that outsiders pay nothing for the expected NPV of the new project. The entire NPV accrues to "old" shareholders.

[16]It is puzzling to understand why "old" shareholders do not provide all investment funds if they know the good state will occur. These funds can come from cash (what Myers and Majluf call slack) or via a rights offering.

issuing common stock or other risky securities so that they do not run into the dilemma of either passing up positive NPV projects or issuing stock at a price they think is too low.

The pecking order theory is a dynamic story. The observed capital structure of each firm will depend on its history. For example, an unusually profitable firm in an industry with relatively slow growth (few investment opportunities) will end up with an unusually low debt-to-equity ratio. It has no incentive to issue debt and retire equity. An unprofitable firm in the same industry will end up with a high debt ratio.

CALCULATING THE FIRM'S COST OF CAPITAL

In this section we will ignore the question of whether a firm is at its optimum capital structure and focus on the practical question of how to estimate the cost of capital given the existing capital structure. Our hypothetical company, the United Corporation, has three sources of financing: debt, preferred stock, and common equity. The first part of this section will show how to estimate the weighted average cost of capital by analyzing the component costs and their market value weights. The remainder of the section will discuss related issues: what is the cost of depreciation-generated funds, the cost of retained earnings, the effect of flotation costs, the cost of hybrid securities, and the cost of capital for a division?

The Weighted Average Cost of Capital for United Corporation

Table 15.16 shows the book value balance sheet for United Corporation, a hypothetical company, in 199X.

Among the liabilities we observe that some carry an interest cost explicitly while others do not. Since there are no "free lunches" in this world, we know that all of the liabilities that do not carry an explicit cost must surely have an implicit cost. For example, accounts payable typically represent the largest single category of current liabilities and carry no interest charge explicitly. To the firm extending credit, the loss of interest on

TABLE 15.16   Balance Sheet for United Corporation, 199X

Assets		Liabilities and Stockholders' Equity	
Current assets	$2,080	Accounts payable	$ 360
Fixed assets	2,490	Accruals	400
		Notes payable @ 12%	400
		Deferred taxes	110
		Minority interests	120
		Long-term debt @ 10%	1,000
		Preferred stock	200
		Stockholders' equity	1,980
Total	$4,570	Total	$4,570

funds tied up in receivables represents a cost of doing business. It is likely that the costs of carrying accounts receivable are reflected in the prices charged by supplier firms. Hence accounts payable does not represent "free financing" but rather a source of financing whose costs have already been levied and reflected in the income statement. We will, therefore, focus only on those liabilities and equity claims for which an explicit cost can be calculated.

This case study illustrates how the cost of capital can actually be measured for a firm. The concepts previously developed will now be put to practical application. Although we shall attempt to make the procedures specific and numerically precise, we must recognize that considerable judgment must be exercised. Because of the crucial role of cost of capital measurements in guiding a firm's investment decisions, and because the valuation of a firm is highly sensitive to the applicable cost of capital employed, the judgments must be arrived at with great care. We shall use a stylized case example to keep the presentation within reasonable bounds. Our own experience in making such calculations for individual firms has involved reports that are quite lengthy. Final judgments involve comparisons with firms similar to the one for which the analysis is made. To make the comparisons, the same cost of capital calculations have to be made for the 7 to 10 other firms for which the comparisons may be made. The purpose of the example is to provide a road map of the main procedures that should be employed.

We shall illustrate calculations of the cost of capital of the three major types of financing — debt, preferred stock, and common equity — and employ the following symbols throughout the discussion:

k_b = the before-tax opportunity cost of debt

k_{ps} = the before- and after-tax opportunity cost of preferred stock

k_s = the before- and after-tax return required by the market for equity capital

k_r = the before- and after-tax cost of internally generated equity capital

WACC = the weighted average cost of capital, represents a weighted marginal cost of capital.

Our ultimate objective is to obtain the firm's marginal cost of capital for use in capital budgeting decisions and for application in valuation analysis. The firm's marginal cost of capital is a weighted average of the opportunity costs of its financing sources. In calculating WACC, all costs are expressed on an after-tax basis. This provides consistency with the after-tax cash flows utilized in our previous capital budgeting analysis. In using the marginal cost of capital for decision-making purposes, we are assuming that the risks of individual projects are similar to the riskiness of the firm's present portfolio of assets. This is required for utilization of the WACC in both capital budgeting and valuation analysis.

We shall first estimate the marginal cost of each source of capital, then the market value weights of each source, and finally the weighted average cost of capital. United Corporation has short-term debt, long-term debt, preferred stock, and common equity. As we already discussed, the implicit cost of accounts payable is already reflected in the cash flows of the income statement. The same is true of accruals and deferred taxes. Minority interests occur when a third party owns some percentage of one of the company's consolidated subsidiaries. Since the cash flows paid to minority interests are not part of the value of the company, the opportunity cost of funds provided by minority interests is not included in the WACC.

Cost of Debt

Although accounting statements distinguish between notes payable (short-term debt) and long-term debt it is important to remember that they are perfect substitutes — one is *not* cheaper than the other. Short-term debt must be rolled over. If the term structure of interest rates is upward sloping, the market expects that future short-term rates will be higher than the current short-term rate. Therefore, except for liquidity premiums, the product of n short-term rates equals the n-year rate. For this reason we combine short-term and long-term debt in the capital structure and assume they have the same long-term marginal cost, *ex ante*.

The cost of debt should be on an after-tax basis because interest payments are tax deductible. Therefore, the cost of debt capital is calculated as follows:

$$k_b(1 - T) = \text{the after-tax cost of debt.}$$

Here T is the corporate tax rate as used previously. Thus, if the before-tax cost of debt were 15 percent and the firm's effective corporate tax rate were 40 percent, the after-tax cost of debt would be 9 percent.

We start with the firm's before-tax cost of debt and multiply it by the $(1 - T)$ factor to obtain the relevant after-tax cost. How do we obtain the before-tax cost of debt in practice for an actual firm? Two main procedures may be used. We can look in any of the investment manuals to determine the rating of the firm's outstanding publicly held bonds. Various government agencies and investment banking firms periodically publish promised yields to maturity of debt issues by rating categories.

For our United Corporation example, its bonds were rated AA. At the time, we find that seasoned AA industrial debt issues of 10-year maturity (the remaining years to maturity of most of UC's long-term corporate debt) were 13.5 percent.

We can check this by calculating the promised yield to maturity on the cash flows from UC's long-term debt in relation to its current price. For its major issue of long-term debt, UC pays a coupon of 10 percent based on $1,000 par value per bond. Coupons are paid semiannually. UC's bonds are rated AA rather than Aaa, so there is some very slight risk associated with them. We can obtain the current price of the UC bonds by looking in the daily newspaper or from various quote machines. We find that the price is $810.95. We can estimate the promised yield to maturity of UC's bonds by solving for k_b in Equation 15.30:

$$\$810.95 = \sum_{t=1}^{20} \frac{50}{\left(1 + \dfrac{k_b}{2}\right)^t} + \frac{(1,000)}{\left(1 + \dfrac{k_b}{2}\right)^{20}}. \tag{15.30}$$

When we make the calculation, we find that the k_b that solves this equation is very close to the 13.5 percent cost of AA seasoned industrial bond issues. We shall, therefore, use 13.5

percent as the before-tax cost of long-term debt. Let us postulate that the firm's effective corporate tax rate is 40 percent. The after-tax cost of long-term debt would, therefore, be as follows:

$$k_b(1 - T) = .135(.6) = .081.$$

Thus, the after-tax cost of debt would be 8.1 percent. We had indicated that the coupon payment actually promised by the long-term debt of UC was 10 percent. But the coupon rate simply indicates what the cost was at the time the debt was issued. What is relevant for present decision making is the current cost of the debt, which we calculated.

Cost of Preferred Stock

Preferred stock is a hybrid between debt and common stock. Like debt, preferred stock carries a fixed commitment on the part of the corporation to make periodic payments; in liquidation, the claims of the preferred stockholders take precedence over those of the common stockholders. However, failure to make the preferred dividend payments does not result in bankruptcy as nonpayment of interest on bonds does. Thus, to the firm, preferred stock is somewhat less risky than common stock but riskier than bonds. To the investor, preferred stock is also less risky than common but riskier than bonds.

From the standpoint of the issuing firm, preferred stock has the disadvantage that its dividend is not deductible for tax purposes. On the other hand, the tax law provides that 85 percent of all dividends received by one corporation from another are not taxable. This 85 percent dividend exclusion makes preferred stock a potentially attractive investment to other corporations such as commercial banks and stock insurance companies. This attractiveness on the demand side pushes the yields on preferred stock to slightly below yields on bonds of similar companies. Although preferred issues may be callable and may be retired, most are perpetuities. If the preferred issue is a perpetuity, then its yield is calculated as follows:

$$\text{Preferred yield} = \frac{\text{Preferred dividend}}{\text{Price of preferred stock}} = \frac{d_{ps}}{p_{ps}}. \qquad \textbf{(15.31)}$$

Returning to our example for United Corporation, we find that its only preferred stock issue outstanding carries a $9 dividend. The current price of the preferred stock obtained from newspapers or other sources is $69.23. Hence, the preferred stock yield or its cost will be

$$\frac{d_{ps}}{p_{ps}} = \frac{\$9}{\$69.23} = .13 = 13\%.$$

The result is 13 percent. Since preferred stock dividends paid by the issuing corporation are not deductible for tax purposes, this 13 percent is therefore already on an after-tax basis. No further tax adjustment need be made. It stands on the same basis as the 8.1 percent after-tax cost of long-term debt whose before-tax cost was 13.5 percent.

Cost of Common Equity

The cost of common equity is the most difficult of the major sources of financing to be determined. Four major methods will be employed. They are

1. The Capital Asset Pricing Model (CAPM)
2. The bond yield plus equity risk premium
3. Realized investor yield
4. The dividend growth model

The first three are based fundamentally on financial market data. The fourth, the dividend growth model, has some theoretical problems but is so widely used that we include it as one of the inputs.

Capital Asset Pricing Model (CAPM) Approach.   Recall that the CAPM approach states that the investors' required rate of return on common stock is equal to a risk-free rate plus a risk premium. The risk premium is the market risk premium (which is the market return minus a risk-free rate) multiplied by the applicable beta of the firm. The Security Market Line equation is

$$k_s = R_F + (\bar{R}_M - R_F)\beta_j.$$

The market risk premium has been calculated in a number of studies. Over long periods of time it appears to average out for the United States between 6 and 8 percent. We will use 7.5 percent in our calculations here. Theory calls for using the short-term Treasury bill rate as an estimate of the risk-free rate. For our example we can readily determine that the short-term Treasury bill rate is 10 percent. The only information specific to the firm that is required in the use of the CAPM is the beta or the risk measure. Various investment advisory services publish beta estimates for a large number of companies. Drawing on these we find that the beta for the common stock of United Corporation is 1.05.

Short-term interest rates fluctuate with greater volatility than longer-term interest rates. This is true of short-term T-bill rates as well as other short-term interest rates. Some analysts, therefore, find it useful to use a longer-term Treasury bond rate as a check in developing a CAPM estimate of the firm's cost of equity capital. For the 199X period we would find that the 10-year T-bill rate was 12.5 percent so that we would have

$$k_s = 12.5 + 7.875 = 20.375 \text{ percent.}$$

For 199X use of the 10-year T-bill rate would yield a somewhat higher cost of equity capital. For some prior periods such as early 1982, the reverse would have been true. Thus, we have some initial estimates of the firm's cost of equity capital, but we need to test these estimates by using other procedures as well.

Bond Yield Plus Equity Risk Premium.   Under the CAPM method described, the required return on equity represents a premium over the risk-free rate measured by yields on government securities. This second method also involves a risk premium. However, in this case it represents a premium over the firm's own long-term debt cost. This method provides a logical test check since the cost of common equity should be greater than the cost of debt. Debt represents a fixed legal claim giving bondholders a senior position over holders of preferred stock or common stock. The beta of long-term debt for a firm is typically much lower than the beta of its common stock. Hence we would expect a premium over the debt return in the required return to common stock.

This method is in the same spirit as the CAPM placing both the debt and the equity on a Security Market Line with the debt having a lower beta. If we had a good estimate of the beta of the debt, the differential between the required yield on the debt and the required yield on the equity would be given by the Security Market Line. The premium of the required equity return over the long-term debt return would represent the indicated risk premium. We have estimated this to be 4.5 percent for the United Corporation. Hence given the cost of long-term debt that we have calculated to be 13.5 percent, the indicated required return to common equity by this method would be 18 percent.

Realized Investor Yield. The realized investor yield is the average dividend yield plus the average capital gain over some prior period such as 10 years. This measure represents what investors have, in fact, required as a return from this company's common stock. This method captures the readjustments that investors make in the price of the firm's stock to take account of changes in the outlook for the firm. However, the measure for an individual firm may be unstable. To make the measure more reliable, another test check is to make the calculation for a group of similar firms, where random individual firm instabilities may be averaged out.

This calculation of the average dividend yield plus the average capital gain represents the average return realized by investors. This can be related to the Security Market Line, which gives us the required return on equity. In the long run we would expect the average return to equal the required return since stock prices will be adjusted to move the two toward equality. For the previous 10 years for United Corporation we have calculated the average dividend yield to be 4.1 percent and the average capital gain to be 14.1 percent. Thus, by this method the indicated required return on equity is 18.2 percent.

Dividend Growth Model. The dividend valuation model can be expressed as follows:

$$p_o = \frac{d_1}{k_s - g} = \frac{d_o(1 + g)}{k_s - g} = \frac{EPS_o(1 + g)(1 - b)}{k_s - br}. \tag{15.32}$$

The required return on equity can be derived from this dividend valuation expression. In Equation 15.32, b is the percent of earnings retained by the firm, r is the expected marginal return on new capital invested, and d_o and d_1 are the current and expected dividends per share, respectively. A number of assumptions underlying the dividend valuation model should be noted to understand how it may be used to estimate the required return on equity for a firm. The growth rate (g) refers to the growth in dividends. Since g is the product of the retention rate times the internal profitability rate, this indicates that the model is an all internal equity financing model. Retained earnings is the only source of financing investment in this model. Furthermore, constant growth is required. There is no period of supernormal or subnormal growth and the constant growth continues through infinity.

The logic of the model indicates that the g refers to the growth rate in dividends, but under the assumptions of the model everything else also grows at the same rate. If dividends grow at 12 percent, and the payout ratio and retention rate are constant, earnings must be growing at the same 12 percent. Since retained earnings are the only source of growth, the total assets of the firm will also be growing at 12 percent. And over time, the value of the firm or the price of its common stock will be growing at a 12 percent rate as well. Clearly there is a relationship between p, the price of the common stock, and the growth rate in earnings, dividends, and the total assets of the firm. Thus, the model does not provide an unambiguous basis for estimating k_s.

Nevertheless, the dividend valuation model is widely used in practice both for valuing common stock and for estimating the cost of equity capital. In estimating the cost of equity capital for United Corporation the valuation expression is solved for k_s as shown in Equation 15.33:

$$k_s = \frac{d_1}{p_o} + g. \tag{15.33}$$

Equation 15.33 states that the required return on equity is the expected dividend yield plus the expected growth rate in dividends. The expected dividend is obtained by taking the current dividend, d_o, and applying the expected growth rate. For United Corporation the current dividend is $2.75. It is difficult to arrive at a reliable figure for the expected growth rate. One approach is to begin with the growth over some previous period. But the position of the firm is likely to be affected by developments of the economy as a whole as well as in its own industry. Nevertheless, various financial services provide estimates of expected growth in earnings and dividends for individual firms. In addition, an independent analysis can be made by the analyst attempting to make a calculation of the cost of capital for the firm. Suppose that by a combination of all of these methods we arrive at an expected growth rate in dividends for the firm of 12 percent. Then d_1 would be $2.75 multiplied by 1.12 to give us a d_1 or expected next year's dividend of $3.08. The current price of UC's stock is $62.44. The $3.08 divided by $62.44 represents a 4.9 percent dividend yield. When this is added to the 12 percent expected growth rate, we obtain a 16.9 percent estimate of the required return on equity.

Summarizing our results thus far we have the following results for the four methods:

1. CAPM — 20.4 percent
2. Bond yield plus equity risk premium — 18.0 percent
3. Realized investor yield — 18.2 percent
4. Dividend growth model — 16.9 percent.

Note that the first three methods of estimating the cost of equity capital use information generated by the financial markets. Therefore they may be reasonably regarded as the required rates of return on equity by external investors. Hence they represent an estimate of the cost of external equity funds. Since the dividend valuation model is an all internal equity financing model it may be reasonably regarded as providing the cost of internal funds. It is interesting to note that the three methods that provide estimates of external equity financing cluster at a little more than 18 percent, whereas the dividend valuation model gives a somewhat lower figure at approximately 17 percent as a cost of internal equity financing.

We now have estimates of all of the costs of the individual components in financing. We next consider how we can pull all of this information together to calculate the weighted marginal cost of capital for the firm as a whole, an expression that is referred to as WACC or MCC (marginal cost of capital).

Determining Market Value Weights and WACC

Column (1) in Table 15.17 represents the book value of the liabilities and stockholders' equity accounts for which an explicit charge can be calculated. The first item is notes payable on a short-term basis. Short-term notes payable would carry an interest cost relatively close to current interest rate levels. Hence their market value would approximate their face value. Therefore, in Column (2), the market price factor of the notes payable is shown at 100 percent. In calculating the effective cost of long-term debt we indicated that with a coupon rate of 10 percent and a current required market rate of 13.5 percent on United Corporation's AA debt, the current price per $1,000 bond for United Corporation would be approximately $800. Hence the market price would be about 80 percent of their maturity value. We made a similar calculation for preferred stock arriving at a 70 percent factor. For common equity we would employ the price of $62.44 previously used, which is 120 percent of the $52.04 book value per share.

Applying the market prices to the book value figures, we obtain the indicated market values shown in Column (3). When we sum the market value figures we obtain $3,716 million as compared with book values of the four items of a somewhat smaller amount. From the market value figures we can calculate the proportions of financing, shown in Column (4). These are proportions at market values. The use of book value weights would have been inappropriate because they are less likely to indicate what the proportions would be in the future financing of the firm. Market proportion weights provide a better estimate of the target financing mix of the firm than book value weights. In the financial planning models of the firm, target financing proportions would be employed. These

TABLE 15.17   Calculation of Market Value Weights and Proportions for United Corporation

	Book Value (millions) (1)	Market Price Factor (2)	Market Value (millions) (3)	Proportions (4)	Targets (5)
Notes payable	$ 400	100%	$ 400	.108	10%
Long-term debt	1,000	80	800	.215	20
Preferred stock	200	70	140	.038	5
Common equity*	1,980	120	2,376	.639	65
	$3,580		$3,716	1.000	

*38.05 million shares.

TABLE 15.18   United Corporation's Cost of Capital with Internal Equity Financing

	Before-Tax Cost	After-Tax Cost	Target Proportions	Weighted Cost
Notes payable	13.5%	8.1%	.10	.81%
Long-term debt	13.5	8.1	.20	1.62
Preferred stock	13.0	13.0	.05	.65
Common equity	18.0	18.0	.65	11.70
			1.00	WACC = 14.78%

would be the best indicator of the appropriate proportions to use in calculating the firm's weighted cost of capital. In Column (5) we assume that we have access to such information. The figures are closely related to the current market proportions. It is assumed that the target proportion of common equity financing would increase slightly with the expected future rise in the price of the firm's common equity shares.

We now have the component costs of financing and the target proportions. We can bring these together to calculate the marginal cost of capital or the WACC (see Table 15.18). Recall that we assumed a 40 percent tax rate for United Corporation so that the after-tax cost of notes payable and the after-tax cost of long-term debt represent their before-tax cost multiplied by $(1 - .40)$. We obtain a weighted average marginal cost of financing of 14.78 percent for United Corporation as of the early part of 199X.

RELATED ISSUES

The United Corporation example covers the cost of the main sources of external funds, but practitioners have to consider other topics as well. What is the cost of internally generated funds? How do flotation costs affect the cost of capital? What is the cost of hybrid securities — those that are convertible or callable? And how does one calculate the cost of capital for a division or business unit?

There are two main sources of internally generated funds: depreciation and retained earnings. How should one think about their costs?

Cost of Depreciation-Generated Funds

The first increment of cash flow used to finance any year's capital budget is depreciation-generated funds. In their statements of changes in financial position, corporations generally show depreciation charges to be a very substantial noncash charge. For capital budgeting purposes, should depreciation be considered free capital, should it be ignored completely, or should a charge be assessed against it? The answer is that a charge should be assessed against these funds, and that this cost is the weighted cost of capital before outside equity is used.

The reasoning here is that the firm could, if it so desired, distribute the depreciation-generated funds to its creditors and stockholders, the parties who financed the assets in the first place. For example, if $10 million of depreciation-generated funds were available, the firm could either reinvest them or distribute them. If the funds are to be distributed, the distribution must be to both bondholders and stockholders in proportion to their shares of the capital structure; otherwise, the capital structure will change. Obviously, this distribution should take place if the funds cannot be invested to yield the cost of capital. However, retention should occur if the internal rate of return exceeds the cost of capital. Since the cost of depreciation-generated funds is equal to the weighted cost of capital, depreciation does not enter the calculation of the weighted cost of capital.

Depreciation may, however, affect the cost of capital *schedule*. If we are concerned with gross capital expenditures — including replacement as well as expansion investments — then the cost of capital schedule that includes depreciation is the relevant one. The flat part of the marginal cost of capital curve, before it is increased by using external equity funds at higher rates, would be extended by the inclusion of depreciation. But if we are concerned with the effects of *net increases* in assets, then the schedule without depreciation is appropriate.

Cost of External Equity Funds versus Retained Earnings

It is useful to recognize and to avoid a fallacy that is sometimes encountered. This is the argument that retained earnings in a given year or accumulated retained earnings have no cost. This view is wrong. Retained earnings represent capital invested in the firm just as much as funds obtained externally do. So retained earnings definitely have a cost. The question is, how is their cost measured?

The traditional approach has been to begin with the dividend growth valuation model to illustrate the difference between the cost of internal versus external equity financing. If we let k_r represent the cost of retained earnings, and consider an all equity financed firm to set aside the leverage issue, we could express its determinants either on a per share basis (that is, dividends per share, d_1, divided by price per share, p_o) or for the firm as a whole (for example, total dividends, D_1, divided by total value, V_o), as shown in Equation 15.34.

$$k_r = \frac{d_1}{p_o} + g = \frac{D_1}{V_o} + g \tag{15.34}$$

The g should be interpreted as the growth in dividends per share or in total dividends for the company, given the assumptions of the dividend valuation model. A weakness in this approach is that the value of the firm or its value per share depends upon the growth rate. Hence it is not valid to treat the growth term as though it were independent of the current price per share or value of the firm.

Setting aside these problems, the traditional approach in using the dividend valuation model is to argue that flotation costs reduce the net proceeds from any external equity offering. If we express the flotation costs as a percentage of the gross proceeds on any particular offering, it would reduce the denominator in the dividend yield expression by a factor of $(1 - f)$ where f represents the equity flotation cost percentage. We would have the expression shown in Equation 15.35 for the cost of external equity financing.

$$k_s = \frac{d_1}{p_o(1 - f)} + g = \frac{D_1}{V_o(1 - f)} + g \tag{15.35}$$

We can illustrate the application of the expression in Equation 15.35 using the per share relationship. For example, if p_o is $20, d_1 is $2, and f is 10 percent, then the firm receives $18 for each new share sold. Hence the net proceeds are $18 per share. Assuming a constant future growth in dividends per share of 5 percent, the cost of new outside equity would be

$$k_s = \frac{\$2}{\$20(1 - 0.10)} + 5\% = 16.11\%.$$

Without the influence of flotation costs, the required return would be 15 percent. However, because of flotation costs, the required return on external equity financing would be 16.11 percent. Since the cost of equity capital is defined as the rate of return that must be earned to prevent the price of the stock from falling, we observe that the company's cost of external equity financing is 16.11 percent.[17]

If this approach is used to calculate the cost of external equity financing, we would have the situation depicted in Figure 15.12. The flotation cost factor is used to gross up the cost of internal equity funds to arrive at the cost of equity funds obtained externally. This also provides a basis for determining the availability of dividends. In Figure 15.12(a) the marginal efficiency of the firm's investment schedule crosses the marginal cost of capital function at a point where internal equity funds available are not fully used. Hence dividends could be paid equal to the total internal equity funds available less the amount required for investment. In Figure 15.12(b), the marginal efficiency of investment schedule intersects the marginal cost of capital schedule at a point beyond funds available from internal sources. A firm characterized by the situation in Panel (b) would not pay dividends, but would only be raising external funds. Or if the firm paid dividends it would have to raise external funds to meet investment needs plus pay whatever amount of dividends were paid.

Another view holds that flotation costs should not affect the opportunity costs of funds supplied to the firm. It is proposed that the costs of investment projects be grossed up by the weighted average flotation costs on all sources of financing (cf. Copeland and Weston [1988], pp. 534–536). This approach is reflected in Equation 15.36:

$$NPV = \sum_{t=1}^{N} \frac{CF_t}{(1 + k)^t} - \frac{\Delta I}{(1 - f)}. \tag{15.36}$$

---

[17]The cost of external equity is sometimes defined as

$$k_s = \frac{k_r}{1 - f}.$$

This equation is correct only if the firm's expected growth rate is zero. In other cases it overstates k_s.

FIGURE 15.12   Cost of Internal versus External Funds

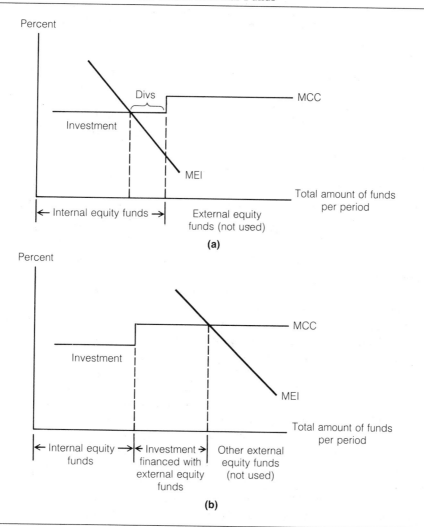

In Equation 15.36 the standard NPV expression in capital budgeting has the investment term grossed up by the (1 − flotation cost) factor.

If the tax deductibility of flotation costs is taken into account, then the burden of flotation costs is reduced by the factor of $(1 - T)$. This is illustrated in Equation 15.37:

$$NPV = \sum_{t=1}^{N} \frac{CF_t}{(1 + k)^t} - \frac{\Delta I}{[1 - f(1 - T)]}. \qquad (15.37)$$

If the tax deductions can all be taken at the time of the outlay, then Equation 15.37 expresses the tax influence correctly. If, however, some of the tax deductions have to be amortized over the life of the project, then the tax benefits for reducing flotation costs would also have to be amortized over time. If the assumptions that flotation costs and their tax effects are associated with the time period over which the investment outlays for projects are made, the newer approach is correct. An argument that has been made in support of the older method is that it may be difficult for a going concern to associate individual projects with their sources of financing. The business firm represents a pool of funds used to finance a stream of project activities. Thus, although applying the gross-up factor to the investment outlay may be correct theoretically, as a practical matter it may be more appropriate to apply the gross-up factor for flotation costs to the relevant cost of capital.

Cost of Capital for Hybrid Securities

Firms sometimes issue bonds or preferred stock that have implied options as part of the financing. They may be convertible into common stock as the option of their owner or they may be callable for early repayment by the firm. Conversion is a benefit to the security holder and therefore reduces the coupon rate or the preferred dividend. And the call feature is a cost because high coupon bonds might be called if interest rates drop. Consequently, the coupons on callable bonds are higher than on equivalent noncallable bonds. In either case, one must be careful to recognize that the stated coupon rate or preferred dividend yield are not good estimates of the true cost of capital because these hybrid securities are combinations of straight debt or preferred and risky options that are imbedded in the conversion or call feature.

A convertible bond is equivalent to a portfolio of two securities: straight debt with the same coupon rate and maturity as the convertible bond, and a warrant written on the value of the firm. The coupon rate on convertible bonds is usually lower than comparable straight debt because the right to convert is worth something. For example, in February 1982, the LS Company wanted to raise $50 million by using either straight debt or convertible bonds. An investment banking firm informed the company's treasurer that straight debt with a 25-year maturity would require a 17 percent coupon. Alternately, convertible debt with the same maturity would require only a 10 percent coupon. Both instruments would sell at par (i.e., $1,000), and the convertible debt could be converted into 35.71 shares (i.e., on exercise price of $28 per share). The stock of the LS Company was selling for $25 per share at the time. After using the option pricing model to figure out the cost of the implied conversion option (23.74 percent), the before-tax cost of the convertible bond was estimated to be 19.56 percent — an answer that is nearly double the 10 percent coupon rate on the bond.[18]

Brigham [1966] received responses from chief financial officers of 22 firms that had issued convertible debt. Of them, 68 percent said they used convertible debt because they believed the stock price would rise over time and that convertibles would provide a way of selling common stock at a price above the market price on the date of issue. Another 27

---

[18]The calculations are illustrated in Copeland and Weston [1988, pp. 475–478].

percent said their company wanted straight debt but found conditions to be such that a straight bond issue could not be sold at a "reasonable" rate of interest. The problem is that neither reason makes much sense. Convertible bonds are not "cheap debt." Because convertible bonds are riskier, their true cost of capital is greater than the cost of straight debt. Also, convertible bonds are not deferred sale of common stock at an attractive price. The uncertain sale of shares for $28 at some future date can hardly be compared with a current share price of $25. The cost of convertible debt is discussed at greater length in Chapter 25.

Cost of Capital for Projects or a Division

Calculating the cost of capital for a project or for a division encounters some common problems. First, the data are in dollars rather than rates of return. Second, different projects and different divisions are likely to have different risks and risks different from those of the firm as a whole. Fortunately we can solve both types of problems based on relationships derived from the basic Security Market Line. We shall illustrate the procedure.[19] We start with the Security Market Line as repeated in Equation 15.38:

$$E(R_j) = R_F + \lambda COV(R_j, R_M), \tag{15.38}$$

where

$$\lambda = \frac{\bar{R}_M - R_F}{\sigma_M^2}.$$

We then recognize that

$$E(R_j) = \frac{E(X_j)}{V_j}. \tag{15.39}$$

We substitute Equation 15.39 in the SML and solve for V_j, which gives us Equation 15.40:

$$V_j = \frac{E(X_j) - \lambda COV(X_j, R_M)}{R_F}. \tag{15.40}$$

We now have a relationship between the covariance expressed in terms of the net operating income (after taxes) of an unlevered activity. This we can obtain from the available data for an individual division of a firm or for a firm even if its securities are not traded publicly. If the division or nonpublicly traded firm has a historical record, we could develop a calculation of $COV(X_j, R_M)$. Even if we had no historical record or sometimes as a check on historical data we may also formulate subjective estimates of net operating income under alternative future states-of-the-world. Using either the historical data or subjective estimates under alternative future states-of-the-world we are thereby enabled to calculate the expected net operating income and its covariance. Suppose we have made these calculations and obtain the following:

---

[19]This procedure was described in Weston and Lee [1977], pp. 1779–1780.

$$\overline{X}_j = \$240$$
$$COV(X_j, R_M) = \$11.60.$$

We postulate further the market parameters, which are

$$R_F = 10\%$$
$$\lambda = 8 \qquad VAR(R_M) = .01.$$

We can now use these data inputs in Equation 15.40:

$$V_j = \frac{\$240 - 8(\$11.60)}{.10}$$
$$= \$1,472.$$

We thus obtain an estimate of the value of the division or the firm whose securities are not publicly traded of \$1,472. We can now express the covariance in rate of return form using the following relationship:

$$COV(R_j, R_M) = \frac{COV(X_j, R_M)}{V_j}.$$

Inserting the numbers, we have

$$COV(R_j, R_M) = \frac{\$11.60}{\$1,472} = .0079.$$

Since the variance of the market has been given as 1 percent, we can readily express the risk relationship in the form of beta.

$$\beta_U = \frac{COV(R_j, R_M)}{VAR(R_M)} = \frac{.0079}{.01} = .79$$

To this point we have assumed no leverage, so the beta of .79 we have obtained represents an unlevered beta. Let us postulate further that after careful assessment of the operations of the division under analysis we determine the applicable leverage to be applied is a ratio of debt to equity of one-half and that the effective corporate tax rate that would be applicable to this division's activities is 40 percent. We can then calculate the indicated levered beta by using Equation 15.6:

$$\beta_j = \beta_U[1 + B/S(1 - T)]. \tag{15.6}$$

Inserting the numerical values calculated, we would have

$$\beta_j = .79[1 + .5(.6)]$$
$$\beta_j = 1.027 \approx 1.03.$$

We have thus obtained a levered beta of 1.03 that would be applicable to the activities of the division. Before utilizing the beta calculated in the Security Market Line to obtain the cost of equity capital and related measures, we check the number we have obtained. One way to do so would be to observe the betas of publicly traded companies whose activities are similar to the individual division we have under analysis. Suppose we find a publicly traded company that is very similar. We observe that it has a beta of .85. But we also observe that for a long period of time this company has had a leverage ratio measured by the market value of debt to the market value of equity of .1. This is much lower than the .5 target leverage ratio of our division. We, therefore, have to releverage the comparable company to see what its beta would be at the target leverage for our division. First, we calculate its unlevered beta based on our knowledge of its current leverage. We solve Equation 15.6 for β_U to obtain Equation 15.41:

$$\beta_U = \frac{\beta_j}{[1 + B/S(1 - T)]}. \tag{15.41}$$

Inserting our numerical values we have

$$\beta_U = \frac{.85}{1.06} = .80.$$

We obtain an unlevered beta of .80, which is very close to the .79 we estimated for our particular division. This gives us some assurance that the company that we have chosen as similar in its activities to our division is indeed comparable since its unlevered beta is approximately the same as the unlevered beta we have calculated for our division. We now releverage the external similar company. We would then have

$$\beta_k = .80[1 + .5(.6)]$$
$$= 1.04.$$

We obtain a levered beta for our comparable company of 1.04. This is very close to the 1.03 that we had calculated using internal data. Giving greater weight to the market determined number, we will use the beta of 1.04 in the subsequent analysis. First, we apply this to the Security Market Line parameters. Since we know that the variance of the market is 1 percent, Equation 15.38 can be rewritten in beta form as shown in Equation 15.42:

$$E(R_j) = R_F + [E(R_M) - R_F]\beta_j. \tag{15.42}$$

We now have all the information we need to solve Equation 15.42 to estimate the cost of equity capital for the division or for the nonpublicly traded firm. This would be

$$E(R_j) = 10\% + 8\%(1.04)$$
$$= 18.32\%.$$

We obtain a cost of equity capital for our division of 18.32 percent. We can now proceed finally to calculate an applicable weighted marginal cost of capital that would represent the appropriate investment hurdle rate for projects undertaken by the division. Recall that in calculating the levered beta we indicated that the appropriate debt-equity ratio was 50 percent. This means that the leverage ratio expressed in terms of the total value of the firm is one-third debt and two-thirds equity. For this division the applicable cost of debt is 15 percent. We can, therefore, proceed to calculate the weighted marginal cost of capital.

Source	After-Tax Cost	Financing Proportions	Marginal Cost of Capital
Debt	9%	.33	3.00%
Equity	18.32	.67	12.27
		Divisional Cost of Capital	15.27%

We find that the cost of capital for this division would be slightly more than 15 percent. This is the appropriate investment hurdle rate to use for new projects of the division that are not greatly different from its existing product market mix. In a similar fashion we could calculate the cost of capital for each of the divisions of the firm. In addition to the application of these divisional investment hurdle rates in capital budgeting, these estimates would provide a check on the firm's overall beta and cost of capital. This is because the firm's beta is simply a value-weighted average of the betas of its individual divisions. Therefore, the value-weighted average of the betas of the individual divisions should be reasonably close to the publicly available estimates of the beta for the firm as a whole.[20]

The same problems are involved in analyzing a project. Indeed, in the foregoing analysis we could always substitute "project" for "division." The results are estimates of investment hurdle rates by division or project for use in capital budgeting decisions. Without these estimates of investment hurdle rates for individual projects or divisions, highly risky activities would be allocated too much financing and less risky activities would not receive the requisite funds. If a single marginal weighted cost of capital were applied to all risky activities, some projects that should not be financed would be adopted. For less risky activities, projects that should be accepted would be rejected.

SUMMARY

Under the Modigliani and Miller assumptions, a firm's cost of capital is not affected by leverage when there are no taxes. However, even without taxes, the firm's cost of equity capital rises linearly. With taxes, the firm's cost of equity capital still rises linearly but at a reduced rate. The firm's marginal weighted cost of capital under the MM theory would decline, implying that firms would all be highly leveraged. However, we do not observe this in actuality. A number of factors could limit leverage, including agency problems, information asymmetry and signaling, and bankruptcy costs. Any of these could result in limiting the amount of leverage employed so that a firm would have an "optimal capital structure." The foregoing framework provided a basis for analyzing the influence of leverage on the cost of capital of a firm, the subject of the remainder of the chapter.

The rate of return required or expected on any security, $E(R_j)$, is the minimum rate of return necessary to induce investors to buy or to hold the security; it is a function of the riskless rate of interest and the investment's risk characteristics:

$$E(R_j) = R_F + [E(R_M) - R_F]\beta_j.$$

This equation is called the Security Market Line (SML). Because investors generally dislike risk, the required rate of return is higher on riskier securities. As a class, bonds are

[20]This has actually been done for a sample of multidivision firms using the "pure-play technique," which involves matching each division of a multidivision firm with a publicly traded company having only one business line. See Fuller and Kerr [1981].

b. A preferred stock issue is refina pected current dividend, p_o = the current
c. Bonds are sold for cash.   owth in dividends, is sometimes used to
d. The firm repurchases 10 percent in the implications of the formula.
e. An issue of convertible bonds is ebt to increase with financial leverage?

15.2 From an economic and social standp rate of return on common equity (k_s) and
Explain by listing some advantages a

15.3 Financial leverage and operating lev tal and the average cost of capital be likely
What is this similarity, and why is it to a new, riskier industry?

15.4 How does the use of financial leverag at its low for the year, but management

15.5 Would you expect risk to increase pr depressed because of investor pessimism.
than proportionately with added finar that the firm is contemplating the use of
es not want to sell new stock at the current

15.6 What are some reasons for variations arture from its "optimal" capital structure

15.7 Why is the following statement true? 've raised in the equity markets. Does this
stable sales and profits are able to in

15.8 Why do public utility companies usua nal cost of capital is an average in some
trade firms?

15.9 The use of financial ratios and industry
a firm should be approached with cau ————————————————————

15.10 Suppose that basic business risks to a
a. Would you expect all firms in the any are identical except for their leverage
capital?   as $10 million in assets, each earned $2
b. How would the averages differ a each has a 40 percent corporate tax rate.
t/total assets) of 30 percent and pays 10
15.11 Are internally generated retained earn s a 50 percent leverage ratio and pays 12
stock? Why or why not?

15.12 Prior to the 1930s, the corporate inco et income/equity) for each firm.
were fairly low. Also prior to the 1930 n on equity, Bonner's treasurer decides to
it has been since that time. Is there a r cent. This will increase Bonner's interest
taxes and the decline in importance o new rate of return on equity for Bonner.

15.13 The firm's covariance is 0.014, the ris t year's return on equity under different
($\bar{R}_M - R_F$) is 5 percent, and the varia million and its tax rate is 40 percent. The
a. With no bankruptcy costs, what gs for three possible states-of-the-world. It
b. What is the beta of the firm?   and taxes will be $3 million with a 0.2

15.14 Assume that the information in Quest ty, and $500,000 with a 0.3 probability.
corporate tax rate is 50 percent, and th the standard deviation, and the coefficient
percent, with a debt cost of 10 percen ge ratios:
a. What is the new beta of the firm?
b. What is its return on equity?
c. What is the cost of capital for the

15.15 An unlevered firm has a beta of 0.8. H
tax rate is 50 percent and it aims to ha

15.3 The beta for the Hume Company is 0.8 if it employs no leverage, and its tax rate is 40 percent. The financial manager of Hume uses the following expression to calculate the influence of leverage on beta:

$$\beta_L = \beta_U[1 + (B/S)(1 - T)].$$

a. Several alternative target leverage ratios are being considered. What will be the beta on the common stock of Hume Company if the following alternative leverage ratios are employed — that is, $B/S = 0.4$? 0.8? 1.0? 1.2? 1.6?

b. If the financial manager of Hume uses the SML to estimate the required return on equity, what are the required rates of return on equity at each of the above leverage ratios? (The estimated risk-free return is 6 percent, and the market risk premium is 5 percent.)

c. The financial manager wants to keep the beta at 1.5 or below. What is the maximum leverage ratio which can be employed? What is the required rate of return on equity at this leverage ratio?

15.4 The Shuman Company plans to raise a net amount of $240 million for new equipment financing and working capital. Two alternatives are being considered. Common stock may be sold to net $40 per share, or debentures yielding 10 percent may be issued. The balance sheet and income statement of the Shuman Company prior to financing are:

The Shuman Company Balance Sheet as of December 31, 1985 (Millions of Dollars)

Current assets	$ 800	Accounts payable	$ 150
Net fixed assets	400	Notes payable to bank	250
		Other current liabilities	200
		Total current liabilities	$ 600
		Long-term debt	250
		Common stock, $2 par	50
		Retained earnings	300
Total assets	$1,200	Total claims	$1,200

The Shuman Company Income Statement for Year Ended December 31, 1985 (Millions of Dollars)

Sales	$2,200
Earnings before interest and taxes (10%)	$ 220
Interest on debt	40
Earnings before taxes	$ 180
Tax (40%)	72
Net income after tax	$ 108

Annual sales are expected to be distributed according to the following probabilities:

Annual Sales	Probability
$2,000	0.30
2,500	0.40
3,200	0.30

a. Assuming that earnings before interest and taxes remain at 10 percent of sales, calculate earnings per share under both the stock financing and the debt financing alternatives at each possible level of sales.

b. Calculate expected earnings per share under both debt and stock financing.

15.5 CME Corporation produces one product, a small calculator. Last year, 50,000 calculators were sold at $20 each. CME's income statement is shown below.

CME Corporation Income Statement for Year Ended December 31, 1985

Sales		$1,000,000
Less: variable costs	$400,000	
fixed costs	200,000	600,000
EBIT		$ 400,000
Less: interest		125,000
Net income before tax		$ 275,000
Less: income tax ($T = 0.40$)		110,000
Net income		$ 165,000
EPS (100,000 shares)		$1.65

a. Calculate the following for CME's 1985 level of sales:
   (1) the degree of operating leverage
   (2) the degree of financial leverage
   (3) the combined leverage effect.

b. CME is considering changing to a new production process for manufacturing the calculators. Highly automated and capital intensive, the new process will double fixed costs to $400,000 but will decrease variable costs to $4 a unit. If the new equipment is financed with bonds, interest will increase by $70,000; if it is financed by common stock, total stock outstanding will increase by 20,000 shares. Assuming that sales remain constant, calculate for each financing method:
   (1) earnings per share
   (2) the combined leverage effect.

c. Under what conditions would you expect CME to want to change its operations to the more automated process?

d. If sales are expected to increase, which alternative will have the greatest impact on EPS? Illustrate with an example.

15.6 You are given the following information about the Richardson Company, which manufactures small hot plates:

Price	$35
Variable costs	$19 per unit
Fixed costs	$200,000
Debt (B)	$300,000
Interest rate	12%
T	40%

In 1989, Richardson's net income was $600,000.

a. How many hot plates were sold in 1989?

   b. Calculate the degrees of operating, financial, and combined leverage for Richardson.
   c. Suppose that Richardson restructures its balance sheet, increasing debt to $1 million. Prepare a pro forma income statement and calculate the degree of the combined leverage assuming the same level of sales calculated in Part (a).

15.7 The Lewis Corporation plans to expand assets by 50 percent. To finance the expansion, it is choosing between a straight 11 percent debt issue and common stock. Its current balance sheet and income statement are shown below. If Lewis Corporation finances the $350,000 expansion with debt, the rate on the incremental debt will be 11 percent, and the price/earnings ratio of the common stock will be 8 times. If the expansion is financed by equity, the new stock can be sold at $25. The price/earnings ratio of all the outstanding common stock will remain at 10 times.

Lewis Corporation Balance Sheet as of December 31, 1989

	Debt (at 8%)	$140,000
	Common stock, $10 par	350,000
	Retained earnings	210,000
Total assets $700,000	Total claims	$700,000

Lewis Corporation Income Statement for Year Ended December 31, 1989

Sales	$2,100,000	Earnings per share:
Total costs		$\dfrac{\$103,600}{35,000} = \$2.96$
(excluding interest)	1,881,600	
Earnings before interest and taxes	$ 218,400	Price/earnings ratio: $10 \times$ [a]
Debt interest	11,200	
Income before taxes	$ 207,200	Market price:
Taxes (at 50%)	103,600	$10 \times \$2.96 = \$29.60$
Net income	$ 103,600	

[a]The price/earnings ratio is the market price per share divided by earnings per share. It represents the amount of money an investor is willing to pay for $1 of current earnings. The higher the riskiness of a stock, the lower its P/E ratio, other things held constant.

   a. Assuming that earnings before interest and taxes (EBIT) are 10 percent of sales, what are the earnings per share at sales levels of $0; $700,000; $1,400,000; $2,100,000; $2,800,000; $3,500,000; and $4,200,000, when financing is with common stock? When financing is with debt? (Assume no fixed costs of production.)
   b. Make a chart for EPS indicating the crossover point in sales (where EPS using bonds = EPS using stock).
   c. Using the price/earnings ratio, calculate the market value per share of common stock for each sales level for both the debt and the equity financing.
   d. Using data from Part (c), make a chart of market value per share for the company indicating the crossover point.
   e. Which form of financing should be used if the firm follows the policy of seeking to maximize

(1) EPS?

(2) market price per share?

   f. Now assume that the following probability estimates of future sales have been made: 5 percent chance of $0, 7.5 percent chance of $700,000, 20 percent chance of $1,400,000, 35 percent chance of $2,100,000, 20 percent chance of $2,800,000, 7.5 percent chance of $3,500,000, and 5 percent chance of $4,200,000. Calculate expected values for EPS and market price per share under each financing alternative.

   g. What other factors should be taken into account in choosing between the two forms of financing?

   h. Would it matter if the presently outstanding stock was all owned by the final decision maker (the president) and that this represented his entire net worth? Would it matter if he was compensated entirely by a fixed salary? If he had a substantial number of stock options?

15.8 Companies U and L are identical in every respect except that U is unlevered while L has $10 million of 5 percent bonds outstanding. Assume (1) that all of the MM assumptions are met, (2) that the tax rate is 40 percent, (3) that EBIT is $2 million, (4) that the equity capitalization rate for Company U is 10 percent, and (5) that the coupon rate is equal to the risk-free rate, i.e., 5 percent.

   a. What value would MM estimate for each firm?

   b. Suppose V_U = $8 million and V_L = $18 million. According to MM, do these represent equilibrium values? If not, explain the process by which equilibrium will be restored. No calculations are necessary.

15.9 You are provided the following information: The firm's expected net operating income (X) is $600. Its value as an unlevered firm (V_U) is $2,000. The tax rate is 40 percent. The cost of debt is 10 percent. The ratio of debt to equity for the levered firm, when it is levered, is 1. Use the MM propositions to:

   a. Calculate the after-tax cost of equity capital for both the levered and the unlevered firm.

   b. Calculate the after-tax weighted average cost of capital for each.

   c. Why is the cost of equity capital higher for the levered firm, but the weighted average cost of capital lower?

15.10 The Gorman Company is unlevered. Its balance sheet can be summarized as follows:

Gorman Company Balance Sheet, 12/31/X0 (Millions of Dollars)

Total assets	$500	Common stock (par value = $1)	$100
		Paid-in capital	100
		Retained earnings	300
		Total claims	$500

Net operating earnings for the year ending December 31, 19X0 were $100 million and the effective tax rate was 50 percent. The common stock has a market price of $5 per share. To finance additional projects, $100 million of long-term debt is sold at par with an 8 percent coupon rate. Earnings rise to $120 million per year. Alternatively, the expansion may be financed by the sale of an additional 20 million shares of common stock. Use the Modigliani-Miller model to answer the following questions.

     a. Before the new financing,
       (1) What are earnings per share of common stock?
       (2) What is the price/earnings ratio on the common stock?
       (3) What is the relationship between book value and market value?
       (4) What is the cost of capital?
     b. After the new financing by debt,
       (1) What is the new value of the firm?
       (2) What are the new earnings per share?
       (3) What is the new price per share of common stock?
       (4) What is the new price/earnings ratio on the common stock?
       (5) What is the new required return on the common equity?
       (6) What is the new cost of capital for the firm?
       (7) What is the market/book relationship?
     c. After financing by equity, answer Questions 1 through 7 in Part (b).
     d. Comment on the implications of the above analysis.

15.11 The earnings, dividends, and stock price of the Abbott Company are expected to grow at 9 percent per year. Abbott's common stock sells for $30 per share, and the company will pay a year-end dividend of $2.40 per share. What is the cost of retained earnings?

15.12 The Crothers Company has a beta of 1.5. It has no debt in its capital structure.
     a. The expected market rate of return is 14 percent and the risk-free rate is 6 percent. What is the cost of equity capital for Crothers?
     b. Should Crothers accept a project that earns a rate of return of 15 percent and has a beta of 0.9?

15.13 The Graham Company's financing plans for next year include the sale of long-term bonds with a 9 percent coupon. The company believes it can sell the bonds at a price that will give a yield to maturity of 10 percent. If the tax rate is 40 percent, what is Graham's after-tax cost of debt?

15.14 The Brandon Company plans to issue 20-year bonds that have a 10 percent coupon, a par value of $1,000, and can be sold for $920. Interest is paid semiannually. Brandon's tax rate is 40 percent.
     a. What is the after-tax cost of this debt to Brandon?
     b. What would be the after-tax cost if this were a perpetual bond issue?

15.15 Infinity Industries has just issued some $100 par preferred stock with a 10 percent dividend. The stock is selling on the market for $96.17, and Infinity must pay flotation costs of 6 percent of the market price. What is the cost of the preferred stock for Infinity?

15.16 The Iversen Company earns $5 per share. The expected year-end dividend is $1.60, and price per share is $40. Iversen's earnings, dividends, and stock price have been growing at 8 percent per year, and this growth rate is expected to continue indefinitely. New common stock can be sold to net $38. What is Iversen's cost of retained earnings?

15.17 The Longwell Company is expected to pay a year-end dividend of $4.40. Longwell earns $7.70 per share, and its stock sells at $55 per share. Stock price, earnings, and dividends are expected to grow 6 percent per year indefinitely.
     a. Calculate the stockholders' rate of return.

b. If the firm has a zero growth rate and pays out all its earnings as dividends, what is the stockholders' rate of return?

15.18 The Riley Company has $200 million in total net assets at the end of 19X0. It plans to increase its production machinery in 19X1 by $50 million. Bond financing, at an 11 percent rate, will sell at par. Preferred will have an 11.5 percent dividend payment and will be sold at a par value of $100. Common stock currently sells for $50 per share and can be sold to net $45 after flotation costs. There is $10 million of internal funding available from retained earnings. Over the past few years, dividend yield has been 6 percent and the firm's growth rate is 8 percent. The tax rate is 40 percent. The present capital structure shown below is considered optimal:

Debt:		
4% coupon bonds	$40,000,000	
7% coupon bonds	40,000,000	$ 80,000,000
Preferred stock		20,000,000
Common stock ($10 par)	$40,000,000	
Retained earnings	60,000,000	
Equity		100,000,000
		$200,000,000

a. How much of the $50 million must be financed by equity capital if the present capital structure is to be maintained?
b. How much of the equity funding must come from the sale of new common stock?
c. Calculate the component cost of:
  (1) New debt
  (2) New preferred stock
  (3) Retained earnings
  (4) New equity
d. What is Riley's average cost of equity for 19X1?
e. What would be Riley's weighted average cost of capital if only retained earnings were used to finance additional growth — that is, if only $20 million were raised?
f. What is the weighted average cost of capital when $50 million is raised?
g. What is the weighted average cost of capital on the $30 million raised over the $20 million?

15.19 The Tanner Company's cost of equity is 18 percent. Tanner's before-tax cost of debt is 12 percent, and its tax rate is 40 percent. Using the following balance sheet, calculate Tanner's after-tax weighted average cost of capital. (Assume that this accounting balance sheet also represents Tanner's target capital structure.)

Assets		**Liabilities**	
Cash	$ 100	Accounts payable	$ 200
Accounts receivable	200	Accrued taxes due	200
Inventories	300	Long-term debt	400
Plant and equipment, net	1,800	Equity	1,600
Total assets	$2,400	Total liabilities	$2,400

15.20 Parnelli Products' stock is currently selling for $45 a share. The firm is earning $5 per share and is expected to pay a year-end dividend of $1.80.

a. If investors require a 12 percent return, what rate of growth must be expected for Parnelli?

b. If Parnelli reinvests retained earnings to yield the expected rate of return, what will be next year's EPS?

15.21 You are planning to form a new company, and you can use several different capital structures. Investment bankers indicate that debt and equity capital will cost the following under different debt ratios (debt/total assets):

Debt Ratio	20% and below	21 to 40%	41 to 50%	51 to 65%
Before-tax cost of debt	8%	9%	11%	14%
Cost of equity capital	12	13	18	25

a. Assuming a 40 percent tax rate, what is the after-tax weighted cost of capital for the following capital structures?

	(1)	(2)	(3)	(4)	(5)	(6)	(7)	(8)
Debt	0%	20%	21%	40%	41%	50%	51%	65%
Equity	100	80	79	60	59	50	49	35

b. Which capital structure minimizes the weighted average cost of capital?

15.22 On January 1, 19X0, the total assets of the Rossiter Company were $60 million. By the end of the year total assets are expected to be $90 million. (Assume there is no short-term debt.) The firm's capital structure, shown below, is considered to be optimal:

Debt (10% coupon bonds)	$24,000,000
Preferred stock (at 10.5%)	6,000,000
Common equity	30,000,000
	$60,000,000

New bonds will have an 11 percent coupon rate and will be sold at par. Preferred stock will have an 11.5 percent rate and will also be sold at par. Common stock, currently selling at $30 a share, can be sold to net the company $27 a share. Stockholders' required rate of return, estimated to be 12 percent, consists of a dividend yield of 4 percent and an expected growth of 8 percent. Retained earnings are estimated to be $3 million (ignoring depreciation). The marginal corporate tax rate is 40 percent.

a. Assuming all asset expansion (gross expenditures for fixed assets plus related working capital) is included in the capital budget, what is the dollar amount of the capital budget (ignoring depreciation)?

b. To maintain the present capital structure, how much of the capital budget must be financed by equity?

c. How much of the new equity funds needed must be generated internally? How much externally?

d. Calculate the cost of each of the equity components.

e. At what level of capital expenditures will there be a break in the MCC schedule?

f. Calculate the MCC both below and above the break in the schedule.

g. Plot the MCC schedule. Also, draw in an IRR or MEI schedule that is consistent with the MCC schedule and the projected capital budget.

15.23 (*Use the computer diskette, File name: 15 FINLEV, Financial Structure and the Use of Leverage.*)

a. Given three alternative future states with sales and cost function as given and total assets of $10,000, what is the range of before-tax return on total assets?

b. Given the range of before-tax return on total assets, what is the range of return on equity (ROE) and earnings per share (EPS) across the three states as capital structure changes? Examine debt/total assets ratios of 0%, 20%, 50%, and 80%. (Note: The cost of debt increases with increased leverage.)

c. Two forecasting firms, Polyana Predictions and Deyer Prospects, project different probabilities for the three future states. How are expected ROE and standard deviation affected by alternative capital structures? Which financial structure should be chosen if management agrees with the Polyana forecast? If management agrees with the Deyer forecast?

d. Assuming an unlevered beta of 1.4, how does beta change with increases in leverage? Once again, examine debt/total assets ratios of 0%, 20%, 50%, and 80%. (Note: We must also make assumptions about the debt-to-equity ratio at market values (B/S) corresponding to each debt/total assets ratio at book value.)

e. Examine the effects of leverage in more detail by varying any assumptions shown in Screen #3.

15.24 (*Use the computer diskette, File name: 15 WACC, Cost of Capital.*)

a. Assume a world of Modigliani and Miller where the after-tax debt cost does not change with leverage because there are no bankruptcy costs, and the equity cost function is a straight line reflecting the equation of Modigliani and Miller's Proposition II, which is $k_s = k_u + (k_u - k_b)(B/S)(1 - T)$.

(1) What happens to the cost of equity as the debt-to-firm-value ratio at market value, B/V, rises from 0 to 60 percent in increments of 10 percent? (The before-tax cost of debt is 10 percent, the unlevered cost of equity is 12 percent, and the tax rate is 40 percent.) Hint: Translate debt-to-value ratios into debt-to-equity ratios for use in MM Proposition II.

(2) What happens to the weighted cost of capital (WCC) as B/V rises? Is there a minimum weighted cost of capital? What does this imply for the value of the firm? For optimum leverage?

b. An alternative to the MM world postulates that the cost of debt rises with leverage, and that the cost of equity rises with leverage curvilinearly, not as a straight line as implied by MM Proposition II. The following figures reflect this alternative:

Leverage	Before-Tax Cost of Debt	Cost of Equity
0-10%	10.00%	12.00%
10-20	10.20	12.30
20-30	10.80	12.75
30-40	11.00	13.29
40-50	12.00	15.00
50-60	16.00	20.00
Over 60%	27.00	30.00

(1) Compare the weighted cost of capital for each alternative capital structure under the Modigliani-Miller assumptions to the weighted cost of capital with bankruptcy costs.

(2) Is there a minimum cost of capital in the non-MM world? What is the optimum capital structure?

c. Now you are free to change any of the decision variables: leverage ratio, initial cost of debt, unlevered cost of equity, tax rate. Note, however, that the costs of debt and equity in the world with bankruptcy costs are dependent upon the leverage ratio and cannot be changed independently.

SELECTED REFERENCES

Aivazian, Varouj, and Callen, Jeffrey L., "Investment, Market Structure, and the Cost of Capital," *Journal of Finance*, 34 (March 1979), pp. 85–92.

Alberts, William W., and Hite, Gailen L., "The Modigliani-Miller Leverage Equation Considered in a Product Market Context," *Journal of Financial and Quantitative Analysis*, 18 (December 1983), pp. 425–437.

Altman, Edward I., "A Further Empirical Investigation of the Bankruptcy Cost Question," *Journal of Finance*, 39 (September 1984), pp. 1067–1089.

———, "Corporate Bankruptcy Potential, Stockholder Returns, and Share Valuation," *Journal of Finance*, 24 (December 1969), pp. 887–900.

Arditti, Fred D., "The Weighted Average Cost of Capital: Some Questions on Its Definition, Interpretation and Use," *Journal of Finance*, 28 (September 1973), pp. 1001–1007.

———, "Risk and the Required Return on Equity," *Journal of Finance*, 22 (March 1967), pp. 19–36.

———, and Pinkerton, John M., "The Valuation and the Cost of Capital of the Levered Firm with Growth Opportunities," *Journal of Finance*, 33 (March 1978), pp. 65–73.

Arditti, Fred D., and Tysseland, Milford S., "Three Ways to Present the Marginal Cost of Capital," *Financial Management*, 2 (Summer 1973), pp. 63–67.

Auerbach, Alan J., "Wealth Maximization and the Cost of Capital," *Quarterly Journal of Economics*, 43 (August 1979), pp. 433–446.

Barnea, Amir; Haugen, Robert A.; and Senbet, Lemma W., "Market Imperfections, Agency Problems, and Capital Structure: A Review," *Financial Management*, 10 (Summer 1981), pp. 7–22.

Beranek, William, "The Weighted Average Cost of Capital and Shareholder Wealth Maximization," *Journal of Financial and Quantitative Analysis*, 12 (March 1977), pp. 17–32.

Black, F., and Scholes, M., "The Pricing of Options and Corporate Liabilities," *Journal of Political Economy*, 81 (May-June 1973), pp. 637–654.

Boness, A. James, and Frankfurter, George M., "Evidence of Non-homogeneity of Capital Costs within 'Risk-Classes,'" *Journal of Finance*, 32 (June 1977), pp. 775–787.

Brennan, M. J., and Schwartz, E. S., "Corporate Income Taxes, Valuation, and the Problem of Optimal Capital Structure," *Journal of Business*, 51 (January 1978), pp. 103–114.

Castanias, Richard, "Bankruptcy Risk and Optimal Capital Structure," *Journal of Finance*, 38 (December 1983), pp. 1617–1635.

Chambers, Donald R.; Harris, Robert S.; and Pringle, John J., "Treatment of Financing Mix in Analyzing Investment Opportunities," *Financial Management*, 11 (Summer 1982), pp. 24–41.

Chen, Andrew, "Recent Developments in the Cost of Debt Capital," *Journal of Finance*, 33 (June 1978), pp. 863–883.

———, and Kim, E. Han, "Theories of Corporate Debt Policy: A Synthesis," *Journal of Finance*, 34 (May 1979), pp. 371–384.

Constantinides, George M., and Ingersoll, Jonathan E., Jr., "Tax Effects and Bond Prices," *Journal of Finance*, 37 (May 1982), pp. 349–352.

Cooper, Ian, and Franks, Julian R., "The Interaction of Financing and Investment Decisions When the Firm has Unused Tax Credits," *Journal of Finance*, 38 (May 1983), pp. 571–583.

Copeland, Thomas E., and Weston, J. Fred, *Financial Theory and Corporate Policy*, 3d Ed., Reading, Mass.: Addison-Wesley, 1987.

Cordes, Joseph J., and Sheffrin, Steven M., "Estimating the Tax Advantage of Corporate Debt," *Journal of Finance*, 38 (March 1983), pp. 95–105.

Davidson, Wallace N., III., "The Effect of Rate Cases on Public Utility Stock Returns," *Journal of Financial Research*, 7 (Spring 1984), pp. 81–93.

DeAngelo, H., and Masulis, R., "Optimal Capital Structure under Corporate and Personal Taxation," *Journal of Financial Economics*, 8 (March 1980), pp. 3–30.

Draper, Dennis W., and Findlay, M. Chapman, III., "A Note on Vickers' Marginal Cost of Debt Capital," *Journal of Business Finance & Accounting*, 9 (Winter 1982), pp. 579–582.

Dyl, Edward A., and Joehnk, Michael D., "Sinking Funds and the Cost of Corporate Debt," *Journal of Finance*, 34 (September 1979), pp. 887–893.

Ezzell, John R., and Porter, R. Burr, "Flotation Costs and the Weighted Average Cost of Capital," *Journal of Financial and Quantitative Analysis*, 11 (September 1976), pp. 403–414.

Fama, Eugene F., "Risk, Return, and Equilibrium: Some Clarifying Comments," *Journal of Finance*, 23 (March 1968), pp. 29–40.

———, and Miller, Merton H., *The Theory of Finance*, New York: Holt, Rinehart and Winston, 1972.

Feldstein, Martin; Green, Jerry; and Sheshinski, Eytan, "Corporate Financial Policy and Taxation in a Growing Economy," *Quarterly Journal of Economics*, 43 (August 1979), pp. 411–431.

———, "Inflation and Taxes in a Growing Economy with Debt and Equity Finance," *Journal of Political Economy*, 86 (April 1978), pp. S53–S70.

Fuller, Russell J., and Kerr, Halbert S., "Estimating the Divisional Cost of Capital: An Analysis of the Pure-Play Technique," *Journal of Finance*, 36 (December 1981), pp. 997–1009.

Gordon, M. J., "Leverage and the Value of a Firm Under a Progressive Personal Income Tax," *Journal of Banking and Finance*, 6 (December 1982), pp. 483–493.

Gordon, M. J., and Kwan, Clarence C. Y., "Debt Maturity, Default Risk, and Capital Structure," *Journal of Banking and Finance*, 3 (December 1979), pp. 313–329.

Grier, Paul, and Strebel, Paul, "An Implicit Clientele Test of the Relationship Between Taxation and Capital Structure," *Journal of Financial Research*, 6 (Summer 1983), pp. 163–174.

Gup, Benton E., and Norwood, Samuel W., III., "Divisional Cost of Capital: A Practical Approach," *Financial Management*, 11 (Spring 1982), pp. 20–24.

Hamada, Robert S., "Portfolio Analysis, Market Equilibrium and Corporation Finance," *Journal of Finance*, 24 (March 1969), pp. 13–32.

Harris, John M., Jr.; Roenfeldt, Rodney L.; and Cooley, Philip L., "Evidence of Financial Leverage Clienteles," *Journal of Finance*, 38 (September 1983), pp. 1125–1132.

Harris, Milton, and Raviv, Artur, "The Theory of Capital Structure," *Journal of Finance*, 46, No. 1 (March 1991), pp. 297–355.

Haugen, R. A., and Senbet, L. W., "New Perspectives on Informational Asymmetry," *Journal of Financial and Quantitative Analysis*, 14 (November 1979), pp. 671–694.

Heinkel, Robert, "A Theory of Capital Structure Relevance under Imperfect Information," *Journal of Finance*, 37 (December 1982), pp. 1141–1150.

Higgins, Robert C., "Growth, Dividend Policy and Capital Costs in the Electric Utility Industry," *Journal of Finance*, 29 (September 1974), pp. 1189–1201.

Hirshleifer, Jack, "Investment Decisions under Uncertainty: Applications of the State-Preference Approach," *Quarterly Journal of Economics*, 83 (May 1966), pp. 252–277.

Hite, Gailen L., "Leverage, Output Effects, and the M-M Theorems," *Journal of Financial Economics,* 4 (March 1977), pp. 177–202.

Hong, Hai, "Inflation and the Market Value of the Firm: Theory and Tests," *Journal of Finance,* 32 (September 1977), pp. 1031–1048.

Hsia, Chi-Cheng, "Optimal Debt of a Firm: An Option Pricing Approach," *Journal of Financial Research,* 4 (Fall 1981), pp. 221–231.

Huffman, Lucy, "Operating Leverage, Financial Leverage, and Equity Risk," *Journal of Banking and Finance,* 7 (June 1983), pp. 197–212.

Ibbotson, Roger G.; Diermeier, Jeffrey J.; and Siegel, Laurence B., "The Demand for Capital Market Returns: A New Equilibrium Theory," *Financial Analysts Journal,* 40 (January/February 1984), pp. 22–33.

Jensen, M. C., and Meckling, W., "Theory of the Firm: Managerial Behavior, Agency Costs and Capital Structure," *Journal of Financial Economics,* 3 (October 1976), pp. 11–25.

Keenan, Michael, "Models of Equity Valuation: The Great Serm Bubble," *Journal of Finance,* 25 (May 1970), pp. 243–273.

Kim, E. Han, "Miller's Equilibrium, Shareholder Leverage Clienteles and Optimal Capital Structure," *Journal of Finance,* 37 (May 1982), pp. 301–319.

———, "A Mean-Variance Theory of Optimal Capital Structure and Corporate Debt Capacity," *Journal of Finance,* 33 (March 1978), pp. 45–63.

———; Lewellen, Wilbur G.; and McConnell, John J., "Financial Leverage Clienteles: Theory and Evidence," *Journal of Financial Economics,* 7 (March 1979), pp. 83–109.

———; McConnell, John J.; and Greenwood, Paul R., "Capital Structure Rearrangements and Me-First Rules in an Efficient Capital Market," *Journal of Finance,* 32 (June 1977), pp. 789–810.

Krainer, Robert E., "Interest Rates, Leverage, and Investor Rationality," *Journal of Financial and Quantitative Analysis,* 12 (March 1977), pp. 1–16.

Kraus, Alan, and Litzenberger, Robert, "A State-Preference Model of Optimal Financial Leverage," *Journal of Finance,* 28 (September 1973), pp. 911–922.

Krouse, Clement G., "Optimal Financing and Capital Structure Programs for the Firm," *Journal of Finance,* 27 (December 1972), pp. 1057–1072.

Lee, Wayne Y., and Barker, Henry H., "Bankruptcy Costs and the Firm's Optimal Debt Capacity: A Positive Theory of Capital Structure," *Southern Economic Journal,* 43 (April 1977), pp. 1453–1465.

Leland, H. E., and Pyle, D. H., "Informational Asymmetries, Financial Structure, and Financial Intermediation," *Journal of Finance,* 32 (May 1977), pp. 371–387.

Lewellen, Wilbur G., "A Conceptual Reappraisal of Cost of Capital," *Financial Management,* 3 (Winter 1974), pp. 63–70.

———, *The Cost of Capital,* Belmont, Calif.: Wadsworth, 1969, Chapters 3–4.

———, and Ang, James S., "Inflation, Security Values, and Risk Premia," *Journal of Financial Research,* 5 (Summer 1982), pp. 105–123.

Lewellen, Wilbur G., and McConnell, John J., "Utility Rate Regulation," *Journal of Business Research,* 7, No. 2 (1979), pp. 117–138.

Litzenberger, Robert H., and Sosin, Howard B., "A Comparison of Capital Structure Decisions of Regulated and Non-Regulated Firms," *Financial Mangement,* 8 (Autumn 1979), pp. 17–21.

Marsh, Paul, "The Choice Between Equity and Debt: An Empirical Study," *Journal of Finance,* 37 (December 1982), pp. 121–144.

Masulis, Ronald W., "The Impact of Capital Structure Change on Firm Value: Some Estimates," *Journal of Finance,* 38 (March 1983), pp. 107–126.

———, "The Effects of Capital Structure Change on Security Prices: A Study of Exchange Offers," *Journal of Financial Economics,* 8 (June 1980), pp. 139–177.

Morris, James R., "Taxes, Bankruptcy Costs and the Existence of an Optimal Capital Structure," *Journal of Financial Research,* 5 (Fall 1982), pp. 285–299.

Myers, Stewart C., "Determinants of Corporate Borrowing," *Journal of Financial Economics,* 5 (November 1977), pp. 147–175.

Merton, Robert C., "On the Pricing of Corporate Debt: The Risk Structure of Interest

Rates," *Journal of Finance*, 29 (May 1974), pp. 449–470.

Miller, Merton H., "Debt and Taxes," *Journal of Finance*, 32 (May 1977), pp. 261–275.

———, and Modigliani, Franco, "Cost of Capital to Electric Utility Industry," *American Economic Review*, 56 (June 1966), pp. 333–391.

Modigliani, Franco, and Miller, Merton H., "The Cost of Capital, Corporation Finance and the Theory of Investment," *American Economic Review*, 48 (June 1958), pp. 261–297.

Myers, Stewart C., "The Capital Structure Puzzle," *Journal of Finance*, 39 (July 1984), pp. 575–592.

———, "Interactions of Corporate Financing and Investment Decisions — Implications for Capital Budgeting," *Journal of Finance*, 29 (March 1974), pp. 1–25.

Penrose, E. T., *The Theory of the Growth of the Firm*, New York: John Wiley and Sons, 1959.

Petry, Glenn H., "Empirical Evidence on Cost of Capital Weights," *Financial Management*, 4 (Winter 1975), pp. 58–65.

———, "An Unidentified Corporate Risk — Using the Wrong Cost of Funds," *MSU Business Topics*, Graduate School of Business Administration, Michigan State University, (Autumn 1975), pp. 57–65.

———, and Fuller, Russell J., "Inflation and Stock Prices," *American Association of Individual Investors Journal*, VI (January 1984), pp. 11–15.

Pettway, Richard H., and Jordan, Bradford D., "Diversification, Double Leverage, and the Cost of Capital," *Journal of Financial Research*, 6 (Winter 1983), pp. 289–300.

Phillips, Paul D.; Groth, John C.; and Richards, R. Malcolm, "Financing the Alaskan Project: The Experience at Sohio," *Financial Management*, 8 (Autumn 1979), pp. 7–16.

Protopapadakis, Aris, "Some Indirect Evidence on Effective Capital Gains Tax Rates," *Journal of Business*, 56 (April 1983), pp. 127–138.

Reilly, Raymond R., and Wecker, William E., "On the Weighted Average Cost of Capital," *Journal of Financial and Quantitative Analysis*, 8 (January 1973), pp. 123-126.

Reinganum, Marc R., "Abnormal Returns in Small Firm Portfolios," *Financial Analysts Journal*, 37 (March/April 1981), pp. 52–56.

Robichek, Alexander A., and Myers, Stewart C., *Optimal Financial Decisions*, Englewood Cliffs, N. J.: Prentice-Hall, 1965.

Ross, S. A., "The Determination of Financial Structure: The Incentive-Signalling Approach," *Bell Journal of Economics*, 8 (Spring 1977), pp. 23–40.

Rubinstein, Mark E., "A Mean-Variance Synthesis of Corporate Financial Theory," *Journal of Finance*, 28 (March 1973), pp. 167–181.

Scott, J. H., "Bankruptcy, Secured Debt, and Optimal Capital Structure," *Journal of Finance*, 32 (March 1977), pp. 1–19.

———, "A Theory of Optimal Capital Structure," *Bell Journal of Economics*, 7 (Spring 1976), pp. 33–54.

Scott, David F., Jr., and Johnson, Dana J., "Financing Policies and Practices in Large Corporations," *Financial Management*, 11 (Summer 1982), pp. 51–59.

Scott, David F., Jr., and Martin, John D., "Industry Influence on Financial Structure," *Financial Management*, 4 (Spring 1975), pp. 67–73.

Senbet, Lemma W., and Taggart, Robert A., Jr., "Capital Structure Equilibrium under Market Imperfections and Incompleteness," *Journal of Finance*, 39 (March 1984), pp. 93–103.

Shiller, Robert J., and Modigliani, Franco, "Coupon and Tax Effects on New and Seasoned Bond Yields and the Measurement of the Cost of Debt Capital," *Journal of Financial Economics*, 7 (September 1979), pp. 297–318.

Sosin, Howard B., "Neutral Recapitalizations: Predictions and Tests Concerning Valuation and Welfare," *Journal of Finance*, 33 (September 1978), pp. 1228–1234.

Stapleton, R. C., and Subrahmanyam, M. G., "Market Imperfections, Capital Market Equilibrium, and Corporation Finance," *Journal of Finance*, 32 (May 1977), pp. 307–319.

Taggart, Robert A., Jr., "A Model of Corporate Financing Decisions," *Journal of Finance*, 32 (December 1977), pp. 1467–1484.

Thompson, H., "Estimating the Cost of Equity Capital for Electric Utilities: 1958–1976," *Bell Journal of Economics,* 10 (Autumn 1979), pp. 619–635.

Titman, S., "The Effect of Capital Structure on a Firm's Liquidation Decision," *Journal of Financial Economics,* 13 (1984), pp. 137–183.

Turnbull, Stuart M., "Debt Capacity," *Journal of Finance,* 34 (September 1979), pp. 931–940.

————, "Debt Capacity: Erratum," *Journal of Finance,* 37 (March 1981), p. 197.

Vickers, Douglas, "The Cost of Capital and the Structure of the Firm," *Journal of Finance,* 25 (March 1970), pp. 35–46.

Warner, J., "Bankruptcy Costs: Some Evidence," *Journal of Finance,* 32 (May 1977), pp. 337–348.

Weinstein, Mark, "The Systematic Risk of Corporate Bonds," *Journal of Financial and Quantitative Analysis,* 16 (September 1981), pp. 257–278.

Weston, J. Fred, "A Test of Cost of Capital Propositions," *Southern Economic Journal,* 30 (October 1963), pp. 105–112.

————, and Lee, Wayne Y., "Cost of Capital for a Division of a Firm: Comment," *Journal of Finance,* 32 (December 1977), pp. 1779–1780.

Wippern, Ronald F., "Financial Structure and the Value of the Firm," *Journal of Finance,* 21 (December 1966), pp. 615–634.

APPENDIX A TO CHAPTER 15

The Modigliani-Miller Propositions: Some Extensions

COST OF CAPITAL FOR FINITE LIVES

Three equivalent formulas were set forth in Chapter 15 for measuring the weighted cost of capital. The one that brings out most clearly the effect of the tax benefits of using debt is Equation 15.23:

$$k = k_U (1 - TL). \qquad (15.23)$$

Thus, if $T = .4$ and $L = .5$, then $TL = .2$. Hence the weighted average cost of capital would be .8 of the unlevered cost of capital or

$$k = .8k_U.$$

Thus, if k_U were 15 percent, the weighted cost of capital would be 12 percent. The three percentage points by which the weighted cost of capital is below the unlevered cost of capital represent the tax benefit of the leverage employed. The expressions in Equation 15.23 and in the related MM valuation relationships are based on constant or unchanging cash flows, a perpetuity. Alternatively these could be considered one-period models. The question arises with respect to uneven cash flows from year to year in the setting of a finite project life. A number of materials have been developed on the subject. They are brought together very well in an analysis by Miles and Ezzell (ME) [1980]. Making no assumptions with regard to either the time pattern or the duration of the unlevered cash flows, ME developed the relationship between the unlevered cost of capital and the weighted cost of capital. The relationship depends on maintaining a constant leverage ratio throughout the project life. This means that as the value of the firm changes as a consequence of the investments made, the amount of debt outstanding has to be readjusted to maintain the constant leverage ratio. When these conditions are met, we obtain Equation 15A.1:

$$k = k_U - rTL\left(\frac{1 + k_U}{1 + r}\right), \tag{15A.1}$$

where

$$r = k_b = \text{cost of debt.}$$

Thus, the original MM relationship is modified somewhat. Let us explore its characteristics. For a corporate tax rate equal to .4 and a leverage ratio of .5 as before, TL is again .2. The expression then becomes

$$k = k_U - .2r\left(\frac{1 + k_U}{1 + r}\right).$$

In the previous example we had assumed k_U to be 15 percent. If the cost of debt were also 15 percent, then the last expression becomes 1 and the weighted cost of capital would again be 12 percent. This is a very special case, however. Normally we would expect the unlevered cost of equity capital to be somewhat higher than the cost of debt. If so, the ratio expression would be greater than 1. Continuing the previous example but with a cost of debt of 10 percent, we would have

$$k = k_U - .2(.1)\left(\frac{1.15}{1.10}\right)$$

$$= .1291.$$

In this case the weighted cost of capital would be somewhat higher than the weighted cost of capital under the infinite horizon case. On the other hand, if the cost of debt were greater than the unlevered cost of capital we would have

$$k = k_U - .2(.20)\left(\frac{1.15}{1.20}\right)$$

$$= .11167 \approx .112.$$

In this case the weighted cost of capital would be lower than the weighted cost of capital under the infinite horizon example. For finite project lives, the weighted cost of capital would be somewhat different from the result under the infinite horizon case. The advantage of the ME procedure is that the cash flow for each year of the finite life project would be discounted by the weighted cost of capital based on that year's data as calculated by the expression that ME have developed.

THE MM PROPOSITIONS WITH DEPRECIABLE ASSETS

Levy and Arditti (LA) [1973] presented an analysis which argued that MM propositions must be modified to recognize a reduction in the value of the firm when assets are depreciable. The issue of leverage is not involved, so we will focus on their unlevered firm case. In the basic LA equation for the unlevered firm, the firm's annual post-tax cash flows are

$$X^t = (1 - T)X + K - K, \tag{15A.2}$$

where $-K$ is the annual investment and $+K$ the depreciation charge, assumed to be equal in LA's model.

LA then state, "We claim that one cannot cancel the $+K$ and $-K$ terms and then apply the appropriate discount rates to the expected value of the resulting cash flow expression. The reason is that while the replacement outlay $(-K)$ is a certain amount, only a part of the $+K$ term is certain."[1] They reformulate Equation 15A.2 as

$$X^t = (1 - T)C + TK - K, \tag{15A.3}$$

where C is the annual pretax flow before depreciation and interest.

They observe:

> Thus, X^t is separated into two distinct components: (a) an uncertain stream equal to $(1 - T)C$, and (b) a certain stream equal to . . . $TK - K$ in the unlevered case. . . . So TK is a certain stream and should be capitalized by the riskless rate r. The annual investment flow, $-K$, must also be treated as a certain amount, since our model requires the firm to invest an amount equal to its depreciation expense in order to assure perpetual asset lives. Hence $TK - K$ may be treated as a certain stream.[2]

Their resulting valuation relationship is

$$V_U = \frac{(1 - T)\overline{C}}{\rho^t} - \frac{(1 - T)K}{r}, \tag{15A.4}$$

where "C denotes the expected cash flow . . . and ρ^t denotes . . . the required rate of return on a pure equity stream." They point out that their resulting valuation expression is smaller than the MM values by

$$\frac{1}{r} - \frac{1}{\rho^t}(1 - T)K,$$

and that the MM valuation expressions must be correspondingly reduced for the case of depreciable assets.

Paul [1975] commented that the LA results assume that their ρ^t is the same ρ^t used by MM to discount the unlevered firm's EBIT. All of LA's modifications assume that the same rate would be used to discount both the expected pretax operating cash flow ($\overline{C}$) and the expected EBIT ($\overline{X}$). Paul demonstrates the basic LA assumption cannot be made, consistent with the underlying nature of the models under analysis. The example she presents is reproduced in Table 15A.1.

Since the two firms have the same EBIT, they must have the same value. But if 10 percent is the applicable discount rate for Firm A, it has a value of $1,500. Using LA Equation 3, reproduced as Equation 15A.4, not changing ρ^t and using a 5 percent riskless

---

[1] See Levy and Arditti [1973], p. 688.
[2] Ibid., pp. 688–689.

TABLE 15A.1   Comparisons of Two Firms with Equal EBIT

Distribution of Annual Flows for Firm A with No Depreciable Assets

P	C = Pretax Operating Cash Flow	K = Depreciation	X = EBIT	Yᵃ = Net Cash Flow
0.2	150	0	150	90
0.5	200	0	200	120
0.3	400	0	400	240
1.0	$\bar{C} = 250$	$K = 0$	$\bar{X} = 250$	$\bar{Y} = 150$

Distribution of Annual Flows for Firm B with Depreciable Assets

P	C = Pretax Operating Cash Flow	K = Depreciation	X = EBIT	Yᵃ = Net Cash Flow
0.2	225	75	150	90
0.5	275	75	200	120
0.3	475	75	400	240
1.0	$\bar{C} = 325$	$K = 75$	$\bar{X} = 250$	$\bar{Y} = 150$

ᵃ$Y = [X(1 - T) + K] - K$, where the bracketed term represents after-tax operating cash flow and the $-K$ represents the capital outflow necessary to maintain the operating cash flow at its present level.
Source: R. S. Paul, "Comment," *Journal of Finance,* 30 (March 1975), p. 212.

rate gives a value of $1,050 for Firm B. This suggests that the discount rate for discounting $\bar{C}$ is not the same discount rate applicable to $\bar{X}$. Paul then demonstrates this analytically, using the symbol $\hat{\rho}^t$ (rho with a hat) to indicate the appropriate capitalization rate for $\bar{C}$. For the firms to have the same value, it follows that

$$\frac{(1 - T)\bar{C}_b}{\hat{\rho}^t} = \frac{(1 - T)\bar{C}_a}{\rho^t} + \frac{(1 - T)K}{r}. \tag{15A.5}$$

But C_a is the same as X_b with the same probability distributions, so with substitution we have the following relationship for any Firm B with depreciable assets:

$$\frac{(1 - T)\bar{C}_b}{\hat{\rho}^t} = \frac{(1 - T)\bar{X}_b}{\rho^t} + \frac{(1 - T)K}{r}. \tag{15A.6}$$

When we solve Equation 15A.6 for the first term on the right-hand side, we have the following result:

$$V_U = \frac{(1 - T)\bar{X}_b}{\rho^t} = \frac{(1 - T)\bar{C}_b}{\hat{\rho}^t} - \frac{(1 - T)K}{r}. \tag{15A.7}$$

The first equality is MM's original Proposition I. The second equality is LA's Equation 3 for depreciable assets, shown to be the same as MM's expression if $\hat{\rho}^t$ is changed appropriately. The basic point is that once $\bar{C}_b$ contains both the uncertain and certain cash flow stream components, it would be capitalized by a lower discount rate than $\bar{X}_b$, which contains only the uncertain cash flow streams. In their reply, LA acknowledged that $\hat{\rho}^t$ had to be 0.081 (below 0.10) for the equality to hold.[3] In so doing, they acknowledged the validity of the clarification presented by Paul. It appears that LA misinterpreted Paul's analysis since they concluded their reply to her as follows:

> It appears that Paul believes that the discount rate (in her example, 10 percent) is independent of the probability distribution of returns. Why else would she apply the same discount rate of 10 percent to stream C_a as well as stream C_b?[4]

But Paul did this only to emphasize that it resulted in unequal values for the two firms, which could not be the case, given the underlying facts and assumptions. In doing so, she established that $\hat{\rho}^t$ has to be lower than ρ^t. When this is recognized, MM's Proposition I applies as fully to the valuations of firms with depreciable assets as to firms with nondepreciable assets.

THE WEIGHTED AVERAGE COST OF CAPITAL AS A CUTOFF RATE

Another criticism is that the application of the weighted average cost of capital as derived in the MM propositions is incorrectly specified as an investment hurdle rate or for deriving the value of the firm. The expression we developed from the MM materials and now generally referred to as the "traditional textbook theory" is

$$V_L = \frac{\overline{X}(1 - T)}{k_s(S/V) + (1 - T)r(B/V)}. \tag{15A.8}$$

Here we again use r for k_b. But in developing other relationships, MM also have

$$V = \frac{\overline{X}(1 - T)}{k_U} + TB = \frac{\overline{X}(1 - T)}{k_U} + \frac{TrB}{r}. \tag{15A.9}$$

Building on the Equation 15A.9 relationship, Arditti and Levy (AL) [1977] proposed that the true valuation formula is

$$V_L^* = \frac{(\overline{X} - rB)(1 - T) + rB}{k(S/V) + r(B/V)} = \frac{\overline{X}(1 - T) + rBT}{k^*}. \tag{15A.10}$$

In the AL expression, the capitalization factor uses the before-tax cost of debt rather than the after-tax cost of debt and adds the interest tax shelter to the cash flows in the numerator to be capitalized. We shall demonstrate that the AL formulation is actually the same as the "traditional textbook" formulation and that when appropriately applied to projects gives the same results.[5]

We shall develop a proof that

$$V_L^* = V_L.$$

---

[3]See Levy and Arditti [1975].

[4]Ibid., p. 222.

[5]See similar demonstrations in the group of articles on the "Weighted Average Cost of Capital" in *Financial Management*, 8 (Summer 1979) by Boudreaux and Long; Ezzell and Porter; Ben-Horim, and Shapiro.

As before, let

$$L = B/V_L.$$

Then

$$k = rL(1 - T) + k_s(1 - L)$$
$$= rL - rLT + k_s(1 - L).$$

AL define $k*$ as

$$k* = rL + k_s(1 - L).$$

Thus,

$$k* = k + TrL$$
$$V_L^* = \frac{\bar{X}(1 - T) + rTLV_L^*}{k + rTL}. \tag{15A.11}$$

Multiply by the denominator of the right-hand side of Equation 15A.11:

$$V_L^*(k + rTL) = \bar{X}(1 - T) + rTLV_L^*$$
$$kV_L^* + rTLV_L^* = kV_L + rTLV_L^*. \tag{15A.12}$$

Cancel common terms on each side of Equation 15A.12:

$$V_L^* = V_L.$$

Therefore it has been established that the AL expression in Equation 15A.10 is identical to the MM formulation.

A numerical illustration can be provided from an example where:

$$\bar{X} = \$200,000$$
$$T = 40\%$$
$$k_s = 12.8571\%$$
$$k_b = r = 10\%$$
$$B = \$500,000$$
$$S = \$700,000$$
$$V_L = B + S = \$1,200,000$$
$$k_U = 12\%$$
$$k = 10\%.$$

For $k*$ we would have

$$k* = k + \frac{rBT}{V_L} = 0.10 + \frac{0.10(500,000)0.4}{1,200,000} = 0.10 + \frac{20,000}{1,200,000}$$
$$= 0.10 + 0.01667 = 0.11667 = 11.667\%.$$

Using the AL expression for V_L:

$$V_L^* = \frac{\overline{X}(1 - T) + rBT}{k^*} = \frac{120{,}000 + 0.10(500{,}000)0.4}{0.11667}$$

$$= \frac{120{,}000 + 20{,}000}{0.11667} = \frac{140{,}000}{0.11667} = \$1{,}200{,}000.$$

This is, of course, the same as the V_L we obtained before.

Project Evaluation

AL next evaluate a project with an investment cost, I, and an earnings annuity of Y in perpetuity. The standard NPV approach states:

$$\text{NPV} = \frac{\overline{Y}(1 - T)}{k} - I. \tag{15A.13}$$

AL state that the actual net present value is NPV* defined as:

$$\text{NPV*} = \frac{\overline{Y}(1 - T) + Tr(B/V)I}{k^*} - I. \tag{15A.14}$$

But this NPV* formulation is inconsistent in shifting to a book (investment) basis for leverage, while the market value of the firm increases by $(I + \text{NPV*})$. To maintain a constant leverage ratio, the firm must increase debt by an amount equal to $(I + \text{NPV*})(B/V)$. When we make the necessary adjustment to the NPV* formulations, we obtain Equation 15A.14a:

$$\text{NPV*} = \frac{\overline{Y}(1 - T) + Tr(B/V)(I + \text{NPV*})}{k^*} - I. \tag{15A.14a}$$

Expand the second term in the numerator:

$$\text{NPV*} = \frac{\overline{Y}(1 - T)}{k^*} + \frac{rT(B/V)I}{k^*} + \frac{rT(B/V)(\text{NPV*})}{k^*} - I.$$

Move NPV* term to left side of equation and factor out NPV*.

$$NPV*\left(1 - \frac{rTB}{k^*V}\right) = \frac{\overline{Y}(1 - T) + rT(B/V)I}{k^*} - I.$$

Multiply both sides by k^*.

$$NPV*\left(k^* - \frac{rTB}{V}\right) = \overline{Y}(1 - T) + rT(B/V)I - k^*I.$$

But the last two terms in the above equation are equal to kI, since $[k^* - rT(B/V)] = k$. Then we have

$$k\text{NPV*} = \overline{Y}(1 - T) - kI.$$

Next divide by k to obtain:

$$NPV^* = \frac{\overline{Y}(1 - T)}{k} - I = NPV.$$

Thus, when the target leverage ratio is maintained by applying it to the increase in the market value of the firm, instead of to the book value of the new investment, NPV* is equal to the traditional NPV.

We can continue our previous numerical example to illustrate the formal proof. Let I be $10,000 and $\overline{Y} = \$2,500$. Using the traditional measure of NPV, we have

$$NPV = \frac{\$2,500(0.6)}{0.10} - \$10,000 = \frac{1,500}{0.10} - \$10,000 = \$5,000.$$

The same data can be applied to the NPV* formulation as corrected in Equation 15A.14a. The value of NPV* that satisfies the corrected equation is $5,000:

$$NPV^* = \frac{\$1,500 + 0.4(0.10)(5/12)(15,000)}{0.116667} - \$10,000$$

$$= \$12,857 + \frac{5/12(600)}{0.116667} - \$10,000$$

$$= \$12,857 + \frac{250}{0.116667} - \$10,000$$

$$= \$5,000 = NPV.$$

Again, the proposed reformulation actually reinforces the MM relationships when used in a manner consistent with the underlying theory.

SELECTED REFERENCES

Arditti, F. D., and Levy, H., "The Weighted Average Cost of Capital as a Cutoff Rate: A Critical Analysis of the Classical Textbook Weighted Average," *Financial Management,* 6 (Fall 1977), pp. 24–34.

Boudreaux, K. J., et al., "The Weighted Average Cost of Capital: A Discussion," *Financial Management,* 8 (Summer 1979), pp. 7–14.

Hite, Gailen L., "Leverage, Output Effects, and the M-M Theorems," *Journal of Financial Economics,* 4 (March 1977), pp. 177–202.

Levy, H., and Arditti, F. D., "Valuation, Leverage, and the Cost of Capital in the Case of Depreciable Assets," *Journal of Finance,* 28 (June 1973), pp. 687–693.

———, "Reply," *Journal of Finance,* 30 (March 1975), pp. 221–223.

Martin, John D.; Scott, David F., Jr.; and Vandell, Robert F., "Equivalent Risk Classes: A Multidimensional Examination," *Journal of Financial and Quantitative Analysis,* 14 (March 1979), pp. 101–118.

Miles, J. A., and Ezzell, J. R., "The Weighted Average Cost of Capital, Perfect Capital Markets, and Project Life: A Clarification," *Journal of Financial and Quantitative Analysis,* 15 (September 1980), pp. 719–729.

Miller, Merton H., "Debt and Taxes," *Journal of Finance,* 32 (May 1977), pp. 261–275.

———, and Modigliani, Franco, "Cost of Capital to Electric Utility Industry," *American*

Economic Review, 56 (June 1966), pp. 333–391.

Modigliani, Franco, and Miller, Merton H., "The Cost of Capital, Corporation Finance and the Theory of Investment," *American Economic Review,* 48 (June 1958), pp. 261–297.

————, "Taxes and the Cost of Capital: A

Correction," *American Economic Review,* 53 (June 1963), pp. 433–443.

Paul, R. S., "Comment," *Journal of Finance,* 30 (March 1975), pp. 211–213.

Stiglitz, Joseph E., "A Re-examination of the Modigliani-Miller Theorem," *American Economic Review,* 59 (December 1969), pp. 784–793.

APPENDIX B TO CHAPTER 15

The State-Preference Model[1]

Three important recent developments in finance are the Capital Asset Pricing Model (CAPM), the State-Preference Model (SPM), and the Option Pricing Model (OPM). The Capital Asset Pricing Model is presented in Chapters 10 and 11. The Option Pricing Model is set forth in Chapter 12. In this appendix we describe the State-Preference Model to conclude the discussion of financial leverage.

ALTERNATIVE FUTURE STATES-OF-THE-WORLD

The State-Preference Model provides a useful way of looking at the world and the nature of securities. One way of describing uncertainty about the future is to say that one of a set of possible states-of-the-world will occur. Definition of a set of states provides a means of describing characteristics of securities, since any security can be regarded as a contract to pay an amount that depends on the state that actually occurs.

For example, the decision to invest in the securities of a machinery manufacturer or the decision of a machinery manufacturer to issue securities under a favorable set of conditions will depend on the potential future states of the economy. Will the economy be sufficiently strong that the demand for capital goods will provide favorable demand factors for a machinery manufacturer? Similarly, in the production plans of an automobile manufacturer, or in an investor's decision to buy securities of an automobile company, will the future state of the economy be sufficiently strong to stimulate consumer optimism, resulting in a high volume of automobile purchases? Some of the main factors influencing the future states-of-the-world that will influence the sales of a firm or the prospects for investments in a firm are set forth in Table 15B.1.

As a practical matter, a person will explicitly consider only a small number of factors in making a decision. Hence individual decision makers are likely to select those variables

---

[1]This section was written with the valuable counsel of Professor Harry DeAngelo.

TABLE 15B.1   Central Factors Influencing Estimates of Future States-of-the-World for Use in Forecasting the Sales of the Firm

A. Economy

1. Growth rate of GNP—real terms
2. Growth rate of GNP—inflation
3. Growth rate of monetary base (availability)
4. Long-term interest rates
5. Short-term interest rates

B. Competition

1. Prices of rival products
2. New products by rivals
3. Changes in products by rivals
4. New advertising campaigns by rivals
5. Salesperson and other selling efforts by rivals
6. Prices of industry-substitute products
7. Quality of industry-substitute products

C. Cultural and political factors

1. Externalities and their influences on sales of our products
2. Product liabilities

judged to be most critical for influencing the payoff possibilities of securities in which a position or investment is contemplated. For practical reasons, therefore, alternative future states-of-the-world might be summarized into forecasts of alternative levels or rates of growth in the gross national product. Ultimately, a wide variety of the factors listed in Table 15B.1 are likely to be reflected in levels of gross national product. Furthermore, the rate of growth and the performance of most individual industries in the economy are greatly influenced by movements in gross national product. Thus, alternative future states-of-the-world may be characterized in terms of four possibilities with respect to gross national product: a strong rate of growth, a moderate rate of growth, a moderate decline, or a substantial decline.

While for practical problems we might limit the number of alternative future states-of-the-world, from another standpoint—that of personal portfolio construction—we would like to provide for all possible future states-of-the-world. If we could always find a security that provided some payoff under one of the many possible future states-of-the-world, we could hedge by combining a large number of securities so that regardless of the future state-of-the-world that occurs, we would receive some payoff. The securities we encounter in the real world are complex securities in the sense that their payoffs are generally different under alternative states-of-the-world. If we could obtain some payoff for every possible future state-of-the-world by appropriately combining long and short positions in actual complex securities, we could create a pure, or primitive, security.

TABLE 15B.2   Payoffs in Relation to Prices of Baskets of Fruit

	Bananas	Apples	Prices
Basket #1	10	20	$8
Basket #2	30	10	$9

THE CONCEPT OF A PURE SECURITY

A pure, or primitive, security is one that pays off $1 if one particular future state-of-the-world occurs and pays off nothing if any other state-of-the-world occurs. This seems like an abstract concept, so let us develop the idea further by means of an example. We shall take the case of the Mistinback Company, which sells baskets of fruit. This particular company limits its sales to only two types of baskets. Basket 1 is composed of 10 bananas and 20 apples and sells for $8. Basket 2 is composed of 30 bananas and 10 apples and sells for $9. The question is posed: What is the price of one banana or one apple only? The situation may be summarized by the payoffs set forth in Table 15B.2.

To calculate the value of a banana or an apple, we set up two equations:

$$10\ V_b + 20\ V_a = \$8$$
$$30\ V_b + 10\ V_a = \$9.$$

Solving simultaneously, we obtain:

$$V_a = \$.30$$
$$V_b = \$.20.$$

We may now apply this same analysis to securities. Any individual security is similar to a mixed basket of goods with regard to alternative future states-of-the-world. Recall that a pure security is a security that pays $1 if a specified state occurs and nothing if any other state occurs.[2]

We can determine the price of a pure security in a manner analogous to that used for the fruit baskets. Consider Security j, which pays $10 if State 1 occurs and $20 if State 2 occurs. The current price of Security j is $8. Security k pays $30 if State 1 occurs and $10 if State 2 occurs. Its current price is $9. Note that State 1 might be a GNP growth during the year of 8 percent in real terms, while State 2 might represent a growth in real national product of only 1 percent. In Table 15B.3 the payoff for the two securities is set forth. Here, F_{j1} is the payoff in State 1 to Security j, F_{k1} is the payoff in State 1 to Security k,

---

[2]Observe that this is a clear form of nondiversification. It represents putting all of one's financial resources into one state-basket.

TABLE 15B.3 Payoff Table for Securities 1 and 2

	State 1	State 2	
Security j	$F_{j1} = \$10$	$F_{j2} = \$20$	$p_j = \$8$
Security k	$F_{k1} = \$30$	$F_{k2} = \$10$	$p_k = \$9$

and so on. The equations for determining the prices for the two pure securities related to the situation described are

$$p_1 F_{j1} + p_2 F_{j2} = p_j$$
$$p_1 F_{k1} + p_2 F_{k2} = p_k.$$

Proceeding analogously to the situation for the fruit baskets, we insert the value of security payoffs into the two equations to obtain the price of Pure Security 1 as $.20 and the price of Pure Security 2 as $.30.

$$10p_1 + 20p_2 = \$8$$
$$30p_1 + 10p_2 = \$9$$
$$p_1 = \$.20$$
$$p_2 = \$.30.$$

It should be emphasized that the p_1 of $.20 and the p_2 of $.30 are not assigned to Securities j and k.

In sum, Securities j and k represent bundles of returns under alternative future states. Any actual security provides different payoffs for different future states. But under appropriately defined conditions, the prices of pure securities can be determined from the prices of actual securities. The concept of a pure security is useful for analytical purposes as well as for providing a useful point of view in financial analysis as illustrated in the following section, which provides an application of the State-Preference Model to leverage decisions.

USE OF THE SPM TO DETERMINE THE OPTIMAL FINANCIAL LEVERAGE

The State-Preference Model has been used to analyze the question of optimal financial leverage.[3] The ideas will be conveyed by a specific example. It is assumed that there are four possible states-of-the-world and that the capital markets are complete in that there exists at least one security for every possible state-of-the-world such that there is a full set

---

[3]See Kraus and Litzenberger [1973].

of primitive securities. The symbols that will be utilized are listed in Table 15B.4, and the data that will be analyzed in this example are summarized in Table 15B.5.

TABLE 15B.4   Symbols Used in the SPM Analysis of Optimal Financial Leverage

p_s = Market price of the primitive security that represents a claim on one dollar in State s and zero dollars in all other states
X_s = Earnings before interest and taxes that the firm will achieve in State s (EBIT)
B = Nominal payment to debt, representing a promise to pay Fixed Amount B, irrespective of the state that occurs
$S(B)$ = Market value of the firm's equity as a function of the amount of debt issued by the firm
$V(B)$ = Market value of the firm as a function of the amount of debt issued
f_s = Costs of failure in State s; $0 < f_s \leq X_s$
T = Corporate tax rate = 50%

TABLE 15B.5   Data for SPM Analysis of Optimal Financial Leverage

s (1)	X_s (2)	p_s (3)	f_s (4)
1	$ 100	$0.30	$ 100
2	500	0.50	400
3	1,000	0.20	500
4	2,000	0.10	1,200

In Table 15B.5 we have ordered the states by the size of the EBIT that the firm will achieve under alternative states. Column (3) of the table lists the prices of primitive securities for each of the four states. In Column (4) we list the failure or bankruptcy costs associated with the inability to meet debt obligations.

In this state-preference framework, let us analyze the position of debtholders and equity holders. Table 15B.6 analyzes the amounts received under alternative conditions. Under Condition 1 the EBIT is equal to or exceeds the debt obligation. Under that condition, debtholders will receive B and equity holders will receive the income remaining after deduction of B and of taxes. Under Condition 2, the EBIT is positive but less than the amount of the debt obligation, B. The debtholders will receive whatever EBIT remains after payment of the failure or bankruptcy costs. Equity holders will receive nothing. If the EBIT is negative, neither the debtholders nor equity holders receive anything. These relationships are quite logical and straightforward.

The amounts received under alternative conditions as outlined in Table 15B.7 are multiplied by the prices of the primitive securities to obtain the value of debtholders' receipts and of equity holders' receipts as well as the value of the firm under alternative conditions. The value of debtholders' receipts is obtained by simply multiplying what the

TABLE 15B.6   Amounts Received under Alternative Conditions

Condition	Amount of X_s in Relation to B (1)	Debtholders Receive (2)	Equity Holders Receive (3)
1	$X_s \geq B$	B	$(X_s - B)(1 - T)$
2	$0 \leq X_s < B$	$(X_s - f_s)$	0
3	$X_s < 0$	0	0

TABLE 15B.7   Formulas for the Value of the Firm under Alternative Conditions

Condition	Amount of X_s in Relation to B (1)	Debt-holders Receive (2)	Value of Debtholders' Receipts in State s (3)	Equity Holders Receive (4)	Value of Equity Holders' Receipts in State s (5)	Value of the Firm in State s (6)
1	$X_s \geq B$	B	Bp_s	$(X_s - B)(1 - T)$	$(X_s - B)(1 - T)p_s$	$Bp_s + (X_s - B)(1 - T)p_s$
2	$0 \leq X_s < B$	$(X_s - f_s)$	$(X_s - f_s)p_s$	0	0	$(X_s - f_s)p_s$
3	$X_s < 0$	0	0	0	0	0

debtholders receive by p_s and similarly for the value of equity holders' receipts. The value of the firm is obtained by adding the value of the debtholders' receipts to the value of the equity holders' receipts.

In Table 15B.8 we utilize the preceding information to calculate the value of the firm under alternative debt levels. On the left-hand side of the table we begin by specifying the amount of debt and the resulting relationships between X_s, the EBIT under alternative states, and the promised debt payment. The subsequent lines on the left then set forth the applicable formulas for calculating the state contingent value of the firm depending upon the level of debt utilized. For example, when the firm is unlevered, its value is equal to EBIT times (1 minus the tax rate) times the price of the primitive security for each state summed over all the states. Using the illustrative data from Table 15B.5, we obtain the amounts on the right-hand column of Table 15B.8.

When debt is 100, EBIT is equal to or greater than debt for all states-of-the-world. The formula employed, therefore, is set forth in Table 15B.7 under Condition 1 and shown in Column (6). Again, the numbers from Table 15B.5 are inserted to obtain a current market value of the firm, $V(100)$, of $395 for Debt Level 2 in Table 15B.8.

We shall discuss the pattern for debt of $1,000 as illustrative of the remaining sections of Table 15B.8. When B is equal to $1,000 the EBIT is less than the promised debt payment for States 1 and 2 and equal to or greater than debt for States 3 and 4. As Table 15B.7 indicates, Condition 2, therefore, obtains for States 1 and 2, while Condition 1 obtains for States 3 and 4. The applicable formulas are therefore utilized to obtain a $V(1,000)$ of $400, as shown in Table 15B.8.

TABLE 15B.8   Calculations of the Value of the Firm under Alternative Debt Levels

Condition	State	Value of Firm's State s Payoff
1. $\underline{B = 0, \ X_s > B \text{ for all } s}$ $V_s(0) = \sum_{s=1}^{4} X_s(1 - T)p_s$	1 2 3 4	$100(0.5)0.3 = \quad 15$ $500(0.5)0.5 = \quad 125$ $1{,}000(0.5)0.2 = \quad 100$ $2{,}000(0.5)0.1 = \quad 100$ $\overline{}$ $V(0) = \$340$
2. $\underline{B = 100, \ X_s \geq B \text{ for all } s}$ $V_s(100) = \sum_{s=1}^{4} Bp_s + \sum_{s=1}^{4}(X_s - B)(1 - T)p_s$	1 2 3 4	$100(0.3) + (100 - 100)0.3 = \quad 30$ $100(0.5) + (500 - 100)(0.5)0.5 = \quad 150$ $100(0.2) + (1{,}000 - 100)(0.5)0.2 = \quad 110$ $100(0.1) + (2{,}000 - 100)(0.5)0.1 = \quad 105$ $\overline{}$ $V(100) = \$395$
3. $\underline{\begin{array}{l} B = 500, \ X_s < B \text{ for } s = 1 \\ X_s \geq B \text{ for } s = 2, 3, 4 \end{array}}$ $V_s(500) = (X_s - f_s)p_s \text{ for } s = 1$ $V_s(500) = \sum_{s=2}^{4} Bp_s + \sum_{s=2}^{4}(X_s - B)(1 - T)p_s$	1 2 3 4	$(100 - 100)0.3 = \quad 0$ $500(0.5) + (500 - 500)(0.5)0.5 = \quad 250$ $500(0.2) + (1{,}000 - 500)(0.5)0.2 = \quad 150$ $500(0.1) + (2{,}000 - 500)(0.5)0.1 = \quad 125$ $V(500) = \$525$
4. $\underline{\begin{array}{l} B = 1{,}000, \ X_s < B \text{ for } s = 1, 2 \\ X_s \geq B \text{ for } s = 3, 4 \end{array}}$ $V_s(1{,}000) = \sum_{s=1}^{2} (X_s - f_s)p_s$ $V_s(1{,}000) = \sum_{s=3}^{4} Bp_s + \sum_{s=3}^{4}(X_s - B)(1 - T)p_s$	1 2 3 4	$(100 - 100)0.3 = \quad 0$ $(500 - 400)0.5 = \quad 50$ $1{,}000(0.2) + (1{,}000 - 1{,}000)(0.5)0.2 = \quad 200$ $1{,}000(0.1) + (2{,}000 - 1{,}000)(0.5)0.1 = \quad 150$ $V(1{,}000) = \$400$
5. $\underline{\begin{array}{l} B = 2{,}000, \ X_s < B \text{ for } s = 1, 2, 3 \\ X_s \geq B \text{ for } s = 4 \end{array}}$ $V_s(2{,}000) = \sum_{s=1}^{3} (X_s - f_s)p_s$ $V_s(2{,}000) = Bp_s + (X_s - B)(1 - T)p_s \text{ for } s = 4$	1 2 3 4	$(100 - 100)0.3 = \quad 0$ $(500 - 400)0.5 = \quad 50$ $(1{,}000 - 500)0.2 = \quad 100$ $2{,}000(0.1) + (2{,}000 - 2{,}000)(0.5)0.1 = \quad 200$ $V(2{,}000) = \$350$

An analysis of Table 15B.8 shows that the highest value of the firm is obtained when debt leverage of $500 is employed by the firm. For any other level of debt obligations the value of the firm is lower. This example illustrates that with taxes and bankruptcy costs, there exists an optimal amount of leverage.[4]

---

[4]Kraus and Litzenberger conclude with regard to their analysis as follows: "Contrary to the traditional net income approach to valuation, if the firm's debt obligation exceeds its earnings in some states the firm's market value is not necessarily a concave (from below) function of its debt obligation." Ibid., p. 918. However, this result follows only from their formulation of the problem in discontinuous terms. The problem could equally well be formulated with continuous functions in such a way that the resulting value of the firm would be a continuous and concave (from below) function of B.

IMPLICATIONS FOR LEVERAGE DECISIONS

Our use of the State-Preference Model has enabled us to analyze some conditions under which an optimal capital leverage exists.[5] This result is, of course, not perfectly general since it was based on a specific illustration. Some more general relationships will now be set forth. First, we need to introduce the concept of complete capital markets. *Complete capital markets* are those in which a security exists for every possible state-of-the-world, so that it is possible to create a full set of primitive securities. In complete capital markets, in the absence of such imperfections as taxes, agency costs, and bankruptcy costs, capital structure would not matter (the Modigliani-Miller propositions would obtain).

The leverage policy of a firm consists of repackaging the claims on its EBIT. The only reason why repackaging of claims on the firm's EBIT would have an effect on the value of the firm would be that the firm had thereby provided investors with a new set of market opportunities for forming portfolios or taking a position with regard to future states-of-the-world. But if the capital markets are already complete, the firm has added nothing by a repackaging of claims on EBIT since no new independent investment opportunities can be provided. All possible future states-of-the-world have already been covered by existing securities.

The proof of the Modigliani-Miller independence thesis does not depend on the assumption that the firm will always meet its debt obligations. For some debt levels the firm may not meet its debt obligations in some states-of-the-world and would be bankrupt. If there are no bankruptcy penalties or bankruptcy costs (the situation in a perfect market), the *nature* of the claims on the firm's EBIT have been fundamentally unaltered. Thus, the value of the firm remains unchanged.

Thus, complete and perfect capital markets constitute sufficient conditions for the Modigliani-Miller propositions to hold. But as the foregoing example illustrated, the taxation of corporate profits and the existence of bankruptcy-agency penalties represent market imperfections under which the capital structure choice will affect the value of the firm. We conclude that Modigliani and Miller are correct under properly specified conditions.

Furthermore, it is the absence of complete and perfect capital markets that makes capital structure matter. It is not clear whether the actual number of securities approximates the condition of completeness of the capital markets. However, without question there are corporate income taxes as well as agency and bankruptcy costs. The extent to which agency and bankruptcy costs significantly affect capital structure is an empirical matter.

PROBLEMS

15B.1 Security A pays $30 if State 1 occurs and $10 if State 2 occurs. Security B pays $20 if State 1 occurs and $40 if State 2 occurs. The price of Security A is $5 and the price of Security B is $10.

---

[5]Problems 15B.4 and 15B.5 illustrate that the production decisions and capital structure decisions of the firm can be interdependent, given the presence of imperfections.

    a. Set up the payoff table for Securities A and B.

    b. Determine the prices of pure Securities 1 and 2.

15B.2 The common stock of GM will pay $70 if State 1 occurs, in which the U.S. economy is in an upswing and GM's production volume of small cars causes the volume of imports to decline. In State 2, the U.S. economy experiences stagflation, with real growth at 1 percent per year and inflation near the two-digit rate. In State 2, the common stock of GM pays $35. In State 2, Control Data pays $68. In State 1, Control Data pays $55. The current price of GM is $53, and the current price of Control Data is $60.

    a. Set up the payoff tables for GM and Control Data.

    b. Determine the prices of the two pure securities.

15B.3 The Sand Corporation is evaluating alternatives for financing its production. There are essentially three possible levels of production, depending on which state-of-the-world occurs. Costs of failure and earnings before interest and taxes are different for each state. The company is considering use of debt in the amount of $0, $1,000, $3,000, or $6,000 and would like to know which alternative will maximize the expected value of the firm, given the primitive security prices associated with each state. The tax rate is 40 percent.

State	Planned Production EBIT	Price of Primitive Security	Cost of Failure
(s)	(X_s)	(p_s)	(f_s)
1	$2,000	0.30	$ 500
2	4,000	0.50	1,500
3	8,000	0.20	4,000

15B.4 The Kendrick Company is evaluating three alternative production plans $(X_s, Y_s,$ and $Z_s)$, as follows. Cost of failure is the same for each plan. Prices of primitive securities for the four possible states are as indicated.

State	Price of Primitive Security	Cost of Failure	Planned Production EBIT		
(s)	(p_s)	(f_s)	(X_s)	(Y_s)	(Z_s)
1	0.10	$ 100	$ 200	$ 600	$ 100
2	0.40	600	1,200	1,500	800
3	0.30	1,500	3,000	2,800	3,200
4	0.20	2,000	3,500	3,000	3,800

Assuming the production will be financed with funds including $3,000 of debt, which of the three production plans would maximize the value of the firm? The tax rate is 40 percent.

15B.5 Under production Plan A, the EBIT of the firm for alternative states-of-the-world is indicated by the X_s column. The price of the primitive pure securities in State s is p_s. The failure or bankruptcy costs are f_s. Under production Plan B, the EBIT of the firm is indicated by X_s'. Production Plan B involves giving up $300 in State 3 to add $300 in State 2. Since the prices of pure securities and bankruptcy costs are given by the market, they remain unchanged under production Plan B. The tax rate is 40 percent.

s	X_s	p_s	f_s	X_s'
1	$ 500	0.20	$100	$ 500
2	600	0.40	300	900
3	1,400	0.30	500	1,100
4	2,000	0.10	800	2,000

a. What is the optimal financial leverage for production Plan A by the criterion of maximizing the value of the firm? Calculate the value for debt levels of $0, $500, $600, $1,400, and $2,000.

b. Is the optimal financial leverage changed by new production Plan B? Answer for debt levels of $0, $500, $900, $1,100, and $2,000.

c. What implications do the results under Plans A and B have for the interdependence between production plans and financial structure?

SELECTED REFERENCES

Arrow, K. J., "The Role of Securities in the Optimal Allocation of Risk-Bearing," *Review of Economic Studies,* 31 (April 1964), pp. 91–96.

Dyl, Edward A., "A State Preference Model of Capital Gains Taxation," *Journal of Financial and Quantitative Analysis,* 14 (September 1979), pp. 529–535.

Hirshleifer, J., "Investment Decisions under Uncertainty: Application of the State-Preference Approach," *Quarterly Journal of Economics,* 80 (May 1966), pp. 262–277.

Kraus, Alan, and Litzenberger, Robert, "A State-Preference Model of Optimal Financial Leverage," *Journal of Finance,* 28 (September 1973), pp. 911–922.

CHAPTER 16

Dividend Policy

Dividend policy determines the division of earnings between payments to stockholders and reinvestment in the firm. Retained earnings are one of the most significant sources of funds for financing corporate growth, but dividends constitute the cash flows that accrue to stockholders. This chapter analyzes the factors that influence the allocation of earnings to dividends or retained earnings. It also discusses the relationship between dividend payouts and share prices.

DIVIDEND PAYMENTS

Dividends are normally paid quarterly. For example, suppose Liggett Group pays annual dividends of $2.50. In financial parlance we say that Liggett Group's regular quarterly dividend is 62.5 cents, or that its regular annual dividend is $2.50. The management of a company such as Liggett Group conveys to stockholders, sometimes by an explicit statement in the annual report and sometimes by implication, an expectation that the regular dividend will be maintained if at all possible. Furthermore, management conveys its belief that earnings will be sufficient to maintain the dividend.

Many variables influence dividends, however. For example, a firm's cash flows and investment needs may be too volatile for it to set a very high regular dividend. Yet, it may desire a high dividend payout to distribute funds not necessary for reinvestment. In such a case, the directors can set a relatively low regular dividend — low enough that it can be maintained even in low profit years or in years when a considerable amount of reinvestment is needed — and supplement it with an extra dividend in years when excess funds are available. General Motors, whose earnings fluctuate widely from year to year, often followed the practice of supplementing its regular dividend with an extra dividend paid in addition to the regular fourth quarter dividend.

Payment Procedure

The actual payment procedure is of some importance, and the following is an outline of the payment sequence.

1. *Declaration date*. The directors meet, say, on November 15 and declare the regular dividend. On this date, they issue a statement similar to the following: "On November 15, 19X0, the directors of the XYZ Company met and declared the regular quarterly dividend of 50 cents a share, plus an extra dividend of 75 cents a share, to holders of record on December 15, payment to be made on January 2, 19X1."

2. *Holder-of-record date*. On December 15, the *holder-of-record date,* the company closes its stock transfer books and makes up a list of the shareholders as of that date. If XYZ Company is notified of the sale and transfer of some stock before December 16, the new owner receives the dividend. If notification is received on or after December 16, the old stockholder gets the dividend.

3. *Ex-dividend date*. Suppose Irma Jones buys 100 shares of stock from Robert Noble on December 13. Will the company be notified of the transfer in time to list her as new owner and pay her the dividend? To avoid conflict, the brokerage business has set up a convention of declaring that the right to the dividend remains with the stock until four days prior to the holder-of-record date; on the fourth day before the record date, the right to the dividend no longer goes with the shares. The date when the right to the dividend leaves the stock is called the *ex-dividend date*. In this case, the ex-dividend date is four days prior to December 15, or December 11. Therefore, if Jones is to receive the dividend, she must buy the stock by December 10. If she buys it on December 11 or later, Noble will receive the dividend. The total dividend, regular plus extra, amounts to $1.25, so the ex-dividend date is important. Barring fluctuations in the stock market, we would normally expect the price of a stock to drop by approximately the amount of the dividend on the ex-dividend date.

4. *Payment date*. The company actually mails the checks to the holders of record on January 2, the payment date.

FACTORS INFLUENCING DIVIDEND POLICY

What factors determine the extent to which a firm will pay out dividends instead of retaining earnings? As a first step toward answering this question, we shall consider some of the factors that influence dividend policy. Note that although they may affect the payment of dividends, there is no necessary relationship between these factors and actual dividend policy.

Legal Rules

Although some statutes and court decisions governing dividend policy are complicated, their essential nature can be stated briefly. The legal rules provide that dividends must be paid from earnings — either from the current year's earnings or from past years' earnings as reflected in the balance sheet account "retained earnings."

State laws emphasize three rules: (1) the net profits rule, (2) the capital impairment rule, and (3) the insolvency rule. The *net profits rule* provides that dividends can be paid from past and present earnings. The *capital impairment rule* protects creditors by forbidding the payment of dividends from capital. (Paying dividends from capital would be distributing the investment in a company rather than earnings.)[1] The *insolvency rule* provides that corporations cannot pay dividends while insolvent. (*Insolvency* is defined here, in the bankruptcy sense, as liabilities exceeding assets. To pay dividends under such conditions would mean giving stockholders funds that rightfully belong to creditors.)

Legal rules are significant in that they provide the framework within which dividend policies can be formulated. Within their boundaries, however, financial and economic factors have a major influence on policy.

Liquidity Position

Profits held as retained earnings (which show up on the right-hand side of the balance sheet) are generally invested in assets required for the conduct of the business. Retained earnings from preceding years are already invested in plant and equipment, inventories, and other assets; they are not held as cash. Thus, even if a firm has a record of earnings, it may not be able to pay cash dividends because of its liquidity position. Indeed, a growing firm, even a very profitable one, typically has a pressing need for funds. In such a situation the firm may elect not to pay cash dividends.

Need to Repay Debt

When a firm has issued debt to finance expansion or to substitute for other forms of financing, it is faced with two alternatives. It can refund the debt at maturity by replacing it with another form of security, or it can make provisions for paying off the debt. If the decision is to retire the debt, this will generally require the retention of earnings.

Restrictions in Debt Contracts

Debt contracts, particularly when long-term debt is involved, frequently restrict a firm's ability to pay cash dividends. Such restrictions, which are designed to protect the position of the lender, usually state that (1) future dividends can be paid only out of earnings generated *after* the signing of the loan agreement (that is, they cannot be paid out of past retained earnings) and (2) that dividends cannot be paid when net working capital (current

---

[1]It is possible, of course, to return stockholders' capital; when this is done, however, the procedure must be clearly stated as such. A dividend paid out of capital is called a *liquidating* dividend.

assets minus current liabilities) is below a specified amount. Similarly, preferred stock agreements generally state that no cash dividends can be paid on the common stock until all accrued preferred dividends have been paid.

Rate of Asset Expansion

The more rapidly a firm is growing, the greater its needs for financing asset expansion. The greater the future need for funds, the more likely the firm is to retain earnings rather than pay them out. If a firm seeks to raise funds externally, natural sources are the present shareholders, who already know the company. But if earnings are paid out as dividends and are subjected to high personal income tax rates, only a portion of them will be available for reinvestment.

Profit Rate

The expected rate of return on assets determines the relative attractiveness of paying out earnings in the form of dividends to stockholders (who will use them elsewhere) or using them in the present enterprise.

Stability of Earnings

A firm that has relatively stable earnings is often able to predict approximately what its future earnings will be. Such a firm is therefore more likely to pay out a higher percentage of its earnings than is a firm with fluctuating earnings. The unstable firm is not certain that in subsequent years the hoped-for earnings will be realized, so it is likely to retain a high proportion of current earnings. A lower dividend will be easier to maintain if earnings fall off in the future.

Access to the Capital Markets

A large, well-established firm with a record of profitability and stability of earnings has easy access to capital markets and other forms of external financing. A small, new, or venturesome firm, however, is riskier for potential investors. Its ability to raise equity or debt funds from capital markets is restricted, and it must retain more earnings to finance its operations. A well-established firm is thus likely to have a higher dividend payout rate than is a new or small firm.

Control

Another important variable is the effect of alternative sources of financing on the control situation of the firm. As a matter of policy, some corporations expand only to the extent of their internal earnings. This policy is defended on the ground that raising funds by selling additional common stock dilutes the control of the dominant group in that company. At the same time, selling debt increases the risks of fluctuating earnings to the present owners of the company. Reliance on internal financing in order to maintain control reduces the dividend payout.

Tax Position of Stockholders

The tax position of a corporation's owners greatly influences the desire for dividends. For example, a corporation closely held by a few taxpayers in high income tax brackets is likely to pay a relatively low dividend. The owners prefer taking their income in the form of capital gains rather than as dividends, which are subject to higher effective personal income tax rates.[2] However, the stockholders of a large, widely held corporation might prefer a high dividend payout.

At times there is a conflict of interest in large corporations between stockholders in high income tax brackets and those in low tax brackets. The former may prefer to see a low dividend payout and a high rate of earnings retention in the hope of an appreciation in the capital stock of the company. The latter may prefer a relatively high dividend payout. The dividend policy in such firms may be a compromise between a low and a high payout — an intermediate payout ratio. If one group comes to dominate the company and sets, say, a low payout policy, those stockholders who seek income are likely to sell their shares over time and shift into higher-yielding stocks. Thus, to at least some extent, a firm's payout policy determines the type of stockholders it has — and vice versa. This has been called the "clientele influence" on dividend policy.

Tax on Improperly Accumulated Earnings

To prevent wealthy stockholders from using the corporation as an "incorporated pocketbook" by which they can avoid high personal income tax rates, tax regulations applicable to corporations provide for a special surtax on improperly accumulated income. However, Section 531 of the Revenue Act of 1954 places the burden of proof on the Internal Revenue Service to justify penalty rates for accumulation of earnings. That is, earnings retention is justified unless the IRS can prove otherwise.

GENERAL DIVIDEND PATTERNS IN THE ECONOMY

Table 16.1 presents after-tax profits, dividends, and dividend payouts for 1960–1990. In years such as 1982 and 1990, after-tax profits declined. These were both recession years. Dividends, however, increased in both years so that the dividend payout ratios increased sharply. Note that the dividend payout ratio was 41 percent for the first time segment, 1960–1966. Dividend payouts have risen in each successive time period. The time seg-

---

[2]At the time this edition was written, the statutory nominal capital gains rate was only slightly lower than the ordinary income tax rate in the United States. Even so, the effective capital gains rate was lower for two reasons. First, capital gains can be deferred. Second, investors with portfolios of assets can use capital losses to offset capital gains.

TABLE 16.1 Dividend Payout Patterns, 1960–1990 ($ billions)

Year	After-Tax Profits	Dividends	Dividend Payout
1960	26.8	12.9	0.48
1961	27.6	13.3	0.48
1962	34.3	14.4	0.42
1963	37.4	15.5	0.41
1964	42.7	17.3	0.41
1965	50.4	19.1	0.38
1966	52.9	19.4	0.37
1967	51.4	20.2	0.39
1968	51.4	22.0	0.43
1969	47.7	22.5	0.47
1970	40.3	22.5	0.56
1971	49.3	22.9	0.47
1972	58.8	24.4	0.41
1973	64.1	27.0	0.42
1974	49.9	29.7	0.60
1975	66.7	29.6	0.44
1976	81.0	34.6	0.43
1977	101.8	39.5	0.39
1978	113.7	44.7	0.39
1979	112.1	50.1	0.45
1980	92.4	54.7	0.59
1981	106.8	63.6	0.60
1982	86.9	66.9	0.77
1983	136.5	71.5	0.52
1984	173.0	79.0	0.46
1985	185.9	83.3	0.45
1986	175.8	91.3	0.52
1987	181.4	98.2	0.54
1988	201.4	110.0	0.55
1989	176.5	123.5	0.70
1990	163.0	133.9	0.82
1960–1966	272.1	111.9	0.41
1967–1972	298.6	134.5	0.45
1973–1982	875.4	440.4	0.50
1983–1990	1,393.5	790.7	0.57

Note: The second column shows corporate profits with inventory valuation and capital consumption adjustments.
Source: President's Council of Economic Advisers, *Economic Report of the President,* (Washington, D.C.: Government Printing Office, 1991), Table B-87.

ment 1983–1990 shows a rise in the dividend payout to 57 percent. This includes the years 1989 and 1990 during which after-tax profits had declined. Thus the dividend payout ratios were quite high.

Another perspective is obtained by comparing the behavior of the growth of after-tax profits and dividends for selected time periods as shown in Table 16.2. After-tax profits grew faster than gross national product (GNP) in the first and fourth time segments.

TABLE 16.2 Compound Annual Growth Rates in Selected Series, 1960–1990

	1960–1966	1966–1972	1972–1982	1982–1990
GNP	6.97%	7.82%	10.07%	7.06%
After-tax profits	12.00	1.78	3.98	8.18
Dividends	7.04	3.90	10.61	9.06
CPI	1.52	4.34	8.73	3.86

Source: President's Council of Economic Advisers, *Economic Report of the President*, (Washington, D.C., Government Printing Office, 1991) Tables B-1, B-60, B-87.

Dividends grew faster than after-tax profits in time segments when the growth of after-tax profits was low. Only in the time segment 1960–1966 when after-tax profits grew at a strong 12 percent rate was dividend growth lower. Only when profit growth was strong did it outpace the growth in the consumer price index (CPI). Similarly, only when the growth in dividends was strong did that growth outpace the growth in the CPI.

Dividend Policy Behavior

Figure 16.1 shows that corporate after-tax profits are subject to wide cyclical fluctuations, while generally trending upward. The absolute amount of dividends has grown at a steady upward rate. In no year did they decline. In 1970 they leveled off at $22.5 billion, but increased in all of the other years. This trend indicates most corporations' desire to avoid reducing dividends, because a dividend cut signals a future permanent decline in earnings. Thus, dividends increase only with a lag after earnings rise. That is, they are increased only after an increase in earnings appears clearly sustainable and relatively permanent. When dividends have been increased, strenuous efforts are made to maintain them at the new level. If earnings decline, the existing dividend generally is maintained until it is clear that an earnings recovery will not take place.

Figure 16.2 illustrates these ideas by showing the earnings and dividend patterns for the Walter Watch Company over a 30-year period. Initially, earnings are $2 and dividends $1 a share, providing a 50 percent payout ratio. Earnings rise for four years, while dividends remain constant; thus, the payout ratio falls during this period. During 1965 and 1966, earnings fall substantially; however, the dividend is maintained, and the payout ratio rises above the 50 percent target. During the period between 1966 and 1970 earnings experience a sustained rise. Dividends are held constant for a time, while management seeks to determine whether the earnings increase is permanent. By 1971, the earnings gains seem permanent, and dividends are raised in three steps to reestablish the 50 percent target payout. During 1975 a strike causes earnings to fall below the regular dividend; expecting the earnings decline to be temporary, management maintains the dividend. Earnings fluctuate on a fairly high plateau from 1976 through 1982, during which time dividends remain constant. A new increase in earnings induces management to raise the dividend in 1983 to reestablish the 50 percent payout ratio.

FIGURE 16.1   Corporate Earnings after Taxes and Dividends, 1960–1990

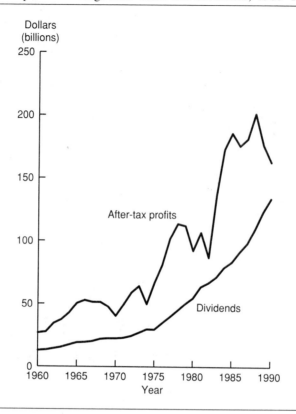

FIGURE 16.2   Dividends and Earnings Patterns for the Walter Watch Company

Different Dividend Payout Schemes

Even though most firms seem to have a policy of paying stable dollar dividends, this is not the only policy. The three major types of dividend payout schemes are:

1. *Stable dollar amount per share.* The policy of a stable dollar amount per share, followed by most firms, is the policy implied by the words *stable dividend policy.*

2. *Constant payout ratio.* Very few firms follow a policy of paying out a constant percentage of earnings. Since earnings fluctuate, following this policy necessarily means that the dollar amount of dividends will fluctuate. This policy is not likely to maximize the value of a firm's stock because it results in unreliable signals to the market about the future prospects of the firm and because it may interfere with investment policy. Before its bankruptcy, Penn Central Railroad followed the policy of paying out half its earnings — "A dollar for the stockholders and a dollar for the company," as one director put it.

3. *Low regular dividend plus extras.* The low regular dividend plus extras policy is a compromise between the first two. It gives the firm flexibility, but it leaves investors somewhat uncertain about what their dividend income will be. If a firm's earnings are quite volatile, however, this policy may well be its best choice.

In addition to these policies that describe how a target payout is achieved across the years, there is also the question of what the target payout should be in the first place. Should a firm's target dividend payout be 10 percent of earnings or 50 percent? We turn to this question next.

THEORIES OF DIVIDEND POLICY

The central issue of dividend policy is whether it is possible to affect shareholders' wealth by changing the firm's target dividend payout ratio — its dividend policy. If we compare two firms that are alike in every way, except for their current dividend payout, will the shares of the firms be valued differently? If so, then dividend policy matters. To answer this question we begin in the simplest possible world — one with no taxes. Then we move to a more realistic world of personal and corporate taxes. Finally, we consider the relationship between investment policy (capital budgeting) and dividend policy.

Dividend Policy in a World without Taxes

Consider two firms that are alike in every way except for their dividend policies. They have the same portfolio of risky assets, the same cash flows, and the same earnings each year. In addition, assume they have no debt at all so that we don't confuse the effect of capital structure (the mixture of debt and equity financing) with dividend policy. Finally, assume a world without taxes, just to keep things simple. Miller and Modigliani [1961] formalized these assumptions in a multiperiod model as follows:

$$\text{NOI}_1(t) = \text{NOI}_2(t) \qquad t = 0, 1, \ldots, \infty \qquad \textbf{(16.1a)}$$

$$I_1(t) = I_2(t) \qquad t = 0, 1, \ldots, \infty \qquad \textbf{(16.1b)}$$

$$d_1(t) = d_2(t) \qquad t = 1, \ldots, \infty \qquad \textbf{(16.1c)}$$
$$d_1(0) \neq d_2(0) \qquad t = 0. \qquad \textbf{(16.1d)}$$

Assumptions (16.1a) and (16.1b) say that the cash flows from operations, NOI(t), as well as both firms' investment plans, $I(t)$, are identical in every time period from now, $t = 0$, to infinity, $t = \infty$.[3] They imply that each firm's investment decisions are separate from its dividend policy (and other financing decisions). No matter what level of current cash flows is paid out in the form of dividends, the firm will make the same investment decisions. As we shall see later on, this assumption is absolutely critical. If the firm were to forego positive net present value projects because it wanted to pay high dividends, then the value of the firm would surely be affected not by dividend policy per se, but by the refusal to take profitable investments. Assumptions (16.1c) and (16.1d) state that current dividend payout will be different for the two firms, that is, $d_1(0) \neq d_2(0)$, but all future dividends will be identical.

The important question is whether or not the two firms will have different values if their current dividend payouts are different. To supply an answer we need a simple valuation model. Start by noting that the two firms have the same risk because their streams of operating cash flows are identical. Hence the cash flows of the two firms can be discounted at the same risk-adjusted rate, k_U, the cost of capital for an unlevered firm. The one-period rate of return, k_U, for a share of stock is

$$k_U(t + 1) = \frac{d_i(t + 1) + p_i(t + 1) - p_i(t)}{p_i(t)}, \qquad \textbf{(16.2)}$$

where

$$k_U(t + 1) = \text{the cost of capital for an unlevered firm in time period } t$$
$$d_i(t + 1) = \text{dividends per share paid at the end of time period } t$$
$$p_i(t + 1) = \text{the price per share at the end of time period } t$$
$$p_i(t) = \text{the price per share at the beginning of period } t.$$

If the numerator and denominator of Equation 16.2 are multiplied by the current number of shares outstanding, $n_i(t)$, and if we rearrange terms, we obtain

$$n_i(t)p_i(t) = S_i(t) = \frac{D_i(t + 1) + n_i(t)p_i(t + 1)}{1 + k_U(t + 1)}, \qquad \textbf{(16.3)}$$

where

$$D_i(t + 1) = \text{total dollar dividend payment} = n_i(t)d_i(t + 1)$$
$$S_i(t) = \text{the market value of the all-equity firm.}$$

The value of the firm is seen to be equal to the discounted sum of two cash flows: dividends paid out, $D_i(t + 1)$, and the end-of-period value of the firm, $S_i(t + 1) = n_i(t)p_i(t + 1)$.

---

[3]Net operating income, NOI, is defined as earnings from operations before interest and taxes. If there are no nonrecurring items on the income statement, then NOI equals EBIT, earnings before interest and taxes. We have also previously used the symbol X to designate operating income. For this chapter, we assume that NOI = EBIT = X.

The key to understanding why dividend payout does not affect the value of the firm, given our current set of assumptions, is the firm's sources and uses of funds. The major sources are internal funds provided by cash flows from operations, $NOI_i(t + 1)$; and external funds provided by issuing new shares, $m_i(t + 1)p_i(t + 1)$, where $m_i(t + 1)$ is the number of new shares. The major uses of funds are investment expenditures, $I_i(t + 1)$, and dividends, $D_i(t + 1)$.[4] By definition, sources and uses must be equal, therefore we can write the following:

$$NOI_i(t + 1) + m_i(t + 1)p_i(t + 1) \equiv I_i(t + 1) + D_i(t + 1). \qquad (16.4)$$

The sources and uses identity shows why investment decisions can be independent of dividend policy. For example, suppose a firm has $100 in cash flow from operations, wishes to invest $80, and to pay $40 in dividends. Equation 16.4 becomes

$$\$100 + m_i(t + 1)p_i(t + 1) = \$80 + \$40$$
$$m_i(t + 1)p_i(t + 1) = \$20.$$

The firm must issue enough new shares to raise $20. On the other hand, suppose the firm wishes to invest only $20. The sources and uses equation becomes

$$\$100 + m_i(t + 1)p_i(t + 1) = \$20 + \$40$$
$$m_i(t + 1)p_i(t + 1) = -\$40.$$

In this case the firm uses its excess cash flow to repurchase $40 worth of its outstanding stock. These two examples serve to illustrate that external sources and uses of funds (sale or repurchase of equity) can be used to balance the sources and uses equation without affecting planned investments.

To continue the proof of dividend policy irrelevancy, solve the sources and uses identity (Equation 16.4) for dividend payments:

$$D_i(t + 1) = NOI_i(t + 1) - I_i(t + 1) + m_i(t + 1)p_i(t + 1),$$

then substitute the result into the numerator of our one-period valuation equation (Equation 16.3).

$$S_i(t) = \frac{NOI_i(t + 1) - I_i(t + 1) + m_i(t + 1)p_i(t + 1) + n_i(t)p_i(t + 1)}{1 + k_U(t + 1)}$$

Next, we know that if new shares are issued, the total number of shares outstanding at the end of the period, $n_i(t + 1)$, will be the sum of current shares, $n_i(t)$, and new shares, $m_i(t + 1)$:

$$n_i(t + 1) = n_i(t) + m_i(t + 1).$$

Rearranging this expression, the current number of shares is

$$n_i(t) = n_i(t + 1) - m_i(t + 1).$$

---

[4] We have assumed, for the sake of convenience, that sources and uses of funds from the balance sheet (for example, changes in inventory, accounts payable, etc.) are negligible.

Finally, substituting this into our valuation equation we have

$$S_i(t) = \frac{\text{NOI}_i(t+1) - I_i(t+1) + m_i(t+1)p_i(t+1) + n_i(t+1)p_i(t+1) - m_i(t+1)p_i(t+1)}{1 + k_U(t+1)}$$

$$= \frac{\text{NOI}_i(t+1) - I_i(t+1) + n_i(t+1)p_i(t+1)}{1 + k_U(t+1)}$$

$$= \frac{\text{NOI}_i(t+1) - I_i(t+1) + S_i(t+1)}{1 + k_U(t+1)}. \tag{16.5}$$

It is no accident that dividends do not appear in the valuation Equation 16.5. The firm can choose any dividend policy whatsoever without affecting the stream of cash flows available to shareholders. Because we have assumed that there are no taxes, shareholders are indifferent as to whether they receive their cash flows as dividends, if the cash is paid out, or as capital gains if the cash is kept as retained earnings. The firm could, as illustrated earlier, elect to pay current dividends in excess of cash flows from operations and still be able to undertake any planned investment. The extra funds needed are supplied by issuing new equity. It is the availability of external financing in a world without transactions costs that makes the value of the firm independent of dividend policy, because all profitable investments can be undertaken regardless of the extent of dividend payout.

Note that Equation 16.5 has four variables. All are identical for both firms even though they have different current dividend payouts. First, the market-determined cost of equity for the unlevered firms, k_U, must be the same because both firms have identical risk. Second, current cash flows from operations and current investment outlays for the two firms have been assumed to be identical:

$$\text{NOI}_1(1) = \text{NOI}_2(1); \ I_1(1) = I_2(1).$$

Finally, the end-of-period values of the two firms depend only on *future* investments, dividends, and cash flows, which have also been assumed to be identical. Therefore, the end-of-period values of the two firms must be the same

$$S_1(1) = S_2(1).$$

Consequently, the present values of the two firms must be identical regardless of their current dividend payout. Dividend policy is irrelevant in a world without taxes or transactions costs.

Dividend Policy in a World with Taxes

As before, we want to assume that the firm's investment policy is unaffected by its dividend policy and that there are no transactions costs associated with raising external capital. However, the analysis is made more realistic if we allow taxes to enter the picture. Assume there are three different tax rates. First there is a proportional corporate tax, T_c. Second is a personal tax rate on income from bonds, dividends, and wages, T_p. And finally there is a tax on capital gains, T_g. Furthermore, assume that all firms and all investors actually pay these tax rates, that is, there are no loopholes.

The 1986 Tax Reform Act requires that individuals pay the ordinary personal income tax rate on all dividends and capital gains. Before 1986, the capital gains rate (on long-term gains) was half of the ordinary personal income rate. The difference between ordinary and capital gains rates is crucial for dividend policy. Therefore, we shall present all arguments two ways: first, assuming that the ordinary rate exceeds the capital gains rate and second, assuming they are equal. Even though the tax rates are normally the same, there is good reason to believe that the *effective* rate on capital gains is lower than on ordinary income because the offset of capital gains by capital losses in a diversified investment strategy creates a *tax-timing option*. The idea, first modeled by Constantinides (1983), shows that the effective capital gains tax is lowered because the tax law does not require that all capital gains and losses be realized at the end of each year, hence capital losses can be realized as they are incurred while gains can be deferred at the option of the taxpayer.

As long as the personal tax rate on income received in the form of dividends is greater than the personal tax rate on capital gains ($T_p > T_g$), then shareholders will prefer that the firm pay no dividends. They would be better off if the funds remained in the firm or were paid out via repurchase of shares.[5] Either way, the stock price per share would be higher than it would be had dividends been paid out. If dividends are not paid out, shareholders who need cash can always sell off a fraction of their holdings. In doing so, they pay capital gains taxes that are lower than the ordinary income taxes they would have paid had they received dividends.

Formal analysis of this idea was provided in a partial equilibrium context by Farrar and Selwyn [1967] and in a market equilibrium framework by Brennan [1970]. The idea is that shareholders maximize their after-tax income. They have two choices. They can own shares in an all equity firm and borrow to provide personal leverage, or they can buy shares in a levered firm. Either way they have the same risk. Their first choice is the amount of personal versus corporate leverage that is desired. The second choice is the form of payment to be made by the firm. It can pay out earnings as dividends or it can retain earnings and allow shareholders to take their income in the form of capital gains.

Let's consider two cases as they relate to dividend policy. Either the firm pays out all of its income as dividends (Case 1) or it pays out no dividends at all (Case 2).

Case 1. If a firm pays out all of its cash flows as dividends, the ith shareholder will receive the following after-tax income, Y_{di}:

$$Y_{di} = [(\text{NOI} - rD_c)(1 - T_c) - rD_{pi}](1 - T_{pi}), \tag{16.6}$$

where

Y_{di} = after-tax stream of income to the ith individual if all corporate income is paid out as dividends

NOI = cash flows from operations of the firm (net operating income) = $1,000

r = borrowing rate that is assumed identical for individual and firms = 10%

D_c = corporate debt = $6,000

---

[5]Later on we shall see that the repurchase of shares is an important alternative to paying out cash dividends — so important that the Internal Revenue Service can declare regular stock repurchases (on a pro rata basis) to be taxable as dividends.

D_{pi} = personal debt held by the ith individual = \$2,000

T_c = corporate tax rate = 40%

T_p = personal tax rate on income (wages, rents, interest received, and dividends) received by the ith individual = 30%.

The first term within the brackets in Equation 16.6 is the after-tax cash flow of the firm, which is $(NOI - rD_c)(1 - T_c) = \$240$. All of this is assumed to be paid out as dividends. The before-tax income to the shareholder is the dividends received minus the interest on debt used to buy shares, $(NOI - rD_c)(1 - T_c) - rD_{pi} = \$40$. After subtracting personal income taxes, $\$40 T_{pi} = \$12$, we are left with after-tax income, \$28.

Case 2. Alternatively, the firm can decide to pay no dividends, in which case we assume that all capital gains are realized *immediately* by investors and taxed at the capital gains rate.[6] In this case, the after-tax income of a shareholder is

$$Y_{gi} = (NOI - rD_c)(1 - T_c)(1 - T_{gi}) - rD_{pi}(1 - T_{pi}), \qquad (16.7)$$

where

Y_{gi} = after-tax income to the ith individual if the firm pays no dividends

T_{gi} = capital gains rate for the ith individual = 15%.

Now the individual pays a capital gains tax rate on the firm's income and deducts after-tax interest expenses on personal debt. The capital gain after taxes is

$$(NOI - rD_c)(1 - T_c)(1 - T_{gi}) = (\$1,000 - \$600)(1 - .4)(1 - .15) = \$204.$$

From this we subtract the after-tax cost of interest on personal debt, $rD_{pi}(1 - T_{pi}) = \$140$. Altogether the individual's after-tax income is \$64. Clearly, the individual is better off if the firm pays no dividends. If the firm pays dividends the individual's after-tax income is $Y_{di} = \$28$. If the firm retains the cash flows or uses them to repurchase shares, the individual realizes a capital gain and an after-tax income of $Y_{gi} = \$64$, which is better than if the firm pays dividends. This result will be true as long as the personal tax rate on dividends is higher than the capital gains rate $(T_{pi} > T_{gi})$. If the rates are the same $(T_{pi} = T_{gi})$, then the individual is indifferent between corporate and personal savings.

Miller and Scholes [1978] modified the preceding argument by demonstrating that even with earlier tax laws (where the tax on ordinary personal income was greater than the capital gains tax) many individuals did not pay more than the capital gains rate on dividends. The implication is that many individuals were indifferent between payments in the form of dividends or capital gains. Thus, the firm's value may have been unrelated to its dividend policy even in a world with differential tax rates.

The Miller and Scholes argument can be illustrated with an example. Suppose we have an initial net worth of \$25,000, which is represented wholly by an investment in 2,500 shares worth \$10 each in a company that earns \$1.00 per share. At the end of the

---

[6]Obviously there is the third possibility that earnings are translated into capital gains and the capital gains are deferred to a later date. This possibility is considered in Farrar and Selwyn [1967]. It does not change their conclusions.

TABLE 16.3   A Technique for Sheltering Dividend Income

Opening Balance Sheet				Closing Balance Sheet			
Assets		**Liabilities**		**Assets**		**Liabilities**	
2,500 shares at $10	= $25,000	Loan	$16,667	2,500 shares at $10.60	= $26,500	Loan accrued	= $16,667
Insurance	= 16,667	Net worth	25,000	Accrued dividends	= 1,000	Accrued interest	= 1,000
	$41,667		$41,667	Insurance	= 16,667	Net worth	= 26,500
					$44,167		$44,167

Ordinary Income		**Capital Gains**	
Dividends received	$1,000	Sale of 2,500 shares at $10.60 = $26,500	
Less: interest expense	1,000	Less: original basis	25,000
	0	Capital gain	$ 1,500
Nontaxable income	$1,000		
	$1,000		

year the company pays $.40 per share in dividends and retains $.60. Consequently, its end-of-year price per share is $10.60. In order to neutralize dividend income for tax purposes, we borrow $16,667 at 6 percent and invest the proceeds in a risk-free project (such as life insurance or a retirement account), which pays 6 percent of tax-deferred interest. Our opening and closing balance sheets and our income statement are shown in Table 16.3. Note that by investing in risk-free assets we have not increased the risk of our wealth position. The riskless cash inflows from insurance exactly match the required payments on debt. Our true economic income would be $1,500 in *unrealized* capital gains plus the $1,000 of tax-deferred interest from life insurance or our retirement account.

Of course, federal tax laws are complex and tax sheltering investments cannot be carried out without some transactions costs. Also, Feenberg [1981] has shown that the maximum amount of dividends or interest income that could be sheltered in this way was $10,000. Nevertheless, the above argument is a clever way to demonstrate the fact that ordinary income taxes on dividends could be legally avoided.

In a world with personal and corporate taxes, dividends are undesirable to most taxpaying shareholders, or at best shareholders are indifferent between dividends and capital gains. Of course there are also many institutional investors, such as pension funds, which pay no taxes on either dividends or capital gains; or corporations that pay taxes on only 15 percent of the dividends they receive. There is nothing in the theory to suggest that dividends are desirable. Why, then, do corporations pay any dividends at all?

INGREDIENTS FOR OPTIMAL DIVIDEND POLICY

For an optimal dividend policy to exist, there must be benefits from paying dividends as well as costs due to their payment. There are three different approaches to optimal dividend policy that identify benefits as well as costs. The first two theories work as well in a world without as in a world with taxes. The third extends our intuition of how taxes affect dividend policy.

Dividends, Agency Costs, and External Financing

Rozeff [1982] suggests that optimal dividend policy may exist even without considering tax implications. Systematic patterns in corporate dividend payout ratios may be explained by a trade-off between the flotation costs of raising external capital and the benefit of reduced agency costs when the firm increases its dividend payout.

The more dividends a firm chooses to pay, the greater the probability that the supply of retained earnings (internally generated capital) will be exhausted, thus making it necessary to seek external funds (debt or equity) in order to undertake new investment. But the flotation costs associated with raising external capital make it a more expensive source of financing. Consequently, dividend payout is costly because it increases the probable need to raise more expensive external capital.

A possible benefit of dividend payments is that they may reduce agency costs between owner-managers and outside owners of a firm. To see how agency costs might arise (in an all equity firm) let's begin with an owner-managed firm. Because the owner-manager (Mr. Jones) owns all of the firm's common stock, any decision he makes will maximize his utility. For example, if he decides to play golf on Wednesday afternoons he bears all of the costs and benefits of that decision. If he sells part of his common stock to some outsiders, the situation changes. Now, if he plays golf, the outsiders share in the cost of his actions. This creates a principal-agent problem. The owner-manager can shirk his duties or pay himself more perquisites at the expense of outsiders. Consequently, the outsiders must charge, *ex ante,* for the potential agency problem that owner-managers may increase their personal wealth in lieu of maximizing the wealth of all shareholders. They do this by demanding a higher rate of return on the equity capital that they invest in the firm. To decrease this *ex ante* charge, owner-managers find it in their own interest to agree to incur monitoring or bonding costs if such costs are less than the *ex ante* charge that outsiders would be forced to request. Thus, a wealth-maximizing firm will adopt an optimal monitoring/bonding policy that minimizes agency costs.

Dividend payments may well serve as a means of monitoring or bonding management performance. Although greater dividend payout results in costly external financing, the very fact that the firm must go to the capital markets implies that it will come under greater scrutiny. For example, banks will require a careful analysis of the credit-worthiness of the firm and the Securities and Exchange Commission will require prospectus filings for new equity issues. Thus, outside suppliers of capital help to monitor the owner-manager on behalf of outside equity owners. Of course, audited financial statements are a substitute means for supplying the same information, but they may not be a perfect substitute for the "adversary" relationship between the firm and new suppliers of capital.

Because of the transactions costs of external financing, Rozeff also argues that the variability of a firm's cash flows will affect its dividend payout. Consider two firms with the same average cash flows across time but different variability. The firm with greater volatility will borrow in bad years and repay in good. It will need to finance externally more often. Consequently, it will have a lower payout ratio.

TABLE 16.4   Cross-Sectional Dividend Payout Regressions

	CONSTANT	INS	GROW1	GROW2	BETA	STOCK	R^2	D.W.	F-Statistic
(1)	47.81	−0.090	−0.321	−0.526	−26.543	2.584	0.48	1.88	185.47
	(12.83)	(−4.10)	(−6.38)	(−6.43)	(−17.05)	(7.73)			
(2)	24.73	−0.068	−0.474	−0.758	—	2.517	0.33	1.79	123.23
	(6.27)	(−2.75)	(−8.44)	(−8.28)		(6.63)			
(3)	70.63	—	−0.402	−0.603	−25.409	—	0.41	1.88	231.46
	(40.35)		(−7.58)	(−6.94)	(−15.35)				
(4)	39.56	−0.116	—	—	−33.506	3.151	0.39	1.80	218.10
	(10.02)	(−4.92)			(−21.28)	(8.82)			
(5)	1.03	−0.102	—	—	—	3.429	0.12	1.60	69.33
	(0.24)	(−3.60)				(7.97)			

Note: *t*-statistics are shown in parentheses under estimated values of the regression coefficients. R^2 is adjusted for degrees of freedom. *D.W.* is Durbin-Watson statistic.
Source: Rozeff, M., "Growth, Beta, and Agency Costs as Determinants of Dividend Payout Ratios," *Journal of Financial Research*, Vol. 5, No. 3, Fall 1982, pp. 249–259.

Rozeff [1982] selected a sample of 1,000 nonregulated firms in 64 different industries and examined their average dividend payout ratios during the years 1974–1980. Five proxy variables were used in a multiple regression equation to test his theory. The results are shown in Table 16.4. The independent variables *GROW1* and *GROW2* are an attempt to measure the effect of costly external financing. Firms that grow faster can reduce their need to use external financing by paying lower dividends. *GROW1* measures the growth rate in revenues between 1974 and 1979, while *GROW2* is Value Line's forecast of the growth in sales revenue over the five-year period 1979–1984. Both variables are negatively related to dividend payout and are statistically significant. The variables *INS* and *STOCK* are proxies for the agency relationship. *INS* is the percentage of the firm held by insiders. Dividend payout is negatively related to the percentage of insiders because given a lower percentage of outsiders there is less need to pay dividends to reduce agency costs.[7] On the other hand, if the distribution of outsider holdings is diffuse, then agency costs will be higher, hence one would expect *STOCK,* the number of stockholders, to be positively related to dividend payout. Both *INS* and *STOCK* are statistically significant and of the predicted sign. Finally, the variable *BETA* measures the systematic risk of the firm. The prediction that riskier firms have lower dividend payout is verified by the regression.

The best regression in Table 16.4 explains 48 percent of the cross-sectional variability on dividend payout across individual firms. All of the explanatory variables are statistically significant with the predicted signs. Although the results cannot be used to distinguish among various theories of optimal dividend policy, they are consistent with Rozeff's predictions. Furthermore, the very existence of strong cross-sectional regularities suggests that there is an optimal dividend policy.

[7]This relationship is also consistent with the tax argument that assumes high tax bracket insiders prefer to take their return in the form of capital gains rather than dividends.

Dividends as Signals

Dividend signaling is more a story about how information may be transmitted to the marketplace than it is a theory about optimal dividend policy. The announcement that a firm has decided to increase dividends per share may be interpreted by investors as good news because higher dividends per share imply that the firm believes future cash flows will be large enough to support the higher dividend level.

Managers, as insiders who have monopolistic access to information about the firm's cash flows, will choose to establish unambiguous signals about the firm's future if they have the proper incentive to do so. Ross [1977] proved that an increase in dividends paid out (or in the usage of debt) can represent an inimitable and unambiguous signal to the marketplace that a firm's prospects have improved. In order for a signal to be useful, four conditions must be met:

1. Management must always have the right incentive to send a truthful signal, even if the news is bad.

2. The signal of a successful firm cannot be easily mimicked by less successful competitors.

3. The signal must be significantly correlated with observable events (for example, higher dividends today must be correlated with higher future cash flows).

4. There cannot be a more cost effective way of sending the same message.

To show how these conditions are met by Ross' [1977] signaling equilibrium, assume a one-period world. Managers' compensation, M, paid at the end of the period, depends on the market's current assessment of the value of the firm, V_0, and on its end-of-period value, V_1. In general, managers' compensation can be expressed as

$$M = (1 + r)\gamma_0 V_0 + \gamma_1 \begin{cases} V_1 & \text{if } V_1 \geq D \\ V_1 - L & \text{if } V_1 < D, \end{cases} \tag{16.8}$$

where

$\gamma_0,\ \gamma_1$ = positive fractions of the value of the firm which are paid to managers

r = the one-period interest rate

$V_0,\ V_1$ = the current and future value of the firm

D = the face value of debt

L = a penalty paid by managers if bankruptcy occurs, that is, if $V_1 < D$.

The first term in Equation 16.8 is the end-of-period value of the managers' fraction of the current price of the firm. The second term is the managers' fraction of the end-of-period value. Note that if the firm goes bankrupt (because its value is less than the face value of debt obligations), managers experience a decrease, L, in the value of their human capital.

Suppose we have two firms that have the same size and the same amount of debt, D, but have different earnings prospects, which are known by management, but not by the marketplace in general. The successful firm (which will have higher future cash flows) can pay out greater dividends today and still have enough cash left at the end of the period to pay off its debt obligations $(V_1 \geq D)$.[8] The unsuccessful firm cannot pay high current dividends without going bankrupt at the end of the period $(V_1 < D)$. Assume that div^* is the maximum amount of dividends that the unsuccessful firm can pay out without going bankrupt. If a firm elects to pay out current dividends greater than div^*, then the market perceives the firm to be successful and vice versa.

To show that managers have the incentive to provide truthful signals to the market, begin by assuming the end-of-period value of the successful firm is V_{1a} and V_{1b} is the value of the unsuccessful firm. Compensation of the management of the successful firm depends on the type of dividend signal it sends to the market. If it tells the truth it will signal $div > div^*$ and the market will assign a current market value that is

$$V_0 = \frac{V_{1a}}{1 + r}.$$

If the successful firm wants to lie, the managers will signal $div < div^*$ and the market will assign a current value

$$V_0 = \frac{V_{1b}}{1 + r} < \frac{V_{1a}}{1 + r}.$$

For the successful firm, we can summarize the managers' compensation using Equation 16.8 as follows:

$$M_a = \begin{cases} \gamma_0(1 + r) \dfrac{V_{1a}}{1 + r} + \gamma_1 V_{1a} & \text{if } div \geq div^* \text{ (tell the truth)} \\[2mm] \gamma_0(1 + r) \dfrac{V_{1b}}{1 + r} + \gamma_1 V_{1b} & \text{if } div < div^* \text{ (lie).} \end{cases}$$

Clearly, the management of the successful firm has the incentive to pay a high level of dividends $(div > div^*)$ to earn maximum compensation. Therefore, it will give the correct signal. But what about the management of the unsuccessful firm? Doesn't it have an incentive to lie by falsely signaling with high dividends? The answer is found by looking at the management incentive scheme:

$$M_b = \begin{cases} \gamma_0(1 + r) \dfrac{V_{1a}}{1 + r} + \gamma_1(V_{1b} - L) & \text{if } div \geq div^* \text{ (lie)} \\[2mm] \gamma_0(1 + r) \dfrac{V_{1b}}{1 + r} + \gamma_1(V_{1b}) & \text{if } div < div^* \text{ (tell the truth).} \end{cases}$$

In order for management of an unsuccessful firm to have incentive to signal that the firm will be unsuccessful, the payoff from telling the truth must be greater than that produced by telling lies. Mathematically,

$$\gamma_0 V_{1a} + \gamma_1(V_{1b} - L) < \gamma_0 V_{1b} + \gamma_1 V_{1b},$$

---

[8]Miller and Rock [1984] have suggested that D may be interpreted as *net* dividends, the difference between cash dividends and borrowing. Thus, a firm that borrows $1 million to pay $1 million in dividends will have a net dividend of $0. This interpretation links dividend and debt signals into a unified concept.

which can be rewritten as

$$\gamma_0(V_{1a} - V_{1b}) < \gamma_1 L.$$

This condition says that management will provide a truthful signal if the marginal gain from a false signal, $V_{1a} - V_{1b}$, weighted by management's share γ_0, is less than the penalty paid by management, $\gamma_1 L$, if the firm goes bankrupt. Managers of unsuccessful firms who falsely signal success by paying a higher current dividend can benefit because the market assigns a higher current value to the firm, but they ultimately lose because the value of their human capital declines (by $\gamma_1 L$) when the firm goes bankrupt due to cash flow insufficiency.

The incentive-signaling approach suggests that management might choose real financial payouts such as dividends (or debt payments) as a means of sending unambiguous signals to the public about the future performance of the firm. These signals cannot be mimicked by unsuccessful firms because such firms do not have sufficient cash flow to back them up and because managers have correct incentives to tell the truth.

Bhattacharya [1979] develops a dividend signaling model closely related to that of Ross [1977], which can be used to explain why firms may use dividends for signaling despite the tax disadvantages of doing so. If investors believe that firms that pay greater dividends per share have higher values, then an unexpected dividend increase will be taken as a favorable signal. Presumably dividends convey information about the value of the firm that cannot be fully communicated by other means such as annual reports, earnings forecasts, or presentations before security analysts. It is expensive for less successful firms to mimic the signal because they must incur extra costs associated with raising external funds in order to pay the cash dividend. Hence, the signaling value of dividends is positive and can be traded off against the tax loss associated with dividend income (as opposed to capital gains).

If dividend changes are to have an impact on share values, it is necessary that they convey information about future cash flows, but it is not sufficient. The same information may be provided to investors via other sources. Therefore, it becomes an empirical question whether announcements of dividend changes actually affect share value.

There have been many studies of the effect of the announcement of an unexpected change in dividends.[9] Most of the results strongly support the conclusion that unanticipated changes in dividends are, indeed, interpreted by the marketplace as signals about the future prospects of the firm. Figure 16.3 shows the dividend announcement effects for a sample of firms studied by Aharony and Swary [1980]. Because firms often announce earnings and dividends at about the same time, Aharony and Swary were careful to select only those dividend announcements that were separated from earnings announcements by at least ten trading days. Figure 16.3 shows the average residual rates of return attributable to the announced dividend changes taken from a sample of 2,610 dividend announcements that were preceded by earnings announcements (representative of 149 firms over the period January 1963 to December 1976). Even though the dividend change announcements were preceded by earlier announcements of earnings changes, there was a strong

---

[9]For example, see Fama, Fisher, Jensen, and Roll [1969]; Pettit [1972]; Watts [1973]; Kwan [1981]; and Aharony and Swary [1980].

FIGURE 16.3   Daily Cumulative Average Abnormal Returns: Cases Where Earnings Announcements Precede Dividend Announcements

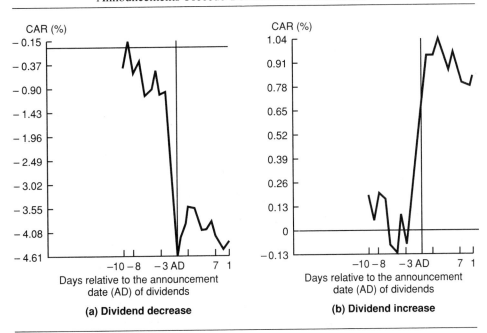

Source: Aharony, J., and I. Swary, "Quarterly Dividend and Earnings Announcements and Stockholder Returns: An Empirical Analysis," *Journal of Finance*, (March 1980), p. 8.

market reaction to dividend signals. When dividends decreased, the average stock price decrease was −3.76 percent and when they rose the stock price increased .72 percent. Both results were statistically significant. These findings strongly support the hypothesis that dividend changes contain information about changes in management's assessment of the future prospects of the firm. Furthermore, dividend announcements contain useful information beyond that already provided by earnings announcements.

Dividends, Investment, and Taxes

The complex individual and corporate tax system in the United States may be an important part of the dividend puzzle. Masulis and Trueman [1988] model the investment and dividend decision under fairly realistic assumptions and show that the costs of deferring dividends may be large enough to induce firms to optimally pay cash dividends. The tax system that they model assumes:

1. Corporations pay an effective marginal tax rate, T_c.
2. Individuals pay different personal tax rates on dividend income, T_{di}.
3. There are no capital gains taxes, $T_g = 0$.

4. The IRS taxes regular corporate repurchases of equity in the same way as dividend payments.

5. There is an 80 percent dividend exclusion from taxes on all dividends paid by one corporation to another.

In addition, to keep capital structure questions separate from dividend policy, they assume no debt.

Figure 16.4 illustrates the effect of taxes on the supply and demand for investment funds. Internal capital (retained earnings) and external equity capital (proceeds from new issues) have different costs to the firm. If retained earnings are not reinvested, then the ith shareholder receives the following after-tax return for each dollar paid out as dividends:

$$r_b(1 - T_c)(1 - T_{di}) = \text{cost of internal funds} \qquad (16.9)$$

where r_b = the pretax return on investments in real assets.

For example, if the pretax return required on investments of equal risk is $r_b = 15\%$, the corporate tax rate is $T_c = 50\%$, and the individual's tax rate is 40 percent, then the individual will be indifferent between (1) earning 9.0 percent before taxes on a corporate investment and (2) receiving dividends.[10] If the individual's tax rate is 20 percent, a 12 percent before-tax rate on investment will be required. The higher an individual's tax bracket, the more likely he or she is to want the firm to invest cash flows internally instead of paying dividends, even when investment returns decline with more investment. The line segment WX in Figure 16.4 represents the cost of capital to current shareholders in different tax brackets. In Panel (a) it represents a high tax bracket shareholder and in Panel (b), a low tax bracket shareholder. At Point Y are shareholders who pay no personal taxes at all (for example, pension funds). They are indifferent between earnings retention and dividend payout because their opportunity cost is the same as the cost of external capital to the firm.

$$r_b(1 - T_c) = \text{cost of external funds} \qquad (16.10)$$

External funds are more expensive to the firm because investors do not pay double taxes (corporate and personal) on funds put to other uses. It is assumed that alternative investments earn capital gains only and are not taxed at the personal level. The cost of external capital is illustrated by the horizontal line segment YZ in Figure 16.4 (both panels).

The firm has two categories of investment opportunity. First are investments in real assets, represented by line segment AB, and assumed to have diminishing returns to scale. Second are investments in securities of other firms. These securities investments have

---

[10]Given an individual tax rate of 40 percent, and a 15 percent before-tax rate on investment, the after-tax rate on a dollar paid out as dividends would be

$$r_b(1 - T_c)(1 - T_{di}) = .15(1 - .5)(1 - .4) = .045.$$

If the money is kept in the firm, the before-tax return can fall to 9.0 percent and should give the same after-tax yield, assuming there is no capital gains tax;

$$r_b(1 - T_c) = .09(1 - .5) = .045.$$

See Equation 16.10 for the cost of external equity capital.

FIGURE 16.4   Corporate Investment and Dividend Decisions
with Differing Personal Tax Rates

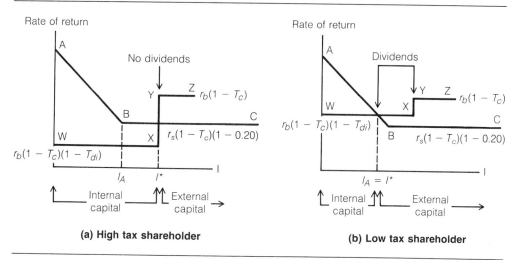

(a) **High tax shareholder**   (b) **Low tax shareholder**

constant returns to scale as illustrated by line segment BC. The before-tax return on
investments in securities of other firms is defined as r_s. There is a virtually infinite amount
of security investments (in assets of equivalent risk) but their after-tax rate of return to the
firm is affected by the fact that it must pay corporate taxes on 20 percent of the dividends
paid to it by other firms. Thus, the after-tax return on security investments is

$$r_s(1 - T_c)(1 - .20).   (16.11)$$

To reach its optimal investment/dividend decision the firm in Figure 16.4(a), uses internal
funds to undertake all investments in real assets, I_A, and then invests in securities of other
firms up to an amount I^*. At this point it stops because the after-tax return on investing in
securities is less than the opportunity cost of capital for externally supplied equity, and we
see that the investment in real assets, I_A, is less than total investment, I^*. Since all internal
funds have been used, dividends will not be paid out. The high tax bracket shareholders,
in Panel (a), prefer low (or zero) dividend payout.

In Panel (b), however, low tax bracket shareholders have a higher opportunity cost
for internally generated funds. They will want investment in real assets to stop at $I_A = I^*$.
At this point, not all internally generated capital has been spent on real investment and
dividends are paid out. For low tax bracket shareholders the cost of deferring dividends is
sufficiently high that they prefer dividend payout.

One of the implications of this model is that shareholders with different tax rates, T_{di},
will not unanimously agree on the firm's investment/dividend decision. High tax bracket
shareholders would prefer the firm to invest more and low tax bracket shareholders would

prefer less investment. This lack of unanimity can be diminished somewhat if investors self-select into clienteles with low tax bracket individuals purchasing shares of high dividend firms and vice versa.[11]

There are five other implications of the Masulis-Trueman model.

1. Firms are predicted not to externally finance security purchases for investment purposes. However, they are likely to purchase stocks with the internally generated funds which remain after financing their own profitable production opportunities.

2. Firms with many profitable production opportunities (high growth firms) will use up all of their internally generated funds without paying dividends, but older more mature firms will pay dividends because not all internally generated funds will be exhausted by investment opportunities.

3. Mergers are predicted between firms where one is internally financing its profitable investments and the other is externally financing.

4. While a decrease in current earnings should leave unchanged the investment expenditures of externally financed firms, it is likely to decrease investment expenditures of firms that initially planned to internally finance all of their investments rather than to make up the shortfall of funds through external financing.

5. Shareholder disagreement over internally financed investment policy will be more likely the greater the amount of internally generated funds relative to the firm's investment opportunities.

In these cases, firms are more likely to experience takeover attempts, proxy fights, and efforts to "go private." Given these tax-induced shareholder conflicts, diffuse ownership is more likely for externally financed firms than internally financed firms.

STOCK DIVIDENDS, STOCK SPLITS, AND REPURCHASES

Another aspect of dividend policy is stock dividends and stock splits. A *stock dividend* is paid in additional shares of stock instead of in cash and simply involves a bookkeeping transfer from retained earnings to the capital stock account.[12] In a *stock split* there is no change in the capital accounts; instead, a larger number of shares of common stock is issued. In a two-for-one split, stockholders receive two shares for each one previously held. The book value per share is cut in half; and the par, or stated, value per share of stock is similarly changed.

From a practical standpoint there is little difference between a stock dividend and a stock split. The New York Stock Exchange considers any distribution of stock totaling less than 25 percent of outstanding stock to be a stock dividend and any distribution of 25

---

[11]See Appendix 16A for empirical evidence on dividend clientele effects.

[12]The transfer from retained earnings to the capital stock account must be based on market value. In other words, if a firm's shares are selling for $100 and it has 1 million shares outstanding, a 10 percent stock dividend requires the transfer of $10 million (100,000 × $100) from retained earnings to capital stock. Stock dividends are thus limited by the size of retained earnings. The rule was put into effect to prevent the declaration of stock dividends unless the firm has had earnings.

percent or more a stock split. Since the two are similar, the issues outlined below are discussed in connection with both stock splits and stock dividends.

Stock Splits and Stock Dividends

Many hypotheses have been put forth to explain why corporations have stock splits. Logically, a paper transaction that doubles the number of shares outstanding without changing the firm in any other way should not create shareholder wealth out of thin air. The exact effect of stock splits on shareholder wealth has been studied extensively. The pioneering study by Fama, Fisher, Jensen, and Roll [1969] measured unexpected stock price changes around split ex dates. Monthly data for 940 splits between 1927 and 1959 revealed no significant changes in shareholder wealth in the split month. However, for a subsample of firms that split and increased their dividends, they found an increase in shareholders' wealth in the months following the split. For a dividend decrease subsample they found a decrease in shareholders' wealth. These results are consistent with the idea that splits are interpreted as messages about dividend increases, or about higher future cash flows.

A more recent study by Grinblatt, Masulis, and Titman [1984] used daily data and looked at shareholder returns on the split announcement date as well as the split ex date. They examined a special subsample of splits where no other announcements were made in the three-day period around the split announcement and where no cash dividends had been declared in the previous three years.[13] For this sample of 125 "pure" stock splits they found a statistically significant announcement return of 3.44 percent. They interpret stock split announcements as favorable signals about the firm's future cash flows. Surprisingly, they also find statistically significant returns (for their entire sample of 1,360 stock splits) on the split ex date. There is no good explanation for this result.

In the same study, Grinblatt, Masulis, and Titman [1984] confirm earlier work on stock dividends by Foster and Vickrey [1978] and Woolridge [1983a, 1983b]. The announcement effects for stock dividends are large, 4.90 percent for a sample of 382 stock dividends and 5.89 percent for a smaller sample of 84 stock dividends with no other announcements in a three-day period around the stock dividend announcement. One possible reason for the larger announcement effect of a stock dividend is that retained earnings must be reduced by the dollar amount of the stock dividend. Only those companies that are confident they will not run afoul of debt restrictions that require minimum levels of retained earnings will willingly announce a stock dividend. As with stock splits, there was a statistically significant positive return on the stock dividend ex date (and the day before). No explanation is offered for why the ex-date effect is observed.

One often hears that stocks split because there is an "optimal" price range for common stocks. Moving the security price into this range is alleged to make the market for trading in the security "wider" or "deeper," hence there is more trading liquidity. Copeland [1979] reports that contrary to the above argument, market liquidity is actually lower following a stock split. Trading volume is proportionately lower than its presplit level, brokerage revenues (a major portion of transactions costs) are proportionately higher, and

---

[13]However, 11 percent of the pure samples declared a dividend within one year of the stock split.

TABLE 16.5 Effect of Stock Dividends on Stock Ownership

	Percentage Increase in Ownership, 1950–1953
Stock split, 5 for 4 or higher	30
Stock dividend, 5–25%	17
No stock dividends or splits	5

Source: C. Austin Barker, ''Evaluation of Stock Dividends,'' *Harvard Business Review*, 36 (July/August 1958), pp. 99–114.

bid-ask spreads are higher as a percentage of the bid price.[14] Taken together, these empirical results point to lower post-split liquidity.

Table 16.5, from a study by Barker [1958], shows the effect of stock dividends and stock splits on common stock ownership during a four-year period. Stock splits resulted in the largest percentage increases in stock ownership. For companies and industries that did not offer stock splits or stock dividends, the increase was only 5 percent. Furthermore, the degree of increase itself increased with the size of the stock dividend or split. This evidence suggests that regardless of the effect on the total market value of the firm, the use of stock dividends and stock splits effectively increases the number of shareholders by lowering the price at which shares are traded to a more popular range.

Brennan and Copeland [1988] present a signaling model of stock splits. Because transactions costs are a higher percentage of the value of a share traded for low-priced stocks than for high-priced stocks, stock splits are a costly signal. If two companies are alike in every way except that managers of the first company believe that their firm will experience higher cash flows in the future, then the first company can benefit from a stock split because the price increase from signaling higher future cash flows will exceed the cost of (temporarily) lower liquidity. This theory predicts that the target split price, and not the split factor, will be related to the announcement date return. In other words, the market will react more favorably to a $50 stock that splits two-for-one down to the $25 price range than to a $200 stock that splits four-for-one to the $50 price range. This is exactly the empirical result that Brennan and Copeland find. In addition, McNichols and Dravid [1990] report that after the event there are unexpected positive increases in the earnings of companies that have stock splits. It seems, therefore, that stock splits are best explained as signals about better future prospects for the firm.

Stock Repurchases

A corporation's repurchase of its own stock can serve as a tax advantageous substitute for dividend payout. Repurchases have the effect of raising share prices so that shareholders can be taxed at the capital gains rate instead of the ordinary dividend rate on cash dividends.[15]

---

[14]The bid price is the price that a potential buyer offers, say $20, and the ask price is what the seller requires, suppose it's $20\frac{1}{2}$. The bid-ask spread is the difference, specifically, $\frac{1}{2}$.

[15]The following material is similar to Copeland and Weston [1988] pp. 596–600.

Corporations can repurchase their own shares in two ways: on the open market or via tender offer. Open market repurchases usually (but not always) involve gradual programs to buy back shares over a period of time. In a tender offer, the company usually specifies the number of shares it is offering to repurchase, a tender price, and a period of time during which the offer is in effect. If the number of shares actually tendered by shareholders exceeds the maximum number specified by the company, then purchases are usually made on a *pro rata* basis.[16] Alternatively, if the tender offer is undersubscribed the firm may decide to cancel the offer or extend the expiration date. Shares tendered during the extension may be purchased on either a *pro rata* or first-come, first-served basis.

Tender offers are usually significant corporate events. Dann [1981] reports that for a sample of 143 cash tender offers by 122 different firms between 1962 and 1976, the average cash distributions proposed by the tender represented almost 20 percent of the market value of the company's pre-tender equity value. The announcement effects of tender offers on the market values of corporate securities have been studied by Masulis [1980], Dann [1981], and Vermaelen [1981].[17] Share repurchases are not just a simple alternative to cash dividends. Tender offers for repurchase are related to (at least) five separate, but not mutually exclusive, hypotheses:

1. *The information or signaling hypothesis.* The cash disbursed to shareholders in a tender offer may represent a signal that the firm is expected to have increased future cash flows but it may also imply that the firm has exhausted profitable investment opportunities. Therefore, the signal may be interpreted as either good or bad news by shareholders.

2. *The leverage hypothesis.* If the repurchase is financed by issuing debt rather than paying out cash, the leverage of the firm may increase — and if there is a gain to leverage as suggested by Modigliani and Miller [1963], then shareholders may benefit.

3. *The dividend tax avoidance hypothesis.* The tender for share repurchase will be taxed as a capital gain rather than a dividend if the distribution is "essentially not equivalent to paying a dividend" (according to Section 302 of the U.S. Internal Revenue Code) or if the redemption is "substantially disproportionate" to the extent that the individual shareholder must have sold more than 20 percent of his or her holdings in the tender.[18] These criteria are rarely violated, consequently there may be a tax incentive for repurchases as opposed to large extraordinary dividends.

4. *The bondholder expropriation hypothesis.* If the repurchase unexpectedly reduces the asset base of the company, then bondholders are worse off because they have less collateral. Of course, bond indentures serve to protect against this form of expropria-

---

[16]To avoid taxation of repurchases as dividends, the repurchase usually excludes corporate officers, directors, and other insiders. Hence, most repurchases are not strictly *pro rata*.

[17]The reader is also referred to studies by Woods and Brigham [1966]; Bierman and West [1966]; Young [1967]; Elton and Gruber [1968]; Stewart [1976]; Coates and Fredman [1976]; and Lane [1976].

[18]According to Vermaelen [1981] only 3 out of 105 tender offers that he studied actually were subject to ordinary income taxes.

FIGURE 16.5   Schematic Representation of Average Price Changes
Surrounding Tender Offers for Repurchase

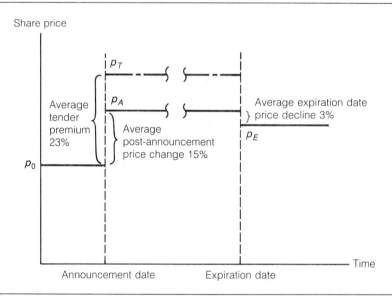

tion. A direct test of this hypothesis is to look at bond price changes on the repurchase announcement date.

5. *Wealth transfers among shareholders.* Wealth transfers between tendering and nontendering stockholders may occur when there are differential constraints and/or costs across groups of owners. Even when the tender price is substantially above the pre-tender stock price, some shareholders may voluntarily decide not to tender their shares.

A great deal can be learned about these hypotheses if we focus on the price effects on shares, bonds, and preferred stock. Figure 16.5 shows the average pattern of share price changes around the tender announcement date and the expiration date. More or less the same results were reported by Masulis [1980], Dann [1981], and Vermaelen [1981]. The average tender price, p_T, is roughly 23 percent above the announcement price, p_0. If all shares tendered were actually purchased by the firm, then the tender price, p_T, would equal the average post-announcement price, p_A. But because of *pro rata* repurchases given oversubscribed tenders we observe that on average $p_A < p_T$. The post-announcement price, p_A, averages 15 percent above the pre-announcement price, p_0. Finally, note that the average post-expiration price, p_E, is only 3 percent below the average post-announcement price, p_A, and is above the pre-announcement price, p_0. This suggests that the tender offer may have increased the market value of the firm's equity.

Unfortunately, the difference between the pre-announcement price and the post-expiration price does not measure the information effect of the tender offer. We have to look deeper. Begin by noting that the market value of the firm's equity after expiration, $p_E n_E$, is equal to the pre-announcement value, $p_0 n_0$, minus the cash paid out in the tender, $p_T(n_0 - n_E)$, plus the tender offer effect, ΔW:

$$p_E n_E = p_0 n_0 - p_T(n_0 - n_E) + \Delta W, \qquad (16.12)$$

where

p_E = the post-expiration share price

n_E = the number of shares outstanding after repurchase

p_0 = the pre-announcement share price

n_0 = the pre-announcement number of shares outstanding

p_T = the tender price

ΔW = the shareholder wealth effect attributable to the tender offer.

Note that the change in value attributable to the tender, ΔW, may be caused by (1) personal tax savings, (2) a leverage effect, (3) expropriation of bondholder wealth, or (4) the reassessment of the firm's earnings prospects.

If we define the fraction of shares repurchased, F_P, as

$$F_P = 1 - \frac{n_E}{n_0}, \qquad (16.13)$$

and divide Equation 16.12 by n_0, we have

$$p_E(1 - F_P) = p_0 - p_T F_P + \frac{\Delta W}{n_0}. \qquad (16.14)$$

Solving for $\Delta W/n_0$ and dividing by p_0 gives

$$\frac{\Delta W}{n_0 p_0} = (1 - F_P)\frac{p_E - p_0}{p_0} + F_P\frac{p_T - p_0}{p_0}. \qquad (16.15)$$

Thus, the rate of return created by the tender offer has two components. First is the rate of return received by nontendering shareholders weighted by the percent of untendered shares, $1 - F_P$; and second is the rate of return received by tendering shareholders weighted by the percent of shares purchased, F_P.

Vermaelen [1981] found that the average wealth effect, $\Delta W/n_0 p_0$, was 15.7 percent and that only 10.7 percent of the tender offers experienced a wealth decline. On average, both nontendered shares and tendered shares experienced a wealth increase, although not by equal amounts.

What causes the average 15.7 percent wealth gain from tender offers? Personal tax savings are a possibility but seem too small to explain the large wealth gain. The leverage hypothesis suggests that if the repurchase is financed with debt, and if there is a tax gain from leverage, then the shareholders will benefit. Both Masulis [1980] and Vermaelen [1981] find evidence consistent with a leverage effect. Masulis divided his sample into offers with more than 50 percent debt financing where the average announcement return was 21.9 percent, and offers with less than 50 percent debt where the average announcement return was only 17.1 percent. Vermaelen finds similar results and concludes that while it is not possible to reject the leverage hypothesis outright, it is possible to conclude that it is not the predominant explanation for the observed abnormal returns following the tender offer. Also, if leverage is a signal, then it is not possible to separate the leverage signaling effect from the leverage tax effect.

The best explanation for the shareholder wealth gain from the tender offer is that the offer represents a favorable signal. Vermaelen [1981] finds that the per-share earnings of tendering firms are above what would have been predicted by a time series model using pre-announcement data. Thus, the tender offer may be interpreted as an announcement of favorable earnings prospects. Also, the size of the tender premium, the fraction of shares repurchased, and the fraction of insider holdings are all positively related to the wealth gain, ΔW, and explain roughly 60 percent of its variance. These results are also consistent with interpreting the tender offer as a signal.

Evidence on the bondholder wealth expropriation hypothesis is provided by looking at bond price changes around the announcement date. Dann [1981] found 122 publicly traded debt and preferred stock issues for 51 tender offers. There were 41 issues of straight debt, 34 issues of convertible debt, 9 issues of straight preferred stock, and 38 issues of convertible preferred stock. An analysis of abnormal returns around the announcement date revealed significant positive rates of return for the convertible securities and rates that were insignificantly different from zero for straight debt and preferred. Furthermore, the correlation between common stock returns and straight debt (and preferred) returns was positive. Thus, the evidence seems to contradict bondholder expropriation as the dominant effect.

Repurchases via tender offer represent an interesting and significant corporate event. The empirical evidence, although not rejecting leverage effects or dividend tax avoidance effects, seems to most strongly support the hypothesis that the tender offer for repurchase is interpreted by the marketplace as favorable information regarding future prospects of the firm.

SUMMARY

Dividend policy remains a puzzle. The earliest model of dividend policy, by Miller and Modigliani [1961], shows that, in a world without taxes, dividends have no effect on shareholders' wealth. Later models, which include corporate and individual taxes (Farrar and Selwyn [1967] and Brennan [1970]), suggest that the best policy is to pay no dividends at all — that shareholders are better off selling their shares a few at a time and paying the lower capital gains rate.

Corporations do pay dividends and their payout patterns seem to have a great deal of cross-sectional regularity (as shown by Rozeff, 1981). Theories of optimal dividend policy include signaling (Ross [1978], Bhattacharya [1979], Hakansson [1982]), agency costs (Rozeff [1981]), and taxation (Masulis and Trueman [1988]). As yet, none of these theories is completely satisfactory, but together they seem to shed some light on why corporations pay dividends.

The empirical evidence on dividends, which has been voluminous, suggests that the following conclusions are warranted.

1. On average, shareholders require higher risk-adjusted returns for those firms that have higher dividend yields. These results (which are reported in Appendix 16A) have to be tempered somewhat by the fact that the studies have looked at average effects and have not attempted to look at departures from "optimal" dividend policy.

2. Dividend *changes* are clearly interpreted as signals about the future prospects of the firm. The market reacts strongly and immediately to announcements of positive dividend increases.

3. Repurchases, and to a lesser extent stock dividends and stock splits, are interpreted by the market as good news.

4. There is evidence that shareholders do self-select into clienteles, with high tax bracket shareholders migrating toward low payout firms and low tax bracket shareholders selecting high payout firms. (See Appendix A to this chapter for more on clientele effects.)

QUESTIONS

16.1 As an investor, would you rather invest in a firm with a policy of maintaining a constant payout ratio, a constant dollar dividend per share, or a constant regular quarterly dividend plus a year-end extra when earnings are sufficiently high or corporate investment needs are sufficiently low? Explain your answer.

16.2 How would each of the following changes probably affect aggregate payout ratios? Explain your answer.
  a. An increase in the personal income tax rate
  b. A liberalization in depreciation policies for federal income tax purposes
  c. A rise in interest rates
  d. An increase in corporate profits
  e. A decline in investment opportunities

16.3 Discuss the pros and cons of having the directors formally announce what a firm's dividend policy will be in the future.

16.4 Most firms would like to have their stock selling at a high price-earnings ratio with extensive public ownership (many different shareholders). Explain how stock dividends or stock splits may be compatible with these aims.

16.5 What is the difference between a stock dividend and a stock split? As a stockholder, would you prefer to see your company declare a 100 percent stock dividend or a two-for-one split?

16.6 In theory, if we had perfect capital markets, we would expect investors to be indifferent about whether cash dividends were issued or an equivalent repurchase of stock outstanding were made. What factors might in practice cause investors to value one over the other?

16.7   Discuss this statement: The cost of retained earnings is less than the cost of new outside equity capital. Consequently, it is totally irrational for a firm to sell a new issue of stock and to pay dividends during the same year.

16.8   Would it ever be rational for a firm to borrow money to pay dividends? Explain.

16.9   Unions have presented arguments similar to the following: "Corporations such as General Foods retain about half their profits for financing needs. If they financed by selling stock instead of by retaining earnings, they could cut prices substantially and still earn enough to pay the same dividend to their shareholders. Therefore, their profits are too high." Evaluate this statement.

16.10   If executive salaries are tied more to the size of the firm's sales or its total assets rather than to profitability, how might managers' policies be adverse to the interests of stockholders?

PROBLEMS

16.1   The Bane Engineering Company has $2 million of backlogged orders for its patented solar heating system. Management plans to expand production capacity by 30 percent with a $6 million investment in plant machinery. The firm wants to maintain a 45 percent debt-to-total-asset ratio in its capital structure; it also wants to maintain its past dividend policy of distributing 20 percent of after-tax earnings. In 19X0 earnings were $2.6 million. How much external equity must the firm seek at the beginning of 19X1?

16.2   Lifton Company expects next year's after-tax income to be $5 million. The firm's current debt-equity ratio is 80 percent. If Lifton has $4 million of profitable investment opportunities and wishes to maintain its current debt-equity ratio, how much should it pay out in dividends next year?

16.3   After a three-for-one stock split, Novak Company paid a dividend of $4. This represents an 8 percent increase over last year's pre-split dividend. Novak Company's stock sold for $80 prior to the split. What was last year's dividend per share?

16.4   The following is an excerpt from a 1977 *Wall Street Journal* article:

> General Motors Corp., confident of its outlook for auto sales and profit, boosted its quarterly dividend to $1 a share from 85 cents and declared a special year-end dividend of $2.25 a share. Both the quarterly and the special are payable Dec. 10 to stock of record Nov. 17.
>
> The sizeable fourth quarter payout, totaling $3.25 a share, is a record for any GM dividend in the final quarter. Last year, the No. 1 auto maker, buoyed by strong sales and sharply improved earnings, paid $3 a share in the fourth quarter.
>
> The $3.25-a-share fourth quarter will bring GM's total cash dividend on common stock for 1977 to a record $6.80 (*sic*) a share, up from the previous record, set last year, of $5.55 a share.
>
> Yesterday's action by GM directors underscored the wave of higher profit that most of the auto makers have been riding for almost two years. Moreover, in raising its quarterly dividend to $1 a share, GM indicated that it expects strong sales and earnings to

continue into 1978. In announcing the board's action, Thomas A. Murphy, Chairman, and Elliott M. Estes, President, said the dividends "reflect GM's strong earnings and capital position and our confidence in the fundamental strength of the U.S. economy and the automotive market."

The 85-cents-a-share quarterly dividend was instituted by GM in 1966; it was scaled back in 1974 when the auto industry entered a prolonged slump. The 85-cent rate was restored in the third quarter of 1976.[19]

a. Did GM appear to be following a stable dividend payout ratio or a policy of a stable dollar amount of dividends per quarter? What role did the fourth-quarter year-end "extras" perform in this policy?

b. Some authors have suggested that dividends have "announcement effects," performing the role of signaling investors that a change in underlying earning power has taken place. Is there anything in the article relevant to the concept that dividend changes convey information to investors?

16.5 In 19X0 the Odom Company paid dividends totaling $1,125,000. For the past ten years, earnings have grown at a constant rate of 10 percent. After-tax income was $3,750,000 for 19X0. However, in 19X1, earnings were $6,750,000 with investment of $5,000,000. It is predicted that Odom Company will not be able to maintain this higher level of earnings and will return to its previous 10 percent growth rate. Calculate dividends for 19X1 if Odom Company follows each of the following policies.

a. Its dividend payment is stable and growing.

b. It continues the 19X0 dividend payout ratio.

c. It uses a pure residual dividend policy (30 percent of the $5,000,000 investment was financed with debt).

d. The investment in 19X1 is financed 90 percent with retained earnings and 10 percent with debt. Any earnings not invested are paid out as dividends.

e. The investment in 19X1 is financed 30 percent with external equity, 30 percent with debt, and 40 percent with retained earnings. Any earnings not invested are paid out as dividends.

16.6 Raffer Company stock earns $7 per share, sells for $30, and pays a $4 dividend per share. After a two-for-one split, the dividend will be $2.70 per share. By what percentage has the payout increased?

16.7 Barnes Company has 500,000 shares of common stock outstanding. Its capital stock account is $500,000, and retained earnings are $2 million. Barnes is currently selling for $10 per share and has declared a 10 percent stock dividend. After distribution of the stock dividend, what balances will the retained earnings and capital stock accounts show?

16.8 The directors of Northwest Lumber Supply have been comparing the growth of their market price with that of one of their competitors, Parker Panels. Their findings are summarized in Table P16.8.

[19]"General Motors Boosts Payout to $1 a Share," *The Wall Street Journal*, November 8, 1977. Reprinted by permission of *The Wall Street Journal*, Dow Jones & Company, Inc., 1977. All Rights Reserved Worldwide.

TABLE P16.8 Northwest Lumber Supply and Parker Panels: Comparative Statements

Northwest Lumber Supply

Year	Earnings	Dividend	Payout	Price	P-E
19X9	$4.30	$2.58	60%	$68	15.8
19X8	3.85	2.31	60	60	15.6
19X7	3.29	1.97	60	50	15.2
19X6	3.09	1.85	60	42	13.6
19X5	3.05	1.83	60	38	12.5
19X4	2.64	1.58	60	31	11.7
19X3	1.98	1.19	60	26	13.1
19X2	2.93	1.76	60	31	10.6
19X1	3.48	2.09	60	35	10.1
19X0	2.95	1.77	60	30	10.2

Parker Panels

Year	Earnings	Dividend	Payout	Price	P-E
19X9	$3.24	$1.94	60%	$70	21.6
19X8	2.75	1.79	65	56	20.4
19X7	2.94	1.79	61	53	18.0
19X6	2.93	1.73	59	48	16.4
19X5	2.90	1.65	57	44	15.2
19X4	2.86	1.57	55	41	14.3
19X3	2.61	1.49	57	35	13.4
19X2	1.66	1.50	97	20	12.9
19X1	2.24	1.50	67	34	15.2
19X0	2.19	1.49	68	30	13.7

Both companies are in the same markets, and both are similarly organized (approximately the same degree of operating and financial leverage). Northwest has been consistently earning more per share; yet for some reason, it has not been valued at as high a P-E ratio as Parker. What factors would you point out as possible causes for this lower market valuation of Northwest's stock?

16.9 Associated Engineers has experienced the sales, profit, and balance sheet patterns found in Table P16.9. Identify the financial problem that has developed, and recommend a solution for it.

TABLE P16.9 Associated Engineers Financial Data, 19X0–19X9 (Millions of Dollars)

Income Statements	19X0	19X1	19X2	19X3	19X4	19X5	19X6	19X7	19X8	19X9
Sales	$100	$140	$180	$200	$240	$400	$360	$440	$480	$680
Profits after tax	10	14	18	20	24	40	36	44	48	68
Dividends	8	10	12	12	14	20	20	28	36	48
Retained earnings	$ 2	$ 4	$ 6	$ 8	$ 10	$ 20	$ 16	$ 16	$ 12	$ 20
Cumulative retained earnings	$ 2	$ 6	$ 12	$ 20	$ 30	$ 50	$ 66	$ 82	$ 94	$114

TABLE P16.9 Associated Engineers Financial Data, 19X0–19X9 (Millions of Dollars)

Balance Sheets	19X0	19X1	19X2	19X3	19X4	19X5	19X6	19X7	19X8	19X9
Current assets	$ 20	$ 30	$ 40	$ 50	$ 60	$100	$ 80	$110	$120	$160
Net fixed assets	30	40	50	50	60	100	100	110	120	180
Total assets	$ 50	$ 70	$ 90	$100	$120	$200	$180	$220	$240	$340
Trade credit	$ 8	$ 12	$ 16	$ 18	$ 20	$ 36	$ 30	$ 40	$ 40	$120
Bank credit	8	12	20	20	26	58	28	40	40	40
Other	2	10	12	12	14	16	16	18	16	16
Total current liabilities	$ 18	$ 34	$ 48	$ 50	$ 60	$110	$ 74	$ 98	$ 96	$176
Long-term debt	0	0	0	0	0	10	10	10	20	20
Total debt	$ 18	$ 34	$ 48	$ 50	$ 60	$120	$ 84	$108	$116	$196
Common stock	30	30	30	30	30	30	30	30	30	30
Retained earnings	2	6	12	20	30	50	66	82	94	114
Net worth	$ 32	$ 36	$ 42	$ 50	$ 60	$ 80	$ 96	$112	$124	$144
Total claims on assets	$ 50	$ 70	$ 90	$100	$120	$200	$180	$220	$240	$340

16.10 Babco Industries has earnings this year of $16.5 million, 50 percent of which is required to take advantage of the firm's excellent investment opportunities. The firm has 206,250 shares outstanding, selling currently at $320 a share. Ralph Miller, a major stockholder (18,750 shares), has expressed displeasure with a great deal of managerial policy. Management has approached him with the prospect of selling his holdings back to the firm, and he has expressed a willingness to do this at a price of $320 a share. Assuming that the market uses a constant P-E ratio of 4 in valuing the stock, answer the following questions.

   a. Should the firm buy Miller's shares? Assume that dividends will not be paid on them if they are repurchased.

   b. How large a cash dividend should be declared?

   c. What is the final value of Babco Industries' stock after all cash payments to shareholders?

16.11 Consider two firms in a world without taxes. They both initially have $100 of assets and both can earn 10 percent on assets with certainty. Both are all equity firms with a 10 percent cost of equity capital. One pays out all of its earnings in dividends while the other has a 50 percent dividend payout.

   a. What is the market value of equity for each firm?

   b. What does your answer to Part (a) tell you about the effect of dividend policy decisions on the market value of the firm in a world without taxes?

16.12 Firms A and B carry no debt, have the same current earnings before interest and taxes (EBIT = $1,000), the same tax rate ($T = 40\%$), and the same unlevered cost of capital ($k_U = 10\%$). However, their growth rates and dividend policies are dramatically different. Firm A retains 80 percent of its net income for future investment and its dividends grow (forever) at 8 percent per year ($g = .08$). Firm B retains only 20 percent of its net income and its dividends grow at 4 percent per year ($g = .04$).

a. Which firm is worth more?

b. Explain the intuition behind your answer to Part (a).

SELECTED REFERENCES

Aharony, J., and Swary, I., "Quarterly Dividend and Earnings Announcements and Stockholders' Returns: An Empirical Analysis," *Journal of Finance,* (March 1980), pp. 1–12.

Asquith, Paul, and Mullins, David W., Jr., "The Impact of Initiating Dividend Payments on Shareholders' Wealth," *Journal of Business,* 56 (January 1983), pp. 77–96.

Barker, C. Austin, "Evaluation of Stock Dividends," *Harvard Business Review,* (July/August, 1958), pp. 99–114.

Bhattacharya, S., "Imperfect Information, Dividend Policy, and 'The Bird in the Hand' Fallacy," *Bell Journal of Economics,* 10 (Spring 1979), pp. 259–270.

Bierman, Harold, Jr., and West, Richard, "The Acquisition of Common Stock by the Corporate Issuer," *Journal of Finance,* 21 (December 1966), pp. 687–696.

Black, F., "The Dividend Puzzle," *Journal of Portfolio Management,* (Winter 1976), pp. 5–8.

Blume, M., "Stock Returns and Dividend Yields: Some More Evidence," *Review of Economics and Statistics,* (1980), pp. 567–577.

Brennan, Michael, "Taxes, Market Valuation and Corporate Financial Policy," *National Tax Journal,* (December 1970), pp. 417–427.

———, and Copeland, T., "Stock Splits, Stock Prices, and Transaction Costs," *Journal of Financial Economics,* 22 (October 1988), pp. 83–101.

———, "Beta Changes around Stock Splits: A Note," *Journal of Finance,* 43 (September 1988), pp. 1009–1013.

Brennan, M., and P. Hughes, "Stock Prices and the Supply of Information," working paper, UCLA, 1990.

Brickley, James A., "Shareholder Wealth, Information Signaling and the Specially Designated Dividend: An Empirical Study," *Journal of Financial Economics,* 12 (August 1983), pp. 187–209.

Brittan, J. A., *Corporate Dividend Policy,* Washington, D. C.: Brookings Institute, 1966.

Charest, Guy, "Dividend Information, Stock Returns and Market Efficiency, I, II," *Journal of Financial Economics,* 6 (June-September 1978), pp. 265–296, 297–330.

Coates, C., and Fredman, A., "Price Behavior Associated With Tender Offers to Repurchase Common Stock," *Financial Executive,* (April 1976), pp. 40–44.

Constantinides, G. M., "Capital Market Equilibrium with Personal Tax," *Econometrica,* (May 1983), pp. 611–636.

Copeland, Thomas E., "Liquidity Changes Following Stock Splits," *Journal of Finance,* 34 (March 1979), pp. 115–141.

———, and Weston, J. Fred, *Financial Theory and Corporate Policy,* 3d ed., Reading, Mass.: Addison-Wesley Publishing Company, 1988.

Dann, Larry Y., "Common Stock Repurchases: An Analysis of Returns to Bondholders and Stockholders," *Journal of Financial Economics,* 9 (June 1981), pp. 113–138.

Eades, Kenneth M., "Empirical Evidence on Dividends as a Signal of Firm Value," *Journal of Financial and Quantitative Analysis,* 17 (November 1982), pp. 471–502.

———; Hess, P.; and Kim, E. H., "On Interpreting Security Returns During the Ex-Dividend Period," *Journal of Financial Economics,* (March 1984), pp. 3–34.

Elton, Edwin J., and Gruber, Martin J., "The Cost of Retained Earnings — Implications of Share Repurchase," *Industrial Management Review,* 9 (Spring 1968), pp. 68–74.

Fama, Eugene F., "The Empirical Relationships between the Dividend and Investment Decisions of Firms," *American Economic Review,* 64 (June 1974), pp. 304–318.

———, and Babiak, Harvey, "Dividend Policy: An Empirical Analysis," *Journal of the American Statistical Association,* 63 (December 1968), pp. 1132–1161.

Fama, Eugene F.; Fisher, Lawrence; Jensen, Michael; and Roll, Richard, "The Adjustment of Stock Prices to New Information," *International Economic Review,* 10 (February 1969), pp. 1–21.

Farrar, D., and Selwyn, L., "Taxes, Corporate Financial Policy and Return to Investors," *National Tax Journal,* (December 1967), pp. 444–454.

Feenberg, Daniel, "Does the Investment Interest Limitation Explain the Existence of Dividends?", *Journal of Financial Economics,* 9 (September 1981), pp. 265–269.

Foster, T., and Vickrey, D., "The Information Content of Stock Dividend Announcements," *The Accounting Review,* (1978), pp. 360–370.

Friend, Irwin, and Puckett, Marshall, "Dividends and Stock Prices," *American Economic Review,* 54 (September 1964), pp. 656–682.

Grinblatt, M.; Masulis, R.; and Titman, S., "The Valuation Effects of Stock Splits and Stock Dividends," *Journal of Financial Economics,* (December 1984), pp. 461–490.

Hakansson, Nils H., "To Pay or Not to Pay," *Journal of Finance,* (May 1982), pp. 415–428.

Handjinicolaou, G., and Kalay, A., "Wealth Redistributions or Changes in Firm Value: An Analysis of Returns to Bondholders and Stockholders Around Dividend Announcements," *Journal of Financial Economics,* (March 1984), pp. 35–64.

Hess, P., "The Ex-Dividend Behavior of Stock Returns: Further Evidence on Tax Effects," *Journal of Finance,* 37 (May 1982), pp. 445–456.

Kalay, Avner, "Stockholder-Bondholder Conflict and Dividend Constraints," *Journal of Financial Economics,* 10 (June 1982), pp. 211–233.

———, "Signaling, Information Content, and the Reluctance to Cut Dividends," *Journal of Financial and Quantitative Analysis,* 15 (November 1980), pp. 855–870.

Khoury, N., and Smith, K., "Dividend Policy and the Capital Gains Tax in Canada," *Journal of Business Administration,* (Spring 1977).

Kim, E. H.; Lewellen, W.; and McConnell, J., "Financial Leverage Clienteles: Theory and Evidence," *Journal of Financial Economics,* (March 1979), pp. 83–110.

Kwan, C., "Efficient Market Tests of the Informational Content of Dividend Announcements: Critique and Extension," *Journal of Financial and Quantitative Analysis,* 16 (June 1981), pp. 193–206.

Lane, W., "Repurchase of Common Stock and Managerial Discretion," unpublished Ph.D. dissertation, University of North Carolina, Chapel Hill, N.C., 1976.

Lintner, John, "Distribution of Incomes of Corporations among Dividends, Retained Earnings, and Taxes," *American Economic Review,* 46 (May 1956), pp. 97–113.

Long, John B., Jr., "Efficient Portfolio Choice with Differential Taxation of Dividends and Capital Gains," *Journal of Financial Economics,* 5 (August 1977), pp. 25–53.

Masulis, R., "Stock Repurchase via Tender Offer: An Analysis of the Causes of Common Stock Price Changes," *Journal of Finance,* 35 (May 1980), pp. 305–318.

———, and Trueman, B., "Corporate Investment and Dividend Decisions under Differential Personal Taxation," *Journal of Financial and Quantitative Analysis,* 23, 4 (December 1988), pp. 369–383.

McNichols, M., and Dravid, A., "Stock Dividends, Stock Splits, and Signaling," *Journal of Finance,* 45 (July 1990), pp. 857–879.

Miller, Merton H., and Modigliani, Franco, "Dividend Policy, Growth, and the Valuation of Shares," *Journal of Business,* 34 (October 1961), pp. 411–433.

———, "Dividend Policy and Market Valuation: A Reply," *Journal of Business,* 36 (January 1963), pp. 116–119.

Miller, Merton H., and Rock, Kevin, "Dividend Policy under Asymmetric Information," working paper, University of Chicago, 1984.

Miller, Merton H., and Scholes, Myron S., "Dividends and Taxes," *Journal of Financial Economics,* 6 (December 1978), pp. 333–364.

Modigliani, F., and Miller, M., "Taxes and the Cost of Capital: A Correction," *American Economic Review,* (June 1963), pp. 433–443.

Penman, Stephen H., "The Predictive Content of Earnings Forecasts and Dividends," *Journal of Finance,* 38 (September 1983), pp. 1181–1199.

Peterson, Pamela P., and Benesh, Gary A., "A Reexamination of the Empirical Relationship between Investment and Financing Decisions," *Journal of Financial and Quantitative Analysis,* 18 (December 1983), pp. 439–453.

Pettit, R. Richardson, "The Impact of Dividend and Earnings Announcements: A Reconciliation," *Journal of Business,* 49 (January 1976), pp. 86–96.

———, "Dividend Announcements, Security Performance, and Capital Market Efficiency," *Journal of Finance,* 27 (December 1972), pp. 993–1007.

Ross, S. A., "Some Notes on Financial Incentive-Signalling Models, Activity Choice and Risk Preferences," *Journal of Finance,* 33 (June 1978), pp. 777–792.

———, "The Determination of Financial Structure: The Incentive-Signalling Approach," *Bell Journal of Economics,* (Spring 1977), pp. 23–40.

Rozeff, Michael S., "Growth, Beta and Agency Costs as Determinants of Dividend Payout

Ratios," *Journal of Financial Research,* 5 (Fall 1982), pp. 249–259.

Shefrin, Hersh M., and Statman, Meir, "Explaining Investor Preference for Cash Dividends," *Journal of Financial Economics,* (June 1984), pp. 253–282.

Stewart, Samuel S., Jr., "Should a Corporation Repurchase Its Own Stock?", *Journal of Finance,* 31 (June 1976), pp. 911–921.

Vermaelen, Theo, "Common Stock Repurchases and Market Signalling: An Empirical Study," *Journal of Financial Economics,* 9 (June 1981), pp. 139–183.

Watts, Ross, "The Information Content of Dividends," *Journal of Business,* 46 (April 1973), pp. 191–211.

West, Richard R., and Brouilette, Alan B., "Reverse Stock Splits," *Financial Executive,* 38 (January 1970), pp. 12–17.

Woods, Donald H., and Brigham, Eugene F., "Stockholder Distribution Decisions: Share Repurchase or Dividends," *Journal of Financial and Quantitative Analysis,* 1 (March 1966), pp. 15–28.

Woolridge, J. Randall, "Ex-Date Stock Price Adjustment to Stock Dividends: A Note," *Journal of Finance,* (1983a), pp. 247–255.

———, "Stock Dividends as Signals," *Journal of Financial Research,* (1983b), pp. 1–12.

Young, Allan E., "The Performance of Common Stock Subsequent to Repurchase," *Financial Analysts Journal,* (September-October 1967), pp. 117–121.

APPENDIX A TO CHAPTER 16

Dividend Policy: Stock Prices and Clientele Effects

The chapter on dividend policy covered most managerial decisions. However, there are two important related issues. First is the matter of how stock prices are affected by dividend policy. Do firms with higher dividend yields have higher or lower stock prices? This question is different from whether or not changes in dividends have signaling effects. The issue is whether a firm with 50 percent of its earnings paid out in dividends has a higher stock price than the same firm with a 20 percent dividend payout. The second issue is whether or not dividend policy affects the type of shareholder who is attracted to hold the firm's stock. We might guess that low dividend firms attract high tax bracket investors and that high dividend firms attract widows and orphans with low tax brackets, and the empirical evidence seems to support this supposition.[1]

DIVIDENDS AND VALUE

In a world with no taxes, Miller and Modigliani [1961] proved that dividend payout has no effect on shareholders' wealth. When corporate and personal taxes are introduced into the model, Farrar and Selwyn [1967] and Brennan [1970] proved that if the effective capital gains rate is lower than the ordinary personal income tax rate, then shareholders' wealth decreases when dividends are paid out. Finally, Chapter 16 gave three possible arguments for optimal dividend policies: agency costs, signaling, and taxes. The empirical research on the relationship between dividend yields and common stock prices has, in most cases, not looked at the effect of departures from an optimal dividend payout. All of the studies mentioned below are tests of the general question — do investors require higher rates of return on common stocks with high dividend yields? They are based on various versions of Brennan's [1970] model:

$$E(R_{jt}) - R_{ft} = a_1 + a_2\beta_j + a_3(d_{jt} - R_{ft}), \tag{16A.1}$$

where

$E(R_{jt})$ = the expected before-tax return on the jth security

R_{ft} = the before-tax return on the risk-free asset

β_j = the systematic risk of the jth security (its "beta")

a_1 = the constant term

a_2 = the marginal effect of systematic risk

a_3 = the marginal effective tax differences between ordinary income and capital gains rates

d_{jt} = the dividend yield, that is, the dividend divided by the price of the jth security.

Equation 16A.1 is analogous to the standard Capital Asset Pricing Model discussed in Chapter 11 except that the last term looks at the possibility of a dividend effect. If a_3 is significantly positive, then we can conclude that investors do not like dividends and therefore require higher before-tax returns, R_{jt}, in order to compensate them. All other things held constant, stocks with greater dividend payout would have lower prices.

Black and Scholes [1974] tested for the relationship between security returns and dividend yield by forming well-diversified portfolios and ranking them on the basis of their systematic risk (their "beta") and then by dividend yields within each risk class. They concluded that dividend yield had no effect on security returns.

---

[1]This appendix is similar to material found in Copeland and Weston [1988] pp. 578–583 and 590–596.

Litzenberger and Ramaswamy [1979, 1980, and 1982] also test the relationship between dividends and security returns. Using the Brennan model, Equation 16A.1, they conclude that risk-adjusted returns are higher for securities with higher dividend yields. The implication is that dividends are undesirable, hence higher returns are necessary to compensate investors in order to induce them to hold high dividend yield stocks.

There are (at least) three serious problems with testing for the dividend effect predicted by Equation 16A.1. The first is that investors use dividend announcements to estimate expected returns, $E(\tilde{R}_{jt})$, that is, there is an information effect. The second is that measures of systematic risk, $\hat{\beta}_j$, are subject to a great deal of error. And the third is that individual security returns (rather than portfolio returns) are needed to obtain statistically powerful results. Litzenberger and Ramaswamy [1979] largely solved the second and third problems, but were criticized by Miller and Scholes [1983] for their handling of the information effect of dividend announcements. When using monthly data, about two-thirds of the firms in the sample will have a zero yield because most firms pay dividends on a quarterly basis. Of the firms that pay their dividend (that is, go ex dividend) in month t, about 30 to 40 percent also announce the dividend in the same month. When the announcement date and the ex-dividend date occur in the same month, the monthly return will contain both the information effect and the tax effect (if any). In order to avoid confusing these effects, Litzenberger and Ramaswamy computed dividend yields in the following way:

- If a firm declared its dividend prior to month t and went ex dividend in month t, then the dividend yield, d_{jt}, was computed using the actual dividend paid in t divided by the share price at the end of month $t - 1$.

- If a firm both declared and went ex dividend in month t, then the yield, d_{jt}, was computed using the last regular dividend, going back as far as one year.

Table 16A.1 shows the results of regressions run by Miller and Scholes [1983] using Equation 16A.1. Regressions using the actual dividend yield in month t show that the

TABLE 16A.1   Cross-Sectional Estimates of the Dividend Yield Effect (Equation 16A.1), 1940–1978

Definition of Expected Dividend Yield	Regression Coefficients		
	a_1	a_2	a_3
Actual dividend yield	.0059	.0024	.3173
	(4.5)	(1.6)	(10.2)
Level-revised monthly dividend yield	.0065	.0022	.1794
	(4.9)	(1.4)	(6.1)
Dividend yield of 12 months ago	.0038	.0019	.0376
	(2.9)	(1.3)	(1.3)
Only firms with dividends declared in advance	.0043	.0035	.0135
	(2.5)	(2.2)	(0.1)

t-Statistics in parentheses.
Source: Miller, M., and M. Scholes, "Dividends and Taxes: Some Empirical Evidence," *The Journal of Political Economy*, (December 1983), pp. 1118–1141.

dividend variable has a coefficient of .317 and is highly significant, but recall that the actual yield confuses announcement effects with dividend tax effects. When the Litzenberger-Ramaswamy measure of dividend yield (called the level-revised yield) was duplicated by Miller and Scholes, the dividend coefficient dropped from .317 to .179 and also dropped in significance.

The third regression in Table 16A.1 corrects for a bias not contemplated in the two prior regressions. Namely, some firms are expected to pay a dividend in month t but, for some reason, the board of directors suspends the dividend. Miller and Scholes call this the case of the "dog that didn't bark." Suppose that a $10 stock has a 50-50 chance of either announcing a $2 dividend (in which case the stock price doubles to $20) or suspending the dividend (thereby causing the stock price to fall to $5). The *ex ante* rate of return (and the average *ex post* return) is 35 percent, and the *ex ante* dividend yield is 10 percent.[2] However, if the level-revised measure of dividend yield is used, then if the firm actually pays the $2 dividend the yield is 20 percent and the return is 120 percent. But if the dividend is passed, the yield is 0 percent and a -50 percent return is recorded. Thus, the regressions with the level-revised measure tend to show what appears to be a positive association between returns and dividend yields. However, the correlation is spurious. A simple way to correct for the problem is to use the dividend yield of 12 months ago. Shown in the third regression in Table 16A.1, the results indicate a small, statistically insignificant relationship between dividend yields and returns.

Another approach, shown in the fourth regression in Table 16A.1, is to drop from the sample all firms except those that both paid dividends in month t and announced them in advance. Again the dividend coefficient is insignificant.

Litzenberger and Ramaswamy [1982] have responded to the Miller-Scholes criticism by rerunning their regressions. Table 16A.2 shows their results. The level-revised dividend yield gave the highest coefficient (a_3) and it is slightly higher than the Miller-Scholes estimate. Instead of using a dividend 12 months ago Litzenberger and Ramaswamy built a more sophisticated model to predict dividends. Their "predicted dividend yield" model avoids the Miller-Scholes criticism and continues to give a statistically significant estimate of the dividend effect. So, too, does a restricted subsample designed to avoid the Miller-Scholes criticism. Thus, the empirical evidence, at this point in time, points toward the conclusion that shareholders express their displeasure with corporate dividend payments by requiring a higher risk-adjusted return (that is, by paying a lower price) for those stocks that have higher dividend yields.[3]

----

[2]The *ex ante* return is computed as

$$.5\left(\frac{20-10}{10}+\frac{2}{10}\right) + .5\left(\frac{5-10}{10}\right) = .35,$$

and the *ex ante* dividend yield is

$$.5\left(\frac{2}{10}\right) + .5\left(\frac{0}{10}\right) = .10.$$

[3]The only empirical study that has found evidence shareholders prefer dividends is a paper by Long [1978], which carefully examines the case of Citizens Utilities, a company that has two classes of stock that are alike in every way except one pays cash dividends and the other pays stock dividends.

TABLE 16A.2   Pooled Time Series and Cross-Section Test of
the Dividend Effect, 1940–1980

Definition of Expected Dividend Yield	a_1	a_2	a_3
Level-revised monthly dividend yield	.0031	.0048	.233
	(1.81)	(2.15)	(8.79)
Predicted dividend yield	.0034	.0047	.151
	(1.95)	(2.08)	(5.39)
Restricted subsample	.0010	.0053	.135
	(0.52)	(2.33)	(4.38)

Source: Litzenberger, R., and K. Ramaswamy, "The Effects of Dividends on Common Stock Prices: Tax Effects or Information Effects?", *Journal of Finance*, (May 1982), p. 441.

DIVIDEND CLIENTELE EFFECTS

The clientele effect was originally suggested by Miller and Modigliani [1961]:

> If, for example, the frequency distribution of corporate payout ratios happened to correspond exactly with the distribution of investor preferences for payout ratios, then the existence of these preferences would clearly lead ultimately to a situation whose implications were different, in no fundamental respect, from the perfect market case. Each corporation would tend to attract to itself a "clientele" consisting of those preferring its particular payout ratio, but one clientele would be as good as another in terms of the valuation it would imply for firms.

The clientele effect is a possible explanation for management reluctance to alter established payout ratios because such changes might cause current shareholders to incur unwanted transactions costs.

Elton and Gruber [1970] attempt to measure clientele effects by observing the average price decline when a stock goes ex dividend. If we were current shareholders and sold our stock the instant before it went ex dividend, we would receive its price, p_B, and pay the capital gains rate, T_g, on the difference between the selling price and the price at which it was purchased, p_C. Alternatively, we could sell the stock after it went ex dividend. In this case we would receive the dividend, d, and pay the ordinary tax rate, T_0, on it. In addition, we would pay a capital gains tax on the difference between its ex-dividend price, p_A, and the original purchase price, p_C. To prevent arbitrage profits, our gain from either course of action must be the same, namely,

$$p_B - T_g(p_B - p_C) = p_A - T_g(p_A - p_C) + d(1 - T_0). \qquad \text{(16A.2)}$$

Rearranging (16A.2), we obtain

$$\frac{p_B - p_A}{d} = \frac{1 - T_0}{1 - T_g}. \qquad \text{(16A.3)}$$

Therefore the ratio of the decline in stock price to the dividend paid becomes a means of estimating the marginal tax rate of the average investor if we assume that the capital gains rate is half the ordinary tax rate.

Using 4,148 observations between April 1, 1966 and March 31, 1967, Elton and Gruber discovered that the average price decline as a percent of dividend paid was 77.7 percent. This implied that the marginal tax bracket of the average investor was 36.4 percent. They continued by arguing

> . . . the lower a firm's dividend yield the smaller the percentage of his total return that a stockholder expects to receive in the form of dividends and the larger the percentage he expects to receive in the form of capital gains. Therefore, investors who hold stocks that have high dividend yields should be in low tax brackets relative to stockholders who hold stocks with low dividend yield.

Table 16A.3 shows the dividend payout ranked from the lowest to highest deciles along with (1) the average drop in price as a percent of dividends and (2) the implied tax bracket. Note that the implied tax bracket decreases when dividend payout increases. Elton and Gruber conclude that the evidence suggests that Miller and Modigliani were right in hypothesizing a clientele effect.

A possible counterargument to this interpretation is that arbitrage may also be carried out by traders who do not own the stock initially. They would not receive favored capital gains treatment but would have to pay ordinary income taxes on short-term gains. Their arbitrage profit, Π, may be stated mathematically as

$$\Pi = -p_B + d - T_0 d + p_A + T_0(p_B - p_A). \tag{16A.4}$$

TABLE 16A.3 Dividend Yield Statistics Ranked by Decile

| | | $(p_B - p_A)/d^*$ | | | | |
Decile	d/p Mean	Mean	Standard Deviation	Z Value	Probability: True Mean Is One or More	Implied Tax Bracket
1	.0124	.6690	.8054	.411	.341	.4974
2	.0216	.4873	.2080	2.465	.007	.6145
3	.0276	.5447	.1550	2.937	.002	.5915
4	.0328	.6246	.1216	3.087	.001	.5315
5	.0376	.7953	.1064	1.924	.027	.3398
6	.0416	.8679	.0712	1.855	.031	.2334
7	.0452	.9209	.0761	1.210	.113	.1465
8	.0496	.9054	.0691	1.369	.085	.1747
9	.0552	1.0123	.0538	.229	.591	**
10	.0708	1.1755	.0555	3.162	.999	**

*Spearman's rank correlation coefficient between d/p and $(p_B - p_A)/d$ is .9152, which is significant at the 1 percent level.
**Indeterminate.
Source: Elton, E. J., and M. J. Gruber, "Marginal Stockholders' Tax Rates and the Clientele Effect," reprinted from *The Review of Economics and Statistics*, (February 1970), p. 72.

They spend p_B to acquire the stock before it goes ex dividend, then receive the dividend and pay ordinary income taxes on it, and finally sell the stock after it goes ex dividend (receiving p_A dollars) and receive a tax shield from their short-term loss. Rearranging Equation 16A.4 we see that their profit is

$$\Pi = (1 - T_0)[p_A - p_B + d].\qquad\qquad\text{(16A.5)}$$

To prevent arbitrage profits, the price decline must equal the amount of dividend payout, that is, $p_B - p_A = d$.

The above condition is completely different from Equation 16A.3 proposed by Elton and Gruber. Of course, neither model has taken transactions costs into account, nor have we considered other classes of investors, such as tax-free investors. Therefore no strong conclusion can be made regarding the existence of a clientele effect.

Pettit [1977] tested for clientele effects by examining the portfolio positions of approximately 914 individual accounts handled by a large retail brokerage house between 1964 and 1970. He argues that stocks with low dividend yields will be preferred by investors with high income, by younger investors, by investors whose ordinary and capital gains tax rates differ substantially, and by investors whose portfolios have high systematic risk. His model is

$$DY_i = a_1 + a_2\beta_i + a_3 AGE_i + a_4 INC_i + a_5 DTR_i + \epsilon_i,\qquad\text{(16A.6)}$$

where

DY_i = dividend yield for the ith individual's portfolio in 1970

β_i = the systematic risk of the ith individual's portfolio

AGE_i = the age of the individual

INC_i = the gross family income averaged over the last three years

DTR_i = the difference between the income and capital gains tax rates for the ith individual

ϵ_i = a normally distributed random error term.

He finds that[4]

$$DY_i = \underset{(11.01)}{.042} - \underset{(-16.03)}{.021\beta_i} + \underset{(6.15)}{.031 AGE_i} - \underset{(-2.25)}{.037 INC_i} + \underset{(1.57)}{.006 DTR_i}.$$

The evidence suggests that there is a clientele effect because a significant portion of the observed cross-sectional variation in individual portfolio dividend yields can be explained. However, the study in no way suggests that the market price of a security is determined by the dividend policy followed by the firm.

A second study by Lewellen, Stanley, Lease, and Schlarbaum [1978] was drawn from the same data base as the Pettit study, but reached different conclusions. They ran a multiple regression to explain the dividend yields of investor portfolios as a function of

---

[4]The numbers in parentheses are t-statistics. The r^2 was .3 for 914 observations.

TABLE 16A.4   Pooled Time Series and Cross-Section Test of Tax Clientele, 1940–1980, Using Predicted Dividends

Dividend Yield Group	a_1	$t(a_1)$	a_2	$t(a_2)$	a_3	$t(a_3)$
1 (low yield)	.0048	(2.22)	.0050	(2.06)	.555	(2.83)
2	.0021	(1.01)	.0047	(1.97)	.486	(4.18)
3	.0034	(1.69)	.0043	(1.78)	.339	(5.32)
4	.0018	(0.98)	.0067	(2.70)	.212	(4.74)
5 (high yield)	.0037	(1.94)	.0062	(2.62)	.022	(0.65)

Source: Litzenberger, R., and K. Ramaswamy, "The Tax Effects of Dividends on Common Stock Prices: Tax Effects or Information Effects?" *Journal of Finance*, (May 1982), p. 438.

various investor characteristics. Although the tax rate variable was negatively related to dividend yield and was statistically significant, it implied that a 10 percent increase in an investor's marginal (imputed) tax bracket was associated with only a .1 percent decline in the yield of securities held. This suggests only a very weak clientele effect.

Finally, the Litzenberger-Ramaswamy study [1982] reports results that may be interpreted as consistent with dividend clienteles. They ranked all NYSE stocks on the basis of their dividend yield and then divided the entire sample into quintiles based on market value. Companies in the first quintile comprised the one-fifth of total market value with the lowest dividend yield, and so on. They then ran a regression based on Equation 16A.1. The results are given in Table 16A.4. Note that the dividend yield coefficient, a_3, decreases as the dividend yield in each quintile becomes larger. The lowest dividend yield stocks had the most severe return penalty for dividend payments and the highest yield stocks had no statistically significant penalty at all. These results are consistent with the interpretation that high tax bracket clientele hold low yield stocks while low bracket clientele hold high yield stocks.

SUMMARY

The empirical evidence on the relationship between dividends and share prices is mixed. Some researchers such as Litzenberger and Ramaswamy [1979, 1980, 1982] report that investors dislike dividends and that they require higher returns to compensate them for dividend taxes. However, Miller and Scholes [1983] find no dividend effect. Only one study by Long [1978] provides evidence for shareholder preference for dividends.

Although the empirical evidence on dividend clientele effects is also mixed, most studies do find evidence in support of a clientele effect. High tax bracket investors seem to prefer low dividend stocks, presumably because they pay lower taxes when receiving their return in the form of capital gains.

SELECTED REFERENCES

Black, F., and Scholes, M., "The Effects of Dividend Yield and Dividend Policy on Common Stock Prices and Returns," *Journal of Financial Economics,* 1 (May 1974), pp. 1–22.

Brennan, Michael, "Taxes, Market Valuation and Corporate Financial Policy," *National Tax Journal,* (December 1970), pp. 417–427.

Copeland, Thomas E., and Weston, J. Fred, *Financial Theory and Corporate Policy,* 3d ed., Reading, Mass.: Addison-Wesley, 1988.

Elton, Edwin J., and Gruber, Martin J., "Marginal Stockholder Tax Rates and the Clientele Effect," *Review of Economics and Statistics,* 52 (February 1970), pp. 68–74.

Farrar, D., and Selwyn, L., "Taxes, Corporate Financial Policy and Return to Investors," *National Tax Journal,* (December 1967), pp. 444–454.

Lewellen, Wilbur G.; Stanley, Kenneth L.; Lease, Ronald C.; and Schlarbaum, Gary G., "Some Direct Evidence on the Dividend Clientele Phenomenon," *Journal of Finance,* 33 (December 1978), pp. 1385–1399.

Litzenberger, R., and Ramaswamy, K., "The Effects of Dividends on Common Stock Prices: Tax Effects or Information Effects?"

Journal of Finance, 37 (May 1982), pp. 429–444.

———, "Dividends, Short-Selling Restrictions, Tax-Induced Investor Clienteles and Market Equilibrium," *Journal of Finance,* 35 (May 1980), pp. 462–482.

———, "The Effect of Personal Taxes and Dividends on Capital Asset Prices: Theory and Empirical Evidence," *Journal of Financial Economics,* (June 1979), pp. 163–196.

Long, John B., Jr., "The Market Valuation of Cash Dividends: A Case to Consider," *Journal of Financial Economics,* 6 (June-September 1978), pp. 235–264.

Miller, Merton H., and Modigliani, Franco, "Dividend Policy, Growth, and the Valuation of Shares," *Journal of Business,* 34 (October 1961), pp. 411–433.

Miller, Merton H., and Scholes, Myron S., "Dividends and Taxes: Some Empirical Evidence," *Journal of Political Economy,* (December 1983), pp. 1118–1141.

Pettit, R. Richardson, "Taxes, Transactions Costs and the Clientele Effect of Dividends," *Journal of Financial Economics,* 5 (December 1977), pp. 419–436.

CHAPTER 17

Value-Based Management

Stated simply, the theme of this book is that all managerial decisions should serve to maximize the value of the firm on behalf of its stakeholders. In the earlier chapters, we studied decisions across time, risk-return trade-offs, and contingent claims. When these frameworks were applied to the liabilities side of the balance sheet (capital structure and dividend policy) we saw that opportunities to increase value were limited or possibly nonexistent. In this chapter, we focus on the entire firm to show (1) how value-based management systems provide superior understanding for maximizing the value of the firm, (2) how to value companies, and (3) that the valuation methodology works well when discounted cash flow valuations are compared with actual market values.

VALUE-BASED MANAGEMENT

One of the surprising facts of life is that the top management of most companies uses the analysis of the net present value (NPV) for major capital budgeting decisions, but when setting corporate strategy or evaluating managerial performance it almost never analyzes value created. This pattern is surprising because the NPV of a single project is an estimate of the value created at the project level. At the company level, however, management does not seem to study the value creation at all. This section of the chapter illustrates why top management should abandon traditional accounting-based decision-making tools — e.g., return on equity (ROE), return on assets (ROA), return on sales (ROS), and growth in earnings per share — and why it should focus on value creation. Having established value creation as the appropriate goal, we then discuss how it can be used in value-based management systems: to provide quick diagnostics, to restructure companies, to implement value-based planning, and to compensate executives—especially at the business unit level.

Using Value to Measure Performance and Set Strategy

There is no good reason to use ROS, ROE, ROA, or growth in earnings per share as corporate goals or measures of performance. Their only virtue is that, being accounting based, they are easy to calculate. As we shall see, however, each of them can be inconsistent with value creation. Later on, when we review formula approaches for estimating value, we shall establish that three factors work together to create value:

1. *ROIC > WACC.* The return on invested capital (ROIC) must exceed the weighted average cost of capital (WACC). This is absolutely a necessary condition for creating value.

2. *The amount of investment.* Business units with high rates of return cannot create much value unless a great deal of capital can be invested in them. For example, the return on capital for bank trust departments is always high, because their capital requirements are low. However, they do not create much value because they cannot grow rapidly.

3. *The interval of competitive advantage.* This is the period of time when the ROIC is expected to exceed the WACC before competition drives the rate of return down to long-term equilibrium levels. For example, a new product might be sold at a relatively high price to "skim" the market, but with the expectation that the resulting high profits will quickly attract competition, or, alternatively, a lower price might be chosen with the expectation that competitors might find other opportunities more attractive. Without further analysis it is not clear which of these strategies creates greater value.

Various combinations of these three ingredients work together to create value. It should be made clear that they are fundamentally forward-looking and that they are based on expected future cash flows. Cash flows use both income statement and balance sheet information.

To contrast expected cash flows with earnings per share, take a look at the projected income statements for the Longlife and Shortlife companies in Table 17.1. To keep the example as simple as possible, we have assumed no debt or taxes. Consequently, earnings before interest and taxes, EBIT, equals net income, NI. Which company has the better value-maximizing strategy? This is not a trick question. It is, however, a question with insufficient information to answer it. Our point is this—there is not enough information on the income statement alone to make value-based decisions. Both companies have exactly the same net income. Earnings, or earnings growth, are inadequate measures of performance because they ignore critical balance sheet information and because they can never be used to understand whether or not ROIC > WACC.

Table 17.2 combines information from the income statement and the balance sheet to project expected cash flows for the two (all equity) companies. Cash flows are defined as operating cash flows (after taxes if any) plus depreciation, a noncash operating charge,

TABLE 17.1   Projected Income Statements ($ in Millions)

Longlife Company	Year 1	Year 2	Year 3	Year 4	Year 5	Year 6
Sales	$1,000	$1,050	$1,100	$1,200	$1,300	$ 1,450
Cash expenses	(700)	(745)	(790)	(880)	(970)	(1,105)
Depreciation	(200)	(200)	(200)	(200)	(200)	(200)
EBIT = NI	100	105	110	120	130	145
Shortlife Company						
Sales	$1,000	$1,050	$1,100	$1,200	$1,300	$ 1,450
Cash expenses	(700)	(745)	(790)	(880)	(970)	(1,105)
Depreciation	(200)	(200)	(200)	(200)	(200)	(200)
EBIT = NI	100	105	110	120	130	145

Source: T. Copeland; T. Koller; and J. Murrin, *Valuation: Measuring and Managing the Value of Companies*, New York: John Wiley & Co., 1990, p. 76.

minus capital expenditures, minus increases in working capital. In other words, the cash flows provided by a company are its operating cash flows less cash flows needed to grow the balance sheet. The major differences between Longlife and Shortlife are found on the balance sheet, not the income statement. Longlife uses manufacturing equipment that must be replaced every three years, while Shortlife uses equipment that must be replaced every year but costs only one-third as much. In addition, Shortlife does a much better job of collecting its receivables.

TABLE 17.2   Projected Cash Flow ($ in Millions)

Longlife Company	Year 1	Year 2	Year 3	Year 4	Year 5	Year 6	Cumulative
Net income = EBIT	$ 100	$ 105	$ 110	$ 120	$ 130	$ 145	$ 710
Depreciation	200	200	200	200	200	200	1,200
Capital expenditures	(600)	0	0	(600)	0	0	(1,200)
Increase in receivables	(250)	(13)	(13)	35	45	(23)	(219)
Cash flow	(550)	292	297	(245)	375	322	491
Shortlife Company							
Net income = EBIT	$ 100	$ 105	$ 110	$ 120	$ 130	$ 145	$ 710
Depreciation	200	200	200	200	200	200	1,200
Capital expenditures	(200)	(200)	(200)	(200)	(200)	(200)	(1,200)
Increase in receivables	(150)	(8)	(8)	(15)	(15)	(23)	(219)
Cash flow	(50)	97	102	105	115	122	491

Source: T. Copeland, T. Koller, and J. Murrin, *Valuation: Measuring and Managing the Value of Companies*, New York: John Wiley & Co., 1990, p. 77.

TABLE 17.3   Value of Longlife and Shortlife ($ in Millions)

	Longlife CF	NPV @10%	Shortlife CF	NPV @10%
Year 1	$(550)	$(500.00)	$ (50)	$ (45.45)
Year 2	292	241.32	97	80.17
Year 3	297	223.14	102	76.63
Year 4	(245)	(167.34)	105	71.72
Year 5	375	232.85	115	71.41
Year 6	322	181.76	122	68.87
Total	491	211.73	491	323.35

Table 17.3 contrasts the present value of Longlife and Shortlife, assuming that they have the same risk and, therefore, that their WACC is 10 percent. Clearly, anyone with a 10 percent opportunity cost of capital would find Shortlife to be the superior company. Shortlife is worth $323 million while Longlife is worth only $212 million. This simple numerical example clearly demonstrates why top level management should not base strategic decisions nor measure performance by relying on earnings, earnings per share, or earnings per share growth.

Figure 17.1 compares the earnings per share of Giant Food versus Albertson's for the decade 1978–1987. Which is better? Giant Food has a slightly higher growth rate, *but* it also has less stability. The right-hand panel of Figure 17.1 shows the value in 1987 of one dollar invested in 1978 for the two companies (including reinvested dividends). The

FIGURE 17.1   EPS Growth versus Shareholder Value

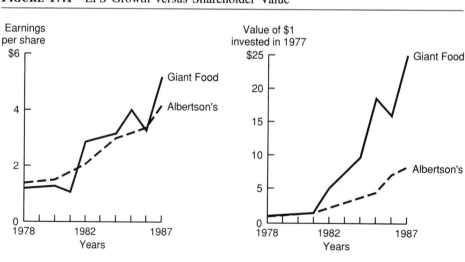

differences are remarkable. At the end of the decade, one dollar invested in Albertson's was worth $8 while the same dollar invested in Giant Food had grown to be worth $25. The differences can be traced to fundamental business improvements by Giant relative to Albertson's. Giant's operating margin improved while Albertson's declined. Consequently Albertson's sales had to grow faster to generate the same earnings growth. Giant's inventory turnover improved while Albertson's deteriorated. Giant increased its financial leverage while Albertson's reduced its debt levels. This comparison of Giant versus Albertson's provides additional evidence that value creation is fundamentally different from earnings per share or growth in earnings per share.

Another commonly used metric of performance is return on equity, ROE. It, too, is seriously flawed. Table 17.4 shows the return on equity for four business units of a multinational conglomerate. If one were to use return on equity as a means for allocating resources to the business units, then the bank would be the top candidate. Fortunately, the senior management of this company asked a different question — "Which business units have the greatest projected increases in value?" Using this point of view, a completely different picture emerges. Now the steel company, which had earned less than its cost of equity, turned out to have the greatest value creation potential. This example illustrates a common problem with accounting-based measures of performance — they tend to be backward-looking. One should care less about how a business unit did last year than how it is expected to do in the future.

Even if a company is trying to forecast the ROE of its business units, there is often a great difference between forecasted ROE and value created. Figure 17.2 shows the forecasted ROE for a major business unit of a bank using a three-year horizon — the standard forecast period for the bank. Two strategies were being compared. The first was to treat the business unit as a cash cow while the second, a growth strategy, was to recapture market share by investing heavily in advertising, refurbishment of branches, and installation of newer automatic teller machines. The ROE of the two strategies was quite similar, but as shown in Figure 17.3, the value created by the more aggressive growth strategy to recapture market share was 130 percent greater than the cash flow alternative. It would have been easy for management to reject the growth strategy because its ROE was about the same and because it required a substantial amount of investment. However, by focusing on value creation the correct decision became obvious.

We have focused on the most common measures of performance, earnings per share, and return on equity; but other measures are also flawed. Companies that focus on return

TABLE 17.4   ROE versus Value-Creation Potential

Business Unit	1989 ROE	1989 Value	Value Creation	As a % of Value in 1989
Steel Co.	10.6%	$510 million	$163 million	32%
Bank	41.1	787	75	10
Building materials	2.2	204	24	12
Development and construction	5.6	258	82	32

FIGURE 17.2 Projected ROE for Two Strategies

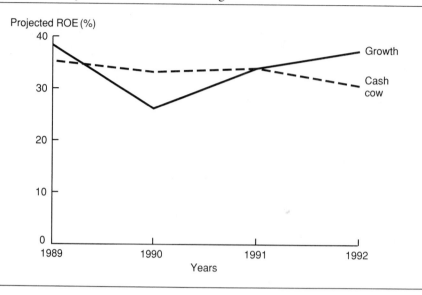

on sales (ROS) completely ignore management of their balance sheets, e.g., working capital management. And companies that use return on assets (ROA) fall into the usual problems that accounting-based measures are heir to. For example, the ROA on a business unit may be artificially high because the assets of the unit are depreciated, or because the unit does not require many assets in the first place.

FIGURE 17.3 Value Created by Two Strategies

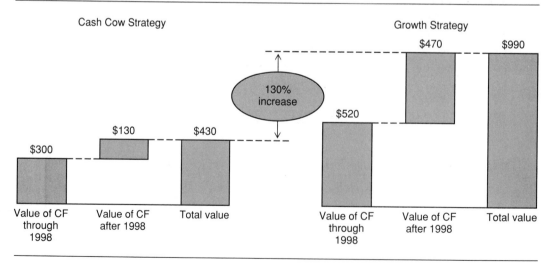

Using Value-Based Management to Restructure Companies

Later on in the chapter, we shall go into great detail about how to value companies and their business units. But, before doing that, let's take a look at how value-based management can be used to change companies. Figure 17.4 shows the normal evolutionary track that managements seem to follow as they shake off bad habits (like using ROE to measure business unit performance) and adopt value-based management. The first step is usually an experiment—a diagnostic scan—that is driven by top-level management as a quick and dirty value-based analysis to attempt to surface major new value-creating opportunities or to better understand the differences in point of view when value creation is contrasted with older metrics like ROE. The next step in the evolution is generally a strategic restructuring of the company. Like most strategic exercises this event takes place only when needed and it generally has a major impact on the company. When the restructuring has been completed, the firm usually implements value-based planning as an annual event designed to get the maximum value out of the company. Finally, once top-level and business unit managers are familiar and comfortable with value-based planning, it is time to tie a portion of executive compensation to value creation.

Since restructuring is a major strategic event, let's use a disguised real example to illustrate the tremendous impact it can have. The framework used here was developed at McKinsey & Co. and is called the restructuring pentagon. It is illustrated in Figure 17.5. It provides an exhaustive list of all of the actions that can maximize the value of a company. It starts by looking at the current market-determined value of the company. The company in Figure 17.6 had 17 different business units and the market value of its equity was roughly $1 billion before restructuring. Its stock price performance had been lacklus-

---

FIGURE 17.4 Value-Based Management System

Diagnostic scan	Restructuring	Value-based planning	Value-based compensation
• Top management • Quick and dirty analysis • Surface major hypotheses	• Value the company and each business unit • Surface all strategic and operating improvements • Evaluate all acquisition and divestiture opportunities • Understand financial engineering opportunities • Monitor headquarters costs	• Annual cycle • Dialogue between top management and business units • Understand value drivers within each business unit • Allocate capital based on value-creation potential	• Tie compensation to value captured • Separate factors under management control from external factors • Focus on business units

FIGURE 17.5   McKinsey Restructuring Pentagon Framework

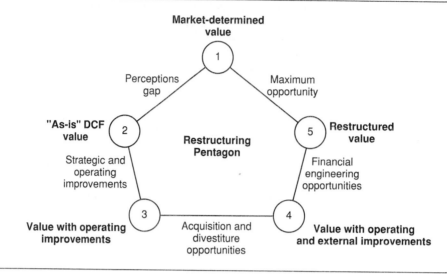

ter and it had made several acquisitions that had not paid off as expected. Top management decided to undertake a value-based restructuring exercise. The first step was to value each business unit as well as corporate headquarters. When aggregated, the value of the company if operated "as is," according to its own plans, was approximately $975 million. Consequently, the perceptions gap, i.e., the difference between the market value of the company and its discounted cash flow value (DCF value), was quite small. This is not always the case. Sometimes the company is a takeover target and the market value is well above the "as is" value. When this happens the best way for management to avoid the raider threat is to change course to increase the "as is" value of the company. Sometimes the market value of the company is higher than the "as is" value. This may be due to inside information that needs to be disclosed to the market to increase the market's perception about the value of the company, or to the fact that management's forecast about future cash flows is too optimistic.

After understanding its "as is" value, the company in Figure 17.6 took a careful look at the operations of each business unit to discover improvements that could be made — for example, discontinuing unprofitable product lines, consolidating operations, cutting headquarters costs, improving the management of working capital, focusing research and development efforts, and improving marketing, sales, and distribution. When added together, these strategic and operating improvements were worth $350 million. If all of the value from these improvements could be captured, the company's value would rise to $1,275 billion (at Vertex 3 of the pentagon).

The company also had two money-losing business units that had subpar performance relative to competition and were not anticipated to become first-quartile performers. Their

FIGURE 17.6 Disguised Example of Restructuring

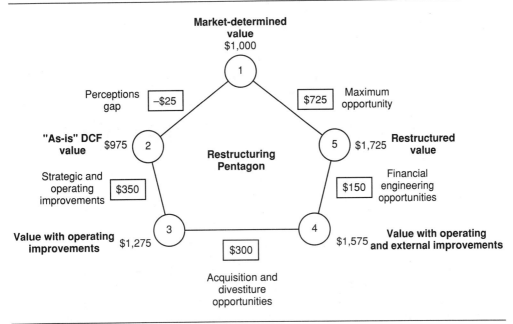

Market-determined
value
$1,000

Perceptions
gap   −$25

$725   Maximum
opportunity

"As-is" DCF $975
value

Restructuring
Pentagon

$1,725   Restructured
value

Strategic and
operating $350
improvements

$150   Financial
engineering
opportunities

Value with operating $1,275
improvements

$1,575   Value with operating
and external improvements

$300

Acquisition and
divestiture
opportunities

value if sold exceeded their "as is" value by $300 million. Management decided they should be sold.

Finally, the company was underutilizing its debt capacity. The present value of the tax shield from prudent use of debt was estimated to be worth about $150 million—a financial engineering opportunity.

Altogether the company found $750 million of value-creation opportunities and it began to implement its plans. Over a three-year period its stock price increased 70 percent *relative to comparables* in its own industry. In other words, it actually captured nearly all of the value from restructuring. This is not a fairy tale—it actually happened. We have seen it happen dozens of times. On average, about 64 percent of the value-creation opportunities come from strategic and operating opportunities directly under management's control, another 22 percent come from acquisitions or divestitures, and the balance—about 14 percent—from financial engineering opportunities.

Value-Based Planning

Restructuring is a strategic event that takes place on an as-needed basis. Value-based planning is an annual event that is part of a company's culture. It focuses on the value-creation potential of each business unit and on the value drivers that the business unit managers have under their control. As part of the planning cycle, business unit managers establish specific objectives during a dialogue with top management and capital is allocated based on the value-creation potential of each business unit.

FIGURE 17.7   ROIC Comparisons

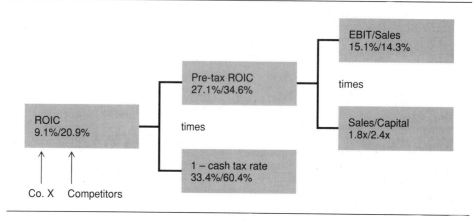

Part of the value-based planning exercise is a competitive analysis of each business unit. It is not always easy to find "pure play" comparables, but some comparisons, even if not perfect, usually lead to profitable insights. The relevant question is whether or not a business unit is a first-quartile performer against competition, and if not, why not. Figure 17.7 shows a return on invested capital (ROIC) tree for a publishing company compared with the averages for about a half-dozen competitors. For planning purposes the company had focused on return on sales as its primary performance criterion. Based on ROS, they were doing fine. They earned 15.1 percent while their average competitor earned 14.3 percent. But their stock price had been falling and their return on invested capital was well below their competition, 9.1 percent versus 20.9 percent. Why? There were two reasons. The first, and most obvious, was that the company was paying more taxes. The second reason, and the one that we want to focus on here, was poor management of their working capital and of their plant capacity utilization. Their capital turnover was low. They had a ratio of 1.8 versus an average of 2.4 for their competitors. This does not seem like much to worry about, but when we put a value to the opportunity of improving capital management, it turned out to be $500 million. This opportunity had been missed (1) because the company had been focusing on return on sales instead of value creation and (2) because it had never done a thorough competitive analysis.

Another significant part of value-based planning is understanding value drivers.[1] Headquarters needs to understand that the relevant value drivers differ among business units, and business unit managers need to understand which of the value drivers under their control can be changed to create the greatest effect on value. Figure 17.8 illustrates a simplified analysis of value drivers for three business units of a large consumer products company. Consumerco, the largest business unit, could benefit almost equally from sales growth and operating-margin improvements. An implication was that price increases to

---

[1] For an excellent presentation of value drivers see A. Rappaport, *Creating Shareholder Value*.

FIGURE 17.8   Value Drivers for Three Business Units

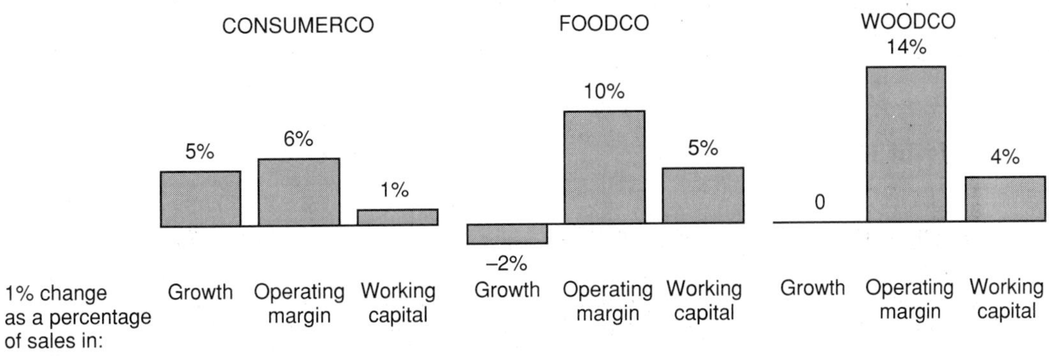

Source: T. Copeland; T. Koller; and J. Murrin, *Valuation: Measuring and Managing the Value of Companies,* New York: John Wiley & Co., 1990.

raise operating margins are useless if sales growth erodes as a result. Foodco was a restaurant operation. The parent company's plan was to spend capital to grow this business unit. What they learned from an analysis of the value drivers was that growing the business would actually destroy value because ROIC < WACC. Instead, what they needed to do was work hard to increase operating margins. A similar story unfolded for Woodco—a furniture business.

As the above-mentioned examples have illustrated, the objective of value-based planning is not merely to value business units, but to help business unit managers understand how their actions affect the value of the company, and to focus continually on value-creation opportunities. Value-based planning is particularly useful for multibusiness companies because value is an easily understood least common denominator for performance comparisons across business units. Other performance measures, e.g., ROE or ROA, are not.

VALUING COMPANIES

There are many methodologies for valuing companies. The one that we will focus on is discounted cash flows. The procedure requires a good forecast of expected future cash flows and a theoretically sound estimate of the risk-adjusted discount rate that is consistent with the cash flow definition. This section is divided into two parts: (1) formula approaches and (2) spreadsheet approaches for valuing companies. Before explaining the details of DCF, however, it is useful to describe the market value of a company as the maximum of three alternatives:

Market value = MAX [liquidation, going concern, sale to third party]

The *liquidation value* is the amount that can be realized if an asset or group of assets is sold separately from the organization that has been using it. It may imply selling off inventory and equipment, or it may be the *break-up value* that results from selling business units as separate entities. The *going-concern value* is the worth of a company when operated "as is" by current management. The valuation of W. R. Grace and Company that follows is a going-concern value. The final way of looking at value is *sale to a third party,* and it may exceed the "as is" value if a third party is willing to pay more — presumably because they can improve the way the business is being operated.

The marketplace will value a company as the higher of the liquidation or going-concern value as long as the market believes that the company will be operated "as is" by incumbent management. However, if the company is worth more if it were operated by someone else, and if the company is not takeover-proof, then the market value will exceed the "as is" or going-concern value. The premium above the "as is" value will depend on the probability of a change in control, the timing of the change, and the magnitude of the value enhancements that can be made. Separate from these market value estimates is the book value of a company — the historical record of the book value of the company's assets as represented on its balance sheet.

The remainder of this chapter is devoted to the implementation of valuing companies. For convenience, we separate the material into sections on "formula" approaches and a "spreadsheet" approach. Both use discounted cash flow methods as described in Chapter 9 on capital budgeting. Each approach has advantages and limitations. The formula approaches provide insight into the critical factors that affect value. But if a large number of variables must be taken into consideration, the formulas become cumbersome. In addition, it is often necessary to make restrictive assumptions to keep a formula compact.

The spreadsheet approach facilitates the consideration of a larger number of factors or variables that may impact the value of a company. The spreadsheet approach, therefore, relates factors affecting value drivers to the efforts for enhancing the value of the firm. The two approaches are complementary in that spreadsheets are often used to analyze data patterns that facilitate the use of formulas. In turn, formulas are used in arriving at valuations of data elaborated in spreadsheets. Since valuation requires forecasts of the future, the valuations by either approach depend upon forecasts or projections of the critical factors determining value — the value drivers.

We present both approaches because spreadsheets permit a wider range of variables to be considered. With the increased use of computer spreadsheets, company valuations are now widely performed on personal computers. (We will use Lotus 1-2-3.) We begin with an explanation of formula approaches since a formula is used in the spreadsheet approach to determine the continuing value of a company beyond the explicit forecast period. Also it is always possible to reformulate a problem into a small number of critical value drivers as a check on the spreadsheet valuations. This provides a test as to whether the increased complexity introduced by the spreadsheet approach has any significant impacts on valuation. Reformulating a problem for use in formulas often sharpens understanding of the key or critical factors influencing value. In addition, the formula approach and the spreadsheet approach provide mutual checks on the reasonableness of the procedures and the accuracy of the resulting valuations.

FORMULA APPROACHES FOR VALUING COMPANIES

At first, we will derive a valuation formula assuming that a company has no debt and that there are no taxes, then we will extend it to include taxes and debt capital as a source of financing. Table 17.5 shows the cash flows for a company. In the first year, for example, cash flows are equal to net operating income, NOI, less new capital expenditures, I_1. We have assumed that depreciation and replacement investment are equal so that they cancel out and are not shown in the table. Therefore, I_1 represents only net new investment in capital expenditures and working capital and r_1 is the rate of return on new capital expenditures. Since the firm is all equity, the appropriate discount rate is the unlevered cost of equity, k_u, and the value of the firm is:

$$V_o = \frac{NOI_1 - I_1}{1 + k_u} + \frac{NOI_2 - I_2}{(1 + k_u)^2} + \cdots + \frac{NOI_N - I_N}{(1 + k_u)^N}. \tag{17.1}$$

The amount of operating income in Year 2 depends on the level of income in Year 1, NOI_1, which is maintained by replacement investment equal to depreciation, and on the return on new capital invested times the amount of new capital, $r_1 I_1$. This is illustrated in Row 2 of Table 17.5. Mathematically, the present value of the growing firm, given in Equation 17.1, can be rewritten as:

$$V_o = \frac{NOI_1 - I_1}{1 + k_u} + \frac{NOI_1 + r_1 I_1 - I_2}{(1 + k_u)^2} + \frac{NOI_1 + r_1 I_1 + r_2 I_2 - I_3}{(1 + k_u)^3}$$

$$\tag{17.2}$$

$$+ \cdots + \frac{NOI_1 + \sum\limits_{t=1}^{N-1} r_t I_t - I_N}{(1 + k_u)^N}.$$

TABLE 17.5   Cash Flows

Time Period	Cash Inflow	Cash Outflow
1	NOI_1	$-I_1$
2	$NOI_2 = NOI_1 + r_1 I_1$	$-I_2$
3	$NOI_3 = NOI_1 + r_1 I_1 + r_2 I_2$	$-I_3$
•	•	•
•	•	•
•	•	•
N	$NOI_N = NOI_1 + \sum\limits_{t=1}^{N-1} r_t I_t$	$-I_N$

To simplify this expression, first rearrange terms as follows:

$$V_o = \frac{NOI_1}{1 + k_u} + \frac{NOI_1}{(1 + k_u)^2} + \cdots + \frac{NOI_1}{(1 + k_u)^N}$$

$$+ I_1\left[\frac{r_1}{(1 + k_u)^2} + \frac{r_1}{(1 + k_u)^3} + \cdots + \frac{r_1}{(1 + k_u)^N} - \frac{1}{(1 + k_u)}\right]$$

$$+ I_2\left[\frac{r_2}{(1 + k_u)^3} + \frac{r_2}{(1 + k_u)^4} + \cdots + \frac{r_2}{(1 + k_u)^N} - \frac{r_1}{(1 + k_u)^2}\right] + \cdots$$

The result can be generalized as:

$$V_o = \sum_{t=1}^{N} \frac{NOI_1}{(1 + k_u)^t} + \sum_{t=1}^{N} I_t\left[\left(\sum_{\tau=t+1}^{N} \frac{r_t}{(1 + k_u)^\tau}\right) - \frac{1}{(1 + k_u)^t}\right]. \tag{17.3}$$

The first term in Equation 17.3 is an infinite annuity with constant payments so its present value is

$$\lim_{N \to \infty} \sum_{t=1}^{N} \frac{NOI_1}{(1 + k_u)^t} = \frac{NOI_1}{k_u}. \tag{17.4}$$

Next, the second term can be simplified as follows:

$$\sum_{\tau=t+1}^{N} \frac{r_t}{(1 + k_u)^\tau} = \frac{1}{(1 + k_u)^t} \sum_{\tau=1}^{N-t} \frac{r_t}{(1 + k_u)^\tau},$$

and

$$\frac{1}{(1 + k_u)^t} \lim_{N \to \infty} \frac{r_t}{(1 + k_u)^\tau} = \frac{1}{(1 + k_u)^t} \frac{r_t}{k_u}. \tag{17.5}$$

Substituting (17.4) and (17.5) back into (17.3), we obtain a simplified expression for the present value of the firm.

$$V_o = \lim_{N \to \infty} \left\{\frac{NOI_1}{k_u} + \sum_{t=1}^{N} I_t\left[\left(\frac{r_t}{k_u(1 + k_u)^t}\right) - \frac{1}{(1 + k_u)^t}\right]\right\}$$

$$= \frac{NOI_1}{k_u} + \sum_{t=1}^{\infty} \frac{I_t(r_t - k_u)}{k_u(1 + k_u)^t} \tag{17.6}$$

$$= \text{value of assets in place} + \text{value of future growth}$$

One of the implications of Equation 17.6 is that the value of any company can be separated into two parts: (1) the value of assets in place, assuming that the company does not grow in real terms, and (2) the present value of future growth which, in turn, depends on the rate of return on new investment, r, and the amount of new investment, I. Note also, that there is no value to growth unless the return on new capital invested is greater than the

TABLE 17.6 The Difference between Value and Earnings Growth

	Investment	Return	Change in NOI	Change in Value
Company 1	$ 100,000	20%	$20,000	$ 90,909
Company 2	300,000	10	30,000	0
Company 3	1,000,000	5	50,000	−454,545

cost of capital (i.e., no value is created unless $r > k_u$). For a firm with no debt, this is equivalent to the requirement that ROIC > WACC that we discussed earlier. Table 17.6 illustrates by comparing three hypothetical companies whose opportunity cost of capital is 10 percent. Company 3 has the highest growth in earnings, $50,000, but the greatest value destruction. Using the second term in Equation 17.6 and assuming one time period, we have

$$\text{Change in value} = \frac{I(r - k_u)}{k_u(1 + k_u)} = \frac{\$1,000,000\ (.05 - .10)}{.1\ (1 + .1)} = -\$454,545.$$

Value is destroyed, even though earnings grow, because the investment by Company 3 earns less than its cost of capital.

The amount of net new investment, I_t, in Equation 17.6 can be measured as a constant proportion, b, of operating cash flows.

$$I_t = b(\text{NOI}_t) \tag{17.7}$$

We shall refer to b as the *investment rate*. It is also sometimes called the retention rate because it measures the percentage of cash flows retained in the company for investment purposes. However, since it can be greater than 100 percent of the cash flows from operations, we prefer to call it the investment rate.

If the rate of return is assumed to be the same for all new investments, then

$$\text{NOI}_t = \text{NOI}_{t-1} + rI_{t-1}. \tag{17.8}$$

$$\text{NOI}_t = \text{NOI}_{t-1} + rb\,\text{NOI}_{t-1}$$
$$= \text{NOI}_{t-1}(1 + rb) \tag{17.9}$$

Note that the rate of return, r, multiplied by the investment rate, b, is equal to the rate of growth in operating cash flows, $rb = g$, so that

$$\text{NOI}_t = \text{NOI}_{t-1}(1 + g), \text{ since } g = br. \tag{17.10}$$

If we take this relationship all the way back to NOI_1, we have

$$\text{NOI}_t = \text{NOI}_1(1 + g)^{t-1}. \tag{17.11}$$

Substituting 17.9 into 17.6 we have

$$V_o = \frac{\text{NOI}_1}{k_u} + \sum_{t=1}^{\infty} \frac{b(\text{NOI}_1)(1+g)^{t-1}(r-k_u)}{k_u(1+k_u)^t}$$

$$= \frac{\text{NOI}_1}{k_u} \left[1 + \frac{b(r-k_u)}{1+g} \sum_{t=1}^{\infty} \left(\frac{1+g}{1+k_u}\right)^t \right]. \tag{17.12}$$

As long as the long-run rate of growth is less than the cost of capital ($g < k_u$), then the last term in Equation 17.12 has a finite limit.[2]

$$\lim_{N \to \infty} \sum_{t=1}^{N} \left(\frac{1+g}{1+k_u}\right)^t = \frac{1+g}{k_u - g} \tag{17.13}$$

When we substitute 17.13 into 17.12, we obtain a simple equation for the value of a firm that grows forever at a constant rate, g.

$$V_o = \frac{\text{NOI}_1}{k_u} \left[1 + \frac{b(r-k_u)}{1+g} \frac{1+g}{k_u - g} \right]$$

$$= \frac{\text{NOI}_1(1-b)}{k_u - g} \tag{17.14}$$

Equation 17.14 can be extended to a world with taxes and to companies that use debt in their capital structures as follows:

$$V_o = \frac{\text{NOI}_1(1-T)(1-b)}{\text{WACC} - g}. \tag{17.15}$$

The numerator is the after-tax free cash flow from operations

$$\text{FCF} = \text{NOI}_1(1-T)(1-b),$$

and since the investment rate, b, is equal to the growth rate divided by the return on investment, Equation 17.15 can be rewritten as:

$$V_o = \frac{\text{NOI}_1(1-T)(1-g/r)}{\text{WACC} - g}. \tag{17.16}$$

We will use Equation 17.16 as the terminal value (or continuing value) formula a little later on when we show how to use spreadsheets to value companies. It makes the

---

[2]For proof, let $(1+g)/(1+k_u) = U$. The last term in Equation 17.12 can be written as the sum of an infinite series

$$S = U + U^2 + \cdots + U^N$$

Multiplying this by U and subtracting the result from the above, we have

$$S = U/(1-U) - U^{N+1}/(1-U)$$

Since $U < 1$ the second term approaches zero in the limit as N approaches infinity. Substituting back the definition of U we obtain Equation 17.13.

simplifying assumptions that (1) the rate of return on all new investments is constant and (2) the company invests a constant proportion of its cash flows, b. The result is a constant perpetual rate of growth, $g = br$.

Before moving on to spreadsheet approaches to valuation, it is also important to show how Equation 17.12 can be generalized to a world with debt and taxes and to discuss the intuition behind management actions that create value. Equation 17.12 is rewritten below:

$$V_o = \frac{NOI_1}{k_u} + \frac{NOI_1 b(r - k_u)}{k_u(1 + g)} \sum_{t=1}^{\infty} \left(\frac{1 + g}{1 + k_u}\right)^t. \tag{17.12}$$

When it is extended to a world with debt and taxes, it becomes:

$$V_o = \frac{NOI_1(1 - T)}{WACC} + \frac{NOI_1(1 - T)b(r - WACC)}{WACC(1 + g)} \sum_{t=1}^{\infty} \left(\frac{1 + g}{1 + WACC}\right)^t. \tag{17.17}$$

Although this expression is complicated in appearance, it is actually straightforward to implement, as shown by the following case example.

The Koller Company has a free cash flow (NOI_o) of $10 million, expected to grow at a rate of 26.5 percent for the next 10 years. Its ratio of investment to after-tax net operating income (b) is .5. The applicable tax rate is 40 percent; the applicable cost of capital is 10 percent. After the period of supernormal growth, Koller will have no further growth in NOI.

Since the growth period is 10 years, Equation 17.17 would be modified slightly as shown in Equation 17.17a, in which n in the summation term is 10 years.

$$V_o = \frac{NOI_1(1 - T)}{WACC} + \frac{NOI_1(1 - T)b(r - WACC)}{WACC(1 + g)} \sum_{t=1}^{n} \left(\frac{1 + g}{1 + WACC}\right)^t \tag{17.17a}$$

We can readily solve this equation by inserting the numbers from our case example. They are shown in Equation 17.17b. Since $g = .265$ and $g = br$, we have $.5r = .265$; so $r = .53$.

$$V_o = \frac{10(1.265)(.6)}{.10} + \frac{10(1.265)(.6)(.5)(.53 - .10)}{.10(1 + .265)} \sum_{t=1}^{10} (1.15)^t$$

$$= \frac{7.59}{.10} + \frac{7.59(.5)(.43)}{.1265} [1.15(20.304)] \tag{17.17b}$$

$$V_o = 75.90 + 301.21 = \$377.11$$

Equation 17.17 can be further analyzed by breaking it into its components.

Note that the first term is the value of assets in place, assuming no growth, and the second term is the value of growth.

$$V_o = \text{value of assets in place} + \text{value of growth}$$

Also, the value of growth depends on exactly the same three components that we emphasized in the first part of the chapter.

1. *ROIC > WACC*. In Equation 17.17, the value of growth cannot be positive unless the rate of return on new investment is greater than the weighted average cost of capital, r > WACC.

2. *The amount of investment*. In Equation 17.17, the amount of investment is the proportion of after-tax operating cash flows that can be invested to earn the rate of return, r. The amount of investment is

$$I = \text{NOI}(1 - T)b.$$

3. *The interval of competitive advantage* is expressed in Equation 17.17a as the relationship between the growth rate, g, and the length of time, t, that the growth rate can be maintained. In Equation 17.17, we assumed that the growth rate was maintained forever.

SPREADSHEET APPROACH FOR VALUING COMPANIES

Before the advent of personal computers the amount of work needed to complete a thorough discounted cash flow analysis of a company was too time-consuming to be practical in most applications. Very few companies actually tried to implement value-based planning, and most DCF valuations utilized primitive versions of the formula approach that was described in the prior section of this chapter. In the 1990s, given the easy access to spreadsheets on personal computers, more and more managers are using value-based approaches to planning and control because the greater complexity of managing value has been overcome. This section of the chapter provides sufficient detail to allow the reader to value a company using explicitly forecasted spreadsheets.[3] Figure 17.9 shows the steps involved.

The Entity Approach

We are using *the entity approach* to valuation. We first value the free cash flows from operations by discounting them at the weighted average cost of capital. The result is the value of the entity that arises from normal operations. To this is added the present value of nonoperating cash flows, for example, marketable securities. The result is the total entity value. We then subtract the market value of debt and other liabilities (e.g., unfunded pension plan liabilities and preferred stock) in order to estimate the market value of equity (see Figure 17.10).

The entity approach to valuing a company is the same as the capital budgeting approach for valuing projects that was described in Chapter 9. Free cash flows are after-tax operating cash flows net of gross investment and net increases in working capital. They are completely independent of choices about how the company (or the project) is fi-

---

[3]For a more complete presentation, the reader is referred to T. Copeland, T. Koller, and J. Murrin, *Valuation: Measuring and Managing the Value of Companies*, New York: John Wiley & Co., 1990.

FIGURE 17.9 Steps in Performing a Spreadsheet DCF Valuation

Forecast free cash flow	Estimate the cost of capital	Estimate the continuing value	Calculate the result
• Collect historical data for the company and its comparables • Decide on an explicit forecast interval • Use the correct definition of FCF • Use the expected cash tax rate	• Calculate market-determined opportunity costs of capital • Use market value weights • Use the statutory marginal tax rate	• Choose appropriate continuing value assumptions • Match the formula used to the assumptions	• Triangulate the DCF value using other indicators • Test and evaluate scenarios

nanced. The value impact of financing, if any, is reflected entirely in the weighted average cost of capital.

Free Cash Flows

Table 17.7 gives the income statements for a hypothetical company and Table 17.8 gives its balance sheets.

FIGURE 17.10 The Entity Approach to Valuation

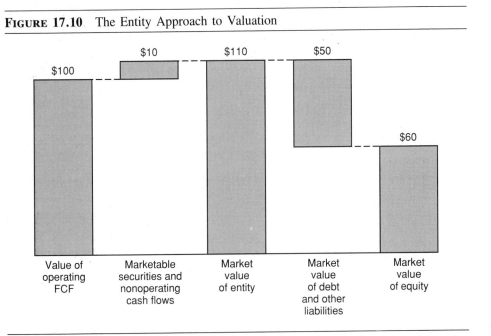

TABLE 17.7   ABC Company Income Statements

	1991	1992
Revenues	$14,500	$ 15,000
− Cost of goods sold	(9,667)	(10,000)
− Selling, general, and administrative expense	(2,996)	(3,100)
− Depreciation	(387)	(400)
− Goodwill amortization*	(20)	(20)
= Operating income	$ 1,430	$ 1,480
+ Interest income	15	17
− Interest expense	(434)	(431)
= Income before income taxes	$ 1,011	$ 1,066
− Provision for income taxes	(495)	(426)
= Net income	$ 516	$ 640
− Dividends	(161)	(200)
= Addition to retained earnings	$ 355	$ 440

*Not a deductible expense for tax purposes; therefore, in 1992, EBIT = operating income plus goodwill = $1,500.

TABLE 17.8   ABC Company Balance Sheets

	1990	1991	1992
Cash	$ 87	$ 90	$ 100
+ Excess marketable securities	308	320	300
+ Accounts receivable	2,800	2,900	3,000
+ Inventories	3,200	3,310	3,400
= Short-term assets	$ 6,395	$ 6,620	$ 6,800
+ Gross property, plant, and equipment	7,000	7,500	8,000
− Accumulated depreciation	(2,400)	(2,700)	(3,000)
= Net property, plant, and equipment	$ 4,600	$ 4,800	$ 5,000
+ Goodwill	540	520	500
+ Other assets	920	950	1,000
= Total assets	$12,455	$12,890	$13,300
Short-term debt	$ 1,060	$ 1,030	$ 1,000
+ Accounts payable	1,980	2,050	2,000
+ Accrued liabilities	880	900	1,000
= Short-term liabilities	$ 3,920	$ 3,980	$ 4,000
+ Long-term debt	3,400	3,500	3,500
+ Accumulated deferred taxes	380	400	500
+ Common shares	1,250	1,150	1,000
+ Retained earnings	3,505	3,860	4,300
= Total shareholders' equity	$ 4,755	$ 5,010	$ 5,300
Total liabilities and shareholders' equity	$12,455	$12,890	$13,300

These statements are used to estimate free cash flows, both historically and during the explicit forecast period that is chosen for analysis. Table 17.9 shows the estimated free cash flows. Note that the cash flows are estimated two ways. First are free cash flows from operations and second are financial flows. These two independent estimates must equal each other. Cash flows from operations are used to make financial payments to providers of debt and equity. Financial flows include all interest-earning or interest-paying financial securities as well as equity. The following paragraphs define each of the major components of free cash flows.

Earnings Before Interest and Taxes (EBIT). EBIT is the pretax income that a company would have earned if it had no debt. It includes all types of "operating" income (the distinction between operating and nonoperating cash flows is described later). It is often

TABLE 17.9 ABC Company Free Cash Flows

Operating Cash Flows	1991	1992
Earnings before interest and taxes (EBIT)	$1,450	$1,500
− Taxes on EBIT	(701)	(600)
+ Change in deferred taxes	20	100
= Net operating profit less adjusted taxes	$ 769	$1,000
+ Depreciation	387	400
= Gross cash flow	$1,156	$1,400
Increase in working capital	123	150
+ Capital expenditures	587	600
+ Investment in goodwill	0	0
+ Increase in net other assets	30	50
= Gross investment	$ 740	$ 800
Gross cash flow	1,156	1,400
− Gross investment	(740)	800
= Free cash flow from operations	$ 416	$ 600
+ Nonoperating cash flow	0	0
= Total free cash flow	$ 416	$ 600
Financial Flows		
Change in excess marketable securities	$ 12	$ (20)
− After-tax interest income*	(8)	(10)
+ Decrease in debt	(70)	30
+ After-tax interest expense*	221	250
+ Dividends	161	200
+ Share repurchase	100	150
= Total financial flow	$ 416	$ 600

*Marginal tax rates of 49 percent in 1991 and 42 percent in 1992 were used to calculate after-tax interest income and expense.

equal to the line "operating income" on the company's income statement. Depreciation should be subtracted in calculating EBIT but goodwill amortization should not.

Taxes on EBIT. Taxes on EBIT represent the income taxes that are attributable to EBIT. They are the taxes the company would pay if it had no debt or excess marketable securities. They equal the total income tax provision (current and deferred) adjusted for the income taxes attributed to interest expense, interest income, and nonoperating items. Using figures for our ABC Company, 1992 taxes on EBIT are calculated as follows:

Total income tax provision from income statement	$426
+ Tax shield on interest expense	181
− Tax on interest income	(7)
− Tax on nonoperating income	0
= Taxes on EBIT	$600

The taxes related to interest expense, interest income, and nonoperating items are calculated by multiplying the marginal tax rate by the item. (The marginal tax rate is generally the statutory marginal rate, including state and local taxes. However, companies with tax loss carry-forwards or those subject to the alternative minimum tax may have different marginal rates.)

Change in Deferred Taxes. For valuation purposes, taxes should be stated on a cash basis. The provision for income taxes in the income statement generally does not equal the actual taxes paid in cash by the company due to differences between GAAP accounting and accounting for taxes. The adjustment to a cash basis can be calculated from the change in accumulated deferred income taxes on the company's balance sheet. An increase in deferred taxes is a source of cash.

Net Operating Profit Less Adjusted Taxes (NOPLAT). NOPLAT represents the after-tax operating profits of the company after adjusting the taxes to a cash basis. It is important because it is used in the calculation of the rate of return on invested capital. NOPLAT is equal to $EBIT(1 - T)$ or to $NOI(1 - T)$ in the formula valuation model discussed in the previous section of this chapter.

Depreciation. Depreciation includes all the noncash charges deducted from EBIT except goodwill amortization (which is not added back to NOPLAT because it was not deducted in calculating NOPLAT). It also includes the amortization of intangible assets with definite lives such as patents and franchises.

Gross Cash Flow. Gross cash flow represents the total cash flow thrown off by the company. It is the amount available to reinvest in the business for maintenance and growth without relying on additional capital.

Change in Working Capital. The change in working capital is the amount the company invested in working capital during the period. Only operating working capital should be included. Nonoperating assets, excess marketable securities, and interest-bearing liabilities (short-term debt and the current portion of long-term debt) are excluded because they are financing flows, not operating cash flows. The measure is the change in current assets (excluding marketable securities) less current liabilities (excluding short-term debt and the current portion of long-term debt).

Capital Expenditures.   Capital expenditures include expenditures on new and replacement property, plant, and equipment. Capital expenditures can be calculated as the increase in *net* property, plant, and equipment on the balance sheet plus depreciation expense (taken from the income statement) for the period. (Technically, this calculation results in capital expenditures less the net book value of retired assets.)

Investment in Goodwill.   The investment in goodwill equals the amount of expenditure to acquire another company in excess of the book value of its net assets. Theoretically, goodwill has an indefinite life and should always be stated on a gross basis — that is, before accumulated amortization. In any year, the investment in goodwill is best calculated as the net change in the goodwill account on the balance sheet plus the amortization of goodwill in that period. This ensures that goodwill amortization does not affect free cash flow in either gross cash flow or gross investment.

Increase in Net Other Assets.   The increase in net other assets equals the expenditure on all other operating assets including capitalized intangibles (patents, trademarks), deferred expenses, and net of increases in noncurrent, noninterest-bearing liabilities. These can be calculated directly from the change in the balance sheet accounts plus any amortization included in depreciation.

Gross Investment.   Gross investment is the sum of a company's expenditures for new capital, including working capital, capital expenditures, goodwill, and other assets.

Nonoperating Cash Flow.   Nonoperating cash flow represents the after-tax cash flow from items not related to operations.

Free cash flow explicitly does not include nonoperating cash flow. Caution must be exercised, however, in considering an item to be nonoperating. Any nonoperating cash flow must be reflected in the value of the company explicitly. We do this by defining the total value of the company as the discounted present value of the company's free cash flow plus the value of its after-tax nonoperating cash flow.

$$\begin{matrix} \text{Present value of} \\ \text{company's free} \\ \text{cash flow} \end{matrix} \quad + \quad \begin{matrix} \text{Present value of} \\ \text{after-tax nonoper-} \\ \text{ating cash flow} \end{matrix} \quad = \quad \begin{matrix} \text{Total value of} \\ \text{company} \end{matrix}$$

Cash flow items that are sometimes considered nonoperating include cash flow from discontinued operations, extraordinary items, and the cash flow from investments in unrelated subsidiaries. Remember, though, that the present value of any nonoperating cash flow must be reflected in the total value of the company.

It is generally not advisable to consider a recurring cash flow as nonoperating. The company's risk and therefore its cost of capital reflects all its assets and its cash flow.

Arbitrarily excluding items from free cash flow may violate the principle of consistency between free cash flow and cost of capital.

Change in Excess Marketable Securities. Changes in excess marketable securities and the related interest income are considered financial cash flows for two reasons:

1. Excess marketable securities generally represent temporary imbalances in the company's cash flow. For example, the company may build up cash while deciding what to do with it. These excess marketable securities are not generally directly related to the company's operating decisions.

2. Considering these changes as financial cash flow makes valuation easier. Marketable securities are generally much less risky than the operations of the firm. As marketable securities grow or decline in relation to the size of the company, the company's overall level of risk and its cost of capital should rise or fall. Modeling the change in the cost of capital is complex. It is much easier to consider the value of a company as the sum of the value of its operating free cash flow plus the present value of the cash flow related to its excess marketable securities, where the risk of each component is relatively stable over time.

Excess marketable securities are the short-term cash investments that the company holds over and above its target cash balances to support operations. The target balances can be estimated by observing the variability in the company's cash and marketable security balances over time and by comparing against similar companies.

Excess marketable securities and their counterpart, unscheduled debt, are used as "plug" figures in the balance sheet forecasts. When your forecasts imply that the company is generating positive cash flows then excess marketable securities will build up. Conversely, if your forecasts imply that the company is in trouble then excess marketable securities will fall to zero and unscheduled debt will build up.

Recognize also that the investment in marketable securities or the buildup of unscheduled debt (government securities and commercial paper) is a zero-net-present-value investment. The return on this investment just compensates for its risk. Therefore, the present value of the cash flow related to these marketable securities must equal the market value of the excess marketable securities on the company's books at the time of the valuation.

After-Tax Interest Income. The after-tax interest income on excess marketable securities equals the pretax income times 1 minus the appropriate marginal income tax rate. The marginal tax rate should be consistent with the rate used for the adjustment of taxes on EBIT.

Change in Debt. The change in debt represents the net borrowing or repayment on all the company's debt, including short-term debt.

After-Tax Interest Expense. The after-tax interest expense equals the pretax interest expense times 1 minus the company's marginal income tax rate. The marginal tax rate should be consistent with the rate used for the adjustment of taxes on EBIT.

Dividends. Dividends include all cash dividends on common and preferred shares.

Share Issues/Repurchases. Share issues/repurchases include both preferred and common shares and the effects of conversions of debt to equity. This figure can be calculated by taking the change in total equity plus dividends less net income.

Special Items. The foregoing items are fairly standard for most companies. A number of special items may also be relevant, including operating leases, pensions, minority interest, investments in unconsolidated subsidiaries, and foreign currency translation gains/losses.

Operating leases are any lease obligations that the company has not capitalized. Operating leases represent a type of financing and should be treated as such. Therefore, we adjust the company's financial statements to treat operating leases as if they were capitalized. First, reclassify the implied interest expense portion of the lease payments from an operating expense (usually in cost of goods sold, or selling, general, and administrative expense) to an interest expense. This increases EBIT by the amount of implied interest. Do not forget to adjust the EBIT taxes as well.

Also, reflect changes in the implied principal amount of the leases in gross investment and the change in debt. This mimics the effects that would have occurred had the leases been capitalized. The principal amount of the leases must be estimated by discounting expected future operating lease expenses at the before-tax cost of debt. (See Chapter 24 for more about leases.) The implied interest expense is the principal amount times an appropriate interest rate.

The company's *pension costs* are included in the cost of goods sold, or selling, general, and administrative expense. Normally, nothing special need be done in the free cash flow or the valuation related to pensions. If the company has a significantly over-funded or underfunded plan, however, care must be taken to ensure that the related cash flow is treated consistently in the valuation. Overfunded or underfunded pension plans can be handled in one of two ways:

1. Adjust the forecasted pension expense so that the overfunded or underfunded pension is eliminated over time. Do not treat the current amount of overfunding or underfunding as a separate item in the valuation, because that would be double counting.

2. Do not reflect the overfunding or underfunding in the pension expense forecast. The current amount of the after-tax overfunding or underfunding must be included as a separate item added to or subtracted from the valuation.

A *minority interest* occurs when a third party owns some percentage of one of the company's consolidated subsidiaries. The related cash flow should be included as part of the company's financial flow since a minority interest is simply another form of financing. The relevant cash flow amount equals the income statement amount less the change in the minority interest on the balance sheet. This should equal the dividends paid to the minority shareholder less any capital contributions received by the company from the minority shareholders.

The cash flow associated with *unconsolidated subsidiaries* can be handled in one of two ways:

1. Include the cash flow in free cash flow.
2. Exclude the cash flow from free cash flow but include the present value of the cash flow as a separate item in the valuation.

The first approach is simpler and should be used unless the amount of the cash flow is material in size, and the operations of the subsidiary are not related to the core operations of the company. The first approach is recommended because the company's cost of capital probably reflects its holdings in these subsidiaries. Excluding the subsidiaries could violate the consistency between free cash flow and cost of capital.

The related cash flow can be calculated by subtracting the balance sheet increases in the investment-in-subsidiaries account from the income related to the subsidiaries (this works whether they are accounted for on the equity or cost method). The cash flow should also be adjusted for related income taxes.

The change in the cumulative *foreign currency translation gains or losses* account is driven by the changes in translation rates applied to both assets and debt. As a practical matter, you generally cannot separate the asset and debt gains or losses without good historical internal information. Therefore, treat these gains/losses as nonoperating cash flow in the free cash flow. If you have the information needed to separate the asset from the debt effects, treat the gains/losses on assets as adjustments to free cash flow and the gains/losses on debt as financial cash flow. (See Financial Accounting Standards Board Statement No. 52 for a complete discussion of foreign currency accounting.)

Your forecast of expected future foreign exchange gains or losses should be zero. If you really can make an accurate forecast of foreign exchange gains or losses you do not need to worry about valuing companies because you can make a fortune speculating in FC markets. If markets are reasonably efficient it should not be possible to forecast abnormal returns.

AN EXAMPLE: W.R. GRACE

We now illustrate the valuation of W.R. Grace using spreadsheets to estimate discounted cash flows. If you want to construct your own valuation model all that needs to be done is to copy our format and fill in the numbers for the company or companies that are of interest to you. During the course of discussion, we will cover:

- Forecasts of free cash flows during a 10-year explicit forecast period
- Continuing value calculations for cash flows beyond the explicit forecast period
- Computation of the weighted average cost of capital.

Forecasting Free Cash Flows

Although primarily a specialty chemical company, W.R. Grace also has significant investments in natural resources, health care, and specialty businesses (e.g., cocoa, textiles, book distribution, and breeding services). In 1986, it got out of the restaurant and the agricultural chemicals businesses. Tables 17.10 through 17.12 show the income statements, the balance sheets, and the free cash flow statements for W.R. Grace. Our valuation was done as of September 1990. Our explicit forecast period was 10 years (1990 to 1999). Note that we chose to treat operating leases as a financial flow. Therefore, on the statement of free cash flows, we added our estimate of operating lease expenses back to operating income, and treated increases in the capitalized value of operating leases as a source of funds.

Figure 17.11 shows the results of our valuation. First, we explicitly forecasted free cash flows from 1990 to 1999. Their present value was $1.216 billion. Next, we used a formula to estimate the present value of free cash flows from the year 2000 onward. This continuing value was worth $2.667 billion in 1989 dollars. We also added in the present value of the company's excess marketable securities, $109 million, since their interest income is not included in the definition of free cash flows. And finally, we added on the present value of nonoperating assets, $408 million of investments and advances. The result of summing these numbers is the company's entity value. From this, we subtracted the market value of debt, $2.017 billion; our estimate of the capitalized value of operating leases, $262 million; preferred stock, $8 million; and minority interest, $153 million. The result is the market value of equity, $1.96 billion or $22.80 per share. The actual market price per share at the time was $22.00 per share, 3.5 percent lower.

FIGURE 17.11   Valuation Summary for W.R. Grace ($ millions)

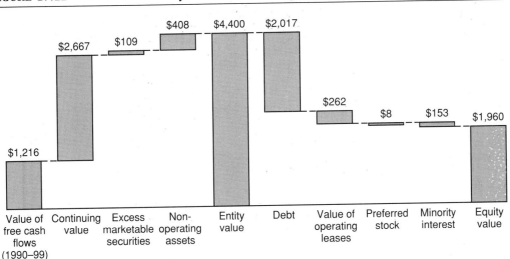

TABLE 17.10   Income Statements for W.R. Grace, 1985–1999 ($ millions)

	Historic						
	1985	1986	1987	1988	1989	1990	1991
Income Statement							
Revenues	$5,193.0	$3,725.7	$4,515.4	$5,786.1	$6,114.6	$6,550.0	$6,899.7
Cost of Goods Sold	(3,586.7)	(2,554.9)	(3,107.3)	(4,013.4)	(4,241.8)	(4,543.8)	(4,786.5)
Selling, G&A Expenses	(1,120.0)	(782.7)	(902.9)	(1,158.4)	(1,245.3)	(1,334.0)	(1,393.7)
Depreciation	(271.3)	(201.0)	(192.4)	(224.1)	(252.4)	(248.2)	(261.6)
Operating Income	$ 215.0	$ 187.1	$ 312.8	$ 390.2	$ 375.1	$ 424.0	$ 457.9
Amort. of Goodwill	0.0	0.0	0.0	0.0	0.0	(12.9)	(12.9)
Non-Op. Income	71.6	49.6	57.8	55.0	73.0	73.0	73.0
Interest Income	0.0	0.0	0.0	34.7	36.2	10.9	15.3
Interest Expense	(187.0)	(191.8)	(122.9)	(167.9)	(213.3)	(230.2)	(244.0)
Special Items	75.0	(368.8)	0.0	4.6	114.4	0.0	0.0
Minority Interest	0.0	0.0	0.0	0.0	0.0	0.0	0.0
Earnings Before Taxes	$ 174.6	$ (323.9)	$ 247.7	$ 316.6	$ 385.4	$ 264.8	$ 289.3
Income Taxes	(46.8)	(51.5)	(105.8)	(124.6)	(128.8)	(84.1)	(91.8)
Income Before Extra Items	$ 127.8	$ (375.4)	$ 141.9	$ 192.0	$ 256.6	$ 180.7	$ 197.6
Extraordinary Items	19.1	(96.9)	31.2	41.6	(3.4)	0.0	0.0
Net Income	$ 146.9	$ (472.3)	$ 173.1	$ 233.6	$ 253.2	$ 180.7	$ 197.6
Statement of Retained Earnings							
Beginning Ret. Earnings	$1,824.7	$1,829.3	$1,238.9	$1,292.8	$1,407.3	$1,540.8	$1,635.9
Net Income	146.9	(472.3)	173.1	233.6	253.2	180.7	197.6
Common Dividends	(142.0)	(117.6)	(118.7)	(118.6)	(119.2)	(85.1)	(93.0)
Preferred Dividends	(0.7)	(0.5)	(0.5)	(0.5)	(0.5)	(0.5)	(0.5)
Adj. for Splits and Repurchases	0.4	(0.0)	(0.0)	(0.0)	0.0	0.0	0.0
Ending Ret. Earnings	$1,829.3	$1,238.9	$1,292.8	$1,407.3	$1,540.8	$1,635.9	$1,740.0

			Forecast				
1992	1993	1994	1995	1996	1997	1998	1999
$7,368.9	$7,870.0	$8,405.2	$8,976.7	$9,515.3	$10,086.2	$10,691.4	$11,332.9
(5,091.9)	(5,438.2)	(5,808.0)	(6,193.9)	(6,565.6)	(6,959.5)	(7,377.1)	(7,819.7)
(1,488.5)	(1,581.9)	(1,681.0)	(1,795.3)	(1,903.1)	(2,017.2)	(2,138.3)	(2,266.6)
(277.9)	(296.6)	(316.6)	(337.9)	(360.6)	(382.5)	(390.4)	(414.0)
$ 510.5	$ 553.4	$ 599.6	$ 649.6	$ 686.0	$ 727.0	$ 785.7	$ 832.6
(12.9)	(12.9)	(12.9)	(12.9)	(12.9)	(12.9)	(12.9)	(12.9)
73.0	73.0	73.0	73.0	73.0	73.0	73.0	73.0
15.3	15.3	15.3	15.3	15.3	15.3	15.3	15.3
(249.1)	(257.9)	(266.8)	(276.1)	(285.4)	(291.8)	(298.4)	(306.3)
0.0	0.0	0.0	0.0	0.0	0.0	0.0	0.0
0.0	0.0	0.0	0.0	0.0	0.0	0.0	0.0
$ 336.9	$ 370.8	$ 408.2	$ 448.9	$ 476.0	$ 510.5	$ 562.6	$ 601.6
(107.4)	(118.2)	(130.2)	(143.3)	(151.7)	(162.9)	(179.9)	(192.5)
$ 229.5	$ 252.6	$ 278.0	$ 305.6	$ 324.3	$ 347.6	$ 382.7	$ 409.2
0.0	0.0	0.0	0.0	0.0	0.0	0.0	0.0
$ 229.5	$ 252.6	$ 278.0	$ 305.6	$ 324.3	$ 347.6	$ 382.7	$ 409.2
$1,740.0	$1,861.0	$1,994.1	$2,140.8	$2,302.0	$ 2,473.1	$ 2,656.6	$ 2,858.7
229.5	252.6	278.0	305.6	324.3	347.6	382.7	409.2
(108.0)	(118.9)	(130.9)	(143.9)	(152.7)	(163.7)	(180.2)	(192.6)
(0.5)	(0.5)	(0.5)	(0.5)	(0.5)	(0.5)	(0.5)	(0.5)
0.0	0.0	0.0	0.0	0.0	0.0	0.0	0.0
$1,861.0	$1,994.1	$2,140.8	$2,302.0	$2,473.1	$ 2,656.6	$ 2,858.7	$ 3,074.7

TABLE 17.11 Balance Sheets for W.R. Grace, 1985–1999 ($ millions)

	Historic						
	1985	1986	1987	1988	1989	1990	1991
Balance Sheet							
Operating Cash	$ 0.0	$ 0.0	$ 0.0	$ 0.0	$ 0.0	$ 0.0	$ 0.0
Excess Mkt. Secs.	151.6	92.5	151.4	132.7	108.7	153.0	153.0
Accounts Receivable	703.7	665.6	826.5	1,068.9	1,163.2	1,246.0	1,312.6
Inventories	607.6	563.0	629.5	751.5	762.5	816.8	860.4
Other	560.6	175.3	115.3	60.8	131.9	141.3	148.8
Current Assets	$2,023.5	$1,496.4	$1,722.7	$2,013.9	$2,166.3	$2,357.1	$2,474.8
Gross PPE	4,829.1	3,575.3	3,917.4	4,412.3	4,682.4	4,935.8	5,244.1
Accum. Depreciation	(2,088.2)	(1,868.8)	(2,072.3)	(2,238.7)	(2,401.1)	(2,569.7)	(2,747.4)
Net PPE	$2,740.9	$1,706.5	$1,845.1	$2,173.6	$2,281.3	$2,366.2	$2,496.8
Goodwill	133.1	104.2	112.1	405.1	516.1	503.2	490.3
Other Assets	147.6	323.5	306.5	185.9	247.2	264.8	278.9
Investments & Advances	375.8	466.6	487.2	531.8	408.2	408.2	408.2
Total Assets	$5,420.9	$4,097.2	$4,473.6	$5,310.3	$5,619.1	$5,899.5	$6,149.0
Short-term Debt	$ 294.2	$ 152.6	$ 148.4	$ 307.5	$ 379.0	$ 343.3	$ 361.1
Accounts Payable	408.1	431.6	521.1	589.6	619.6	663.7	699.2
Other Current Liabs.	333.0	534.5	495.1	586.9	590.5	632.5	666.3
Total Current Liabs.	$1,035.3	$1,118.7	$1,164.6	$1,484.0	$1,589.1	$1,639.5	$1,726.6
Long-term Debt	1,524.1	1,095.3	1,222.5	1,509.1	1,637.7	1,637.7	1,637.7
New Long-term Debt	0.0	0.0	0.0	0.0	0.0	148.4	176.6
Deferred Income Taxes	262.5	94.5	101.4	84.4	89.5	95.2	101.4
Other Noninterest-Bearing Liabilities	194.5	480.1	521.8	681.7	419.4	449.3	473.3
Minority Interest	0.0	0.0	0.0	0.0	153.0	153.0	153.0
Preferred Stock	10.3	7.7	7.5	7.5	7.5	7.5	7.5
Common Stock	670.6	697.4	125.8	123.5	132.9	132.9	132.9
Retained Earnings	1,829.3	1,238.9	1,292.8	1,407.3	1,540.8	1,635.9	1,740.0
Foreign Currency Adj.	(105.7)	(635.4)	37.2	12.8	49.2	0.0	0.0
Total Common Equity	$2,394.2	$1,300.9	$1,455.8	$1,543.6	$1,722.9	$1,768.8	$1,872.9
Total Liabs. and Equity	$5,420.9	$4,097.2	$4,473.6	$5,310.3	$5,619.1	$5,899.5	$6,149.0
Validation Test:							
Assets − (Liability + Equity)	0	0	0	(0)	(0)	0	0

				Forecast				
	1992	1993	1994	1995	1996	1997	1998	1999
	$ 0.0	$ 0.0	$ 0.0	$ 0.0	$ 0.0	$ 0.0	$ 0.0	$ 0.0
	153.0	153.0	153.0	153.0	153.0	153.0	153.0	153.0
	1,401.8	1,497.1	1,598.9	1,707.7	1,810.1	1,918.7	2,033.9	2,155.9
	918.9	981.4	1,048.1	1,119.4	1,186.6	1,257.8	1,333.2	1,413.2
	159.0	169.8	181.3	193.6	205.3	217.6	230.6	244.5
	$2,632.7	$2,801.3	$2,981.4	$3,173.7	$3,355.0	$3,547.1	$3,750.7	$3,966.6
	5,596.4	5,972.7	6,374.8	6,804.4	7,217.3	7,654.8	8,118.4	8,609.7
	(2,936.1)	(3,137.6)	(3,352.6)	(3,582.1)	(3,806.7)	(4,044.8)	(4,282.1)	(4,533.8)
	$2,660.2	$2,835.1	$3,022.2	$3,222.3	$3,410.7	$3,610.0	$3,836.3	$4,075.8
	477.4	464.5	451.6	438.7	425.8	412.9	400.0	387.1
	297.9	318.2	339.8	362.9	384.7	407.8	432.2	458.2
	408.2	408.2	408.2	408.2	408.2	408.2	408.2	408.2
	$6,476.4	$6,827.3	$7,203.2	$7,605.8	$7,984.3	$8,385.9	$8,827.4	$9,295.9
	$ 352.2	$ 356.7	$ 354.4	$ 355.5	$ 355.0	$ 355.3	$ 355.1	$ 355.2
	746.7	797.5	851.7	909.6	964.2	1,022.0	1,083.4	1,148.4
	711.6	760.0	811.7	866.9	918.9	974.0	1,032.5	1,094.4
	$1,810.5	$1,914.2	$2,017.8	$2,132.1	$2,238.1	$2,351.4	$2,471.0	$2,598.0
	1,637.7	1,637.7	1,637.7	1,637.7	1,637.7	1,637.7	1,637.7	1,637.7
	260.1	332.3	413.1	492.3	547.5	603.4	671.2	741.4
	108.3	115.8	123.9	132.6	141.8	151.6	162.2	173.4
	505.4	539.8	576.5	615.7	652.7	691.8	733.3	777.3
	153.0	153.0	153.0	153.0	153.0	153.0	153.0	153.0
	7.5	7.5	7.5	7.5	7.5	7.5	7.5	7.5
	132.9	132.9	132.9	132.9	132.9	132.9	132.9	132.9
	1,861.0	1,994.1	2,140.8	2,302.0	2,473.1	2,656.6	2,858.7	3,074.7
	0.0	0.0	0.0	0.0	0.0	0.0	0.0	0.0
	$1,993.9	$2,127.0	$2,273.7	$2,434.9	$2,606.0	$2,789.5	$2,991.6	$3,207.6
	$6,476.4	$6,827.3	$7,203.2	$7,605.8	$7,984.3	$8,385.9	$8,827.4	$9,295.9
	0	0	0	0	(0)	0	(0)	0

TABLE 17.12 Free Cash Flows and Financial Flows for W.R. Grace, 1985–1999 ($ millions)

	Historic					1990	1991
	1985	1986	1987	1988	1989	1990	1991
Free Cash Flow							
Revenues	$5,193.0	$ 3,725.7	$4,515.4	$5,786.1	$6,114.6	$6,550.0	$6,899.7
Cost of Goods Sold	(3,586.7)	(2,554.9)	(3,107.3)	(4,013.4)	(4,241.8)	(4,543.8)	(4,786.5)
Selling, G&A Expenses	(1,120.0)	(782.7)	(902.9)	(1,158.4)	(1,245.3)	(1,334.0)	(1,393.7)
Depreciation	(271.3)	(201.0)	(192.4)	(224.1)	(252.4)	(248.2)	(261.6)
Adj. for Operating Leases	49.6	30.8	15.2	17.6	24.2	26.2	27.0
Amortization of Goodwill	0.0	0.0	0.0	0.0	0.0	12.9	12.9
EBIT	$ 264.6	$ 217.9	$ 328.0	$ 407.8	$ 399.3	$ 450.2	$ 484.9
Taxes on EBIT	(83.7)	(273.7)	(138.7)	(162.0)	(134.2)	(151.3)	(163.0)
Change in Def. Taxes	(38.5)	(168.0)	6.9	(17.0)	5.1	5.7	6.2
NOPLAT	$ 142.4	$ (223.7)	$ 196.2	$ 228.8	$ 270.2	$ 304.6	$ 328.1
Depreciation	271.3	201.0	192.4	224.1	252.4	248.2	261.6
Gross Cash Flow	$ 413.7	$ (22.7)	$ 388.6	$ 452.9	$ 522.6	$ 552.8	$ 589.7
Change in Working Capital	$ 340.2	$ (693.0)	$ 117.3	$ 149.6	$ 142.8	$ 60.3	$ 48.5
Capital Expenditures	167.3	(833.4)	331.0	552.6	360.1	333.0	392.2
Incr. in Cap. Op. Leases	(188.0)	(156.0)	23.2	66.4	19.6	8.0	14.4
Investment in Goodwill	(1.0)	(28.9)	7.9	293.0	111.0	0.0	0.0
Incr. in Other Assets	17.1	175.9	(17.0)	(120.6)	61.3	17.6	14.1
(Incr.) in Other Liabs.	(32.1)	(285.6)	(41.7)	(159.9)	262.3	(29.9)	(24.0)
Gross Investment	$ 303.5	$(1,821.0)	$ 420.7	$ 781.1	$ 957.1	$ 389.2	$ 445.2
Operating Free Cash Flow	$ 110.2	$ 1,798.3	$ (32.1)	$ (328.2)	$ (434.5)	$ 163.6	$ 144.5
Non-Op. Cash Flow	37.7	(376.0)	44.7	32.2	234.5	44.5	44.5
FC Translation Adj.	45.1	(529.7)	672.6	(24.4)	36.4	(49.2)	0.0
Total Free Cash Flow	$ 193.0	$ 892.6	$ 685.2	$ (320.5)	$ (163.6)	$ 158.9	$ 189.0
Financial Flows							
Incr./(Decr.) Excess Mkt. Sec.	$ (5.2)	$ (59.1)	$ 58.9	$ (18.7)	$ (24.0)	$ 44.3	$ 0.0
AT Interest Income	0.0	0.0	0.0	(20.5)	(22.1)	(6.6)	(9.3)
Decr./(Incr.) in Debt	(114.3)	570.4	(123.0)	(445.7)	(200.1)	(112.7)	(46.0)
Decr./(Incr.) in Minority Interest	0.0	0.0	0.0	0.0	(153.0)	0.0	0.0
(Incr.)/Decr. in Cap. Oper. Leases	188.0	156.0	(23.2)	(66.4)	(19.6)	(8.0)	(14.4)
AT Interest Expense	110.3	113.2	72.5	99.1	130.1	140.4	148.8
Implied Int. Exp. on Op. Leases	29.3	18.2	9.0	10.4	14.8	16.0	16.4
Common Dividends	142.0	117.6	118.7	118.6	119.2	85.1	93.0
Preferred Dividends	0.7	0.5	0.5	0.5	0.5	0.5	0.5
Decr./(Incr.) in Preferred	0.0	2.6	0.2	0.0	0.0	0.0	0.0
Decr./(Incr.) in Common	(157.8)	(26.8)	571.6	2.3	(9.4)	0.0	0.0
Financing Flows	$ 193.0	$ 892.6	$ 685.2	$ (320.5)	$ (163.6)	$ 158.9	$ 189.0
Validation Test:							
Free Cash Flows – Financing Flows	(0)	(0)	0	0	(0)	(0)	0

			Forecast				
1992	1993	1994	1995	1996	1997	1998	1999

$7,368.9	$7,870.0	$8,405.2	$8,976.7	$9,515.3	$10,086.2	$10,691.4	$11,332.9
(5,091.9)	(5,438.2)	(5,808.0)	(6,193.9)	(6,565.6)	(6,959.5)	(7,377.1)	(7,819.7)
(1,488.5)	(1,581.9)	(1,681.0)	(1,795.3)	(1,903.1)	(2,017.2)	(2,138.3)	(2,266.6)
(277.9)	(296.6)	(316.6)	(337.9)	(360.6)	(382.5)	(390.4)	(414.0)
28.4	30.3	32.4	34.6	37.0	39.2	41.5	44.0
12.9	12.9	12.9	12.9	12.9	12.9	12.9	12.9
$ 538.9	$ 583.7	$ 632.0	$ 684.2	$ 723.0	$ 766.1	$ 827.2	$ 876.6
(181.2)	(196.2)	(212.4)	(230.0)	(243.0)	(257.5)	(278.0)	(294.7)
6.9	7.5	8.1	8.7	9.2	9.8	10.6	11.2
$ 364.7	$ 394.9	$ 427.6	$ 462.9	$ 489.2	$ 518.4	$ 559.7	$ 593.1
277.9	296.6	316.6	337.9	360.6	382.5	390.4	414.0
$ 642.6	$ 691.5	$ 744.2	$ 800.8	$ 849.8	$ 900.9	$ 950.1	$ 1,007.2
$ 65.0	$ 69.5	$ 74.2	$ 79.2	$ 74.7	$ 79.1	$ 83.9	$ 88.9
441.4	471.5	503.6	538.0	549.0	581.9	616.7	653.6
19.3	20.6	22.0	23.5	22.2	23.5	24.9	26.4
0.0	0.0	0.0	0.0	0.0	0.0	0.0	0.0
19.0	20.3	21.6	23.1	21.8	23.1	24.5	25.9
(32.2)	(34.4)	(36.7)	(39.2)	(36.9)	(39.2)	(41.5)	(44.0)
$ 512.5	$ 547.5	$ 584.8	$ 624.6	$ 630.7	$ 668.4	$ 708.4	$ 750.9
$ 130.1	$ 144.1	$ 159.4	$ 176.2	$ 219.2	$ 232.5	$ 241.7	$ 256.3
44.5	44.5	44.5	44.5	44.5	44.5	44.5	44.5
0.0	0.0	0.0	0.0	0.0	0.0	0.0	0.0
$ 174.6	$ 188.6	$ 204.0	$ 220.7	$ 263.7	$ 277.0	$ 286.2	$ 300.8
$ 0.0	$ (0.0)	$ 0.0	$ 0.0	$ (0.0)	$ (0.0)	$ 0.0	$ (0.0)
(9.3)	(9.3)	(9.3)	(9.3)	(9.3)	(9.3)	(9.3)	(9.3)
(74.6)	(76.7)	(78.6)	(80.3)	(54.6)	(56.2)	(67.6)	(70.3)
0.0	0.0	0.0	0.0	0.0	0.0	0.0	0.0
(19.3)	(20.6)	(22.0)	(23.5)	(22.2)	(23.5)	(24.9)	(26.4)
151.9	157.3	162.8	168.4	174.1	178.0	182.0	186.9
17.3	18.5	19.8	21.1	22.5	23.9	25.3	26.8
108.0	118.9	130.9	143.9	152.7	163.7	180.2	192.6
0.5	0.5	0.5	0.5	0.5	0.5	0.5	0.5
0.0	0.0	0.0	0.0	0.0	0.0	0.0	0.0
0.0	0.0	0.0	0.0	0.0	0.0	0.0	0.0
$ 174.6	$ 188.6	$ 204.0	$ 220.7	$ 263.7	$ 277.0	$ 286.2	$ 300.8
(0)	(0)	0	0	0	(0)	0	(0)

Forecasting the income statement and the balance sheet so that they are mutually consistent can be quite a challenge. Tables 17.13 to 17.15 show most of our forecast assumptions. For example, we assumed sales growth would be 7.1 percent for 1990, 5.3 percent for 1991 (a recession year), 6.8 percent for 1992 to 1995, and 6 percent long run. By way of contrast, Value Line Investor Service forecasts 5 percent growth in sales out to 1995. Our operating margin is 11 percent long term. Value Line estimates 12 percent. The consistency between the income statement and the balance sheet is measured by the turnover ratio of sales revenues to invested capital. In Table 17.15 we see that, in our forecast, the ratio stays relatively stable at 1.8. A common forecasting error is the failure to adequately tie capital requirements to sales growth. When this happens the turnover ratio increases rapidly, implying that sales is supported with inadequate capital — either that, or else the company is becoming inordinately efficient in its capital utilization. The result is that the company will be overvalued because cash outflows for capital investment are underestimated.

One of the "tricks" to building the balance sheet is the addition of two special lines. On the assets portion of Table 17.11, excess marketable securities has been set at a

TABLE 17.13   Forecast Assumptions and Operating Ratios for W.R. Grace, 1985–1999

	Historic						
	1985	1986	1987	1988	1989	1990	1991
Operating Ratios + Assumptions							
Operations							
Revenue Growth	−22.8%	−28.3%	21.2%	28.1%	5.7%	7.1%	5.3%
COGS/Revenues	69.1	68.6	68.8	69.4	69.4	69.4	69.4
SG&A/Revenues	21.6	21.0	20.0	20.0	20.4	20.4	20.2
EBDIT Margin	9.4	10.4	11.2	10.6	10.3	10.3	10.4
Depreciation/Revenues	5.2	5.4	4.3	3.9	4.1	3.8	3.8
Operating Margin	4.1	5.0	6.9	6.7	6.1	6.5	6.6
Working Capital/Revenues							
Operating Cash	0.0%	0.0%	0.0%	0.0%	0.0%	0.0%	0.0%
Accounts Receivable	13.6	17.9	18.3	18.5	19.0	19.0	19.0
Inventories	11.7	15.1	13.9	13.0	12.5	12.5	12.5
Other Current Assets	10.8	4.7	2.6	1.1	2.2	2.2	2.2
Accounts Payable	7.9	11.6	11.5	10.2	10.1	10.1	10.1
Other Current Liabilities	6.4	14.3	11.0	10.1	9.7	9.7	9.7
Net Working Capital	21.8	11.8	12.3	12.2	13.9	13.9	13.9
PPE							
Gross PPE/Revenues	93.0%	96.0%	86.8%	76.3%	76.6%	75.4%	76.0%
Net PPE/Revenues	52.8	45.8	40.9	37.6	37.3	36.1	36.2
Depr./Gross PPE	5.6	4.2	5.4	5.7	5.7	5.3	5.3
Retirements/Gross PPE	3.4	8.7	−0.3	1.5	2.0	1.7	1.7
Capital Expend./Sales	3.2	−22.4	7.3	9.6	5.9	6.3	6.9

minimum of $153 million. If the forecast showed W.R. Grace to be generating a lot of cash after financing charges, Excess Marketable Securities would be used as a ''plug'' figure that would grow over time. Future increases in marketable securities do not contribute to the present value of the company, however, because any investment in marketable securities has zero net present value, *ex ante*. The ''plug'' figure on the liabilities portion of the balance sheet in Table 17.11 is New Long-term Debt. For W.R. Grace, this line is growing in size because the company is not earning enough cash flows to be self-financing. Since debt is a financing flow, any forecasted increase has no effect on entity free cash flows and no effect on the weighted average cost of capital unless we believe that the target capital structure should change over time. Consequently, there is no effect on value.

Tables 17.16 and 17.17 are backup calculations that show the details for estimating some of the key variables, e.g., the EBIT, tax rate, changes in working capital, capital expenditures, investment in goodwill, nonoperating cash flow, and invested capital. Note that short-term debt is not part of our working capital definition because it is a financing flow, not an operating flow.

	Forecast						
1992	1993	1994	1995	1996	1997	1998	1999
6.8%	6.8%	6.8%	6.8%	6.0%	6.0%	6.0%	6.0%
69.1	69.1	69.1	69.0	69.0	69.0	69.0	69.0
20.2	20.1	20.0	20.0	20.0	20.0	20.0	20.0
10.7	10.8	10.9	11.0	11.0	11.0	11.0	11.0
3.8	3.8	3.8	3.8	3.8	3.8	3.7	3.7
6.9	7.0	7.1	7.2	7.2	7.2	7.3	7.3
0.0%	0.0%	0.0%	0.0%	0.0%	0.0%	0.0%	0.0%
19.0	19.0	19.0	19.0	19.0	19.0	19.0	19.0
12.5	12.5	12.5	12.5	12.5	12.5	12.5	12.5
2.2	2.2	2.2	2.2	2.2	2.2	2.2	2.2
10.1	10.1	10.1	10.1	10.1	10.1	10.1	10.1
9.7	9.7	9.7	9.7	9.7	9.7	9.7	9.7
13.9	13.9	13.9	13.9	13.9	13.9	13.9	13.9
75.9%	75.9%	75.8%	75.8%	75.8%	75.9%	75.9%	76.0%
36.1	36.0	36.0	35.9	35.8	35.8	35.9	36.0
5.3	5.3	5.3	5.3	5.3	5.3	5.1	5.1
1.7	1.7	1.7	1.7	2.0	2.0	2.0	2.0
7.2	7.2	7.2	7.2	7.2	7.2	7.2	7.2

TABLE 17.14   Financing and Other Ratios for W.R. Grace, 1985–1999

	Historic						
	1985	**1986**	**1987**	**1988**	**1989**	**1990**	**1991**
Financing and Other Ratios and Values + Forecast Assumptions							
Taxes							
EBIT Tax Rate	31.6%	125.6%	42.3%	39.7%	33.6%	33.6%	33.6%
Marginal Tax Rate	41.0	41.0	41.0	41.0	39.0	39.0	39.0
Incr. Def. Tax/Tax on EBIT	−46.0	−61.4	5.0	−10.5	3.8	3.8	3.8
Financing							
Int. Rate on Excess Mkt. Secs.						10.0%	10.0%
Int. Rate on Existing Debt	11.0%	10.5%	9.8%	12.2%	11.7%	11.7	11.7
Int. Rate on Short-term Debt				12.2	11.7	10.0	10.0
Int. Rate on New Long-term Debt						11.7	11.7
Dividend Payout Ratio	96.7	−24.9	68.6	50.8	47.1	47.1	47.1
Rate on Operating Leases	10.0	10.0	10.0	10.0	10.0	10.0	10.0
Other Ratios							
Non-Op. Income Growth	6.2%	−30.7%	16.5%	−4.8%	32.7%	0.0%	0.0%
Goodwill/Revenues	2.6	2.8	2.5	7.0	8.4	7.7	7.1
Other Assets/Revenues	2.8	8.7	6.8	3.2	4.0	4.0	4.0
Non-Op. Assets Growth Rate	22.1	24.2	4.4	9.2	−23.2	0.0	0.0
Other Liabs./Revs.	3.7	12.9	11.6	11.8	6.9	6.9	6.9
Capitalized Op. Leases	$ 308.4	$ 152.4	$ 175.6	$ 242.0	$ 261.6	$ 269.6	$ 284.0
Cap. Op. Leases/Revenues	5.9%	4.1%	3.9%	4.2%	4.3%	4.1%	4.1%
Other Values							
Amort. of Goodwill	$ 0.0	$ 0.0	$ 0.0	$ 0.0	$ 0.0	$ 12.9	$ 12.9
Special Items	75.0	(368.8)	0.0	4.6	114.4	0.0	0.0
Extraordinary Items	19.1	(96.9)	31.2	41.6	(3.4)	0.0	0.0
Short-term Debt	294.2	152.6	148.4	307.5	379.0	343.3	361.1
Long-term Debt	1,524.1	1,095.3	1,222.5	1,509.1	1,637.7	1,637.7	1,637.7
Preferred Stock	10.3	7.7	7.5	7.5	7.5	7.5	7.5
Preferred Dividends	(0.7)	(0.5)	(0.5)	(0.5)	(0.5)	(0.5)	(0.5)

			Forecast				
1992	**1993**	**1994**	**1995**	**1996**	**1997**	**1998**	**1999**
33.6%	33.6%	33.6%	33.6%	33.6%	33.6%	33.6%	33.6%
39.0	39.0	39.0	39.0	39.0	39.0	39.0	39.0
3.8	3.8	3.8	3.8	3.8	3.8	3.8	3.8
10.0%	10.0%	10.0%	10.0%	10.0%	10.0%	10.0%	10.0%
11.7	11.7	11.7	11.7	11.7	11.7	11.7	11.7
10.0	10.0	10.0	10.0	10.0	10.0	10.0	10.0
11.7	11.7	11.7	11.7	11.7	11.7	11.7	11.7
47.1	47.1	47.1	47.1	47.1	47.1	47.1	47.1
10.0	10.0	10.0	10.0	10.0	10.0	10.0	10.0
0.0%	0.0%	0.0%	0.0%	0.0%	0.0%	0.0%	0.0%
6.5	5.9	5.4	4.9	4.5	4.1	3.7	3.4
4.0	4.0	4.0	4.0	4.0	4.0	4.0	4.0
0.0	0.0	0.0	0.0	0.0	0.0	0.0	0.0
6.9	6.9	6.9	6.9	6.9	6.9	6.9	6.9
$ 303.3	$ 324.0	$ 346.0	$ 369.5	$ 391.7	$ 415.2	$ 440.1	$ 466.5
4.1%	4.1%	4.1%	4.1%	4.1%	4.1%	4.1%	4.1%
$ 12.9	$ 12.9	$ 12.9	$ 12.9	$ 12.9	$ 12.9	$ 12.9	$ 12.9
0.0	0.0	0.0	0.0	0.0	0.0	0.0	0.0
0.0	0.0	0.0	0.0	0.0	0.0	0.0	0.0
352.2	356.7	354.4	355.5	355.0	355.3	355.1	355.2
1,637.7	1,637.7	1,637.7	1,637.7	1,637.7	1,637.7	1,637.7	1,637.7
7.5	7.5	7.5	7.5	7.5	7.5	7.5	7.5
(0.5)	(0.5)	(0.5)	(0.5)	(0.5)	(0.5)	(0.5)	(0.5)

TABLE 17.15   Key Operating Ratios for W.R. Grace, 1985–1999

	Historic						
	1985	1986	1987	1988	1989	1990	1991
Key Operating Ratios							
Return on Invested Cap. (YE)*							
COGS/Revenues	69.1%	68.6%	68.8%	69.4%	69.4%	69.4%	69.4%
SG&A/Revenues	21.6%	21.0%	20.0%	20.0%	20.4%	20.4%	20.2%
Depreciation/Revenues	5.2%	5.4%	4.3%	3.9%	4.1%	3.8%	3.8%
EBIT/Revenues	5.1%	5.8%	7.3%	7.0%	6.5%	6.9%	7.0%
Net PPE/Revenues	52.8%	45.8%	40.9%	37.6%	37.3%	36.1%	36.2%
Working Capital/Revenues	21.8%	11.8%	12.3%	12.2%	13.9%	13.9%	13.9%
Net Other Assets/Revenues	7.6%	2.7%	1.6%	2.6%	9.9%	9.0%	8.4%
Revenues/Invested Capital	1.2	1.7	1.8	1.9	1.6	1.7	1.7
Pretax ROIC	6.2%	9.7%	13.3%	13.5%	10.7%	11.7%	12.0%
Operating Tax Rate	46.2%	202.6%	40.2%	43.9%	32.3%	32.3%	32.3%
After-Tax ROIC	3.3%	−10.0%	7.9%	7.6%	7.2%	7.9%	8.1%
After-Tax ROIC (ex. Goodwill)	3.4%	−10.5%	8.3%	8.7%	8.4%	9.1%	9.3%
Return on Invested Cap. (Avg.)							
Net PPE/Revenues	53.8%	59.7%	39.3%	34.7%	36.4%	35.5%	35.2%
Working Capital/Revenues	18.5%	21.1%	11.0%	10.9%	12.7%	13.4%	13.5%
Net Other Assets/Revenues	9.6%	6.6%	1.9%	1.9%	6.2%	9.1%	8.5%
Revenues/Invested Capital	1.2	1.1	1.9	2.1	1.8	1.7	1.7
Pretax ROIC	6.2%	6.7%	13.9%	14.8%	11.8%	11.9%	12.3%
After-Tax ROIC	3.4%	−6.9%	8.3%	8.3%	8.0%	8.0%	8.3%
After-Tax ROIC (ex. Goodwill)	3.5%	−7.1%	8.7%	9.2%	9.2%	9.3%	9.5%
Increm. Pretax ROIC	−121.6%	−145.0%	−5.4%	34.9%	−1.5%	7.2%	24.6%
Increm. After-Tax ROIC	−82.1%	−1,137.1%	−20.8%	14.3%	7.4%	4.9%	16.7%
(Five-Year Rolling Avg.)		−85.7%	11.9%	1.1%	2.0%	−32.4%	−141.1%
Investment Rates							
Gross Investment Rate	73.4%	8,017.0%	108.3%	172.5%	183.1%	70.4%	75.5%
Net Investment Rate	22.6%	903.8%	116.4%	243.5%	260.8%	46.3%	56.0%
(Five-Year Cum. Avg.)	52.3%	−202.0%	−245.7%	−161.4%	−81.4%	−50.4%	136.7%
Growth Rates							
Sales	−22.8%	−28.3%	21.2%	28.1%	5.7%	7.1%	5.3%
NOPLAT	−51.0%	−257.1%	−187.7%	16.6%	18.1%	12.7%	7.7%
Financing							
Coverage (EBIT/Interest)	111.8%	97.9%	237.5%	219.9%	168.1%	175.6%	179.0%
Debt/Total Cap. (Book)	44.4%	50.0%	49.7%	55.7%	55.6%	56.2%	55.4%
Debt/Total Cap. (Market)					54.5%		

*YE = Year End.

	Forecast							
	1992	1993	1994	1995	1996	1997	1998	1999
	69.1%	69.1%	69.1%	69.0%	69.0%	69.0%	69.0%	69.0%
	20.2%	20.1%	20.0%	20.0%	20.0%	20.0%	20.0%	20.0%
	3.8%	3.8%	3.8%	3.8%	3.8%	3.8%	3.7%	3.7%
	7.3%	7.4%	7.5%	7.6%	7.6%	7.6%	7.7%	7.7%
	36.1%	36.0%	36.0%	35.9%	35.8%	35.8%	35.9%	36.0%
	13.9%	13.9%	13.9%	13.9%	13.9%	13.9%	13.9%	13.9%
	7.8%	7.2%	6.7%	6.2%	5.8%	5.4%	5.0%	4.7%
	1.7	1.8	1.8	1.8	1.8	1.8	1.8	1.8
	12.7%	13.0%	13.3%	13.6%	13.7%	13.8%	14.1%	14.2%
	32.3%	32.3%	32.3%	32.3%	32.3%	32.3%	32.3%	32.3%
	8.6%	8.8%	9.0%	9.2%	9.3%	9.3%	9.6%	9.6%
	9.7%	9.8%	10.0%	10.1%	10.1%	10.1%	10.3%	10.2%
	35.0%	34.9%	34.8%	34.8%	34.9%	34.8%	34.8%	34.9%
	13.4%	13.4%	13.4%	13.4%	13.5%	13.5%	13.5%	13.5%
	7.8%	7.2%	6.7%	6.2%	5.8%	5.4%	5.1%	4.7%
	1.8	1.8	1.8	1.8	1.8	1.9	1.9	1.9
	13.0%	13.3%	13.7%	14.0%	14.0%	14.1%	14.5%	14.6%
	8.8%	9.0%	9.3%	9.5%	9.5%	9.6%	9.8%	9.9%
	10.0%	10.1%	10.3%	10.4%	10.4%	10.4%	10.6%	10.5%
	29.4%	19.1%	19.3%	19.5%	13.5%	16.0%	21.4%	15.5%
	19.9%	12.9%	13.0%	13.2%	9.2%	10.8%	14.4%	10.5%
	9.3%	9.1%	10.4%	14.7%	13.2%	11.7%	12.1%	11.6%
	79.8%	79.2%	78.6%	78.0%	74.2%	74.2%	74.6%	74.6%
	64.3%	63.5%	62.7%	61.9%	55.2%	55.2%	56.8%	56.8%
	121.7%	91.1%	59.2%	61.9%	61.3%	59.4%	58.1%	57.1%
	6.8%	6.8%	6.8%	6.8%	6.0%	6.0%	6.0%	6.0%
	11.1%	8.3%	8.3%	8.3%	5.7%	6.0%	8.0%	6.0%
	194.2%	202.5%	211.2%	220.2%	224.3%	231.4%	243.3%	250.2%
	54.8%	54.1%	53.4%	52.6%	51.6%	50.5%	49.5%	48.6%

TABLE 17.16   Calculation of Key Variables for W.R. Grace, 1985–1999

	Historic						
	1985	**1986**	**1987**	**1988**	**1989**	**1990**	**1991**
Taxes on EBIT and EBIT Tax Rate							
Total Tax Provision	$ 46.8	$ 51.5	$105.8	$124.6	$128.8	$ 84.1	$ 91.8
Tax Shield on Interest Exp.	76.7	78.6	50.4	68.8	83.2	89.8	95.2
Tax: Implied Int. Op. Leases	20.4	12.6	6.2	7.2	9.4	10.2	10.5
Less Taxes on Int. Income	0.0	0.0	0.0	(14.2)	(14.1)	(4.2)	(6.0)
Less Taxes on Non-Op. Income	(60.1)	130.9	(23.7)	(24.4)	(73.1)	(28.5)	(28.5)
Taxes on EBIT	$ 83.7	$ 273.7	$138.7	$162.0	$134.2	$151.3	$163.0
divided by EBIT	264.6	217.9	328.0	407.8	399.3	450.2	484.9
= EBIT Tax Rate	31.63%	125.56%	42.29%	39.72%	33.61%	33.61%	33.61%
Change in Working Capital							
Incr. in Oper. Cash	$ 0.0	$ 0.0	$ 0.0	$ 0.0	$ 0.0	$ 0.0	$ 0.0
Incr. in Accts. Receivable	51.2	(38.1)	160.9	242.4	94.3	82.8	66.5
Incr. in Inventories	(436.7)	(44.6)	66.5	122.0	11.0	54.3	43.6
Incr. Other Current Assets	503.6	(385.3)	(60.0)	(54.5)	71.1	9.4	7.5
(Incr.) in Accts. Payable	209.0	(23.5)	(89.5)	(68.5)	(30.0)	(44.1)	(35.4)
(Incr.) Other Current Liabs.	13.1	(201.5)	39.4	(91.8)	(3.6)	(42.0)	(33.8)
Net Change in Working Capital	$ 340.2	$ (693.0)	$117.3	$149.6	$142.8	$ 60.3	$ 48.5
Capital Expenditures							
Increase in Net PPE	$(104.0)	$(1,034.4)	$138.6	$328.5	$107.7	$ 84.9	$130.6
Depreciation	271.3	201.0	192.4	224.1	252.4	248.2	261.6
Cap. Exp. (Net of Disposals)	$ 167.3	$ (833.4)	$331.0	$552.6	$360.1	$333.0	$392.2
Investment in Goodwill							
Incr./(Decr.) Bal. Sheet Goodwill	$ (1.0)	$ (28.9)	$ 7.9	$293.0	$111.0	$ (12.9)	$ (12.9)
Amort. of Goodwill	0.0	0.0	0.0	0.0	0.0	(12.9)	(12.9)
Investment in Goodwill	$ (1.0)	$ (28.9)	$ 7.9	$293.0	$111.0	$ (25.8)	$ (25.8)
Non-Op. Cash Flow							
Extraordinary Items	$ 19.1	$ (96.9)	$ 31.2	$ 41.6	$ (3.4)	$ 0.0	$ 0.0
AT Non-Op. Income	86.5	(188.3)	34.1	35.2	114.3	44.5	44.5
Chg. in Investments & Advances	(67.9)	(90.8)	(20.6)	(44.6)	123.6	0.0	0.0
Non-Op. Cash Flow	$ 37.7	$ (376.0)	$ 44.7	$ 32.2	$234.5	$ 44.5	$ 44.5

	Forecast							
	1992	1993	1994	1995	1996	1997	1998	1999
	$107.4	$118.2	$130.2	$143.3	$151.7	$162.9	$179.9	$192.5
	97.1	100.6	104.1	107.7	111.3	113.8	116.4	119.5
	11.1	11.8	12.6	13.5	14.4	15.3	16.2	17.2
	(6.0)	(6.0)	(6.0)	(6.0)	(6.0)	(6.0)	(6.0)	(6.0)
	(28.5)	(28.5)	(28.5)	(28.5)	(28.5)	(28.5)	(28.5)	(28.5)
	$181.2	$196.2	$212.4	$230.0	$243.0	$257.5	$278.0	$294.7
	538.9	583.7	632.0	684.2	723.0	766.1	827.2	876.6
	33.61%	33.61%	33.61%	33.61%	33.61%	33.61%	33.61%	33.61%
	$ 0.0	$ 0.0	$ 0.0	$ 0.0	$ 0.0	$ 0.0	$ 0.0	$ 0.0
	89.3	95.3	101.8	108.7	102.5	108.6	115.1	122.0
	58.5	62.5	66.7	71.3	67.2	71.2	75.5	80.0
	10.1	10.8	11.5	12.3	11.6	12.3	13.1	13.8
	(47.5)	(50.8)	(54.2)	(57.9)	(54.6)	(57.9)	(61.3)	(65.0)
	(45.3)	(48.4)	(51.7)	(55.2)	(52.0)	(55.1)	(58.4)	(61.9)
	$ 65.0	$ 69.5	$ 74.2	$ 79.2	$ 74.7	$ 79.1	$ 83.9	$ 88.9
	$163.5	$174.9	$187.1	$200.1	$188.4	$199.3	$226.3	$239.6
	277.9	296.6	316.6	337.9	360.6	382.5	390.4	414.0
	$441.4	$471.5	$503.6	$538.0	$549.0	$581.9	$616.7	$653.6
	$ (12.9)	$ (12.9)	$ (12.9)	$ (12.9)	$ (12.9)	$ (12.9)	$ (12.9)	$ (12.9)
	(12.9)	(12.9)	(12.9)	(12.9)	(12.9)	(12.9)	(12.9)	(12.9)
	$ (25.8)	$ (25.8)	$ (25.8)	$ (25.8)	$ (25.8)	$ (25.8)	$ (25.8)	$ (25.8)
	$ 0.0	$ 0.0	$ 0.0	$ 0.0	$ 0.0	$ 0.0	$ 0.0	$ 0.0
	44.5	44.5	44.5	44.5	44.5	44.5	44.5	44.5
	0.0	0.0	0.0	0.0	0.0	0.0	0.0	0.0
	$ 44.5	$ 44.5	$ 44.5	$ 44.5	$ 44.5	$ 44.5	$ 44.5	$ 44.5

TABLE 17.17   Invested Capital Calculations for W.R. Grace, 1985–1999

	Historic					1990	1991
	1985	1986	1987	1988	1989		
Invested Capital							
Current Assets	$1,871.9	$1,403.9	$1,571.3	$1,881.2	$2,057.6	$2,204.1	$2,321.8
Noninterest Current Liabs.	(741.1)	(966.1)	(1,016.2)	(1,176.5)	(1,210.1)	(1,296.3)	(1,365.5)
Working Capital	$1,130.8	$ 437.8	$ 555.1	$ 704.7	$ 847.5	$ 907.8	$ 956.3
Net PPE	2,740.9	1,706.5	1,845.1	2,173.6	2,281.3	2,366.2	2,496.8
Capitalized Op. Leases	308.4	152.4	175.6	242.0	261.6	269.6	284.0
Goodwill	133.1	104.2	112.1	405.1	516.1	503.2	490.3
Other Assets	147.6	323.5	306.5	185.9	247.2	264.8	278.9
Other Noninterest Liabs.	(194.5)	(480.1)	(521.8)	(681.7)	(419.4)	(449.3)	(473.3)
Total Invested Capital	$4,266.3	$2,244.3	$2,472.6	$3,029.6	$3,734.3	$3,862.4	$4,033.1
Total Debt	$1,818.3	$1,247.9	$1,370.9	$1,816.6	$2,016.7	$2,129.4	$2,175.4
Capitalized Op. Leases	308.4	152.4	175.6	242.0	261.6	269.6	284.0
Deferred Income Taxes	262.5	94.5	101.4	84.4	89.5	95.2	101.4
Common Equity	2,394.2	1,300.9	1,455.8	1,543.6	1,722.9	1,768.8	1,872.9
Preferred Stock	10.3	7.7	7.5	7.5	7.5	7.5	7.5
	$4,793.7	$2,803.4	$3,111.2	$3,694.1	$4,098.2	$4,270.6	$4,441.3
Less: Excess Mkt. Secs.	(151.6)	(92.5)	(151.4)	(132.7)	(108.7)	(153.0)	(153.0)
Less: Non-Op. Assets	(375.8)	(466.6)	(487.2)	(531.8)	(255.2)	(255.2)	(255.2)
Total Invested Capital	$4,266.3	$2,244.3	$2,472.6	$3,029.6	$3,734.3	$3,862.4	$4,033.1
Validation Test: Asset Side – Liability Side	0	0	0	(0)	(0)	0.0	0.0
Invested Capital (Ex. Goodwill)	$4,133.2	$2,140.1	$2,360.5	$2,624.5	$3,218.2	$3,359.2	$3,542.8

The Weighted Average Cost of Capital

Table 17.18 shows our calculation of the weighted average cost of capital for W.R. Grace. Noninterest-bearing liabilities, accounts payable for example, are given no weight in the calculation because their costs, if any, are already included in the estimation of free cash flows. Although trade credit pays no specific financing charges, its cost is implicit in the price being charged for the goods — the trade credit discount. We make no distinction between short- and long-term debt because 1-year debt has approximately the same cost as 10-year debt when it is rolled over 10 times during the explicit forecast period. The before-tax cost of all interest-bearing debt capital was about 10.4 percent for new long-term debt at the margin (i.e., if reissued) in 1990. W.R. Grace had no convertible debt outstanding, however, if it did, it would have been necessary to use the option pricing model to estimate its true opportunity cost (see Chapter 25 on warrants and convertibles). The coupon rate on convertible securities is not a good estimate of their opportunity cost.

			Forecast				
1992	**1993**	**1994**	**1995**	**1996**	**1997**	**1998**	**1999**
$2,479.7	$2,648.3	$2,828.4	$3,020.7	$3,202.0	$3,394.1	$3,597.7	$3,813.6
(1,458.3)	(1,557.5)	(1,663.4)	(1,776.5)	(1,883.1)	(1,996.1)	(2,115.9)	(2,242.8)
$1,021.4	$1,090.8	$1,165.0	$1,244.2	$1,318.8	$1,398.0	$1,481.9	$1,570.8
2,660.2	2,835.1	3,022.2	3,222.3	3,410.7	3,610.0	3,836.3	4,075.8
303.3	324.0	346.0	369.5	391.7	415.2	440.1	466.5
477.4	464.5	451.6	438.7	425.8	412.9	400.0	387.1
297.9	318.2	339.8	362.9	384.7	407.8	432.2	458.2
(505.4)	(539.8)	(576.5)	(615.7)	(652.7)	(691.8)	(733.3)	(777.3)
$4,254.8	$4,492.7	$4,748.1	$5,021.9	$5,279.0	$5,552.0	$5,857.1	$6,181.1
$2,250.0	$2,326.6	$2,405.2	$2,485.5	$2,540.2	$2,596.4	$2,664.0	$2,734.2
303.3	324.0	346.0	369.5	391.7	415.2	440.1	466.5
108.3	115.8	123.9	132.6	141.8	151.6	162.2	173.4
1,993.9	2,127.0	2,273.7	2,434.9	2,606.0	2,789.5	2,991.6	3,207.6
7.5	7.5	7.5	7.5	7.5	7.5	7.5	7.5
$4,663.0	$4,900.9	$5,156.3	$5,430.1	$5,687.2	$5,960.2	$6,265.3	$6,589.3
(153.0)	(153.0)	(153.0)	(153.0)	(153.0)	(153.0)	(153.0)	(153.0)
(255.2)	(255.2)	(255.2)	(255.2)	(255.2)	(255.2)	(255.2)	(255.2)
$4,254.8	$4,492.7	$4,748.1	$5,021.9	$5,279.0	$5,552.0	$5,857.1	$6,181.1
(0.0)	0.0	(0.0)	(0.0)	0.0	0.0	(0.0)	0.0
$3,777.4	$4,028.3	$4,296.5	$4,583.2	$4,853.2	$5,139.1	$5,457.2	$5,794.0

Preferred stock was a trivial portion of W.R. Grace capital structure, only 0.2 percent, so we used a rough estimate for its opportunity cost, i.e., 11.3 percent.

The cost of equity was estimated by using the Capital Asset Pricing Model (CAPM).

$$k_s = R_F + [E(R_M) - R_F]\beta_s$$

where for W.R. Grace in 1990:

$$R_F = \text{the rate on 10-year Treasury bonds} = 8.7\%$$

$$E(R_M) - R_F = \text{the market risk premium} = 6.0\%$$

$$\beta_s = \text{the beta for the levered equity of W.R. Grace} = 1.00.$$

Therefore, the cost of equity estimate is

$$k_s = .087 + (.06)1.0 = 14.7\%.$$

TABLE 17.18   Weighted Average Cost of Capital Calculation

	Market Value	Percent of Total Market Capitalization	Cost of Capital	After-Tax Cost*	Contribution to WACC
Debt and Capitalized Operating Leases	$2,279	54.5%	10.4%	6.3%	3.46%
Preferred Stock	8	0.2	11.5	11.5	.02
Common Stock	1,893	45.3	14.7	14.7	6.66
	$4,180	100.0%			10.14%

*Assumes a 39 percent marginal tax rate (local, state, and federal).

The end result of our cost of capital calculations was a weighted average cost of capital estimate of 10.14 percent. This was the discount rate that was used both for the 10 years of explicit cash flows and for the continuing value calculation.

Estimating the Continuing Value

To estimate the value of free cash flows beyond the explicit forecast period we use a formula approach that embodies only broad assumptions about rates of return, growth rates, and the cost of capital. Equation 17.16 is the basis of our analysis.

$$V_0 = \frac{NOI_1(1 - T)(1 - g/r)}{WACC - g} \qquad (17.16)$$

It makes the simplifying assumptions that (1) the rate of return on all new investments, r, is constant; (2) the company invests a constant proportion of its cash flows, b; and therefore (3) the long-run nominal rate of growth in cash flows, g, is constant and less than the weighted average cost of capital, WACC. Recall that the growth rate is equal to the return on new capital invested multiplied by the investment rate.

$$g = br \qquad (17.18)$$

If we use Equation 17.16 to value cash flows beyond the explicit forecast period we will use our estimate of net operating profit less adjusted taxes (NOPLAT) for the eleventh year in the numerator because

$$NOI_1(1 - T) = NOPLAT_{10}(1 + g).$$

Net operating income after taxes in the formula approach to valuation is equal to earnings before interest and taxes (EBIT) minus taxes on EBIT plus the change in deferred taxes.

There are a variety of assumptions that can be used when applying the continuing value formula. The most common, and most conservative, is that competition will drive the company's rate of return on new invested capital (ROIC = r) down to equal its weighted average cost of capital. If r = WACC, then Equation 17.16 reduces to:

$$V_N = \frac{\text{NOI}_{N+1}(1-T)}{\text{WACC}} = \frac{\text{NOPLAT}_N(1+g)(1-T)}{\text{WACC}}$$

$$= \frac{\text{NOPLAT}_{N+1}}{\text{WACC}}. \tag{17.19}$$

This is called the *perpetuity model* for estimating the continuing value of the company beyond the 10-year explicit forecast period. Note that it does not make any difference what the nominal rate of growth in cash flows is because WACC = r and consequently the net present value of all investments is zero given this assumption. For W.R. Grace, the continuing value as of the end of the explicit forecast period is:

$$V_{10} = \frac{\$593.1 \ (1.06)}{0.1013} = \$6.206 \text{ billion}$$

The last step is to discount this value at the end of Year 10 back to the present. In Figure 17.11 the result is a continuing value estimate of $2.667 billion.

An *aggressive model* for estimating the continuing value, an approach that we do not recommend, assumes that the cash flows of the company can grow at a constant rate forever without investing any capital. Solving Equation 17.18 for the investment rate we have $b = g/r$. Substituting this into Equation 17.16:

$$V_0 = \frac{\text{NOI}_1(1-T)(1-b)}{\text{WACC} - g},$$

and if we assume that the investment rate is zero, $b = 0$, then:

$$V_0 = \frac{\text{NOI}_1}{\text{WACC} - g}. \tag{17.20}$$

Had we used the aggressive approach for W.R. Grace, our continuing value estimate would have been:

$$V_{10} = \frac{\$593.1 \ (1.06)}{0.1013 - 0.06} = \$15.222 \text{ billion}.$$

This is more than double the result from the more conservative perpetuity approach. The aggressive approach almost always overvalues companies.

The third way of looking at continuing value is to use Equation 17.16 for companies where the forecasted ROIC is greater than WACC perpetually. Few companies actually attain this lofty goal. We do not believe that W.R. Grace will. In fact, even by the end of the explicit forecast period our forecast of ROIC is only 9.6 percent compared with a 10.1 percent WACC. Companies where ROIC > WACC for long intervals are usually those with sustainable competitive advantages that take the form of established brand names (e.g., Pepsi or Coke), research and development programs that result in a stream of patents (pharmaceutical companies), or unique management skills that cannot be duplicated by competition.

Suppose that we call Equation 17.16 the *competitive advantage model,* and compute the effect on W.R. Grace's continuing value had we been willing to assume that (1) it could earn a 12 percent ROIC in the long run and (2) it could reinvest about 60 percent of its cash flows. These two facts mean that we must revise our estimated growth rate upward from 6 percent to

$$g = br = 0.6(0.12) = 7.2\%.$$

Using these facts in the competitive advantage model we have

$$V_0 = \frac{\mathrm{NOI}_1(1 - T)(1 - g/r)}{\mathrm{WACC} - g}$$

$$= \frac{\$593.1(1.072)(1 - 0.072/0.12)}{0.1013 - 0.72} = \$8.680 \text{ billion.}$$

The result, of course, is a continuing value estimate that lies between the other two. For the W.R. Grace case, however, we believe that the conservative perpetuity model is best because it implicitly assumes that the company will earn a rate of return on new investment just equal to its cost of capital.

EMPIRICAL RESULTS

With the advent of personal computers and user-friendly spreadsheets, the time needed to do a detailed discounted cash flow valuation has decreased dramatically. Furthermore, the models are no longer "black boxes" that reside on mainframe computers, but are under the direct control of top management and its staff. Consequently, DCF is used much more often as a planning and performance evaluation tool. But the question remains — how well do DCF valuations of companies compare with the actual market values? A major issue is whether the marketplace is using the same forecasts of cash flows as the internally generated forecasts that management is using.

To test the validity of the DCF model, we used forecasts made by the *Value Line Investment Survey* (sales growth, operating margins, capital expenditures, and working capital needs) to construct DCF models for 35 large companies in 1988. We estimated the DCF values in a blind test, i.e., we did not look at the actual market prices until after our valuations were completed. We did not try to force fit our valuations to make them come close to the market values and we did not spend much time working on each company. Table 17.19 shows the results. The absolute value of our average error rate was 9.2 percent. Figure 17.12 plots the ratio of the market price per share to the book value per share (market/book) against the discounted cash flows per share divided by the book value per share (DCF/book). If the DCF value provided a perfect fit against the market value, the result would be a 45 degree line (the solid line) and it would go through the origin. The actual regression was

$$\text{Market/book} = -0.0309 + 0.9805 \text{ (DCF/book)}.$$
$$(-0.08) \quad\quad (23.55)$$

The numbers in parentheses are t-statistics. They indicate that the intercept is not significantly different from zero and that the slope is significantly above zero (but not signifi-

---

TABLE 17.19   Discounted Cash Flow Valuations of 35 Companies, 1988

| Company | Price/Share | | Book Value/ Share | Ratios | | Error | Percent of Mkt. Price |
	Market	DCF		Mkt./ Book	DCF/ Book		
Abbott Laboratories	$ 44.63	$ 44.52	$ 9.23	4.83	4.82	$ 0.11	0.25%
American Home Products Corp.	73.13	75.18	17.42	4.20	4.32	−2.05	−2.80
AMP Inc.	47.88	51.62	12.54	3.82	4.12	−3.74	−7.81
Anheuser Busch	29.75	29.23	9.87	3.01	2.96	0.52	1.75
Automatic Data Processing, Inc.	38.38	42.09	12.71	3.02	3.31	3.71	−9.67
Baxter International, Inc.	20.63	23.83	11.79	1.75	2.02	−3.20	−15.51
Bristol-Myers Company	40.13	38.77	11.23	3.57	3.45	1.36	3.39
Deluxe Corporation	22.88	25.57	5.77	3.96	4.43	−2.69	−11.76
Dow Jones & Co., Inc.	33.13	37.26	8.80	3.76	4.23	−4.13	−12.47
Dun & Bradstreet Corp.	47.63	51.41	10.95	4.35	4.69	−3.78	−7.94
EG&G, Inc.	33.38	27.07	9.79	3.41	2.77	6.31	18.90
Eli Lilly and Co.	84.25	79.65	21.83	3.86	3.65	4.60	5.46
Emerson Electric Co.	29.75	25.38	11.68	2.55	2.17	4.37	14.69
Gannett Company, Inc.	32.00	39.26	9.94	3.22	3.95	−7.26	−22.69
General Electric Co.	44.13	40.45	18.25	2.42	2.22	3.68	8.34
Genuine Parts Company	36.75	36.98	9.84	3.73	3.76	−0.23	−0.63
H.J. Heinz Company	40.50	37.23	12.48	3.25	2.98	3.27	8.07
Hewlett-Packard Company	52.50	50.67	19.52	2.69	2.60	1.83	3.49
International Business Machines Corp.	127.63	129.58	64.09	1.99	2.02	−1.95	−1.53
Johnson & Johnson	77.50	69.77	20.25	3.83	3.45	7.73	9.97
Masco Corporation	27.50	22.87	10.34	2.66	2.21	4.63	16.84
The Maytag Corp.	22.13	16.20	5.43	4.07	2.98	5.93	26.80

TABLE 17.19   (*continued*)

| Company | Price/Share | | Book Value/ Share | Ratios | | Error | Percent of Mkt. Price |
	Market	DCF		Mkt./ Book	DCF/ Book		
McGraw-Hill, Inc.	60.88	52.40	17.11	3.56	3.06	8.48	13.93
Merck & Co., Inc.	54.63	53.59	5.37	10.17	9.98	1.04	1.90
Minnesota Mining & Manufacturing Co.	64.75	62.21	22.24	2.91	2.80	2.54	3.92
Nalco Chemical Company	36.50	36.17	11.41	3.20	3.17	0.33	0.90
Northern Telecom Ltd.	18.88	16.36	9.84	1.92	1.66	2.52	13.35
PepsiCo, Inc.	36.00	31.72	9.63	3.74	3.29	4.28	11.89
Pfizer Inc.	50.38	46.78	23.60	2.13	1.98	3.60	7.15
SmithKline Beckman Corp.	45.50	52.29	12.74	3.57	4.10	−6.79	−14.92
Syntex Corporation	38.63	39.49	6.38	6.05	6.19	−0.86	−2.23
Wal-Mart Stores, Inc.	32.75	30.75	3.99	8.21	7.71	2.00	6.11
The Washington Post Co.	191.50	189.09	47.80	4.01	3.96	2.41	1.26
Waste Management, Inc.	34.38	30.39	8.39	4.10	3.62	3.99	11.61
Worthington Industries	24.00	18.70	7.04	3.41	2.66	5.30	22.08

Source: McKinsey analysis.

cantly different from 1). The *r*-squared for the regression was 0.94, indicating that 94 percent of the variance in the market/book ratios was captured by the DCF valuations. Overall, our quick and dirty valuations provided an excellent fit for this set of companies. In general, if the market is efficient and the model is correct, we should expect to see a good fit. We conclude that the spreadsheet DCF model is very good indeed.

SUMMARY

We began the chapter by describing the uses for a value-based management system and by showing that value-based performance measures are superior to their accounting-based counterparts, for example, return on sales, return on assets, return on equity, or earnings per share growth. We then shifted to focus on how to do valuations. First, we covered formula approaches to show the relationship between earnings and free cash flows and to derive the formula that was used in estimating the continuing value of a company. Second, we showed the details involved in applying a discounted cash flow approach. Then we illustrated the approach with a case example — W.R. Grace Co. Finally, we validated the DCF approach by using it in a blind test to value 35 companies. In general, the

---

FIGURE 17.12   Market to Book Regressed Against DCF to Book

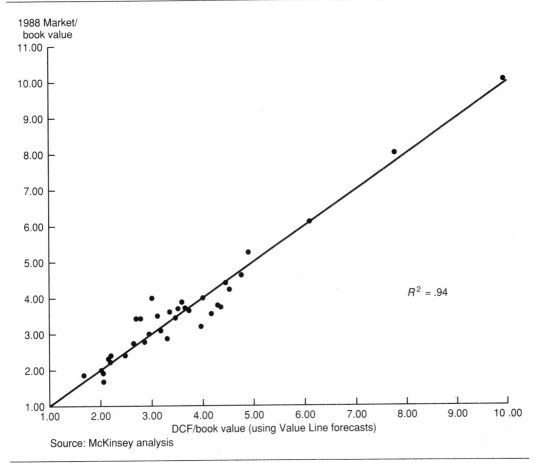

1988 Market/
book value

$R^2 = .94$

DCF/book value (using Value Line forecasts)

Source: McKinsey analysis

---

approach works quite well. It is not difficult to come within plus or minus 10 percent of the market value of a company.

Although using discounted cash flows to value companies is a complicated task (certainly much more complicated than using ratios like price-earnings multiples), the extra complexity is more than offset by the insights that can be provided to management.

QUESTIONS

17.1 What are the different kinds of growth that are likely to have an influence on the valuation relationship?

17.2 Explain why a share of no growth common stock is similar to a share of preferred stock. Use one of the equations developed in the chapter as part of your explanation.

17.3 Explain the importance in common stock valuation of
   a. dividend policy
   b. net operating income
   c. current market price
   d. the expected future growth rate
   e. the market capitalization rate.

17.4 Describe the factors that determine the market rate of return on a particular stock at a given point in time.

17.5 Explain how the following influence stock and bond prices:
   a. interest rates
   b. investors' aversion to risk.

17.6 Why must the balance sheet information be considered in addition to income statement information for valuing companies?

17.7 Why is EPS growth an unsatisfactory basis for achieving value creation?

17.8 Why is there often a difference between forecasted return on equity and the amount of value created?

17.9 Compare and contrast the "formula" approaches versus the "computer spreadsheet" approach in valuing companies.

PROBLEMS

17.1 The reader is likely to encounter two leading variations on Equation 17.17 that was derived in the text. In this and the following problem, we will illustrate the use of the variations on Equation 17.17. Equation 17.17p was developed by two Nobel Prize winners in financial economics, Merton Miller and Franco Modigliani (see Miller and Modigliani, [1961]). Using the same facts as in the Koller Company example in connection with Equation 17.17, calculate value using an equivalent expression for Equation 17.17a, the following Equation 17.17p.

$$V_o = \frac{X(1-T)}{k}\left\{1 + \frac{b(r-k)}{g-k}\left[\left(\frac{1+g}{1+k}\right)^n - 1\right]\right\}(1+g) \qquad \textbf{(17.17p)}$$

17.2 Another expression for Equation 17.17a is 17.17q below. This is associated with the name of another leading financial economist, Burton Malkiel (Malkiel, [1963]). Use it to solve for value using the facts of the previous problem.

$$V_o = X_o(1-T)(1-b)\sum_{t=1}^{n}\left(\frac{1+g}{1+k}\right)^t + \frac{X_o(1-T)(1+g)^{n+1}}{k(1+k)^n} \qquad \textbf{(17.17q)}$$

17.3 The Smith Company has a beta of 1.2. The expected return on the market is 12 percent, the risk-free rate is 7 percent, and the market variance is 1 percent. The net operating income of the Smith Company for the year just completed was $8 million, with an applicable corporate tax rate of 40 percent.

a. Assuming no growth in Smith's NOI is expected, what would be the value of the firm?

b. Next assume that the profitability rate of Smith is 15 percent and that the ratio of investment to net operating income averages 0.60. What would be the value of Smith under these new assumptions?

17.4 The Pelman Company has a required return of 12 percent. Its free cash flow (X), now $5 million, is expected to grow at a rate of 28.8 percent for the next eight years, with a ratio of investment to after-tax net operating income of .90. The applicable tax rate is 40 percent. If, after the period of supernormal growth, the net operating income of Pelman has zero growth, what is the current value of the firm?

17.5 The Murrin Company has a free cash flow (X) of $10 million, expected to grow at a rate of 32 percent for the next seven years. Its ratio of investment to after-tax net operating income (b) is 60 percent. The applicable tax rate is 40 percent; the applicable cost of capital is 10 percent. After the period of supernormal growth, Murrin will have no further growth in X.

a. What is the value of Murrin? What is the implied r?

b. If g drops to 26.5 percent, with b the same, what is the new value?

c. If b changes to 90 percent, with r the same, what is the new value?

d. If b changes to 20 percent, with r the same, what is the new value?

17.6 Equation 17.15 in the text (which values the entity) can be modified to provide a dividend constant growth valuation model (to value the firm's equity) as shown in Equation 17.15a below.

$$p_o = \frac{d_o(1 + g)\,(1 - b)}{k_s - g} \tag{17.15a}$$

where:

p_o = price per share

d_o = initial dividends per share

g = growth rate in dividends per share (to infinity)

b = retention rate (investment rate as a fraction of earnings per share)

k_s = cost of equity capital

While subject to limitations, this dividend growth valuation model is widely used, so we provide some problems to develop familiarity with its implications. Note that this formula provides for the valuation of the equity portion of the firm's value. We now illustrate its use: An investor requires a 15 percent return on the common stock of the M Company. During its most recent complete year, the M Company stock earned $4 and paid $2 per share. Its earnings and dividends are expected to grow at 8 percent per year. At what value of the M Company stock would the investor earn a required 20 percent return?

TABLE P17.7

Relationships	Bonden (per share)	Seeger (per share)	Ellis (totals)
Earnings per share, 19X6	$ 5.00	$ 8.00	$ 1,500,000
Average, 19X0-19X6	4.00	5.00	1,000,000
Price per share, 19X6	48.00	65.00	—
Dividends per share, 19X6	3.00	4.00	700,000
Average, 19X0-19X6	2.50	3.25	500,000
Book value per share	45.00	70.00	12,000,000

17.7 The Ellis Company is a small jewelry manufacturer. The company has been successful and has grown. Now, Ellis is planning to sell an issue of common stock to the public for the first time, and it faces the problem of setting an appropriate price on its common stock. The company feels that the proper procedure is to select firms similar to it, with publicly traded common stock, and to make relevant comparisons.

The company finds several jewelry manufacturers similar to it with respect to product mix, size, asset composition, and debt/equity proportions. Of these, Bonden and Seeger are most similar, with data as shown in Table P17.7.

a. Calculate the per share data for Ellis assuming that 500,000 shares of stock will be sold.

b. Calculate the P/E, dividend yield, and market to book relations for Bonden and Seeger.

c. Apply the relationships in Part (b) to the Ellis per share data to establish boundaries for the indicated market price for the Ellis stock.

d. Using the boundaries, and taking trend patterns into account, what is your recommendation for an issuing price for the Ellis stock?

17.8 After six years as vice president of a New York bank, Henry Thorson has decided to simplify his lifestyle and become a small-town shopkeeper. He has found an apparently successful variety store in rural Pennsylvania for sale at a price of $120,000. The most recent balance sheet is given in Table P17.8.

TABLE P17.8

Assets		Liabilities	
Cash	$ 18,000	Notes payable, bank	$ 6,000
Receivables, net	6,000	Accounts payable	12,000
Inventories	39,000	Accruals	3,000
Net fixed assets	42,000	Net worth	84,000
Total assets	$105,000	Total liabilities and net worth	$105,000

Annual pretax earnings (after rent, interest, and salaries) have averaged $24,000 for the preceding three years. The store has been in business in the same community for 20 years and has 6 years remaining on a 10-year lease. The purchase price includes all assets, except for cash, and Thorson would have to assume all debts.

    a. Is the price of $120,000 reasonable?

    b. What other factors should be considered in arriving at a purchase price?

    c. What is the significance, if any, of the lease?

17.9 The Blue Company has free cash flows (X) of $19 million, and is expected to grow at a rate of 26.5 percent for the next five years. Its ratio of investment to after-tax NOI (b) is 0.5. The applicable tax rate is 30 percent; Blue's cost of capital is 10 percent. After the period of supernormal growth, Blue Company is not expected to grow any further.

    a. What is the value of Blue Company?

    b. What is the implied profitability rate (r)?

    c. If Blue has $110 in interest-bearing debt, what is the value of Blue's equity?

17.10 The Brown Company has the same parameters as the Blue Company in Problem 17.9, except that its investment rate (b) is 1.0, and its profit rate is 26.5 percent.

    a. What is the value of Brown Company?

    b. If Brown Company has $68 million in interest-bearing debt, what is the value of Brown's equity?

17.11 Given the following information on the Pink Company and the Red Company, as well as the Blue and Brown Companies, use the investment banker comparables method to value the equity of Blue and Brown. All four firms are roughly similar in size and have similar product-market mix characteristics. In performing the comparables analysis, use the ratios on the following page.

	Pink Co.	Red Co.	Blue Co.	Brown Co.
Revenues	$600	$400	$500	$400
EBDIT	40	40	33	40
Depreciation	6	8	7	13
EBIT	34	32	26	27
Interest expense	10	10	8	8
EBT	24	22	18	19
Current taxes	7	6	5	6
Net income	17	16	13	13
Current ratio	2/1	2/1	2/1	2/1
Interest-bearing debt/NW	50%	50%	55%	45%
Fixed-charge coverage	3 times	3 times	3 times	3 times
Revenue growth	25%	30%	24%	31%
EBIT growth	30%	30%	26.5%	26.5%
Net income growth	30%	30%	28%	28%
Marginal free cash flow to total investment capital, net (r)	50%	25%	53%	26.5%
Marginal investment requirements to free cash flow, net (b)	0.6	1.2	0.5	1.0
Market value	$400	$350		
Book value	300	200	150	100
Replacement cost	500	400	300	300

    a. Market to book value
    b. Market to replacement cost
    c. Market to sales
    d. Price to earnings (P/E)
    e. Market to after-tax EBIT; in other words, EBIT $(1 - T)$

17.12 *(Use the computer diskette, File name: 17VALUE, Valuation.)*

    a. You are given the following information on the key input parameters that determine the value of a firm:

$$X_0 = \$600,000 = \text{NOI}$$
$$T = .40 = \text{tax rate}$$
$$b = .50 = \text{ratio of net investment to after-tax NOI}$$
$$g_s = .30 = \text{rate of supernormal growth}$$
$$k = .15 = \text{cost of capital}$$

Assuming that the firm experiences zero growth following the five-year supernormal growth period, what is the value of the firm? What do these inputs imply about the internal profitability rate (r)?

    (1) What is the multiplier, defined as value divided by after-tax net operating income?

    (2) We will now investigate the effects on the value of the firm as g, b, and r are changed. Recall the relationship, $g = br$. It is important when we change one of the three terms in that equation to make consistent changes as required in the other terms. Although r was not stated in the facts given above, the implicit r is 60 percent, which is quite high. If b rises to 1, what g would be required to keep r constant at .60? Does the value of the firm rise or fall?

    (3) If b rises to 1 while g remains at 30 percent, does the value of the firm rise or fall in relation to what it was originally? (Be sure to notice what this change implies has happened to the value of r.)

    (4) Suppose that the value of b declines to .2; if g remains the same at .30, what does this imply for the value of r? Does the value of the firm rise or fall?

    b. Going back to the original conditions, lower and increase k, the cost of capital, by increments of .02, and observe what happens to the value of the firm. Also see Graph A.

    c. Going back to the original conditions, now lower and increase n, the supernormal growth period, by increments of 1 and observe what happens to the value of the firm. See Graph B.

    d. Now raise and lower the tax rate upward and downward in increments of .02, and observe the effects on value. See Graph C.

    e. Now you are free to explore the effects of varying the input parameters during the supernormal growth period as well as the growth assumptions at the end of the supernormal growth period. To which variables is firm value most sensitive?

SELECTED REFERENCES

Banz, Rolf W., "The Relationship Between Return and Market Value of Common Stocks," *Journal of Financial Economics,* 9 (March 1981), pp. 3–18.

Basu, Sanjoy, "The Relationship Between Earnings' Yield, Market Value and Return for NYSE Common Stocks: Further Evidence," *Journal of Financial Economics,* 12 (June 1983), pp. 129–156.

Brennan, Michael, "A Note on Dividend Irrelevance and the Gordon Valuation Model," *Journal of Finance,* 26 (December 1971), pp. 1115–1123.

Copeland, T.; Koller, T.; and Murrin, J., *Valuation: Measuring and Managing the Value of Companies,* New York: John Wiley & Co., 1990.

Fuller, Russell J., and Hsia, Chi-Cheng, "A Simplified Common Stock Valuation Model," *Financial Analysts Journal,* 40 (September-October 1984), pp. 49–56.

Graham, B.; Dodd, D. L.; and Cottle, S., *Security Analysis,* New York: McGraw-Hill, 1961, p. 28.

Haugen, Robert A., "Expected Growth, Required Return, and the Variability of Stock Prices," *Journal of Financial and Quantitative Analysis,* 5 (September 1970), pp. 297–308.

Hakansson, Nils H., "Changes in the Financial Market: Welfare and Price Effects and the Basic Theorems of Value Conservation," *Journal of Finance,* 37 (September 1982), pp. 977–1004.

Holt, Charles C., "The Influence of Growth Duration on Share Prices," *Journal of Finance,* 17 (September 1962), pp. 465–475.

Malkiel, Burton G., "Equity Yields, Growth, and the Structure of Share Prices," *American Economic Review,* 53 (December 1963), pp. 467–494.

Miller, Merton H., and Modigliani, Franco, "Dividend Policy, Growth, and the Valuation of Shares," *Journal of Business,* 34 (October 1961), pp. 411–433.

Modigliani, Franco, "Debt, Dividend Policy, Taxes, Inflation and Market Valuation," *Journal of Finance,* 37 (May 1982), pp. 255–273.

Morris, James R., "The Role of Cash Balances in Firm Valuation," *Journal of Financial and Quantitative Analysis,* 18 (December 1983), pp. 533–545.

Rappaport, A., *Creating Shareholder Value,* New York: The Free Press, 1986.

Robichek, Alexander A., and Bogue, Marcus C., "A Note on the Behavior of Expected Price/Earnings Ratios over Time," *Journal of Finance,* 26 (June 1971), pp. 731–736.

Salmi, Timo, "Estimating the Internal Rate of Return from Published Financial Statements," *Journal of Business Finance & Accounting,* 9 (Spring 1982), pp. 63–74.

Senbet, Lemma W., and Thompson, Howard E., "Growth and Risk," *Journal of Financial and Quantitative Analysis,* 17 (September 1982), pp. 331–340.

Stapleton, Richard C., "Portfolio Analysis, Stock Valuation, and Capital Budgeting Decision Rules for Risky Projects," *Journal of Finance,* 26 (March 1971), pp. 95–118.

Stewart, G. B., III, *The Quest for Value,* New York: Harper Collins, 1991.

Stone, B. K., "The Conformity of Stock Values Based on Discounted Dividends to a Fair-Return Process," *Bell Journal of Economics,* 6 (Autumn 1975), pp. 698–702.

Turnbull, Stuart M., "Market Value and Systematic Risk," *Journal of Finance,* 32 (September 1977), pp. 1125–1142.

Walter, James E., *Dividend Policy and Enterprise Valuation,* Belmont, Calif.: Wadsworth, 1967.

Wendt, Paul F., "Current Growth Stock Valuation Methods," *Financial Analysts Journal,* 33 (March-April 1965), pp. 3–15.

Financial Strategies for Working Capital Management

In Part Three, we covered financial planning and control from the standpoint of the firm as a whole. In Parts Four and Five, we developed the analytical framework for dealing with uncertainty. With this background, we now turn to aspects of financial management of the firm in more detail. Part Six begins with a focus on the top half of the balance sheet analyzing current assets, current liabilities, and the interrelationships between them. This type of analysis was historically called working capital management and more recently has been called short-term financial management. In broad perspective, short-term financial management represents the efforts of the firm to make adjustments to short-run changes. These represent the developments to which the firm must make prompt and effective responses. These decision areas are of vital importance because they occupy the major portion of the financial manager's time and represent areas in which activity takes place on a continuing basis.

Chapter 18 examines short-term financial planning and the critical area of cash management, including cash disbursements, management of the firm's marketable securities portfolio, and cash management models. In Chapter 19, we analyze credit management decisions by calculating the net present values of alternative credit management policies, utilizing the capital budgeting framework developed earlier. Chapter 19 also includes an overview of inventory models, a subject with broad implications since all investments represent an inventory decision to some degree. Chapter 20 begins with a risk-return trade-off analysis of current asset investments. After developing a borrowing model, the major sources of short-term financing are described.

CHAPTER 18

Short-Term Financial Planning
and Cash Management

Thus far this book has discussed planning for investment decisions and the determination of the appropriate discount factors to apply to the cash flows from investors, including the impact of capital structure and dividend policy. We discussed these within the framework of long-term financial strategy and planning and control systems within a long-term horizon. We now turn to financial strategies for working capital management, beginning with short-term financial planning. Short-term financial planning is important because it involves the liquidity and solvency of the firm — its ability to pay its bills. In a broader sense this means being able to meet its financial obligations to all of its stakeholders including suppliers, employees, sources of funds, its customers, as well as its expanded social obligations. The key objective of short-term financial planning is managing the cash flows of the firm effectively.

Cash management took on increased importance in the 1970s when the high level of interest rates on short-term investments raised the opportunity cost of holding cash balances. Even with lower rates, managing cash will remain important given the active market for takeovers. Financial managers, therefore, have developed and refined techniques of cash collection and disbursement enabling them to optimize the availability of funds and to reduce the interest costs of outside financing. Closely allied with the cash management function is the management of marketable securities, the portfolio of highly liquid, near-cash assets that serves as a back-up to the cash account.

Computerization has increased the sophistication of the techniques employed. In addition to access to large-scale computer systems, many financial managers use desk-top personal computers with the capabilities of continuously accessing information on financial markets as well as on internal developments of the firm. We shall seek to emphasize the concepts that guide the use of modern developments in information management.

CASH BUDGETS

In Chapter 2, entitled ''Financial Statements and Cash Flows,'' we analyzed the statement of cash flows as prescribed by the November 1987 Statement of Financial Accounting Standards No. 95 issued by the Financial Accounting Standards Board (FASB 95). We also reviewed the older approach reflected in the Statement of Sources and Uses of Funds. These statements are typically based on historical data. But they could also be made forward looking as projections, forecasts, or pro forma statements. This forward-looking approach is called the cash budget or cash flow forecast — a highly significant tool in the financial planning and control processes of business firms. The cash budget is a projection or forecast of future cash receipts and cash disbursements over some time interval. It provides the financial executive with an overview of probable patterns of cash flows in the future. Collection and disbursement procedures can then be reviewed to determine whether they are maximizing the firm's net cash flows. The cash budget enables the financial executive to determine whether and when additional financing will be required and provides lead time for taking the actions necessary to provide for future financing. The cash budget also supplies information on whether and when the firm may have positive cash inflows available for a number of alternative uses.

In this chapter we shall first describe the procedures for preparing the cash budget. We shall then use the cash budget framework to analyze how cash collections and cash disbursements can be efficiently managed and controlled to optimize the firm's net cash flows.

Procedures for Preparing a Cash Budget

The cash budget is forward looking. It seeks to estimate future cash receipts and cash disbursements. Forecasting is necessarily involved. As we discussed in Chapter 8 on ''Financial Planning and Control,'' the key to financial forecasts must begin with the sales forecast for the firm. In Chapter 8 we summarized alternative approaches to sales forecasting. Developing sales forecasts for product lines and for the firm as a whole is a critical activity in every firm. It is the basis for other forecasts and budgets affecting not only finance but such factors as procurement, production, and employment policies. Since the sales forecasts are so important, all of the key executives of the firm are likely to be involved. Finance is only one of the users of the sales forecast, but it is especially critical to financial planning and control.

The financial manager, in conjunction with other executives, develops a sales forecast. We now describe how this sales forecast is used in developing a cash budget for the next six months. In Table 18.1, we set forth a schedule of sales and cash collections. The sales forecast is given for January through June of the forthcoming year. It is assumed that the sales level for the months prior to January is at the same $600,000 level and that the

TABLE 18.1   Schedule of Sales and Cash Collections —
Sales Forecast One (Thousands of Dollars)

	Jan.	Feb.	Mar.	Apr.	May	June
1. Sales forecast one	$600	$800	$800	$1,000	$1,000	$ 600
2. Collections — 80% of sales (t − 1)	480	480	640	640	800	800
3. Collections — 20% of sales (t − 2)	120	120	120	160	160	200
4. Total cash receipts	$600	$600	$760	$ 800	$ 960	$1,000

sales for the months following June are also at the same $600,000 level since lead-and-lag relationships require forecasts prior to and following the specific six-month period. The firm sells on a 30-day basis (that is, customers have 30 days to pay). Its experience establishes that, on average, 80 percent of the sales are collected in the month following the sales and 20 percent during the second month following the sales. Row 1 in Table 18.1 presents the sales forecast. Row 2 sets forth collections made during the following month. Since it has been assumed that sales for the months prior to January were also at the $600,000 level, the entry in Row 2 would be 80 percent of $600,000, or $480,000. In Row 3, the collections during the second month after sales would be 20 percent of $600,000, which is $120,000. Total cash receipts for January would, therefore, be $600,000. For February, the total cash receipts would be the same. In March, collections during one month following sales would be 80 percent of $800,000, or $640,000. The collections related to sales two months previously would be 20 percent of $600,000, or $120,000. Total cash receipts for March would, therefore, be $760,000. The total cash receipts for the subsequent months would be calculated following the same logic.

In Table 18.2, we consider the schedule of cash expenses based on the sales forecast in Table 18.1, which we refer to as "Sales Forecast One." Row 1 starts with the sales

TABLE 18.2   Schedule of Cash Expenses — Sales Forecast One (Thousands of Dollars)

	Dec.	Jan.	Feb.	Mar.	Apr.	May	June	July
1. Sales forecast one		$600	$800	$800	$1,000	$1,000	$600	
2. Purchases — 50% of sales (t + 1)	$300	400	400	500	500	300	300	$300
3. Payment — purchases (t − 1)		300	400	400	500	500	300	
4. Wages — 60% of purchases (t − 1)		180	240	240	300	300	180	
5. Other expenses — 30% of purchases (t + 1)		120	150	150	90	90	90	
6. Total cash expenses		$600	$790	$790	$ 890	$ 890	$570	

forecast. Purchases have to be made in anticipation of sales. Experience for this firm indicates that purchases on average represent about 50 percent of sales that are expected to be made in the following month. Hence, purchases would represent 50 percent of the sales forecast for the month following. It is assumed further that purchases are paid for on average in the month after they have been made. Hence, taking the Row 2 figures and shifting them forward one month gives us the cash outflows for payment of purchases shown in Row 3.

It is assumed that wages and other expenses in a given month represent the processing of goods which were purchased in the previous month. It is also assumed that wages and other expenses are paid during the month that they are incurred. Hence Row 4, which represents cash outlays for wages, is 60 percent of purchases made in the previous month. It is assumed that other expenses are incurred and paid in the month preceding the month in which purchases are made. Hence Row 5 would be 30 percent of purchases made in the following month. Total cash expenses in Row 6 represent the sum of payments set forth in Rows 3 through 5.

If these were the only receipts and expenses for the firm, the cash budget or schedule of net cash flows would be as depicted in Table 18.3. Rows 2 and 3 of Table 18.3 simply summarize the results of the previous two tables. The difference between total cash receipts and total cash expenses is the net cash flows shown in Row 4. These are accumulated to give us the cumulative cash flow in Row 5. Under the data assumed, the firm has a zero cash flow position at the end of January. Moreover, the cumulative position is negative for the following months through the end of May. It moves into a positive cumulative cash flow position in June. The pattern of cumulative cash flows provides information to the financial manager on the financing needs that will be required during the months that the cumulative cash flows are in a negative position. For the data presented in Table 18.3, the financial manager will have to finance on a temporary short-term seasonal basis the cumulative negative cash flow position during the months from February through May but will be able to repay this short-term loan during the month of June.

As a part of a sensitivity analysis we consider the effect of continuing sales at the $1 million level in June instead of the sales level of $600,000 previously assumed. It is easy to see that total cash receipts would reflect the "steady state" level of sales at $1 million. Hence, total cash receipts in June would be $1 million as shown in Table 18.4. The projection of total cash expenses is somewhat more complicated and is detailed in

TABLE 18.3   Schedule of Net Cash Flows —
Sales Forecast One (Thousands of Dollars)

	Jan.	Feb.	Mar.	Apr.	May	June
1. Sales	$600	$ 800	$ 800	$1,000	$1,000	$ 600
2. Total cash receipts	600	600	760	800	960	1,000
3. Total cash expenses	600	790	790	890	890	570
4. Net cash flow	$ 0	$(190)	$ (30)	$ (90)	$ 70	$ 430
5. Cumulative cash flow	$ 0	$(190)	$(220)	$ (310)	$ (240)	$ 190

TABLE 18.4 Schedule of Net Cash Flows —
Sales Forecast Two (Thousands of Dollars)

	Jan.	Feb.	Mar.	Apr.	May	June
1. Sales	$600	$ 800	$ 800	$1,000	$1,000	$1,000
2. Total cash receipts	600	600	760	800	960	1,000
3. Total cash expenses	600	790	790	890	950	950
4. Net cash flow	$ 0	$(190)	$ (30)	$ (90)	$ 10	$ 50
5. Cumulative cash flow	$ 0	$(190)	$(220)	$ (310)	$ (300)	$ (250)

Table 18.5. Following the same logic that was employed in Table 18.2, we obtain total cash expenses of $950,000 in Row 6 of Table 18.5. This is used as Row 3 in Table 18.4. We can then calculate the net cash flows in Row 4 of Table 18.4. Accumulating the results in Row 5, we observe that from the month of February on, the firm is in a cumulative negative cash flow position. In planning the financing, the financial manager must, therefore, forecast beyond the six months to determine the period for which financing of the negative cash flows shown in Table 18.4 will have to be planned.

Realistically, the firm will have other cash receipts and other cash disbursements in addition to those directly related to sales and purchases. We shall illustrate additional types of cash disbursements as shown in Table 18.6. We start with the total cash expenses that we had obtained in Table 18.2 based on Sales Forecast One. In Row 2 of Table 18.6, we assume capital outlays for machinery to take place in the months of March and June. In addition, we assume in Row 3 interest payments of $50,000 to be made in June. Income taxes are estimated for the months of January and April. Finally, we provide in Row 5 for quarterly dividend payments in the months of March and June. Total cash disbursements are, therefore, the figures shown in Row 6.

In Table 18.7, we present net cash flows and cash balances, taking the additional types of cash disbursements into account. The new net cash flows are shown in Row 3. They are accumulated in Row 4. Assuming an initial cash balance at the beginning of January (the end of December) of 100, we can, therefore, calculate in Row 6 the end-of-

TABLE 18.5 Schedule of Cash Expenses —
Sales Forecast Two (Thousands of Dollars)

	May	June	July
1. Sales	$1,000	$1,000	$1,000
2. Purchases — 50% of sales $(t + 1)$	500	500	500
3. Payment of purchases $(t - 1)$	500	500	
4. Wages — 60% of purchases $(t - 1)$	300	300	
5. Other expenses — 30% of purchases $(t + 1)$	150	150	
6. Total cash expenses	$ 950	$ 950	

TABLE 18.6   Schedule of Cash Disbursements —
Sales Forecast One (Thousands of Dollars)

	Jan.	Feb.	Mar.	Apr.	May	June
1. Total cash expenses (Table 18.2)	$600	$790	$790	$890	$890	$570
2. Capital expenditures			100			200
3. Interest payments						50
4. Income taxes	40			40		
5. Dividends			10			10
6. Total cash disbursements	$640	$790	$900	$930	$890	$830

month cash balance without financing. Again, under the numbers postulated, the firm is in a cumulative negative cash flow position after January. This provides a forewarning to the financial manager of the financing that will be required during the forthcoming six-month period.

The basic methodology for developing the cash budget has been described. Some additional variations will now be indicated. Clearly for longer-term planning, the firm needs a cash budget beyond a six-month period. Typically, cash budgets will be prepared on a one-year basis for annual budgeting and then for periods up to five or ten years for longer-term financial planning. The end objective is the same — to get a picture of what the firm's cash balance position will be regarding the availability of funds or the financing that will be required.

In addition to requiring longer-term plans, the firm needs to take into account the variability that is likely to be experienced in the cash flows actually realized. We have seen that each segment of the cash budget is based on a sales forecast. Sales are obviously subject to variation. Provision must be made for altering the cash budget based on differ-

TABLE 18.7   Net Cash Flows and Cash Balances — Sales Forecast One (Thousands of Dollars)

	Dec.	Jan.	Feb.	Mar.	Apr.	May	June
1. Total cash receipts (Table 18.1)		$600	$600	$760	$800	$960	$1,000
2. Total cash disbursements (Table 18.6)		640	790	900	930	890	830
3. Net cash flow		(40)	(190)	(140)	(130)	70	170
4. Cumulative net cash flow		(40)	(230)	(370)	(500)	(430)	(260)
5. Initial cash balance (end of Dec.)	$100						
6. End-of-month cash balance without financing	100	60	(130)	(270)	(400)	(330)	(160)

ent possible levels of sales. In addition to variability in sales, other receipts and disbursements are subject to error as well. Collections may not actually follow the exact pattern that has been assumed. Expenses and other disbursements may differ because of the performance in controlling material, labor, and other costs.

Variability can be experienced in all elements of the cash budget. This has given rise to sophisticated computer techniques for analyzing the cash budget (as well as other elements of financial planning). No matter how complex the computerized approaches to cash planning and other aspects of financial planning employed, the underlying logic must follow the principles set forth in the previous discussion. If these are understood, they can readily be applied in any sophisticated type of computerized handling of the mechanics of the financial planning processes.

CASH AND MARKETABLE SECURITIES MANAGEMENT

Several issues are involved in the management of the firm's liquidity position. One is to develop efficient systems for the management of cash inflows and cash outflows. Efficient cash gathering and disbursal has become a major area of managerial finance. So many high-level corporate executives are involved and so many conceptual issues are raised that important institutional developments in cash management have taken place. Because the developments in this field are so rapid and the literature has become so substantial, our treatment of the subject will be streamlined to focus on a more generalized framework for approaching the subject. The treatment of more specific techniques and procedures would rapidly become obsolete.

Why Hold Cash and Marketable Securities?

Cash and marketable securities are discussed together because marketable securities can be quickly converted into cash with only small transactions costs and hence can be regarded as a form of back-up cash. When we refer to cash itself, we are using cash in the broad sense of demand deposits and money market accounts as well as currency holdings (of the "green stuff"). Business firms, like individuals, now hold their "cash" mostly in the form of some kind of an account that earns interest in a financial institution.

Since investments in cash and marketable securities represent assets with less risk than product or project investments, they may be expected to have returns less than the weighted average returns on all of the assets of a firm. We would expect investments in marketable securities to cover their proportionate cost of capital in relation to the liquidity function that they perform for the firm. In general, given the highly competitive and efficient nature of the financial markets, we would not expect that investments in marketable securities would be positive NPV investments. It is the investment in projects that hopefully will earn positive NPVs and thereby increase the value of the firm.

Businesses and individuals have four primary motives for holding cash and cash back-up in the form of marketable securities: (1) the transactions motive, (2) the precautionary motive, (3) to meet future needs, and (4) to satisfy compensating balance requirements.

Transactions Motive. The principal motive for holding cash is to enable the firm to conduct its ordinary business — making purchases and sales. In lines of business where billings are predictable (such as the utilities), cash inflows can be scheduled and synchronized with the need for the cash outflows. We expect the cash-to-revenues ratio and cash-to-total-assets ratio for such firms to be relatively low. In retail trade, by contrast, sales are more random, and a number of transactions may actually be conducted with physical currency. A number of large transactions may occur unexpectedly, creating a surge in cash flows. As a consequence, retail trade requires a higher ratio of cash-to-sales and of cash-to-total assets.

The seasonality of a business may give rise to a need for cash to purchase inventories. For example, raw materials may be available only during a harvest season and may be perishable, as in the food-canning business. Or sales may be seasonal, as they are in department stores (with the peaks around the Christmas and Easter holidays), giving rise to an increase in cash needs during the busy periods.

Precautionary Motive. The precautionary motive for holding safety stocks of cash relates primarily to the predictability of cash inflows and outflows. If the predictability is high, less cash need be held against an emergency or any other contingency. Another factor that strongly influences the precautionary motive is the ability to borrow additional cash on short notice. Borrowing flexibility is primarily a matter of the strength of the firm's relationships with banking institutions and other credit sources. The need for holding cash is satisfied in large part by having near-money assets, such as short-term government securities.

Future Needs. The firm's cash and marketable securities accounts may rise to rather sizable levels on a temporary basis as funds are accumulated to meet specific future needs. For example, at the end of 1977, IBM held $252 million in cash and $5.2 billion in marketable securities. Combined, these items represented 38.9 percent of IBM's year-end total assets of $14.0 billion. Whenever IBM introduces a new computer development, the cash requirements are quite substantial, since the total investment and production costs will be recovered over several years in monthly rental receipts. By the end of 1982, IBM's total assets had risen to over $32 billion, representing 232 percent of its 1977 total assets. But cash plus marketable securities had fallen to $3.3 billion, representing only 10 percent of total assets. The level rose to 11.7 percent of 1990 total assets of $38.9 billion. Cash and marketable securities also represent a "war chest" or pool of funds from which a firm may draw quickly to meet a short-term opportunity, including acquisitions. This is sometimes referred to as the *speculative motive* for holding cash.

Compensating Balance Requirements. The commercial banking system performs many functions for business firms. Business firms pay for these services in part by direct fees and sometimes in part by maintaining compensating balances at the bank. Compensating balances represent the minimum levels that the firm agrees to maintain in its checking account with the bank. With this assurance, the bank can loan such funds on a longer basis, earning a return, which is an indirect fee to the bank. This represents an institutional reason why a firm holds cash.

A firm holds cash and marketable securities primarily for transactions purposes. Additional holdings for precautionary purposes and to meet future needs represent in concept a type of a safety stock. With respect to the precautionary motive, the safety stock holdings relate primarily to the fact that cash inflows and cash outflows cannot be predicted perfectly. Holding cash for future needs represents another type of safety stock motive, so that temporarily less favorable conditions in the money and capital markets will not delay or increase the cost of an otherwise favorable positive NPV investment opportunity.

Thus, decisions with regard to holding cash and marketable securities require careful analysis in order to approach optimal holdings. To hold an inadequate amount of cash and marketable securities may interrupt the normal operations of a business. An inadequate safety stock may cause the embarrassment of having inadequate funds to meet emergencies or to seize favorable opportunities. But, the dangers of having inadequate cash are not solved by holding excess amounts of cash and marketable securities. Excess conservatism has disadvantages, although they may be different from those associated with excess aggressiveness. If the amount of cash and marketable securities held is either inadequate or excessive, this area of financial management is not being handled in an optimal fashion. Thus, a number of important functions are involved in cash and marketable securities management. One is effective design and management of cash inflows and outflows. Second, cash and marketable securities should be held in amounts that are close to an optimal level. Third, cash and marketable securities should be placed in the proper institutions and in the proper forms of securities.

Specific Advantages of Adequate Cash

In addition to these general motives, sound working capital management requires maintenance of an ample amount of cash for several other specific reasons.

1. It is essential that the firm have sufficient cash to take trade discounts. The payment schedule for purchases is referred to as the *term of the sale*. A commonly encountered billing procedure, or *term of trade,* is that of a 2 percent discount on a bill paid within 10 days, with full payment required in 30 days, if the discount is not taken. (This is usually stated as 2/10, net 30.) Since the net amount is due in 30 days, failure to take the discount means paying the extra 2 percent for using the money an additional 20 days. The following equation can be used for calculating the cost, on an annual basis, of not taking discounts:

    $$\text{Cost} = \frac{\text{Discount \%}}{(100 - \text{Discount \%})} \times \frac{365}{(\text{Final due date} - \text{Discount period})}.$$

    The denominator in the first term (100 − Discount percent) equals the funds made available by not taking the discount. To illustrate, the cost of not taking a discount and paying on the 30th day when the terms are 2/10, net 30 is computed:

    $$\text{Cost} = \frac{2}{98} \times \frac{365}{20} = 0.0204 \times 18.25 = 37.23\% = \text{Calculated cost}.$$

We then determine the APR or effective interest rate:

$$\text{APR} = r_e = \left(1 + \frac{.3723}{18.25}\right)^{18.25} - 1 = 44.56\%.$$

This represents an annual effective interest rate of about 45 percent. Most firms' cost of capital is substantially lower than 45 percent, so they should borrow funds, if necessary, to take the discount when the implicit interest rates in foregoing cash discounts are this high.

2. Since the current and acid test ratios are key items in credit analysis, it is essential that the firm, in order to maintain its credit standing, meet the standards of the line of business in which it is engaged. A strong credit standing enables the firm to purchase goods from trade suppliers on favorable terms and to maintain its line of credit with banks and other sources of credit.

3. Ample cash is useful for taking advantage of favorable business opportunities that may come along from time to time, such as special cash offers by suppliers or for acquisitions.

4. The firm should have sufficient liquidity to meet emergencies, such as strikes, fires, or marketing campaigns of competitors.

Financial managers may be able to improve the inflow-outflow pattern of cash. They can do so by better synchronization of flows and by reduction of float, explained in the following sections.

Sources of Float

Whenever a customer mails a check, some amount of time passes before the check is received by the seller. This is called *mail-time float*. After the firm receives the check, processing time is involved in crediting the customer's account and in getting the check into the banking system. This kind of time lag is called *processing float*. A third type of lag, related to the clearing time within the banking system, is called *transit float*. The seller's bank may use the Federal Reserve System or a local clearinghouse for clearing its checks. The banks and clearinghouse mechanisms involved may have an availability schedule for checks involving specified distances, and so forth. The time required by the system to communicate the information needed to clear the checks may be longer or shorter than the availability schedule. Thus, *availability time* may differ from *clear time*.

Considerable progress has been made by business firms and the banking system in an attempt to manage the clearing process efficiently. The development of an efficient cash mobilization system requires decisions with respect to (1) collection points, (2) bank-gathering systems, and (3) alternative methods of transferring funds.

If a firm makes sales to distant cities, mail float alone can be as much as three or four days. This can be reduced by setting up collection points and banking relationships in the areas where sales are made. Since the firm is likely to have field sales offices in the major regions in which it sells, it can provide for direct collection by these units. As payments are received by the field office, they are recorded and deposited in a local bank (a field depository bank). Since the local offices are close to the customer, mail-time float is reduced.

A *lockbox system* can significantly reduce all types of float.[1] A firm will set up a lockbox arrangement in a city (or cities) corresponding to the geographic distribution of its customers. Customers are directed to mail payments to the lockbox (a post office box) administered by a local bank which collects checks from the box, sometimes several times a day, and deposits the checks to the firm's account. The bank begins the clearing process and notifies the firm that a check has been received, reducing processing float. The bank charges the receiving firm for the services rendered. To determine whether a lockbox system is advantageous, the firm will compare the bank fees (including compensating balances) against the gains from reducing float. A rule of thumb in estimating potential lockbox savings is that for every $1 million in annual sales, accelerating the collection time by one-quarter of a day results in $1,000 in savings. Thus, the savings can be of significant magnitude.[2]

Cash-Gathering System

Several categories of banks are used when a firm gathers cash. The general relationships are illustrated in Figure 18.1 for local depository banks, regional concentration banks, and a central bank. *Local depository banks* are those into which field collections are channeled. They are not necessarily limited to cities in which the firm has sales offices. A *regional concentration bank* is one to which a firm seeks to channel funds to have them available for disbursements. Firms usually maintain a major disbursing account at such a bank. As illustrated in Figure 18.1, the regional concentration banks are part of the *concentration banking system* of the firm. Figure 18.1 also indicates that the regional concentration banks usually also handle a lockbox arrangement. Since a lockbox system uses data processing, check handling, and other banking services with substantial fixed costs and other expenses, there will be fewer regional concentration banks than local depository banks.

The concentration banking system developed by the firm seeks to mobilize its funds as efficiently as possible. In addition to a cash-gathering system, the firm needs to work out some policies and decision rules for the rapid transfer of funds. These rules are considered next.

Transfer Mechanisms

A *transfer mechanism* is a system for moving funds between accounts at different banks. The three main transfer mechanisms are:

1. Depository transfer checks (DTCs)

2. Electronic depository transfer checks (EDTCs)

3. Wire transfers.

---

[1]The analytics of designing a lockbox system have become quite sophisticated. See, for example, the August 1981 issue of *Management Science,* which carries three articles on the subject by Nauss and Markland, by Stone, and by Fielitz and Fennell; see also Gallinger and Healey [1987], pp. 201–203.

[2]See Ferguson [1983].

FIGURE 18.1   Cash-Gathering System of a National Company

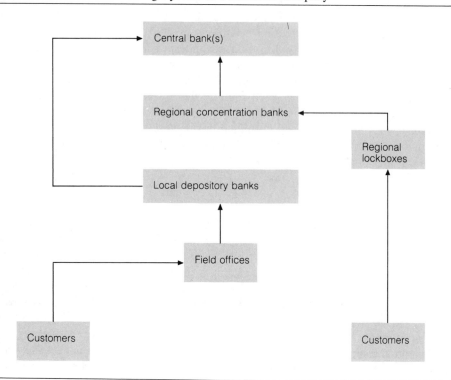

A *depository transfer check (DTC)* is a check restricted for deposit at a particular bank. Except for the deposit-only restriction, a DTC is an ordinary check. DTCs provide a means for moving funds from local depository banks into concentration banks. A DTC is payable only to the bank of deposit for credit to the firm's specific account. In a mail-based initiation procedure, the local office or a company's field unit prepares the DTC and mails it with the deposit slip to a regional concentration bank, which is often a "lockbox bank." (This bank will subsequently transfer the funds to the central bank along with other checks received at the lockbox.) The concentration bank credits the funds to the firm's account, placing the check into the clearing process. While this process is automatic in that no action is required by the firm's cash managers, funds availability is limited by postal and clearing times. DTCs may also be initiated by central company management in response to deposit reports from local offices and/or lockbox banks, or on a pre-arranged schedule.

An *electronic DTC (EDTC)* is a paperless electronic image transfer via the Automated Clearinghouse (ACH) network developed by the Federal Reserve System. The EDTC avoids the use of the mails and has a uniform one-business-day clearing time. EDTCs are generally initiated by central company management.

Wire transfer of funds between banks makes funds collected at one bank immediately available for use at another bank, even in a different city. It is the fastest way to move cash between banks, eliminating transit float. The bank wire method is a private wire service used and supported by about 300 banks in the United States. They use the bank wire system for transferring funds, exchanging credit information, and making securities transactions. The Federal Reserve wire system can be used by commercial banks that are members of the Federal Reserve System. However, commercial banks not on the bank wire or not members of the Federal Reserve System can obtain access to the wire transfer system through their correspondent banks.

Wire transfers are typically initiated on a standing order basis. Company headquarters will make a written authorization to a local depository bank to transfer funds to the firm's concentration bank when the amount exceeds some target level, such as $80,000. The use of standing instructions to transfer funds can be an effective way of managing complex cash-gathering systems, avoiding the need for daily communication with distant locations.

An efficient cash management system must consider the timing and amount of cash transfers which will minimize costs while conforming to bank balance requirements and company policy. The majority of companies (80 percent of the largest 1,200 industrial firms) simply make daily transfers of each day's reported deposits, leaving a minimum required balance in the account.[3] Other firms use simple rules of thumb, for example, the anticipation of deposits, so that the firm reduces float by initiating the transfer before being notified that deposits have been made; firms also take advantage of weekend timing and another form of float termed "dual balance." *Dual balance* refers to the balances resulting when the DTC clearing time is longer than the availability time specified. Dual balances involve only DTCs, since both wires and EDTCs have the same clear time and availability time. For example, availability time at the concentration bank may be one business day, while the actual DTC clearing time back to the depository bank upon which the DTC is written is *two* business days. Thus, a $15,000 DTC deposited in the concentration bank on Tuesday would result in a $15,000 available balance addition at the concentration bank on Wednesday, but with $15,000 still not charged at the depository bank until Thursday. Thus, the same $15,000 is an available balance in both the concentration bank and the depository bank on Wednesday — hence the term *dual balance*.

Comparing the Costs of Alternative Transfer Mechanisms

The use of a wire transfer is the quickest transfer mechanism but the most expensive. There is no delay on a wire transfer, but the typical cost range is $18 to $25. A mail depository transfer check (DTC) may cost only $2 to $5 but may involve delays from two to seven days. An evaluation of the alternatives has conventionally involved a comparison of the value of the extra interest from the faster transfer related to the extra cost involved. The conventional cost comparisons are giving way to more sophisticated programming techniques.[4] The conventional formula for the breakeven transfer size is as follows:

$$S* = \Delta COST/r\Delta T, \tag{18.1}$$

[3]See Stone and Hill [1980a].

[4]This discussion is based on Stone and Hill [1980b].

where

S^* = the breakeven size of transfer above which the faster, higher cost mechanism is preferred

ΔCOST = the incremental cost of the faster mechanism

r = the applicable daily interest rate

ΔT = the difference in transfer time in days.

If the cost difference between a wire and a DTC is $15, with a time difference of two days and an interest value of funds at the concentration bank of 0.03 percent per day, the breakeven transfer size would be

$$S^* = \frac{\$15.00}{.0003(2)} = \$25,000. \tag{18.2}$$

Thus, on amounts above $25,000, a wire transfer would be used. If the time saved is only one day, the breakeven size is $50,000.

Stone and Hill criticize the above conventional procedure on a number of grounds.[5] They argue that the conventional breakeven analysis assumes no value for funds in the depository bank. They observe that compensating balances are recognized by banks in assigning "service credits" to the firm in the bank's analysis of the profitability of the account and the need to make service charges to the company. Hence, it is argued that the opportunity cost of not having funds in the concentration bank is not the full interest rate but rather the *difference* between the interest rate and the earnings credit rate at the depository bank.

A number of other considerations must be taken into account in evaluating the cost/benefit trade-offs of alternative transfer systems. The benefit of one system over another may be small relative to the cost of disrupting existing relationships. These different trade-offs, plus the service credits earned by leaving some funds in the gathering system as compensating balances, result in the use of a variety of transfer mechanisms under different circumstances. Systematic decision models are under development, but the judgment of the financial manager still plays a key role.

MANAGING DISBURSEMENTS

Just as expediting the collection process conserves cash, slowing disbursements accomplishes the same thing by keeping cash on hand for longer periods. An obvious way to do this is simply to delay payments, but this involves equally obvious difficulties. Firms have, in the past, devised rather ingenious methods for "legitimately" lengthening the collection period on their own checks, ranging from maintaining disbursement accounts in remote banks to using slow, awkward payment procedures. Since such practices are usually recognized for what they are, their use should be avoided.

---

[5]Stone and Hill [1980b], pp. 46–57.

One procedure for delaying disbursements is the use of drafts. While a check is written by the payer and, once written, payable on demand, a draft is, in theory, drawn by the recipient. It is submitted to the payer who must approve it and deposit funds to cover it. Only then can it be collected.

AT&T has used drafts in the following way: In handling its payrolls, for instance, AT&T can pay an employee by draft on Friday. The employee cashes the draft at his local bank, which sends it on to AT&T's New York bank. It may be Wednesday or Thursday before the draft arrives. The bank then sends it to the company's accounting department, which has until 3 P.M. that day to inspect and approve it. Not until then does AT&T deposit funds in its bank to pay the draft.[6] Insurance companies also use drafts to pay claims.

Using Float

Checks written by firms (or individuals) are not deducted from bank records until they are actually received by the bank, possibly a matter of several days. The lag between the time the check is written and the time the bank receives it is also known as *float*.

Some firms are able to exploit float to create what is effectively an interest-free loan. For example, a firm with only a moderate balance in its business checking account (which does not pay interest) and $100,000 in its savings account may write a check for $100,000, knowing that it will not clear for six or seven days. After six days, it can move the $100,000 from the savings account to the checking account so the check will be covered. In the meantime, six days of interest will have been earned on the savings account. This is the gain from float.

In reality, the problem is more complex. The check-writing firm in the illustration also receives checks, which it deposits in its savings account. Historically, banks have considered these deposits to be available to the company when they are deposited. If the firm is slow to deposit such checks, float is reduced.

Suppose a firm writes checks totaling about $5,000 each day. It takes about six or seven days for these checks to clear and to be deducted from the firm's bank account. Thus, the firm's own checking records show a balance $30,000 less than that shown by the bank's records. If the firm receives checks in the amount of $5,000 daily and loses only four days while these checks are being deposited, its own books show a balance that is $20,000 larger than the bank's balance. Thus, the firm's float — the difference between the $30,000 and the $20,000 — is $10,000.

Bank Charge Analysis

In the past, banks have compensated for funds lost through float by raising prices of other services, which are paid for by all customers. They have, for example, offset float costs by higher interest rates on loans or higher service charges. Thus, other customers of the bank bore part of the cost if a firm used float successfully. Clearly, this was not desirable

---

[6]"More Firms Substitute Drafts for Checks to Pay, Collect Bills," *The Wall Street Journal*, August 29, 1971.

for either the bank or the other customers, and efforts to reduce the gains from using float have intensified in recent years.

One method banks would like to employ to reduce these gains is the electronic funds transfer system. EFTS, as it is called, would create a nationwide computer network that would substantially reduce float time. It presently takes several days to clear checks across the country. Under EFTS, the time could be reduced to hours or even minutes. As yet, no nationwide system exists, but developments in that direction are moving rapidly.

In addition to reducing the actual time it takes to clear a check, banks are attempting to more accurately match costs and revenues on individual accounts. One effect of this matching is a further reduction in the gains from using float. Table 18.8 depicts a typical commercial checking account service charge analysis. In the earnings credit section, the customer is credited for the average collected balance at the interest rate of 5 percent. The collected balance is the daily balance adjusted for the typical time it takes for the bank to collect on checks deposited. Thus, the estimated days of float will be low for a business dealing mostly with local customers and high for a business that receives payments from out-of-state customers. In this way, the individual firm bears the cost of float directly. The expense part of the analysis is straightforward. In reality, there are many more expense classifications than the few itemized here — among them lockbox charges, computer service billings, and required compensating balances. In Table 18.8, the service charge to the firm is $10.98 after allowing for the earnings credit.

Cost of Cash Management

We have described a number of procedures that can be used to hold down cash balance requirements.[7] Implementing these procedures, however, is not a costless operation. How far should a firm go in making its cash operations more efficient? As a general rule, a firm should incur these expenses so long as its marginal returns exceed its marginal expenses.

For example, suppose that by establishing a lockbox system and increasing the accuracy of cash inflow and outflow forecasts, a firm can reduce its investment in cash by $1.2 million. Further suppose that the firm borrows at an effective rate of 10 percent.[8] The steps taken release $1.2 million, and the cost of capital required to carry this $1.2 million investment in cash is $120,000. If the costs of the procedures necessary to release the $1.2 million are less than $120,000, the move is a good one; if the costs exceed $120,000, the greater efficiency is not worth the cost. It is clear that larger firms, with larger cash balances, can better afford to hire the personnel necessary to maintain tight control over their cash positions. Cash management is one element of business operations in which economies of scale are clearly present. In sum, the value of careful cash management depends on the cost of funds invested in cash, which, in turn, depends on the current rate of interest. With high interest rates during the 1970s, firms began devoting more care than

---

[7]We are abstracting from the security aspects of cash management — the prevention of fraud and embezzlement. These topics are better covered in accounting than in finance courses.

[8]The borrowing rate, 10 percent, is used rather than the firm's average cost of capital, because cash is a less risky investment than the firm's average assets. Notice also that before-tax figures are used here; the analysis can employ either before-tax or after-tax figures so long as consistency is maintained.

TABLE 18.8   State National Bank Commercial Service Charge Analysis
Mail Order Supply Company, September 19X0

Earnings Credit		
1. Days in month	31	
2. Less average days float	6	
3. Basis for earnings credit	25	
4. Average daily balance	$21,300.00	
5. Daily rate factor (@ 5%)	0.000139	
6. Earnings credit ($3 \times 4 \times 5$)		$74.02
Service Debits		
7. 20 deposits (@ $.25 each)	$ 5.00	
8. 3,200 checks deposited (@ $.02 each)	64.00	
9. 200 checks written (@ $.08 each)	16.00	
10. Total service debits (7 + 8 + 9)		85.00
Service charge (10 − 6)		$10.98

ever to cash management. This increased emphasis has continued during periods of lower interest rates as well.

Electronic Payments

FEDWIRE is the wire transfer system operated by the Federal Reserve System. It has been available to transfer money for the same-day settlement for many years, but high costs restrict its use to large dollar amounts. Sartoris and Hill [1989] note that in 1986 wire transactions were only 0.11 percent of the number of transactions but 78.5 percent of the dollar amount. The Automated Clearing House (ACH) system described above is used for electronic transfers for next-day settlement for small transactions.

Sartoris and Hill [1989] also describe the General Motors electronic payment system, which seeks to convert all suppliers to electronic payments, thereby eliminating paper checks that involved an average 3.6 days of disbursement float. Under the electronic payment system, GM moved the payment date back three days, thereby retaining three days of float while passing 0.6 days on to suppliers. This is an illustration of a shift in emphasis in the management of cash flow systems. Efficiency is more important than gimmicks such as float. Information availability and cost savings are balanced against float gains and costs.

ELECTRONIC DATA INTERCHANGE

The increased use of computer-related systems is moving the economy toward electronic data interchange (EDI), which is the movement of business information electronically both within and between firms in computer-processable format [Sartoris and Hill, 1989].

EDI is distinguished from facsimile transmission (FAX) or electronic mail. FAX messages do not permit entering the image directly into a business application. Electronic mail moves data electronically but its free format makes it difficult to accept the input directly without manual editing. Sartoris and Hill [1989] note that the infrastructure for EDI has been developing rapidly. Four main elements are involved: (1) formatting standards, (2) the requisite software, (3) communication networks, and (4) related low-cost computer hardware. The key requirement for EDI is the development of widely accepted data format and communications standards. Various trade associations have developed committees for the further development of the requisite national standards. They note that the impact of wide EDI implementation would be substantial. Efforts in "float management" will increasingly shift to coordinating the activities involved in short-term financial management. It will be possible to forecast the timing of cash flows with greater accuracy. Traditional practices in areas such as credit terms based on paper/mail/manual processing are likely to be subject to change.

MARKETABLE SECURITIES

Firms sometimes report sizable amounts of short-term marketable securities such as Treasury bills or bank certificates of deposit among their current assets. Why are marketable securities held? The two primary reasons — the need for a substitute for cash and the need for a temporary investment — are considered in this section.

Substitute for Cash

Some firms hold portfolios of marketable securities in lieu of large cash balances, liquidating part of the portfolio to increase the cash account when cash outflows exceed inflows. Data are not available to indicate the extent of this practice, but our impression is that it is not common. Most firms prefer to let their banks maintain such liquid reserves, and they borrow to meet temporary cash shortages.

Temporary Investment

In addition to using marketable securities as a buffer against cash shortages, firms also hold them on a strictly temporary basis. Firms engaged in seasonal operations, for example, frequently have surplus cash flows during a part of the year and deficit cash flows the rest of the time. Such firms may purchase marketable securities during their surplus periods and then liquidate them when cash deficits occur. Other firms, particularly those in capital goods industries, where fluctuations are violent, attempt to accumulate cash or near-cash securities during a downturn in volume in order to be ready to finance an upturn.

Firms also accumulate liquid assets to meet predictable financial requirements. For example, if a major modernization program is planned for the near future, or if a bond issue is about to mature, the marketable securities portfolio may be increased to provide the required funds. Marketable securities holdings are also frequently increased immediately before quarterly corporate tax payments are due.

Some firms accumulate resources as a protection against a number of contingencies. When they make uninsurable product warranties, for example, companies must be ready to meet any claims that may arise. Firms in highly competitive industries must have resources to carry them through substantial shifts in the market structure. And firms in an industry in which new markets are emerging — for example, foreign markets — need to have resources to meet developments. These funds may be on hand for fairly long periods.

Criteria for Selecting Securities

The applicable criteria for selection among the wide range of securities available include (1) financial risk, (2) interest rate risk, (3) purchasing power risk, (4) liquidity or marketability, (5) taxability, and (6) relative yields. Each will be considered in turn.

Financial Risk. The greater the degree to which the price and returns of a security fluctuate, the greater is the financial risk. Many factors may influence the size and frequency of a security's price changes, but the greater the fluctuations, the greater is the risk that a loss may be incurred. In the extreme, the most serious unfavorable event is that the issuer cannot meet interest payments or principal payments — the risk of default. U.S. government securities do not carry the risk of default and, therefore, are considered "safer" than other securities. Bonds issued by state and local governments, as well as corporate securities, are considered to be subject to some degree of default risk. Rating agencies such as Moody's Investors Service and the Standard & Poor's Corporation assign quality ratings to securities. Among the factors influencing a security's rating is the degree of likelihood that default may occur. These quality assessments can and do change with time. For many years, the securities of utility companies were regarded as of the highest quality with minimum risk of default. In recent years, however, some utility securities have been downgraded to lower quality ratings.

Interest Rate Risk. Changes in the general level of interest rates will cause the prices of securities to fluctuate. This is especially true of such securities as notes or bonds, which carry a fixed rate of interest. In general, the shorter the maturity of a debt instrument, the smaller is the size of fluctuations in its price. A partial exception to this generalization should be noted. For bonds selling at 20 to 30 percent below maturity value with maturities of less than 30 years, the degree of fluctuation in their prices reaches a maximum around a maturity of about 15 to 18 years and then declines with longer maturities.[9]

In general, long-term bonds are riskier than short-term securities for a firm's marketable securities portfolio. However, partly because of this risk differential, higher yields are more frequently available on long-term than on short-term securities.

Given the motives most firms have for holding marketable securities portfolios, it is generally not feasible for them to be exposed to a high degree of risk from interest rate fluctuations. Accordingly, firms usually confine their portfolios to securities with short

---

[9]For the mathematics and reasons for this result, see Hsia and Weston [1981].

maturities. Only if the securities are expected to be held for a long period and not be subject to forced liquidation on short notice will long-term securities be chosen. Additional protection from interest rate fluctuations is provided by the use of the interest rate futures markets described in Chapter 14.

Purchasing Power Risk. Changes in general price levels will affect the purchasing power of both the principal and the income from investments in securities. The total return from a security is measured by the capital gain or loss plus the income yield. Varied relationships have developed for different types of assets during the prolonged inflation since the late 1960s in the United States. Bonds with fixed dollar amounts of income and a fixed dollar amount at maturity have declined in value as inflation caused interest rate levels to rise. But common stocks whose dividends theoretically are not fixed in amount have also declined in value because the underlying earning power of corporations appears to have been impaired during persistent inflation. Commodities such as gold and diamonds have value even though they pay no interest or other forms of income. Real estate is a hybrid case in that rentals have not risen as fast as the general price level, but the values of homes and commercial properties have outpaced the rise in the general price level. The 1980s combined moderate inflation with strong securities markets.

Liquidity or Marketability Risk. The potential decline from a security's quoted market price when the security is sold is its liquidity or marketability risk. Liquidity risk is related to the breadth or thinness of the market for a security. U.S. Treasury bonds or AT&T securities will be more widely held and have greater liquidity than the securities of the Podunk Printing Company.

Taxability. The tax position of a firm's marketable securities portfolio is influenced by the overall tax position of a firm. A firm with prior years' losses to carry forward can postpone taxability. A firm that pays the full 34 percent marginal corporate tax rate must take taxability into account. The market yields on a security will reflect the total demand and supply of tax influences. Yet, the position of the individual firm may be different from the overall pattern. To the extent that a firm may have a need for tax protection different from the overall pattern of the market, it might find that taxability considerations are either favorable or unfavorable. A number of kinds of securities, such as the bonds of state and local governments, have varying degrees of tax exemption. In addition, securities that sell at a discount offer opportunities for taking returns in the form of capital gains rather than ordinary income.

Returns on Securities. The higher the risk, the higher is the required return. Thus, in building a marketable securities portfolio, corporate treasurers must evaluate the risk-return trade-offs. Since the motive for holding marketable securities is protection against uncertain and fluctuating inflows and outflows, the dominant policy is to choose relatively less risky alternatives at the sacrifice of some return. Accordingly, corporate treasurers will emphasize relatively short-term, highly liquid assets in constructing the marketable securities portfolio.

Investment Alternatives

The main kinds of investments meeting the objectives just set forth are listed in Table 18.9. These represent the highly liquid, short-term securities issued by the U.S. government and by the very strongest domestic and foreign banks and other business corporations.

The financial manager decides on a suitable maturity pattern for the holdings on the basis of how long the funds are to be held. The numerous alternatives can be selected and balanced in such a way that maturities and risks appropriate to the financial situation of the firm are obtained. Commercial bankers, investment bankers, and brokers provide the financial manager with detailed information on each of the forms of investment listed. The yields on these marketable securities change with shifts in financial market conditions. The financial manager should keep up to date on these characteristics and follow the principle of making investment selections that offer maturities, yields, and risks appropriate to the firm.

In several previous chapters we have discussed financial engineering as innovative ways of dealing with the risks of financial instruments. Financial engineering has greatly

TABLE 18.9   Alternative Marketable Securities for Investment

Treasury bills (T-bills)	Obligations of the U.S. government. Exempt from state and local income taxes.
U.S. Treasury notes and bonds	Original maturities of more than one year, but maturing issues have high liquidity. Also exempt from state and local income taxes.
Federal agency issues	Notes issued by corporations and agencies created by the U.S. government.
Short-term tax exempts	Notes issued by states, municipalities, local housing agencies, and urban renewal agencies. Exempt from state and local taxes and from the federal income tax.
Commercial paper	Unsecured notes issued by finance companies, bank holding companies, and industrial firms.
Bonds of domestic and foreign corporations (highest grade)	Original maturities of more than one year, but issues near maturity behave similarly to short-term instruments.
Negotiable certificates of deposit (CDs)	Receipts for time deposits at commercial banks that can be sold before maturity.
Bankers' acceptances	Time drafts (or orders to pay) issued by a business firm (usually an importer) that have been accepted by a bank that guarantees payment.
Eurodollars	Dollar-denominated time deposits at overseas banks.
Repurchase agreements (repos)	Sale of government securities by a bank or securities dealer with a simultaneous agreement to repurchase.
Money market mutual funds	Investment companies whose portfolios are limited to short-term money market instruments.
Money market preferred stock	Duration is relatively short with dividends paid at maturity. Seventy percent of dividend income can be excluded from income for tax purposes by corporations.

Note: The marketable securities listed on this table are illustrative of a much larger range of available alternatives. For a more complete listing, see the financial sections of most major newspapers and the publications of investment banking firms.

expanded the number of alternative marketable securities in which business firms may invest. Some of the new instruments obtain wide acceptance. Others are not widely adopted and evolve into different kinds of instruments. For example, adjustable rate preferred stock did not receive wide acceptance and led to the development of auction-rate preferred stock. The advantage of the adjustable rate preferred stock was the 70 percent tax exclusion on its dividends to corporations. The floating rate dividends set at the time of issue often fail to provide adequate compensation for the credit risks associated with the issuers. Many issues traded below par and led to the wider use of auction-rate preferred stock. The dividend rate for auction-rate preferred stock is set by a *Dutch auction*. Each bidder submits to the seller in charge of the auction the number of shares desired and a specified dividend level. The lowest rate that enables the available shares to be completely sold will be the dividend for the 49 days until the new auction, which resets the dividend. The 49-day period means that the auctions will always take place on the same day of the week for the life of individual issues. To be eligible for the 70 (or 80) percent dividend exclusion a corporation must hold the dividend paying stock for at least 45 days according to IRS rules. The risk of auction-rate preferred stock is that the credit quality of the issuer may change between reset periods. One method of dealing with this risk is through diversification of issuers. This has been supplemented by individual large brokers who have been willing to guarantee to retain auction-rate preferred at par between reset periods.

Because financial engineering has created a wide range of instruments with numerous variations in provisions, the financial manager must continue to maintain contact with developments in the money markets and markets for longer-term financial instruments. Even longer-term financial instruments can be used as marketable securities either because of their relative stable, built-in protection or because their remaining time to maturity is relatively short.

The Price of Securities Quoted on a Discount Basis

Some securities are quoted on a discount basis. The relation between the discount and price can be illustrated using U.S. Treasury bills with maturities of less than one year. The computation is based on the actual number of days to maturity, using 360 days per year.[10] The following expressions are used to compute the discount basis and dollar price:

$$D = \frac{M}{360}B,$$

$$P = \$100 - D,$$

where

$$D = \text{full discount}$$

$$M = \text{days to maturity}$$

---

[10]The number of days in the year used in interest rate calculations varies in different applications. The number 360 had been widely used for many years. For some uses, 365 has begun to be assumed. But the established practice for calculations related to Treasury bills is still 360 days.

$$B = \text{discount basis in percent}$$
$$P = \text{dollar price.}$$

For example, calculate the dollar price for a Treasury bill due in 275 days on an 8 percent discount basis.

$$D = \frac{275}{360} \times 8\%$$
$$= 6.111\%$$
$$P = \$100 - D$$
$$= \$100 - \$6.111$$
$$= \$93.889 \text{ (the dollar price on an 8\% discount basis)}$$

Note that the price is greater than simply deducting the 8 percent discount factor from $100. Income from Treasury bills is subject to all federal taxes. The difference between the purchase price and the sale price or maturity value is treated as ordinary income, not a capital gain or loss.

Effects of Inflation

Inflation devalues money, making the careful investment of cash essential to the health of the firm. An improved cash management system keeps track of idle cash; but once this cash has been found, it can act as a hedge against inflation only if it is invested appropriately. During periods of tight money, neither small nor large firms can be confident of receiving bank loans to meet cash shortages. Therefore, it is imperative for them to keep cash reserves for future contingencies.

To protect these cash reserves against inflation, companies have begun to invest the funds aggressively, seeking higher yields. Idle cash is no longer merely kept in the bank or invested exclusively in Treasury bills. Certificates of deposit, municipal securities, and commercial paper offer higher rates of return and, therefore, are gaining in popularity. Firms are even using foreign instruments. For example, NCR invests in commercial paper, the Euromarket, and both domestic and Japanese certificates of deposit to increase pretax earnings by about $1 million per year. Litton Industries invests part of its portfolio in Swiss franc- and German mark-denominated time deposits and in foreign certificates of deposit. AT&T trades Treasury bills, looking for the best yield, rather than holding them to maturity. Its other investments include commercial paper, bankers' acceptances, certificates of deposit, and overnight repurchase agreements. *Repurchase agreements,* or repos, have a very short maturity of one or a few days.[11] Therefore, they are especially appropriate for investing money for short periods of time while avoiding most types of risks.

---

[11]The repurchase time and price are specified in advance. Thus, the return to the seller and the yield to the buyer are "locked in" with no interest rate fluctuation risk.

CASH MANAGEMENT MODELS

Investment in cash and marketable securities is analogous to investment in inventory. (All asset investments represent an inventory decision to some degree.) First, a basic stock must be on hand to balance inflows and outflows of the items, the size of the stock depending on the patterns of flows, whether regular or irregular. Second, because the unexpected may always occur, it is necessary to have safety stocks on hand, representing the little extra to avoid the costs of not having enough to meet current needs. Third, additional amounts may be required to meet future growth needs; these are called *anticipation stocks*. Related to anticipation stocks is the recognition that there are optimum purchase sizes, defined as *economic ordering quantities*.

Both rising and falling costs are associated with maintaining various levels of stocks or balances (cash, inventories, or any other asset); that is, there are costs associated with levels that are both too high and too low, and thus some optimal level exists at which these costs are balanced. In cash management, the basic stock is the minimum cash balance, which may be determined, in part, by bank compensating balance requirements. This cash stock must be sufficient to cover at least the transactions needs of the firm. Inflows come principally from receipts, borrowing, and sales of securities; outflows are represented by cash disbursements. The marketable securities portfolio acts as a reserve, or safety stock, against anticipated (or unanticipated) future needs and opportunities.

The primary cost associated with too high a level of cash is the opportunity cost of having funds tied up in a nonpositive NPV asset. The costs of too low a level of cash include the costs of running short (including the inability to take cash discounts) and the more quantifiable transactions costs associated with borrowing funds or converting marketable securities to cash. Since the opportunity costs rise with holding more cash, and the transactions costs rise with less cash (and thus more frequent transfers from marketable securities to cash), there is some optimal level of cash and size of transfer which minimizes the total cost of cash management.

Several types of mathematical models have been developed to help determine optimal cash balances. An early model developed by William Baumol [1952] essentially applies a basic inventory model to cash management. In this model, it is assumed that the firm on average is growing and is a net user of cash. Marketable securities represent a buffer stock between episodes of external financing, which is drawn down as required periodically. Ordering costs are represented by the clerical and transactions costs of making transfers between the investment portfolio and the cash account. The holding cost is the interest foregone on cash balances held. Assuming that expenditures occur evenly over time and that cash replenishments come in lump sums at periodic intervals, the optimal size of the cash transfer is formulated as follows:

$$C^* = \sqrt{\frac{2bT}{i}},$$

where

C^* = the optimal size of the cash transfer

T = the total cash usage for the period of time involved

b = the cost of the transaction in the purchase or sale of marketable securities

i = the applicable interest rate on marketable securities.

The formula can be illustrated in a specific numerical example. The total demand for cash (T) over the period of time involved (one year) is $1.8 million. The cost per transaction is $25. The applicable interest rate is 10 percent.

Using the data in the formula, we obtain

$$C^* = \sqrt{\frac{2bT}{i}} = \sqrt{\frac{2(\$25)(\$1,800,000)}{.10}} = \$30,000.$$

Having calculated C^*, the optimal amount of cash transfer, the average cash balance for the period will be

$$\frac{C^*}{2} = \frac{\$30,000}{2} = \$15,000.$$

The total number of transactions or transfers required per year can also be readily determined:

$$\frac{\$1,800,000}{\$30,000} = 60, \text{ or somewhat more than one transaction per week.}$$

Finally, the total cost per year of maintaining cash balances can be calculated:

$$TC = b\left(\frac{T}{C}\right) + i\left(\frac{C}{2}\right)$$
$$= \$25(60) + .10(\$15,000) = \$1,500 + \$1,500$$
$$= \$3,000.$$

On the basis of the data of the example, the total cost is $3,000 per year. Under the assumptions of the analysis, this minimizes the costs of managing the inventory of cash.

MILLER-ORR MODEL

Miller and Orr [1966] expanded the Baumol model by incorporating a stochastic generating process for periodic changes in cash balances so that the cash pattern resembles that shown in Figure 18.2. In contrast to the completely deterministic assumptions of the Baumol model, Miller and Orr assume that net cash flows behave as if they were generated by a "stationary random walk." This means that changes in the cash balance over a given period are random in both size and direction and that they form a normal distribution as the number of periods observed increases. The model allows for *a priori* knowledge, however, that changes at a certain time have a greater probability of being either positive or negative.[12]

---

[12]See Miller and Orr [1966], pp. 418, 419, 422.

FIGURE 18.2   Miller-Orr Cash Management Model

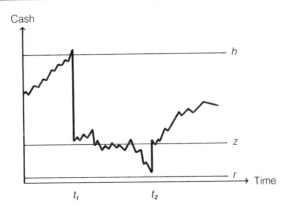

The Miller-Orr model is designed to determine the time and size of transfers between an investment account and the cash account according to a decision process illustrated in Figure 18.2. Changes in cash balances are allowed to go up until they reach some level h at time t_1; they are then reduced to level z, the *return point*, by investing $(h - z)$ dollars in the investment portfolio. Next, the cash balance wanders aimlessly until it reaches the minimum balance point, r, at t_2. At this time, enough earning assets are sold to return the cash balance to its return point, z. Miller and Orr define t so that $1/t$ is "some small fraction of a working day such as $\frac{1}{8}$," or, equivalently, "the number of operating cash transactions per day." We suppose that during any such hour, the cash balance will either increase by m dollars with probability p or decrease by m dollars with probability $q = 1 - p$. Most of their analysis is based on the "special symmetric or zero-drift case in which $p = q = \frac{1}{2}$." For this special case, the variance of daily changes in the cash balance is equal to $m^2 t$. The model is based on a cost function similar to Baumol's, and it includes elements for the cost of making transfers to and from cash and for the opportunity cost of holding cash. The upper limit, h, which cash balances should not be allowed to surpass, and the return point, z, to which the balance is returned after every transfer either to or from the cash account, are computed so as to minimize the cost function. The lower limit is assumed to be given, and it could be the minimum balance required by the banks in which the cash is deposited.

The cost function for the Miller-Orr model can be stated as $E(c) = bE(N)/T + iE(m)$, where $E(N) =$ the expected number of transfers between cash and the investment portfolio during the planning period; $b =$ the cost per transfer; $T =$ the number of days in the planning period; $E(m) =$ the expected average daily cash balance; and $i =$ the daily rate of interest earned on the investments. The objective is to minimize $E(c)$ by choice of the variables h and z, the upper control limit and the return point, respectively.

The solution as derived by Miller and Orr becomes

$$z^* = \left(\frac{3b\sigma^2}{4i}\right)^{1/3} \tag{18.3}$$

The variance of the daily changes in the cash balance is represented by σ^2. As would be expected, a higher transfer cost, b, or variance, σ^2, would imply a greater spread between the upper and lower control limits. For the special case where p (the probability that cash balances will increase) equals 0.5, and q (the probability that cash balances will decrease) equals 0.5 (and $r = 0$), the upper control limit will always be three times greater than the return point, z:

$$h^* = 3z^*. \tag{18.4}$$

To illustrate the Miller-Orr model, let $b = \$25$, $m = \$10$, $t = 8$, $i = 20\%$, $r = 0$, and $\sigma^2 = m^2 t = 800$. Given Equation 18.4:

$$z^* = \left[\frac{3(\$25)(800)}{4(0.20/365)}\right]^{1/3} = \left(\frac{\$60,000}{0.0021917808}\right)^{1/3}$$

$$= (\$27,375,000)^{1/3}$$

$$= \$301.38 \approx \$300$$

$$h^* = 3(\$301.38) = \$904.14 \approx \$900$$

For $r = 100$, h^* would be $1,000 and z would be $400.

Miller and Orr tested their model by applying it to nine months of data on the daily cash balances and purchases and sales of short-term securities of a large industrial company. When the decisions of the model were compared to those actually made by the treasurer of the company, the model was found to produce an average daily cash balance that was about 40 percent *lower* ($160,000 for the model and $275,000 for the treasurer). Looking at it from another side, the model would have been able to match the $275,000 average daily balance with only 80 transactions, as compared to the treasurer's 112 actual transactions.

As with most inventory control models, the Miller-Orr model's performance depends not only on how well the conditional predictions (in this case, the expected number of transfers and the expected average cash balance) conform to actuality but also on how well the parameters are estimated. In this model, b, the transfer cost, is sometimes difficult to estimate. In Miller and Orr's study, the order costs included such components as "(a) making two or more long-distance phone calls plus 15 minutes to a half-hour of the assistant treasurer's time, (b) typing up and carefully checking an authorization letter with four copies, (c) carrying the original of the letter to be signed by the treasurer, and (d) carrying the copies to the controller's office where special accounts are opened, the entries are posted and further checks of the arithmetic are made."[13] These clerical procedures were thought to be in the magnitude of $20 to $50 per order. In the application of

---

[13]Miller and Orr [1967].

their model, however, Miller and Orr did not rely on their estimate for order costs; instead, they tested the model through the use of a series of "assumed" order costs until the model used the same number of transactions as did the treasurer. They could then determine the order cost implied by the treasurer's own action. The results were then used to evaluate the treasurer's performance in managing the cash balances and so provided valuable information to the treasurer.

The treasurer found, for example, that his action in purchasing securities was often inconsistent. Too often, he made small-lot purchases well below the minimum of $(h - z)$ computed by the model, while, at other times, he allowed cash balances to drift to as much as double the upper control limit before making a purchase. If it did no more than give the treasurer some perspective about his buying and selling activities, the model was used successfully.[14]

The Miller-Orr model has a valuable element of flexibility. Expectations that cash balances are more likely to either increase or decrease over a given period can be incorporated into the calculation of the optimal values for the decision variables. Thus, if a business is subject to seasonal trends, the optimal control limits can be adjusted for each season by using different values for p and q, the respective probabilities that cash will increase and decrease.

The decision models (Baumol, Miller-Orr) are not intended to be applied blindly. Difficulties often arise in estimating parameters and probabilities. Even more important, the financial manager may have information not directly incorporated into the model. But despite their sometimes restrictive assumptions, decision models perform effectively if they capture the essential elements in a decision problem. Cash management models should be used as a guide to intelligent decision making, tempered by the manager's own good judgment.

Estimating the Firm's Daily Cash Balance

The cash management models of the type just described call for transfers from the marketable securities portfolio to the firm's demand deposit accounts (cash) when the firm's cash balances reach predetermined levels. This requires that the firm seek to anticipate the levels of its cash balances on a continuing basis. With the aid of computerization, some firms develop daily cash forecasts [Stone and Miller, 1981]. The procedures for doing this can be outlined. The monthly cash budgets provide the initial framework. The items in the cash budget can be broken into daily repetitive transactions that can be modeled into patterns of daily inflows and outflows. Weekly, monthly, and seasonal influences can be taken into account. In addition, major outflows and inflows are scheduled. The major scheduled outflows would be taxes, lease payments, debt service obligations, and so forth. The major scheduled inflows would be the maturing of investments, sales of assets, and so on. The timing of major scheduled inflows and outflows can be superimposed on the pattern of repetitive flows.

---

[14]For a cash planning approach related to credit decisions by the use of a financial simulation model, see Stone [1973]; see also Hill and Sartoris [1988].

Taking both repetitive flows and scheduled flows into account permits the formulation of projections of expected daily cash balances. Computerization permits closely tracking the projected balances against the actual daily cash balances. Analysis of the divergences between the two should enable the financial manager to improve the estimating model, to improve cash gathering and cash disbursing practices, and to provide dependable lead times for adjustments of the actual cash balances by transfers into and from the marketable securities portfolio. Here, as in many other aspects of the responsibilities of financial managers, computerization permits a rapid flow of information and prompt adjustments to change. These adjustments call for improvements in policies and procedures and in the refinement of forecasting models.

CASH MANAGEMENT IN INTERNATIONAL ENTERPRISE

The general principles that apply to the management of cash on an international basis are very similar to those used successfully by many firms on a domestic basis. Multinational firms try to speed up the collection of cash by having bank accounts in the banking system of each country. In many countries, customers pay their bills by requesting their bank or postal administration to deduct the amount owed from their account and to transfer it to the other firm's account.

Multinational commercial banks, particularly those that have branches or affiliates in a large number of countries, can be very helpful to multinational firms. Several of the larger U.S. multinational commercial banks have foreign departments whose sole purpose is to help U.S. multinational firms solve their problems of international cash management. An international bank can speed the flow of funds of a multinational firm and thereby decrease the exposure of these funds to foreign exchange rate risk. It can suggest the routing of the transfers as well as the national currency to be used. While in the United States, the average time between the initiation and completion of a financial transaction is two to three days, the time interval for foreign transactions can be as long as two to three weeks. The long delays unnecessarily tie up large amounts of funds and should be avoided. In this area, the multinational commercial banks are particularly helpful, since they can transfer funds from one country to another (provided government restrictions do not interfere) on a same-day basis if they have branches or affiliates in the two countries involved.

Increasingly, the arena for business finance is the global market. At the start of each day, the corporate treasurer determines whether to borrow or to lend in the international financial market. The investment activity takes place in both domestic and foreign countries.

The financial manager of the multinational corporate enterprise must consider the form and extent of protection against currency fluctuations on sales and purchases. If the firm has surplus cash, the financial manager must compare the returns from investing in the domestic money market with those from investing in the international market. Similarly, if short-term financing needs arise, the manager must make comparisons between domestic and foreign financing sources. Among the considerations are the advantages and disadvantages of using the impersonal international financial market versus those of developing long-term financing relations with international commercial banks or financial groups in the United States, London, Paris, Zurich, Bonn, and Tokyo.

SUMMARY

Relatively high levels of interest rates have increased the importance of cash management, while, at the same time, advances in technology have changed the nature of the cash management function. Financial managers have developed new techniques for optimizing cash balances and determining the appropriate relation between holding cash and holding investments in marketable securities.

The four primary reasons for holding cash are the transactions motive, the precautionary motive, to meet future needs, and to satisfy bank compensating balance requirements. The two major aspects of a cash flow system involve the gathering and disbursement of cash, with the firm's objective to speed collections and legitimately slow disbursements.

Float arises from lags in the payment process (mail, processing, and bank clearing delays). Float is an advantage to the firm as a buyer and a disadvantage to the firm as a seller. An efficient cash-gathering system will focus on reducing negative mail float with decentralized collections and a lockbox system. The use of the lockbox also reduces processing time by starting checks through the bank clearing process before they have been recorded in the firm's accounting system.

A concentration banking system seeks to speed the cash-gathering process by mobilizing funds efficiently through a hierarchy of local depository banks, regional concentration banks, and a central bank. The local depository banks are used to channel field office collections. The concentration banks, which usually handle the lockbox arrangement, channel funds to a major disbursement account. A key element in the selection of concentration banks is their location relative to a firm's customers and to Federal Reserve System check-clearing facilities and their access to the bank wire system to facilitate the transfer of funds to the firm's central bank, where greater control can be exercised over a single cash pool.

The financial manager has a range of mechanisms from which to choose for the rapid transfer of funds and must balance speed against cost. The conventional model for the cost comparison arrives at a breakeven size of transfer (above which a more rapid, more expensive method would be preferred) by comparing the value of the extra interest which would be earned in the central bank with the incremental cost of the faster mechanism. This method has been criticized for failing to consider any other value for the funds than the interest foregone by not transferring them to the central bank. For example, balances left in the concentration banks can earn service credits, reducing the cost to the firm using the bank's services. Timing considerations further complicate the cost-benefit analysis of transfer mechanisms, and systematic models which reflect these considerations are under development.

With respect to disbursements, several methods can be used to lengthen the payment period. However, banks seek to offset the gains from float; they attempt to charge for their services in such a way that firms bear the cost of the float directly.

Companies' liquidity policies vary with individual circumstances and needs. In selecting the firm's portfolio of marketable securities, the financial manager must consider financial risk, interest rate risk, purchasing power risk, liquidity or marketability, taxability, and relative yields. The securities which have best suited the financial manager's objectives are short-term U.S. government issues, plus those of the very strongest domestic and foreign banks and corporations. The effects of inflation, however, with its rapid devaluation of the purchasing power of idle cash, have led firms to be somewhat more aggressive in their efforts to seek out the highest yielding opportunities for given levels of risk.

The performance of mathematical models designed to determine the optimal cash balance depends on how well the firm's patterns of cash flows conform to the assumptions of the model. The Baumol model applies the EOQ inventory model to cash management (with an assumption of continuous expenditures) to determine the economic quantity of cash to have on hand.

The Miller-Orr model incorporates a stochastic generating process for periodic changes in cash balances in contrast to the deterministic assumptions of the Baumol model by assuming that net cash flows behave as if they were generated by a "stationary random walk." Changes in the cash balance form a normal distribution as the number of periods observed increases. This permits a probabilistic approach to be taken.

International cash management involves minimizing exposure of foreign-located funds to exchange rate risks and avoiding restrictions on the movement of funds from one country to another. International banks provide many services that facilitate effective international working capital management by multinational firms.

QUESTIONS

18.1 How can better methods of communication reduce the necessity for firms to hold large cash balances?

18.2 Discuss this statement: Improved communications and the many different near-cash assets have greatly reduced a firm's needs for demand deposits for transactions balances.

18.3 Would you expect a firm with a high growth rate to hold more or fewer precautionary and speculative cash balances than a firm with a low growth rate? Explain.

18.4 Many firms that find themselves with temporary surplus cash invest these funds in Treasury bills. Since Treasury bills frequently have the lowest yield of any investment security, why are they chosen as investments?

18.5 Discuss the differences between financial risk and interest rate risk. Which has the greater effect on the selection of marketable securities?

18.6 Explain the possible effects on a firm's cash balance of each of the following factors (other things held constant):
  a. The level of interest rates rises
  b. The cost of trading in marketable securities rises
  c. The cost of trading in marketable securities falls
  d. Sales forecasts are improved through the use of a more accurate forecasting technique.

18.7 Discuss possible sources of resistance to a concentration banking system instituted in a decentralized firm.

PROBLEMS

18.1 Hayes Associates is short on cash and is attempting to determine whether it would be advantageous to forego the discount on this month's purchases or to borrow funds to take advantage of the discount. The discount terms are 2/10, net 45.
  a. What is the maximum annual interest rate that Hayes Associates should pay on borrowed funds? Why?
  b. What are some of the intangible disadvantages associated with foregoing the discount?

18.2 Scott, Inc., currently has a centralized billing system located in New York City. However, over the years, its customers gradually have become less concentrated on the East Coast and now cover the entire United States. On average, it requires five days from the time customers mail payments until Scott is able to receive, process, and deposit their payments. To shorten this time, Scott is considering the installation of a lockbox collection system. It estimates that the system will reduce the time lag from customer mailing to deposit by three and one-half days. Scott has a daily average collection of $700,000.
  a. What reduction in cash balances can Scott achieve by initiating the lockbox system?
  b. If Scott has an opportunity cost of 8 percent, how much is the lockbox system worth on an annual basis?
  c. What is the maximum monthly charge Scott can pay for the lockbox system?

18.3 A firm issues checks in the amount of $1 million each day and deducts them from its own records at the close of business on the day they are written. On average, the bank receives and clears the checks (deducts them from the firm's bank balance) the evening of the fourth day after they are written; for example, a check written on Monday will be cleared on Friday afternoon. The firm's loan agreement with the bank requires it to maintain a $750,000 minimum average compensating balance; this is $250,000 greater than the cash safety stock the firm would otherwise have on deposit.
  a. Assuming that the firm makes its deposit in the late afternoon (and the bank includes the deposit in the day's transactions), how much must the firm move to its demand deposit account each day to maintain a sufficient balance once it reaches a steady state?
  b. How many days of float does the firm carry?
  c. What ending daily balance should the firm try to maintain at the bank and on its own records?
  d. Explain how float can help increase the value of the firm's common stock. Use a partial balance sheet and the du Pont system concept (Chapter 8) in your answer.

18.4 The New York field office of the Metallux Corporation has sold a quantity of silver ingots for $15,000. Metallux wants to transfer this amount to its concentration bank in San Francisco as economically as possible. Two means of transfer are being considered.
  (1) A mail depository transfer check (DTC) costs 50 cents and takes three days.

(2) A wire transfer costs $7.50 and funds are immediately available in San Francisco. Metallux earns 14.5 percent annual interest on funds in its concentration bank. Which transfer method should be used?

18.5 Warrior Industries projects that annual cash usage of $3.75 million will occur uniformly throughout the forthcoming year. Warrior plans to meet these demands for cash by periodically selling marketable securities from its portfolio. The firm's marketable securities are invested to earn 12 percent, and the cost per transaction of converting funds to cash is $40.

    a. Use the Baumol model to determine the optimal transaction size for transfers from marketable securities to cash.

    b. What will be Warrior's average cash balance?

    c. How many transfers per year will be required?

18.6 (*Use the computer diskette, File name: 18CASBUD, Cash Budgeting.*)

    a. Given the initial assumptions (Screen #3), what is the amount owed to banks or excess cash available at the end of June (Screen #4)?

    b. If the share of sales collected in the first month drops from 30 percent to 20 percent, expenses rise from 50 percent to 60 percent of current month's sales, and purchases rise from 40 percent to 50 percent of the following month's sales, what is the effect on the cash position at the end of June?

    c. Go back to the initial assumptions. If the beginning cash balance is doubled, and the minimum cash balance tripled, what is the effect on the cash position at the end of June?

    d. Assume the following alternative sales forecast instead of the one given: Sales will rise faster and level off, so February sales are $15,000, March sales are $17,000, April sales are $20,000, and then sales remain at $20,000. What is the effect on the cash position at the end of June?

    e. Now assume that sales start high, at $30,000, and continuously decrease by $2,000 each month. What is the effect on the cash position at the end of June?

    f. Now suppose that sales started at $8,000 and rose by $2,000 each month. What is the effect on the cash position?

    g. Make any desired changes with respect to inputs, such as time patterns of expenses or collections or minimum cash requirements to determine effects of cash needed or required each month.

REFERENCES

Baumol, William J., "The Transactions Demand for Cash: An Inventory Theoretic Approach," *Quarterly Journal of Economics*, 66 (November 1952), pp. 545–556.

Ferguson, Daniel, "Optimize Your Firm's Lockbox Selection System," *Financial Executive*, (April 1983), p. 19.

Gallinger, George W., and Healey, P. Basil, *Liquidity Analysis and Management*, Reading, Mass.: Addison-Wesley, 1987.

Hill, Ned C., and Sartoris, William L., *Short-Term Financial Management*, New York: Macmillan, 1988.

Maier, S. F., and Vander Weide, J. H., "What Lockbox and Disbursement Models Really Do," *Journal of Finance*, 38 (May 1983), pp. 361–371.

Miller, Merton H., and Orr, Daniel, "An Application of Control-Limit Models to the Management of Corporate Cash Balances," in *Fi-*

nancial Research and Management Decisions, A. A. Robichek ed., New York: Wiley, 1967, pp. 133–151.

———, "A Model of the Demand for Money by Firms," *Quarterly Journal of Economics,* 80 (August 1966), pp. 413–435.

Sartoris, William L., and Hill, Ned C., "Innovations in Short-Term Financial Management," *Business Horizons,* 32 (November/December 1989), pp. 56–64.

Stone, Bernell K., "Cash Planning and Credit-Line Determination with a Financial Statement Simulator: A Cash Report on Short-Term Financial Planning," *Journal of Financial and Quantitative Analysis,* 8 (November 1973), pp. 711–730.

———, and Hill, Ned C., "Cash Transfer Scheduling for Efficient Cash Concentration," *Financial Management,* (Autumn 1980a), pp. 35–43.

———, "The Evaluation of Alternative Cash Transfer Mechanisms and Methods," *Proceedings of the Nineteenth Annual Meeting of the Southwestern Finance Association,* 1980b, pp. 39–58.

———, and Miller, Tom W., "Daily Cash Forecasting: A Structuring Framework," *Journal of Cash Management,* 1 (October 1981), pp. 35, 38–50.

CHAPTER 19

Receivables and Inventory Management

Inventory and accounts receivable are the two largest current asset accounts. Of approximately equal magnitude, together they comprise almost 80 percent of current assets and over 30 percent of total assets for all manufacturing industries. We first discuss credit management and policy—the basis for making decisions on extending credit. Such decisions involve credit standards, credit terms, and the determination of who shall receive credit. A framework for evaluating decisions on changing credit policies is also presented.

While the complexities of inventory decision modeling may be more appropriately the province of operations management, financial managers must also be concerned with inventory as part of the overall cycle of cash flows; the financial manager must understand the logic of the inventory control model, which is one of the most widely used mathematical models in business and which has more general applicability beyond inventory (for example, in cash management).[1]

CREDIT MANAGEMENT POLICIES

In our view credit management involves the following decision areas: (1) analyzing credit risk, (2) setting standards for accepting or rejecting the credit risk, (3) specifying credit terms, (4) deciding how to finance accounts receivable—the credit extended, (5) determining who bears the credit risk, (6) establishing collections policies and practices, and (7) avoiding suboptimization by individual departments. The foregoing seven items provide an outline for our discussion of credit management and policy.

---

[1] In rewriting this chapter, we incorporated many suggestions from Professor C. C. Hsia of Portland State University.

Credit Analysis

Credit analysis seeks to determine who shall receive credit and under what conditions. Two aspects of the process should be distinguished: the new customer versus continuing accounts. The second is much less difficult because experience provides considerable information. Credit analysis obviously is a tougher problem for new customers. Two main approaches are taken. One is to determine how the prospective customer has behaved with other suppliers. This kind of information can be obtained at a price from specialized financial information agencies, such as Dun & Bradstreet. Also, local associations for credit managers often compile information on the credit experience of sellers in individual product lines. It obviously makes sense to benefit from the experience of other firms with the prospective customer.

In addition, the firm will perform its own analysis to make its own independent decision. When trade credit is involved, the firm is both selling goods and extending credit. The two activities are intertwined. How the customer behaves may depend in part on how the sales organization has been treating the customer. In addition, the collections policies and practices of the seller may adversely affect customers. Hence a selling firm may decide not to rely completely on the experience of other selling firms. There may be an opportunity to develop a new customer relationship.

In making its own independent assessment, a firm traditionally considers the five Cs of credit: character, capacity, capital, collateral, and conditions.

Character has to do with the probability that a customer will try to honor his or her obligations. This factor is of considerable importance because every credit transaction implies a promise to pay. Will the creditor make an honest effort to pay the debts, or is this credit applicant likely to try to get away with something? Experienced credit managers frequently insist that character is the most important issue in a credit evaluation.

Capacity describes a subjective judgment of the customer's ability to pay. It is gauged by the customer's past business performance record, supplemented by physical observation of the plant or store and business methods.

Capital is measured by the general financial position of the firm as indicated by a financial ratio analysis, with special emphasis on the tangible net worth of the enterprise.

Collateral is represented by assets the customer offers as a pledge for security of the credit extended.

The fifth C, *conditions,* has to do with the impact of general economic trends on the firm or special developments in certain areas of the economy that may affect the customer's ability to meet the obligation.

When judging credit risk, information on the five Cs of credit is obtained from a number of sources, including the firm's prior experience with the customer. If it is a new account, audited financial statements for the three previous years may be requested. (Applicants sometimes submit income tax returns in lieu of other statements.)

Sources of Information. Two major sources of external information are available. First, by periodic meetings of local groups and by correspondence, information on experience with debtors is exchanged through the credit associations. More formally, Credit Interchange, a system developed by the National Association of Credit Management for assembling and distributing information on debtors' past performance, is provided. The interchange reports show the paying record of the debtor, the industries from which the debtor firm is buying, and the trading areas in which the purchases are being made.

The second source of external information is the credit-reporting agencies, the best known of which is Dun & Bradstreet. Agencies that specialize in coverage of a limited number of industries also provide information. Representative of these are the National Credit Office and Lyon Furniture Mercantile Agency. These agencies provide data that can be used by the credit manager in the credit analysis; they also provide ratings similar to those available on corporate bonds.

Another source of credit information is the customer's commercial bank. While the bank cannot disclose account balances and loan balances without the applicant's consent, some general information can be provided. Typically, the bank will express the magnitude of the customer's account balance (for example, a "medium six-figure" balance). The extent to which the bank will disclose information will also depend in part on the creditor firm's past dealings with the bank and the personal relationships of the executives involved.

Analysis of Credit Information. The evaluation will start with a relatively standard financial ratio analysis, placing emphasis on the liquidity, leverage, and profitability ratios. The ratios will be compared to composites for the lines of business in which the firm operates.

In addition to a general financial analysis, some specific tests related to credit activity will be performed. Information on the payment practices of the prospective customer will be factored into the analysis. This is done by taking the accounts payable data from the financial statements and calculating an average age of accounts payable. This average payment period can then be used in two comparisons. The first one relates the actual payment period to the terms of credit. For example, if credit terms are net 30 days and the average payment period is 55 days, a slippage of 25 days is involved. The second comparison examines the customer's payment period against the average for its line of business. The average payment period might be 40 days. Continuing the assumption of credit terms of net 30 days, this represents a lag of 10 days as general practice and is therefore "normal" in some sense. The additional 15 days beyond the 40 days represents a further "abnormal" lag.

Formal Evaluation Systems. After analysis of the credit information, the firm may seek to express the results in quantitative terms. This is generally referred to as credit scoring. It involves a numerical measure to predict the probability that a customer will pay on time. Sometimes the analysis is turned around to predict the probability that the customer will *not* pay on time or will actually go bankrupt. For example, in evaluating consumers' credit, scoring might include annual income, home ownership, married or single, number of years on the current job, number of years living at current residence, and age. The higher the annual income the better. Home ownership indicates a stronger position than renting, on average. The number of years at the current job indicates the probability of continued income. A greater length of time at the current residence indicates a greater degree of stability, as does marriage. Age is a consideration because in some cases lending to minors would be ruled out. Whether being 40 or 70 is better is a judgmental factor best determined in conjunction with the other variables. This suggests an important point. The variables are likely to be interrelated. While credit scoring is convenient it is important to consider interactions and use judgment as well. When desired characteristics are given higher ratings, then the scoring system will specify a minimum number that must be achieved before extending credit.

When the concepts of credit scoring are used for business firms, they are based on some set of financial ratios. For a firm selling to a large number of customers, relatively simple rules may be employed. For example, if a firm has a current ratio of less than one to one and if ownership equity is less than what is owed to creditors, the customer is likely to be a slow pay. If profitability ratios are satisfactory, then the customer might be accepted depending upon further analysis. If profitability ratios are low, the customer would not be extended credit. But even more formal statistical techniques are also employed including various forms of regression analysis and discriminant analysis.[2] Edward Altman used discriminant analysis to develop a measure of credit risk he called the Z score.[3] Its nature and application are similar to credit scoring.

Either on the basis of judgment or by more formal credit scoring, a firm may set up risk classes, grouped according to the probability of loss associated with sales to a customer. The combination of rating and supplementary information might lead to the groupings of probable loss experience below.

Risk Class Number	Probable Loss Ratio (in %)
1	None
2	0–1/2
3	1/2–1
4	1–2
5	2–5
6	5–10
7	10–20
8	Over 20

If the selling firm has a 20 percent margin over the sum of direct operating costs and all delivery and selling costs, and if it is producing at less than full capacity, it may adopt the following credit policies: selling on customary credit terms to Groups 1 through 5; selling to Groups 6 and 7 under more stringent credit terms, such as cash on delivery; and requiring advance payment from Group 8. As long as the bad debt loss ratios are less than 20 percent, the additional sales are contributing something to overhead. However, the opportunity costs of the increased investment in receivables also must be taken into account in the analysis, as will be shown in the examples later in the chapter.

---

[2]Discriminant analysis, discussed in Appendix B of Chapter 7, partitions a sample into two or more components on the basis of a set of characteristics. The sample, for instance, might be loan applicants at a consumer loan company. The components into which they are classified might be those likely to make prompt repayment and those likely to default. The characteristics might be whether the applicant owns a home, how long the person has been with the current employer, level of income, and so on.

[3]Altman, Edward I., "Financial Ratios, Discriminant Analysis and the Prediction of Corporate Bankruptcy," *Journal of Finance*, 23 (September 1968), pp. 589–609.

Credit Standards

Credit standards represent the specification of scores or characteristics that determine whether a customer will receive credit. A number of variables are involved and some weak customers may be granted credit under specified conditions. If a firm makes credit sales to only the strongest of customers, it will experience only small amounts of bad debt losses. On the other hand, it will probably lose sales, and the profit it foregoes on these lost sales may be greater than the costs it avoids. To determine the optimal credit standard, the firm relates the marginal costs of credit to the marginal profits on the increased sales.

Marginal costs include production and selling costs; here however, we will consider only those costs associated with the quality of the marginal accounts, or *credit quality costs*. These costs include (1) default, or bad debt losses, (2) higher investigation and collection costs, and (3) higher amounts tied up in receivables, resulting in higher costs of capital, due to less creditworthy customers who delay payment.

Since credit costs and credit quality are correlated, the quality of an account needs to be determined. Perhaps the best way to do this is in terms of the probability of default. Probability estimates are for the most part subjective; but credit rating is a well-established practice, and a good credit manager can make reasonably accurate judgments of the probability of default by different classes of customers. One decision may be the approval or disapproval of a particular sale on the firm's standard credit terms. Also, a line of credit may be determined for a customer. One rule of thumb for a line of credit is a percentage of the customer's net worth (or "estimated financial strength") related to the number of its major suppliers. For example, if the credit-supplying firm has a general standard of trying to keep total trade credit below 60 percent of the customer's net worth and it is determined that there are four other major suppliers, the credit limit may be established at no more than 12 percent of the customer's net worth (60% ÷ 5 total suppliers). Or, the figure may be set at 10 percent to provide a margin of safety and to allow for fluctuations in the volume of business among the customer's major suppliers.

Credit Terms

The terms of credit specify the period for which credit is extended and the discount, if any, for early payment. For example, if a firm's credit terms to all approved customers are stated as 2/10, net 30, then a 2 percent discount from the stated sales price is granted if payment is made within 10 days, and the entire amount is due 30 days from the invoice date if the discount is not taken. If the terms are stated "net 60," this indicates that no discount is offered and that the bill is due and payable 60 days after the invoice date.

If sales are seasonal, a firm may use seasonal dating. Jensen, Inc., a bathing suit manufacturer, sells on terms of 2/10, net 30, May 1 dating. This means that the effective invoice date is May 1, so the discount can be taken until May 10, or the full amount must be paid on May 30, regardless of when the sale was made. Jensen produces output throughout the year, but retail sales of bathing suits are concentrated in the spring and early summer. Because of its practice of offering seasonal datings, Jensen induces some customers to stock up early, saving Jensen storage costs and also nailing down sales.

The following discussion outlines five aspects of credit terms: the economic nature of the product, the seller's circumstances, the buyer's circumstances, credit period, and cash discounts.[4]

Economic Nature of the Product. Commodities with high sales turnover are sold on relatively short credit terms; buyers resell the products rapidly, generating cash that enables them to pay the suppliers. Groceries have a high turnover, but perishability also plays a role. The credit extended for fresh fruits and vegetables might run from 5 to 10 days, whereas the credit extended on canned fruits and vegetables could be 15 to 30 days. Terms for items that have a slow retail turnover, such as jewelry, may run six months or longer.

Seller Circumstances. Financially weak sellers require cash or exceptionally short credit terms. For example, farmers sell livestock to meat-packing companies on a cash basis. In many industries, variations in credit terms can be used as a sales promotion device. Although the use of credit as a selling device could endanger sound credit management, the practice does occur, especially when the seller's industry has excess capacity. Also, large sellers can use their position to impose relatively short credit terms. However, the reverse appears more often in practice; that is, financially strong sellers are suppliers of funds to small firms.

Buyer Circumstances. In general, financially sound retailers who sell on credit may, in turn, receive slightly longer terms. Some classes of retailers regarded as selling in particularly risky areas (such as clothing) receive extended credit terms but are offered large discounts to encourage early payment.

Credit Period. Lengthening the credit period stimulates sales, but there is a cost to tying up funds in receivables. For example, if a firm changes its terms from net 30 to net 60, the average receivables for the year may rise from $100,000 to $300,000 — the increase caused partly by the longer credit terms and partly by the larger volume of sales. The optimal credit period is determined by the point where marginal profits on increased sales are offset by the costs of carrying the higher amounts of accounts receivable.

Cash Discounts. A *cash discount* is a reduction in price based on payment within a specified period. The costs of not taking cash discounts often exceed the rate of interest at which the buyer can borrow, so it is important that a firm be cautious in its use of trade credit as a source of financing; it could be quite expensive. If the customer borrows and takes the cash discount, the period during which accounts payable remain on the books is reduced. The effective length of credit is thus influenced by the size of discounts offered.

Why should the seller offer large financial inducements for the buyer to take the cash discount? The traditional explanations were mainly financial. The seller receives the funds earlier. If the buyer pays within the cash discount period, the risk of subsequent default is

---

[4]For a discussion of the determinants of credit policy, see Hill, Wood, and Sorenson [1981].

reduced to zero. Another possible reason is to enable the seller to engage in price discrimination by varying credit terms such as cash discounts.

Theory of Trade Credit

But it is not likely that the size of the trade credit gains explains the large implicit interest difference involved in offering and taking the cash discounts. A further set of reasons has been offered by Janet K. Smith [1987]. She views trade credit as a contractual device for dealing with informational asymmetry. Credit terms are used to cause the buyers to signal their creditworthiness; buyers sort themselves as low risk or high risk by their decisions to take cash discounts or to forego them. Credit terms thereby perform as a screening device.

Trade credit provides valuable default risk information to the sellers who have made nonsalvageable investments in the buyer. These investments consist of the decline in value of a product if it is necessary to repossess it, the costs of acquiring information about the buyer, training sales and credit personnel to understand the characteristics of the business of the buyer, product demonstrations, entertainment of the buyer to establish relationships, etc. Early detection of the credit risk of the buyer may enable the seller to take actions to control and protect these nonsalvageable investments.

Trade credit also provides informational benefits to the buyers. Credit terms that call for a net payment after 30 days, for example, provide the buyer with the opportunity to evaluate the quality of the merchandise received. Thus when a seller extends trade credit, it is a signal that the firm is confident of its ability to provide reliable merchandise and will carry out its implicit promises and guarantees. In these ways trade credit reduces contracting costs between sellers and buyers and supplies financing as a joint product with other services, which makes the financing involved in trade credit more attractive (lower price and/or quality) than financing supplied from alternative institutions.

Financing Receivables

The fourth topic in credit management is how the receivables are to be financed. At least four alternatives are available: general credit, secured debt financing, factoring, or a captive finance subsidiary. With respect to general credit, one view is that all sources of financing on the right-hand side of the balance sheet are used in financing the investments on the left-hand side. From this perspective, receivables are on the same basis as inventories or any other asset to be financed.

However, if the financial position of the firm is weak, it may be necessary to provide the lender with a guarantee in the form of financing secured by the receivables. It may be the expansion of sales and associated receivables increase that have created the need for additional financing.

Other institutions may be employed. A factoring company is defined as a specialist firm that performs the credit analysis. It may also extend credit. If the factor extends credit, it may take on the risk of nonpayment by the customer—called nonrecourse financing. If the seller still bears the risk, it is recourse financing. A full evaluation of the role of the factor is made in the following chapter, which deals with alternative sources of financing.

Another method of financing receivables is the captive financing subsidiary. Usually larger firms with large volumes of transactions or large unit transactions are the ones that employ captive finance subsidiaries. A number of considerations may be involved — some good, some dubious. Financing is a specialist activity, so the firm may separate the specialist finance group from its basic business operations. As a separate legal subsidiary, the managers may be evaluated more effectively and, in turn, may be motivated more strongly by accountability related to rewards for levels of performance. Formerly, an alleged advantage was off-balance sheet financing, but current FASB rules require consolidated reporting. The literature is in disagreement about whether captive finance companies are used to impair the position of prior creditors. (Compare Kim, McConnell, and Greenwood [1977] versus Mian and Smith [1990].) On the positive side, Mian and Smith [1990, p. 9] hold that captive finance subsidiaries provide a means for segregating cash flows for payments to creditors and help control other types of agency problems.

Who Bears the Credit Risk?

Ultimately the seller firm bears the risk of nonpayment when credit is extended. When a firm employs a captive finance subsidiary, the parent still is involved in some kind of guarantee, either explicitly or implicitly. When a factor is used with nonrecourse financing, the factor appears to bear the risk. The factor is a specialist firm that bears the risks of unexpected departures from default rate patterns. The seller firm, however, pays a fee to the factor for the expected or actuarial levels of losses for the line or lines of business involved.

Another type of specialist firm may be utilized — commercial credit insurance companies. Credit insurance covered sales of an amount estimated at slightly over $50 billion in 1985, representing about 1.3 percent of final sales in the economy in that year. A credit insurance policy will specify a deductible aggregate amount and contain a coinsurance provision, which requires the insured to bear a 10 to 20 percent portion of the loss. Again the seller firm, the insured, pays an insurance premium which represents expected losses; the insurer provides protection against unexpected or catastrophic losses. The leading carriers providing credit insurance in the United States are American Credit Indemnity, a subsidiary of the Commercial Credit Company, and The London Guarantee and Accident Company. To cover export sales an association of insurance companies formed the Foreign Credit Insurance Association (FCIA). The U.S. Export-Import Bank (Eximbank) performs a cooperative and facilitating role with the FCIA. To the extent that the Eximbank provides credits for export sales and participates in the credit insurance activities of the FCIA, some element of government subsidy is provided in covering credit expense and losses.

Collections Policies

A sixth aspect of credit management is collecting the bills. The prescriptions are to be tough, informed, and creative. When payments are delinquent, the temptation is to follow standard collections patterns. These include sending letters of increasing insistence, making phone calls, seeking intervention by the firm's legal department, using outside collection agencies, and instigating lawsuits. Such methods may succeed in collecting all or part of the money. But the credit manager's larger objective is to build a broad and increasing base of profitable sales.

Credit executives have a substantial positive function in a firm. They are not simply "heavies," whose job it is to bully delinquent accounts. The basic objective of credit management is to add value to the firm by contributing to an optimal amount of profitable sales. Especially in the evaluation of credit information and in the collections functions, credit managers can perform a valuable role for the firm. If a potential borrower does not meet credit standards, one simple approach is to turn down the order. This could probably be justified by comparing probable gain with probable loss on the order. But in analyzing the applicant's credit information, the credit manager may identify causes of or factors in the firm's poor financial performance that could alter the credit decision.

A good credit manager will strive to learn the business of the firm's customers as well as (or better than) the executives of those firms. He or she should seek to keep current on customers' sales trends, management performance, liquidity, leverage, and profitability. The creative credit manager keeps abreast of external factors affecting customers' businesses and is in continuous communication with the large accounts. He or she should seek to serve as a valued sounding board for discussions of trends affecting customers' industries as well as of important policy decisions in the individual firms. A credit manager should provide a source of counsel on important policy and decision areas affecting customers' future well-being. To be sure, these recommendations reflect the ideal and must be balanced with practical considerations of time and cost. But to the degree that these potentials are realized, a credit manager can help customers' businesses expand profitably and can increase sales volume for his or her own firm. Thus, the credit granting and collection functions can be part of an effective sales activity strategy.

Avoid Suboptimization

The sales department may seek to maximize sales especially if salespeople are paid on a commission basis. The credit department may seek to minimize loss ratios. Both goals are wrong. Both departments should seek to maximize the value of the firm, which involves cooperation between the two departments. Both the sales and credit activities can be sources of market research and information on customers as well as provide creative counseling to customers. Sales and credit departments can develop close relations with customers and help them achieve successful operations. This will help build a loyal and financially strong customer list. Credit analysis, credit standards, terms and collections are not enough. Credit situations provide opportunities for creative interactions with customers.

EVALUATING CHANGES IN CREDIT POLICY

Thus far in our treatment of current asset management, we have dealt with each area individually, and in actual practice, similar compartmentalization is often reinforced by organizational structures in which cash managers manage cash, payables managers man-

FIGURE 19.1   The Cash Flow Timeline

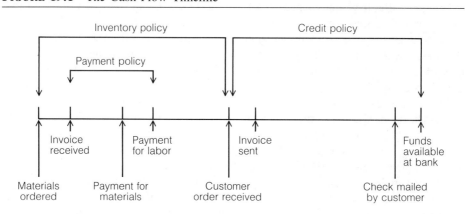

age payables, credit managers manage receivables, and operations managers manage inventories. However, such fragmentation is illusory and may lead to erroneous decision criteria in any one area unless consideration is given to the decision's impact on other areas. For example, a decision to deny credit to slow-paying customers would likely reduce the collection period but would also reduce total sales and production volume, thus altering the level of cash flows in these areas, and perhaps their timing as well. An integrated model must consider the interrelationships between both the timing and the amount of all cash flows involved in current asset policy decisions.

A number of authors have attempted to formulate decision models that integrate several elements of working capital management, for example, the relationship between inventory control and payables and receivables management. By concentrating on cash flows over time (rather than accounting measures) in an NPV framework, the Sartoris-Hill [1981] credit policy decision model discussed below goes a long way towards integrating all of the elements of current asset management to the goal of maximizing the value of the firm. Sartoris and Hill (building on the earlier work of Kim and Atkins [1978], of Hill and Riener [1979], and of Dyl [1977]) formulate a net present value cash flow approach to the analysis of alternative credit policies. Their decision model is based on calculating the net gain or loss resulting from a change in credit policy. It is sufficiently flexible to account for differences of price, cost, trade discount, bad debt loss rate, timing of cash flows, inventory effects, and growth rate of sales, all simultaneously or in any combination.

Their cash flow timeline, in Figure 19.1, is a useful tool for illustrating that evaluation of a change in credit policy extends beyond its impact on the level of accounts receivable. The timeline shifts the focus to changes in the timing and amount of cash flows over the entire cycle, which encompasses inventory and payables management, credit management, and cash collections.

An example will illustrate how the Sartoris-Hill model incorporates the interrelation of current asset variables into the evaluation of a credit policy. The Halbard Company manufactures electric typewriters. Credit sales are constant throughout the year, averaging 200 units per day at $500 each; costs are $350 per unit. Based on a weighted average, cash collections are received 40 days from the date of sale. (Terms of sale are net 30; however, some customers delay payment.) The current bad debt loss rate is 2 percent, and Halbard estimates its daily interest rate to be 0.05 percent.[5] Halbard is considering extending its terms of sale to net 45 days. It is estimated that sales will rise to 250 units per day, but the bad debt loss rate will also rise to 3 percent and the average collection period will rise to 50 days.

Using the Sartoris-Hill notation, in which the subscripts "0" and "1" refer to the current and proposed credit policies respectively, we have

Factors	Current Policy	Proposed Policy
P = price per unit	P_0 = $500	P_1 = $500
C = cost per unit	C_0 = $350	C_1 = $350
Q = daily sales	Q_0 = 200 units	Q_1 = 250 units
b = bad debt loss rate	b_0 = 2%	b_1 = 3%
t = average collection period	t_0 = 40 days	t_1 = 50 days
k = daily interest rate	k_0 = 0.05%	k_1 = 0.05%

The net present value under the current policy consists of net revenues discounted for t_0 days, less costs (inventory is assumed to be purchased or produced and paid for on the date of sale).

$$NPV_0 = \left[\frac{P_0 Q_0 (1 - b_0)}{(1 + k_0)^{t_0}} \right] - C_0 Q_0$$

$$= \frac{\$500(200)(1 - .02)}{(1.0005)^{40}} - \$350(200)$$

$$= \frac{\$98,000}{1.0202} - \$70,000$$

$$= \$96,060 - \$70,000$$

$$= \$26,060$$

Likewise, the NPV of one day's operations under the proposed new policy will be

$$NPV_1 = \left[\frac{P_1 Q_1 (1 - b_1)}{(1 + k_1)^{t_1}} \right] - C_1 Q_1$$

$$= \frac{\$500(250)(1 - .03)}{(1.0005)^{50}} - (\$350)(250)$$

$$= \frac{\$121,250}{1.0253} - \$87,500$$

$$= \$118,258 - \$87,500$$

$$= \$30,758.$$

---

[5]This amounts to 18.25 percent per 365-day year.

The decision criterion for the change in credit policy should be to adopt the policy with the higher net present value; in this case, NPV_1 is greater than NPV_0 by \$4,698, and thus the proposed change in credit policy should be adopted.

For simplicity, we have excluded until now the impact on the NPV analysis of changes in working capital resulting from changes in credit terms. As the amount of sales increases so does the amount of working capital required to support that level of sales. Cash, inventories, and accounts receivables all increase. For our example, we will assume other working capital (receivables are already reflected in the model) to be a constant percentage, w, of sales. Assume $w = 25$ percent. In evaluating the proposed credit policy, we need to subtract an additional cost due to the additional working capital. Thus, NPV_0 becomes

$$NPV_0 = \left[\frac{P_0Q_0(1 - b_0)}{(1 + k_0)^{t_0}}\right] - C_0Q_0 - w\left[P_0Q_0 - \frac{P_0Q_0}{(1 + k_0)^{t_0}}\right]$$

$$= \frac{\$500(200)(1 - .02)}{(1.0005)^{40}} - \$350(200) - .25\left[\$500(200) - \frac{\$500(200)}{(1.0005)^{40}}\right]$$

$$= \$96,060 - \$70,000 - \$495 = \$25,565.$$

The term wP_0Q_0 represents our outlay for the current level of working capital, and the term

$$\frac{wP_0Q_0}{(1 + k_0)^{t_0}}$$

represents what we get back in 40 days collection time. We do the same for NPV_1, which becomes

$$NPV_1 = \left[\frac{P_1Q_1(1 - b_1)}{(1 + k_1)^{t_1}}\right] - C_1Q_1 - w\left[P_1Q_1 - \frac{P_1Q_1}{(1 + k_1)^{t_1}}\right].$$

Again, the term wP_1Q_1 represents the working capital outlay for the proposed level of receivables, and the term

$$\frac{wP_1Q_1}{(1 + \cdot k_1)^{t_1}}$$

represents what we get back after the increase in collection time to 50 days.

$$NPV_1 = \frac{\$500(250)(1 - .03)}{(1.0005)^{50}} - \$350(250) - .25\left[\$500(250) - \frac{\$500(250)}{(1.0005)^{50}}\right]$$

$$= \$118,258 - \$87,500 - \$771 = \$29,987$$

The result for $NPV_1 - NPV_0$ is \$4,422; hence, the new credit policy remains favorable.

Thus, additional working capital requirements such as additional inventories occur when credit policy changes result in increased sales and the NPV calculation of the credit change is affected.

This example demonstrates the interrelation of aspects of current asset management. Credit policy affects not only accounts receivable but also sales and working capital requirements. Other examples could show how production costs might change, or the optimum inventory level might change. Still others might incorporate changing prices or the timing of cash flows. The model is capable of including all effects of the credit policy by focusing on cash flow impacts and the resulting NPV of a given credit policy change.

As with any analytical tool, the results can only be as valid as the data inputs. Estimates of the effects of a policy change might be made on the basis of market research or by comparison with existing product line/credit policy combinations within the firm or in other firms. Alternatively, the model can be used in a sensitivity framework to calculate the change in sales or bad debt loss rate (for example) required to justify a change in credit policy, in conjunction with an analysis of the probabilities of various changes occurring.[6]

USE OF COMPUTERS IN CREDIT MANAGEMENT

By nature, credit management lends itself to the use of computer controls. Credit management requires the collection, compilation, storage, analysis, and retrieval of information. Since accurate information on fund flows is critical to good credit management, efficient information processing is important.

All of the accounts receivable materials can be organized into a computer record system giving the credit manager current information on the status of accounts. Records will include the date the account was opened, the amount currently owed, the customer's maximum credit line, and a record of the customer's past payments. The credit rating assigned to the customer by Dun & Bradstreet or other rating agencies can be noted. Periodically, the credit manager may draw off various types of analyses of the customer accounts.

In addition, particular controls can be set up to monitor account delinquency. The computer can periodically flag past-due accounts for the credit manager's attention. The computer may be programmed to provide information on how close the account balance is to the established maximum line of credit. Such information provides the credit manager with the opportunity to contact the customer on a timely basis.

Indeed, the computer can be programmed to perform selected credit decisions. Based on credit limits set in advance, credit standards can be expressed quantitatively, and the computer can approve or reject credit applications or flag them for further analysis. Aided by a computer, a relatively small staff can manage a greatly increased volume of credit activity.

In addition to information on individual accounts, the computer can provide the credit manager with information on groups of companies. Periodically, the credit manager may receive a summary of all receivable accounts with respect to each account individually and in total. Information can be provided on billings, payments, discounts taken, and amounts owed. In addition, the computer can prepare special reports to provide analytical information that may be useful in making credit decisions. For example, the payment history of companies in the same industry may be compared. Do companies in a particular industry tend to pay slowly during certain months of the year? If this appears to be a trend, the

---

[6]Sartoris and Hill [1983]. Also, see Copeland and Khoury [1981].

credit manager should analyze the economic factors that cause firms in a particular industry to respond in similar ways. On the other hand, if a customer performs differently from most firms in the industry, the credit manager can examine the circumstances behind the firm's behavior. The credit manager may also analyze, before the problems escalate, any management or operating problems that may be developing in a firm making the account a serious credit risk.

Using a computer increases both the amount and frequency of information available to the credit manager. This information facilitates interaction with the customer and enables the credit management department to communicate promptly and effectively with other divisions in its own company as well as with general management. Thus, the effectiveness of the credit department has been greatly enhanced by making feasible computer-generated information flows that would otherwise be too expensive and time consuming to develop.

MONITORING RECEIVABLES MANAGEMENT

Two key issues facing the financial executive in accounts receivable management are the forecasting and the control of accounts receivable. We first examine two methods widely used by corporations, namely, the Days' Sales Outstanding (DSO) and the Aging Schedule (AS). We then focus our attention on the payments pattern approach, which offers a better means of monitoring accounts receivable.

According to a survey by Stone [1976], out of the companies that reported the use of some systematic procedures to project accounts receivable, a great majority used either a pro forma projection of DSO or some other ratio of receivables to a measure of sales. In the control of receivables, the AS is reportedly the popular method.

Days' Sales Outstanding

The average Days' Sales Outstanding (DSO) at a given time t is usually calculated as the ratio of receivables to a measure of daily sales:

$$DSO_t = \frac{\text{Total } AR_t}{\text{Daily sales}}.$$

The daily sales figure is obtained by averaging sales over a recent time period. The averaging period may be 30 days, 60 days, 90 days, or another relevant period. Clearly, DSO is affected by both the level of sales and the averaging period used.

The Aging Schedule

The Aging Schedule (AS) is the percentage of end-of-quarter accounts receivable in different age groups. Here, the phrase *age group* refers to the period of time that receivables have been outstanding from the time of sales. A strong AS shows only a small percentage of end-of-quarter receivables based on old sales, with the highest percentage based on the most recent month's sales.

Problems with DSO and AS

Both the DSO and the AS are affected by the pattern of sales within a quarter. Table 19.1 shows the end-of-quarter DSO for three different sales patterns. Total sales for the three quarters are identical at $180,000; only the monthly distributions differ from quarter to quarter. The payments pattern is assumed to be constant, with collections of 10 percent of sales during the month that sales are made and 30 percent, 40 percent, and 20 percent in the three months that follow. As a result, end-of-quarter receivables are 20 percent of the first month's sales, 60 percent of the second, and 90 percent of the third. If sales were level at $60,000 per month, the DSO would be constant at 51 days, as shown for the first quarter in Table 19.1 (look in the 30 Days column under End-of-Quarter DSO). With changing sales patterns, the DSO varies, changing to 41 for the second quarter and 81 for the third when the averaging period is for 30 days.

Table 19.2 shows the aging schedule for the same sales and collections data. If sales were level at $60,000 monthly, the AS would be constant, with 53 percent in the 0 to 30 days group, 35 percent in the 31 to 60 days group, and 12 percent in the 61 to 90 days group (shown for the first quarter in the Percent of Total column). But with a changing sales pattern, the AS becomes erratic. If sales are rising, as in the second quarter, the uncollected receivables from the first two months make up a relatively small portion (34 percent) of end-of-quarter receivables. Consequently, the payments experience appears to be improving. When sales are falling, as in the third quarter, uncollected receivables based on heavy sales for the first two months make up 67 percent of end-of-quarter receivables, and the payments experience appears to be worsening. Thus, seasonal variations in sales can send false signals to the credit manager, even though the true collection experience is unchanged.

TABLE 19.1 DSO with Varying Sales Patterns and Varying Averaging Periods (Dollars in Thousands)

Month	Sales	Receivables at End of Quarter	Daily Sales if Averaging Period Is the Most Recent:			End-of-Quarter DSO (in Days) if Averaging Period Is:		
			30 Days	60 Days	90 Days	30 Days	60 Days	90 Days
January	$60	$ 12						
February	60	36						
March	60	54						
		$102	$2	$2	$2	51	51	51
April	$30	$ 6						
May	60	36						
June	90	81						
		$123	$3	$2.50	$2	41	49	62
July	$90	$ 18						
August	60	36						
September	30	27						
		$ 81	$1	$1.50	$2	81	54	41

TABLE 19.2   Aging Schedules (Dollars in Thousands)

Month	Sales	Total Receivables at End of Quarter	Age Group (in Days)	Percent of Total
January	$60	$ 12	61-90	12%
February	60	36	31-60	35
March	60	54	0-30	53
		$102		100%
April	$30	$ 6	61-90	5%
May	60	36	31-60	29
June	90	81	0-30	66
		$123		100%
July	$90	$ 18	61-90	22%
August	60	36	31-60	45
September	30	27	0-30	33
		$ 81		100%

Other factors can also cause DSO and AS figures to shift. The DSO figures can be further distorted when alternative averaging periods are used to calculate daily sales. For the data in Table 19.1, third quarter daily sales rise from $1,000 based on a 30-day average to $2,000 based on a 90-day average. The corresponding end-of-quarter DSO falls from an alarming 81 days to a healthy 41 days. The way the credit manager perceives the collection experience as measured by the DSO will depend on which averaging period is chosen.

The AS figures can be further distorted if payments on the most recent month's sales are unusually high or low. A high proportion of payments on the most recent month's sales means that receivables for the previous two months will make up a higher percentage of end-of-quarter receivables, even though the old receivables may be normal in relation to the sales for those months. For instance, if receivables from September sales were $10,000 (instead of the $27,000 shown in Table 19.2) because customers paid $20,000 during September instead of the normal $3,000, the proportion of receivables in the three age groups would have been:

Month	Receivables	Age Groups	Percent of Total
July	$18	61-90	28%
August	36	31-60	56
September	10	0-30	16
	$64		100%

In this example, the exceptionally high collections on September sales—a condition favorable to the firm—distort the percentages to create the impression that the aging schedule has deteriorated.

TABLE 19.3   Payments Pattern of $60,000 of Credit Sales in January

Month	Collections from January Sales during Month		Receivables from January Sales Outstanding at End of Month	
	Percent	In Thousands	In Thousands	Percent
January	10	$ 6	$54	90
February	30	18	36	60
March	40	24	12	20
April	20	12	0	0

Payments Pattern Approach

We have seen that the DSO and AS procedures can be unreliable in the forecasting and control of accounts receivable. The major deficiency of both methods lies in their aggregation of sales and accounts receivable over a particular time period, a quarter in the above example. The payments pattern approach, suggested by Lewellen and Johnson [1972] and by Stone [1976], overcomes this difficulty to produce an analysis of payments behavior which is, of course, the real issue of interest to management.

A (monthly) payments pattern is characterized by the proportions of credit sales in a given month that are paid in that month and a number of subsequent months. Table 19.3 gives the monthly cash flows and accounts receivable arising from $60,000 of credit sales in January. The payments pattern is reflected in the last column: We see that 90 percent of payments for January sales remains outstanding at the end of that month, 60 percent at the end of February, and 20 percent at the end of March. A graphical representation of the payments pattern is given in Figure 19.2; the rectangles represent the accounts receivable

FIGURE 19.2   Graph of Payments Pattern of $60,000 of Credit Sales in January

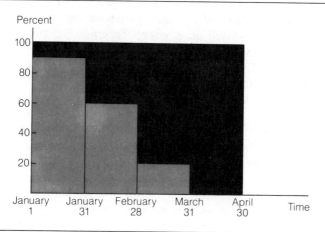

TABLE 19.4   Accounts Receivable as Percentages of Original Sales

Month of Origin	Sales during That Month (in Thousands)	Receivables at End of Quarter (in Thousands)	Percentage Outstanding (Receivables/Sales in Month of Origin)
January	$60	$ 12	20%
February	60	36	60
March	60	54	90
		$102	
April	$30	$ 6	20%
May	60	36	60
June	90	81	90
		$123	
July	$90	$ 18	20%
August	60	36	60
September	30	27	90
		$ 81	

proportions and the accumulated paid proportions of January sales at different points in time.

When the payments pattern remains unchanged from month to month, it is said to be constant. For example, using the same data as in Table 19.1, we observe a constant payments pattern (0.1, 0.3, 0.4, 0.2) and, consequently, a constant accounts receivable pattern (0.9, 0.6, 0.2) as exhibited in Table 19.4.

The major deficiency of the DSO and AS methods is due to the aggregation of sales and accounts receivable over a number of time periods. This aggregation makes it difficult to detect changes in the payments behavior. In the payments pattern approach, the problem is overcome by matching accounts receivable to sales in the month of origin. As a consequence, the payments pattern approach, in contrast to the DSO and AS, is not sales-level dependent. No matter what the sales pattern may be, the last column in Table 19.4 remains unchanged, provided the payments pattern is constant. Conversely, any change in payments behavior would be immediately reflected and recognized. Thus, the payments proportions and the balance proportions provide efficient means of control for the credit manager. For example, assume that a firm's historical accounts receivable pattern was (0.9, 0.6, 0.2). In early March, assume that the report on actual payments for January and February credit sales showed a current balance fraction for January sales of $F_1 = 0.70$ versus the pro forma value of 0.60, and a balance fraction for February sales of $F_0 = 0.95$ versus the pro forma value of 0.90. A problem, created by two consecutive adverse and large deviations from the normal pattern, is indicated.

The procedures proposed by Carpenter and Miller [1979] build on the payments pattern framework. (For brevity, their study will be referred to by the initials CM.) The emphasis of the sales pattern approach presented by Lewellen and Johnson and by Stone was to express receivables as a percent of sales in the month of origin. Control standards are developed from the percentages based on the payments pattern and corresponding receivables pattern. CM built upon the payments pattern concept to develop some additional evaluation relations. The key measure is the weighted DSO (WDSO). The changes in the WDSO, or changes in the average daily sales (ADS) in relation to the WDSO of the previous reference period, enable them to calculate efficiency and volume variances in receivables. The resulting data enable the credit executive to separate the changes in collection experience from changes in the sales patterns. The executive is thus better able to evaluate the current state of collections and receivables investment. Since he or she can now distinguish between changes in credit experience and in sales volume, the credit executive can plan to work on changing collection performance or to alter the credit-related variables that influence the volume of sales.

THEORY AND TESTS OF RECEIVABLES MANAGEMENT POLICIES

Mian and Smith developed a theory of accounts receivable management policy including empirical tests of their framework.[7] In analyzing the interrelationships between functions to be performed and the determination of the agency to perform them, they set out a theory of the determinants of alternative policies. First they consider incentives to extend trade credit to customers rather than cash sales with the buyer obtaining credit elsewhere. They argue that trade credit is more likely to be used if the cost of supplying both merchandise and credit from a single source can be lower than using separate transactions. They point out that this is similar to the basic problem of the theory of the firm in which the decision must be made between using external markets for transactions versus performing them internally within the firm. They examine the cost advantages for a firm to combine selling with extending trade credit. Potential cost advantages include the following:

1. The merchandise sold may be more valuable if repossessed by the seller than if repossessed by a financial institution. For example if a computer manufacturer sells a large batch of personal computers to a retailer and has to repossess them for nonpayment, the manufacturer has the sales organization to resell them. A bank or a finance company does not have the same facilities and could experience a substantial loss in a resale market.

2. The seller may save costs in credit evaluation by combining it with the information obtained in the selling activity.

3. If the buyer is more vulnerable to opportunistic behavior at the hands of the seller, the extension of credit by the seller bonds the buyer in good faith to behavior by the seller. If the converse relationship obtains, a cash sale is more likely.

In addition to cost advantages, another reason given for the use of trade credit is tax deferral, particularly when the item can be financed as an installment sale. Market power is another variable discussed. Some argue that market power can be exploited through

---

[7]Shehzad L. Mian and Clifford W. Smith, Jr., "Accounts Receivable Management Policy: Theory and Evidence," ms., August 1, 1990.

opportunities for price discrimination in formulating credit terms. If market power is held by financial intermediaries, their monopoly rents can be avoided if the firm extends credit itself.

After discussing incentives to extend trade credit, Mian and Smith next analyze the influence of the structure of sales. An industry with many firms selling to a large number of buyers would involve duplication of the credit analysis of individual buyers. The use of an external factoring concern, which performs the credit analysis, avoids duplication and, therefore, achieves economies. Similarly, there are cost advantages to a credit information firm such as Dun & Bradstreet from selling credit reports on an individual firm to multiple buyers. Larger firms are more likely to establish their own specialized credit department. Similarly, the use of an internal credit department is more likely if the seller uses its own sales force rather than employing outside sales organizations.

Mian and Smith next discuss agency problem aspects of credit management. They argue that secured debt helps avoid stockholder expropriation of creditors. They argue that the use of a captive finance subsidiary is an alternative to secured debt as a means of segregating the relevant cash flows for payments to creditors and other potential agency problems. The passage of the Uniform Commercial Code (UCC) enables a firm to issue a ''floating'' or ''blanket'' lien against a pool of assets and provides a continuing security interest in all present and future collateral of the categories named in the contract.

Mian and Smith then subject the foregoing hypotheses to empirical tests. Their data suggest that the larger, more creditworthy firms establish captive finance companies, but smaller, riskier firms issue accounts receivable secured debt. They conclude that their evidence suggests that the use of captive finance companies allows more flexible contracting opportunities. In contrast to some earlier studies, they find no evidence of bondholder wealth expropriation associated with the formation of captive finance companies.

INVENTORY MANAGEMENT

Manufacturing firms generally have three kinds of inventories: (1) raw materials, (2) work in process, and (3) finished goods. The level of *raw materials inventories* is influenced by anticipated production, seasonality of production, reliability of sources of supply, and the efficiency of scheduling purchases and production operations. *Work-in-process inventory* is strongly influenced by the length of the production period, which is the time between placing raw material in production and completing the finished product. Inventory turnover can be increased by decreasing the production period. One means of accomplishing this is new techniques such as just-in-time (JIT) inventory management. Another means is to buy items rather than make them.

The level of *finished goods inventory* is a matter of coordinating production and sales. The financial manager can stimulate sales by changing credit terms or by granting credit to marginal risks. But whether the goods remain on the books as inventories or as receivables, the financial manager has to finance them. Many times, firms find it desirable to make the sale so that they are one step nearer to realizing cash. The potential profits can outweigh the additional collection risk.

Our primary focus in this section is control of investment in inventories. Inventory models, developed as an aid in this task, have proved extremely useful in minimizing inventory costs. Any procedure that can reduce the investment required to generate a given sales volume will have a beneficial effect on the firm's rate of return and hence on the value of the firm.

Controlling Investments in Inventories

Although wide variations occur, inventory to sales ratios are generally concentrated in the 12 to 20 percent range. The major determinants of investment in inventory are (1) level of sales, (2) length and technical nature of the production processes, and (3) durability versus perishability (the style factors) in the end product. Inventories in the tobacco industry, for example, are large because of the long curing process. Similarly, in the machinery manufacturing industries, inventories are large because of the long work-in-process period. However, inventories in oil and gas production are low, because raw materials and goods in process are small in relation to sales. In the canning industry, average inventories are large because of the seasonality of the raw materials.

With respect to durability and style factors, large inventories are found in the hardware and the precious metals industries because durability is great and the style factor is small. Inventories are small in baking because of the perishability of the final product and in printing because the items are manufactured to order.

Managing assets of all kinds is basically an inventory problem; the same method of analysis applies to cash and fixed assets as to inventories themselves. In borrowing money, in buying raw materials for production, or in purchasing plant and equipment, it is cheaper to buy more than just enough to meet immediate needs.

Within limits set by the economics of a firm's industry, there exists a potential for improvement in inventory control from the use of computers and operations research. Although the techniques are far too diverse and complicated for a complete treatment in this text, the financial manager should be prepared to use the contributions of specialists who have developed effective procedures for minimizing the investment in inventory.

We shall limit ourselves to the discussion of the standard model for determining the optimal size of the purchase order, which also implies the optimal investment in inventory and the choice of the time to reorder. This is called the *economic ordering quantity (EOQ)*. The model involves a trade-off between rising and declining costs. Costs such as those related to storage rise with larger inventories, which result from larger orders placed less frequently. But with larger orders placed less frequently, the costs of placing orders would be lower. The goal is to balance these two types of influences to minimize the costs of ordering and of inventory investment. Since entire books and courses are devoted to inventory management, we will not cover the total subject. The model we illustrate, however, is the most widely used and can be developed to encompass any desired extensions.

Classification of Costs

The first step in the process of building an EOQ model is to specify those costs that rise and those that decline with the size and frequency of orders and the resulting levels of inventory. Table 19.5 lists some typical costs associated with ordering goods and with carrying inventories. Part A involves carrying costs. Obviously, the larger the inventory,

Table 19.5 Costs Associated with Inventories

A. Carrying Costs	B. Ordering Costs	C. Costs Related to Safety Stocks
1. Storage costs	1. Cost of placing order or production setup costs	1. Loss of sales
2. Insurance	2. Shipping and handling costs	2. Loss of customer goodwill
3. Property taxes	3. Quantity discounts taken or lost	3. Disruption of production schedules
4. Cost of capital tied up		
5. Depreciation and obsolescence		

the larger will be storage costs, insurance, and property taxes. Warehousing costs are likely to be more directly related to the size of the inventory item rather than to the value of the item purchased. However, all of the other carrying costs vary with the value of the item. For example, both insurance costs and property taxes are related to the value of inventories. In addition, more valuable items in inventory may require extra protection and extra safeguards. Therefore, storage costs and carrying costs are generally expressed as a percentage of inventory value. Since carrying cost is usually measured as some percentage of inventory value, carrying costs are a type of variable cost. As in economics, when a cost is a fixed amount per quantity produced or sold, this is generally regarded as a "variable cost." To the extent that a firm has safety stocks (discussed later), the carrying costs related to a fixed amount of safety stocks may be regarded as a fixed cost.

The second category of costs set forth in Table 19.5 is ordering costs. Ordering costs are the costs of placing an order if the items are purchased from others or production setup costs if produced within the firm. Ordering costs include the costs of running a purchasing department, personnel and telephone or letter writing expenses associated with placing orders, and the costs of preparing specifications. Ordering costs would also include the related costs of receiving and inspecting the material and the costs of paying invoices. Another type of ordering cost is represented by quantity discounts (negative cost), which may be available if the size of the purchase order is large enough.

In practice, it is difficult to draw the line between variable and fixed ordering costs. The basic costs of running an order department, including the salary of the purchasing agent and the cost of typewriters, desks, and telephones, may be regarded as fixed. Given this basic purchasing facility, the cost of increasing the number of orders over a moderate range may be relatively small. As the number of orders increases, it may be necessary at some point to increase the space allocated to the purchasing department, to acquire additional personnel, and so forth. In these situations, the ordering costs become variable.

The third category of costs presented in Table 19.5 is costs related to safety stocks. Safety stocks represent the inventories held by the firm in the effort to avoid running short of goods to meet sales opportunities. If safety stocks are inadequate, the firm will incur lost sales and the loss of customer goodwill. If we are considering an inventory production system, running short may require overtime and other disruptions of production schedules.

Having classified costs associated with inventories, we are now in a position to present the basic inventory model. We shall do this by a specific numerical example for purposes of clarity. We will assume that the Emerson Company expects to achieve a sales volume of 3,600 widgets during 19X0 and that Emerson is quite confident of hitting this target. Further, these sales are expected to be evenly distributed over the year, so inventories will decline smoothly and gradually. The widgets are purchased for $40 each.

The notation and illustrative numerical amounts that we shall use in the analysis are shown in Table 19.6.

Carrying Costs. Field studies indicate that carrying costs vary among companies but are likely to be in the range of 20 to 25 percent of inventory value. Storage and insurance costs are likely to vary with the type of product as well as product value. Obsolescence, shrinkage, and spoilage will be especially influenced by the type of product. For standard, staple items, such costs may be relatively low. For perishables or products with a very important element of style (for example, clothing), obsolescence costs may be very substantial.

We will assume that this is a warehousing model in which the company is not producing the products it sells. Supplies appear all at once and are used uniformly over time. We will assume initially that there is no safety stock. Thus, carrying costs will rise in direct proportion to the average amount of inventory carried. For example, Emerson's cost of capital is 10 percent, and depreciation is estimated to amount to 5 percent per year. Lumping together these and Emerson's other costs of carrying inventory produces a total cost of 25 percent of the investment in inventory.

Defining the percentage cost as C, we can, in general, find the total carrying costs as the percentage carrying cost (C) times the price per unit (P) times the average number of units (A) (which is $Q/2$ since inventory falls evenly to zero during the inventory cycle).

$$\text{Total carrying costs} = (C)(P)(A).$$

If Emerson elects to order only once a year, average inventories will be $3,600/2 = 1,800$ units, and the cost of carrying the inventory will be $0.25 \times \$40 \times 1,800 = \$18,000$. If the company orders twice a year and hence has average inventories that are half as large, total carrying costs will decline to $9,000, and so on. For our example, total carrying costs will equal $\$10 \times Q/2$, or $\$5Q$.

TABLE 19.6   Notation and Data Inputs for EOQ Example

A = average inventory
C = carrying cost expressed as a percentage of inventory purchase price = 25% per year
CP = carrying cost expressed in dollars per unit of inventory = $10 per year
EOQ = economic order quantity
F = fixed ordering costs = $5,400 per year
N = number of orders placed per year = U/Q
P = purchase price per unit of inventory = $40
Q = order quantity
S = safety stock
T = total inventory costs
U = annual usage in units = 3,600
V = variable ordering costs per order = $125

Ordering Costs. The fixed costs of the order department in our example are estimated to be $5,400. There are in addition costs of placing an order — for example, preparing specifications, telephone calls, and delivery charges. Total variable ordering costs will be the cost of placing an order (V) times the number of orders placed (N). The company's cost of ordering, shipping, and receiving, which we define as V, is $125 per order.

$$\text{Total ordering costs} = F + (V)(N)$$
$$= \$5,400 + \$125(U/Q)$$
$$= \$5,400 + \$125(3,600)/Q$$

The EOQ Model

The economic order quantity (EOQ) model can be developed algebraically and graphically. Although total inventory costs are affected by both fixed and variable ordering and carrying costs, the EOQ is determined solely by variable inventory costs. The intersection point of the (rising) variable carrying costs curve with the (declining) variable ordering costs curve lies directly below the minimum point of the total inventory costs curve, as illustrated in Figure 19.3, where T^* is the minimum level of total inventory costs, and Q^* is the optimal quantity of inventory for periodic reordering, that is, the EOQ.

We can also determine the optimal order quantity algebraically. This is the quantity, Q, that minimizes total costs, T. Total inventory costs (T) can be defined as the sum of variable carrying costs, variable ordering costs, and fixed ordering costs.

$$T = CPA + VN + F \tag{19.1}$$

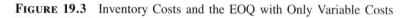

FIGURE 19.3   Inventory Costs and the EOQ with Only Variable Costs

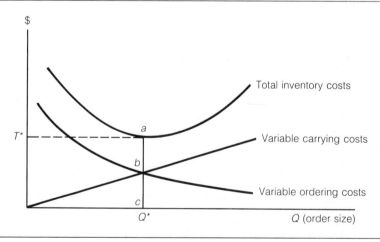

Recognizing that $A = Q/2$ and $N = U/Q$, Equation 19.1 can be written as an explicit function of Q:

$$T = CP\left(\frac{Q}{2}\right) + V\left(\frac{U}{Q}\right) + F \qquad (19.2)$$

$$= CP\left(\frac{Q}{2}\right) + VUQ^{-1} + F.$$

We differentiate Equation 19.2 with respect to Q, set the result equal to zero, and solve for Q. We thereby minimize total costs and obtain the basic economic order quantity model:[8]

$$\frac{dT}{dQ} = \frac{CP}{2} - \frac{VU}{Q^2} = 0 \qquad (19.3)$$

$$\frac{CP}{2} = \frac{VU}{Q^2}$$

$$Q^2 = \frac{2VU}{CP}$$

$$Q = \sqrt{\frac{2VU}{CP}} = Q^* = \text{EOQ}.$$

In the Emerson case, we find

$$\text{EOQ} = \sqrt{\frac{2(\$125)(3,600)}{(0.25)(\$40)}}$$

$$= \sqrt{\frac{\$900,000}{\$10}}$$

$$= \sqrt{90,000}$$

$$= 300 \text{ units per order.}$$

If the EOQ is ordered 12 times a year ($3,600/300 = 12$), or every 30 days, the total costs of ordering and carrying inventories will be minimized.

Relationship between Sales and Inventories

Intuitively, we would suppose that the higher the ordering or processing costs, the less frequently orders should be placed. However, the higher the carrying costs of inventory, the more frequently stocks should be ordered. These two features are incorporated in the EOQ formula. Notice also that if Emerson's sales had been estimated at 900 units, the EOQ would have been 150, while the average inventory would have been 75 units instead of the 150 called for with sales of 3,600 units. Thus, a quadrupling of sales leads to only a doubling of inventories. The general rule is that the EOQ increases with the *square root* of sales, so any increase in sales results in a less than proportionate increase in inventories.

---

[8]When we differentiate, fixed costs do not vary with Q, so they drop out.

FIGURE 19.4   Inventory Costs and the EOQ with Fixed Ordering Costs

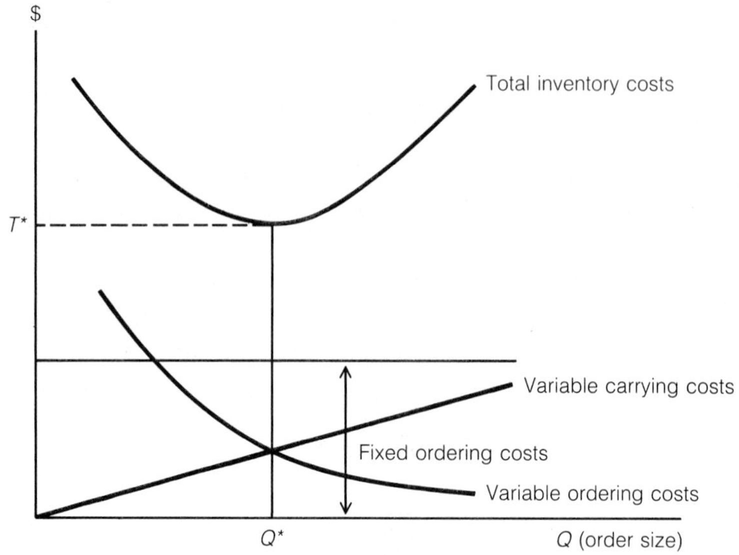

The financial manager should keep this in mind in establishing standards for inventory control.

We will now examine the effect of fixed ordering costs on the properties of the EOQ model. From the derivation of the EOQ model, we know that

$$Q^{*2} = 2VU/CP.$$

Rearranging terms yields

$$CP(Q^*/2) = V(U/Q^*). \qquad (19.4)$$

Note that $(Q^*/2) = A^*$, the optimal average inventory, and that $(U/Q^*) = N^*$, the optimal number of orders placed. Thus, Equation 19.4 can be written as

$$CPA^* = VN^*. \qquad (19.5)$$

Equation 19.5 indicates that, at the order quantity where the total inventory costs are minimized, the variable carrying costs equal the variable ordering costs. Figure 19.3 illustrates this case. It can be proved that point b, the intersection between the variable ordering costs curve and the variable carrying costs curve, lies midway between points a and c, and is directly below the minimum point on the total inventory costs curve.

Note that the fixed ordering costs are not a function of the order size Q. The existence of F merely raises the level of the total inventory costs as shown in Figure 19.4. It has nothing to do with the determination of EOQ, and, thus, the minimum point on the total cost curve can still be proved to lie directly above the intersection of the variable carrying and variable ordering costs curves.

FIGURE 19.5   Demand Forecast with Certainty

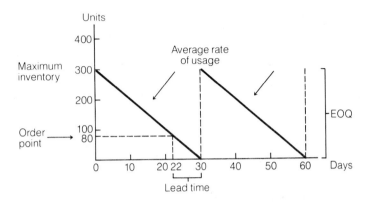

For the Emerson example with fixed ordering costs, the total costs of ordering and carrying inventories are shown in Equation 19.6.

$$T = CPA + VN + F \qquad\qquad\qquad (19.6)$$

$$= CP\left(\frac{Q}{2}\right) + V\left(\frac{U}{Q}\right) + F$$

$$= (.25)(40)\left(\frac{300}{2}\right) + \$125\left(\frac{3,600}{300}\right) + \$5,400$$

$$= \$1,500 + \$1,500 + \$5,400$$

$$= \$8,400$$

This is Emerson's lowest possible cost of ordering and carrying inventories.

The EOQ model gives us the optimum, or cost minimizing, order quantity for given levels of usage (U) and inventory carrying cost (C). Knowing the EOQ and continuing our assumption that the pattern of inventory across time is a sawtooth as shown in Figure 19.5, we can find the optimal average inventory as

$$A = \frac{EOQ}{2} = \frac{300}{2} = 150 \text{ units.} \qquad\qquad (19.7)$$

Emerson will thus have an average inventory investment of 150 units at $40 each, or $6,000.

The basic EOQ model assumes a predictable sales activity, a constant usage over the year, and an immediate replenishment of the inventory stocks. For the Emerson Company, with an annual demand of 3,600 units and an EOQ of 300 units, there is a need to order 12 times each year, once every 30 days. If the beginning and ending inventory balances are zero, the maximum inventory would be 300 units, with an average of 150 units. The slope of the daily usage line is 10 units. We now can extend the analysis to see what happens (1) if inventory stocks are not replenished instantaneously and (2) if inventory usage is uncertain instead of constant throughout the year.

Inventory Policy with Lead Time

We can relax the assumption of instantaneous order and delivery. Let us assume Emerson requires eight days to place an order and receive the delivery. In order not to interrupt its sales activities, Emerson must keep an eight-day stock, or 80 units, on hand whenever it places an order (Daily usage × Lead time = 10 × 8 = 80). The stock that must be on hand at the time of ordering is defined as the order point; whenever inventory falls below this point, a new order will be placed. If Emerson's inventory control process is automated, the computer will generate an order when the stock on hand falls to 80 units.[9] These conditions are reflected in Figure 19.5.

EOQ Model with Uncertainty: Safety Stocks

To this point, we have assumed that usage (demand) is known with certainty and is uniform throughout time and that order lead time never varies. Either or both of these assumptions could be incorrect, so it is necessary to modify the EOQ model to allow for this possibility. This modification generally takes the form of adding a *safety stock* to average inventories.

An optimal policy will minimize the total cost of the safety stock. The increased carrying costs of the safety stock must be traded off against the costs of stockout. The increased carrying costs are the annual carrying costs per unit (CP) times the safety stock (S).[10] The annual stockout cost depends on four factors:

Expected (E) annual stockout cost = Unit stockout cost × Units of stockout
× Probability of stockout in a cycle
× Number of inventory cycles per year.

If we return to our initial assumption that inventory is delivered, not produced, then the number of inventory cycles per year for the Emerson Company is $N = U/\text{EOQ} = 3,600/300 = 12$. Thus, Emerson Company would order every 30 days if there were no uncertainty about the rate of inventory usage. We assume, for the time being, that the order lead time is also 30 days. Suppose that the Emerson Company sales force has provided estimates of the usage rate during one inventory cycle as shown in Table 19.7. Note that the EOQ in a world without any uncertainty was 300 units. This is the unweighted average usage rate in Table 19.7, but actual usage could be as high as 450 units or as low as 150 units in a 30-day period.

---

[9]If a new order must be placed before a prior order is received — that is, the normal delivery lead time is longer than the time between orders — then what is called a "goods in transit inventory" builds up. This complicates matters somewhat, but the simplest solution to the problem is to deduct goods in transit when calculating the order point. In other words, the order point would be calculated as (Order point = Lead time × Daily usage − Goods in transit).

[10]Note that we have multiplied CP by the *entire* safety stock, not by one-half of the safety stock. The reason is that the EOQ represents the expected (or average) usage rate. There is a 50-50 chance of using more or less (see Table 19.7). Hence, the entire safety stock is also the average safety stock.

TABLE 19.7   The Distribution of Usage during One 30-Day Inventory Cycle

Usage/30-Day Period	Daily Usage	Probability
150 units	5.00 units	.04
200	6.67	.08
250	8.33	.20
300	10.00	.36
350	11.67	.20
400	13.33	.08
450	15.00	.04

If we are also told that the stockout cost is $5.21 per unit, it should be possible to determine the optimal safety stock. For example, suppose we decide to carry 150 units of safety stock. Then, as shown in Table 19.8, we start with 450 units at the beginning of the inventory cycle (that is, the sum of an EOQ of 300 units and the 150-unit safety stock). There is no chance of stockout, and hence the expected (E) stockout cost is zero. However, the expected carrying cost is

$$E(\text{Carrying cost per 30-day cycle}) = \left(\frac{\$10 \text{ per year}}{12 \text{ cycles per year}}\right) \times \text{Safety stock}$$

$$= \left(\frac{\$10}{12}\right)150 = \$125.$$

Thus, the total cost of a 150-unit safety stock is $125. Alternately, we could choose a 100-unit safety stock. As shown in Table 19.8, the expected stockout cost in this case is $10.42 because the company expects to stockout 4 percent of the time at a cost of $260.50. Carrying costs have decreased to $83.33, and hence the 100-unit safety stock is superior to the 150-unit policy because total costs have dropped from $125 to $93.75.

TABLE 19.8   Safety Stock Computations (30-Day Inventory Cycle)

Safety Stock	Total Inventory	Stockout Quantity	Stockout Cost	Probability	Expected Stockout Cost	Expected Carrying Cost	Expected Total Cost
150	450	0	0	0	0	$125.00	$125.00
100	400	50	$260.50	.04	$ 10.42	83.33	93.75
50	350	50	260.50	.08	20.84		
		100	521.00	.04	20.84		
					$ 41.68	41.67	83.35
0	300	50	260.50	.20	$ 52.10		
		100	521.00	.08	41.68		
		150	781.50	.04	31.26		
					$125.04	0	125.04

The optimal policy is the one where expected stockout costs equal expected carrying costs. In our example, this is a safety stock of 50 units. Emerson Company expects to stockout 12 percent of the time under this policy. Emerson's initial order would be 350 units instead of 300 units, and subsequent orders would be for 300 units each.

The lead time is important in this type of analysis. For example, suppose we reduce the assumed lead time from 30 days (equal to the inventory cycle) to only 5 days.[11] The maximum usage is 15 units per day, so if we set our order point at $5 \times 15 = 75$ units, we will never stockout. When the lead time is less than the inventory cycle, it is necessary to compute the optimal safety stock using the lead time instead of the inventory cycle.

Note that even with a safety stock, the EOQ remains at 300 units. The increase in total carrying costs resulting from an addition of a fixed amount for carrying the safety stocks of 50 units at $10 per unit does not affect the cost minimizing quantity. And, as we shall demonstrate, the minimum point of the total inventory cost curve still lies directly above the intersection of the variable ordering and variable carrying costs curves.

Given a safety stock (S), which has annual expected stockout costs of K, total inventory costs are

$$T = CPA + VN + F + CPS + K.$$

Since the EOQ is not a function of the fixed ordering costs, nor a function of the costs for carrying the safety stock, the existence of expected stockout costs and the costs for carrying the safety stock merely raises further the level of the total inventory costs. Therefore, the same principle as shown for the simplest case with no fixed costs remains valid for this case, which is illustrated in Figure 19.6.

For our example, with a safety stock of 50 units, Emerson's total inventory costs will increase to

$$
\begin{aligned}
T = \quad & CPA && + && VN && + && F && + && CPS && + && K \\
= \;& (.25)(40)\left(\frac{300}{2}\right) + \$125\left(\frac{3,600}{300}\right) + \$5,400 + (.25)(40)(50) + 44.68(12) \\
= \;& \quad \$1,500 \quad + \quad \$1,500 \quad + \$5,400 + \quad \$500 \quad + \quad \$500 \\
= \;& \quad \$9,400.
\end{aligned}
$$

Effects of Inflation on EOQ

During inflation, formal models such as the EOQ must be adjusted. As freight costs rise, the cost of placing an order may increase rapidly. Purchase prices may also rise abruptly and repeatedly. Also, in recent years, the cost of capital has changed rapidly. Therefore, the values used in the EOQ equation may not remain constant for any appreciable length of time. If so, the optimal order quantity will not remain fixed. Some companies will need greater flexibility in the timing of their orders than that afforded by the automatic order point because they may be able to buy marginal production at reduced prices. Also, certain companies may stockpile inventories, taking advantage of the opportunity to purchase supplies before major price increases and gaining protection against shortages.

---

[11]The assumed lead time is known with certainty.

FIGURE 19.6   Inventory Costs and EOQ with Two Types of Fixed Costs

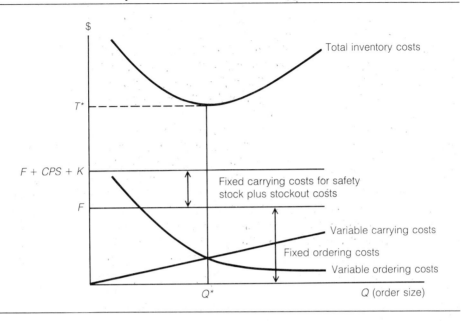

Therefore, during periods of inflation and tight money, a firm may need more flexible inventory management as it attempts to take advantage of bargains and to provide for future contingencies. The basic logic of the inventory model remains intact: Some costs will rise with larger inventories, and others will fall. Although an optimum is still there to be found, it may change and require repeated reassessments.

New Inventory Control Developments

Our emphasis thus far has been on the relatively formal EOQ model of the optimal order quantity, which also implies the investment in inventories. This provides a useful framework for inventory management. However, important developments impacting the fundamental philosophy of inventory management and manufacturing methods generally have taken place. During the last two decades, the increasing pressures of international competition have forced U.S. companies to attempt to imitate the management practices that have made foreign firms formidable competitors.

Production methods and philosophy have been undergoing fundamental changes, altering manufacturing facilities and methods of operations. The assembly line system with long production runs for a given product setup has been yielding to an emphasis on flexible manufacturing systems. More intense competition to produce better products coupled with consumer desires for increased variety and product change have led to an emphasis on flexible manufacturing systems. Financial management of receivables and inventories has had to join in the effort of firms seeking to improve their competitive position.

As manufacturing methods have changed, changes in the philosophy of inventory control have also occurred. The shift in philosophic approach has been supported by the use of computer-based control systems that enable companies to achieve fast reaction time in providing information on all aspects of their operating activities. These computer systems seek to relate inventory management to production operations. One well-known form of computerized inventory control systems has been termed material requirements planning (MRP). Improved inventory information control systems have supported innovations in the nature of inventory management itself. One of these is the development of the just-in-time (JIT) system called *kanban* by the Japanese. The JIT system emphasizes a planned and controlled manufacturing system, which enables the amount of investment in inventory to be substantially reduced. JIT requires an understanding of the total manufacturing flow process.

JIT was introduced at General Motors when, in a joint venture with Toyota, it reopened its Fremont, California production facility to manufacture a modified version of the Toyota Corolla. The entire manufacturing flow system was revamped. Less than half of the factory floor space was required compared with the previous assembly line system. An additional building was erected to house huge presses for turning out the body shells. The setup for these huge presses to produce a different form of body shell could be accomplished within a matter of one or two hours. The relationships with suppliers of materials and parts were reformulated. More information exchange had to take place and with greater frequency. Suppliers had to change their methods of operation so that with better coordination they could provide materials and parts in a more timely fashion without having to increase their own inventory investments excessively. Since suppliers did not produce large quantities for long production runs, JIT enabled the manufacturer to provide more prompt feedback on defects or specification changes to which the supplier, in turn, could quickly make adjustments.

We emphasize that what is involved is an entire philosophic approach to manufacturing processes rather than inventory management alone. Changes in inventory methods could not have been made without rethinking the entire approach to manufacturing methods. In turn, these new approaches to manufacturing processes, including inventory planning and control methods, require a change in practices and attitudes of workers and plant supervision. Fundamental changes in the approach to human resource management are, therefore, also involved. Much new learning in management systems is required. Here is another example of our basic approach to managerial finance. Models are useful tools. But much more important is the broader philosophic approach to management systems. It is essential that financial management be integrated with the broader aspects of operating management as well as with the broader framework of the firm's strategic planning.

SUMMARY

In establishing a credit policy, a firm formulates its credit standards and its credit terms. Credit standards that are too strict will lose sales; credit standards that are too easy will result in excessive bad debt losses. To determine optimal credit standards, the firm relates the marginal costs of credit to the marginal profits on the increased sales. Individual customers are evaluated on the five Cs of credit: character, capacity, capital, collateral, and conditions, all of which indicate the likelihood that the buyer will pay its obligations. Credit analysis and the evaluation of prospective customers typically include analysis of financial ratios, the average age of accounts receivable, and record of past payments. They also incorporate the experience of the credit manager in similar situations.

The terms of credit specify the credit period and the use of cash discounts. Longer credit periods stimulate sales, but the optimal credit period balances the marginal profits on increased sales against the costs of carrying the higher amounts of accounts receivable. Similarly, an optimal cash discount policy balances the benefit of increased sales and the costs of discounts taken.

Our discussion of evaluating alternative credit policies recognized the interdependence of current asset variables. Credit policy changes can involve overall changes in the level and composition of all current assets. The Sartoris-Hill credit policy decision model uses a capital budgeting framework to determine the effects of alternative credit policies on the value of the firm.

Computerized accounts receivable can provide a valuable information tool to credit managers. Computer records include such information as the amount currently owed, the customer's maximum credit line, and record of past payments. The computer can flag past-due accounts, make note of accounts approaching their credit limit, and even perform some selected credit decisions. It can also provide summary information on all accounts or help analyze customers in a specific industry. Credit terms and policies are likely to be impacted by these developments.

New theoretical approaches are reinterpreting credit management practices and testing their effectiveness. Fresh insights are likely to bring new developments in the theory and practice of receivables management. We have emphasized the importance of relating both sales and credit policies to the goals of enhancing enterprise value.

Inventories — raw materials, work-in-process, and finished goods — are necessary in most businesses. New systems for controlling the level of inventories have been designed. These systems frequently use computers for keeping records of all the items in stock. An inventory control model that considers anticipated sales, ordering costs, and carrying costs can be used to determine EOQs for each item.

The basic inventory model recognizes that certain costs (carrying costs) rise as average inventory holdings increase but that certain other costs (ordering costs and stockout costs) fall as these holdings increase. The two sets of costs make up the total cost of ordering and carrying inventories, and the EOQ model is designed to locate an optimal order size that will minimize total inventory costs.

Recent developments include material requirements planning (MRP) and just-in-time (JIT) inventory planning and control systems. They require sophisticated computer backup as well as closer relationships with suppliers and more enlightened human resource utilization. In addition, fundamental changes in manufacturing facilities, production methods, and philosophy have been stimulated.

Accounts receivable and inventories together represent the major portion of a manufacturing firm's current assets and hence a significant proportion of total assets. Their effective management is essential to control of costs and investments. Equally important are their broader impacts. Receivables management can be used to build good relationships with customers and to stimulate increased profitable sales. New developments in inventory management have been associated with a reorientation of management of human resources and a new philosophy of manufacturing processes.

QUESTIONS

19.1   Assume that a firm sells on terms of net 30 and that its accounts are, on the average, 30 days overdue. What will its investment in receivables be if its annual credit sales are approximately $720,000?

19.2   Evaluate this statement: It is difficult to judge the performance of many of our employees but not that of the credit manager. If the credit manager is performing perfectly, credit losses are zero; the higher our losses (as a percent of sales), the worse is the performance.

19.3   Apco Corporation's 19X1 sales were $990,000. In April 19X1, the accounts receivable balance was $41,250; by July 19X1, accounts receivable had more than doubled to $96,250. Calculate the Days' Sales Outstanding for each period. Did the increase necessarily represent a problem for Apco?

19.4   How would a new business go about setting up credit standards? Would its credit policies be likely to vary from those of established firms in the same line of business?

19.5   Explain how the credit terms of a firm's suppliers can affect the terms offered to the firm's customers.

19.6   Inventory decision models are designed to help minimize the cost of obtaining and carrying inventory. Describe the basic nature of the fundamental inventory control model and specifically discuss the nature of increasing costs, decreasing costs, and total costs.

19.7   What are the probable effects of the following on inventory holdings?
   a.   Manufacture of a part formerly purchased from an outside supplier
   b.   Greater use of air freight
   c.   Increase, from 7 to 17, in the number of styles produced
   d.   Large price reductions to your firm from a manufacturer of bathing suits if the suits are purchased in December and January

19.8   What factors are likely to reduce the holdings of inventory in relation to sales in the future? What factors will tend to increase the ratio? What, in your judgment, is the net effect?

19.9   Explain how a firm can reduce its investment in inventory by having its supplier hold raw materials inventories and its customers hold finished goods inventories. What are the limitations of such a policy?

19.10   Discuss new developments in inventory management systems and their implications for production techniques and philosophy.

PROBLEMS

19.1   The Fulton Company has been reviewing its credit policies. The credit standards it has been applying have resulted in annual credit sales of $5 million. Its average collection period is 30 days, with a bad debt loss ratio of 1 percent. Because persistent inflation has caused deterioration in the financial position of many of its customers, Fulton is considering a reduction in its credit standards. As a result, it expects incremental credit sales of $400,000, on which the average collection period (ACP) would be 60 days and on which the bad debt loss (BDL) ratio would be 3 percent. The variable cost ratio (VCR) to sales for Fulton is 70 percent. The required return on investment in receivables is 15 percent. Evaluate the relaxation in credit standards that Fulton is considering. (Use .04 percent per 365 days/year.)

19.2   Instead of relaxing credit standards, Fulton is considering simply lengthening credit terms from net 20 to net 50, a procedure that would increase the average collection period from 30 days to 60 days. Under the new policy, Fulton expects incremental sales to be $500,000 and the new bad debt loss ratio to rise to 2 percent on *all* sales. Assume all other returns hold. Evaluate the lengthening in credit terms that Fulton is considering.

19.3   Gulf Distributors makes all sales on a credit basis; once each year, it routinely evaluates the creditworthiness of all its customers. The evaluation procedure ranks customers from 1 to 5, in order of increasing risk. Results of the ranking are given below.

Category	Percentage Bad Debts	Average Collection Period (Days)	Credit Decision	Annual Sales Lost through Credit Restrictions
1	None	10	Unlimited credit	None
2	1.0	12	Unlimited credit	None
3	3.0	20	Limited credit	$360,000
4	9.0	60	Limited credit	$180,000
5	30.0	90	No credit	$360,000

The variable cost ratio is 75 percent. The opportunity cost of investment in receivables is 15 percent. What will be the effect on profitability of extending full credit to Category 3? To Category 4? To Category 5? (Use a 360-day year.)

19.4   Milburn Auto Parts is considering changing its credit terms from 2/15, net 30 to 3/10, net 30 in order to speed collections. At present, 60 percent of Milburn's customers take the 2 percent discount. Under the new terms, this number is expected to rise to 70 percent, reducing the average collection period from 25 to 22 days. Bad-debt losses are expected to rise from 1 percent to the 2 percent level. However, the more generous cash discount terms are expected to increase credit sales from $800,000 to $1 million per year. Milburn's variable cost ratio is 80 percent, and its cost of accounts receivable is 15 percent. Evaluate the change. (Use .04 percent per 365 days/year.)

19.5   Charles Roberts, the new credit manager of the Baskin Corporation, was alarmed to find that Baskin sells on credit terms of net 90 days, when industrywide credit terms are net 30 days. On annual credit sales of $2.5 million, Baskin currently averages 95 days' sales in accounts receivable. Roberts estimates that tightening the credit terms to 30 days will reduce annual sales to $2,375,000 but that accounts receivable will drop to 35 days sales and the bad debt loss ratio drop from 3 percent of sales to 1 percent of sales. Baskin's variable cost ratio is 85 percent. If Baskin's opportunity cost of funds is 18 percent, should the change be made? (Use .05 percent per 365 days/year.)

19.6   You are given the following information:

Annual demand: 2,800 units
Cost per order placed: $5.25
Carrying cost: 20%
Price per unit: $30

a.   Fill in the blanks in the table below.

Order size	35	56	70	140	200	2,800
Number of orders	___	___	___	___	___	___
Average inventory	___	___	___	___	___	___
Carrying cost	___	___	___	___	___	___
Order cost	___	___	___	___	___	___
Total cost	___	___	___	___	___	___

b.   What is the EOQ?

19.7   The following relationships for inventory purchase and storage costs have been established for the Norman Corporation.
   (1) Orders must be placed in multiples of 100 units.
   (2) Requirements for the year are 180,000 units (U). (Use 50 weeks in a year for calculations.)
   (3) The purchase price per unit (P) is $2.
   (4) The carrying cost (C) is 50 percent of the purchase price of goods.
   (5) The cost per order placed (V) is $400.
   (6) Desired safety stock (S) is 10,000 units (on hand initially).
   (7) One week is required for delivery.
   a.   What is the most economical order quantity?
   b.   What is the optimal number of orders to be placed?
   c.   At what inventory level should a reorder be made?

19.8   The following relationships for inventory purchase and storage costs have been established for the Lomer Fabricating Corporation.
   (1) Orders must be placed in multiples of 100 units.
   (2) Requirements for the year are 400,000 units (U). (Use 50 weeks in a year for calculations.)
   (3) The purchase price per unit (P) is $2.
   (4) The carrying cost (C) is 20 percent of the purchase price of goods.
   (5) The cost per order placed (V) is $50.
   (6) Desired safety stock (S) is 10,000 units (on hand initially).
   (7) One week is required for delivery.
   a.   What is the most economical order quantity?
   b.   What is the optimal number of orders to be placed?
   c.   At what inventory level should a reorder be made?

19.9 The following relationships for inventory purchases and storage costs have been established for the Milton Processing Corporation.

    (1) Orders must be placed in multiples of 100 units.

    (2) Requirements for the year are 500,000 units (U). (Use 50 weeks in a year for calculations.)

    (3) The purchase price per unit (P) is $5.

    (4) The carrying cost (C) is 20 percent of the purchase price of goods.

    (5) The cost per order placed (V) is $25.

    (6) Desired safety stock (S) is 10,000 units (on hand initially).

    (7) One week is required for delivery.

  a. What is the most economical order quantity?

  b. What is the optimal number of orders to be placed?

  c. At what inventory level should a reorder be made?

  d. If annual unit sales double, what is the percent increase in the EOQ? What is the elasticity of EOQ with respect to sales (percent change in EOQ/percent change in sales)?

  e. If the purchase price per unit doubles, what is the percent change in EOQ? What is the elasticity of EOQ with respect to purchase price per unit?

19.10 Professors Tiernan and Tanner have identified the variables which determine the degree of sensitivity of total inventory costs to order quantity.[12] Their model can be briefly summarized within our framework. Recall Equation 19.2 reproduced below:

$$T = CP(Q/2) + V(U/Q) + F. \qquad (19.2)$$

This can be slightly rearranged as shown in Equation 19.2a:

$$T = F + VU/Q + \frac{CP}{2}(Q). \qquad (19.2a)$$

Their numerical example illustrates the factors that determine the sensitivity of inventory costs to order size. To illustrate, assume that fixed costs are $20 and that total usage (U) is 1,000 units. One set of curves is defined by Cases A and B, where ordering costs and carrying costs are as follows:

	V	CP
A	.10	.01
B	50.00	.01

  a. What are the resulting equations in the format of Equation 19.2a for Cases A and B?

  b. In contrast are Cases C and D, the data for which are presented below:

	V	CP
C	.10	20
D	.50	20

What are the resulting equations?

---

[12]Tiernan and Tanner [1983].

    c. Graph the four sets of equations identifying the EOQ.

    d. Comment on the sensitivity of total costs to order size for each case.

19.11 (*Use the computer diskette, File name: 19CRDTMG, Credit Management.*)

    a. Firm A is proposing to relax its credit terms so that its average collection period rises from 40 days to 50 days, while its daily sales rise from 200 to 260 units. Price per unit remains the same at $500; cost per unit remains the same at $350. The bad debt loss ratio rises from 2 percent to 3 percent. The daily interest rate is 0.05 percent. Enter these proposed changes in the table. Is the NPV of this change in credit terms positive or negative?

        (1) If the bad debt loss ratio had risen to 4 percent, how would the NPV be affected?

        (2) If the bad debt loss ratio had risen to 10 percent, how would the NPV be affected?

        (3) If daily sales had increased to 350 units, but all other conditions were as in Part (a), how would NPV be affected?

        (4) If the relaxation of credit terms had enabled the firm to raise its price from $500 to $550 per unit, and all other conditions were as in the original Part (a), how would NPV be affected?

    b. Now, going back to the original situation, Firm A changes its credit standards, so that it now accepts customers with financial profiles that are much weaker. As a consequence, it is able to increase its sales by 100 units (from 200 units to 300 units). The bad debt loss ratio, however, becomes 5 percent, and the average collection period on the incremental sales now becomes 60 days. Is the NPV of the policy change positive or negative? (Hint: For incremental sales, use only "Proposed Policy" and NPV$_1$ equation to test whether incremental NPV is positive or negative.)

        (1) To what would the bad debt loss ratio have to rise in order for the NPV of relaxing credit standards to become negative?

        (2) How does this bad debt loss ratio compare to the contribution margin?

    c. Suppose we now consider Firm B, for which the contribution margin is $50 per unit, instead of $150 per unit as in the above questions. Do the same analysis as in Part (b).

    d. Hamilton Fixtures is rethinking its credit policies. It has collected credit data on each of its major customers and wonders to which categories of customers it should relax credit restrictions. First, its customers must be sorted in order of their credit worthiness. Next, it must analyze the change in NPV from extending credit to credit categories 1–4. Which categories of customers should be offered credit?

    e. Now repeat the same analysis for Brandon's Deli and Jones's Van Detailing. Replace with new customers, sort in order of creditworthiness, and analyze resulting NPVs for each of the four credit categories. Which categories of customers should be offered credit?

    f. Now make up your own question. You may vary price, cost, sales, bad debt rate, collection period, and interest rate. Compare current policy with any changes you might consider, as entered in "Proposed Policy."

19.12 (*Use the computer diskette, File name: 19INVMGT, Inventory Management.*)

a. For each of firms A, B, C, and D, do the following:

(1) Look at the calculation of EOQ (Screen #3).

(2) Call up the graph.

(3) Look at the table of total inventory costs and its components (Screen #4). At the lowest total inventory costs, what is the relation between variable ordering costs and variable carrying costs?

b. For which firm is EOQ the largest? Smallest? Why?

c. For which firm is the EOQ relatively insensitive to order quantity (flat total cost of inventory)? Why is this so?

d. Suppose that for Firm A, the estimate of variable ordering costs is off by 50 percent. (Replace variable ordering costs of 400 with 600. Then replace with 267.) How is EOQ affected?

e. Use four examples to determine the sensitivity of EOQ. First, set variable ordering costs to 60 and carrying costs to 25. Then use 45 and 15, 60 and 15, 45 and 25, respectively.

f. If variable ordering costs are high (for example, 200) and variable carrying costs are low (for example, 2), what is EOQ? Now reverse the numbers. Compare the EOQs.

g. Could you make a similar prediction, if both costs were high (500 and 500, for example) or both were low (2 and 2, for example)?

h. Make up your own questions by varying any assumptions.

SELECTED REFERENCES

Altman, Edward I., "Financial Ratios, Discriminant Analysis and the Prediction of Corporate Bankruptcy," *Journal of Finance*, 23 (September 1968), pp. 589–609.

Carpenter, Michael D., and Miller, Jack E., "A Reliable Framework for Monitoring Accounts Receivable," *Financial Management*, 8 (Winter 1979), pp. 37–40.

Copeland, Thomas E., and Khoury, Nabil, "A Theory of Credit Extensions with Default Risk and Systematic Risk," *The Engineering Economist*, (1981), pp. 35–51.

Dyl, Edward A., "Another Look at the Evaluation of Investments in Accounts Receivable," *Financial Management*, 6 (Winter 1977), pp. 67–70.

Hill, Ned C., and Riener, Kenneth D., "Determining the Cash Discount in the Firm's Credit Policy," *Financial Management*, 8 (Spring 1979), pp. 68–73.

Hill, Ned C.; Wood, Robert A.; and Sorenson, Dale R., "Factors Influencing Credit Policy:

A Survey," *Journal of Cash Management*, 1 (December 1981), pp. 38–47.

Kim, E. Han; McConnell, John J.; and Greenwood, Paul R., "Capital Structure Rearrangement and Me-First Rules in an Efficient Capital Market," *Journal of Finance*, 32 (June 1977), pp. 789–810.

Kim, Yong H., and Atkins, Joseph C., "Evaluating Investments in Accounts Receivable: A Maximizing Framework," *Journal of Finance*, 33 (May 1978), pp. 403–412.

Kim, Yong H., and Chung, Kee H., "Inventory Management Under Uncertainty: A Financial Theory for the Transactions Motive," *Managerial and Decision Economics*, 10 (December 1989), pp. 291–298.

Lewellen, W. G., and Johnson, R. W., "Better Way to Monitor Accounts Receivable," *Harvard Business Review*, 50 (May-June 1972), pp. 101–109.

Mian, Shehzad, and Smith, Clifford W., Jr., "Accounts Receivable Management Policy: Theory and Evidence," ms., August 1, 1990.

Sartoris, William, and Hill, Ned C., "A Generalized Cash Flow Approach to Short-Term Financial Decisions," *Journal of Finance,* 38 (May 1983), pp. 349–360.

————, "Evaluating Credit Policy Alternatives: A Present Value Framework," *The Journal of Financial Research,* 4 (Spring 1981), pp. 81–89.

Smith, Janet K., "Trade Credit and Information Asymmetry," *Journal of Finance,* (September 1987), pp. 863–872.

Stone, B. K., "Payments-Pattern Approach to Forecasting and Control of Accounts Receivable," *Financial Management,* 5 (1976), pp. 65–82.

Tiernan, Frank M., and Tanner, Dennis A., "How Economic Order Quantity Controls Inventory Expense," *Financial Executive,* 51 (July 1983), pp. 46–52.

CHAPTER 20

Short-Term Financial Management

In Chapters 18 and 19 we began with a discussion of short-term planning with emphasis on the role of cash budgeting. We then analyzed policies for managing cash, marketable securities, accounts receivable, and inventories. These comprise the current assets section of the balance sheet. In this chapter we treat the relations between current assets and current liabilities and their financing. Formerly, this was called working capital policy. While usage varies, working capital is generally defined in financial reports as current assets minus current liabilities. Some refer to this measure as net working capital, but if working capital is what remains after deducting current liabilities, it is redundant to add the word, "net."

Working capital policy was defined to encompass all aspects of the management of both current assets and current liabilities. Short-term financial management is the term now widely used in place of working capital management. The concept of "short-term financial management" covers all decisions of an organization involving cash flows in the short run with emphasis on the management of investments in current assets and their financing.[1]

Short-term financing is defined as debt originally scheduled for repayment within one year. A variety of short-term credits are available to the firm, and the financial manager must know the advantages and disadvantages of each. In this chapter, we evaluate the three major sources of funds with short maturities. Ranked in descending order by volume of credit supplied, they are (1) trade credit among firms, (2) loans from commercial banks, and (3) commercial paper.

---

[1]William L. Sartoris and Ned C. Hill, "Innovations in Short-Term Financial Management," *Business Horizons*, 32 (November-December 1989), pp. 56–64.

Short-term credits are often secured with some form of collateral. Hence, we will also discuss two common methods for securing loans: accounts receivable financing and inventory financing.

In addition, exotic new financial instruments and sources have been developed in seeking to create provisions attractive to issuers and investors with different desired patterns of investment, returns, and risk. These financial innovations associated with financial engineering have taken place in both domestic and international financing markets.

Short-term financial management includes a number of aspects that make it an important topic for study:

1. Surveys indicate that the largest portion of a financial manager's time is devoted to the day-by-day internal operations of the firm, which can appropriately be subsumed under the heading of short-term financial management.

2. Characteristically, current assets represent more than half the total assets of a business firm. Because they represent such a large investment and because this investment tends to be relatively volatile, current assets are worthy of the financial manager's careful attention.

3. Working capital management is particularly important for small firms. Although such firms can minimize their investment in fixed assets by renting or leasing plant and equipment, they cannot avoid investment in cash, receivables, and inventories. Therefore, current assets are particularly significant for the financial manager of a small firm. Further, because a small firm has relatively limited access to the long-term capital markets, it must necessarily rely heavily on trade credit and short-term bank loans, both of which affect working capital by increasing current liabilities.

4. The relationship between sales growth and the need to finance current assets is close and direct. For example, if the firm's average collection period is 40 days and its credit sales are $1,000 a day, it has an investment of $40,000 in accounts receivable. If credit sales rise to $2,000 a day, the investment in accounts receivable rises to $80,000. Sales increases produce similar immediate needs for additional inventories and, perhaps, for cash balances. All such needs must be financed; since these needs are so closely related to sales volume, the financial manager must be aware of developments in the working capital segment of the firm. Of course, continued sales increases require additional long-term assets, which must also be financed. However, fixed asset investments, while critically important to the firm in a strategic, long-run sense, generally have more lead time in financing than do current asset investments.

We begin with a discussion of central issues of the amount of investments in current assets and broad issues of their sources and methods of financing.

RISK-RETURN TRADE-OFF FOR CURRENT ASSET INVESTMENTS

If it could forecast perfectly (the assumption of certainty), a firm would hold exactly enough cash to make disbursements as required, exactly enough inventories to meet production and sales requirements, exactly the accounts receivable called for by an opti-

FIGURE 20.1   Relationship between Current Assets and Output
under Certainty and Uncertainty

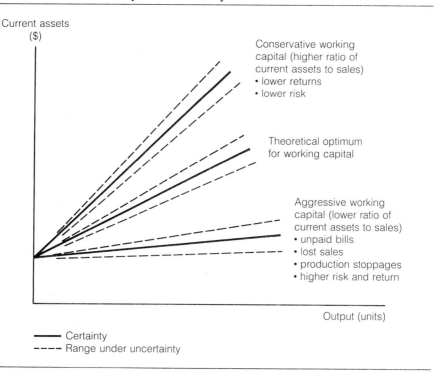

mal credit policy, and no marketable securities unless the interest returns on such assets exceeded the cost of capital (an unlikely occurrence). The current asset holdings under the perfect foresight case would be the theoretical optimum for a profit-maximizing firm. The middle solid line in Figure 20.1 shows the theoretical optimum at different output levels. Any holdings larger than the optimum would increase the firm's assets without a proportionate increase in its returns, thus lowering its rate of return on investment. Any smaller holdings would mean the inability to pay bills on time, lost sales and production stoppages because of inventory shortages, and lost sales because of an overly restrictive credit policy.

When uncertainty is introduced into the analysis, current asset management involves (1) determination of the minimum required balances of each type of asset and (2) addition of a safety stock to account for the fact that forecasts are imperfect. The broken lines in Figure 20.1 illustrate variations in alternative current asset policies. The lines with the steepest slopes represent conservative policies. Under conservative current asset policies, relatively large balances of cash and marketable securities are maintained, large amounts of inventories are kept on hand, and sales are stimulated by the use of a credit policy that provides liberal financing to customers and that results in a high level of accounts receiva-

TABLE 20.1   Effects of Alternative Current Asset Policies on Rates of Return

	Conservative	Middle-Ground	Aggressive
Part A			
Sales	$110,000,000	$105,000,000	$100,000,000
EBIT @15%	16,500,000	15,750,000	15,000,000
Current assets	70,000,000	55,000,000	40,000,000
Fixed assets	50,000,000	50,000,000	50,000,000
Total assets	$120,000,000	$105,000,000	$ 90,000,000
Rate of return on assets (EBIT/assets)	13.75%	15%	16.7%
Part B			
Sales	$115,000,000	$105,000,000	$ 80,000,000
EBIT rate	15%	15%	12%
EBIT amount	17,250,000	15,750,000	9,600,000
Total assets	$120,000,000	$105,000,000	$ 90,000,000
Rate of return on assets (EBIT/assets)	14.4%	15%	10.7%

ble. The lowest of the lines in Figure 20.1 have the smallest slopes, representing the most aggressive current asset policy in which holdings of cash, receivables, and inventories are sharply restricted. The intermediate lines represent a middle-ground approach.

Current asset holdings are the highest at any output level under the conservative policy and the lowest under the aggressive policy. For example, a firm that follows a conservative current asset policy holds relatively large safety stocks. If it follows an aggressive policy, its safety stocks are minimal. The aggressive policy requires the smallest investment, but the return on investment in current assets depends upon the degree to which the more restrictive asset management policies reduce sales levels below those that would be achieved under other policies. Numerical illustrations of some possibilities are presented in Table 20.1.

In Part A, it is assumed that the less aggressive current asset investment policies stimulate sales to a slight degree by having more variety in inventory, fewer stockout problems, and so forth. But the indicated rate of return on assets is highest for the current asset policy of greatest aggressiveness under the assumptions.

In Part B of Table 20.1, an alternative set of assumptions is illustrated. It is assumed that the aggressive current asset investment policy results in a larger adverse sales effect and also lowers the earnings rate. As a consequence, the most aggressive policy now results in the lowest indicated return on assets. It is assumed that the middle-ground policy produces the same results as before. The results of the conservative policy are assumed to improve somewhat. Still the outcome for the middle-ground policy represents the highest return on assets for the relationships postulated.

Table 20.1 illustrates the general idea that the kind of current asset policy a firm follows may result in a stimulus to sales and profitability or in negative effects on both the volume of sales and profitability. In actual practice and experience, matters are considerably more complex than this simple example suggests. For one thing, different types of current assets affect both risk and returns differently. Increased holdings of cash do more to improve the firm's risk posture than a similar dollar increase in receivables or inventories; idle cash penalizes earnings more severely than does the same investment in marketable securities. Generalizations are difficult when we consider accounts receivable and inventories, because it is difficult to measure either the earnings penalty or the risk reduction that results from increasing the balances of these items beyond their theoretical optimum levels.

FINANCING CURRENT ASSETS

Capital budgeting decisions involve estimating the stream of benefits expected from a given project and then discounting the expected cash flows back to the present to find the present value of the project. Although current asset investment analysis is similar to fixed asset analysis in the sense that it also requires estimates of the effects of such investments on profits, it is different in two key respects:

1. The cash and marketable securities portion of current assets provides liquidity to the firm and reduces its vulnerability to adverse patterns of cash flows. This increased liquidity reduces the risk that the firm would not have cash assets to meet maturing obligations from the liability side of the balance sheet. In this respect, the riskiness of the firm is reduced. But to the extent that liquid assets earn less than other assets and to the extent that having large safety stocks of cash and marketable securities increases the current and total assets over what they might otherwise be, the overall return on assets is reduced.

2. Although both fixed and current asset holdings are functions of *expected* sales, only current assets can be adjusted to *actual* sales in the short run. Adjustments to short-run fluctuations in sales level are made primarily by current asset investment policies and by short-term financing adjustments.

Agricultural Models of Financing Current Assets

Up to now, we have been focusing on the asset side of the balance sheet, assuming that the liability structure was being held constant. Now we turn to the liability side of the balance sheet and assume that the asset pattern is being held constant.

The term *working capital* originated at a time when most industries were closely related to agriculture. Processors would buy crops in the fall, process them, sell the finished product, and end up just before the next harvest with relatively low inventories. Bank loans with maximum maturities of one year were used to finance both the purchase and the processing costs, and these loans were retired with the proceeds from the sale of the finished products.

This situation is depicted in Figure 20.2, where fixed assets are shown to be growing steadily over time, while current assets jump at harvest season and then decline during the year, ending at zero just before the next crop is harvested. Current assets are financed with short-term credit, and fixed assets are financed with long-term funds. Thus, the top segment of the graph deals with working capital.

FIGURE 20.2 Fixed and Current Asset Patterns in Agriculture

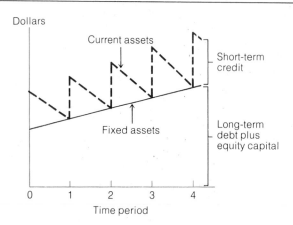

The figure represents, of course, an idealized situation for agriculture. In manufacturing and distribution, current assets may build up gradually and decline in various patterns. Nevertheless, the example does illustrate the general nature of seasonal patterns in working capital. Working capital management consists of decisions relating to the top section of the graph — managing current assets and arranging the short-term credit used to finance them.

Links between Long-Term and Short-Term Financing

As the economy became less oriented toward agriculture, the production and financing cycles of typical businesses changed. Although seasonal patterns still exist and business cycles cause asset requirements to fluctuate, current assets are less likely to drop to zero. As sales increase, the investment in cash, receivables, and inventories must grow proportionately. A steadily rising level of sales over the years will result in permanent increases in current assets. Although individual receivables accounts are paid off and individual inventory items become embodied in completed products and are sold, the continuous operations of the firm will result in rising investments in receivables and inventories as sales increase. Temporary seasonal fluctuations in sales would be followed by similar fluctuations in current asset requirements.

Lines A through H in Figure 20.3 illustrate alternative policies of financing current and fixed assets. Policy A is to finance only a portion of fixed assets with long-term financing. We shall define long-term financing as equity and long-term debt. Policy A relies on short-term financing for a portion of fixed assets, all of permanent current assets, and current assets as they rise and fall. Policy A clearly invites financial disaster. Prudent leaders should not finance long-term investments with short-term financing. This represents mismatching of the duration of assets and of claims as discussed in Chapter 14 on "Managing Financial Risk." The Policy B line coincides with the time trend line of total

TABLE 20.3   Fixed Rate versus Flexible Rate Financing, Recession

	Fixed Rate Financing	Flexible Rate Financing
Total assets	$ 800,000	$ 800,000
Flexible rate debt @8%		400,000
Fixed rate debt @12%	400,000	
Equity	400,000	400,000
Total claims	$ 800,000	$ 800,000
Sales	$1,000,000	$1,000,000
Net operating income @10%	100,000	100,000
Less interest	48,000	32,000
Taxable income	$ 52,000	$ 68,000
Less taxes @40%	20,800	27,200
Net income	$ 31,200	$ 40,800
Return on equity	7.8%	10.2%

The decline in return on equity is 6.6 percentage points for fixed rate financing, but only 2.4 percentage points for flexible rate financing.

Thus, the firm's profitability, given flexible rate financing, is more stable and less influenced by overall economic conditions than under fixed rate financing. This example shows the relative degree to which the profitability of a firm covaries with general market conditions. As long as interest rates are positively correlated with the health of the firm and the economy, we will have the result that flexible rate financing (or the rollover of short-term debt) is less risky than long-term financing. We next consider sources and forms of short-term funds.

TRADE CREDIT

In the ordinary course of events, a firm buys its supplies and materials on credit from other firms, recording the debt as an *accounts payable*. Accounts payable, or *trade credit,* is the largest single category of short-term credit, representing about one-third of the current liabilities of nonfinancial corporations.[2] This percentage is somewhat larger for small firms. Because these firms may not qualify for financing from other sources, they rely rather heavily on trade credit.

Trade credit is a spontaneous source of financing in that it arises from ordinary business transactions. For example, suppose a firm makes average purchases of $2,000 a

---

[2]In Chapter 18, we discussed trade credit from the viewpoint of minimizing investment in current assets. In the present chapter, we look at the other side of the coin — trade credit as a source, rather than a use, of financing. In Chapter 18, the use of trade credit by customers resulted in an asset investment called *accounts receivable*. In the present chapter, the use of trade credit gives rise to short-term obligations, generally called *accounts payable*.

day on terms of net 30. On the average, it will owe 30 times $2,000, or $60,000, to its suppliers. If its sales and, consequently, its purchases double, accounts payable will also double — to $120,000. The firm will have spontaneously generated an additional $60,000 of financing. Similarly, if the terms of credit are extended from 30 to 40 days, accounts payable will expand from $60,000 to $80,000; thus, lengthening the average payment period generates additional financing.

Concept of Net Credit

Trade credit has double-edged significance for the firm. It is a source of credit for financing purchases, and it is a use of funds to the extent that the firm finances credit sales to customers. For example, if, on the average, a firm sells $3,000 worth of goods a day and has an average collection period of 40 days, at any balance sheet date, it will have accounts receivable of approximately $120,000.

If the same firm buys $2,000 worth of materials a day and the balance is outstanding for 20 days, accounts payable will average $40,000. The firm is thus extending net credit of $80,000 — the difference between accounts receivable and accounts payable.

Large firms and well-financed firms of all sizes tend to be net suppliers of trade credit; small firms and undercapitalized firms of all sizes tend to be net users of trade credit. It is impossible to generalize about whether it is better to be a net supplier or a net user; the choice depends on the firm's circumstances and on the various costs and benefits of receiving and using trade credit.

Advantages of Trade Credit as a Source of Financing

Trade credit, a customary part of doing business in most industries, is convenient and informal. A firm that does not qualify for credit from a financial institution may receive trade credit because previous experience has familiarized the seller with the creditworthiness of the customer. The seller knows the merchandising practices of the industry and is usually in a good position to judge the capacity of the customer and the risk of selling on credit. The amount of trade credit fluctuates with the buyer's purchases, subject to any credit limits that may be operative.

Whether trade credit costs more or less than other forms of financing is a moot question. The buyer often has no alternative form of financing available, and the costs may be commensurate with the risks to the seller. But in some instances, trade credit is used simply because the buyer does not realize how expensive it is. In such circumstances, careful financial analysis may lead to the substitution of alternative forms of financing.

At the other extreme, trade credit may represent a virtual subsidy or sales promotion device offered by the seller. For example, in certain cases, manufacturers quite literally supplied *all* the financing for new firms by selling on credit terms substantially longer than those of the new company. In one instance, a manufacturer, eager to obtain a dealership in a particular area, made a loan to the new company to cover operating expenses during the initial phases and geared the payment of accounts payable to cash receipts. Even in such instances, however, the buying firm must be careful that it is not really paying a hidden financing cost in the form of higher product prices than could be obtained elsewhere. Extending credit involves a cost to the selling firm, and this firm may well be increasing its prices to offset the apparently ''free'' credit it extends to buyers.

Importance of Good Supplier Relations

During periods of uncertainty and tight money, firms raise their standards for extending trade credit to their customers. Since cleaning up accounts receivable is one way to obtain a more favorable liquidity position, suppliers become more selective when extending trade credit. This shows that it is important for a firm to earn the confidence of its suppliers. Showing good financial ratios and paying promptly are excellent ways to achieve this goal. But even if these indicators are unfavorable, a firm may still be able to obtain trade credit by offering realistic plans for improving its situation. Illustrative was the W. T. Grant Company experience in 1975. After it announced policy changes and a program for improvement, W. T. Grant's suppliers were willing to continue to extend trade credit for a period of time. The more recent experience of the Wickes Companies in 1982 is similar. Sanford Sigoloff, who had a record of success in rehabilitating bankrupt companies, was appointed to turn around the Wickes Companies. Mr. Sigoloff's appointment, and the subsequent program for rehabilitation that he announced, enabled the company to maintain relationships with an important number of its suppliers.

SHORT-TERM FINANCING BY COMMERCIAL BANKS

Commercial bank lending, which appears on the balance sheet as *notes payable,* is second in importance to trade credit as a source of short-term financing. Banks occupy a pivotal position in the short-term and intermediate-term money markets. Their influence is greater than it appears to be from the dollar amounts they lend, because the banks provide nonspontaneous funds. As a firm's financing needs increase, it requests additional funds from banks. If the request is denied, often the alternative is to slow down the rate of growth or to cut back operations.

Characteristics of Loans from Commercial Banks

In the following sections, the main characteristics of lending patterns of commercial banks are briefly described.

Forms of Loans. A single loan obtained from a bank by a business firm is not different in principle from a loan obtained by an individual. In fact, it is often difficult to distinguish a bank loan to a small business from a personal loan. The loan is obtained by signing a conventional promissory note. Repayment is made in a lump sum at maturity (when the note is due) or in installments throughout the life of the loan.

A *line of credit* is a formal or informal understanding between the bank and the borrower concerning the maximum loan balance the bank will allow the borrower. For example, a bank loan officer may indicate to a financial manager that the bank regards the firm as "good" for up to $80,000 for the forthcoming year. Subsequently, the manager signs a promissory note for $15,000 for 90 days, thereby "taking down" $15,000 of the total line of $80,000 in credit. This amount is credited to the firm's checking account at the bank. At maturity, the checking account is charged for the amount of the loan. Interest may be deducted in advance or may be paid at maturity. Before repayment of the $15,000, the firm may borrow additional amounts up to the total of $80,000. The borrower may be required to pay 1/4 percent to 1/2 percent per annum for the unused line of credit. To illustrate, Chrysler Corporation arranged a line of credit for over $100 million with a group of banks. The banks were formally committed to lend Chrysler the funds if they were needed. Chrysler, in turn, paid a commitment fee of approximately one-quarter of 1 percent of the unused balance of the commitment to compensate the banks for making the funds available.

Size of Customers.   Banks make loans to firms of all sizes. By dollar amount, the major proportion of loans from commercial banks is obtained by large firms. But by number of loans, small- and medium-sized firms account for over one-half of bank loans. Local commercial banks are the main suppliers of most financial services used by such firms.[3] These services include lines of credit, mortgage lending, leasing, motor vehicle loans, and equipment loans.

Maturity.   Commercial banks concentrate on the short-term lending market. Short-term loans make up about two-thirds of bank loans by dollar amount, whereas term loans (loans with maturities longer than one year) make up only one-third.

Security.   If a potential borrower is a questionable credit risk, or if the firm's financing needs exceed the amount that the loan officer of the bank considers prudent on an unsecured basis, some form of security is required. More than half the dollar value of bank loans is secured. (The forms of security are described later in this chapter.) In terms of the number of bank loans, two-thirds are secured through the endorsement of a third party, who guarantees payment of the loan in the event the borrower defaults.

Compensating Balances.   Banks typically require that a regular borrower maintain an average checking account balance equal to 15 or 20 percent of the outstanding loan. These balances, commonly called *compensating balances,* are a method of raising the effective interest rate. For example, if a firm needs $80,000 to pay off outstanding obligations but must maintain a 20 percent compensating balance, it must borrow $100,000 in order to obtain the required $80,000. If the stated interest rate is 5 percent, the effective cost is actually $6\frac{1}{4}$ percent ($5,000 divided by $80,000). These *loan* compensating balances are, of course, added to any *service* compensating balances that the firm's bank may require.

Repayment of Bank Loans.   Because most bank deposits are subject to withdrawal on demand, commercial banks seek to prevent firms from using bank credit for permanent

---

[3]Gregory E. Elliehausen and John D. Wolkers, "Banking Markets and the Use of Financial Services by Small and Medium-Sized Businesses," *Federal Reserve Bulletin,* (October 1990), pp. 801–817.

financing cost in the form of higher product prices than could be obtained elsewhere. Extending credit involves a cost to the selling firm, and this firm may well be increasing its prices to offset the apparently "free" credit it extends to buyers.

Importance of Good Supplier Relations

During periods of uncertainty and tight money, firms raise their standards for extending trade credit to their customers. Since cleaning up accounts receivable is one way to obtain a more favorable liquidity position, suppliers become more selective when extending trade credit. This shows that it is important for a firm to earn the confidence of its suppliers. Showing good financial ratios and paying promptly are excellent ways to achieve this goal. But even if these indicators are unfavorable, a firm may still be able to obtain trade credit by offering realistic plans for improving its situation. Illustrative was the W. T. Grant Company experience in 1975. After it announced policy changes and a program for improvement, W. T. Grant's suppliers were willing to continue to extend trade credit for a period of time. The more recent experience of the Wickes Companies in 1982 is similar. Sanford Sigoloff, who had a record of success in rehabilitating bankrupt companies, was appointed to turn around the Wickes Companies. Mr. Sigoloff's appointment, and the subsequent program for rehabilitation that he announced, enabled the company to maintain relationships with an important number of its suppliers.

SHORT-TERM FINANCING BY COMMERCIAL BANKS

Commercial bank lending, which appears on the balance sheet as *notes payable,* is second in importance to trade credit as a source of short-term financing. Banks occupy a pivotal position in the short-term and intermediate-term money markets. Their influence is greater than it appears to be from the dollar amounts they lend, because the banks provide nonspontaneous funds. As a firm's financing needs increase, it requests additional funds from banks. If the request is denied, often the alternative is to slow down the rate of growth or to cut back operations.

Characteristics of Loans from Commercial Banks

In the following sections, the main characteristics of lending patterns of commercial banks are briefly described.

Forms of Loans. A single loan obtained from a bank by a business firm is not different in principle from a loan obtained by an individual. In fact, it is often difficult to distinguish a bank loan to a small business from a personal loan. The loan is obtained by signing a conventional promissory note. Repayment is made in a lump sum at maturity (when the note is due) or in installments throughout the life of the loan.

   A *line of credit* is a formal or informal understanding between the bank and the borrower concerning the maximum loan balance the bank will allow the borrower. For example, a bank loan officer may indicate to a financial manager that the bank regards the firm as "good" for up to $80,000 for the forthcoming year. Subsequently, the manager signs a promissory note for $15,000 for 90 days, thereby "taking down" $15,000 of the total line of $80,000 in credit. This amount is credited to the firm's checking account at the bank. At maturity, the checking account is charged for the amount of the loan. Interest may be deducted in advance or may be paid at maturity. Before repayment of the $15,000, the firm may borrow additional amounts up to the total of $80,000. The borrower may be required to pay 1/4 percent to 1/2 percent per annum for the unused line of credit. To illustrate, Chrysler Corporation arranged a line of credit for over $100 million with a group of banks. The banks were formally committed to lend Chrysler the funds if they were needed. Chrysler, in turn, paid a commitment fee of approximately one-quarter of 1 percent of the unused balance of the commitment to compensate the banks for making the funds available.

Size of Customers. Banks make loans to firms of all sizes. By dollar amount, the major proportion of loans from commercial banks is obtained by large firms. But by number of loans, small- and medium-sized firms account for over one-half of bank loans. Local commercial banks are the main suppliers of most financial services used by such firms.[3] These services include lines of credit, mortgage lending, leasing, motor vehicle loans, and equipment loans.

Maturity. Commercial banks concentrate on the short-term lending market. Short-term loans make up about two-thirds of bank loans by dollar amount, whereas term loans (loans with maturities longer than one year) make up only one-third.

Security. If a potential borrower is a questionable credit risk, or if the firm's financing needs exceed the amount that the loan officer of the bank considers prudent on an unsecured basis, some form of security is required. More than half the dollar value of bank loans is secured. (The forms of security are described later in this chapter.) In terms of the number of bank loans, two-thirds are secured through the endorsement of a third party, who guarantees payment of the loan in the event the borrower defaults.

Compensating Balances. Banks typically require that a regular borrower maintain an average checking account balance equal to 15 or 20 percent of the outstanding loan. These balances, commonly called *compensating balances,* are a method of raising the effective interest rate. For example, if a firm needs $80,000 to pay off outstanding obligations but must maintain a 20 percent compensating balance, it must borrow $100,000 in order to obtain the required $80,000. If the stated interest rate is 5 percent, the effective cost is actually $6\frac{1}{4}$ percent ($5,000 divided by $80,000). These *loan* compensating balances are, of course, added to any *service* compensating balances that the firm's bank may require.

Repayment of Bank Loans. Because most bank deposits are subject to withdrawal on demand, commercial banks seek to prevent firms from using bank credit for permanent

---

[3]Gregory E. Elliehausen and John D. Wolkers, "Banking Markets and the Use of Financial Services by Small and Medium-Sized Businesses," *Federal Reserve Bulletin,* (October 1990), pp. 801–817.

financing. A bank, therefore, may require its borrowers to "clean up" their short-term bank loans for at least one month each year. If a firm is unable to become free of bank debt at least part of each year, it is using bank financing for permanent needs and should develop additional sources of long-term or permanent financing.

Cost of Commercial Bank Loans. Loans from commercial banks vary in cost, with the effective rate depending on the characteristics of the firm and the level of interest rates in the economy. If the firm can qualify as a prime risk because of its size and financial strength, the rate of interest will be one-half to three-quarters of a percent above the discount rate charged by Federal Reserve banks to commercial banks. This is called the *prime interest rate*. On the other hand, a small firm with below-average financial ratios may be required to provide collateral security and to pay an effective rate of interest of 2 to 3 points above the prime rate.

"Regular" Interest. Determination of the effective, or true, rate of interest on a loan depends on the stated rate of interest and the lender's method of charging interest. If the interest is paid at the maturity of the loan, the stated rate of interest is the effective rate of interest. For example, on a $20,000 loan for one year at 10 percent, the interest is $2,000.

$$\text{"Regular" loan, interest paid at maturity} = \frac{\text{Interest}}{\text{Borrowed amount}}$$

$$= \frac{\$2,000}{\$20,000} = 10\%$$

Discounted Interest. If the bank deducts the interest in advance (discounts the loan), the effective rate of interest is increased. On the $20,000 loan for one year at 10 percent, the discount is $2,000, and the borrower obtains the use of only $18,000. The effective rate of interest is 11.1 percent (versus 10 percent on a "regular" loan):

$$\text{Discounted loan} = \frac{\text{Interest}}{\text{Borrowed amount} - \text{Interest}} = \frac{\$2,000}{\$18,000} = 11.1\%.$$

Installment Loan. The "regular" and discounted interest loans above are both characterized by repayment of the loan principal at maturity. Under the installment method, principal payments are made periodically (for example, monthly) over the term of the loan; on a one-year loan, the borrower has the full amount of the money only during the first month and by the last month has already paid back eleven-twelfths of the loan. Thus, the effective rate (that is, the annual percentage rate, or APR) of interest on an installment loan is significantly higher than the stated rate. Installment loans can be arranged in two ways. In an add-on installment loan, net loan proceeds are the same as the face amount of the loan, but interest is added to the loan principal to calculate the monthly installments. In a discounted installment loan, interest is subtracted from the principal to obtain the net loan proceeds while the installments are based on the full face value of the loan. The add-on installment loan results in higher monthly payments but a lower effective interest rate; the discounted installment loan results in lower monthly payments but a higher effective interest rate. Examples will illustrate the calculation of the effective interest rate under the two methods for a one-year installment loan of $20,000 at a 10 percent nominal interest rate.

1. Add-on Installment Loan

Amount borrowed	$20,000.00
Stated interest rate	10%
Add-on interest	$2,000.00
Total	$22,000.00
Monthly installment ($22,000/12)	$1,833.33

The computed interest rate, r_c, implicit in these terms can be found as

$$\text{Borrowed amount} = \text{Periodic payment} \times \text{PVIFA}(r_c, n \text{ periods}).$$

Substituting the numerical values and using the formula for the PVIFA, we have

$$\$20,000 = \$1,833.33 \left[\frac{1 - \dfrac{1}{\left(1 + \dfrac{r}{q}\right)^q}}{r/q} \right].$$

Solving for (r/q) (on a programmed hand-calculator), we find that (r/q) is approximately equal to .015 on a monthly basis, implying a computed annual interest rate of 18 percent compounded monthly and an effective or annual percentage rate of 19.56 percent, computed from $(1 + .015)^{12} - 1$.

2. Discounted Installment Loan

Amount borrowed	$20,000.00
Stated interest rate	10%
Subtract interest	$2,000.00
Amount received	$18,000.00
Monthly installment ($20,000/12)	$1,666.67

Again, the computed interest rate can be found as

$$\text{Amount received} = \text{Periodic payment} \times \text{PVIFA}(r/q, n \text{ periods}),$$

or

$$\$18,000 = \$1,666.67 \left[\frac{1 - \dfrac{1}{\left(1 + \dfrac{r}{q}\right)^q}}{r/q} \right].$$

Solving, we find $r/q = .01659$ for a computed annual rate of approximately 19.91 percent, compounded monthly, and an APR of 21.83 percent, computed from $(1.01659)^{12} - 1$.

In both cases, the interest is calculated on the original amount of the loan, not on the amount actually outstanding (the declining balance), and this causes the effective interest rate to be almost double the stated rate. Interest is calculated by the installment method on most consumer loans (for example, automobile loans), but the installment method is not often used for business loans larger than about $15,000.

Choice of Banks

Banks have direct relationships with their borrowers. Because of the personal association over the years, business prospects and problems of the borrower are frequently discussed. Thus, banks often provide informal management counseling services. A potential borrower seeking such a relationship should consider the following important differences among banks:

1. Banks have different policies towards risk. Some are inclined to follow relatively conservative lending practices; others engage in what may be termed creative banking practices. The policies reflect partly the personalities of the bank officers and partly the characteristics of the bank's deposit liabilities. Thus, a bank with fluctuating deposit liabilities in a static community tends to be a conservative lender. A bank whose deposits are growing with little interruption may follow liberal credit policies. A large bank with diversification over broad geographical regions or among several industries can obtain the benefit of combining and averaging risks. Thus, marginal credit risks that may be unacceptable to a small bank or to a specialized unit bank can be pooled by a branch banking system to reduce the overall risks of a group of marginal accounts.

2. Some bank loan officers are active in providing counsel and in stimulating development loans to firms in their early and formative years. Certain banks even have specialized departments to make loans to firms expected to become growth firms. Bankers in such departments can provide much counseling to customers.

3. Banks differ in the extent to which they support a borrower's activities in bad times. This characteristic is referred to as the bank's degree of loyalty. Some banks put great pressure on a business to liquidate its loans when the firm's outlook becomes clouded, whereas others stand by the firm and work diligently to help it return to healthy, profitable operations.

4. Another characteristic by which banks differ is the degree of deposit stability. Instability arises not only from fluctuations in the level of deposits but also from the composition of deposits. Deposits can take the form of *demand deposits* (checking accounts) or *time deposits* (savings accounts, certificates of deposit, Christmas clubs). Total deposits tend to be more stable when time deposits are substantial. Differences in deposit stability go a long way toward explaining differences in the extent to which banks are willing or able to help borrowers work their way out of difficulties or even crises.

5. Banks differ greatly in the degree of loan specialization. Larger banks have separate departments specializing in different kinds of loans, such as real estate, installment, and commercial loans. Within these broad categories, they may specialize by line of business, such as steel, machinery, or textiles. Smaller banks are likely to reflect the

nature of the business and economic areas in which they operate. They tend to become specialists in specific lines, such as oil, construction, or agriculture. The borrower can obtain more creative cooperation and more active support at the bank that has the greatest experience and familiarity with the borrower's particular type of business. The financial manager, therefore, should choose a bank with care. The bank that is excellent for one firm may be unsatisfactory for another.

6. The size of a bank can be an important characteristic. Since the maximum loan a bank can make to any customer is generally limited to 10 percent of the bank's capital accounts (capital stock plus retained earnings), it generally is not appropriate for large firms to develop borrowing relationships with small banks.

7. With the heightened competition among commercial banks and other financial institutions, the aggressiveness of banks has increased. Modern commercial banks now offer a wide range of financial and business services. Most large banks have business development departments that provide counseling to firms and serve as intermediaries on a wide variety of their requirements.

8. A potential borrower must also consider the financial strength of the bank. By the early 1990s, some banks had been weakened by loans to less developed countries (LDC debt), loans to highly leveraged companies, and commercial real estate loans in weak markets.

COMMERCIAL PAPER

Commercial paper consists of unsecured promissory notes issued by firms to finance short-term credit needs. In recent years, the issuance of commercial paper has become an increasingly important source of short-term financing for many types of corporations, including utilities, finance companies, insurance companies, bank holding companies, and manufacturing companies. It is used not only to finance seasonal working capital needs but also as a means of interim financing of major projects such as buildings, ships, pipelines, nuclear fuel cores, and plant expansion. Worldwide the total commercial paper market in late 1990 was $740 billion.[4] Between December 1979 and July 1990, the amount of commercial paper outstanding in the United States increased from $113 billion to $546 billion. The total of the commercial and industrial loans of all commercial banks in July 1990 was $653 billion. So commercial paper outstanding has grown to be almost as large as direct bank business loans.[5]

Some commercial paper—especially the large volume of it issued by finance companies—is sold directly to investors, including business corporations, commercial banks, insurance companies, and state and local government units. As of December 1984, about 50 percent of the commercial paper outstanding had been directly placed with investors. The remainder represented that sold through commercial paper dealers, who function as intermediaries in the commercial paper market.

[4]Commercial paper markets abroad are described in Chapter 4 and in the last section of this chapter.
[5]*Federal Reserve Bulletin,* November 1990, pp. A16, A23.

Maturity and Cost

Maturities of commercial paper generally vary from two months to one year, with an average of about five months. The rates on prime commercial paper vary, but they are generally about half a percent below those on prime business loans. And since compensating balances are not required for commercial paper, the *effective* cost differential is still wider. However, this factor is offset to some extent by the fact that firms issuing commercial paper are sometimes required by commercial paper dealers to have unused bank lines of credit to back up their outstanding commercial paper, and fees must be paid on these lines.

Effects of Inflation

During periods of inflation and tight money, many commercial paper sellers are pushed out of the market because the sources of purchasing commercial paper do not have the ability to expand their assets as does a fractional reserve commercial banking system. Ryder System, a Florida trucking company, was forced to turn to bank loans for $10 million of financing during 1974 because it was able to find buyers for only $15 million of its commercial paper. Thus, during inflationary periods, firms may be forced to seek the more expensive bank loans since they can no longer sell the cheaper commercial paper.

Advantages and Disadvantages

The commercial paper market has some significant advantages:

1. It permits a broader and more advantageous distribution of debt.
2. It provides more funds at lower rates than do other methods.
3. The borrower avoids the inconvenience and expense of financing arrangements with a number of institutions, each of which requires a compensating balance.
4. Publicity and prestige accrue to the borrower as its product and paper become more widely known.
5. The commercial paper dealer frequently offers valuable advice to clients.

A disadvantage of the commercial paper market is that a debtor who is in temporary financial difficulty receives little help because commercial paper dealings are impersonal. Banks are much more personal and traditionally much more likely to help a good customer weather a financial storm.[6] But in the early 1990s banks have faced their own difficulties and have limited their lending activity.

---

[6]This point was emphasized dramatically in the aftermath of the Penn Central bankruptcy. Penn Central had a large amount of commercial paper that went into default, embarrassing corporate treasurers who had been holding the paper as part of their liquidity reserves. Immediately after the bankruptcy, the commercial paper market dried up to a large extent, and some companies that had relied heavily on this market found themselves under severe liquidity pressure as their commercial paper matured and could not be refunded. Chrysler, for example, had to seek bank loans of over $500 million because it could not sell commercial paper for a time. Without adequate bank lines, Chrysler might well have been forced into bankruptcy itself, even though it was then basically sound, because of the Penn Central panic. Incidentally, the Federal Reserve Board recognized that many other firms would be in the same position as Chrysler and so expanded bank reserves in order to enable the banking system to take up the slack caused by the withdrawal of funds from the commercial paper market.

TABLE 20.4 Commercial Paper Ratings

Standard & Poor's		Moody's
A-1	The degree of safety regarding timely payment is very strong. Those issues determined to possess overwhelming safety characteristics are denoted with a plus (+) sign.	P-1
A-2	Capacity for timely payment is strong.	P-2
A-3	Satisfactory capacity for timely payment. These issues are somewhat more vulnerable to adverse developments.	P-3
B	Only adequate capacity for timely payment. However, such capacity may be damaged by changing circumstances.	
C	Capacity for payment is doubtful.	
D	The issue is either in default or is expected to be in default.	

Uses and Recent Developments[7]

Over 1,000 companies borrow in the commercial paper market. Traditionally, these companies were mainly larger firms whose commercial paper carried high ratings. The ratings on commercial paper are described in Table 20.4. As of late 1990, companies with A-1 or P-1 ratings accounted for 84 percent of the commercial paper market worldwide. The top five companies near the end of 1990 accounted for almost $100 billion. The companies and their amounts (in billions) outstanding were General Electric Capital, $33; General Motors Acceptance, $26; Ford Motor Credit, $17; Sears Roebuck Acceptance, $10; American Express Credit, $7.

Companies with A-2 or P-2 ratings account for only about 13 percent of the market. Companies in the lowest investment grade levels, A-3 or P-3, are 2 percent of the market. Companies rated below investment grade or unrated represent the remaining 1 percent. Unrated commercial paper was an innovation by Drexel Burnham in the early 1980s. By the end of 1988 this market was estimated at about $7 billion. As the credit crunch of 1990 and 1991 developed, the volume of unrated paper dropped to about $5 billion with about 75 unrated issuers.

A credit crunch was associated with a recession that began in the United States in late 1990. Companies experienced reductions in their commercial paper ratings. For example, Chrysler Financial in June 1990 had its commercial paper rating dropped to the third level. In early February 1991, Chrysler withdrew its rating (a company has to pay to receive a rating) because it feared a further lowering. During 1990 Chrysler's commercial paper

---

[7]This section is based on a lengthy article by Jonathan Fuerbringer, "Commercial Paper Has Troubles, Too," *New York Times,* February 10, 1991, Sec. 3, p. 4.

Maturity and Cost

Maturities of commercial paper generally vary from two months to one year, with an average of about five months. The rates on prime commercial paper vary, but they are generally about half a percent below those on prime business loans. And since compensating balances are not required for commercial paper, the *effective* cost differential is still wider. However, this factor is offset to some extent by the fact that firms issuing commercial paper are sometimes required by commercial paper dealers to have unused bank lines of credit to back up their outstanding commercial paper, and fees must be paid on these lines.

Effects of Inflation

During periods of inflation and tight money, many commercial paper sellers are pushed out of the market because the sources of purchasing commercial paper do not have the ability to expand their assets as does a fractional reserve commercial banking system. Ryder System, a Florida trucking company, was forced to turn to bank loans for $10 million of financing during 1974 because it was able to find buyers for only $15 million of its commercial paper. Thus, during inflationary periods, firms may be forced to seek the more expensive bank loans since they can no longer sell the cheaper commercial paper.

Advantages and Disadvantages

The commercial paper market has some significant advantages:

1. It permits a broader and more advantageous distribution of debt.
2. It provides more funds at lower rates than do other methods.
3. The borrower avoids the inconvenience and expense of financing arrangements with a number of institutions, each of which requires a compensating balance.
4. Publicity and prestige accrue to the borrower as its product and paper become more widely known.
5. The commercial paper dealer frequently offers valuable advice to clients.

A disadvantage of the commercial paper market is that a debtor who is in temporary financial difficulty receives little help because commercial paper dealings are impersonal. Banks are much more personal and traditionally much more likely to help a good customer weather a financial storm.[6] But in the early 1990s banks have faced their own difficulties and have limited their lending activity.

---

[6]This point was emphasized dramatically in the aftermath of the Penn Central bankruptcy. Penn Central had a large amount of commercial paper that went into default, embarrassing corporate treasurers who had been holding the paper as part of their liquidity reserves. Immediately after the bankruptcy, the commercial paper market dried up to a large extent, and some companies that had relied heavily on this market found themselves under severe liquidity pressure as their commercial paper matured and could not be refunded. Chrysler, for example, had to seek bank loans of over $500 million because it could not sell commercial paper for a time. Without adequate bank lines, Chrysler might well have been forced into bankruptcy itself, even though it was then basically sound, because of the Penn Central panic. Incidentally, the Federal Reserve Board recognized that many other firms would be in the same position as Chrysler and so expanded bank reserves in order to enable the banking system to take up the slack caused by the withdrawal of funds from the commercial paper market.

TABLE 20.4 Commercial Paper Ratings

Standard & Poor's		Moody's
A-1	The degree of safety regarding timely payment is very strong. Those issues determined to possess overwhelming safety characteristics are denoted with a plus (+) sign.	P-1
A-2	Capacity for timely payment is strong.	P-2
A-3	Satisfactory capacity for timely payment. These issues are somewhat more vulnerable to adverse developments.	P-3
B	Only adequate capacity for timely payment. However, such capacity may be damaged by changing circumstances.	
C	Capacity for payment is doubtful.	
D	The issue is either in default or is expected to be in default.	

Uses and Recent Developments[7]

Over 1,000 companies borrow in the commercial paper market. Traditionally, these companies were mainly larger firms whose commercial paper carried high ratings. The ratings on commercial paper are described in Table 20.4. As of late 1990, companies with A-1 or P-1 ratings accounted for 84 percent of the commercial paper market worldwide. The top five companies near the end of 1990 accounted for almost $100 billion. The companies and their amounts (in billions) outstanding were General Electric Capital, $33; General Motors Acceptance, $26; Ford Motor Credit, $17; Sears Roebuck Acceptance, $10; American Express Credit, $7.

Companies with A-2 or P-2 ratings account for only about 13 percent of the market. Companies in the lowest investment grade levels, A-3 or P-3, are 2 percent of the market. Companies rated below investment grade or unrated represent the remaining 1 percent. Unrated commercial paper was an innovation by Drexel Burnham in the early 1980s. By the end of 1988 this market was estimated at about $7 billion. As the credit crunch of 1990 and 1991 developed, the volume of unrated paper dropped to about $5 billion with about 75 unrated issuers.

A credit crunch was associated with a recession that began in the United States in late 1990. Companies experienced reductions in their commercial paper ratings. For example, Chrysler Financial in June 1990 had its commercial paper rating dropped to the third level. In early February 1991, Chrysler withdrew its rating (a company has to pay to receive a rating) because it feared a further lowering. During 1990 Chrysler's commercial paper

---

[7]This section is based on a lengthy article by Jonathan Fuerbringer, ''Commercial Paper Has Troubles, Too,'' *New York Times,* February 10, 1991, Sec. 3, p. 4.

outstanding dropped from over $10 billion to $1.1 billion. It substituted bank borrowing in the amount of $6.2 billion and sold some of its automobile loan paper in the secondary market. It was reported that the use of bank borrowing increased Chrysler's cost in 1990 by about $25 million.

During the period between June 1989 and the end of 1990, 11 companies had defaulted on a total of $1.1 billion in commercial paper. Seven of the 11 defaults took place in the commercial paper markets in London, Japan, and France. Concern about the increasing risks associated with commercial paper led the SEC in July of 1990 to propose regulatory limits on the purchase of commercial paper by money market funds which have become major buyers. For example, the Webster Cash Reserve Fund associated with Kidder Peabody reported that 74 percent of its investments in 1990 were in commercial paper. The SEC proposed that no more than 5 percent of a money market fund's assets could be invested in commercial paper without the highest grade rating and that 5 percent would have to be in paper with the second highest rating. Commercial banks have always provided a backup to the commercial paper market. Their inability or unwillingness to do so during the credit crunch that began in late 1990 has raised doubts as to whether this backup can always be relied upon.

BANKERS' ACCEPTANCES

A *banker's acceptance* is a debt instrument created by the creditor and arises out of a self-liquidating business transaction, mainly from import and export activity. For example, a U.S. coffee processor may arrange with a U.S. commercial bank for the issuance of an irrevocable letter of credit in favor of a Brazilian exporter with whom the U.S. processor has negotiated a transaction. The letter of credit covers the details of the shipment and states that the Brazilian exporter can draw a draft for a specified amount on the U.S. bank.[8] On the basis of the letter of credit, the exporter draws a draft on the bank and negotiates the draft with a local Brazilian bank, receiving immediate payment. The Brazilian bank then forwards the draft to the United States for presentation to the bank that issued the letter of credit. When this bank stamps the draft "accepted," it accepts the obligation to pay the draft at maturity, thereby creating an acceptance. Typically, the acceptance is then sold to an acceptance dealer, and the proceeds are credited to the account of the Brazilian bank. The shipping documents are released to the U.S. importer against a trust receipt, enabling the U.S. company to process and sell the coffee.

The proceeds of the coffee sales are deposited by the importer at the accepting bank in time to meet the required payment on the draft at maturity. The holder of the acceptance at maturity presents it to the accepting bank for payment, completing the transaction. The cost of the acceptance reflects the discount in the acceptance dealer's bid plus the accepting bank's commission rate. The cost can be borne by either the seller or buyer of the goods in accordance with the agreement made with the accepting bank. It reflects the

---

[8]A *draft* is similar to an ordinary check. A check is drawn up by those *making* the payment, but a draft is drawn up by those who are to *receive* payment. Also a draft can be a sight draft which, like a check, is to be paid when received by the bank on which it is drawn. But a time draft will specify payment at a future date. This is similar to a post-dated check, except that time drafts represent a customary procedure, unlike post-dated checks.

trade-offs involved in the selling price of the goods (which is related to provisions for bearing the risks that may be involved in the transaction) and the payment of fees for various instruments created by the transaction (such as the acceptance itself).

Bankers' acceptances are an effective method of short-term financing since the drawer gains time before funds are due. The appeal of bankers' acceptances, which are traded in an active secondary market, results from two basic characteristics. First, they are safe. Since they usually finance the shipment and storage of goods, the inventory can be pledged as collateral. Return to investors is usually comparable to the return on a good certificate of deposit. During periods of inflation, when investors become increasingly selective, a banker's acceptance may look safer than commercial paper or even the certificates of deposit of some banks. Second, when an acceptance is backed by readily marketable goods and a warehouse receipt has been issued, the acceptance is eligible for rediscount with the Federal Reserve.

SECURED SHORT-TERM FINANCING

Given a choice, it is ordinarily better to borrow on an unsecured basis, since the bookkeeping costs of secured loans are often high. However, a potential borrower's credit rating may not be sufficiently strong to justify the loan. If the loan can be secured by some form of collateral to be claimed by the lender in the event of default, then the lender may extend credit to an otherwise unacceptable firm. Similarly, a firm that can borrow on an unsecured basis may elect to use security if it finds that this will induce lenders to quote a lower interest rate.

Several different kinds of collateral can be employed — marketable stocks or bonds, land or buildings, equipment, inventory, and accounts receivable. Marketable securities make excellent collateral, but few firms hold portfolios of stocks and bonds. Similarly, real property (land and buildings) and equipment are good forms of collateral, but they are generally used as security for long-term loans. The bulk of secured short-term business borrowing involves the pledge of short-term assets — accounts receivable or inventories.

In the past, state laws varied greatly with regard to the use of security in financing. By the late 1960s, however, most states had adopted the *Uniform Commercial Code (UCC),* which standardized and simplified the procedure for establishing loan security.

The heart of the UCC is the *security agreement,* a standardized document, or form, on which are stated the specific pledged assets. The assets can be items of equipment, accounts receivable, or inventories. Procedures for financing under the UCC are described in the following sections.

ACCOUNTS RECEIVABLE FINANCING

Accounts receivable financing involves either the assigning of receivables or the selling of receivables (factoring). Assigning, or pledging, or discounting of accounts receivable is characterized by the fact that the lender not only has a lien on the receivables but also has

recourse to the borrower (seller of the goods); if the person or firm that bought the goods does not pay, the selling firm must take the loss. In other words, the risk of default on the accounts receivable pledged remains with the borrower. Also, the buyer of the goods is not ordinarily notified about the pledging of the receivables. The financial institution that lends on the security of accounts receivable is generally either a commercial bank or one of the large industrial finance companies.

Factoring, or selling accounts receivable, involves the purchase of accounts receivable by the lender without recourse to the borrower (seller of the goods). The buyer of the goods is notified of the transfer and makes payment directly to the lender. Since the factoring firm assumes the risk of default on bad accounts, it must do the credit checking. Accordingly, factors provide not only money but also a credit department for the borrower.

Procedure for Pledging Accounts Receivable

The financing of accounts receivable is initiated by a legally binding agreement between the seller of the goods and the financing institution. The agreement sets forth in detail the procedure to be followed and the legal obligations of both parties. Once the working relationship has been established, the seller periodically takes a batch of invoices to the financing institution. The lender reviews the invoices and makes an appraisal of the buyers. Invoices of companies that do not meet the lender's credit standards are not accepted for pledging. The financial institution seeks to protect itself at every phase of the operation. Selection of good invoices is the essential first step. If the buyer of the goods does not pay the invoice, the lender still has recourse against the seller of the goods. However, if many buyers default, the seller may be unable to meet the obligation to the financial institution. Additional protection afforded the lender is that the loan is generally for less than 100 percent of the pledged receivables; for example, the lender may advance the selling firm 75 percent of the amount of the pledged receivables.

An example will illustrate how the effective cost of accounts receivable financing is a function of accounts receivable turnover and the nominal interest rate: The Commerce Electronics Company has annual credit sales of $1 million, and its average accounts receivable balance is $200,000. Thus, its receivables turn over five times per year. Commerce is considering the use of accounts receivable financing to provide needed funds. The proposed pledging agreement specifies that a 15 percent reserve be deducted from funds advanced to protect against returns on disputed items. The annual interest rate is 16 percent (a 2 percent premium over the [then current] prime rate), charged on the amount of receivables less the reserve requirement. Interest is deducted in advance.

The formula for calculating the computed interest rate, r_c, is

$$r_c = \frac{1}{\left(\frac{1}{r}\right) - \left(\frac{1}{n}\right)},$$

where

$$r_c = \text{the computed interest rate}$$
$$r = \text{the nominal interest rate} = 16 \text{ percent}$$
$$n = \text{the annual accounts receivable turnover} = 5 \text{ times.}$$

Thus,

$$r_c = \frac{1}{\left(\dfrac{1}{.16}\right) - \left(\dfrac{1}{5}\right)}$$

$$= \frac{1}{6.25 - 0.2}$$

$$= \frac{1}{6.05}$$

$$= 16.53\%.$$

We can verify this computed rate using a worksheet methodology:

Average duration of advance	360/5 = 72 days
Periodic interest rate	16%/5 = 3.2%
Reserve	(.15)$200,000 = $30,000
Periodic interest charge	.032($200,000 − $30,000) = $5,440
Annual interest charge	(5)$5,440 = $27,200
Net amount received	$200,000 − $30,000 − $5,440 = $164,560
Computed interest rate	$27,200/$164,560 = 16.53%.

Thus, the computed annual interest rate is 16.53 percent, the same result achieved above based solely on the nominal interest rate and turnover. The reserve requirement does not impact the computed interest rate since interest is calculated after deducting the reserve. Nor does the level of sales affect the computed interest rate, so long as the accounts receivable turnover remains constant. However, given the nominal interest rate, a higher turnover will result in a lower computed interest rate, and conversely. For example, with an accounts receivable turnover of 3, the computed rate for Commerce would be

$$r_c = \frac{1}{\left(\dfrac{1}{.16}\right) - \left(\dfrac{1}{3}\right)}$$

$$= \frac{1}{6.25 - .33}$$

$$= 16.90\%.$$

And with a turnover of 7, the computed cost would be

$$r_c = \frac{1}{6.25 - .143}$$

$$= 16.37\%.$$

Procedure for Factoring Accounts Receivable

The procedure for factoring is somewhat different from that for simply using accounts receivable as collateral for a loan. Again, an agreement between the seller and the factor is made to specify legal obligations and procedural arrangements. When the seller receives an order from a buyer, a credit approval slip is written and immediately sent to the factoring company for a credit check. If the factor does not approve the sale, the seller generally refuses to fill the order. This procedure informs the seller, prior to the sale, about the buyer's creditworthiness and acceptability to the factor. If the sale is approved, shipment is made and the invoice is stamped to notify the buyer to make payment directly to the factoring company.

The factor performs three functions in carrying out the procedure outlined above: (1) credit checking, (2) lending, and (3) risk bearing. The seller can select various combinations of these functions by changing provisions in the factoring agreement. For example, a small- or medium-sized firm can avoid establishing a credit department. The factor's service may well be less costly than a department that has a capacity in excess of the firm's credit volume. Also, if the firm uses a part-time noncredit specialist to perform credit checking, the person's lack of education, training, and experience may result in excessive losses. In some situations, the seller may have the factor perform the credit-checking and risk-taking functions but not the lending function.

To illustrate the more typical situation in which the factor also performs a lending function by making payment in advance of collection, we return to the Commerce Electronics Company example. Instead of pledging or using its accounts receivable as collateral, Commerce is now considering a factoring arrangement. The factor would approve Commerce's invoices and advance funds as soon as the goods are shipped. The factoring commission or fee for credit checking is $1\frac{1}{2}$ percent of the invoice amount, deducted in advance. As in pledging, the factor sets up a 15 percent reserve against returns on disputed items. Interest expense is computed at a 16 percent annual rate on the invoice amount less the reserve and is deducted in advance. Recall that Commerce has annual sales of $1 million, with an average accounts receivable balance of $200,000; thus, the receivables turnover is five times, implying an average collection period of 72 days. This is the length of time the factor's funds will be at risk. (This 72-day collection period is approximately double the average collection period for all manufacturing firms and may be the reason that Commerce is motivated to consider pledging or factoring receivables in the first place.) We can calculate the effective cost of the factoring arrangement using the worksheet method:

Factoring commission	$(.015)\$200,000 = \$\ \ \ 3,000$
Reserve	$(.15)\$200,000 = \$\ 30,000$
Interest expense	$(.16)\left(\dfrac{72}{360}\right)(\$200,000 - \$30,000) = \$\ \ \ 5,440$
Funds advanced	$\$200,000 - \$3,000 - \$30,000 - \$5,440 = \$161,560$
Annual interest expense	$5 \times \$5,440 = \$\ 27,200$
Annual factoring commission	$5 \times \$3,000 = \underline{\$\ 15,000}$
Total annual expense	$\$\ 42,200$
Computed interest rate	$\$42,200/\$161,560 = 26.12\%.$

Note that this is much higher than the effective interest rate in the pledging scenario (16.53 percent); this is due solely to the addition of the factoring commission or credit-checking fee, since other variables were not altered.[9] But since the use of factoring may reduce the firm's costs of a credit department, it may still be cost-efficient.

Once a factoring arrangement is established, a continuous circular flow of goods and funds takes place among the seller, the buyers, and the factor. The seller of the goods receives orders and transmits the purchase orders to the factor for approval; on approval, the goods are shipped; the factor advances the money to the seller; the buyers pay the factor; and the factor periodically remits any excess reserve to the seller of goods. Thus, once the agreement is in force, funds from this source are "spontaneous."

Evaluation of Receivables Financing

Accounts receivable financing occurs because the seller needs to borrow, but its credit position isn't strong enough to borrow on an unsecured basis. Pledging of accounts receivable involves this financing aspect alone, with the receivables treated as collateral for the loan. Pledging would be appropriate where a firm's buyers tend to be high-quality companies. Factoring, on the other hand, involves both the financing aspect and credit evaluation and assumption of credit risk by the factor. Thus, in a sense, it is misleading to include the factoring commission in calculating the effective financial cost of factoring as in the worksheet above.

The key issue for this "insurance" element of the cost is whether the credit-checking and risk-bearing functions can be carried out more cheaply by the factor or by the firm itself. An efficient factor has the advantage that having done a credit evaluation of a buyer firm, it can "sell" its evaluation to, for example, ten different selling firms for as little as one-tenth of the cost of the evaluation. In contrast, each individual seller would have to bear the entire cost of the evaluation alone, and the evaluation would have to be duplicated as many times as there are sellers. (It is not surprising that we find factoring companies specializing in particular seller industry groups.) This raises the question why a company would ever do a credit evaluation on its own. The answer may be that, when done properly, credit evaluation involves continuing interaction between the sales and credit departments of the selling firm with the buyers, which can benefit follow-on sales. Also, the cost difference may not be large, so that the issue comes down to the relative efficiency of the selling company versus the factoring company. For example, where the number of buyers is large but the dollar amount of sales to each is relatively small, the efficiency aspect may hinge on the sheer mechanics of handling the paperwork.

Accounts receivable financing also has disadvantages. First, when invoices are numerous and relatively small in dollar amount, the administrative costs involved may render this method of financing inconvenient and expensive. Second, the firm is using a highly liquid asset as security. For a long time, accounts receivable financing was

---

[9]There can be considerable variation in the terms of accounts receivable financing contracts; for example, a factoring agreement may call for interest to be computed on the invoice price less both the reserve and the factoring commission. The worksheet methodology is flexible enough to handle these variations, while, for example, the compact formula used in the pledging analysis is not.

frowned on by most trade creditors; it was regarded as confession of a firm's unsound financial position. It is no longer regarded in this light, however, and many sound firms engage in receivables pledging or factoring. Still, the traditional attitude causes some trade creditors to refuse to sell on credit to a firm that is factoring or pledging its receivables, on the ground that this practice removes one of the most liquid of the firm's assets and, accordingly, weakens the position of other creditors.

In the future, accounts receivable financing is likely to continue to increase in relative importance. Computer technology is rapidly advancing towards the point where credit records of individuals and firms can be kept in computer memory. Systems already have been devised whereby a retailer can insert an individual's magnetic credit card into a box and receive a signal showing whether the person's credit is good and whether a bank is willing to buy the receivable created when the store completes the sale. The cost of handling invoices will be greatly reduced from present-day costs because the new systems will be so highly automated. This will make it possible to use accounts receivable financing for very small sales, and it will reduce the cost of all receivables financing. This suggests a continued expansion of accounts receivable financing.

INVENTORY FINANCING

If a firm is a relatively good credit risk, the mere existence of the inventory may be a sufficient basis for receiving an unsecured loan. If the firm is a relatively poor risk, the lending institution may insist on security, which often takes the form of a blanket lien against the inventory. Alternatively, trust receipts, field warehouse financing, or collateral certificates can be used to secure loans. These methods of using inventories as security are discussed below.

Blanket Inventory Lien

The *blanket inventory lien* gives the lending institution a lien against all inventories of the borrower. However, the borrower is free to sell the inventories; thus, the value of the collateral can be reduced. This fact often makes an inventory lien a less desirable arrangement to a bank.

Trust Receipts

Because of the weaknesses of the blanket lien for inventory financing, another kind of security is often used — the trust receipt. A *trust receipt* is an instrument acknowledging that the borrower holds the goods in trust for the lender. On receiving funds from the lender, the borrowing firm conveys a trust receipt for the goods. The goods can be stored in a public warehouse or held on the borrower's premises. The trust receipt provides that the goods are held in trust for the lender or are segregated on the borrower's premises on behalf of the lender and that proceeds from the sale of such goods are transmitted to the lender at the end of each day. Automobile dealer financing is the best example of trust receipt financing.

One defect of this form of financing is the requirement that a trust receipt must be issued for specific goods. For example, if the security is bags of coffee beans, the trust receipts must indicate the bags by number. In order to validate its trust receipts, the lending institution must send someone to the borrower's premises to see that the bag numbers are correctly listed. Furthermore, complex legal requirements for trust receipts require the attention of a bank officer. Problems are compounded if borrowers are widely separated geographically from the lender. To offset these inconveniences, warehousing is coming into wide use as a method of securing loans with inventory.

Field Warehouse Financing

Like trust receipts, field warehouse financing uses inventory as security. A public warehouse represents an independent third party engaged in the business of storing goods. Sometimes the warehouse is not practical because of the bulkiness of goods and the expense of transporting them to and from the borrower's premises. Field warehouse financing represents an economical method of inventory financing in which the "warehouse" is established on the borrower's premises. To provide inventory supervision, the lending institution employs a third party in the arrangement, the field warehousing company. This company acts as the control (or supervisory) agent for the lending institution.

Field warehousing is illustrated by a simple example. Suppose a potential borrower has stacked iron in an open yard on its premises. A field warehouse can be established if, say, a field warehousing concern places a temporary fence around the iron and erects a sign stating: "This is a field warehouse supervised and conducted by the Smith Field Warehousing Corporation."

The example illustrates the two elements in the establishment of a warehouse: (1) public notification of the field warehouse arrangement and (2) supervision of the warehouse by a custodian of the field warehouse concern. When the field warehousing operation is relatively small, the second condition is sometimes violated by hiring an employee of the borrower to supervise the inventory. This practice is viewed as undesirable by the lending institution because there is no control over the collateral by a person independent of the borrowing concern.[10]

The field warehouse financing operation is described best by a specific illustration. Assume that a tomato canner is interested in financing operations by bank borrowing. The canner has funds sufficient to finance 15 to 20 percent of operations during the canning season. These funds are adequate to purchase and process an initial batch of tomatoes. As the cans are put into boxes and rolled into the storerooms, the canner needs additional funds for both raw materials and labor.

---

[10]This absence of independent control was the main cause of the breakdown that resulted in the huge losses connected with loans to the Allied Crude Vegetable Oil Company headed by Anthony (Tino) DeAngelis. American Express Field Warehousing Company hired men from Allied's staff as custodians. Their dishonesty was not discovered because of another breakdown — the fact that the American Express touring inspector did not actually take a physical inventory of the warehouses. As a consequence, the swindle was not discovered until losses running into the hundreds of millions of dollars had been suffered. See Norman C. Miller, *The Great Salad Oil Swindle* (Baltimore, Md.: Penguin Books, 1965), pp. 72–77.

Because of the canner's poor credit rating, the bank decides that a field warehousing operation is necessary to secure its loans. The field warehouse is established, and the custodian notifies the lending institution of the description, by number, of the boxes of canned tomatoes in storage and under his control. Thereupon, the lending institution establishes for the canner a deposit on which it can draw. From this point on, the bank finances the operations. The canner needs only enough cash to initiate the cycle. The farmers bring more tomatoes; the canner processes them; the cans are boxed and the boxes put into the field warehouse; field warehouse receipts are drawn up and sent to the bank; the bank establishes further deposits for the canner on the basis of the receipts; and the canner can draw on the deposits to continue the cycle.

Of course, the canner's ultimate objective is to sell the canned tomatoes. As the canner receives purchase orders, it transmits them to the bank, and the bank directs the custodian to release the inventories. It is agreed that, as remittances are received by the canner, they will be turned over to the bank. These remittances pay off the loans made by the bank.

Typically, a seasonal pattern exists. At the beginning of the tomato harvesting and canning season, the canner's cash needs and loan requirements begin to rise, and they reach a maximum by the end of the canning season. It is hoped that, just before the new canning season begins, the canner has sold a sufficient volume to have paid off the loan completely. If for some reason the canner has had a bad year, the bank may carry the company over another year to enable it to sell off its inventory.

Acceptable Products. In addition to canned foods, which account for about 17 percent of all field warehouse loans, many other product inventories provide a basis for field warehouse financing. Some of these are miscellaneous groceries, which represent about 13 percent; lumber products, about 10 percent; and coal and coke, about 6 percent.

These products are relatively nonperishable and are sold in well-developed, organized markets. Nonperishability protects the lender who has to take over the security. For this reason, a bank will not make a field warehousing loan on perishables such as fresh fish. However, frozen fish, which can be stored for a long time, can be field warehoused. An organized market also aids the lender in disposing of inventory that it takes over. Banks are not interested in going into the canning or the fish business. They want to be able to dispose of an inventory with the expenditure of a minimum amount of their own time.

Cost of Financing. The fixed costs of a field warehousing arrangement are relatively high; such financing, therefore, is not suitable for a very small firm. If a field warehouse company sets up the warehouse itself, it typically sets a minimum fixed charge, plus about 1 or 2 percent of the amount of credit extended to the borrower. Furthermore, the financing institution charges interest at a rate somewhat above the prevailing prime rate. The minimum size of an efficient warehousing operation requires an inventory of about $100,000.

Appraisal. The use of field warehouse financing as a source of funds for business firms has many advantages. First, the amount of funds available is flexible because the financing is tied to the growth of inventories, which, in turn, is related directly to financing needs. Second, the arrangement increases the acceptability of inventories as loan collateral. Some inventories are not accepted by a bank as a security without a field warehousing arrangement. Third, the necessity for inventory control, safekeeping, and the use of specialists in warehousing has resulted in improved warehouse practices. The services of the field warehouse companies have often saved money for the firm, in spite of the financing costs mentioned above. The field warehouse company may suggest inventory practices that reduce both the number of people the firm has to employ and inventory damage and loss as well.

The major disadvantage of a field warehousing operation is the fixed cost element, which reduces the feasibility of this form of financing for small firms.

Collateral Certificates

A *collateral certificate* guarantees the existence of the amount of inventory pledged as loan collateral. It is a statement issued periodically to the lender by a third party, who certifies that the inventory exists and that it will be available if needed.

This method of bank financing is becoming increasingly popular, primarily because of its flexibility. First, there is no need for physical segregation or possession of inventories. Therefore, collateral certificates can even be used to cover work-in-progress inventories, facilitating more freedom in the movement of goods. Second, the collateral certificate can provide for a receivables financing plan, allowing financing to continue smoothly as inventories are converted into receivables. Third, the certificate issuer usually provides a number of services to simplify loan administration for both the borrower and the lender.

INTERNATIONAL FORMS AND SOURCES OF SHORT-TERM FINANCING

With the globalization of financial markets, international short- and medium-term financing has become increasingly important. International commercial banking is increasingly involved in deposit-taking and lending activities. Much international banking activity takes place in offshore banking centers generally referred to as the Euromarkets. Euromarkets consist of Eurocurrency deposits, Eurocommercial paper, and Eurobonds. Eurocurrency deposits are bank deposits denominated in any foreign currency, not just those of European countries; they account for 86 percent of the foreign-owned deposits of banks [Pavel and McElravey, 1990, p. 5]. Also recall, as defined in Chapter 4, that Eurocommercial paper is a short-term debt instrument issued and sold outside the country of the currency in which it is denominated. Eurobonds are the long-term debt counterpart. The international banks make unsecured Eurodollar loans with maturities on the shorter end. Interest rates on Eurodollar loans are tied to the London Interbank Offer Rate (LIBOR) — the rate at which banks lend Eurodollars to one another. U.S. branches and agencies of foreign banks allocate over half of their assets to loans.

Because the amounts may be very large, Eurodollar loans are likely to be made by a syndicate of banks. In syndicated Eurobank loans each bank has a separate loan agreement with the borrower. However, there has been a trend toward a shift by borrowing firms from syndicated bank loans to floating rate notes (FRNs).[11] Floating rate notes are medium-term securities carrying a floating rate of interest reset at regular intervals such as quarterly or half-yearly in relation to some reference rate, usually LIBOR.

Another innovation is the development of note issuance facilities (NIFs). An individual NIF is a line of credit or revolving facility that enables a borrower to issue a series of "Euronotes" over the medium term. The market for NIFs is a type of Eurocommercial paper market which is a mechanism for high-grade borrowers to raise funds cheaply. These Euronotes are marketed by one or more commercial banks or investment banks. This financing activity is supported by a group of banks, which underwrite the NIF by contracting to buy up any unsold notes. The firm pays an initial fee and an annual underwriting fee for this note issuance facility.

The NIF technique separates the functions performed by a single bank in a traditional syndicated credit permitting each function to be performed by a different institution. The function of financing the firm is transferred from one of lending money into one of setting up a borrowing mechanism. The credit risk is shared between the holders of the notes, who carry default risk, and the underwriters, who will have to take up an increasing proportion of the notes issued by a borrower if investors lose confidence in the firm. The popularity of NIFs results from the cost savings of unbundling but also from the trend toward securitization in which lending to high-grade borrowers takes place through securities rather than by bank loans.

SUMMARY

Short-term financial management encompasses *working capital management* and involves all aspects of the administration of current assets and current liabilities.

The first policy question deals with the determination of the level of total current assets to be held. Current assets vary with sales, but the ratio of current assets to sales is a policy matter. A firm that elects to operate aggressively will hold relatively small stocks of current assets, a policy that will reduce the required level of investment and increase the expected rate of return on investment. However, an aggressive policy also increases the likelihood of running out of inventories or losing sales because of an excessively tough credit policy.

The second policy question concerns the relationships among types of assets and the way these assets are financed. One policy calls for matching asset and liability maturities by financing current assets with short-term debt and fixed assets with long-term debt or equity. But this policy is unsound, because current assets include "permanent" investments that increase as sales grow. In our judgment, the financing of current assets should recognize that some portion bears a constant relationship to sales, so that this portion represents "permanent" investment. This would call for financing the permanent portion

---

[11]Bank for International Settlements, *Recent Innovations in International Banking*, April 1986, p. 130.

of current assets with the permanent portion of short-term debt (the spontaneous portion provided by accounts payable and accruals) and by long-term debt and equity financing to the extent required.

Short-term credit is debt originally scheduled for repayment within one year. The three major sources of short-term credit are trade credit among firms, loans from commercial banks, and commercial paper.

Trade credit (represented by accounts payable) is the largest single category of short-term credit; it is especially important for smaller firms. Trade credit is a *spontaneous source of financing* in that it arises from ordinary business transactions; as sales increase so does the supply of financing from accounts payable.

Bank credit occupies a pivotal position in the short-term money market. Banks provide the marginal credit that allows firms to expand more rapidly than is possible through retained earnings and trade credit. A denial of bank credit often means that a firm must slow its rate of growth.

Bank interest rates are quoted in three ways — regular compound interest, discount interest, and installment interest. Regular interest needs no adjustment. Discount interest requires a small upward adjustment to make it comparable to regular compound interest rates. Installment interest rates require a large adjustment, and, frequently, the true interest rate is double the quoted rate for an installment loan.

Bank loans are personal in the sense that the financial manager meets with the banker, discusses the terms of the loan, and reaches an agreement that requires direct and personal negotiation. Commercial paper, however, although it is physically similar to a bank loan, is sold in a broad, impersonal market. A California firm might, for example, sell commercial paper to a manufacturer in the Midwest.

The highest rated firms are the main users of the commercial paper markets. The nature of these markets is such that the firm selling the paper must have a reputation so good that buyers of the paper are willing to buy it without any sort of credit check. Interest rates in the commercial paper market are the lowest available to business borrowers.

The most common forms of collateral used for short-term credit are inventories and accounts receivable. Accounts receivable financing can be done either by pledging the receivables or by selling them outright (often called factoring). When the receivables are pledged, the borrower retains the risk that the person or firm owing the receivables will not pay; in factoring, this risk is typically passed on to the lender. Because factors take the risk of default, they investigate the purchaser's credit; therefore, factors can perform three functions: lending, risk bearing, and credit checking. When receivables are pledged, the lender typically performs only the first of these functions.

Loans secured by inventories are not satisfactory under many circumstances. For certain kinds of inventory, however, the technique known as field warehousing is used to provide adequate security to the lender. Under a field warehousing arrangement, the inventory is physically controlled by a warehouse company, which releases the inventory only on order from the lending institution. Canned goods, lumber, steel, coal, and other standardized products are goods usually covered in field warehouse arrangements. Blanket inventory liens, trust receipts, and collateral certificates are also used in securing loans with inventories.

With the globalization of financial markets, short-term international financing sources have grown. Eurodollar loans and Eurocommercial paper involve activity outside the country of the currency in which the debt is denominated. Eurodollar loans are likely to be made by a syndicate of banks. Floating rate notes are increasingly used. A note issuance facility (NIF) enables a borrower to issue a series of medium-term Euronotes, a type of Eurocommercial paper.

QUESTIONS

20.1   Give your reaction to this statement: Merely increasing the level of current asset holdings does not necessarily reduce the riskiness of the firm. Rather, the composition of the current assets, whether highly liquid or highly illiquid, is the important consideration.

20.2   How does the seasonal nature of a firm's sales influence the decision about the amount of short-term credit in the financial structure?

20.3   What is the advantage of matching the maturities of assets and liabilities? What are the disadvantages?

20.4   There have been times when the term structure of interest rates has been such that short-term rates were higher than long-term rates. Does this necessarily imply that the best financial policy for a firm is to use all long-term debt and no short-term debt? Explain.

20.5   It is inevitable that firms will obtain a certain amount of their financing in the form of trade credit, which is (to some extent) a free source of funds. What are some other reasons for firms to use trade credit?

20.6   Discuss the statement: Commercial paper interest rates are always lower than bank loan rates to a given borrower. Nevertheless, many firms perfectly capable of selling commercial paper employ higher-cost bank credit. Explain (a) why commercial paper rates are lower than bank rates and (b) why firms might use bank credit in spite of its higher cost.

20.7   Discuss these statements: Trade credit has an explicit interest rate cost if discounts are available but not taken. There are also some intangible costs associated with the failure to take discounts.

20.8   The availability of bank credit is more important to small firms than to large ones. Why?

20.9   What variables should a firm consider in selecting its primary bank?

20.10   Indicate whether each of the following changes will raise or lower the cost of a firm's accounts receivable financing and explain why this occurs:
   a.   The firm eases up on its credit standards in order to increase sales.
   b.   The firm institutes a policy of refusing to make credit sales if the amount of the purchase (invoice) is below $100. Previously, about 40 percent of all invoices were below $100.
   c.   The firm agrees to give recourse to the finance company for all defaults.

d. A firm without a recourse arrangement changes its terms of trade from net 30 to net 90.

20.11 Would a firm that manufactures specialized machinery for a few large customers be more likely to use a form of inventory financing or a form of accounts receivable financing? Why?

20.12 Discuss the statement: A firm that factors its accounts receivable will have a stronger current ratio than one that discounts its receivables.

20.13 Why would it not be practical for a typical retailer to use field warehouse financing?

Problems

20.1 Indicate the effects of the transactions listed below on each of the following: total current assets, working capital, current ratio, and net profit. Use "+" to indicate an increase, "−" to indicate a decrease, and "0" to indicate no effect. State necessary assumptions and assume an initial current ratio of more than 1 to 1.

	Total Current Assets	Working Capital[a]	Current Ratio	Net Profit
1. Cash is acquired through issuance of additional common stock.				
2. Merchandise is sold for cash.				
3. Federal income tax due for the previous year is paid.				
4. A fixed asset is sold for less than book value.				
5. A fixed asset is sold for more than book value.				
6. Merchandise is sold on credit.				
7. Payment is made to trade creditors for previous purchases.				
8. A cash dividend is declared and paid.				
9. Cash is obtained through short-term bank loans.				
10. Short-term notes receivable are sold at a discount.				
11. A profitable firm increases its fixed assets depreciation allowance account.				
12. Marketable securities are sold below cost.				
13. Uncollectible accounts are written off against the allowance account.				
14. Advances are made to employees.				
15. Current operating expenses are paid.				
16. Short-term promissory notes are issued to trade creditors for prior purchases.				
17. Ten-year notes are issued to pay off accounts payable.				
18. A wholly depreciated asset is retired.				
19. Accounts receivable are collected.				
20. A stock dividend is declared and paid.				

21. Equipment is purchased with short-term notes.
22. The allowance for doubtful accounts is increased.
23. Merchandise is purchased on credit.
24. The estimated taxes payable are increased.

ᵃWorking capital is defined as current assets minus current liabilities.

20.2   The Warner Flooring Corporation is attempting to determine the optimal level of current assets for the coming year. Management expects sales to increase to approximately $1.2 million as a result of asset expansion presently being undertaken. Fixed assets total $500,000, and the firm wishes to maintain a 60 percent debt ratio. Warner's interest cost is currently 10 percent on both short-term debt and longer-term debt (which the firm uses in its permanent capital structure). Three alternatives regarding the projected current asset level are available to the firm: (1) an aggressive policy requiring current assets of only 45 percent of projected sales, (2) an average policy of 50 percent of sales in current assets, and (3) a conservative policy requiring current assets of 60 percent of sales. The firm expects to generate earnings before interest and taxes at a rate of 12 percent on total sales.

   a.   What is the expected return on equity under each current asset level? (Assume a 40 percent tax rate.)

   b.   In this problem, we have assumed that the earnings rate and the level of expected sales are independent of current asset policy. Is this a valid assumption?

   c.   How would the overall riskiness of the firm vary under each policy? Discuss specifically the effect of current asset management on demand, expenses, fixed charge coverage, risk of insolvency, and so on.

20.3   Three companies—Aggressive, Between, and Conservative—have different working capital management policies as implied by their names. For example, Aggressive employs only minimal current assets and finances entirely with current liabilities and equity. The "tight-ship" approach has a dual effect. It keeps total assets low, and this tends to increase return on assets. But for reasons such as stockouts, total sales are reduced; and since inventory is ordered more frequently and in smaller quantities, variable costs are increased. Condensed balance sheets for the three companies are presented below.

Balance Sheets

	Aggressive	Between	Conservative
Current assets	$150,000	$200,000	$300,000
Fixed assets	200,000	200,000	200,000
Total assets	$350,000	$400,000	$500,000
Current liabilities (@12%)	$200,000	$100,000	$ 50,000
Long-term debt (@10%)	0	100,000	200,000
Total debt	$200,000	$200,000	$250,000
Equity	150,000	200,000	250,000
Total claims on assets	$350,000	$400,000	$500,000
Current ratio	0.75:1	2:1	6:1

The cost of goods sold functions for the three firms are as follows:

$$\text{Cost of goods sold} = \text{Fixed costs} + \text{Variable costs}$$

Aggressive: Cost of goods sold = $200,000 + 0.70 (Sales)

Between: Cost of goods sold = $270,000 + 0.65 (Sales)

Conservative: Cost of goods sold = $385,000 + 0.60 (Sales)

Because of the working capital differences, sales for the three firms under different economic conditions are expected to vary as indicated below:

	Aggressive	Between	Conservative
Strong economy	$1,200,000	$1,200,000	$1,200,000
Average economy	900,000	1,000,000	1,150,000
Weak economy	700,000	800,000	1,050,000

a. Make out income statements for each company for strong, average, and weak economies using the following pattern:

Sales

Less cost of goods sold

Earnings before interest and taxes (EBIT)

Less interest expense

Taxable income

Less taxes (@40%)

Net income

b. Compare the rates of return (EBIT/Total Assets and Return on Equity). Which company is best in a strong economy? In an average economy? In a weak economy?

c. What considerations for management of working capital are indicated by this problem?

20.4 Wilber Corp. is negotiating with the Citizen's Bank for a $500,000 one-year loan. Citizen has offered Wilber the following three alternatives:

(1) A 15 percent interest rate, no compensating balance, and interest due at the end of the year.

(2) A 13 percent interest rate, a 20 percent compensating balance, and interest due at the end of the year.

(3) An 11 percent interest rate, a 15 percent compensating balance, and the loan discounted.

If Wilber wishes to minimize the effective interest rate, which alternative will it choose?

20.5 Mark Industries is having difficulty paying its bills and is considering foregoing its trade discounts on $300,000 of accounts payable. As an alternative, Mark can obtain a 60-day note with a 14 percent annual interest rate. The note will be discounted, and the trade credit terms are 2/10, net 60.

a. Which alternative has the lower effective cost?

b. If Mark does not take its trade discounts, what conclusions may outsiders draw?

20.6 Best Catsup Company is considering the following two alternatives for financing next year's canning operations:

(1) Establishing a $1 million line of credit with a 1 percent interest rate on the used amount at the end of each month and a 1 percent per annum commitment fee rate on the unused portion (.0833 percent on unused amount at the end of each month). A $150,000 compensating balance will be required at all times on the entire $1 million line.

(2) Using field warehousing to finance the inventory. Financing charges will be a flat fee of $500, plus 2 percent of the maximum amount of credit extended, plus a 10 percent annual interest rate (.833 percent on amount outstanding at the end of each month) on all outstanding credit.

Best has $150,000 of funds available for inventory financing. All financing is done on the first of the month and is sufficient to cover the value of the expected inventory at the end of the month. Expected month-end inventory levels are given below.

Month	Amount	Month	Amount
July 19X0	$ 150,000	January 19X1	$600,000
August	400,000	February	450,000
September	600,000	March	350,000
October	800,000	April	225,000
November	1,000,000	May	100,000
December	750,000	June	0

Which financing plan has the lower cost? (Hints: Under the bank loan plan, borrowings in July are $150,000 and in December $750,000; under the field warehousing plan, July borrowings are zero and December borrowings are $600,000.)

20.7 Collins Manufacturing needs an additional $100,000. The financial manager is considering two methods of obtaining this money: a loan from a commercial bank or a factoring arrangement. The bank charges 12 percent per annum interest, discount basis. It also requires a 15 percent compensating balance. The factor is willing to purchase Collins's accounts receivable and to advance the invoice amount less a 3 percent factoring commission on the invoices purchased each month. (All sales are on 30-day terms.) A 10 percent annual interest rate will be charged on the total invoice price and deducted in advance. Also, under the factoring agreement, Collins can eliminate its credit department and reduce credit expenses by $2,000 per month. Bad debt losses of 10 percent on the factored amount can also be avoided.

a. How much should the bank loan be in order to net $100,000? How much accounts receivable should be factored to net $100,000?

b. What are the computed interest rates and the annual total dollar costs, including credit department expenses and bad debt losses, associated with each financing arrangement?

c. Discuss some considerations other than cost that may influence management's choice between factoring and a commercial bank loan.

20.8 Sunlight Sailboats estimates that due to the seasonal nature of its business, it will require an additional $200,000 of cash for the month of July. Sunlight has four options available to provide the needed funds. It can

(1) Establish a one-year line of credit for $200,000 with a commercial bank. The commitment fee will be 0.5 percent, and the interest charge on the used funds will be 15 percent per annum. The minimum time the funds can be used is 30 days.

   (2) Forego the July trade discount of 2/10, net 40 on $200,000 of accounts payable.
   (3) Issue $200,000 of 30-day commercial paper at a 13.8 percent per annum interest rate.
   (4) Issue $200,000 of 60-day commercial paper at a 14 percent per annum interest rate. Since the funds are required for only 30 days, the excess funds ($200,000) can be invested in 13 percent per annum marketable securities for the month of August. The total transaction fee on purchasing and selling the marketable securities is 0.5 percent of the fair value.

   a. Which financial arrangement results in the lowest cost?
   b. Is the source with the lowest expected cost necessarily the source to select? Why or why not?

20.9 The balance sheet of the Pacific Finance Corporation is shown below.

Pacific Finance Corporation Balance Sheet
(Millions of Dollars)

Assets		Liabilities	
Cash	$ 75	Bank loans	$ 250
Net receivables	2,400	Commercial paper	825
Marketable securities	150	Others	375
Repossessions	5	Total due within a year	$1,450
Total current assets	$2,630	Long-term debt	1,000
Other assets	170	Total shareholders' equity	350
Total assets	$2,800	Total claims	$2,800

   a. Calculate commercial paper as a percentage of short-term financing, as a percentage of total-debt financing, and as a percentage of all financing.
   b. Why do finance companies such as Pacific Finance use commercial paper to such a great extent?
   c. Why do they use both bank loans and commercial paper?

20.10 Wilkins Manufacturing needs an additional $250,000, which it plans to obtain through a factoring arrangement. The factor would purchase Wilkins's accounts receivable and advance the invoice amount, less a 2 percent commission, on the invoices purchased each month. (Wilkins sells on terms of net 30 days.) In addition, the factor charges 16 percent annual interest on the total invoice amount, to be deducted in advance.
   a. What amount of accounts receivable must be factored to net $250,000?
   b. If Wilkins can reduce credit expenses by $1,500 per month and avoid bad-debt losses of 3 percent on the factored amount, what is the total dollar cost of the factoring arrangement?

20.11 The Shandow Insulation Company has been growing rapidly, but because of insufficient working capital, it has now become slow in paying bills. Of its total accounts payable, $96,000 is overdue. This threatens Shandow's relationship with its main supplier of powders used in the manufacture of various kinds of insulation materials for aircraft and

missiles. Over 75 percent of its sales are to six large, financially strong defense contractors. The company's balance sheet, sales, and net profit for the past year are shown
below.

Balance Sheet
Shandow Corporation

Cash	$ 28,800	Trade credit[a]	$240,000
Receivables	320,000	Bank loans	192,000
Inventories		Accruals[a]	48,000
Raw material	38,400	Total current debt	$480,000
Work in process	192,000	Mortgages on equipment	288,000
Finished goods	57,600	Capital stock	96,000
Total current assets	$ 636,800	Retained earnings	96,000
Equipment	323,200		
Total assets	$ 960,000	Total liabilities/net worth	$960,000
Sales	$1,920,000		
Profit after taxes	96,000		

[a]Increases spontaneously with sales increases.

Shandow is considering two alternative methods to solve its payments problem: factoring and receivables financing. Additional information follows.

    Receivables turn over six times a year. (Sales/receivables = 6.) All sales are made
on credit. The factor requires a 15 percent reserve for returns on disputed items. The
factor also requires a 1.5 percent commission on average receivables outstanding, payable at the time the receivable is purchased, to cover the costs of credit checking. There is
an interest charge by the factor at the prime rate (12 percent) plus 3 percent based on
receivables *less* any reserve requirements and commissions. This payment is made at the
beginning of the period and is deducted from the advance. Receivables financing would
involve the same costs as factoring except the factoring commission and a 20 percent
reserve rather than 15 percent under factoring.

a. When sales are $1,920,000, on average, what is the total amount of receivables
outstanding?

b. What is the average duration of advances, on the basis of 360 days a year?

c. How much cash does the firm actually receive under factoring as compared with
receivables financing?

d. What is the total annual dollar cost of financing under factoring as compared with
receivables financing?

e. What is the annual effective percentage financing cost paid on the money received
under factoring as compared with receivables financing?

f. Which method of financing should Shandow utilize?

20.12 The Morton Plastics Company manufactures plastic toys. It buys raw materials, manufactures the toys in the spring and summer, and ships them to a large number of department stores and toy stores by late summer or early fall. The company factors its receivables. If it did not, Morton's balance sheet would have appeared as follows:

Morton Company
Pro Forma Balance Sheet as of March 31, 19X0

Cash	$ 40,000	Accounts payable	$1,200,000
Receivables	1,200,000	Notes payable	800,000
Inventory	800,000	Accruals	80,000
Total current assets	$2,040,000	Total current debt	$2,080,000
		Mortgages	200,000
		Common stock	400,000
Fixed assets	800,000	Retained earnings	160,000
Total assets	$2,840,000	Total claims	$2,840,000

Morton provides dating on its sales; thus, its receivables are not due for payment until 90 days after purchase. Also, the company would have been overdue on some $800,000 of its accounts payable if the above situation actually existed.

Morton has an agreement with a finance company to factor the receivables for the quarterly periods. The factoring company charges a flat commission of 1.5 percent, plus interest at 3 points over the prime rate (15 percent) on the outstanding balance. It deducts a reserve of 15 percent for returned and damaged materials. Interest and commission are paid in advance. No interest is charged on the reserved funds or on the commission.

a. Show the balance sheet of Morton on March 31, 19X0, giving effect to the purchase of all the receivables by the factoring company and the use of the funds to pay accounts payable.

b. If the $1.2 million is the average level of outstanding receivables and if they turn over four times a year (hence, the commission is paid four times a year), what are the total dollar costs of financing and the computed annual interest rate?

c. What are the advantages to Morton Plastics of using factoring, as opposed to discounting its receivables?

20.13 *(Use the computer diskette, File name: 20WRKPOL, Working Capital Policy.)*

a. Given the initial conditions and assumptions, which working capital policy achieves the highest return on equity?

(1) Assuming that sales rise to $2 million, and that the investment in current assets remains unchanged under each policy, what happens to the Sales/Current Assets multiple? Which working capital policy now has the highest return on equity?

(2) Suppose sales drop to $960,000 and the investment in current assets remains the same. What happens to the Sales/Current Assets multiple? Which policy achieves the highest return on equity?

b. Given the investment in current assets in Part (a) and given a level of sales for the alternative policies of $960,000 for Aggressive, $1,200,000 for Average, and $1,400,000 for Conservative, what does this imply for the Sales/Current Assets multiple? Under which policy will return on equity be greatest?

c. Given the conditions of Part (b) and given a total cost function high in fixed costs ($500,000) and relatively low in variable costs (.4 × Sales), which working capital policy will achieve the highest return on equity?

d. Going back to the conditions assumed in Part (b), but with a total cost function of $250,000 + (.7 × Sales), which policy will have the highest return on equity?

e. Now you are free to explore any set of relationships that interests you, by changing current assets, sales, fixed assets, and the cost function.

SELECTED REFERENCES

Barlev, Benzion; Livnat, Joshua; and Yoran, Aharon, "Advance Payments During Inflationary Periods," *Journal of Business Finance & Accounting*, 9 (Autumn 1982), pp. 413–426.

Heller, Lucy, ed., *Eurocommercial Paper,* London: Euromoney Publications, 1988.

Hill, Ned C., and Sartoris, William L., *Short-Term Financial Management*, New York: Macmillan Publishing Company, 1988.

Hill, Ned C.; Wood, Robert A.; and Sorenson, Dale R., "Factors Influencing Credit Policy: A Survey," *Journal of Cash Management*, 1 (December 1981), pp. 38–47.

James, Christopher, "An Analysis of Bank Loan Rate Indexation," *Journal of Finance*, 37 (June 1982), pp. 809–825.

Loosigian, Allan M., "Hedging Commercial Paper Borrowing Costs with Treasury Bill Futures," *Journal of Cash Management*, 2, no. 2, (June 1982), pp. 50–57.

Maier, Steven F., and Vander Weide, James H., "A Practical Approach to Short-Run Financial Planning," *Financial Management*, 7 (Winter 1978), pp. 10–16.

Merville, L. J., and Tavis, L. A., "Optimal Working Capital Policies: A Chance-Constrained Programming Approach," *Journal of Financial and Quantitative Analysis*, 8 (January 1973), pp. 47–60.

Nelson, Robert E., Jr., "The Practice of Business Liquidity Improvement: A Management Approach," *Business Horizons*, 20 (October 1977), pp. 54–60.

Pavel, Christine, and McElravey, John N., "Globalization in the Financial Services Industry," *Economic Perspectives,* Federal Reserve Bank of Chicago, (May/June 1990), pp. 3–18.

Santomero, Anthony M., "Fixed Versus Variable Rate Loans," *Journal of Finance*, 38 (December 1983), pp. 1363–1380.

Sartoris, William L., and Hill, Ned C., "A Generalized Cash Flow Approach to Short-Term Financial Decisions," *Journal of Finance*, 38 (May 1983), pp. 349–360.

Smith, Keith V., *Readings on the Management of Working Capital*, 2d ed., New York: West Publishing Company, 1980.

———, *Guide to Working Capital Management*, New York: McGraw-Hill, 1975.

Stancill, James M., *The Management of Working Capital*, Scranton, Pa.: Intext Educational Publishers, 1971.

Stone, Bernell K., "The Cost of Bank Loans," *Journal of Financial and Quantitative Analysis*, 7 (December 1972), pp. 2077–2086.

Walker, Ernest W., "Towards a Theory of Working Capital," *Engineering Economist*, 9 (January-February 1964), pp. 21–35.

Yardini, Edward E., "A Portfolio-Balance Model of Corporate Working Capital," *Journal of Finance,* 33 (May 1978), pp. 535–552.

The Treasurer's Long-Range
Financial Strategies

Part Seven takes the point of view of the treasurer of the firm. It covers mainly the lower right side of the balance sheet, considering the various types of funds available to the firm when it seeks long-term, external capital. Within the framework of the relationship between financial structure and the cost of capital, decisions on individual financing episodes can be made to help the firm toward its objective of achieving an optimal mix of financing. The aim is to maximize the value of the firm. We have previously discussed investment decisions and other methods for increasing the cash inflow stream of the firm which in conjunction with minimizing financing costs enhances the value of the firm.

Chapter 21 presents an overview of the institutional material essential to an understanding of the use of the financial markets by business firms. Chapter 22 analyzes the conditions under which common stock financing is used. Chapter 23 describes the nature of long-term debt and preferred stocks and their role in the financing of the firm. Chapter 24 analyzes leasing decisions, which involve the issue of choosing the applicable discount rate. Chapter 25 discusses the nature of warrants, convertibles, and options and describes how their use helps resolve the problem of pricing the uncertain risk of corporate debt. Chapter 26 deals with pension fund management, with emphasis on decision making about alternative types of pension plans, performance evaluation, and tax aspects.

CHAPTER 21

Sources of Long-Term Financing

Our central theme has been minimizing the cost of capital and maximizing the value of the firm for its stakeholders. The present chapter deals with a number of aspects of the institutions of the capital markets that business firms use in seeking to develop sound strategies for financing. We begin with observations on the dramatic impacts of the changes associated with the wave of mergers, takeovers, and restructuring activities of the 1980s. We next present an overview of financing sources. Taking a life cycle perspective, we discuss the role of venture capital financing. We go on to describe the practice of direct financing from institutions such as insurance companies and banks called "private placement." We then cover the investment banking mechanisms by which funds are mobilized for use by business firms. We consider the issues of going public and initial public offerings (IPOs). We analyze the use of rights in financing. We discuss the implications of securities laws and regulations for financing. We conclude the chapter with a review of recent developments in financial markets and practices.

IMPACT OF MERGERS, TAKEOVERS, AND CORPORATE RESTRUCTURING

As we shall discuss more fully in Chapter 27, a new wave of mergers, acquisitions, and corporate restructuring took place beginning in the early 1980s. Debt was used to replace equity and more lower grade debt was employed. Innovative changes were made in the characteristics of debt so that the distinctions between short- and long-term debt and between debt and equity became blurred. New forms of financing instruments were developed. The roles of commercial banks and other financing institutions were changed. New regulations were promulgated by government agencies. These developments affected all the remaining topics of this chapter.

OVERVIEW OF FINANCING SOURCES

The data in Table 21.1 show that internal financing accounts for about three-quarters of the total sources of funds for U.S. corporations. The percentage is higher when profits are depressed and lower when profits are high. Studies show that internal funds are a high percentage of total sources in other developed countries as well [Remolona, 1990]. For the period mostly between 1983–1988, the ratio of internal funds was somewhat higher in France, Germany, and the United Kingdom, but somewhat lower in Japan — 63.2 percent for years 1984–1988 [Remolona, Table 3, p. 38].

The data patterns suggest some generalizations. Internal financing appears generally to have advantages over external financing — less taxes, less monitoring by external financing sources. External financing is used when investment requirements are high in relation to profitability levels. The role of internal financing by Japanese companies was even lower in earlier periods when they were aggressively expanding market share by a low price strategy resulting in large investments and narrow profit margins. The success of this strategy has paid off in higher profit margins in more recent years so that the role of internal financing has expanded in Japan as well. This further reinforces the conclusion of the advantages of internal financing in developed nations.

Another pattern observed across countries is that short-term debt is used for external financing when investment requirements are large in relation to internal sources as a short-term adjustment mechanism. When profits are high in relation to investment requirements, the short-term debt is paid off. As retained earnings accumulate, equity in the capital structure rises to offset increases in debt.

A rise in the ratio of long-term debt-to-equity represents a decision to increase the leverage ratio. Between 1983 and 1987, leverage ratios decreased in France, Germany,

TABLE 21.1   Sources of Funds for Business Corporations, 1950–1989 (Billions of Dollars)

		Internal		Securities & Mortgage		Loans & Short-term Paper		Other[1]	
					External				
Year	Total	Amount	Percent	Amount	Percent	Amount	Percent	Amount	Percent
1950	$ 42	$ 18	42%	$ 4	10%	$ 4	10%	$16	38%
1960	48	36	75	8	16	4	8	1	2
1970	102	62	60	26	26	8	8	4	4
1980	324	200	62	30	10	40	12	54	16
1985	458	352	76	−3	0	54	12	54	12
1989	512	380	74	−45	−10	80	16	98	20

[1]Consists of tax liabilities, trade debt, and direct foreign investment in the United States.
Source: President's Council of Economic Advisers, *Economic Report of the President,* (Washington, D.C.: Government Printing Office, 1991), Table B–92.

and Japan accompanied by a decline in the use of both short-term and long-term debt. During these years leverage increased slightly in the United Kingdom, but sharply in the United States where the ratio of long-term debt-to-total-assets (both at book) increased [Remolona, Chart 1, p. 33]. The increases in book ratios of debt in the United States during this period were associated with the merger and restructuring activities. Net external equity financing (i.e., proceeds from the sale of equity less repurchases and reductions due to mergers and takeovers) in the United States has long been negligible; between 1983 and 1990, the cumulative total was a negative $600 billion [Crabbe, Pickering, and Prowse, 1990, p. 594].

Statistics on the three broad sources of funds used by business corporations have been presented. The sources are internal cash flows, short-term external funds, and long-term external funds. The first two categories of financing were discussed in previous chapters. The third is the subject of the present chapter, which provides an overview of the market mechanisms for raising long-term funds. This overview is intended as a framework for the discussions of individual forms of long-term financing presented in the following chapters.

Another generalization to be emphasized is the increased participation and competition among the various types of financial institutions. Legislative changes enacted during the 1980s have blurred the distinction between investment banks and commercial banks. In addition, other financial intermediaries have increasingly provided a wide variety of financial services [Aguilar, 1990]. A mere listing of the types of banks and nonbanks is sufficient to convey the many types of intermediaries competing in the financial markets. A partial list of competing institutions in the different segments of the market is shown by Table 21.2.

Another perspective is to view financing sources in relation to the stage of development of the firm. This is suggested by Table 21.3.

In its formative stage, the new, small firm must rely most heavily on personal savings, trade credit, and government agencies. During its period of rapid growth, internal financing will become an important source of meeting its financing requirements, although continued reliance will be placed on trade credit. At this stage, its record of accomplishment also makes it possible to obtain bank credit to finance seasonal needs; and if the loan can be paid off on an amortized basis over two or three years, the firm may qualify for a term loan as well. If it has the potential for really strong growth, the firm may also be able to attract equity from a venture capital company.

A particularly successful firm may reach the stage where going public becomes feasible — this leads to access to the broader money and capital markets, and it represents a true coming-of-age for the small firm. Even at this point, however, the firm must look ahead, analyzing its products and their prospects. Because every product has a life cycle, the firm must be aware that without the development of new products, growth will cease, and eventually the firm will decline. Accordingly, as product maturity approaches, the firm must plan for the possibility of share repurchases, mergers, or other longer-term strategies. The best time to look ahead and plan for this is while the firm has energy, momentum, and a high price-earnings ratio.

In the following section we focus on financing the firm during its rapid growth stages.

TABLE 21.2   List of Well-Known Nonbanks and Large Bank Holding Companies

A. Bank Holding Companies
 1. Consumer:
   Citicorp
   Security Pacific Corp.
   Wells Fargo & Co.
   First Interstate Bancorp.
   Bank of New England Corp.
   NCNB Corp.
   Barnett Banks, Inc.
   Banc One Corp.
   First Union Corp.
   Citizens and Southern Corp.

 2. Commercial:
   Chase Manhattan Corp.
   Manufacturers Hanover Corp.
   Chemical New York Corp.
   J.P. Morgan & Co.
   First Chicago Corp.
   Bankers Trust New York Corp.
   Bank of Boston Corp.
   Marine Midland Banks, Inc.
   Mellon Bank Corp.
   Bank of New York Co.

B. Investment Banks:
 1. Merrill Lynch
 2. Goldman, Sachs
 3. Morgan Stanley
 4. Shearson Lehman
 5. PaineWebber
 6. Salomon Brothers
 7. First Boston
 8. Kidder, Peabody
 9. Dean Witter
 10. Smith Barney
 11. Donaldson Lufkin & Jenrette
 12. Drexel Burnham Lambert

C. Other Nonbanks
 1. Auto companies:
   General Motors Acceptance Corp.
   Ford Motor Credit Co.
   Chrysler Financial Corp.

 2. Consumer finance companies:
   American Express Co.
   Sears, Roebuck & Co.
   J.C. Penney Co.
   Associates
   Household International
   Beneficial Corp.
   Avco Financial Services
   Commercial Credit

 3. Commercial finance companies:
   General Electric Financial Services
   ITT Financial Corp.
   IBM Credit
   Westinghouse Credit
   Weyerhauser Financial Services
   Heller International
   Transamerica Corp.

 4. Insurance companies:
   The Prudential
   Aetna
   The Travelers
   Metropolitan Life
   Teachers Insurance and Annuity Association
   The Equitable
   Cigna
   John Hancock
   CNA Financial Corp.
   American General

FINANCING GROWTH FIRMS

After the firm's inception, a successful firm with growth potential will enter Stage 2 of its financial cycle. Here, the firm has achieved initial success—it is growing rapidly and is reasonably profitable. Cash flows and working capital management have become increasingly important. Also, at this stage the firm will have an extraordinary need for additional outside financing; this is shown in Table 21.4, which compares rapid and moderate growth firms. The growth company (Firm 1) expands from $800,000 in sales to $1.2 million in one year; Firm 2 grows by the same amount, but over a four-year period. The

---

TABLE 21.3   Financing Sources at Four Stages of a Firm's Development

Stage	Financial Patterns
1. Formation	Personal savings, trade credit, government agencies
2. Rapid growth	Internal financing, trade credit, bank credit, venture capital
3. Growth to maturity	Going public, money and capital markets
4. Maturity and industry decline	Internal financing, share repurchase, diversification, mergers

---

percentages in parentheses following the asset-liability accounts indicate the assumed relationships between asset items and the spontaneous sources of funds, which we discussed in Chapter 8 in the section on the percent of sales forecasting method. Note also that profits are assumed to be 6 percent of sales during the year, and that all earnings are retained. Let us further assume that notes payable are increased to cover the financing required — notes payable function as the balancing item. If the firm grows by 50 percent in one year, notes payable almost double. However, if the firm grows from $800,000 to

---

TABLE 21.4   Financial Effects of Different Rates of Growth (Thousands of Dollars)

	Firm 1		Firm 2				
	Year 1	Year 2	Year 1	Year 2	Year 3	Year 4	Year 5
Sales	$800	$1,200	$800	$900	$1,000	$1,100	$1,200
Current assets (30%)	240	360	240	270	300	330	360
Fixed assets (20%)	160	240	160	180	200	220	240
Total assets	$400	$ 600	$400	$450	$ 500	$ 550	$ 600
Accounts payable (10%)	80	120	80	90	100	110	120
Notes payable	96	172	96	79	56	27	(8)
Other accruals (3%)	24	36	24	27	30	33	36
Current liabilities	$200	$ 328	$200	$196	$ 186	$ 170	$ 148
Common stock	100	100	100	100	100	100	100
Retained earnings[a]	100	172	100	154	214	280	352
Net worth	$200	$ 272	$200	$254	$ 314	$ 380	$ 452
Total claims	$400	$ 600	$400	$450	$ 500	$ 550	$ 600
Key ratios							
Current ratio (times)	1.2	1.1	1.2	1.4	1.6	1.9	2.4
Debt ratio (percentage)	50	55	50	44	37	31	25
Sales to total assets (times)	2	2	2	2	2	2	2
Profit to net worth (percentage)	24.0	26.5	24.0	21.3	19.1	17.4	15.9

[a]Profit is 6 percent of sales; retained earnings are equal to profit plus retained earnings from the previous year.

$1.2 million over a four-year period, then notes payable not only do not increase at all, but they can actually be paid off. Hence, current liabilities decline from $200,000 to $148,000, while net worth increases from $200,000 to $452,000.

There is considerable doubt whether the growth firm could actually obtain short-term bank loans of the amount required. Such a large amount of short-term bank financing would cause its current ratio to drop to 1.1, and its debt ratio to rise to 55 percent. This situation develops even with the very favorable 24 percent rate of return on net worth. If the profit rate were lower, the firm's financing problem would be even more serious. When the firm uses four periods to achieve the same amount of growth, the financial ratios indicate a less risky situation. The current ratio never declines — it actually improves over the period. The debt ratio drops from 50 to 25 percent, which is very low compared with the average for all manufacturing firms.

If the rapid growth firm continues to grow at the 50 percent rate, the situation will further deteriorate, and it will become increasingly clear that the firm requires additional equity financing. The debt ratio will become much too high, yet the firm may well be reluctant to bring in additional outside equity money because the original owners are unwilling to share control. At this juncture, some financial pitfalls should be recognized and avoided. These are illustrated by the actual experiences of two individual small business owners who explained to the authors the difficulties they encountered. In one instance, the former owner of a firm described the problems that occurred after he obtained additional funds to support growth. He originally owned 100 percent of his company, but the firm needed capital. When two potential suppliers of the necessary funds each requested 30 percent ownership, the founder of the enterprise agreed, figuring that he would still have control with 40 percent, the largest block of the common stock. However, the two new equity owners joined forces, interfered with the creative management of the company, and caused it to fail. It may seem that this was a rather elementary error, since a person in business might be expected to look ahead to exactly this kind of move. However, production in new businesses tends to consume owner interest, and it is not uncommon for innovative entrepreneurs to fail as financial managers when more than one owner enters and changes the balance of power.

It is also an error to incur debt with an unrealistically short maturity. The former owner of another small firm borrowed on one- and two-year terms, but he failed to realize that if his firm continued to grow at a rapid rate, its needs for financing would increase, not decrease. Subsequently, he simply could not meet his debt maturities. It was convenient to borrow funds that were critically needed for growth on a relatively short-term basis, but when he was unable to make payments as the loans matured, he was forced to give up the controlling share of the equity. Thus, failure to plan properly again caused the founder to lose control of his company.

A number of sources of funds are available for growth firms. They include individuals, commercial banks, factoring companies, venture capital firms, alliances with larger companies, foreign companies, the Small Business Administration (SBA), and the SBA-sponsored Small Business Investment Corporations (SBICs).

Many small business firms have found that as they grow, commercial bankers are unwilling to finance them as their needs become relatively high multiples of their net worth. Often such small firms will use factoring services provided either by a specialized company or as a division of a commercial bank. The work of the factors was discussed in Chapter 20. The factor service began in the textile business over 200 years ago in the American colonies. In more recent years, the industries covered by the factor companies have been extended to toy, shoe, and furniture manufacturers, in particular, but also a wide range of other industries. Venture capital firms are also another important source of financing growth.

Venture Capital Financing

Firms that have growth potential face greater risks than almost any other type of business, and their higher risks require special types of financing. This has led to the development of specialized venture capital financing sources. Some venture capital companies are organized as partnerships; others are more formal corporations termed *investment development companies*. The American Research and Development Corporation, one of the first investment development companies, is widely traded in the financial markets; it and other publicly owned investment companies permit individuals and institutions, such as insurance companies, to participate in the venture capital market. Other venture capital companies represent the activities of individuals or partnerships. From time to time the operations of these individual companies are described in the financial press.

The pool of funds available for venture capital investments reached $31 billion by 1989, as compared with about $3 billion at the beginning of the 1980s and small annual inflows of only $10 million in the mid-1970s.[1] Although venture capital activity began in the United States almost immediately after World War II, a stimulus to growth took place in 1978 when (1) the capital gains tax was reduced and (2) rules that prevented pension funds from investing in venture capital funds were relaxed. Some venture capital funds became involved in leveraged buyouts (LBOs) during the 1980s which also stimulated their growth. Pension funds that accounted for 31 percent of the sources of venture capital in 1983 increased their share to 46 percent in 1988. The role of individuals and families dropped from 21 percent in 1983 to only 8 percent in 1988. Between 1983 and 1988 the share of endowments and foundations grew from 8 to 12 percent while the other major sources — foreign investors, corporations, and insurance companies — declined slightly.

The great influx of funds into venture capital funds caused their returns to decline. A study by Venture Economics Inc. calculated the median rates of return on venture capital investments as of year-end 1987.[2] Funds started in the period 1977 to 1979 earned a median annual return of 25.4 percent. The comparable figure for funds started in 1980 was 15.1 percent. Funds started from 1982 on through 1987 earned mostly less than 2 percent. However, it should be recognized that it takes about 10 years for venture fund investments to mature. Also, it is one or two big winners that return 10 to 20 times the investment that make up for the majority of the investments whose returns are quite modest. Nevertheless, in the early 1990s, many venture funds were "sitting with a lot of puppies in their portfolios that appeared to be emerging dogs."

---

[1]Andrew Pollack, *New York Times*, October 8, 1989, Section 3, p. 1, 6.

[2]Udayan Gupta, "Recent Venture Funds Perform Poorly As Unrealistic Expectations Wear Off," *Wall Street Journal*, November 8, 1988, p. B2.

Because of the increased competition among venture funds during the 1980s, some began to specialize. Many early venture funds were in high-technology areas following the example of the American Research and Development Corporation in Boston which in the late 1950s invested $60,000 in the Digital Equipment Corporation. Some 12 years later that investment was worth more than $500 million. Many venture funds located near Silicon Valley near San Francisco, California. In recent years, some funds have specialized in the bio-technology or health care areas. Some venture funds have sought to revitalize firms in the "rust belt."[3]

Investment banking firms and commercial banks have also established venture capital subsidiaries. Related to these are some venture capital investments by firms whose owners often have had prior investment banking or commercial banking experience. Some of these firms engage in raising financing for leveraged buyouts, discussed in Chapter 27. Still other venture capital firms represent investment activities by wealthy individuals. By 1990 there were probably over 2,000 venture capital firms. Another longtime source of venture capital is represented by large, well-established business firms. A number of large corporations have invested both money and various types of know-how to start or to help develop small business firms. The owner of the small firm is usually a specialist, frequently a technically oriented person who needs both money and help in such administrative services as accounting, finance, production, and marketing. The small firm's owner contributes entrepreneurship, special talents, a taste for risk taking, and "the willingness to work 18 hours a day for peanuts." A number of major corporations have found that there is a mutual advantage for this form of venture capital investment.

When a new business makes an application for financial assistance from a venture capital firm, it receives a rigorous examination. Some development companies use their own staffs for this investigation, while others depend on a board of advisers acting in a consultative capacity. A high percentage of applications is rejected, but if the application is approved, funds are provided. Venture capital companies generally take an equity position in the firms they finance, but they may also extend debt capital. However, when loans are made, they generally involve convertibles or warrants or are tied in with the purchase of stock by the investment company. Often the venture capital firm will take convertible preferred stock for its investment. This avoids burdening the new capital-hungry firm with a requirement to pay interest on debt or technically be in default. The convertible preferred stock also provides the venture capital firm with a prior position in liquidation and the opportunity to obtain a substantial equity position if the venture turns out well [Sahlman, 1988].

Another technique is the use of a staged capital commitment. In staged capital commitment (SCC), the venture capitalist agrees to provide capital in various stages in the future as opposed to providing all expected capital requirements up front. For example, the venture capitalist might agree to provide $1 million today (first round) for the purpose of assembling a managerial team, writing a business plan, completing engineering specifi-

---

[3]Ruth Simon, "Diamonds in the Rust Belt," *Forbes,* November 13, 1989, pp. 134, 136; *Venture,* June/July 1989, pp. 36–39. Before it ceased publication in mid-1991, *Venture* magazine annually compiled a list of Venture Capital 100 largest and another list of the next 150, both rankings based on the dollar value of investments during the year. Other information including Paid-In-Capital of each firm and types of investments (such as buyouts) was also provided.

cations, conducting market research, and testing the feasibility of the process; $4 million nine months from now (second round) for the purpose of building a prototype manufacturing plant; and $15 million three years from now (third round) for the purpose of building a full-scale manufacturing facility and beginning to market the product. Also, the venture capitalist typically reserves the option to abandon, revalue, or increase his or her capital commitment to the project at each future round of financing.

SCC reduces the perceived risk to the venture capitalist, since the venture capitalist receives a wealth of information about the company (e.g., how has the company performed relative to its initial business plan, does the management team work well together, does the market research reveal adequate demand, has new competition surfaced?) before the next round of financing arrives. This new information reduces the uncertainty of the value of the company and aids in the venture capitalist's decision as to how to proceed. Also, the knowledge that the company is scheduled to run out of cash is a powerful motivator for management to focus its energies on creating value from its limited resources.

The option to abandon helps the entrepreneur by (1) increasing the value of the company to the venture capitalist, thereby lowering the share of the company that needs to be awarded to the venture capitalist initially (holding all other things constant) and (2) focusing the entrepreneur's energies on creating value (a portion of which accrues to the entrepreneur).

Properly structured options to revalue and increase capital commitment aid both the entrepreneur and the venture capitalist by (1) allowing the venture to continue when performance is not as favorable as expected, (2) giving the entrepreneur the opportunity to raise capital at a higher valuation (necessitating less dilution), and (3) allowing the company to grow at an accelerated pace (and at terms acceptable to both the venture capitalist and the original venture capitalist) when performance exceeds initial expectations.

Venture capital companies perform a continuing and active role in the enterprise. Typically, they do not insist on voting control, but they usually have at least one member on the board of directors of the new enterprise. The matter of control has *not* been one of the crucial considerations in investment companies' decisions to invest — indeed, if the management of a small business is not sufficiently strong to make sound decisions, the venture capital firm is not likely to be interested in the first place. However, the investment company does want to maintain continuous contact, provide management counsel, and monitor the progress of its investment.

The Small Business Administration and SBICs

The Small Business Administration (SBA) is an important source of venture capital to small firms. The SBA guarantees, up to 90 percent, loans made by banks to small business firms.

Another important source of venture capital financing for small business is the Small Business Investment Company (SBIC). The Small Business Investment Company Act of 1958 empowered the Small Business Administration (SBA) to license and regulate SBICs and to provide them with financial assistance.

To qualify as a Small Business Investment Company (SBIC), a firm must have at least $1 million in private equity capital. An SBIC can borrow up to four times its private equity capital from the Small Business Administration (SBA) in government debentures or 100 percent loan commitments both of which can be renewed. The program started in the late 1950s. Among the companies receiving start-up capital from SBICs were Apple Computer and Federal Express. The SBIC program is said to have helped stimulate the private venture-capital industry. Commercial banks have been active in establishing their own SBICs which in 1991 accounted for 38 percent by number, 74 percent of private capital, and 61 percent of investments and loans.[4]

In their operations, SBICs have followed two policies similar to venture capital companies. First, their investments are generally made by the purchase of convertible securities or bonds with warrants, thus giving the SBICs a residual equity position in the companies to which funds are provided. Second, SBICs emphasize management counsel, for which a fee is charged. In 1971, Public Law 92-213 amended the Small Business Investment Company Act and clarified the SBA's authority to guarantee debentures issued by the SBICs, thus providing the SBIC industry with an expanded source of funding at interest rates somewhat below prevailing market levels.

By mid-1991, 368 SBICs were operating with over $1 billion of funds provided through the SBA; but 165 SBICs were being liquidated with 94 failures occurring since 1986. The SBA estimated that its loss exposure had reached some $800 million. In response to Congressional pressure, the SBA began tightening its regulation of SBICs. In July 1991 alone, the SBA published 15 regulatory changes for SBICs in the Federal register.[5]

DIRECT FINANCING

Venture capital financing is a form of direct financing. Other forms of direct long-term financing are term lending by commercial banks and insurance companies and the private placement of securities with insurance companies and pension funds. *Term loans* are direct business loans with a maturity of more than one year but less than 15 years, with provisions for systematic repayment (amortization during the life of the loan). *Private placements* are direct business loans with a maturity of more than 15 years. The distinction is, of course, arbitrary. Private placement differs from the term loan only in its arbitrary maturity length; this distinction becomes even fuzzier when we discover that some private placements call for repayment of a substantial portion of the principal within 5 to 10 years. Thus, term loans and private placements represent about the same kind of financing arrangements.

---

[4]Jeanne Saddler, "Rate of SBIC Liquidations Reaches 'Crisis Proportions,'" *Wall Street Journal*, July 16, 1991, p. B2.

[5]Jeffrey A. Tannenbaum, "SBICs Say Tight Rules Will Limit Flow of Funds to Small Companies," *Wall Street Journal*, August 9, 1991, p. B2.

Characteristics of Term Loans and Private Placements

Amortization. Most term loans are repayable on an amortized basis. The purpose of amortization, of course, is to have the loan repaid gradually over its life rather than fall due all at once; this protects both the lender and the borrower against the possibility that the borrower will not make adequate provisions for retirement of the loan during its life. Amortization is especially important for a loan used to purchase a specific item of equipment; here, the schedule of repayment will be geared to the productive life of the equipment, and payments will be made from cash flows resulting from use of the equipment. The mechanics of preparing an amortization schedule were illustrated in Chapter 3.

Maturity. For commercial banks, the term loan runs 5 years or less (typically 3 years). For insurance companies, typical maturities have been 5 to 15 years. This difference reflects the fact that liabilities of commercial banks are shorter term than those of insurance companies. Banks and insurance companies occasionally cooperate in their term lending. For example, if a firm (usually a large one) seeks a 15-year term loan, a bank may take the loan for the first 5 years and an insurance company for the last 10 years.

Collateral. Commercial banks require security on about 60 percent of the dollar amount and 90 percent of the number of term loans made. They take as security mainly stocks, bonds, machinery, and equipment. Insurance companies also require security on nearly one-third of their loans, frequently using real estate as collateral on the longer term ones.

Options. In recent years, institutional investors have increasingly taken compensation in addition to fixed interest payments on directly negotiated loans. The most popular form of additional compensation is an option to buy common stock, the option being in the form of detachable warrants permitting the purchase of the shares at stated prices over a designated period. (See Chapter 25 for more details on warrants.)

Terms of Loan Agreements

A major advantage of a term loan is that it assures the borrower of the use of the funds for an extended period. On a 90-day loan, since the commercial bank has the option to renew or not renew, it has frequent opportunities to reexamine the borrower's situation. If it has deteriorated unduly, the loan officer simply does not renew the loan. On a term loan, however, the bank or insurance company has committed itself for a period of years. Because of this long-term commitment, restrictive provisions are incorporated into the loan agreement to protect the lender for the duration of the loan. The most important of these provisions (though by no means all of them) are listed below:

1. *Current ratio.* The current ratio must be maintained at some specified level — $2\frac{1}{2}$ to 1; 3 to 1; $3\frac{1}{2}$ to 1, depending on the borrower's line of business. Working capital (net) must also be maintained at some minimum dollar amount.

2. *Additional long-term debt.* Typically, there are prohibitions against (a) incurring additional long-term indebtedness, except with the permission of the lender; (b) the

pledging of assets; (c) the assumption of any contingent liabilities, such as guaranteeing the indebtedness of a subsidiary; and (d) the signing of long-term leases beyond specified amounts.

3. *Management.* The loan agreement may require that (a) any major changes in management personnel be approved by the lender; (b) life insurance be taken out on the principals, or key people, in the business; and (c) a voting trust be created or proxies be granted for a specified period to ensure that the management of the company will be under the control of the group on which the lender has relied in making the loan.

4. *Financial statements.* The lender will require the borrower to submit periodic financial statements for review.

Costs

As with other forms of lending, the interest rate on term loans varies with the level of interest rates generally, the size of the loan, and the quality of the borrower. Surveys show that on small term loans, the effective interest rate may run up to as much as six to eight percentage points above the prime rate. On loans of $1 million and more, term loan rates have been close to the prime rate.

The interest rate may be fixed for the life of the loan, or it may vary. Often the loan agreement specifies that the interest rate will be based on the average of the rediscount rate in the borrower's Federal Reserve district during the previous three months — generally 1 or 2 percent above the rediscount rate.[6] It may also be geared to the published prime rate charged by New York City banks.

Hays, Joehnk, and Melicher [1979] analyzed risk premiums when corporate debt was issued in public offerings versus private placements during the 1970–1975 time period. Risk premiums were measured for 376 public issues and 314 private placements by relating their yields to maturity to the yield to maturity on U.S. Treasury securities of comparable maturities. On public offerings, risk premiums were smaller when the issue size was large, the issue was secured, the EBIT trend was favorable, and the times interest earned ratio was favorable. Risk premiums were larger when the years to maturity were longer and the long-term debt-to-total-asset ratio higher. For private placements, only the issue size and times interest earned ratio were significant and negatively related to risk premiums. For both public and private offerings, risk premiums were negatively related to the level of economic activity as measured by industrial production. They were also negatively related to market factors such as the level of free reserves. In addition, for private placements, the risk premium was positively related to plant and equipment expenditure expectations and negatively related to the amount of life insurance funds available for direct placements.

While the model was able to explain approximately 50 percent of the variation in risk premiums, the variables that were important in doing so differed. Risk premiums for public offerings were largely explained by default risk measures in the form of issue and issuing firm characteristics. Risk premiums in the private market were explained more by

---

[6]The rediscount rate is the rate of interest at which a bank can borrow from a Federal Reserve bank.

economic and market-related factors. The authors conclude that investors in the public market used different measures to assess investment attractiveness than did investors in the private placement market.

On private placements, the interest rate generally runs from about 10 to 50 basis points higher than that on comparable public issues. In the Hays-Joehnk-Melicher study, the yield to maturity on the private placements was 46 basis points higher than on the public offerings. Thus, to some extent, the economies of using private placements are offset by their somewhat higher interest rates, in turn reflecting the higher risk characteristics of the borrowing firms.

Evaluation of Direct Financing

From the standpoint of the borrower, the advantages of direct financing are:

1. Much seasonal short-term borrowing can be dispensed with, thereby reducing the danger of nonrenewal of loans.
2. The borrower avoids the expenses of SEC registration and investment bankers' distribution.
3. Less time is required to complete arrangements for obtaining a loan than is involved in a bond issue.
4. Since only one lender is involved, rather than many bondholders, it is possible to modify the loan indenture.

The disadvantages to a borrower of direct financing are:

1. The interest rate may be higher on a term loan than on a short-term loan because the lender is tying up money for a longer period and, therefore, does not have the opportunity to review the borrower's status periodically (as is done whenever short-term loans are renewed).
2. The cash drain is large. Since the loans provide for regular amortization or sinking fund payments, the company experiences a continuous cash drain. From this standpoint, direct loans are less advantageous than equity funds (which never have to be repaid), a preferred stock without maturity, or even a bond issue without a sinking fund requirement.
3. Since the loan is a long-term commitment, the lender employs high credit standards, insisting that the borrower be in a strong financial position and have a good current ratio, a low debt-equity ratio, good activity ratios, and good profitability ratios.
4. Because of the long-term exposure of the lender, the loan agreement has restrictions that are not found in a 90-day note.
5. Investigation costs may be high. The lender stays with the company for a longer period. Therefore, the longer-term outlook for the company must be reviewed, and the lender makes a more elaborate investigation than would be done for a short-term note. For this reason, the lender may set a minimum on any loan (for example, $50,000) in order to recover the costs of investigating the applicant.

In addition, there are some advantages to the public distribution of securities that are not achieved by term loans or private placement, including:

1. The firm establishes its credit and achieves publicity by having its securities publicly and widely distributed. Because of this, it will be able to engage in future financing at lower rates.

2. The wide distribution of debt or equity may enable its repurchase on favorable terms at some subsequent date if the market price of the securities falls.

Thus, direct long-term financing has both advantages and limitations. Its use has fluctuated over the years.

Recent Trends in Usage — Rule 144A

The private placement market has grown since the early 1980s. In 1988 and 1989 the volume of privately placed bonds has been greater than the new issues of publicly offered bonds as shown in Figure 21.1. Data for 1990 from IDD Information Services show that U.S. private placement financing dropped from $165 billion in 1989 to $121 billion in 1990. This downturn was surprising since private placements were expected to be stimulated by the adoption in 1989 of the Securities and Exchange Commission's Rule 144A. The rule exempts U.S. and foreign corporations from registration requirements for bonds and stock sold to large institutional investors. Furthermore, it permits the resale of these privately placed securities to qualified institutions at any time. Before the new rule, private placements could not be resold for two years. In 1990, 37 issues, $3.7 billion in

FIGURE 21.1   New Issues of Securities by Nonfinancial Corporations

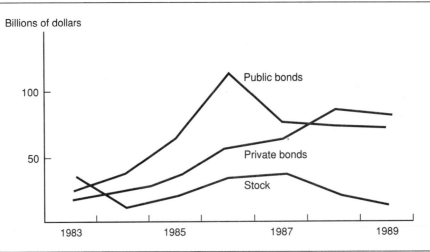

Source: Crabbe, Pickering, and Prowse, 1990, p. 602.

amount, were placed with institutional buyers in the United States. Foreign companies were major participants.

Event Analysis

A number of studies have shown small but significant negative price reactions to public offerings of both bonds and equities [C. W. Smith, 1986]. However, most studies of the private placement of debt and equity securities have found small but significantly positive market reactions [James, 1987; Wruck, 1989; Szewczyk and Varma, 1991]. Szewczyk and Varma compared a sample of public utility debt offerings for the period 1963–1986. They observed a significant positive window of average returns for the four days covering two days before and after the first public report of the placement. Public offerings of debt over the same time period experienced a significant negative window average abnormal return. Szewczyk and Varma attribute the advantages of private placement to (1) attenuation of information asymmetries between sellers and buyers, (2) quality certification by purchasing institutions, and (3) closer monitoring of the managers provided by blockholders.

NVESTMENT BANKING

In the U.S. economy, saving is done by one group of persons and investing by another. (*Investing* is used here in the sense of actually putting money into plant, equipment, and inventory, and not in the sense of buying securities.) Savings are placed with financial intermediaries, who, in turn, make the funds available to firms wishing to acquire plants and equipment and to hold inventories.

One of the major institutions performing this channeling role is the *investment banking* institution. The term *investment banker* is somewhat misleading, since investment bankers are neither investors nor bankers. That is, they do not invest their own funds permanently, nor are they repositories for individuals' funds, as are commercial banks or savings banks. What, then, is the nature of investment banking?

The many activities of investment bankers can be described first in general terms and then with respect to specific functions. The traditional function of the investment banker has been to act as the middleman in channeling individuals' savings and funds into the purchase of business securities. The investment banker does this by purchasing and distributing the new securities of individual companies while performing the functions of underwriting, distribution of securities, and advice and counsel.

Underwriting

Underwriting is the insurance function of bearing the risks of adverse price fluctuations during the period in which a new issue of securities is being distributed. The nature of the investment banker's underwriting function can best be conveyed by example: A business firm needs $10 million. It selects an investment banker, holds conferences, and decides to issue $10 million of bonds. An underwriting agreement is drawn up. On a specific day, the investment banker presents the company with a check for $10 million (less commission). In return, the investment banker receives bonds in denominations of $1,000 each to sell to the public.

The company receives the $10 million before the investment banker has sold the bonds. Between the time the firm is paid the $10 million and the time the bonds are sold, the investment banker bears all the risk of market price fluctuations in the bonds. Conceivably, it can take the investment banker days, months, or longer to sell bonds. If the bond market deteriorates in the interim, the investment banker carries the risk of loss on the sale of the bonds.

There have been dramatic instances of bond market collapses within one week after an investment banker has bought $50 million or $100 million of bonds. For example, an issue of New Jersey Sporting Arena bonds dropped $140 per $1,000 bond during the underwriting period, costing the underwriters an estimated $8 million. The issuing firm, however, does not need to be concerned about the risk of market price fluctuations while the investment banker is selling the bonds, since it has received its money. One fundamental economic function of the investment banker, then, is to underwrite the risk of a decline in the market price between the time the money is transmitted to the firm and the time the bonds are placed in the hands of their ultimate buyers. For this reason, investment bankers are often called underwriters; they underwrite risk during the distribution period.

Distribution

The second function of the investment banker is marketing new issues of securities. The investment banker is a specialist with a staff and organization to distribute securities and, therefore, the capacity to perform the physical distribution function more efficiently and more economically than can an individual corporation. A corporation that wished to sell an issue of securities would find it necessary to establish a marketing or selling organization—a very expensive and ineffective method of selling securities. The investment banker has a permanent, trained staff and dealer organization available to distribute securities. In addition, the investment banker's reputation for selecting good companies and pricing securities fairly builds up a broad clientele over time, and this further increases the efficiency with which securities can be sold.

Advice and Counsel

The investment banker, engaged in the origination and sale of securities, through experience becomes an expert adviser about terms and characteristics of securities that will appeal to investors. This advice and guidance is valuable. Furthermore, the person's reputation as a seller of securities depends on the subsequent performance of the securities. Therefore, investment bankers often sit on the boards of firms whose securities they have sold. In this way, they can provide continuing financial counsel.

The Certification Function

A number of factors give rise to the certification function of investment bankers. Information asymmetry may exist—the managers may know more about the company than the prospective buyers of its securities. Since investment bankers conduct continuing in-depth studies of the companies they are in a position to reduce information asymmetry. In addition, they are likely to provide monitoring of the company's performance as well. The ability of the underwriter to maintain the confidence of a syndicate of other underwriters as well as selling firms depends on its reputation for both knowledge and unquestionable integrity. Thus, the reputation of the investment banker depends on being informed and honest. The investment banker thereby has the ability to perform as a guarantor of issue quality and fair pricing.

INVESTMENT BANKING OPERATIONS

Probably the best way to gain a clear understanding of the investment banking function is to trace the history of a new issue of securities.[7] Accordingly, this section describes the steps necessary to issue new securities.

Preunderwriting Conferences

First, the members of the issuing firm and the investment banker hold preunderwriting conferences, at which they discuss the amount of capital to be raised, the type of security to be issued, and the terms of the agreement. Memoranda describing proposals suggested at the conferences are written by the treasurer of the issuing company to the firm's directors and other officers. Meetings of the board of directors of the issuing company are held to discuss the alternatives and to attempt to reach a decision.

At some point, the issuer and the investment banker enter an agreement that a flotation will take place. The investment banker then begins to conduct an underwriting investigation. If the company is proposing to purchase additional assets, the underwriter's engineering staff may analyze the proposed acquisition. A public accounting firm is called upon to make an audit of the issuing firm's financial situation and also helps prepare the registration statements in connection with these issues for the SEC.

A firm of lawyers is called in to interpret and judge the legal aspects of the flotation. In addition, the originating underwriter (who is the manager of the subsequent underwriting syndicate) makes an exhaustive investigation of the company's prospects.

When the investigations are completed, but before registration with the SEC is made, an underwriting agreement is drawn up by the investment banker. Terms of the tentative agreement may be modified through discussions between the underwriter and the issuing company, but the final agreement will cover all underwriting terms except the price of the securities.

---

[7]The process described here relates primarily to situations where the firm doing the financing picks an investment banker and then negotiates over the terms of the issue. An alternative procedure, used extensively only in the public utility industry, is for the selling firm to specify the terms of the new issue and then to have investment bankers bid for the entire new issue with sealed bids. The very high fixed costs that an investment banker must incur to thoroughly investigate the company and its new issue rule out sealed bids except for the largest issues. The operation described in this section is called *negotiated underwriting*. Competition is keen among underwriters, of course, to develop and maintain working relations with business firms.

Registration Statement

A registration statement containing all relevant financial and business information on the firm then is filed with the SEC. The statutes set a 20-day waiting period (which, in practice, may be shortened or lengthened by the SEC), during which the SEC staff analyzes the registration statement to determine whether there are any omissions or misrepresentations of fact. During the examination period, the SEC can file exceptions to the registration statement or can ask for additional information from the issuing company or the underwriters. Also during this period, the investment bankers are not permitted to offer the securities for sale, although they can print a preliminary prospectus with all the customary information except the offering price.

Pricing the Securities

The actual price the underwriter pays the issuer is not generally determined until the end of the registration period. There is no universally followed practice, but one common arrangement for a new issue of stock calls for the investment banker to buy the securities at a prescribed number of points below the closing price on the last day of registration. For example, the stock of Wilcox Chemical Company had a current price of $38.00 and had traded between $35.00 and $40.00 a share during the previous three months. The firm and the underwriter agreed that the investment banker would buy 200,000 new shares at $2.50 below the closing price on the last day of registration. The stock closed at $36.00 on the day the SEC released the issue, so the firm received $33.50 a share. Typically, such agreements have an escape clause that provides for the contract to be voided if the price of the securities falls below some predetermined figure. In the case of Wilcox, this *upset price* was set at $34.00 a share. Thus, if the closing price of the shares on the last day of registration had been $33.50, Wilcox would have had the option of withdrawing from the agreement.

The investment banker has an easier job if the issue is priced relatively low, but the issuer of the securities naturally wants as high a price as possible. Some conflict on price, therefore, arises between the investment banker and the issuer. If the issuer is financially sophisticated and makes comparisons with similar security issues, the investment banker is forced to price close to the market. On seasoned issues with a good historical record of prices, pricing is related to recent patterns. The problem is more difficult on initial public offerings with no prior public trading.

Underwriting Syndicate

The investment banker with whom the issuing firm has conducted its discussions does not typically handle the purchase and distribution of the issue alone, unless the issue is a very small one. If the sums of money involved are large and the risks of price fluctuations are substantial, the investment banker forms a syndicate in an effort to minimize the amount of personal risk. A *syndicate* is a temporary association for the purpose of carrying out a specific objective. The nature of the arrangements for a syndicate in the underwriting and

FIGURE 21.2   Diagram of Sales of $100 Million of Bonds
through Investment Bankers

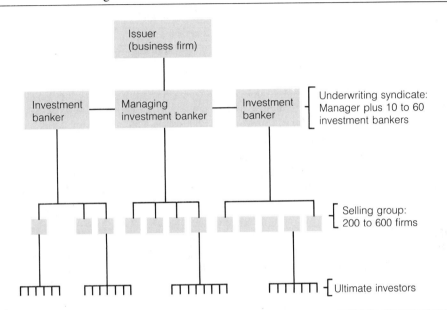

sale of a security through an investment banker can best be understood with the aid of Figure 21.2.

The managing underwriter invites other investment bankers to participate in the transaction on the basis of their knowledge of the particular kind of offering to be made and their strength and dealer contacts in selling securities of this type. Each investment banker has business relationships with other investment bankers and dealers and thus has a selling group composed of these people.

Some firms combine all these characteristics. For example, Merrill Lynch, Pierce, Fenner & Smith underwrites some issues and manages the underwriting of others. On still other flotations, it is invited by the manager to join in the distribution of the issue. It also purchases securities as a dealer, carries an inventory of those securities, and publishes lists of securities it has for sale. In addition to being a dealer, Merrill Lynch, of course, carries on substantial activity as a broker. Any individual investment firm may also carry on all these functions.

There are also firms with a narrower range of functions — specialty dealers, specialty brokers, and specialty investment counselors. Thus, in the financial field, there is often specialization of financial functions. A *dealer* purchases securities outright, holds them in inventory, and sells them at whatever price can be obtained. The dealer may benefit from price appreciation or may suffer a loss on declines, as any merchandiser does. A *broker,* on the other hand, takes orders for purchases and transmits them to the proper exchange; the gain is the commission charged for the service.

Syndicates are used in the distribution of securities for three reasons:

1. A single investment banker may be financially unable to handle a large issue alone.
2. The originating investment banker may desire to spread the risk even if it is financially able to handle the issue alone.
3. The utilization of several selling organizations (as well as other underwriters) permits an economy of selling expense, limits risk, and encourages nationwide distribution.

Participating underwriters and dealers are provided with full information on all phases of these financing transactions, and they share in the underwriting commission. Suppose that an investment banker buys $10 million worth of bonds to be sold at par, or $1,000 each. If this banker receives a two-point spread, the banker pays the issuer $9.8 million. Typically, on a two-point spread, the managing underwriter receives the first one-quarter of one percent for originating and managing the syndicate. Next, the entire underwriting group receives about 0.75 percent. Members of the selling group receive about 1 percent as a sales commission.

The manager of the underwriting group who makes a sale to an ultimate purchaser of the securities receives the 0.25 percent as manager, 0.75 percent as underwriter, and 1 percent as seller — the full 2 percent. If the manager wholesales some of the securities to members of the selling group who make the ultimate sale, they receive the 1 percent selling commission and the manager receives the other 1 percent for managing and underwriting the issue. Variations take place around these patterns.

Ordinarily, each underwriter's liability is limited to the agreed-upon commitment. For example, an investment banker who participates in a $20 million offering agreeing to sell $5 million of the securities is no longer responsible after that firm sells the $5 million of securities.

Selling Group

The selling group is formed primarily for the purpose of distributing securities; it consists of dealers, who take relatively small participations from the members of the underwriting group. The underwriters act as wholesalers; members of the selling group act as retailers. The number of investment banking houses in a selling group depends partly on the size of the issue. A selling group may have as many as 300 to 400 dealers. The operation of the selling group is controlled by the *selling group agreement,* which usually covers the following major points.

1. *Description of the issue.* The description is set forth in a report on the issue — the prospectus — which fully describes the issue and the issuer.
2. *Concession.* Members of the selling group subscribe to the new issue at a public offering price less the *concession* given to them as a commission for their selling service. The selling commission is generally greater than the sum of the managing and underwriting fees.
3. *Handling purchased securities.* The selling group agreement provides that no member of the selling group will be permitted to sell the securities below the public

offering price. The syndicate manager invariably "pegs" the quotation in the market by placing continuous orders to buy at the public offering price. A careful record is kept of bond or stock certificate numbers, so that repurchased securities can be identified with the member of the selling group who sold them. The general practice is to cancel the commission on such securities. Repurchased securities are then placed with other dealers for sale.[8]

4. *Duration of selling group.* The most common provision in selling group agreements is that the group has an existence of 30 days, subject to earlier termination by the manager. The agreement may be extended, however, for an additional 80 days by members representing 75 percent of the selling group (by volume).

Offering and Sale

After the selling group has been formed, the actual offering takes place. Publicity for the sale is given in advance of the offering date. Advertising material is prepared for release as soon as permitted. The actual day of the offering is chosen with a view to avoiding temporary congestion in the security market and other unfavorable events or circumstances.

The formal public offering is called *opening the books,* an archaic term reflecting ancient customs of the investment banking trade. When the books are opened, the manager accepts subscriptions to the issue from both selling group participants and outsiders who wish to buy. If the demand is great, the books may be closed immediately and an announcement made that the issue is oversubscribed; the issue is said to "fly out the window." If the reception is weak, the books may remain open for an extended period.

Market Stabilization

During the period of the offering and distribution of securities, the manager of the underwriting group typically stabilizes the price of the issue. The duration of the price-pegging operation is usually 30 days. The price is pegged by placing orders to buy at a specified price in the market. The pegging operation is designed to prevent a cumulative downward movement in the price, which would result in losses for all members of the underwriting group. The manager of the underwriting group has the major responsibility for pegging the price.

If the market deteriorates during the offering period, the investment banker carries a substantial risk. For this reason, the pegging operation may not be sufficient to protect the underwriters. In one Pure Oil Company issue of $44 million convertible preferred stock, only $1 million of shares were sold at the $100 offering price. At the conclusion of the underwriting agreement, initial trading took place at $74, incurring for the investment bankers a loss of over $11 million ($43 million × 26 percent). In a Textron issue the offering was reduced from $100 million to $50 million because of "market congestion,"

---

[8]Without these repurchase arrangements, members of the selling group could sell their share of the securities on the market instead of soliciting new purchasers. Since the pegging operation is going on, there will be a ready market for the securities; consequently, a penalty is necessary to avoid thwarting the syndicate operation.

and 5 percent of the bonds still were unsold after the initial offering. A *Wall Street Journal* article of December 13, 1984, stated that "investment bankers are stuck with a lot of unsold bonds on their shelves and $40 million of potential losses." As one investment banker expressed it: "There's a lot of blood on the floor." Reference was also made to the craters that the offerings that "bombed" had made on the corporate finance landscape.

It has been charged that pegging the price during the offering period constitutes a monopolistic price-fixing arrangement. Investment bankers reply, however, that not to peg the price would increase the risk and, therefore, the underwriting cost to the issuer. On balance, it appears that the pegging operation has a socially useful function. The danger of monopolistic pricing is avoided, or at least mitigated substantially, by competitive factors. If an underwriter attempts to set a monopolistic price on a particular issue of securities, the investor can turn to thousands of other securities. The degree of control over the market by the underwriter in a price-pegging operation seems negligible.

COSTS OF FLOTATION

The costs of selling new issues of securities are conveyed by Table 21.5. The underwriting fees represent the spread or difference between the price at which the issue is offered to the public and the net proceeds received by the issuer. For large issues of over $100 million, the underwriter fee as a percentage of gross proceeds is likely to be a modest 2 to 3 percent. For issues of less than $2 million, the direct flotation costs may run as high as 8 to 10 percent.

A second type of flotation cost is represented by those costs incurred by the issuing firm, but not part of the compensation paid to the investment banking firm. These direct expenses include legal fees, accounting fees, filing fees, and taxes. While large in dollar amount, as a percentage of gross proceeds they are less than 1 percent for large issues. For smaller issues, the percentage can be more substantial. Indirect expenses (item 3) represent indirect costs incurred by the issuer representing time and other expenses of management and other employees involved in negotiating with the investment bankers, lawyers, and accountants, during the process of issuing new securities.

TABLE 21.5   Costs of Underwritten Sales of Seasoned Equity Securities to the Public

	Seasoned Issues[a]	
	Large Issues	**Small Issues**
1. Underwriter fees	2-3%	8-10%
2. Other direct expenses	0.5	4-6
3. Indirect expenses	1-2	2-4
4. Event adjustments	1-2	1-2
5. Underpricing	?	?
6. Green-shoe option	?	?

[a]Large issues are over $100 million, small issues are less than $2 million.

The fourth category expense is represented by event adjustments. In issues of seasoned stocks or bonds, a significant 1 to 2 percent price drop takes place. Miller and Reilly [1987] suggest this may be due to a signal of an adverse change in the flows of internal financing sources. Another explanation is asymmetric information. The managers are selling securities which they feel are undervalued on the basis of the future prospects for the firm. Another possibility is that the initial negative abnormal return is due to a temporary demand-supply imbalance. Finally, it may be that studies of the longer-term performance of seasoned issues of securities may find that positive abnormal returns are associated with financing favorable growth opportunities.

Underpricing refers to abnormal returns that may be earned by buyers within a few weeks or days after issue. The negative event abnormal returns make substantial underpricing unlikely for seasoned issues.

Another potential cost is the green-shoe option (so named because the Green-Shoe Co. was the first to provide this option to underwriters). It gives underwriters the right to buy additional shares at the offer price to cover possible over-allotments. But since the price in the immediate aftermarket for a seasoned issue may reflect negative abnormal returns, the underwriter would have no incentive to buy at the higher offer price.

A number of conclusions can be drawn from Table 21.5. The flotation costs for small issues can be a substantial portion of the gross proceeds. Clearly, the fixed costs involved in selling seasoned equity or bond issues are large so that there are economies of scale involved. Reasons for the variation in cost with the size of issue are also easily found. First, certain fixed expenses are associated with any distribution of securities: the underwriting investigation, the preparation of the registration statement, legal fees, and so on. Since these expenses are relatively large and fixed, their percentage of the total cost of flotation runs high on small issues. Second, small issues are typically those of relatively less well-known firms, so underwriting expenses may be larger than usual because the danger of omitting vital information is greater. Furthermore, the selling job is more difficult; salespeople must exert greater effort to sell the securities of less well-known firms. For these reasons, the underwriting commission, as a percentage of the gross proceeds, is relatively high for small issues.

Studies also find that the costs of flotation for common stock are greater than for preferred stock, and the costs of both are greater than the cost of flotation for bonds. The explanations for these relationships are found in the amount of risk involved and in the job of physical distribution. Bonds are generally bought in large blocks by relatively few institutional investors, whereas stocks are bought by millions of individuals. For this reason, the distribution job for common stock is more involved and the expenses of marketing it are greater. Similarly, stocks are more volatile than bonds, so underwriting risks are larger for stock than for bond flotations.

Negotiated versus Multiple Bids

The general practice is for a long-term relationship to develop between a business firm and its investment banker. The investment banking firm builds up a cumulative background of knowledge and understanding through its continuous counseling with the firm over a period of years. On a particular financing, the firm's historical investment banker already has considerable background knowledge. It takes much more time and expense for another investment banking firm to develop a comparable fund of knowledge. The business firm, therefore, is likely to look to its traditional investment banker on any new financing requirement. The terms and arrangements on any particular issue will be worked out in direct negotiations between the firm and its investment banker. These are called "negotiated underwritings."

However, for public utility firms, more than one investment banker is likely to be competing for the business of underwriting a particular issue. The SEC Rule U-50 makes competitive bidding mandatory on new issues of securities by public utility holding companies. Whether required by law or not, it is more likely that competitive bidding will be used by public utilities than by industrial firms. The characteristics of public utilities are more uniform, with fewer special circumstances than for industrial firms in a wide variety of business activities. Also, as regulated industries, the utilities have long been required to provide substantial amounts of information on a relatively uniform basis. Hence, the kinds of information that the historical investment banker develops for an industrial firm over a longer period of time are more easily developed for utility firms.

The question of the relative costs of negotiated versus "competitive" underwritings has been raised. The terms *negotiated* and *competitive* are sometimes misleading. Negotiated underwritings are as fully competitive as underwritings with bidding by more than one investment banker. The performance of the historical investment banker must assure the firm that no other investment banker could do the job better. Hence, the potential competition from others waiting in the wings for the opportunity of displacing the historical investment banker assures that competition is as effective on single bids as on multiple bidding. Thus, the empirical studies are measuring not only the effects of multiple bidding on the costs of underwriting but also the characteristics of the firms and the nature of the general financial market conditions that are likely to result in negotiated versus multiple bidding underwritings in particular cases.

Several articles have studied the relative costs of negotiated versus multiple-bidding underwritings. In their studies, Tallman, Rush, and Melicher (TRM) [1974] concluded that "competitive offerings appeared to be less costly during stable market conditions, but that negotiated offerings might be more advantageous during unstable markets." Their empirical results indicated that underwriter compensation was a positive function of "default risk" and a negative function of "market preference for utility bonds" in the case of competitive issues only. In their paper on utility debt, Dyl and Joehnk [1976] found that competitive offerings result in lower underwriting charges, attempting to hold all other factors constant. But they also found a significant fixed cost element in the flotation charges for competitive issues. With different data sets, Ederington [1976] reached conclusions similar to TRM: Competitive offerings might be more desirable during stable markets and negotiated offerings superior during troubled markets. Ederington found that the negotiated offering variable was significant in explaining yield spreads and implied a yield eight basis points higher than a similar competitive issue. He came to the conclusion that some relaxation of SEC Rule U-50, at least during periods of great market uncertainty, might be appropriate.

A study made by Findlay, Johnson, and Morton (FJM) [1979] used the independent variables of (1) issuer size, (2) type of utility, (3) seasoning, (4) maturity, (5) sinking fund, (6) type of offering, (7) issue size, (8) stock market ebullience, (9) bond market interest rate, (10) volume conditions, (11) AT&T ownership, and (12) S&P's rating class. The dependent variable employed was the ratio of total direct issuance cost (underwriter fees plus other direct expenses) to gross total dollar amount raised in the issue. Regressions were run on the total sample of 628 issues and on the subsamples of 135 communications and 493 electric, gas, and water issues.

A low bond rating had a positive influence on flotation costs, while a high bond rating had a negative influence. These results would seem to be a proxy for selling effort and/or risk effect. The implication is that even after taking account of the yield differential, Aaa utility bonds were viewed as fast or easy sales, and Bbb bonds were seen as slow or hard sales. These results are consistent with earlier studies, which found default risk premium to be the most important influence on issuing costs.

The next variable to enter the regression was issuer size, which had a negative impact on flotation costs. This variable undoubtedly acts as a proxy for any economies of scale in the underwriting process. Besides that, issuer size may also proxy a repeat business effect from the underwriter's perspective. Finally, the level of interest rates, as depicted by the Aaa utility bond average, had a significantly positive influence on flotation costs.

The FJM study demonstrated that the traditional competitive-negotiated issue question is far more complex than it would appear. At least four reasons why high interest rates might lead to high flotation costs were discussed—higher inventory carrying costs, reduction in underwriter competition, higher interest rate risk, and negotiated offerings. Only the last was related to the mode of issue, and it had perhaps the least convincing economic rationale. Where the firm and its situation are stable, this facilitates a competitive bidding process. Where the situation is more complex, a negotiated transaction is more likely. As the previous studies indicate, even where competitive bids have been used, a shift may be made to a negotiated transaction when the markets themselves become unsettled. Apparently, for this reason, the FJM study concluded that "the data and methodology employed in all studies to date are simply too crude to determine whether an inefficiency exists with respect to mode of banker compensation which can be exploited by a purchaser of intermediation services."

GOING PUBLIC AND IPOS

We have described how firms may be aided during the early stages of their growth by sources such as venture capital. We have also described the nature of investment banking in bringing seasoned issues of debt and equity to the market. We can draw on this background to discuss going public and initial public offerings.

Going public represents a fundamental change in lifestyle in at least four respects: (1) the firm moves from informal, personal control to a system of formal controls, and the need for financial techniques such as ratio analysis and the du Pont system of financial planning and control greatly increases; (2) information must be reported on a timely basis to the outside investors, even though the founders may continue to have majority control; (3) the firm must have breadth of management in all the business functions if it is to operate its expanded business effectively; and (4) the publicly owned firm typically draws on a board of directors, which should include representatives of the public owners and other external interest groups, to help formulate sound plans and policies.

The timing of the decision to go public is also especially important, because small firms are more affected by variations in money market conditions than larger companies. During periods of tight money and high interest rates, financial institutions, especially commercial banks, find that the quantity of funds demanded exceeds the supply available at legally permissible and conventionally acceptable rates. One important method employed to ration credit is to raise credit standards. During tight money periods, both a stronger balance sheet record and a longer and more stable record of profitability are required in order to qualify for bank credit. Since financial ratios for small and growing firms tend to be less strong, such firms bear the brunt of credit restraint. Obviously, the small firm that goes public and raises equity capital before a money squeeze is in a better position to ride it out. This firm has already raised some of its needed capital, and its equity cushion enables it to present a stronger picture to the banks, thus helping it to obtain additional capital in the form of debt.

The Securities and Exchange Commission (SEC) has made a number of changes to make it easier for small firms to sell their stock to the public. Under Regulation A offerings, a firm is not required to meet standard SEC securities registration requirements. In 1978, the SEC raised the dollar ceiling for Regulation A offerings from $500,000 to $1.5 million. In late May 1979, the SEC announced that underwriters of Regulation A stock offerings will be able to use a preliminary offering circular as a sales tool, rather than waiting until a final offering circular has been cleared by the SEC staff. Securities firms had told the SEC that their inability to use the preliminary circular had hampered their ability to make firm underwriting commitments for such issues.

Also in May 1979, the SEC announced that a new and simplified registration form would be available to smaller firms with assets of less than $1 million and fewer than 500 shareholders. Such firms will be permitted to raise up to $5 million in the public market by using a new S-18 simplified registration form instead of the standard S-1. The companies may also register the sale at any of the commission's nine regional offices rather than in Washington only. This will enable them to use their local accounting and legal firms, holding down costs.

TABLE 21.6   Costs of Underwritten Sales of Initial Public Offerings (Percentage)

| | Initial Public Offerings[a] | | | |
| | Firm-Commitment Offerings | | Best Efforts Offerings | |
	Large Issues	Small Issues	Large Issues	Small Issues
1. Underwriter fees	7%	10%	8%	11%
2. Other direct expenses	2	10	2	10
3. Indirect expenses	1-2	2-4	1-2	2-4
4. Underpricing	10	25	5-15	40
5. Green-shoe option	varies	varies	varies	varies

[a]Large issues are over $100 million, small issues are less than $2 million. The numbers are percentages of gross proceeds.

Costs of IPOs

The apparent costs of initial public offerings (IPOs) are high. But recent evidence on their aftermarket underperformance suggests these costs may represent a bargain to the issuer. Let's first look at the data, then interpret their implications.

Table 21.6 summarizes the costs of underwritten sales of initial public offerings. It distinguishes between ''firm-commitment offerings'' and ''best efforts offerings.'' The differences can be summarized by nine main criteria:

Characteristic	Firm Commitment	Best Efforts
1. Size of issuer	Larger	Smaller
2. Size of issue	Larger	Smaller
3. Offer price assured	Yes	Yes
4. Minimum number of shares specified	Yes	Yes
5. Offer withdrawn if minimum not sold	No	Yes
6. Underwriters	Majors	Usually not
7. Purchasers	More institutional investors	More individual investors
8. Initial value of issue	More certain	Less certain
9. Volatility in the aftermarket	Lower	Higher

In a firm-commitment cash offer the investment banker agrees to underwrite and distribute the issue at an agreed upon price for a specified number of shares to be bought by the underwriters. The issuer still bears some risk with regard to both price and number of shares sold. These are subject to revision by the investment banker between the date a preliminary agreement is signed and the actual issue date after SEC clearance and other procedures have been completed. Typically, a day before the actual issue date in a conference between the investment banker, lawyers, accountants, and the issuer, the number of shares to be sold may be adjusted downward (depending on the strength of the market) and an issue price is set.

A best efforts offering is subject to the additional risk that if a minimum number of shares is not sold, the offering is withdrawn by the investment banker. Best efforts offerings generally involve smaller issuers and smaller size of issue. They also involve industries or activities where future performance of the firm is difficult to predict. The volatility of price movements in the market after issue is likely to be greater. Thus the investment banker may find it difficult to make a good estimate of the potential market. In a best efforts offering, the issuer has no assurance that the offer will succeed.

As Table 21.6 indicates, the greater uncertainty involved in best efforts offerings results in higher cost to the issuer. The underwriter fees are somewhat higher than for firm-commitment offerings. Other direct expenses and the indirect expenses explained previously run about the same and probably are not greatly different as compared with seasoned issues. It is on the underpricing where IPOs apparently involve very high expenses. The apparent underpricing averages about 15 percent for firm-commitment IPO offerings, somewhat lower for large issues and as high as 25 percent for small issues. The underpricing for best efforts IPOs is even greater [Ritter, 1987]. The effect of Green-shoe options is likely to be greater also.

A number of explanations have been suggested for the underpricing of IPOs. One theoretical explanation is based on two categories of investors, informed and uninformed [Rock, 1986]. The informed investors know when an issue is relatively underpriced or overpriced. On underpriced issues, the informed investor seeks to buy a high percentage of the shares. The uninformed investor allocates about the same amount of investment funds for each issue. The large investments by the informed cause the issue to be oversubscribed. The underwriters allocate the shares on a *pro rata* basis. Hence, on an issue that the informed investor recognizes as underpriced, the uninformed investor is allocated a relatively small percentage of desired purchases.

On the issues that informed investors recognize as overpriced, they make no bid. The uninformed investors receive all the shares they bid for, so receive a higher percentage. In time the uninformed investor would learn from experience and stop bidding. To attract all categories of investors the underwriters underprice on average.

A related type of explanation is provided by Benveniste and Spindt [1989]. They model the IPOs as an option designed to induce informed investors to convey their information to the underwriter. This model implies that IPOs will be underpriced and that the underwriters will give priority in allocations to their regular investors.

Beatty and Ritter [1986] relate underpricing of an IPO to the degree of uncertainty of investors with respect to its value. They explain that an underpricing equilibrium is enforced by investment bankers to preserve their reputation capital. Investment bankers who don't underprice enough will lose potential investors; if they underprice too much they lose issuers.

The opinion that IPO underpricing takes place is widely held. For example, the April 29, 1991 issue of *Business Week* carries an article which states, "The IPO market is red-hot." It lists the names of companies whose price by late April 1991 had risen substantially over prices at offerings that had taken place a month or two earlier. But despite this widespread belief of the underpricing of IPOs, a study by Ritter [1991] presents evidence that "indicates that the offering price is not too low, but that the first aftermarket price is too high" [p. 24]. For a sample of 1,526 IPOs of common stock in 1975–1984, IPOs earned investors only 83 percent of the returns that would have been earned from investing in a group of matching firms over the same time period. The holding period return is measured from the closing market price on the first day of public trading to the market price three years later. Of the possible explanations for the subsequent underperformance, Ritter gives greatest weight to the overoptimism associated with periodic hot new issue markets. Other studies have found that when the studies are extended beyond three years, underperformance does not continue. Rao [1989] found no underperformance in years four through six. Ibbotson [1975] found no underperformance in the fifth year (his last year) after going public.

The Decision to Go Public

With all the foregoing as background, what are the pros and cons for a firm going public? A number of advantages can be stated:

1. Obviously, additional funds are raised.

2. The disclosure and outside monitoring may make it easier to raise additional funds in the future.

3. A public price is established and its subsequent behavior is a test of the performance of the firm.

4. It is often useful to have public prices, which establish values for tax purposes.

5. Increased liquidity is provided because of the market that may develop in the stock.

A number of potential disadvantages of going public must be considered:

1. Some loss of control is involved in sharing ownership.

2. The activities of the firm are now more fully disclosed.

3. More formal reporting to public agencies is required. This can be costly.

4. If the firm's shares do not attract a following, the market for them may be relatively inactive thereby losing the potential benefits of performance evaluation and aligning incentives.

5. Outside investors may push for short-term performance results to an excessive degree.

6. A public firm must publish information that may disclose vital and competitively sensitive information to rival firms.

7. Stockholders' servicing costs and other related expenses may also be a consideration for smaller firms.

8. An advantage of *not* going public is that major programs do not have to be justified by detailed studies and reports to the board of directors. Action can be taken more speedily, and sometimes getting a new investment program under way early is critical for its success.

Generalization is not possible. The going-public decision depends on the circumstances of the firm and the preferences of its major owners.

The advantages and disadvantages of going public may be so closely balanced that the decision may be reversed as time, circumstances, and preferences change. An early comprehensive study of going-private decisions was made by DeAngelo, DeAngelo and Rice [1984]. Their sample consisted of 72 firms that made 72 initial and 9 subsequent (revived) going-private proposals during the period 1973–1980. The median market value of total equity was about $6 million for the sample of 45 pure going-private proposals. Thus the firms were relatively small. In addition, management held a relatively large ownership position. In 72 going-private proposals management's mean preoffer ownership fraction was 45 percent with a median measure of 51 percent. Going-private transactions are also involved in management buyouts (MBOs) and leveraged buyouts (LBOs), which will be treated more fully in Chapter 27. Later studies of going-private transactions reflected the increased MBO and LBO activity. For example, the Lehn-Poulsen [1988] study, which covered 284 going-private transactions during 1980–1987, found a mean equity value of $191 million. The increase in going-private activity demonstrates that the going-public decision may be reversed as the economic and financial environments change.

USE OF RIGHTS IN FINANCING

If the preemptive right is contained in a firm's charter, then the firm must offer any new common stock to existing stockholders. If the charter does not prescribe a preemptive right, the firm has a choice of making the sale to its existing stockholders or to an entirely new set of investors. If it sells to the existing stockholders, the stock flotation is called a *rights offering*. Each stockholder is issued an option to buy a certain number of the new shares, and the terms of the option are contained on a piece of paper called a *right*. Each stockholder receives one right for each share of stock owned. The advantages and disadvantages of rights offerings are described in the following section.

The value of rights amendments *per se* was investigated by Bhagat [1983]. For a sample of 211 proposals to remove charter provisions that required rights offerings, he found that (1) in only four instances did shareholders turn down the proposal and that (2) stock prices declined by an average of −.34 percent when the proposal was announced (statistically significant at the 10 percent confidence level). The evidence indicates that removal of the rights provision from corporate charters has the effect of decreasing shareholders' wealth but leaves the puzzle of why shareholders would vote in favor of the removal in the first place.

We first consider some theoretical relationships in rights offerings. Several issues confront the financial manager who is deciding on the details of a rights offering. The various considerations can be shown by the use of illustrative data on the Southeast Company, whose balance sheet and income statement are given in Table 21.7. Southeast earns $4 million after taxes and has 1 million shares outstanding, so earnings per share are $4. The stock sells at 25 times earnings, or for $100 a share. The company plans to raise $10 million of new equity funds through a rights offering and decides to sell the new stock to shareholders for $80 a share. This present analysis will not take into account the NPV from the new investment. A positive NPV would increase the value of the firm. We here

---

TABLE 21.7   Southeast Company Financial Statements before Rights Offering

Partial Balance Sheet

		Total debt (at 5%)	$ 40,000,000
		Common stock	10,000,000
		Retained earnings	50,000,000
Total assets	$100,000,000	Total liabilities and capital	$100,000,000

Partial Income Statement

Total earnings	$10,000,000
Interest on debt	2,000,000
Income before taxes	$ 8,000,000
Taxes (50% assumed)	4,000,000
Earnings after taxes	$ 4,000,000
Earnings per share (1 million shares)	$4
Market price of stock (price-earnings ratio of 25 assumed)	$100

consider only the pure "stock split" effects of the issue of rights. Under these assumptions, the questions posed to the financial manager are:

1. How many rights will be required to purchase a share of the newly issued stock?
2. What is the value of each right?
3. What effect will the rights offering have on the price of the existing stock?

Number of Rights Needed to Purchase a New Share

As stated, Southeast plans to raise $10 million in new equity funds and to sell the new stock at a price of $80 a share. Dividing the subscription price into the total funds to be raised gives the number of shares to be issued:

$$\text{Number of new shares} = \frac{\text{Funds to be raised}}{\text{Subscription price}} = \frac{\$10,000,000}{\$80}$$
$$= 125,000 \text{ shares.}$$

The next step is to divide the number of new shares into the number of previously outstanding shares to get the number of rights required to subscribe to one share of the new stock. Note that stockholders always receive one right for each share of stock they own:

$$\text{Number of rights needed to buy a share of the stock} = \frac{\text{Old shares}}{\text{New shares}} = \frac{1,000,000}{125,000} = 8 \text{ rights.}$$

Therefore, a stockholder will have to surrender eight rights plus $80 to receive one of the newly issued shares. If the subscription price had been set at $95 a share, 9.5 rights would have been required to subscribe to each new share; if the price had been set at $10 a share, only one right would have been needed. If the number of new shares exceeds the number of old shares, the number of rights required to subscribe to each new share would be a fraction of one. For example, if the number of old shares is 1 million and 1.6 million new shares are to be issued, the number of rights required to subscribe to each new share would be five-eighths of one right. Trading in the rights would take place so that exact, not fractional, numbers of new shares could be purchased by the exercise of rights plus the required cash.

Value of a Right

It is clearly worth something to be able to pay less than $100 for a share of stock selling for $100. The right provides this privilege, so it must have a value. To see how the theoretical value of a right is established, we continue with the example of the Southeast Company, assuming that it will raise $10 million by selling 125,000 new shares at $80 a share.

Notice that the *market value* of the old stock was $100 million: $100 a share times 1 million shares. (The book value is irrelevant.) When the firm sells the new stock, it brings in an additional $10 million. As a first approximation, assume that the market value of the common stock increases by exactly this $10 million. Actually, the market value of all the common stock will go up by more than $10 million if investors think the company will be able to invest these funds at a yield substantially in excess of the cost of equity capital, but it will go up by less than $10 million if investors are doubtful of the company's ability to put the new funds to work profitably in the near future.

Under the assumption that market value exactly reflects the new funds brought in, the total market value of the common stock after the new issue will be $110 million. Dividing this new value by the new total number of shares outstanding, 1.125 million, gives a new market value of $97.78 a share. Therefore, after the financing has been completed, the price of the common stock will have fallen from $100 to $97.78.

Since the rights give the stockholders the privilege of paying only $80 for a share of stock that will end up being worth $97.78, thereby saving them $17.78, is $17.78 the value of each right? The answer is no, because eight rights are required to buy one new share. The $17.78 must be divided by 8 to get the value of each right. In the example, each one is worth $2.22.

Ex Rights

The Southeast Company's rights have value that accrues to the holders of the common stock. But what happens if stock is traded during the offering period? Who will receive the rights — the old owners or the new? The standard procedure calls for the company to set a *holder of record date* and for the stock to go *ex rights* after that date. If the stock is sold prior to the ex rights date, the new owner receives the rights; if it is sold on or after the ex rights date, the old owner receives them. For example, on October 15, Southeast Company announces the terms of the new financing; the company states that rights will be mailed out on December 1 to stockholders of record as of the close of business on November 15. Anyone buying the old stock on or before November 15 will receive the rights; anyone buying the stock on or after November 16 will *not* receive them. Thus, November 16 is the *ex rights date*; before November 16, the stock sells *rights-on*. In the case of Southeast Company, the rights-on price is $100, and the ex rights price is expected to be $97.78.

Formula Value of a Right

Rights On. Equations have been developed for determining the value of rights equivalent to the reasoning process above. While the stock is still selling rights-on, the value at which the rights will sell when they are issued can be found by use of the following formula:

$$\text{Value of one right} = \frac{\text{Market value of stock, rights-on} - \text{Subscription price}}{\text{Number of rights required to purchase 1 share} + 1}$$

$$v_r = \frac{p_0 - p^s}{\# + 1}, \tag{21.1}$$

where

p_0 = rights-on price of the stock

p^s = subscription price

$\#$ = number of rights required to purchase a new share of stock

v_r = value of one right.

Substituting the appropriate values for the Southeast Company:

$$v_r = \frac{\$100 - \$80}{8 + 1} = \frac{\$20}{9} = \$2.22.$$

This agrees with the value of the rights found by looking at the overall relationships.

Ex Rights. Suppose you are a stockholder in the Southeast Company who did not sell your shares when they were selling rights-on. The stock is now selling ex rights for $97.78 a share. How can you calculate the theoretical value of a right? By using the following formula, which follows the logic described in preceding sections, you can determine the value of each right:

$$\text{Value of one right} = \frac{\text{Market value of stock, ex rights} - \text{Subscription price}}{\text{Number of rights required to purchase 1 share}}$$

$$v_r = \frac{p_e - p^s}{\#}$$

$$= \frac{\$97.78 - \$80}{8} = \frac{\$17.78}{8} = \$2.22. \qquad \textbf{(21.2)}$$

Here, p_e is the ex rights price of the stock.[9]

To this point, we have developed the value of a right under some simplifying assumptions, which we now relax. First we took a static approach. We assumed that the total

---

[9]We developed Equation 21.2 directly from the verbal explanation given in the immediately preceding section. Equation 21.1 can be derived from Equation 21.2 as follows:

$$p_t = p_0 - v_r. \qquad \textbf{(21.3)}$$

Substituting Equation 21.3 into Equation 21.2:

$$v_r = \frac{p_0 - v_r - p^s}{\#}. \qquad \textbf{(21.4)}$$

Rearranging Equation 21.4:

$$v_r = \frac{p_0 - p^s}{\#} - \frac{v_r}{\#}$$

$$v_r + \frac{v_r}{\#} = \frac{p_0 - p^s}{\#}$$

$$v_r \left(\frac{\# + 1}{\#} \right) = \frac{p_0 - p^s}{\#}$$

$$v_r = \frac{p_0 - p^s}{\#} \cdot \frac{\#}{\# + 1}$$

$$v_r = \frac{p_0 - p^s}{\# + 1}.$$

The result is Equation 21.1.

value of the equity was increased only by the amount of additional funds raised from the rights offering. If we take a longer-term view, and postulate that the additional funds will be used in positive net present value investments, then the value of equity would increase by more than the new funds raised. If so, the value of the rights would be above the level we had illustrated in the example of $2.22.

Another approach would be to treat each right as a call option. This is because a right is an option to buy the stock of the company at the subscription price (the exercise price) for a specified period of time. The maturity of a right is typically around 30 days while the maturity of a warrant is more likely to be two to ten years. But the valuation methodology would be the same for both. Galai and Schneller [1978] have shown that a right or a warrant is valued exactly as a call divided by $(1 + q)$, where q is the ratio of the additional rights or warrants issued to the number of shares previously outstanding. In our symbols, q would be equal to $1/\#$. We can now illustrate this procedure. Recall that the relevant option pricing equations we will need to evaluate are the following:

$$C_0 = S_0 N(d_1) - X_0 \, e^{-R_f T} \, N(d_2)$$

$$d_1 = \frac{ln(S_0/X_0) + [R_F + (\sigma^2/2)]T}{\sigma\sqrt{T}}$$

$$d_2 = d_1 - \sigma\sqrt{T}.$$

To utilize the above expressions, we already were given that S, the stock price before the rights offering, was $100 and that the subscription price (exercise price) is $80. We will further assume that the risk-free rate is 10 percent, the variance of the returns on equity is 16 percent, and the time to maturity is 0.1 of a year. We can then make the calculations as follows:

$$d_1 = \frac{.223 + [.10 + .08].1}{.4(.316)} = \frac{.223 + .018}{.1264} = \frac{.241}{.1264} = 1.9066$$

$$N(d_1) = .9719$$

$$d_2 = 1.9066 - .1264 = 1.7802 = 1.78$$

$$N(d_2) = .9625$$

$$C_0 = 100(.9719) - 80(.9625).99$$

$$= 97.19 - 76.23$$

$$= 20.96.$$

The value of the rights as a call is $20.96. Since eight rights are required to purchase one share of stock, the value per right will be $20.96 ÷ 8, which is $2.62. We now apply the dilution factor effect on the value of the right, so we divide further by $(1 + q)$, which is 1.125 here. We obtain $2.33 for the value of each right. This is somewhat above the $2.22 obtained when the right is valued in the traditional way. Although these numbers are only illustrative, the order of the relationships is plausible. This is because we would expect that the value of a right should be higher than when its option value properties are taken into account.

EFFECTS ON POSITION OF STOCKHOLDERS

Stockholders have the choice of exercising their rights or selling them. If they have sufficient funds and want to buy more shares of the company's stock, they will exercise the rights. If they do not have the money or do not want to buy more stock, they will sell the rights. In either case, provided the formula value of the rights holds true, stockholders will neither benefit nor lose by the rights offering. This statement can be illustrated by considering the position of an individual stockholder in the Southeast Company.

The stockholder has eight shares of stock before the rights offering. Each share has a market value of $100, so the stockholder has a total market value of $800 in the company's stock. If, after the rights offering, a shareholder exercises the rights, this individual will be able to purchase one additional share at $80 — a new investment of $80. With a total investment of $880, the stockholder will own nine shares of the company's stock, which now has a value of $97.78 a share. The value of the nine shares will be $880, exactly what was invested in it.

Alternatively, by selling the eight rights, which have a value of $2.22 each, the holder will receive $17.76 and will thus have the original eight shares of stock plus $17.76 in cash. But, the original eight shares of stock now have a market price of $97.78 a share. The $782.24 market value of this stock plus the $17.76 in cash is the same as the $800 market value of stock with which the investor began.

Oversubscription Privilege

Even though the rights are valuable and should be exercised, some stockholders neglect to do so. Still, all the stock is sold because of the *oversubscription privilege* contained in most rights offerings. This privilege gives subscribing stockholders the right to buy, on a pro rata basis, all shares not taken in the initial offering. To illustrate: If Jane Doe owns 10 percent of the stock in Southeast Company, and if 20 percent of the rights offered by the company are not exercised (or sold) by the stockholders to whom they were originally given, then she can buy an additional 2.5 percent of the new stock.[10] Since this stock is a "bargain" — $80 for stock worth $97.78 — Jane Doe and other stockholders will use the oversubscription privilege, thereby assuring the full sale of the new stock issue.

Exercise of Rights

Interestingly enough, it is expected that a small percentage of stockholders will neglect to exercise or to sell their rights. In a GM offering, the holders of $1\frac{1}{2}$ percent of GM's common stock did not exercise their rights. The loss experienced by these stockholders was $1.5 million. In an AT&T issue, the loss to shareholders who neglected to exercise their rights was $960,000.

---

[10]Eighty percent of the stock was subscribed. Since Jane Doe subscribed to 10/80, or 12.5 percent, of the stock that was taken, she can obtain 12.5 percent of the unsubscribed stock. Therefore, her oversubscription allocation is 12.5 percent × 20 = 2.5 percent of the new stock.

Market Price and Subscription Price

Measured from the registration date for the new issue of the security, the average percentage by which the subscription prices of new issues were below their market prices has been about 15 percent in recent years. Examples of price concessions of 40 percent or more can be observed in a small percentage of issues, but the most frequently encountered discounts are from 10 to 20 percent.

Effect on Subsequent Behavior of Market Price

It is often said that issuing new stock through rights will depress the price of the company's existing common stock. To the extent that a subscription price, in connection with the rights offering, is lower than the market price, there will be a "stock-split effect" on the market price of the common stock. With the prevailing market price of Southeast Company's stock at $100 and a $10 subscription price, the new market price will probably drop to about $55.

But whether, because of the rights offering, the actual new market price will be $55 or lower or higher is unknown. Again, empirical analysis of the movement in stock prices during rights offerings indicates that generalization is not practical. What happens to the market prices of the stock ex rights and after the rights trading period depends on the future earnings prospects of the issuing company.

Relative Costs

The relative costs of underwritten versus rights offerings are indicated by Table 21.8. The underwriting and other direct expenses of a public new issue of securities are lower for a pure rights offering than for offerings in which investment bankers participate. Rights offerings in which underwriters perform in a standby capacity probably do not lower costs greatly for large issues, but do so for small issues. In an early study, Smith [1977]

TABLE 21.8   Costs of Underwritten versus Rights Offerings as a Percent of Gross Proceeds

	Underwriting		Rights with Standby Underwriting		Rights Offering	
	Large Issues[a]	Small Issues	Large Issues	Small Issues	Large Issues	Small Issues
1. Underwriter fees	2-3	10	2-3	4-6	—	—
2. Other direct expenses	.15-.40	5-7	.15-.40	4-5	—	—
3. Total expenses	2-3+	15-17	2-3+	8-11	0.5	5-7

[a]Large issues are over $100 million, small issues are less than $2 million.

reported that the flotation costs of common stock issues during the period 1971–1975 were 6.17 percent on public issues compared with 2.45 percent on the pure rights offerings. Yet during this period only 38 of 578 common stock issues were pure rights offerings. Smith considered a number of explanations, which he rejected.

Possible Reasons for Underwritten Issues

We think that a number of factors are worth consideration for providing at least a partial explanation why issues are underwritten. One, management may prefer to avoid burdening shareholders with the necessity of using funds to invest more in the company by exercising their rights or selling them. Some time is also involved in handling the tax implications. The certainty of obtaining the funds is not a compelling reason for using underwriting because by setting the subscription price low enough the rights will have value either exercised or sold, in which case a buyer will exercise the rights.

Two, the use of an underwriter can provide a wider distribution of the securities — the underwriting agreement may specify that efforts will be made to sell the shares to new shareholders. But thousands of brokers are already trying to sell this company's stock widely if it is a good buy. Yet the underwriting effort may be compared to a special promotion to widen the distribution of the stock. So broader ownership is a possible advantage of an underwritten issue.

Three, underwriters may provide continuing advice and counsel between issues difficult to price directly so compensation is provided in connection with periodic issues. In pure theory advice and counsel could be paid for by direct fees. But long traditions and customs may prevail in practice. Stronger theoretical reasons are the certification and monitoring roles of underwriters. Booth and R. Smith [1986] suggest a certification role for investment bankers who put their reputation on the line that managers are not using inside information to the disadvantage of outside investors. C. Smith [1986] recognizes a role for monitoring of the firm by investment bankers which also represents a service to investors. Heinkel and Schwartz [1986] propose a signaling role for underwritten offerings. They distinguish between high-quality firms whose managers believe true value exceeds current market value and low-quality firms whose managers fear that their stock is currently overvalued by the market. High-quality firms can use a rights offering with a high ratio of subscription price to prevailing market price. Low-quality firms would have to set a relatively low subscription price, which would signal their low quality. Because an attempt at a rights offering with a high subscription price would carry the risk of failing, they prefer underwritten new offers.

Appraisal of the Use of Rights

The preemptive right gives shareholders the protection of preserving their pro rata share in the earnings and control of the company. It also benefits the firm. By offering new issues of securities to existing stockholders, the firm increases the likelihood of a favorable reception for the stock. By their ownership of common stock in the company, investors have already evaluated the company favorably. They, therefore, may be receptive to the purchase of additional shares.

Other factors can offset the tendency towards a downward pressure on the price of the common stock occurring at the time of a new issue.[11] With the increased interest in (and advantages afforded by) the rights offering, the "adjusted" downward price pressure may be mitigated.

REGULATION OF SECURITY TRADING

The operations of investment bankers, exchanges, and over-the-counter markets are significantly influenced by a series of federal statutes enacted during and after 1933. The financial manager is affected by these laws for several reasons:

1. Corporate officers are subject to personal liabilities.

2. The laws affect the ease and costs of financing and the behavior of the money and capital markets in which the corporation's securities are sold and traded.

3. Investors' willingness to buy securities is influenced by the existence of safeguards provided by these laws.

Securities Act of 1933

The first of the securities acts, the Securities Act of 1933, followed congressional investigations of the stock market collapse of 1929–1932. Motivating the act were (1) the large losses to investors, (2) the failures of many corporations on which little information had been provided, and (3) misrepresentations that had been made to investors.

The basic objective of the Securities Act of 1933 is to provide for both *full disclosure* of relevant information and a *record of representations*. The act seeks to achieve these objectives by the following means:

1. It applies to all interstate offerings to the public in amounts of $1.5 million or more. (Some exemptions are government bonds and bank stocks.)

2. Securities must be registered at least 20 days before they are publicly offered. The registration statement provides financial, legal, and technical information about the company. A prospectus summarizes this information for use in selling the securities. If information is inadequate or misleading, the SEC will delay or stop the public offering. (Obtaining the information required to review the registration statement may result in a waiting period that exceeds 20 days.)

3. After the registration has become effective, the securities can be offered if accompanied by the prospectus. Preliminary, or "red herring," prospectuses can be distributed to potential buyers during the waiting period.

---

[11]The downward pressure develops because of an increase in the supply of securities without a necessarily equivalent increase in the demand. Generally, it is a temporary phenomenon, and the stock tends to return to the theoretical price after a few weeks. Obviously, if the acquired funds are invested at a very high rate of return, the stock price benefits; if the investment does not turn out well, the stock price suffers.

4. If the registration statement or prospectus contains misrepresentations or omissions of material facts, any purchaser who suffers a loss can sue for damages. Liabilities and severe penalties can be imposed on the issuer and its officers, directors, accountants, engineers, appraisers, and underwriters and on all others who participated in preparing the registration statement.

Securities Exchange Act of 1934

The Securities Exchange Act of 1934 extends the disclosure principle applied to new issues by the Securities Act of 1933 to trading in already issued securities (the secondhand securities market). It seeks to accomplish this by the following measures:

1. It establishes the Securities and Exchange Commission. (The Federal Trade Commission had been administering the Securities Act of 1933.)

2. It provides for registration and regulation of national securities exchanges. Companies whose securities are listed on an exchange must file reports similar to registration statements with both the SEC and the stock exchange and must provide periodic reports as well.

3. It establishes control over corporate "insiders." Officers, directors, and major stockholders of a corporation must file monthly reports of changes in holdings of the corporation's stock. Any short-term profits from such transactions are payable to the corporation.

4. It gives the SEC the power to prohibit manipulation by such devices as pools (aggregations of funds used to affect prices artificially), wash sales (sales among members of the same group to record artificial transaction prices), and pegging the market other than during stock flotations.

5. It gives the SEC control over the proxy machinery and practices.

6. It establishes control over the flow of credit into security transactions by giving the board of governors of the Federal Reserve System the power to control margin requirements.

The Securities Acts Amendments of 1975

The Securities Acts Amendments of 1975 were passed after four years of research and investigation into the changing nature of securities markets. Secondary markets were seen as being under stress due to overall increased trading volume and increased dominance by large institutional investors. In particular, the NYSE system of fixed minimum percentage rate brokerage commissions was seen as inequitable, resulting in unreasonably high transactions costs on a per-share basis when applied to large block trades. This system had led many large traders to move away from the NYSE to the over-the-counter market and the regional exchanges, resulting in market fragmentation and nondisclosure of significant trading on the NYSE tape. The study recommended the abolition of fixed minimum brokerage commissions and increased automation of trading by utilizing electronic communication and data processing technology to link markets. The wording of the amendments is general, speaking of fostering efficiency, enhancing competition, increasing available information, and so forth. The Securities and Exchange Commission was mandated to work with the securities industry to develop an operational framework for a national market system to achieve the goal of nationwide competition in securities trading, with centralized reporting of price quotations and transactions and a central order routing system to find the best available price.

Empirical studies have demonstrated that both higher trading volume and more dealer competition result in narrower bid-ask spreads in stock trading. Among the benefits to corporate financial managers which might be expected from the new securities legislation are:

1. Broader exposure to the public, since both listed and unlisted firms are included in the national market system.

2. Stronger secondary markets, which should encourage individual investors to commit capital on new issues.

3. More liquid securities markets, leading to lower transactions costs.

Changes in SEC Rules

The mechanisms of selling securities in the public markets have been greatly influenced by some recent changes in the rules of the Securities and Exchange Commission. In 1978, the SEC began to streamline the securities registration process. Large well-known corporations were permitted to abbreviate registration statements, to disclose information by reference to other documents that had already been made public, and to be subject to only selective reviews of documents by the SEC staff. Before these changes, the registration process sometimes took several weeks to be completed. With the changes made after 1978, a registration statement can be approved in as short a time as two days.

A further development took place in March 1982, when the Securities and Exchange Commission by Rule 415 authorized shelf registration. Larger corporations (with stock outstanding exceeding $150 million in market value) can register the full amount of debt or equity they plan to sell over a two-year period. After this initial registration has been completed, the firm can sell up to the specified amount of debt or equity without further delay. The firm can choose the time when the funds are needed or when market conditions appear favorable. With the increased volatility in financial markets in recent years, shelf registration gives firms the flexibility to act quickly when market conditions appear favorable. Shelf registration reduces the costs of issuing securities because of the savings achieved on accounting, legal, and printing expenses. It appears to have introduced increased competition among investment bankers, and this, in turn, may lower underwriting fees. But the method of distribution may also be involved. When securities are sold from a shelf registration, a large investment banking firm often quickly places them with a relatively small number of buyers. Thus, extensive syndication, as described earlier in the chapter, does not take place, and the securities are not as broadly distributed, at least initially.

The use of shelf registration thus far has been quite different in the bond market as compared with the issue of new equity shares. Shelf registration has been very popular in the sale of bonds. Since 1982, on average, 50 to 60 percent of all debt sales made use of shelf registration. It has been noted that financial firms such as commercial banks have made use of shelf registration to a greater degree than have manufacturing corporations, for example. Financial firms have traditionally raised funds quickly in a number of receptive markets. Hence, shelf registration permits them to extend their traditional financing practices. In contrast to the very considerable use of shelf registration in the bond market, in the equity market less than 10 percent of total issuance has been accounted for by shelf registration.

Regulation of Insider Trading

Associated with the increase of merger and acquisition activity of the 1980s has been increased regulation by the SEC and the courts of insider trading activity. A summary of insider trading laws and regulations is presented in Table 21.9.

Takeovers are often accompanied by large increases in the stock price and trading volume of the target firm. The insider trading cases that have achieved the most notoriety in the last few years have involved outsiders in possession of inside information, specifically risk arbitrageurs (such as Ivan Boesky) and officers in the merger and acquisitions

---

TABLE 21.9   Summary of Securities Laws and Regulations

Rule 10b-5	Prohibits fraud, misstatements, or omission of material facts in connection with the purchase or sale of any security.
Section 13(d)	Provides early warning to target firms of acquisitions of their stock by potential acquirers: 5 percent threshold, ten-day filing period. Applies to all large stock acquisitions.
Section 14(d) (1)	Requirements of Section 13(d) extended to *all public tender offers.* Provides for full disclosure to SEC by any group making recommendations to target shareholders.
Section 14(d) (4)–(7)	Regulates terms of tender offers. Length of time offer must be held open (twenty days), right of shareholders to withdraw tendered shares, and so on.
Section 14(e)	Prohibits fraud, misrepresentation in context of tender offers. Rule 14e-3 prohibits trading on nonpublic information in tender offers.
Section 16(a)	Provides for reporting by corporate insiders on their transactions in their corporations' stocks.
Section 16(b)	Allows the corporation or its security holders to sue for return of profits on transactions by corporate insiders completed within a six-month period.
Insider Trading Sanctions Act of 1984	Provides for triple damages in insider trading cases.
Racketeer Influenced and Corrupt Organizations Act of 1970 (RICO)	Provides for seizure of assets upon accusation and triple damages upon conviction for companies that defraud consumers, investors, and so on.

and takeover defense departments of prestigious investment banking firms (such as Michael Milken). Some investment banking firms have both M&A and risk arbitrage departments under the same roof, in theory separated by a so-called "Chinese wall" to prevent information leaks. Some have argued that these walls have been somewhat less impermeable than the original, and there has been growing criticism of having both functions within the same firm.

Interpreting very general existing legislation, the courts have found it wrong for outsiders to trade on inside information under three kinds of circumstances:

1. *Outsider buys information.* It is wrong to trade if the outsider "buys" information from insiders who breached their fiduciary duty to their company by divulging the information. This includes not only outright purchases of information, but information given in exchange for business or other favors. In Texas Gulf Sulphur, the SEC sought to overturn the trades of those who had received information from insiders on this basis.

   Manne [1966] suggested that bartering of information may be a way of coping with Section 16 disclosure requirements. Although insiders may effectively be barred from trading on inside information about their own firms, they may engage in information exchanges with associates who are insiders in another firm, and each would trade on the other's inside information. The Boesky case involved outright purchases, although the purchases were not from insiders in the classical sense, but from "temporary" insiders, employed by investment banking firms assisting their clients in takeover contests, and thus privy to inside information.

2. *The "misappropriation" doctrine.* Court decisions in classic insider trading cases tend to rely heavily on the principle of the fiduciary duty of insiders to the outside shareholders of their own firms. And the principle of fiduciary duty has been extended to include temporary insiders such as accountants, lawyers, and investment bankers whose jobs require that they have access to privileged information, and who are similarly prohibited from using the information at the expense of their client. However, beyond this group the definition of insider begins to become a bit strained, and the SEC has had to stretch to include those who have no fiduciary duty to the firm in whose stock they are trading. Under the misappropriation doctrine, outsiders are prohibited from trading on the basis of information which they misappropriate, or steal.

3. *Insider trading in tender offers.* Finally, the SEC adopted Rule 14e-3 to apply to insider trading within the context of tender offers specifically.

   One argument for insider trading is that it results in more efficient pricing of securities and in the more efficient operation of securities markets. Another is that insider trading produces more effective compensation of insiders. Opponents of insider trading question the validity of these arguments and suggest that insider trading activities could undermine confidence in the securities markets themselves. Unless the playing field (the market) is perceived as being level and equally fair to all, they argue, trading would diminish.

THE EMERGING DEVELOPMENTS

There are three major emerging developments that affect the preceding materials covered in the chapter: (1) increased rivalry among financing sources; (2) the blurring of traditional categories of forms of financing; and (3) increased globalization of financial markets.

Increased Rivalry among Financing Sources

A series of legislative enactments gave increased powers to financial intermediaries to invade the turf of others. Table 21.2, earlier in this chapter, described seven categories of financial intermediaries and leading firms in each category. Financial deregulation has intensified their rivalry to increase market share. In addition, excess capacity in financial services has developed in the attempt to maintain or improve market share as eroded profit margins for many of these companies.

Table 21.10 shows the market share of sources and forms of funds between 1983 and 1989. The share of total funds raised in credit markets by nonfinancial corporations represented by loans from U.S. banks dropped by 56 percent during the six-year period. The share of bank loans from foreign banks increased by almost 40 percent. Finance company loans have dropped greatly. Securitization has increased so that bonds, notes, and mortgages represented over 60 percent of the market in 1989.

TABLE 21.10   Distribution of Funds Raised in Credit Markets by Nonfinancial Corporations, by Type of Instrument, 1983, 1989

Type of Instrument	1983	1989
Bank loans		
U.S. banks	32.1%	14.2%
Foreign banks	4.9	6.8
Commercial paper	−1.5	10.6
Finance company loans	14.1	5.4
Bonds and notes[a]	46.5	57.7
Mortgages	−8.0	3.1
Bankers' acceptances and U.S. government loans	11.9	2.2
Total	100.0%	100.0%
MEMO		
Total funds raised in credit markets (billions of dollars)	$54.8	$196.0

[a]Includes bonds and notes issued abroad by U.S. corporations and tax-exempt bonds issued for the benefit of nonfinancial corporations.
Source: Crabbe, et al., [1990], p. 600.

Blurring of Some Traditional Distinctions

In the past, bank loans and commercial paper were considered short-term debt while corporate bonds and mortgages were regarded as long-term debt. Interest rates on short-term debt were regarded as variable and interest rates on long-term debt were regarded as fixed. This distinction was the basis for evaluating exposure to interest rate and liquidity risk. But interest rate swaps can convert variable interest payments to fixed and vice versa. In foreign currency swaps, the nature of foreign exchange risks is altered. Caps, floors, and collars have changed the nature of floating- and fixed-rate debt. A cap places a maximum on the interest rate paid on floating debt. A floor places a minimum. A collar combines a cap and a floor to establish a range. The smaller the range, the closer floating-rate debt becomes to fixed-rate. The issue of a fixed-rate security may include flexible caps, floors, and collars to mimic short-term debt.

Extendable notes give the issuer the option of extending the maturity of an issue. This blurs the difference between intermediate and long-term securities. The option to extend may be associated with reset notes, which provide for resetting coupon rates under specified conditions. Similarly, the introduction of medium-term notes that are continuously offered through agents on a "best efforts" basis and their continued rollover provides longer-term financing programs. As this market has matured, both the dollar amounts and maturities have increased. Initially, medium-term notes represented an extension of the commercial paper market. Growth in the late 1980s, however, was stimulated by a shift away from bond issuance by U.S. firms in foreign markets.

Increased Globalization of Financial Markets

With the increased globalization of financial markets, corporations shift between domestic and foreign sources based on relative tax conditions and regulations and changing foreign exchange rate expectations. The Eurobond market can be used as an illustration. Recall that Eurobonds are bonds issued outside of the home market. Eurobonds are issued in bearer form, and hence involve no registration to record the identity of the owners. This enables investors to collect interest on Eurobonds without paying taxes. This resulted in lower yields on the bearer Eurobonds.

However, in 1984, the United States repealed the withholding tax on interest paid on bonds held by foreign investors. Domestic U.S. Treasury and corporate bonds became more attractive to foreign investors. The yield advantages of Eurobonds have diminished and, relative to U.S. Treasuries, have been reversed. Since 1986 U.S. firms have reduced their borrowing in foreign markets. The demand for U.S. corporate issues in the Euromarket decreased as a consequence of "event risk" shocks. Event risks refers to takeovers or defensive recapitalizations of U.S. firms that resulted in smaller equity protection for the debt. A decline in the market prices of such bonds caused some unpleasant shocks to the bondholders. Increasingly, bonds of U.S. corporations have been required to add covenants that protect against event risk. Such a covenant might provide, for example, that in the event of a substantial change in leverage ratios, the bonds can be "put" to the issuing company at par.

The above examples illustrate how the financial markets have become globalized. Sometimes it is more favorable to finance domestically. Sometimes the advantage is in financing outside the home market. The countries or financial markets in which funds are raised change as the relative attractiveness of home versus foreign markets shifts. As a consequence, horizons of financial managers have had to be expanded to international dimensions.

SUMMARY

In this chapter we seek to provide an overview of sources of long-term financing. Data on sources of funds for business corporations since 1950 show that internal financing in the United States accounts for about 75 percent of the total sources of funds. Internal funds are also a high percentage of total sources in most of the other developed countries except Japan, where they have risen to the 63 percent level for the years 1984–1988. Another pattern observed across countries is that short-term debt is used as an adjustment mechanism. A change in the relative use of long-term debt is more likely to represent a change in the capital structure target.

Venture capital financing has taken on increased importance in recent years. Venture capital firms typically use convertible preferred stock in staged financing as the good performance of the recipient firm is demonstrated. Venture capital is a form of direct financing. Two other major forms of direct financing are term lending by commercial banks and the private placement of securities with insurance companies and pension funds. Term loans and private placements represent similar financing arrangements. Their advantages are avoidance of SEC registration procedures, flexibility in renegotiation of terms, and the assurance of availability of financing provided by long-term arrangements as compared with short-term bank borrowing.

Ordinarily, direct loans are retired by systematic repayments (amortization payments) over the life of the loan. Security, generally in the form of a chattel mortgage on equipment, is often employed, although the larger, stronger companies are usually able to borrow on an unsecured basis. Commercial banks typically make smaller, shorter-term loans; life insurance companies and pension funds grant larger, longer-term loans.

Like rates on other credits, the cost of direct loans varies with general interest rate levels, the size of the loan, and the strength of the borrower. For small loans to small companies, rates may be as high as six to eight percentage points above the prime lending rate; for large loans to large, stable firms, they will probably be close to the prime rate. Since these loans run for long periods, during which interest rates can change radically, many of them have variable interest rates, with the rate set at a certain level in relation to the domestic prime rate or above the Federal Reserve rediscount rate or an international rate such as the LIBOR. Often, direct loans include a "kicker" in the form of warrants to purchase the borrower's equity securities near the price prevailing at the time of the loan transaction.

The investment banker provides middleman services to both the seller and the buyer of new securities, helping plan the issue, underwriting it, and handling the job of selling the issue to the ultimate investor. The cost of this service to the issuer is related to the magnitude of the total job that must be performed to place the issue. The investment banker must also look to the interests of the brokerage customers; if these investors are not satisfied with the banker's products, they will deal elsewhere. Thus the investment banker performs a certification role for the issuer.

For seasoned public offerings, flotation costs are lowest for bonds, higher for preferred stock, and highest for common stock. For each type of security, flotation costs are lower for larger companies than for smaller ones, and most companies can cut their stock flotation costs by issuing the new securities to stockholders through rights offerings.

Going public and initial public offerings represent a fundamental change in the lifestyle of business firms. Costs of flotation are higher for initial public offerings than for seasoned issues. Flotation costs are higher for best efforts offerings than for firm-commitments. Best efforts offerings typically involve smaller firms whose share prices exhibit greater volatility in the aftermarket. Public offerings have advantages and disadvantages. The benefits and drawbacks appear to change with time since public firms may subsequently go private. The going-private phenomenon has become of increased importance in recent years as manifested in the increased use of MBOs and LBOs.

Rights offerings can be used effectively by financial managers. The use of rights will permit shareholders to preserve their share of ownership positions. However, if investors feel that the new financing is not well-advised, the rights offering may cause the price of the stock to decline even after adjustments. Because rights offerings are directed to existing shareholders, their use can reduce the costs of floating the new issue.

A major decision for financial managers in a rights offering is setting the subscription price. Formulas reflecting the static effects of a rights offering indicate that neither the company nor the stockholders gain or lose from the price changes. The rights offering has the effect of a stock split; the level set for the subscription price reflects, to a great degree, the objectives and effects of a stock split.

The subsequent price behavior of the rights and the common stock in the associated new offering reflects the earnings and dividends prospects of the company as well as underlying developments in the securities markets. The new financing associated with the rights offering can be an indicator of prospective growth in the company's sales and earnings.

The financial manager should be familiar with the federal laws regulating the issuance and trading of securities, because they influence liabilities and affect financing methods and costs. Regulation of securities trading seeks (1) to provide information that investors can utilize as a basis for judging the merits of securities, (2) to control the volume of credit used in securities trading, and (3) to provide orderly securities markets. The laws do not, however, prevent either purchase of unsound issues or wide price fluctuations. They raise the costs of flotation somewhat, but they also probably decrease the costs of trading by increasing public confidence in the securities markets.

The time and costs of SEC regulation have been reduced by some of its new rules. Rule 144A exempts U.S. and foreign corporations from registration requirements for bonds and stocks sold to large investors who, in turn, can resell them to qualified institutions. Rule 415 provides for shelf registration, which permits companies to make continuous securities offerings covered by a single initial filing.

Three emerging developments were summarized: the increased rivalry among financing sources, the blurring of traditional categories of forms of financing, and the increased globalization of financial markets.

QUESTIONS

21.1 What is the difference between a venture capital firm and an investment banking firm?

21.2 Why are convertible preferred stock and a staged capital commitment employed by venture capital firms?

21.3 Define these terms: *brokerage firm, underwriting, selling group,* and *investment banking.*

21.4 Before entering a formal agreement, investment bankers carefully investigate the companies whose securities they underwrite; this is especially true of the issues of firms going public for the first time.
  a. Since the bankers do not themselves plan to hold the securities but intend to sell them to others as soon as possible, why are they so concerned about making careful investigations?
  b. Does your answer to the question have any bearing on the fact that investment banking is a very difficult field to enter? Explain.

21.5 Since investment bankers price new issues in relation to outstanding issues, should a spread exist between the yields on the new and the outstanding issues? Discuss this matter separately for stocks and bonds.

21.6 **a.** If competitive bidding were required on all security offerings, would flotation costs be higher or lower?
  b. Would the size of the issuing firm be material in determining the effects of required competitive bidding?

21.7 Each month, the Securities and Exchange Commission publishes a report of the transactions made by the officers and directors of listed firms in their own companies' equity securities. Why do you suppose the SEC makes this report?

21.8 Prior to 1933, investment banking and commercial banking were both carried on by the same firm. In that year, however, the Banking Act required that these functions be separated. Discuss the pros and cons of this forced separation.

21.9 Suppose two similar firms are each selling $10 million of common stock. The firms are of the same size, are in the same industry, have the same leverage, and so on — except that one is publicly owned and the other is closely held.
  a. Will their costs of flotation be the same?
  b. If the issue were $10 million of bonds, would your answer be the same?

21.10 Evaluate the following statement: The fundamental purpose of the federal security laws dealing with new issues is to prevent investors, principally small ones, from sustaining losses on the purchase of stocks.

21.11 What issues are raised by the increasing purchase of equities by institutional investors?

21.12 Should the preemptive right entitle stockholders to purchase convertible bonds before they are offered to outsiders?

21.13 What are the reasons for not letting officers and directors of a corporation make short sales in their company's stock?

21.14 It is frequently stated that the primary purpose of the preemptive right is to allow individuals to maintain their proportionate share of the ownership and control of a corporation.

    a. Just how important do you suppose this consideration is for the average stockholder of a firm whose shares are traded on the New York or American Stock Exchange?

    b. Is the preemptive right likely to be of more importance to stockholders of closely held firms? Explain.

21.15 How would the success of a rights offering be affected by a declining stock market?

21.16 What are some of the advantages and disadvantages of setting the subscription price on a rights offering substantially below the current market price of the stock?

21.17 **a.** Is a firm likely to get wider distribution of shares if it sells new stock through a rights offering or directly to underwriters?

    b. Why would a company be interested in getting a wider distribution of shares?

21.18 The Fairmont Company was planning to issue $5 million of new common stock. In reaching the decision as to the form of offering, two alternatives were considered:

    (1) A rights offering, with out-of-pocket cost as a percentage of new capital at 1.4 percent.

    (2) An underwriting, with out-of-pocket cost as a percentage of new capital at 7.0 percent.

Can you think of possible reasons why Fairmont might choose the second alternative?

PROBLEMS

21.1 The common stock of the Nelson Company is selling for $32 a share on the market. Stockholders are offered one new share at a subscription price of $20 for every three shares held. What is the value of each right?

21.2 The Zoom Company common stock is priced at $40 a share on the market. Notice is given that stockholders can purchase one new share at a price of $27.50 for every four shares held.

    a. At approximately what market price will each right sell?

    b. Why will this be the approximate price?

    c. What effect will the issuance of rights have on the original market price?

21.3 Arlene Jackson's total assets consist of 490 shares of Collingwood Corporation and $2,000 in cash. Collingwood now offers stockholders one additional share at a price of $20 for each five shares held. The current market price of the stock is $35.

    a. What is the value of each right?

   b. Prepare statements showing Jackson's total assets after the offering for each of these alternative courses of action.

     (1) She exercises all her rights.

     (2) She sells all her rights.

     (3) She sells 400 rights and exercises 90 rights.

     (4) She neither sells nor exercises the rights.

21.4 The Miller Company has the balance sheet and income statement in Table P21.4. The company plans to raise an additional $5 million through a rights offering; the additional funds will continue to earn 10.5 percent. The price-earnings ratio is assumed to remain at 15 times, the dividend payout will continue to be 56 percent, and the 40 percent tax rate will remain in effect. (Do not attempt to use the formula given in the chapter. Additional information is given here that violates the "other things constant" assumption inherent in the formula.)

   a. Assuming subscription prices of $25, $50, and $80 a share:

     (1) How many additional shares of stock will have to be sold?

     (2) How many rights will be required to purchase one new share?

     (3) What will be the new earnings per share?

     (4) What will be the new market price per share?

     (5) What will be the new dividend per share if the dividend payout ratio is maintained?

   b. Suppose you hold 100 shares of Miller stock before the rights offering. After you exercise your rights, what is the value of your position?

TABLE P21.4 The Miller Company Balance Sheet before Rights Offering

		Total debt (6%)	$ 7,000,000
		Common stock (100,000 shares)	3,000,000
		Retained earnings	4,000,000
Total assets	$14,000,000	Total liabilities and capital	$14,000,000

The Miller Company Income Statement

Earnings rate: 10.5% on total assets	
Total earnings	$1,470,000
Interest on debt	420,000
Income before taxes	$1,050,000
Taxes (40% rate assumed)	420,000
Earnings after taxes	$ 630,000
Earnings per share	$6.30
Dividends per share (56% of earnings)	$3.53
Price-earnings ratio	15 times
Market price per share	$94.50

21.5   The Johnson Company common stock is selling for $60 per share. With its investment bankers the company has formulated a plan to raise additional funds through a common stock rights offering at $50 per share, with 4 rights needed to buy one share at the subscription price.

a.   Using the traditional formula, what is the value of each right?

b.   Assume that the risk-free rate is 9 percent, the variance of returns on equity is 16 percent, and the time to maturity of the rights is 0.1 of a year. Calculate the value of a right using the option pricing approach plus consideration of the dilution factor.

21.6   As the chief financial officer of XTZ Corporation, you are planning to sell $100 million of ten-year bonds to finance the construction of a hot-tub factory. The market rate of interest on debt of this quality and maturity is 12 percent. However, the total costs of the underwriting have been estimated to be 10.5 percent of the gross proceeds.

a.   Calculate the effective cost of this debt to your firm, before taxes. (Hint: Let the coupon rate be 12 percent, so that the bonds will sell at face value; then solve for the IRR, which will make the future payments on the bond equal to the face value less 10.5 percent — that is, to $895 per bond.)

b.   Your investment banker advises you that a 10 percent interest rate may be obtained by establishing a sinking fund provision whereby one-tenth of the original debt principal will be retired at the end of each year. What is the effective cost of debt for this issue? (Underwriting costs remain at 10.5 percent.)

c.   Why might an investment banker prefer you to finance by (b) rather than (a)?

21.7   If your firm sells preferred stock in the amount of $100 million, the total flotation expense will be about 11.5 percent of gross proceeds. If the going rate on preferred stock of the same quality as your firm's is 12 percent, what is the effective cost of the preferred stock issue? (Assume the stock will remain outstanding in perpetuity.)

21.8   Three executives of the Hughes Aircraft Company, one of the largest privately owned corporations in the world, have decided to break away from Hughes and to set up a company of their own. The principal reason for this decision was capital gains; Hughes Aircraft stock is all privately owned, and the corporate structure makes it impossible for executives to be granted stock purchase options. Hughes's executives receive substantial salaries and bonuses, but this income is all taxable at normal tax rates, and no capital gains opportunities are available.

The three men, Jim Adcock, Robert Goddard, and Rick Aiken, have located a medium-size electronics manufacturing company available for purchase. All the stock of this firm, Baynard Industries, is owned by the founder, Joseph Baynard. Although the company is in excellent shape, Baynard wants to sell it because of his failing health. A price of $5.7 million has been established, based on a price/earnings ratio of 12 and annual earnings of $475,000. Baynard has given the three prospective purchasers an option to purchase the company for the agreed price; the option is to run for six months, during which time the three men are to arrange financing with which to buy the firm.

Adcock has consulted with Jules Scott, a partner in the New York investment banking firm of Williams Brothers and an acquaintance of some years' standing, to seek his assistance in obtaining the funds necessary to complete the purchase. Adcock, Goddard, and Aiken each have some money available to put into the new enterprise, but they need a substantial amount of outside capital. There is some possibility of borrowing part of the money, but Scott has discouraged this idea. His reasoning is, first, that Baynard Industries is already highly leveraged, and if the purchasers were to borrow additional funds, there would be a very severe risk that they would be unable to service this debt in the event of a recession in the electronics industry. Although the firm is currently earning $475,000 a year, this figure could quickly turn into a loss in the event of a few cancelled defense contracts or cost miscalculations.

Scott's second reason for discouraging a loan is that Adcock, Goddard, and Aiken plan not only to operate Baynard Industries and seek internal growth but also to use the corporation as a vehicle for making further acquisitions of electronics companies. This being the case, Scott believes that it would be wise for the company to keep any borrowing potential in reserve for use in later acquisitions. Scott proposes that the three partners obtain funds to purchase Baynard Industries in accordance with the figures shown in Table P21.8.

TABLE P21.8   Baynard Industries

Price paid to Joseph Baynard		$5,700,000
(12 × $475,000 earnings)		
Authorized shares	5,000,000	
Initially issued shares	1,125,000	
Initial distribution of shares:		
Adcock	100,000 shares at $1	$ 100,000
Goddard	100,000 shares at $1	100,000
Aiken	100,000 shares at $1	100,000
Williams Brothers	125,000 shares at $7	875,000
Public stockholders	700,000 shares at $7	4,900,000
	1,125,000	$6,075,000
Underwriting costs: 5% of $4,900,000	$ 245,000	
Legal fees, and so on, associated with issue	45,000	290,000
		$5,785,000
Payment to Joseph Baynard		5,700,000
Net funds to Baynard Industries		$ 85,000

Baynard Industries would be reorganized with an authorized 5,000,000 shares, with 1,125,000 to be issued at the time the transfer takes place and the other 3,875,000 to be held in reserve for possible issuance in connection with acquisitions. Adcock, Goddard, and Aiken would each purchase 100,000 shares at a price of $1 a share, the par value. Williams Brothers would purchase 125,000 shares at a price of $7. The remaining 700,000 shares would be sold to the public at a price of $7 a share.

Williams Brothers' underwriting fee would be 5 percent of the shares sold to the public, or $245,000. Legal fees, accounting fees, and other charges associated with the issue would amount to $45,000, for a total flotation cost of $290,000. After deducting the underwriting charges and the payment to Baynard from the gross proceeds of the stock sale, the reorganized Baynard Industries would receive funds in the amount of $85,000, which would be used for internal expansion purposes.

As a part of the initial agreement, Adcock, Goddard, and Aiken each would be given options to purchase an additional 80,000 shares at a price of $7 a share for one year. Williams Brothers would be given an option to purchase an additional 100,000 shares at $7 a share in one year.

a. What is the total flotation cost, expressed as a percentage of the funds raised by the underwriter? Does this charge seem reasonable in the light of published statistics on the cost of floating new issues of common stock?

b. Suppose that the three men estimate the following probabilities for the firm's stock price one year from now:

Price	Probability
$ 1	0.05
5	0.10
9	0.35
13	0.35
17	0.10
21	0.05

Assuming Williams Brothers exercises its options, calculate the following ratio based on the expected stock price (ignore time-discount effects):

$$\frac{\text{Financial benefits to Williams Brothers}}{\text{Funds raised by underwriter}}.$$

Disregard Williams Brothers' profit on the 125,000 shares it bought outright at the initial offering. Comment on the ratio.

c. Are Adcock, Goddard, and Aiken purchasing their stock at a "fair" price? Should the prospectus disclose the fact that they would buy their stock at $1 a share whereas public stockholders would buy their stock at $7 a share?

d. Would it be reasonable for Williams Brothers to purchase its initial 125,000 shares at a price of $1?

e. Do you foresee any problems of control for Adcock, Goddard, and Aiken?

f. Would the expectation of an exceptionally large need for investment funds next year be a relevant consideration in deciding on the amount of funds to be raised now?

21.9 Beatty and Ritter [1986] set forth the proposition that the greater the *ex ante* uncertainty about a new issue the greater will be its expected underpricing. Their equation for the issuing firm's optimal offering price (OP) is their Equation (5) on page 230:

$$\text{OP}^2 - 2[a + (b - a)C]\text{OP} + a^2 = 0$$

where $C \equiv c/(W - c)$. C is the cost of becoming informed as a fraction of the investable wealth of the informed, and a and b represent, for this problem, the terms in a probability density function distributed uniformly on $[a, b]$ where $a \leq 0 < b$. Let $W = 10$ and $c = 1$. Compare the OP for $(a, b) = (0, 4)$ with OP for $(a, b) = (1, 3)$. Hint: $C = \frac{1}{9}$.

21.10 On 6/6/91 Time Warner (TW) announced a rights offering. Each shareholder would receive .6 of a right for each share. Each right could buy one share of common stock.

The subscription price would be $63 if 60 percent of rights were exercised; $105 if 100 percent of rights were exercised, in which case TW would raise $3.5 billion in new equity. Shareholders, especially institutional holders, objected on two grounds: (1) The uncertain terms were confusing and (2) the advisory fees to six investment bankers totaling $179 million, or between 1.91 percent and 5.24 percent of the proceeds, were considered excessive. The SEC reviewed the proposal, objecting to its "coercive nature" in that it might force shareholders to buy TW stock at prices above the then current market. The price of the TW stock just before the 6/6/91 announcement was $125. After the announcement, the stock traded down to just below $90 by 7/12/91. The reason given for the sliding scale price was to minimize dilution of the TW stock and to avoid a price decline. On 7/15/91, TW announced a new rights offer to shareholders with the ex-rights trading date 7/16/91. TW had closed on Friday 7/12/91 at $87\frac{5}{8}$. The stock closed 7/15/91 at $88\frac{3}{4}$ (equivalent to $85\frac{3}{4}$ ex-rights). The rights were trading at $7\frac{3}{8}$ on 7/16/91. Each right could purchase 0.6 shares of TW at a subscription price of $80. TW had 57.5 million shares outstanding. Comment on the TW strategy in this mini-case study.

SELECTED REFERENCES

Aguilar, Linda, "Still Toe-to-Toe: Banks and Nonbanks at the End of the '80s," *Economic Perspectives,* 14 (January-February 1990), Federal Reserve Bank of Chicago, pp. 12–23.

Beatty, Randolph P., and Ritter, Jay R., "Investment Banking, Reputation, and the Underpricing of Initial Public Offerings," *Journal of Financial Economics,* 15 (1986), pp. 213–232.

Benveniste, Lawrence M., and Spindt, Paul A., "How Investment Bankers Determine the Offer Price and Allocation of New Issues," *Journal of Financial Economics,* 24 (1989), pp. 343–361.

Bhagat, Sanjai, "The Effect of Pre-emptive Right Amendments on Shareholder Wealth," *Journal of Financial Economics,* (November 1983), pp. 289–310.

Booth, James R., and Smith, Richard L., II, "Capital Raising, Underwriting and the Certification Hypothesis," *Journal of Financial Economics,* 15 (January-February 1986), pp. 261–281.

Brown, J. Michael, "Post-Offering Experience of Companies Going Public," *Journal of Business,* (January 1970), pp. 10–18.

Crabbe, L. E.; Pickering, M. H.; and Prowse, S. D., "Recent Developments in Corporate Finance," *Federal Reserve Bulletin,* 76 (August 1990), pp. 593–603.

DeAngelo, Harry; DeAngelo, Linda; and Rice, Edward, "Going Private: Minority Freezeouts and Stockholder Wealth," *Journal of Law and Economics,* (October 1984), pp. 367–401.

Dyl, Edward, and Joehnk, Michael, "Competitive versus Negotiated Underwriting of Public Utility Debt," *Bell Journal of Economics,* 7 (Autumn 1976), pp. 680–689.

Ederington, Louis, "Negotiated versus Competitive Underwritings of Corporate Bonds," *Journal of Finance,* 31 (March 1976), pp. 17–28.

Findlay, M. Chapman, III; Johnson, Keith B.; and Morton, T. Gregory, "An Analysis of the Flotation Cost of Utility Bonds, 1971–76," *Journal of Financial Research,* 2 (Fall 1979), pp. 133–142.

Galai, D., and Schneller, M., "The Pricing of Warrants and the Value of the Firm," *Journal of Finance,* 33 (December 1978), pp. 1333–1342.

Hayes, S. L., III, and Hubbard, P. M., *Investment Banking,* Boston, Mass.: Harvard Business School Press, 1990.

Hays, Patrick A.; Joehnk, Michael D.; and Melicher, Ronald W., "Differential Determinants of Risk Premiums in the Public and Private Corporate Bond Markets," *Journal of Financial Research,* 2 (Fall 1979), pp. 143–152.

Heinkel, Robert, and Schwartz, Eduardo S., "Rights Versus Underwritten Offerings: An Asymmetric Information Approach," *Journal of Finance,* (March 1986), pp. 1–18.

Ibbotson, Roger G., and Jaffe, Jeffrey F., "'Hot Issue' Markets," *Journal of Finance,* 30 (September 1975), pp. 1027–1042.

James, C., "Some Evidence on the Uniqueness of Bank Loans," *Journal of Financial Economics,* 19 (1987), pp. 217–235.

Lehn, Kenneth, and Poulsen, Annette, "Free Cash Flow and Stockholder Gains in Going Private Transactions," *Journal of Finance,* 44, 3 (July 1989), pp. 771–787.

Miller, R. E., and Reilly, F. K., "An Examination of Mispricing, Returns, and Uncertainty for Initial Public Offerings," *Financial Management,* 16 (1987), pp. 33–38.

Rao, Gita, "The Relation between Stock Returns and Earnings: A Study of Newly-Public Firms," unpublished working paper, University of Illinois, 1989.

Remolona, Eli M., "Understanding International Differences in Leverage Trends," *FRBNY Quarterly Review,* 15 (Spring 1990), pp. 31–42.

Ritter, Jay R., "The Long-Run Performance of Initial Public Offerings," *Journal of Finance,* 46 (March 1991), pp. 3–27.

———, "The Costs of Going Public," *Journal of Financial Economics,* 19 (1987), pp. 269–281.

Rock, Kevin, "Why New Issues are Underpriced," *Journal of Financial Economics,* 15 (1986), pp. 187–212.

Sahlman, W. A., "Aspects of Financial Contracting in Venture Capital," *Journal of Applied Corporate Finance,* 1 (Summer 1988), pp. 23–36.

Smith, C. W., "Investment Banking and the Capital Acquisition Process," *Journal of Financial Economics,* 15 (1986), pp. 3–29.

———, "Alternative Methods for Raising Capital: Rights Versus Underwritten Offerings," *Journal of Financial Economics,* 5 (December 1977), pp. 273–307.

Stover, Roger D., "The Interaction between Pricing and Underwriting Spread in the New Issue Convertible Debt Market," *Journal of Financial Research,* 6 (Winter 1983), pp. 323–332.

Szewczyk, S. H., and Varma, R., "Raising Capital with Private Placements of Debt," *The Journal of Financial Research,* 14 (Spring 1991), pp. 1–13.

Tallman, Gary; Rush, David; and Melicher, Ronald, "Competitive versus Negotiated Underwriting Costs for Regulated Industries," *Financial Management,* 3 (Summer 1974), pp. 49–55.

Wruck, K. H., "Equity Ownership Concentration and Firm Value: Evidence from Private Equity Financings," *Journal of Financial Economics,* 23 (1989), pp. 3–28.

CHAPTER 22

Common Stock Financing

Common equity in a corporation or partnership or proprietorship interests in an unincorporated firm constitute the first source of funds to a new business and the base of support for borrowing by existing firms. Accordingly, our discussion of specific forms of long-term financing will begin with an analysis of various attributes of common stock. We also set forth an analytical framework for decisions choosing between common stock versus other forms of financing.

COMMON STOCK FINANCING

The nature of equity ownership depends on the form of the business or organization. The central problem of such ownership revolves around an apportionment of certain rights and responsibilities among those who have provided the funds necessary for the operation of the business. The rights and responsibilities attached to equity consist of positive considerations (income potential and control of the firm) and negative considerations (loss potential, legal responsibility, and personal liability).

Apportionment of Income, Control, and Risk

Two important positive considerations are involved in equity ownership: income and control. The right to income carries the risk of loss. Control also involves responsibility and liability. In an individual proprietorship that uses funds supplied only by the owner, the owner has a 100 percent right to income and control and to loss and responsibility. As soon as the proprietor incurs debt, however, he or she has entered into contracts that limit the freedom to control the firm and to apportion the firm's income. In a partnership, these

TABLE 22.1   Balance Sheets for Corporations A and B

Corporation A				Corporation B			
		Debt	$ 20			Debt	$ 60
		Equity	80			Equity	40
Total assets	$100	Total claims	$100	Total assets	$100	Total claims	$100

rights are apportioned among the partners in an agreed-upon manner. In the absence of a formal agreement, a division is made by state law. In a corporation, more significant issues arise concerning the rights of the owners.

Through the right to vote, holders of common stock have legal control of the corporation. As a practical matter, however, in many corporations, the principal officers constitute all, or a majority, of the members of the board of directors. In this circumstance, the board may be controlled by the management rather than by the owners. However, numerous examples demonstrate that stockholders can reassert their control if they are dissatisfied with the corporation's policies. In recent years, proxy battles with the aim of altering corporate policies have occurred with increasing frequency, and firms whose managers are unresponsive to stockholders' desires are subject to takeover bids by other firms.

Another consideration involved in equity ownership is risk. On liquidation, holders of common stock are last in the priority of claims. Therefore, the portion of capital they contribute provides a cushion for creditors, if losses occur on dissolution. The equity-to-total-assets ratio indicates the percentage by which assets may shrink in value on liquidation before creditors will incur losses.

For example, compare two corporations, A and B, whose balance sheets are shown in Table 22.1. The ratio of equity to total assets in Corporation A is 80 percent. Total assets, therefore, will have to shrink by 80 percent before creditors will lose money. By contrast, in Corporation B, the extent to which assets will have to shrink in value on liquidation before creditors lose money is only 40 percent.

RIGHTS OF HOLDERS OF COMMON STOCK

The rights of holders of common stock in a business corporation are established by the laws of the state in which the corporation is chartered and by the terms of the charter granted by the state. Charters are relatively uniform on many matters, including collective and specific rights. Certain collective rights are usually given to the holders of common stock: (1) the right to amend the charter with the approval of the appropriate officials in the state of incorporation, (2) the right to adopt and amend bylaws, (3) the right to elect the directors of the corporation, (4) the right to authorize the sale of fixed assets, (5) the right to enter into mergers, (6) the right to change the amount of authorized common stock, and (7) the right to issue preferred stock, debentures, bonds, and other securities. Holders of common stock also have specific rights as individual owners: (1) the right to

vote in the manner prescribed by the corporate charter, (2) the right to sell their stock certificates (their evidence of ownership) and, in this way, to transfer their ownership interest to other persons, (3) the right to inspect the corporate books,[1] and (4) the right to share residual assets of the corporation on dissolution. (However, the holders of common stock are last among the claimants to the assets of the corporation.)

Nature of Voting Rights and Proxy Contests

For each share of common stock owned, the holder has the right to cast one vote at the annual meeting of stockholders or at such special meetings as may be called.

Proxy. Provision is made for the temporary transfer of the right to vote by an instrument known as a *proxy*. The transfer is limited in its duration; typically, it applies only to a specific occasion, such as the annual meeting of stockholders.

The SEC supervises the use of the proxy machinery and frequently issues rules and regulations to improve its administration. SEC supervision is justified for at least two reasons:

1. If the proxy machinery is left wholly in the hands of management, there is a danger that the incumbent management will be self-perpetuated.

2. If it is made easy for minority groups of stockholders and opposition stockholders to oust management, there is a danger that they will gain control of the corporation for temporary advantages to place themselves or their friends in management positions.

Dodd and Warner [1983] found that proxy contests perform a useful economic function. In 96 proxy contests over a 16-year sample period beginning in 1962, they observed that the challenges were often led by former company insiders, suggesting that proxy contests, to some degree, are an outgrowth of competition in the managerial labor market. They found that the challenges obtained a majority of seats on the board of directors in about one-fifth of the 96 contests. Dissidents gained some board representation in over half the sample contests. Dissidents usually feel that they have "won" if they obtain two seats on the board — one person to make motions and another to second them, so that the resulting discussion is included in the board minutes.

Dodd and Warner found that proxy contests stimulate expectations of improved corporate performance. During the 40-day period prior to the date of the initial public contest announcement, their estimate of the average positive abnormal performance was 10.5 percent. They found that a portion of the positive share price changes taking place in early stages of proxy contests was not permanent. Dodd and Warner found some price declines just after record date, which establishes who has the right to vote shares. Thus, negative excess returns found in the later stages of proxy contests are at least partially attributable to declines in the market value of the vote.

---

[1]Obviously, a corporation cannot have its business affairs disturbed by allowing every stockholder to go through any records the stockholder wants to inspect. Furthermore, a corporation cannot wisely permit a competitor who buys shares of its common stock to look at all the corporation records. There must be, and there are, practical limitations to this right.

A later study by DeAngelo and DeAngelo [1989] of 60 proxy contests from 1978–1985 corroborated many of Dodd and Warner's [1983] results. They found significant abnormal returns from 40 days before the contest through the outcome announcement of 6.02 percent, significant returns of 18.76 percent in the 40 days preceding any public indication of dissident activity. They also found negative returns at the contest outcome when the dissidents failed to win any seats on the board. The negative returns were larger when the dissidents were defeated by the expenditure of corporate assets to buy off the dissidents, a white knight acquisition of the target, or court approval of the validity of the incumbent's defense in the face of which the dissidents withdrew. This result suggests that when the incumbent management is securely entrenched or the probability of future control contests is reduced, the value of vote and/or the expected takeover premium capitalized in the share price declines.

Cumulative Voting

A method of voting that has come into increased prominence is cumulative voting. Cumulative voting for directors is required in 22 states, including California, Illinois, Michigan, Ohio, and Pennsylvania. It is permissible in 18, including Delaware, New Jersey, and New York. Ten states make no provision for it.

Cumulative voting permits multiple votes for a single director. For example, suppose six directors are to be elected. The owner of 100 shares can cast 100 votes for each of the six openings. Cumulatively, then, the stockholder has 600 votes. When cumulative voting is permitted, the stockholder can accumulate the votes and cast all of them for one director, instead of 100 each for six directors. Cumulative voting is designed to enable a minority group of stockholders to obtain some voice in the control of the company by electing at least one director to the board.

The nature of cumulative voting is illustrated by use of the following formula:

$$\text{req.} = \frac{\text{des.}(N)}{\# + 1} + 1, \qquad \text{(22.1)}$$

where

req. = number of shares required to elect a desired number of directors

des. = number of directors stockholder desires to elect

N = total number of shares of common stock outstanding and entitled to be voted[2]

\# = total number of directors to be elected.

The formula can be made more meaningful by an example. The ABC Company will elect six directors. There are 15 candidates and 100,000 shares entitled to be voted. If a group desires to elect two directors, how many shares must it have?

---

[2]An alternative that may be agreed to by the contesting parties is to define N as the number of shares *voted*, not *authorized to be voted*. This procedure, which in effect gives each group seeking to elect directors the same percentage of directors as their percentage of the voted stock, is frequently followed. When it is used, a group that seeks to gain control with a minimum investment must estimate the percentage of shares that will be voted and then obtain control of more than 50 percent of that number.

$$\text{req.} = \frac{2 \times 100,000}{6 + 1} + 1 = 28,572$$

Observe the significance of the formula. Here, a minority group wishes to elect one-third of the board of directors. It can achieve its goal by owning less than one-third the number of shares of stock.[3]

Alternatively, assuming that a group holds 40,000 shares of stock in the company, how many directors can it elect following the rigid assumptions of the formula? The formula can be used in its present form or can be solved for des. and expressed as

$$\text{des.} = \frac{(\text{req.} - 1)(\# + 1)}{N}. \qquad \textbf{(22.2)}$$

Inserting the figures, the calculation is

$$\text{des.} = \frac{39,999 \times 7}{100,000} = 2.8.$$

The 40,000 shares can thus elect 2.8 directors. Since directors cannot exist as fractions, the group can elect only two directors.

As a practical matter, suppose that, in the above situation, the total number of shares is 100,000; hence, 60,000 shares remain in other hands. The voting of all 60,000 shares may not be concentrated. Suppose the 60,000 shares (cumulatively 360,000 votes) not held by the minority group are distributed equally among ten candidates, with 36,000 shares held by each candidate. If the minority group's 240,000 votes are distributed equally among each of six candidates, it can elect all six directors even though it does not have a majority of the stock.

Actually, it is difficult to make assumptions about how the opposition votes will be distributed. What is shown here is a good example of game theory. One rule in this theory is to assume that your opponents will do the worst they can do to you and to counter with actions to minimize the maximum loss. This is the kind of assumption followed in the formula. If the opposition concentrates its votes in the optimum manner, what is the best you can do to work in the direction of your goal? Other plausible assumptions can be substituted if there are sufficient facts to support alternative hypotheses about the opponents' behavior.

Preemptive Right

The financial effects of rights offering were discussed in some detail in the preceding chapter. Here we simply discuss the pros and cons of preemptive rights. The preemptive right gives holders of common stock the first option to purchase additional issues of common stock. In some states, the right is made part of every corporate charter; in others, the right must be specifically inserted in the charter.

The purpose of the preemptive right is twofold. First, it protects the power of control of present stockholders. If it were not for this safeguard, the management of a corporation

---

[3]Note also that at least 14,286 shares must be controlled to elect one director.

under criticism from stockholders could prevent stockholders from removing it from office by issuing a large number of additional shares at a very low price and purchasing these shares itself. Management would thereby secure control of the corporation to frustrate the will of the current stockholders.

The second, and by far the more important, protection that the preemptive right affords stockholders concerns dilution of value. For example, assume that 1,000 shares of common stock, each with a price of $100, are outstanding, making the total market value of the firm $100,000.[4] An additional 1,000 shares are sold at $50 a share, a total of $50,000, thereby raising the market value of the firm to $150,000. When the total market value is divided by the new total shares outstanding, a value of $75 a share is obtained. Thus, selling common stock at below market value will enable new shareholders to buy stock on terms more favorable than those that had been extended to the old shareholders. The preemptive right prevents such occurrences.

The above views are not held by everyone. For example, in 1981 the shareholders of General Motors approved a charter amendment to eliminate preferential subscription rights. A shareholder proposal to restore limited preemptive rights was opposed in GM's proxy statement in relation to its annual meeting of May 24, 1991. The reason given was: "Wherever a broad base of corporate ownership and an active market for a corporation's shares exist, preferential subscription rights serve no useful purpose" [p. 17].

Voting Rights and Value of Control

The distribution of voting and cash flow rights among common stockholders on other than a one-to-one basis can be done in a number of ways. With different classes of common stock, one class may be barred from voting in elections for the board of directors or permitted to elect only a minority of the board. The inferior-vote class of stock may have fewer votes per share, or may have no voting rights at all. Even without different classes of stock, the distribution of shares can alter effective voting rights; especially where cumulative voting is not enforced, the vote of minority stockholders may be rendered virtually meaningless.

Contractual arrangements such as voting trusts and standstill agreements can also impact nominally equal voting rights. In a voting trust, stockholders retain cash flow rights to their shares while giving the right to vote those shares to another entity. Standstill agreements require a shareholder (often a threatening raider) to refrain from acquiring additional stock and to vote with management over a specified period of time. There may be contingent voting rights for preferred stockholders in the event of missed dividends or, more rarely, for bondholders. Convertible securities as well as warrants and options may also be viewed as conferring contingent voting rights, that is, contingent upon conversion or exercise.

Lease, McConnell, and Mikkelson [1983] hypothesized that any voting rights premium, that is, the incremental value of superior-vote stock over inferior-vote stock, must reflect differences in payoffs in future states of nature. The evidence from their sample of

---

[4]What is relevant is market value not par value, which is a purely arbitrary designation, nor book value, which reflects only historical accounting numbers.

dual-class stock firms over the period 1940–1978 supports a price premium for superior voting rights. The average premium was 5.44 percent. The authors find a partial explanation for the price premium in the possibility of indirect cash and noncash payments in the form of higher than warranted compensation and/or perquisites for superior-vote stockholders who are also employees (managers) of the corporation. If the incremental value of control is based to a great extent on the possibility of incremental payoffs to superior-vote stockholders who also happen to be employee/managers of the issuing firm, then we would expect to find ownership of superior-vote stock concentrated in management.

DeAngelo and DeAngelo [1985] focused on ownership concentration of dual-class stock and confirmed that management does, indeed, seem to place a higher value on voting rights over cash flow rights. For 45 firms with dual-class stock in 1980, 96 percent of all shareholders held inferior-vote stock, with superior-vote stock concentrated in the hands of management. Sixty to 75 percent of the firms were classified as majority controlled by management (depending on whether the definition of management was extended to include nonofficer directors). Management's median voting rights ownership was 56.9 percent, while median cash flow ownership was only 24 percent.

Other benefits of managerial voting control in addition to incremental salary and perquisites are identified. Vote ownership encourages managers to invest in organization-specific human capital. Management performance evaluation costs may be high if it is difficult to communicate the information necessary to evaluate performance to outside shareholders; managerial vote ownership protects managers from being removed from office by mistake. For example, a potentially successful long-term strategy may be causing havoc with short-term performance indicators; or an accurate assessment of management performance might require dissemination of proprietary information.

This insulation from competition by other management teams in the market for corporate control is also the primary cost of managerial vote ownership; however, other substitute discipline mechanisms operate to keep management discretion within bounds. Consistently poor management will result in excessive costs of external capital as well as adverse cash flow consequences for the managers themselves. The significant family involvement in many of these dual-class stock firms provides another potent disciplinary force in the form of social sanctions against family member/managers. Many of these firms started as family businesses, but as growth continued, family wealth constraints would have meant foregoing profitable investment opportunities in the absence of external equity. By going public with inferior-vote stock, these companies raise the needed capital without relinquishing control for themselves, and exchanges of stock among family members provide a means to transfer control across generations. (The Ford Company is a notable example.)

Why should a voting rights premium exist for marginal (noncontrol block) shares of superior voting rights stock? Megginson [1990] posed three hypotheses. The "extra merger premium hypothesis" involves the possibility that a firm may become the target in a takeover attempt and that a higher price will be paid for the superior voting rights shares. The differential price is a premium for the power to sell control of a company. The rational capital market will capitalize the discounted value of the extra merger premium into the current market price of the superior voting rights stock. Under this hypothesis, the premium will be related to (1) the probability that the firm will become a takeover target and (2) the likelihood that a higher price will be paid for the superior voting shares. One difficulty of the hypothesis is that the observed voting rights premium (such as the 45 percent premium reported by Levy, [1983]) appears too large for a discounted expected value of some future takeover premium.

Thus, Megginson [1990] explored a second hypothesis — the "ownership structure hypothesis." Managerial shareholdings can have both incentive and entrenchment effects. When managerial shareholdings are large, managers are effectively entrenched in office and it is difficult to discipline them (even through a takeover). As noted earlier, DeAngelo and DeAngelo [1985] document very large shareholdings of insiders in dual-class firms. Further, managers increase their holdings of voting rights after recapitalizations that introduce a dual-class common stock structure, even as they reduce their fractional ownerships of cash flow rights [Partch, 1987]. The entrenchment effect may lower the market value of dual-class firms. Empirical evidence consistent with this proposition is reported by Jarrell and Poulsen [1988], who document a significant and negative stock price reaction to the announcement by NYSE firms of plans to adopt dual-class equity capitalization after June 1984.

The third hypothesis is based on the observation that the stability of the controlling coalition of insider shareholders will impact the market value of noncontrol-block shares. Coalition stability affects the probability of a control contest occurring in the future and thus determines the probability that noncontrol-block shares will participate in any premium payment made to establish voting control. Thus the "voting power hypothesis" is very similar to the extra merger premium hypothesis. It predicts that marginal superior voting shares will sell at a greater premium when control of a corporation is more contestable, that is, when the control coalition is less stable.

To provide empirical evidence on the three alternative, but related, hypotheses, Megginson [1988] examined a sample of 152 British firms with two or more common share classes with differential voting rights outstanding at some time during the period 1955–1982. Over 16,000 monthly price pairs were examined. The superior voting rights shares had an average price premium of 13.3 percent over an otherwise equivalent class of restricted voting rights. Liquidity was not causing the premium, because the restricted voting shares traded much more frequently. Liquidity, if anything, attenuated the premium.

Regression analyses showed that the voting rights premium was directly related to insider holdings of superior voting shares and inversely related to insider holdings of restricted voting shares. This result is consistent with the ownership structure hypothesis, but appears inconsistent with the voting power hypothesis (because greater insider holdings of superior voting shares should increase the stability of coalition and thus reduce the voting power of marginal shares and their premium). Thus, the empirical evidence generally supports the extra merger premium and ownership structure hypotheses.

Dual-class recapitalizations can be used to consolidate control of the corporation by insiders, protecting them from displacement by a hostile takeover. To test this hypothesis, Jarrell and Poulsen [1988] examined shareholder wealth effects of 94 firms recapitalizing with dual classes of common stock with disparate voting rights. The sample firms recapitalized in the period 1976–1986 by either the dividend method (55 percent of the sample), the exchange method (35 percent), or the length of time method (10 percent). The dividend method starts with a stock split or a stock dividend involving distribution of low-vote stock. The previously existing common stock is redesignated as high-vote class B stock usually entitled to ten votes per share and/or to elect a majority of the board of directors. The low-vote stock is usually entitled to one vote per share and/or to elect a minority of the board and sometimes receives a higher dividend. The exchange method issues high-vote stock in exchange for the currently outstanding (low-vote) stock. The low-vote stock generally receives a higher dividend. The length of time method involves a change in voting rights of the existing common stock which becomes entitled to ten votes per share. Newly issued or traded shares become ''short term'' and are entitled to only one vote. The short-term shares become ''long-term'' shares and entitled to ten votes per share after being held continuously for a substantial period, such as four years.

Sixty-seven of the 94 firms recapitalized since 1983, and over half of the recent cases represent NYSE-listed firms. For the 62 firms recapitalizing after the NYSE imposed a moratorium in June 1984 on the delisting of dual-class equity firms, the announcement effect of recapitalization was insignificantly negative 0.72 percent for the two-day window of the announcement day and the following day, but was significantly negative 0.55 percent for the day following the announcement. In addition, the fraction of firms with negative abnormal returns was 61 percent (and significantly different from 50 percent) on each of the two days. However, for the premoratorium sample, the abnormal return was insignificant. This latter result was also observed by Partch [1987], who studied 44 dual-class recapitalizations in the premoratorium period and concluded these recapitalizations do not harm shareholders.

Evaluation of Common Stock as a Source of Funds

We will now appraise common stock from both the viewpoint of the issuer and from a social viewpoint.

From the Viewpoint of the Issuer

Advantages. The advantages of financing with common stock include:

1. Common stock does not entail fixed charges. If the company generates the earnings, it can pay common stock dividends. In contrast to bond interest, however, there is no legal obligation to pay dividends.

2. Common stock carries no fixed maturity date.

3. Since common stock provides a cushion against losses of creditors, the sale of common stock increases the creditworthiness of the firm.

4. Common stock can, at times, be sold more easily than debt. It appeals to certain investor groups because (a) it typically carries a higher expected return than does preferred stock or debt; and (b) since it represents the ownership of the firm, it

provides the investor with a better hedge against inflation than does straight preferred stock or bonds. Ordinarily, common stock increases in value when the value of real assets rises during an inflationary period.[5]

5. Returns from common stock in the form of capital gains may be subject to a lower personal income tax rate on capital gains. Hence, the effective personal income tax rates on returns from common stock may be lower than the effective tax rates on the interest on debt. Recent tax law changes have reduced this advantage.

Disadvantages. Disadvantages to the issuer of common stock include the following:

1. The sale of common stock may extend voting rights or control to the additional stock owners who are brought into the company. For this reason, among others, additional equity financing is often avoided by small and new firms, whose owner-managers may be unwilling to share control of their companies with outsiders.

2. The use of debt may enable the firm to utilize funds at a fixed low cost, whereas common stock gives equal rights to new stockholders to share in the future net profits of the firm.

3. As we saw in Chapter 21, the costs of underwriting and distributing common stock are usually higher than those for underwriting and distributing preferred stock or debt. Flotation costs for selling common stock are characteristically higher because (a) costs of investigating an equity security are higher than those of investigating the feasibility of a comparable debt security; and (b) stocks are more risky, which means equity holdings must be diversified, which, in turn, means that a given dollar amount of new stock must be sold to a greater number of purchasers than the same amount of debt.

4. As we saw in Chapter 15, if the firm has more equity or less debt than is called for in the optimum capital structure, the average cost of capital will be higher than necessary.

5. Common stock dividends are not deductible as an expense for calculating the corporation's income subject to the federal income tax, but bond interest is deductible. The impact of this factor is reflected in the relative cost of equity capital vis-à-vis debt capital.

From a Social Viewpoint

From a social viewpoint, common stock is a desirable form of financing because it renders business firms (a major segment of the economy) less vulnerable to the consequences of declines in sales and earnings. Common stock financing involves no fixed charges, the payment of which might force a faltering firm into reorganization or bankruptcy.

---

[5]However, during the inflation of the 1970s, the lags of product price increases behind the rise of input costs depressed corporate earnings and increased the uncertainty of earnings growth, causing price-earnings multiples to fall, so that common stock prices were depressed.

TABLE 22.2   Chemical Industry Financial Ratios

Current ratio: 2.0 times	Coverage of fixed charges: 7 times
Sales to total assets: 1.6 times	Cash flow coverage: 3 times
Current debt to total assets: 30%	Net income to sales: 5%
Long-term debt to net worth: 40%	Return on total assets: 9%
Total debt to total assets: 50%	Net income to net worth: 13%

CHOOSING AMONG ALTERNATIVE FORMS OF FINANCING

A pattern of analysis can be formulated for choosing among alternative forms of financing. This framework applies to the decision choices involved in evaluating the other major forms of financing covered: various forms of debt, preferred stock, lease financing, and financing in international markets, among others. Thus, the pattern of analysis has broad applications.

To make the application of the concepts more concrete, a case will be used to illustrate and exemplify the procedures involved. Stanton Chemicals, having estimated that it will need to raise $200 million for an expansion program, discusses with its investment bankers whether it should raise the $200 million through debt financing or through selling additional shares of common stock. The bankers are asked to make their recommendation to Stanton's board of directors using the information on industry financial ratios and the company's 19X1 balance sheet and income statement found in Tables 22.2, 22.3, and 22.4, respectively.

Stanton's dividend payout has averaged about 30 percent of net income. At present, its cost of debt is 10 percent (with an average maturity remaining of ten years), and its cost of equity is 14 percent. If the additional funds are raised by debt, the cost of debt will rise

TABLE 22.3   Stanton Chemicals Company Balance Sheet as of December 31, 19X1 (Millions of Dollars)

Assets		Liabilities		
Total current assets	$1,000	Notes payable (at 10%)	$300	
Net fixed assets	800	Other current liabilities	400	
		Total current liabilities		$ 700
		Long-term debt (at 10%)		300
		Total debt		$1,000
		Common stock, par value $1		100
		Paid-in capital		300
		Retained earnings		400
Total assets	$1,800	Total claims on assets		$1,800

TABLE 22.4   Stanton Chemicals Company Income Statement for Year Ended
December 31, 19X1 (Millions of Dollars)

	1984	Pro Forma after Financing
Total revenues	$3,000	$3,400
Depreciation expense	200	220
Other costs	2,484	2,820
Net operating income	$ 316	$ 360
Interest expense	60	
Net income before taxes	$ 256	
Income taxes (at 50%)	128	
Net income	$ 128	

to 12 percent, and the cost of equity will rise to 16 percent. If the funds are raised by equity, the cost of debt will remain at 10 percent, and the cost of equity will fall to 12 percent; new equity will initially be sold at $9 per share.

Stanton's common stock is widely held; there is no strong control group. The market parameters are a risk-free rate of 6 percent and an expected return on the market of 11 percent. The debt will carry a maturity of ten years and will require a sinking fund of $20 million per year in addition to the present $20 million annual sinking fund requirement.

In their analysis of which form of financing should be chosen, the management and investment bankers consider the following factors:

A. Risk
   1. Financial structure
   2. Fixed charge coverage
   3. Coverage of cash flow requirements
   4. Level of systematic risk (beta)

B. Relative costs
   1. Effects on market value per share of common stock
   2. Effects on cost of capital

C. Effects on control

The solution proceeds as follows. First, the two forms of financing are examined with reference to the firm's risk as measured by its financial structure (see Table 22.5). Stanton fails to meet the industry standards on both the short-term and total debt ratios. If it finances with debt, its financial structure ratios will be further deficient. If it finances with equity, its long-term debt to net worth ratio will be strengthened, and it will meet the industry standard for the total debt to total assets ratio. Stanton, therefore, should seek to fund some short-term debt into longer-term debt in the future, and it should try to build up its equity base further from retained earnings.

Stanton's fixed charge coverage is analyzed next, in Table 22.6. The table shows that the company's fixed charge coverage is below the industry standard. The use of debt

TABLE 22.5   Stanton Financial Structure (Millions of Dollars)

| | Present | | Pro Forma | | | | Industry Standard |
| | | | Debt | | Equity | | |
	Amount	Percent	Amount	Percent	Amount	Percent	Percent
Current debt	$ 700	39	$ 700	35	$ 700	35	30
Long-term debt	300	17	500	25	300	15	20
Total debt	$1,000	56	$1,200	60	$1,000	50	50
Equity	800	44	800	40	1,000	50	
Total assets	$1,800	100	$2,000	100	$2,000	100	
Long-term debt to net worth		38		63		30	40

financing will further aggravate the weakness in this area. The use of equity financing will move the company towards the industry standard.

Stanton's cash flow coverage is analyzed in Table 22.7. To obtain the cash inflow, depreciation expense is added to net operating income. To obtain the cash outflow requirements, the before-tax sinking fund payment is added to the interest expenses. The sinking fund payments must be placed on a before-tax basis because they are not a tax-deductible expense.

The resulting cash flow coverage ratios appear satisfactory when measured against the industry standard of 3.00. However, this result has to be qualified by the recognition that a full analysis of cash flow coverage must consider other cash outflow requirements. These will include scheduled principal repayments on debt obligations, preferred stock dividends, payments under lease obligations, and probably some capital expenditures that are regarded as essential for the continuity of the firm. Within the broader definition of cash outflow requirements, Stanton's cash flow coverage would undoubtedly be lowered.

The next consideration is the effect of the various forms of financing on the level of the firm's systematic risk, that is, its beta. As indicated earlier, Stanton's cost of equity is

TABLE 22.6   Stanton's Fixed Charge Coverage (Millions of Dollars)

| | Present | Pro Forma | | Industry Standard |
		Debt	Equity	
Net operating income	$316	$360	$360	
Interest expenses	$ 60	$ 90[a]	$ 60	
Coverage ratio	5.27	4.00	6.00	7.00

[a]See Table 22.8 and related discussion.

TABLE 22.7   Stanton's Cash Flow Coverage (Millions of Dollars)

	Present	Pro Forma		Industry Standard
		Debt	Equity	
Net operating income	$316	$360	$360	
Depreciation expense	200	220	220	
Cash inflow	$516	$580	$580	
Interest expense	60	90	60	
Sinking fund payments	20	40	20	
Before-tax sinking fund payments	40	80	40	
Cash outflow requirements	$100	$170	$100	
Cash flow coverage ratio	5.16	3.41	5.80	3.00

14 percent at present. Using the Security Market Line and additional data on the market parameters already provided, Stanton's present level of beta can be determined as follows:

$$k_s = R_F + [E(R_M) - R_F]\beta$$
$$0.14 = 0.06 + (0.11 - 0.06)\beta$$
$$\beta_s = 1.6 \text{ at present.}$$

Stanton's present equity beta is 1.6. As stated earlier, if the additional funds are raised by debt, the cost of equity will rise to 16 percent. The implied new equity beta, therefore, will be

$$0.16 = 0.06 + (0.05)\beta$$
$$\beta = 2.0.$$

Stanton's beta will rise to 2 with debt financing. With equity financing, the cost of equity will fall to 12 percent. The implied new beta will thus be 1.2.

Four measures of risk have been used to assess the effect of choosing between equity financing and debt financing. Each measure has covered different aspects of risk, and the results for Stanton have all pointed in the same direction. If debt financing is used, the financial structure ratios will be above the industry standards, the deficiency in the fixed charge coverage ratio will be further aggravated, and the cash flow coverage will decline toward the industry standard (and, by a broader measure, may even fall below it). The existing 1.6 beta level is relatively high. The use of debt financing will push the beta level to 2, which is high for an industrial firm. The use of equity financing will move the beta level toward the average beta level of the market, which is 1. Clearly, therefore, from the standpoint of the four different measures of risk, equity financing is the more favorable.

The next consideration is the relative costs of the different forms of financing. Relative costs are measured by the effects of each form of financing on the market value per share of common stock and by the effects on the firm's cost of capital. To apply these two criteria, it is first necessary to calculate the amount of interest expense (in Table 22.8) for use in the income statements (Table 22.9).

TABLE 22.8   Calculation of the Amount of Debt Interest for Stanton (Millions of Dollars)

Form of Debt	No Expansion		Expansion with Debt		Expansion with Equity	
	Amount	Rate	Amount	Rate	Amount	Rate
$300 million short-term notes payable	$30	10%	$36	12%	$30	10%
$300 million existing long-term debt[a]	30	10	30	10	30	10
$200 million new long-term debt			24	12		
Total interest expense	$60		$90		$60	

[a]If debt financing is used, the current market value of the debt (with an average life of ten years remaining), when the interest rate rises from the coupon rate of 10 percent to a market rate of 12 percent, would become $885 per bond, or for the 300,000 bonds outstanding, it would become $265.5 million. Note that the interest payment would be .12 × $265.5, which equals $31.86 million. This is approximately the same as the 10 percent interest on the $300 million existing long-term debt, illustrating that $rD = k_b B$.

The total amount of interest expense without expansion is $60 million. Interest expense will remain unchanged if the expansion is financed by equity funds. If the expansion is financed by long-term debt, the facts of the problem state that the cost of debt will rise to 12 percent. The opportunity cost of all debt funds, therefore, is 12 percent, and an argument can be made that all forms of debt should bear the higher 12 percent rate. However, the actual rate paid on the long-term debt will remain at 10 percent, while the short-term notes payable must be renewed periodically at the higher 12 percent rate (as shown in Table 22.8). If the expansion is financed by debt, the total interest expense will be $90 million. The total interest expense amounts needed for the income statements in Table 22.9 are now available. With the information developed in the income statements, the market value of equity can be calculated (see Table 22.10).

The net income under each alternative is capitalized by the applicable cost of equity to obtain the total market value of equity. The price per share can also be determined. The

TABLE 22.9   Stanton's Income Statements (Millions of Dollars)

	No Expansion	Expansion with Debt	Expansion with Equity
Net operating income	$316	$360	$360
Interest expense	60	90	60
Net income before taxes	$256	$270	$300
Income taxes (at 50%)	128	135	150
Net income	$128	$135	$150

TABLE 22.10　Stanton's Market Value of Equity (Millions of Dollars)

	No Expansion	Expansion with Debt	Expansion with Equity
Net income (NI)	$ 128	$ 135	$ 150
Cost of equity (k_s)	0.14	0.16	0.12
Value of equity (S)	$ 914	$ 844	$1,250
Number of shares	100	100	122.2
Price per share	$9.14	$8.44	$10.23

total number of shares of common stock outstanding remains unchanged with no expansion or with expansion financed by debt. The facts of the case stated that if equity were sold, the price would be $9 per share; the $200 million of new financing divided by the $9 equals 22.2 million shares. Thus, the total number of shares is 122.2 million (the original 100 million plus the additional 22.2 million). The indicated new price per share of common stock is obtained by dividing the total value of equity by the total number of shares of common stock outstanding. The resulting new price per share declines with expansion by debt financing and increases with expansion by equity financing — which means that equity financing is more favorable than debt financing. If debt financing were used, the criterion of maximizing share price would recommend that the expansion program not be adopted.

This result can be checked further by calculating the total market value of the firm (see Table 22.11). The total market value is obtained by adding the amount of interest-bearing debt to the market value of equity. It is increased by expansion with either debt or equity. However, as shown in Table 22.10, the market price per share of common stock is decreased by expansion with debt.

We calculate the total market value of the firm to determine the firm's capital structure proportions for use in the cost of capital calculations. In the process, we also find that the value of the firm is greatest when expansion is financed with equity funds. The leverage ratios are calculated in Table 22.12. The leverage ratio is increased if debt is employed but decreased if equity financing is employed. Using the capital structure proportions from Table 22.12, the weighted average cost of capital can be calculated:

TABLE 22.11　Stanton's Market Value (Millions of Dollars)

	No Expansion	Expansion with Debt	Expansion with Equity
Market value of equity	$ 914	$ 844	$1,250
Amount of debt[a]	600	766	600
Value of the firm	$1,514	$1,610	$1,850

[a]Since the market value of the long-term debt has fallen by $34 million, the total amount of debt is $800 million less $34 million, or $766 million, as shown in the table.

TABLE 22.12   Calculation of Stanton's Leverage Ratios

	No Expansion	Expansion with Debt	Expansion with Equity
Total debt	$ 600	$ 766	$ 600
Market value of the firm	$1,514	$1,610	$1,850
Debt to value ratio	0.40	0.48	0.32

$$k_b(1 - T)(B/V) + k_s(S/V) = k$$

No expansion $0.10(0.5)(0.40) + 0.14(0.60) = 10.4\%$

Expansion with debt $0.12(0.5)(0.48) + 0.16(0.52) = 11.2\%$

Expansion with equity $0.10(0.5)(0.32) + 0.12(0.68) = 9.8\%.$

Expansion with debt will raise Stanton's cost of capital from 10.4 percent to 11.2 percent. Expansion with equity will lower the company's cost of capital from 10.4 percent to 9.8 percent. These results are consistent with the findings for the market value per share of common stock, where debt financing caused a decrease and equity financing an increase. Thus, the cost of capital and market price per share of common stock criteria provide consistent findings.[6] For example, we could also obtain the value of the firm using:

$$V_L = \frac{X(1 - T)}{k_U} + TB.$$

For the no expansion case, we have

$$k = k_b(1 - T)(L) + k_s(1 - L), \text{ where } L = B/V$$
$$= 0.10(0.5)(0.4) + 0.14(0.6)$$
$$= 0.02 + 0.084 = 0.104.$$

Since $k = k_U(1 - TL)$,

$$0.104 = k_U(1 - 0.2),$$

and

$$k_U = 0.13.$$

Hence,

$$V_L = \frac{\$316(0.5)}{0.13} + 0.5(\$600)$$
$$= \$1,515.$$

---

[6]We are here using the Modigliani and Miller valuation framework and the three equations for calculating the weighted cost of capital developed in Chapter 15 on financial structure and the cost of capital.

The final item on the checklist of factors for evaluating alternative forms of financing is "effects on control." The problem states that the common stock is already widely held so that there is no control problem to militate against the use of equity financing.

The investment bankers summarize the evidence with respect to the two forms of financing as follows. Risks are already high and will be further increased if debt financing is used. As a result of this substantial increase in risk, the costs of both debt and equity funds will rise. With equity financing, the value per share of common stock is increased and the cost of capital reduced. There is no control issue. On the basis of all the factors considered, the common stock financing is recommended.

The Stanton case illustrates the application of a checklist of key factors to evaluate alternative forms of financing. Four measures of risk and several measures of costs to the firm (returns to investors) are employed. Relative costs of financing can be evaluated by reference to effects on market value per share of common stock, on the cost of capital, and on control of the firm. Thus, the analysis is essentially a risk-return evaluation and reflects a basic theme that runs through all of the chapters of this book.

SUMMARY

Common stock involves the balancing of risk income and control. We analyzed various dimensions of the rights of common stockholders. We discussed voting rights and proxy contests for membership on the board of directors. We reviewed issues connected with the value of control. In particular, we discussed the motivations and effects of using dual classes of common stock. Class B typically has superior voting rights and is a mechanism for maintaining control. Class A common stock typically has inferior voting rights, but superior claims to dividends.

The announcements of proxy contests generally result in a stock price increase. The reason is that the market expects improvements in management performance to result. If the dissident group obtains membership on the board of directors, control and operations changes are likely to be stimulated. Even if dissidents do not obtain board membership, incumbent management realizes that good performance will be required to reduce the likelihood of future proxy contests.

We set forth a framework for analyzing decisions for choosing between different forms of debt, preferred stock, and common stock. The evaluation is based on the analysis of the trade-offs between risk, relative costs, and effects on control. Relative costs are measured primarily in terms of effects on market share pricing consistent with maximizing the value of the firm. Analysis of relative costs incorporates the effects of risk. However, control considerations may sometimes be more important to owners and managers than differences in relative risks and costs.

QUESTIONS

22.1 By what percentage could total assets shrink in value on liquidation before creditors incur losses in each of the following cases:

a. Equity-to-total-asset ratio of 50 percent?

b. Debt-to-equity ratio of 50 percent?

c. Debt-to-total-asset ratio of 40 percent?

22.2 How many shares must a minority group own in order to assure election of two directors if nine new directors will be elected and 200,000 shares are outstanding? Assume cumulative voting exists.

22.3 Why does the SEC supervise the proxy voting process?

22.4 Why does the announcement of a proxy contest cause the price of the firm's stock to rise?

22.5 In proxy contests, dissidents obtain a majority of seats in about one-fifth of the contests. Does this mean that proxy contests generally fail?

22.6 In a company with dual-class stock, does the stock with superior voting rights sell in the market at a premium or discount as compared with the other class of stock, which generally has superior income payments?

22.7 Compare management's voting rights ownership with cash flow ownership.

22.8 Explain the three hypotheses for the voting rights premium:

a. Extra merger premium

b. Ownership structure

c. Coalition stability.

PROBLEMS

22.1 The Nevada Corporation plans to expand assets by 25 percent. It can finance the expansion with straight debt or with common stock. The interest rate on the debt would be 12 percent. Nevada's current balance sheet and income statement are given in Table P22.1.

   If Nevada Corporation finances the $200,000 expansion with debt, the rate on the incremental debt will be 12 percent, and the price-earnings ratio of the common stock will drop to nine times. If the expansion is financed with equity, the new stock will sell for $8 per share, the rate on debt will be 10 percent, and the price-earnings ratio will remain at ten times. (The opportunity cost of debt is 12 percent. However, use the 10 percent rate on the debt already on the balance sheet, because this is the rate actually being paid.)

a. Assume that the net income before interest and taxes (EBIT) is 10 percent of sales. Calculate EPS at sales levels of $0, $600,000, $2,400,000, $2,800,000, $3,000,000, $3,600,000, and $4,800,000 for financing with (1) debt and (2) common stock. Assume no fixed costs of production.

b. Make a companion chart for EPS and indicate the crossover point in sales (that is, where EPS using bonds equals EPS using stock).

c. Using the price-earnings ratio, calculate the market value per share of common stock for each sales level for both the debt and the equity financing.

d. Using data from Part (c), plot market value per share against level of sales and indicate the crossover point.

e. If the firm follows the policy of seeking to maximize (1) EPS or (2) market price per share, which form of financing should be used?

TABLE P22.1   Nevada Corporation Balance Sheet as of
December 31, 19X0 (Thousands of Dollars)

Assets		Liabilities	
		Debt (at 10%)	$300
		Common stock, $1 par (100,000 shares outstanding)	100
		Retained earnings	400
Total assets	$800	Total claims	$800

Nevada Corporation Income Statement for Year Ended
December 31, 19X0 (Thousands of Dollars)

Sales	$2,300
Total costs (excluding interest)	2,070
Net operating income	$ 230
Debt interest	30
Income before taxes	$ 200
Taxes (at 50%)	100
Net income	$ 100

Earnings per share: $\dfrac{\$100,000}{100,000} = \$1.$

Price-earnings ratio = 10.[a]

Market price = P-E × EPS = 10 × 1 = $10.

---

[a]The P-E ratio is the market price per share divided by earnings per share. It represents the amount of money an investor is willing to pay for $1.00 of current earnings. The higher the riskiness of a stock, the lower its P-E ratio, other things held constant.

f. The probability estimates of future sales are the following: 5 percent chance of $0; 10 percent chance of $600,000; 20 percent chance of $2,400,000; 30 percent chance of $2,800,000; 20 percent chance of $3,000,000; 10 percent chance of $3,600,000; and 5 percent chance of $4,800,000. Calculate expected values for EPS, market price per share, the standard deviation, and the coefficient of variation for each alternative.

g. What other factors should be taken into account in choosing between the two forms of financing?

h. Would it matter if the presently outstanding stock were all owned by the final decision maker — the president — and that this represented that individual's entire net worth? Would it matter if the president were compensated entirely by a fixed salary? If the president had a substantial number of stock options?

22.2 The Brock Food Company is engaged principally in the business of growing, processing, and marketing a variety of frozen vegetables. A major company in this field, it produces and markets high quality food at premium prices. Its profitability is expected to rise to industry standards.

During each of the past several years, the company's sales have increased and the needed inventories have been financed from short-term sources. The officers have discussed the idea of refinancing their bank loans with long-term debt or common stock. A common stock issue of 310,000 shares sold at this time (present market price $72 a share) will yield $21 million after expenses. The same sum can be raised by selling 12-year bonds with an interest rate of 10 percent. Assume a marginal 40% tax rate. (See financial ratios and statements in Tables P22.2a, P22.2b, and P22.2c.)

a. Should Brock Food refinance the short-term loans? Why?

b. If the bank loans should be refinanced, what factors should be considered in determining which form of financing to use?

TABLE P22.2a   Food Processing Industry Financial Ratios

Current ratio: 2.2 times
Sales to total assets: 2.0 times
Sales to inventory: 5.6 times
Average collection period: 22.0 days
Current liabilities/total assets: 30%
Long-term debt/total assets: 15%
Preferred/total assets: 0.5%
Net worth/total assets: 50%
Profits to sales: 5%
Operating income to total assets: 14%
Net income to net worth: 16%
Expected growth rate of earnings and dividends: 9%

TABLE P22.2b   Brock Food Company Consolidated Balance Sheet as of March 31, 19X3 (Millions of Dollars)[a]

Current assets	$141	Accounts payable	$12	
Fixed plant and equipment	57	Notes payable (at 10%)	36	
Other assets	12	Accruals	15	
		Total current liabilities		$ 63
		Long-term debt (at 5%)		63
		Preferred stock		9
		Common stock (par $6)	$12	
		Retained earnings	63	
		Shareholders' equity		75
Total assets	$210	Total claims on assets		$210

[a]The majority of harvesting activities do not begin until late April or May.

TABLE P22.2c   Brock Food Company Consolidated Income Statement for
Year Ended March 31 (Millions of Dollars)

	19X0	19X1	19X2	19X3
Net sales	$225.0	$234.6	$292.8	$347.1
Cost of goods sold	146.1	156.6	195.3	230.4
Gross profit	$ 78.9	$ 78.0	$ 97.5	$116.7
Other expenses	61.8	66.0	81.0	88.5
Operating income	$ 17.1	$ 12.0	$ 16.5	$ 28.2
Interest expense	3.3	4.2	5.7	9.3
Earnings before tax	$ 13.8	$ 7.8	$ 10.8	$ 18.9
Taxes	7.2	3.3	5.4	9.6
Net profit	$ 6.6	$ 4.5	$ 5.4	$ 9.3
Preferred dividend	0.3	0.3	0.3	0.3
Earnings available to common stock	$ 6.3	$ 4.2	$ 5.1	$ 9.0
Earnings per share	$3.15	$2.10	$2.55	$4.50
Cash dividends per share	$1.29	$1.44	$1.59	$1.80
Price range for common stock:				
High	$66.00	$69.00	$66.00	$81.00
Low	$30.00	$42.00	$51.00	$63.00
Average (for calculations)	$48.00	$55.50	$58.50	$72.00

22.3 Inland Steel is planning an expansion program. It estimates that it will need to raise an additional $200 million. Inland discussed with its investment banker whether to raise the $200 million through debt financing or through selling additional shares of common stock. The banker's recommendation was based on the following background information. The dividend payout has averaged about 50 percent of net income. The cost of debt is 10 percent, and the cost of equity is 14 percent. If the additional funds are raised by debt, the cost of debt will be 12 percent and the cost of equity will rise to 16 percent. If the additional funds are raised by equity, the cost of debt will remain at 10 percent, and the cost of equity will fall to 12 percent. Equity will be sold at $9 per share. (See also the steel industry standards in Table P22.3a and Inland's balance sheet and income statement in Table P22.3b.)

TABLE P22.3a   Steel Industry Standards

Long-term liabilities to shareholders' equity: 35%
Shareholders' equity to total assets: 55%
Fixed charge coverage: 7 times
Current ratio: 2.1 times
Return on net worth: 11%

TABLE P22.3b   Inland Steel Balance Sheet as of December 31, 19X0 (Millions of Dollars)

Assets		Liabilities	
Total current assets	$ 600	Notes payable (at 10%)	$100
Net fixed assets	1,200	Other current liabilities	100
		Total current liabilities	$ 200
		Long-term debt (at 10%)	500
		Other liabilities	300
		Total debt	$1,000
		Common stock, par value $1	100
		Paid-in capital	300
		Retained earnings	400
Total assets	$1,800	Total claims on assets	$1,800

Inland Steel Income Statement for Year Ended December 31, 19X0 (Millions of Dollars)

	Current Year	With Expansion, Pro Forma
Total revenues	$2,000	$2,400
Net operating income	231	260
Interest expense	60	—
Net income before taxes	$ 171	—
Income taxes (at 25%)	43	—
Net income to equity	$ 128	—

a. Make a financial risk analysis using financial structure ratios.

b. Complete the pro forma income statements under the two forms of financing and compare fixed charge coverage under the two alternatives.

c. Calculate the market value of equity and the indicated market price per share before and after financing by the two methods.

d. Calculate the value of the firm and the B/S, B/V, and S/V percentages.

e. Calculate the weighted cost of capital at present and under the two financing alternatives.

f. Recommend the best form of financing for Inland.

22.4 *(Use the computer diskette, File name: 22DTEQTY, Debt Equity Financing.)*

a. Given the initial values of the decision variables, we analyze the effects on the six valuation factors (the four measures of risk and the two measures of cost). This will be done in five subsections of each question.

   (1) How does the firm compare with the industry standards under the debt versus equity financing alternative?

(2) How does the firm perform in relation to the industry standard with regard to the coverage ratio under the two financing alternatives?

(3) Evaluate the performance of the firm in relation to the industry standard for cash flow coverage under the two financing alternatives.

(4) How is the level of beta affected by the two alternative forms of financing?

(5) Under what financing alternative is the firm's weighted cost of capital lower? Market price per share higher?

b. Suppose the cost of debt is .10 and the cost of equity is .15 under both financing alternatives. Go to Screen #5 (Summary of Key Quantitative Factors) and determine whether the effects on financial risk are consistent with the indicated effects on costs. To see how summary measures of risk and cost are calculated, see Screen #6.

c. Suppose the tax rate is 30 percent rather than 40 percent. Answer subquestions (1) through (5) in Question (a).

d. You can now vary the amounts of capital to be raised and your assumptions about how the choice of debt versus equity financing will affect the respective costs of debt and equity to see the effects on the cost of capital and the value of common per share. (NOTE: Press the ''Esc'' key to enter Screen 4, and make changes to any highlighted assumptions. To bring back the list of screens, hold down the ''Alt'' key, then press the ''S'' key.)

SELECTED REFERENCES

DeAngelo, Harry, and DeAngelo, Linda, ''The Role of Proxy Contests in the Governance of Publicly-Held Corporations,'' *Journal of Financial Economics*, 23 (June 1989), pp. 29–59.

———, ''Managerial Ownership of Voting Rights,'' *Journal of Financial Economics*, (1985), pp. 33–69.

Dodd, P., and Warner, J. B., ''On Corporate Governance: A Study of Proxy Contests,'' *Journal of Financial Economics*, 11 (April 1983), pp. 401–438.

Jarrell, G. A., and A. B. Poulsen, ''Dual-Class Recapitalizations as Antitakeover Mechanisms: The Recent Evidence,'' *Journal of Financial Economics*, (1988), pp. 129–152.

Kalay, A., ''Toward a Theory of Corporate Dividend Policy,'' unpublished Ph.D. thesis, University of Rochester, Rochester, New York, 1979.

Lease, Ronald C.; McConnell, John J.; and Mikkelson, Wayne H., ''The Market Value of Control in Publicly-Traded Corporations,'' *Journal of Financial Economics*, 11 (1983), pp. 439–471.

Levy, H., ''Economic Evaluation of Voting Power of Common Stock,'' *Journal of Finance*, (1983), pp. 79–93.

Megginson, W. L., ''Restricted Voting Stock, Acquisition Premiums, and the Market Value of Corporate Control,'' *The Financial Review*, 25 (May 1990), pp. 175–198.

Partch, M. M., ''The Creation of Limited Voting Common Stock and Shareholder Wealth,'' *Journal of Financial Economics*, (1987), pp. 313–339.

CHAPTER 23

Debt and Preferred Stock Financing

There are many classes of fixed-income securities: long-term and short-term, secured and unsecured, marketable and nonmarketable, participating and nonparticipating, senior and junior, and so on. Financial managers, with the counsel of investment bankers and other financial advisers, seek to package securities with characteristics that will make them attractive to the widest range of different types of investors. By relating the design of securities effectively to the tastes and needs of potential investors, financial managers can hold the firm's cost of financing to the lowest possible levels. This chapter deals with the two most important types of long-term, fixed-income securities — bonds and preferred stocks.

LONG-TERM DEBT FINANCING

An understanding of long-term forms of financing requires some familiarity with technical terminology. The discussion of long-term debt, therefore, begins with an explanation of several important instruments and terms.

Instruments of Long-Term Debt Financing

Most people have had some experience with promises to pay. A *bond* is simply a long-term promissory note. A *mortgage* represents a pledge of designated property for a loan. Under a *mortgage bond*, a corporation pledges certain real assets as security for the bond. The pledge is a condition of the loan. A mortgage bond, therefore, is secured by real property. *Real property* is defined as real estate — land and building. A *chattel mortgage* is secured by personal property; but this is generally an intermediate-term instrument.

Personal property is defined as any other kind of property, including equipment, inventories, and furniture. A *debenture* is a long-term bond that is *not* secured by a pledge of any specific property. However, like other general creditors, it has a claim on any property not otherwise pledged. *Funded debt* is simply long-term debt. *Funding* does not imply placing money with a trustee or other repository. A firm planning to "fund" its floating debt will replace short-term securities by long-term securities.[1]

Trustee

Bonds are not only of long duration but also, usually, of substantial size. Before the rise of large aggregations of savings through insurance companies or pension funds, no single buyer was able to buy an issue of such size. Bonds, therefore, were issued in denominations of $1,000 each and were sold to a large number of purchasers. To facilitate communication between the issuer and the numerous bondholders, a trustee was appointed to represent the bondholders. The trustee is still presumed to act at all times for the protection of the bondholders and on their behalf.

Any legal person, including a corporation, is considered competent to act as a trustee. Typically, however, the duties of the trustee are handled by a department of a commercial bank.

Trustees have three main responsibilities:

1. They certify the issue of bonds. This duty involves making certain that all the legal requirements for drawing up the bond contract and the indenture have been carried out.

2. They police the behavior of the corporation in its performance of the responsibilities set forth in the indenture provisions.

3. They are responsible for taking appropriate action on behalf of the bondholders if the corporation defaults on payment of interest or principal.

It is said that in many corporate bond defaults in the early 1930s, trustees did not act in the best interests of the bondholders. They did not conserve the assets of the corporation effectively, and often they did not take early action, thereby allowing corporation executives to continue their salaries and to dispose of assets under conditions favorable to themselves but detrimental to the bondholders. In some cases, assets pledged as security for the bonds were sold, and thus specific security was no longer available. The result, in many instances, was that holders of mortgage bonds found themselves more in the position of general creditors than of secured bondholders.

As a consequence of such practices, Congress passed the Trust Indenture Act of 1939 in order to give more protection to bondholders. The act provides that (1) trustees must be given sufficient power to act on behalf of bondholders; (2) the indenture must fully disclose rights and responsibilities and must not be deceptive; (3) bondholders may make

---

[1]Tampa Electric Company provides a good example of funding. This company has a continuous construction program. Typically, it uses short-term debt to finance construction expenditures. However, once short-term debt has built up to about $100 million, the company sells a stock or bond issue, uses the proceeds to pay off its bank loans, and starts the cycle again. The high flotation costs of small security issues make this process desirable.

changes in the indenture; (4) prompt, protective action be taken by the trustee for bond-holders if default occurs; (5) an arm's-length relationship exist between the issuing corporation and the trustee; and (6) the corporation must make periodic reports to its trustee to enable that person to carry out the protective responsibilities.

Indenture

The long-term relationship between the borrower and the lender of a long-term promissory note is established in a document called an *indenture*. In the case of an ordinary 60- or 90-day promissory note, few developments that will endanger repayment are likely to occur in the life or affairs of the borrower. The lender looks closely at the borrower's current position, because current assets are the main source of repayment. A bond, however, is a long-term contractual relationship between the bond issuer and the bondholder; over this extended period, the bondholder has cause to worry that the issuing firm's position may change materially.

The bond indenture can be a document of several hundred pages that discusses a large number of factors important to the contracting parties, such as (1) the form of the bond and the instrument, (2) a complete description of property pledged, (3) the authorized amount of the bond issue, (4) detailed protective clauses, or *covenants,* (5) a minimum current ratio requirement, and (6) provisions for redemption or call privileges.

Bond covenants can be divided into four broad categories: (1) those restricting the issuance of new debt, (2) those with restrictions on dividend payments, (3) those with restrictions on merger activity, and (4) those with restrictions on the disposition of the firm's assets. A good description of the multitude of specific provisions in debt contracts can be found in the American Bar Association compendium called *Commentaries on Model Indenture Provisions* [1971]. Smith and Warner [1979] examined a random sample of 87 public issues of debt registered with the Securities and Exchange Commission between January 1974 and December 1975. They observed that fully 90.8 percent of the bonds restricted the issuance of new debt, 23 percent restricted dividend payments, 39.1 percent restricted merger activity, and 35.6 percent constrained the firm's disposition of assets.

Bond covenants that restrict subsequent financing are by far the most common type. The covenant provisions are usually stated in terms of accounting numbers and consequently are easy to monitor. The issuance of debt may carry restrictions that require all new debt to be subordinate or prohibit the creation of new debt with a higher priority unless existing bonds are upgraded to have an equal priority. All these restrictions are designed to prevent the firm from increasing the riskiness of outstanding debt by issuing new debt with a superior or equal claim on the firm's assets. Alternate restrictions may prohibit the issuance of new debt unless the firm maintains minimum prescribed ratios between net tangible assets and funded (long-term) debt, capitalization and funded debt, tangible net worth and funded debt, income and interest charges, or current assets and current liabilities (working capital tests). There may also be "clean-up" provisions that require the company to be debt-free for limited periods.

Other techniques that are used to protect bondholders against subsequent financing include restrictions on rentals, leases, and sale-leaseback agreements; sinking fund requirements (which roughly match the depreciation of the firm's tangible assets); required purchase of insurance; required financial reports and specification of accounting techniques; and required certifications of compliance by the officers of the firm.

Bond covenants that restrict dividend payments are necessary if for no other reason than to prohibit the extreme case of shareholders voting to pay themselves a liquidating dividend that would leave the bondholders holding an empty corporate shell. Kalay [1979] reported that in a random sample of 150 firms, every firm had a dividend restriction in at least one of its debt instruments. Restrictions on dividend policy are relatively easy to monitor, and they protect debtholders against the unwarranted payout of the assets that serve as collateral. Appropriately, most indentures refer not only to cash dividends but to all distributions in respect to capital stock, whether they be dividends, redemptions, purchases, retirements, partial liquidations, or capital reductions, and whether in cash, in kind, or in the form of debt obligations to the company. Without such general provisions, the firm could, for example, use cash to repurchase its own shares. From the bondholders' point of view, the effect would be the same as payment of cash dividends. No matter what the procedure is called, once cash is paid out to shareholders, it is no longer available as a cushion in the event of reorganization or bankruptcy.

The dividend covenant does not prohibit dividends per se; rather, it restricts the financing of the payment of dividends with new debt or by sale of the firm's existing assets. This arrangement is in the interest of stockholders because it does not restrict the payment of earned income. It is also in the interest of bondholders because it prevents any dilution of their claim on the firm's assets.

Bond covenants may also restrict merger activity. The effect of a merger on bondholders can be beneficial if the cash flows of the merged firms are not perfectly correlated. Offsetting cash flow patterns can reduce the risk of default, thereby strengthening the positions of the bondholders of both firms. Mergers can also be detrimental to bondholders. For example, if Firm A has much more debt in its capital structure than Firm B, the bondholders of B will suffer increased risk after the merger. Or if the maturity of debt in Firm A is shorter than for Firm B, the bondholders of B will, for all practical purposes, become subordinate to those of Firm A after the merger. To protect against the undesirable effects that can result from a merger, it is possible to require bond covenants that allow merger only if the net tangible assets of the firm, calculated on a postmerger basis, meet a certain dollar minimum or are at least a specified fraction of long-term debt. The merger can also be made contingent on the absence of default of any indenture provision after the transaction is completed.

Bond covenants that restrict production or investment policies are numerous. They are frequently difficult to enforce, however, given the impossibility of effectively monitoring the investment opportunities that the managers of the firm decide not to undertake. Myers [1977] suggests that a substantial portion of the value of a firm is composed of intangible assets in the form of future investment opportunities. A firm with outstanding debt may have the incentive to reject projects that have a positive net present value if the benefit from accepting the project accrues to the bondholders without also increasing shareholders' wealth.

Direct restrictions on investment-disinvestment policy take the following forms: (1) restrictions on common stock investments, loans, extensions of credit, and advances that cause the firm to become a claimholder in another business enterprise, (2) restrictions on the disposition of assets, and (3) covenants requiring the maintenance of assets. Secured debt is an indirect restriction on investment policy. Assets that provide surety cannot be disposed of under the provisions of the indenture agreement. Collateralization also reduces foreclosure expenses because the lender already has established title via the bond covenant.

Even though covenants are designed to protect bondholders from various actions which can diminish the surety of their position, no set of covenants can eliminate all risk. Consequently, there is considerable interest in accurate information about changes in the riskiness of corporate debt on a firm-by-firm basis.

Bond Ratings

One guide to bond quality is its rating. Ratings are supplied by Standard & Poor's (S&P), Moody's, and Fitch. Moody's ratings range from Aaa to Caa; the corresponding S&P ratings are from AAA to CCC. Weinstein [1978] collected data on the distribution of ratings by risk class for the period 1962–1974. About 40 percent were in the two highest quality ratings, about 55 percent in the next two, and the remaining 5 percent in the below investment grade — below BBB or Baa. These are the high-yield or "junk bonds." Table 23.1 shows that this pattern did not change greatly for the period 1975–1982, but shifted greatly for the period 1983–1988. High-yield or junk bonds jumped to over 20 percent of new issues. About one-half of the high-yield issues were used in financing corporate restructuring.

A comparison of the spreads between the promised yields on junk bonds and long-term government bonds is presented in Table 23.2. The spreads were mostly between 3 to

TABLE 23.1   New Bond Issues by S&P Rating, 1975–1988 ($ Billions)

	1975–1982		1983–1988	
	Amount	Percent	Amount	Percent
AAA	$ 78.78	29.95%	$ 58.81	10.96%
AA	76.83	29.21	152.78	28.48
A	75.85	28.84	128.71	23.99
BBB	21.83	8.30	79.75	14.86
Total Investment Grade	$253.29	96.30%	$420.05	78.29%
BB	$ 3.85	1.46%	$ 24.30	4.53%
B	5.43	2.06	73.39	13.68
CCC	0.45	0.17	18.76	3.50
Total High Yield	$ 9.73	3.70%	$116.45	21.71%
Total	$263.02	100.00%	$536.50	100.00%

Source: Altman, 1989a.

TABLE 23.2 Promised Yields on Long-Term Government Bonds
versus High-Yield Bonds, 1978–1989

		Promised Yield (%)		
	Year	High Yield	Long-Term Government	Spread
	1989	15.41	7.93	7.48
	1988	13.95	9.00	4.95
	1987	12.66	8.75	3.91
	1986	14.45	9.55	4.90
	1985	15.40	11.65	3.75
	1984	14.97	11.87	3.10
	1983	15.74	10.70	5.04
	1982	17.84	13.86	3.98
	1981	15.97	12.08	3.89
	1980	13.46	10.23	3.23
	1979	12.07	9.13	2.94
	1978	10.92	8.11	2.81

Source: Altman, 1990.

4 percent up until 1989 when confidence in the junk bond market was shattered and the spread rose to about 7.5 percent.

The spreads between individual rating categories were shown in Chapter 6 in Table 6.2. The differentials in promised spreads are shown in Table 23.3. We shall refer to the differences in promised yields in terms of basis points where 100 basis points equals one percentage point (1 percent). A bond rated AAA requires a yield spread of about 75 basis points over a U.S. Treasury bond. The increase in yield spreads for the next three shifts in quality ratings averages about 50 basis points each. Movement to the first two

TABLE 23.3 Change in Promised Yield Spreads by Ratings

	Category Change	Additional Promised Yield Spread (basis points)	Cumulative Yield Spread
	T-Bond to AAA	75	
	AAA to AA	50	125
	AA to A	35	160
	A to BBB	65	225
	BBB to BB	100	325
	BB to B	100	425
	B to CCC	300	725

Source: Table 6.2 in Chapter 6.

below-investment-grade categories requires an additional 100 basis points each. A drop from B to CCC required an additional 300 basis points of promised yield spread.

For the period 1978–1989, the promised yield on long-term government bonds averaged 10.24 percent; for high-yield bonds, 14.4 percent. The realized returns over the same period were 10.24 percent for the long-term governments; 11.19 percent for high-yield debt [Altman, 1990]. Thus the realized returns on the governments were virtually the same as the promised yields. For junk bonds, realized yields were 321 basis points below their promised yields, but still almost a full percentage point (99 basis points) above the realized yields on the long-term governments for this particular time period.

One may raise the following question: Do the agencies determine the prices and interest rates paid for bonds or do investors in the capital markets? The evidence collected by Wakeman [1978] and Weinstein [1977] shows that changes in bond ratings are not treated as new information by capital markets. In fact, changes in ratings usually occur several months after the capital markets have already reacted to the fundamental change in the bond's quality. Changes in agency ratings do not cause changes in required yields to maturity. It is the other way around. However, this does not imply that bond ratings are without value. On average, the ratings provide unbiased estimates of bond risk and are, therefore, a useful source of information.

Call Provision

A *call provision* gives the issuing corporation the right to call in the bond for redemption. The provision generally states that the company must pay an amount greater than the par value of the bond; this additional sum is defined as the *call premium*. The call premium is typically equal to one year's interest if the bond is called during the first year, and it declines at a constant rate each year thereafter. For example, the call premium on a $1,000 par value, 20-year, 6 percent bond is generally $60 if called during the first year, $57 if called during the second year (calculated by reducing the $60, or 6 percent, premium by one-twentieth), and so on.

The call privilege is valuable to the firm but potentially detrimental to the investor, especially if the bond is issued in a period when interest rates are thought to be cyclically high. The problem for investors is that the call privilege enables the issuing corporation to substitute bonds paying lower interest rates for bonds paying higher ones. Consider a simple example of consols (bonds with no maturity). Suppose consols are sold to yield 10 percent when interest rates are high. If interest rates drop so that the consols yield 8 percent, the value of the bond, theoretically, could rise to $1,250. Suppose the issuing firm can call the bond by paying a $100 premium. The investor receives $1,100 for a bond whose market value will otherwise be $1,250. The callability of the bond will probably prevent its rising to the full $1,250 in the marketplace.

This disadvantage of the call privilege to the investor is supported by empirical data. Studies indicate that when interest rate levels are high, new issues of callable bonds must bear yields from one-quarter to one-half of 1 percent higher than the yields of noncallable bonds. If callability is deferred for five years (that is, if the issuer cannot exercise the call privilege until the bond has been outstanding for at least five years), in periods of relatively high interest rates, the yields for long-term bonds with five years of call deferment are about 0.13 percent lower than the yields for similar bonds that can be called immediately. During periods of relatively low interest rates, the discount for five years of deferment drops to about 0.04 percent from yields on fully callable bonds.[2] (The procedures for calculating when it is advantageous for the corporation to call or refund a bond or preferred stock issue are presented later in the chapter.)

Almost all corporate bonds are callable and none are puttable. Why? A plausible answer is that whenever the tax rate of the borrower exceeds the tax rate of the lender, there is a tax incentive for issuing callable debt. Since corporations have marginal tax rates of around 34 percent while individuals have lower rates, corporations have had an incentive to issue callable bonds. The opposite is true when the government is lending. The government has a zero tax rate and holders of government debt have positive rates. Consequently, the government has incentive to offer puttable debt and it does. Series E and H savings bonds are redeemable at the lender's option.

From the firm's point of view the coupons paid and the call premium are both deductible as interest expenses. The investor pays ordinary income taxes on interest received and capital gains taxes on the call premium. If the stream of payments on debt is even across time, then low and high tax bracket lenders and borrowers will value it equally. However, if it is decreasing across time, as it is expected to be with a callable bond, then low tax bracket lenders will assign a higher value because they discount at a higher after-tax rate. Near-term cash inflows are *relatively* more valuable to them. A high tax bracket borrower (i.e., the firm) will use a lower after-tax discount rate and will also prefer a decreasing cash flow pattern because the present value of the interest tax shield will be relatively higher. Even though the firm pays a higher gross rate, it prefers callable debt to ordinary debt because of the tax advantages for the net rate of return.

Sinking Fund

A *sinking fund* is a provision that facilitates the orderly retirement of a bond issue (or, in some cases, preferred stock issue). Typically, it requires the firm to buy and retire a portion of the bond issue each year. Sometimes, the stipulated sinking fund payment is tied to the current year's sales or earnings, but usually it is a mandatory fixed amount. If it is mandatory, a failure to meet the payment causes the bond issue to be thrown into default and can lead the company into bankruptcy. Obviously, then, a sinking fund can constitute a serious cash drain on the firm.

In most cases, the firm (through the bond trustee) is given the right to handle the sinking fund in either of two ways: (1) it can call a certain percentage of the bonds at a stipulated price each year (for example, 2 percent of the original amount at a price of $1,050), with the serial numbers of the actual bonds to be called determined by a lottery; or (2) to retire the required face amount of the bonds, it can buy the bonds on the open market. The firm will do whichever results in the required reduction of outstanding bonds for the smallest outlay. Therefore, if interest rates have risen (and the price of the bonds has fallen), the firm will choose the open market alternative. If interest rates have fallen (and bond prices have risen), it will elect the option of calling bonds.

---

[2]See Jen and Wert [1967] and Pye [1967].

The call provision of the sinking fund, at times, works to the detriment of bondholders. If, for example, the bond carries a 7 percent interest rate, and if yields on similar securities are 4 percent, the bond will sell for well above par. A sinking fund call at par thus greatly disadvantages some bondholders. On balance, securities that provide for a sinking fund and continuing redemption are likely to be offered initially on a lower yield basis than are securities without such a fund. Since sinking funds provide additional protection to investors, sinking fund bonds are likely to sell initially at higher prices; hence, they carry a lower interest rate cost to the issuer.

SECURED BONDS

Secured long-term debt can be classified according to (1) the priority of claims, (2) the right to issue additional securities, and (3) the scope of the lien.

Priority of Claims

A senior mortgage has prior claims on assets and earnings. Senior railroad mortgages, for example, have been called the "mortgages next to the rail," implying that they have the first claim on the land and assets of the railroad corporations. A junior mortgage is a subordinate lien, such as a second or third mortgage. It is a lien or claim junior to others.

Right to Issue Additional Securities

Mortgage bonds can also be classified with respect to the right to issue additional obligations pledging already encumbered property.

In the case of a *closed-end mortgage*, a company cannot sell additional bonds (beyond those already issued) secured by the property specified in the mortgage. For example, assume that a corporation with plant and land worth $5 million has a $2 million mortgage on these properties. If the mortgage is closed-end, no more bonds having first liens on this property can be issued. Thus, a closed-end mortgage provides security to the bond buyer. The ratio of the amount of the senior bonds to the value of the property is not increased by subsequent issues.

If the bond indenture is silent on this point, it is called an *open-end mortgage*. Its nature can be illustrated by referring to the example cited above. Against property worth $5 million, bonds of $2 million are sold. If an additional first mortgage bond of $1 million is subsequently sold, the property has been pledged for a total of $3 million of bonds. If, on liquidation, the property sells for $2 million, the original bondholders will receive 67 cents on the dollar. If the mortgage had been closed-end, they would have been fully paid.

Most characteristic is the *limited open-end mortgage*. Its nature can be indicated by continuing the example. A first mortgage bond issue of $2 million, secured by the property worth $5 million, is sold. The indenture provides that an additional $1 million worth of bonds — or an additional amount of bonds to bring the total to 60 percent of the original cost of the property — can be sold. Thus, the mortgage is open only to a certain point.

Scope of the Lien

Bonds can also be classified with respect to the scope of their lien. A lien is granted on certain specified property. When a *specific lien* exists, the security for a first or second mortgage is a specifically designated property. On the other hand, a *blanket mortgage* pledges all real property currently owned by the company. Real property includes only land and those things affixed thereto; thus, a blanket mortgage is not a mortgage on cash, accounts receivables, or inventories, which are items of personal property. A blanket mortgage gives more protection to the bondholder than does a specific mortgage because it provides a claim on all real property owned by the company.

UNSECURED BONDS

Debentures

The reasons for a firm's use of unsecured debt are diverse. Paradoxically, the extremes of financial strength and weakness may give rise to its use. Also, tax considerations and great uncertainty about the level of the firm's future earnings have given rise to special forms of unsecured financing. A *debenture* is an unsecured bond and, as such, provides no lien on specific property as security for the obligation. Debenture holders, therefore, are general creditors whose claim is protected by property not otherwise pledged. The advantage of debentures from the issuer's standpoint is that the property is left unencumbered for subsequent financing. However, in practice, the use of debentures depends on the nature of the firm's assets and its general credit strength.

A firm whose credit position is exceptionally strong can issue debentures; it simply does not need specific security. However, the credit position of a company may be so weak that it has no alternative to the use of debentures; all its property may already be encumbered. The debt portion of American Telephone & Telegraph's vast financing program for many years after World War II has been mainly through debentures. AT&T is such a strong institution that it does not have to provide security for its debt issues.

Debentures are also issued by companies in industries where it is not practical to provide a lien through a mortgage on fixed assets. Examples of such companies are large mail order houses and finance companies, which characteristically do not have large fixed assets in relation to their total assets. The bulk of their assets is in the form of inventory or receivables, neither of which is satisfactory security for a mortgage lien.

Subordinated Debentures

The term *subordinate* means below or inferior. Thus, *subordinated debt* has claims on assets after unsubordinated debt in the event of liquidation. Debentures can be subordinated to designated notes payable — usually bank loans — or to any or all other debt. In the event of liquidation or reorganization, the debentures cannot be paid until senior debt *as named in the indenture* has been paid. Senior debt, typically, does not include trade accounts payable. How the subordination provision strengthens the position of senior debtholders is shown in Table 23.4.

TABLE 23.4   Illustration of Bankruptcy Payments to Senior Debt, Other Debt, and Subordinated Debt

Financial Structure	Book Value (1)	Percent of Total Debt (2)	Initial Allocation (3)	Actual Payment (4)	Percent of Original Claim Satisfied (5)
$200 available for claims on liquidation					
Bank debt	$200	50%	$100	$150	75%
Other debt	100	25	50	50	50
Subordinated debt	100	25	50	0	0
Total debt	$400	100%	$200	$200	50%
Net worth	300				0
Total	$700				29%
$300 available for claims on liquidation					
Bank debt	$200	50%	$150	$200	100%
Other debt	100	25	75	75	75
Subordinated debt	100	25	75	25	25
Total debt	$400	100%	$300	$300	75%
Net worth	300				0
Total	$700				43%

Steps:
1. Express each type of debt as a percentage of total debt (Column 2).
2. Multiply the debt percentages (Column 2) by the amount available to obtain the initial allocations (Column 3).
3. The subordinated debt is subordinate to bank debt. Therefore, the initial allocation to subordinate debt is added to the bank debt allocation until it has been exhausted or until the bank debt is finally paid off (Column 4).

In Table 23.4, where $200 is available for distribution, the subordinated debt has a claim on 25 percent of $200, or $50. However, this claim is subordinated to the bank debt (the only senior debt) and is added to the $100 claim of the bank. As a consequence, 75 percent of the bank's original claim is satisfied.

Where $300 is available for distribution, the $75 allocated to the subordinated debt is divided into two parts; $50 goes to the bank, and the other $25 remains for the subordinated debtholders. In this situation, the senior bank debtholders are fully paid off, 75 percent of other debt is paid, and only 25 percent of subordinated debt is paid.

Subordination is frequently required. Alert credit managers of firms supplying trade credit or commercial bank loan officers typically insist on subordination, particularly where debt is owed to the principal stockholders or officers of a company. Subordinated debt was widely used in leveraged buyouts during the 1980s. Often, subordinated debentures are also convertible into the common stock of the issuing company.

In comparison to subordinated debt, preferred stock suffers from the disadvantage that its dividends are not deductible as an expense for tax purposes. Subordinated debentures have been referred to as being like a special kind of preferred stock, the dividends of which *are* deductible as an expense for tax purposes. Subordinated debt has, therefore, become an increasingly important source of corporate capital.

The reasons for the use of subordinated debentures are clear. They offer a tax advantage over preferred stock; yet, they do not restrict the borrower's ability to obtain senior debt, as would be the case if all debt sources were on an equal basis. The use of subordinated debentures is further stimulated by periods of tight money, when commercial banks tend to require a greater equity base for short-term financing. These debentures provide a greater equity cushion for loans from commercial banks or other forms of senior debt. Their use also illustrates the development of hybrid securities that emerge to meet the changing situations that develop in the capital market.

Income Bonds

Income bonds provide that interest must be paid only if the earnings of the firm are sufficient to meet the interest obligations. The principal, however, must be paid when due. Thus, the interest itself is not a fixed charge. Income bonds, historically, have been issued because a firm has been in financial difficulties and its history suggests that it may be unable to meet a substantial level of fixed charges in the future. More generally, however, income bonds simply provide flexibility to the firm in the event that earnings do not cover the amount of interest that would otherwise have to be paid. Income bonds are like preferred stock in that the firm will not be in default if current payments on the obligations are not made. They have an additional advantage over preferred stock in that the interest is a deductible expense for corporate income tax computations, while the dividends on preferred stock are not.

The main characteristic and distinct advantage of the income bond is that interest is payable only if the company achieves earnings. Since earnings calculations are subject to differing interpretations, the indenture of the income bond carefully defines income and expenses. If it did not, litigation might result. Some income bonds are cumulative indefinitely (if interest is not paid, it accumulates, and it must be paid at some future date); others are cumulative for the first three to five years, after which they become noncumulative.

Income bonds usually contain sinking fund provisions to provide for their retirement. The annual payments to the sinking funds range between $\frac{1}{2}$ and 1 percent of the face amount of the original issue. Because the sinking fund payment requirements are typically contingent on earnings, a fixed cash drain on the company is avoided. Typically, income bondholders do not have voting rights when the bonds are issued. Sometimes, bondholders are given the right to elect some specified number of directors if interest is not paid for a certain number of years.

Sometimes, income bonds are convertible; there are sound reasons for convertibility if the bonds arise out of a reorganization. Creditors who receive income bonds in exchange for defaulted obligations have a less desirable position than they had previously. Since they have received something based on an adverse and problematical forecast of the company's future, it is appropriate that if the company does prosper, income bondholders are entitled to participate. When income bonds are issued in situations other than reorgani-

zation, the convertibility feature is likely to make the issue more attractive to prospective bond buyers.

Floating-Rate Notes

When inflation forces interest rates to high levels, borrowers are reluctant to commit themselves to long-term debt. Yield curves are typically inverted at such times, with short-term interest rates higher than long-term. One factor is that borrowers would rather pay a premium for short-term funds than lock themselves into high long-term rates for two or three decades.

Two risks are faced by those who defer long-term borrowing in hope that interest rates will soon fall. First, there is no assurance that rates will not rise even higher and remain at unexpectedly high levels for an indefinite period. If long-term rates rise to 15 percent, for example, debt that looked expensive at 12 percent will seem like a bargain to a borrower who passed it up in the hope of waiting out the rate crisis. Second, the short-term money may simply become unavailable.

The floating-rate note (FRN) was developed to decrease the risks of interest rate volatility at high levels.[3] In an FRN, the coupon rate varies at a given percentage above prevailing short- or long-term Treasury debt yields. The FRN rate is typically either fixed or guaranteed to exceed a stated minimum for an initial period and then adjusted at specified intervals to movements in the Treasury rates. FRNs were first issued in the United States by Citicorp in 1974. The rate was set at a minimum of 9.7 percent for ten months and then adjusted semiannually to 1 percent above the current three-month Treasury bill rate. Other firms followed Citicorp's lead. These early issues carried rates based on T-bill yields, and most allowed investors to "put" the FRN to the issuer at face value after a given date.[4] Initial rates on the notes were well below the going rate on such short-term borrowing as commercial paper. In July 1974, the rate on three-month prime commercial paper was 11.9 percent, while Treasury bills of comparable maturity were yielding 7.6 percent. Because interest rates were generally expected to decline, borrowers hoped that FRNs would also cost less over the life of the notes than fixed-rate long-term debt.

The terms of FRNs are not fixed by law. A variety of features have been employed by issuing companies:

1. *Convertibility.* Either to common stock or to fixed-rate notes or to both, at either the issuer's option, the holder's option, or both. The note may state particular dates or time periods when conversion is allowed and may set other conditions, such as a given Treasury bill rate at the time of conversion. The rate on the fixed-rate note may be preset or may depend on Treasury rates at conversion.

---

[3]See the survey by Marks and Law [1980].

[4]Remember that a *call* gives the holder the option to buy at a specified price. For example, a security may be selling for $50, but you may have a call to buy it for $45. By symmetry, a *put* gives the owner the option to sell the security to the issuer at a specified price. For example, a bond may have a market price of $900, but you may own a put to sell the bond to the issuing corporation for $1,050.

2. *Put option.* This feature allows the holder to redeem the note at face value, generally at stated times or under other given conditions.

3. *Minimum rate.* This feature prevents the note rate from floating below a stated minimum.

4. *Drop-lock rate.* If the note rate has dropped to a stated rate, it becomes locked at that rate until maturity.

5. *Sinking fund provision.* Permits the issuer to repay stated portions of the principal amount before maturity.

6. *Declining spread.* The spread between the note rate and the Treasury rate decreases by given amounts at specified times.

7. *Declining minimum rate.* The minimum rate decreases in a similar manner.

8. *Call option.* The issuer has the right to call the note, usually at a moderate premium, and sometimes within a short time after issuance.

Since certain features benefit the issuer while others favor potential buyers, the choice of terms for a particular offering influences the market value of the note. For example, convertibility at the issuer's option gives the issuer control over the cost of debt should Treasury rates remain at high levels; lenders will charge a premium for this right. Conversely, convertibility by the holder allows lenders to lock into higher rates of return if Treasury rates begin to fall. Lenders will accept a lower mark-up, or spread, over Treasury rates in return for this option. One important consideration for issuers is the complexity of the offering. If the FRN includes too many options, investors may conclude they are unable to evaluate it accurately and reduce the amount they are willing to pay.

FRNs are particularly useful for financial institutions which hold a large percentage of assets bearing floating-rate returns. These institutions can issue FRNs to establish a constant spread between their return on investments and cost of debt. But FRNs are not always advantageous. For example, they can create a substantial interest rate mismatch if the bank's asset portfolio has a long duration. Nonfinancial companies whose revenues tend to vary more than their costs with the rate of inflation can also use FRNs to stabilize their cost-revenue spread. Capital-intensive companies, whose depreciation expenses vary little with inflation, are one example.

FRNs give investors two important guarantees during periods of high and unpredictable inflation:

1. Returns on investment will follow changes in Treasury rates.

2. Because FRN rates vary with the market, the market value of the note will remain relatively stable.

The convertibility and minimum rate features found in most FRNs give investors additional assurance and flexibility in an unstable investment environment.

Floating-rate notes provide another illustration of the flexibility of financial markets and instruments. The increased volatility of fluctuations in interest rates has brought forth debt instruments with new types of provisions. Additional new efforts by lenders to achieve protection against inflation include a provision that the principal will also float—

that it will be tied to the value of real assets such as oil or silver. Other inflation hedges by lenders include such claims on equity as warrants, convertibility into common stock, or add-on contingent interest fees based on some measure of company performance such as sales or income. Such hedges are added to a fixed interest rate that will be lower than it would otherwise have to be to provide protection against uncertain inflation. Thus, the lender trades off some inflation protection against some near-term interest income.

BOND VALUATION AND THE COST OF DEBT

Bond valuation and the cost of debt are so important that we found it necessary to discuss both of these topics in earlier chapters. In Chapter 3 on Decisions Across Time and in Chapter 14 on Managing Financial Risk, we explained the valuation of bonds. In Chapter 12 on options we discussed the yield to maturity on risky bonds. In Chapter 14 we also developed the concept of duration, which conveys how the value or price of bonds depends on the time weighted values of the cash flows promised. In Chapter 15 we discussed how to measure the cost of debt — both long and short term. These significant aspects of debt should be kept in mind as we turn to an evaluation of the role of debt in long-term financing decisions.

DECISIONS ON THE USE OF DEBT

From the viewpoint of long-term debtholders, debt is less risky than preferred or common stock, has limited advantages in regard to income, and is weak in regard to control. To elaborate:

1. In the area of risk, debt is favorable (relative to preferred or common stock) because it gives the holder priority both in earnings and in liquidation. Debt also has a definite maturity and is protected by the covenants of the indenture.

2. In the area of income, the bondholder has a fixed return, except in the case of income bonds or floating rate notes. Interest payments are not contingent on the company's level of earnings or current market rates of interest. However, debt does not participate in any superior earnings of the company, and gains are limited in magnitude. Bondholders actually suffer during inflationary periods. A 20-year, 6 percent bond pays $60 of interest each year. Under inflation, the purchasing power of this $60 is eroded, causing a loss in real value to the bondholder.[5] Frequently, long-term debt is callable. If bonds are called, the investor receives funds that must be reinvested to be kept active.

3. In the area of control, the bondholder usually does not have the right to vote. However, if the bonds go into default, then bondholders, in effect, take control of the company.

---

[5]Recognizing this fact, investors demand higher interest rates during inflationary periods.

From the viewpoint of long-term debt issuers, there are several advantages and disadvantages to bonds. The advantages are:

1. The cash cost of debt is definitely limited. Bondholders do not participate in superior profits (if earned).

2. Not only is the cost limited, but, typically, the required return is lower than that of common stock.

3. The owners of the corporation do not share their control when debt financing is used.

4. The interest payment on debt is deductible as a tax expense.

5. Flexibility in the financial structure of the corporation can be achieved by inserting a call provision in the bond indenture.

The disadvantages are:

1. Debt has committed charges whose nonpayment is a default.

2. As seen in Chapter 15, higher financial leverage brings higher required rates of return on equity earnings. Thus, even though leverage may be favorable and may raise earnings per share, the higher required rates attributable to leverage may drive the common stock value down. An indirect cost of using more debt is possibly a higher cost of equity.

3. Debt usually has a fixed maturity date, and the financial officer must make provision for repayment of the debt.

4. Since long-term debt is a commitment for a long period, it involves risk. The expectations and plans on which the debt was issued may change, and the debt may prove to be a burden. For example, if income, employment, the price level, and interest rates all fall greatly, the prior assumption of a large amount of long-term debt may have been an unwise financial policy. The railroads are always given as an example in this regard. They were able to meet their ordinary operating expenses during the 1930s but were unable to meet the heavy financial charges they had undertaken earlier, when their prospects looked more favorable than they turned out to be.

5. In a long-term contractual relationship, the indenture provisions are likely to be much more stringent than they are in a short-term credit agreement. Hence, the firm may be subject to much more disturbing and crippling restrictions than if it had borrowed on a short-term basis or had issued common stock.

6. There is a limit on the extent to which funds can be raised through long-term debt. Generally accepted standards of financial policy dictate that the debt ratio shall not exceed certain limits. When debt goes beyond these limits, its cost rises rapidly.

How the above considerations are balanced in decisions on the proportions of debt, preferred stock, and common stock in the financing mix will be analyzed after we discuss the nature of the financing alternatives.

THE USE OF PREFERRED STOCK IN FINANCING DECISIONS

Preferred stock has claims and rights ahead of common stock but behind all bonds. The preference may be a prior claim on earnings, a prior claim on assets in the event of liquidation, and/or a preferential position with regard to both earnings and assets.

The hybrid nature of preferred stock becomes apparent when we try to classify it in relation to bonds and common stock. The priority feature and the (generally) fixed dividend indicate that preferred stock is similar to bonds. Payments to preferred stockholders are limited in amount, so that common stockholders receive the advantages (or disadvantages) of leverage. However, if the preferred dividends are not earned, the company can forego paying them without danger of bankruptcy. In this characteristic, preferred stock is similar to common stock. Moreover, failure to pay the stipulated dividend does not cause default of the obligation, as does failure to pay bond interest.

In some types of analysis, preferred stock is treated as debt. This occurs, for example, when the analysis is being made by a *potential stockholder* considering the earnings fluctuations induced by fixed charge securities. Suppose, however, that the analysis is by a *bondholder* studying the firm's vulnerability to failure brought on by declines in sales or income. Since the dividends on preferred stock are not a fixed charge (in the sense that failure to pay them represents a default of an obligation), preferred stock represents a cushion; it provides an additional equity base. For *stockholders,* it is a leverage-inducing instrument much like debt. For *creditors,* it constitutes additional net worth. Preferred stock, therefore, can be treated as either debt or equity, depending on the nature of the problem under consideration.[6]

The dividend stream on preferred stock, which is not convertible into common stock or callable, represents a perpetuity. Therefore, the valuation and cost of preferred stock measures are based on the perpetuity formulation.

$$k_{ps} = \frac{d_{ps}}{p_{ps}} \tag{23.1}$$

Preferred stock with a maturity would be valued as a bond to maturity, but its cost would not be a tax deduction. Equation 23.1 would not be appropriate for measuring the cost of convertible preferred, which would be measured by the principles discussed in Chapter 25.

MAJOR PROVISIONS OF PREFERRED STOCK ISSUES

Because the possible characteristics, rights, and obligations of any specific security vary so widely, a point of diminishing returns is quickly reached in a descriptive discussion of the different kinds of securities. As economic circumstances change, new kinds of securities are manufactured. Their number and variety are limited chiefly by the imagination

---

[6]Accountants generally include preferred stock in the net worth portion of the capital structure. But preferred is different from common equity.

and ingenuity of the managers formulating the terms of the issues. It is not surprising, then, that preferred stock can be found in many forms. The following sections will look at the main terms and characteristics in each case and examine the possible variations in relation to the circumstances in which they could occur.

Priority in Assets and Earnings

Many provisions in a preferred stock certificate are designed to reduce the purchaser's risk in relation to the risk carried by the holder of common stock. Preferred stock usually has priority with regard to earnings and assets. Two provisions designed to prevent undermining this priority are often found. The first states that, without the consent of the preferred stockholders, there can be no subsequent sale of securities having a prior or equal claim on earnings. The second seeks to keep earnings in the firm. It requires a minimum level of retained earnings before common stock dividends are permitted. In order to assure the availability of liquid assets that can be converted into cash for the payment of dividends, the maintenance of a minimum current ratio may also be required.

Cumulative Dividends

A high percentage of preferred stock issues provide for cumulative dividends — that is, all past preferred dividends must be paid before common dividends can be paid. The cumulative feature, therefore, is a protective device. If the preferred stock were not cumulative, preferred and common stock dividends could be passed by for a number of years. The company could then vote a large common stock dividend but only the stipulated payment to preferred stock. Suppose that preferred stock with a par value of $100 carried a 7 percent dividend and that the company did not pay dividends for several years, thereby accumulating funds that would enable it to pay in total about $50 in dividends. It could pay a single $7 dividend to the preferred stockholders and a $43 dividend to the common stockholders. Obviously, this device could be used to evade the preferred position that the holders of preferred stock have tried to obtain. The cumulative feature prevents such evasion.[7]

Large arrearages on preferred stock make it difficult to resume dividend payments on common stock. To avoid delays in beginning common stock dividend payments again, a compromise arrangement with the holders of preferred stock is likely to be worked out. A package offer is one possibility; for example, a recapitalization plan may provide for an exchange of shares. The arrearage will be wiped out by the donation of common stock with a value equal to the amount of the preferred dividend arrearage, and the holders of preferred stock will thus be given an ownership share in the corporation. Alternately, resumption of current dividends on the preferred may be promised. Whether these provisions are worth anything depends on the future earnings prospects of the company.

The advantage to the company of substituting common stock for dividends in arrears is that it can start again with a clear balance sheet. If earnings recover, dividends can be

---

[7]Note, however, that compounding is absent in most cumulative plans. In other words, the arrearages themselves earn no return.

paid to the holders of common stock without making up arrearages to the holders of preferred stock. The original common stockholders, of course, will have given up a portion of their ownership of the corporation.

Convertibility

A substantial portion of preferred stock issued is convertible into common stock. For example, one share of preferred stock might be convertible into 2.5 shares of the firm's common stock at the option of the preferred stock shareholder. The rationale for the use of the convertibility provision for both debt and preferred stock is set forth in Chapter 25. We may note at this point that convertible preferred stock is frequently used by venture capital firms, as discussed in Chapter 21. The main reasons are that the venture capital firm receives income if earned by the firm, has priority in liquidation, and if the firm does well, can convert to an equity position and participate in the position.

Other Provisions

Other provisions encountered in preferred stocks include the following:

1. *Voting rights.* Sometimes preferred stockholders are given the right to vote for directors. When this feature is present, it generally permits the preferred stockholders to elect a *minority* of the board, say three out of nine directors. The voting privilege becomes operative only if the company has not paid the preferred dividend for a specified period, say six, eight, or ten quarters.

2. *Participating.* A rare type of preferred stock is one that participates with the common stock in sharing the firm's earnings. The following factors generally relate to participating preferred stocks: (a) the stated preferred dividend is paid first — for example, $5 a share; (b) next, income is allocated to common stock dividends up to an amount equal to the preferred dividend — in this case, $5; and (c) any remaining income is shared equally between the common and preferred stockholders.

3. *Sinking fund.* Some preferred issues have a sinking fund requirement. When they do, the sinking fund ordinarily calls for the purchase and retirement of a given percentage of the preferred stock each year.

4. *Maturity.* Preferred stocks almost never have maturity dates on which they must be retired. However, if the issue has a sinking fund, this effectively creates maturity dates. Convertibility may also shorten the life of preferred stock.

5. *Call provision.* A call provision gives the issuing corporation the right to call in the preferred stock for redemption, as for bonds. If it is used, the call provision states that the company must pay an amount greater than the par value of the preferred stock, the additional sum being defined as the *call premium*. For example, a $100 par value preferred stock might be callable at the option of the corporation at $108 a share.

6. *Adjustable-rate preferred stock (ARPS).* Under unexpected inflation, preferred stock with fixed dividend rates becomes undesirable from the investor's point of view because of the risk that the market value of the preferred will fall. In order to share the

risk and to make preferred issues more attractive to investors, many companies, particularly utilities, have begun to issue preferred stock with dividends tied to rates on various U.S. government obligations. This form of preferred stock as well as auction-rate preferred stock were already discussed more fully in Chapter 20.

7. *Auction-rate preferred stock.* Both ARPS and auction-rate preferred stock have a floating dividend rate and tax advantages. They differ in that while the dividend rate on the ARPS is typically tied to a government obligation, the auction-rate preferred stock is set by Dutch auctions as described in Chapter 20.

Evaluation of Preferred Stock

There are both advantages and disadvantages to selling preferred stock. Among the advantages are:

1. In contrast to bonds, the obligation to make committed interest payments is avoided.

2. A firm wishing to expand because its earning power is high can obtain higher earnings for the original owners by selling preferred stock with a limited return rather than by selling common stock.

3. By selling preferred stock, the financial manager avoids the provision of equal participation in earnings that the sale of additional common stock would require.

4. Preferred stock also permits a company to avoid sharing control through participation in voting.

5. In contrast to bonds, it enables the firm to conserve mortgageable assets.

6. Since preferred stock typically has no maturity and no sinking fund, it is more flexible than bonds.

Among the disadvantages are:

1. Characteristically, preferred stock must be sold on a higher yield basis than that for bonds.[8]

2. Preferred stock dividends are not deductible as a tax expense, a characteristic that makes their cost differential very great in comparison with that of bonds.

3. As shown in Chapter 15, the after-tax cost of debt is approximately half the stated coupon rate for profitable firms. The after-tax cost of preferred, however, is frequently the full percentage amount of the preferred dividend.[9]

---

[8]Historically, a given firm's preferred stock generally carried higher rates than its bonds because of the preferred's greater risk from the holder's viewpoint. However, as is noted below, the fact that preferred dividends are largely exempt from the corporate income tax has made preferred stock attractive to corporate investors. From time to time the dividend yields required on preferred stock may be somewhat below the required yields on long-term debt.

[9]By far the most important issuers of nonconvertible preferred stocks are the utility companies. For these firms, taxes are an expense for rate-making purposes — that is, higher taxes are passed on to the customers in the form of higher prices — so tax deductibility is not an important issue. This explains why utilities issue about 85 percent of all nonconvertible preferreds.

In fashioning securities, the financial manager needs to consider the investor's point of view. Frequently, it is asserted that preferred stocks have so many disadvantages to both the issuer and the investor that they should never be issued. Nevertheless, preferred stock is issued in substantial amounts. Preferred stock provides the following advantages to the investor:

1. It provides reasonably steady income.

2. Preferred stockholders have a preference over common stockholders in liquidation; numerous examples can be cited where the preference position of holders of preferred stock saved them from losses incurred by holders of common stock.

3. Many corporations (for example, insurance companies) like to hold preferred stocks as investments because 70 or 80 percent of the dividends received on these shares is not taxable.

Preferred stock also has some disadvantages to investors:

1. Although the holders of preferred stock bear a substantial portion of ownership risk, their returns are limited.

2. Price fluctuations in preferred stock may be greater than those in bonds; yet, yields on bonds are sometimes higher than those on preferred stock.

3. The stockholders have no legally enforceable right to dividends.

4. Accrued dividend arrearages are seldom settled in cash comparable to the amount of the obligation that has been incurred.

Basically, preferred stock enables a firm to use leverage without fixed charges. For corporate investors at least 70 percent of the dividends can be excluded from taxable income, so that the 34 percent tax rate becomes only 10.2 percent. Generally, preferred stocks had been sold mostly by utility companies for whom the non-deductibility of dividends as an expense for tax purposes is less of a disadvantage because of the nature of the regulatory ratemaking process which essentially treats taxes paid as an expense to be considered in setting allowable rates of return.

During 1991 a resurgence in the use of preferred stock took place with sales of over $16 billion by early December. Offerings in the $2 billion range each were made by Ford, GM, and RJR Nabisco; Kmart's was over $1 billion. Many banks sold large amounts of preferred to strengthen their capital base in response to regulatory pressure. Some corporations sold preferred to reduce excessive debt levels (like RJR); other companies whose business is cyclical and/or subject to increased global competition (like the auto companies) were seeking to strengthen their equity base particularly because of the 1991 economic downturn.

Another new development was the use of Preference Equity Redemption Cumulative Stock (PERCS), used by GM, RJR, and Kmart in 1991. PERCS pay a higher dividend than the common stock. They are callable by the issuer at prices starting at the issue price, declining each year by the dollar amount by which the dividend on the PERCS exceeds the dividend on the common. At the end of a 3- to 4-year period, the PERCS convert into common at a predetermined price.

REFUNDING DEBT OR PREFERRED[10]

In an era of falling interest rates, a firm may find itself with bonds or preferred stock outstanding that pay a coupon rate higher than the prevailing market rate. A net present value analysis will reveal whether the outstanding securities should be called or, if they are not callable, repurchased on the open market.[11] Almost all public bond issues and many preferred stock issues have a call provision allowing the firm to force recall of the security at a call premium. Although the following example is for a bond refinancing, the same analysis applies equally well to a preferred stock refinancing.

To provide a focus for the analysis, consider the following facts. The L and S Company has a $10 million bond issue outstanding with five years to maturity, a coupon rate of 16 percent, and annual interest payments. The current market rate on debt of equivalent risk is 10 percent. The call price on the $1,000 face value debt is $1,050, and the firm has a 40 percent tax rate. What is the net present value of calling the outstanding bonds and replacing them with new bonds of equivalent maturity and risk? Assume no transactions costs.

This is a capital budgeting decision and the usual procedures apply. The changes in the after-tax cash flows should be discounted at the appropriate after-tax discount rate. In this case, the appropriate rate is the after-tax rate on debt of equivalent risk; that is, $(1 - T_c)k_b = (1 - .4).10 = .06$. We use the after-tax rate because all refunding costs (such as the call premium) are assumed to be financed with debt capital. This debt provides an interest tax shield; hence, the relevant discount rate is the after-tax rate.

The after-tax cash flows have three components (in a world without transactions costs).

1. The *call premium* will cost $500,000. It is deductible as an expense; therefore, its after-tax cost is $500,000(1 - .4) = $300,000$. We assume that the cash flow from the tax shield is available immediately.

2. The new debt issue will have to be $10,300,000, and it will pay a 10 percent coupon $(r_2 = 10\%)$; thus, the new interest will be $1,030,000 per year. The old interest was 16 percent $(r_1 = 16\%)$ of $10,000,000, or $1,600,000 per year. Therefore, the *after-tax interest saving* amounts to $(1 - T_c)(r_1 - r_2)D - (1 - T_c)r_2\Delta D$, where D is the original book value and ΔD is the change in book value. Numerically, the annual interest savings is:

$$(1 - .4)(.16 - .10)(10,000,000) - (1 - .4)(.10)(300,000) = 342,000.$$

---

[10]The methodology described in this section is consistent with the treatments found in Lewellen and Emery [1981] and in Finnerty, Kalotay, and Farrell [1988] whose Equation (3.1) on p. 21 is the same as our (23.1) for the same after-tax refunding transactions costs.

[11]The accounting treatment of bond repurchase when bonds are selling at a discount can cause extremely perverse behavior. Suppose that interest rates have risen, thereby causing fixed-rate outstanding debt to sell at a discount. Repurchase of this debt at market value has no economic gain or loss before taxes because the firm is paying the fair market price. However, the accounting treatment allows the firm to record the difference between the face value and the market value as profit. Therefore, firms that desire to increase their reported earnings per share may decide to repurchase discounted debt. Unfortunately, this is a negative present value decision because the firm has to pay (1) ordinary income taxes on its paper gain and (2) higher coupons on replacement debt.

3. *Incremental principal* on the new debt, namely $300,000, must be paid off at maturity.

The net present value of these components can be calculated by using Equation 23.1.

$$
\text{NPV} = \sum_{t=1}^{n} \frac{(1 - T_c)(r_1 - r_2)D}{[1 + (1 - T_c)k_b]^t} - \sum_{t=1}^{n} \frac{(1 - T_c)r_2\Delta D}{[1 + (1 - T_c)k_b]^t}
$$

$$
- \frac{\Delta D}{[1 + (1 - T_c)k_b]^n} \tag{23.1}
$$

$$
= \sum_{t=1}^{5} \frac{(1 - .4)(.16 - .10)10,000,000}{[1 + (1 - .4)(.10)]^t} - \sum_{t=1}^{5} \frac{(1 - .4).10(300,000)}{[1 + (1 - .4)(.10)]^t}
$$

$$
- \frac{300,000}{[1 + (1 - .4)(.10)]^5}
$$

$$
= 1,516,464 - 75,823 - 224,190
$$

$$
= 1,216,451
$$

Therefore, the debt should be refunded.

Two additional issues are pertinent. First, the debt refinancing may slightly alter the capital structure of the firm because the market value of the new debt issue exceeds the market value of the outstanding debt. This may create a tax gain from leverage.[12] The second issue is that callable debt should never sell for more than the call price plus a small premium approximately equal to the flotation costs of exercising the call. No investor would rationally pay $1,100 for a bond which might be called (any minute) at $1,050.

SUMMARY

A *bond* is a long-term promissory note. A *mortgage bond* is secured by real property. An *indenture* is an agreement between the firm issuing the bond and the numerous bondholders, represented by a *trustee*. *Secured long-term debt* differs with respect to (1) the priority of claims, (2) the right to issue additional securities, and (3) the scope of the lien provided. These characteristics determine the amount of protection provided to the bondholder by the terms of the security. Giving investors more security will induce them to accept a lower yield but will restrict the future freedom of action of the issuing firm. The main classes of unsecured bonds are (1) *debentures*, (2) *subordinated debentures*, and (3) *income bonds*. Holders of debentures are unsecured general creditors. Subordinated debentures are junior in claim to bank loans. Income bonds are similar to preferred stock in that interest is paid only when earned.

[12]Cf. Ofer and Taggart [1977].

The nature of long-term fixed rate debt encourages its use under the following circumstances:

1. Sales and earnings are relatively stable.
2. Profit margins are adequate to make leverage advantageous.
3. A rise in profits or in the general price level is expected.
4. The existing debt ratio is relatively low.
5. Common stock price–earnings ratios are low in relation to the levels of interest rates.
6. Control considerations are important.
7. Cash flow requirements under the bond agreement are not burdensome.
8. Restrictions of the bond indenture are not onerous.

While the characteristics of preferred stock vary, some patterns persist. Preferred stocks usually have priority over common stocks with respect to earnings and claims on assets in liquidation. Preferred stocks are usually cumulative; they have no maturity but are sometimes callable. They are typically nonparticipating and offer only contingent voting rights.

The advantages to the issuer are limited dividends and no maturity. These advantages may outweigh the disadvantages of higher cost and nondeductibility of the dividends as an expense for tax purposes. Companies sell preferred stock when they seek the advantages of financial leverage but fear the dangers of the fixed charges on debt in the face of potential fluctuations in income. If debt ratios or the cost of common stock financing are relatively high, these advantages of preferred stock are reinforced.

Other advantages of preferred stock include: (1) 70 or 80 percent of preferred stock dividends received by other corporations are exempt from taxable income; (2) convertible preferred is used by venture capital firms because it gives them priority in claims plus an option to obtain equity; (3) when used as payment in a takeover or merger, the transaction may qualify as a tax-free exchange.

If a bond or preferred stock issue was sold when interest rates were higher than they are at present, and if the issue is callable, it may be profitable to call the old issue and refund it with a new, lower-cost issue. An analysis similar to capital budgeting is required to determine whether a refunding operation should be undertaken.

Questions

23.1 Explain what is meant by the term *yield to maturity* in reference to (a) bonds and (b) preferred stocks. Is it appropriate to talk of a yield to maturity on a preferred stock that has no specific maturity date?

23.2 A sinking fund is set up in one of two ways:

    a. The corporation makes annual payments to the trustee, who invests the proceeds in securities (frequently government bonds) and uses the accumulated total to retire the bond issue on maturity.

b. The trustee uses the annual payments to retire a portion of the issue each year, either calling a given percentage of the issue by a lottery and paying a specified price per bond or buying bonds on the open market, whichever is cheaper.

Discuss the advantages and disadvantages of each procedure from the viewpoint of both the firm and the bondholders.

23.3 Since a corporation often has the right to call bonds, do you believe individuals should be able to demand repayment at any time they so desire? Explain.

23.4 Bonds are less attractive to investors during periods of inflation because a rise in the price level reduces the purchasing power of the fixed interest payments and of the principal. Discuss the advantages and disadvantages to a corporation of using a bond whose interest payments and principal would fluctuate in direct proportion to fluctuations in the price level (a floating rate bond).

23.5 If preferred stock dividends are passed for several years, the preferred stockholders are frequently given the right to elect several members of the board of directors. In the case of bonds that are in default on interest payments, this procedure is not followed. Why does the difference exist?

23.6 Preferred stocks are found in almost all industries, but one industry is the really dominant issuer of preferred shares. What is this industry, and why are firms in it so disposed to using preferred stock?

23.7 If the corporate income tax were abolished, would this raise or lower the amount of new preferred stock issued?

23.8 Investors buying securities have some expected or required rate of return in mind. Which would you expect to be higher — the required rate of return (before taxes) on preferred stocks or that on common stocks?

23.9 Do you think the before-tax required rate of return is higher on very high-grade preferred stocks or on bonds in the following instances:
a. for individual investors?
b. for corporate investors?

23.10 For purposes of measuring a firm's leverage, should preferred stock be classified as debt or as equity? Does it matter if the classification is being made by (a) the firm itself, (b) creditors, or (c) equity investors?

23.11 A firm is seeking a term loan from a bank. Under what conditions would it want a fixed interest rate, and under what conditions would it want the rate to fluctuate with the prime rate?

PROBLEMS

23.1 Three years ago, your firm issued some 18-year bonds with 10.5 percent coupon rates and a 10 percent call premium. You have called these bonds. The bonds originally sold at their face value of $1,000. (Use semiannual compounding.)
a. Compute the realized rate of return for investors who purchased the bonds when they were issued.
b. Given the rate of return in Part (a), did investors welcome the call? Explain.

TABLE P23.2   Cash Flows on Three Bonds with Five-Year Maturities

Year	Fully Amortized	Balloon	Pure Discount
Current value	$1,000.00	$1,000.00	$1,000.00
1	277.41	120.00	0
2	277.41	120.00	0
3	277.41	120.00	0
4	277.41	120.00	0
5	277.41	1,120.00	1,762.34

23.2 A fully amortized bond, a balloon payment bond, and a pure discount bond, each with five years to maturity were newly issued today. Each has a 12 percent promised yield to maturity. Their annual cash flows and current market values are provided in Table P23.2.
  a. If current market yields are 12 percent, what is the duration of each bond?
  b. If current market yields were 20 percent, what would the duration of each bond be? (Don't forget that their current values decrease if the interest rate rises from 12 percent to 20 percent; use annual compounding.)

23.3 Carson Electronics, a leading manufacturer in its field, is planning an expansion program. It has estimated that it will need to raise an additional $100 million. Carson is discussing with its investment banker the alternatives of raising the $100 million through debt financing or through selling additional shares of common stock.
  The prevailing cost of Aaa debt is 8 percent, while the prevailing cost of Baa debt is 9.6 percent. New equity would be sold at $10 per share. The corporate tax rate is 40 percent. The industry's financial ratios, followed by Carson's balance sheet and income statement, are provided in Table P23.3.
  a. Estimate Carson Electronics' cost of equity capital by using the Security Market Line. The risk-free rate is 6 percent, the expected return on the market is 11 percent, and the beta based on Carson's present leverage is 1.2.
  b. What is the value of Carson's total equity? What is its indicated price per share?
  c. On the basis of a cost of debt of 8 percent and the cost of equity that you have calculated, determine the weighted average cost of capital for Carson at the present time. (The company has no short-term interest-bearing debt.)
  d. If Carson finances its expansion by the use of debt, calculate the new financial structure and coverage relationships and present your conclusion on whether the new debt issue will be risky or relatively risk-free. (Assume that the same percentage of net operating income is earned on the increase in assets as was earned on the total assets before the financing.)
  e. If Carson finances with debt, the cost of debt will be 8 percent, while the cost of equity will reflect the rise in beta to 1.25. If the company finances with equity, the cost of debt will be 8 percent, while the cost of equity will reflect a drop in beta to 1.19. Compare the cost of equity under the two methods of financing.

TABLE P23.3   Electronics Industry Financial Ratios

Current ratio: 2.1 times	Coverage of fixed charges: 7 times
Sales to total assets: 1.8 times	Net income to sales: 5%
Current liabilities to total assets: 30%	Return on total assets: 9%
Long-term debt to net worth: 40%	Net income to net worth: 12%
Total liabilities to total assets: 50%	

Carson Electronics Balance Sheet as of December 31, 19X0 (Millions of Dollars)

Assets		**Liabilities**		
Total current assets	$ 600	Total current liabilities	$200	
Net fixed assets	400	Long-term debt (at 8%)	100	
		Total debt		$ 300
		Common stock, par value $1		100
		Additional paid-in capital		200
		Retained earnings		400
Total assets	$1,000	Total claims on assets		$1,000

Carson Electronics Income Statement for Year Ended
December 31, 19X0 (Millions of Dollars)

Total revenues	$2,000
Net operating income	208
Interest expense	8
Net income before taxes	$ 200
Income taxes (at 40%)	80
Net income to equity	$ 120

f.   Under each of the two methods of financing, what will be the total value of the equity, and what will be the new value per share of common stock?

g.   Under the same assumptions as in the preceding questions, calculate the value of the firm under the two methods of financing.

h.   Compare the weighted cost of capital under the two methods of financing.

i.   Summarize your recommendation about which form of financing Carson should employ for raising the additional $100 million.

23.4   In late 19X8, the Gallaway Gas & Electric Company sought to raise $6 million for expansion of facilities and services. The company could have sold additional debt at 9 percent, preferred stock at 8.84 percent, or common stock at $50 a share. Growth in earnings and dividends was expected to be 4.5 percent. How should the company have raised the money? Relevant financial information is provided in Table P23.4. (Ignore flotation costs.)

TABLE P23.4   Public Utilities Financial Ratios

Current ratio: 1.0 times	Preferred/total assets: 10-15%
Interest earned (before taxes): 4.0 times	Common equity/total assets: 30-35%
Sales to total assets: 0.3 times	Earnings before interest and taxes to total
Average collection period: 28.0 days	assets: 8.9%
Current debt/total assets: 5-10%	Profits to common equity: 12.1%
Long-term debt/total assets: 45-50%	

Gallaway Gas & Electric Company Balance Sheet as of
July 31, 19X8 (Thousands of Dollars)

Assets		Liabilities	
Cash	$ 750	Current liabilities	$ 3,000
Receivables	1,500	Long-term debt (at 8%)	30,000
Materials and supplies	1,200	Preferred stock (at 10%)	3,000
Total current assets	$ 3,450	Common stock, $25 par value	11,250
Net property	56,550	Capital surplus	6,600
		Retained earnings	6,150
Total assets	$60,000	Total claims	$60,000

Gallaway Gas & Electric Company Income Statement for Year
Ended July 31, 19X8 (Thousands of Dollars)

Operating revenues	$18,900
Operating expenses	12,000
Earnings before interest and taxes	$ 6,900
Interest deduction	2,400
Earnings before taxes	$ 4,500
Income taxes (at 40%)	1,800
Earnings after taxes	$ 2,700
Preferred dividends	300
Net income available to common	$ 2,400

Earnings per share = $5.33
Expected dividends per share = $4.25

23.5 a.   A manufacturing firm with $60 million of assets judges that it is at the beginning of a three-year growth cycle. It has a total debt-to-assets ratio of 16 percent, and it expects sales and net earnings to grow at a rate of 10 percent a year and stock prices to rise 30 percent a year over the three-year period. The firm will need $6 million at the beginning of the three-year period and another $3 million by the middle of the third year. It is at the beginning of a general business upswing, when money and capital costs are what they generally are after about a year of recession and at the beginning of an upswing. By the middle of the third year, money and capital costs will show their characteristic pattern near the peak of an upswing. How should the firm raise the $6 million and the $3 million?

b. An aerospace company with sales of $25 million a year needs $5 million to finance expansion. It has a debt-to-total-assets ratio of 65 percent; and its common stock, which is widely held, is selling at a price-earnings ratio of 25 times. It is comparing the sale of common stock and convertible debentures. Which do you recommend? Explain.

c. A chemical company has been growing steadily. To finance a growth of sales from $40 million a year to $50 million over a two-year period, it needs $2 million in additional equipment. When additional working capital needs are taken into account, the total additional financing required during the first year is $5 million. Profits will rise by 50 percent after the first ten months. The stock is currently selling at 20 times earnings. The company can borrow on straight debt at $7\frac{1}{2}$ percent or with a convertibility or warrant "sweetener" for $\frac{3}{4}$ percent less. The present debt-to-total-assets ratio is 25 percent. Which form of financing should it employ?

23.6 The Rubik Company is trying to decide whether or not it should call its outstanding debt. It has a $25,000,000 bond issue outstanding which has eight years to maturity and pays a 14 percent annual coupon. The call price on each $1,000 face value bond is $1,100, and the firm has a 40 percent tax rate. If the current market rate on bonds of equivalent risk is 9 percent, what is the net present value of calling the bonds and financing the deal with new bonds of equivalent risk and maturity?

23.7 *(Use the computer diskette, File name: 23RFDNG, Refunding.)*

a. The components of the refunding decision are the initial cash outlay and the future cash flows over time. Initial cash outlays determine the amount of new financing required (assuming that all refunding costs are financed with the incremental debt).
   (1) Calculate the dollar amount of the call premium, after-tax.
   (2) Calculate the immediate tax savings from writing off the unamortized flotation costs remaining on the old issue.
   (3) Calculate the flotation costs on the new issue.

b. There are two steps in the analysis of future cash flows. First, determine the annual cash inflows and outflows:
   (1) Calculate the annual tax savings from amortizing flotation costs on the new issue.
   (2) Calculate the future annual tax savings lost due to the immediate write-off of old flotation costs. This is a negative inflow.
   (3) Calculate the interest savings as a result of the interest rate differential.
   Then discount future cash flows at the after-tax cost of new debt over the life of the new bond, adjusting for semiannual compounding where necessary.

c. Suppose, as some people argue, that the before-tax cost of new debt is the appropriate discount rate. How does this affect the present values calculated in Question (b)?

d. As in any capital budgeting decision, the NPV of refunding equals cash inflows minus cash outflows. (Return to the initial assumptions to answer the following questions.)

(1) How would NPV be affected if the interest rate on the new debt were 11 percent instead of 10 percent?

(2) How would NPV be affected if we assume that the old bond has only 5 years to maturity (and the new bond has a 5-year life)?

(3) What gross proceeds would be required if the flotation costs on the new issue were 3 percent? How would this affect the NPV of refunding?

(4) What would be the effect on the NPV of refunding of a higher call premium? Try 6 percent.

(5) How would NPV be affected if the firm were in a lower tax bracket? Try 20 percent.

e. Now you are free to explore other changes that might affect the NPV of refunding.

SELECTED REFERENCES

Agmon, T.; Ofer, A. R.; and Tamir, A., "Variable Rate Debt Instruments and Corporate Debt Policy," *Journal of Finance*, 36 (March 1981), pp. 113–125.

Altman, Edward I., "Setting the Record Straight on Junk Bonds: A Review of the Research on Default Rates and Returns," *Journal of Applied Corporate Finance*, 3 (Summer 1990), pp. 82–95.

———, *Default Risk, Mortality Rates, and the Performance of Corporate Bonds*, Charlottesville, Va.: The Research Foundation of The Institute of Chartered Financial Analysts, 1989a.

———, "Measuring Corporate Bond Mortality and Performance," *Journal of Finance*, 44 (September 1989b), pp. 909–922.

Dyl, Edward A., and Joehnk, Michael D., "Sinking Funds and the Cost of Corporate Debt," *Journal of Finance*, 34 (September 1979), pp. 887–893.

Emanuel, David, "A Theoretical Model for Valuing Preferred Stock," *Journal of Finance*, 38 (September 1983), pp. 1133–1155.

Finnerty, John D.; Kalotay, Andrew J.; and Farrell, Francis X., *The Financial Manager's Guide to Evaluating Bond Refunding Opportunities*, Cambridge, Mass.: Ballinger, 1988.

Jen, Frank C., and Wert, James E., "The Effects of Call Risk on Corporate Bond Yields," *Journal of Finance*, 22 (December 1967), pp. 637–652.

Kalay, A., "Toward a Theory of Corporate Dividend Policy," unpublished Ph.D. thesis, University of Rochester, Rochester, New York, 1979.

Lewellen, Wilbur G., and Emery, Douglas R., "On the Matter of Parity Among Financial Obligations," *Journal of Finance*, 36 (March 1981), pp. 97–111.

Marks, Kenneth R., and Law, Warren A., "Hedging against Inflation with Floating-Rate Notes," *Harvard Business Review*, 58 (March-April 1980), pp. 106–112.

McConnell, J., and Schlarbaum, G., "The Income Bond Puzzle," *Chase Financial Quarterly*, (Summer 1982), pp. 8–28.

———, "Returns, Risks and the Pricing of Income Bonds, 1956–1976 (Does Money Have an Odor?)," *Journal of Business*, 54 (January 1981), pp. 33–63.

Myers, S., "Determinants of Corporate Borrowing," *Journal of Financial Economics*, (November 1977), pp. 147–176.

Ofer, Ahron R., and Taggart, Robert A., Jr., "Bond Refunding: A Clarifying Analysis," *Journal of Finance*, 32 (March 1977), pp. 21–30.

Pinches, George E., and Singleton, J. Clay, "The Adjustment of Stock Prices to Bond Rating Changes," *Journal of Finance*, 33 (March 1978), pp. 29–44.

Pye, Gordon, "The Value of Call Deferment on a Bond: Some Empirical Results," *Journal of Finance*, 22 (December 1967), pp. 623–636.

Smith, Clifford W., and Warner, Jerold B., "On Financial Contracting: An Analysis of Bond Covenants," *Journal of Financial Economics*, 7 (June 1979), pp. 117–161.

Wakeman, L., "Bond Rating Agencies and Capital Markets," working paper, Graduate School of Management, University of Rochester, Rochester, New York, 1978.

Weinstein, Mark I., "The Seasoning Process of New Corporate Bond Issues," *Journal of Finance*, 33 (December 1978), pp. 1343–1354.

———, "The Effect of a Rating Change Announcement on Bond Price," *Journal of Financial Economics*, (December 1977), pp. 329–350.

APPENDIX A TO CHAPTER 23

Refunding Decisions

Many articles have appeared on bond refunding, as indicated by the Selected References to this appendix. These articles — and the broad interest in refunding — were stimulated by large fluctuations in the interest rates during recent decades. This appendix discusses the debate about whether the appropriate discount rate is the before- or after-tax cost of debt. It also discusses debt refunding in an era of rising interest rates.

CHOOSING A DISCOUNT RATE FOR THE BOND REFUNDING DECISION

Bond refunding, which takes place when interest rates have fallen, may yield future cash benefits to the firm as the result of the reduction in bond interest payments. Once the contractual terms under which the new bonds will be sold have been established, the interest saving is known with certainty. Therefore, it is generally agreed that the discount rate should be the cost of debt. However, disagreement has arisen on whether the before-tax cost of debt or the after-tax cost of debt should be used, and this is a central question to be addressed in the materials which follow.

The net present value from a bond refunding can be expressed logically by Equation 23A.1:

$$\text{NPV} = \overset{(1)}{\underbrace{\sum_{t=1}^{n} \frac{(1 - T)(r_1 - r_2)D}{(1 + r_2)^t}}} - \overset{(2)}{\underbrace{\sum_{t=1}^{n} \frac{(1 - T)r_2 \Delta D}{(1 + r_2)^t}}}$$

$$\overset{(3)}{\underbrace{- \frac{\Delta D}{(1 + r_2)^n}}} - \overset{(4)}{\underbrace{[(1 - T)RC - \Delta D]}}, \tag{23A.1}$$

where

T = corporate income tax rate

RC = cost of refunding

r_1 = coupon rate on old issue

r_2 = coupon rate on new issue (also assumed to be the current yield on bonds of equivalent risk)

D = par value (or face value) of debt

n = remaining years to maturity on the old issue

ΔD = the incremental debt needed to pay for refunding costs.

The four numbered terms on the right-hand side of the equation represent the following:

1. Present value of after-tax interest savings on the old bond issue
2. Present value of interest that will be paid on incremental debt
3. Present value of repayment of the incremental debt at maturity
4. Present value of financing issued, the difference between after-tax refunding costs (such as the call premium and flotation costs) and the new financing issued to cover these costs. Later on, we shall assume that all new financing is via new debt.

The sense of each of the terms can also be readily explained. In the first term, the difference in the expression $(r_1 - r_2)(1 - T)$ is the after-tax interest savings, which is multiplied times the value of the old bonds and discounted to arrive at the present value of the interest savings (PVS). In the second term, the after-tax cost of whatever increase in debt is used to finance the refunding costs is also discounted back to the present. The third term is the present value of the incremental debt. In the fourth term, we start with the after-tax refunding costs and deduct the incremental debt. The difference must be the amount of financing needed to refund the debt issue. We have not thus far discussed the discount factor used in the present value calculations. We shall do that in the following analysis.

We begin by simplifying the second term, with the results shown in Equation 23A.2:

$$\sum_{t=1}^{n} \frac{(1-T)(r_2)\Delta D}{(1+r_2)^t} = \left[\frac{(1-T)(r_2)\Delta D}{(1+r_2)}\right] \sum_{t=0}^{n-1} \frac{1}{(1+r_2)^t}$$

$$= \left[\frac{(1-T)r_2\Delta D}{(1+r_2)}\right] \frac{1 - \dfrac{1}{(1+r_2)^n}}{1 - \dfrac{1}{(1+r_2)}}$$

$$= (1-T)\Delta D[1 - (1+r_2)^{-n}]. \qquad (23A.2)$$

First, we factored a $1/(1 + r_2)$ from the denominator. We were then able to evaluate the denominator, using a standard geometric series, to arrive at the results shown. Having the second term in this simplified form permits the equation to be simplified still further. By multiplying through and regrouping terms, we arrive at the results shown in Equation 23A.3:

$$\begin{aligned}
\text{NPV} &= PVS - \Delta D(1 - T)[1 - (1 + r_2)^{-n}] - \Delta D(1 + r_2)^{-n} - [(1 - T)RC - \Delta D] \\
&= PVS - \Delta D + \Delta D(1 + r_2)^{-n} + T\,\Delta D[1 - (1 + r_2)^{-n}] - \Delta D(1 + r_2)^{-n} \\
&\quad - [(1 - T)RC] + \Delta D \\
&= PVS + T\,\Delta D[1 - (1 + r_2)^{-n}] - (1 - T)RC.
\end{aligned}
\tag{23A.3}$$

If the net present value expression is to be greater than zero, then the after-tax refunding costs must be exceeded by the sum of the other terms in the expression. To show this relationship, we formulate the inequality shown in Equation 23A.4:

$$\sum_{t=1}^{n} \frac{(1 - T)(r_1 - r_2)D}{(1 + r_2)^t} + T\,\Delta D[1 - (1 + r_2)^{-n}] > (1 - T)RC.
\tag{23A.4}$$

Thus far, the analysis has been within the framework of debt with a finite time to maturity. If we let n go to infinity, Equation 23A.4 becomes 23A.5:

$$\frac{(1 - T)(r_1 - r_2)D}{r_2} + T\,\Delta D > (1 - T)RC.
\tag{23A.5}$$

The first term represents the standard capitalization of an infinite stream. In the second term, the value of $1/(1 + r_2)^n$ becomes zero.

Additionally, if the total after-tax refunding costs are financed by debt so that we have $\Delta D = (1 - T)RC$, we obtain Equation 23A.6:[1]

$$\frac{(1 - T)(r_1 - r_2)D}{r_2} > (1 - T)RC - T(1 - T)RC$$

$$\frac{(1 - T)(r_1 - r_2)D}{r_2} > (1 - T)RC(1 - T)$$

$$\frac{(1 - T)(r_1 - r_2)D}{(1 - T)r_2} > (1 - T)RC.
\tag{23A.6}$$

The result in 23A.6 is the same as that obtained by Ofer and Taggart [1977] when all new financing is via incremental debt. The significance of this result is that if the refunding costs are financed entirely by debt, the incremental debt generates a tax shelter on the full amount of the financing. Hence, the relevant cost becomes the after-tax cost of debt.[2]

Gordon [1974] argued for the use of after-tax cash flows with the before-tax cost of debt as the discount factor. However, his proof is flawed by the use of the valuation model for risky returns in his analysis of nonrisky returns. Also, when bonds are used to finance the refunding costs, additional tax shelter is achieved so that the discount rate is the after-tax rate on the refunding bonds.

---

[1]See Laber [1979b].

[2]Note, however, that 23A.6 is also equivalent to discounting the before-tax cash flows at the before-tax cost of debt.

Livingston [1980] criticized the Ofer and Taggart results as well as equivalent text-book procedures developed under the same financing assumptions. To view the nature of the criticism, first define the gain in the value of shareholders' equity as the excess of the gains from refunding over the after-tax refunding costs, as shown in Equation 23A.7:

$$\frac{(1 - T)(r_1 - r_2)D}{(1 - T)r_2} - (1 - T)RC = \Delta S. \tag{23A.7}$$

Next, cancel the $(1 - T)$ expressions in the first term and separate the elements of the numerator.

$$\left(\frac{r_1 D}{r_2} - D\right) - (1 - T)(RC) = \Delta S. \tag{23A.8}$$

Livingston argued that the gain from refunding appears to be the market value of the old bond less the par value of the new bond. But, he objected that the old bond cannot sell for more than its call price plus other (relatively small) refunding costs. Technically, Livingston is correct. But, the $D(r_1 - r_2)/r_2$ term still measures the value of the interest "saving" from refunding the old bond. The original r_1 and the new r_2 on callable bonds are higher than the rates on noncallable bonds since the issuer must compensate investors for the call option.

REFUNDING WHEN INTEREST RATES HAVE RISEN

Widely fluctuating interest rates give rise to opportunities for bond refunding. Bonds sold at high interest rates in the late sixties and early seventies provided opportunities for refunding when interest rates fell in the mid-1970s. The resumption of the sharp rise in interest rates caused those bonds, which were sold at lower interest levels, to go to a discount by the late 1970s. This raised questions about the profitability of advanced refunding of discounted bonds. The early 1980s and 1990s experienced declines in interest rates.

Interest rate fluctuations in which interest rates go either lower or higher are said to provide opportunities for bond refunding. Lower interest rates may provide opportunities for interest rate savings. Higher interest rates may provide opportunities for buying in bonds at a discount. Before becoming immersed in the details of the following analysis, we should like first to present as an overview some general principles that should be kept in mind as a framework for the subsequent detailed computations.

In the absence of special characteristics or restrictions, neither falling interest rates nor rising interest rates provide an obvious basis for savings to corporate financial managers. Lower or higher interest rates simply represent the costs of funds at a particular time, and without special restrictions provide no opportunities for gains or losses. What makes refunding at lower interest rates advantageous is the call option that is inserted in corporate bond indentures. For example, if the bond is issued at a 9 percent interest rate and if interest rates subsequently fall to 6 percent, a noncallable perpetual bond issued at a par value of 100 would sell at 150 at the lower 6 percent interest yield basis. If the company has a call option which permits it to buy in the bond at 105, for example, the firm can achieve interest savings with a substantial present value.

On the other hand, if the market had accurately priced the value of the call privilege, then the bond refunding would not represent a net gain. In such a case, the bond refunding would represent only the interest savings that the company would have to realize in order to be compensated for the higher yield it was required to offer on callable bonds.

With respect to bonds that sell at a discount because interest rates have risen substantially, there is no special privilege analogous to the call option. The firm simply goes into the market and buys its bonds at a discount because the going yield is higher than the coupon rates paid on its existing bonds. One attractive feature to business firms is that the difference between the value of the bond shown on its books and the market price at which the bonds are purchased can be recorded as a realized profit from the standpoint of reporting income. The firm is thus able to report higher income than it otherwise would. However, from a cash flow standpoint, this is a disadvantage, not an advantage. The reported profit is subject to income taxation. The gain is simply a paper gain. It has not produced an increment of positive cash flows for the company. The net effect of reporting the income and the taxation of it is to reduce the cash flows for the firm, not to increase them. Thus, unless the taxation can be avoided, net cash flows are reduced by buying in the discount bonds.

Consider the situation where interest rates have risen substantially above the coupon rates on the firm's outstanding bonds. For example, suppose that Firm F had sold ten $1,000 perpetual bonds at 6 percent, but the prevailing yield on such bonds is now 10 percent. The old bonds now sell for $600 each. Firm F can retire the bonds at $6,000, reporting a profit of $4,000. The interest paid on the old bonds is $600. The total interest on the $6,000 of new bonds issued at 10 percent to buy up the old bonds would also be $600. Thus, Firm F experiences no change in interest costs. If the gain of $4,000 is taxed at, say, 40 percent, the net cash flow to the firm is reduced by $1,600. Thus, from a pure cash flow standpoint, all that has really happened is that the firm has an additional cash outflow required by the amount of taxes it has to pay on the increase in reported income.

The Internal Revenue Code provides that a corporation may elect to have excluded from gross income the gain when it buys its own bond at a discount.[3] But, if a corporation does make this election, the basis of the property against which the obligations were issued is reduced by the amount of the gain.[4] This may more than offset the advantage of not reporting the gain from the repurchase of the discount bond, since the depreciation basis is reduced and the basis for determining the gain or loss on a subsequent sale is also reduced. Thus, it is difficult to envisage how the negative effects of the tax payments on the actual cash flows of the firm can be avoided.

A superior strategy would be to buy a bond of the same quality at par that pays 10 percent. The interest income will just cancel with the interest expense of the old bond, but there will be no tax liability. From a cash flow standpoint, the firm avoids the $1,600 cash tax payment.

---

[3]Internal Revenue Code, Secs. 108(a); 1.108(a)-1.

[4]Ibid., Secs. 1017; 1.1017-1.

An article in *Business Week* of November 12, 1979, described the very active operations of investment bankers in arranging for helping clients buy up bonds at a discount. The context of this presentation was that the firms were going to have to make purchases for bond sinking funds in one, two, three, or five years anyhow. In other words, the firms had decided that it was a good strategy to make anticipatory purchases, since when the purchases would have to be made in subsequent years, the bonds might not be at such deep discounts. The bonds could be purchased at a saving and used to meet future sinking fund requirements as they became effective.

We believe that this analysis also requires qualification. By buying its own bonds at a discount, a firm would have reported profits and taxable income. The basis for the anticipatory bond purchases appears to be the expectation that interest rates would be lower in the future. If the firm really believed that interest rates were going to be lower, it could buy bonds of equal quality (or a portfolio of bonds) and then hold them until it was required to purchase bonds for its own sinking fund. If interest rates fell in the meantime, the firm would have realized capital gain on the bonds that it had purchased. It would have an equal paper loss on its own bonds that it did not purchase. At the same time, it would be receiving a higher yield on the bonds that it purchased at the market when interest rates were higher. Furthermore, it would have obtained protection against a rise in the required yield on its own bonds through quality deterioration. But, the fundamental point is that at a minimum, it would defer the taxes on the capital gain involved in the interest rate change by buying bonds other than its own.

These general observations provide the foundation for a key to understanding some of the literature in this area. Ang [1975] made a presentation in which he sought to demonstrate that refunding was advantageous not only when current interest rates fell below interest rates at issue but also possibly when current interest rates rose above the interest rate at issue. Single-period and multiperiod models were used along with the hypothetical application using dynamic programming.

However, Mayor and McCoin [1978] demonstrated (following the general logic set forth in this analysis) that refunding when interest rates have risen cannot be profitable unless implementation costs are negative. Implementation costs are measured by brokerage commissions plus the difference between the average purchase price and the current market price. Implementation costs cannot be reasonably assumed to be negative. In the multiperiod model, refunding when interest rates have risen again depends upon very extreme assumptions. First, implementation costs are assumed to be very small. Second, implicit in the analysis is that interest rates will subsequently fall, and the firm will realize a capital gain from the interest rate change. This second assumption then means that the firm is able to forecast future interest rates correctly, and part of the gain from refunding is to buy the bonds when interest rates are high and sell them when interest rates are lower. If the firm is able to forecast future interest rates, it does not have to engage in refunding to make a profit. It will simply buy bonds when interest rates are high and sell them when interest rates have fallen.

This general result for refunding criteria when interest rates have risen can be made more explicit with reference to the general points made by employing the framework developed by Kalotay [1978]. The most general expression for the advanced refunding of discounted debt is set forth by Kalotay in Equation 23A.9, where NPV is expressed as a percentage of the debt issue.

$$\text{NPV} = -p + \sum_{t=1}^{n} \frac{(1 - T)r_1}{[1 + (1 - T)r_2]^t} + \frac{1}{[1 + (1 - T)r_2]^n}$$

$$- \sum_{t=0}^{M} \frac{T(1 - p)}{M + 1} \times \frac{1}{[1 + (1 - T)r_2]^t} - (1 - T)RC'. \qquad \textbf{(23A.9)}$$

The symbols are the same as defined earlier, with the exception of p and M; p is the price at which the discounted bond can be purchased, expressed as a decimal ratio of its par value. M is the number of years over which the taxable gain can be amortized. The second term on the right-hand side of the equation is the discounted interest payments. The third term is the discounted principal payment. The fourth term is represented by the tax obligations associated with the gain $(1 - p)$. The RC' term represents other refunding costs that have not been explicitly dealt with to this point. In Equation 23A.10, the same equation is rewritten with the summation expressions carried out.

$$\text{NPV} = -p + \frac{r_1}{r_2}\left\{1 - [1 + (1 - T)r_2]^{-n}\right\} + [1 + (1 - T)r_2]^{-n} - \frac{T(1 - p)}{M + 1}$$

$$\times \left\{ \frac{[1 + (1 - T)r_2] - [1 + (1 - T)r_2]^{-(M-1)}}{(1 - T)r_2} \right\} - (1 - T)RC'. \qquad \textbf{(23A.10)}$$

The nature of the expressions in the above equation can be shown by using illustrative values for the variables involved. Let $p = 0.57$, $r_1 = 0.0425$, $r_2 = 0.11$, $n = 18$, $RC' = 0.02$, $T = 0.5$, and $M = 18$. Under the assumptions in the illustration, the value of the discounted interest payments and the discounted principal payments was 0.62, while the purchase price of the bond was assumed to be 0.57. This represented a gain of 0.05. The taxable income, however, is the difference between the par value of the bond at one and the purchase price of 0.57. Thus, the taxable gain is 0.43. The present value of the tax obligations then turns out to be -0.13. The difference between the 0.05 gain from buying a bond with a value of 0.62 at 0.57 is offset by the additional tax obligations of 0.13. The result is a negative 9 percent $(-0.57 + 0.24 + 0.38 - 0.13 - 0.01 = -0.09)$.

Kalotay emphasizes that profitable refunding when interest rates have risen is probably plausible only if for some reason there are no tax obligations or if the tax obligations are amortized over an extremely long period of time. To illustrate this, Kalotay takes the extreme case where the firm discounts interest payments and principal payments at the after-tax cost of debt while the individual investor in the market uses the before-tax rate of interest as the discount factor. This results in an even lower value of p. Under the numerical values previously assumed, the value of p becomes 0.48. Or, alternatively, the underlying determinants of p are shown in Equation 23A.11. Suppose

$$p = \sum_{t=1}^{n} \frac{r_1}{(1 + r_2)^t} + \frac{1}{(1 + r_2)^n} = \frac{r_1}{r_2}[1 - (1 + r_2)^{-n}] + \frac{1}{(1 + r_2)^n}. \qquad \textbf{(23A.11)}$$

If these underlying determinants of *p* are substituted in Equation 23A.10, and if we use the numerical values previously assumed plus the assumption that *p* is determined by the before-tax cost of debt, the NPV becomes −2 percent ($-0.48 + 0.24 + 0.38 - 0.15 - 0.01 = -0.02$). Kalotay comments that the assumption that *p* is determined by discounting at the before-tax cost of debt is more favorable to the refunding decision at higher interest rates. Yet, under plausible relationships, the NPV is still negative.

The thrust of the logic set forth above and the concrete framework presented by Kalotay is this: To initiate the possibility of favorable refunding requires that the price at which the bond can be purchased be lower than the appropriately discounted interest payments plus the discounted principal payment. Second, the difference between the par value of the bond and its purchase price is taxable income. Profitable refunding requires either that this differential is for some reason not taxable or, alternatively, that the amortization period for the taxable income be extremely long.

SUMMARY

We reiterate our general conclusions. When declines in the general level of interest rates have occurred, the call privilege appears to provide an opportunity for reducing interest expenses. But, if the call privilege had been correctly priced, then, on average, the exercise of this option simply compensates the firm for the higher interest rates that it paid by having the call provision in the indenture of the bonds it sold. The firm paid a higher interest rate differential that it can recoup only by exercising the option it has purchased. The refunding operation then is required to "balance the books" in some sense.

The other face of bond refunding is considered when interest rates have risen. Unless the taxes on the gain from buying back the bonds can be avoided, the net cash flow effects are negative. The absolute amount of interest costs would be essentially unchanged. Therefore, unless the taxes can be avoided without other disadvantages, the effects of refunding when interest rates have risen would appear to be unfavorable. The conclusion seems to be that bond refunding has but one face, not two.

SELECTED REFERENCES

Ang, James S., "The Two Faces of Bond Refunding," *Journal of Finance*, 30 (June 1975), pp. 869–874.

———, "The Two Faces of Bond Refunding: Reply," *Journal of Finance*, 33 (March 1978), pp. 354–356.

Bierman, Harold, "The Bond Refunding Decision," *Financial Management*, 1 (Summer 1972), pp. 22–29.

Gordon, M. J., "A General Solution to the Buy or Lease Decision: A Pedagogical Note," *Journal of Finance*, 29 (March 1974), pp. 245–250.

Kalotay, A. J., "On the Advanced Refunding of Discounted Debt," *Financial Management*, 7 (Summer 1978), pp. 7–13.

Kolodny, Richard, "The Refunding Decision in Near Perfect Markets," *Journal of Finance*, 29 (December 1974), pp. 1467–1477.

Laber, Gene, "The Effect of Bond Refunding on Shareholder Wealth: Comment," *Journal of Finance*, 34 (June 1979a), pp. 795–799.

————, "Implications of Discount Rates and Financing Assumptions for Bond Refunding Decisions," *Financial Management,* 8 (Spring 1979b), pp. 7–12.

Livingston, Miles, "Bond Refunding Reconsidered: Comment," *Journal of Finance,* 35 (March 1980), pp. 191–196.

————, "The Effect of Bond Refunding on Shareholder Wealth: Comment," *Journal of Finance,* 34 (June 1979), pp. 801–804.

Mayor, Thomas H., and McCoin, Kenneth G.,

"Bond Refunding: One or Two Faces?" *Journal of Finance,* 33 (March 1978), pp. 349–353.

Ofer, Ahron R., and Taggart, Robert A., Jr., "Bond Refunding: A Clarifying Analysis," *Journal of Finance,* 32 (March 1977), pp. 21–30.

————, "'Bond Refunding Reconsidered': Reply," *Journal of Finance,* 35 (March 1980), pp. 197–200.

CHAPTER 24

Lease Financing

Firms are generally interested in using buildings and equipment. One way of obtaining their use is to buy them, but an alternative is to lease them. Prior to the 1950s, leasing was most often associated with real estate — land and buildings — but today, virtually any kind of fixed asset can be leased. We estimate that from 15 to 20 percent of all new capital equipment put in use by business each year is leased. In many cases, our analysis will show that leasing is a perfect substitute for borrowing. Hence, managers should think of the lease/borrow decision rather than the lease/buy decision.

Leasing simultaneously provides for the use of assets and their financing. One advantage over debt is that the lessor has a better position than a creditor if the user firm experiences financial difficulties. If the lessee does not meet the lease obligations, the lessor has a stronger legal right to take back the asset, because the lessor still legally owns it. A creditor, even a secured creditor, encounters costs and delays in recovering assets that have been directly or indirectly financed. Since the lessor has less risk than other financing sources used in acquiring assets, the riskier the firm seeking financing, the greater is the reason for the supplier of financing to formulate a leasing arrangement rather than a loan. The relative tax positions of lessors and users of assets may also affect the lease versus borrow decision.

TYPES OF LEASES

Leases take several different forms, the most important of which are sale and leaseback, service or operating leases, and straight financial leases. These three major types of leases are described below.

Sale and Leaseback

Under a sale and leaseback arrangement, a firm owning land, buildings, or equipment sells the property to a financial institution and simultaneously executes an agreement to lease the property back for a certain period under specific terms.

Note that the seller, or *lessee,* immediately receives the purchase price put up by the buyer, or *lessor.* At the same time, the seller-lessee retains the use of the property. This parallel is carried over to the lease payment schedule. Under a mortgage loan arrangement, the financial institution receives a series of equal payments just sufficient to amortize the loan and to provide the lender with a specified rate of return on investment. Under a sale and leaseback arrangement, the lease payments are set up in the same manner. The payments are sufficient to return the full purchase price to the financial institution in addition to providing it with some return on its investment.

Operating Leases

Operating, or service, leases include both financing and maintenance services. IBM is one of the pioneers of the service lease contract. Computers and office copying machines, together with automobiles and trucks, are the primary types of equipment covered by operating leases. The leases ordinarily call for the lessor to maintain and service the leased equipment, and the costs of this maintenance are either built into the lease payments or contracted for separately.

Another important characteristic of the operating lease is that, frequently, it is not fully amortized. In other words, the payments required under the lease contract are *not* sufficient to recover the full cost of the equipment. Obviously, however, the lease contract is written for considerably less than the expected life of the leased equipment, and the lessor expects to recover the cost either in subsequent renewal payments or on disposal of the equipment.

A final feature of the operating lease is that, frequently, it contains a cancellation clause, giving the lessee the right to cancel the lease and return the equipment before the expiration of the basic agreement. This is a put option that allows return of the equipment if technological developments render it obsolete or if it simply is no longer needed, which is an important consideration for the lessee.

Financial Leases

A strict financial lease is one that does not provide for maintenance services, is not cancellable, and is fully amortized (that is, the lessor contracts for rental payments equal to the full price of the leased equipment). The typical arrangement involves the following steps:

1. The firm that will use the equipment selects the specific items it requires and negotiates the price and delivery terms with the manufacturer or distributor.

2. Next, the user firm arranges with a bank or leasing company for the latter to buy the equipment from the manufacturer or distributor, simultaneously executing an agreement to lease the equipment from the financial institution. The terms call for full

amortization of the financial institution's cost, plus a return on the lessor's investment. The lessee generally has the option to renew the lease at a reduced rental on expiration of the basic lease but does not have the right to cancel the basic lease without completely paying off the financial institution.

Financial leases are almost the same as sale and leaseback arrangements, the main difference being that the leased equipment is new and the lessor buys it from a manufacturer or a distributor instead of from the user-lessee. A sale and leaseback can thus be thought of as a special type of financial lease.

Internal Revenue Service Requirements for a Lease

The full amount of the annual lease payments is deductible for income tax purposes, provided the Internal Revenue Service agrees that a particular contract is a genuine lease and not simply an installment loan called a lease. This makes it important that the lease contract be written in a form acceptable to the IRS. Following are the major requirements for bona fide lease transactions from the standpoint of the IRS.

1. The term must be less than 30 years; otherwise, the lease is regarded as a form of sale.
2. The rent must represent a reasonable return to the lessor — in the range of 7 to 12 percent on the investment.
3. The renewal option must be bona fide, and this requirement can best be met by giving the lessee the first option to meet an equal bona fide outside offer.
4. There must be no repurchase option; if there is, the lessee should merely be given parity with an equal outside offer.

ACCOUNTING FOR LEASES

In November 1976, the Financial Accounting Standards Board issued its Statement of Financial Accounting Standards No. 13, *Accounting for Leases*. Like other FASB statements, the standards set forth must be followed by business firms if their financial statements are to receive certification by auditors. FASB Statement No. 13 has implications both for the utilization of leases and for their accounting treatment. The elements of FASB Statement No. 13 most relevant for financial analysis of leases are summarized below.

For some types of leases, this FASB statement requires that the obligation be capitalized on the asset side of the balance sheet with a reduced lease obligation on the liability side. The accounting treatment depends on the type of lease. The classification is more detailed than the two categories of operating and financial leases described above.

From the standpoint of the lessee:
1. Capital leases
2. Operating leases (all leases other than capital leases)

From the standpoint of the lessor:

1. Sales-type leases
2. Direct financing leases
3. Leveraged leases
4. Operating leases (all leases other than the first three)

A lease is classified in Statement No. 13 as a capital lease if it meets one or more of four Paragraph 7 criteria:

1. The lease transfers ownership of the property to the lessee by the end of the lease term.
2. The lease gives the lessee the option to purchase the property at a price sufficiently below the expected fair value of the property that the exercise of the option is highly probable.
3. The lease term is equal to 75 percent or more of the estimated economic life of the property.
4. The present value of the minimum lease payments exceeds 90 percent of the fair value of the property at the inception of the lease. The discount factor to be used in calculating the present value is the implicit rate used by the lessor or the lessee's incremental borrowing rate, whichever is lower. (Note that the lower discount factor represents a higher present value factor and, therefore, a higher calculated present value for a given pattern of lease payments. It thus increases the likelihood that the 90 percent test will be met and that the lease will be classified as a capital lease.)

From the standpoint of the lessee, if a lease is not a capital lease, it is classified as an operating lease. From the standpoint of the lessor, four types of leases are defined: (1) sales-type leases, (2) direct financing leases, (3) leveraged leases, and (4) operating leases representing all leases other than the first three types. Sales-type leases and direct financing leases meet one or more of the four Paragraph 7 criteria and both of the Paragraph 8 criteria, which are:

1. Collectibility of the minimum lease payments is reasonably predictable.
2. No important uncertainties surround the amount of unreimbursable costs yet to be incurred by the lessor under the lease.

Sales-type leases give rise to profit (or loss) to the lessor — the fair value of the leased property at the inception of the lease is greater (or less) than its cost of carrying amount. Sales-type leases normally arise when manufacturers or dealers use leasing in marketing their products. Direct financing leases are leases other than leveraged leases for which the cost-of-carrying amount is equal to the fair value of the leased property at the inception of the lease. Leveraged leases are direct financing leases in which substantial financing is provided by a long-term creditor on a nonrecourse basis with respect to the general credit of the lessor.

Accounting by Lessees

For operating leases, rentals must be charged to expense over the lease term, with disclosures of future rental obligations in total as well as by each of the following five years. For lessees, capital leases are to be capitalized and shown on the balance sheet both as a fixed asset and a noncurrent obligation. Capitalization represents the present value of the minimum lease payments minus that portion of lease payments representing executory costs such as insurance, maintenance, and taxes to be paid by the lessor (including any profit return in such charges). The discount factor is as described in Paragraph 7(4) — the lower of the implicit rates used by the lessor and the incremental borrowing rate of the lessee.

The asset must be amortized in a manner consistent with the lessee's normal depreciation policy for owned assets. During the lease term, each lease payment is to be allocated between a reduction of the obligation and the interest expense to produce a constant rate of interest on the remaining balance of the obligation. Thus, for capital leases, the balance sheet includes the items in Table 24.1.

In addition to the balance sheet capitalization of capital leases, substantial additional footnote disclosures are required for both capital and operating leases. These include a description of leasing arrangements, an analysis of leased property under capital leases by major classes of property, a schedule by years of future minimum lease payments (with executory and interest costs broken out for capital leases), and contingent rentals for operating leases.

FASB Statement No. 13 sets forth requirements for capitalizing leases and for standardizing disclosures by lessees for both capital leases and operating leases. Lease commitments, therefore, do not represent ''off-balance-sheet'' financing for capital assets, and standard disclosure requirements make general the footnote reporting of information on operating leases. Hence, the argument that leasing represents a form of off-balance-sheet financing that lenders may not take into account in their analysis of the financial position of firms seeking financing is simply invalid.

It is unlikely that sophisticated lenders were ever fooled by off-balance-sheet leasing obligations. However, the capitalization of capital leases and the standard disclosure requirements for operating leases will make it easier for general users of financial reports to obtain additional information on firms' leasing obligations. Hence, the requirements of FASB Statement No. 13 are useful. Probably, the extent or use of leasing will remain

TABLE 24.1   Company X Balance Sheet

Assets	December 31, 1992	1993	Liabilities	December 31, 1992	1993
Leased property under capital leases, less accumulated amortization	XXX	XXX	Current: Obligations under capital leases	XXX	XXX
			Noncurrent: Obligations under capital leases	XXX	XXX

substantially unaltered, since the particular circumstances that have provided a basis for its use in the past are not likely to be greatly affected by the increased disclosure requirements.

THE FINANCING DECISION: LEASE VERSUS BORROW

We next consider the framework for the analysis of the cost of owning with the cost of leasing. The form of leasing to be analyzed initially will be a pure financial lease that is fully amortized, noncancellable, and without provision for maintenance services. Furthermore, we assume that the asset's salvage value is zero and that there is no investment tax credit.

In concept, the first screening test is whether, from a capital budgeting standpoint, the project passes the investment hurdle rate. The second question is then whether leasing or some other method of financing, namely borrowing, is the least expensive method of financing the project.

Alternatively, it could be argued that we do not know what the cost of capital (and, therefore, the investment screening rate) is until we have determined the least expensive method of financing. Having determined this method, we can determine the applicable investment screening hurdle rate for the decision of whether to undertake the project from a capital budgeting standpoint.

The Lessor's Point of View. To lay a foundation for the leasing versus owning cost comparison, the lessor's point of view will first be considered. The leasing company, or lessor, could be a commercial bank, a subsidiary of a commercial bank, or an independent leasing company. These various types of lessors are considered to be providing financial intermediation services of essentially the same kind. Each form of financial intermediary is considered to be providing a product, which represents a form of senior debt financing to the company that uses the equipment. Since the product that is being sold by the financial intermediary is a debt instrument, the income to that intermediary is considered to be a return on debt that earns the intermediary's cost of capital. This is equivalent to the judgment that the financial intermediary's cost of capital, composed of both debt and equity capital, is approximately equal to the rate charged on the debt (or equivalent) instruments that comprise its assets (the assets of the lessor in our analysis).

We can then proceed to calculate the required lease-rental charge that must be made by the lessor to obtain a fair rate of return for a lending position. To illustrate the analysis, assume the following data:

$$I_0 = \text{cost of an asset} = \$20,000$$

$$\text{Dep} = \text{annual economic and tax depreciation charge}$$

$$k_b = \text{before-tax cost of debt} = 8\%$$

$$T = \text{lessor's corporate tax rate} = 40\%$$

$$n = \text{economic life and tax depreciation life of the asset} = 5 \text{ years}$$

$$\text{NPV}_{LOR} = \text{net present value of the lease-rental income from the assets to the lessor}$$

With the above facts, the equilibrium lease-rental rate in a competitive market of lessors can be calculated. What has been posed is a standard capital budgeting question: What cash flow return from the use of an asset will earn the applicable cost of capital? The investment in the capital budgeting project is $-I_0$. The return is composed of two elements: the cash inflow from the lease rental and the tax shelter from depreciation. The discount factor is the lessor's weighted cost of capital, which, as we have indicated, will be equal to the applicable rate on debt instruments of the risk of the cash flows involved. As Myers, Dill, and Bautista [1976] have pointed out, the weighted average cost of capital of the financial intermediary is

$$k_L = k_{UL}(1 - \lambda T). \tag{24.1}$$

For the financial intermediary, the lambda (λ) is the debt per dollar of assets leased. In other words, it is the capital structure employed in the leasing project. Equation 24.1 is the Modigliani-Miller definition of the weighted average cost of capital, which was discussed in Chapter 15. For the data assumed in the example, we can compute the cost of capital of the lessor by using Equation 24.1 as shown below. Here we postulate that the all-equity financing rate for the lessor (k_{UL}) is 8.57 percent and that the debt-to-assets ratio, λ, is 0.75.

$$\begin{aligned} k_L &= k_{UL}(1 - \lambda T) \\ &= 8.57\%[1 - 0.75(0.4)] \\ &= 6\% \end{aligned}$$

The after-tax weighted cost of capital to the lessor is 6 percent. In other words, the bank or leasing company has to earn at least 6 percent after taxes in order for the lease to have a positive net present value. Note that the before-tax rate of return, which is also the lessor's lending rate, will be

$$k_b = \frac{k_L}{1 - T} = \frac{.06}{1 - .4} = 10\%.$$

Next, we can compute the minimum competitive lease fee which would be charged by the lessor. Equation 24.2 discounts the lease cash flows at the lessor's after-tax cost of capital. The cash flows are the after-tax lease payments received plus the depreciation tax shield provided because the lessor owns the asset. The NPV of the lease to the lessor is

$$\begin{aligned} \text{NPV}_{LOR} &= -I_0 + \sum_{t=1}^{n} \frac{L_t(1 - T) + T\text{Dep}_t}{(1 + k_L)^t} \\ &= -I_0 + \text{PVIFA}(6\%, 5 \text{ yrs.})[L_t(1 - T) + T\text{Dep}_t], \tag{24.2} \end{aligned}$$

where

L_t = periodic lease payment (assumed to be paid at the end of each period)

Dep_t = amount of depreciation expense in Period t. Using straight line depreciation, $\text{Dep}_t = \$4,000$.

We can now solve for the equilibrium lease-rental rate required by the lessor by utilizing the data inputs we have provided.[1] The NPV of the lease is set equal to zero so that we can compute the minimum lease payment required by the lessor. The minimum fee will also be the competitive fee if the leasing industry is perfectly competitive.

$$0 = -\$20,000 + (4.2124)[0.6L_t + 0.4(\$4,000)]$$
$$L_t = \$5,246$$

The Lessee's Point of View. Presented with a lease-rental rate of $5,246, the user firm takes the lease fee as an input in making a comparison of the cost of leasing with the cost of borrowing. The analysis of the possible benefits of leasing as compared with borrowing involves the analysis of the following cash flows:

1. A cash savings equal to the dollar amount of the investment outlay, I_0, which the firm does not have to incur if it leases.

2. A cash outflow amounting to the present value of the after-tax lease dollars which must be paid out, $PV[L_t(1 - T)]$.

3. The present value of the opportunity cost of the lost depreciation tax shield, $PV(T\text{Dep}_t)$.

4. The present value of the *change* in the interest tax shield on debt which is displaced by the lease financing, $PV[T\Delta(k_bB_t)]$.

These four terms are presented in Equation 24.3, which gives the net advantage of leasing, NAL, as compared with borrowing in present value terms:

$$\text{NAL} = I_0 - PV[L_t(1 - T)] - PV[T\text{Dep}_t] + PV[T\Delta(k_bB_t)]. \qquad \textbf{(24.3)}$$

We shall assume that from the standpoint of the user firm, debt and lease financing are perfect substitutes. This is certainly true for strict financial leases. Therefore, the fourth term in Equation 24.3 reflects a dollar-for-dollar substitution of debt tax shield for leasing tax shield applied to the portion of the asset which would be debt-financed at the project's optimal capital structure.

Since both the lease payments and the foregone depreciation tax shields have the same risk for the lessee as for the lessor, they can be discounted at the before-tax cost of debt, that is, 10 percent. Alternatively, as shown by Myers, Dill, and Bautista [1976], we can discount the cash flows exclusive of interest tax shields at the after-tax cost of capital (which is 6 percent). In order to see why, note that the fourth term in Equation 24.3 is the opportunity cost of the interest tax shield which is lost because the firm decides to lease rather than borrow to finance ownership. Throughout the text, we have explicitly excluded interest costs from our definition of cash flows because the effect of these costs as well as their tax shield is accounted for by discounting at the after-tax cost of capital. Given our assumptions, discounting the first three terms in Equation 24.3 at the after-tax

---

[1] We have assumed that all lease payments are made in arrears, that is, at the end of each year. However, most actual lease contracts require lease payments to be made at the beginning of each time period.

cost of debt is the same as discounting all four terms at the before-tax cost of debt. Therefore, we can write the NPV of the lease from the lessee's point of view as

$$\text{NAL} = I_0 - \sum_{t=1}^{n} \frac{L_t(1 - T) + T\text{Dep}_t}{[1 + (1 - T)k_b]^t}. \tag{24.4}$$

Note that Equation 24.4 is exactly the same as Equation 24.2, the value of the lease from the lessor's point of view, if two conditions are met: (1) The lessee and the lessor have the same tax rate, T, and (2) the after-tax weighted average cost of capital to the lessor, k_L, is equal to the after-tax cost of borrowing to the lessee. For the time being, we have assumed the tax rates of the lessee and lessor are equal, but they need not be. The discount rates have to be the same because the cash flows in the numerators of Equations 24.2 and 24.4 are identical and have the same risk. The rate earned by the lessor is the rate paid by the lessee. Substituting the numbers from our example into Equation 24.4, we have

$$\begin{aligned}
\text{NAL} &= I_0 - \text{PVIFA}(6\%,5 \text{ yrs.})[L_t(1 - T)] - \text{PVIFA}(6\%,5 \text{ yrs.})[T\text{Dep}_t] \\
&= 20{,}000 - 4.2124(5{,}246)(1 - 0.4) - 4.2124(0.4)(4{,}000) \\
&= 20{,}000 - 13{,}259 - 6{,}740 \\
&= 20{,}000 - 19{,}999 \cong 0.
\end{aligned}$$

This result tells us that the firm is indifferent between the two methods of financing the project, namely leasing or borrowing. The first and last terms on the right-hand side of the equation represent the costs of borrowing in order to own the asset. The investment outlay is $\$I$ and the lost depreciation tax shield is $T\text{Dep}_t$. The second term is the cost of leasing.

$$\begin{aligned}
\text{Cost of borrowing} &= I_0 - \text{PVIFA}(6\%,5 \text{ yrs.})[T\text{Dep}_t] = 20{,}000 - 6{,}740 \\
&= \$13{,}260. \\
\text{Cost of leasing} &= \text{PVIFA}(6\%,5 \text{ yrs.})[L_t(1 - T)] \\
&= \$13{,}259
\end{aligned}$$

In our example, the cost of borrowing equals the cost of leasing; hence, the net advantage of leasing is zero. Thus, there is equilibrium between the lessor market and the user market. The lessor earns its cost of capital, which determines the lease-rental charge that it must make. At this lease-rental rate, and given that the lessee and lessor have identical tax rates, then the lessee is indifferent between borrowing to own the asset or leasing it.

Note that in determining the lessor's cost of capital, we started with the all-equity financing rate for the lessor, k_{UL}, that would be applicable to the debt instrument portfolio, or lease portfolio, of the financial intermediary. Given the appropriate leverage ratio for the lessor, λ, we arrived at the after-tax cost of capital of the lessor. When this is placed on a before-tax basis, it represents the cost of debt borrowing or the implicit capital cost in the lease financing contract. All the required conditions for indifference between leasing and borrowing are obtained.

The Effect of Taxes.   Whenever the lessor has a higher tax rate than the lessee, there is a possibility (but not necessity) of a financial advantage of leasing over borrowing in order to finance a project. In order to illustrate this result, let us assume that the numbers from the lessor's point of view are unchanged. With a 40 percent tax rate, the lessor would require a lease fee of $L_t = \$5,246$ in order to earn 6 percent after taxes. But, suppose the lessee's tax rate is 20 percent rather than 40 percent as assumed earlier. If so, the after-tax cost of debt to the lessee increases from $(1 - T)k_b = (1 - .4).10 = 6\%$ to $(1 - .2).10 = 8\%$. Substituting the lease fee and depreciation opportunity costs into Equation 24.4, along with the lower 20 percent tax rate and the higher after-tax borrowing rate (8 percent), we have

$$NAL = I_0 - PVIFA(8\%,5 \text{ yrs.})[L_t(1 - T)] - PVIFA(8\%,5 \text{ yrs.})T Dep_t$$
$$= 20,000 - 3.9927(5,246)(1 - .2) - 3.9927(.2)(4,000)$$
$$= 20,000 - 16,757 - 3,194$$
$$= \$49.$$

Now the net advantage of leasing is positive because the cost of borrowing is greater than the cost of leasing. The lease has a positive NPV. Therefore, from the lessee's point of view, leasing is preferred to borrowing as a means of financing the project. The increased value to the lessee results from the fact that the lessor can take better advantage of the tax shelters (depreciation, interest expenses, and investment tax credits) because of the lessor's higher tax rate.

THE INVESTMENT DECISION

So far, we have analyzed leasing as a perfect substitute for borrowing. The issue has been how to finance the project. But now, we must turn to the central issue, namely, whether the investment should be undertaken in the first place. If the project has a large negative net present value, it will not make any difference how we finance it. Any value added by financing can be easily outweighed by unfavorable cash flows from the project itself. Also, remember that the strict financial leases we have been analyzing are not cancellable, except via bankruptcy.

Owning an asset exposes one to more risk than simply taking a lending or a lease position. Owning and operating a project involves the total risk of its cash flows, not merely the relatively secure risk of a debt position. Suppose we define k_U as the all-equity financing rate of return required on the project. We know that the risk-adjusted rate of return on the project, k_U, is greater than the before-tax borrowing rate, k_b, and that, in turn, this is greater than the lessor's after-tax cost of capital, k_L (that is, $k_U > k_b > k_L$). Suppose that the all-equity financing rate, given the operating risks of the project, is $k_U = 13.33\%$, that the project can carry 50 percent debt to total assets, and that the firm's tax rate is 20 percent. Given these facts, we can use the Modigliani-Miller definition of the weighted average cost of capital, Equation 24.1, to compute the discount rate for the project's cash flows:

$$k(\text{project}) = k_U(1 - \lambda T)$$
$$= .1333[1 - .5(.2)]$$
$$= 12\%.$$

Suppose that the project costs $20,000 as before, that it has a five-year life, that the firm uses straight-line depreciation, that the project increases annual revenues by $10,000 and costs by $4,068. Using the capital budgeting techniques of Chapter 9 the NPV of the project is

$$\text{NPV} = -I_0 + \sum_{t=1}^{n} \frac{(R - C)(1 - T) + T\text{Dep}}{[1 + k(\text{project})]^t}$$

$$= -20,000 + \text{PVIFA}(12\%,5 \text{ yrs.})[(10,000 - 4,068)(1 - .2) + .2(4,000)]$$

$$= -20,000 + 3.6048[(5,932)(.8) + .2(4,000)]$$

$$= -20,000 + 19,991$$

$$= -\$9.$$

Under our assumptions, the project should be rejected. However, since an additional $49 is added if we lease, the value added by lease financing is enough to raise the project to a positive NPV. Note, however, that if there were other projects which are mutually exclusive with the one under consideration and which can be leased, then one of them should be accepted if its NPV is higher.

ALTERNATIVE COMPUTATION PROCEDURES IN THE LEASING ANALYSIS

Thus far, we have made the leasing versus owning analysis using compact equations. The same results can be obtained when the flows are tabulated by years. To illustrate, we shall use data similar to the previous example. The cost of the asset is $20,000, and the required lease-rental rate is calculated to be $5,246 under straight-line depreciation. The earlier analysis treated leasing and borrowing as substitutes; so under the ownership scenario, the $20,000 is assumed to be borrowed at a 10 percent before-tax cost of debt by the user of the asset.[2]

It is assumed that the loan of $20,000 is paid off at a level annual amount that covers annual interest charges plus amortization of the principal. The amount is an annuity that can be determined by the use of the present value of an annuity formula, shown in Equation 24.5.

---

[2] The implicit assumption here is that the entire investment amount, $I_0 = \$20,000$, is financed with the lease and that this is not a change in the firm's target capital structure. This assumption is valid if one compares the firm's balance sheet when financing the project with debt with the alternative of financing the project with leasing. For example, suppose the firm had $100,000 in assets and a 50 percent debt to total assets ratio before the project. If the $20,000 investment is financed with debt and equity, assets will increase to $120,000 and debt to $60,000. If the project is leased, debt will fall to $40,000 and leasing increase from zero to $20,000. Equity will be $60,000 either way. Comparing the two balance sheets, we see that debt is $20,000 less if the asset is leased.

TABLE 24.2 Schedule of Debt Payments

End of Year (1)	Balance of Principal Owed at End of Year (2)	Principal plus Interest Payments (3)	Annual Interest 10% × (2): (4)	Reduction of Principal (5)
1	$20,000	$ 5,276	$2,000	$ 3,276
2	16,724	5,276	1,672	3,604
3	13,120	5,276	1,312	3,964
4	9,156	5,276	916	4,360
5	4,796	5,276	480	4,796
Totals		$26,380	$6,380	$20,000

$$\$20,000 = \sum_{t=1}^{n} \frac{a_t}{(1 + k_b)^t}$$

$$a_t = \frac{\$20,000}{(\text{PVIFA})(10\%, 5 \text{ yrs.})}$$

$$= \frac{\$20,000}{3.7908} = \$5,276 \tag{24.5}$$

Solving Equation 24.5 for the level annual annuity results in $5,276, which represents the principal plus interest payments set forth in Column (3) of Table 24.2. The sum of these five annual payments is shown to be $26,380, which represents repayment of the principal of $20,000 plus the sum of the annual interest payments. The interest payments of each year are determined by multiplying Column (2), the balance of principal owed at the end of the year, by 10 percent, the assumed cost of borrowing. The sum of the annual interest payments does, in fact, equal the total interest of $6,380, obtained by deducting the principal of $20,000 from the total of the five annual payments shown in Column (3).

A schedule of cash outflows for the borrow-own alternative is then developed to determine the present value of the after-tax cash flows. This is illustrated in Table 24.3.

The analysis of cash outflows begins with a listing of the loan payments, as shown in Column (2). Next, the annual interest payments from Table 24.2 are listed in Column (3). Since straight-line depreciation is assumed, the annual depreciation charges are $4,000 per year, as shown in Column (4). The tax shelter to the owner of the equipment is the sum of the annual interest plus depreciation multiplied by the tax rate. The amounts of the annual tax shield are shown in Column (5). Column (6) is cash flow after taxes, obtained by deducting Column (5) from Column (2).

Since the cost of borrowing is 10 percent, its after-tax cost with a 40 percent tax rate is 6 percent. The present value factors at 6 percent are listed in Column (7). They are multiplied by the after-tax cash flows to obtain Column (8), the present value of the after-tax costs of owning the asset.

TABLE 24.3   Costs of Borrowing

End of Year (1)	Loan Payment (2)	Annual Interest (3)	Depreciation (4)	Tax Shield: [(3) + (4)]0.4 (5)	Cash Flows after Taxes: (2) − (5) (6)	Present Value Factor (at 6%) (7)	Present Value of Costs (8)
1	$ 5,276	$2,000	$ 4,000	$ 2,400	$ 2,876	0.9434	$ 2,713
2	5,276	1,672	4,000	2,269	3,007	0.8900	2,676
3	5,276	1,312	4,000	2,125	3,151	0.8396	2,646
4	5,276	916	4,000	1,966	3,310	0.7921	2,622
5	5,276	480	4,000	1,792	3,484	0.7473	2,603
Totals	$26,380	$6,380	$20,000	$10,552	$15,828		$13,260

The costs of leasing the asset can be obtained in a similar manner, as shown in Table 24.4. The uniform annual lease payments are shown in Column (2). By multiplying 0.6 times the Column (2) figures, the after-tax cost of leasing is obtained and shown in Column (3). The present value factors for 6 percent are listed in Column (4) and multiplied times the figures in Column (3). Column (5) presents the after-tax costs of leasing by year, which total to $13,260.

The result is the same as for the costs of borrowing in order to own the asset. Thus, in formulating the problem to make the positions of the lessors and users symmetrical, indifference between the costs of borrowing and the costs of leasing is obtained once again. A number of factors could change this result: differences in costs of capital, differences in applicable tax rates or usability of tax subsidies, differences in patterns of payments required under leasing versus owning, and so on. But in order to measure the effects of factors which cause the costs of leasing and owning to be different, it is helpful to start with an equality relation to understand better what is causing a divergence.

TABLE 24.4   Costs of Leasing

End of Year (1)	Lease Payments (2)	After-Tax: 0.6 × (2) (3)	Present Value Factor (at 6%) (4)	Present Value of Costs: (3) × (4) (5)
1	$ 5,246	$ 3,147.6	0.9434	$ 2,970
2	5,246	3,147.6	0.8900	2,802
3	5,246	3,147.6	0.8396	2,643
4	5,246	3,147.6	0.7921	2,493
5	5,246	3,147.6	0.7473	2,352
Totals	$26,230	$15,738.0		$13,260

Cost Comparison for Operating Leases

Under an operating lease, the lessor must bear the risk involved in the use of the asset because the lease is cancellable and, therefore, may be returned by the lessee. Operating leases are virtually equivalent to having the lessor own the equipment and operate it. In these circumstances, the required rate of return is not the rate on a portfolio of assets of loaned funds. Rather, it is something higher. The operating lease, from the lessor's point of view, has three elements: (1) the cash flows received from the lease contract, (2) the expected market or salvage value of the asset, and (3) the value of an American put option. The put option captures the present value of the lessee's right to cancel the lease and return the asset whenever the value of the economic rent on the asset falls below the lease fee. This may happen if the asset wears out faster than anticipated or if the asset (for example, a computer) becomes obsolete faster than expected. Equation 24.6 shows how the NPV of the lease to the lessor must be adjusted for operating leases:

$$\text{NPV}_{LOR} = -I_0 + \sum_{t=1}^{n} \frac{L_t(1-T) + T\text{Dep}_t}{[1+(1-T)k_b]^t} + \frac{E(MV)}{(1+k_1)^n} - P, \qquad \textbf{(24.6)}$$

where

$$\text{NPV}_{LOR} = \text{present value to the lessor}$$

$$L_t = \text{lease rental fee without the cancellation feature}$$

$$E(MV) = \text{expected market value of the asset}$$

$$k_1 = \text{the risk-adjusted discount rate for the salvage value}$$

$$P = \text{the value of the American put implied by the cancellation feature.}$$

Because the lessor is giving up something by allowing the lease to be cancelled, it is necessary to charge a higher lease fee. How much higher depends on the value of the American put, P.[3] As the risk of obsolescence increases so does the value of the put option held by the lessee. Since there are no free lunches, the lease fee charged by the lessor will rise to reflect the extra risk being undertaken. An internal rate of return analysis of a cancellable operating lease which uses only the first three terms of Equation 24.6, thereby leaving out the put option, will show that the lessor sets the lease fee such that a high rate of return is being charged. The lessee would be badly mistaken to compare the rate required on a cancellable operating lease with the rate required on a straight (noncancellable) financial lease (or comparable debt financing).

Additional Influences on the Leasing versus Owning Decision

A number of other factors can influence the user firm's costs of leasing versus owning capital assets. These include (1) different costs of capital for the lessor versus the user firm, (2) financing costs higher in leasing, (3) differences in maintenance costs, (4) the

---

[3] See Copeland and Weston [1982] for an analysis of cancellable operating leases and Lee, Martin, and Senchack [1982] for an analysis of the salvage value problem.

benefits of residual values to the owner of the assets, (5) the possibility of reducing obsolescence costs by the leasing firms, (6) the possibility of increased credit availability under leasing, (7) more favorable tax treatment, such as more rapid write-off, and (8) possible differences in the ability to utilize tax reduction opportunities. A number of arguments exist with respect to the advantages and disadvantages of leasing, given these factors. Many of the arguments carry with them implicit assumptions, thus their applicability to real-world conditions is subject to considerable qualification.

Different Costs of Capital for the Lessor versus the User Firm

If the lessor has a lower cost of capital than the user, the cost of leasing is likely to be lower than the cost of owning to the user. But is it realistic to assume that the cost of capital would be different? To answer this question, the basic risks involved in using capital assets must be considered. It has been demonstrated that two broad types of risks are present.

One risk is that an asset's economic rate of depreciation and obsolescence will vary, in some systematic way with the level of the economy, from the rate expected when the lease-rental rate was determined. That is, the risk is that the agreed-upon lease payments, which are based on expected depreciation, will be insufficient to cover the subsequent realized depreciation. This risk is borne by the owner, whether it is a leasing firm or a user-buyer.

The other risk is associated with the uncertain future net cash flows to be derived from employing the capital services of the asset. This risk is borne by the leasing company if the lease contract is cancellable at any time with no penalty, borne by the user firm if the lease contract is noncancellable over the life of the asset, and shared by them under any contractual arrangement between these two extremes. But, competitive capital markets will ensure that the implicit discount rate in the leasing arrangement, as negotiated, will reflect the allocation of the risks under the particular sharing arrangement specified. Under the standard price equals marginal cost condition of competitive markets, it is the project's cost of capital that is the relevant discount rate. Hence, it is difficult to visualize why the risk in use of a capital asset will be different whether the asset is owned by a leasing company or by the user firm.[4]

Another possibility is that the user firm may have a lower cost of capital than the leasing company. This possibility has been evaluated as follows: "It is true that such a company, looking only at the conventional formulas, might find it profitable to buy rather than rent. But it would find it even more profitable, under those circumstances, to enter the leasing business."[5] This would eliminate any divergence.

Under competitive market conditions, it is unlikely that the disequilibrium conditions implied by the different costs of capital will long persist. The supply of financial intermediaries as lessors will either increase or decrease to restore equilibrium in the benefits to a user firm from leasing versus owning an asset.

---

[4] Miller and Upton [1976].

[5] Ibid., p. 767.

Financing Costs Higher in Leasing

A familiar view is that leasing always involves higher implicit financing costs. This argument is also of doubtful validity. First, when the nature of the lessee as a credit risk is considered, there may be no difference. Second, it is difficult to separate the money costs of leasing from the other services embodied in a leasing contract. If, because of its specialized operations, the leasing company can perform nonfinancial services such as maintenance of the equipment at a lower cost than the lessee or some other institution can perform them, then the effective cost of leasing may be lower than the cost of funds obtained from borrowing or other sources. The efficiencies of performing specialized services may thus enable the leasing company to operate by charging a lower total cost than the lessee would have to pay for the package of money plus services on any other basis.

Differences in Maintenance Costs

Another argument frequently encountered is that leasing may be less expensive because no explicit maintenance costs are involved. But, this is because the maintenance costs are included in the lease-rental rate. The key question is whether the maintenance can be performed at a lower cost by the lessor or by an independent firm that specializes in performing maintenance on capital assets of the type involved. Whether the costs will differ if supplied by one type of specialist firm rather than another is a factual matter, depending on the industries and particular firms involved.

Residual Values

One important point that must be mentioned in connection with leasing is that the lessor owns the property at the expiration of the lease. The value of the property at the end of the lease is called the *residual value*. Superficially, it appears that where residual values are large, owning is less expensive than leasing. However, even this apparently obvious advantage of owning is subject to substantial qualification. On leased equipment, the obsolescence factor may be so large that it is doubtful whether residual values will be of a great order of magnitude. If these values appear favorable, competition between leasing companies and other financial sources, as well as competition among leasing companies themselves, will force leasing rates down to the point where the potentials of residual values are fully recognized in the leasing contract rates. Thus, the existence of residual values is unlikely to result in materially lower costs of owning.

However, in decisions about whether to lease or to own land, the obsolescence factor is involved only to the extent of deterioration in areas with changing population or use patterns. In a period of optimistic expectations about land values, there may be a tendency to overestimate their rates of increase. As a consequence, the current purchase of land may involve a price so high that the probable rate of return on owned land will be relatively small. Under this condition, leasing may well represent the more economical way of obtaining the use of land. Conversely, if the probable increase in land values is not fully reflected in current prices, it will be advantageous to own the land.

Thus, it is difficult to generalize about whether residual value considerations are likely to make the effective cost of leasing higher or lower than the cost of owning. The results depend on whether the individual firm has opportunities to take advantage of overoptimistic or overpessimistic evaluations of future value changes by the market as a whole and whether the firm or market is correct on average.

Obsolescence Costs

Another popular notion is that leasing costs will be lower because of the rapid obsolescence of some kinds of equipment. If the obsolescence rate on equipment is high, leasing costs must reflect that rate. Thus, in general terms, it can be argued that neither residual values nor obsolescence rates can basically affect the relative cost of owning versus leasing.

However, it is possible that certain leasing companies are well equipped to handle the obsolescence problem. For example, the Clark Equipment Company is a manufacturer, reconditioner, and specialist in materials handling equipment, with its own sales organization and system of distributors. This may enable Clark to write favorable leases for equipment. If the equipment becomes obsolete to one user, it may be satisfactory for other users with different materials handling requirements, and Clark is well situated to locate the other users. The situation is similar in computer leasing.

This illustration indicates how a leasing company, by combining lending with other specialized services, may reduce the social costs of obsolescence and increase effective residual values. By such operations, the total cost of obtaining the use of such equipment is reduced. Possibly other institutions that do not combine financing and specialist functions (such as manufacturing, reconditioning, servicing, and sales) may, in conjunction with financing institutions, perform the overall functions as efficiently and at as low a cost as do integrated leasing companies. However, this is a factual matter depending on the relative efficiency of the competing firms in different lines of business and different kinds of equipment.

Increased Credit Availability

Two possible situations that give leasing an advantage to firms seeking the maximum degree of financial leverage may exist. First, it is frequently stated that firms wishing to purchase a specific piece of equipment can obtain more money for longer terms under a lease arrangement than under a secured loan agreement. Second, leasing may not have as much of an impact on future borrowing capacity as does borrowing to buy the equipment.

This point is illustrated by the balance sheets of two hypothetical firms, A and B, in Table 24.5. Initially, the balance sheets of both firms are identical, with both showing debt ratios of 50 percent. Next, each company decides to acquire assets costing $100. Firm A borrows $100 to make the purchase, so an asset and a liability go on its balance sheet, and its debt ratio is increased to 75 percent. Firm B leases the equipment. The lease may call for fixed charges as high as or even higher than the loan, and the obligations assumed under the lease can be equally (or more) dangerous to other creditors; but the fact that its reported debt ratio is lower may enable Firm B to obtain additional credit from

TABLE 24.5 Balance Sheet Effects of Operating Leases

Before Asset Increase Firms A and B			After Asset Increase Firm A				Firm B		
	Debt	$ 50		Debt	$150			Debt	$ 50
	Equity	50		Equity	50			Equity	50
Total assets $100	Total	$100	Total assets $200	Total	$200	Total assets $100		Total	$100

other lenders. The amount of the annual rentals is shown as a note to Firm B's financial statements, so credit analysts are aware of it; but many of them may still give less weight to Firm B's lease than to Firm A's loan.

This illustration indicates quite clearly a weakness of the debt ratio. If two companies are being compared, and if one leases a substantial amount of equipment, then the debt ratio as calculated here does not accurately show their relative leverage positions.[6]

Rapid Write-Off

If the lease is written for a period that is much shorter than the depreciable life of the asset (with renewals at low rentals after the lessor has recovered costs during the basic lease period), then the deductible depreciation which the lessee could take if the asset were owned is small in relation to the deductible lease payment in the early years. In a sense, this amounts to a very rapid write-off, which is advantageous to the lessee. However, the Internal Revenue Service disallows the deductibility of lease payments that provide for an unduly rapid amortization of the lessor's costs and have a relatively low renewal or purchase option.

Differences in Tax Rates or Tax Subsidies

An advantage to leasing or to buying may occur when the tax rates of lessors and user firms are different. But, even here, unambiguous predictions are not always possible. The effects of differential taxes depend upon the relationships among earnings from the capital assets and their interactions with differential tax rates and tax subsidies.

But, the inability of a user firm to utilize tax benefits may make it advantageous for it to enter a lease arrangement. In this situation, the lessor (a bank or a leasing company) can utilize the tax shield, and competition with other lessors may result in lower leasing rates.

---

[6]Three comments are appropriate here. First, financial analysts frequently attempt to reconstruct the balance sheets of firms such as B by capitalizing the lease payments — that is, estimating the value of both the lease obligation and the leased assets and transforming B's balance sheet into one comparable to A's. Second, as indicated in Chapter 7, lease charges are included in the fixed charge coverage ratio; and this ratio is approximately equal for Firms A and B, thereby revealing the true state of affairs. Thus, it is unlikely that lenders will be fooled into granting more credit to a company with a lease than to one with a conventional loan having terms similar to those of the lease. Third, FASB Statement No. 13 provides for including capital leases in the firm's balance sheet.

If a firm is unprofitable, or if it is expanding so rapidly and generating such large tax credits that it cannot use them all, then it may be profitable for it to enter a lease arrangement. In this situation, the lessor (a bank or a leasing company) can use the tax shield and give the lessee a corresponding reduction in lease charges. In recent years, railroads and airlines have been large users of leasing for this reason, as have industrial companies faced with similar situations. Anaconda, for example, financed most of the cost of a $138 million aluminum plant built in 1973 through a lease arrangement.[7] Anaconda had suffered a $365 million tax loss when Chile expropriated its copper mining properties, and the carry-forward of this loss would hold taxes down for years. Thus, the firm could not use the tax shields associated with the new plant. By entering a lease arrangement, the company was able to pass the shields on to the lessors, who, in turn, gave it lease payments lower than would have existed under a loan arrangement. Anaconda's financial staff estimated that financial charges over the life of the plant would be $74 million less under the lease arrangement than under a borrow-and-buy plan.

Incidentally, the Anaconda lease was set up as a leveraged lease.[8] A group of banks and Chrysler Corporation provided about $38 million of equity and were the owner-lessors. They borrowed the balance of the required funds from Prudential, Metropolitan, and Aetna, large life insurance companies. The banks and Chrysler received not only an investment tax credit but also the tax shelter associated with accelerated depreciation on the plant. Such leveraged leases, often with wealthy individuals seeking tax shelters acting as owner-lessors, are an important part of the financial scene today and help explain why leasing has reached a total volume of over $100 billion.

SUMMARY

Leasing has long been used in connection with the acquisition of equipment by railroad companies. In recent years, it has been extended to a wide variety of equipment, such as computers and airplanes.

The most important forms of lease financing are (1) sale and leaseback, in which a firm owning land, buildings, or equipment sells the property and simultaneously executes an agreement to lease it for a certain period under specific terms; (2) service leases or operating leases, which include both financing and maintenance services and are often cancellable and call for payments under the lease contract that may not fully recover the cost of the equipment; and (3) financial leases, which do not provide for maintenance services, are not cancellable, and do fully amortize the cost of the leased asset during the basic lease contract period.

It is important to remember that lease financing is a substitute for debt. There is no such thing as a company which is 100 percent lease financed. Lease financing, like debt financing, requires an equity base. The first step in a lease versus buy analysis is to discount the cash flows of the project under consideration at the appropriate weighted

---

[7] Vanderwicken [1973].

[8] Technically, a *leveraged lease* is one in which the financial intermediary (a bank or other lessor) uses borrowed funds to acquire the assets it leases.

average cost of capital. Then, if the project makes sense, the second step is to decide whether it should be financed with a mixture of debt and equity or with a lease. As shown in Equation 24.4, the net present value of the lease is determined by discounting the after-tax lease fees and the lost depreciation tax shield at the lessee's after-tax cost of debt. If the NPV of the lease is positive, then leasing is preferred to borrowing as a means of financing the project. Always be sure that the NPV of the project plus the NPV of the lease is positive.

In the absence of major tax advantages and other "market imperfections," there should be no advantage to either leasing or owning. A wide range of factors that may influence the indifference result can be introduced. These possible influences include tax differences, differences in maintenance costs, differences in obsolescence, and differences in the contractual positions in leasing versus other forms and sources of financing. Whether these other factors will actually give an advantage or disadvantage to leasing depends on the facts and circumstances of each transaction analyzed.

QUESTIONS

24.1 Discuss this statement: The type of equipment best suited for leasing has a long life in relation to the length of the lease; is a removable, standard product that could be used by many different firms; and is easily identifiable. In short, it is the kind of equipment that could be repossessed and sold readily. However, we would be quite happy to write a ten-year lease on paper towels for a firm such as Eastman Kodak or Owens-Illinois.

24.2 Leasing is often called a hedge against obsolescence. Under what conditions is this actually true?

24.3 Is leasing in any sense a hedge against inflation for the lessee? For the lessor?

24.4 One alleged advantage of leasing is that it keeps liabilities off the balance sheet, thus making it possible for a firm to obtain more leverage than it otherwise could. This raises the question of whether both the lease obligation and the asset involved should be capitalized and shown on the balance sheet. Discuss the pros and cons of capitalizing leases and related assets.

PROBLEMS

24.1 a. The Clarkton Company produces industrial machines, which have five-year lives. Clarkton is willing to either sell the machines for $30,000 or lease them at a rental that, because of competitive factors, yields an after-tax return to Clarkton of 6 percent — its cost of capital. What is the company's competitive lease-rental rate? (Assume straight-line depreciation, zero salvage value, and an effective corporate tax rate of 40 percent.)

b. The Stockton Machine Shop is contemplating the purchase of a machine exactly like those rented by Clarkton. The machine will produce net benefits of $10,000 per year. Stockton can buy the machine for $30,000 or rent it from Clarkton at the competitive lease-rental rate. Stockton's cost of capital is 12 percent, its cost of debt 10 percent, and $T = 40$ percent. Which alternative is better for Stockton?

c. If Clarkton's cost of capital is 9 percent and competition exists among lessors, solve for the new equilibrium rental rate. Will Stockton's decision be altered?

24.2 The Norton Company is faced with the decision of whether it should purchase or lease a new forklift truck. The truck can be leased on an eight-year contract for $4,641.44 a year or it can be purchased for $26,000. The salvage value (Z_n) of the truck after eight years is $2,000. The company uses straight-line depreciation. The discount rate applied is its after-tax cost of debt. The company can borrow at 15 percent and has a 40 percent marginal tax rate and a 12 percent cost of capital.

a. Analyze the lease versus purchase decision using the firm's after-tax cost of debt as the discount factor.

b. Discuss your results.

24.3 The Barrington Company seeks to acquire the use of a rolling machine at the lowest possible cost. The choice is either to lease one at $21,890 annually or to purchase one for $54,000. The company's cost of capital is 14 percent, its cost of debt is 10 percent, and its tax rate is 40 percent. The machine has an economic life of six years and no salvage value. The company uses straight-line depreciation. The discount rate applied is the after-tax cost of debt. Which is the less costly method of financing?

24.4 The Scott Brothers Department Store is considering a sale and leaseback of its major property, consisting of land and a building, because it is 30 days late on 80 percent of its accounts payable. The recent balance sheet of Scott Brothers is as shown in Table P24.4.

Profit before taxes is $36,000; after taxes, $20,000. Annual depreciation charges are $57,600 on the building and $72,000 on the fixtures and equipment. The land and building could be sold for a total of $2.8 million. The annual net rental will be $240,000.

a. How much capital gains tax will Scott Brothers pay if the land and building are sold? (Assume all capital gains are taxed at a capital gains tax rate, 34 percent; disregard such items as recapture of depreciation, tax preference treatment, and so on.)

TABLE P24.4 Scott Brothers Department Store Balance Sheet as of December 31, 19X0 (Thousands of Dollars)

Assets		Liabilities	
Cash	$ 288	Accounts payable	$1,440
Receivables	1,440	Bank loans (at 8%)	1,440
Inventories	1,872	Other current liabilities	720
Total current assets	$3,600	Total current debt	$3,600
Land	1,152	Common stock	1,440
Building	720	Retained earnings	720
Fixtures and equipment	288		
Net fixed assets	2,160		
Total assets	$5,760	Total claims	$5,760

b. Compare the current ratio before and after the sale and leaseback if the after-tax net proceeds are used to clean up the bank loans and to reduce accounts payable and other current liabilities.

c. If the lease had been in effect during the year shown in the balance sheet, what would Scott Brothers' profit for that year have been?

d. What are the basic financial problems facing Scott Brothers? Will the sale and lease-back operation solve them?

24.5 *(Use the computer diskette, File name: 24LESNG, Leasing.)*

a. Given the assumptions in Screen #3, what is the lessor's required lease rental rate? If the user/lessee employs his after-tax cost of debt at the discount rate in his lease versus purchase analysis, is the cost of owning higher or lower than the cost of leasing?

(1) How is your answer to Question (a) affected if the user lessee uses his cost of capital as the discount rate in both the leasing and purchase analyses?

(2) How is your answer affected if the user/lessee employs the cost of capital in the purchase analysis, and the after-tax cost of debt in the lease analysis?

b. Now suppose that the lessor's cost of capital rises to 8 percent. How will this affect the lease rental rate the lessor must charge?

(1) If the user/lessee uses his after-tax cost of debt as the discount rate, is the cost of owning higher or lower than the cost of leasing?

(2) Suppose the lessor's cost of capital rises to 12 percent, and the user/lessee uses his cost of capital as the discount rate. Is the cost of owning higher or lower than the cost of leasing?

(3) If the lessor's cost of capital is 12 percent, and the user/lessee uses his after-tax cost of debt in the leasing analysis, but his cost of capital in the purchase analysis, which alternative will be chosen?

c. Return to the original assumptions, except now assume that the lessor's tax rate is 20 percent. How will this affect the required lease/rental rate and the user/lessee's decision to lease or purchase, assuming that he discounts at after-tax cost of debt?

d. Return to the original assumptions, except that the user/lessee's cost of debt has risen to 15 percent, and his cost of capital is 20 percent.

(1) If he uses the after-tax cost of debt as the discount rate, which alternative will he choose?

(2) If he uses his cost of capital as the discount rate, which alternative will he choose?

e. You are now free to change any of the parameters in the model to explore the relationships involved in lease analysis. (Note: The model uses the tax rate in the calculations of lease payments and the costs of leasing versus buying. It does not automatically calculate an after-tax discount rate; if you intend to use an after-tax discount rate, it must be entered as such.)

Selected References

Abdel-Khalik, A. R., "The Economic Effects on Lessees of FASB No. 13 — Accounting for Leases," Stanford: FASB, 1981.

Ang, James, and Peterson, Pamela, "The Leasing Puzzle," *Journal of Finance*, (September 1984), pp. 1055–1066.

Athanasopoulos, Peter J., and Bacon, Peter W., "The Evaluation of Leveraged Leases," *Financial Management,* 9 (Spring 1980), pp. 76–80.

Bowman, R. G., "The Debt Equivalence of Leases: An Empirical Investigation," *Accounting Review,* (April 1980), pp. 237–253.

Copeland, Thomas E., and Weston, J. Fred, "A Note on the Evaluation of Cancellable Operating Leases," *Financial Management,* 11 (Summer 1982), pp. 60–67.

Flath, D., "The Economics of Short-Term Leasing," *Economic Inquiry,* (April 1980), pp. 247–259.

Johnson, Robert W., and Lewellen, Wilbur G., "Analysis of the Lease-or-Buy Decision," *Journal of Finance,* 27 (September 1972), pp. 815–823.

Kim, E. Han; Lewellen, Wilbur G.; and McConnell, John J., "Sale-and-Leaseback Agreements and Enterprise Valuation," *Journal of Financial and Quantitative Analysis,* 13 (December 1978), pp. 871–883.

Lee, Wayne Y.; Martin, John D.; and Senchack, Andrew J., "The Case for Using Options to Evaluate Salvage Values in Financial Leases," *Financial Management,* 11 (Autumn 1982), pp. 33–41.

Levy, Haim, and Sarnat, Marshall, "Leasing, Borrowing, and Financial Risk," *Financial Management,* 8 (Winter 1979), pp. 47–54.

Lewellen, Wilbur G.; Long, Michael S.; and McConnell, John J., "Asset Leasing in Competitive Capital Markets," *Journal of Finance,* 31 (June 1976), pp. 787–798.

McConnell, John J., and Schallheim, James S., "Valuation of Asset Leasing Contracts," *Journal of Financial Economics,* 12 (August 1983), pp. 237–261.

Miller, Merton H., and Upton, Charles W., "Leasing, Buying and the Cost of Capital Services," *Journal of Finance,* 31 (June 1976), pp. 761–786.

Myers, Stewart C.; Dill, David A.; and Bautista, Alberto J., "Valuation of Financial Lease Contracts," *Journal of Finance,* 31 (June 1976), pp. 799–819.

Schall, Lawrence D., "The Lease-or-Buy and Asset Acquisition Decisions," *Journal of Finance,* 29 (September 1974), pp. 1203–1214.

Vanderwicken, P., "Powerful Logic of the Leasing Boom," *Fortune,* (November 1973), pp. 136–140.

CHAPTER 25

Warrants and Convertibles

In Chapter 12, the theory of options was set forth. In the present chapter, we discuss two particular forms of options: warrants and convertibles. The ordinary options discussed in Chapter 12 do not directly raise funds for the firm. Indeed, the firm may not be involved in the purchase and sale of call and put options. But, warrants and convertibles are used to assist in raising additional funds for the firm. Warrants are used in connection with the sale of other securities in order to make their purchase more attractive. Convertibles give the holder the right to exchange a form of debt or preferred stock for common stock. Since both warrants and convertibles are used to facilitate financing by the firm, they are discussed here where we deal with alternative methods of raising funds as a part of the responsibilities of financial managers.

WARRANTS

A *warrant* is an option to buy a stated number of shares of common stock at a specified exercise price. Warrants are similar to the call options we discussed in Chapter 12 except that they are issued by the firm itself and, typically, have longer maturities. When debt, preferred stock, or common stock is issued, it may be sold in units, which include one or more warrants to purchase common stock or other securities. Warrants, thus, are often used as "sweeteners" to make it easier to sell the associated security.

Characteristics

A warrant states an exercise price at which the common stock may be purchased and the number of shares of common stock which may be purchased per warrant. In Table 25.1, the characteristics of an illustrative group of warrants are listed. In Column (1), the name

TABLE 25.1 Characteristics of Warrants

Company Name (1)	Expiration Date (2)	Exercise Price per Share (3)	Current Common Price (4)	Number of Common (5)	Formula Value of Warrant* (6)	Actual Warrant Price (7)	Percent Premium** (8)
Anacomp	11/11/00	$ 1.84	$ 4.00	1.00	$ 2.16	$ 2.25	2.25
Atlas Corp.	None	15.63	7.25	1.00	0.00	3.25	44.83
Biogen	6/30/94	20.00	32.38	1.00	12.38	18.88	20.07
Cetus	6/30/93	30.00	16.00	1.00	0.00	1.75	10.94
Genesco	10/15/93	11.75	4.50	1.00	0.00	0.63	14.00
Global Marine	3/15/96	3.00	4.13	1.00	1.13	2.13	24.02
Navistar Intl.	12/15/93	5.00	3.75	1.00	0.00	1.25	33.33
Safeway	11/24/96	3.77	20.38	0.28	4.63	4.88	4.40
Sunshine Mining	6/30/91	4.38	1.38	1.00	0.00	0.25	18.12

*Formula Value of Warrant = (Market price of common − Exercise price) × (Conversion ratio:ratio)
**Percent Premium = (Actual price of warrant − Formula value)/(Price of common stock × Number of common)
Source: Various financial publications for the date of April 22, 1991.

of the issuing company is set forth. Column (2) lists the expiration date. The warrants in this random sample all have a maturity of greater than one year, and some have maturities of almost ten years. Some warrants have no expiration date and so may be exercised without a time limit. For example, the Atlas Corp. has warrants outstanding to purchase its common at $15.63 with no expiration date.

In Column (3), the exercise price per share for each of the warrants is set forth. This may be compared in Column (4) with the current market price of the common stock that the warrant may be used to acquire. Column (5) lists the number of common shares that each warrant enables the holder to obtain. The remaining columns of the table will be discussed in connection with the valuation of warrants.

Warrants may be nondetachable from the security they accompany (for example, bonds) or detachable so that they can be traded separately. Since a warrant is an option to buy common stock, it does not carry the rights of common stockholders until it is exercised. Thus, cash dividends are not paid on warrants. Warrants do not have voting power. If the position of the underlying common stock is altered through a stock dividend or through a stock split, provision is usually made to adjust the exercise price of the warrant appropriately.

Generally accepted accounting principles now require that a company with warrants outstanding (this applies to convertibles also) report its earnings per share in two ways. The first method is called the *primary* earnings per share, which is simply the total earnings available to shareholders divided by the actual number of common shares of stock outstanding. The second method of reporting is on a *fully diluted* basis. This represents earnings available to common shareholders divided by the total number of shares actually outstanding plus the additional number of shares that would come into being if all warrants were exercised or all convertible securities were converted. This makes it possible to take into account the impact on the company's earnings per share if all of the options were exercised.

Valuation of Warrants

Since a warrant is fundamentally a call option, its value can be determined by the methods described in Chapter 12. However, in the publications of various financial services, a "formula value" is usually calculated for the warrant. The formula value is found by use of the following expression:

$$\begin{matrix} \text{Formula} \\ \text{value} \end{matrix} = \left(\begin{matrix} \text{Market price} \\ \text{of common stock} \end{matrix} - \begin{matrix} \text{Exercise} \\ \text{price} \end{matrix} \right) \times \left(\begin{matrix} \text{Number of shares each warrant} \\ \text{entitles owner to purchase} \end{matrix} \right).$$

The calculation of the formula value starts by comparing the exercise price of the warrant with the current price of the common stock. By reference to Table 25.1, this would represent subtracting Column (3), the exercise price of the warrant, from Column (4), the current market price of the stock. Hence the "formula value" is the value received if the warrant were exercised immediately. If the exercise price of the warrant is greater than the current market price of the common stock, in the terminology of Chapter 12, the warrant is "out-of-the-money," and the formula value would be defined as zero. To illustrate, we will use the Biogen warrants, which are in the third row of Table 25.1. The exercise price is $20.00 while the price of the common stock on the date of analysis (April 22, 1991) was $32.38. Hence, the warrant was "in-the-money" and its formula value was $12.38. The actual warrant price at the close of trading on April 22, 1991, was $18.88. The "percent premium" is then calculated by deducting the formula value from the actual price and dividing by the price of the common stock in Column (4). This results in a 20.07 percent premium in Column (8) of Table 25.1 for the Biogen warrants expiring June 30, 1994.

The percent premium of the actual price of a warrant in excess of its formula value relates to the elements that give value to any option as discussed in Chapter 12. Hence, the size of the percent premium will reflect the five underlying determinants of the value of an option. Other things being equal, the value of an option will be higher (the percent premium of a warrant larger) if (1) the price of the underlying common stock is higher, (2) the exercise price of the option is lower, (3) the variance of the returns of the underlying asset is higher, (4) the time to maturity of the option is longer, and (5) the risk-free interest rate is higher. Thus, the percent premium of the actual price of a warrant in relation to its formula value reflects the underlying determinants of the warrant value as an option.

Use of Warrants in Financing

Warrants are often used as sweeteners to improve the terms of financing by the issuing firm. They are used by firms of different sizes in different circumstances. The list of firm names in Table 25.1 represents relatively large and well-known firms. Large, strong corporations may sell bonds with warrants, for example, in order to be able to sell the bonds at an interest rate lower than otherwise would be required. The amount of interest

TABLE 25.2   Use of Warrants in Financing (Thousands of Dollars)

Financing Source (1)	Before Financing (2)	Sale of Debentures (3)	Exercise Warrants (4)
Debentures		$ 25,000	$ 25,000
Common stock ($1 par value)	$ 4,000	4,000	5,000
Paid-in capital	16,000	16,000	20,000
Retained earnings	80,000	80,000	80,000
Net worth	$100,000	$100,000	$105,000
Total capitalization	$100,000	$125,000	$130,000

saved would depend upon the circumstances of the firm as well as the state of the financial markets at the time of issues. Firms as large as AT&T have sold bonds with warrants to obtain lower interest rates.

Firms that are relatively new and still in their development stage have uncertain futures. Since their outlook is uncertain, investors would be reluctant to purchase straight debt issues without extremely high, burdensome rates of interest. The high rates of interest can be moderated by selling debt with warrants, which give the purchaser the opportunity to obtain a higher rate of return if the small, rapidly growing firm succeeds and the value of its common stock increases. The warrant is especially attractive to investors in high-income tax brackets because they can take part of their return on the bonds in the form of capital gains rather than interest subject to ordinary personal income tax rates. Warrants are also used as additional compensation to investment bankers to induce them to risk their reputation in bringing out an issue of common stock for a new firm whose track record has not been firmly established.

Another characteristic of warrants is that when they are exercised, the firm receives additional funds. This can be shown by an illustrative example. Consider the situation of the ABC Company. Its situation before financing is depicted in Column (2) of Table 25.2. It has 4 million shares of common stock outstanding at $1 par value. Its paid-in capital is $16 million and its retained earnings are $80 million. Its net worth is $100 million and its total capitalization is the same.

Column (3) then depicts the results of selling $25 million of debentures with warrants. Column (3) is the same as Column (2), except that we add the $25 million of debentures, so that total capitalization increases to $125 million. The debentures carry a 10 percent coupon interest rate, with each debenture of $1,000 face value carrying 40 warrants permitting the purchase of one share of common stock at $5 per share. Since 25,000 debentures are outstanding, each carrying 40 warrants, one million new shares would be sold if the warrants were exercised. With a par value of $1, $1 million would be added to common stock and $4 million to paid-in capital. Net worth would increase from $100 million to $105 million. The total capitalization would rise to $130 million.

The example in Table 25.2 illustrates how warrants can be used to facilitate the sale of a security. A further advantage of the use of the warrants is that when they are exercised, additional funds flow into the corporation. All this, of course, depends upon the company growing and prospering so that the market price of its stock goes up. This is because the exercise price set when the warrants are issued is typically from 15 to 25 percent higher than the prevailing market price of the common stock.

The value of a warrant, or in its short maturity form, a right, has been developed under simplifying conditions by Galai and Schneller [1978]. They postulate a one-period model for a 100 percent equity-financed firm which distributes the proceeds from issuing warrants as dividends to the old shareholders and the warrants are assumed to be exercised as a block. The following summarizes the symbols and illustrative magnitudes for the variables in the analysis.

V = value of the firm without warrants = $1 million

N = current number of shares = 10,000

q = ratio of warrants to shares = .25

X = exercise price of warrant = $80

S = price per share without warrants = $100

S_x = price per share warrants exercised

W = value of a right or a warrant.

The price per share of the stock without warrants will be

$$S = \frac{V}{N} = \frac{\$1,000,000}{10,000} = \$100.$$

Next, postulate that warrants are issued and that they are exercised. The resulting price per share is determined by adding the proceeds from the warrants, NqX, to the value of the firm, V, and dividing by the new number of shares outstanding, $N(1 + q)$,

$$S_x = \frac{V + NqX}{N(1 + q)} = \frac{\$1,000,000 + 10,000(.25)\$80}{10,000(1 + .25)} = \frac{\$1,200,000}{12,500} = \$96.$$

Since $V = NS$ the stock price given that the warrants are exercised, S_x, can also be written as:

$$S_x = \frac{S + qX}{1 + q} = \frac{100 + .25(80)}{1.25} = \frac{120}{1.25} = \$96.$$

The warrants will be exercised if their value after conversion is greater than the exercise price. But, it must also be true that the firm's end-of-period stock price without the warrants must exceed the warrant exercise price as well. Hence, the warrant will be exercised in the same states of nature as a call option with the same exercise price. When we analyze the end-of-period payoffs, we observe the following relationships:

End-of-Period Payoffs

	If $S \leq X$	If $S > X$
Call on firm without warrants, C	0	$S - X$
Warrant on firm with warrants, W	0	$\frac{S + qX}{1 + q} - X = \frac{1}{1 + q}(S - X)$

We see that the payoffs to the warrant are a constant proportion of the payoffs to a call written on a firm without warrants. A call option would pay nothing when $S \leq X$ and $S - X$ when $S > X$. The returns on the warrant, therefore, are perfectly correlated with the returns on a call option written on the firm without warrants. Hence, the value of a warrant will be related to the value of the call in the following way:

$$W = \frac{1}{1 + q}C.$$

In addition, because the warrant and the call are perfectly correlated, they will have the same systematic risk and, consequently, the same required rate of return.

We have now described the characteristics of warrants. We shall next treat the nature of convertibles, which are similar. The rationale for the use of these options sold by the firm will then be discussed.

CONVERTIBLES

Convertible securities are bonds or *preferred stocks* that are exchangeable into common stock at the option of the holder and under specified terms and conditions. The most important of the special features relates to how many shares of stock a convertible holder receives by converting. This feature is defined as the *conversion ratio,* and it gives the number of shares of common stock the holder of the convertible receives on surrender of the security. Related to the conversion ratio is the *conversion price* — the effective price paid for the common stock when conversion occurs. In effect, a convertible is similar to a bond with an attached warrant.

Some illustrative convertible debt issues are listed in Table 25.3. In Column (1) is the company name. Column (2) sets forth the coupon rates. These vary widely. One influence on the coupon rate is the conversion premium at the time the security is issued. The conversion premium is the percent by which the conversion price at the time of issue exceeds the prevailing price of the common stock into which the debt or preferred stock will be converted. Other influences on the coupon level will be discussed below. Column (3) contains the maturity dates, which also vary. On convertible preferred stocks, often there will be no maturity. Column (4) is the conversion ratio, the number of shares of common stock received on conversion. Column (5) is the prevailing price of the common stock as of the date of the analysis, which was April 29, 1991. Column (6) is the product of the previous two columns divided by 10, since the conversion ratio times the current price of the common stock gives the current conversion value per $100 of the convertible bond (not per $1,000 face value). For example, for the first bond in the list, the Avnet's 8 percent coupon convertible bonds maturing in 2013, the conversion ratio was 19.230. This multiplied times the applicable current price of the common stock gives $528.875, divided by 10, to give the current conversion value shown in Column (5) of $52.88. The price of the convertible bond per $100 of par value of the bond was $92.50 on April 29, 1991. The conversion price premium on the date of analysis was 75 percent. This is the percent by which the current price of the convertible exceeds its current conversion value.

TABLE 25.3   Characteristics of Convertible Debt

Company Name (1)	Coupon (2)	Maturity (3)	Conversion Ratio (4)	Price of Common (5)	Current Conversion Value* (6)	Price of Convertible (7)	Conversion Price Premium** (8)
Avnet	8.000%	2013	19.230	$ 27.500	$52.880	$ 92.500	75%
Baker Hughes	9.500	2006	16.975	26.630	45.200	102.000	126
Carolina Frt.	6.250	2011	21.053	17.500	36.840	69.000	88
Hercules	8.000	2010	22.371	34.250	76.620	94.000	23
IBM	7.875	2004	6.508	106.880	69.560	101.630	47
Travelers	8.320	2015	19.500	24.250	47.290	91.000	93
Xerox	6.000	1995	10.870	57.880	62.920	92.500	47

*Conversion Value = (Conversion ratio)(Price of common)/10
**Conversion Price Premium = [(Price of convertible/Current conversion value) − 1] × 100
Source: Various financial publications for the date of April 29, 1991.

Note that there is a distinction between the conversion price and the current conversion value. The conversion price is akin to the exercise price on a call option. It is, of course, determined by the conversion ratio. Thus, for Avnet, the conversion price would be

$$\text{Conversion price} = \frac{\text{Par value of bond}}{\text{Shares received}} = \frac{\$1,000}{19.230} = \$52.002.$$

Since the stock price is $27.50 and the conversion price is $52.002, the call option implied in Avnet's convertible bond is way out-of-the-money. The conversion price and conversion ratio are established at the time the convertible bond is sold. Generally, these values are fixed for the life of the bond, although sometimes a stepped-up conversion price is used.

Another factor that may cause a change in the conversion price and ratio is a standard feature of almost all convertibles — the clause protecting the convertible against dilution from stock splits, stock dividends, and the sale of common stock at low prices (as in a rights offering). The typical provision states that no common stock can be sold at a price below the conversion price and that the conversion price must be lowered (and the conversion ratio raised) by the percentage amount of any stock dividend or split. For example, if Avnet had a two-for-one split, the conversion ratio would be adjusted to 38.46 and the conversion price lowered to $26.00. If this protection were not contained in the contract, a company could completely thwart conversion by the use of stock splits and dividends. Warrants are similarly protected against dilution.

Like warrant exercise prices, the conversion price is characteristically set from 15 to 20 percent above the prevailing market price of the common stock at the time the convertible issue is sold. How the conversion price is established can best be understood after considering the rationale for the use of convertibles.

FIGURE 25.1   Debt Value and Risk

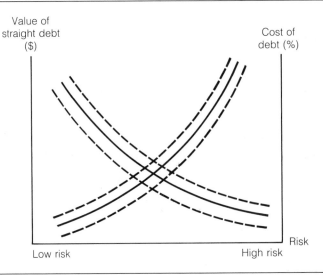

The Rationale for the Use of Convertibles

The traditional reasons for selling convertibles were that the coupon rate was low and that the conversion price represented a premium over the current price of the common stock. But, our previous discussion of options in Chapter 12 should indicate that this older view is incomplete at best. Convertible debt is not a free lunch. The convertible bond may be viewed as a package of straight debt plus an associated warrant. Since a convertible bond is a hybrid between straight debt and equity, its cost is a weighted average of the cost of straight debt and the cost of equity. More precisely, it is a weighted average of the explicit interest charges on straight debt and the value of the associated option.

Recall from Chapter 15 on capital structure and the cost of capital that the value of straight debt would decline with risk as depicted in Figure 25.1. The cost of debt would, of course, rise with risk, also shown in Figure 25.1. Since the assessment of risk is uncertain, both the value of straight debt and the cost of debt are also uncertain. Hence, the value of straight debt is depicted as varying within some range. In contrast, we established in Chapter 12 that the value of an option rises with the variance or the riskiness of the underlying security into which the option is exercised. This relationship is depicted in Figure 25.2. Again, the value of the option is shown as a band since both the assessment of the risk and the related value would be uncertain.

High uncertainty would decrease the value and increase the cost of straight debt. With high risk or uncertainty for a company or project, the likelihood of establishing a value or cost that is fair both to the issuer and the buyer is improved by attaching an option. Combining an option with a straight debt security makes its value and cost less sensitive to the uncertainty associated with the outlook for a firm or a project.

FIGURE 25.2   Option Value and Risk

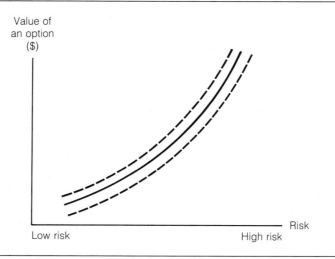

The foregoing provides a basis for predictions of the characteristics of firms and the circumstances under which convertibles or securities with warrants are likely to be employed. These are listed below:

1. Firms with uncertain operating risks characterized by low stock and bond ratings
2. Concern about agency problems
   a. Uncertain investment programs
   b. Other divergences of interest between shareholders and bondholders
3. Periods of general uncertainty in the economy
4. Firms with investment activities in international markets or other environments of high uncertainty
5. Firms with less need for tax shelter.

The reasons why options may perform a useful role when combined with other securities under the conditions listed above will next be briefly summarized.

Low stock and bond ratings indicate a high uncertainty with regard to the outlook for the firm. Hence, when such firms sell debt, we might expect to find some form of option associated with it in order to reduce agency problems. The managers of a company with straight debt outstanding may have an incentive to increase the riskiness of the firm's investment programs. Increasing the risk of the firm hurts the bondholders and helps the common stockholders. This is because if risky projects turn out well, the bondholders do not receive any more than the fixed return originally promised, and the stockholders reap all of the rewards. The buyers of straight debt must take this possibility into account and require compensation in the form of a higher promised coupon rate. The higher cost of straight debt can be avoided by attaching a warrant which enables bondholders to participate in any actions that increase the value of the common stock.

This is an example of the agency problem reflecting the divergence of interest with respect to investment programs. A wide range of divergent interests may be present. For example, a high dividend payout or selling off the assets of the company reduces the asset security for the bondholders. All of these potentially adverse actions by shareholders will be taken into account by bondholders and cause the cost of straight debt to be higher. One way of avoiding these higher costs is to use bond covenants or bond agreements, which restrict the discretion of shareholders. But, this represents a cost also in that it restricts the flexibility and freedom of action of the firm. Hence, using options instead of bond covenants may be a way of reducing the cost of dealing with agency problems.

Periods of general uncertainty in the economy are likely to be particularly adverse to bondholders. For example, a severe recession will decrease the ability of a firm to pay the interest on its debt. At the other extreme, a high rate of inflation will reduce the purchasing power of the fixed return provided by straight debt. Thus, periods of high uncertainty are likely to be associated with the increased use of debt with some form of options such as warrants or convertibility.

For similar reasons, firms with considerable activity in international markets or other environments of high uncertainty impose greater risks on bondholders. International activities involve new risks such as adverse policies by foreign governments, including, in the extreme, the possibility of expropriation. Fluctuating exchange rates impose additional risks.

Finally, there is also a tax aspect. When an option feature is included in straight debt, the nominal interest expense is lowered. Hence, the tax shield provided by interest payments is reduced for the firm. This is a disadvantage unless the firm has less need for interest-type shields because of previous losses or large tax shields in the form of investment tax credits or accelerated depreciation. Hence, firms with less need for interest tax shields are more likely to use the lower interest-bearing debt with options in the form of warrants or convertibility.

Empirical Evidence Consistent with the Foregoing Rationale for the Use of Convertibles

In his early study, Brigham [1966] found that firms using convertible debt, on average, had lower bond ratings relative to firms generally. In a more recent study, Mikkelson [1980] found that firms with high debt leverage and high growth companies were active users of convertibles. High leverage increases financial risks. High growth is subject to the risks of building an effective organization, competitive reactions by rivals, and changes in investment programs. Longer maturities were also found to increase the likelihood of adding convertibility to a debt issue. Investment programs are subject to change over longer periods, and, in addition, it is simply more difficult to forecast the outlook for a firm over longer periods of time.

The basic rationale for associating options with straight debt is that while greater uncertainty increases the cost of debt, it increases the value of an associated warrant. Brennan and Schwartz [1982] provide a numerical illustration. Table 25.4 conveys the

TABLE 25.4 Illustrative Benefit of Convertible Debt

	Company Risk	
	Average	High
Straight debt coupon	13%	16%
Convertible debt coupon	10%	10.25%

nature of their example. Table 25.4 suggests that the rate on the straight debt of a firm of high risk might be three percentage points higher than the rate a firm of average risk would pay. The use of convertible debt, however, would reduce the *coupon* for both firms. But, it would be reduced relatively more for the firm of high risk. The suggested spread is only one-fourth of 1 percent for the high-risk firm over the firm of average risk. Although the coupon is relatively lower, these results do not imply that the risk-adjusted opportunity cost of capital is lower. Remember, there are no free lunches. These numerical relationships, of course, are purely illustrative. The actual figures would depend upon the state of the security markets and the terms of the individual issues.

It should be emphasized that these nominal coupon rates do not represent the actual opportunity cost of convertible debt. Since convertible debt is a hybrid between straight debt and equity, the cost of convertible debt must necessarily be higher than the cost of straight debt. The 10 percent coupon on convertible debt shown for the firm of average risk is only part of the compensation to the investor. The other portion is the value of the option that the investor has received through the convertibility feature.

Furthermore, the total opportunity cost of convertible debt to the firm of high risk is not the one-fourth of 1 percent coupon differential shown in Table 25.4. In the high-risk firm, the convertible debt will necessarily have a cost higher than that for the firm of average risk. Since the nominal coupon is only slightly higher for the firm of higher risk, the value of the option attached to its convertible debt must be even greater than for the firm of average risk. Thus, the investor in the convertible debt of the high-risk firm will be taking an even larger portion of compensation in the form of the value of the option received. Table 25.5 illustrates the differences between the coupon rate and the true before-tax opportunity cost of capital for two samples of callable-convertible bonds, one in March 1988 and the other in October 1990. The true opportunity cost of capital averaged 4.89 percent *above* the average coupon rate, 7.83 percent. Not only is the true opportunity cost of convertible debt significantly higher than the coupon rate, but also the opportunity cost is not constant over the life of the instrument because the value of call option implied in the convertibility feature changes as the option comes closer to expiration.

In spite of its high opportunity cost, the use of convertible debt is still a logical option for some firms. Necessarily, a high-risk company must pay more for financing than a firm of average risk. By combining straight debt with an option, the penalty of the higher risk may be mitigated to some degree by two influences. First, the lower coupon rate may reduce the probability of default and the bankruptcy costs that are associated with it.

TABLE 25.5   Comparison of the Coupon Rate with the Opportunity
Cost of Callable, Convertible Debt

	Coupon Rate	True Opportunity Cost of Capital	Spread
March 1988			
American Medical	9.50%	12.53%	3.03%
Ashland Oil	4.75	10.20	5.45
Baker Hughes	9.50	10.21	0.71
Bally	6.00	12.89	6.89
Bank of Boston	7.75	15.45	7.70
General Instrument	7.25	13.42	6.17
Humana	8.50	10.55	2.05
Loral	10.75	12.44	1.69
October 1990			
Kerr-McGee Corporation	7.25	13.70	6.45
Noble Affiliates	7.25	12.90	5.65
Petrie Stores	8.00	15.80	7.80
Union Carbide	7.50	12.70	5.20

Source: McKinsey analysis.

Second, convertible debt reduces the cost of information asymmetries between the firm and its creditors.

THE VALUATION OF CALLABLE-CONVERTIBLE BONDS

In concept, a convertible bond is a combination of a straight bond plus a warrant. Thus, in one sense, a convertible bond could be valued by calculating the value of the option expressed in the convertibility features. This would represent an oversimplification, however. In practice, additional factors must be taken into account. In their seminal work in this area, Brennan and Schwartz [1977, 1980] included consideration of call provisions, bankruptcy risk, and relations between the value of the underlying stock and the convertible bond value near maturity. Their formula involves a system of partial differential equations solved by numerical methods on the computer.

The complex model used by Brennan and Schwartz does not permit an easy numerical illustration of the valuation of convertible bonds. We will use, instead, a simple binomial option pricing approach (BOP). The value of a callable, convertible bond will depend on two types of uncertainty: changes in the stock price and changes in interest rates. We will take the uncertainty in interest rates into account first and show how to value a bond. Then we will extend the analysis to a callable bond, and finally to a callable-convertible bond.

FIGURE 25.3 Binomial Representation of the Term Structure

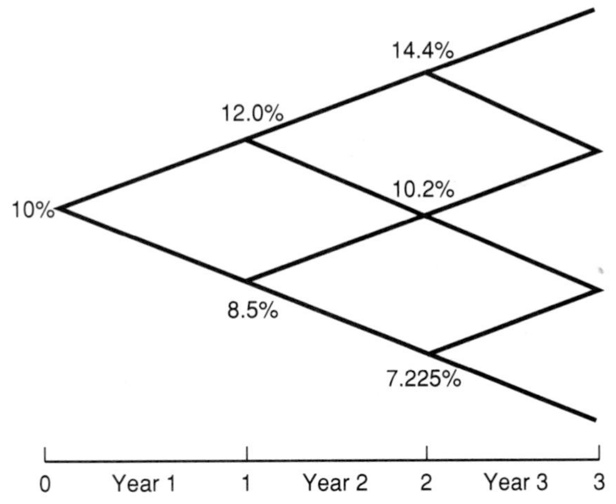

Valuing a Default-Free Bond

Figure 25.3 illustrates a binomial model of the term structure of interest rates. We assume that the bond is default free, that interest rates can move up or down with equal probability, and that upward movements increase the rate by 120 percent while downward movements decrease it by a factor of 0.85.

Figure 25.4 shows the cash flows for a default-free 12 percent bond. Regardless of the change in interest rates, the bond will repay $100 of principal plus $12 of interest at the end of the last time period. However, if interest rates have risen to 14.4 percent by then, the present value of these cash flows at the end of Year 2 is only

$$PV(\text{year } 2|r = 14.4\%) = \frac{.5(\$112) + .5(\$112)}{(1.144)} = \$97.90.$$

Thus, we see that the value of the bond, ex coupon, at the end of Year 2 depends on the level of one-year interest rates at that time. Its value is $97.90 when the rate is 14.4 percent, $101.63 when the rate is 10.2 percent, and $104.45 when the rate is 7.225 percent. By starting with the payoffs at maturity and working backward, we can solve for the present value of the bond, $104.46. Note that this is not the same result that would be obtained if we had assumed a constant 10 percent interest rate. With that (unrealistic) assumption, the present value of the bond would have been

$$B_o = \frac{\$12}{1.10} + \frac{\$12}{1.10^2} + \frac{\$100 + \$12}{1.10^3}$$

$$= \$10.91 + \$9.92 + \$84.15 = \$104.98.$$

FIGURE 25.4 Valuing a Default-Free, Straight Bond

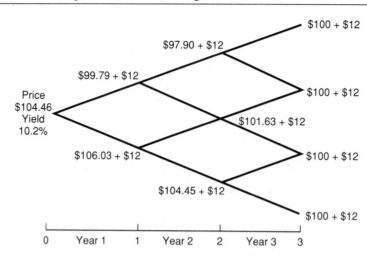

Given that the price of the bond is $104.46 with the term structure of interest rates shown in Figure 25.3, we can also compute the expected yield to maturity, y, by solving Equation 25.1:

$$B_o = \$104.46 = \frac{\$12}{(1 + y)} + \frac{\$12}{(1 + y)^2} + \frac{\$100 + \$12}{(1 + y)^3} \tag{25.1}$$

$$y = 10.2\%.$$

Valuing a Callable Bond

Suppose that the bond illustrated in Figure 25.5 is callable at a price of $104. The call provision is equivalent to a call option written by the investors who buy the bonds from the firm. The bonds may be repurchased by the firm at the exercise or call price anytime during the life of the bond. If interest rates fall, the market price of the outstanding bonds may exceed the call price, thereby making it advantageous for the firm to exercise its option to call in the debt. Since the option is valuable to the firm, it must compensate the bondholders by offering a higher interest rate on callable bonds than on similar ordinary bonds that do not have the call feature. New issues of callable bonds often bear yields that are from one-quarter to one-half of a percent higher than the yields of noncallable bonds. In our numerical example the yield in the callable bond is 10.56 percent versus 10.2 percent for its noncallable counterpart.

We can see from Figure 25.5 that the bond would be called at the end of the first year if the interest rate falls to 8.5 percent. When called, the bond is worth only $104 and if

FIGURE 25.5 Valuing a Callable Bond

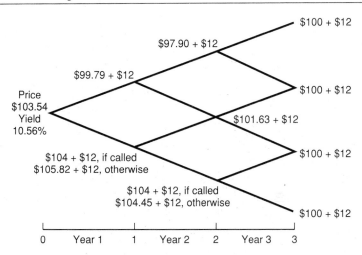

uncalled it is worth $105.82.[1] From the firm's point of view, it is better off if the bonds are called and new debt is issued at the lower 8.5 percent interest rate. As interest rates change the market value of the callable bond is compared with the call price and if the call price is lower, the firm will exercise its right. This rule will change somewhat if there are nontrivial transaction costs involved in calling and then reissuing debt. The firm might allow the market price of the callable debt to rise somewhat above the call price before exercising the call privilege.

Valuing Callable-Convertible Debt

The callable-convertible bond, C, in Figure 25.6 is modeled in a world with only one source of uncertainty, the price of the underlying common stock. We no longer assume uncertain interest rates. The risk-free rate is assumed to be constant at 8 percent. The company is assumed to be worth $400,000 right now, but there is a 60 percent chance its value may go up by 50 percent and a 40 percent chance it might go down by 50 percent each period. The company has two securities outstanding: 150 shares of common stock and 100 callable-convertible bonds that can be converted into shares at a ratio of one-half share per bond. If converted, the bondholders will own $50/(150 + 50) = 25$ percent of the company. Each $1,000 face value bond pays a $100 per period coupon. At any time

---

[1]It is worth $105.82 if not called because the model assumes that it will be called at the end of the second year for $104, therefore

$$B(\text{year } 1 | r = 8.5\%) = \frac{.5(113.63) + .5(116)}{(1.085)} = \$105.82.$$

FIGURE 25.6   Value of a Callable-Convertible Bond (Thousands of Dollars)

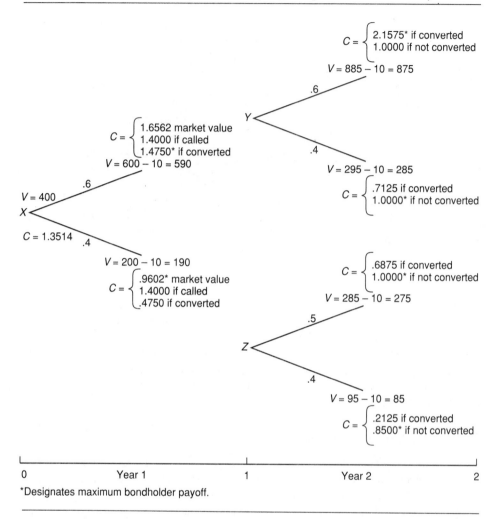

0   Year 1   1   Year 2   2

*Designates maximum bondholder payoff.

before maturity, the stockholders have the right to call the bonds for $1,400. We assume the firm pays no dividends and that the first bond coupon has just been paid.

To value the callable-convertible bonds, we start with their final payouts, determine the optimal action (call, convert, or do nothing), and compute their value at the end of Year 1 conditional on the value of the company. For example, if the value of the company goes up in the first year, the final company value can be $875 (thousand) or $285 (thousand), ex coupon. If it is $875 (thousand), the bondholders each receive $2,187.50 if they convert, and $1,000 otherwise. Obviously, they will convert. If the company value is

FIGURE 25.7   Payoffs at End of Year 1, Favorable State of Nature
(Node Y) (Thousands of Dollars)

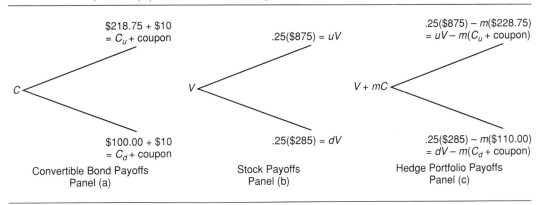

Convertible Bond Payoffs
Panel (a)

Stock Payoffs
Panel (b)

Hedge Portfolio Payoffs
Panel (c)

$285 (thousand) they will not convert, preferring to receive the $1,000 face value rather than the conversion value of $712.50. With these facts in hand, we can determine the market value of the bond at the end of Year 1. To do so we must work through an algebraic solution similar to the binomial option pricing model that was introduced in Chapter 12.

The logic of the binomial model is to write down the end-of-period payoffs for the contingent claim asset, in this case the convertible bond; then create a hedge portfolio composed of a long position in the underlying risky asset and a short position of m convertible bonds. Since the hedge portfolio earns the risk-free rate, we can use the value of the hedge portfolio to solve for the value of the convertible bond. Take the favorable state of nature at the end of Year 1 as an example. Panel (a) of Figure 25.7 shows the end-of-period payoffs for the convertible bondholders, (C) . If the stock price goes up they will convert and receive 25 percent of the value of the company ex coupon, or $218.75 (thousand). They also receive the coupon, $10 (thousand). If the stock price declines, they will not convert and will receive the face value of the bond plus the coupon, or $110 (thousand). The value of the company, V, is illustrated in Panel (b).

A risk-free hedge portfolio can be constructed with one share of stock and by shorting m convertible bonds. Its payoffs are given in Panel (c) of Figure 25.7. We can figure out the necessary number of convertible bonds by equating the end-of-period payoffs in the "up" and "down" states of nature and solving for m.

$$uV - m(C_u + \text{coupon}) = dV - m(C_d + \text{coupon})$$

$$m = \frac{V(u - d)}{C_u - C_d}$$

$$= \frac{.25(590)(1.5 - .5)}{218.75 - 100.00} = \frac{147.50}{118.75}$$

$$= 1.2421$$

A hedge portfolio consisting of one share of stock and a short position in 1.2421 convertible bonds will yield exactly the same dollar payoff regardless of the state of nature. Therefore, the present value of the hedge portfolio will earn the risk-free rate, r_f:

$$(V - mC)(1 + r_f) = uV - m(C_u + \text{coupon})$$

$$C = \frac{(u - r_f - 1)V - m(C_u + \text{coupon})}{-m(1 + r_f)}$$

$$= \frac{(1.5 - .08 - 1).25(590) - 1.2421[.25(875) + 10]}{-1.2421(1.08)}$$

$$= \frac{61.95 - 284.1304}{-1.3415}$$

$$= \$165.62 \text{ thousand.}$$

There are 100 bonds outstanding, therefore the market value per bond (at node Y) is $1,656.20 in the favorable state at the end of Year 1. When confronted with this market value, the company will decide to exercise its call option by paying only $1,400 for each bond. However, the bondholders, knowing that the company will exercise its call option, will decide to exercise their right to convert before the bonds are called. Taking all of this into consideration, the maximum bondholder payoff, given the favorable state of nature at the end of Year 1, is $1,475 per bond. (This is marked with an asterisk in Figure 25.6.)

The present value of the convertible bond is determined by repeating the aforementioned procedure for each branch of the payoff tree in Figure 25.6. By working backward from the set of final payouts, we find that the current market value of the bond is $1,258.10. The company will not call the bond immediately since it would have to pay $1,400 per bond to do so, and the bondholders will not convert because the current conversion value is .25($400,000)/100 = $1,000 per bond. Consequently, the bond will not be called or converted immediately. Similar calculations can be performed to show that the present value of the same bond, if callable but not convertible, is $1,012.98. So the value of the conversion feature is $245.12 per bond. (See Problem 25.13.)

It is important to bear in mind that there are a number of thorny problems we have not taken into account in our simple approach to valuing callable, convertible debt. For example, we have assumed the following:

- The term structure of interest rates is flat and rates are not random.

- The dividend payout is zero; usually it is growing and is variable across time.

- The company does not have a portfolio of many different convertible securities outstanding; if there were other convertible securities outstanding then as the first of them matures, if it is in-the-money, its conversion will dilute the value of "subordinate" convertible issues, thereby affecting their value.

- We have not explicitly shown how to model the effect of bankruptcy on the convertible bond payouts

- We have assumed that the company rationally exercises its call privilege.

In the next section we focus on companies' call policies.

CALL POLICY ON CONVERTIBLE BONDS

The call policy on convertible bonds performs a critical role. The effective return to the investor depends on how much the issuer permits the market price of a convertible bond to rise before calling it. For example, suppose that a convertible bond with a face value of $1,000 can be converted into 40 shares of common stock. The conversion price is, therefore, $25. If the market price of the common stock were $20, there would be no immediate incentive to convert into the common stock. However, as the common stock rises above $25, there will be some incentive to convert. For example, if the common stock were to rise in value to $35, the market value of the stock into which the bond can be converted is $1,400, which is 40 percent above the face value of the bond. Suppose that the bond carries a call provision which gives the company the right to call the bond at $105, or a value of $1,050. When the market price of the stock rises sufficiently above $25 to give the bond a value of more than $1,050, the company is in a position to call the bond at the $1,050.

Purchasers of convertible bonds would obviously prefer to have the company permit the price of the stock to rise well above the $25 before the company forced conversion. Otherwise, the holders of the convertible bonds would be faced with the choice of exercising their conversion privilege or accepting the $1,050 call price for their bond. A number of alternative company policies would be possible. Companies could establish the reputation for calling convertibles as soon as the market value of the convertible rises a small amount above the call price. Other companies might seek to establish a reputation for waiting until the market price of the stock is substantially above its conversion price to allow more generous returns to investors in their convertibles. Or a company might follow a pattern which made it difficult to discern whether or not it had a definite policy on conversion. These are the kinds of issues that have stimulated a literature on the optimal call policy for a company to follow.

Ingersoll [1977a] has set forth the optimal call point. He states, "Under the optimal call policy, the bond is called when its conversion value equals its call price." [pp. 465-466]. From a practical standpoint, Ingersoll observes that bondholders must be given 30-day notice of a call. During this delayed period, there is some risk of price fluctuations. The firm will want to have some margin of safety that conversion will take place rather than having to use cash to redeem the bonds. Ingersoll suggests that a cushion of about 6 to 8 percent above the call price would be prudent. This will give management reasonable assurance that fluctuations in the stock price after notice has been given will not create incentives for redemption rather than conversion.

The actual call policies of companies diverge widely from the theoretical boundaries. Ingersoll found that for the period between 1968 and 1975, the average ratio of conversion value of the bonds was 43.9 percent above the call price. For convertible preferreds, on average, the conversion value exceeded the call price by 38.5 percent.

The prevailing literature has found it difficult to provide a satisfactory explanation of this wide divergence between theory and practice with respect to call policy. One possible explanation is that management seeks to avoid dilution in reported earnings per share. But this is not plausible since earnings must be reported on both a diluted and undiluted basis.

If management compensation is tied to undiluted reported earnings, this, of course, would make a difference.

Another possible explanation has been termed ''fair play'' by some and ''market memory'' by others. The idea that management imposes self-restrictions on call policy out of some notion of fair play has not received much support. A more plausible view is that on successive issues of convertibles, the market will form an expectation of the company's call policies by its past behavior. Anecdotal evidence can be found in the financial press that companies have had to pay a somewhat higher interest rate on a new issue of convertibles because of a past history of calling convertibles as soon as their conversion value has risen modestly above their call price. The market will penalize erratic behavior; what appears optimal is the adoption by the company of a consistent call policy. Whether the policy is to call at a conversion value substantially above call price or at a conversion value close to call price will be ''priced out'' by the market. This is not a matter of ''fairness'' or self-imposed restrictions. It is a matter of providing investors with a basis for forming expectations.

The reason that the call policy of a company takes on significance is that it has a major influence on what investors will earn by purchasing a convertible (which also, of course, represents the cost to the issuing firm). But, the convertible is a straight bond plus an option. The idea behind an option is that there will be variations in the price of the underlying stock. Upside fluctuations provide opportunities for converting into the common stock. One way of portraying these relationships is expressed in Equation 25.2.

$$C_t = p_o(1 + g)^t q, \tag{25.2}$$

where

C_t = the conversion value of the bond at Time t

p_o = the initial price of the underlying common stock = \$44.02

g = the growth rate in the price of the common stock = .06

q = the conversion ratio = 18.52.

Equation 25.2 is an oversimplification in a number of respects. The idea of an option is that there are fluctuations in both directions. Equation 25.2 ignores the downside fluctuations and postulates upside movements expressed as a constant rate of growth. Also, the formula implies certainty, but a number of uncertainties are involved. The actual rate of growth is uncertain, its duration is not known, and the call policy of the company may not be clear.

But, Equation 25.2 is a useful oversimplification for illustrating how the return to the investor and the cost to the issuing firm depend upon the price of the underlying stock which is obtained if the option is exercised. In the present illustration, the convertible bond was not callable until five years after issuance. Let us consider some possibilities of what the conversion value of the bond might be after five years have elapsed. Suppose that during the five-year period, the stock averaged a growth rate of 6 percent and that the call price at the end of five years is $1,080. First, calculate the conversion value as shown in Equation 25.2a:

$$C_5 = \$44.02(1 + .06)^5 18.52$$
$$= \$44.02(1.3382)(18.52) \qquad \textbf{(25.2a)}$$
$$= \$1,090.97.$$

Suppose the call value at the end of five years is $1,080. The conversion value is only about 1 percent above its call value. On the other hand, if the underlying stock price had grown at an average rate of 12 percent for the five years, we would have the situation depicted in Equation 25.2b:

$$C_5 = \$44.02(1 + .12)^5 18.52$$
$$= \$44.02(1.7623)(18.52) \qquad \textbf{(25.2b)}$$
$$= \$1,436.72.$$

Here, the conversion value would be $1,436.72, which is about 33 percent above the $1,080 call value.

The return that investors actually realize on a convertible, therefore, is heavily dependent on the performance of the stock price in relation to the exercise price, which is, of course, implicit in the conversion ratio used in Equation 25.2. For example, using the data assumed for Equation 25.2b, we can calculate the return realized by the investor if the company followed the policy of calling a convertible as soon as callability is permitted when its conversion value is substantially above the call price. We shall define the expected rate of return on a convertible, k_c, by solving for k_c in Equation 25.3.

$$B_{co} = \sum_{t=1}^{n} \frac{c}{(1 + k_c)^t} + \frac{C_n}{(1 + k_c)^n}. \qquad \textbf{(25.3)}$$

The equation is purely definitional; it simply states that if an investor pays B_{co} dollars for a convertible bond, holds it for n years, and receives a series of interest payments plus a conversion value, then the return on the investment will be equal to k_c.[2]

The *ex ante* yield on a convertible (k_c) is probabilistic — dependent on a set of variables subject to probability distributions and, hence, itself a random variable. It is possible, however, to define each of the determinants of k_c in terms of its mean expected value; $E(g)$, for example, is the expected value of the growth rate in the stock's price over n years. For simplicity, $E(g)$ and other random variables are shortened to g, C_n, and so on.

For example, we have a bond paying a coupon of $80 a year and we are analyzing the effect if the company calls the bond as soon as possible at the end of five years when the

---

[2]Three simplifications are made in this analysis. First, taxes are ignored. Second, the problem of reinvestment rates is handled by assuming that all reinvestment is made at the internal rate of return. Third, it is assumed that bondholders do not hold stock after conversion; they cash out, as do some institutional investors precluded from holding common stock.

provisions of the bond indenture permit the company to do so. Using semiannual compounding, we can express the relationships in Equation 25.3a:

$$B_{co} = \sum_{t=1}^{10} \frac{40}{(1 + .07)^t} + \frac{1,436.72}{(1 + .07)^{10}}$$ (25.3a)

$$997 = 7.0236(40) + .5083(1,436.72)$$

$$= 280.94 + 730.28$$

$$997 \approx 1,011.22.$$

With semiannual compounding, the coupon would be $40 at each semiannual payment for ten periods. We find that using a semiannual rate of 7 percent, we obtain a bond value approximating the assumed price paid for the convertible bond, $997. Hence, the effective yield to the investor and the effective cost to the issuer is slightly over 14 percent. This represents 2.5 percentage points higher than the then-prevailing market rate on straight debt of otherwise similar characteristics. This illustrates how the effective return on a convertible bond is likely to be greater than the return on straight debt. The relationships depicted here are purely illustrative. What is actually realized depends upon the resolution of a wide range of uncertainties that are involved as to the performance of the company and its common stock during the time period under analysis.

Studies of convertible bond calls find a negative effect on market prices [Mikkelson, 1981]. Convertible bond calls are associated with an average 2 percent decline in stock prices. Forced conversions of preferred stock issues are associated with an average market decline of 0.33 percent. One possible explanation for this negative market reaction to forced conversion is that debt leverage has been decreased and some of the firm's interest tax shelter has been lost. However, if only a pure tax effect were involved, then managers would not be acting in the best interest of shareholders to reduce the tax advantage from which they had been benefiting. This suggests that management had been pressured by some other developments or factors which caused it to sacrifice some tax shelter. Thus, forced conversions may convey an "information effect." The market may interpret forced conversions as a judgment by management that less-favorable developments are facing the firm. This activity by managers in reducing the amount of debt on the balance sheets may be regarded as getting the firm ready to meet some future adversity. Thus, forced conversion may be viewed as a harbinger of unfavorable things to come and cause the market price of the firm's common stock to decline.

The relationships among the coupon, purchase price, call policy, and investor cash-out policy determine the return on an investment in a convertible security. This represents the cost of convertible debt. The required return or cost of convertible debt is composed of two parts. One is the interest return based on the coupon on the convertible debt. This is, typically, lower than the return on straight debt. The second component of return is based on the expected rise in the price of the common stock into which a conversion may be made. This component of return carries risk associated with a security junior to straight debt. Hence, the required return on convertibles would, on average, be higher than the cost of straight debt.

SUMMARY

Both warrants and convertibles are forms of options used in financing business firms. When warrants are exercised, they bring in additional funds to the firm. When convertibles are exchanged for common stock, no increase in funds is provided to the firm. Only the form of its financing has been changed. The time to maturity on warrants issued by a company is usually much longer than the maturity of puts and calls traded on the options exchanges. A warrant is a call option plus a provision for the issuance of more securities for cash. The return and risk of a warrant are correlated with the return and risk of a call. The value of a warrant is the value of the equivalent call divided by the dilution factor $(1 + q)$, where q is the ratio of warrants to shares.

In concept, a convertible bond represents straight debt plus a warrant. Hence, the value of a convertible bond may be viewed as a package of straight debt plus the value of the associated option. Since a convertible bond usually includes a call feature which is adjusted over time, and since the maturity characteristics as well as bankruptcy possibilities must be taken into account, the precise calculation of the value of a convertible can be quite complex.

But, the rationale for both warrants and convertibles has now been well established. The value of straight debt falls with risk, or, equivalently, its required cost rises with risk. But, the value of the associated warrant or option rises with risk. Hence, it is easier for sellers and buyers of a security which combines both features to arrive at a mutually agreeable price. Thus, warrants and convertibles perform a particularly useful role in selling the securities of firms with high or uncertain operating risks. They also provide control of agency problems with respect to the possibility of changing investment programs and other areas where there may be a divergence of interests between shareholders and bondholders. Warrants and convertibles are also likely to be used to an increased degree during periods of high uncertainty in the economy.

In theory, convertibles should be called when the conversion value of the bond equals its call price plus a cushion of about 6 to 8 percent above the call price. However, the practice is much different. On average, companies call convertibles when they are about 40 percent above their call price. The reasons for this divergence are still in dispute.

It is clear, however, that a call policy which delays until a substantial premium of conversion value over call price has developed increases the return to holding a convertible. The basic reason is that the value of any option is increased as its maturity is increased. Delaying the call until a substantial premium has developed will generally involve a longer time for investors to exercise the conversion option. The expected return on a convertible can be calculated from Equation 25.3. The cost of a convertible will generally be found to be above the cost of straight debt. It will represent a weighted average between the cost of straight debt and the cost of equity capital.

In brief, warrants and convertibles may perform a useful role in reducing monitoring costs of controlling agency problems. Also, combining an option with a straight debt security makes its value and cost less sensitive to the uncertainty associated with a firm or a project. Thus, warrants and convertibles are likely to be used when agency problems may be of high concern and when uncertainty due either to external economy factors or to conditions specific to the firm may be particularly large.

QUESTIONS

25.1 Why do warrants typically sell at prices greater than their formula values?

25.2 Why do convertibles typically sell at prices greater than straight debt with the same coupon, maturity, and call provisions?

25.3 What effect does the trend in stock prices (subsequent to issue) have on a firm's ability to raise funds through convertibles? Through warrants?

25.4 If a firm expects to have additional financial requirements in the future, would you recommend that it use convertibles or bonds with warrants? Why?

25.5 Evaluate the following statement: Issuing convertible securities represents a means by which a firm can sell common stock at a price above the existing market.

25.6 Why do corporations often sell convertibles on a rights basis?

25.7 Why might an investor prefer a bond with a warrant attached, over a convertible bond?

PROBLEMS

25.1 A convertible bond has a face value of $1,000 and a 10 percent coupon rate. It is convertible into stock of $50; that is, each bond can be exchanged for 20 shares. The current price of the stock is $43 per share.
   a. If the price per share grows at 6 percent per year for five years, what will the approximate conversion value be at the end of five years?
   b. If dividends on the stock are presently $2 per share, and if these also grow at 6 percent per year, will bondholders convert after five years, or will they tend to hold onto their bonds? Explain.
   c. If the bonds are callable at a 10 percent premium, about how much would you lose per bond if the bonds were called before you converted? (Assume the same conversion value as in Part (a) above, at the end of five years.)

25.2 Warrants attached to a bond entitle the bondholder to purchase one share of stock at $10 per share. Compute the approximate value of a warrant if
   a. The market price of the stock is $9 per share
   b. The market price of the stock is $12 per share
   c. The market price of the stock is $15 per share
   d. Each warrant entitles you to purchase two shares at $10, and the current price of the stock is $15 per share.

25.3 The Schuller Chemical Company's net income for 1992 was $2,450,000. Schuller's capital stock consists of 500,000 shares of common stock, and 175,000 warrants, each good for buying two shares of common stock at $25. The warrants are protected against dilution; that is, the exercise price must be adjusted downward in the event of a stock dividend or if Schuller sells common stock at less than the $25 exercise price. On June 1, 1993, Schuller issued rights to buy one new share of common stock for $15 for every four shares held. The market price of Schuller stock on June 1 was $45 per share.
   a. Compute primary and fully diluted EPS as of December 31, 1992.

b. What is the theoretical value of the rights before the stock sells ex rights?

c. What is the adjusted exercise price of the warrants after the rights offering? (Hint: Adjust the exercise price of the warrant so that the formula value of the warrant based on the ex rights stock price is the same as the formula value before the rights offering.)

d. Net income for 1993 is $2,800,000. All of the rights and none of the warrants have been exercised. Compute primary and fully diluted EPS for 1993.

25.4 The Ironhill Manufacturing Company was planning to finance an expansion in the summer of 1992. The principal executives of the company were agreed that an industrial company such as theirs should finance growth by means of common stock rather than debt. However, they felt the price of the company's common stock did not reflect its true worth, so they were desirous of selling a convertible security. They considered a convertible debenture but feared the burden of fixed interest charges if the common stock did not rise in price to make conversion attractive. They decided on an issue of convertible preferred stock.

The common stock was selling at $48.00 a share. Management projected earnings for 1993 at $3.60 a share and expected a future growth rate of 12 percent a year. It was agreed by the investment bankers and management that the common stock would sell at 13.3 times earnings, the current price-earnings ratio.

a. What conversion price should be set by the issuer?

b. Should the preferred stock include a call price provision? Why?

25.5 The Durham Forge has the following balance sheet:

Balance Sheet 1

Current assets	$125,000	Current debt (free)	$ 50,000
Net fixed assets	125,000	Common stock, par value $2	50,000
		Retained earnings	150,000
Total assets	$250,000	Total claims	$250,000

Durham plans to sell $150,000 of debentures in order to finance its expected sales growth. It is trying to decide whether to sell convertible debentures or debentures with warrants. With spontaneous financing and retained earnings, next year's balance sheet is projected as follows:

Balance Sheet 2

Current assets	$250,000	Current debt	$100,000
Net fixed assets	250,000	Debentures	150,000
		Common stock, par value $2	50,000
		Retained earnings	200,000
Total assets	$500,000	Total claims	$500,000

The convertible debentures will pay 7 percent interest and will be convertible into 40 shares of common stock for each $1,000 debenture. The debentures with warrants will carry an 8 percent coupon and entitle each holder of a $1,000 debenture to buy 25 shares of common stock at $50.

a. Assume that convertible debentures are sold and that all are later converted. Show the new balance sheet, disregarding any changes in retained earnings.

Balance Sheet 3

	Current debt	_____
	Debentures	_____
	Common stock, par value $2	_____
	Paid-in capital	_____
	Retained earnings	_____
Total assets _____	Total claims	_____

b. Assume that instead of convertibles, debentures with warrants were issued. Assume further that the warrants were all exercised. Show the new balance sheet figures:

Balance Sheet 4

	Current debt	_____
	Debentures	_____
	Common stock, par value $2	_____
	Paid-in capital	_____
	Retained earnings	_____
Total assets _____	Total claims	_____

c. Durham's earnings before interest and taxes are 30 percent of total assets, its P-E ratio is 16, and its corporate tax rate is 40 percent. Prepare income statements corresponding to balance sheets 3 and 4. What is the effect of each alternative on Durham's EPS and market price per share?

d. Should Durham choose convertible debentures or debentures with warrants?

25.6 On July 2, 1984, it was announced that the Dana Corporation was issuing $150 million face amount of debt at $500 for each $1,000 face amount of securities. The debentures carry a $5\frac{7}{8}$ percent coupon, maturing in 2009. They are convertible until December 15, 1996, at $75.64 face amount of debentures for each common share. The common closed on July 2, 1984, at $32.

a. How many shares of common stock would be received upon conversion?

b. What is the conversion price based on the $500 issuing price of the bonds?

c. What percentage premium does this represent over the $32 common stock price?

d. What is the yield to maturity of the bonds based on the data given? (Assume semiannual compounding.)

e. Assume that the common stock of Dana increases in price by 10 percent per year and that the bonds sell at the higher of 12 percent above their conversion value or at their "intermediate face value," which is the $500 issue price increased by 4 percent per year. Assume that for a number of reasons, a purchaser of the bonds sells the bonds at the end of ten years. Based on the higher of the two prices, what return has the investor earned?

25.7 The Printomat Company has grown rapidly during the past five years. Recently, its commercial bank has urged the company to consider increasing permanent financing. Its bank loan under a line of credit has risen to $175,000, carrying 15 percent interest. Printomat has been 30 to 60 days late in paying trade creditors.

Discussions with an investment banker have resulted in the suggestion to raise $350,000 at this time. Investment bankers have assured the company that the following alternatives will be feasible (ignoring flotation costs):

(1) Sell common stock at $7.

(2) Sell convertible bonds at a 7 percent coupon, convertible into common stock at $8.

(3) Sell debentures at a 7 percent coupon, each $1,000 bond carrying 125 warrants to buy common stock at $8.

Additional information is given in the company's balance sheet and income statement below:

Printomat Company Balance Sheet

		Current liabilities	$315,000
		Common stock, par $1	90,000
		Retained earnings	45,000
Total assets	$450,000	Total liabilities and capital	$450,000

Printomat Company Income Statement

Sales	$900,000
All costs except interest	810,000
Net operating income	$ 90,000
Interest	26,250
Income before taxes	$ 63,750
Taxes (at 40%)	25,500
Net income	$ 38,250
Shares	90,000
Earnings per share	$0.43
Price-earnings ratio	17 times
Market price of stock	$7.31

Mary Anderson, the president, owns 70 percent of Printomat's common stock and wishes to maintain control of the company; 90,000 shares are outstanding.

a. Show the new balance sheet under each alternative. For alternatives 2 and 3, show the balance sheet after conversion of the debentures or exercise of warrants. Assume that half the funds raised will be used to pay off the bank loan and half to increase total assets.

b. Show Anderson's control position under each alternative, assuming that she does not purchase additional securities.

c. What is the effect on earnings per share of each alternative if it is assumed that profits before interest and taxes will be 20 percent of total assets?

d. What will be the debt ratio under each alternative?

e. Which of the three alternatives would you recommend to Anderson? Explain.

25.8 Vaught Engineering plans to sell a 6 percent coupon, $1,000 par value, 20-year convertible bond issue. The bond is callable at $1,050 in the first year, and the call price declines by $2.50 each year thereafter. The bond may be converted into 18 shares of stock with a current market price of $46 per share. The stock price is expected to grow at a rate of 7 percent per year. Nonconvertible bonds of the same risk as Vaught's would yield 9 percent. In the past, Vaught's policy has been to call convertible securities when the conversion value exceeds the call price by 20 percent.

a. Determine the straight debt value (B_t) at $t = 0$, $t = 6$, and $t = 10$. Use these three points and the maturity value (M) to graph the straight debt value of the convertible.

b. Graph the conversion value (C_t) on the same graph for $t = 0$, $t = 6$, and $t = 10$.

c. What is the minimum the convertible can sell for at $t = 0$? At $t = 6$? At $t = 10$? Assume the stock value increases as predicted.

d. Show the call price, D_{ct}, of the debt on the same graph at $t = 0$, $t = 5$, $t = 6$, and $t = 10$.

e. In what year is the debt expected to be called?

f. On the graph, locate on C_t the point where the expected call policy forces conversion (M'). Draw a curve between the issue price B_{co} and M' with curvature similar to the C_t curve.

g. What would debtholders do if the bond was called at $t = 0$? At $t = 5$? At $t = 6$?

h. What return on investment is earned by bondholders who purchased the convertibles at par value on the date they were issued if the bonds are called in four years?

25.9 Olympic Lumber Company is planning to raise $10 million by selling convertible debentures. It recently sold an issue of nonconvertible debentures yielding 10 percent. Investment bankers have informed the treasurer that she can sell convertibles at a lower interest yield; they have offered her these two choices:

(1) convertible bond price = $55.55 ($q = 18$)
coupon = $70 (7% coupon yield)
face value = $1,000
25-year maturity

(2) convertible bond price = $58.82 ($q = 17$)
coupon = $80 (8% coupon yield)
face value = $1,000
25-year maturity

In each case, the bonds are not callable for two years; but, thereafter, they are callable at $1,000. Investors do not expect the bonds to be called unless $C_t = $1,354; but they do expect the bonds to be called if $C_t = $1,354.

Olympic's current stock price (p_o) is $50, and its growth is expected to continue at an annual rate of 6 percent. Olympic's current dividend is $4.50 per share, so investors appear to have an expected (and required) rate of return of 15 percent ($k = d/p_o + g = $4.50/$50 + 6%$) on investments as risky as the company's common stock. Olympic's tax rate is 40 percent.

a. Determine the expected yield on Bond A and on Bond B.

b. Do the terms offered by the investment bankers seem consistent? Which bond would an investor prefer? Which would Olympic's treasurer prefer?

c. Suppose the company decided on Bond A but wanted to step up the conversion price from $55.55 to $58.82 after ten years. Should this stepped-up conversion price affect the expected yield and the other terms on the bonds?

d. Suppose, contrary to investors' expectations, Olympic called the bonds after two years. What would the *ex post* (after-the-fact) effective yield be on Bond A? Would this early call affect the company's credibility in the financial markets?

e. What would happen to the wealth position of an investor who bought Olympic bonds the day before the announcement of the unexpected two-year call?

f. Suppose the expected yield on the convertible had been less than that on straight debt (actually, it was higher). Would this appear logical? Explain.

25.10 The Wright Corporation has a current market value of $40 million with 1 million shares of common stock outstanding. If the firm's current investment policy is successful, its value at the end of one period is expected to be $60 million; if unsuccessful, end-of-period value is expected to be $20 million. The firm has debt outstanding on which the face value of $25 million must be repaid at the end of the period. The risk-free rate is 10 percent.

a. Use the binomial option pricing approach to find the present value of Wright's debt if the debt is nonconvertible.

b. If the debt is convertible with a conversion price of $25 per share, what is the present value of the convertible debt?

25.11 In the text, we have described the methodology and the procedures for valuing a default-free straight bond with a three-year maturity. To economize on space we omitted a number of intermediate steps. As a problem exercise, write out the solution processes indicated by Figure 25.3 and Figure 25.4 including all the steps and verifying the results shown in the text for arriving at the value of the bond and the computation of the expected yield to maturity, y.

25.12 The bond in Problem 25.11 was a straight bond. We now postulate that it is a callable bond, callable at any time at a price of $104. Verify the data in Figure 25.5 by writing out all of the intermediate steps. You need only write the bottommost branch of the binomial tree representing nodes A, C, F, and J. Also, verify for Figure 25.5 at node A the price of the bond and its yield to maturity.

25.13 In this problem, verify in systematic, detailed fashion the numerical results presented in Figures 25.6 and 25.7 based on the facts of the problem as given in the text.

25.14 *(Use the computer diskette, File name: 25CNVRT, Convertibles.)*

a. Given the initial assumptions (Screen #3), what is the relationship between the theoretical conversion value and the straight-debt value over the life of the bond (Screen #4)? (The theoretical conversion value does not include the implicit option premium which would increase the market price of the convertible.)

(1) What is the lowest price the bond could sell for in year 0? In year 4? In year 10?

b. Suppose the growth rate of the stock price is 5 percent. How does this affect the relationship between theoretical conversion value and straight-debt value? (Note: Calculations may be somewhat slow due to the complexity of the model.)

(1) What if the growth rate of the stock price is 10 percent?

c. Investors expect the bond to be called at the end of the year in which its conversion value exceeds its call price by 10 percent. What is the ex ante expected return for an investor who bought the bond at issuance for $1,000 if the expected growth rate in the price of stock is 7 percent?

(1) What is the ex post return if the growth rate turns out to be 5 percent?

(2) What is the ex post return if the growth rate turns out to be 10 percent? (Assume the call policy remains the same.)

d. Answer the same questions as in Question (c) above assuming that the firm follows, and is expected to follow, a call policy which allows the conversion value to exceed the call price by 40 percent before conversion is forced.

e. You are now free to use the model to test the sensitivity of convertible return to the underlying variables.

SELECTED REFERENCES

Alexander, Gordon J., and Stover, Roger D., "The Effect of Forced Conversion on Common Stock Prices," *Financial Management,* 9 (Spring 1980), pp. 39–45.

————, "Pricing in the New Issue Convertible Debt Market," *Financial Management,* 6 (Fall 1977), pp. 35–39.

————, and Kuhnau, David B., "Market Timing Strategies in Convertible Debt Financing," *Journal of Finance,* 34 (March 1979), pp. 143–155.

Black, Fischer, and Scholes, Myron, "The Valuation of Option Contracts and a Test of Market Efficiency," *Journal of Finance,* 27 (May 1972), pp. 399–417.

Brennan, M. J., "The Pricing of Contingent Claims in Discrete Time Models," *Journal of Finance,* 24 (March 1979), pp. 53–68.

————, and Schwartz, E., "The Case for Convertibles," *Chase Financial Quarterly,* 1 (1982), pp. 27–46.

————, "Analyzing Convertible Bonds," *Journal of Financial and Quantitative Analysis,* 15 (November 1980), pp. 907–929.

————, "Convertible Bonds: Valuation and Optimal Strategies for Call and Conversion," *Journal of Finance,* 32 (December 1977), pp. 1699–1715.

Brigham, Eugene F., "An Analysis of Convertible Debentures: Theory and Some Empirical Evidence," *Journal of Finance,* 21 (March 1966), pp. 35–54.

Courtadon, G. R., and Merrick, J. J., "The Option Pricing Model and the Valuation of Corporate Securities," *Chase Financial Quarterly,* 1 (Fall 1983), pp. 43–56.

Emanuel, David C., "Warrant Valuation and Exercise Strategy," *Journal of Financial Economics,* 12 (August 1983), pp. 211–235.

Frankle, A. W., and Hawkins, C. A., "Beta Coefficients for Convertible Bonds," *Journal of Finance,* 30 (March 1975), pp. 207–210.

Galai, Dan, and Schneller, Mier I., "Pricing of Warrants and the Value of the Firm," *Journal of Finance,* 33 (December 1978), pp. 1333–1342.

Hettenhouse, G. W., and Puglisi, D. J., "Investor Experience with Options," *Financial Analysts Journal,* 31 (July-August 1975), pp. 53–58.

Ingersoll, J., "An Examination of Corporate Call Policies on Convertible Securities," *Journal of Finance,* (May 1977a), pp. 463–478.

————, "A Contingent-Claims Valuation of Convertible Securities," *Journal of Financial Economics,* (May 1977b), pp. 289–322.

Loy, L. David, and Toole, Howard R., "Accounting for Discounted Convertible Bond Exchanges: A Survey of Results," *Journal of Accounting, Auditing and Finance,* 3 (Spring 1980), pp. 227–243.

Mikkelson, Wayne H., "Convertible Calls and Security Returns," *Journal of Financial Economics,* 9 (September 1981), pp. 237–264.

————, "Convertible Debt and Warrant Financing: A Study of the Agency Cost Motivation and the Wealth Effects of Calls of Convertible Securities," MERC monograph and theses series MT-80-03, University of Rochester, Rochester, N.Y., 1980.

Schwartz, Eduardo S., "The Valuation of Warrants: Implementing a New Approach," *Journal of Financial Economics,* 4 (January 1977), pp. 79–93.

Stone, Bernell K., "Warrant Financing," *Journal of Financial and Quantitative Analysis,* 11 (March 1976), pp. 143–154.

CHAPTER 26

Pension Fund Management

Corporate pension plan liabilities have grown rapidly during the last several decades. For many companies, pension plan liabilities are larger than the book value of all long-term assets. This chapter describes various types of pension plans, publicly accepted accounting principles which govern pension plan reporting, the regulation of pension plans by ERISA, and management decision making about various pension plan problems, such as how to evaluate the performance of pension fund assets and how to use pension fund assets to reduce taxes.

PENSION PLAN OVERVIEW: HISTORICAL DATA AND FINANCIAL STATEMENTS

A *pension plan* is a promise by an employer to provide benefits to employees upon their retirement. Contractual pension fund commitments are a liability of the employer and must be disclosed in the firm's financial statements. A pension fund is established on behalf of the employees and is managed by a trustee, who collects cash from the firm, manages the assets owned by the fund, and makes disbursements to retired employees. The firm is able to expense pension fund contributions for tax purposes. The fund pays no taxes on its earnings. However, beneficiaries must pay personal taxes upon receiving retirement payments from the fund. Hence, pension funds are a tax-favored form of employee compensation because taxes are deferred until retirement.

Table 26.1 shows the rapid growth of pension fund assets in the United States over the past two decades. Private pension plans have grown at a rate of 14.6 percent per year and government plans at 13.2 percent per year. The rapid growth of private plans is explained, in part, by the fact that corporate contributions are tax deductible while em-

TABLE 26.1 Private and Public Pension Funds, by Type of Fund: Selected Years (1970–1988) (Billions of Dollars)

	1970	1980	1988
Private funds			
Insured	$ 41.0	$172.0	$ 631.7
Noninsured[a]	112.0	469.6	1,140.0
Public funds			
Railroad retirement	4.5	2.5	7.8
Federal civil service[b]	23.0	73.9	200.3
State and local government	60.3	198.1	605.1
Total	$240.8	$916.1	$2,584.9

[a]Covers all pension funds of corporations, nonprofit organizations, unions, and multi-employer groups. Also includes deferred profit-sharing plans; excludes health, welfare, and bonus plans.
[b]Includes U.S. Foreign Service Retirement and Disability Trust Fund and the Federal Employees Retirement System.
Source: U.S. Department of Commerce. Bureau of the Census. *Statistical Abstract of the United States, 1990.* Table No. 591.

ployee benefits are tax deferred until retirement, when payments are then taxed at the individual's ordinary tax rate. Table 26.1 also shows that in 1988, $2,584.9 billion was invested in pension funds, with 68.5 percent of this total in the private sector. Pension fund management involves huge sums of money. Corporations often make their pension contributions to insurance companies, which then guarantee the benefits, or else firms manage their own funds. In 1988, 35.6 percent of the private pension fund assets were with insurance companies, but the majority, 64.3 percent, was controlled by the corporation via a pension fund trustee. It is also worth noting that in 1987, there were 48.1 million people who were members of pension plans. They represent roughly 41 percent of the work force in the United States.

Table 26.2 shows the format of a pension fund income statement and balance sheet. Cash inflows to the fund are provided by corporate contributions, employee contributions, dividends and interest earned by the fund's stocks and bonds, and capital gains. Cash outflows are management fees, brokerage expenses, disbursements to beneficiaries, and capital losses. The change in the net fund balance is the difference between inflows and outflows. The fund's profit is not taxable.

Turning to the balance sheet in Table 26.2, most pension funds hold their assets in the form of marketable securities: money market accounts, bonds, and stock. Because pension fund earnings are not taxed, it never pays to hold municipal bonds because their low tax-exempt interest rates are always dominated by the higher interest paid by taxable bonds of similar risk. Direct investment in real estate (with the possible exception of undeveloped land) is also not advisable because most real estate investments are priced such that the investor must be in a relatively high tax bracket in order to receive a positive after-tax return. Pension funds are in a zero tax bracket. Although the pension fund can profitably hold taxable securities, it is not immediately clear what percentage of the fund's investment should be held in the form of interest-bearing securities (money market funds and bonds) or common stock. This choice will be discussed later in the chapter. Mean-

TABLE 26.2 Format for Pension Fund Income Statement and Balance Sheet

Pension Fund Income Statement	Pension Fund Balance Sheet
Funds received	Assets
From employer(s)	Marketable securities (market value)
From employees	Cash (money market accounts)
From dividends, interest, and capital gains (losses)	Bonds
	Stock
Funds expended	PV of future contributions
Management fees and brokerage costs	Deficit (surplus)
Disbursements to beneficiaries	
Change in net fund balance	Liabilities
	PV of benefits for past service
	PV of benefits for future service

while, Table 26.3 shows the actual portfolio composition of private pension plans not held with insurance companies at the end of each of the last five decades. The most striking change in portfolio composition is the decline in the proportion invested in bonds from 74.3 percent in 1950 to 28.18 percent in 1988 and the increase in stocks (common and preferred) from 17.1 percent in 1950 to 47.6 percent in 1988.

Returning to the pension fund balance sheet in Table 26.2, marketable securities is the only item which is not the result of a present value calculation. The present value of future contributions to the fund is the other major asset. Contributions are received in two forms: cash from the firm and earnings on the fund's assets. A major issue is: What rate of return will be generated from the fund's assets? If the return is high, then the firm can reduce the amount of cash which it puts into the fund. As we shall see, later in the chapter, the rate of return assumption is a tricky decision.

Liabilities are subdivided into two categories. The present value of benefits from past service is handled one of two ways. Some companies calculate the present value of *vested*

TABLE 26.3 Assets of Private and Public Pension Funds, by Type of Fund: Selected Years (1950–1988)

	1950	1960	1970	1980	1988
U.S. government securities	30.50%	8.10%	2.68%	10.78%	12.25%
Corporate bonds[a]	43.80	47.40	26.25	16.55	15.83
Corporate equities[b]	17.10	34.70	60.63	49.11	47.59
Other	8.60	9.80	10.45	23.57	24.32
Total	100.00%	100.00%	100.00%	100.00%	100.00%

[a]Includes mutual fund shares.
[b]Includes foreign bonds.
Source: U.S. Department of Commerce. Bureau of the Census. *Statistical Abstract of the United States, 1990.* Table No. 591.

TABLE 26.4   Hypothetical 1984 Consolidated Year-End Balance Sheet for du Pont Showing Vested Pension Liabilities (Billions of Dollars)

Assets		Liabilities	
Pension fund	$ 8.4	Pension liability	$ 7.6
Plant and equipment	14.4	Long-term debt	3.4
Other long-term assets	1.0	Equity	13.0
Current assets	8.7	Other long-term liabilities	3.3
		Current liabilities	5.2
Total assets	$32.5	Total liabilities	$32.5

benefits only. These are the benefits which would be paid if all employees left the firm immediately. It is typical that employees become vested in the pension plan only after accumulating a minimum period of seniority, say five years. If they leave prior to five years, they receive none of their promised pension benefits. An alternative procedure is to calculate the present value of all benefits accrued for past service whether employees are fully vested or not. Hence, *accrued benefits* will usually be larger than vested benefits because not all employees are fully vested. Regardless of how the present value of benefits from past service is handled, total pension liabilities remain unchanged. If only vested benefits are included in the present value of benefits for past service, then unvested benefits are included in the second liability category.

The second major liability item is the present value of benefits for future service. Its computation is complex and depends on actuarial assumptions about the amount of employee turnover, the age and seniority of retiring employees, their life expectancy, and the choice of a discount rate for present value computations.

Of major concern to all parties is the size of the pension fund deficit or surplus. An unfunded deficit is an asset of the pension fund (as shown in Table 26.2) and a liability of the firm, and it can be enormous. For example, had the pension liabilities of du Pont been included, its balance sheet for the end of its 1984 fiscal year would have looked like Table 26.4. The $7.6 billion pension liability represents the vested liabilities of du Pont, that is, the liability which would be incurred if all of the employees left the firm at the end of 1984. Du Pont's pension was overfunded by $800 million. In principle, this money "belongs" to shareholders. Even though the pension was overfunded, the addition of pension assets and liabilities to the balance sheet raised du Pont's debt-to-total-assets ratio from 49 percent to 60 percent.[1] Clearly, pension fund liabilities are important enough to require full disclosure.

---

[1]The effect of the pension fund on the balance sheet is to increase assets by $8.4 billion, to increase pension liabilities by $7.6 billion, and to increase equity by $0.8 billion (the amount of the overfunding). Note that Table 26.4 is purely hypothetical and does not conform to the generally accepted accounting practices which are discussed later in the chapter.

PENSION FUND REGULATIONS: ERISA, FASB 36, AND THE IRS

With the rapid growth of pensions as a form of deferred compensation (as documented in Table 26.1), it became more and more important that firms fully disclose their pension commitments in their financial statements and that various pension practices become regulated by law. The Financial Accounting Standards Board (FASB) has established the generally accepted accounting practices for reporting by pension funds (FASB No. 35, issued in 1980) and by firms (APB No. 8, issued in 1966, and FASB No. 36, issued in 1980). In September 1974, President Ford signed into law the Employment Retirement Income Security Act (ERISA), which regulates various aspects of pension plans, including eligibility, vesting, funding, fiduciary responsibility, reporting and disclosure, and plan termination insurance.

There are two types of pension plans. *Defined contribution plans* consist of funds built up over time via employee and employer contributions, but benefits are not predetermined. Employees are simply paid out the market value of their portion of the pension fund when they retire. The firm has no responsibilities other than paying its share of the contributions and prudent management of the pension fund assets. The second, and more common type, is a *defined benefit plan*. Corporations are required to pay a contractual benefit upon the retirement of a vested employee. When ERISA was signed, defined benefit pensions were converted from corporate promises to liabilities enforceable by law.

The provisions of ERISA are many. No employee older than 25 years and with more than one year of service with a company, or hired more than five years before normal retirement age, may be excluded from participation in that company's pension plan. Prior to ERISA, unusual vesting practices resulted in many injustices. For example, some plans required 20 or more years of uninterrupted service before an employee became vested. Sometimes, workers would be fired in their nineteenth year simply to prevent vesting them in a pension plan. With the advent of ERISA, all plans must choose from one of three vesting schedules for the corporate portion of the contributions to the pension plan:

1. Ten-year vesting: 100 percent vesting after ten years of service.

2. Graded vesting: 25 percent vesting after 5 years of service and then increasing by 5 percent per year to 50 percent vesting after 10 years of service; thereafter, increasing by 10 percent a year up to 100 percent vesting after 15 years.

3. Rule of 45: 50 percent vesting when a participant's age and years of service add up to 45 and then increasing by 10 percent a year up to 100 percent vesting 5 years later.

All employee contributions to a pension fund, and investment returns on such contributions, are fully vested from the beginning.

ERISA legislates minimum corporate funding of defined benefit plans while the IRS (Internal Revenue Service) sets limits on the maximum corporate contribution. According to ERISA, the minimum contribution is determined as follows: (1) All *normal costs* attributable to benefit claims deriving from employee services in a given year must be paid that year; (2) any *experience losses* (caused by a decline in the value of the securities in the fund, by unexpected changes in employee turnover, or by changes in actuarial assumptions about the discount rate) must be amortized over a period not to exceed 15 years; and (3) *supplemental liabilities* resulting from increased benefits or unfunded past service costs must be amortized over a period not to exceed 30 years (40 years for companies with pre-ERISA supplemental liabilities). On the other hand, the IRS defines the maximum corporate pension contribution as the actuarially determined normal cost of the plan plus any amount necessary to amortize supplemental and experience losses over a 10-year period. The ERISA and IRS restrictions limit corporate discretion over the amount of funds contributed to a plan.

One of the most important provisions of ERISA was the creation of the Pension Benefit Guaranty Corporation (PBGC). It is a pension insurance fund operated under the supervision of the U.S. Department of Labor. Corporations must pay the PBGC a fixed annual premium, currently $19, for each employee in a pension plan; and an additional variable amount of $9 per $1,000 of unfunded vested benefit, capped at $53 per participant. This central fund is then used to guarantee pension benefits even if a plan fails. A pension plan may be terminated voluntarily by the corporation or involuntarily by the PBGC upon court order. The PBGC may terminate a plan (1) if the plan fails to meet minimum funding standards, (2) if the plan is unable to pay benefits when due, (3) if the plan is administered improperly, or (4) if the liability of the PBGC for fulfilling claims deriving from the plan is likely to increase unreasonably.

If a plan is terminated because it is underfunded, the company is liable for 100 percent of the deficit up to 30 percent of the company's net worth. Furthermore, the PBGC may place a lien on corporate assets, which has the same priority as federal taxes. Hence, unfunded pension liabilities are equivalent to the most senior debt. A bankrupt firm may have few assets to pay to the PBGC; hence, a worthy public policy question is whether the PBGC has enough resources of its own to adequately insure the pensioners in a major corporate bankruptcy.

Perhaps the best way to understand corporate pension accounting is to use a realistic example. Assume that a 52-year-old worker is fully vested, has already accumulated 20 years of work experience, and is expected to retire after 10 additional years. We want to illustrate the calculations for how the normal cost of her defined benefits will increase for each additional year that she works. Her salary, which is currently $30,000 per year, is expected to increase at a rate of 10 percent per year. The formula for her annual pension, starting when she reaches age 62, is

$$\text{Annual pension} = (.25 + .01N)[\text{MAX } S],$$

where N is the number of years worked and MAX S is her maximum salary. Table 26.5 shows the pension calculations, assuming that her life expectancy is 20 years when she retires. Column (3) shows her expected salary each year. Column (4) is her annual pension, starting at the end of Year 10 but assuming she stops work after only N years of seniority. For example, if she only works two additional years (if she stops work after her twenty-second year of seniority, that is, $N = 22$), her expected maximum salary is $33,000 and her annual pension will be

$$\text{Annual pension} = [.25 + .01(22)][\$33,000] = (.47)(\$33,000)$$
$$= \$15,510.$$

TABLE 26.5 Defined Benefit Pension Cost Computations

Current Year (1)	N (2)	Expected Salary (3)	Annual Pension Starting at End of Year 10 (4)	PV of Benefits at End of Year 10 (5)	Accumu- lated Benefits (6)	Normal Cost (7)
1	21	$30,000	$13,800	$158,285	$ 93,689	$15,084[a]
2	22	33,000	15,510	177,898	111,615	17,926
3	23	36,300	17,424	199,852	132,913	21,298
4	24	39,930	19,565	224,409	158,199	25,286
5	25	43,923	21,962	251,902	188,236	30,037
6	26	48,315	24,641	282,630	223,869	35,633
7	27	53,147	27,636	316,982	266,144	42,275
8	28	58,462	30,985	355,396	316,301	50,157
9	29	64,308	34,726	398,304	375,758	59,457
10	30	70,738	38,906	446,249	446,249	70,491

[a]Accumulated benefits for Year 0 are assumed to be $78,605.

Column (5) is the present value, at the end of Year 10, of the assumed 20 annual pension payments. The discount rate is assumed to be 6 percent. Therefore, Column (5) is the present value of an annuity (her annual pension) discounted at 6 percent for 20 years. The annuity factor is PVIFA = 11.4699. Hence, the present value of her pension, as of the end of Year 10, is

PV of benefits at the end of Year 10 = (Annual pension)PVIFA

$$= \$15,510(11.4699) = \$177,898.$$

Column (6), the accumulated benefits, is computed as the present value in the current year of the amount in Column (5). For example, in Year 2, the accumulated benefits are

Accumulated benefits (Year 2) = $\$177,898(1.06)^{-8}$

$$= \$177,898(.6274)$$

$$= \$111,615.$$

Finally, the normal cost, Column (7), represents the amount by which the present value of the accumulated benefits increased because the employee worked for the year just ended. In our example, the normal cost in current Year 2 is $111,615 − $93,689 = $17,926. Normal costs increase with employee seniority because (1) her salary has increased; (2) another 1 percent has been added to her pension formula; and (3) the pension is one year closer to being paid, so that its present value increases.

Remember that ERISA requires that firms must contribute (at least) normal costs [Column (7)] into the pension fund each year and that the IRS allows these costs to be expensed on the firm's income statement. There are a variety of techniques for computing projected pension fund benefits. The technique used in Table 26.5 is called the *accrued benefit* method. Other methods are the entry age normal method, the attained age normal method, the aggregate cost method, and the individual level premium method.[2] All four of these methods have the effect of accelerating corporate contributions to the pension fund at a rate faster than the accrued benefit method. They are analogous to accelerated depreciation methods, except pension contributions involve cash flows while depreciation does not. In the next section of this chapter, we will discuss the economic implications of accelerated cost methods and of changes in the assumed discount rate.

Accounting regulations (APB No. 8 and FASB No. 36) require that companies with defined benefit plans provide the following information:

1. The actuarial present value of vested accumulated plan benefits, [Column (6) in Table 26.5, assuming 100 percent vesting].

2. The actuarial present value of nonvested accumulated plan benefits [a fraction of Column (6) in Table 26.5 if not 100 percent vesting].

3. The plan's net assets available for benefits.

4. The assumed actuarial rates of return used in determining the actuarial present values of vested and nonvested accumulated plan benefits.

5. The date as of which the benefit information was determined.

The actuarial present value of plan benefits was explained by the previous example (Table 26.5). The plan's net assets available for benefits are computed from the records of the pension fund. If the firm is contributing to the fund more rapidly than pension expenses accumulate, then the plan's net assets available for benefits will be positive and vice versa if contributions build slower than expenses.[3]

In 1987, the Omnibus Budget Reconciliation Act (OBRA) introduced changes in pension regulation that had the effect of reducing managerial discretion regarding the funding of defined benefit plans. Prior to OBRA it was easier for financially strong companies to employ conservative actuarial assumptions, thereby increasing their cash contributions to the plan as well as the associated tax shelter. It was also easier for financially weak companies to decrease pension fund contributions when they could not benefit from the tax shelter. Alderson [1990] estimates that OBRA significantly reduced companies' flexibility, and thereby reduced the value of the implied tax shelter option.

MANAGERIAL DECISIONS

Most of the foregoing discussion has been descriptive in nature. We have discussed the rapid growth of pension funds, their asset composition, the pension plan financial statements, pension fund regulation by ERISA, the IRS, and the FASB, and we have looked at a simple pension fund example. Now, it is time to ask what types of pension fund

---

[2]See Dreher [1967] for a complete discussion. Note that the pension plan administrator *must* use the accrued benefit method when computing the liabilities of the pension plan.

[3]For details on the computation of net assets available for benefits, see Davidson, Stickney, and Weil [1980], pp. 19.18 through 19.22.

decisions confront financial managers and how these decisions affect the value of share-holders' wealth. Listed by order of presentation, the decisions are

1. What are the effects of changing the actuarial assumptions of a pension plan?
2. What is the optimal mix of pension plan investments?
3. How should pension fund investment performance be measured?
4. When, if ever, is it optimal to voluntarily terminate a pension plan? How can termination legally be accomplished?
5. Should the firm manage its pension plan or enter into a contract with an insurance company?

These are common pension plan problems, and every chief financial officer should understand the impact which pension plan decisions will have on the corporation's shareholders.

CHANGING THE ACTUARIAL ASSUMPTIONS

In 1973, U.S. Steel increased its reported profits by $47 million by "reducing" its pension costs. This was accomplished by recognizing some appreciation in its $2 billion pension fund. Presumably, cash was then diverted from pension contributions to other uses. In the fourth quarter of 1980, Chrysler changed its assumed discount rate on its employee pension plan from 6 percent to 7 percent. Pension costs were reduced, and $50 million was added to profits. Also in 1980, Bethlehem Steel changed the assumed discount rate for its pension benefits [similar to Column (6) in Table 26.5] to 10 percent from 7 percent.[4] This 3 percent increase had the effect of decreasing accumulated pension plan benefits by $713 million (22.5 percent of the total benefits). Before the change, pension plan net assets totaled $1.952 billion and the plan was underfunded by $1.215 billion. After the change, underfunding fell to $502 million, a 58.7 percent decline. *Accounting Trends and Techniques*, an annual survey of reporting practices of 600 companies, showed that roughly 25 percent of the companies sampled voluntarily changed their pension fund accounting assumptions between 1986 and 1990.

The economic effect on shareholders' wealth depends on how the accounting changes revised shareholders' expectations about the level and riskiness of the future cash flows of the firm. The value of shareholders' wealth is equal to the market value of the firm, V, minus the market value of its liabilities. For convenience, we shall divide liabilities into pension fund liabilities, PFL, and all other debt, B. When ERISA was signed, defined pension liabilities became senior debt of the firm. Equation 26.1 shows S, the value of shareholders' wealth.

$$S = V - \text{PFL} - B. \tag{26.1}$$

---

[4]FASB Statement No. 36 allows companies to use different interest rate assumptions for disclosure in the annual report and for funding purposes; for example, Bethlehem used 7 percent for funding and 10 percent for disclosure. See Regan [1982].

We are interested in the market value of pension fund liabilities and how they are affected by accounting changes. The market value is the way the marketplace will view the true pension fund deficit and does not have any necessary relationship to the accounting or book value deficit. The market value of the pension fund deficit (or surplus) is given in Equation 26.2:

$$\text{PFL} = -\text{Market value of pension fund assets} \qquad (26.2)$$
$$- [\text{PV(Expected contributions)}](1 - T)$$
$$+ \text{PV(Expected pension fund benefits from}$$
$$\text{past and future service)}.$$

There are two major pension fund assets. First is the current market value of the stocks, bonds, mortgages, and so forth, held by the pension fund. Second is the present value of the expected pension fund contributions, which are multiplied by one minus the corporate tax rate $(1 - T)$ in order to reflect the fact that pension fund contributions are tax deductible by the firm. As long as the firm is making profits, then pension contributions are "shared" with the government because more contributions mean lower taxes.[5] Expected contributions, as we have discussed earlier, include (1) normal costs [for example, Table 26.5 Column (7)], (2) experience costs (caused by a decline in the market value of securities in the fund, by unexpected changes in employee turnover, or by changes in actuarial assumptions about the discount rate), which are amortized over a period not to exceed 15 years, and (3) supplemental liabilities (resulting from increased benefits or unfunded past service costs), which must be amortized over a period not to exceed 30 years. Balancing the pension fund assets is the pension fund liability, the present value of expected pension fund benefits to be paid to employees. Column (6) in Table 26.5 showed how this number is calculated by the actuaries.

The main difference between the book value of the pension fund deficit and its market value, or true economic value, PFL, is reflected in the rates of return. Equation 26.3 further elaborates Equation 26.2 by showing the present value of the pension fund along with the appropriate market-determined discount rates.

$$\text{PFL} = -\text{Market value of pension fund assets} \qquad (26.3)$$
$$- \sum_{t=1}^{n} \frac{E(\text{Contributions in Year } t)(1 - T)}{[1 + k_b(1 - T)]^t}$$
$$+ \sum_{t=1}^{n} \frac{E(\text{Benefits in Year } t)}{(1 + k_b)^t}$$

The expected pension benefits are discounted at the pre-tax cost of senior debt, k_b, because ERISA has made the payment of pension benefits a senior obligation of the firm,

---

[5]If one considers Social Security to be a pension plan, then recent changes in the Social Security tax law which requires nonprofit organizations to pay Social Security for their employees are burdensome. Because nonprofit organizations have no tax shelter, they must bear the full cost of Social Security expenses.

second only to tax liabilities.[6] Pension contributions are also discounted at the rate, k_b, but on an after-tax basis. Prior to ERISA, the expected benefits would have been discounted at the cost of junior, or subordinated debt, k_j, which is higher than k_b, the cost of senior debt. One of the major effects of ERISA was to transfer wealth from shareholders to pension beneficiaries by increasing the present value of pension deficits, PFL. The transfer was especially large for plans which were seriously underfunded.

The real effect of a change in pension plan actuarial assumptions depends on the cash flow consequences. If the *actuarial* discount rate assumption is raised, then the present value of accumulated benefits in book value terms [Column (6) of Table 26.5] decreases, as do the normal costs which have to be paid into the fund. This has the effect of decreasing the annual expected contributions into the fund and, hence, decreasing their present value in Equation 26.3 because expected contributions decrease while the *market-determined* discount rate, k_b, does not change. The present value of expected benefits, however, remains unchanged. The net effect is to increase the market value of pension liabilities, PFL. There is usually no effect on the firm as a whole because the cash flow not put into pension fund contributions may be used either to decrease other liabilities or to increase assets. Either way, the increased pension liability is exactly offset.[7] Thus, we see that, from the shareholders' point of view, changing the actuarial assumptions in order to change pension contributions is usually an exercise in futility. Even worse, if the funds generated by cutting pension contributions are used for a purpose that is not expensed (for example, repaying the principal on debt), the effect is to increase taxable income and decrease net cash flows to shareholders. Accounting profits have increased, but the firm has sacrificed the pension contribution tax shield. The net effect (assuming the firm is paying taxes) is to benefit the IRS at the expense of shareholders. Finally, changing actuarial assumptions for disclosure in the annual report but not for funding purposes is chicanery at best and stupid at worst. If taxes are based on income reported in the annual report, the effect of such a maneuver is to increase tax liabilities without decreasing cash contributions to the pension fund. If taxes are based on actual contributions, then, at best, managers think they can somehow fool the marketplace.

THE MIX OF PENSION PLAN ASSETS

As with any other portfolio decision, the choice of assets for a pension plan involves a selection of risk and return. Furthermore, tax considerations and pension fund insurance through ERISA are paramount.

---

[6]Some have argued that promised pension benefits are subordinated to other debt claims in spite of ERISA because other debt comes due before pension obligations. Pension beneficiaries cannot force the firm into bankruptcy while debtholders can. The existence of large unfunded pension deficits will, in our opinion, cause debtholders to force bankruptcy sooner than they might if there were no pension obligations. Nevertheless, pension liabilities will still be senior claims at the time of bankruptcy.

[7]One sometimes hears that pension contributions can be legitimately cut if the funds are alternatively used to invest in positive net present value projects. This argument confuses the investment decision (take the profitable project) with the way it is financed (cut pension fund contributions). The project can be financed either by cutting pension contributions, which increases pension liabilities, or by borrowing, which increases debt liabilities. Either way, the effect on shareholders' wealth is the same.

FIGURE 26.1   End-of-Period Pension Fund Payoffs

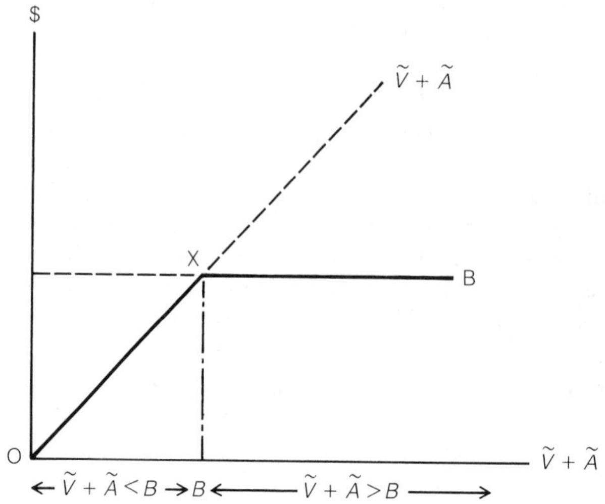

A World without Taxes and without ERISA

Before turning to the effect of ERISA and taxes on pension fund investments, let us build a more complete understanding of their risk and return characteristics. Before the passage of ERISA, corporate pension liabilities were analogous to risky debt, and the shareholders' position was equivalent to a call option on a levered firm.[8] To illustrate this, assume a one-period framework, an all-equity firm which has an uncertain end-of-period market value, V_1, and a world with no taxes. The pension fund holds some risky assets with an end-of-period value, A_1, and the pension beneficiaries have been promised an end-of-period benefit, B.

Figure 26.1 shows the end-of-period payoffs to the pension beneficiaries, assuming that the pension fund is uninsured. Along the horizontal axis, we have the market value of the firm plus the market value of the pension assets, $V + A$, while dollars of end-of-period payoff are graphed along the vertical axis. The pension beneficiaries will receive the full promised amount if the market value of total assets, $V + A$, exceeds the promised benefits, B. But, if not, the pension beneficiaries receive $V + A < B$. The solid line OXB in Figure 26.1 shows the pension beneficiaries' payoff. Because we have assumed the firm has no debt, the shareholders' payoff is simply the residual, as shown in the equation below:

$$\text{Shareholders' payoff} = \text{MAX}[0,(V + A) - B]. \qquad (26.4)$$

---

[8]For a more complete presentation of pension fund liabilities as options, see Sharpe [1976] and Treynor, Priest, and Regan [1976].

FIGURE 26.2 The Pension Beneficiaries' Position Is Equivalent to Risky Debt
(Long in a Riskless Bond and Short in a Put Option)

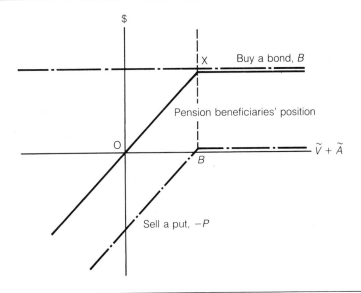

Referring back to Chapter 12 on options on risky assets, we see that the shareholders' payoff is identical to a call option on a levered firm. The pension beneficiaries' position is equivalent to owning a risk-free bond with an end-of-period value equal to the promised pension benefits, B, and selling a put option, P, on the assets of the firm.[9] In other words, they have a risky debt claim. Figure 26.2 shows that if we vertically sum the payoff from holding a riskless bond and selling a put option (at no cost to shareholders), we do, indeed, arrive at the pension beneficiaries' position.

The claims of all parties can be summarized by referring to the put-call parity equation (discussed in Chapter 12). Put-call parity said that the current market value of an underlying risky asset plus the value of a put option written on it (with maturity T periods hence and X as the exercise price) is equal to the value of a riskless bond plus a call option on the risky asset (with the same maturity and exercise price as the put). Using our current notation, the put-call parity expression becomes

$$(V_0 + A_0) + P_0 = B_0 + S_0$$
$$S_0 = (V_0 + A_0) - (B_0 - P_0). \tag{26.5}$$

The shareholders' position, S_0, is equivalent to a call option on a levered firm. On the right-hand side of Equation 26.5, we note that $(V_0 + A_0)$ is the present value of the firm

---

[9]Given that this is a one-period model and that pension benefits are not payable until employees retire at the end of the period, all options in the model are European options. They cannot be exercised before maturity.

and pension fund assets and that $(B_0 - P_0)$ is the present value of risky debt, that is, the pension benefits.

Considerable insight into pension fund asset mix can be provided by this simple option pricing approach. For example, what happens to shareholders' wealth if the pension trustees change the mix of pension assets from a well-diversified portfolio of equity to being 100 percent invested in shares of the firm?[10] The effect would be to increase the correlation between V, the value of the firm, and A, the value of the pension assets. Consequently, the variance of the underlying portfolio of assets increases and the value of shareholders' wealth, S_0, which is a call option on the assets, will also increase. Thus, the effect of any decision that unexpectedly increases the risk of $(V + A)$ is to shift wealth to shareholders and away from pension beneficiaries. The only mitigating circumstance, which was pointed out by Sharpe [1976], is that employees may be able to demand higher wages to compensate them for the higher risk they must bear when pension assets are invested in the firm's own stock. Or they might require pension fund insurance.[11]

The Effect of ERISA and the PBGC

Now let us look at the effect of government pension fund insurance on the pension fund asset mix but maintain our assumption that there are no taxes. As was mentioned earlier, the Pension Benefit Guaranty Corporation (PBGC) insures pension fund liabilities. Corporations contribute into PBGC a fixed insurance premium per employee each year plus a portion that varies with the amount of underfunding. In the event that an underfunded pension plan is terminated, the firm is liable up to 30 percent of its net worth and the PBGC guarantees the remainder of the pension liability.

If the PBGC were a privately owned insurance company, it might charge premiums based on the probability of corporate default on a pension fund. However, as a government organization, it charges all firms exactly the same insurance premium regardless of the likelihood of bankruptcy, the risk of assets in the pension fund, or the average length of employment in the firm. One implication, of course, is that firms with overfunded pension funds and safe assets are paying too much to the PBGC relative to other firms. Another implication is that firms threatened with bankruptcy can decide to change their pension plan asset mix to maximize the value of the call option that represents their shareholders' wealth. If they go bankrupt, shareholders receive nothing, and although the PBGC can claim 30 percent of each firm's net worth, 30 percent of nothing is still nothing. The PBGC claim on equity is worthless in both Chapter 7 bankruptcy or Chapter 11 reorganization (discussed in Chapter 28). Consequently, the optimal strategy from the point of view of shareholders, is to put all of the pension assets into very risky stocks. If they are lucky, the risky portfolio may do well and even result in overfunding of the pension fund. If they are unfortunate, then they end up with nothing, which is where they would have been anyway, and the PBGC has to pay off the pension beneficiaries.

---

[10]This situation is not unusual. For example, at one time, Sears's pension fund had over 50 percent of its assets invested in its stock.

[11]For more on the economics of insuring portfolios of risky assets, see Gatto, Geske, Litzenberger, and Sosin [1980].

Given that the PBGC undercharges for pension fund insurance for underfunded plans, then there is the distinct possibility that corporations facing potential bankruptcy can game the PBGC by shifting pension plan assets to being 100 percent invested in risky stocks.

An interesting case history of a company in trouble is International Harvester. In May of 1982, *The Wall Street Journal* reported that International Harvester Company's pension fund abruptly switched at least $250 million of stock holdings into bonds, chiefly U.S. government issues. Pension industry executives suggested that the company was pursuing a strategy which would let it reduce pension contributions. As of October 31, 1981, Harvester's combined pension assets totaled $1.35 billion.

What are the real economic consequences of Harvester's decision? First, since the company had negative earnings, it is not likely that the tax consequences of the decision were important.[12] Second, by changing the actuarial assumptions of the plan either (1) by realizing gains on the stocks which were sold or (2) by raising the fund rate of return assumption due to the shift from stocks to bonds, Harvester could reduce its planned cash contributions to the fund. We have already seen (in the previous section of this chapter) that the change in actuarial assumptions has no effect on shareholders' wealth at best and a negative effect at worst. Finally, the analysis in this section of the chapter suggests that a shift from stocks to bonds (in the absence of tax benefits) decreases shareholders' wealth and benefits pension beneficiaries (and debtholders of the firm). Although we have insufficient information to draw a definite conclusion about the Harvester decision, it looks like the net effect was to diminish shareholders' wealth.

Tax Effects of the Pension Fund Asset Mix

For most firms, pension fund contributions reduce taxes because they are immediately deductible. At the same time, the pension plan pays no taxes on its earnings. Hence, the rapid growth of pensions is largely attributable to the fact that they are a form of tax-deferred compensation.

The pension assets should be invested in those securities that have the most favorable pre-tax rates of return. Obvious examples of securities in which pension managers should *not* invest are those used as tax shelters by investors with high marginal tax rates, such as municipal bonds or real estate with depreciable assets like buildings.

Perhaps the most interesting tax implication for the pension fund asset mix is that pension plans should be fully funded and invested totally in bonds as opposed to equities.[13] The logic is developed in two parts. The first argument is that the return on debt held in a corporate pension fund is passed through the firm to its shareholders in the form of higher share prices because an overfunded pension plan is an asset of the firm.[14] The implication is that the return on debt held in the pension fund is ultimately taxed at the

---

[12]The next section of this chapter provides the only rational tax explanation for why Harvester shareholders may have benefited from switching pension assets to bonds.

[13]For proof of this proposition, the reader is referred to Tepper and Affleck [1974], Black [1980], and especially to Tepper [1981].

[14]The next section of this chapter discusses ways that shareholders can gain access to the assets of overfunded pension plans.

TABLE 26.6   Beginning Balance Sheets for Two Pension Investment Strategies

100 Percent Stock Strategy
(Millions of Dollars)

Assets		Liabilities	
Pension plan		Pension plan	
Bonds, B	$ 0	PV of Benefits, PFB	$ 200
Stock, S	200	Corporate	
Corporate, A	800	Debt, D	300
		Equity, E	500
	$1,000		$1,000

100 Percent Bond Strategy
(Millions of Dollars)

Assets		Liabilities	
Pension plan		Pension plan	
Bonds, B	$ 200	PV of Benefits, PFB	$ 200
Stock, S	0	Corporate	
Corporate, A	800	Debt, D	400
		Equity, E	400
	$1,000		$1,000

lower personal tax rate on equities. Shareholders will pay less tax than if the debt were held in their personal portfolios. Consequently, shareholders are better off if the pension funds of corporations are invested in bonds while their personal portfolios are invested in equities. This conclusion is based on the fact that pension plan earnings are not taxed and that bond income is taxed at a higher effective rate than capital gains. It does not depend on any theoretical gain to leverage (for example, Chapter 15). While capital gains preferential rates have been eliminated, deferral of realization is still a tax benefit.

The second reason for investing pension assets in bonds is the potential value of the tax shelter involved when the firm borrows to invest pension assets in bonds. The following example compares two pension investment strategies, the first with all pension assets in stock and the second with all assets in bonds. For the sake of simplicity, we assume a one-period world with two equally likely states of nature. If the economy is good, stocks will yield a 100 percent rate of return while bonds will yield 10 percent. If the economy is bad, stocks yield −50 percent and bonds yield 10 percent. The risk-free rate is 10 percent. Note that the expected (or average) return on stocks is 25 percent while bonds are expected to yield only 10 percent. Even so, we will see that the bond investment strategy is better for shareholders.

Table 26.6 shows a beginning-of-period market value balance sheet which combines the firm and pension fund assets and liabilities for each of the two pension investment strategies: all stock and all bonds. The firm's defined benefit pension plan promises to pay $220 million at the end of the period. The present value of this liability is $200 million, and it appears on the liabilities side of the corporate balance sheet. On the assets side, the

TABLE 26.7 Payoffs for the 100 Percent Stock Pension
Investment Strategy (Millions of Dollars)

	State of Nature	
	Good Economy	Bad Economy
Sell stock and receive	$400	$100
Payoff defined benefits	−220	−220
Cash to the firm	$180	−$120
Less taxes at 50 percent	−90	60
Net cash to shareholders	90	−60

current market value of pension assets is $200 million (either in bonds or in stocks). The pension plan is fully funded because the present value of its assets equals that of its liabilities.

If we employ the 100 percent stock investment strategy for our pension plan, the end-of-period payoffs are as shown in Table 26.7. Using the "good economy" as an example, we see that the pension fund stocks can be sold for $400 million at the end of the year. After paying the $220 million of pension benefits, shareholders are left with $180 million pretax and $90 million after taxes. In the "bad economy," they suffer a $60 million loss. The expected gain in shareholders' wealth is $15 million, but they are exposed to a great deal of risk.

The alternative pension investment strategy is to invest $200 million in bonds. If that is all we did, the end-of-period payoff would be exactly $220 million in either economy; the pension benefits would be paid off; and there would be no gain or loss to shareholders. Their expected gain is zero, but they take no risk at all.

In order to present a valid comparison of the stock and bond strategies, we need to keep shareholders' risk constant. Then, we can compare after-tax expected returns to see which strategy is better, given equivalent risk. Table 26.6 shows balance sheets that have the same risk for shareholders.[15] On the assets side, $200 million of bonds is less risky than $200 million of stock. Therefore, in order to offset the decline in risk caused by the 100 percent bond strategy, we increase the firm's financial leverage by borrowing $100 million and using the proceeds to repurchase $100 million in equity.[16] The resulting payoffs are given in Table 26.8.

In the "good economy," the bonds are sold for $220 million and the proceeds are used to pay off the defined benefits. Next, the $100 million of repurchased equity is reissued for $200 million (because the stock has appreciated by 100 percent in the good

---

[15]It really does not make any difference, in our example, how risk is measured. Shareholders' risk is equivalent whether you use the range, the variance, or the beta to measure risk.

[16]In practice, it is not necessary for corporations to actually repurchase shares in order to implement the 100 percent bond pension investment plan. What is important is that when pension assets are invested in bonds rather than stock, the risk of the corporate asset portfolio is lower. Hence, from the point of view of lenders, there is greater debt capacity. More borrowing provides a debt tax shield.

TABLE 26.8 Payoffs for the 100 Percent Bond Pension
Investment Strategy (Millions of Dollars)

	State of Nature	
	Good Economy	**Bad Economy**
Sell bonds and receive	$220	$220
Payoff defined benefits	220	220
	$ 0	$ 0
Sell stock (Book value = $100 million)	200	50
Payoff extra bonds	−100	−100
	$100	−$ 50
Less interest on bonds	−10	−10
	$ 90	−$ 60
Plus tax shield on interest	5	5
Net cash to shareholders	95	−55

economy). Half of the $200 million is used to repay the $100 million of borrowing and $10 million pays the required interest. Note that the interest payments are tax deductible. If the firm is in a 50 percent tax bracket, then taxes are reduced by $5 million below what they otherwise would have been. Net cash available to shareholders in the favorable state of nature is $95 million with the 100 percent bond investment strategy but was only $90 million with the 100 percent equity strategy. The bond strategy also dominates the equity strategy in the unfavorable state of nature (−$55 million versus −$60 million). Hence, our example demonstrates the superiority of the bond strategy from the shareholders' point of view. We have increased their return in both states of nature without changing their risk, because the range of payoffs is $150 million in either case. Regardless of whether the actual return on stock investments is higher or lower than on bonds, the bond strategy is preferable.

Summarizing, we have seen that investing all pension fund assets in bonds benefits shareholders in two ways. First, the pretax bond rate of return is passed through the firm to its shareholders in the form of higher share prices, which are, in turn, taxed at the lower capital gains rate. This argument applies even if there is no gain to leverage. The second reason for favoring bonds over equity is that there may be a gain to firms that can carry more debt without increasing shareholders' risk — a gain to leverage. We have seen that firms choosing to invest pension assets in bonds actually experience lower total asset risk than firms putting pension assets in stock. The lower risk means a greater debt capacity. If the firm uses this debt capacity and if there is a valuable tax shield created by the deductibility of interest payments, then there is a gain to leverage from investing pension assets in bonds while borrowing to hold shareholders' risk constant. [17]

[17]The gain to leverage is most likely to be valuable for those firms which have higher effective tax rates because their tax shelters from other sources (such as investment tax credits, depreciation, research and development expenses, or tax carry-back and carry-forward) are limited.

TABLE 26.9 Fund Balances for Two Pension Funds

| Year | Return on S&P 500 | Fund A | | | Fund B | | |
		Beginning Cash	Beginning of Year Deposit	Ending Cash	Beginning Cash	Beginning of Year Deposit	Ending Cash
1	−50%	$10MM	—	$ 5	$10MM	—	$5
2	100%	$ 5	$10MM	$30	$ 5	−$1MM	$8

MEASURING PENSION PLAN PORTFOLIO PERFORMANCE

If your firm decides to hire a pension plan management firm for a substantial fee, the natural question is what are you getting for your money? The answer comes in two parts. First, how do you calculate the rate of return on monies invested in the pension fund? Second, once you have determined the rate of return, was it higher than could have been expected, given the riskiness of the portfolio of investments? Was it a positive risk-adjusted rate of return?

The first consideration for measuring pension fund return is that it must be a total market value return, which includes all dividends, coupons, and capital gains. Second, it must be a *time-weighted return,* which properly accounts for contributions to and disbursements from the fund.[18] In order to illustrate the difference between time-weighted returns and *dollar-weighted returns*, consider the following example. Two funds have all of their assets continuously invested in the Standard & Poor's 500 Index for a two-year period. They both begin with $10 million. As shown in Table 26.9, Fund A receives an additional $10 million contribution at the beginning of the second year while Fund B disburses $1 million. The only difference between the funds was their pattern of receipts and disbursements, yet, if we use a dollar-weighted return measure, we find that in two years, Fund A appears to have a 200 percent rate of return,

$$\text{Dollar-weighted return on Fund A} = \frac{\$30MM - \$10MM}{\$10MM} = 200\%,$$

while Fund B appears to have a two-year return of −20 percent,

$$\text{Dollar-weighted return on Fund B} = \frac{\$8MM - \$10MM}{\$10MM} = -20\%.$$

A time-weighted return, similar to that used by many mutual funds, begins by dividing the fund into "shares." In Table 26.10, we have divided the initial $10 million

---

[18]The recommendations of the Bank Administration Institute have become a standard for performance measurement. In cooperation with the University of Chicago, they have devised two ways for estimating time-weighted returns.

TABLE 26.10 Time-Weighted Returns for Two Pension Funds (Millions of Dollars)

| Year | S&P Return | Beginning of Period | | | Beginning of Year Deposit | | End of Period | | | Time-Weighted Return |
		Cash	Number of Shares	Price per Share	Cash	Number of Shares	Cash	Number of Shares	Price per Share	
Fund A										
1	−50%	$10	10	$1.0	—	—	$ 5	10	$ .5	−50%
2	+100%	$ 5	10	$ .5	$10	20	$30	30	$1.0	100%
3	+50%	$30	30	$1.0	$10	10	$60	40	$1.5	50%
Fund B										
1	−50%	$10	10	$1.0	—	—	$ 5.0	10	$ .5	−50%
2	+100%	$ 5	10	$ .5	−$1	−2	$ 8.0	8	$1.0	100%
3	+50%	$ 8	8	$1.0	$21	21	$43.5	29	$1.5	50%

investment into 10 shares, each worth $1 million.[19] By the end of the first year, both funds have declined to $5 million because the S&P 500 went down 50 percent. Each share has declined in price to $.5 million. When money is deposited or disbursed, we compute the number of "shares" involved. For example, at the beginning of Year 2, a deposit of $10 million to Fund A represents 20 new shares at $.5 million each. Thus, in Period 2, Fund A has 30 shares and $15 million. When the market goes up 100 percent, Fund A finishes the year with $30 million and 30 shares worth $1 million each. The time-weighted return is computed by using the hypothetical share prices. For example, the Year 2 return for Fund A is

$$\frac{\text{Time-weighted}}{\text{return}} = \frac{(\text{End-of-period share price}) - (\text{Beginning share price})}{\text{Beginning share price}}$$

$$= \frac{1.0\text{MM} - .5\text{MM}}{.5\text{MM}} = 100\%.$$

Since both funds were continuously 100 percent invested in the S&P 500 Index, we know that they must have had exactly the same return. The time-weighted return calculations shown in the last column of Table 26.10 show that the returns for both funds are indeed identical.

Having correctly measured the time-weighted returns, it is necessary to evaluate the risk-adjusted performance of portfolio managers. It is not very hard to invest in the Standard & Poor's 500 Index. The difficult task, the task that should be rewarded, is to select a portfolio which has the same risk but higher returns. The Capital Asset Pricing Model (CAPM) and the Arbitrage Pricing Theory (APT), which were discussed in Chapter 11, provide a sound theoretical basis for measuring risk-adjusted returns. The data

---

[19]The number of "shares" is arbitrary. Usually, the initial investment is divided by enough shares so that each is worth $1.00.

TABLE 26.11   Hypothetical Pension Fund Returns

Year	Hypothetical Pension Fund Returns	S&P 500 Index	90-day T-bill Rate
1973	40.0%	29.1%	7.0%
1974	−15.0	−22.9	7.8
1975	−8.0	4.0	5.8
1976	22.0	18.5	5.0
1977	−10.0	−3.7	5.3
1978	−20.0	−2.2	7.2
1979	10.0	7.1	10.1
1980	25.0	15.5	11.4
1981	7.0	7.9	14.0
Arithmetic average	5.66%	5.92%	8.18%
Standard deviation	20.48%	14.94%	3.05%
Beta	1.22	1.00	.02

given in Table 26.11 show the rates of return on a hypothetical pension portfolio and on the S&P 500 Index from 1973 to 1981, a nine-year interval.

Most pension fund managers report their performance by comparing their portfolio with the Standard & Poor's 500 Index regardless of their portfolio's risk.[20] Figure 26.3 illustrates a typical presentation. The gross rates of return (before management fees and brokerage expenses) on a pension fund (5.66 percent in our example) are compared with the distribution of S&P 500 returns or with the actual performance of other managed funds over the same interval. Our hypothetical pension fund has earned just about the "average" rate of return and is in the 49th percentile.

Unfortunately, it is meaningless to compare gross rates of return, which are unadjusted for risk. In order to illustrate, let us use the Capital Asset Pricing Model, which explains rates of return adjusted for risk. The measure of risk is beta. A perfectly riskless asset has a beta of zero and the market portfolio (in this case, the S&P 500 Index) has a beta which is defined to be $\beta = 1.0$. The *ex post* version of the Capital Asset Pricing Model says that the predicted risk-adjusted rate of return will be equal to the risk-free rate, R_F, plus a risk premium which is equal to the amount of risk, β_j, times a market risk premium which is equal to the difference between the market rate of return, R_M, and the risk-free rate.

$$R_j = R_F + (R_M - R_F)\beta_j. \tag{26.6}$$

Our pension portfolio had a beta of 1.22. In other words, it was 22 percent riskier than the S&P 500 Index. Substituting the appropriate numbers from Table 26.11 into Equation 26.6, we have the predicted return:

$$\hat{R}_j = 8.18\% + (5.92\% - 8.18\%)1.22$$
$$= 5.42\%.$$

---

[20]Bond portfolios are usually compared with the Lehman Brothers government and corporate bond index, which is a weighted average of the rates of return on government and corporate bonds.

FIGURE 26.3   Typical Lay Version of Pension Fund Performance Evaluation

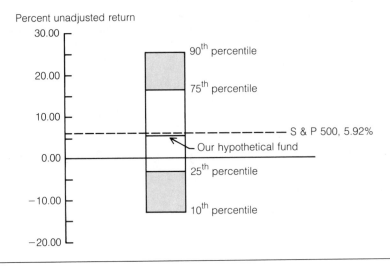

The actual rate of return was 5.66 percent. Hence, our pension fund managers earned a positive risk-adjusted rate of return equal to the difference between the fund's actual return, R_j, and the rate of return which could have been earned in the marketplace for portfolios of equivalent risk, $\hat{R}_j$.

$$\text{Risk-adjusted abnormal return} = R_j - \hat{R}_j$$
$$= 5.66\% - 5.42\% = .24\%.$$

Between 1973 and 1981, the S&P 500 Index actually did worse, on average, than the lower-risk 90-day Treasury bill portfolio. Those were the breaks of the game. In the long run, we expect riskier stock portfolios to outperform low-risk bond portfolios, and they have. However, in shorter time intervals, riskier portfolios can and do underperform bonds. That is what happened in our example. Nevertheless, our pension managers did better than they were expected to do and should be rewarded, even though their gross rate of return was less than the lower-risk S&P 500 Index.[21]

A few rules of thumb for managing and evaluating pension funds are

1. Keep bond and stock funds separate. This makes it easier to evaluate their performance.

2. Keep a record of time-weighted returns.

3. Evaluate pension fund managers' performance by having them first subtract all management and brokerage fees from the fund's gross rate of return and then comparing this net return with the risk-adjusted return expected for portfolios of equivalent risk.

---

[21]Of course, one year of abnormal performance might be attributable to luck rather than skill.

4. You should give the fund manager guidelines for the percentage of the fund which should be invested in bonds or stocks. In so doing, keep in mind the effect your decision will have on the risk of the pension fund and on the value of shareholders' wealth *after taxes*.

VOLUNTARY TERMINATION OF DEFINED BENEFIT PENSION PLANS

In June of 1983, Occidental Petroleum voluntarily terminated four defined benefit pension plans for salaried employees in its oil and chemicals divisions, replacing them with defined contribution plans. All employees covered by the terminated plans received a lump sum payment covering their vested benefits. Because the defined benefit plans were overfunded by approximately $294 million (at the end of 1982), the voluntary termination boosted Occidental's after-tax net income by approximately $100 million, or 64 percent of its 1982 earnings.

Data from the Pension Benefit Guaranty Corporation (PBGC), which has to approve any cancellations of pension funds, indicated that between 1980 and 1987 over $18 billion in excess assets reverted to the sponsors of over 1,600 defined benefit pension plans.

These examples clearly demonstrate that if underfunded pension plans are liabilities of shareholders, then overfunded plans are assets. Although the firm owns the excess assets in the fund, it is restricted greatly in its ability to use them.[22] ERISA states that any residual assets in a terminated plan revert to the employer only if the pension plan explicitly provides for such a distribution upon termination. In many cases, the PBGC has contended that excess assets should go to plan beneficiaries. Consequently, firms must be careful about the process of terminating overfunded pension plans. It should also be noted that ERISA has made it more difficult to borrow against the assets in the pension fund.

Mitchell and Mulherin [1989] have studied a sample of 327 completed reversions of defined benefit plans. Of them, 230 were terminations by parent firms and 97 by subsidiaries. The average amount of excess reversion going to the sponsor was $30.0 million and the ratio of the reversion value to the market value of the firm's equity on the date prior to filing was 8.3 percent. The average abnormal return on the filing date was 0.47 percent and was statistically significant at the one percent confidence level. Therefore, there was a small but significant benefit for shareholders when the reversion petition was filed with the PBGC. This benefit was observed even though only 12.5 percent of the firms in the sample announced their intention to terminate in *The Wall Street Journal* or the Dow Jones News Service ''Broadtape.''

Usually, firms do not consider voluntary termination of underfunded plans because the PBGC can lay claim to 30 percent of their net worth. However, two questions arise: How is net worth to be measured? And, can a subsidiary with negative net worth terminate its pension plan and relinquish the unfunded liabilities to the PBGC? In answer to the second question, the PBGC has denied subsidiaries the right to terminate their plans so long as the parent company shows adequate net worth. Furthermore, the PBGC has argued that in determining net worth, it can look beyond book value and use other infor-

---

[22]For a more complete exposition, the reader is referred to Bulow, Scholes, and Manell [1982].

mation to establish the value of the firm as a going concern. Consequently, voluntary termination of underfunded plans is an unlikely strategy.

Most companies replace their defined benefit with defined contribution plans, thereby shifting the uncertainties of pension performance from themselves to their employees. The company simply promises to pay a fixed percentage of each employee's salary or wages into the defined contribution plan. Benefits upon retirement depend on the return on pension assets. Sometimes, the defined contribution plans are coupled with the 401K tax-deferred savings plan authorized by the Internal Revenue Act of 1978. Employee contributions to the plan reduce their tax liabilities and earn tax-free returns until retirement. One drawback, from the company's perspective, is that its contribution to the 401K plan is vested immediately.

INSURANCE COMPANY CONTRACTS

As noted in Table 26.1, about 36 percent of all nongovernment pension plans were invested with insurance companies. The usual insurance company contract (called a guaranteed investment contract, GIC) provides "guaranteed" rates of return for a fixed period of time. For example, you may be guaranteed an 8 percent return for a ten-year period. The insurance companies can provide the guarantee because they invest your pension fund contributions in ten-year government bonds, which, if held to maturity, yield exactly 8 percent. The catch is that you cannot withdraw your pension plan assets if interest rates change. When market rates of interest rose rapidly during the late 1970s and early 1980s, many firms suddenly realized that a guaranteed rate of return was very different from a riskless return. Market rates of interest of 14 percent on long-term bonds were not unusual, but those companies whose pension assets were committed to insurance company contracts found they were locked into an 8 percent return. This is the hard way to learn about opportunity cost.

If your company is large enough to provide its own pension fund accounting for employees, then there is no difference between contributing pension funds to an insurance company plan and directly investing in 8 percent ten-year bonds yourself. Just bear in mind that long-term bonds are riskier than short-term bonds or money market assets. Some companies have decided to immunize their defined benefit pension liabilities by purchasing long-term bonds which mature with the same pattern as employee retirements. They know for sure that the maturing bonds will pay promised benefits.

SUMMARY

The rapid growth of pension funds in the last two decades has made their management one of the primary responsibilities of corporate chief financial officers. CFOs must be familiar with accounting regulations governing pension fund reporting practices, with government regulation of defined benefit plans under ERISA, and with a wide range of managerial decisions. We discussed the economic implications of changing the pension fund actuarial assumptions, the choice of asset mix, the problem of measuring pension fund portfolio performance, the implications of voluntary termination of defined benefit plans, and the economics of investing pension plan assets with guaranteed insurance company plans.

There are still some as yet unanswered questions. For example, why were 50.5 percent of all noninsured pension fund assets invested in common stocks in 1980? The tax advantage of investing in bonds (at least for fully funded plans) seems obvious. Another question is why the industry standard for measuring pension fund portfolio performance is not risk-adjusted. And finally, why are actuarial changes so frequent when they have no impact on shareholders' wealth?

QUESTIONS

26.1 What is the difference between accrued benefits and vested benefits?

26.2 What are the differences between defined contribution pension plans and defined benefit plans?

26.3 Why should a pension fund never invest its assets in nontaxable municipal bonds?

26.4 How does a change in the actuarial assumptions of a pension plan affect shareholders' wealth?

26.5 What effect did the implementation of ERISA have on the distribution of wealth between shareholders and employees
   a.   for underfunded defined benefit plans and
   b.   for overfunded defined benefit plans?

26.6 Using an option pricing approach, describe how a firm's shareholders might be affected if a large fraction of its pension assets are shifted
   a.   from bonds to a well-diversified stock portfolio
   b.   from a well-diversified stock portfolio to owning the firm's own stock.

26.7 There are two tax-related reasons why pension fund assets should be invested in bonds rather than stock. What are they?

PROBLEMS

26.1 Suppose that Mr. Brandon, a 60-year-old worker, is fully vested in his pension plan and has accumulated 35 years of work experience. He is expected to retire in 5 years at age 65. His current salary of $40,000 is expected to increase at the rate of 5 percent per year, and the annual pension formula is

$$\text{Annual pension} = (.25 + .01N)[\text{MAX } S].$$

If his life expectancy is 15 years when he retires, what is the normal pension cost next year and the following year if the company discounts benefits at 8 percent? (The present value of Brandon's accumulated benefits is currently $139,811.)

26.2 Table 26.2 in the text shows a pension fund income statement and balance sheet. Where in the balance sheet would you enter the following items:

  a. $500 million in U.S. government bonds which are held in trust for the members of the pension plan?

  b. An amount of $200 per month which the firm plans to put aside to pay the pension of an existing employee?

  c. A $15,000 per year pension which you expect to pay an employee who is currently not vested?

  d. A $10,000 per year pension, which the plan is currently paying to a retired employee?

26.3 Table P26.3 shows the cash positions of the Megabucks pension fund over a six-year period. Compute its dollar-weighted and time-weighted returns.

TABLE P26.3   Fund Balances for the Megabucks Pension (Millions of Dollars)

Year	Beginning Cash	Beginning of Period Deposit	Ending Cash
1	$ 90	$ 0	$ 97
2	97	−12	85
3	85	10	100
4	100	10	102
5	102	−5	117
6	117	0	121

26.4 Table P26.4 shows the time-weighted rates of return on the Bigload Pension Fund, the S&P 500 Index, and the 90-day T-bill rate (annualized). Did Bigload have a successful investment strategy?

TABLE P26.4   Returns on the Bigload Fund

Year	Bigload Returns	S&P 500 Returns	90-day T-bill Rate
19X5	8.4%	4.0%	5.8%
19X6	42.1	18.5	5.0
19X7	−1.0	−3.7	5.3
19X8	−10.4	−2.2	7.2
19X9	5.6	7.1	10.1

SELECTED REFERENCES

Alderson, M. J., "Corporate Pension Policy Under OBRA 1987," *Financial Management*, (Winter 1990), pp. 87–95.

Bagehot, W. (pseud.), "Risk and Reward in Corporate Pension Funds," *Financial Analysts Journal*, (January/February 1972), pp. 80–84.

Bank Administration Institute, *Measuring the Investment Performance of Pension Funds*, Park Ridge, Illinois, 1968.

Bicksler, J., and Chen, A., "The Integration of Insurance and Taxes in Corporate Pension Strategy," *Journal of Finance*, (July 1985), pp. 943–955.

Black, F., "The Tax Consequences of Long-run Pension Policy," *Financial Analysts Journal*, (July/August 1980), pp. 21–28.

Bodie, Z.; Light, J.; Morck, R.; and Taggart, R., Jr., "Corporate Pension Policy: An Empirical Investigation," *Financial Analysts Journal*, (September/October 1985), pp. 10–16.

Bulow, J.; Scholes, M.; and Manell, P., "Economic Implications of ERISA," working paper, Graduate School of Business, University of Chicago, March 1982.

Davidson, S.; Stickney, C.; and Weil, R., *Intermediate Accounting*, Hinsdale, Ill.: Dryden Press, 1980.

Dreher, W., "Alternatives Available under APB Opinion No. 8: An Actuary's View," *The Journal of Accountancy*, (September 1967), pp. 37–51.

Feldstein, M., and Seligman, Stephanie, "Pension Funding, Share Prices and National Savings," *Journal of Finance*, 36 (September 1981), pp. 801–824.

Frances, J., and Reiter, S., "Determinants of Corporate Pension Funding Strategy," *Journal of Accounting and Economics*, (January 1987), pp. 35–39.

Gatto, M.; Geske, R.; Litzenberger, R.; and Sosin, H., "Mutual Fund Insurance," *Journal of Financial Economics*, (September 1980).

Ippolito, R., "The Labor Contract and True Economic Pension Liabilities," *American Economic Review*, (December 1985), 1031–1043.

———, "The Role of Risk in a Tax-Arbitrage Pension Portfolio," *Financial Analysts Journal*, (January/February 1990), pp. 24–32.

Marcus, A., "Spinoff/Terminations and the Value of Pension Insurance," *Journal of Finance*, (July 1985), pp. 911–924.

Miller, M., and Scholes, M., "Pension Funding and Corporate Valuation," working paper, Graduate School of Business, University of Chicago, 1981.

Mitchell, M., and Mulherin, J.H., "The Stock Price Response to Pension Terminations and the Relation of Terminations with Corporate Takeovers," *Financial Management*, (Autumn 1989), pp. 41–56.

Regan, P., "Reasons for the Improving Pension Figures," *Financial Analysts Journal*, (March/April 1982), pp. 14–15.

Sharpe, W., "Corporate Pension Funding Policy," *Journal of Financial Economics*, (June 1976), pp. 183–194.

Tepper, I., "The Future of Private Pension Funding," *Financial Analysts Journal*, (1982), pp. 25–31.

———, "Taxation and Corporate Pension Policy," *Journal of Finance*, 36 (March 1981), pp. 1–13.

———, and Affleck, A. R. P., "Pension Plan Liabilities and Corporate Financial Strategies," *Journal of Finance*, 29 (December 1974), pp. 1549–1564.

Thomas, J., "Corporate Taxes and Defined Benefit Pension Plans," *Journal of Accounting and Economics*, (July 1988), pp. 199–238.

Treynor, J., "The Principles of Corporate Pension Finance," *Journal of Finance*, (May 1977), pp. 627–638.

———; Priest, W.; and Regan, P., *The Financial Reality of Pension Funding Under ERISA*, Homewood, Ill.: Dow Jones-Irwin Inc., 1976.

Van Der Hei, J., and Joanette, F., "Economic Determinants for the Choice of Actuarial Cost Methods," *Journal of Risk and Insurance*, (September 1988), pp. 59–74.

PART EIGHT

Dynamic Strategies for Increasing Value

This final part of the book is entitled, "Dynamic Strategies for Increasing Value." Previous chapters have treated individual aspects of this subject. In this concluding part we are in a position to focus on two integrating subjects. Chapter 27 covers the merger and takeover areas. We draw upon the background of the previous chapters to focus on "mergers and acquisitions, restructuring, and corporate control." We are dealing with the growth and adjustment of business firms in relation to their broad financial economic environments and in relation to their competition, which has become global. Mergers and acquisitions enlarge the investment horizons of firms. Financial reconstructuring involves a review and reformulation of financial strategies. The corporate control aspect represents rethinking the implications of the separation of ownership and control, characteristic of large-scale enterprise.

Chapter 28 is entitled, "Financial Distress." A large body of new materials and much new analysis has appeared on this subject within the last two years. This increased attention results in part from the need to repair the excesses of the 1980s and in part from the longer-run effects of the new bankruptcy laws which were enacted at the end of the 1970s. Financial distress may stimulate a firm to rethink all of the subjects covered in this book and begin a new and sometimes even more successful life cycle. Financial distress need not represent a "final chapter" but rather a stimulus for a needed repositioning and restructuring in the broadest dimensions.

Mergers and Acquisitions, Restructuring, and Corporate Control

Growth is vital to the well-being of a firm. Growth is needed to compete for the best managerial talent by offering rapid promotions and broadened responsibilities. Without able executives, the firm is likely to decline and die. Much of the previous material dealing with analysis, planning, and financing has a direct bearing on the financial manager's potential contribution to the firm's growth. This chapter focuses on strategies for promoting growth through mergers and on the role of financial managers in evaluating prospective merger partners and making decisions on which parts of the company to sell.

MERGERS AND TAKEOVERS

Distinctions are made between types of mergers and takeovers. Most generally, *mergers* mean any transaction that forms one economic unit from two or more previous ones. *Horizontal mergers* are in the same industry. *Vertical mergers* are between different stages in a given industry — steel companies could integrate backward into mining iron ore and coal, or forward into fabrication and distribution of steel products. *Conglomerate mergers* involve companies in unrelated industries.

Two major forms of combination have been recognized in compiling data — mergers and acquisitions. In fact, the department of an investment banking firm engaged in providing advice on these activities is usually referred to as the mergers and acquisitions (M&As) department.

TABLE 27.1   Illustrative Large Mergers

	Partners	Combined Market Value (in Billions)
Beecham Group	SmithKline Beckman	$16.1
Nabisco	Standard Brands	2.0
Dart Industries	Kraft	2.4
Schering	Plough	1.4

Acquisitions usually take the form of a tender offer. In a *tender offer*, one party — generally a corporation seeking a controlling interest in another corporation — asks the stockholders of the firm it is seeking to control to sell (tender) their shares of stock in the target firm. An acquiring firm typically seeks prior approval from the other firm's management and board of directors. An alternative approach is the "bear hug." In this approach, a company mails to the directors of the takeover target a letter announcing the acquisition proposal and requiring the directors to make a quick decision on the bid. If approval cannot be obtained, the acquiring company can appeal directly to the stockholders by means of the tender offer, unless the management and the directors of the target firm hold enough stock to retain control. The technique of going directly to the shareholders has been called a *Saturday night special*. The term implies that a gun has been aimed at the directors, since if the shareholders respond favorably to the tender offer, the acquiring company will gain control and have the power to replace the directors who have not cooperated in the takeover effort. (This is also referred to as a *hostile takeover*.) The target firm may seek to avoid being acquired or may seek to elicit a competitive offer from a firm it considers more desirable — a *white knight*.

Another distinction is made, from an accounting standpoint, between a purchase and a pooling of interests (see the appendix to this chapter). A *purchase* generally refers to the acquisition of a much smaller entity that is absorbed into the acquiring firm. A *pooling of interests* represents the joining of two firms of not greatly unequal size, followed by operations in which their identities are continued to a considerable degree.

Examples of large *mergers* in recent years are shown in Table 27.1. Examples of large *acquisitions* completed or pending are given in Table 27.2.

Empirical studies find that in about 50 percent of takeovers, a negotiated agreement has already been worked out between the bidder and the management and board of directors of the target company [Comment and Jarrell, 1987]. When an agreement has already been reached between bidder and target, the tender offer or takeover is almost certainly a friendly one. A takeover can also be a friendly one even if a negotiated agreement had not been worked out in advance. An example would be a takeover "made in heaven" where the price is right and obvious benefits accrue to all parties to the transaction.

In studying mergers and takeovers, it is important to recognize the distinction between friendly and hostile takeovers. Table 27.3 summarizes the characteristics of mergers and the two types of takeovers. Mergers are typically negotiated by mutual consent.

TABLE 27.2   Illustrative Large Acquisitions

Buyer	Target	Price (in Billions)
Chevron	Gulf	$13.3
Philip Morris	Kraft	13.1
Bristol-Myers	Squibb	12.0
Time	Warner	11.7
Texaco	Getty Oil	10.1
Du Pont	Conoco	7.5
AT&T	NCR	7.4
Mobil	Superior Oil	5.7
Royal Dutch/Shell	Shell Oil	5.5
Shell Oil	Belridge Oil	3.7
Beatrice Foods	Esmark	2.7
General Motors	Electronic Data Systems	2.5
Standard Oil (Ohio)	Kennecott	2.3
Groupe Schneider	Square D	2.2
Fluor Corp.	St. Joe Minerals	2.0
Manufacturers Hanover	CIT Financial	1.5
American General	Gulf United Insurance	1.2
American Stores	Jewel Companies	1.2
Dun & Bradstreet	A. C. Nielsen	1.1

TABLE 27.3   Takeover Types

Mergers	Tender Offers	
Friendly, Negotiated	Friendly	Hostile
1. Not resisted	1. Not resisted	1. Resisted
2. Payment in stock	2. Payment in cash or stock	2. Payment in cash
3. Single bidder	3. Single bidder	3. Multiple bidders
4. Announcement anticipated	4. Anticipated to some degree	4. Surprise
5. Management ownership higher	5. Management ownership high	5. Management ownership low
6. Bidder firm with surplus cash seeking a target with growth opportunities, needing cash	6. Target above industry average in performance	6. Target below industry average in performance
	7. Target in growth industry	7. Target in mature industry
	8. Industry and firm q ratio equal to average and higher than q for hostile targets	8. Industry and firm q ratios are low
	9. Bidder likely to be another firm seeking new favorable investment opportunities	9. Bidder likely to be a raider

There is usually a single bidder, and payment is made primarily with stock. The bidder is typically in a mature industry, has surplus cash, and is seeking a target with growth opportunities requiring cash. Tender offers may be friendly or hostile. Hostile bids are typically resisted and result in multiple bidders. Management ownership is low in hostile bids but relatively higher in friendly bids. The target firm in a hostile bid is typically below its industry average in performance and the market value of its securities is lower than the replacement costs of its assets. In a friendly merger, the target is often above its industry average in performance with a market value of securities greater than the replacement cost of its assets.

THE MERGER MOVEMENT OF THE EIGHTIES

Despite the many distinctions between mergers and takeovers and between friendly and hostile takeovers, the time series data lump all into the general term, *merger activity*. A widely used data series is presented in Table 27.4. Clearly, 1981 represents a watershed in the rate of merger activity. The level of activity jumped measured by total dollar value paid, number of $100 million transactions, and number of $1 billion transactions. By all three measures, merger activity peaked in 1988. The dollar values of external investments (M&As) are highly correlated with plant and equipment expenditures of business firms [Weston et al., 1990]. Measured by number of transactions, the highest rate of activity was during the years 1968–1973. During this earlier period, antitrust enforcement prevented horizontal and vertical mergers, so many firms attempted small toehold conglomerate acquisitions to test the attractiveness of different areas of business activity.

The takeover and restructuring movement of the 1980s was brought about by two major sets of forces. One relates to fundamental issues of corporate governance. A second force is the changing economic, political, and cultural environments.

Issues of Corporate Governance and Control

The merger and takeover movement of the 1980s laid bare some fundamental problems in the governance and management of corporations. Deficiencies in effective corporate governance and control are summarized in Table 27.5.

Early it became clear that there was a separation of ownership and control in the corporation with potential conflicts of interest between owners and management. Empirical studies showed that through the 1960s, on average, top management owned fewer than 2 percent of the ownership shares in large corporations. That percentage is higher today but only as a consequence of changes, particularly during the 1980s [Demsetz and Lehn, 1985].

The tensions and weaknesses in corporate governance and control processes summarized in Table 27.5 were joined with changing environmental factors.

TABLE 27.4 Merger Activity

Year	Total Dollar Value Paid ($ Billion) (1)	Number Total (2)	Number of Transactions Valued at		GNP Deflator (1982 = 100) (5)	1982 Constant-Dollar Consideration (6)
			$100 Million or More (3)	$1,000 Million or More (4)		
1968	$ 43.6	4,462	46	—	37.7	$115.6
1969	23.7	6,107	24	—	39.8	59.5
1970	16.4	5,152	10	1	42.0	39.0
1971	12.6	4,608	7	—	44.4	28.4
1972	16.7	4,801	15	—	46.5	35.9
1973	16.7	4,040	28	—	49.5	33.7
1974	12.4	2,861	15	—	54.0	23.0
1975	11.8	2,297	14	1	59.3	19.9
1976	20.0	2,276	39	1	63.1	31.7
1977	21.9	2,224	41	—	67.3	32.5
1978	34.2	2,106	80	1	72.2	47.4
1979	43.5	2,128	83	3	78.6	55.3
1980	44.3	1,889	94	4	85.7	51.7
1981	82.6	2,395	113	12	94.0	87.9
1982	53.8	2,346	116	6	100.0	53.8
1983	73.1	2,533	138	11	103.9	70.4
1984	122.2	2,543	200	18	107.7	113.5
1985	179.6	3,001	270	36	110.9	161.9
1986	173.1	3,336	346	27	113.9	152.0
1987	163.7	2,032	301	36	117.7	139.1
1988	246.9	2,258	369	45	121.3	203.5
1989	221.1	2,366	328	35	126.3	171.0
1990	108.2	2,074	181	21	131.5	82.3

Source: Merrill Lynch, *Mergerstat Review, 1990.*

TABLE 27.5 Issues of Corporate Governance and Control

1. Separation of ownership and control. Management domination of board of directors that is supposed to monitor and control management on behalf of shareholders.
2. Agency problems. Conflict of interest between managers and owners. Management perks. Lack of efficiency enforcement.
3. Static planning and control systems. Slack in segment plans—easy targets.
4. Internal cash flows not subject to capital market disciplines. Weak segments often subsidized. Strong segments may not perform up to potentials and their value to others.
5. Excessive conglomeration. Unrelated activities difficult to manage efficiently. Aggravated by lack of incentives to stimulate segment managers to think like entrepreneurial owners.

TABLE 27.6 Changing Environments

---

1. Increased international competition.
2. Changing technologies and increased competition between industries.
3. Changing manufacturing methods shift from economies of scale to flexible manufacturing systems and economies of scope; oil shocks caused repeated adjustments in mix of production input factors.
4. Changed management of human resources from hierarchy to participative management.
5. Fluctuating exchange rates, changing prices of buying and selling goods and companies.
6. Deregulation accelerated in the 1970s in airlines, banking, the S&L industry, other financial services, broadcasting, cable, communications, transportation, oil, and gas. These industries accounted for almost one-half of all M&A activities during the 1980s.
7. Innovations in financial services. Its deregulation stimulated new entry, excess capacity, pressures on profit margins, innovative products, speculative investments.
8. Changed antitrust policy—recognized increased competition reflecting the above 7 factors.
9. Changes in tax policy, revisions almost every year during the 1980s; marginal corporate tax rate changed from 46 percent to 34 percent; marginal personal tax rate changed from 50 percent to 31 percent; capital gains tax rate changed from 20 percent to 28 percent—arbitraging different tax opportunities—further advantages to debt financing with reduction of capital gains advantage to retained earnings.
10. Persistent U.S. government deficits, large balance of payments deficits, continuing uncertainty and fear of inflation and/or high interest rates.

The Changing Environments

Major recent developments in the external environments of business firms are summarized in Table 27.6. These changes in external environments coupled with the weaknesses in corporate governance and control systems interacted with firm characteristics to produce the M&A activity of the 1980s.

THEORIES OF RESTRUCTURING

As a foundation for analyzing the many forms of restructuring and their financial results, we review the alternative theories of restructuring listed in Table 27.7. Each type of theory is briefly summarized to provide a foundation for review of the empirical studies.

1. Inefficient Management

The removal of inefficient management by a merger or tender offer would represent a gain in efficiency. There are at least two aspects involved.

Differential Efficiency. The most general theory of mergers involves differential efficiency. If the management of Firm A is more efficient than the management of Firm B, and if after Firm A acquires Firm B, the efficiency of Firm B is brought up to the level of efficiency of Firm A, efficiency is increased by merger. Note that this outcome would be a social gain as well as a private gain. The level of efficiency in the economy would be raised by such mergers.

TABLE 27.7 Theories of Restructuring

---

1. Inefficient management
2. Operating synergy
3. Financial synergy
4. Strategic realignment
5. Undervaluation
   a. Short-term results versus long-run investment programs
   b. Market below replacement cost
6. Information and signaling
7. Agency problems and managerialism
   a. Protect or build the empire
   b. Free cash flow theory
8. Realignment of managerial incentives
9. Winner's curse — hubris
10. Market power
11. Tax considerations
12. Redistribution

Inefficient Management. Inefficient management may represent management that is inept in an absolute sense. Almost anyone could do better. Or it may mean that management is simply not performing up to its potential. Another control group might be able to manage the assets of this area of activity more effectively.

2. Operating Synergy

Operating synergy or operating economies may be involved in horizontal and vertical mergers. For horizontal mergers, the source of operating economies may represent a form of economies of scale. These economies, in turn, may reflect indivisibilities and better utilization of capacity after the merger. Or important complementarities in organizational capabilities may be present that result in gains not attainable from internal investments in the short run. Economies of scope represent gains from performing related activities.

Another area in which operating economies may be achieved is vertical integration. Combining firms at different stages of an industry may achieve more efficient coordination of the different levels. The argument here is that costs of communication, and various forms of bargaining, and opportunistic behavior can be avoided by vertical integration [Arrow, 1975; Klein, Crawford, and Alchian, 1978; Williamson, 1971].

3. Financial Synergy

The possible financial synergies involve some unsettled issues of finance theory. Financial synergy argues that the cost of capital function may be lowered for a number of reasons. If the cash flow streams of the two companies are not perfectly correlated, bankruptcy probabilities may be lowered; and this consequence may decrease the existing present value of bankruptcy costs. This debt-coinsurance effect benefits debt holders at the expense of shareholders [Higgins and Schall, 1975]. However, this effect can be offset by increasing leverage after the merger, and the result will be increased tax savings on interest payments [Galai and Masulis, 1976]. The increase in debt capacity (defined as the maximum amount of debt that can be raised at any given interest rate) due to merger has been explicitly analyzed by Stapleton [1982] in the context of the option pricing theory. In his theory, the increase in debt capacity does not require the existence of bankruptcy costs.

Another dimension, emphasized by Levy and Sarnat [1970], is economies of scale in flotation and transaction costs that may be realized in conglomerate firms. Arguments may be raised about the potential magnitude of these financial factors. Further questions could be raised as to why joint activities might not be taken by unmerged firms to achieve the same economies of scale in flotation and transaction costs. However, the heterogeneity of firms and the costs of contracting would seem to make such activities prohibitive since such joint activities are not observed in the real world.

Another financial synergy theory holds that bidders have excess cash flows, but lack good investment opportunities. In contrast, targets are said to need additional funds to finance an abundance of good available growth investment opportunities. An example would be the acquisition by Philip Morris of General Foods in 1987 and of Kraft Foods in 1988. Philip Morris had large cash flows from its tobacco operations, which appeared to be shrinking because of the mounting efforts to achieve a ''smoke-free society.'' The food industry offered opportunities for growth, particularly since new product developments are an important source of expansion for such industries.

A related proposition is based on the distinction between internal and external funds. The nontrivial transactions costs associated with raising capital externally and the differential tax treatment of dividends may constitute the condition for more efficient allocation of capital through mergers from low to high marginal returns production activities. Empirical findings appear to support this internal funds effect. Nielsen and Melicher [1973] find that the rate of premium paid to the acquired firm as an approximation to the merger gain is greater when the cash flow rate of the acquiring firm is greater and that of the acquired firm is smaller. This implies that there is redeployment of capital from the acquiring to the acquired firm's industry. Also internal cash flows affect the rate of investment of firms [Nickell, 1978]. This financial synergy proposition is consistent with the empirical evidence reported by Markham [1973, pp. 88–89]. In his sample of 30 large acquisitions, new capital outlays for the acquired companies' operations in the three-year period following acquisitions averaged 220 percent of the premerger outlays for the same time span. This evidence suggests that investment opportunities are improved.

4. Strategic Realignment

The literature on long-range strategic planning has exploded in recent years. This literature is related to diversification and restructuring. The strategic planning approach to mergers appears to imply either the possibilities of economies of scale or utilization of unused capacity in the firm's present managerial capabilities. Another rationale is that by external diversification, the firm acquires management skills for needed augmentation of its present capabilities. [For an elaboration and evaluation of these themes, see also Chung and Weston, 1982; and Chung, 1982.]

5. Undervaluation

Undervaluation has a number of aspects, each with a different nature and different implications.

Short-Term Myopia.   The problem here is said to be that market participants, especially institutional investors, emphasize short-term earnings performance. As a consequence, it is argued that corporations with long-term investment programs are undervalued. When firms are undervalued, they become attractive targets to raiders—other firms or individual investors with large resources at their command.

Market Below Replacement Cost.   One reason that firms have stepped up diversification programs is that in recent years entry into new product market areas could be accomplished on a bargain basis. For various reasons, stock prices were depressed during the 1970s and did not recover until the latter part of 1982 as the level of inflation dropped and business prospects improved. Also current replacement costs of assets were higher than their recorded historical book values. These two effects resulted in a decline of the q ratio, defined as the ratio of the market value of a firm's securities to the replacement costs of its assets.

   In some years the q ratio has been below one. If a company wished to add to capacity in producing a particular product, it could acquire the additional capacity more cheaply by buying a company that produces the product rather than building new plant and equipment. For example, if the q ratio is 0.6 and if in a merger the premium paid over market value is 50 percent, the resulting purchase price is 0.6 times 1.5, which equals 0.9. This outcome would mean that the average purchase price would still be 10 percent below the current replacement costs of the assets acquired. This potential advantage would provide a broad basis for the operation of the undervaluation theory when the q ratio is below one.

6. Information and Signaling

The announcement of restructuring activities may convey information and/or signals to market participants. For example, the announcement of a merger or tender offer may convey information that the target is "sitting on a gold mine" or signal that the old management will receive a "kick in the pants" from the new owners. A variation of this theme is that the announcement of a merger or tender offer signals that future cash flows are likely to increase and that future values will increase accordingly. Thus, announcements of restructuring may signal a potential for future value increases.

7. Agency Problems and Managerialism

Jensen and Meckling [1976] formulated the implications of agency problems. An agency problem arises when managers own only a small fraction of the ownership shares of the firm. Partial ownership may cause managers to work less vigorously than otherwise and/or to consume more perquisites (such as luxurious offices, company cars, memberships in clubs) because the majority owners bear most of the cost. In large corporations with widely dispersed ownership, individual owners do not have sufficient incentive to expend the substantial resources required to monitor the behavior of managers.

Empire Building. A variant of the agency problem is the managerialism theory of conglomerate mergers as set forth by Mueller [1969]. Mueller hypothesized that managers are motivated to further increase the size of their firms. He assumed that management compensation is a function of the size of the firm and argued that managers adopt too low an investment hurdle rate. But Lewellen and Huntsman [1970] presented findings that managers' compensation is significantly correlated with the firm's profit rate in addition to its level of sales. The financial compensation of managers may not motivate a preference for large size. However, other influences such as managerial power and prestige may be related to firm size.

Free Cash Flow Theory. The free cash flow theory of Jensen [1986, 1988] is based on the inherent conflict of interest between managers and shareholders. It adopts Mueller's theory that managers seek to protect or build their empires to increase perks and salaries. Funds beyond what a firm requires to invest in all available positive net present value investments are termed *free cash flow* by Jensen; such excess cash should be paid out. Jensen recommends substituting debt for equity or increasing debt ratios by other methods for such firms. He argues that this form of restructuring provides bonding that the managements of such firms will pay out excess cash flows in the future. Growth firms that have investment opportunities may properly retain cash flows to finance profitable investments.

Agency theory suggests that when the market for managers does not solve the agency problem, restructuring may take place. Merger activity is a method of dealing with the agency problem. Another managerialism theory argues that the agency problem is not solved, and that merger activity is a manifestation of the agency problems of inefficient, external investments by managers.

8. Realignment of Managerial Incentives

Because of the potential divergence of interests between managers and the stockholders (owners of the firm) described by agency theory, performance of the firm may be improved if managers are made to think like owners. If by restructuring or altering managerial compensation contracts the wealth position of managers is substantially impacted by the price level of the firm's stock, the motives of managers to improve common stock values for shareholders may be strengthened.

9. Winner's Curse — Hubris

The winner's curse occurs when bidding takes place for a valuable object, the value of which is uncertain. If the true value of the object is the same to all the bidders (a common value auction), then the winner of the auction is likely to be the bidder who has made the largest positive error in estimating the value of the object. For example, if all bidders' estimates of the value are unbiased so the mean of these estimates equals the common value of the object and all bidders' bid their estimate, then with several bidders the winner will almost always overbid. The positive valuation error represents the winner's curse. Capen, Clapp, and Campbell [1971], based on their analysis of sealed-bid competitive oil lease sales, demonstrate a relation between the high estimate to true value as a function of the degree of uncertainty and the number of bidders. Roll [1986] analyzes the effect in takeover activity. Postulating strong market efficiency in all markets, the prevailing market price of the target already reflects the full value of the firm. The higher valuation of the bidder (over the target's true economic value), he states, results from hubris — the bidder's excessive self-confidence (pride, arrogance). Hubris is one of the factors causing the winner's curse phenomenon to occur.

10. Market Power

The restructuring and control changes have not had a great impact on concentration in the economy. Neither concentration in individual industries nor aggregate concentration measured by the position of the top 100, 200, or 500 firms in the economy has been greatly changed to any significant degree [Golbe and White, 1988]. The increased mobility of firms is likely to decrease concentration in the long run. A strong market position is rapidly eroded by new forms and sources of competition.

11. Tax Considerations

Another theory of mergers suggests that tax effects are an important motivating factor in some instances. The tax synergy argument is that mergers facilitate the utilization of tax shields not fully available in the absence of an acquisition transaction. Even in combinations undertaken for other motives (for example, to achieve operating synergies), transactions are structured to maximize tax benefits and minimize tax liability while complying with Internal Revenue Code regulations. Tax effects can make a marginal investment more profitable or cause an otherwise acceptable transaction to be abandoned, if, for example, the IRS hands down an unfavorable private ruling on a proposed merger plan.

A transaction qualifies as a so-called tax-free reorganization under IRC 368(a) (1) if certain conditions are met. The distinguishing characteristic of tax-free reorganizations is that the primary consideration paid to obtain the voting stock or assets of the target firm must be voting stock of the acquiring firm.

There are three forms of tax-free reorganizations. Type A reorganizations include statutory mergers (in which the target firm is absorbed by the acquiring firm) and consolidations (in which both firms cease to exist as such and a new entity is created) with the approval of a majority of both target and acquiring firm shareholders. Type B reorganizations are similarly stock-for-stock exchanges; following a Type B reorganization, the target may be liquidated into the acquiring firm or maintained as an independent operating entity. Type C reorganizations are stock-for-asset transactions with the requirement that at least 80 percent of the fair market value of the target's property be acquired. Typically, the target firm "sells" its assets to the acquiring firm in exchange for acquiring firm voting stock; the target then dissolves, distributing the acquiring firm stock to its shareholders in return for their (now-cancelled) target stock. In general, Type A and B reorganizations use the pooling of interests method of accounting, while Type C reorganizations use the purchase method.

Acquisitions are taxable when the medium of exchange is cash or nonequity securities of the acquiring firm. The target may be absorbed into the acquiring firm, or maintained as a separate operating entity.

An overview of tax effects of acquisitions can be summarized as follows:

	Acquiring Firm	**Target Firm**
Tax-free reorganizations	NOL carryover Tax-credit carryover Carryover asset basis	Deferred gains for shareholders
Taxable acquisitions	Stepped-up asset basis Loss of NOLs and tax credits	Depreciation recapture of income Immediate gain recognition by target shareholders

Additional Potential Tax Impacts

1. Interest deductions associated with leverage
2. Capital gains taxes paid by target shareholders
3. Capital gains taxes on post-buyout asset sales
4. Tax payments on debt by creditors
5. Tax payments (reductions) on increased (reduced) income from efficiency gains (losses)
6. Tax payments (reductions) on increased (reduced) income from increased (reduced) sales growth
7. Tax changes resulting from an increased (reduced) rate of productive investments
8. Tax changes resulting from a change in dividend policy

The stepped-up asset basis is available to the acquiring firm only in taxable transactions. Thus, target firm shareholders must immediately (that is, in the year of the sale) recognize any resulting capital gains. If, in addition, the target firm has used accelerated depreciation, a portion of any gain that is attributable to excess depreciation deductions will be recaptured to be taxed as ordinary income rather than capital gain, the amount of recapture depending on the nature of the property involved. In tax-free acquisitions, the target's asset basis is transferred intact to the acquiring firm (carryover basis). Thus, if the target's basis were greater than its market value (and purchase price), an acquirer would most likely prefer a tax-free reorganization. In Type C (stock-for-asset) tax-free reorganizations, depreciation recapture is deferred until the assets are subsequently disposed of in a taxable transaction; obviously, this permits the possibility of indefinite deferral.

Net operating losses are available to the acquiring firm only in tax-free reorganizations; and they can only be used to shield future income, not to recapture past taxes paid. Furthermore, even in tax-free reorganizations, if the target is maintained as a separate operating entity within the acquiring firm following a Type B transaction (stock-for-stock), the carryover remains with the "target/subsidiary" rather than transferring to the "acquirer/parent," and can be used only to shelter target earnings; the target must be liquidated following the transaction to make the NOL carryover available to the acquiring firm. Liquidation, in turn, can trigger depreciation recapture and other negative tax consequences for the target firm (now a part of the acquiring firm). Transactions can be structured to utilize NOL carryforward regardless of whether the loss firm is the target or the acquirer, so long as the arrangement is not solely for the purpose of tax avoidance; that is the combination must have a justifiable business purpose. In taxable transactions, the net operating loss carryover simply vanishes and is not available to anyone. Tax credits such as the investment tax credit or foreign tax credits are treated in the same way as net operating losses.

Prior to the 1986 Tax Reform Act (TRA 86) a corporation could liquidate under Section 337, thereby avoiding paying a corporate-level tax on the distribution of appreciated property. This was the General Utilities Doctrine. Ginsburg [1983] provides several case illustrations. The 1980 Mobil-Esmark transaction is one example. Esmark wanted to sell its Vickers Energy Corporation. Mobil Corporation wanted to buy TransOcean Oil, a subsidiary of Vickers. Instead of simply buying TransOcean Oil stock, which would have resulted ultimately in a capital gain for Esmark, Mobil made a cash tender offer to Esmark stock. Mobil then redeemed its Esmark stock in exchange for shares of Vickers Energy Corporation (which by that time held TransOcean Oil stock as its only asset). Esmark was not required to recognize any gain on the distribution of appreciated property (the Vickers stock) to shareholders in a redemption. Esmark shareholders were free to choose whether they wanted to participate in the transaction; presumably those who tendered their shares to Mobil did so willingly, and took their returns in the form of capital gains. Had Esmark sold the TransOcean Oil stock or assets to Mobil more directly, its gain, net of tax, would conceivably have been passed on to Esmark shareholders eventually in the form of dividends, taxable as ordinary income, whether the shareholders wished to receive them or not.

Ginsburg [1983] also describes a similar arrangement involving Dome Petroleum's tender offer purchase of Conoco stock which it then redeemed in exchange for Conoco's interest in the Hudson's Bay Oil and Gas Co. In this case, Conoco was an unwilling participant in the transaction, whereas Esmark, in the previous instance, was cooperative. The results, however, were the same: A parent firm was able to (or forced to) effectively sell appreciated assets without recognizing gain or recapture income; those of its shareholders who wished to participate benefited in the form of capital gains; and the acquiring firm's asset basis reflected the price it paid to tendering parent firm shareholders. On the other hand, many stock redemption transactions have been struck down, the IRS forcing both the parent firm and its shareholders to recognize gain as if the transaction had been carried out as a sale of the subsidiary's assets followed by a cash distribution in redemption of shares (to those shareholders who tendered to acquiring firm). In particular, the IRS has ruled against cases where shell subsidiaries were created and endowed with appreciated assets for the sole purpose of transferring such assets to an interest buyer via a stock redemption.

Thus, under the General Utilities case decided in the 1930s and incorporated in later code sections, corporations did not recognize gains when they sold assets in connection with a complete liquidation if the requirements of Section 337 were met. This required adoption of a plan of liquidation and sale with distribution of assets within a 12-month period. Distribution of assets in kind of liquidation also was not subject to tax. These provisions were repealed by the TRA of 1986.

Scholes and Wolfson [1989] comment on the Section 338 election. If the acquiring corporation makes this election, the transaction is treated as purchase of all of the assets of the selling firm followed by its complete liquidation (Section 337). This results in the tax basis of the assets being stepped up or down to fair market value, but at the cost of a loss of the NOLs and tax credit carryforwards. They "predict that with the 1986 Act, many more stock transactions will be non-Section 338 elections. This will preserve the old basis and depreciation schedule of the assets of the acquired firm, will avoid recapture and capital gains tax on the sale of these assets, and will permit retention of the firm's tax attributes." [p. 31]

TRA 86 also had a number of other impacts on merger and acquisitions transactions. (1) It severely restricted the use of net operating loss carryovers. (2) The preferential rate on corporate capital gains was repealed. (3) A minimum tax was imposed on corporate profits. (4) Greenmail payments could not be deducted.

TRA 86 provided that if there is a greater than 50 percent ownership change in a loss corporation within a three-year period, an annual limit on the use of NOLs will be imposed. The amount of an NOL that may be used to offset earnings is limited to the value of the loss corporation at the date of ownership change multiplied by the long-term tax-exempt bond rate. For example, assume a loss corporation is worth $10 million immediately before an ownership change, the tax-exempt bond rate is 7 percent, and the corporation has a $5 million loss carryforward. Then $700,000 ($10 million × 7%) of the NOL can be used annually to offset the acquiring firm's taxable income. In addition, a loss corporation may not utilize NOL carryovers unless it continues substantially the same business for two years after the change in ownership. If this requirement is not met, all of the losses generally are disallowed.

The corporate capital gains tax rate had been 28 percent. For taxable years beginning on or after July 1, 1987 long-term as well as short-term corporate capital gains are taxed as ordinary income subject to the maximum corporation tax rate of 34 percent. Since many individuals are taxed at less than the top corporate rate of 34 percent, this could stimulate more acquisitions through master limited partnerships (MLPs) or through use of S corporations. The use of MLPs or S corporations enables profits to flow directly to the partners or to the S corporation shareholders. This achieves a lower tax rate and avoids double taxation on both earnings and dividends.

Before TRA 86 a corporation paid a minimum tax on specific tax preferences in addition to its regular tax. The old add-on minimum tax is replaced by an alternative minimum tax with a flat rate of 20 percent. Thus, corporations pay taxes on at least 20 percent of their income above the exemption amount. This has a negative impact on leveraged buyouts and acquisitions of companies where effective tax rates are below 20 percent.

TRA 86 also limited the extent to which amounts paid as greenmail to corporate raiders could be deducted for tax purposes. This change plus the others listed previously move in the direction of being less favorable to merger and acquisition activity. However, there is a long history of tax planners coming up with creative new ideas for avoiding the adverse impact of tax law changes.

12. Redistribution

Tax saving is a form of redistribution from the tax collector to the firm that achieves tax benefits. Other forms of redistribution may be involved. Some argue that the gains to the shareholders represent redistribution from a number of other stakeholders. These include bondholders in the form of reduced values, labor in the form of reduced wages and/or reduced employment, and consumers in the form of restricted supply and/or higher prices.

Including the subcategories, 16 theories of restructuring have been summarized. We next consider the empirical studies that provide tests of the alternative theories.

FORMS OF RESTRUCTURING AND THEIR RESULTS

Empirical studies may potentially elucidate a number of issues and questions. An important objective from a public policy standpoint is to determine whether or not social value is enhanced by mergers. If, for example, mergers improve efficiency, the improvement represents a social gain regardless of the theory that explains how it is achieved.

Table 27.8 provides an overview of the many forms of restructuring activities that have taken place. In addition it sets forth the returns from these activities. Most produced positive returns in excess of predicted levels without the events studied. To explain these results we need to explain each form of restructuring activity and its rationale.

Five major types of corporate change or transformation restructuring are surveyed. They are expansion, sell-offs, changes in ownership structure, issues of corporate control, and merger defenses. Each of these areas will be analyzed.

Expansion

The *Journal of Financial Economics* published a compendium of studies of mergers and tender offers in 1983. In their comprehensive summary article, Jensen and Ruback [1983] reviewed 13 studies with sample data ending mostly in the late 1970s. Six of the studies were on mergers and seven on tender offers. The summary table of Jensen and Ruback shows a 30 percent positive return to target shareholders in successful tender offers and a somewhat lower return of 20 percent to targets in successful mergers. (In mergers usually the larger firm is designated as the acquiring firm and the smaller firm as the acquired or target.) Jarrell, Brickley, and Netter [1988] summarize results for 663 successful tender offers covering the period from 1962 through December 1985. They observe that premiums to targets in successful tender offers averaged 19 percent in the 1960s, 35 percent in the 1970s, and 30 percent for the period 1980–1985 [p. 51]. Similar results were obtained by Bradley, Desai, and Kim [1988]. For the period July 1963 to June 1968, the returns to targets were 19 percent. For the subperiod July 1968 to December 1980, they were 35 percent; for the period January 1981 to December 1984, the returns were 35 percent. Their study covered 236 successful tender offer contests completed between 1963 and 1984.

TABLE 27.8 Forms of Restructuring and Their Financial Results

Form of Restructuring	Event Returns
Expansion	
Merger Studies	
Acquired firms	20%
Acquiring firms	2 to 3
Tender Offer Studies	
Acquired firms	30 to 35
Acquiring firms	−1 to +4
Joint Ventures	
Absolute	2.5
Scaled by investment	23
Sell-offs	
Spin-offs	2 to 4%
Divestitures	
Sellers	0.5 to1
Buyers	0.34
Equity Carve-outs	2
Changes in Ownership Structure	
Exchange Offers	
Debt for equity	14%
Preferred for equity	8
Share Repurchases	16
Going Private	20
Leveraged Buyouts	40 to 50
Leveraged Cash-outs	20 to 30
ESOPs	?
Corporate Control	
Unequal Voting Rights	
Value of control	5 to 6%
Dual-class recapitalizations	−1
Proxy Contests	10
Premium Buy-backs	
Greenmail	−2
Standstill agreements	−4
Merger Defenses	−4 to +4%

Targets in successful tender offers or mergers earn substantial premiums. In addition, the time trend of returns to targets has been upward. The reasons for the upward time trend may be summarized. In July 1968 the Williams Amendment gave the Securities and Exchange Commission (SEC) the power to regulate tender offers. In the same year the first state antitakeover law was passed by Virginia. The effect of government regulation was to require publication that a foothold position had been taken by the acquiring firm. In addition, government regulations provided for a delay before a tender offer could be completed, enabling the targets to develop defenses and counterbids and essentially ensuring the target shareholders a positive return.

In their summary of the evidence, Jensen and Ruback [1983] concluded that the excess returns to *bidder* firms in successful tender offers were a positive 4 percent. They estimated zero returns to bidder firms in mergers. Jarrell, Brickley, and Netter [1988] examined the data on returns to shareholders of acquiring companies for a sequence of decades. For the 1960s, they obtained about the same results as Jensen and Ruback. For the 1970s the excess returns to successful bidders dropped to about 2 percent, which is statistically significant. For the 1980s, the excess returns became negative at about 1 percent but are not statistically significant.

Bradley, Desai, and Kim [1988] found similar results for bidders. For subperiods approximating the 1960s, the excess returns to acquiring firms were slightly over 4 percent. For a period roughly corresponding to the 1970s, the excess returns were 1.3 percent. For the 1980s, the excess returns became negative at slightly under 3 percent. The data for the 1960s and the 1980s were significant at the 1 percent level. The excess returns to acquiring firms for the total period 1960–1985 for Jarrell, Brickley, and Netter and 1963 through 1984 for Bradley, Desai, and Kim were positive and significant. Bradley, Desai, and Kim also calculated the dollar amount of wealth change. They found that the combined results for target and acquiring firms were positive for each of the subperiods, including the 1980s when the excess wealth return to acquirers was negative.

The preceding evidence suggests that the returns to target firms increased over the decades as government regulation increased and as sophisticated defensive tactics by targets were developed. The returns to bidding firms decreased over the decades because the same influences operated in the reverse direction. But even for the most recent period of the 1980s, the total shareholder wealth increase from M&A activity was positive.

Some potential negative effects of merger and takeover activity may have also occurred. These include possible undue pressures on managements to perform well in the short run, unsettling effects of ownership shifts, employment reductions, and excessive leverage with potential increases in instability in the economy as a whole.

The third category under expansion in Table 27.8 is joint venture activity, already covered in Chapter 5. When scaled to the size of investments, joint ventures appear to achieve about a return 23 percent higher than predicted by general capital market return-risk relationships.

Sell-Offs

The two major types are (1) spin-offs and (2) divestitures. A *spin-off* creates a separate new legal entity, with its shares distributed on a pro rata basis to existing shareholders of the parent company. Thus, existing stockholders have the same proportion of ownership in the new entity as in the original firm. There is, however, a separation of control. In some sense, a spin-off represents a form of a dividend to existing shareholders.

In contrast to the class of spin-offs in which only shares are transferred or exchanged, *divestitures* are another group of transactions in which cash comes in to the firm. Basically, a divestiture involves the sale of a portion of the firm to an outside third party. An *equity carve-out* involves the sale of a portion of the firm via an equity offering of shares in the new entity to outsiders. A new legal entity and control group are created.

Spin-Offs. Schipper and Smith [1983] found a positive 2.84 percent abnormal return to the parent (statistically significant) on the spin-off announcement date. The size of the announcement effect is positively related to the size of the spin-off relative to parent size (the average size of the spin-off is about 20 percent of the original parent). Spin-offs motivated by avoidance of regulation experienced an abnormal return of 5.07 percent as compared to 2.29 percent for the remainder of the sample. Examples of regulation avoidance include separating a regulated utility subsidiary from nonutility businesses and spinning off a foreign subsidiary to avoid restrictions by the U.S. Congress.

Hite and Owers [1983] found abnormal returns of 3.8 percent, somewhat higher than for the full sample of Schipper and Smith. They also found a positive relationship between the relative size of the spin-off and the announcement effect. Neither study found an adverse effect on bondholders.

The Copeland, Lemgruber, and Mayers [1987] study extended the earlier studies in a number of dimensions. Particularly, they tested for postselection bias. In their first sample, they did this by including announced spin-offs that were not completed (11 percent of the sample). This led them to study the effects of successive announcements. A second expanded sample, subject to postselection bias, confirmed the impact of successive announcements. They also studied ex-date effects, which they also found to have positive abnormal performance. They found that taxable spin-offs do not have positive abnormal returns, while nontaxable spin-offs do. However, when they controlled for the size of the spin-off, the difference between the two tax categories disappeared.

For their small sample with no postselection bias, the two-day abnormal return from the first announcement was 2.49 percent; for the larger sample it was 3.03 percent. Both results are significant from a statistical standpoint. Thus, avoiding the postselection bias makes a difference; the return is lower for the sample that includes firms with announced spin-offs never consummated. For the eight firms with announced spin-offs that were never made, the two-day average return was a negative (but insignificant) 0.15 percent.

Divestitures. Event studies of divestitures have found significant positive abnormal two-day announcement-period returns of between 1 and 2 percent for selling firm shareholders. The announcement effects on returns to buyers did not appear to be statistically significant [Alexander, Benson, and Kampmeyer, 1984; Jain, 1985; and Linn and Rozeff, 1984]. A later study by Klein [1986] looked at divestitures in greater depth. When the selling firms do not disclose the transaction price at the initial sell-off announcement, no statistically significant effect on share prices for the seller is observed. When firms initially announce the price, the size of effects depends upon the percentage of the firm sold as measured by the price of the sell-off divided by the market value of the equity on the last day of the month prior to the announcement period. There is no significant price effect when the percentage of the equity sold is less than 10 percent. When the percentage of equity sold is between 10 percent and 50 percent, abnormal returns to the seller average a positive 2.53 percent. When the percentage of the equity sold is greater than 50 percent, the percentage abnormal return is 8.09 percent. The results appear to reflect the potential impact on sellers [Klein, 1986].

When the abnormal gains to sellers from divestitures are aggregated, the totals represent substantial dollar amounts. Black and Grundfest [1988] estimated that for the period 1981–1986, the abnormal value increases to sellers in corporate divestitures could be conservatively placed at $27.6 billion.

Equity Carve-Outs. Equity carve-outs on average are associated with positive abnormal returns of almost 2 percent over a five-day announcement period [Schipper and Smith, 1986]. This is in contrast to findings of significant negative returns of about 2 to 3 percent when parent companies publicly offer additional shares of their own (as opposed to their subsidiary's) stock [Smith, 1986a, 1986b].

The main explanations for the positive returns in spin-offs and equity carve-outs relate to management incentives. This explanation argues that more homogeneous organization units may be managed more effectively and be evaluated more accurately by financial analysts. In addition, managers may receive incentives and rewards more closely related to actual performance than when the quality of performance may be obscured in consolidated financial statements or monitored by superiors unfamiliar with the unique problems of a disparate subsidiary. In spin-offs, the creation of a freestanding stock price, reflecting the market's assessment of management's performance on a continual basis, may help assure that management compensation plans based on stock options will more directly measure and reward performance.

For divestitures, the main explanation appears to be that the resources are shifted to higher value uses. The buying company is motivated by the expectation that it can generate greater value from the use of the assets than can the selling firm.

Changes in Ownership Structure

Share repurchases, discussed in Chapter 16, represent an alternative means of making payouts to shareholders. Cash tender offers to repurchase shares result in significant positive abnormal returns to shareholders of about 13 to 15 percent; returns are even higher when they are financed by debt rather than by cash. Both tendering and nontendering shareholders benefit.

Exchange offers are a way for a company to change its capital structure while holding investment policy unchanged. Debt-for-common-stock offers have the effect of increasing leverage, and vice versa.

Copeland and Lee [1991] test six explanations of exchange offers and swaps: (1) short-term effects on earnings per share; (2) signaling; (3) tax savings; (4) free cash flow; (5) bondholders' wealth expropriation; and (6) dynamic movement toward a desired capital structure. They find that their empirical evidence is consistent with the conclusion that exchanges and swaps are repurchases of equity by issuing debt. Insiders thereby increase their ownership position. The market correctly interprets the announcement of the transactions as good news, increasing the wealth of all shareholders at the announcement date, before the transaction is consummated.

Their empirical evidence is strongly consistent with signaling effects. Leverage-increasing exchange offers have positive announcement effects, are preceded by net insider purchases, and are followed by decreases in systematic risk, increases in (fully diluted) earnings, sales, and total assets per share. Leverage-decreasing exchange offers have the opposite effects.

None of the alternative explanations for exchange offers and swaps is entirely consistent with the empirical evidence. The naive accounting hypothesis [(1) above] is inconsistent with the fact that firms with higher earnings following leverage-decreasing exchange offers have statistically significant negative announcement returns accompanied by increases in beta. The tax hypothesis is weak because it cannot explain several findings. It predicts increases in beta following leverage-increasing events, but the opposite actually happens. Furthermore, the tax hypothesis fails to predict positive announcement returns observed in preferred-for-common exchange offers, and it does not predict higher earnings, sales, and total assets per share following leverage-increasing events. It is difficult to reject the tax hypothesis completely because its effects may be masked by signaling [Dann, 1981; Masulis, 1983; Vermaelen, 1981, 1984].

Going Private and Leveraged Buyouts

"Going private" refers to the transformation of a public corporation into a privately held firm.[1] A leveraged buyout (LBO) is the acquisition, financed largely by borrowing, of the stock or assets of a hitherto public company by a small group of investors. The buying group may be sponsored by buyout specialists (for example, Kohlberg, Kravis, Roberts & Co.) or by investment bankers. A variant of the LBO going-private transactions is the unit management buyout (MBO) in which a segment of the company is sold to members of management. Unit MBOs have represented more than 10 percent of total divestitures since 1981.

Increased leverage does not seem to have been a strategic motive in LBOs. While leverage is increased at the formation of LBOs, it is sharply reduced in successive years. Muscarella and Vetsuypens [1990] present data showing the pattern of leverage for a sample of 72 firms that were taken private in LBOs and then about three years later experienced a secondary initial public offering (SIPO). The debt-to-equity ratio pre-LBO was 78 percent, rose to 1,415 percent at the time of the LBO (on a market basis), dropped to 376 percent by pre-SIPO, and declined further to 150 percent post-SIPO. Since equity values are increased, the ending leverage ratios at market could be below 100 percent. Thus, super-leverage does not appear to be a lasting consequence of LBOs. The initial financing is designed to facilitate higher management participation in the equity, which is associated with the subsequent operating improvements, value increases, and leverage reductions.

There is an important economic perspective to bring to LBOs. They were a unique and valuable economic innovation. They combine four important elements. First, they

---

[1]For a more complete analysis see Chapter 16, "Going Private and Leveraged Buy-Outs," in J. Fred Weston, Kwang S. Chung and Susan E. Hoag, *Mergers, Restructuring, and Corporate Control,* Englewood Cliffs, N.J.: Prentice-Hall, 1990.

TABLE 27.9   Growth of LBOs ($ in Billions)

	Total M&As	LBOs	Percent of LBOs to M&As
1981	$ 83	$ 2	2.4%
1982	54	3	5.6
1983	73	7	9.6
1984	122	11	9.0
1985	180	24	13.3
1986	173	20	11.6
1987	164	22	13.4
1988	247	61	24.7
1989	221	19	8.6
1990	108	4	3.7

Source: Merrill Lynch, *Mergerstat Review*, 1990.

used high leverage so the equity segment was reduced in size. Key management personnel could be provided with a significant equity ownership either through their own investments or based on the improvements they achieved in operating performance. The gains to managers would have a significant impact on their wealth position. Second, a turnaround element was always involved in the LBO based on highly qualified management either already on board in the segment or available to be brought in. Third, management personnel possessed the power of unrestricted decision making. They could use their knowledge; they could be flexible and make prompt decisions without several layers of hierarchical review. Fourth, the rewards of successful operations were large and significant. They provided strong motivation to key managers and employees in the new firm.

This innovative concept was sound. Returns to the original shareholders on the initiation of an LBO or MBO were at least on the order of magnitude of 40 to 50 percent. For successful LBOs, within about a three-year period of time, the firm could again go public. Returns to the shareholders including the key personnel involved in the LBO are on the order of magnitude of 50 to 60 percent [Kaplan, 1989a, 1989b].

We need to bring an economic perspective to understand the subsequent history of LBOs. Such significantly high returns inherently attract additional investment. LBOs totaled $20 billion annually by the early 1980s and had reached $61 billion by 1988. The data clearly illustrate the operation of the fundamental economic principle that high returns attract the flow of additional economic resources for investment. But as Table 27.9 shows, LBO activity fell off greatly in 1989 and 1990.

By 1988 there was enough LBO money to finance an additional $250 to $300 billion of LBO entities. By 1989 some LBO funds were reporting that they hadn't done a deal for two years. Many deals offered made no business sense or were overpriced. When they did bid on attractive deals, the winning bid exceeded theirs by very wide margins — often 50 to 75 percent higher than the second highest bid.

Leveraged cash-outs (or defensive recapitalizations) are a relatively new technique of financial restructuring first developed by Goldman Sachs for Multimedia in 1985. They are considered to be a defensive tactic because in most cases leveraged cash-outs (LCOs) have been implemented in response to a takeover bid. In a typical LCO, outside shareholders receive a large one-time cash dividend and insiders (managers) and employee benefit plans receive new shares instead of the cash dividend. The cash dividend is financed mostly by newly borrowed funds, both senior bank debt and mezzanine debt (subordinated debentures). As a result, the firm's leverage is increased to an "abnormally" high level and the proportional equity ownership of management significantly rises through the recapitalization. LCOs are associated with a positive 20 to 30 percent abnormal return during the announcement period. But financial difficulties are often encountered subsequently. In an article entitled, "All That Leverage Comes Home to Roost," in *Business Week* of September 10, 1990, the list of vulnerable companies had a heavy inclusion of defensive leveraged recaps.

ESOPs

An employee stock ownership plan (ESOP), briefly discussed in Chapter 5, is a type of stock bonus plan which invests primarily in the securities of the sponsoring employer firm.[2] A dramatic increase in the use of ESOPs as a takeover defense occurred in 1989. For example, in response to a tender offer by Shamrock Holdings (the investment vehicle for the family of Roy E. Disney, nephew of the late Walt Disney), Polaroid established an ESOP holding 14 percent of Polaroid common stock. Like most large corporations, Polaroid is chartered in Delaware. The Delaware antitakeover statute forbids hostile acquirers from merging with a target for at least three years unless 85 percent of the company's voting shares are tendered. Thus, it is unlikely that Shamrock would be able to obtain 85 percent of Polaroid shares if the ESOP does not tender [Rice and Spring, 1989].

ESOPs have been used in a wide variety of corporate restructuring activities [Bruner, 1988; GAO, 1986]. Fifty-nine percent of leveraged ESOPs were vehicles used to buy private companies from their owners. This enabled the owners to make their gains tax free by investing the funds received into a portfolio of securities. ESOPs have also been used in buyouts of large private companies.

Thirty-seven percent of leveraged ESOPs were employed in divestitures. In a very substantial ESOP transaction the Hospital Corporation of America sold over 100 of its 180 hospitals to HealthTrust, a new corporation created and owned by an employee leveraged ESOP.

Leveraged ESOPs have also been used as rescue operations. An ESOP was formed in 1983 to avoid the liquidation of Weirton Steel, which subsequently became a profitable company. ESOPs used in the attempt to prevent the failure of Rath Packing, McLean Trucking, and Hyatt Clark Industries were followed by subsequent bankruptcies.

A number of leveraged ESOPs were formed as a takeover defense to hostile tender offers. ESOPs were established as takeover defenses by Dan River in 1983, by Phillips Petroleum in 1985, and by Harcourt Brace Jovanovich in 1987. The reason why ESOPs

---

[2]For a more complete discussion see Chapter 15, "ESOPs and MLPs," in J. Fred Weston, Kwang S. Chung, and Susan E. Hoag, *Mergers, Restructuring, and Corporate Control*, Englewood Cliffs, N.J.: Prentice-Hall, 1990.

are a good takeover defense is that although the ESOP trust may control millions of shares, the employees may actually own and vote a small percentage of the shares at first. Often the majority of the shares are voted by management or management representatives as trustees of the portion of shares not directly owned by employees.

The Tax Reform Act of 1986 also permits excess pension assets to be shifted tax free if they are placed into an ESOP. Ashland Oil reverted $200 million and Transco Energy Co. $120 million into new ESOPs.

The view has been set forth that ESOP transactions represent economic dilution. Potentially they transfer shareholders' wealth to employees [Bruner, 1988]. As we observed at the beginning of this chapter, ESOPs represent a form of an employees' pension program. If the ESOP contribution is not offset by a reduction to some degree in other benefit plans, or in the direct wages of workers, employees gain at the expense of shareholders. The argument has also been made that any borrowing by the ESOP uses some of the debt capacity of the firm [Bruner, 1988]. It could also be argued that such borrowing substitutes for other forms of borrowing the firm would use. To the extent that ESOP transactions are believed to represent economic dilution to the original shareholders, the price charged to the ESOP for the company stock transferred to it may be a premium price to compensate for economic dilution. Since the Department of Labor reviews such transactions, this may be a source of its disagreements about the fairness of the price charged by management to the ESOP.

The impact of moving equity shares into the ownership of the employees is apparently an important disadvantage of ESOPs despite their considerable tax advantage. Kaplan [1988, note 12] has expressed this view in the following terms: "The infrequent use of ESOP loans in the sample analyzed in this paper (5 of 76 companies) suggests that the nontax costs of using an ESOP are high. One such cost is the large equity stake that eventually goes to all contributing employees and significantly reduces the equity stake that can be given to managers and the buyout promoter." A potential advantage is that shares can be sold at higher prices over the years as the ESOP contributes to higher earnings through tax advantages and through the increased incentives and improved motivations of employees as a result of their stock ownership through the ESOP.

The broader economic consequences of ESOPs have also been analyzed [Chen and Kensinger, 1988]. If managements also control the ESOPs that are created, no increase in employee influence on the company takes place. While employees may receive stock that may be sold, the additions to their wealth may be relatively small. The amounts received may be insufficient to provide motivation for increased efforts by workers or to achieve harmonious relations between workers and management. On the other hand, if workers did receive substantial increases in control over the company through ESOPs, other harmful results might follow. Workers might use their increased ownership powers to redistribute wealth away from the original shareholders and other shareholders in the firm. The view has also been expressed that reliance can be placed upon market forces to bring about employee ownership where it is appropriate, without the necessity of tax subsidies. The tax subsidies may cause a misallocation of resources.

ESOPs have provided some participation to workers. However, the motivational influences do not appear to have been sufficient to have an effect upon company performance. In addition, the ESOPs appear often to be controlled by managements and to be used as instruments of policy by managements. It has been estimated that the federal revenue losses from ESOPs for the period 1977–1983 were about $13 billion, an average of $1.9 billion per year [GAO, 1986, pp. 28–31]. Questions have been raised whether these tax subsidies are really serving a useful purpose.

Corporate Control Issues

The fourth set of forms of restructuring deals with corporate control issues. We first consider *unequal voting rights*. In many corporations there is a Class A and a Class B stock. Typically the Class A stock has superior rights to dividends but inferior rights to vote. The Class B stock has superior voting rights but limited dividends. One study shows that management's voting rights ownership was almost 60 percent, but their claims to cash flow were only 24 percent [DeAngelo and DeAngelo, 1985]. Often dual classes of stock are observed in corporations where the family founders seek to maintain or increase their control position.

A strong motive for superior voting rights is to enable the management control group to achieve continuity of future plans and operating programs. Some argue that those holding superior voting rights are likely to receive higher benefits in a merger or takeover. Empirical studies indicate that securities with superior voting rights sell at a premium of 5 to 6 percent [Lease, McConnell, and Mikkelson, 1983; DeAngelo and DeAngelo, 1985; Megginson, 1990].

One way to establish two classes of stock is by dual class recapitalizations. In early years firms that established dual classes of stock were delisted from the New York Stock Exchange for violation of the rule of one share-one vote. The New York Stock Exchange (NYSE) placed a moratorium in June 1984 on the delisting of dual-class equity firms. Studies both before and after the moratorium date indicate a small but insignificant effect on the stock with resulting inferior voting privileges. One study provides evidence that the post-moratorium sample had lower insider and higher institutional holdings [Jarrell and Poulsen, 1988]. Their evidence leads them to suggest that dual class recaps are undertaken by firms more susceptible to takeovers and that they serve to entrench managers. In September 1986, the NYSE proposed converting the moratorium into a permanent policy. In response, the SEC adopted Rule 19c-4, which effectively prohibited recaps with multiple classes of stock. In 1990, the Circuit Court of the District of Columbia ruled that the SEC lacked authority to do so. In 1991, the Supreme Court upheld the Circuit Court decision.

Lehn, Netter, and Poulsen [1990] compare dual-class recaps with LBOs. Firms with greater growth opportunities, lower agency costs, and lower tax liability appear more likely to consolidate control through dual-class recaps. They also find significant increases in industry-adjusted operating income for dual-class firms, but less than for a sample of LBOs. Dual-class firms allocate a higher percentage of subsequent cash flows to capital expenditures than do the LBOs. A high proportion of dual-class firms subsequently issue equity securities. The evidence suggests that dual-class firms possess more future growth opportunities than do the LBOs.

A *proxy* contest represents another form of control struggle. Proxy contests are attempts by dissident groups of shareholders to obtain a board representation. Various interpretations of the success of proxy contests have been offered. One is that the dissident group win a majority on the board. Others argue that success means gaining at least two members, one to propose motions, and the other to second them, to get discussions in the minutes of the board meeting. Still a third view holds that a proxy contest as such is sufficient to indicate that changes will have to be made in the management of the firm.

Studies of proxy contests indicate that they are associated with positive abnormal returns ranging from about 6 to 10 percent [Dodd and Warner, 1983; DeAngelo and DeAngelo, 1989]. Even if there is conflict on the board of directors as the result of a proxy contest, the results seem to indicate that the benefits of adversarial mutual monitoring between the two groups outweigh the costs. The positive shareholder gains indicate that the management had agency problems or potential for improved performance.

Proxy contests over the right to control increase the likelihood that corporate assets will be transferred to higher-valued uses. They perform an important and effective disciplinary role in the managerial labor market. Finally, they provide yet another approach to takeover activity. Changes in laws and regulations to effect a reduction in the costs of a proxy fight would increase the use of proxy-contest mechanisms in the market for corporate control.

Premium buy-backs are primarily involved in dealing with outsiders who have purchased a large foothold of shares in the firm. The outsiders who have purchased a large block of the firm's shares are usually referred to as raiders. The concern is that the raiders will take over the firm. Often their motive is to do a "bustup merger." This implies that the raiders feel that they can sell the parts of the firm for amounts that will add up to more than the existing market value of the firm.

Sometimes the raider is bought out at a premium price over the current market. This has been referred to as greenmail. In addition, the buyout may be associated with a so-called "standstill agreement," which provides that the raider will not attack again within a specified 5- to 10-year period of time.

From some standpoints the payment of greenmail and an associated standstill agreement are harmful to current shareholders in that the raider may have been able to provide more short-term value for them. The counterargument is that existing management may see greater value potential in the future. This provides a justification for paying greenmail. Another justification is that management may feel that given sufficient time it can develop multiple offers, initiate a bidding contest for the firm, and obtain higher value for shareholders than if the raider's efforts succeeded. Notable examples can be cited of large increases in shareholder values in subsequent years after raiders had been held off by greenmail and standstill agreements. However, the initial impact of greenmail and standstill agreements may be small negative changes in the value of the firm's shares.

MERGER DEFENSES

Along with the financial innovations that stimulated takeovers and restructuring, a counterforce developed in the form of merger defenses. The many types of merger defenses may be grouped into five categories: (1) defensive restructuring, (2) poison pills, (3) poison puts, (4) antitakeover amendments, and (5) golden parachutes.

Defensive restructuring has taken many forms. One is a scorched earth policy, which means incurring large debt and selling off attractive segments of the company and using the newly acquired funds to declare a large dividend to existing shareholders. A second involves selling off the crown jewels by disposing of those segments of the business in which the bidder is most interested. A third is to consolidate a voting block allied with target management. This may involve dilution of the bidder's voting percentage by issuing substantial new equity. A fourth is share repurchase without management sale. This simultaneously increases leverage and increases the equity position of management, which may enable management to have enough shares to defeat a takeover bid. A fifth method is to issue new securities to parties friendly to management. This includes the creation or expansion of an ESOP that is either allied with or controlled by management. Thus we see both repurchase activities and ESOPs play important roles as takeover defenses.

A sixth method of defensive restructuring is to create barriers specific to the bidder. For example, antitrust suits may be filed against the bidder or the firm may purchase assets that will create antitrust issues for the bidder.

A second major type of defense against takeovers is the use of *poison pills*. Poison pills are warrants or convertible preferred issued to existing shareholders, giving them the right to purchase surviving firm securities at very low prices in the event of a merger. Typical triggering events are the acquisition of 20 percent of the firm's shares or a tender offer for 30 percent or more of the firm's shares. The aim of poison pills is to seriously impair the control and wealth positions of the bidding firm. The risk and expense of a poison pill challenge may induce bidders to make offers conditional on the withdrawal of the poison pill. At a minimum the poison pill gives incumbent management considerable bargaining power since it can also set aside the warrants if, for example, a very attractive price is offered to the shareholders and perhaps other inducements are offered to existing management.

A third type of merger defense was stimulated by the decline in bond values as a result of the RJR-Nabisco leveraged buyout in December 1988. It permits the bondholders to *put* (sell) the bonds to the issuer corporation or its successor at par or at par plus some premium.

A fourth group of merger defenses consists of many types of *antitakeover amendments*. One type is fair price provisions, which provide that all shareholders must receive a uniform, fair price. This is aimed as a defense against two-tier offers. Supermajority amendments require 67-80 percent (or more) shareholder approval for a change of control. A staggered or classified board of directors may be used to delay the effective transfer of control. For example, the provision may require that only one-third of the board is elected each year. Thus obtaining 50 percent or more of the board members will require one or more years. Another type of charter amendment is to provide for reincorporation in a state with laws more protective against takeovers. Or the charter amendment may provide for the creation of a new class of securities (often privately placed) whose approval is required for takeover. In addition, lock-in amendments may be enacted to make it difficult to void the previously passed antitakeover amendments. While the enactment of antitakeover amendments is typically associated with negative impacts on stock prices, shareholders have approved 90 percent of proposed amendments. The passage of antitakeover amendments may also sometimes have positive effects on stock prices.

The fifth major type of merger defense is *golden parachutes*. Golden parachutes are separation provisions of an employment contract that provide for payments to managers under a change-of-control clause. Usually a lump sum payment is involved. The rationale is to help reduce the conflict of interest between shareholders and managers and change-of-control situations. While the dollar amounts are large the cost in most cases is less than 1 percent of the total takeover value. Recent changes in tax laws have limited tax deductions to the corporation for golden parachute payments and have imposed penalties upon the recipient. A theoretical argument for golden parachutes is that they encourage managers to make firm-specific investments of their human capital and encourage them to take the longer-term view for the corporation. One might argue that, when set at the right level, golden parachutes provide management with a disincentive to resist takeovers because management receives a large payment when the firm is taken over. The optimal golden parachute must be designed to motivate managers to resist takeovers long enough to receive the maximum attainable price for shareholders.

The issue of whether takeover defenses benefit shareholders is largely unresolved. Defenses may entrench incompetent managers, foil unscrupulous raiders, or maximize the price target shareholders eventually receive. Apologists for defensive actions suggest that such actions will promote an auction for the target firm by allowing time for potential bidders to enter the takeover contest. They argue that defenses strengthen management's bargaining position for a better deal or eliminate the pressure for shareholders to tender their shares as caused by coercive tender offers. Opponents of defenses argue that defenses increase the costs of takeover, thereby decreasing the incentive for potential bidders to search for profitable takeover targets or causing an outstanding bid to be withdrawn. For opponents, defensive actions are largely a manifestation of a conflict of interest between management and shareholders. In general, they propose a rule of strict managerial passivity. [See, for example, Easterbrook and Fischel, 1981.] Finally, another view points out that measures are needed to reduce the conflict of interest in situations involving a change of control. A case in point is golden parachute contracts providing compensation to managers for the loss of their jobs under a change of control. In this view, shark repellents and other defenses prevent disruption of the contractual relation between managers and shareholders by putting restrictions on hostile tender offers. [See, for example, Knoeber, 1986.]

Negative stock price effects of some antitakeover measures requiring a shareholder vote raise the question of why they are approved by shareholders. Bhagat and Jefferis [1988] argue that the presence of uninformed investors combined with the high costs of "reaching" those investors during the proxy voting process is responsible for the result. Evidence shows that institutional investors who are presumably better informed vote more actively, and harmful measures are instituted in firms with smaller institutional ownership of voting rights. Since February 1988, with the issuance of the "Avon Letter," the Department of Labor has placed increased pressure on pension funds to "take proxy voting seriously" [Brickley, Lease, and Smith, 1990, footnote 28, p. 24].

Jarrell, Brickley, and Netter [1988, p. 66] express concern that "the business judgment rule is operating too broadly as a shield for defensive actions by target managements." Jensen [1988a, 1988b] warns that, ironically, the broad application of the business judgment rule will increase judicial interference in corporate management. Recent pro-acquirer court decisions in cases involving poison pill defenses have been based on an evaluation by the court of the adequacy of the takeover bid.

Evaluation

Some generalizations from the restructuring movement of the 1980s are possible. M&A activity should be a part of a long-run planning strategy. The strategy comes first and the takeover activity should be placed in that appropriate strategic long-range planning framework. The touchstone should be that the acquired firm should be of greater value as a part of the acquiring company than if left standing alone or purchased by another company. This is an important way to help avoid paying too much.

Changes in the environment plus corporate governance tensions produced the restructuring movement of the 1980s. The restructuring movement itself created new turbulence and tensions. These represent broad adjustment processes in an enterprise system. These pressures have made the managements of many firms uncomfortable. But strong competitive pressures harness energies to creative competition, and restructuring movement has made contributions in this direction.

But mistakes and excesses have also occurred. We are engaged in a competition between types of economic systems. The weaknesses of state planning have become clear. The lack of monitoring control and flexibility in adjusting to change stand out as weaknesses of centralized planning. On the other hand, the use of market forces is not without its own types of mistakes. At least in part the M&A activity of the 1980s was a response to tensions and weaknesses associated with the separation of ownership and control in the large corporation with widely dispersed ownership.

HOLDING COMPANIES

In 1889, New Jersey became the first state to pass a general incorporation law permitting corporations to be formed for the sole purpose of owning the stocks of other companies. This law was the origin of the holding company. The Sherman Act of 1890, which prohibits combinations or collusion in restraint of trade, gave an impetus to holding company operations as well as to outright mergers, because companies could do as one company what they were forbidden to do as separate companies.

Many of the advantages and disadvantages of holding companies are no more than the advantages and disadvantages of large-scale operations already discussed in connection with mergers and consolidations. Whether a company is organized on a divisional basis or with the divisions kept as separate companies does not affect the basic reasons for conducting a large-scale, multiproduct, multiplant operation. However, the holding company form of large-scale operations has different advantages and disadvantages from those of completely integrated divisionalized operations.

Advantages of Holding Companies

Control with Fractional Ownership. Through a holding company operation, a firm can buy 5, 10, or 50 percent of the stock of another corporation. Such a fractional ownership may be sufficient to give the acquiring company effective working control of or substantial influence over the operations of the company in which it has acquired ownership. Working control is often considered to entail more than 25 percent of the common stock, but it can be as low as 10 percent if the stock is widely distributed. Also, control on a very slim margin can be held through friendship with large stockholders outside the holding company group. Sometimes, holding company operations represent the initial stages of transforming an operating company into an investment company, particularly when the operating company is in a declining industry. When an industry's sales begin to decline permanently and the firm begins to liquidate its operating assets, it may use the liquid funds to invest in industries having a more favorable growth potential.

Isolation of Risks. Because the various operating companies in a holding company system are separate legal entities, the obligations of any one unit are separate from those of the other units. Catastrophic losses incurred by one unit, therefore, are not transmitted as claims on the assets of the other units.

Although this is the customary generalization of the nature of a holding company system, it is not completely valid. In extending credit to one of the units of a holding company system, an astute financial manager or loan officer will require a guarantee or a claim on the assets of all the elements in the system. To some degree, therefore, the assets in the various elements are joined. The advantage remains to the extent that catastrophes occurring to one unit are not transmitted to the others.

Approval Not Required. A holding company group that seeks to obtain effective working control of a number of companies may quietly purchase a portion of their stock. The operation is completely informal, and the permission or approval of the stockholders of the acquired company or companies is not required. Thus, the guiding personalities in a holding company operation are not dependent on negotiations and approval of the other interest groups in order to obtain their objectives. This feature of holding company operations has, however, been limited somewhat by recent state law and SEC rules governing tender offers.

Disadvantages of Holding Companies

Partial Multiple Taxation. Provided the holding company owns at least 80 percent of a subsidiary's voting stock, Internal Revenue Service regulations permit the filing of consolidated returns, in which case, dividends received by the parent are not taxed. However, if less than 80 percent of the stock is owned, returns cannot be consolidated, although 70 to 80 percent of the dividends received by the holding company can be excluded. With a tax rate of 34 percent, this means that the effective tax on intercorporate dividends is 6.8 to 10.2 percent. This partial double taxation somewhat offsets the benefits of holding company control with limited ownership, but whether the penalty of 6.8 percent of dividends received is sufficient to offset the advantages is a matter that must be decided in individual situations.[3]

Ease of Enforced Dissolution. In the case of a holding company operation that falls into disfavor with the U.S. Department of Justice, it is relatively easy to require dissolution of the relationship by disposal of stock ownership; for instance, in the late 1950s, du Pont was required to dispose of its 23 percent stock interest in General Motors Corporation, acquired in the early 1920s. Because there was no fusion between the corporations, there were no difficulties, from an operating standpoint, in requiring the separation of the two companies. However, if complete amalgamation had taken place, it would have been much more difficult to break up the company after so many years, and the likelihood of forced divestiture would have been reduced.

Risks of Excessive Pyramiding. Financial leverage effects in pyramiding magnify profits if operations are successful, but they also magnify losses. The greater the degree of pyramiding, the greater is the degree of risk involved in any fluctuations in sales or earnings. This potential disadvantage of pyramiding operations through holding companies is discussed in the next section.

Leverage in Holding Companies

The problem of excessive leverage is worthy of further note, for the degree of leverage in certain past instances has been truly staggering. For example, in the 1920s, Samuel Insull and his group controlled electric utility-operating companies at the bottom of a holding company pyramid by a one-twentieth of 1 percent investment. As a ratio, this represents 1/2,000. In other words, $1.00 of capital at the top holding company level controlled $2,000 of assets at the operating level. A similar situation existed in the railroad field. It has been stated that Robert R. Young, with an investment of $254,000, obtained control of the Allegheny system, consisting of total operating assets of $3 billion.

The nature of leverage in a holding company system and its advantages and disadvantages are illustrated by the hypothetical example developed in Table 27.10.[4] As in the previous example, although this case is hypothetical, it illustrates actual situations. Half of the operating company's Class B common stock is owned by Holding Company 1; in fact, it is the only asset of Holding Company 1. Holding Company 2 holds as its total assets half of the Class B common stock of Holding Company 1. Consequently, $500 of Class B common stock of Holding Company 2 could control $2 million of assets at the operating company level. Further leverage could, of course, have been postulated in this situation by setting up a third company to own Class B common stock of Holding Company 2.

---

[3]The 1969 Tax Reform Law also empowers the Internal Revenue Service to prohibit the deductibility of debt issued to acquire another firm where the following conditions hold: (1) the debt is subordinated to a "significant portion" of the firm's other creditors; (2) the debt is convertible or has warrants attached; (3) the debt/assets ratio exceeds 67 percent; and (4) on a pro forma basis, the times interest earned ratio is less than 3. The IRS can use discretion in invoking this power.

[4]Corrections in computations were supplied by Dr. Narendra C. Bhandari, Pace University, New York City.

TABLE 27.10   Leverage in a Holding Company System

Operating Company			
Total assets	$2,000,000	Debt	$1,000,000
		Preferred stock	150,000
		Common stock: Class A[a]	650,000
		Common stock: Class B	200,000
	$2,000,000		$2,000,000
Holding Company 1			
Class B common stock of		Debt	$ 50,000
operating company	$100,000	Preferred stock	10,000
		Common stock: Class A[a]	30,000
		Common stock: Class B	10,000
	$100,000		$100,000
Holding Company 2			
Class B common stock of Holding		Debt	$2,000
Company 1	$5,000	Preferred stock	$1,000
		Common stock: Class A[a]	1,000
		Common stock: Class B	1,000
	$5,000		$5,000

[a]Class A common stock is nonvoting.

Table 27.11 shows the effects of holding company leverage on gains and losses at the top level. In the first column, it is assumed that the operating company earns 16 percent before taxes on its $2 million of assets; in the second column, it is assumed that the return on assets is 12.5 percent. The operating and holding companies are the same as described in Table 27.10.

A return of 16 percent on the operating assets of $2 million represents earnings of $320,000. The debt interest of $100,000 is deducted from this amount, and the 34 percent tax rate applies to the remainder. The amount available to common stock after payment of debt interest, preferred stock dividends, and a 12 percent return to the nonvoting Class A common stock is $52,200. Assuming a $50,000 dividend payout, Holding Company 1, on the basis of its 50 percent ownership of the operating company, earns $25,000. If the same kind of analysis is followed through, the amount available to Class B common stock in Holding Company 2 is $6,638. This return is on an investment of $1,000, and it represents a return on the investment in Class B common stock of Holding Company 2 of about 664 percent. The power of leverage in a holding company system can indeed be great.

On the other hand, if a decline in revenues causes the pretax earnings to drop to 12.5 percent of the total assets of the operating company, the results will be disastrous. The amount earned under these circumstances will be $250,000. After deducting the bond interest, the amount subject to tax will be $150,000, and the tax will be $51,000. The after-tax but before-interest earnings will be $199,000. The total prior changes will be $193,000, leaving $6,000 available to Class B common stock. If all earnings are paid out

TABLE 27.11 Effects of Holding Company Leverage on Gains and Losses

	Earnings before Interest and Taxes	
	at 16%	at 12.5%
Operating Company		
Earnings before interest and taxes	$320,000	$250,000
Less interest on debt (at 10%)	100,000	100,000
Earnings after interest	$220,000	$150,000
Less tax (at 34%)	74,800	51,000
After-tax earnings available for stockholders	$145,200	$ 99,000
Less: Preferred stock (at 10%)	15,000	15,000
Class A common stock (at 12%)	78,000	78,000
Earnings available to Class B common stock	$ 52,200	$ 6,000
Dividends to Class B common stock		
(by management decision)	50,000	6,000
Transferred to retained earnings	$ 2,200	$ 0
Holding Company 1		
Earnings before interest and taxes (received from the operating company)	$ 25,000	$ 3,000
Less 80% of dividends received	20,000	2,400
Intercorporate dividends subject to tax, before interest	$ 5,000	$ 600
Less interest on debt (at 10%)	5,000	5,000
Before-tax earnings	$ 0	$ (4,400)
Less tax (at 34%)	0	(1,496)[a]
After-tax earnings	$ 0	$ (2,904)
Amount of untaxed dividend	$ 20,000	2,400
After-tax earnings available to stockholders	$ 20,000	$ (504)
Less: Preferred stock (at 10%)	1,000	
Class A common stock (at 12%)	3,600	
Earnings available to Class B common stock	$ 15,400	
Less dividends to Class B common stock		
(by management decision)	15,000	
Transferred to retained earnings	$ 400	
Holding Company 2		
Earnings before interest and taxes (received from Holding Company 1)	$ 7,500	
Less 80% of dividends received	6,000	
Intercorporate dividends subject to tax, before interest	$ 1,500	
Less interest on debt (at 10%)	200	
Before-tax earnings	$ 1,300	
Less tax (at 34%)	442	
After-tax earnings	$ 858	
Amount of untaxed dividends	6,000	
After-tax earnings available to stockholders	$ 6,858	
Less: Preferred stock (at 10%)	100	
Class A common stock (at 12%)	120	
Earnings available to Class B common stock	$ 6,638	
Percentage return on Class B common stock	663.8%	

[a]Assumes tax loss can be sold.

in dividends to Class B common stock, the earnings of Holding Company 1 will be $3,000. This is not enough to meet the debt interest. The holding company system, thus, will be forced to default on the debt interest of Holding Company 1 and, of course, Holding Company 2.

This example illustrates the potential for tremendous gains in a holding company system. It also illustrates that a small earnings decline on the assets of the operating companies will be disastrous.[5]

TRADITIONAL APPROACHES TO ACQUISITION PRICES

For every acquisition actually consummated, a number of other potentially attractive combinations fail during negotiations. Negotiations may be broken off when it is revealed that the companies' operations are not compatible or when the parties are unable to agree on terms. The most important of these is the price to be paid by the acquiring firm.

Effects on Price and Earnings

An acquisition carries the potential for either favorable or adverse effects on earnings, on market price of shares, or on both. Previous chapters have shown that investment decisions should be guided by the effects on market values, and this is our approach presented in the following major section. Future events are difficult to forecast, however, so both stockholders and managers have attributed great importance to the immediate effects on earnings per share. The traditional approach was to look at the effects of a proposed merger on earnings per share (EPS).

An example will illustrate the earnings per share approach. Assume the facts in Table 27.12 for two companies. Suppose the firms agree to merge, with B, the surviving firm, acquiring the shares of A by a one-for-one exchange of stock. The exchange ratio is determined by the market prices of the two companies. Assuming no increase in earnings, the effects on earnings per share are shown in Table 27.13.

Since total earnings are $70,000, and since a total of 15,000 shares will be outstanding after the merger has been completed, the new earnings per share will be $4.67.

TABLE 27.12   Basic Information for Analysis of Dilution and Appreciation

	Company A	Company B
Total earnings	$20,000	$50,000
Number of shares of common stock	5,000	10,000
Earnings per share of stock	$4	$5
Price-earnings ratio per share	15 times	12 times
Market price per share	$60	$60

---

[5]An article on the corporate complex and financial cascade in the Edward and Peter Bronfman holdings provides a 1991 example of all aspects of holding companies discussed above [Laing, 1991].

TABLE 27.13   Effects of Differential P-Es When Merger Terms Are at Market Prices

| | Shares of Company B Owned after Merger | Earnings per Share | |
		Before Merger	After Merger
A's stockholders	5,000	$4	$4.67
B's stockholders	10,000	5	4.67
Total	15,000		

Earnings will increase by 67 cents for A's stockholders, but they will decline by 33 cents for B's.

The effects on market values are less certain. If the combined company sells at Company A's price-earnings ratio of 15, the market value per share of the new company will be $70. In this case, shareholders of both companies will have benefited. This result comes about because the combined earnings are now valued at a multiplier of 15, whereas prior to the merger, one portion of the earnings was valued at a multiplier of 15, and another portion at a multiplier of 12. If, on the other hand, the earnings of the new company are valued at B's multiplier of 12, the indicated market value of the shares will be $56, and the shareholders of each company will have suffered a $4 dilution in market value.

Because the effects on market value per share are less certain than those on earnings per share, the impact on earnings per share tends to be given great weight in merger negotiations. The following analysis thus illustrates effects on earnings per share while recognizing that maximizing market value is the valid rule for investment decisions.

As shown below, if a merger takes place on the basis of earnings, neither earnings dilution nor earnings appreciation will take place, as shown in Table 27.14. It is clear that the equivalent earnings per share after the merger are the same as before the merger.[6] The effect on market values, however, will depend on the size of the earnings multiplier that prevails.

Quantitative Factors Affecting Terms of Acquisitions

Five factors have traditionally received emphasis in arriving at acquisition terms: (1) earnings and the growth of earnings, (2) dividends, (3) market values, (4) book values, and (5) net current assets. Analysis was typically based on the per-share values of the foregoing factors. The nature of these potential influences is described below.

---

[6]On the basis of earnings, the exchange ratio is 4:5. That is, Company A's shareholders receive four shares of B stock for each five shares of A stock they own. Earnings per share of the merged company are $5. But, since A's shareholders now own only 80 percent of the number of their old shares, their equivalent earnings per *old* share are the same $4. For example, if one of A's stockholders formerly held 100 shares, that person will own only 80 shares of B after the merger, and the total earnings will be $80 \times \$5 = \$400$. Dividing the $400 total earnings by the number of shares formerly owned, 100, gives the $4 per *old* share.

TABLE 27.14 Effects of Differential P-Es When Merger Terms Are Based on Earnings

	Shares of Company B Owned after Merger	Earnings per Share	
		Before Merger	After Merger
A's stockholders	4,000	$4	$4
B's stockholders	10,000	5	5
Total	14,000		

Earnings and Growth Rates. Both expected earnings and capitalization rates as reflected in P-E ratios were considered. The analysis began with historical data on the firms' earnings; their past growth rates, probable future trends, and variability.

The ways in which future earnings growth rates could be impacted can be illustrated by extending the preceding example. First, high P-E ratios are commonly associated with rapidly growing companies. Since Company A has the higher P-E ratio, it is reasonable to assume that its earnings will grow more rapidly than those of Company B. Suppose A's expected growth rate is 10 percent and B's is 5 percent. Looking at the proposed merger from the viewpoint of Company B and its stockholders, and assuming that the exchange ratio is based on present market prices, it can be seen that B will suffer a dilution in earnings when the merger occurs. However, B will be acquiring a firm with more favorable growth prospects; hence, its earnings after the merger should increase more rapidly than before. In this case, the new growth rate is assumed to be a weighted average of the growth rates of the individual firms—weighted by their respective total earnings before the merger. In the example, the new expected growth rate is 6.43 percent [2/7(10) + 5/7(5)].

With the new growth rate, it is possible to determine how long it will take Company B's stockholders to overcome the earnings dilution as shown in Figure 27.1.[7] Without the merger, B will have initial earnings of $5 a share, and these earnings will grow at a rate of 5 percent a year. With the merger, earnings will drop to $4.67 a share, but the rate of growth will increase to 6.43 percent. Under these conditions, the earnings dilution will be overcome after five years; from the fifth year on, B's earnings will be higher, assuming the merger is consummated. This same relationship can be developed

---

[7]The calculation could also be made algebraically by solving for n in the following equation:

$$E_1(1 + g_1)^n = E_2(1 + g_2)^n,$$

where

E_1 and E_2 = earnings per share before and after the merger, respectively

g_1 and g_2 = growth rates before and after the merger, respectively

n = breakeven number of years.

FIGURE 27.1   Effect of Merger on Future Earnings

from the viewpoint of the faster growing firm, for which there is an immediate earnings increase but a reduced rate of growth.[8]

Dividends. Because they represent the actual income received by stockholders, dividends can influence the terms of merger. As Chapter 16 suggests, however, dividends are likely to have little influence on the market price of companies with a record of high growth and high profitability. Some companies have not yet paid cash dividends, but they nonetheless command market prices representing a high multiple of current earnings. However, for utility companies and for companies in industries where growth rates and

---

[8]Certain companies, especially the conglomerates, are reported to have used mergers to produce a "growth illusion" designed to increase the prices of their stocks. When a high P-E ratio company buys a low P-E ratio company, the earnings per share of the acquiring firm rise *because* of the merger. Thus, mergers can produce growth in reported earnings for the acquiring firm. This growth by merger, in turn, can cause the acquiring firm to keep its high P-E ratio. With this ratio, the conglomerates can seek new low P-E merger candidates and thus continue to obtain growth through mergers. The chain is broken if (1) the merger activity slows or (2) the P-E ratio of the acquiring firm falls. In 1968 and 1969, several large conglomerates reported profit declines caused by losses in certain of their divisions. This reduced the growth rate in EPS, which, in turn, led to a decline in the P-E ratio. A change in tax laws and antitrust suits against some conglomerate mergers also made it more difficult to consummate favorable mergers. These factors, along with tight money and depressed conditions in some industries, caused a further reduction in the P-E ratio and compounded the firms' problems. The net result was a drastic revaluation of conglomerate share prices, with such former favorites as LTV falling from a high of $169 to $7.50 and Litton Industries from $115 to $6.75.

profitability have declined, the dollar amount of dividends paid can have an influence on the market price of the stock.[9]

Market Values. The price of a firm's stock reflects expectations about its future earnings and dividends, so current market values are expected to have a strong influence on the terms of a merger. However, the value placed on a firm in an acquisition may exceed its current market price for a number of reasons:

1. The prospective purchaser may be interested in the company for the contribution that it will make to the purchaser's company. Thus, the acquired company may be worth more to an informed purchaser than it is in the general market.

2. Stockholders are offered more than current market prices for their stock as an inducement to sell.

3. The value of control or ability to realize tax advantages may add values above the current market levels [Lease, McConnell, and Mikkelson, 1983].

For these reasons, the offering price, historically, had been in the range of 10 to 20 percent above the market price before the merger announcement. In recent years, premiums of 50 percent or more have been observed.

Book Value per Share. Book value is generally considered to be relatively unimportant in determining the value of a company, since it represents only the historical investments made in the company — investments that may have little relation to current values or prices. At times, however, especially when it substantially exceeds market value, book value may have an impact on merger terms. Book value is an index of the amount of physical facilities made available in the merger. Despite a past record of low earning power, it is always possible that, under effective management, a firm's assets may once again achieve normal earning power, in which case, the market value of the company will rise. Because of the potential contribution of physical properties to improved future earnings, book value may have an influence on actual merger terms.

Net Current Assets per Share. Net current assets (current assets minus current liabilities) per share could have an influence on merger terms because they represent the amount of liquidity that can be obtained from a company in a merger. In the postwar textile mergers, net current assets were very high, and this was one of the characteristics making textile companies attractive to the acquiring firms. By buying a textile company, often with securities, an acquiring company was in a position to look for still other merger candidates, paying for new acquisitions with the just-acquired liquidity. Similarly, if an acquired company is debt-free, the acquiring firm may be able to borrow the funds re-

---

[9]If a company that does not pay dividends on its stock is seeking to acquire a firm whose stockholders are accustomed to receiving dividends, the exchange can be on a "convertibles for common stock" basis. This will enable the acquired firm's stockholders to continue receiving income.

quired for the purchase, using the acquired firm's assets and earning power to pay off the loan after the merger or to provide security for renewing or even increasing the borrowing.[10]

Qualitative Influences: Synergy

Sometimes, the most important influences on merger prices are considerations not reflected in historical quantitative data. A soundly conceived merger is one in which the combination produces what may be called a *synergistic,* or "two-plus-two-equals-five," effect. By the combination, more profits are generated than could be achieved by the sum of the individual firms operating separately.

To illustrate: In the merger between Merck and Company and Sharp and Dohme, it was said that each company complemented the other in an important way. Merck had a good reputation for its research organization, whereas Sharp and Dohme had an effective sales force. The combination of these two pharmaceutical companies added strength to both. Another example is the merger between Carrier Corporation and Affiliated Gas Equipment. The merger enabled the combined company to provide a complete line of air-conditioning and heating equipment. The merger between Hilton Hotels and Statler Hotels led to economies in the purchase of supplies and materials. One Hilton executive estimated that the savings accruing simply from the combined management of the Statler and Hilton hotels in New York amounted to $700,000 a year. The bulk of the savings was in laundry, food, advertising, and administrative costs. An argument for the AT&T-NCR combination completed on May 6, 1991 was the complementary capabilities of the two companies in the future developments in information technologies.

Qualitative factors may also reflect other influences. The merger or acquisition may enable a company that lacks general management ability or even a specific skill set to obtain it from the other company. Another factor may be the acquisition of a technically competent scientific or engineering staff if one of the companies has fallen behind in the technological race. In such a situation, the company needing the technical competence possessed by the other firm may be willing to pay a substantial premium over previous levels of earnings, dividends, market values, or book values of the acquired firm.

Managerial motives may also be involved. Managers may seek mergers to reduce the diversifiable (unsystematic) risk of the firm. While stockholders can deal with unsystematic risk by diversification (as explained in Chapters 10 and 11), managers are concerned with total risk because a substantial portion of their wealth and their reputations as executives are tied to the performance of one firm.

The foregoing are the kinds of qualitative considerations that may have an overriding influence on the actual terms of merger, and the value of such contributions is never easy to quantify. The all-encompassing question, of course, is how the factors will affect the contribution of each company to future market value of the combined operation. A value-oriented approach is next set forth.

---

[10]By the same token, a firm seeking to *avoid* being acquired may reduce its liquid position and use up its borrowing potential.

TABLE 27.15   Comparative Statistics for the Year Ended 19X0

	Book Value per Share	Price-Earnings Ratio (P/EPS)	Number of Shares (millions)	Debt Ratio, % (D/E)	Beta for Existing Leverage	Internal Profit-ability Rate (r)	Invest-ment Rate (b)	Growth Rate (g)
Adams	$10	5.40	5	30	1.2	.04	0.1	.004
Black	40	11.70	1	30	1.4	.12	1.5	.18
Clark	40	9.88	1	30	1.6	.14	1.0	.14

MANAGERIAL POLICIES IN A VALUATION FRAMEWORK

In the perspective of alternative merger theories and empirical tests, the foundation has been provided to guide managerial policies with respect to merger and acquisition decisions. From an operational standpoint, mergers and acquisitions should be related to a firm's general planning framework. These requirements have been set forth in detail in other studies [Chung and Weston, 1982]. Here, we focus on merger policies in a capital budgeting valuation framework. We make the concepts explicit by using an illustrative case example to convey the ideas.

The Adams Corporation is a manufacturer of materials handling equipment, with heavy emphasis on forklift trucks. Because of a low internal profitability rate and lack of favorable investment opportunities in its existing line of business, Adams is considering a merger to achieve more favorable growth and profitability opportunities. It has made an extensive search of a large number of corporations and has narrowed the candidates to two firms, for a number of considerations. The Black Corporation is a manufacturer of agricultural equipment and is strong in research and marketing. It has had high internal profitability and substantial investment opportunities. The Clark Company is a manufacturer of plastic toys. It has a better profitability record than Black. Some relevant data on the three firms are summarized in Table 27.15. Additional information on market parameters includes a risk-free rate, R_F, of 6 percent and an expected return on the market, $E(R_M)$, of 11 percent. Each firm pays a 10 percent interest rate on its debt. The tax rate, T_c, of each is 50 percent. A period of ten years is estimated for the duration of supernormal growth, n, used in Equation 17.17q in Chapter 17 on value-based management and employed below. From the information provided, we can first formulate the accounting balance sheets for the three firms (Table 27.16).

TABLE 27.16   Accounting Balance Sheets (Millions of Dollars)

	Adams	Black	Clark
Debt	$15	$12	$12
Equity	50	40	40
Total assets	$65	$52	$52

TABLE 27.17 Market Price per Share

	Adams	Black	Clark
1. Total assets (millions)	$65	$52	$52
2. Earning rate, $r \div (1 - T_c)$	.08	.24	.28
3. Net operating income (1) × (2) (millions)	$ 5.2	$12.48	$14.56
4. Interest on debt (millions)	1.5	1.20	1.20
5. Profit before tax (millions)	$ 3.7	$11.28	$13.36
6. Taxes at 50% (millions)	1.85	5.64	6.68
7. Net income (millions)	1.85	5.64	6.68
8. Number of shares of common stock (millions)	5	1	1
9. Earnings per share of common stock, (7) ÷ (8)	$ .37	$ 5.64	$ 6.68
10. Price-earnings ratio (information provided)	5.4 times	11.7 times	9.88 times
11. Market price per share, (9) × (10)	$ 2.00	$66.00	$66.00
12. Total market value of equity, (11) × (8) (millions)	$10	$66	$66

Dividing the internal profitability rate r by $(1 - T_c)$ and multiplying by total assets, we get the net operating income. From the net operating income, we can obtain the market price per share and the total market value that would have to be paid for each of the three companies (Table 27.17). We now have earnings per share, market values per share, and total market values of equity for use in the subsequent analysis.

One popular criterion for evaluating the desirability of making acquisitions from the standpoint of the acquiring company is to determine the effect on its earnings per share. Table 27.18 illustrates these effects based on the data in the present example. It can be seen that the merger would cause the earnings per share of Adams to decline. The percentage dilution in the earnings per share of Adams would be 47 percent if Black were acquired and 39 percent if Clark were acquired. We believe that this widely used criterion is in error. The effects on market values are relevant, and not the effects on earnings per share.

In a valuation framework, it is necessary to make a forecast of the key variables affecting value after the merger has taken place. This requires an in-depth business analysis of each proposed merger in terms of its impact on the key valuation factors. From the background provided, we observe that Adams is a manufacturer of materials handling equipment. Black is a manufacturer of agricultural equipment with strength in research and marketing. Clark is a manufacturer of plastic toys. While Clark has a better profitability record than Black, the toy industry is under the pressure of continuously creating new ideas and concepts if growth and profitability are to continue. In addition, there seems to be less potential for favorable interaction of management capabilities in a merger between Adams and Clark than there would be in a merger between Adams and Black. Black is known to have a strong research organization, which may be able to develop new products in Adams's area of materials handling equipment. This merely sketches the kind of favor-

TABLE 27.18 Effects of Merger on EPS

	Effects on Adams's Earnings per Share if It Merges:	
	With Black	With Clark
1. Number of new shares (millions)[a]	33	33
2. Existing shares (millions)	5	5
3. Total new shares (millions)	38	38
4. Earnings after taxes (millions of dollars)	5.64	6.68
5. *Add* Adams's after-tax earnings (millions of dollars)	1.85	1.85
6. Total new earnings (millions of dollars)	7.490	8.530
7. New earnings per share, (6) ÷ (3), $	.197	.224
8. *Less* Adams's old earnings per share, $	.370	.370
9. Net effect	(.173)	(.146)
10. Percent dilution [(9 ÷ 8)100]	47%	39%

[a]Each share of Black and Clark has a market value 33 times that of Adams. Hence, 33 shares times the 1 million existing shares of Black and Clark is the total number of new Adams shares required.

able carryover of capabilities that may be achieved in a merger between Adams and Black. Reflecting these qualitative considerations, the following estimates are made of the new financial parameters of the combined firms.

	NOI	r	b	g_s
Adams/Black (AB)	18	.1556	.9	.14
Adams/Clark (AC)	16	.1444	.9	.13

We can now proceed to evaluate the two alternative acquisition prospects, using a valuation analysis. First, we calculate the new beta for the merged company under the two alternatives. We assume the beta for the combined companies is a market-value weighted average of the betas of the constituent companies. We use the new betas in the Security Market Line equation to obtain the cost of equity capital for each of the two combined firms:

$$\beta_{AB} = 1.2\left(\frac{10}{10 + 66}\right) + 1.4\left(\frac{66}{10 + 66}\right)$$
$$= .1579 + 1.2158 = 1.374 = 1.37$$
$$k_s(AB) = R_F + [E(R_M) - R_F]\beta_{AB}$$
$$= .06 + [.05]1.37 = .1285 = 12.85\%$$
$$\beta_{AC} = 1.2\left(\frac{10}{10 + 66}\right) + 1.6\left(\frac{66}{10 + 66}\right)$$
$$= .1579 + 1.3895 = 1.547 = 1.55$$
$$k_s(AC) = .06 + .05(1.55)$$
$$= .1375 = 13.75\%.$$

Given the debt cost of 10 percent and the cost of equity capital as calculated, we can then proceed to determine the weighted average cost of capital for the two combined firms.

	AB	AC
Debt, B	27	27
Equity, S	76	76
Value, V	103	103

We now continue our calculations:

$$\text{WACC} = k = k_s(S/V) + k_b(1 - T_c)(B/V)$$

$$k(AB) = .1285\left(\frac{76}{103}\right) + .05\left(\frac{27}{103}\right)$$

$$= .0948 + .0131 = .1079 = 10.8\%$$

$$k(AC) = .1375\left(\frac{76}{103}\right) + .05\left(\frac{27}{103}\right)$$

$$= .1015 + .0131 = .1146 = 11.5\%.$$

We now have all the information required to calculate the valuation of the two alternative combinations.

We use the valuation formula for a period of supernormal growth (10 years in this example) followed by zero growth. From Chapter 17 on valuation, this is Equation 17.17q, reproduced below for a leveraged company.

$$V = X_0(1 - T)(1 - b) \sum_{t=1}^{n} \frac{(1 + g_s)^t}{(1 + k)^t} + \frac{X_0(1 - T)(1 + g_s)^n}{k(1 + k)^n} \qquad \textbf{(17.17q)}$$

We next insert the numerical values to determine the value of the combined firm if Adams merges with Black (AB) or with Clark (AC). The computations are shown below:

$$V_{AB} = \$18(.5)(.1) \sum_{t=1}^{10} \frac{(1.14)^t}{(1.108)^t} + \frac{\$18(.5)(1.14)^{11}}{.108(1.108)^{10}}$$

$$= .9 \sum_{t=1}^{10} (1.029)^t + \frac{9}{.108}(1.029)^{11}$$

$$= .9(1.029)\text{FVIFA}(2.9\%, 10 \text{ yrs.}) + 83.33\text{FVIF}(2.9\%, 10 \text{ yrs.})(1.14)$$

$$= .9261\left[\frac{1.331 - 1}{.029}\right] + 83.33(1.331)(1.14)$$

$$= .9261(11.414) + 126.44$$

$$V_{AB} = 10.57 + 126.44 = \$137.01 \text{ million.}$$

$$V_{AC} = \$16(.5)(.1) \sum_{t=1}^{10} \left(\frac{1.13}{1.115}\right)^t + \frac{\$16(.5)(1.13)^{11}}{.115(1.115)^{10}}$$

$$= .8 \sum_{t=1}^{10} (1.01345)^t + \frac{8}{.115}(1.01345)^{11}$$

$$= .8(1.01345)\left[\frac{1.14294 - 1}{.01345}\right] + 69.5652(1.14294)(1.13)$$

$$= .81076(10.63) + 89.85$$

$$V_{AC} = 8.62 + 89.85 = \$98.47 \text{ million.}$$

Using the results obtained, we make a summary comparison of the gains or losses from the two alternative mergers shown in Table 27.19. The data show that, based on estimates of the key parameters, a gain in value of $34 million would result from a merger between Adams and Black. However, the merger between Adams and Clark would result in a loss in valuation amounting to $5 million. The results of this comparison permit some margin of error yet clearly indicate that a merger between Adams and Black is preferable to a merger between Adams and Clark. Indeed, the gain in value of $34 million could be divided between the shareholders of Adams and those of Black. Adams could pay a 10 to 20 percent premium over the current market price of Black and still achieve a gain in net value that would go to its shareholders.

The foregoing example provides a general methodology for the management analysis of merger activity, which utilizes a number of principles: The acquiring firm is considering other firms as alternative merger candidates. To come up with a rational basis for analysis, prospective returns and risk from alternative merger combinations must be estimated. While historical data may be used as inputs, a forecast or estimate must be made of the returns and risk that may arise after alternative merger combinations have taken place.

Thus, the forecast of the variables that measure prospective returns and risk for alternative postmerger combinations is critical to a sound evaluation of merger alternatives. The estimates of net operating earnings and of their potential growth may or may not reflect synergy between the combining firms depending on the nature and potential of

TABLE 27.19   Comparison of Two Mergers (Dollars in Millions)

	Adams/Black	Adams/Clark
Postmerger value, V	$137	$98
Less amount of debt, B	27	27
Value of equity, S	$110	$71
Less Adams's premerger market value	10	10
Gain in equity value	$100	$61
Cost if acquired at market price	66	66
Gain in value (loss)	$ 34	$ (5)

the combined operations. Studies in depth of the relevant product markets and the results of combining the organizations of the two firms are required. The resulting forecasts are subject to prediction errors, which are sometimes of substantial magnitude.

We may obtain the measures of risk by market-value weighted averages of the betas (the systematic risk) of the combining firms. With the estimates of the new betas, along with a selection of market parameters, we can calculate the new relevant cost of capital for the merged firm, utilizing the Security Market Line relationship. We must also estimate the effect of alternative merger combinations on the cost of debt. With estimates of the cost of equity capital and the cost of debt, we must formulate appropriate capital structure targets for the combined firm and use these to estimate a cost of capital.

Having obtained an estimate of the applicable cost of capital and the estimates of returns discussed earlier, we can apply valuation principles to formulate estimates of the value of alternative merger combinations. From these, we deduct the value of the acquiring firm in the absence of the merger to determine the total value remaining, which we next compare with the cost of acquiring the firm or firms with which a merger is being considered. If the value contributed by the merger exceeds the cost of the acquisition, the acquiring firm has a basis for making an offer that includes a premium to the shareholders of the acquired firm yet still provides an increase in value for the shareholders of the acquiring firm.

SUMMARY

Mergers have played an important part in the growth of firms, and since financial managers are required both to appraise the desirability of a prospective merger and to participate in evaluating the respective companies involved in it, this chapter has emphasized analysis of the terms of merger decisions.

The gains from corporate combinations may come from

1. Increased efficiency

2. Information and signaling effects

3. Reduction of agency problems

4. Realignment of management incentives

5. Stronger market positions

6. Tax benefits

7. Redistribution among stakeholders.

In transactions involving the rearrangement of the ownership structures of firms, the sources of increased value may come from stronger managerial incentives, better performance evaluation, and the reduction in government regulatory constraints.

In leveraged buyouts, experienced managements have the opportunity to achieve large wealth gains by obtaining complete control unfettered by the intervention of public shareholders and less subject to government regulatory agencies. With the backing of outside lenders, they enter into a highly leveraged situation. If the company performs according to projections, the debt is reduced over a period of years and the gains to the equity investors represent a high rate of return.

In mergers, one firm disappears. However, an alternative is for one firm to buy all or a majority of the common stock of another and to run the acquired firm as an operating subsidiary. When this occurs, the acquiring firm is said to be a *holding company*. A number of advantages arise when a holding company is formed, among them:

1. It may be possible to control the acquired firm with a smaller investment than necessary for a merger.

2. Each firm in a holding company is a separate legal entity, and the obligations of any unit are separate from the obligations of the other units.

3. Stockholder approval is required before a merger can take place. This may not be necessary in a holding company situation.

There are also some disadvantages to holding companies, among them:

1. If the holding company does not own 80 percent of the subsidiary's stock and does not file consolidated tax returns, it is subject to taxes on 20 to 30 percent of the dividends received from the subsidiary.

2. The leverage effects possible in holding companies can subject the company to magnification of earnings fluctuations and related risks.

3. The antitrust division of the U.S. Department of Justice can much more easily force the breakup of a holding company than it can bring about the dissolution of two completely merged firms.

In the perspective of alternative merger theories and tests, we developed a framework for managerial analysis of prospective mergers. Basically, good forecasts of postmerger returns and risks are required as a starting point. Standard capital budgeting procedures, cost of capital analysis, and valuation principles presented in the preceding chapters are then applied. The aim is to determine whether the value of the merged firm exceeds the value of the constituent firms. If it does, the merger has a valid social and private justification.

We have shown that the fundamental basis for valuation in merger transactions represents an extension of basic capital budgeting principles. If there is a positive net present value from an external investment in other companies, sound capital budgeting criteria have been met. If the business combination results in synergies or other sources of increases in value, the incremental net present value will provide a basis for paying a premium to the shareholders of the company acquired. Whether the shareholders of acquiring companies gain depends in part on the intensity of competition in the market for acquisitions and in part on the market's view of what will be achieved by the combined companies. In a well-conceived buyout or sellout, increases in value are achieved, which provide a basis for gains to parties on both sides of the transaction.

QUESTIONS

27.1 What are some of the potential benefits that can be expected by a firm that merges with a company in a different industry?

27.2 Distinguish between a holding company and an operating company. Give an example of each.

27.3 Which appears to be riskier — the use of debt in the holding company's capital structure or the use of debt in the operating company's capital structure? Explain.

27.4 Is the public interest served by an increase in merger and tender offer activity? Give both pro and con arguments.

27.5 Is the book value of a company's assets considered the absolute minimum price to be paid for a firm? Explain. Is there any value that qualifies as an absolute minimum? Explain.

27.6 Discuss the situation in which Midwest Motors calls off merger negotiations with American Data Labs because the latter's stock price is overvalued. What assumption concerning dilution is implicit in the above situation?

27.7 There are many methods by which a company can raise additional capital. Can a merger be considered a means of raising additional equity capital? Explain.

27.8 Are the negotiations for merger agreements more difficult if the firms are in different industries or in the same industry? If they are about the same size or quite different in size? If the ages of the firms are about the same or if they are very different? Explain.

27.9 How would the existence of long-term debt in a company's financial structure affect its valuation for merger purposes? Could the same be said for any debt account regardless of its maturity? Explain.

27.10 During the merger activity of recent years, cash was used by the acquiring company to a much greater extent than during the height of the conglomerate merger activity during 1967–1969. What are some reasons for the relatively greater use of cash in the acquisitions of the more recent period?

27.11 Why are lenders willing to permit the 9 to 1 debt ratios sometimes found in leveraged buyouts?

PROBLEMS

27.1 The Niles Company has agreed to merge with the Aruba Company. Table P27.1 gives information about the two companies prior to their merger:

TABLE P27.1

	Aruba	Niles
Total earnings	$1,000,000	$750,000
Shares outstanding	1,000,000	250,000
P/EPS ratio	20 times	18 times

The Aruba Company will buy the Niles Company with a four-for-one exchange of stock. Combined earnings will initially remain at the premerger level.

a. What will be the effect on EPS for Aruba stockholders?

b. What will be the effect on EPS for premerger Niles Company stockholders?

c. Discuss the results.

27.2 The Brunner Company has agreed to merge with the Powell Company. The shareholders of Powell have agreed to accept half a share of Brunner for each of their Powell shares. The new company will have a P/EPS ratio of 40. Table P27.2 gives additional information about the merging companies.

TABLE P27.2

	Brunner	Powell
P/EPS ratio	56	7
Shares outstanding	2,500,000	500,000
Earnings	$1,750,000	$700,000
Earnings per share	$.70	$1.40
Market value per share	$39.20	$9.80

a. After Brunner and Powell merge, what will the new price per share be, assuming that combined earnings remain the same?

b. Calculate the dollar and percent accretion in EPS for Brunner.

c. Calculate the dollar and percent dilution in EPS for Powell.

d. What is the effect on market price for each?

e. Assuming that Brunner has been growing at 24 percent per year, and Powell at 8 percent, what is the weighted growth rate for the merged firm? (There are no synergistic effects.)

f. How long will it be before Powell's EPS recovers from the dilution caused by the merger? Illustrate by means of a graph showing premerger and postmerger EPS.

27.3 Dalton Company acquires Cory Company with a three-for-one exchange of stock. Table P27.3 presents data for the two companies:

TABLE P27.3

	Dalton	Cory
Total earnings	$100,000,000	$1,000,000
Shares outstanding	80,000,000	800,000
Expected growth rate in earnings	10%	25%
P/EPS ratio	8 times	24 times

a. What is the basis for the three-for-one exchange ratio?

b. What is the new EPS for the premerger Dalton and Cory stockholders?

c. If Dalton's P/EPS ratio rises to 15, what is its new market price?

d. What merger concept does this problem illustrate?

27.4 Hempler Company merges with Rider Company on the basis of market values. Hempler pays one share of convertible preferred stock with a par value of $100 and a dividend rate of 6 percent (convertible into two shares of Hempler's common stock) for each four shares of Rider Company. Table P27.4 presents more data:

TABLE P27.4

	Hempler	Rider
Total earnings	$1,000,000	$400,000
Common shares outstanding	200,000	80,000
Expected growth rate in earnings	18%	6%
Dividends per share	$1.80	$1.80
P/EPS ratio	12 times	6 times
Dividend yield	3%	6%

a. (1) What are the new EPS and market price of Hempler if the P/EPS ratio remains at 12 times?

(2) What are the new EPS and market price on a fully diluted basis?

b. Why might Rider Company shareholders agree to the acquisition?

27.5 You are given the balance sheets in Table P27.5a.

TABLE P27.5a Rocky Mountain Services Company Consolidated Balance Sheet (Millions of Dollars)

Cash	$1,500	Borrowings	$1,125
Other current assets	1,125	Common stock	1,875
Net property	1,875	Retained earnings	1,500
Total assets	$4,500	Total claims on assets	$4,500

White Lighting Company Balance Sheet (Millions of Dollars)

Cash	$375	Net worth	$750
Net property	375		
Total assets	$750	Total net worth	$750

a. The holding company, Rocky Mountain, buys the operating company, White Lighting, with "free" cash of $750 million. Show the new consolidated balance sheet for Rocky Mountain after the acquisition, using purchase accounting.